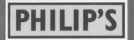

STREE

South Yorks

Barnsley, Doncaster, Rotherham, Sheffield

First published in 1996 by

Philip's, a division of
Octopus Publishing Group Ltd
2-4 Heron Quays, London E14 4JP

Fourth edition 2006
First impression 2006
SYODA

ISBN-10 0-540-08994-X (pocket)
ISBN-13 978-0-540-08994-9 (pocket)

Printed by Toppan, China

Contents

III **Key to map symbols**

IV **Key to map pages**

VI **Route planning**

VIII **Administrative and Postcode boundaries**

1 **Street maps** at 2⅔ inches to 1 mile

160 **Street map of Sheffield city centre** at 5⅓ inches to 1 mile

162 **Index** of towns and villages

164 **Index** of streets, hospitals, industrial estates, railway stations, schools, shopping centres, universities and places of interest

Digital Data

The exceptionally high-quality mapping found in this atlas is available as digital data in TIFF format, which is easily convertible to other bitmapped (raster) image formats.

The index is also available in digital form as a standard database table. It contains all the details found in the printed index together with the National Grid reference for the map square in which each entry is named.

For further information and to discuss your requirements, please contact Philip's on 020 7644 6932 or james.mann@philips-maps.co.uk

Motorway with junction number		◆	**Ambulance station**
Primary route – dual/single carriageway		◈	**Coastguard station**
A road – dual/single carriageway		◆	**Fire station**
B road – dual/single carriageway		◆	**Police station**
Minor road – dual/single carriageway		✚	**Accident and Emergency entrance to hospital**
Other minor road – dual/single carriageway		Ⓗ	**Hospital**
Road under construction		✛	**Place of worship**
Tunnel, covered road		🄸	**Information Centre** (open all year)
Rural track, private road or narrow road in urban area		🛒	**Shopping Centre**
Gate or obstruction to traffic (restrictions may not apply at all times or to all vehicles)		P P&R	**Parking, Park and Ride**
Path, bridleway, byway open to all traffic, road used as a public path		PO	**Post Office**
Pedestrianised area		🏕 🚐	**Camping site, caravan site**
Postcode boundaries DY7		⚑ ✗	**Golf course, picnic site**
County and unitary authority boundaries		Prim Sch	**Important buildings, schools, colleges, universities and hospitals**
Railway, tunnel, railway under construction			**Built up area**
Tramway, tramway under construction			**Woods**
Miniature railway		River Medway	**Water name**
Railway station Walsall			**River, weir, stream**
Private railway station			**Canal, lock, tunnel**
Metro station South Shields			**Water**
Tram stop, tram stop under construction			**Tidal water**
Bus, coach station		Church	**Non-Roman antiquity**
		ROMAN FORT	**Roman antiquity**

Acad	**Academy**	Inst	**Institute**	Recn Gd	**Recreation Ground**
Allot Gdns	**Allotments**	Ct	**Law Court**		
Cemy	**Cemetery**	L Ctr	**Leisure Centre**	Resr	**Reservoir**
C Ctr	**Civic Centre**	LC	**Level Crossing**	Ret Pk	**Retail Park**
CH	**Club House**	Liby	**Library**	Sch	**School**
Coll	**College**	Mkt	**Market**	Sh Ctr	**Shopping Centre**
Crem	**Crematorium**	Meml	**Memorial**	TH	**Town Hall/House**
Ent	**Enterprise**	Mon	**Monument**	Trad Est	**Trading Estate**
Ex H	**Exhibition Hall**	Mus	**Museum**	Univ	**University**
Ind Est	**Industrial Estate**	Obsy	**Observatory**	W Twr	**Water Tower**
IRB Sta	**Inshore Rescue Boat Station**	Pal	**Royal Palace**	Wks	**Works**
		PH	**Public House**	YH	**Youth Hostel**

87	**Adjoining page indicators and overlap bands** The colour of the arrow and the band indicates the scale of the adjoining or overlapping page (see scales below)
237	

Enlarged mapping only

	Railway or bus station building
	Place of interest
	Parkland

■ The small numbers around the edges of the maps identify the 1 kilometre National Grid lines
■ The dark grey border on the inside edge of some pages indicates that the mapping does not continue onto the adjacent page

The scale of the maps on the pages numbered in blue is 4.2 cm to 1 km • 2⅔ inches to 1 mile • 1: 23810

0	¼	½	¾	1 mile
0	250m	500m	750m	1 kilometre

The scale of the maps on pages numbered in red is 8.4 cm to 1 km • 5⅓ inches to 1 mile • 1: 11900

0	220 yards	440 yards	660 yards	½ mile
0	125m	250m	375m	½ kilometre

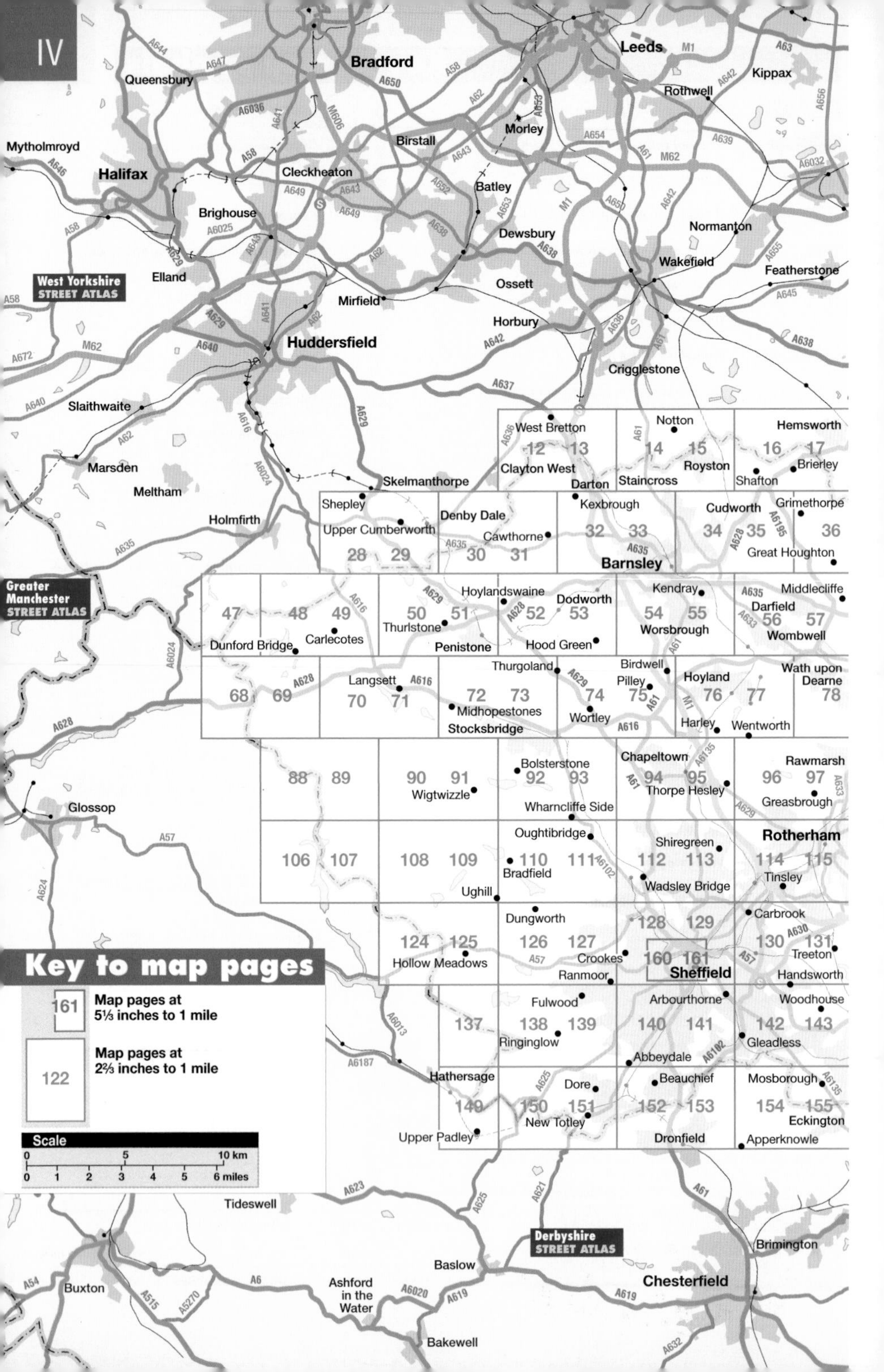
Key to map pages
161
Map pages at 5⅓ inches to 1 mile
122
Map pages at 2⅔ inches to 1 mile
Scale
0 5 10 km
0 1 2 3 4 5 6 miles
West Yorkshire STREET ATLAS
Greater Manchester STREET ATLAS
Derbyshire STREET ATLAS
Bradford
Leeds
Queensbury
Kippax
Rothwell
Mytholmroyd
Halifax
Birstall
Morley
Cleckheaton
Batley
Brighouse
Normanton
Dewsbury
Wakefield
Featherstone
Elland
Ossett
Mirfield
Horbury
Huddersfield
Crigglestone
Slaithwaite
Marsden
Meltham
Holmfirth
Skelmanthorpe
West Bretton
Clayton West
Darton
Notton
Staincross
Royston
Hemsworth
Shafton
Brierley
Shepley
Upper Cumberworth
Denby Dale
Cawthorne
Kexbrough
Barnsley
Cudworth
Grimethorpe
Great Houghton
Dunford Bridge
Carlecotes
Thurlstone
Penistone
Hoylandswaine
Dodworth
Hood Green
Kendray
Worsbrough
Darfield
Middlecliffe
Wombwell
Langsett
Midhopestones
Stocksbridge
Thurgoland
Wortley
Birdwell
Pilley
Hoyland
Harley
Wentworth
Wath upon Dearne
Glossop
Wigtwizzle
Bolsterstone
Wharncliffe Side
Chapeltown
Thorpe Hesley
Rawmarsh
Greasbrough
Rotherham
Oughtibridge
Bradfield
Ughill
Shiregreen
Wadsley Bridge
Tinsley
Carbrook
Dungworth
Hollow Meadows
Crookes
Ranmoor
Sheffield
Treeton
Handsworth
Fulwood
Ringinglow
Arbourthorne
Abbeydale
Woodhouse
Gleadless
Hathersage
Dore
New Totley
Beauchief
Dronfield
Mosborough
Eckington
Apperknowle
Upper Padley
Tideswell
Brimington
Baslow
Buxton
Ashford in the Water
Chesterfield
Bakewell
12 13 14 15 16 17
28 29 30 31 32 33 34 35 36
47 48 49 50 51 52 53 54 55 56 57
68 69 70 71 72 73 74 75 76 77 78
88 89 90 91 92 93 94 95 96 97
106 107 108 109 110 111 112 113 114 115
124 125 126 127 128 129 130 131
160 161
137 138 139 140 141 142 143
149 150 151 152 153 154 155

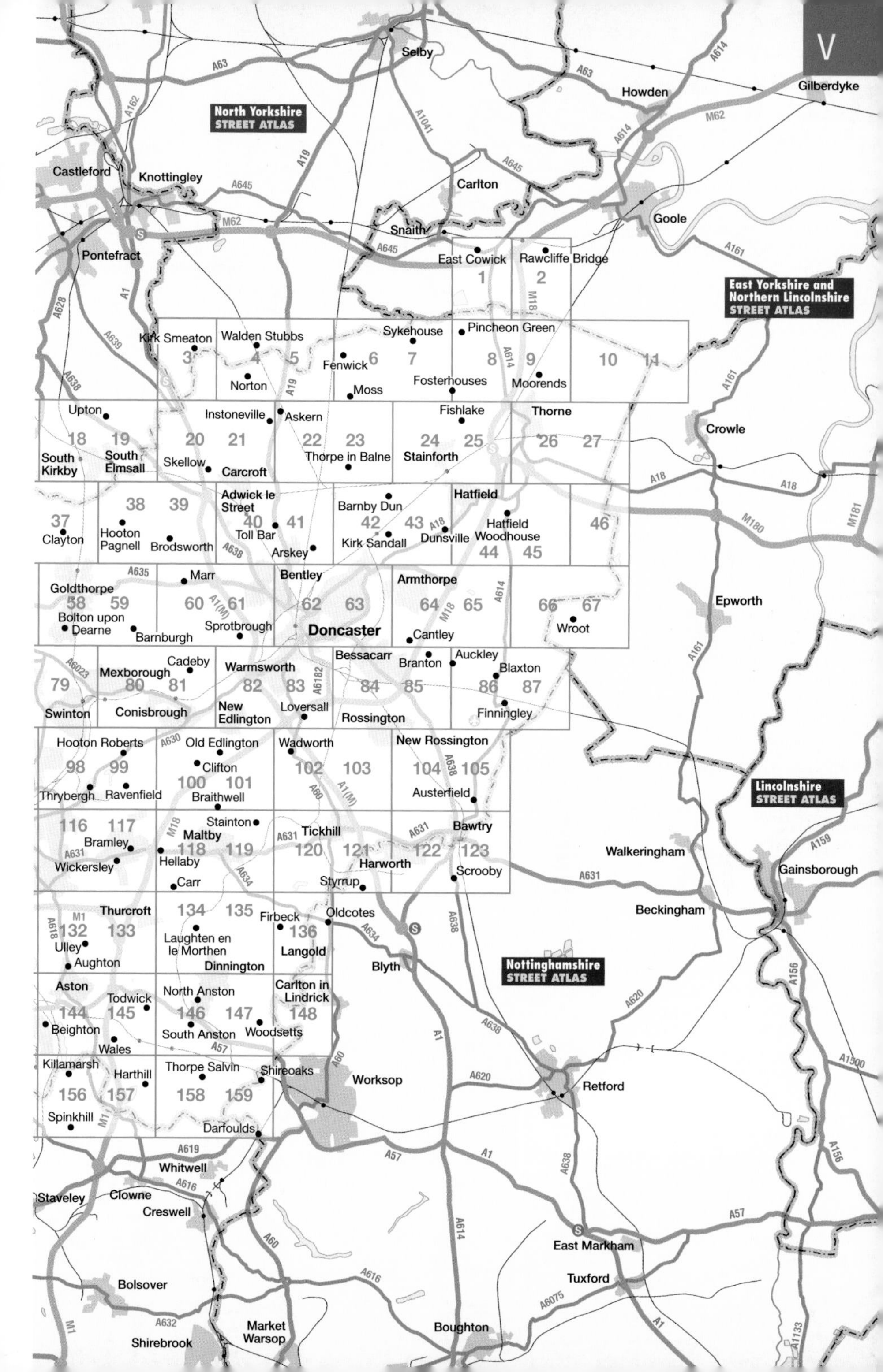
Selby
A63
Howden
Gilberdyke
A614
M62
North Yorkshire STREET ATLAS
A162
A1041
A19
A645
Castleford
Knottingley
Carlton
Goole
M62
Snaith
Pontefract
A645
East Cowick
Rawcliffe Bridge
A161
1
2
East Yorkshire and Northern Lincolnshire STREET ATLAS
A1
M18
A628
A639
Kirk Smeaton
Walden Stubbs
Sykehouse
Pincheon Green
3
4
5
Fenwick
6
7
8
A614
9
10
11
Norton
Moss
Fosterhouses
Moorends
A638
A19
A161
Upton
Instoneville
Askern
Fishlake
Thorne
Crowle
18
19
20
21
22
23
24
25
26
27
South Kirkby
South Elmsall
Skellow
Carcroft
Thorpe in Balne
Stainforth
A18
A18
Adwick le Street
Hatfield
38
39
Barnby Dun
37
40
41
42
43
A18
Hatfield Woodhouse
46
M180
M181
Clayton
Hooton Pagnell
Brodsworth
Toll Bar
Kirk Sandall
Dunsville
A638
Arskey
44
45
A635
Marr
Bentley
Armthorpe
Goldthorpe
A614
Epworth
58
59
60
A1(M)
61
62
63
64
M18
65
66
67
Bolton upon Dearne
Sprotbrough
Doncaster
Wroot
Barnburgh
Cantley
A6023
Cadeby
Bessacarr
Auckley
Mexborough
Warmsworth
Branton
Blaxton
A161
79
80
81
82
83
A6182
84
85
86
87
New Edlington
Loversall
Finningley
Swinton
Conisbrough
Rossington
Hooton Roberts
A630
Old Edlington
Wadworth
New Rossington
Clifton
A638
98
99
100
101
102
103
104
105
Lincolnshire STREET ATLAS
Thrybergh
Ravenfield
Braithwell
A1(M)
Austerfield
A60
Stainton
Bawtry
116
117
M18
Maltby
Tickhill
A631
A159
Bramley
A631
A631
118
119
120
121
122
123
Walkeringham
Hellaby
Harworth
Wickersley
Scrooby
Gainsborough
A634
A631
Carr
Styrrup
Thurcroft
134
135
Oldcotes
Beckingham
M1
Firbeck
A618
132
133
136
A638
Laughten en le Morthen
A634
Ulley
Langold
Aughton
Dinnington
Blyth
Nottinghamshire STREET ATLAS
A156
Aston
North Anston
Carlton in Lindrick
A620
Todwick
144
145
146
147
148
Beighton
Woodsetts
A1
South Anston
A638
Wales
A57
A1500
Killamarsh
Thorpe Salvin
Shireoaks
Harthill
A60
Worksop
A620
156
157
158
159
Retford
M1
Spinkhill
Darfoulds
A619
A57
A1
A156
Whitwell
A638
A616
Staveley
Clowne
Creswell
A57
A60
A614
East Markham
A616
Bolsover
Tuxford
A6075
M1
A632
Market Warsop
A1
Shirebrook
Boughton
A1133

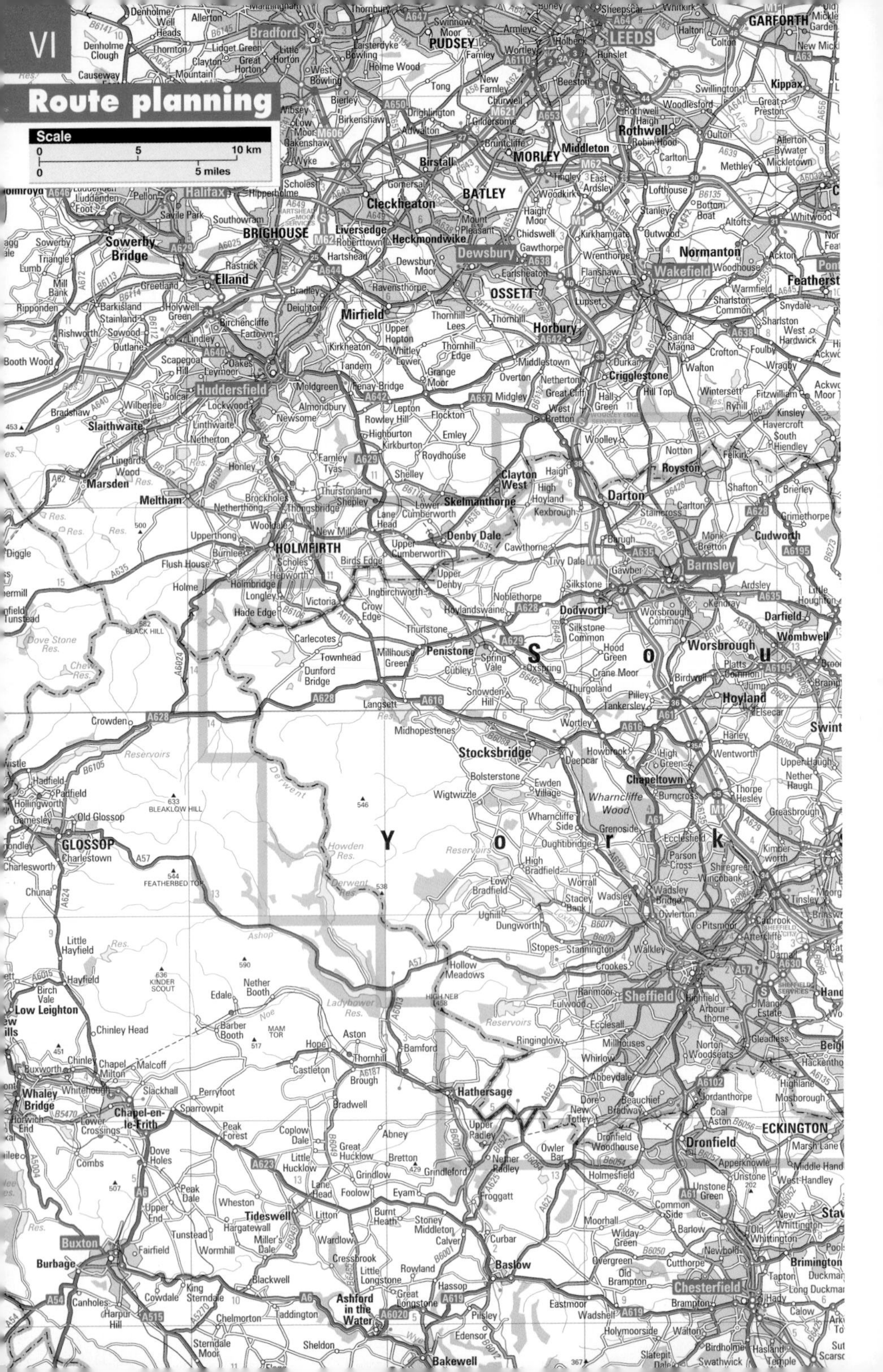
Route planning
Scale
0
5
10 km
0
5 miles
Bradford
LEEDS
PUDSEY
GARFORTH
Halifax
BRIGHOUSE
Cleckheaton
BATLEY
MORLEY
Rothwell
Dewsbury
Wakefield
Normanton
OSSETT
Elland
Mirfield
Horbury
Huddersfield
HOLMFIRTH
Barnsley
Penistone
Stocksbridge
GLOSSOP
Sheffield
Chapel-en-le-Frith
Hathersage
Dronfield
ECKINGTON
Buxton
Tideswell
Baslow
Chesterfield
Bakewell
S o u t h
Y o r k

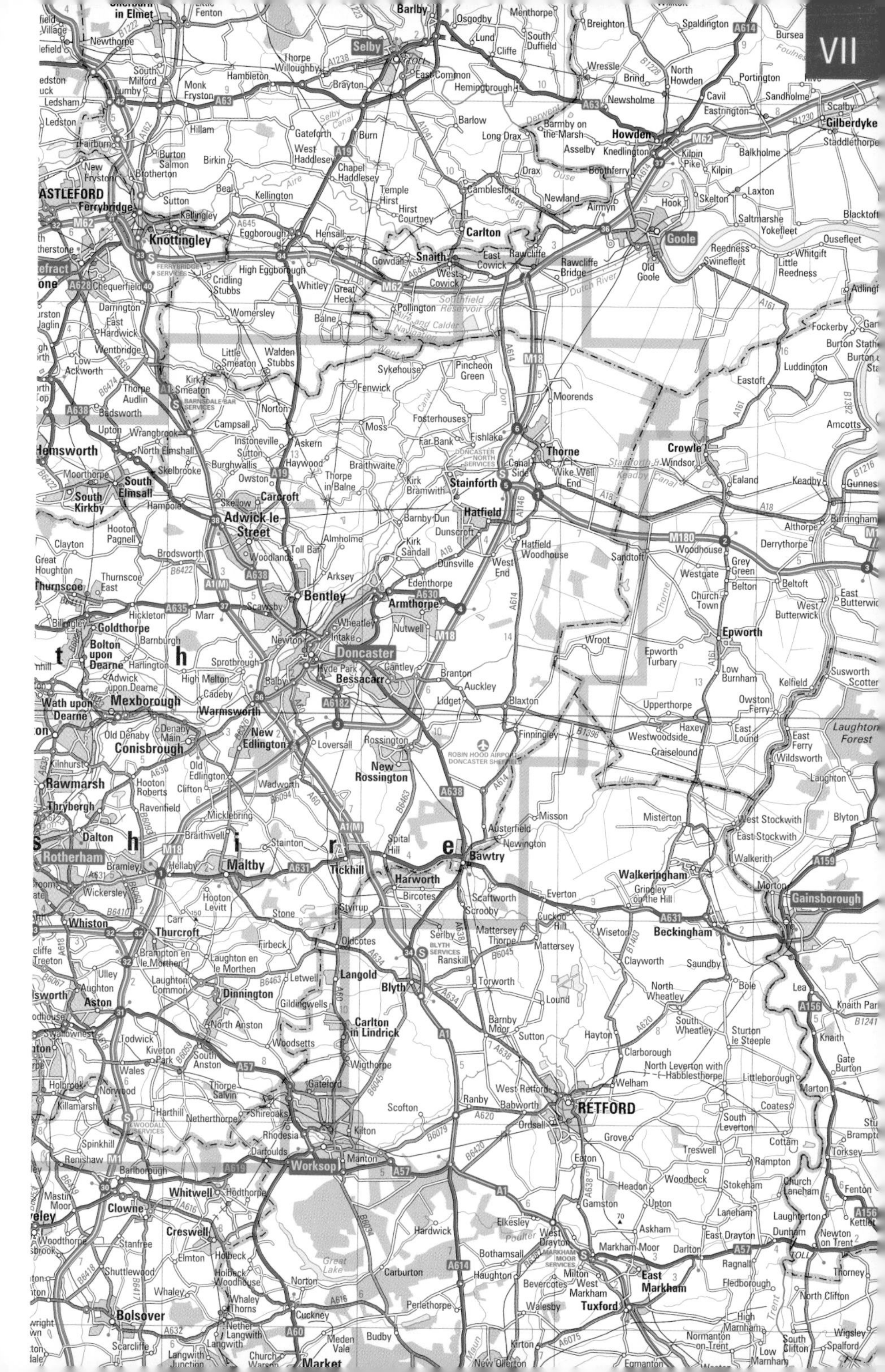
Sherburn in Elmet
Barlby
Osgodby
Menthorpe
Breighton
Spaldington
Bursea
Selby
Lund
South Duffield
Cliffe
Newthorpe
Thorpe Willoughby
Wressle
North Howden
Portington
South Milford
Hambleton
East Common
Brind
Cavil
Sandholme
Monk Fryston
Brayton
Hemingbrough
Newsholme
Eastrington
Scalby
Ledsham
Lumby
Barlow
Barmby on the Marsh
Howden
Gilberdyke
Ledston
Hillam
Gateforth
Burn
Long Drax
Asselby
Knedlington
Staddlethorpe
Fairburn
Burton Salmon
West Haddlesey
Kilpin Pike
Balkholme
Birkin
Chapel Haddlesey
Drax
Boothferry
Kilpin
New Fryston
Brotherton
Temple Hirst
Camblesforth
Laxton
CASTLEFORD
Ferrybridge
Beal
Kellington
Hirst Courtney
Newland
Airmyn
Hook
Skelton
Sutton
Saltmarshe
Blacktoft
Knottingley
Kellingley
Eggborough
Hensall
Carlton
Yokefleet
Goole
Ousefleet
Snaith
East Cowick
Rawcliffe
Gowdall
Reedness
Whitgift
High Eggborough
West Cowick
Rawcliffe Bridge
Old Goole
Swinefleet
Little Reedness
Chequerfield
Cridling Stubbs
Whitley
Great Heck
Pollington
Southfield Reservoir
Darrington
Womersley
Balne
Aire and Calder Navigation
East Hardwick
Wentbridge
Little Smeaton
Walden Stubbs
Sykehouse
Pincheon Green
Fockerby
Burton Stather
Low Ackworth
Eastoft
Luddington
Thorpe Audlin
Kirk Smeaton
Fenwick
Moorends
Badsworth
Norton
Campsall
Fosterhouses
Upton
Wrangbrook
Moss
Amcotts
Hemsworth
North Elmshall
Instoneville
Askern
Far Bank
Fishlake
Thorne
Crowle
Sutton
Burghwallis
Haywood
Braithwaite
Canal Side
Wike Well End
Windsor
Moorthorpe
South Elmsall
Skelbrooke
Owston
Thorpe in Balne
Kirk Bramwith
Stainforth
Ealand
Keadby
Gunness
South Kirkby
Hampole
Carcroft
Skellow
Adwick le Street
Hatfield
Barnby Dun
Dunscroft
Burringham
Althorpe
Hooton Pagnell
Almholme
Clayton
Kirk Sandall
Hatfield Woodhouse
Woodhouse
Derrythorpe
Brodsworth
Woodlands
Toll Bar
Dunsville
West End
Sandtoft
Grey Green
Great Houghton
Westgate
Belton
Beltoft
Thurnscoe
Thurnscoe East
Arksey
Edenthorpe
Church Town
East Butterwick
Hickleton
Marr
Scawsby
Bentley
Armthorpe
West Butterwick
Goldthorpe
Barnburgh
Wheatley
Nutwell
Bolton upon Dearne
Newton
Intake
Wroot
Epworth
Doncaster
Epworth Turbary
Harlington
Sprotbrough
Hyde Park
Cantley
Branton
Low Burnham
Kelfield
Susworth
Scotter
Adwick upon Dearne
High Melton
Balby
Bessacarr
Auckley
Mexborough
Cadeby
Wath upon Dearne
Warmsworth
Lidget
Blaxton
Upperthorpe
Owston Ferry
Old Denaby
Denaby Main
New Edlington
Loversall
Rossington
Finningley
Haxey
Westwoodside
East Lound
East Ferry
Laughton Forest
Conisbrough
Craiselound
Wildsworth
Kilnhurst
Old Edlington
New Rossington
Robin Hood Airport Doncaster Sheffield
Laughton
Rawmarsh
Hooton Roberts
Clifton
Wadworth
Thrybergh
Ravenfield
Micklebring
Misson
Misterton
Blyton
West Stockwith
East Stockwith
Dalton
Braithwell
Stainton
Spital Hill
Austerfield
Newington
Rotherham
Bramley
Hellaby
Maltby
Tickhill
Bawtry
Walkerith
Wickersley
Harworth
Walkeringham
Morton
Gringley on the Hill
Gainsborough
Hooton Levitt
Bircotes
Scaftworth
Everton
Whiston
Carr
Stone
Styrrup
Scrooby
Cuckoo Hill
Thurcroft
Firbeck
Serlby
Mattersey Thorpe
Mattersey
Wiseton
Beckingham
Brampton en le Morthen
Oldcotes
Blyth Services
Ranskill
Treeton
Laughton en le Morthen
Langold
Clayworth
Saundby
Ulley
Letwell
Torworth
Aughton
Laughton Common
Dinnington
Blyth
North Wheatley
Bole
Aston
Gildingwells
Lound
Lea
Knaith Park
North Anston
Carlton in Lindrick
South Wheatley
Barnby Moor
Sturton le Steeple
Knaith
Todwick
Woodsetts
Sutton
Hayton
Kiveton Park
South Anston
Clarborough
Gate Burton
Wales
Wigthorpe
North Leverton with Habblesthorpe
Norwood
Thorpe Salvin
Gateford
Welham
Littleborough
Marton
Killamarsh
West Retford
Harthill
Netherthorpe
Shireoaks
Ranby
Babworth
RETFORD
Coates
Scofton
Ordsall
South Leverton
Rhodesia
Kilton
Spinkhill
Grove
Cottam
Brampton
Torksey
Dartoulds
Renishaw
Barlborough
Worksop
Manton
Eaton
Treswell
Rampton
Woodbeck
Headon
Stokeham
Church Laneham
Fenton
Whitwell
Hodthorpe
Mastin Moor
Gamston
Upton
Laneham
Clowne
Hardwick
Elkesley
Laughterton
Kettlethorpe
Creswell
West Drayton
Askham
East Drayton
Dunham
Newton on Trent
Woodthorpe
Stanfree
Bothamsall
Markham Moor
Darlton
Elmton
Holbeck
Markham Moor Services
Ragnall
Thorney
Shuttlewood
Great Lake
Carburton
Haughton
Milton
East Markham
Holbeck Woodhouse
Norton
Bevercotes
West Markham
Fledborough
Whaley
North Clifton
Whaley Thorns
Perlethorpe
Walesby
Tuxford
Bolsover
Cuckney
High Marnham
Nether Langwith
Budby
Wigsley
Langwith
Meden Vale
Normanton on Trent
South Clifton
Spalford
Scarcliffe
Kirton
Low Marnham
Langwith Junction
Church Warsop
Market
New Ollerton
Egmanton

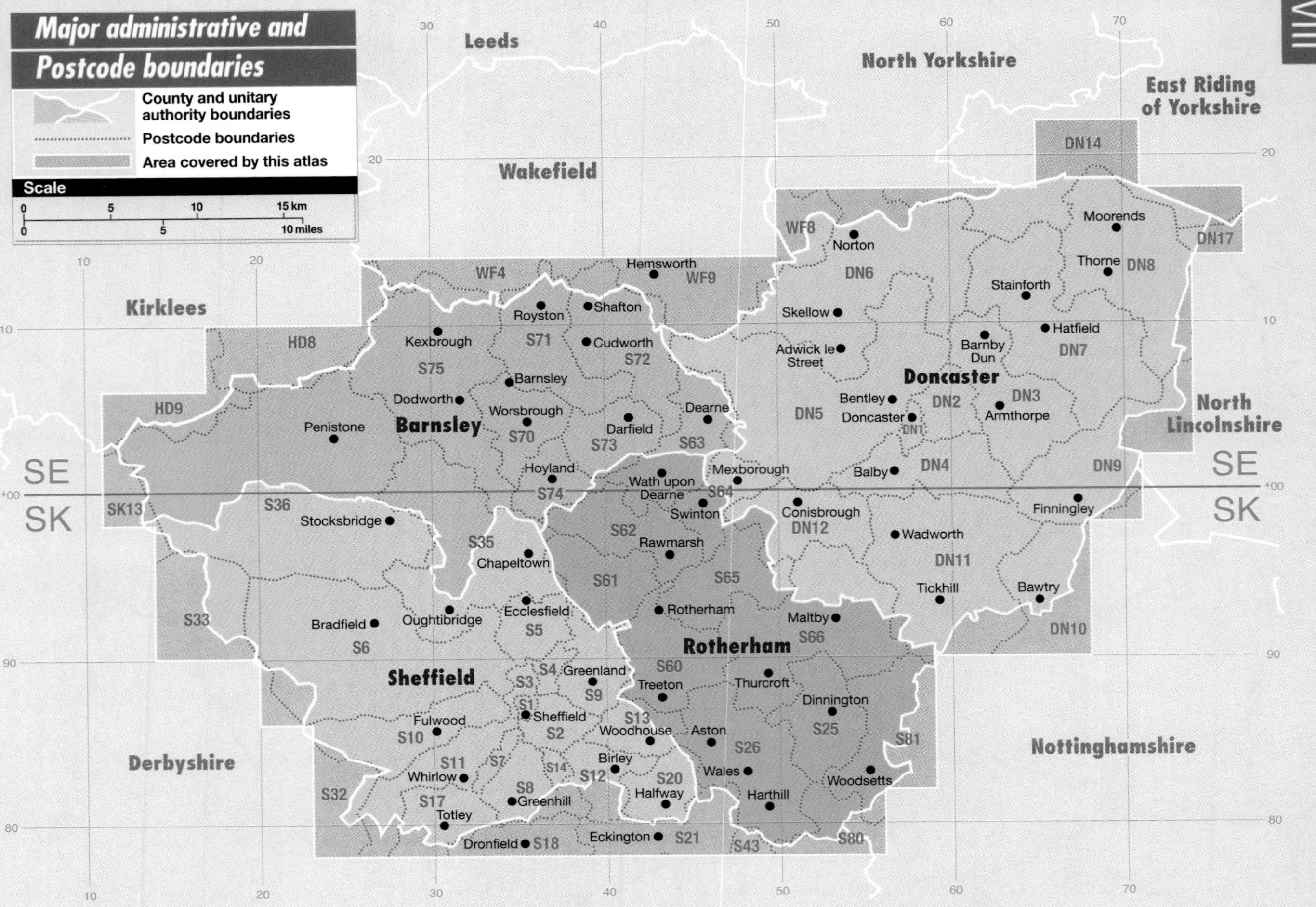

Major administrative and Postcode boundaries

Scale

0   5   10   15 km
0   5   10 miles

County and unitary authority boundaries

Postcode boundaries

Area covered by this atlas

East Riding of Yorkshire

North Lincolnshire

North Yorkshire

Nottinghamshire

Leeds

Wakefield

Kirklees

Derbyshire

Doncaster

Barnsley

Rotherham

Sheffield

DN17
DN14
DN8
DN7
DN9
DN3
DN2
DN1
DN4
DN10
DN11
DN12
DN5
DN6
WF8
WF9
WF4
HD8
HD9
SK13
S36
S33
S32
S6
S75
S71
S72
S73
S70
S74
S63
S64
S62
S61
S65
S66
S60
S35
S1
S2
S3
S4
S5
S7
S8
S9
S10
S11
S12
S13
S14
S17
S18
S20
S21
S25
S26
S43
S80
S1

Moorends
Thorne
Hatfield
Stainforth
Barnby Dun
Armthorpe
Finningley
Bawtry
Norton
Skellow
Adwick le Street
Bentley
Doncaster
Balby
Wadworth
Tickhill
Conisbrough
Maltby
Dinnington
Woodsetts
Mexborough
Thurcroft
Harthill
Swinton
Wath upon Dearne
Dearne
Rawmarsh
Rotherham
Wales
Aston
Woodhouse
Treeton
Hemsworth
Dearne
Darfield
Shafton
Cudworth
Royston
Barnsley
Worsbrough
Hoyland
Kexbrough
Dodworth
Penistone
Stockbridge
Bradfield
Oughtibridge
Chapeltown
Ecclesfield
Greenland
Sheffield
Birley
Greenhill
Fulwood
Whirlow
Totley
Halfway
Eckington
Dronfield

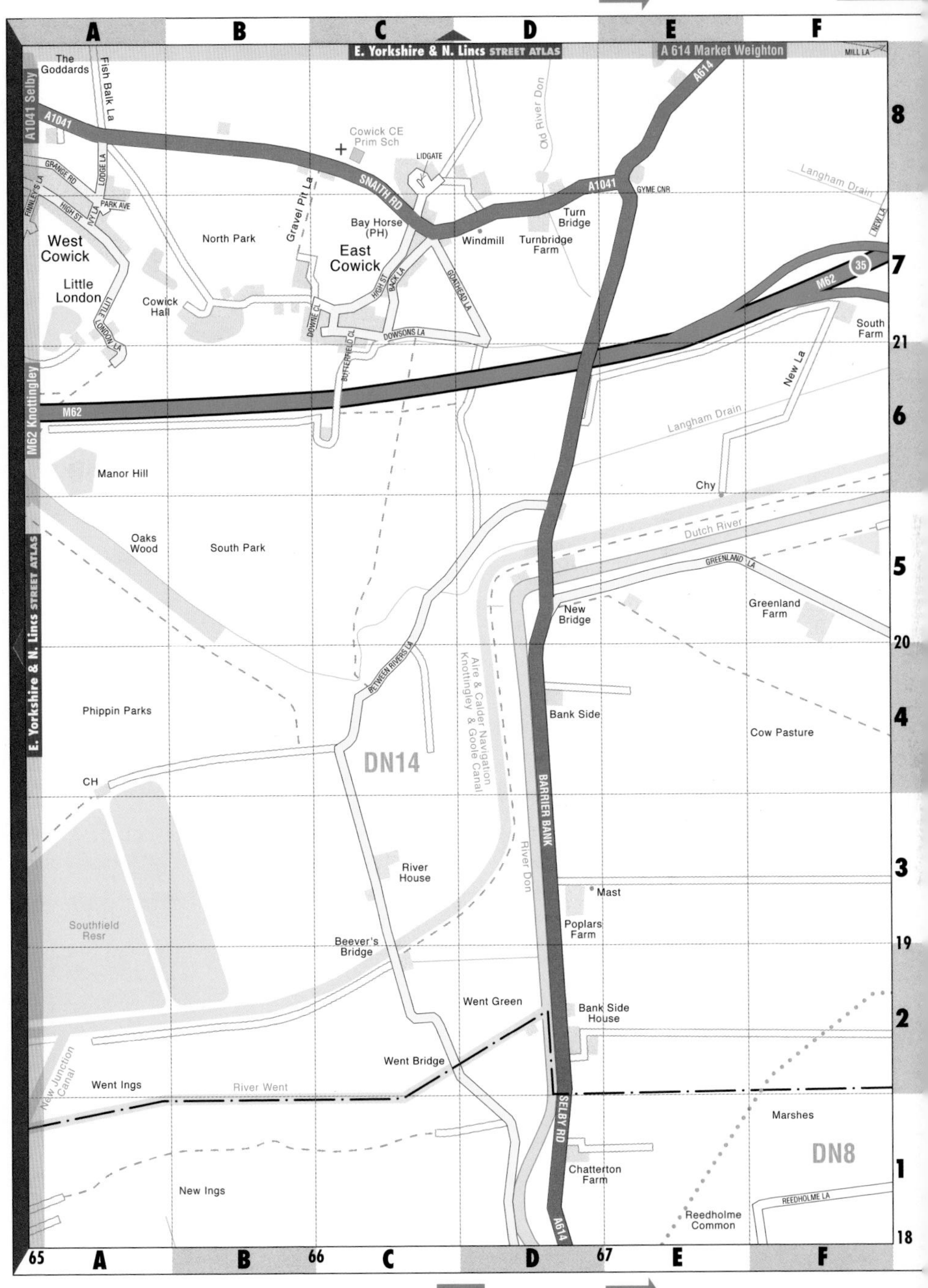

E. Yorkshire & N. Lincs STREET ATLAS

A 614 Market Weighton
MILL LA

A **B** **C** **D** **E** **F**

8

The Goddards

Fish Balk La

A1041 Selby

A1041

Cowick CE
Prim Sch

LIDGATE

SNAITH RD

Turn
Bridge

A1041

GYME CNR

Langham Drain

FINKLE'S LA

GRANGE RD

HIGH ST

PARK AVE

YI PROT

West
Cowick

North Park

Gravel Pit La

Bay Horse
(PH)

East
Cowick

Windmill

Turnbridge
Farm

7

M62

35

Little
London

Cowick
Hall

DOWNE CL

DOWSONS LA

HIGH ST

JACK LA

DONCAS LA

LITTLE JACK LA

M62 Knottingley

M62

South
Farm

New La

21

Manor Hill

BUTTERFIELD CL

Langham Drain

Chy

6

Oaks
Wood

South Park

Dutch River

GREENLAND LA

5

New
Bridge

Greenland
Farm

E. Yorkshire & N. Lincs STREET ATLAS

20

Phippin Parks

BETWEEN RIVERS LA

DN14

Bank Side

Cow Pasture

4

CH

Aire & Calder Navigation
Knottingley & Goole Canal

River Don

BARRIER BANK

River
House

Mast

3

Poplars
Farm

Southfield
Resr

Beever's
Bridge

19

Went Green

Bank Side
House

2

Went Bridge

New Junction Canal

Went Ings

River Went

SELBY RD

Marshes

DN8

New Ings

Chatterton
Farm

A614

Reedholme
Common

REEDHOLME LA

1

65 **A** **B** **66** **C** **D** **67** **E** **F**

18

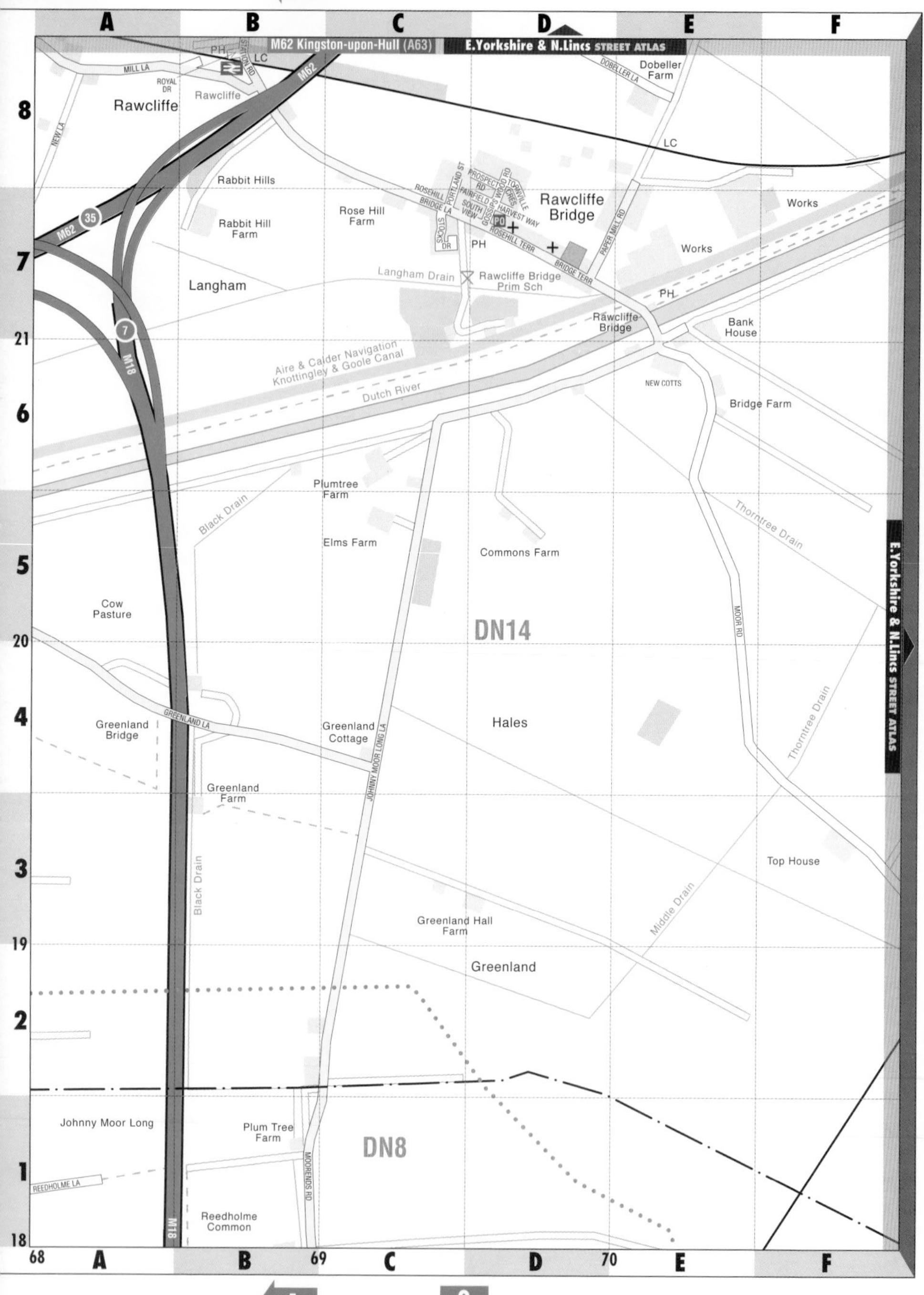

M62 Kingston-upon-Hull (A63)

E.Yorkshire & N.Lincs STREET ATLAS

E.Yorkshire & N.Lincs STREET ATLAS

MILL LA
ROYAL DR
PH
LC
Rawcliffe
Rawcliffe
PENNY LA
PICKHILL

8

M62

Dobeller Farm
DOBELLER LA
LC

Rabbit Hills

Rose Hill Farm

ROSEHILL RD
PROSPECT ST
PORTING ST
PARNELL ST
SOUTH ST
STOCKS DR
BRIDLE LA
LA VIDA
HARVEST WAY
ROSEHILL TERR

Rawcliffe Bridge

Works

Rabbit Hill Farm

35

7

M62

Langham

PH

PAPER MILL RD

Works

BRIDLE TERR

Langham Drain

Rawcliffe Bridge Prim Sch

PH

21

7

M18

Aire & Calder Navigation
Knottingley & Goole Canal

Rawcliffe Bridge

Bank House

Dutch River

NEW COTTS

Bridge Farm

6

Black Drain

Plumtree Farm

Thorntree Drain

Elms Farm

Commons Farm

MOOR RD

5

Cow Pasture

DN14

Thorntree Drain

20

4

Greenland Bridge

GREENLAND LA

Greenland Cottage

JOHNNY MOOR LONG LA

Hales

Greenland Farm

Top House

3

Black Drain

Greenland Hall Farm

Middle Drain

19

Greenland

2

1

Johnny Moor Long

Plum Tree Farm

MOORENDS RD

DN8

M18

REEDHOLME LA

Reedholme Common

18

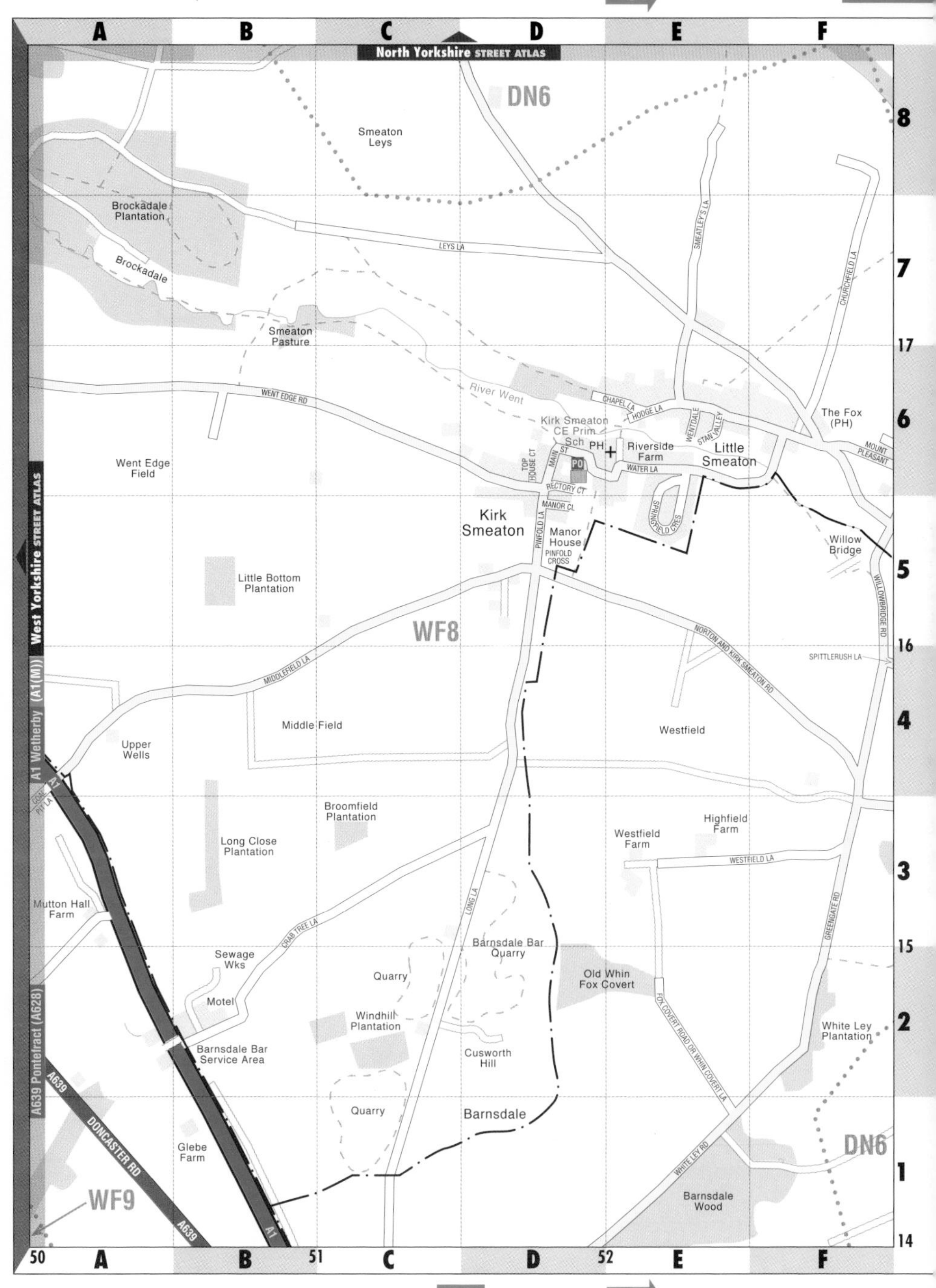

North Yorkshire STREET ATLAS

West Yorkshire STREET ATLAS

DN6

Smeaton Leys

Brockadale Plantation

Brockadale

Smeaton Pasture

LEYS LA

WENT EDGE RD

River Went

SMEATLEY'S LA

CHURCHFIELD LA

8

7

17

Went Edge Field

CHAPEL LA

HODGE LA

WESTDALE

The Fox (PH)

6

Kirk Smeaton CE Prim Sch

PH

Riverside Farm

Little Smeaton

MOUNT PLEASANT

TOP HOUSE CT

MAIN ST

PO

WATER LA

DICKY SYKES LA

Kirk Smeaton

MANOR CL

RECTORY CT

Manor House

PINFOLD CROSS

PINFOLD LA

OLD RD

Willow Bridge

WILLOWBRIDGE RD

5

Little Bottom Plantation

WF8

MORTON AND KIRK SMEATON RD

SPITTLERUSH LA

16

MIDDLEFIELD LA

Middle Field

Westfield

4

Upper Wells

A1 Wetherby (A1(M))

GRANGE LA

PIT LA

Broomfield Plantation

LONG LA

Westfield Farm

Highfield Farm

GREENGATE RD

WESTFIELD LA

3

Mutton Hall Farm

A639 Pontefract (A628)

A638

Long Close Plantation

CRAB TREE LA

Sewage Wks

Motel

Barnsdale Bar Quarry

Quarry

Windhill Plantation

Cusworth Hill

Old Whin Fox Covert

FOX COVERT RD TO WHIN COVERT LA

15

White Ley Plantation

2

Barnsdale Bar Service Area

Glebe Farm

DONCASTER RD

A639

A1

Quarry

Barnsdale

WHITE LEY RD

DN6

Barnsdale Wood

1

WF9

14

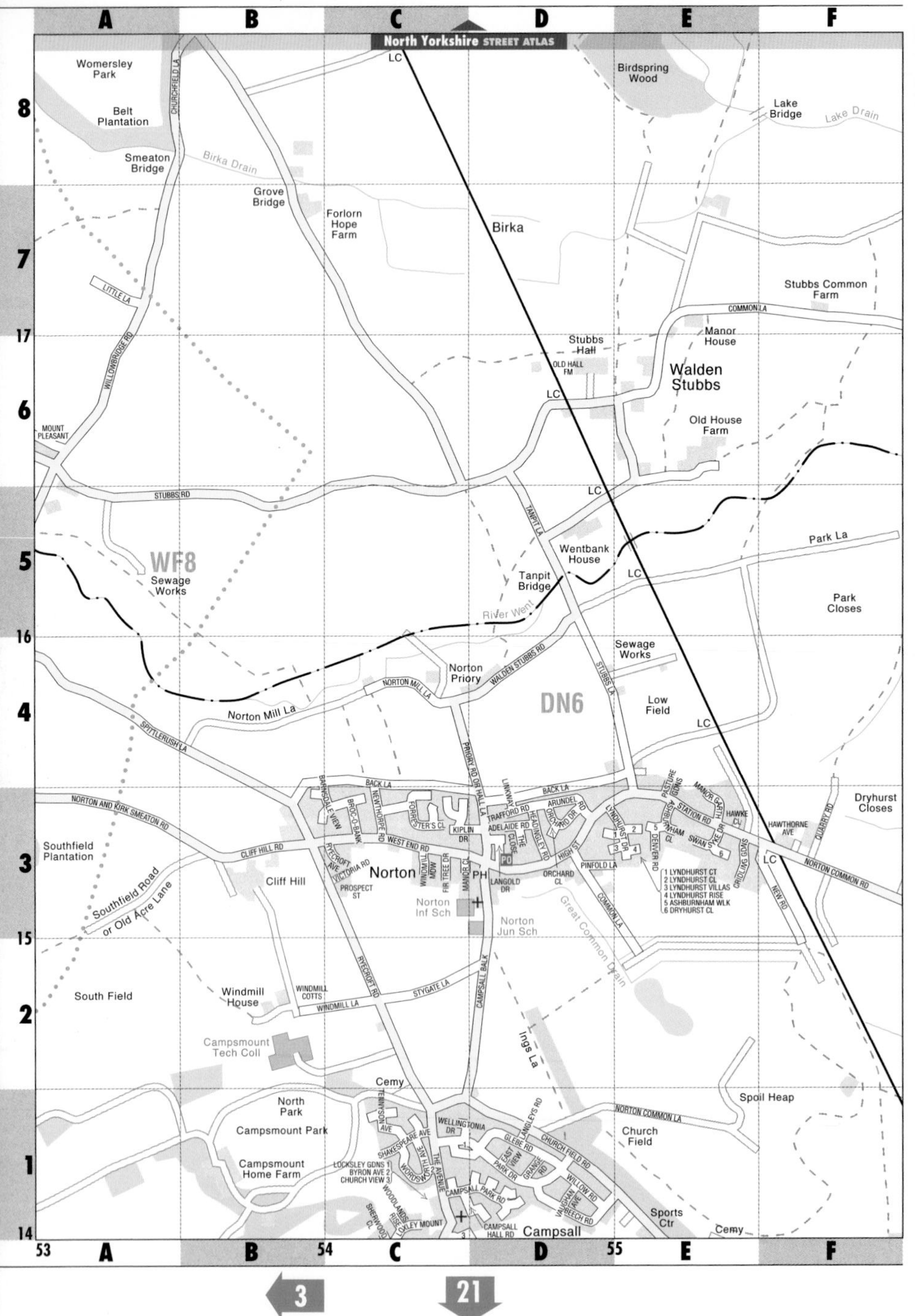

North Yorkshire STREET ATLAS

8

Womersley
Park

Belt
Plantation

Smeaton
Bridge

Birka Drain

Grove
Bridge

Forlorn
Hope
Farm

Birka

Birdspring
Wood

Lake
Bridge

Lake Drain

CHURCH LA

LC

7

LITTLE LA

WILLOWBROOK RD

Stubbs Common
Farm

COMMON LA

Manor
House

17

Stubbs
Hall

OLD HALL
FM

Walden
Stubbs

6

MOUNT
PLEASANT

LC

Old House
Farm

5

STUBBS RD

TANPIT LA

Wentbank
House

Tanpit
Bridge

LC

Park La

WF8

Sewage
Works

River Went

LC

Park
Closes

16

Norton
Priory

WALDEN STUBBS RD

NORTON MILL LA

Sewage
Works

4

SPITTLERUSH LA

Norton Mill La

PRIORY RD OR HALL LA

DN6

Low
Field

LC

3

NORTON AND YORK SMEATON RD

CLIFF HILL RD

BACK LA

NEW RD

BARNSDALE VIEW

FOSTER'S CL

WEST END RD

LINKWOOD DR

BACK LA

TRAFFORD CL

ADELAIDE RD

ARUNDEL

PICTURE RD

MANOR GARTH

STATION RD

HAWNE
CL

SHAM
CL

Dryhurst
Closes

Hawthorne
Ave

NORTON COMMON RD

KIPLIN
DR

FIR TREE DR

MANOR DR

LYNCHGATE RD

SILVER RD

STREAM DR

PINFOLD LA

DEVON DR

GROVE DR

SHAW RD

BELT RD

Southfield
Plantation

Southfield Road
or Old Acre Lane

Cliff Hill

FITZ CROFT

PROSPECT
ST

VICTORIA RD

WINDMILL AVE

ORCHARD
CL

LANGDALE
DR

COMMON LA

LC

1 LYNDHURST CT
2 LYNDHURST CL
3 LYNDHURST VILLAS
4 LYNDHURST RISE
5 ASHBURNHAM WLK
6 DRYHURST CL

15

South Field

Windmill
House

WINDMILL
COTTS

WINDMILL LA

RYECROFT RD

STYGATE LA

CAMPSALL BALK

Great Common Drain

Norton

PH

Norton
Inf Sch

Norton
Jun Sch

2

Campsmount
Tech Coll

Cemy

Ings La

Spoil Heap

1

North
Park

Campsmount Park

Campsmount
Home Farm

Cemy

WENSLEY AVE

SHAKESPEARE AVE

BYRON CT

WOODLAND VIEW

LOCKSLEY GDNS
BYRON AVE 2
CHURCH VIEW 3

LOCKSLEY MOUNT

WELLINGTONIA
DR

GLEBE RD

PARK DR

HANGLERS DR

CHURCH FIELD RD

WILLOW RD

CAMPSALL PARK RD

CAMPSALL
HALL RD

BEECH RD

NORTON COMMON LA

Church
Field

Sports
Ctr

Cemy

Campsall

14

53   **A**   **B**   54   **C**   **D**   55   **E**   **F**

6

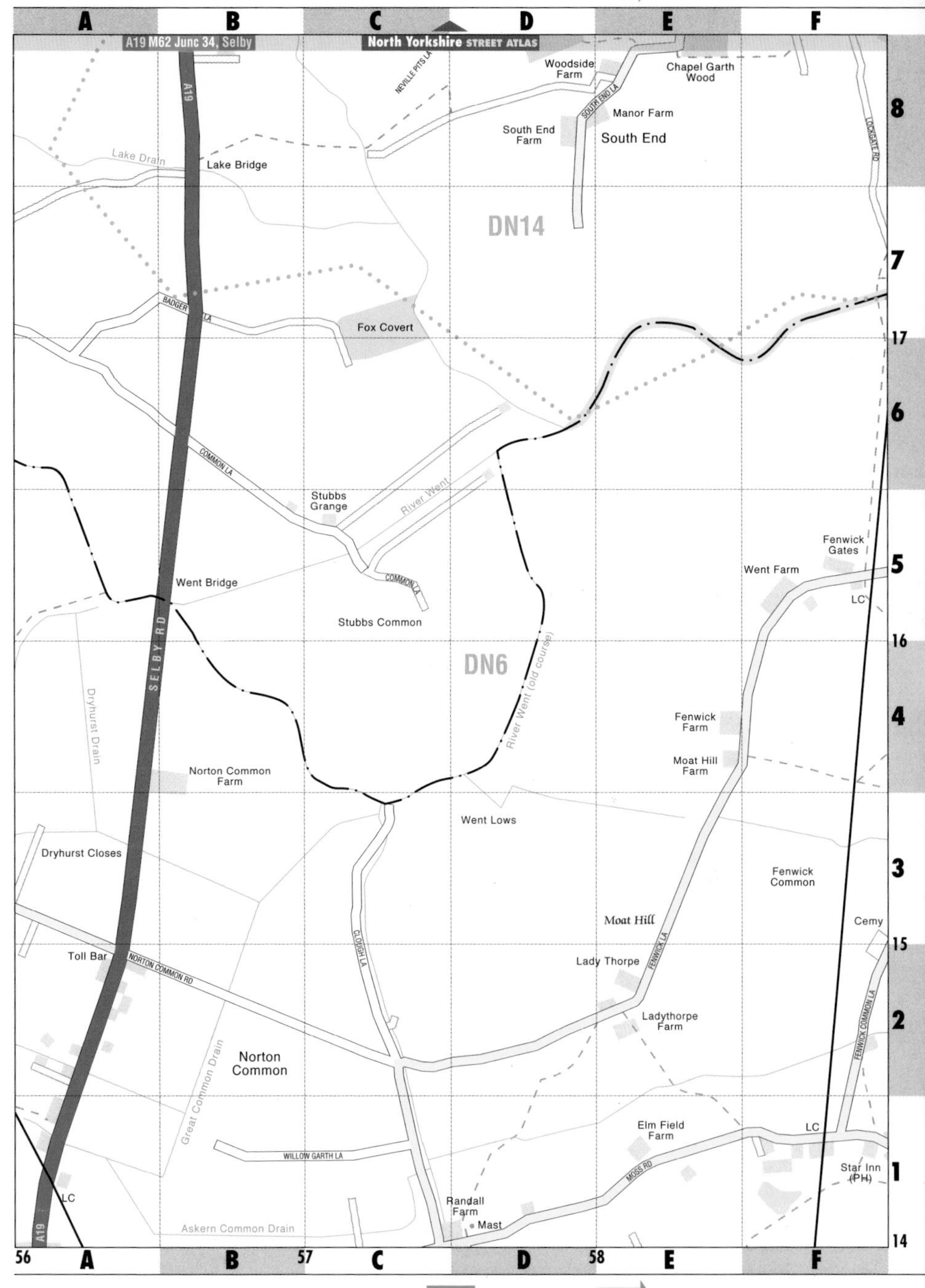

A
B
C
D
E
F
A19 M62 Junc 34, Selby
North Yorkshire STREET ATLAS
NEVILLE PITS LA
Woodside Farm
Chapel Garth Wood
SOUTH END LA
Manor Farm
South End Farm
South End
LOCKGATE RD
A19
Lake Drain
Lake Bridge
DN14
BADGER LA
Fox Covert
COMMON LA
Stubbs Grange
River Went
Went Bridge
COMMON LA
Stubbs Common
Fenwick Gates
Went Farm
LC
SELBY RD
DN6
River Went (old course)
Dryhurst Drain
Fenwick Farm
Moat Hill Farm
Norton Common Farm
Went Lows
Dryhurst Closes
Fenwick Common
Moat Hill
Cemy
CLOUGH LA
FENWICK LA
Toll Bar
NORTON COMMON RD
Lady Thorpe
Ladythorpe Farm
FENWICK COMMON LA
Great Common Drain
Norton Common
Elm Field Farm
LC
WILLOW GARTH LA
MOSS RD
Star Inn (PH)
LC
Randall Farm
Mast
Askern Common Drain
A19
8
7
17
6
5
16
4
3
15
2
1
14
56
57
58

22

6

5

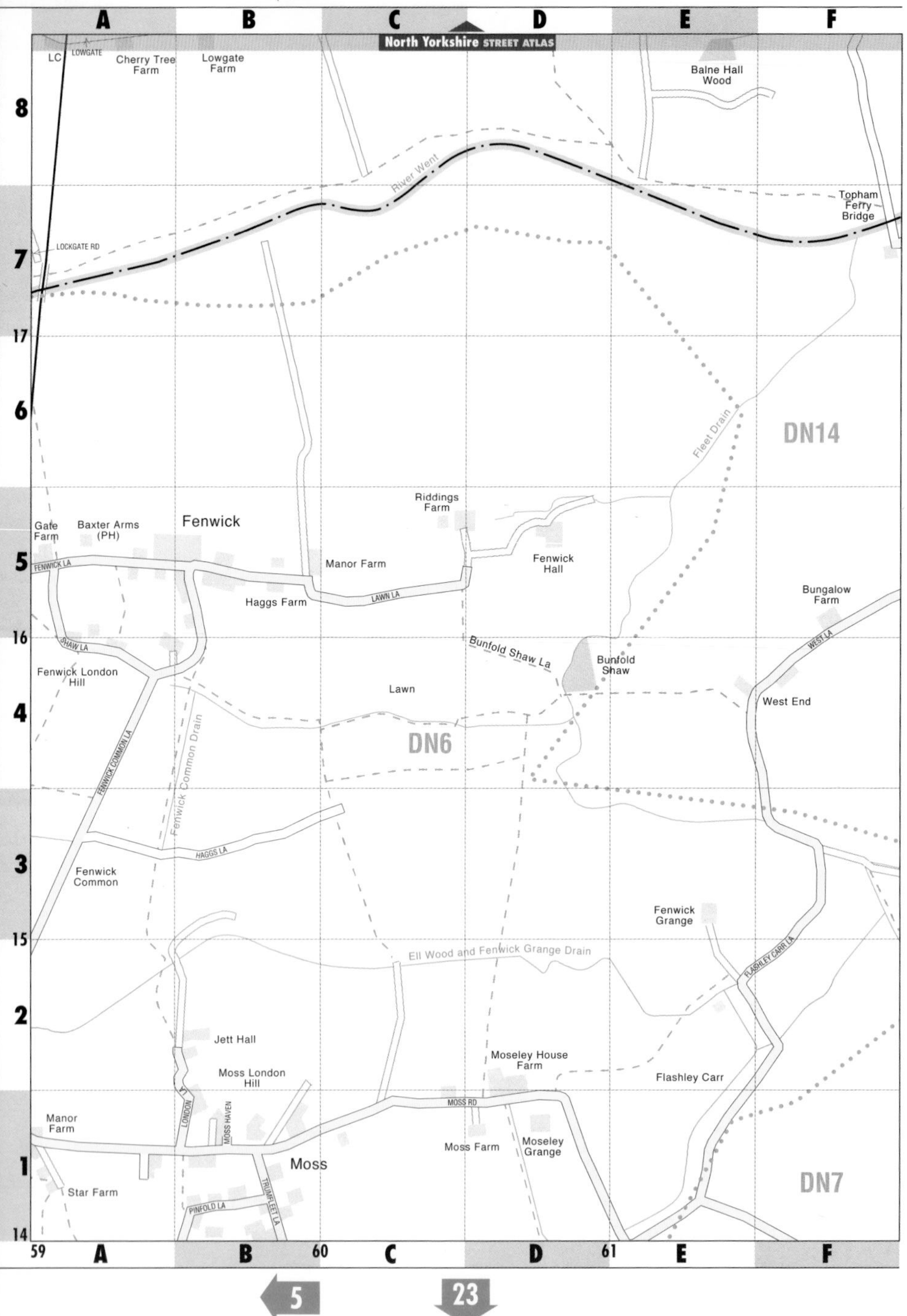

A
B
C
D
E
F
North Yorkshire STREET ATLAS
LC
LOWGATE
Cherry Tree Farm
Lowgate Farm
Balne Hall Wood
8
River Went
Topham Ferry Bridge
LOCKGATE RD
7
17
6
Fleet Drain
DN14
Riddings Farm
Gate Farm
Baxter Arms (PH)
Fenwick
Manor Farm
Fenwick Hall
5
FENWICK LA
Haggs Farm
LAWN LA
Bungalow Farm
16
SHAW LA
Bunfold Shaw La
Bunfold Shaw
WEST LA
Fenwick London Hill
Lawn
West End
4
FENWICK COMMON LA
Fenwick Common Drain
DN6
HAGGS LA
3
Fenwick Common
Fenwick Grange
15
Ell Wood and Fenwick Grange Drain
FLASHLEY CARR LA
2
Jett Hall
Moseley House Farm
Moss London Hill
Flashley Carr
MOSS RD
Manor Farm
LONDON
MOSS HAVEN
Moss Farm
Moseley Grange
1
Moss
DN7
Star Farm
TRUMFLEET LA
PINFOLD LA
14
59
60
61

5
23

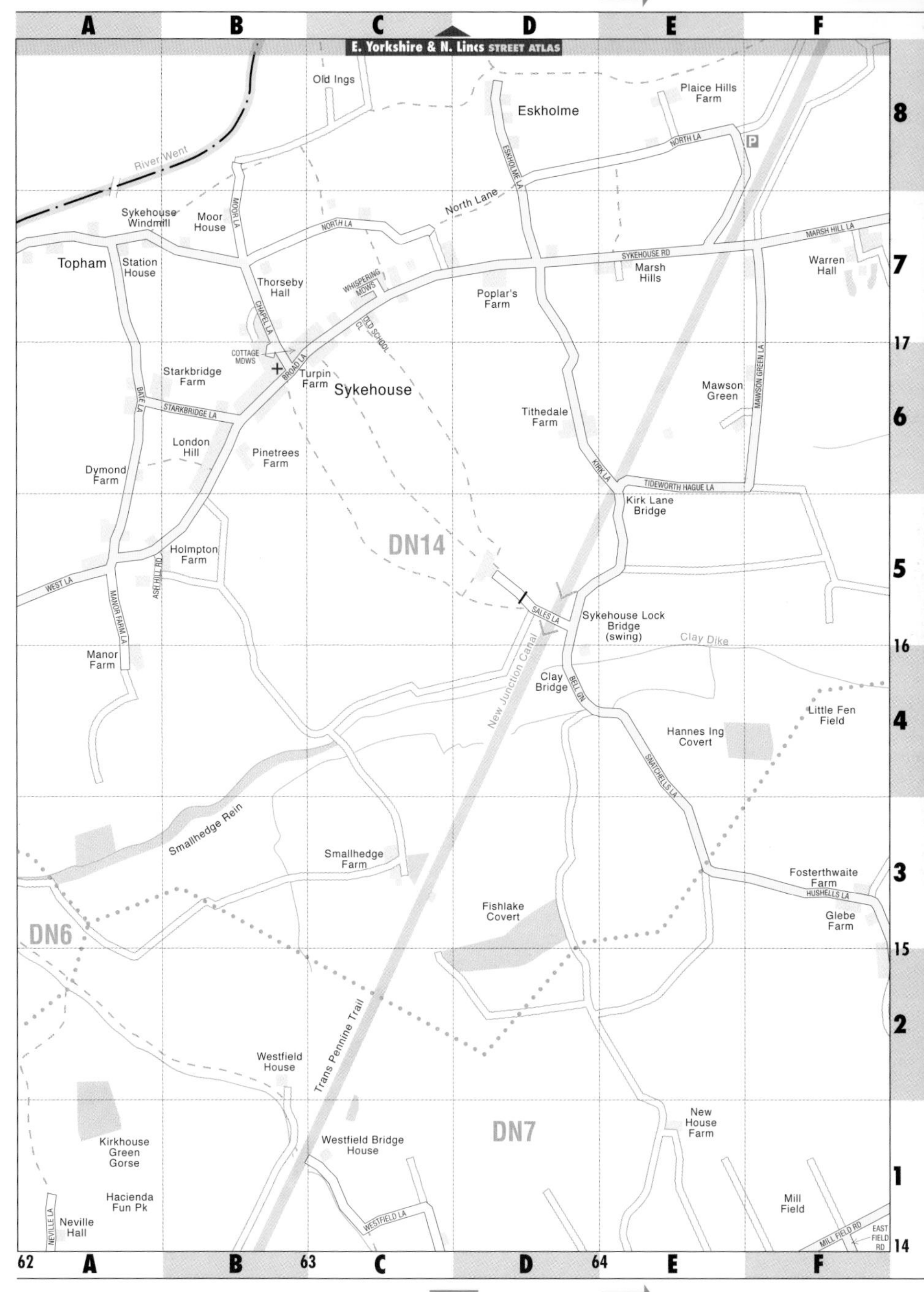

E. Yorkshire & N. Lincs STREET ATLAS

Old Ings

River Went

Eskholme

Plaice Hills Farm

NORTH LA

P

Sykehouse Windmill

Moor House

North Lane

MOOR LA

North Lane

NORTH LA

SYKEHOUSE RD

MARSH HILL LA

Topham

Station House

Thorseby Hall

WHISPERING MEWS

OLD SCHOOL

Poplar's Farm

Marsh Hills

Warren Hall

CHAPEL LA

COTTAGE MDWS

Turpin Farm

Sykehouse

Starkbridge Farm

BRIDGE LA

STARKBRIDGE LA

Tithedale Farm

Mawson Green

MAWSON GREEN LA

Dymond Farm

London Hill

Pinetrees Farm

BALK LA

Kirk Lane Bridge

KIRK LA

TIDEWORTH HAGUE LA

DN14

Holmpton Farm

ASK THE KEY

WEST LA

MANOR FARM LA

SALES LA

Sykehouse Lock Bridge (swing)

Clay Dike

Manor Farm

New Junction Canal

Clay Bridge

BELL DIKE

Little Fen Field

Smallhedge Rein

Hannes Ing Covert

SMITHELLS LA

Fosterthwaite Farm

HUSHELLS LA

DN6

Smallhedge Farm

Fishlake Covert

Glebe Farm

Trans Pennine Trail

Westfield House

DN7

New House Farm

Kirkhouse Green Gorse

Westfield Bridge House

Mill Field

Hacienda Fun Pk

WESTFIELD LA

MILL FIELD RD

EAST FIELD RD

NEVILLE LA

Neville Hall

8

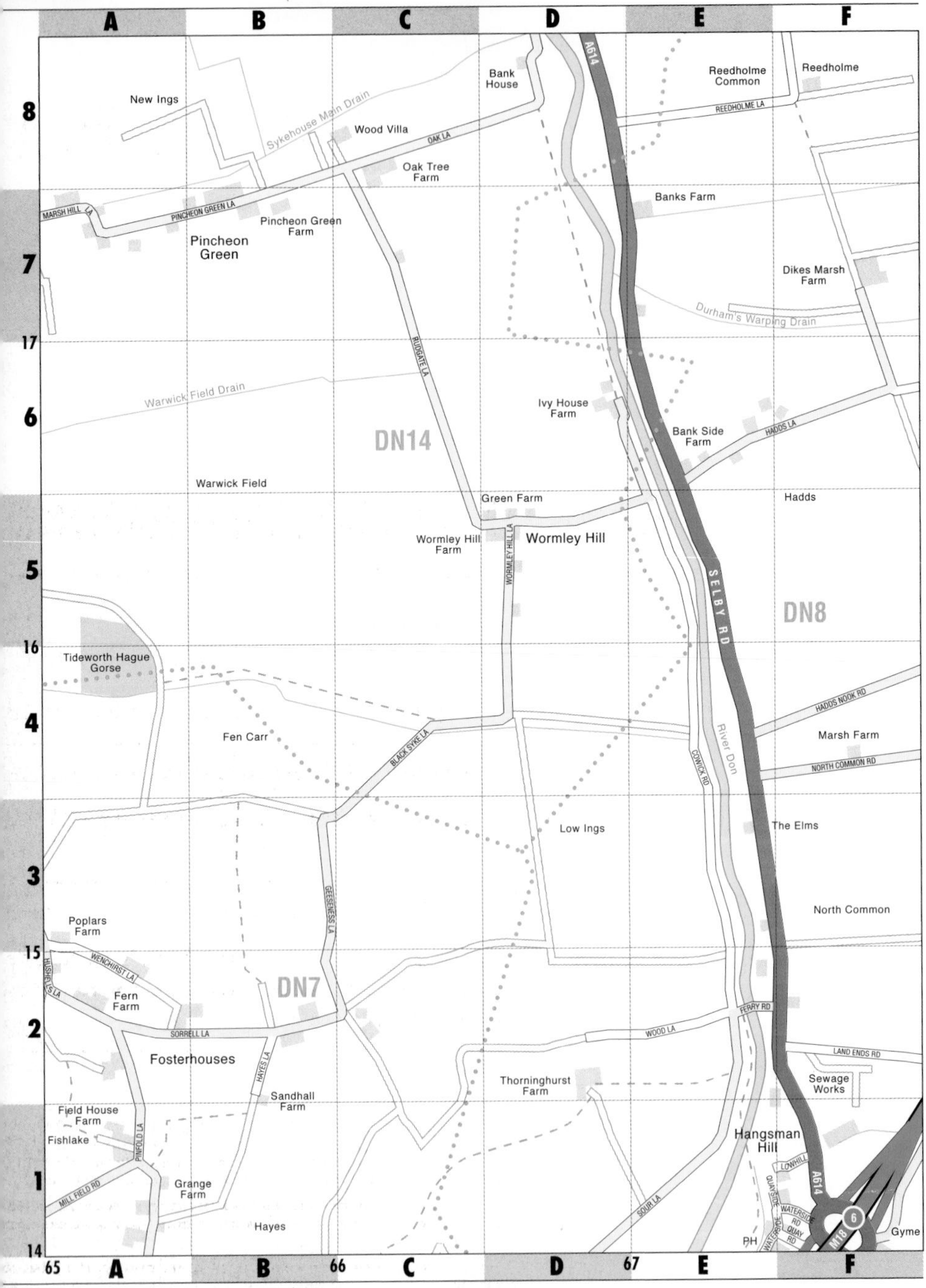

A B C D E F

New Ings

Bank House

Sykehouse Main Drain

Wood Villa Oak LA

Oak Tree Farm

Reedholme Common Reedholme

REEDHOLME LA

MARSH HILL

PINCHEON GREEN LA

Pincheon Green Farm

Pincheon Green

Banks Farm

Dikes Marsh Farm

7

17

Durham's Warping Drain

Warwick Field Drain

DN14

Ivy House Farm

Bank Side Farm HADDS LA

6

Warwick Field

Green Farm

Wormley Hill Farm

Wormley Hill

Hadds

SELBY RD

5

WORMLEY HILL LA

DN8

16

Tideworth Hague Gorse

River Don

Fen Carr

BLACK SYKE LA

HADDS NOOK RD

Marsh Farm

NORTH COMMON RD

4

DANY'S RD

Low Ings

The Elms

3

GREENESS LA

North Common

Poplars Farm

15

WENCHURST LA

DN7

Fern Farm

HARNELS LA

SORRELL LA

HAYES LA

Fosterhouses

WOOD LA

FERRY RD

LAND ENDS RD

2

Thorninghurst Farm

Sewage Works

Field House Farm

Sandhall Farm

Hangsman Hill

Fishlake

PINFOLD LA

Grange Farm

MILL FIELD RD

Hayes

BOUR LA

LONHILL

DUAY'S RD

WATERSIDE RD

DUAY RD

A614

Gyme

PH

1

14

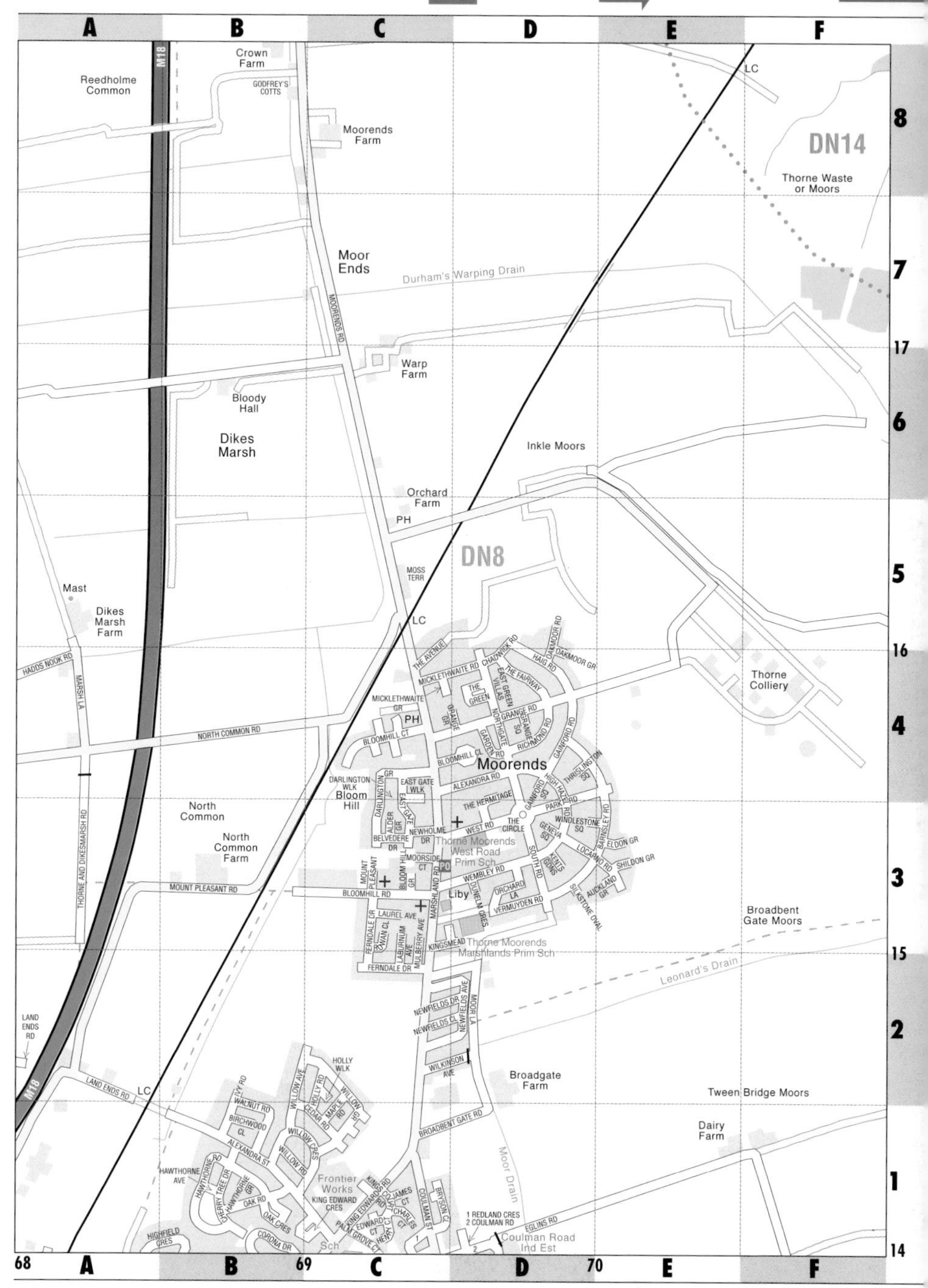

A   B   C   D   E   F

8

Reedholme
Common

Crown
Farm

GODFREY'S
COTTS

M18

DN14

Moorends
Farm

Thorne Waste
or Moors

Moor
Ends

7

Durham's Warping Drain

LC

17

Warp
Farm

Bloody
Hall

6

Dikes
Marsh

Inkle Moors

Orchard
Farm

PH

DN8

MOSS
TERR

5

Mast

Dikes
Marsh
Farm

LC

16

THE AVENUE
MICKLETHWAITE GR

CHADWICK RD

MOORENDS RD
EAST GREEN RD

GARMOOR GR
THE TAVERNA
HAIG RD

Thorne
Colliery

MICKLETHWAITE
GR

PH

THE
GREEN

GRANGE RD
GREEN RD
RICHMOND RD

4

BLOOMHILL RD

North Common Rd

DARLINGTON
Bloom
Hill

EAST GATE
WLK

ALEXANDRA RD

Moorends

THE HERMITAGE

PARK RD
THIRLWELL RD
WINDLESTONE

GEORGE LA
EDWARD ST
LOCKWOOD GR
ELDON GR

ELDON GR
SHELDON GR

North
Common

BELVEDERE
DR

NEWHOLME
DR

WEST RD

THE
CIRCLE

BUCKLAND GR
SILKSTONE OVAL

North
Common
Farm

Mount Pleasant Rd

MOUNT
PLEASANT
BLOOMHILL RD

MOORSIDE
CT

Thorne Moorends
West Road
Prim Sch

WEMBLEY RD
ORCHARD

VERMUYDEN RD

3

Broadbent
Gate Moors

FERNDALE DR
LAUREL AVE
LABURNUM AVE
ALDERBURY AVE

LAURAL CL

Libv

KINGSMEAD
FERNDALE DR

Thorne Moorends
Marshlands Prim Sch

MARSHLAND RD
MOOR RD

Leonard's Drain

15

NEWFIELDS DR
NEWFIELDS CL
WILKINSON
AVE

2

HAGGS HOOK RD

MARSH LA

THORNE AND DIKESMARSH RD

HOLLY
WLK

Broadgate
Farm

Tween Bridge Moors

LAND
ENDS
RD

Land Ends Rd

LC

WALNUT RD
BIRCHWOOD
CL

WILLOW WLK
WILLOW RD

WILLMOT CRES

Dairy
Farm

1

M18

HAWTHORNE
AVE

ALEXANDRA ST
DESERT TREE DR
OAK AVE

WILLOW RD
OAK CRES

Frontier
Works
KING EDWARD
CRES

BROADGATE GATE RD

Moor Drain

HIGHFIELD
DIKES

CORONA DR

JAMES
EDWARD

CHARLES
ST
WADE ST
BRIDGE

CLIFTON RD

1 REDLAND CRES
2 COULMAN RD

EGLINS RD

Coulman Road
Ind Est

14

68   A   B   69   C   D   70   E   F

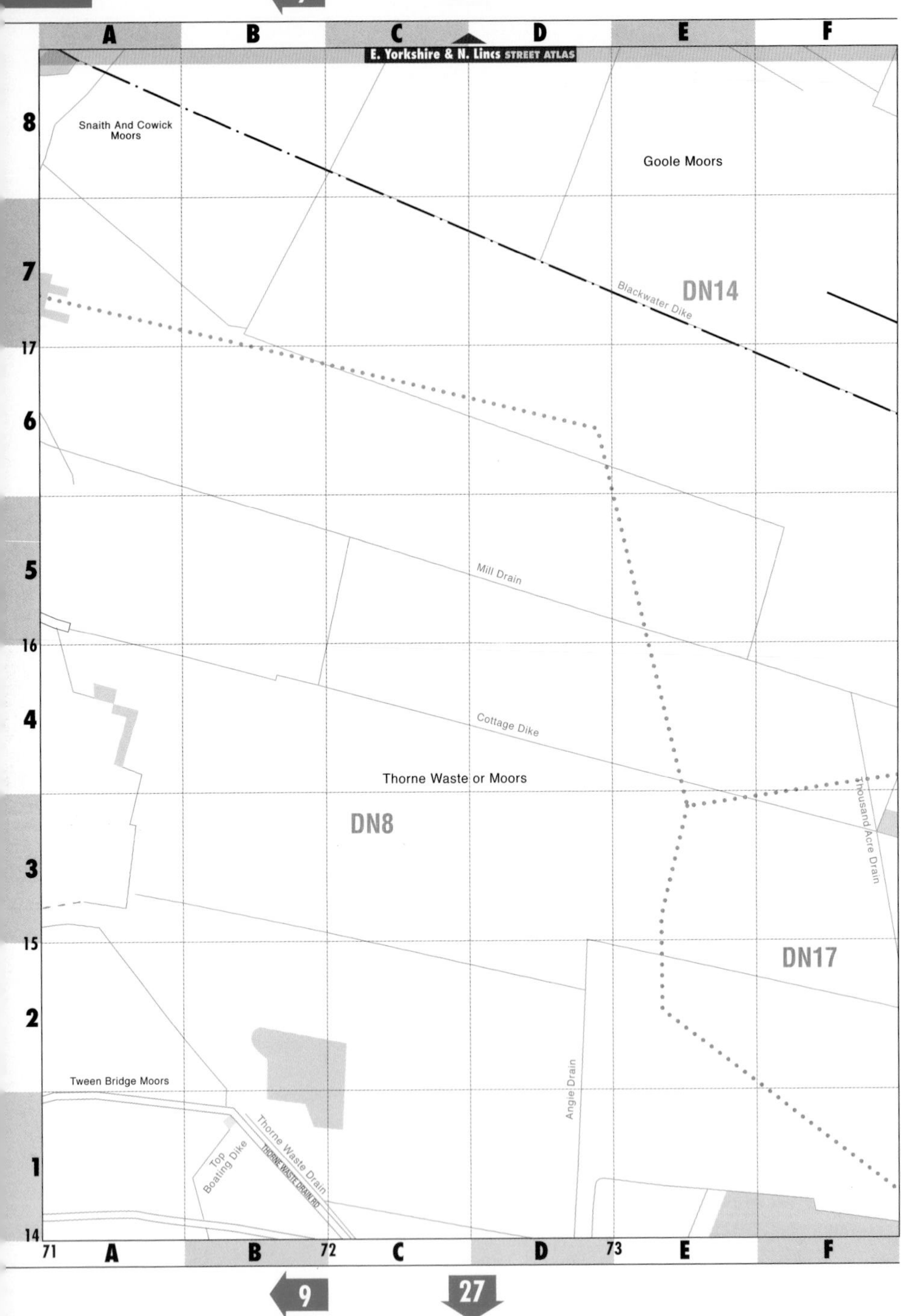

E. Yorkshire & N. Lincs STREET ATLAS

Snaith And Cowick Moors

Goole Moors

DN14

Blackwater Dike

Mill Drain

Cottage Dike

Thorne Waste or Moors

Thousand Acre Drain

DN8

DN17

Tween Bridge Moors

Angle Drain

Thorne Waste Drain

Top Boating Dike

THORNE WASTE DRAIN RD

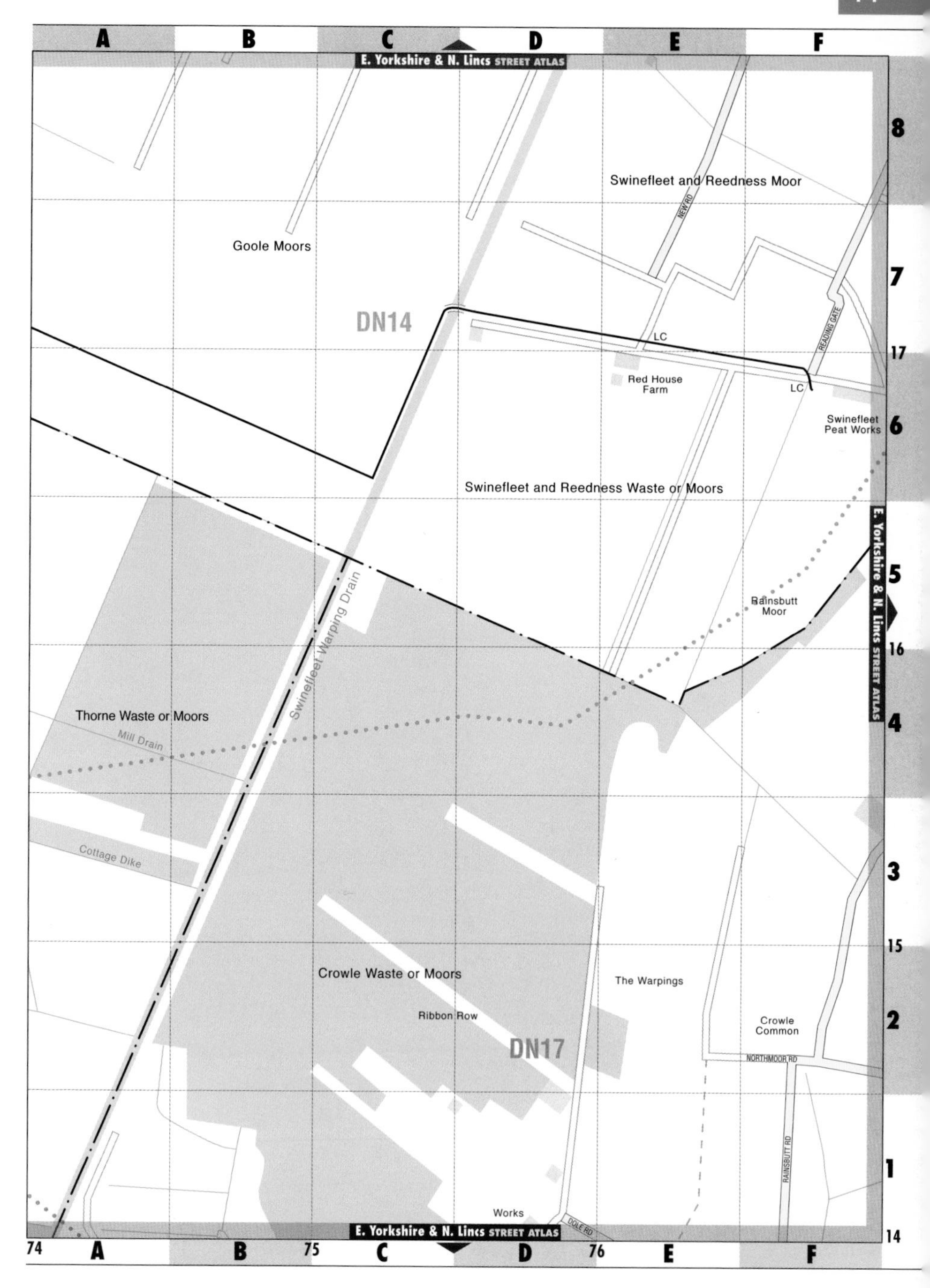

Swinefleet and Reedness Moor

Goole Moors

DN14

LC

Red House Farm

LC

Swinefleet Peat Works

Swinefleet and Reedness Waste or Moors

Rainsbutt Moor

Swinefleet Warping Drain

Thorne Waste or Moors

Mill Drain

Cottage Dike

Crowle Waste or Moors

The Warpings

Ribbon Row

Crowle Common

DN17

NORTHMOOR RD

RAINSBUTT RD

Works

GOOLE RD

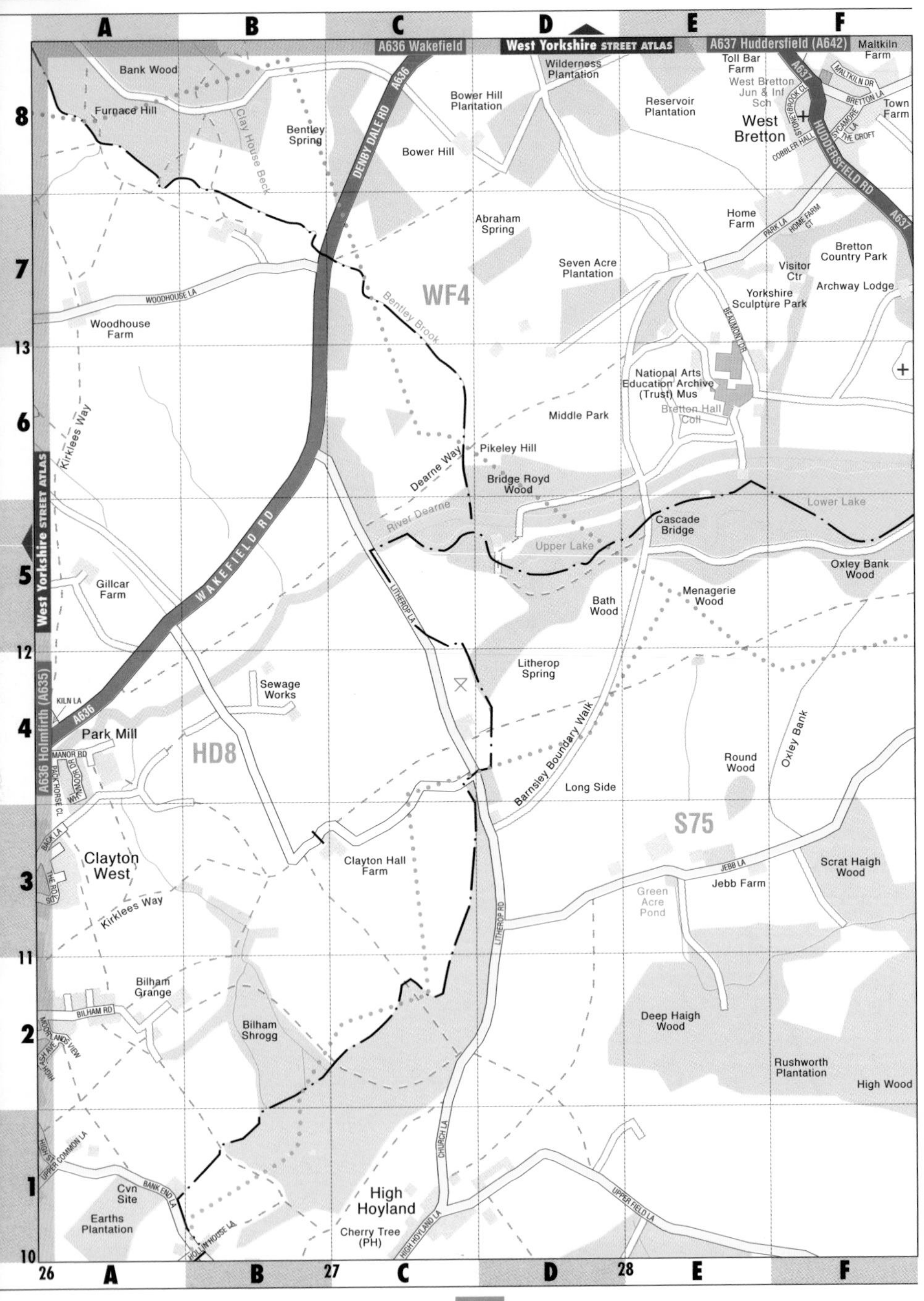
A636 Wakefield
West Yorkshire STREET ATLAS
A637 Huddersfield (A642)
Bank Wood
Furnace Hill
Clay House Beck
Bentley Spring
DENBY DALE RD
A636
Bower Hill Plantation
Bower Hill
Wilderness Plantation
Reservoir Plantation
Toll Bar Farm
West Bretton Jun & Inf Sch
West Bretton
Maltkiln Farm
Town Farm
HUDDERSFIELD RD
A637
Home Farm
Abraham Spring
Seven Acre Plantation
Bretton Country Park
Visitor Ctr
Archway Lodge
Yorkshire Sculpture Park
WF4
Bentley Brook
WOODHOUSE LA
Woodhouse Farm
National Arts Education Archive (Trust) Mus
Bretton Hall Coll
Middle Park
Kirklees Way
Pikeley Hill
Dearne Way
Bridge Royd Wood
River Dearne
Upper Lake
Cascade Bridge
Lower Lake
Oxley Bank Wood
Gillcar Farm
WAKEFIELD RD
LITHEROP LA
Bath Wood
Menagerie Wood
Litherop Spring
Sewage Works
A636 Holmfirth (A635)
KILN LA
Park Mill
HD8
Barnsley Boundary Walk
Oxley Bank
Round Wood
Long Side
S75
Clayton West
Clayton Hall Farm
JEBB LA
Jebb Farm
Scrat Haigh Wood
Green Acre Pond
Kirklees Way
LITHEROP RD
Bilham Grange
BILHAM RD
Bilham Shrogg
Deep Haigh Wood
Rushworth Plantation
High Wood
CHURCH LA
UPPER COMMON LA
Cvn Site
Earths Plantation
BANK END LA
High Hoyland
Cherry Tree (PH)
HIGH HOYLAND LA
UPPER FIELD LA
HOLLIN HOUSE LA
A B C D E F
8 7 13 6 5 12 4 3 11 2 1 10
26 27 28

31

14

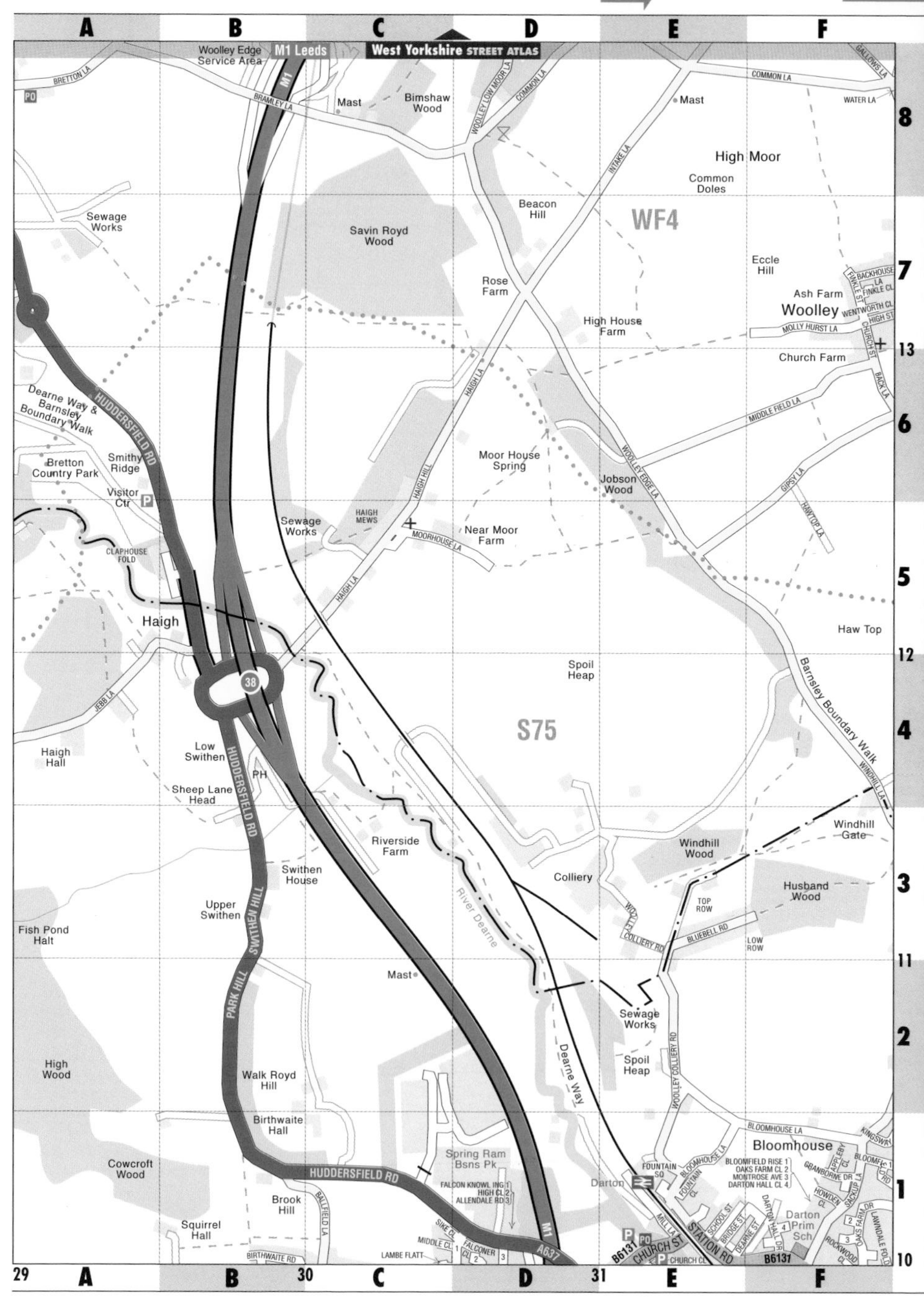

West Yorkshire STREET ATLAS
M1 Leeds
Woolley Edge Service Area
Bimshaw Wood
Mast
High Moor
Common Doles
Beacon Hill
WF4
Savin Royd Wood
Sewage Works
Rose Farm
Eccle Hill
Ash Farm
Woolley
High House Farm
Church Farm
Dearne Way & Barnsley Boundary Walk
Bretton Country Park
Smithy Ridge
Visitor Ctr
Moor House Spring
Jobson Wood
Sewage Works
Near Moor Farm
Haigh
Haw Top
Spoil Heap
S75
Haigh Hall
Low Swithen
Sheep Lane Head
PH
Riverside Farm
Windhill Wood
Windhill Gate
Swithen House
Colliery
Husband Wood
Upper Swithen
River Dearne
Fish Pond Halt
Mast
Sewage Works
Spoil Heap
Dearne Way
High Wood
Walk Royd Hill
Birthwaite Hall
Bloomhouse
Cowcroft Wood
Spring Ram Bsns Pk
Darton
Brook Hill
Squirrel Hall
Darton Prim Sch
HUDDERSFIELD RD
SWITHEN HILL
PARK HILL
HAIGH LA
HAIGH HILL
WOOLLEY EDGE LA
WOOLLEY COLLIERY RD
STATION RD
CHURCH ST
Barnsley Boundary Walk

32
14

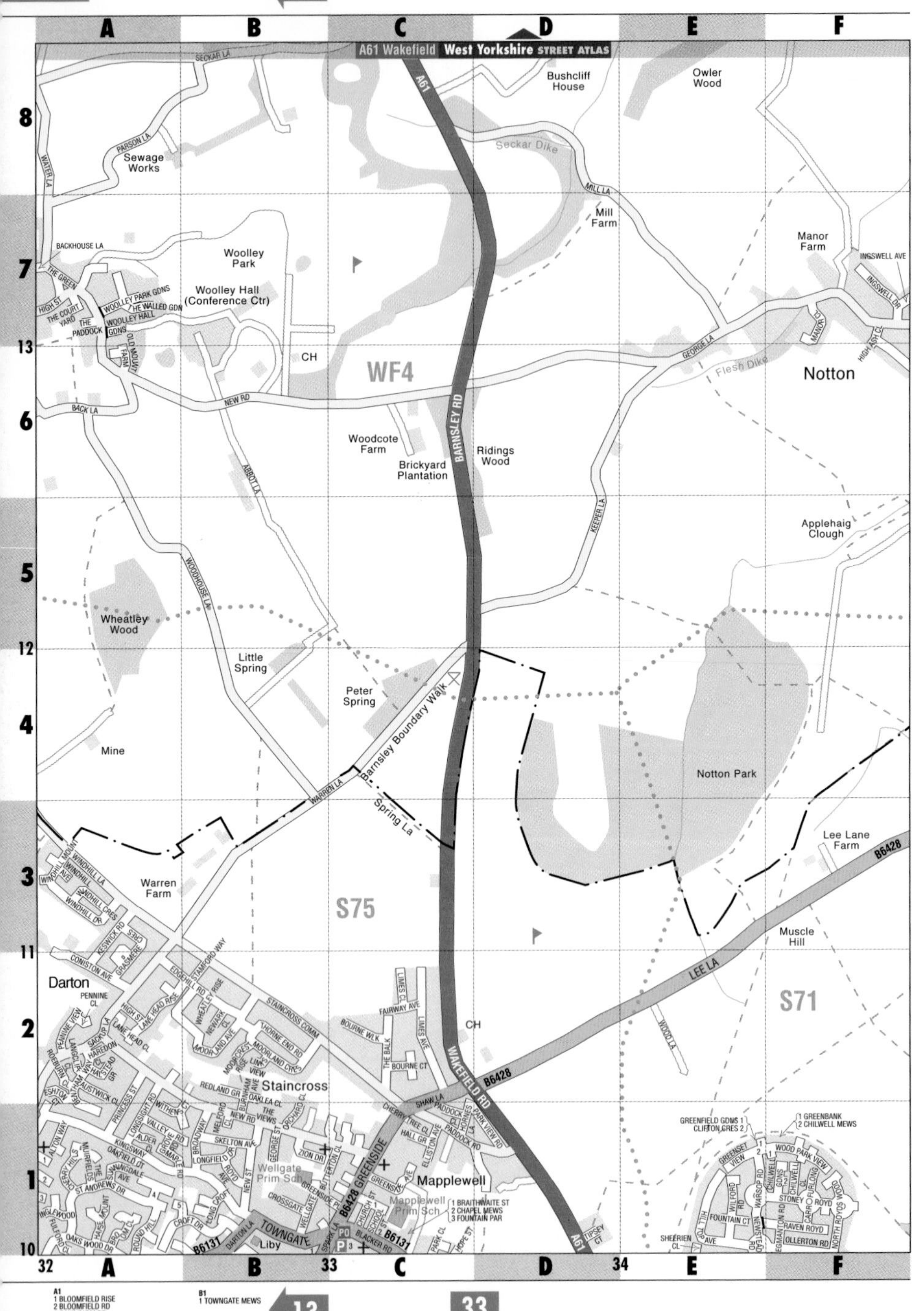

A1
1 BLOOMFIELD RISE
2 BLOOMFIELD RD
3 OAKS FARM DR
4 PRIEST ROYD
5 CROFT CL

B1
1 TOWNGATE MEWS

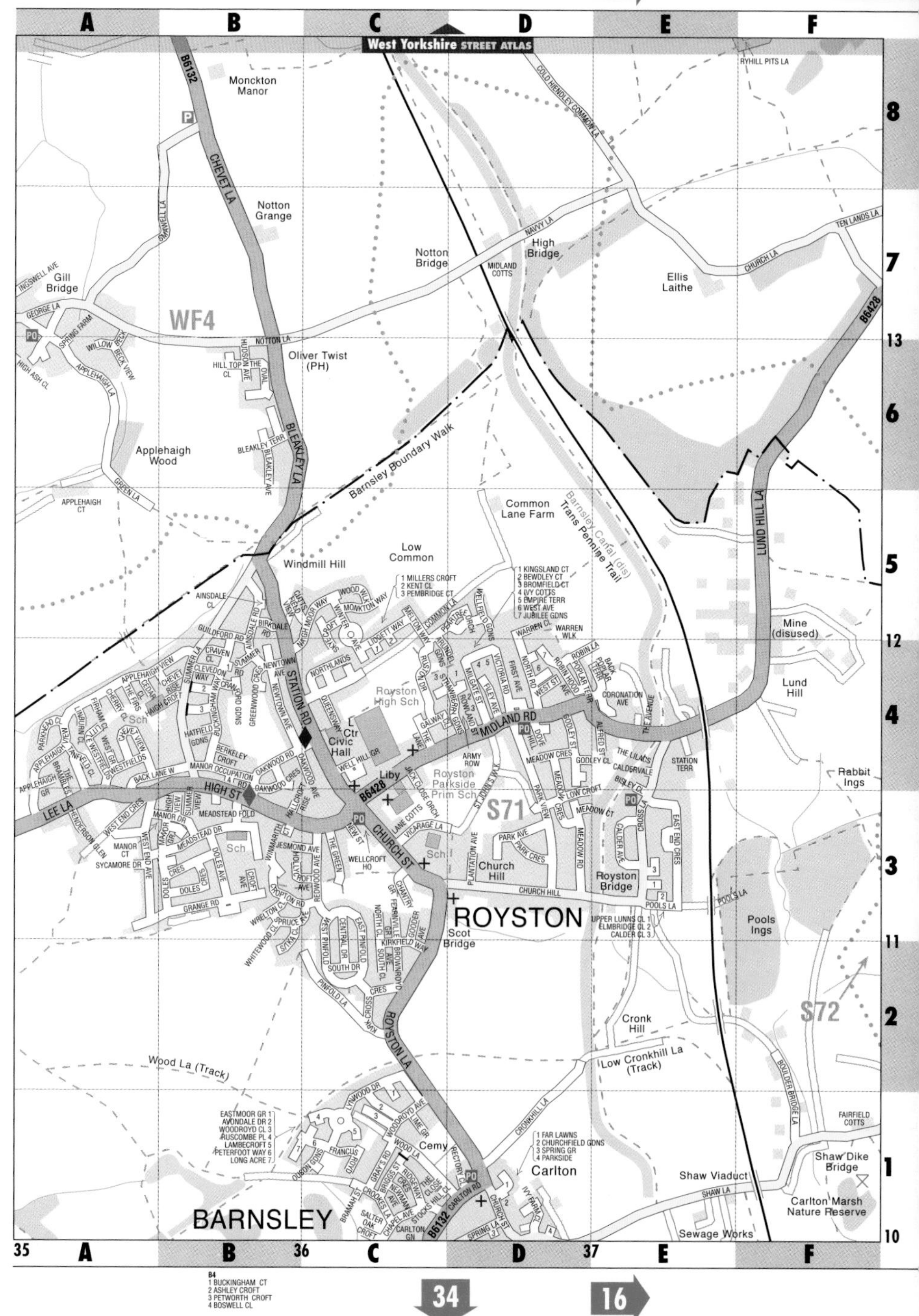
16
A
B
C
D
E
F
West Yorkshire STREET ATLAS
8
7
6
5
4
3
2
1
13
12
11
10
35
36
37
Moncton
Manor
Notton
Grange
Notton
Bridge
High
Bridge
Ellis
Laithe
Gill
Bridge
WF4
Oliver Twist
(PH)
Applehaigh
Wood
Barnsley Boundary Walk
Common
Lane Farm
Barnsley Canal (dis)
Trans Pennine Trail
Low
Common
Windmill Hill
Mine
(disused)
Lund
Hill
Royston
High Sch
Civic
Hall
Ctr
Liby
Royston
Parkside
Prim Sch
S71
Church
Hill
Royston
Bridge
ROYSTON
Scot
Bridge
Rabbit
Ings
Pools
Ings
S72
Cronk
Hill
Low Cronkhill La
(Track)
Wood La (Track)
Cemy
Carlton
Shaw Viaduct
Shaw Dike
Bridge
Carlton Marsh
Nature Reserve
Sewage Works
BARNSLEY
FAIRFIELD
COTTS
CHEVET LA
BLEAKLEY LA
STATION RD
HIGH ST
LEE LA
CHURCH ST
ROYSTON LA
MIDLAND RD
LUND HILL LA
NOTTON LA
NAVVY LA
CHURCH LA
TEN LANDS LA
COLD HIENDLEY COMMON LA
RYHILL PITS LA
CHURCH HILL
POOLS LA
SHAW LA
BOULDER BRIDGE LA
CRONKHILL LA
CARLTON RD
B6132
B6428
1 MILLERS CROFT
2 KENT CL
3 PEMBRIDGE CT
1 KINGSLAND CT
2 BEWDLEY CT
3 BROMFIELD CT
4 IVY COTTS
5 EMPIRE TERR
6 WEST AVE
7 JUBILEE GDNS
UPPER LUNNS CL 1
ELMBRIDGE CL 2
CALDER CL 3
EASTMOOR GR 1
AVONDALE DR 2
WOODROYD CL 3
RUSCOMBE PL 4
LAMBECROFT 5
PETERFOOT WAY 6
LONG ACRE 7
1 FAR LAWNS
2 CHURCHFIELD GDNS
3 SPRING GR
4 PARKSIDE
B4
1 BUCKINGHAM CT
2 ASHLEY CROFT
3 PETWORTH CROFT
4 BOSWELL CL
34
16

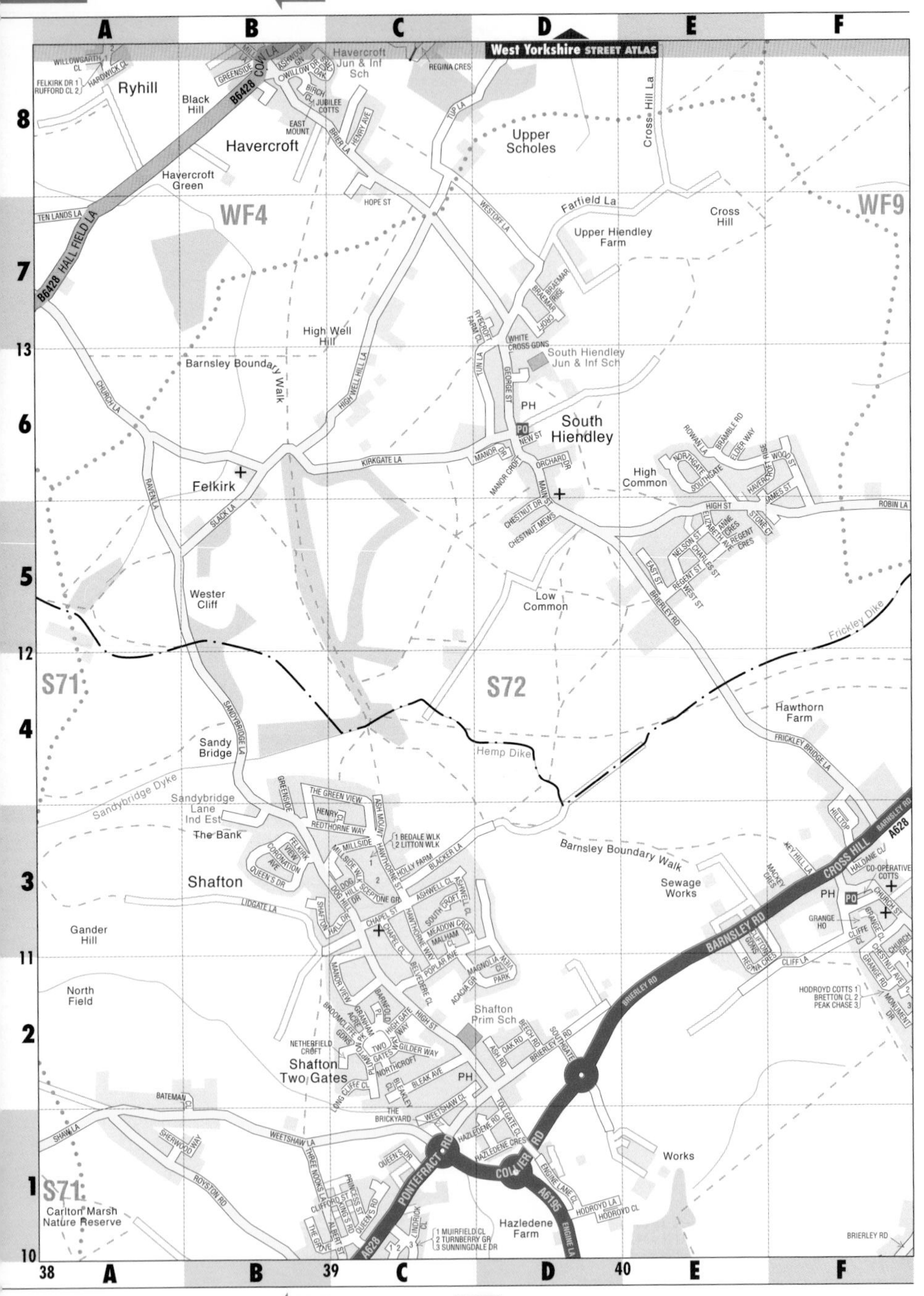

West Yorkshire STREET ATLAS

WF4

WF9

Ryhill

Black Hill

Havercroft

Havercroft Green

Upper Scholes

Farfield La

Upper Hiendley Farm

Cross Hill

High Well Hill

Barnsley Boundary Walk

White Cross Gdns

South Hiendley Jun & Inf Sch

South Hiendley

Felkirk

High Common

Wester Cliff

Low Common

Robin La

S71

S72

Hawthorn Farm

Sandy Bridge

Hemp Dike

Frickley Bridge La

Sandybridge Lane Ind Est

The Bank

Shafton

The Green View

Barnsley Boundary Walk

Sewage Works

A628

Gander Hill

North Field

Shafton Prim Sch

BARNSLEY RD

CROSS HILL

CO-OPERATIVE COTTS

GRANGE HO

HODROYD COTTS 1
BRETTON CL 2
PEAK CHASE 3

Shafton Two Gates

PH

THE BRICKYARD

BRIERLEY RD

Works

S71

Carlton Marsh Nature Reserve

PONTEFRACT RD

COLLIER RD

A628

Hazledene Farm

1 MUIRFIELD CL
2 TURNBERRY GR
3 SUNNINGDALE DR

BRIERLEY RD

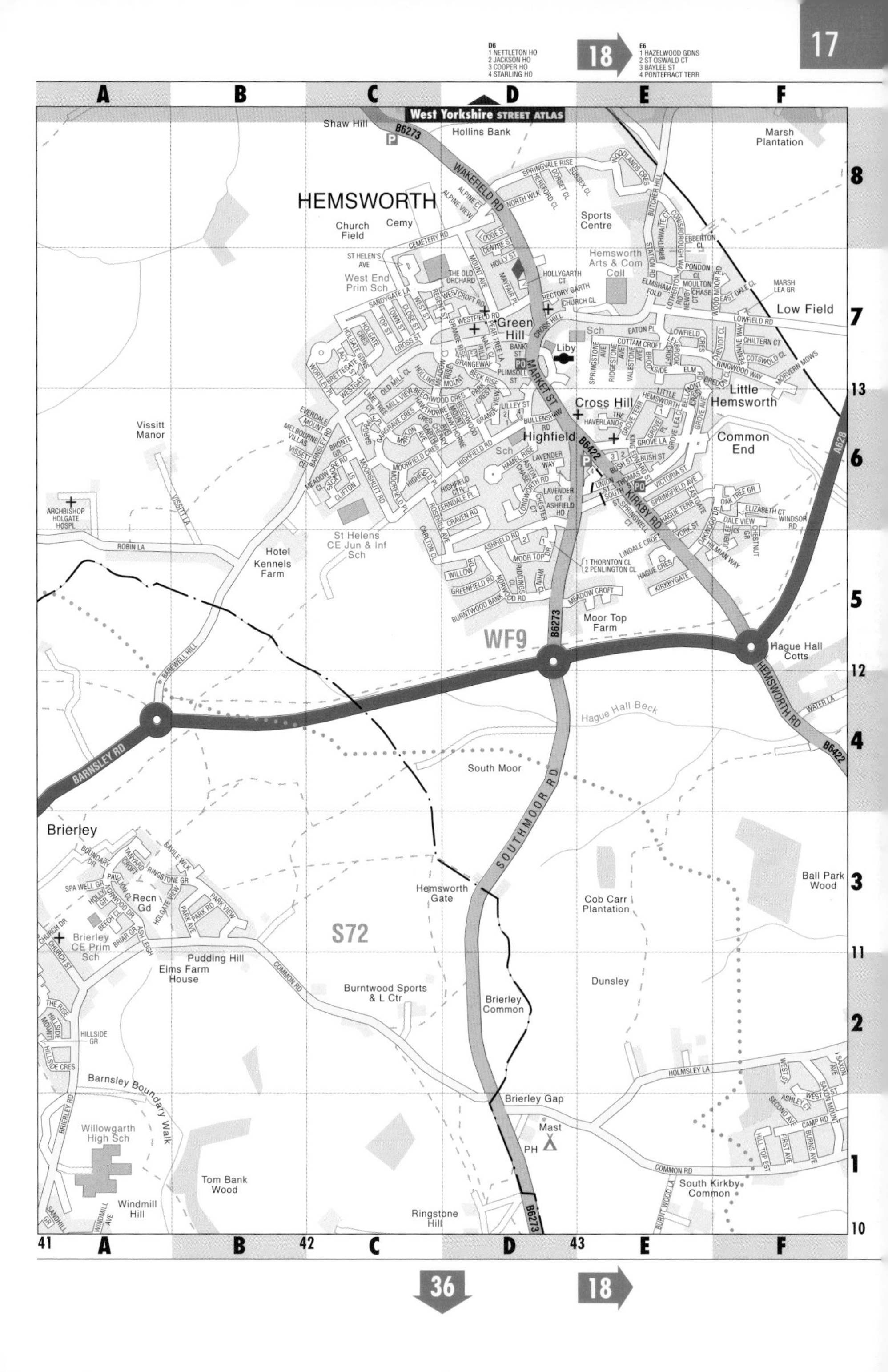
D6
1 NETTLETON HO
2 JACKSON HO
3 COOPER HO
4 STARLING HO
18
E6
1 HAZELWOOD GDNS
2 ST OSWALD CT
3 BAYLEE ST
4 PONTEFRACT TERR
West Yorkshire STREET ATLAS
A
B
C
D
E
F
8
7
13
6
5
12
4
3
11
2
1
10
41
42
43
Shaw Hill
Hollins Bank
Marsh Plantation
B6273
WAKEFIELD RD
HEMSWORTH
Church Field
Cemy
Sports Centre
Hemsworth Arts & Com Coll
West End Prim Sch
Green Hill
Sch
Liby
Low Field
Little Hemsworth
Cross Hill
Highfield
Common End
MARKET ST
B6422
KIRKBY RD
Vissitt Manor
ARCHBISHOP HOLGATE HOSPL
ROBIN LA
VISSITT LA
Hotel Kennels Farm
St Helens CE Jun & Inf Sch
1 THORNTON CL
2 PENLINGTON CL
Moor Top Farm
WF9
Hague Hall Cotts
HEMSWORTH RD
A628
BAREWELL HILL
BARNSLEY RD
Hague Hall Beck
WATER LA
B6422
South Moor
SOUTHMOOR RD
Brierley
Recn Gd
Brierley CE Prim Sch
Hemsworth Gate
S72
Cob Carr Plantation
Ball Park Wood
Pudding Hill
Elms Farm House
COMMON RD
Burntwood Sports & L Ctr
Dunsley
Brierley Common
HOLMSLEY LA
Barnsley Boundary Walk
Brierley Gap
Willowgarth High Sch
Mast
PH
COMMON RD
South Kirkby Common
Tom Bank Wood
Windmill Hill
Ringstone Hill
BRIERLEY RD
B6273
36
18

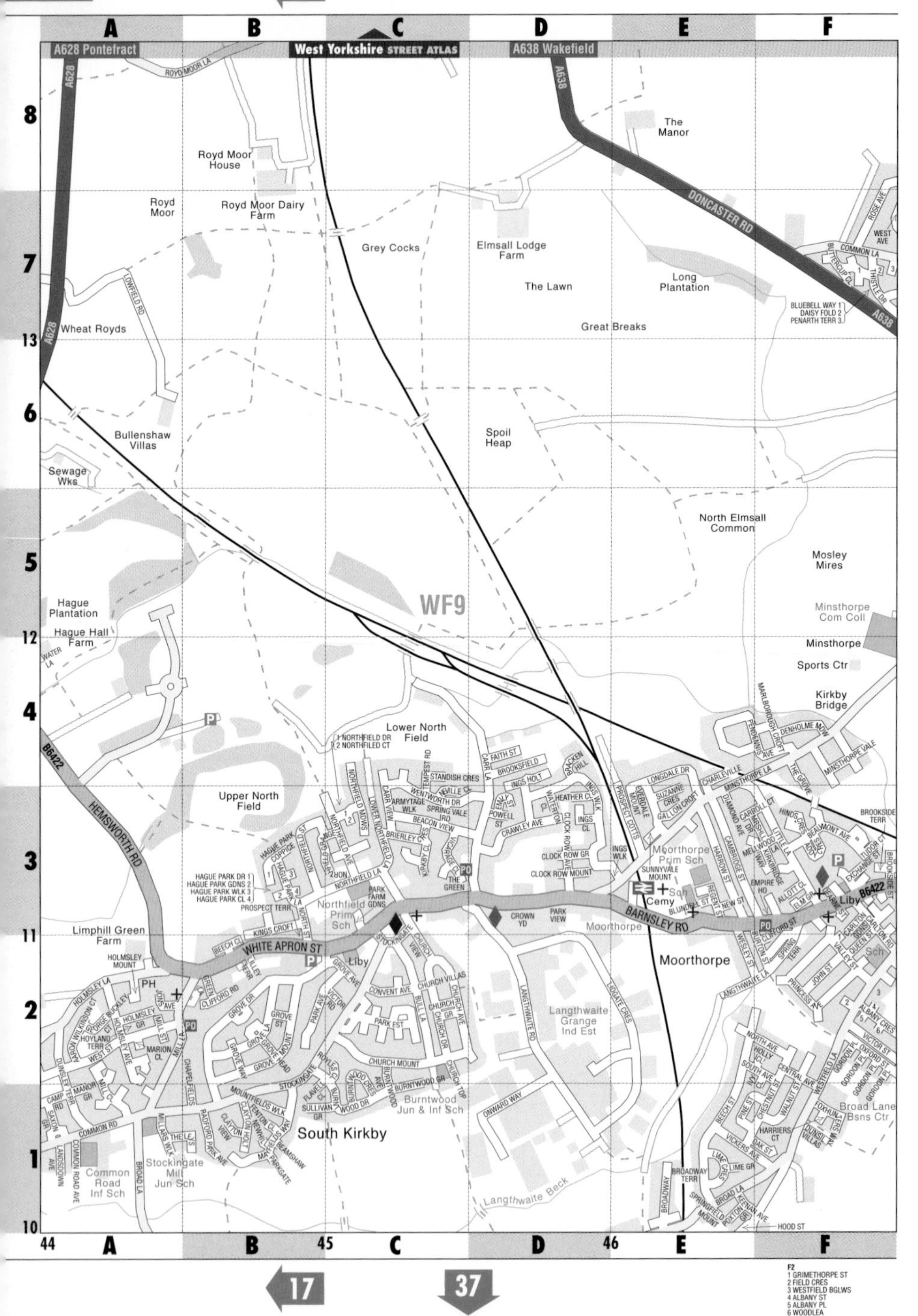

West Yorkshire STREET ATLAS

A628 Pontefract

A638 Wakefield

A **B** **C** **D** **E** **F**

8

7

13

6

5

12

4

3

11

2

1

10

Royd Moor House

Royd Moor

Royd Moor Dairy Farm

Grey Cocks

Elmsall Lodge Farm

The Lawn

Great Breaks

The Manor

DONCASTER RD

Long Plantation

WEST AVE

COMMON LA

BLUEBELL WAY 1
DAISY FOLD 2
PENARTH TERR 3

Wheat Royds

Bullenshaw Villas

Sewage Wks

Hague Plantation

Hague Hall Farm

Spoil Heap

North Elmsall Common

Mosley Mires

Minsthorpe Com Coll

Minsthorpe

Sports Ctr

Kirkby Bridge

WF9

Upper North Field

Lower North Field

1 NORTHFIELD DR
2 NORTHFIELD CT

Limphill Green Farm

Holmsley Mount

PH

Northfield Prim Sch

WHITE APRON ST

Liby

South Kirkby

Common Road Inf Sch

Stockingate Mill Jun Sch

Burntwood Jun & Inf Sch

HEMSWORTH RD

BARNSLEY RD

Moorthorpe

Moorthorpe Prim Sch

Cemy

Langthwaite Grange Ind Est

Langthwaite Beck

BROADWAY

HOOD ST

Broad Lane Bsns Ctr

Liby

Sch

F2
1 GRIMETHORPE ST
2 FIELD CRES
3 WESTFIELD BGLWS
4 ALBANY ST
5 ALBANY PL
6 WOODLEA

20

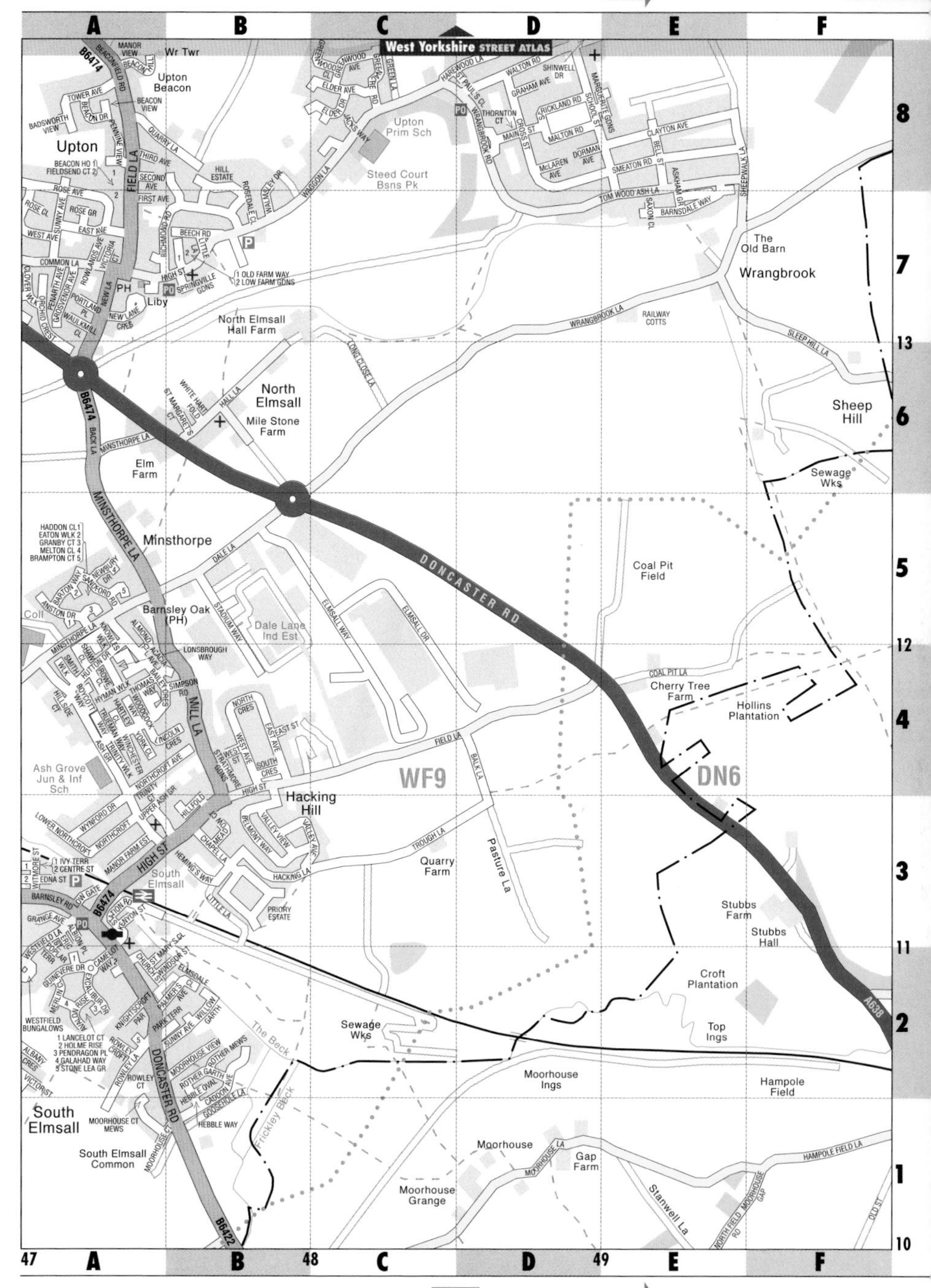
West Yorkshire STREET ATLAS
Upton
Upton Beacon
Wr Twr
Upton Prim Sch
Steed Court Bsns Pk
Hill Estate
The Old Barn
Wrangbrook
Railway Cotts
North Elmsall Hall Farm
North Elmsall
Mile Stone Farm
Elm Farm
Minsthorpe
Sheep Hill
Sewage Wks
Coal Pit Field
Barnsley Oak (PH)
Dale Lane Ind Est
Cherry Tree Farm
Hollins Plantation
Ash Grove Jun & Inf Sch
WF9
DN6
Hacking Hill
Quarry Farm
Pasture La
South Elmsall
Stubbs Farm
Stubbs Hall
Croft Plantation
Top Ings
Sewage Wks
The Beck
Frickley Beck
Moorhouse Ings
Hampole Field
South Elmsall
South Elmsall Common
Moorhouse
Gap Farm
Moorhouse Grange
Stanwell La
DONCASTER RD
FIELD LA
MINSTHORPE LA
MILL LA
HIGH ST
DONCASTER RD
WRANGBROOK LA
HAMPOLE FIELD LA
B6474
B6422
A638
A B C D E F
8 7 6 5 4 3 2 1
13 12 11 10
47 48 49

38
20

19
3

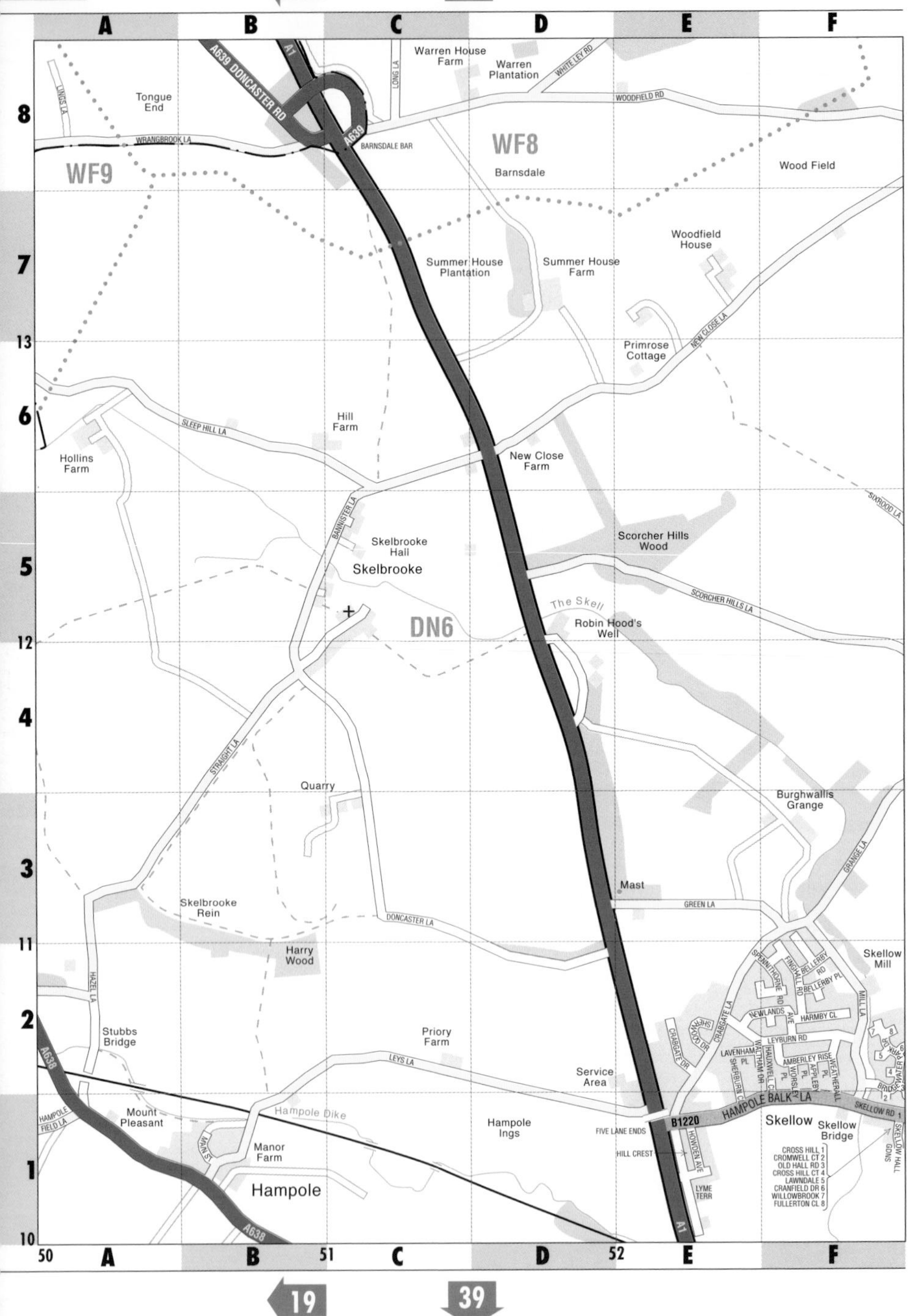
A
B
C
D
E
F
8
7
13
6
5
12
4
3
11
2
1
10
50
51
52
Warren House Farm
Warren Plantation
WHITE LEY RD
LONG LA
A1
A639 DONCASTER RD
Tongue End
LINGS LA
WOODFIELD RD
WRANGBROOK LA
A639
BARNSDALE BAR
WF8
WF9
Barnsdale
Wood Field
Woodfield House
Summer House Plantation
Summer House Farm
Primrose Cottage
NEW CLOSE LA
Hill Farm
SLEEP HILL LA
Hollins Farm
New Close Farm
SIXROOD LA
BANNISTER LA
Skelbrooke Hall
Skelbrooke
Scorcher Hills Wood
SCORCHER HILLS LA
The Skell
DN6
Robin Hood's Well
STRAIGHT LA
Quarry
Burghwallis Grange
GRANGE LA
Mast
GREEN LA
Skelbrooke Rein
DONCASTER LA
Harry Wood
Skellow Mill
HAZEL LA
MILL LA
Stubbs Bridge
Priory Farm
LEYS LA
Service Area
A638
HAMPOLE FIELD LA
Mount Pleasant
Hampole Dike
MAIN ST
Manor Farm
Hampole
Hampole Ings
FIVE LANE ENDS
HILL CREST
B1220
HAMPOLE BALK LA
Skellow
Skellow Bridge
SKELLOW RD
SKELLOW HALL GDNS
HOWDEN AVE
LYME TERR
CROSS HILL 1
CROMWELL CT 2
OLD HALL RD 3
CROSS HILL CT 4
LAWNDALE 5
CRANFIELD DR 6
WILLOWBROOK 7
FULLERTON CL 8
CRABGATE LA
CRABGATE DR
SHERWOOD DR
NEWLANDS AVE
LAVENHAM PL
SHERBURN CL
WALTHAM DR
HAUXWELL CL
LEYBURN RD
HARMBY CL
AMBERLEY RISE
WORSLEY PL
APPLEBY PL
WEATHERALL
SPENNITHORNE RD
FINGHALL RD
BELLERBY RD
BELLERBY PL

19
39

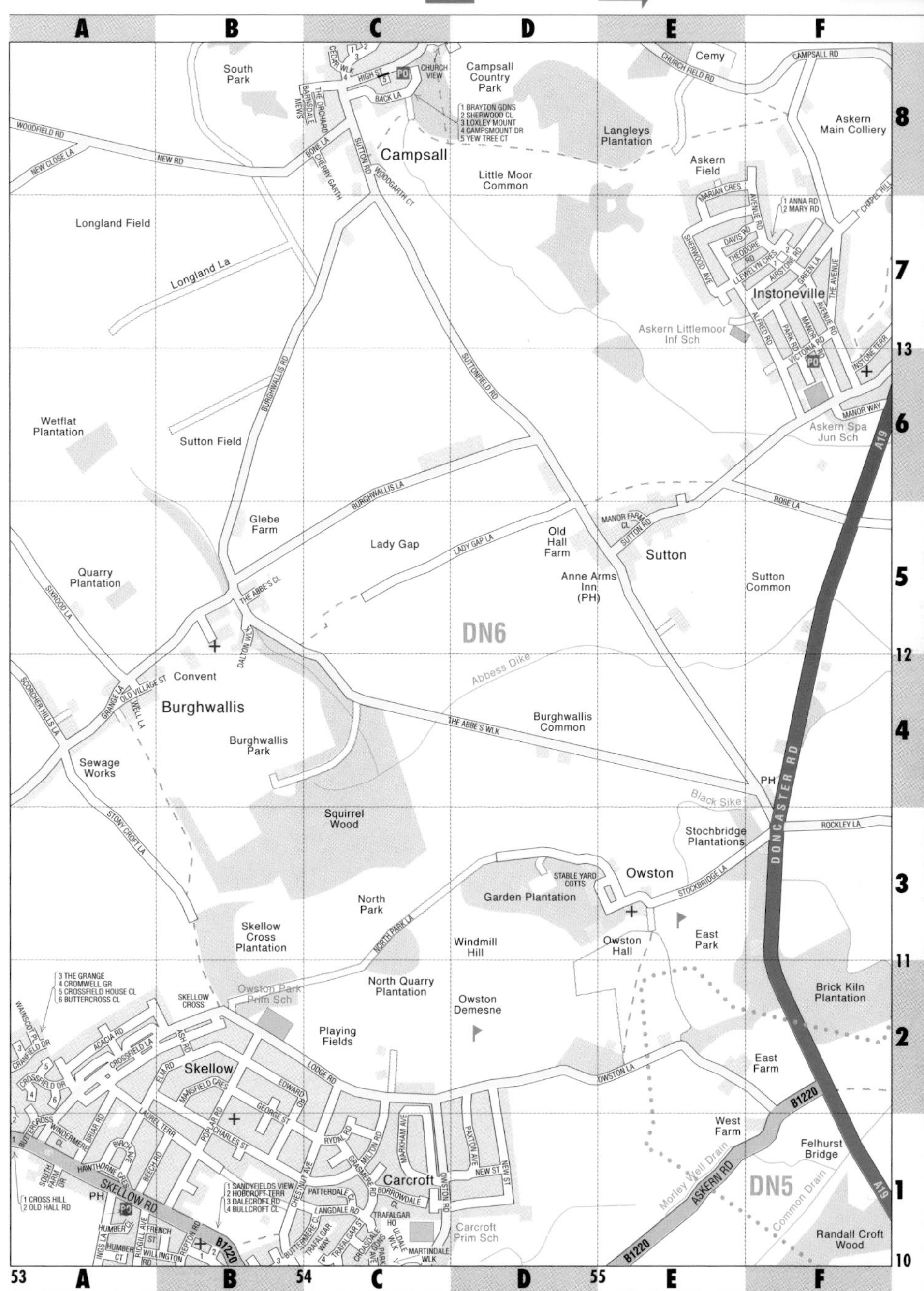
4
22
South Park
Campsall Country Park
Campsall
Little Moor Common
Langleys Plantation
Cemy
Askern Main Colliery
Askern Field
Longland Field
Longland La
Instoneville
Askern Littlemoor Inf Sch
Wetflat Plantation
Sutton Field
Askern Spa Jun Sch
Glebe Farm
Lady Gap
Old Hall Farm
Sutton
Quarry Plantation
Anne Arms Inn (PH)
Sutton Common
DN6
Convent
Burghwallis
Abbess Dike
Burghwallis Park
Burghwallis Common
Sewage Works
Black Sike
Squirrel Wood
Stochbridge Plantations
Owston
Garden Plantation
North Park
Skellow Cross Plantation
Windmill Hill
Owston Hall
East Park
North Quarry Plantation
Owston Park Prim Sch
Owston Demesne
Brick Kiln Plantation
Playing Fields
Skellow
East Farm
West Farm
Felhurst Bridge
Carcroft
DN5
Carcroft Prim Sch
Randall Croft Wood
Morley Well Drain
Common Drain
DONCASTER RD
A19
B1220
ASKERN RD
SKELLOW RD
40
22

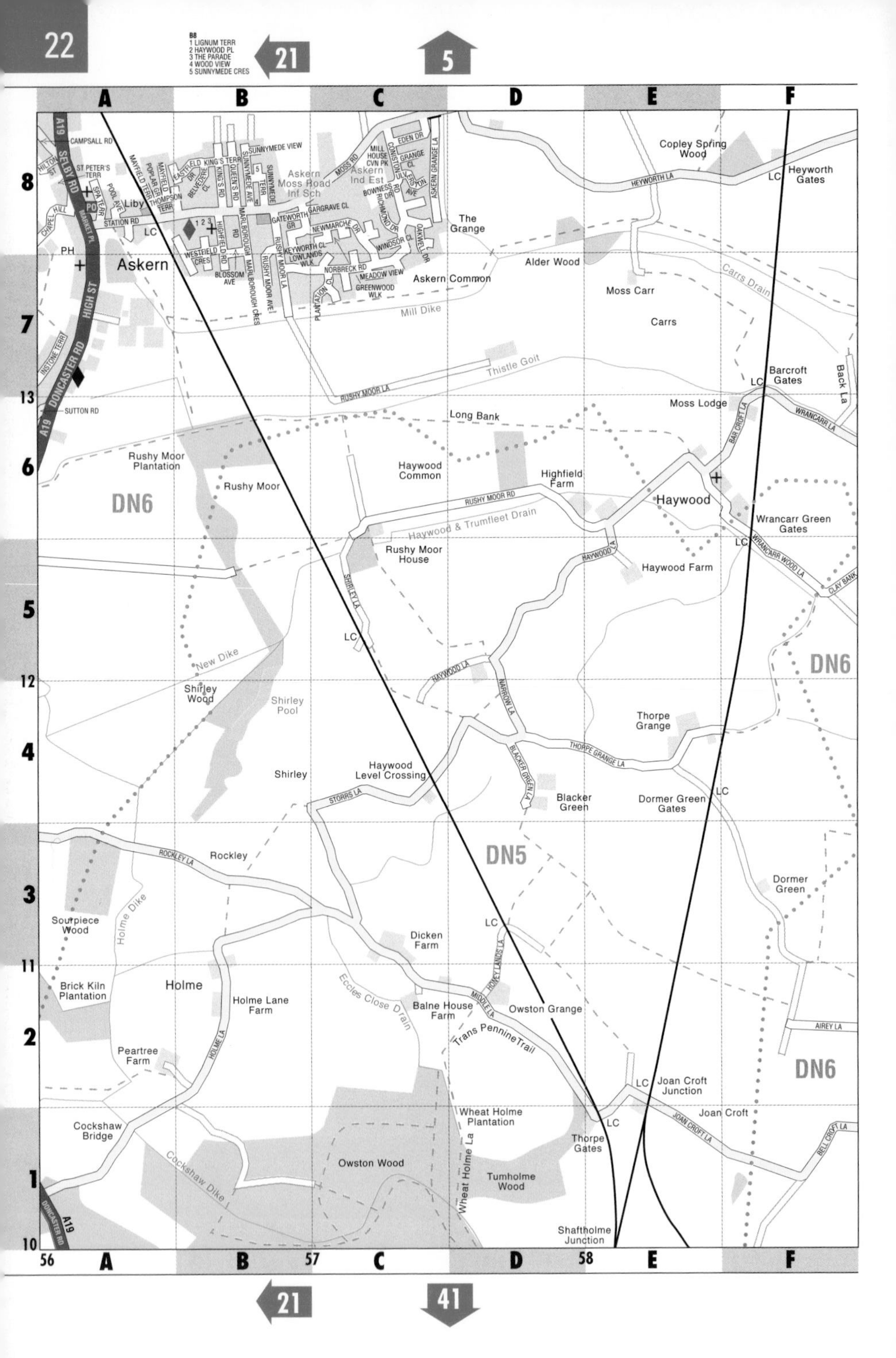

B8
1 LIGNUM TERR
2 HAYWOOD PL
3 THE PARADE
4 WOOD VIEW
5 SUNNYMEDE CRES

21

5

A   B   C   D   E   F

CAMPSALL RD
A19
SELBY RD
ST PETER'S TERR
PO
STATION RD
LC
Liby
PH
Askern
HIGH ST
HISTORIC TERR
A19
SUTTON RD
DONCASTER RD

Copley Spring Wood
HEYWORTH LA
LC
Heyworth Gates

Askern Moss Road Inf Sch
MOSS RD
Askern Ind Est
EDEN DR
MILL HOUSE CVN PK
GRANGE
ASKERN GRANGE LA
The Grange
Alder Wood
Moss Carr
Carrs Drain
Carrs

SUNNYMEDE VIEW
KING'S TERR
QUEEN'S RD
GARGRAVE CL
BOWNESS RD
WINDSOR DR
NEWMARCH
GATEWORTH
HEYWORTH CL
NORBRECK RD
MEADOW VIEW
GREENWOOD WLK
LOWLANDS WLK
WESTFIELD CRES
BLOSSOM AVE
PLANTATION
MARKET
Askern Common

Mill Dike

Thistle Goit
RUSHY MOOR LA

Moss Lodge
LC
Barcroft Gates
Back La
WRANCARR LA

13
SUTTON RD
Long Bank

6
DN6
Rushy Moor Plantation
Rushy Moor
Haywood Common
Highfield Farm
Haywood
Wrancarr Green Gates
HAYWOOD
BALK DRIFT LA

RUSHY MOOR RD
Haywood & Trumfleet Drain
Rushy Moor House
Haywood Farm
WRANCARR WOOD LA
LC
CLAY BANK

5
SHEEPCOT LA
LC
New Dike
HAYWOOD LA
DN6

12
Shirley Wood
Shirley Pool
NARROW LA
Thorpe Grange

4
Shirley
Haywood Level Crossing
THORPE GRANGE LA
Dormer Green Gates
LC
BLACKER GREEN LA
Blacker Green

STORKS LA
DN5
Dormer Green

3
ROCKLEY LA
Rockley
HOLME DIKE

Sourpiece Wood
ECCLES CLOSE DRAIN
Dicken Farm
LC
AIREY LA

11
Brick Kiln Plantation
Holme
Holme Lane Farm
Balne House Farm
Owston Grange
DN6

2
HOLME LA
Peartree Farm
MUCKLE LA
MUCKLE LANES LA
Trans Pennine Trail
LC
Joan Croft Junction
Joan Croft

Cockshaw Bridge
Wheat Holme Plantation
Thorpe Gates
LC
JOAN CROFT LA
BELT CROFT LA

1
A19
Cockshaw Dike
Owston Wood
WHEAT HOLME LA
Tumholme Wood
Shaftholme Junction

10
56   A   B   57   C   D   58   E   F

Kirkhouse Green

The Willows

White Gates Farm

MOSS RD

Flashley Carr Drain

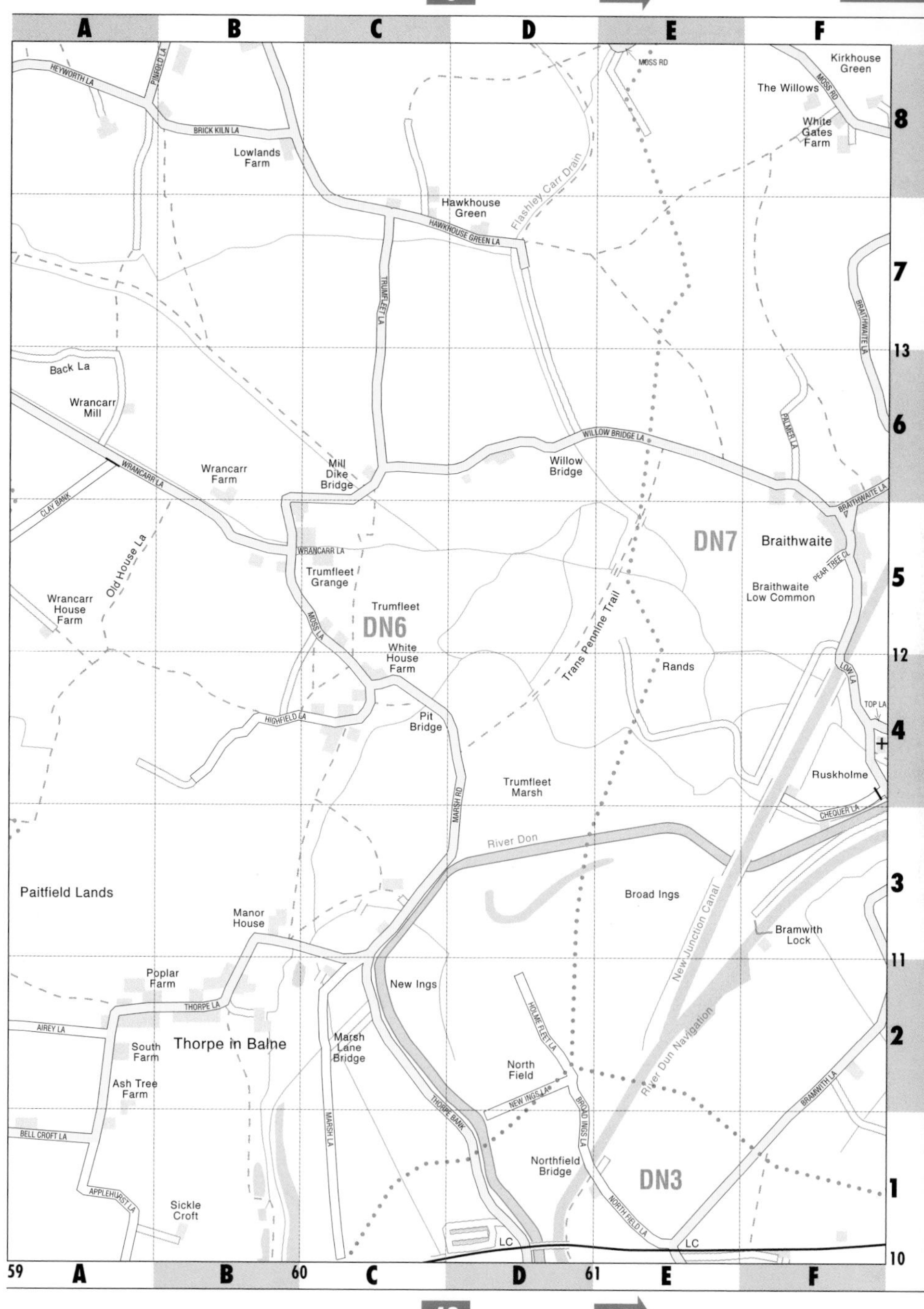

Heyworth La

Pinfold La

Brick Kiln La

Lowlands Farm

Hawkhouse Green

Hawkhouse Green La

Trumfleet La

Back La

Wrancarr Mill

Wrancarr Farm

Mill Dike Bridge

Willow Bridge

Willow Bridge La

Braithwaite La

DN7

Braithwaite

Wrancarr La

Clay Bank

Wrancarr La

Old House La

Wrancarr House Farm

Trumfleet Grange

Trumfleet

DN6

White House Farm

Braithwaite Low Common

Pear Tree Cl

Trans Pennine Trail

Rands

Long La

TOP LA

Highfield La

Pit Bridge

Trumfleet Marsh

Marsh Rd

Ruskholme

Chequer La

River Don

Paitfield Lands

Manor House

Broad Ings

New Junction Canal

Bramwith Lock

Poplar Farm

Thorpe La

New Ings

Holme Fleet La

Airey La

South Farm

Thorpe in Balne

Marsh Lane Bridge

Marsh La

North Field

New Ings La

River Dun Navigation

Bramwith La

Ash Tree Farm

Bell Croft La

Applehurst La

Sickle Croft

Thorpe Bank

Northfield Bridge

Northfield La

DN3

LC

LC

23
7

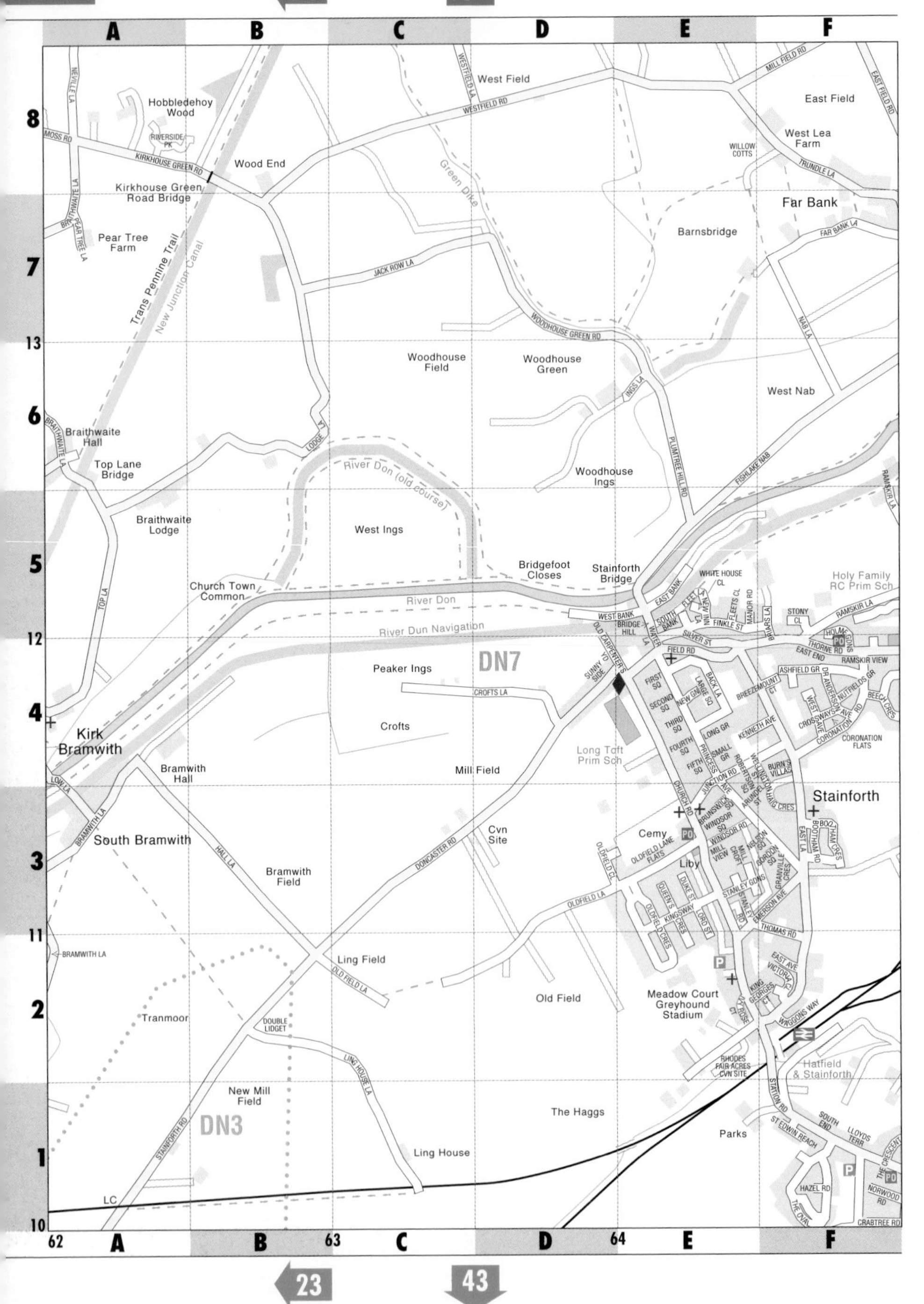
Hobbledehoy Wood
West Field
Westfield Rd
Moss Rd
Kirkhouse Green Rd
Wood End
Kirkhouse Green Road Bridge
Pear Tree Farm
Trans Pennine Trail
New Junction Canal
Green Dike
Jack Row La
East Field
West Lea Farm
Willow Cotts
Trundle La
Far Bank
Barnsbridge
Far Bank La
Woodhouse Green Rd
Woodhouse Field
Woodhouse Green
West Nab
Braithwaite Hall
Top Lane Bridge
River Don (old course)
Woodhouse Ings
Plumtree Hill Rd
Fishlake Nab
Braithwaite Lodge
West Ings
Bridgefoot Closes
Stainforth Bridge
Church Town Common
River Don
River Dun Navigation
Holy Family RC Prim Sch
DN7
Peaker Ings
Crofts La
Crofts
Kirk Bramwith
Bramwith Hall
Long Toft Prim Sch
Mill Field
Stainforth
South Bramwith
Cvn Site
Cemy
Liby
Bramwith Field
Doncaster Rd
Hall La
Oldfield La
Ling Field
Old Field La
Meadow Court Greyhound Stadium
Old Field
Tranmoor
Double Lidget
Ling House La
New Mill Field
DN3
Rhodes Fair Acres Cvn Site
Hatfield & Stainforth
The Haggs
Parks
Ling House
Stainforth Rd
LC

23
43

8
26

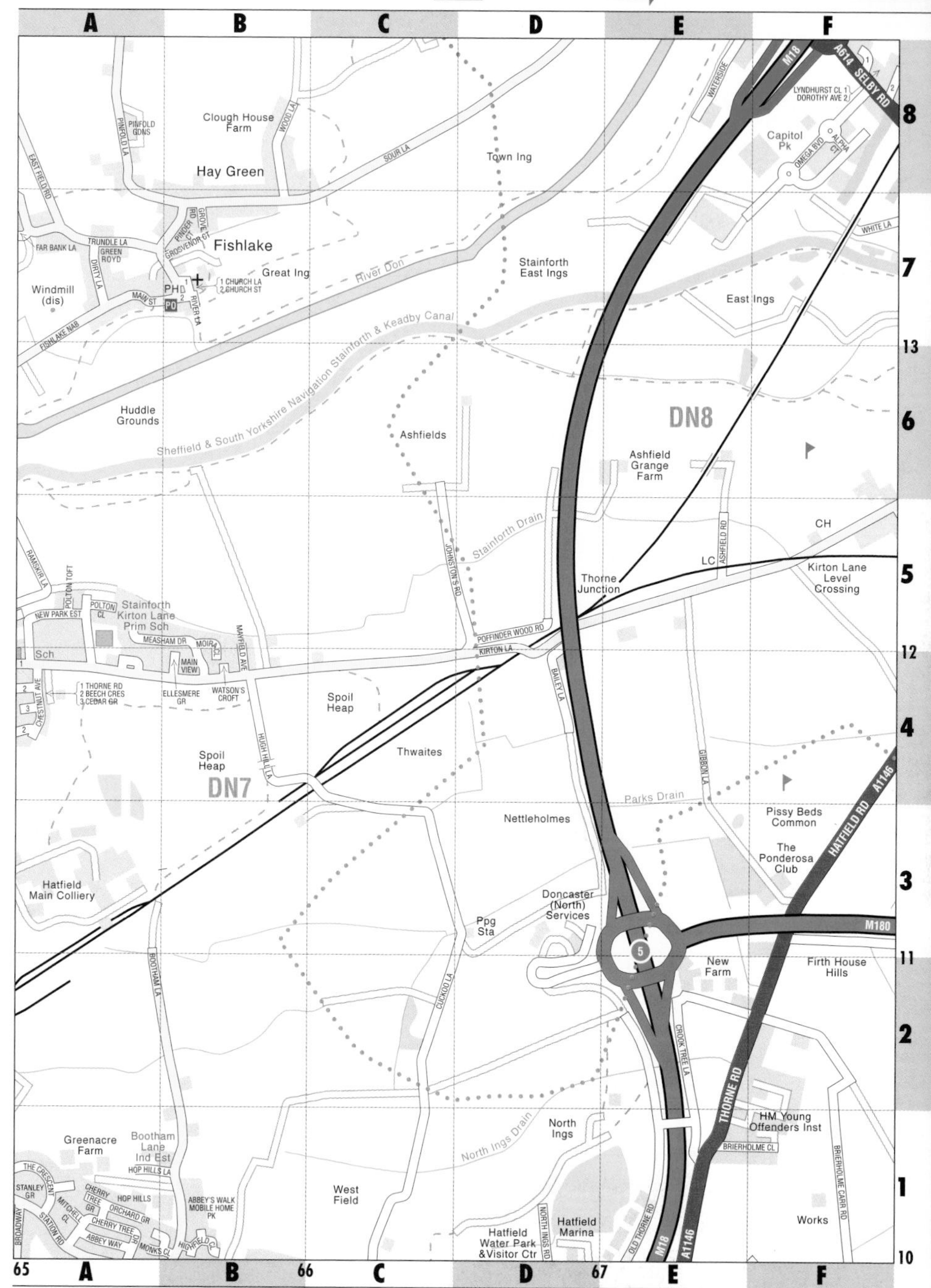

A
B
C
D
E
F
8
7
13
6
5
12
4
3
11
2
1
10
65
66
67
Clough House Farm
Hay Green
WOOD LA
SOUR LA
Town Ing
PINFOLD GDNS
PINFOLD LA
EAST FIELD RD
M18
WATERSIDE
A614 SELBY RD
LYNDHURST CL 1
DOROTHY AVE 2
Capitol Pk
OMEGA BVD
ALPHA CT
WHITE LA
Fishlake
TRUNDLE LA
FAR BANK LA
GREEN ROYD
DIRTY LA
PINDER CT
GROVE RD
GROSVENOR CT
Great Ing
River Don
Stainforth East Ings
Windmill (dis)
PH
PO
MAIN ST
RIVER LA
1 CHURCH LA
2 CHURCH ST
East Ings
FISHLAKE NAB
Stainforth & Keadby Canal
Sheffield & South Yorkshire Navigation
Huddle Grounds
Ashfields
DN8
Ashfield Grange Farm
Stainforth Drain
JOHNSTON'S RD
ASHFIELD RD
CH
LC
Thorne Junction
Kirton Lane Level Crossing
RAMSKIR LA
POLTON TOFT
NEW PARK EST
POLTON CL
Stainforth Kirton Lane Prim Sch
MEASHAM DR
MOIRA CL
MAYFIELD AVE
MAIN VIEW
Sch
POFFINDER WOOD RD
KIRTON LA
CHESTNUT AVE
1 THORNE RD
2 BEECH CRES
3 CEDAR GR
ELLESMERE GR
WATSON'S CROFT
Spoil Heap
BAILEY LA
Thwaites
HUGH HILL LA
Spoil Heap
DN7
GIBBON LA
Parks Drain
Nettleholmes
Pissy Beds Common
The Ponderosa Club
HATFIELD RD
A1146
Hatfield Main Colliery
Doncaster (North) Services
Ppg Sta
M180
5
BOOTHAM LA
CUCKOO LA
New Farm
Firth House Hills
CROOK TREE LA
THORNE RD
HM Young Offenders Inst
BRIERHOLME CL
BRIERHOLME CARR RD
Greenacre Farm
Bootham Lane Ind Est
HOP HILLS LA
North Ings Drain
North Ings
THE CRESCENT
STANLEY GR
CHERRY TREE GR
HOP HILLS
ORCHARD GR
MITCHELL CL
CHERRY TREE DR
STATION RD
BROADWAY
ABBEY WAY
MONKS CL
HIGHFIELD CL
ABBEY'S WALK MOBILE HOME PK
West Field
Hatfield Water Park &Visitor Ctr
NORTH INGS RD
Hatfield Marina
OLD THORNE RD
Works

25 9

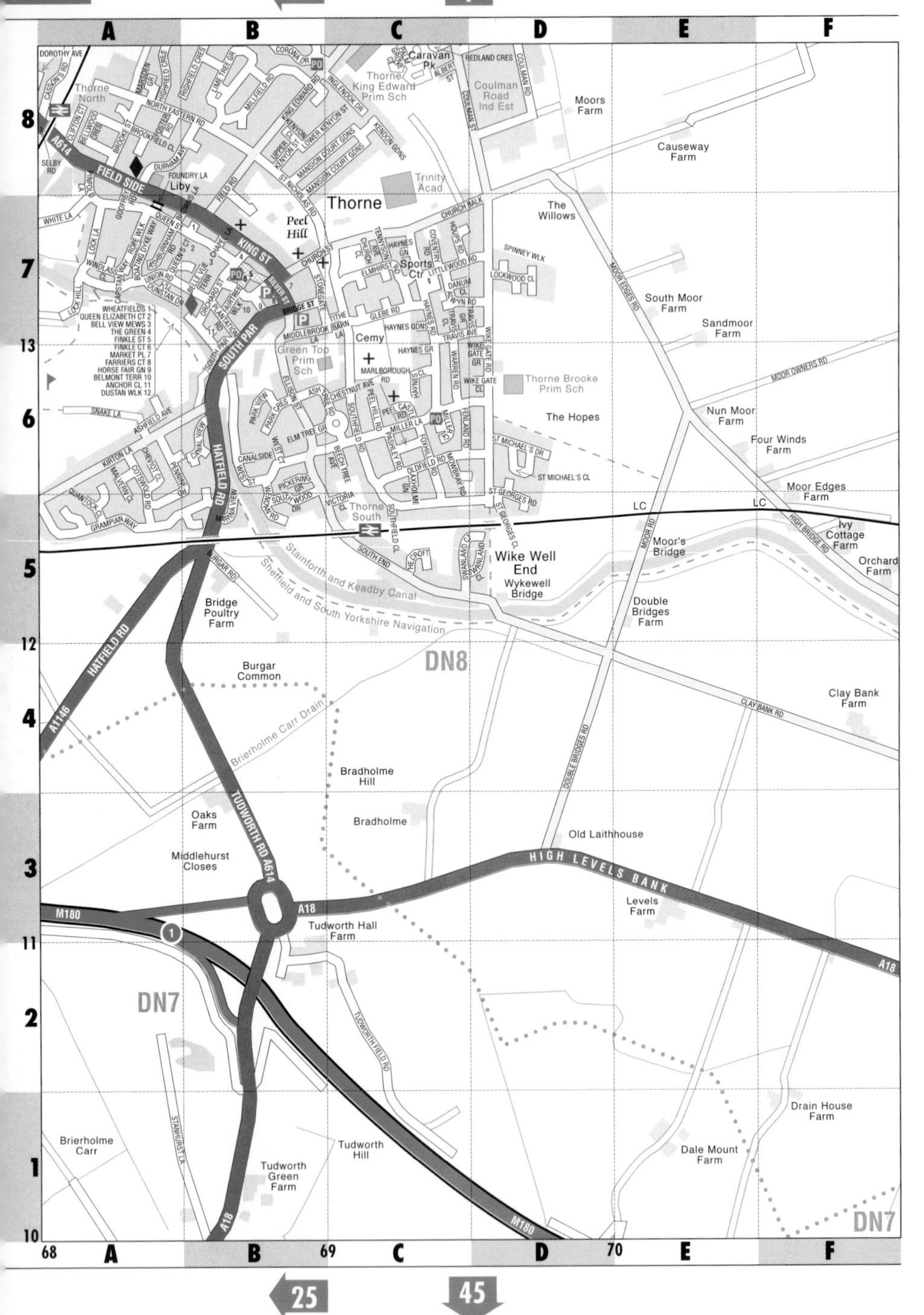

Thorne
Thorne North
Caravan Pk
Thorne King Edward Prim Sch
Coulman Road Ind Est
Moors Farm
Causeway Farm
Trinity Acad
Peel Hill
Liby
The Willows
Sports Ctr
South Moor Farm
Sandmoor Farm
Cemy
Green Top Prim Sch
Thorne Brooke Prim Sch
The Hopes
Nun Moor Farm
Four Winds Farm
Moor Edges Farm
Thorne South
Ivy Cottage Farm
Orchard Farm
Moor's Bridge
Wike Well End
Wykewell Bridge
Bridge Poultry Farm
Double Bridges Farm
Stainforth and Keadby Canal
Sheffield and South Yorkshire Navigation
DN8
Burgar Common
Clay Bank Farm
Brierholme Carr Drain
Bradholme Hill
Bradholme
Oaks Farm
Old Laithhouse
Middlehurst Closes
HIGH LEVELS BANK
Levels Farm
Tudworth Hall Farm
DN7
Drain House Farm
Brierholme Carr
Tudworth Hill
Dale Mount Farm
Tudworth Green Farm
FIELD SIDE
KING ST
SOUTH PAR
HATFIELD RD
TUDWORTH RD A614
A614
A1146
A18
M180
MOOR EDGES RD
MOOR RD
DOUBLE BRIDGES RD
CLAY BANK RD
MOOR OWNERS RD
HIGH BRIDGE RD
TUDWORTH FIELD RD
STAINHURST LA
WHEATFIELDS 1
QUEEN ELIZABETH CT 2
BELL VIEW MEWS 3
THE GREEN 4
FINKLE ST 5
FINKLE CT 6
MARKET PL 7
FARRIERS CT 8
HORSE FAIR GN 9
BELMONT TERR 10
ANCHOR CL 11
DUSTAN WLK 12

25 45

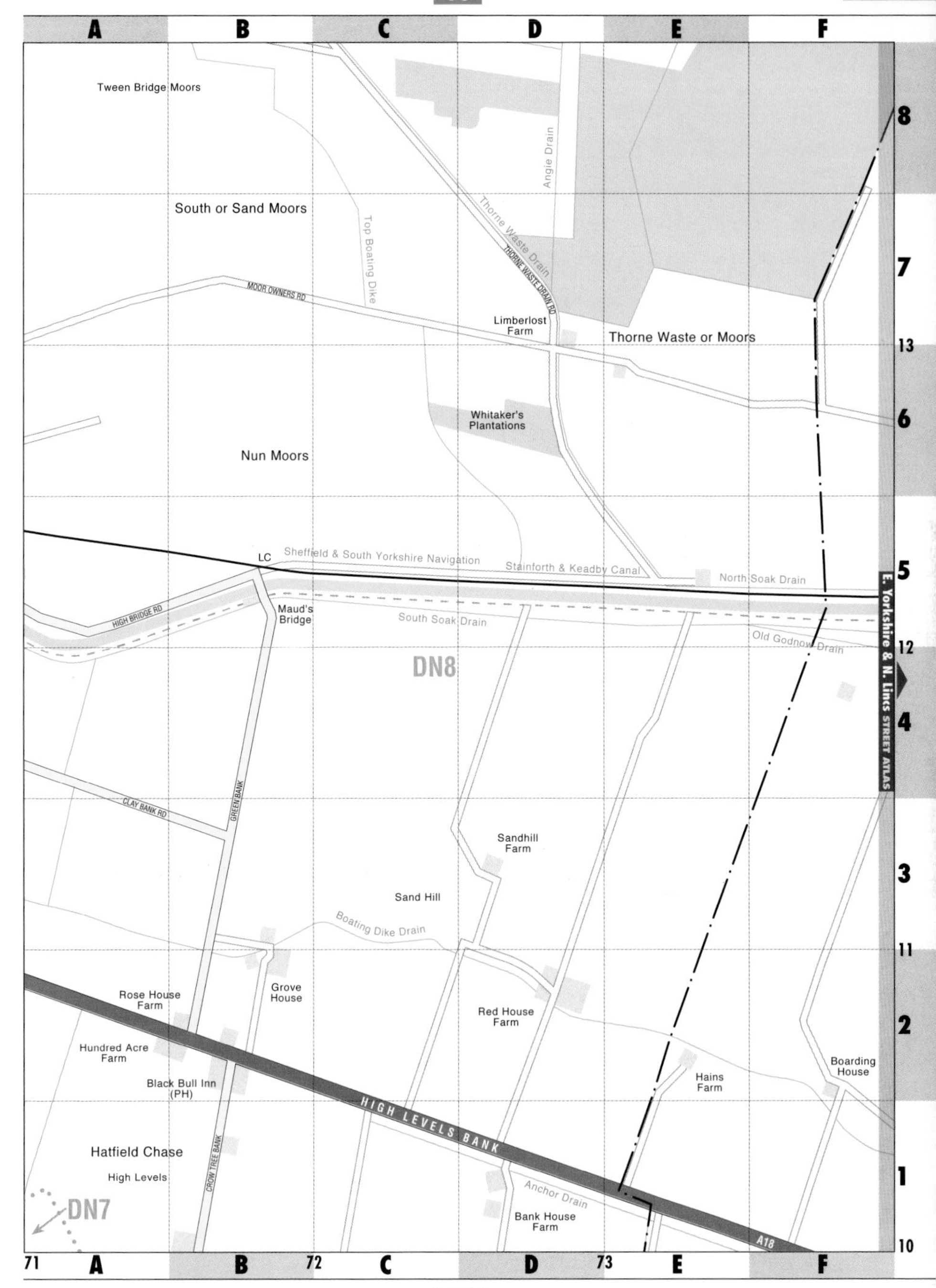

A | **B** | **C** | **D** | **E** | **F**

Tween Bridge Moors

South or Sand Moors

8

Angle Drain

Thorne Waste Drain

7

Top Boating Dike

MOOR OWNERS RD

Limberlost Farm

THORNE WASTE DRAIN RD

13

Thorne Waste or Moors

6

Whitaker's Plantations

Nun Moors

5

LC

Sheffield & South Yorkshire Navigation

Stainforth & Keadby Canal

North Soak Drain

HIGH BRIDGE RD

Maud's Bridge

South Soak Drain

Old Godnow Drain

12

DN8

4

E. Yorkshire & N. Lincs STREET ATLAS

CLAY BANK RD

GREEN BANK

Sandhill Farm

3

Sand Hill

Boating Dike Drain

11

Rose House Farm

Grove House

Red House Farm

2

Hundred Acre Farm

Black Bull Inn (PH)

Boarding House

Hains Farm

CROW TREE BANK

HIGH LEVELS BANK

Hatfield Chase

High Levels

Anchor Drain

1

DN7

Bank House Farm

A18

10

71 | **A** | **B** | 72 | **C** | **D** | 73 | **E** | **F**

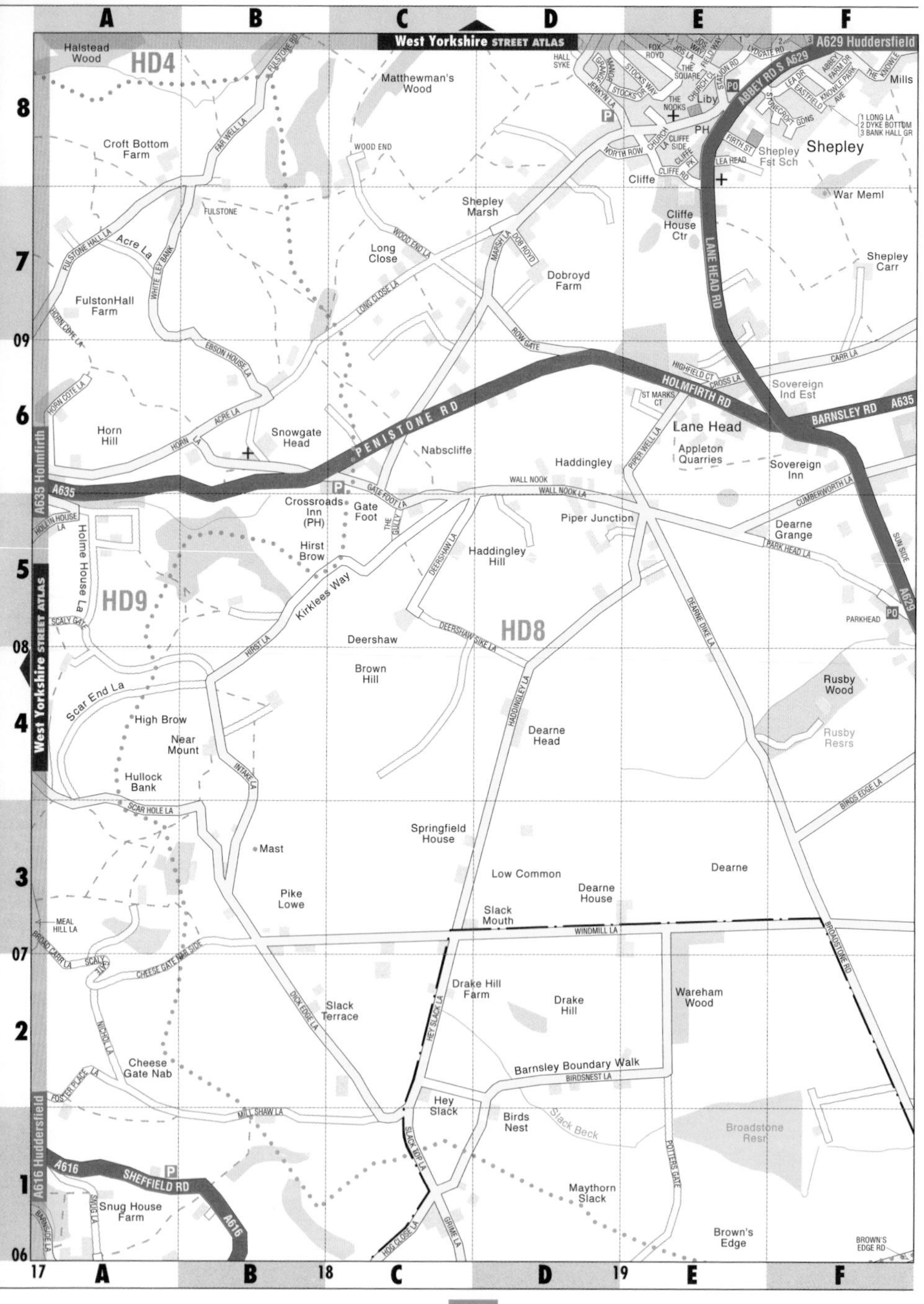

HD4

Halstead Wood

Croft Bottom Farm

Matthewman's Wood

WOOD END

FOX ROYD

HALL SYKE

THE SQUARE

STOCKS WLK

Liby

A629 Huddersfield

Mills

Shepley Fst Sch

Shepley

War Meml

Shepley Carr

FulstonHall Farm

Fulstone

Acre La

Shepley Marsh

Long Close

Dobroyd Farm

Cliffe

Cliffe House Ctr

Horn Hill

Snowgate Head

PENISTONE RD

Nabscliffe

Haddingley

St Marks Ct

Lane Head

Appleton Quarries

Sovereign Ind Est

BARNSLEY RD

A635

Sovereign Inn

A635 Holmfirth

HD9

Crossroads Inn (PH)

Gate Foot

Hirst Brow

Kirklees Way

Deershaw

Brown Hill

Wall Nook

Wall Nook La

Haddingley Hill

Piper Junction

Dearne Grange

PARK HEAD LA

HD8

Dearne Grange

Parkhead

Rusby Wood

Rusby Resrs

Scar End La

High Brow

Near Mount

Hullock Bank

SCAR HOLE LA

Mast

Dearne Head

Springfield House

Pike Lowe

Low Common

Dearne House

Dearne

MEAL HILL LA

Cheese Gate Nab Side

Slack Mouth

WINDMILL LA

Slack Terrace

Drake Hill Farm

Drake Hill

Wareham Wood

Cheese Gate Nab

Barnsley Boundary Walk

BIRDSNEST LA

Broadstone Resr

MILL SHAW LA

Hey Slack

Birds Nest

Slack Beck

A616 Huddersfield

A616

SHEFFIELD RD

Snug House Farm

Maythorn Slack

Brown's Edge

BROWN'S EDGE RD

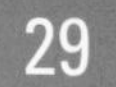

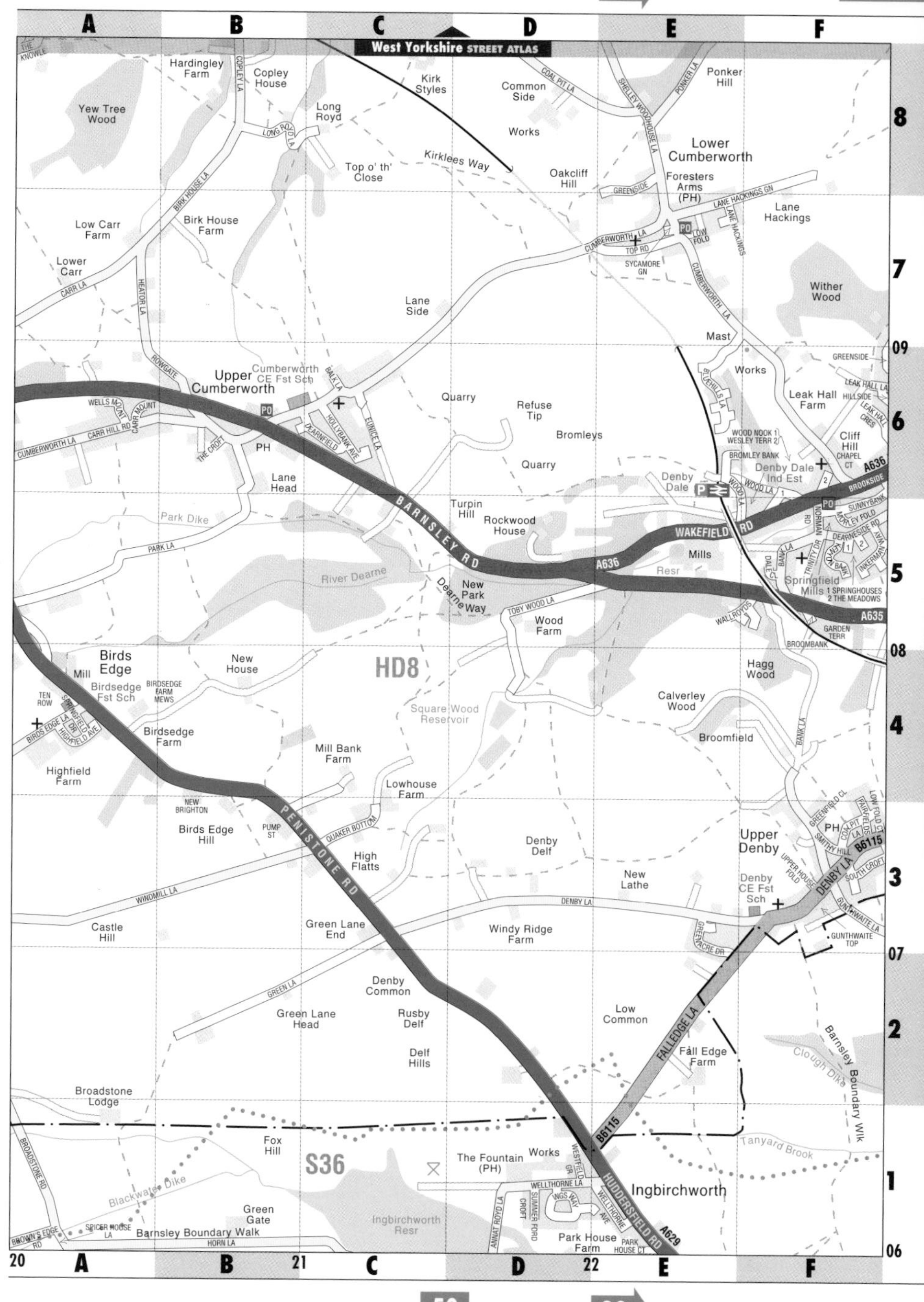

A B C D E F

8

7

09

6

5

08

HD8

4

3

07

S36

2

06

1

20 A B 21 C D 22 E F

50 30

Yew Tree Wood
Hardingley Farm
Copley House
Kirk Styles
Common Side
Works
Ponker Hill
Lower Cumberworth
Long Royd
Top o' th' Close
Kirklees Way
Oakcliff Hill
Foresters Arms (PH)
Lane Hackings GN
Lane Hackings
Low Carr Farm
Birk House Farm
Lower Carr
Lane Side
Cumberworth LA
TOP RD
Wither Wood
SYCAMORE GN
Upper Cumberworth
Cumberworth CE Fst Sch
PO
PH
Lane Head
Quarry
Refuse Tip
Bromleys
Quarry
Works
Leak Hall Farm
GREENSIDE
Cliff Hill
CHAPEL CT
A636
BROOKSIDE
Denby Dale Ind Est
Denby Dale
BARNSLEY RD
A636
WAKEFIELD RD
Turpin Hill
Rockwood House
Mills
Resr
Springfield Mills
1 SPRINGHOUSES
2 THE MEADOWS
GARDEN TERR
A635
BROOMBANK
Park Dike
PARK LA
River Dearne
Dearne Way
New Park Way
TOBY WOOD LA
Wood Farm
Hagg Wood
Birds Edge
Mill
Birdsedge Fst Sch
BIRDSEDGE FARM MEWS
New House
Square Wood Reservoir
Calverley Wood
Broomfield
BARK LA
TEN ROW
Birdsedge Farm
Mill Bank Farm
Highfield Farm
New Brighton
Birds Edge Hill
PUMP ST
QUARMBY BOTTOM
Lowhouse Farm
Denby Delf
Upper Denby
PH
B6115
PENISTONE RD
High Flatts
Denby CE Fst Sch
DENBY LA
Castle Hill
WINDMILL LA
Green Lane End
Windy Ridge Farm
GREENACRE DR
GUNTHWAITE TOP
07
GREEN LA
Denby Common
Low Common
FALL EDGE LA
Clough Dike
Green Lane Head
Rusby Delf
Barnsley Boundary Wlk
Broadstone Lodge
Delf Hills
Fall Edge Farm
Tanyard Brook
Blackwater Dike
Fox Hill
S36
The Fountain (PH)
Works
WESTFIELD LA
B6115
HUDDERSFIELD RD
A629
Ingbirchworth
Green Gate
Barnsley Boundary Walk
HORN LA
Ingbirchworth Resr
Park House Farm
PARK HOUSE CT

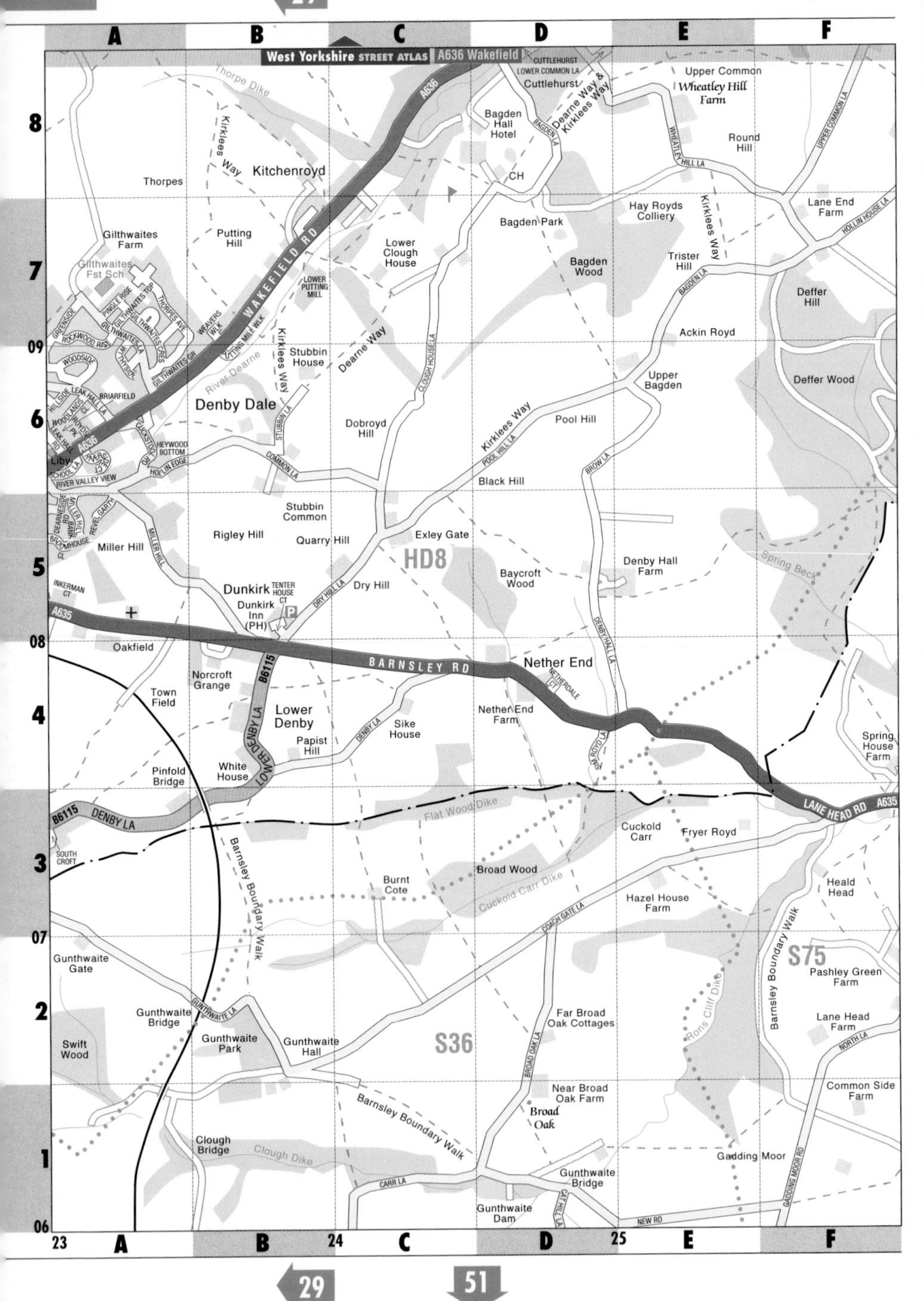

West Yorkshire STREET ATLAS A636 Wakefield

A B C D E F

8

7

09

6

5

08

4

3

07

2

1

06

23 A 24 B C 25 D E F

CUTTLEHURST
LOWER COMMON LA
Cuttlehurst
Upper Common
Wheatley Hill
Farm

Thorpe Dike
Kirklees Way
Kitchenroyd
Thorpes
Way

Bagden
Hall
Hotel
CH
Round
Hill

WAKEFIELD RD
A636

Gilthwaites
Farm
Gilthwaites
Fst Sch
Putting
Hill
LOWER
PUTTING
MILL
Lower
Clough
House
Bagden Park
Hay Royds
Colliery
Lane End
Farm

HILL LA
KIRKLEES WAY
Bagden
Wood
Trister
Hill
Deffer
Hill

HALIN HOUSE LA
UPPER COMMON LA

WEBBS
LINFIT

Stubbin
House
Dearne Way
Ackin Royd

River Dearne
Denby Dale
Dobroyd
Hill
Kirklees Way
Pool Hill
Upper
Bagden

HEYWOOD
BOTTOM
COMMON LA
STUBBIN
Black Hill
BAGDEN LA

Libry
RIVER VALLEY VIEW
Stubbin
Common
Exley Gate
HD8

INKERMAN
CT
Miller Hill
Rigley Hill
Quarry Hill
Baycroft
Wood
Denby Hall
Farm
Spring Beck

MILLER HILL
Dunkirk
TENTER
HOUSE
CT
Dry Hill
DRY HILL LA
Dunkirk
Inn
(PH)
PARTS HILL LA

A635
Oakfield
BARNSLEY RD
Nether End
B6115

Town
Field
Norcroft
Grange
Lower
Denby
Nether End
Farm

DENBY LA
Papist
Hill
Sike
House
NETHERDALE

White
House
DENBY LA
Pinfold
Bridge

B6115
DENBY LA
Flat Wood Dike
SOUTH
CROFT
LANE HEAD RD A635

Barnsley Boundary Walk
Cuckold
Carr
Fryer Royd
Spring
House
Farm

Burnt
Cote
Broad Wood
Cuckold Carr Dike
Hazel House
Farm
Heald
Head

Gunthwaite
Gate
PLOUGH GATE LA
S75
Pashley Green
Farm

GUNTHWAITE LA
Gunthwaite
Bridge
Gunthwaite
Park
Gunthwaite
Hall
Far Broad
Oak Cottages
Lane Head
Farm

Swift
Wood
S36
BROAD OAK LA
Near Broad
Oak Farm
Broad
Oak

NORTH LA

Barnsley Boundary Walk
BARNSLEY MOOR RD
Common Side
Farm

Clough
Bridge
Clough Dike
CARR LA
Gunthwaite
Bridge
Gunthwaite
Dam
NEW RD
Gadding Moor

GADDING MOOR RD

Bagden
Park
Dearne Way
Kirklees Way

8

7

09

6

5

08

4

3

07

2

1

06

HD8

Swallow Hill

Hollin House Farm

Winter Hill
BANK END LA
Hoyland Hill

GREEN LANE

Margery Wood

Cawthorne Park

Dean Hill Farm

Rookery

Deffer Wood

Upper Spring

Cinder Farm

Cinder Hill Bridge

Clay Hall

Tower Cottage

Garden Plantation

Home Farm

Nursery

Cannon Hall House & Mus

The Rowlands

Lower Collier Fold

Cannon Hall Country Park

S75

Sewage Works

Mus

Susannah Spring

Jowett House Farm

Jowett Brook Houre Beck

Cascade Bridge

Barnsley Boundary Walk

Mill

Cawthorne

Alexander Gdns

LION ST

BROOK HOS

A635

Daking Brook

Flash House Plantation

Beet House

Tivy Dale

Windmill Hill

Daw Walls Farm

Daw Hill

Flash House Farm

Clough Green

Raw Green

LANE HEAD RD

Thimble Hall

Hill House Farm

NORCROFT LA

Hill Top Cottages

Works

Pease Grove

UPPER NORCROFT

Dixon Wood

Rawling House

Spoil Heap

Lower Norcroft Farm

Upper House

NORTH LA

Tanyard Beck

Haddon Farmhouse

Banks Hall

Wood Royd

Tanyard Wood

Hattersley Wood

South Lane

SOUTH LA

Banks Bottom Dike

Upper Elmhirst

Wool Greaves

Small Lanes Farm

Banks Wood

Clay Pit

Bull Haw La

WHINMOOR WAY 1
MAYBERRY DR 2
HAWTHORN GR 3

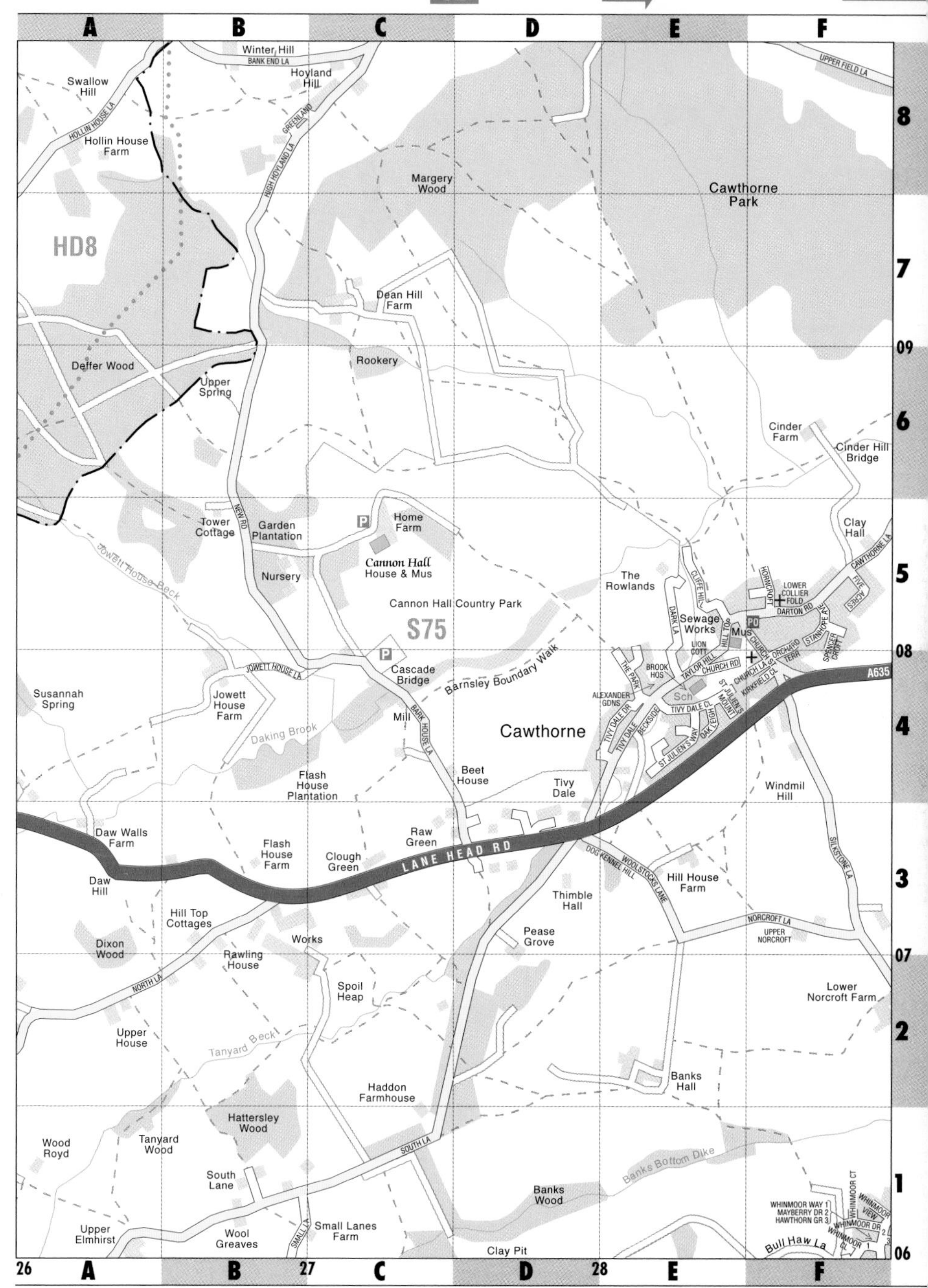

31
13

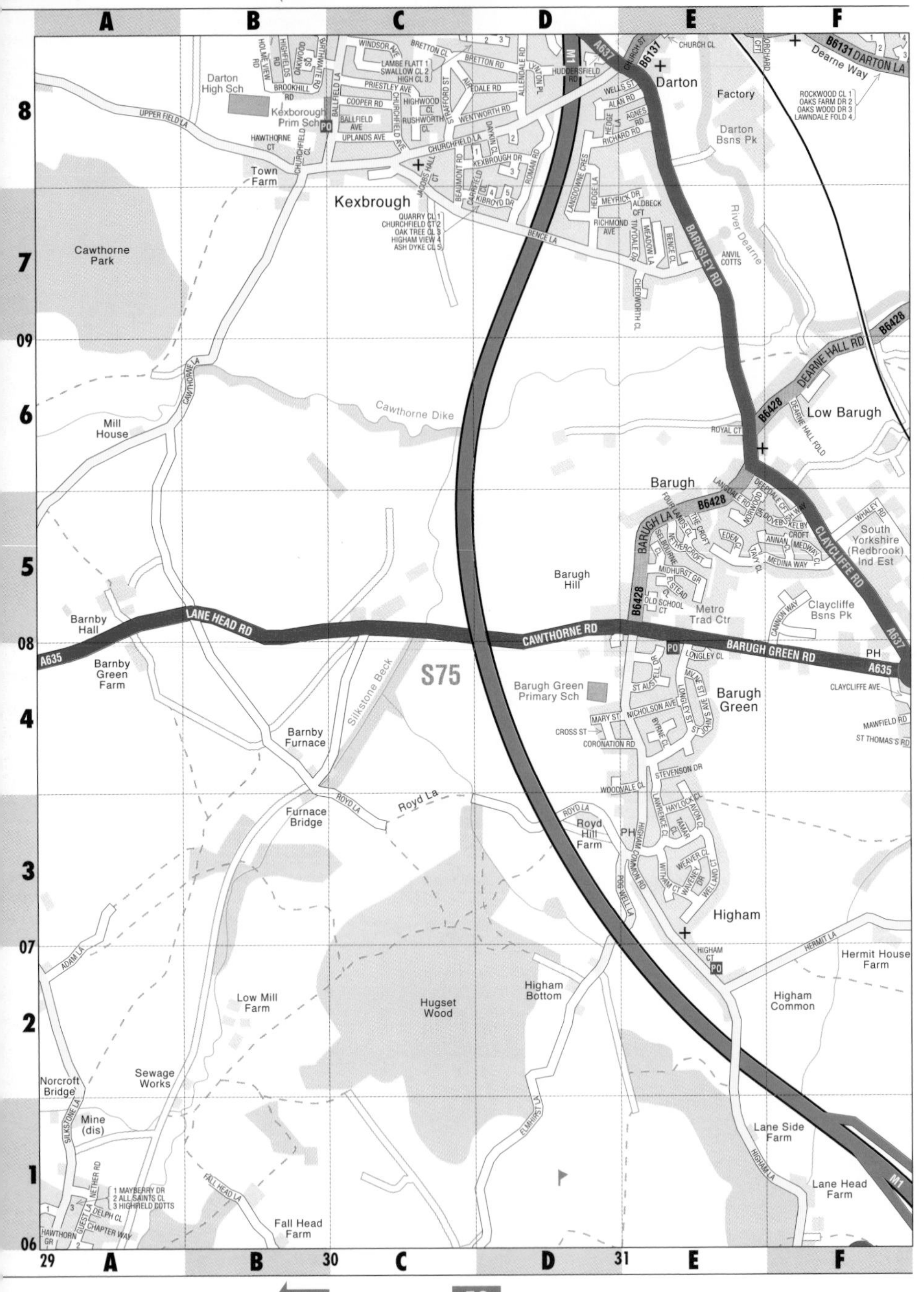
A
B
C
D
E
F
8
7
09
6
5
08
4
3
07
2
1
06
29
30
31
Darton High Sch
Kexborough Prim Sch
UPPER FIELD LA
HOLME VIEW RD
HIGHFIELDS RD
OAKWOOD CL
BIRTHWAITE RD
BROOKHILL RD
BALLFIELD LA
BALLFIELD AVE
HAWTHORNE CT
CHURCHFIELD CL
Town Farm
WINDSOR AVE
BRETTON CL
BRETTON RD
LAMBE FLATT 1
SWALLOW CL 2
HIGH CL 3
PRIESTLEY AVE
COOPER RD
HIGHWOOD CL
RUSHWORTH CL
UPLANDS AVE
CHURCHFIELD AVE
STAFFORD ST
EDALE RD
WENTWORTH RD
ALLENDALE RD
LYNTON PL
HUDDERSFIELD RD
CHURCHFIELD LA
KEXBROUGH DR
BEAUMONT RD
DAYKIN CL
ROMAN RD
KIBROYD DR
JACOBS HALL CT
Kexbrough
QUARRY CL 1
CHURCHFIELD CT 2
OAK TREE CL 3
HIGHAM VIEW 4
ASH DYKE CL 5
BENCE LA
M1
A637
CHURCH ST
B6137
CHURCH CL
Darton
WELLS ST
ALAN RD
AGNES RD
HEDGE LA
RICHARD RD
LANSDOWNE CRES
MEYRICK DR
ALDBECK CFT
RICHMOND AVE
TIVYDALE DR
MEADOW LA
BENCE CL
CHEDWORTH CL
BARNSLEY RD
ANVIL COTTS
River Dearne
Factory
Darton Bsns Pk
ORCHARD CFT
B6131 DARTON LA
Dearne Way
ROCKWOOD CL 1
OAKS FARM DR 2
OAKS WOOD DR 3
LAWNDALE FOLD 4
Cawthorne Park
CAWTHORNE LA
Mill House
Cawthorne Dike
B6428
DEARNE HALL RD
Low Barugh
ROYAL CT
DEARNE HALL FOLD
Barugh
BARUGH LA
FOUR LANDS CL
THE CROFT
NETHERCROFT
SELBOURNE CL
LANGDALE RD
DEEPDALE CFT
NORWOOD
DOVE
KELBY CROFT
EDEN CL
ANNAN CL
TAVY CL
MEDWAY CL
MEDINA WAY
CLAYCLIFFE RD
WHALEY RD
South Yorkshire (Redbrook) Ind Est
Barugh Hill
MIDHURST GR
ELSTEAD CL
OLD SCHOOL CT
Metro Trad Ctr
CANNON WAY
Claycliffe Bsns Pk
Barnby Hall
A635
LANE HEAD RD
CAWTHORNE RD
BARUGH GREEN RD
PH
LONGLEY CL
Barnby Green Farm
S75
Silkstone Beck
Barugh Green Primary Sch
ST AUSTELL
MILNE ST
LONGLEY ST
ST JOHN'S AVE
Barugh Green
CLAYCLIFFE AVE
MAWFIELD RD
ST THOMAS'S RD
MARY ST
NICHOLSON AVE
BYRNE CL
CROSS ST
CORONATION RD
Barnby Furnace
STEVENSON DR
WOODVALE CL
ROYD LA
Royd La
Furnace Bridge
Royd Hill Farm
HAYLOCK CL
AVON CL
LAWRENCE CL
TAMAR CL
HIGHAM COMMON RD
WEAVER CL
WAVENEY DR
WITHAM CT
WELLAND CL
POG WELL LA
Higham
HIGHAM CT
PO
HERMIT LA
Hermit House Farm
ADAM LA
Low Mill Farm
Hugset Wood
Higham Bottom
Higham Common
Norcroft Bridge
Sewage Works
Mine (dis)
SILKSTONE LA
NETHER RD
1 MAYBERRY DR
2 ALL SAINTS CL
3 HIGHFIELD COTTS
GUEST LA
DELPH CL
CHAPTER WAY
HAWTHORN GR
FALL HEAD LA
Fall Head Farm
ELMHIRST LA
HIGHAM LA
Lane Side Farm
Lane Head Farm

31
53

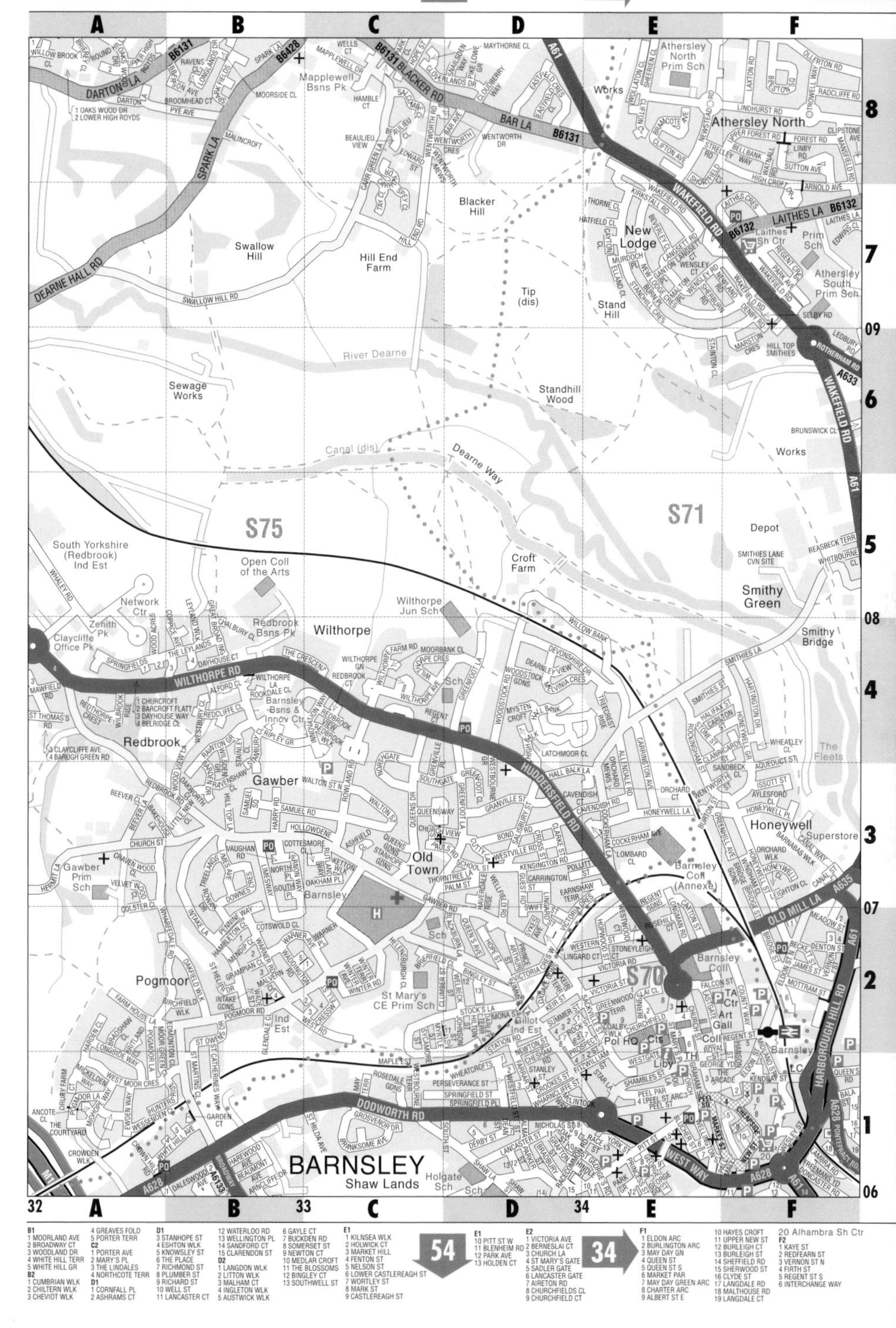

BARNSLEY
Shaw Lands

54 34

B1
1 MOORLAND AVE
2 BROADWAY CT
3 WOODLAND DR
4 WHITE HILL TERR
5 WHITE HILL GR
B2
1 CUMBRIAN WLK
2 CHILTERN WLK
3 CHEVIOT WLK

4 GREAVES FOLD
5 PORTER TERR
C2
1 PORTER AVE
2 MARY'S PL
3 THE LINDALES
4 NORTHCOTE TERR
D1
1 CORNFALL PL
2 ASHRAMS CT

D1
3 STANHOPE ST
4 ESHTON WLK
5 KNOWSLEY CT
6 THE PLACE
7 RICHMOND ST
8 PLUMBER ST
9 RICHARD ST
10 WELL ST
11 LANCASTER CT

4 WATERLOO RD
5 WELLINGTON PL
14 SANDFORD CT
15 CLARENDON ST
D2
1 LANGDON WLK
2 LITTON WLK
3 MALHAM CT
4 AUSTWICK WLK

6 GAYLE CT
7 BUCKDEN RD
8 SOMERSET ST
9 NEWTON CT
10 MEDLAR CROFT
11 THE BLOSSOMS
12 BINGLEY CT
13 SOUTHWELL ST

E1
1 KILNSEA WLK
2 HOLWICK CT
3 MARKET HILL
4 FENTON ST
5 NELSON ST
6 LOWER CASTLEREAGH ST
7 WORTLEY ST
8 MARK ST
9 CASTLEREAGH ST

E1
10 PITT ST W
11 BLENHEIM ST
12 PARK AVE
13 HOLDEN CT

E2
1 VICTORIA AVE
2 BERNESLAI CT
3 CHURCH LA
4 ST MARY'S GATE
5 SADLER GATE
6 LANCASTER GATE
7 AIRETON RD
8 CHURCHFIELDS CT
9 CHURCHFIELD CT

F1
1 ELDON ARC
2 BURLINGTON ARC
3 MAY DAY GN
4 QUEEN ST
5 QUEEN ST S
6 MARKET PAR
7 MAY DAY GREEN ARC
8 CHARTER ARC
9 ALBERT ST E

10 HAYES CROFT
11 UPPER NEW ST
12 BURLEIGH CT
13 BURLEIGH RD
14 SHEFFIELD RD
15 SHERWOOD ST
16 CLYDE ST
17 LANGDALE RD
18 MALTHOUSE RD
19 LANGDALE CT

20 Alhambra Sh Ctr

F2
1 KAYE ST
2 REDFEARN ST
3 VERNON ST N
4 FIRTH ST
5 REGENT ST S
6 INTERCHANGE WAY

33
15

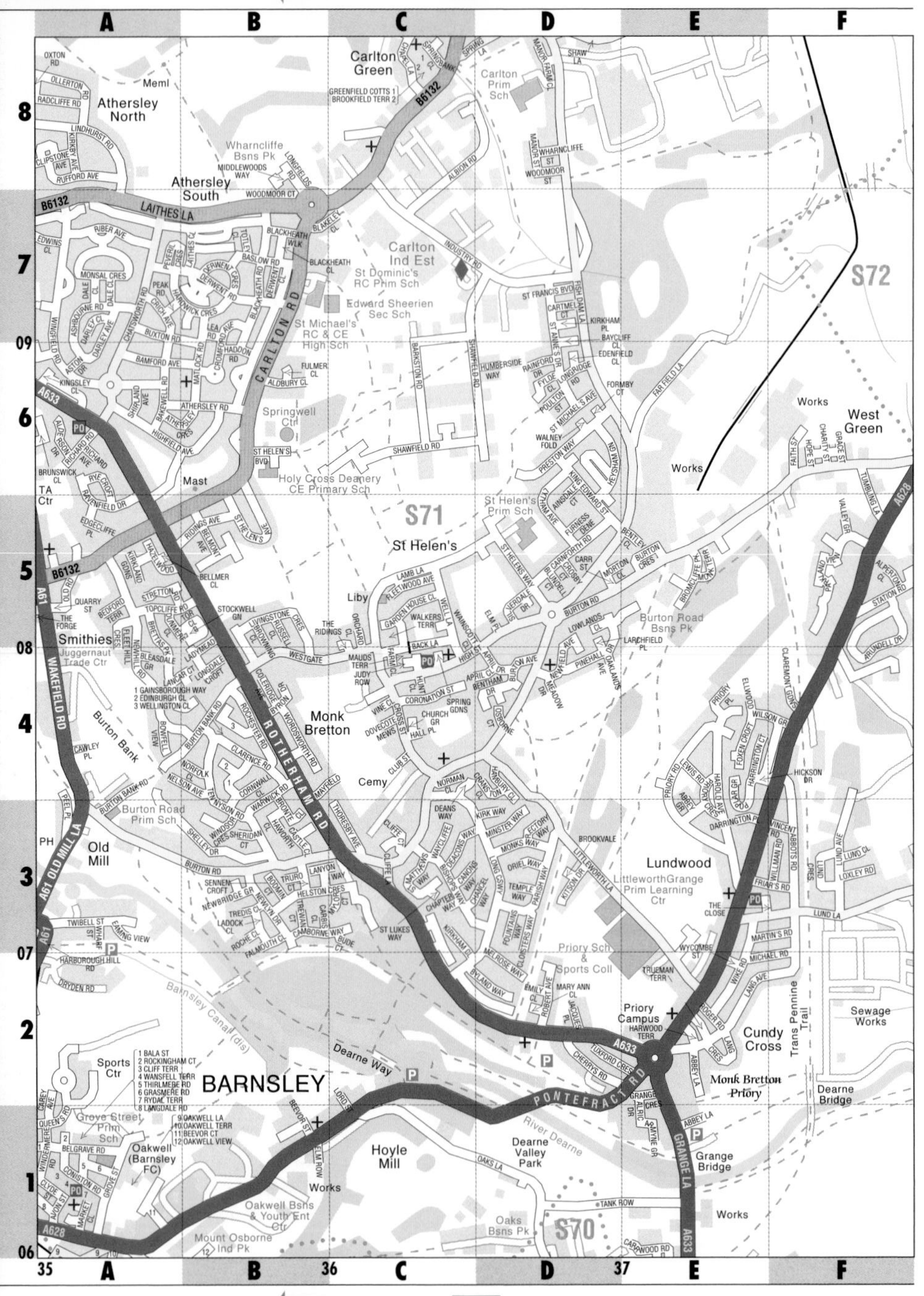
A
B
C
D
E
F
8
7
09
6
5
08
4
3
07
2
1
06
35
36
37
Carlton Green
Athersley North
Meml
Carlton Prim Sch
Wharncliffe Bsns Pk
Athersley South
B6132
LAITHES LA
Carlton Ind Est
St Dominic's RC Prim Sch
Edward Sheerien Sec Sch
St Michael's RC & CE High Sch
CARLTON RD
Springwell Ctr
Holy Cross Deanery CE Primary Sch
S71
S72
St Helen's
St Helen's Prim Sch
Mast
TA Ctr
A633
A61
WAKEFIELD RD
Smithies
Juggernaut Trade Ctr
Liby
Monk Bretton
Burton Road Bsns Pk
Burton Bank
Cemy
ROTHERHAM RD
Burton Road Prim Sch
Old Mill
PH
A61 OLD MILL LA
Lundwood
LittleworthGrange Prim Learning Ctr
Priory Sch & Sports Coll
Priory Campus
Cundy Cross
Trans Pennine Trail
Sewage Works
Works
West Green
A628
Barnsley Canal (dis)
Dearne Way
BARNSLEY
Sports Ctr
Grove Street Prim Sch
Oakwell (Barnsley FC)
PONTEFRACT RD
River Dearne
Monk Bretton Priory
Dearne Bridge
Hoyle Mill
Dearne Valley Park
Grange Bridge
GRANGE LA
Oakwell Bsns & Youth Ent Ctr
Mount Osborne Ind Pk
Oaks Bsns Pk
S70
1 BALA ST
2 ROCKINGHAM CT
3 CLIFF TERR
4 WANSFELL TERR
5 THIRLMERE RD
6 GRASMERE RD
7 RYDAL TERR
8 LANGDALE RD
9 OAKWELL LA
10 OAKWELL TERR
11 BEEVOR CT
12 OAKWELL VIEW
1 GAINSBOROUGH WAY
2 EDINBURGH CL
3 WELLINGTON CL
GREENFIELD COTTS 1
BROOKFIELD TERR 2

33
55

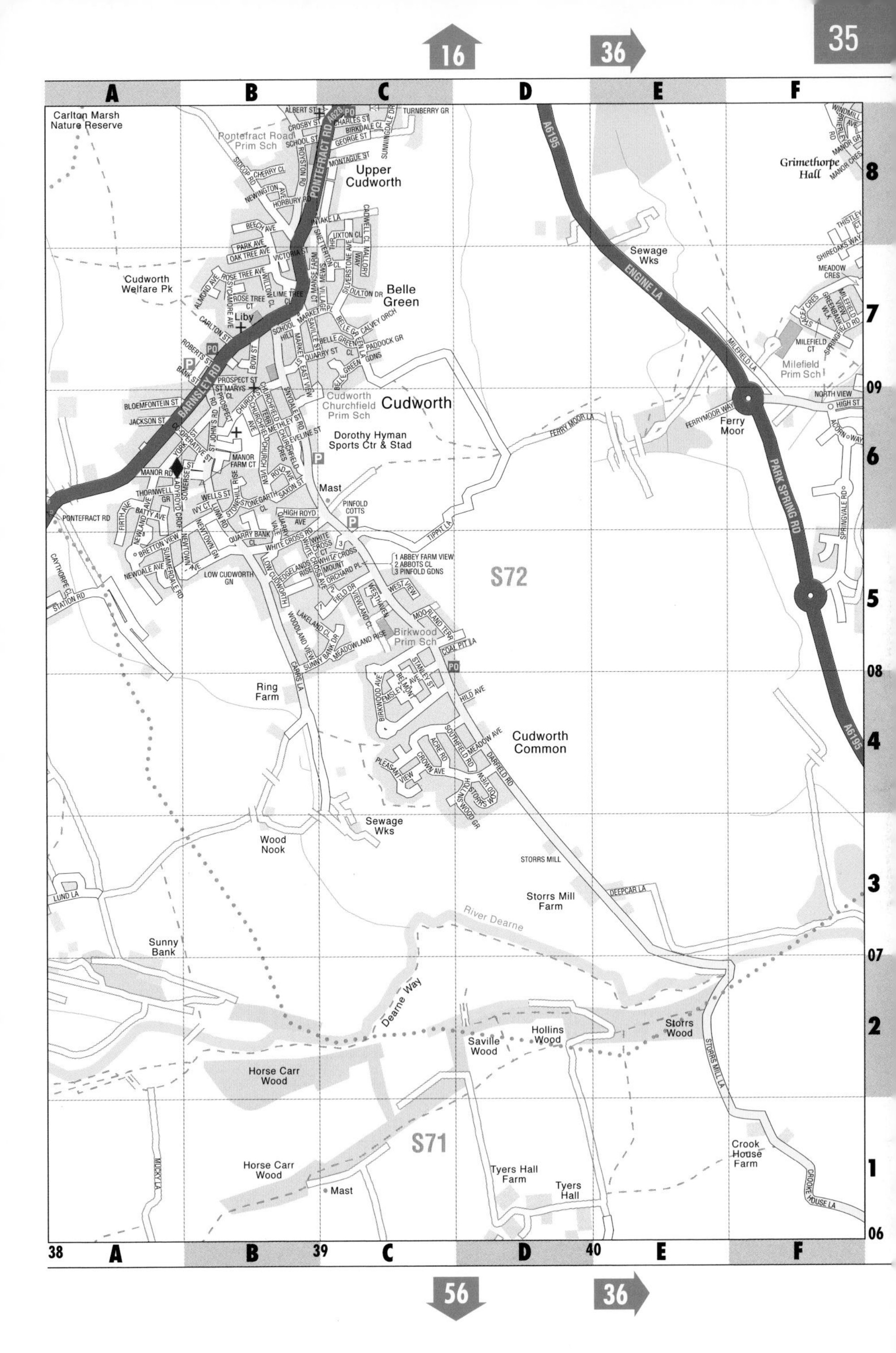
16
36
Carlton Marsh
Nature Reserve
Pontefract Road
Prim Sch
Upper
Cudworth
Cudworth
Welfare Pk
Belle
Green
Cudworth
Cudworth
Churchfield
Prim Sch
Dorothy Hyman
Sports Ctr & Stad
Mast
PINFOLD
COTTS
1 ABBEY FARM VIEW
2 ABBOTS CL
3 PINFOLD GDNS
S72
Birkwood
Prim Sch
Ring
Farm
Cudworth
Common
Sewage
Wks
Wood
Nook
STORRS MILL
Storrs Mill
Farm
River Dearne
Sunny
Bank
Dearne Way
Saville
Wood
Hollins
Wood
Storrs
Wood
Horse Carr
Wood
S71
Horse Carr
Wood
Mast
Tyers Hall
Farm
Tyers
Hall
Crook
House
Farm
Grimethorpe
Hall
Sewage
Wks
ENGINE LA
A6195
PARK SPRING RD
Milefield
Prim Sch
MILEFIELD
CT
Ferry
Moor
FERRY MOOR LA
BARNSLEY RD
PONTEFRACT RD
A628
LUND LA
MUCKY LA
STORRS MILL LA
CROOKE HOUSE LA
DARFIELD RD
CARRS LA
DEEPCAR LA
TIPPIT LA
56
36

35
17

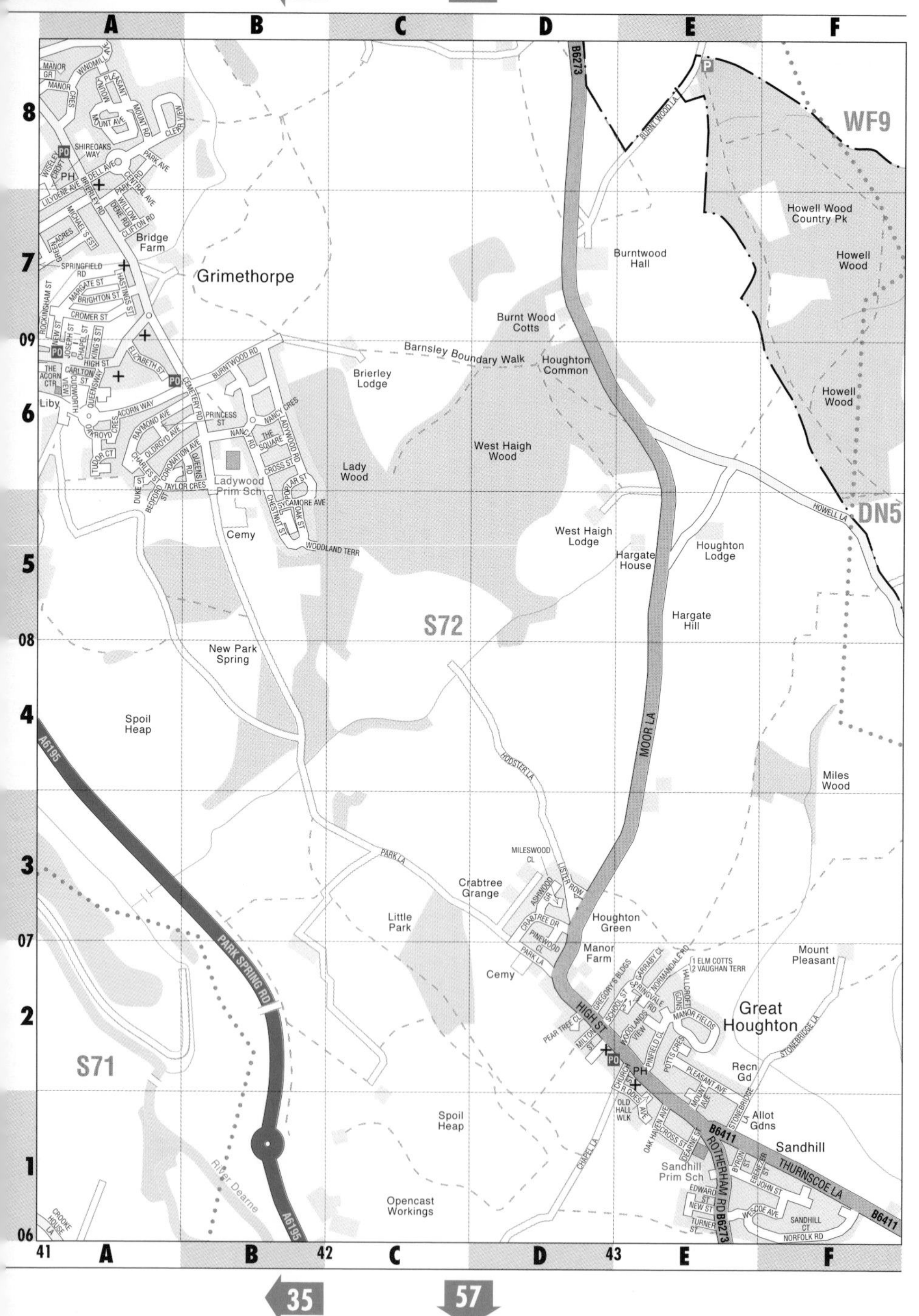
A
B
C
D
E
F
8
7
09
6
5
08
4
3
07
2
1
06
41
42
43
Grimethorpe
Bridge Farm
Burntwood Hall
Burnt Wood Cotts
Barnsley Boundary Walk
Brierley Lodge
Houghton Common
Howell Wood Country Pk
Howell Wood
WF9
West Haigh Wood
Lady Wood
Ladywood Prim Sch
Cemy
West Haigh Lodge
Hargate House
Houghton Lodge
Hargate Hill
DN5
S72
New Park Spring
Spoil Heap
Miles Wood
Crabtree Grange
Little Park
Houghton Green
Manor Farm
Mount Pleasant
Great Houghton
Recn Gd
Allot Gdns
Sandhill
Sandhill Prim Sch
Opencast Workings
S71
River Dearne
A6195
PARK SPRING RD
B6273
MOOR LA
HIGH ST
ROTHERHAM RD
B6411
THURNSCOE LA
HOWELL LA
BURNT WOOD LA
HOOSTER LA
PARK LA
CHAPEL LA
STONEBRIDGE LA
BURNTWOOD RD
CEMETERY RD
WOODLAND TERR
ACORN WAY
Liby
PH
PO
P

35
57

18

38

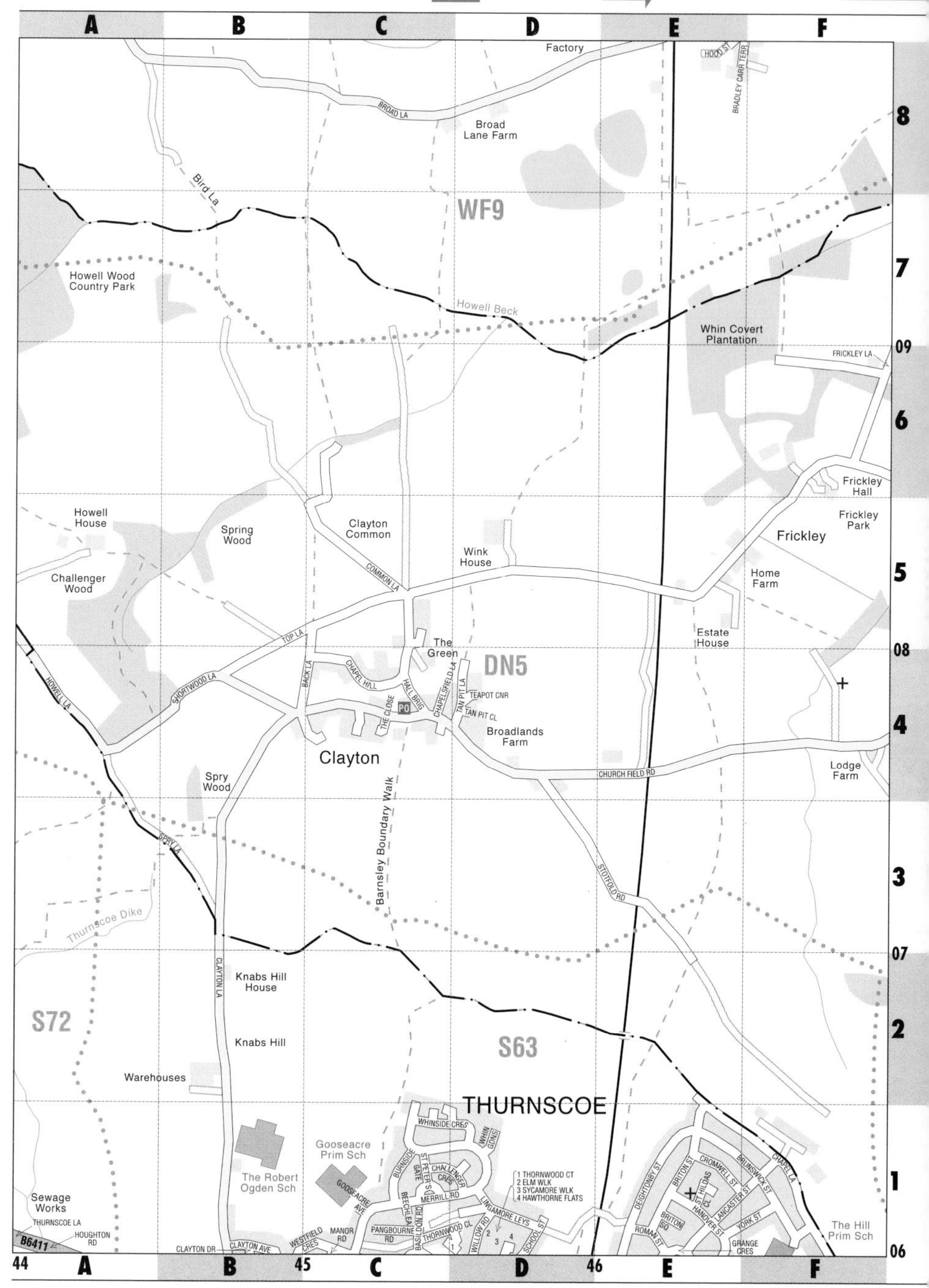

A
B
C
D
E
F
8
7
09
6
5
08
4
3
07
2
1
06
44
45
46
Factory
BROAD LA
Broad
Lane Farm
HOOD ST
BRADLEY CARR TERR
Bird La
WF9
Howell Wood
Country Park
Howell Beck
Whin Covert
Plantation
FRICKLEY LA
Frickley
Hall
Frickley
Park
Frickley
Howell
House
Spring
Wood
Clayton
Common
Wink
House
Challenger
Wood
COMMON LA
Home
Farm
Estate
House
TOP LA
The
Green
DN5
HOWELL LA
SHORTWOOD LA
BACK LA
CHAPEL HILL
HALL BRIG
CHAPELSFIELD LA
TAN PIT LA
TEAPOT CNR
TAN PIT CL
THE CLOSE
PO
Broadlands
Farm
Clayton
CHURCH FIELD RD
Lodge
Farm
Spry
Wood
Barnsley Boundary Walk
SPRY LA
STOTFOLD RD
Thurnscoe Dike
CLAYTON LA
Knabs Hill
House
S72
Knabs Hill
S63
Warehouses
THURNSCOE
WHINSIDE CRES
WHIN GDNS
Gooseacre
Prim Sch
The Robert
Ogden Sch
GOOSEACRE AVE
BURNSIDE
ST PETER'S GATE
CHALLENGER CRES
MERRILL RD
BEECHLEA
1 THORNWOOD CT
2 ELM WLK
3 SYCAMORE WLK
4 HAWTHORNE FLATS
LINGAMORE LEYS
WILLOW RD
SCHOOL ST
THORNWOOD CL
PANGBOURNE RD
MANOR RD
WESTFIELD CRES
CLAYTON AVE
CLAYTON DR
Sewage
Works
THURNSCOE LA
HOUGHTON RD
B6411
DEIGHTONBY ST
BRITON ST
CROMWELL ST
ST HILDAS CL
BRUNSWICK ST
CHAPEL LA
LANCASTER ST
HANOVER ST
BRITON SQ
ROMAN ST
YORK ST
GRANGE CRES
The Hill
Prim Sch

58
38

37
19

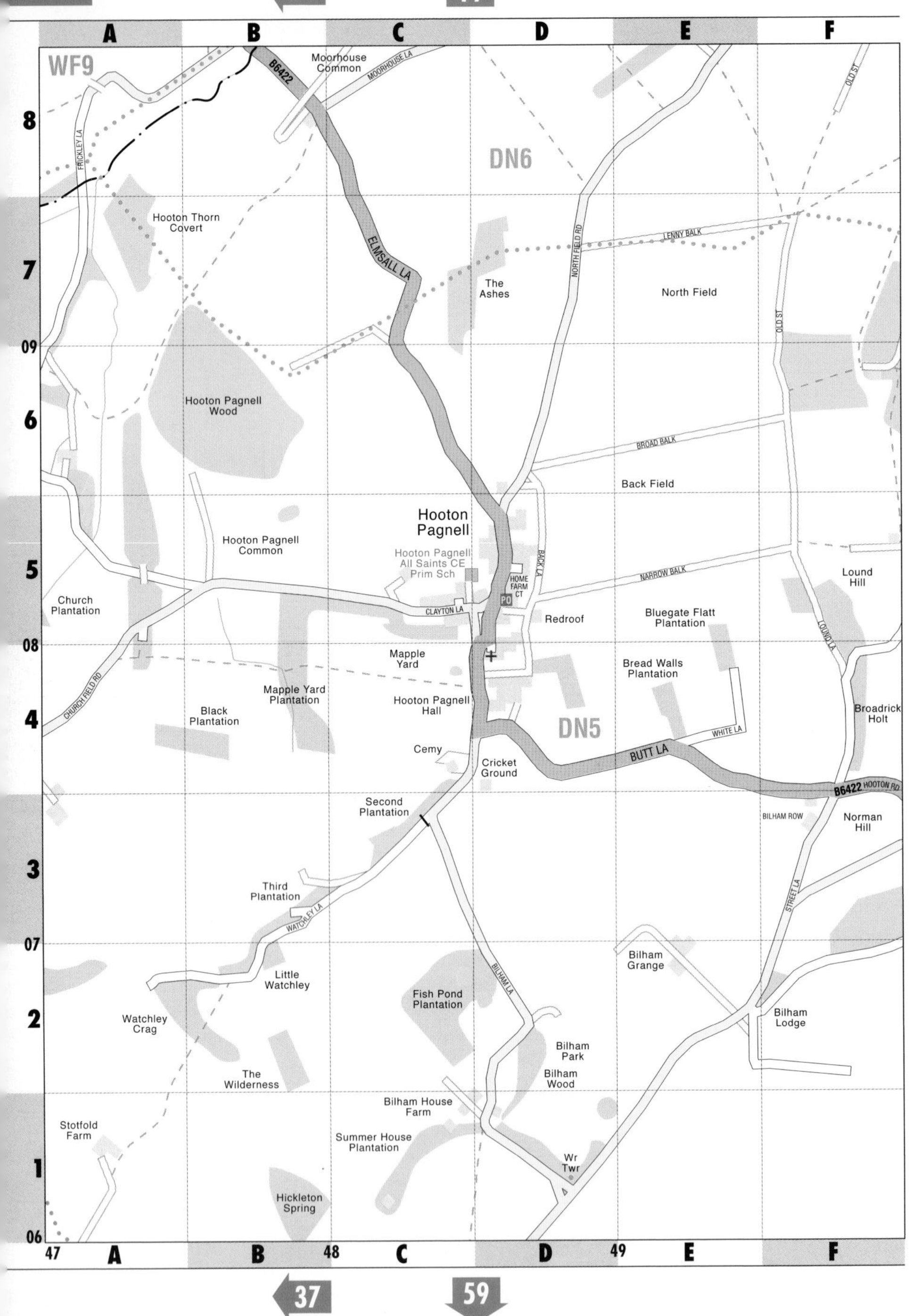
A
B
C
D
E
F
WF9
Moorhouse Common
MOORHOUSE LA
B6422
OLD ST
8
FRICKLEY LA
DN6
Hooton Thorn Covert
ELMSALL LA
LENNY BALK
NORTH FIELD RD
7
The Ashes
North Field
OLD ST
09
Hooton Pagnell Wood
6
BROAD BALK
Back Field
Hooton Pagnell
Hooton Pagnell Common
Hooton Pagnell All Saints CE Prim Sch
BACK LA
5
HOME FARM CT
NARROW BALK
Lound Hill
Church Plantation
PO
CLAYTON LA
Redroof
Bluegate Flatt Plantation
LOUND LA
08
Mapple Yard
Bread Walls Plantation
Mapple Yard Plantation
Hooton Pagnell Hall
CHURCH FIELD RD
Black Plantation
DN5
WHITE LA
Broadrick Holt
4
Cemy
BUTT LA
Cricket Ground
B6422
HOOTON RD
Second Plantation
BILHAM ROW
Norman Hill
3
Third Plantation
WATCHLEY LA
STREET LA
07
Bilham Grange
Little Watchley
BILHAM LA
Fish Pond Plantation
Bilham Lodge
2
Watchley Crag
Bilham Park
Bilham Wood
The Wilderness
Bilham House Farm
Stotfold Farm
Summer House Plantation
1
Wr Twr
Hickleton Spring
06
47
48
49

37
59

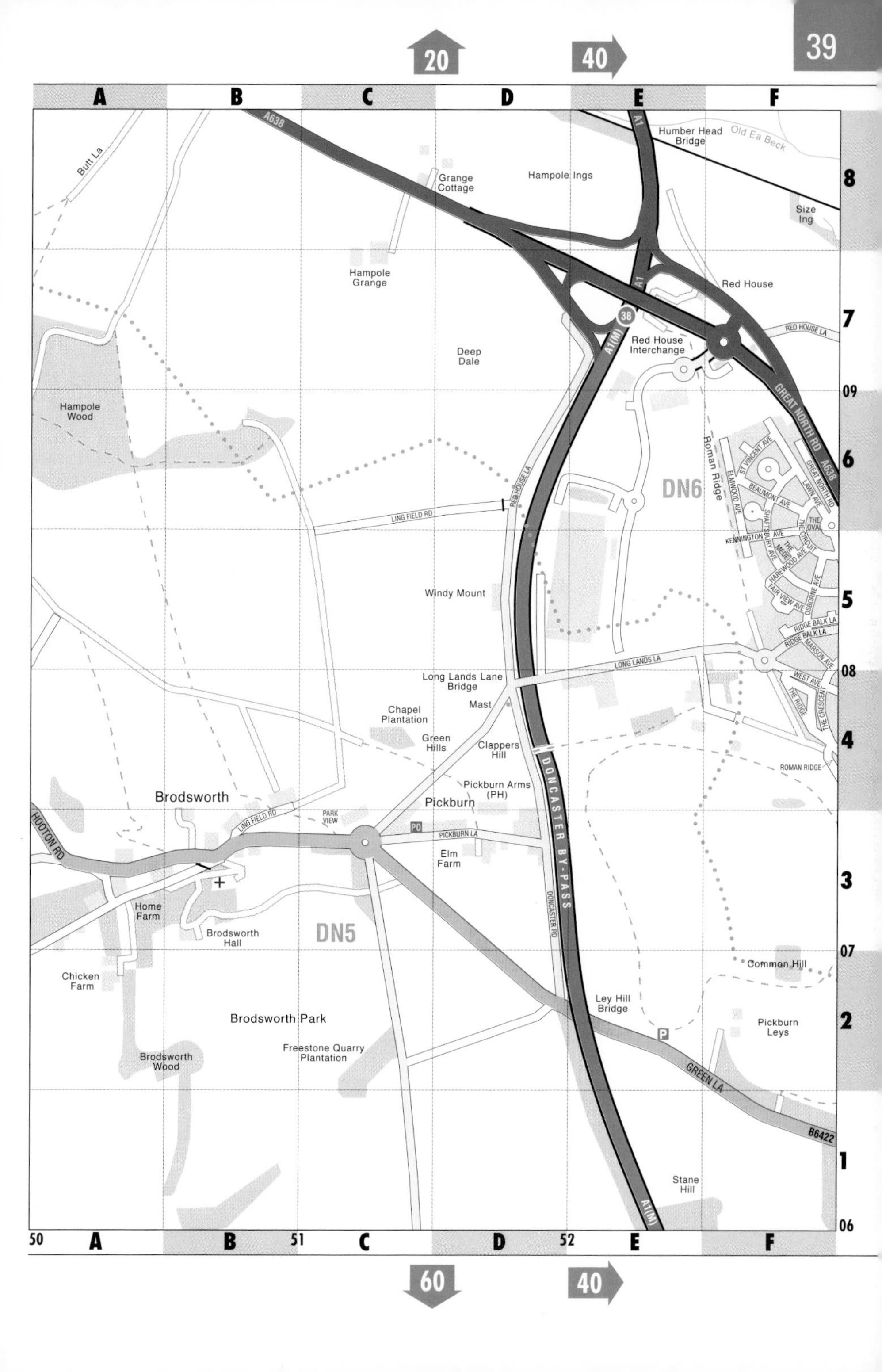
20
40
A638
A1
Butt La
Humber Head Bridge
Old Ea Beck
Grange Cottage
Hampole Ings
Size Ing
Hampole Grange
Red House
38
A1(M)
Red House Interchange
RED HOUSE LA
Deep Dale
Hampole Wood
GREAT NORTH RD
Roman Ridge
DN6
RED HOUSE LA
LING FIELD RD
ST VINCENT AVE
ELMWOOD AVE
BEAUMONT AVE
LAWN AVE
THE OVAL
SHAFTESBURY AVE
THE CIRCUIT
KENNINGTON AVE
THE MEDE
HAREWOOD AVE
FAIR VIEW AVE
OSBORNE AVE
Windy Mount
RIDGE BALK LA
MARSON AVE
LONG LANDS LA
Long Lands Lane Bridge
Mast
WEST AVE
THE RIDGE
THE CRESCENT
Chapel Plantation
Green Hills
Clappers Hill
ROMAN RIDGE
DONCASTER BY-PASS
Pickburn Arms (PH)
Brodsworth
Pickburn
HOOTON RD
LING FIELD RD
PARK VIEW
PO
PICKBURN LA
Elm Farm
Home Farm
DN5
Brodsworth Hall
DONCASTER RD
Common Hill
Chicken Farm
Ley Hill Bridge
Brodsworth Park
P
Pickburn Leys
Freestone Quarry Plantation
Brodsworth Wood
GREEN LA
B6422
Stane Hill
A1(M)
A B C D E F
8 7 09 6 5 08 4 3 07 2 1 06
50 51 52
60
40

39
21

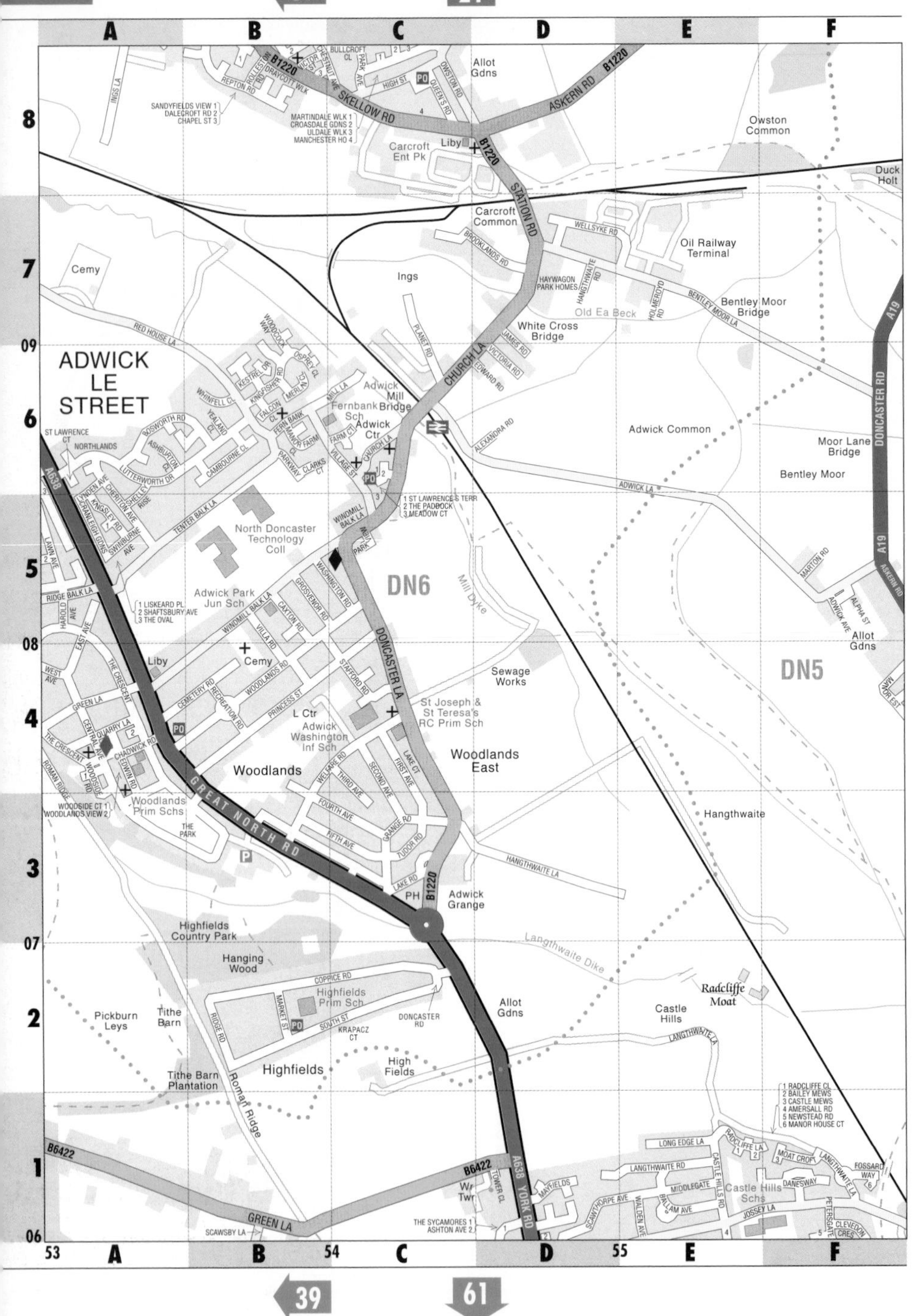
ADWICK
LE
STREET
DN6
DN5
Carcroft
Common
Carcroft
Ent Pk
Owston
Common
Duck
Holt
Oil Railway
Terminal
Ings
Bentley Moor
Bridge
White Cross
Bridge
Adwick Common
Moor Lane
Bridge
Bentley Moor
North Doncaster
Technology
Coll
Adwick Park
Jun Sch
Fernbank
Sch
Adwick
Mill
Bridge
Adwick
Ctr
Sewage
Works
St Joseph &
St Teresa's
RC Prim Sch
Adwick
Washington
Inf Sch
Woodlands
Woodlands
East
Woodlands
Prim Schs
Hangthwaite
Adwick
Grange
Highfields
Country Park
Hanging
Wood
Highfields
Prim Sch
Pickburn
Leys
Tithe
Barn
Allot
Gdns
Castle
Hills
Radcliffe
Moat
Highfields
High
Fields
Tithe Barn
Plantation
Roman Ridge
Castle Hills
Schs
SKELLOW RD
ASKERN RD
STATION RD
CHURCH LA
DONCASTER LA
GREAT NORTH RD
DONCASTER RD
YORK RD
GREEN LA
B1220
B6422
A638
A19
Old Ea Beck
Mill Dyke
Langthwaite Dike
Cemy
Liby
PO
PH
1 LISKEARD PL
2 SHAFTSBURY AVE
3 THE OVAL
1 ST LAWRENCE'S TERR
2 THE PADDOCK
3 MEADOW CT
SANDYFIELDS VIEW 1
DALECROFT RD 2
CHAPEL ST 3
MARTINDALE WLK 1
CROASDALE GDNS 2
ULDALE WLK 3
MANCHESTER HO 4
WOODSIDE CT 1
WOODLANDS VIEW 2
1 RADCLIFFE CL
2 BAILEY MEWS
3 CASTLE MEWS
4 AMERSALL RD
5 NEWSTEAD RD
6 MANOR HOUSE CT
THE SYCAMORES 1
ASHTON AVE 2
A B C D E F
8 7 09 6 5 08 4 3 07 2 1 06
53 54 55

39
61

22

42

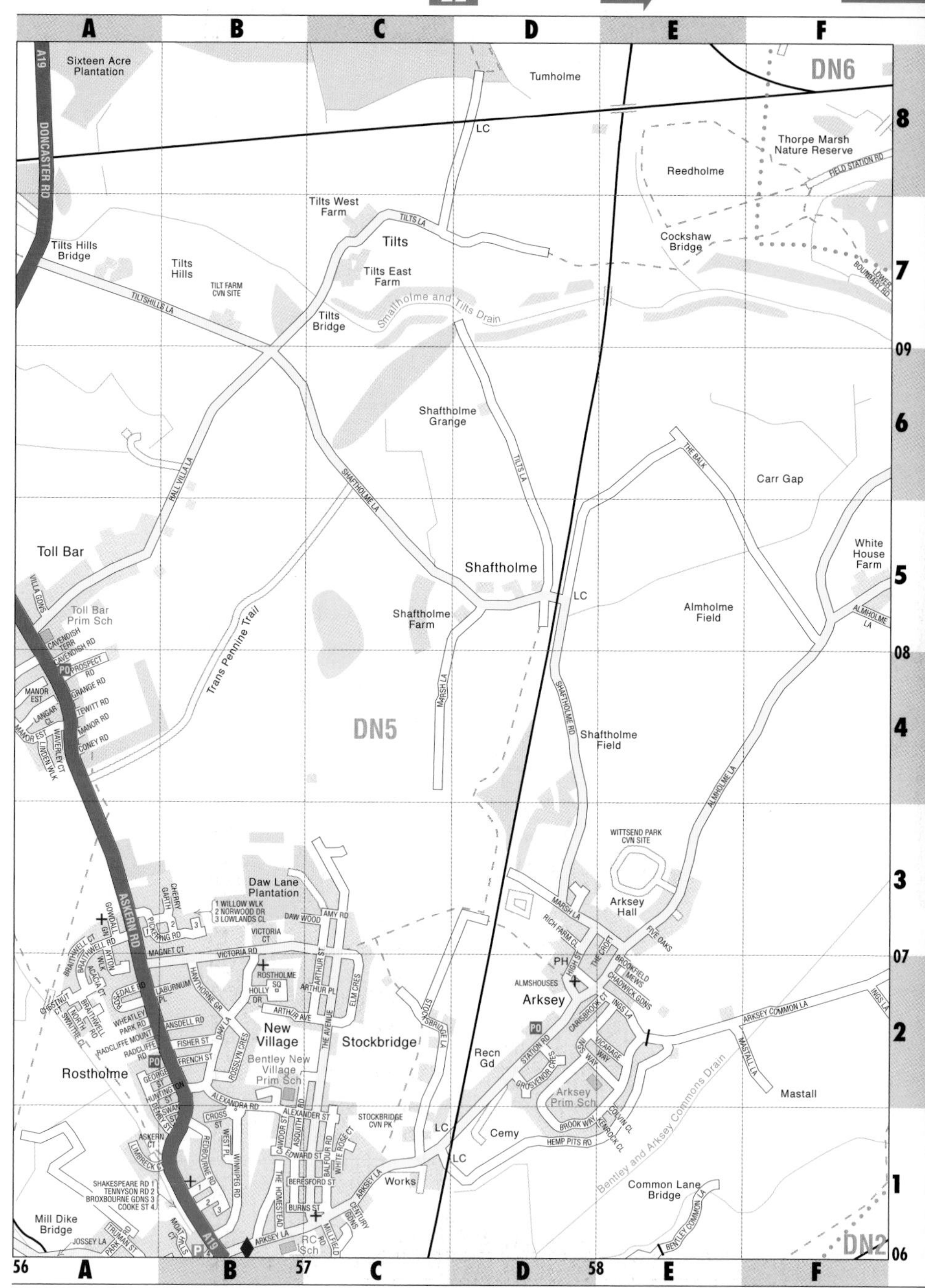

A
B
C
D
E
F
Sixteen Acre Plantation
Tumholme
DN6
A19
DONCASTER RD
LC
Thorpe Marsh Nature Reserve
Reedholme
FIELD STATION RD
Tilts West Farm
TILTS LA
Tilts
Tilts Hills Bridge
Tilts Hills
TILT FARM CVN SITE
Tilts East Farm
Cockshaw Bridge
LOWER BOUNDARY RD
TILTSHILLS LA
Tilts Bridge
Smaltholme and Tilts Drain
Shaftholme Grange
HALL VILLA LA
THE BALK
Carr Gap
TILTS LA
SHAFTHOLME LA
Toll Bar
White House Farm
Shaftholme
LC
VILLA GDNS
Toll Bar Prim Sch
Shaftholme Farm
Almholme Field
ALMHOLME LA
CAVENDISH TERR
CAVENDISH RD
PROSPECT RD
MANOR EST
GRANGE RD
Trans Pennine Trail
MARSH LA
SHAFTHOLME RD
TEWITT RD
LANGAR CL
MANOR RD
MANOR EST
CONEY RD
WAVERLEY CT
LINDEN WLK
DN5
Shaftholme Field
ALMHOLME LA
WITTSEND PARK CVN SITE
Daw Lane Plantation
CHERRY GARTH
1 WILLOW WLK
2 NORWOOD DR
3 LOWLANDS CL
AMY RD
DAW WOOD
ASKERN RD
GOWDALL GN
PICKERING RD
VICTORIA CT
MARSH LA
Arksey Hall
RICH FARM CL
FIVE OAKS
BRAITHWELL CT
BRAITHWELL RD
AYTON WLK
MAGNET CT
VICTORIA RD
ARTHUR ST
THE CROFT
HIGH ST
PH
BROOKFIELD MEWS
ACACIA CT
ROSSDALE RD
LABURNUM PL
HAWTHORNE GR
ROSTHOLME SQ
ELM CRES
ARTHUR PL
CHADWICK GDNS
ALMSHOUSES
CHESTNUT CT
NORTH BRAITHWELL RD
HOLLY DR
ARTHUR AVE
STOCKBRIDGE LA
Arksey
CARISBROOK CT
INGS LA
ARKSEY COMMON LA
INGS LA
WHEATLEY PARK RD
DAW LA
ANSDELL RD
SWAITHE CL
RADCLIFFE MOUNT
ROSSLYN CRES
New Village
THE AVENUE
Stockbridge
PO
MASTALL LA
RADCLIFFE RD
FISHER ST
VICARAGE WAY
PO
FRENCH ST
Bentley New Village Prim Sch
Recn Gd
STATION RD
SIGNS WAY
Rostholme
GEORGE ST
GROSVENOR CRES
Arksey Prim Sch
Bentley and Arksey Commons Drain
Mastall
HUNTINGTON DENBY ST
SWAN ST
ALEXANDRA RD
ALEXANDER ST
CROSS ST
STOCKBRIDGE CVN PK
WHITE ROSE CT
ASKERN CT
WEST PL
WINNIPEG RD
CAMDOR ST
ASQUITH RD
LC
Cemy
COLVIN CL
BROOK WAY
KENROCK CL
HEMP PITS RD
LIMBRECK CT
REDBOURNE RD
EDWARD ST
BALFOUR RD
LC
SHAKESPEARE RD 1
TENNYSON RD 2
BROXBOURNE GDNS 3
COOKE ST 4
THE HOMESTEAD
BERESFORD ST
ARKSEY LA
Works
Common Lane Bridge
BENTLEY COMMON LA
BURNS ST
CENTURY GDNS
Mill Dike Bridge
JOSSEY LA
TRUMAN ST
PARK RD
MOAT HILLS CT
A19
ARKSEY LA
RC Sch
MILLFIELD RD
DN2
8
7
09
6
5
08
4
3
07
2
1
06
56
57
58

62

42

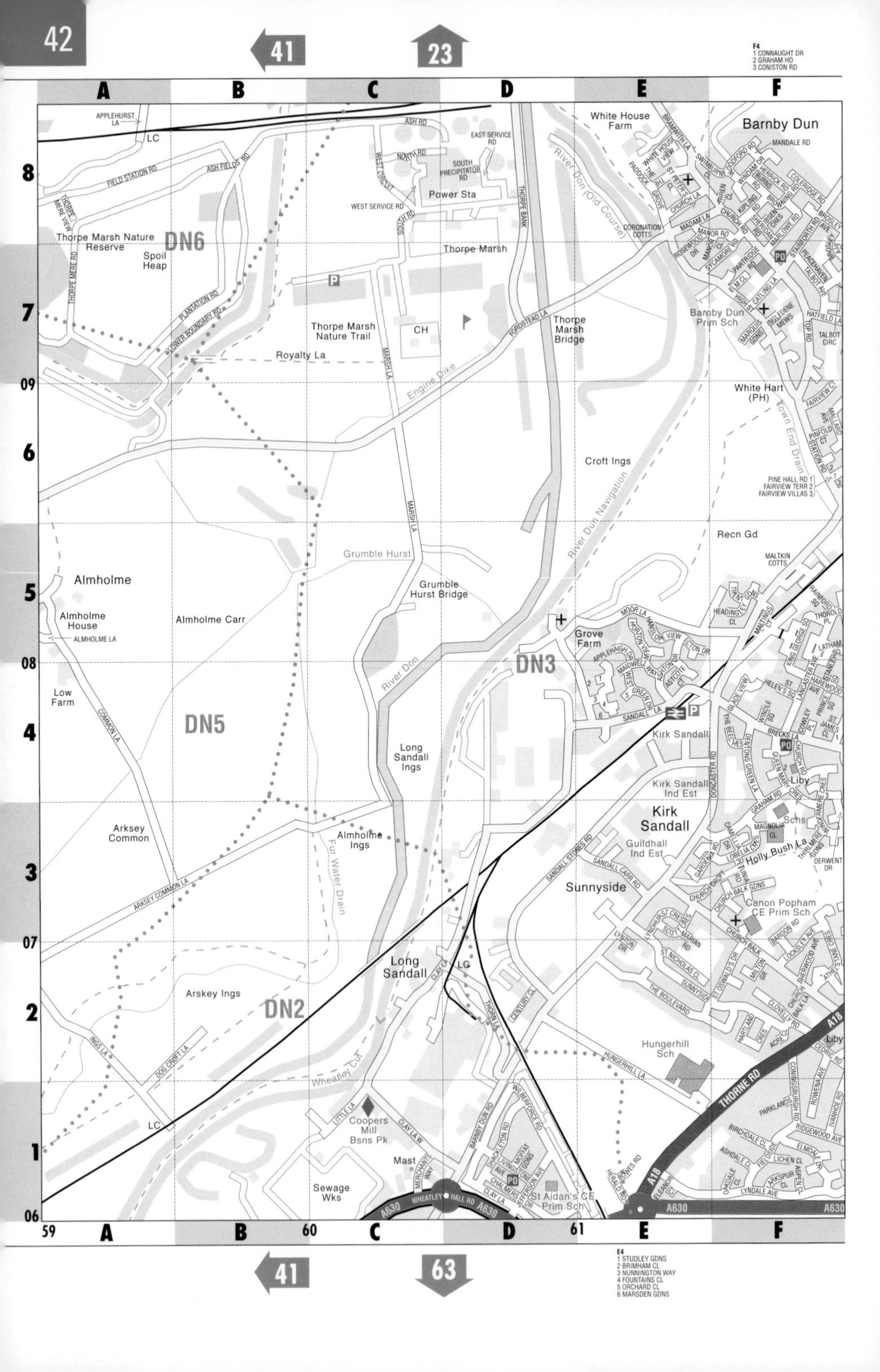

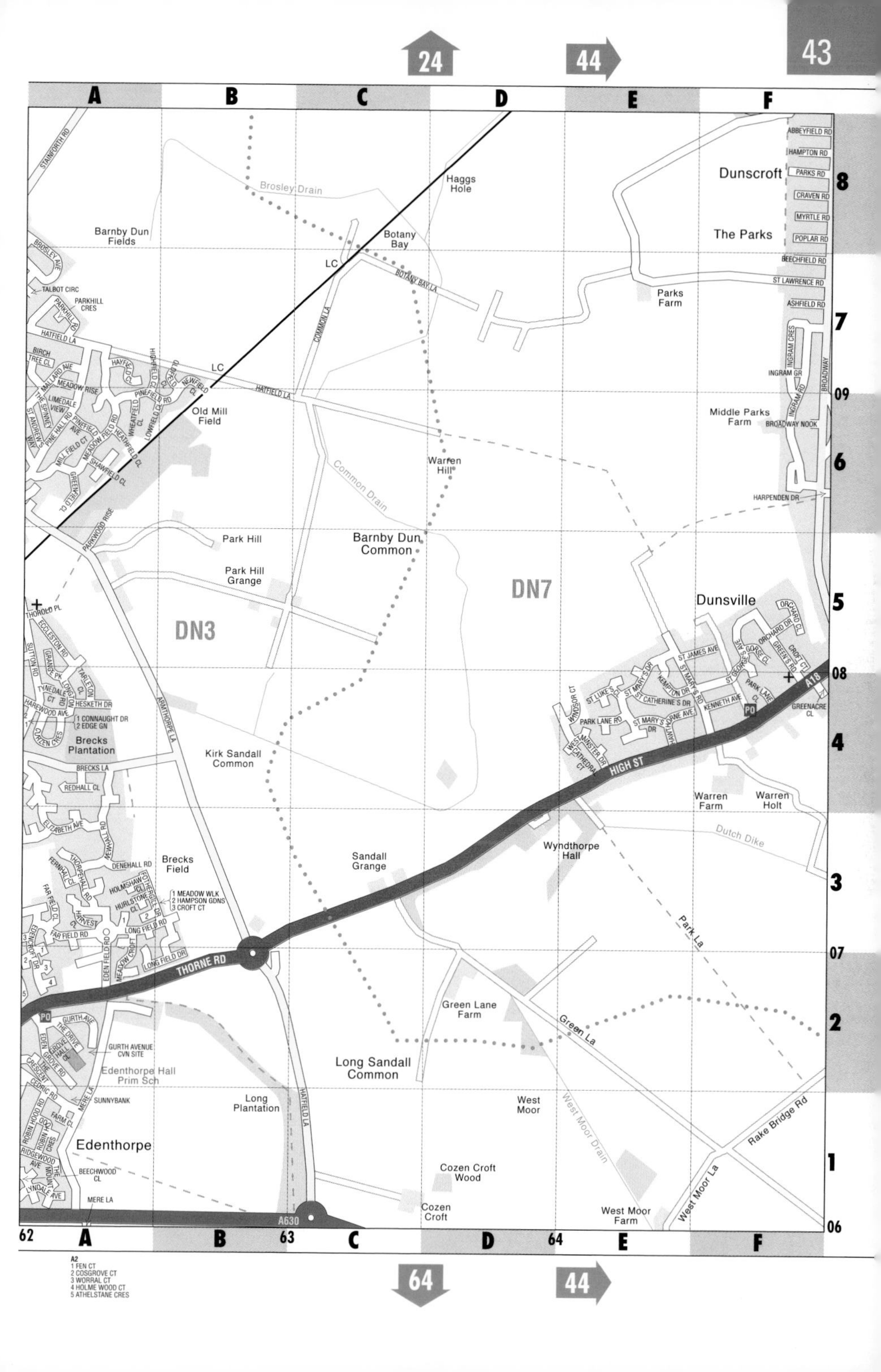

Dunscroft

The Parks

Barnby Dun
Fields

Brosley Drain

Haggs
Hole

Botany
Bay

LC

Talbot Circ

Parkhill
Cres

Parks
Farm

Hatfield La

LC

Old Mill
Field

Middle Parks
Farm

Broadway Nook

Warren
Hill

Harpenden Dr

Park Hill

Barnby Dun
Common

DN7

Dunsville

Park Hill
Grange

DN3

Brecks
Plantation

Kirk Sandall
Common

High St

Warren
Farm

Warren
Holt

Dutch Dike

Brecks
Field

Sandall
Grange

Wyndthorpe
Hall

Park La

Thorne Rd

Green Lane
Farm

Green La

Long Sandall
Common

Edenthorpe

Long
Plantation

West
Moor

West Moor Drain

Rake Bridge Rd

Cozen Croft
Wood

West Moor La

Cozen
Croft

West Moor
Farm

A630

A2
1 FEN CT
2 COSGROVE CT
3 WORRAL CT
4 HOLME WOOD CT
5 ATHELSTANE CRES

43
25

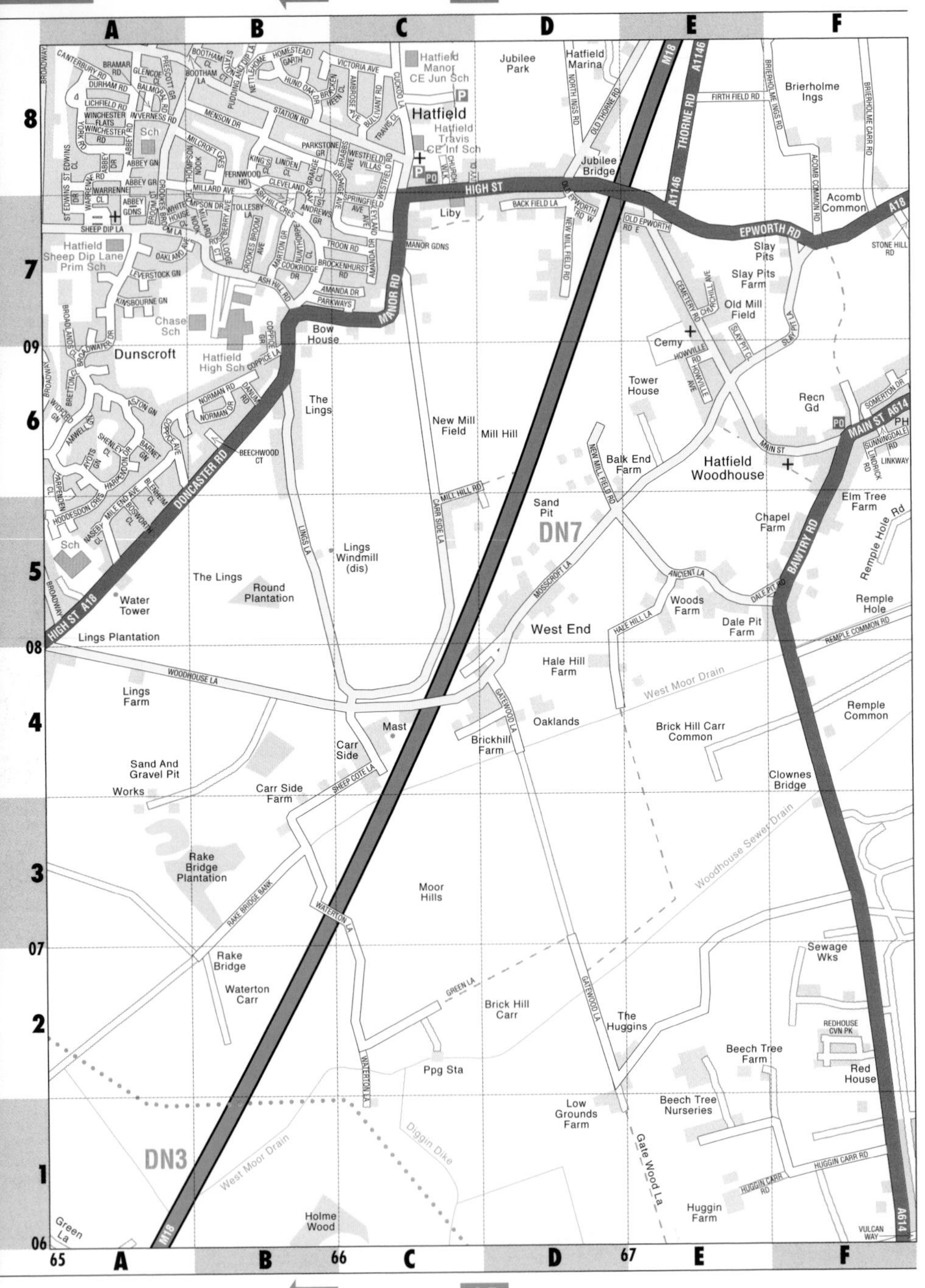
A
B
C
D
E
F
8
7
09
6
5
08
4
3
07
2
1
06
65
66
67
Hatfield Manor CE Jun Sch
Jubilee Park
Hatfield Marina
Brierholme Ings
Hatfield
Hatfield Travis CE Inf Sch
Jubilee Bridge
HIGH ST
Liby
BACK FIELD LA
EPWORTH RD
Acomb Common
Hatfield Sheep Dip Lane Prim Sch
Sch
Chase Sch
Hatfield High Sch
Dunscroft
Bow House
MANOR RD
Slay Pits
Slay Pits Farm
Old Mill Field
Cemy
Tower House
Recn Gd
The Lings
New Mill Field
Mill Hill
DONCASTER RD
Balk End Farm
Hatfield Woodhouse
MAIN ST A614
Elm Tree Farm
Sand Pit
DN7
Chapel Farm
Remple Hole Rd
Lings Windmill (dis)
BAWTRY RD
The Lings
Round Plantation
Water Tower
Woods Farm
Remple Hole
West End
Dale Pit Farm
Lings Plantation
HIGH ST A18
Hale Hill Farm
WOODHOUSE LA
West Moor Drain
Lings Farm
Mast
Oaklands
Brick Hill Carr Common
Remple Common
Carr Side
Brickhill Farm
Sand And Gravel Pit
Works
Carr Side Farm
Clownes Bridge
Woodhouse Sewer Drain
Rake Bridge Plantation
Moor Hills
RAKE BRIDGE BANK
Sewage Wks
Rake Bridge
Waterton Carr
GREEN LA
Brick Hill Carr
The Huggins
REDHOUSE CVN PK
Beech Tree Farm
Ppg Sta
Red House
Low Grounds Farm
Beech Tree Nurseries
Diggin Dike
DN3
West Moor Drain
Gate Wood La
HUGGIN CARR RD
Huggin Farm
Holme Wood
Green La
M18
A1146
THORNE RD
A18
A614
VULCAN WAY

43
65

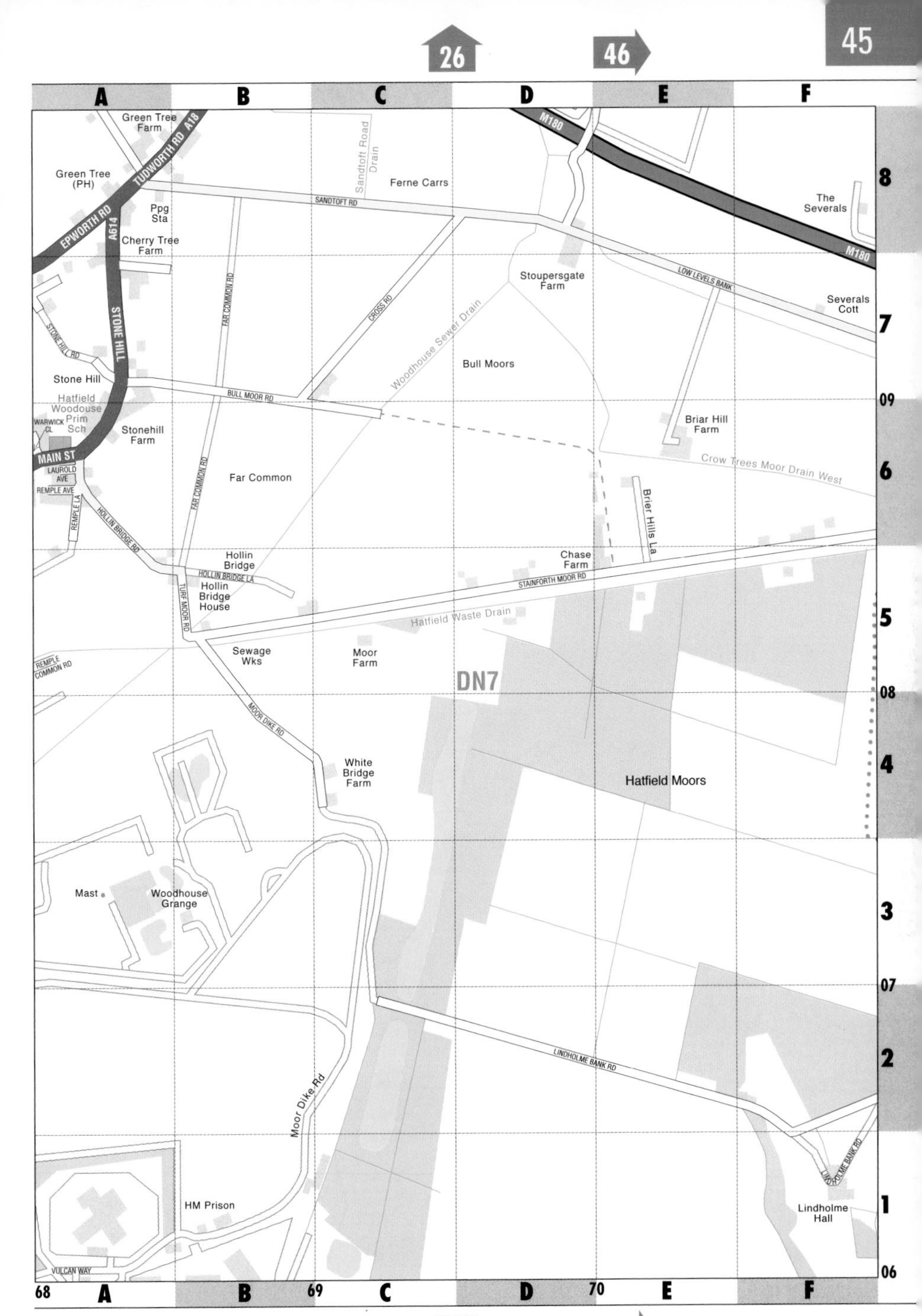

26
46
A
B
C
D
E
F
Green Tree Farm
TUDWORTH RD A18
Green Tree (PH)
EPWORTH RD
Ppg Sta
A614
Cherry Tree Farm
Sandtoft Road Drain
Ferne Carrs
SANDTOFT RD
M180
The Severals
Stoupersgate Farm
LOW LEVELS BANK
Severals Cott
FAR COMMON RD
CROSS RD
STONE HILL
STONE HILL RD
Woodhouse Sewer Drain
Bull Moors
Stone Hill
BULL MOOR RD
Hatfield Woodouse Prim Sch
WARWICK CL
Stonehill Farm
Briar Hill Farm
MAIN ST
LAUROLD AVE
REMPLE AVE
Crow Trees Moor Drain West
Far Common
Brier Hills La
REMPLE LA
HOLLIN BRIDGE RD
Hollin Bridge
HOLLIN BRIDGE LA
Hollin Bridge House
Chase Farm
STAINFORTH MOOR RD
TURF MOOR RD
Hatfield Waste Drain
REMPLE COMMON RD
Sewage Wks
Moor Farm
DN7
MOOR DIKE RD
White Bridge Farm
Hatfield Moors
Mast
Woodhouse Grange
LINDHOLME BANK RD
Moor Dike Rd
HM Prison
Lindholme Hall
VULCAN WAY
8
7
09
6
5
08
4
3
07
2
1
06
68
69
70
66
46

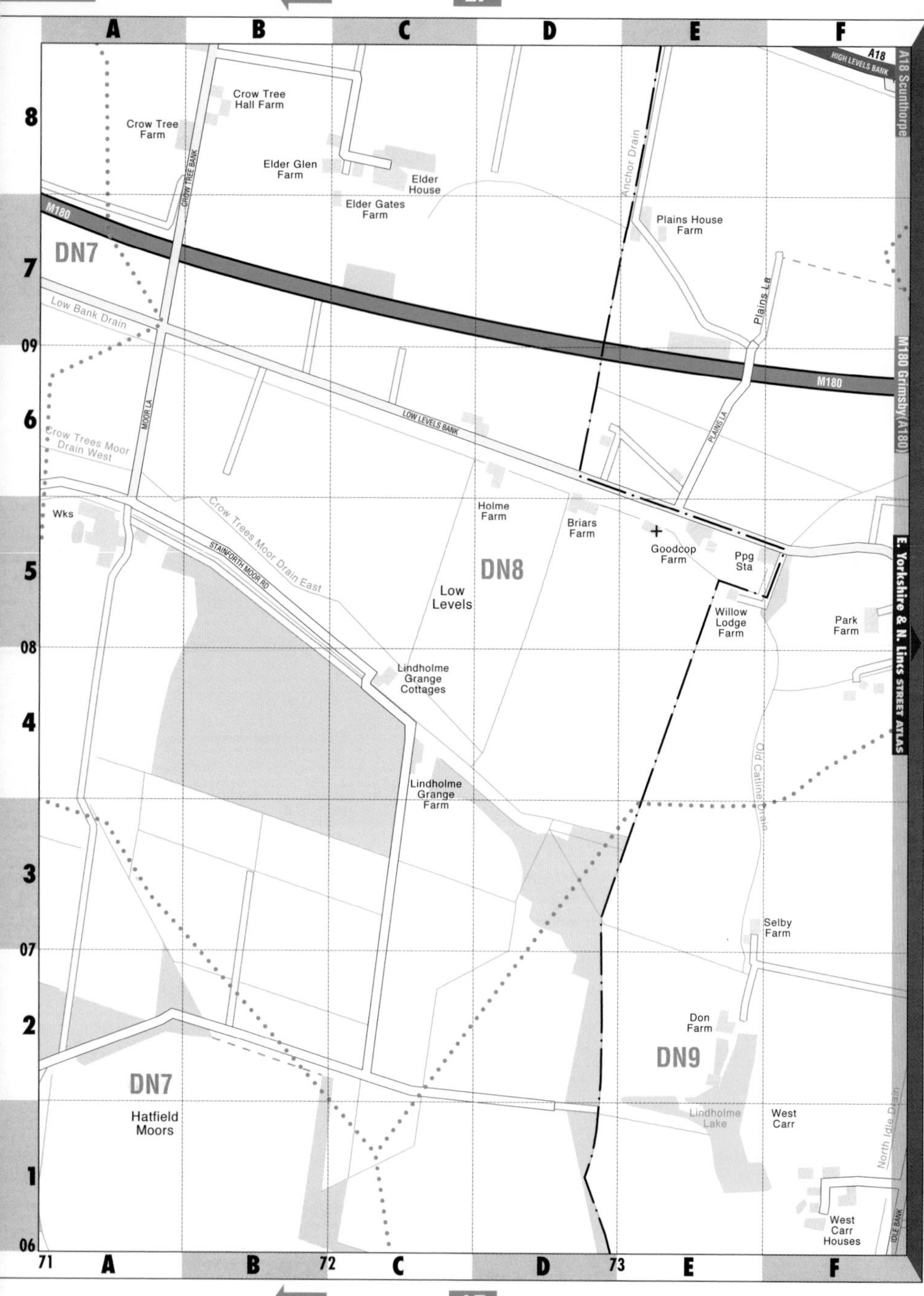

A18 Scunthorpe
HIGH LEVELS BANK
A18

M180 Grimsby/(A180)

E. Yorkshire & N. Lincs STREET ATLAS

8

Crow Tree Farm

Crow Tree Hall Farm

Elder Glen Farm

Elder House

Elder Gates Farm

Anchor Drain

Plains House Farm

Plains La

M180

DN7

7

Low Bank Drain

09

Crow Trees Moor Drain West

LOW LEVELS BANK

M180

6

MOOR LA

CROW TREE BANK

PLAINS LA

Wks

Crow Trees Moor Drain East

Holme Farm

Briars Farm

Goodcop Farm

Ppg Sta

Park Farm

5

STAINFORTH MOOR RD

Low Levels

DN8

Willow Lodge Farm

08

Lindholme Grange Cottages

4

Lindholme Grange Farm

Old Catline Drain

Selby Farm

3

07

Don Farm

DN9

North Idle Drain

2

DN7

Hatfield Moors

Lindholme Lake

West Carr

West Carr Houses

IDLE FDR

1

06

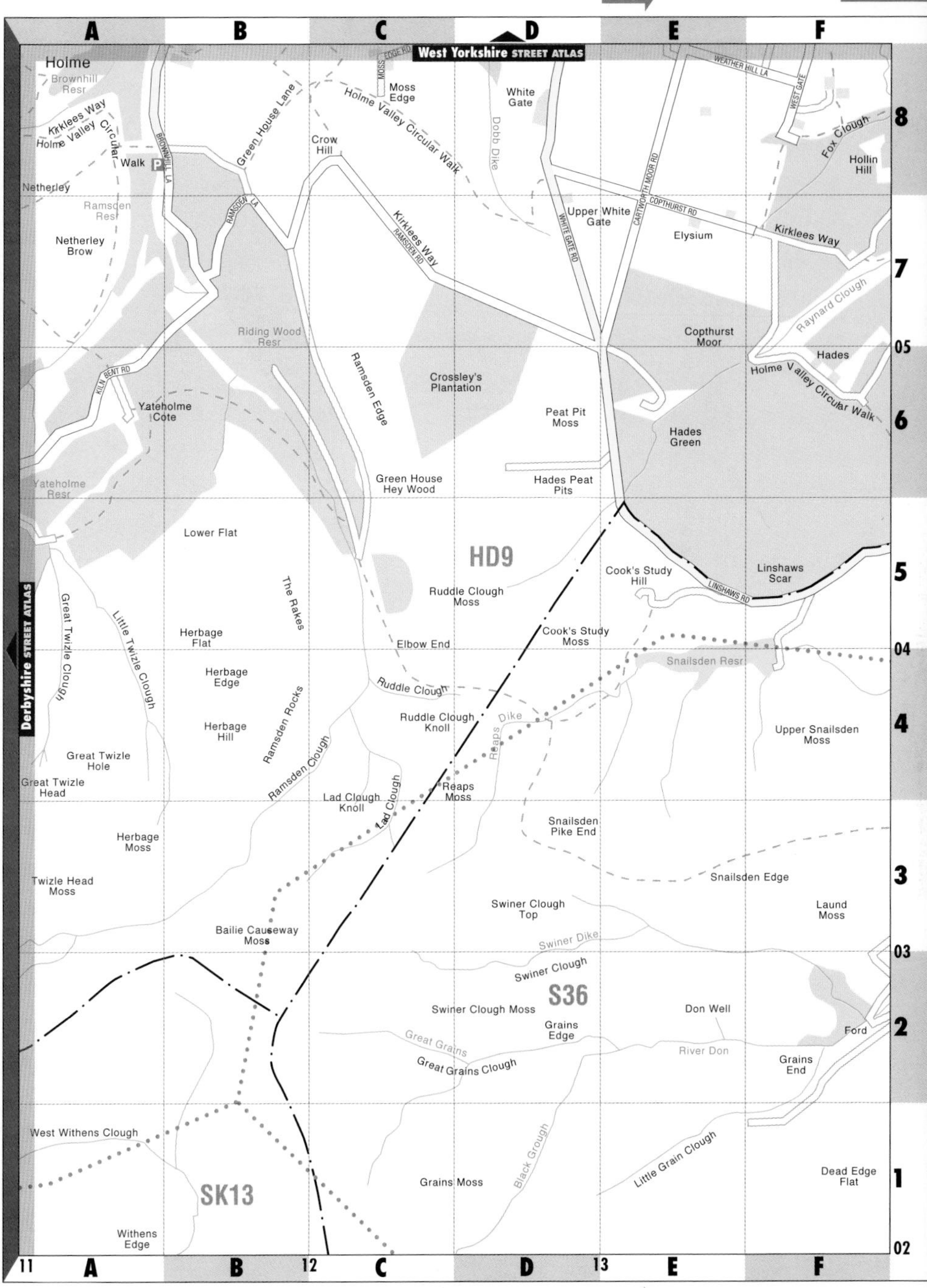

West Yorkshire STREET ATLAS

Holme
Brownhill Resr
Kirklees Way
Holme Valley Circular Walk
Netherley
Ramsden Resr
Netherley Brow
Green House Lane
Moss Edge
Crow Hill
Holme Valley Circular Walk
White Gate
Dobb Dike
WEATHER HILL LA
WEST GATE
Fox Clough
Hollin Hill
Upper White Gate
Elysium
Kirklees Way
CARTWORTH MOOR RD
COPTHURST RD
Kirklees Way
Raynard Clough
Hades
05
Riding Wood Resr
Ramsden Edge
Crossley's Plantation
Peat Pit Moss
Copthurst Moor
Holme Valley Circular Walk
Yateholme Cote
Green House Hey Wood
Hades Peat Pits
Hades Green
Yateholme Resr
Lower Flat
HD9
Ruddle Clough Moss
Cook's Study Hill
Cook's Study Moss
Linshaws Scar
LINSHAWS RD
5
Great Twizle Clough
The Rakes
Herbage Flat
Elbow End
Ruddle Clough
Snailsden Resr
04
Little Twizle Clough
Herbage Edge
Ramsden Rocks
Ruddle Clough Knoll
Reaps Dike
Upper Snailsden Moss
4
Great Twizle Hole
Herbage Hill
Ramsden Clough
Lad Clough Knoll
Lad Clough
Reaps Moss
Snailsden Pike End
Great Twizle Head
Herbage Moss
Snailsden Edge
Twizle Head Moss
Bailie Causeway Moss
Swiner Clough Top
Swiner Dike
Laund Moss
3
03
Swiner Clough
S36
Swiner Clough Moss
Grains Edge
Don Well
River Don
Grains End
Ford
West Withens Clough
Great Grains
Great Grains Clough
Black Clough
Little Grain Clough
2
SK13
Grains Moss
Dead Edge Flat
1
Withens Edge
02

47

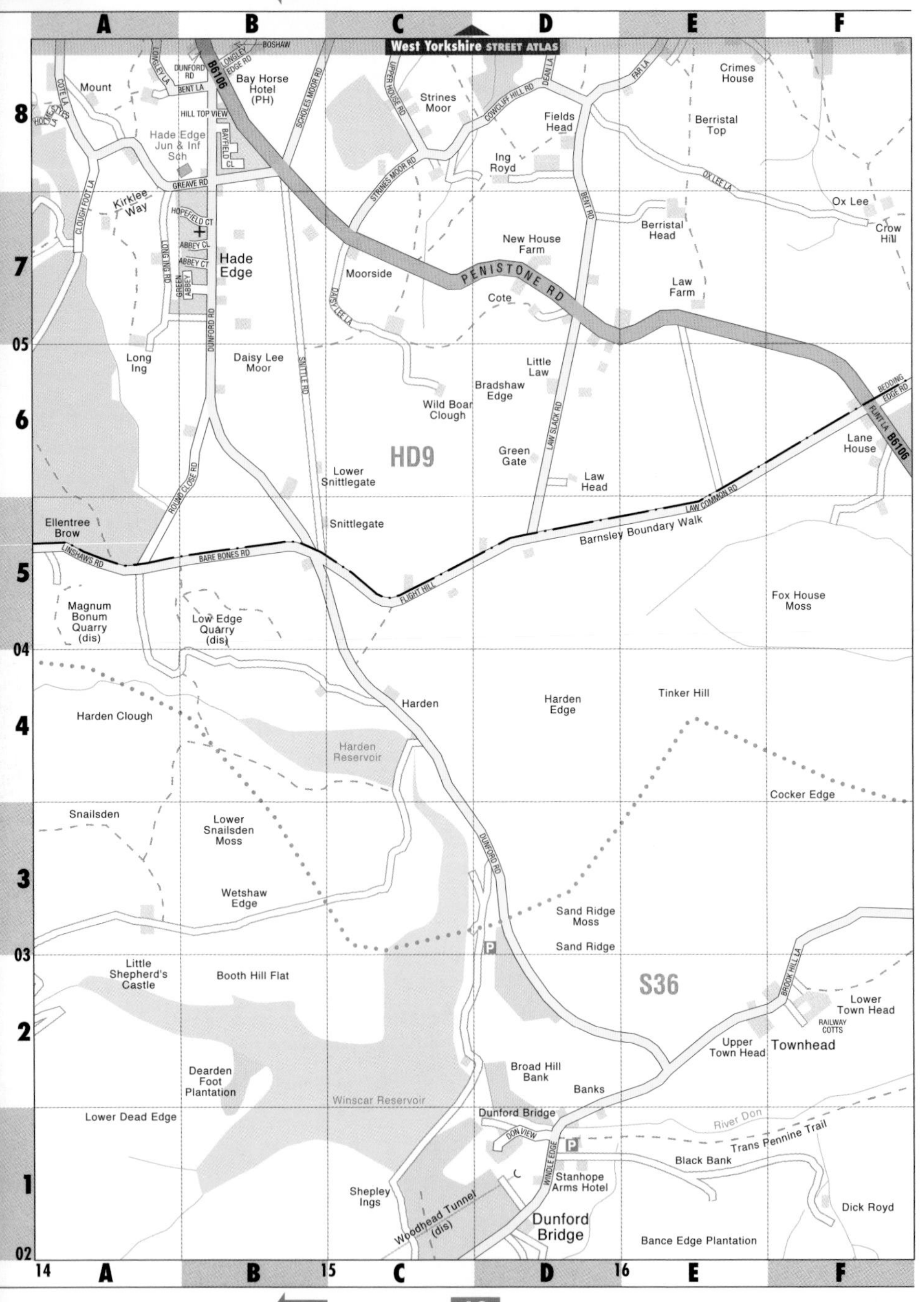

A B C D E F

8

7

05

6

5

04

4

3

03

2

02

14 A B 15 C D 16 E F

47

69

Mount

Hade Edge Jun & Inf Sch

Kirklee Way

Dunford Bridge

Bay Horse Hotel (PH)

Hade Edge

Long Ing

Ellentree Brow

Magnum Bonum Quarry (dis)

Low Edge Quarry (dis)

Harden Clough

Snailsden

Lower Snailsden Moss

Wetshaw Edge

Little Shepherd's Castle

Booth Hill Flat

Dearden Foot Plantation

Lower Dead Edge

Shepley Ings

Woodhead Tunnel (dis)

Winscar Reservoir

Boshaw

Strines Moor

Fields Head

Ing Royd

Moorside

Cote

Daisy Lee Moor

New House Farm

Little Law

Bradshaw Edge

Wild Boar Clough

Lower Snittlegate

Green Gate

Snittlegate

Law Head

Barnsley Boundary Walk

Flight Hill

Harden

Harden Reservoir

Harden Edge

Sand Ridge Moss

Sand Ridge

Broad Hill Bank

Banks

Dunford Bridge

Low View

Stanhope Arms Hotel

Black Bank

Trans Pennine Trail

River Don

Upper Town Head

Townhead

Lower Town Head

RAILWAY COTTS

Brook Hill La

Dick Royd

Bance Edge Plantation

Crimes House

Berristal Top

Berristal Head

Law Farm

Lane House

Fox House Moss

Tinker Hill

Cocker Edge

Ox Lee

Crow Hill

HD9

S36

Penistone Rd

28
50

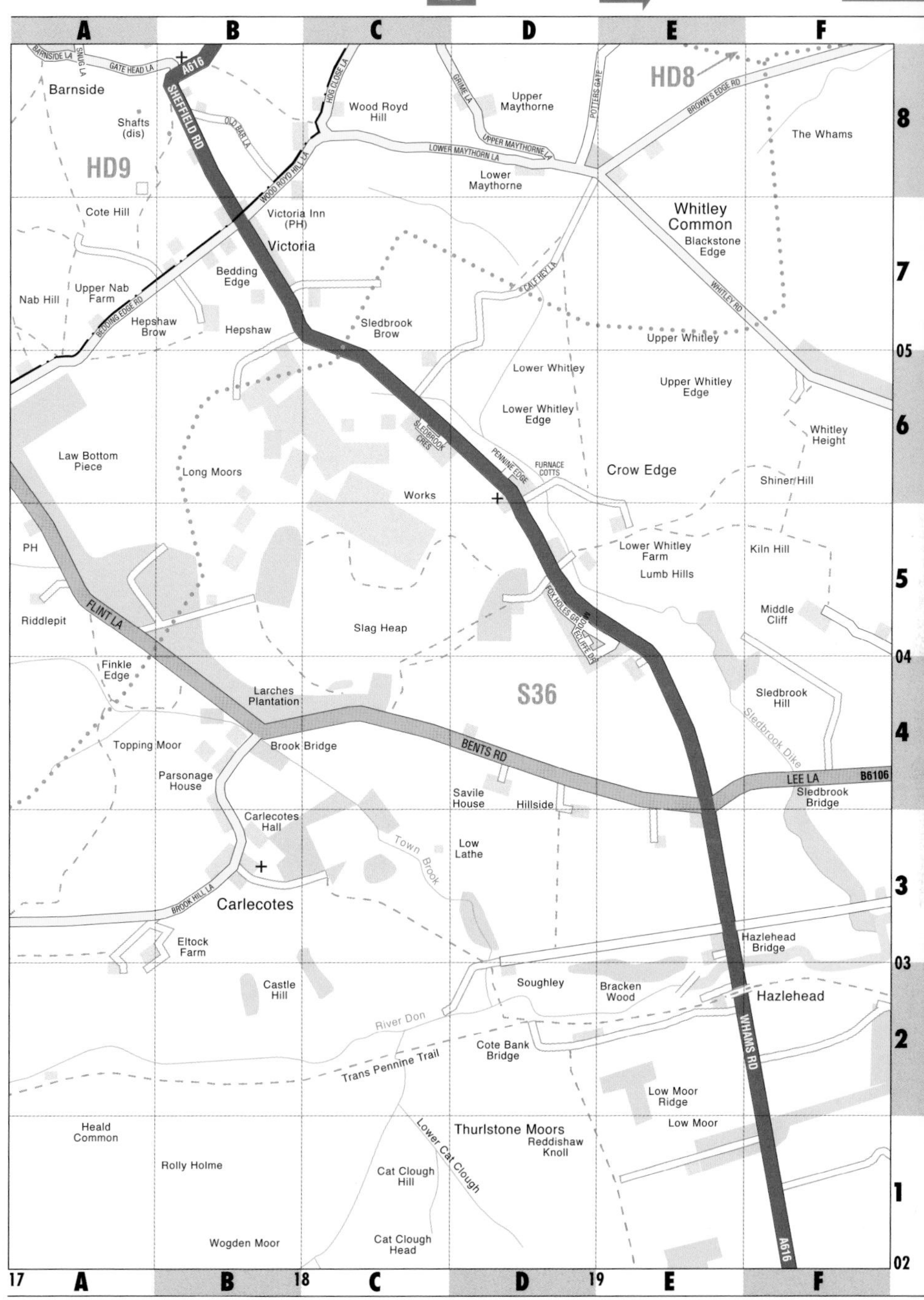

A
B
C
D
E
F
BARNSIDE LA
SNUG LA
GATE HEAD LA
A616
SHEFFIELD RD
Barnside
Shafts (dis)
HD9
OLD BAR LA
HOG CLOSE LA
Wood Royd Hill
GRIME LA
Upper Maythorne
POTTERS GATE
HD8
BROWN'S EDGE RD
The Whams
UPPER MAYTHORNE LA
LOWER MAYTHORN LA
Lower Maythorne
WOOD ROYD HILL LA
Cote Hill
Victoria Inn (PH)
Victoria
Whitley Common
Blackstone Edge
Bedding Edge
Nab Hill
Upper Nab Farm
BEDDING EDGE RD
Hepshaw Brow
Hepshaw
Sledbrook Brow
CALF HEY LA
WHITLEY RD
Upper Whitley
Lower Whitley
Upper Whitley Edge
Lower Whitley Edge
Whitley Height
Law Bottom Piece
Long Moors
SLEDBROOK CRES
PENNINE EDGE
FURNACE COTTS
Crow Edge
Shiner Hill
Works
PH
Lower Whitley Farm
Kiln Hill
Lumb Hills
FOX HOLES GR
ECLIFFE DR
Riddlepit
FLINT LA
Slag Heap
Middle Cliff
Finkle Edge
Larches Plantation
S36
Sledbrook Hill
Sledbrook Dike
Topping Moor
Brook Bridge
BENTS RD
Parsonage House
Savile House
Hillside
LEE LA
B6106
Sledbrook Bridge
Carlecotes Hall
Town Brook
Low Lathe
BROOK HILL LA
Carlecotes
Eltock Farm
Hazlehead Bridge
Castle Hill
Soughley
Bracken Wood
Hazlehead
River Don
WHAMS RD
Cote Bank Bridge
Trans Pennine Trail
Low Moor Ridge
Low Moor
Heald Common
Thurlstone Moors
Reddishaw Knoll
Lower Cat Clough
Rolly Holme
Cat Clough Hill
Wogden Moor
Cat Clough Head
A616
8
7
05
6
5
04
4
3
03
2
1
02
17
18
19
70
50

49
29

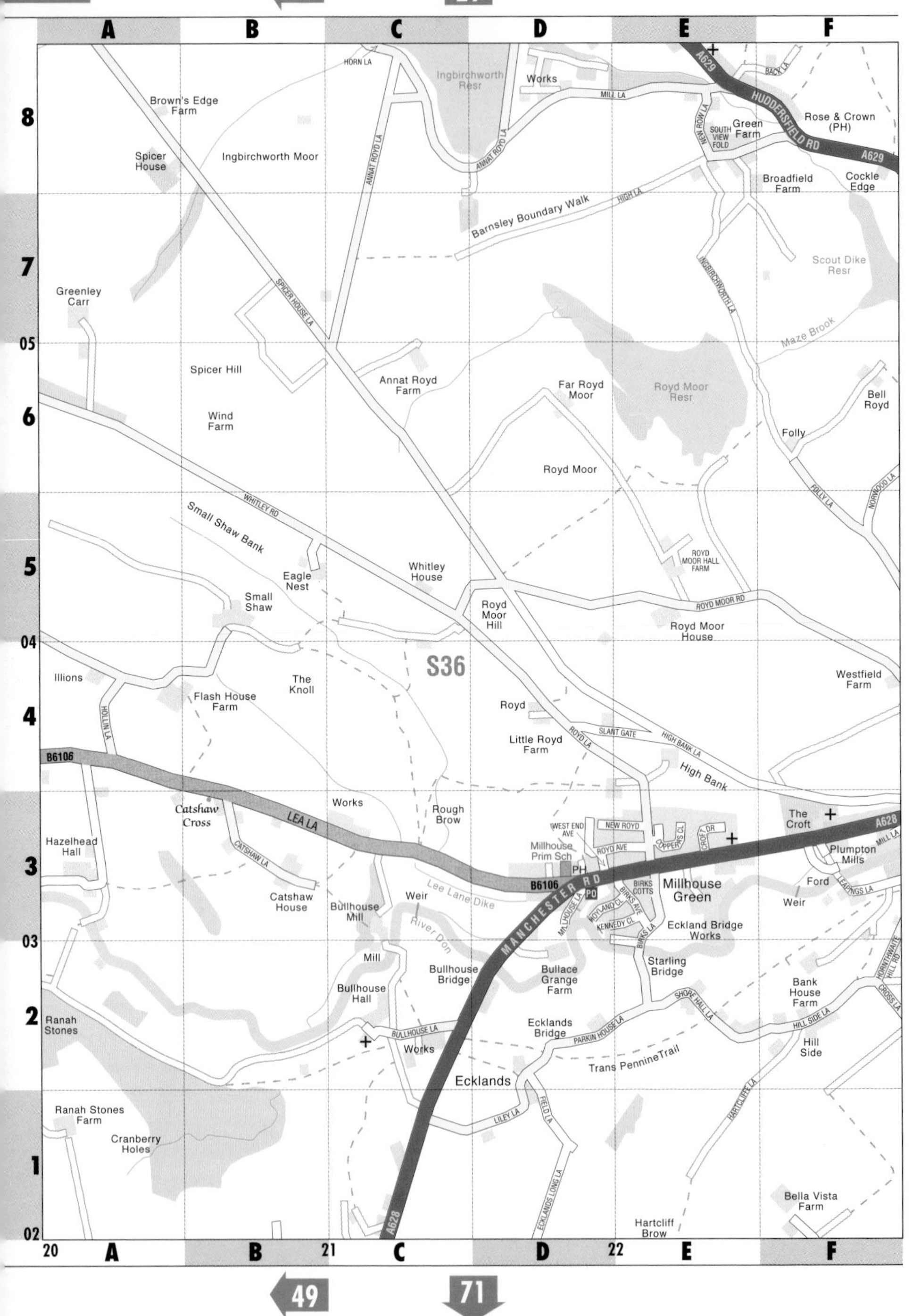
Brown's Edge Farm
Spicer House
Ingbirchworth Moor
Ingbirchworth Resr
Works
MILL LA
HORN LA
ANNAT ROYD LA
HUDDERSFIELD RD
A629
Rose & Crown (PH)
Green Farm
SOUTH VIEW FOLD
NEW ROW LA
BACK LA
Broadfield Farm
Cockle Edge
Barnsley Boundary Walk
HIGH LA
Scout Dike Resr
INGBIRCHWORTH LA
Greenley Carr
SPICER HOUSE LA
Maze Brook
Annat Royd Farm
Spicer Hill
Far Royd Moor
Royd Moor Resr
Bell Royd
Wind Farm
Folly
Royd Moor
FOLLY LA
NORWOOD LA
WHITLEY RD
Small Shaw Bank
ROYD MOOR HALL FARM
Eagle Nest
Whitley House
Small Shaw
Royd Moor Hill
ROYD MOOR RD
Royd Moor House
S36
Illions
The Knoll
Westfield Farm
Flash House Farm
Royd
HOLLIN LA
Little Royd Farm
ROYD LA
SLANT GATE
HIGH BANK LA
B6106
High Bank
Catshaw Cross
LEA LA
Works
Rough Brow
The Croft
A628
WEST END AVE
NEW ROYD
COOPERS CL
CROFT DR
Hazelhead Hall
Millhouse Prim Sch
ROYD AVE
Plumpton Mills
MILL LA
CATSHAW LA
PH
B6106
Catshaw House
MANCHESTER RD
PO
BIRKS COTTS
Millhouse Green
Ford
LEAPINGS LA
Lee Lane Dike
Weir
Weir
Bullhouse Mill
MILLHOUSE LA
BIRKS AVE
HOYLAND CL
KENNEDY CL
Eckland Bridge Works
River Don
BIRKS LA
Mill
Bullhouse Bridge
Bullace Grange Farm
Starling Bridge
HORNTHWAITE HILL RD
Bullhouse Hall
Bank House Farm
CROSS LA
SHORE HALL LA
Ranah Stones
Ecklands Bridge
HILL SIDE LA
BULLHOUSE LA
PARKIN HOUSE LA
Hill Side
Works
Trans PennineTrail
Ecklands
Ranah Stones Farm
LILEY LA
FIELD LA
HARTCLIFFE LA
Cranberry Holes
ECKLANDS LONG LA
Bella Vista Farm
A628
Hartcliff Brow
A
B
C
D
E
F
8
7
05
6
5
04
4
3
03
2
1
02
20
21
22

49
71

30

52

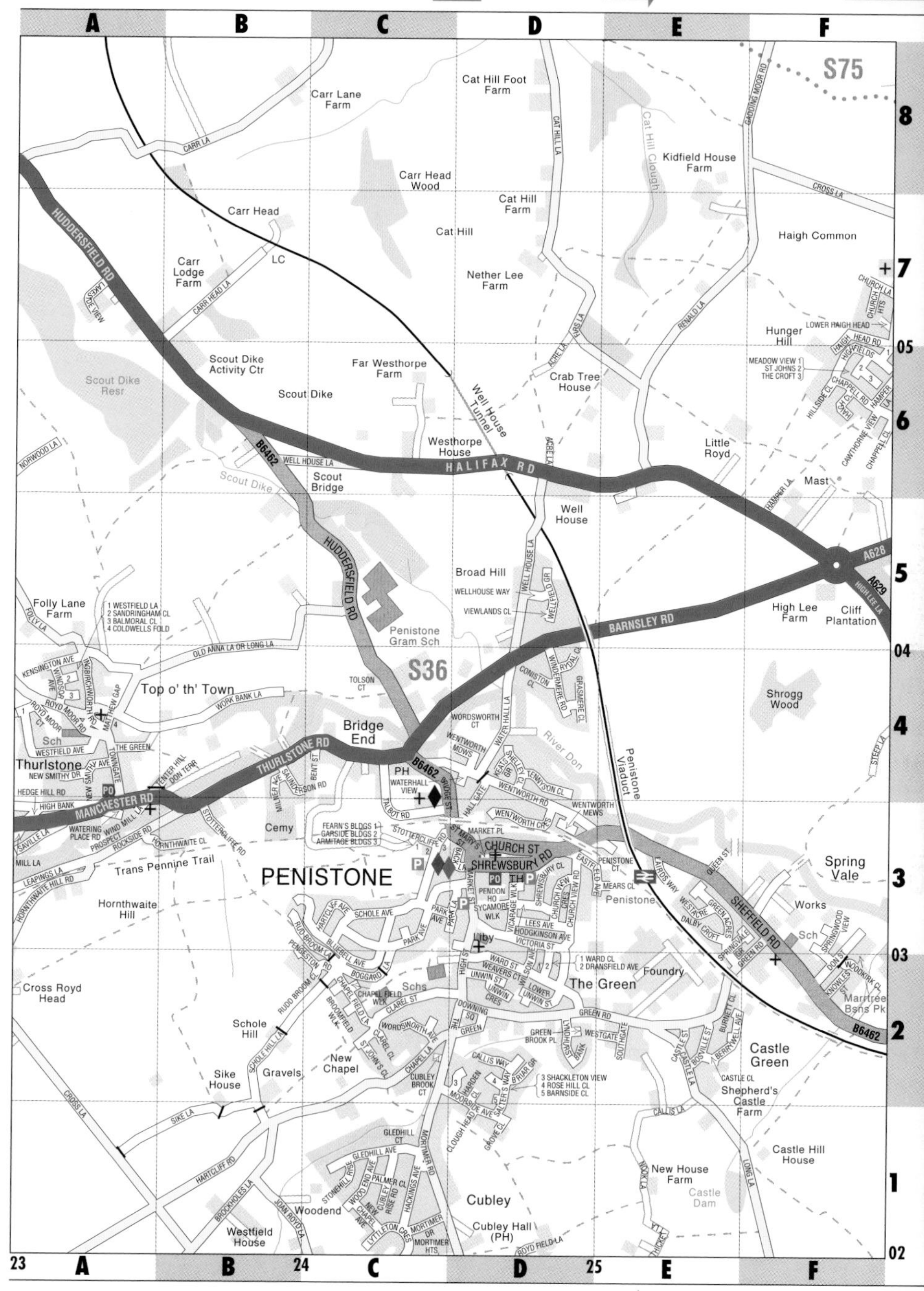

A
B
C
D
E
F
8
7
05
6
5
04
4
3
03
2
1
02
23
24
25
S75
S36
Carr Lane Farm
Cat Hill Foot Farm
Carr Head Wood
Kidfield House Farm
Cat Hill Clough
Cat Hill Farm
Cat Hill
Carr Head
Haigh Common
Carr Lodge Farm
LC
Nether Lee Farm
Hunger Hill
Scout Dike Activity Ctr
Far Westhorpe Farm
Crab Tree House
Scout Dike Resr
Scout Dike
Well House Tunnel
Westhorpe House
Little Royd
Scout Bridge
Mast
Well House
Broad Hill
Folly Lane Farm
High Lee Farm
Cliff Plantation
Penistone Gram Sch
Top o' th' Town
Shrogg Wood
Bridge End
Thurlstone
Sch
PH
River Don
Penistone Viaduct
Cemy
Trans Pennine Trail
PENISTONE
Spring Vale
Works
Hornthwaite Hill
Penistone
Liby
Schs
The Green
Foundry
Marrtree Bsns Pk
Cross Royd Head
Schole Hill
Castle Green
Sike House
Gravels
New Chapel
Shepherd's Castle Farm
Castle Hill House
New House Farm
Castle Dam
Cubley
Woodend
Cubley Hall (PH)
Westfield House
HUDDERSFIELD RD
HALIFAX RD
BARNSLEY RD
THURLSTONE RD
MANCHESTER RD
SHEFFIELD RD
CHURCH ST
SHREWSBURY RD
B6462
A628
A629
CARR LA
CARR HEAD LA
CAT HILL LA
GADDING MOOR RD
CROSS LA
RENALD LA
WELL HOUSE LA
NORWOOD LA
OLD ANNA LA OR LONG LA
WORK BANK LA
WELLHOUSE WAY
VIEWLANDS CL
TOLSON CT
WATER HALL LA
1 WESTFIELD LA
2 SANDRINGHAM CL
3 BALMORAL CL
4 COLDWELLS FOLD
MEADOW VIEW 1
ST JOHNS 2
THE CROFT 3
LOWER HAIGH HEAD
1 WARD CL
2 DRANSFIELD AVE
3 SHACKLETON VIEW
4 ROSE HILL CL
5 BARNSIDE CL
FEARN'S BLDGS 1
GARSIDE BLDGS 2
ARMITAGE BLDGS 3
MARKET PL
WENTWORTH RD
WENTWORTH MEWS
SCHOLE AVE
LEES AVE
HODGKINSON AVE
VICTORIA ST
WARD ST
GREEN RD
WESTGATE
SOUTHGATE
CASTLE CL
CALLIS LA
LONG LA
SIKE LA
HARTCLIFF RD
BROCKHOLES LA
CROSS LA
MORTIMER RD
ROYD FIELD LA
QUEEN ST

72
52

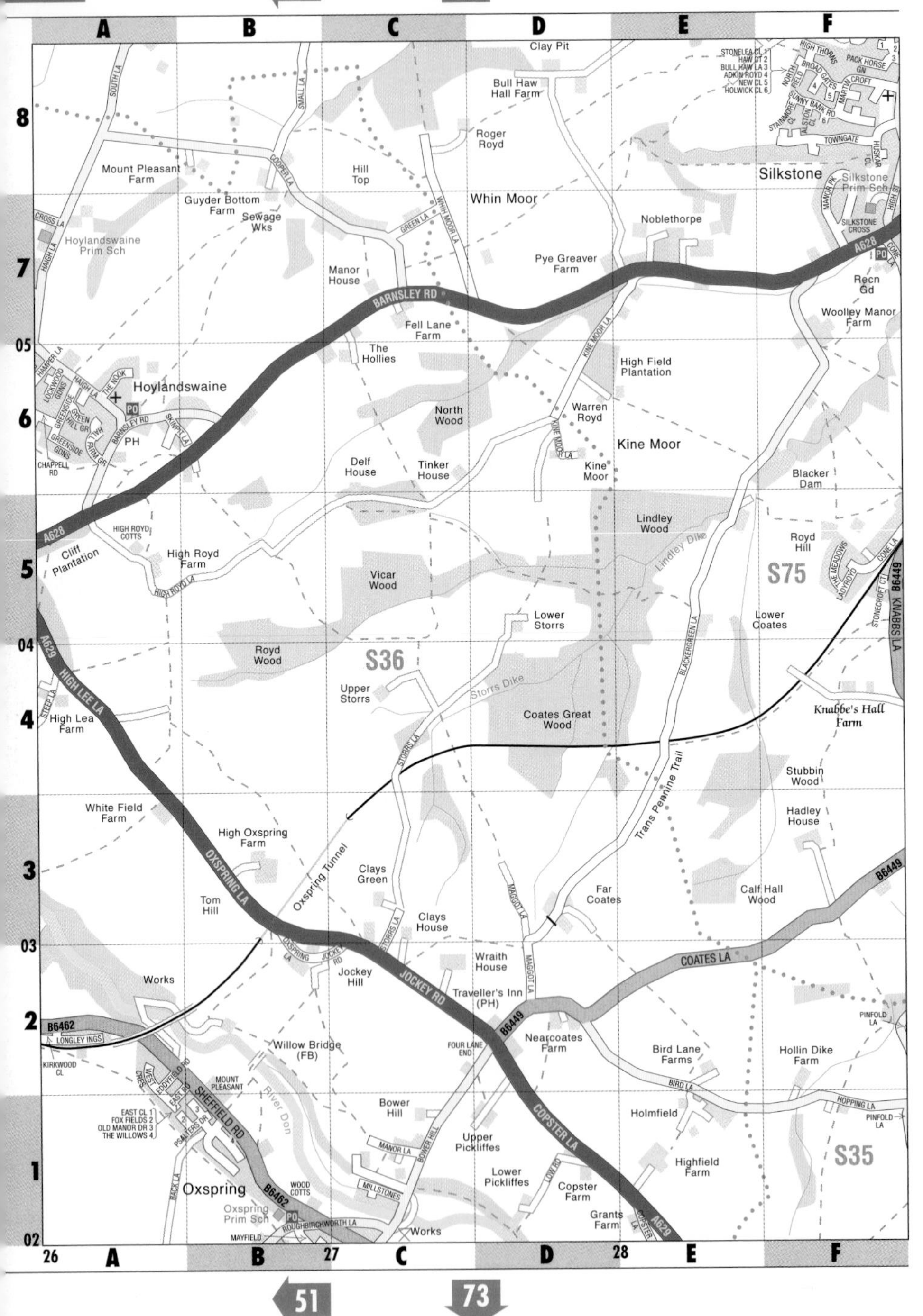

A B C D E F

8

Clay Pit

Bull Haw
Hall Farm

Roger
Royd

Mount Pleasant
Farm

Guyder Bottom
Farm

Hill
Top

Whin Moor

Silkstone

STONELEA CL 1
HAW PT 2
BULL HAW LA 3
ADKIN ROYD 4
NEW CL 5
HOLWICK CL 6.

Silkstone
Prim Sch

Sewage
Wks

Hoylandswaine
Prim Sch

Noblethorpe

SILKSTONE
CROSS

7

Manor
House

Pye Greaver
Farm

A628

Recn
Gd

BARNSLEY RD

Woolley Manor
Farm

05

Fell Lane
Farm

Hoylandswaine

The
Hollies

High Field
Plantation

6

PH

North
Wood

Warren
Royd

Kine Moor

CHAPPELL
RD

Delf
House

Tinker
House

Kine
Moor

Blacker
Dam

A628

Lindley
Wood

Royd
Hill

5

Cliff
Plantation

High Royd
COTTS

High Royd
Farm

Vicar
Wood

Lower
Storrs

Lower
Coates

S75

04

A629

HIGH LEE LA

Royd
Wood

S36

Upper
Storrs

Storrs Dike

Coates Great
Wood

Trans Pennine Trail

Knabbe's Hall
Farm

4

High Lea
Farm

STEEP LA

Stubbin
Wood

White Field
Farm

High Oxspring
Farm

Clays
Green

Far
Coates

Calf Hall
Wood

Hadley
House

B6449

3

OXSPRING LA

Oxspring Tunnel

Tom
Hill

Clays
House

03

Works

Jockey
Hill

Wraith
House

COATES LA

PINFOLD
LA

JOCKEY RD

2

B6462

LONGLEY INGS

Willow Bridge
(FB)

Traveller's Inn
(PH)

FOUR LANE
END

Nearcoates
Farm

Bird Lane
Farms

Hollin Dike
Farm

B6449

KIRKWOOD
CL

MOUNT
PLEASANT

SHEFFIELD RD

River Don

Bower
Hill

COPSTER LA

BIRD LA

HOPPING LA

PINFOLD
LA

1

EAST CL 1
FOX FIELDS 2
OLD MANOR DR 3
THE WILLOWS 4.

Holmfield

Highfield
Farm

S35

Oxspring

B6462

Upper
Pickliffes

Lower
Pickliffes

Copster
Farm

A629

02

Oxspring
Prim Sch

MAYFIELD

WOOD
COTTS

MILLSTONES

Works

Grants
Farm

26 A 27 B C 28 D E F

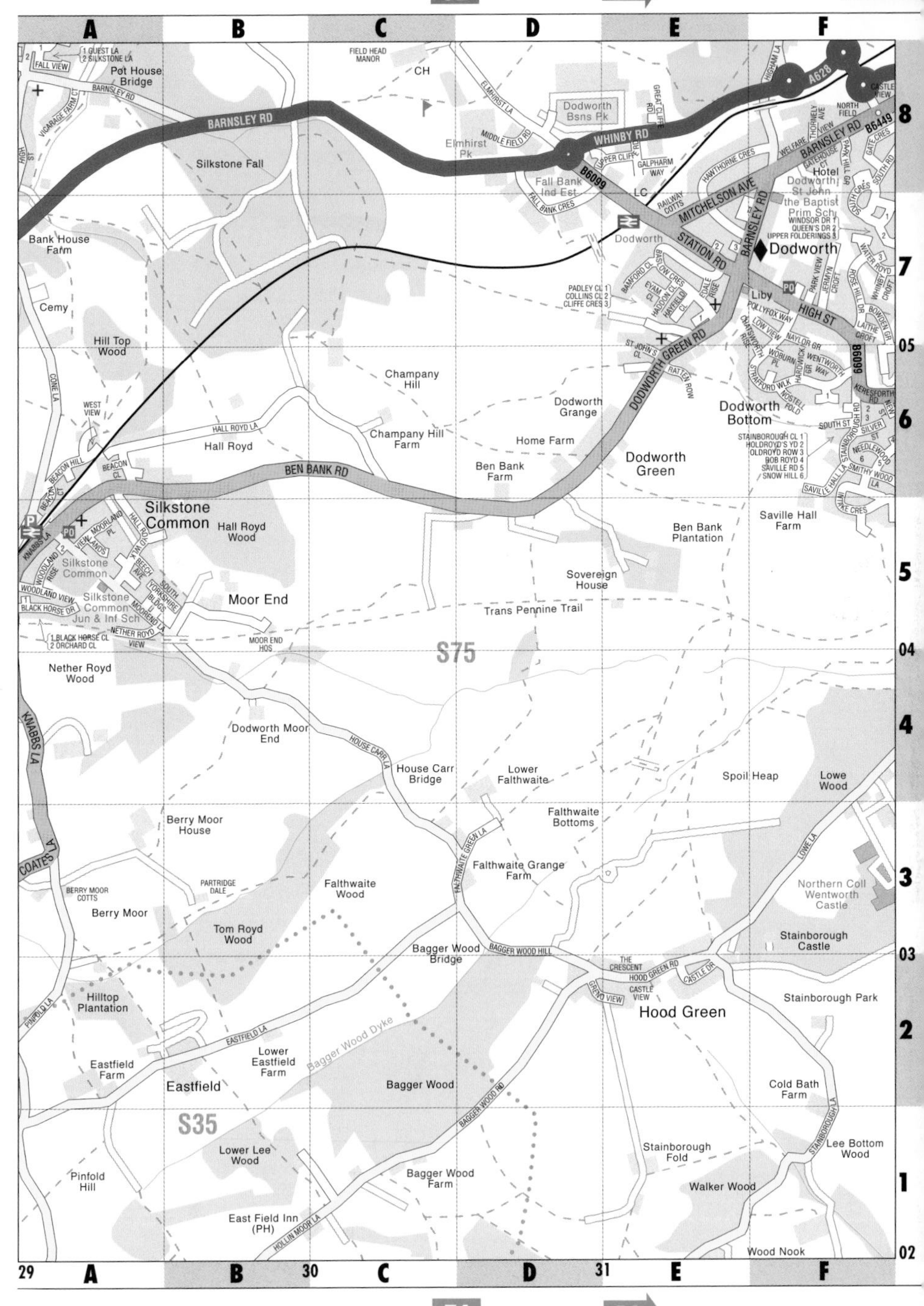

32
54
A
B
C
D
E
F
Pot House Bridge
BARNSLEY RD
Silkstone Fall
FIELD HEAD MANOR
CH
Elmhirst Pk
Dodworth Bsns Pk
WHINBY RD
Fall Bank Ind Est
LC
Dodworth
STATION RD
MITCHELSON AVE
BARNSLEY RD
Dodworth
Hotel
Dodworth St John the Baptist Prim Sch
A628
B6449
B6099
HIGH ST
Bank House Farm
Cemy
Hill Top Wood
Champany Hill
Champany Hill Farm
Hall Royd
BEN BANK RD
Ben Bank Farm
Home Farm
Dodworth Grange
Dodworth Green
DODWORTH GREEN RD
Dodworth Bottom
Liby
Silkstone Common
Hall Royd Wood
Moor End
Silkstone Common Jun & Inf Sch
Saville Hall Farm
Ben Bank Plantation
Sovereign House
Trans Pennine Trail
S75
Nether Royd Wood
KNABBS LA
Dodworth Moor End
House Carr Bridge
Lower Falthwaite
Spoil Heap
Lowe Wood
Berry Moor House
Falthwaite Bottoms
Falthwaite Grange Farm
Falthwaite Wood
Berry Moor
Tom Royd Wood
Northern Coll Wentworth Castle
Stainborough Castle
Bagger Wood Bridge
Hood Green
Stainborough Park
Hilltop Plantation
Eastfield Farm
Eastfield
Lower Eastfield Farm
Bagger Wood
Bagger Wood Dyke
Cold Bath Farm
S35
Lower Lee Wood
Stainborough Fold
Lee Bottom Wood
Pinfold Hill
Bagger Wood Farm
Walker Wood
East Field Inn (PH)
Wood Nook
8
7
6
5
4
3
2
1
05
04
03
02
29
30
31
74
54

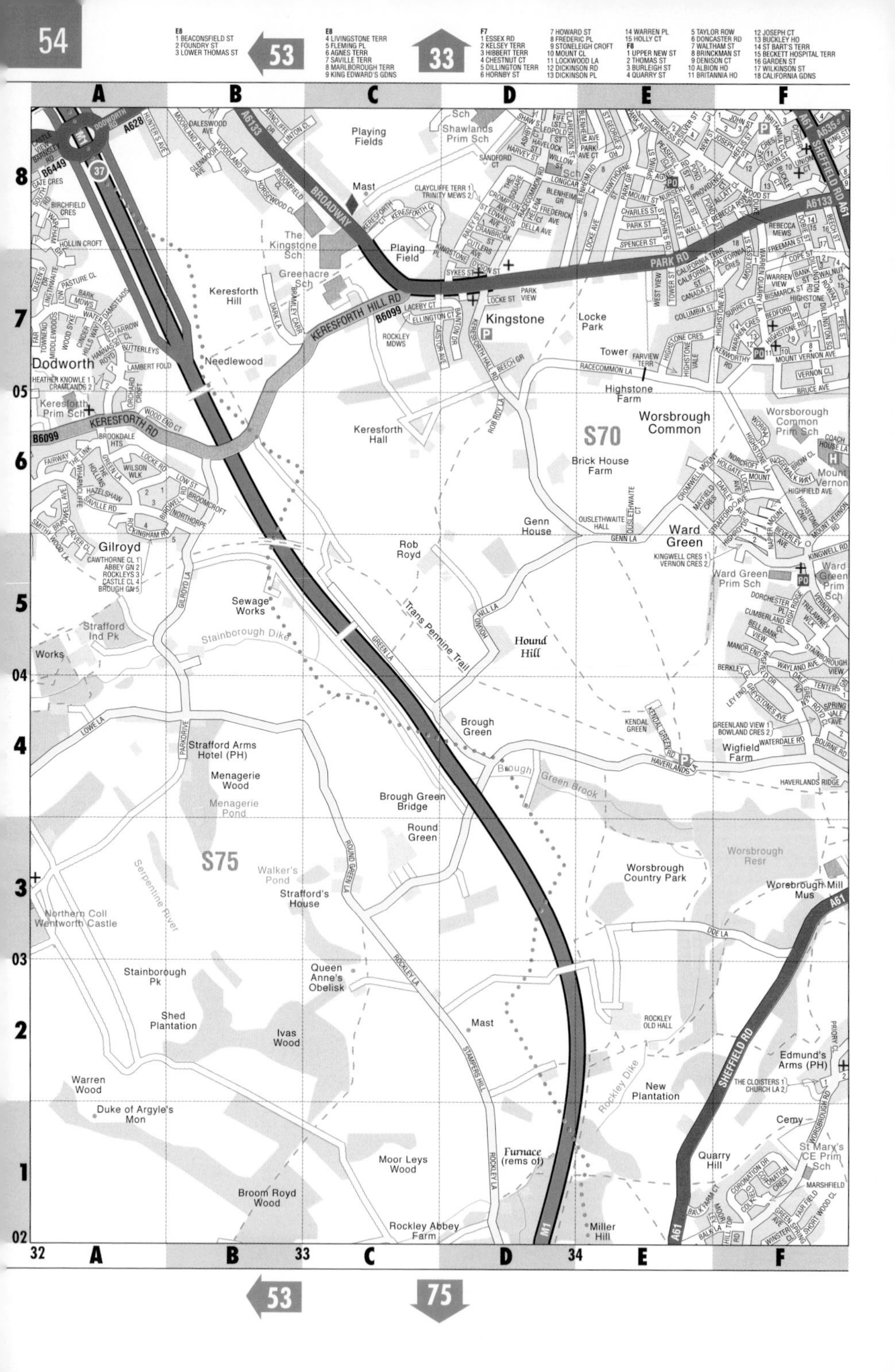
54
E8
1 BEACONSFIELD ST
2 FOUNDRY ST
3 LOWER THOMAS ST
53
E8
4 LIVINGSTONE TERR
5 FLEMING PL
6 AGNES TERR
7 SAVILLE TERR
8 MARLBOROUGH TERR
9 KING EDWARD'S GDNS
33
F7
1 ESSEX RD
2 KELSEY TERR
3 HIBBERT TERR
4 CHESTNUT CT
5 DILLINGTON TERR
6 HORNBY ST
7 HOWARD ST
8 FREDERIC PL
9 STONELEIGH CROFT
10 MOUNT CL
11 LOCKWOOD LA
12 DICKINSON RD
13 DICKINSON PL
14 WARREN PL
15 HOLLY CT
F8
1 UPPER NEW ST
2 THOMAS ST
3 BURLEIGH ST
4 QUARRY ST
5 TAYLOR ROW
6 DONCASTER RD
7 WALTHAM ST
8 BRINCKMAN ST
9 DENISON CT
10 ALBION HO
11 BRITANNIA HO
12 JOSEPH CT
13 BUCKLEY HO
14 ST BART'S TERR
15 BECKETT HOSPITAL TERR
16 GARDEN ST
17 WILKINSON ST
18 CALIFORNIA GDNS
A B C D E F
8 7 6 5 4 3 2 1
05 04 03 02
32 33 34
Playing Fields
Shawlands Prim Sch
Mast
The Kingstone Sch
Greenacre Sch
Playing Field
Keresforth Hill
Kingstone
Locke Park
Tower
Dodworth
Needlewood
Highstone Farm
Worsbrough Common
Keresforth Prim Sch
Keresforth Hall
S70
Worsbrough Common Prim Sch
Brick House Farm
Mount Vernon
Gilroyd
Genn House
Ward Green
Rob Royd
Ward Green Prim Sch
Sewage Works
Strafford Ind Pk
Trans Pennine Trail
Hound Hill
Works
Stainborough Dike
Brough Green
Wigfield Farm
Strafford Arms Hotel (PH)
Menagerie Wood
Menagerie Pond
Brough Green Bridge
Round Green
Brough Green Brook
S75
Walker's Pond
Worsbrough Resr
Worsbrough Country Park
Worsbrough Mill Mus
Serpentine River
Strafford's House
Northern Coll Wentworth Castle
Stainborough Pk
Queen Anne's Obelisk
Shed Plantation
Ivas Wood
Mast
Rockley Old Hall
Edmund's Arms (PH)
Warren Wood
New Plantation
Rockley Dike
Duke of Argyle's Mon
Cemy
St Mary's CE Prim Sch
Furnace (rems of)
Moor Leys Wood
Quarry Hill
Broom Royd Wood
Rockley Abbey Farm
Miller Hill
KERESFORTH HILL RD
KERESFORTH RD
BROADWAY
PARK RD
SHEFFIELD RD
M1
A6133
A628
A61
B6099
B6449
GREEN LA
ROUND GREEN LA
ROCKLEY LA
STAMPERS HILL
LOWE LA
GENN LA
HAVERLANDS LA
DOVE LA
RACECOMMON LA
53
75

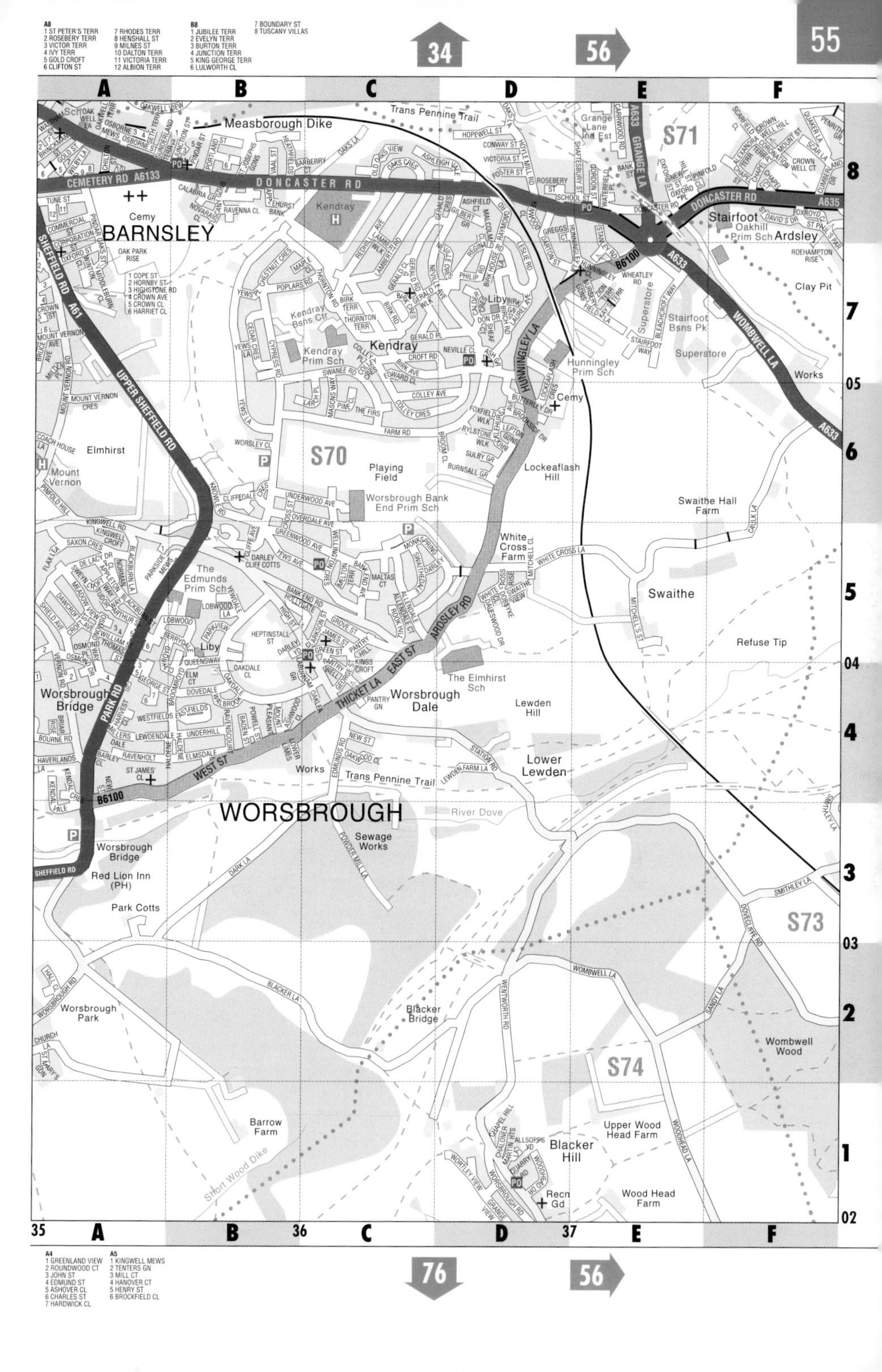

55
34
56
76
A8
1 ST PETER'S TERR
2 ROSEBERY TERR
3 VICTOR TERR
4 IVY TERR
5 GOLD CROFT
6 CLIFTON ST
7 RHODES TERR
8 HENSHALL ST
9 MILNES ST
10 DALTON TERR
11 VICTORIA TERR
12 ALBION TERR
B8
1 JUBILEE TERR
2 EVELYN TERR
3 BURTON TERR
4 JUNCTION TERR
5 KING GEORGE TERR
6 LULWORTH CL
7 BOUNDARY ST
8 TUSCANY VILLAS
A
B
C
D
E
F
Measbrough Dike
Trans Pennine Trail
Grange Lane Ind Est
S71
CEMETERY RD A6133
DONCASTER RD
A633
GRANGE LA
A635
Kendray
Cemy
BARNSLEY
SHEFFIELD RD
A61
UPPER SHEFFIELD RD
Stairfoot
Oakhill Prim Sch
Ardsley
ROEHAMPTON RISE
Clay Pit
B6100
WOMBWELL LA
Superstore
Stairfoot Bsns Pk
Kendray Bsns Ctr
Kendray Prim Sch
Hunningley Prim Sch
HUNNINGLEY LA
Works
OAK PARK RISE
1 COPE ST
2 HORNBY ST
3 HIGHSTONE RD
4 CROWN AVE
5 CROWN CL
6 HARRIET CL
MOUNT VERNON CRES
Elmhirst
Mount Vernon
S70
Playing Field
Worsbrough Bank End Prim Sch
Lockeaflash Hill
Swaithe Hall Farm
White Cross Farm
WHITE CROSS LA
Swaithe
The Edmunds Prim Sch
Refuse Tip
Liby
The Elmhirst Sch
Worsbrough Bridge
Worsbrough Dale
Lewden Hill
PARK RD
THICKET LA
EAST ST
ARDSLEY RD
WEST ST
Lower Lewden
Works
Trans Pennine Trail
WORSBROUGH
River Dove
Sewage Works
Worsbrough Bridge
Red Lion Inn (PH)
Park Cotts
DARK LA
S73
SMITHLEY LA
BLACKER LA
WOMBWELL LA
Worsbrough Park
Blacker Bridge
Wombwell Wood
S74
Barrow Farm
Upper Wood Head Farm
Blacker Hill
Wood Head Farm
Short Wood Dike
Recn Gd
WOODHEAD LA
WENTWORTH RD
8
7
05
6
5
04
4
3
03
2
1
02
35
36
37
A4
1 GREENLAND VIEW
2 ROUNDWOOD CT
3 JOHN ST
4 EDMUND ST
5 ASHOVER CL
6 CHARLES ST
7 HARDWICK CL
A5
1 KINGWELL MEWS
2 TENTERS GN
3 MILL CT
4 HANOVER CT
5 HENRY ST
6 BROCKFIELD CL

55
35

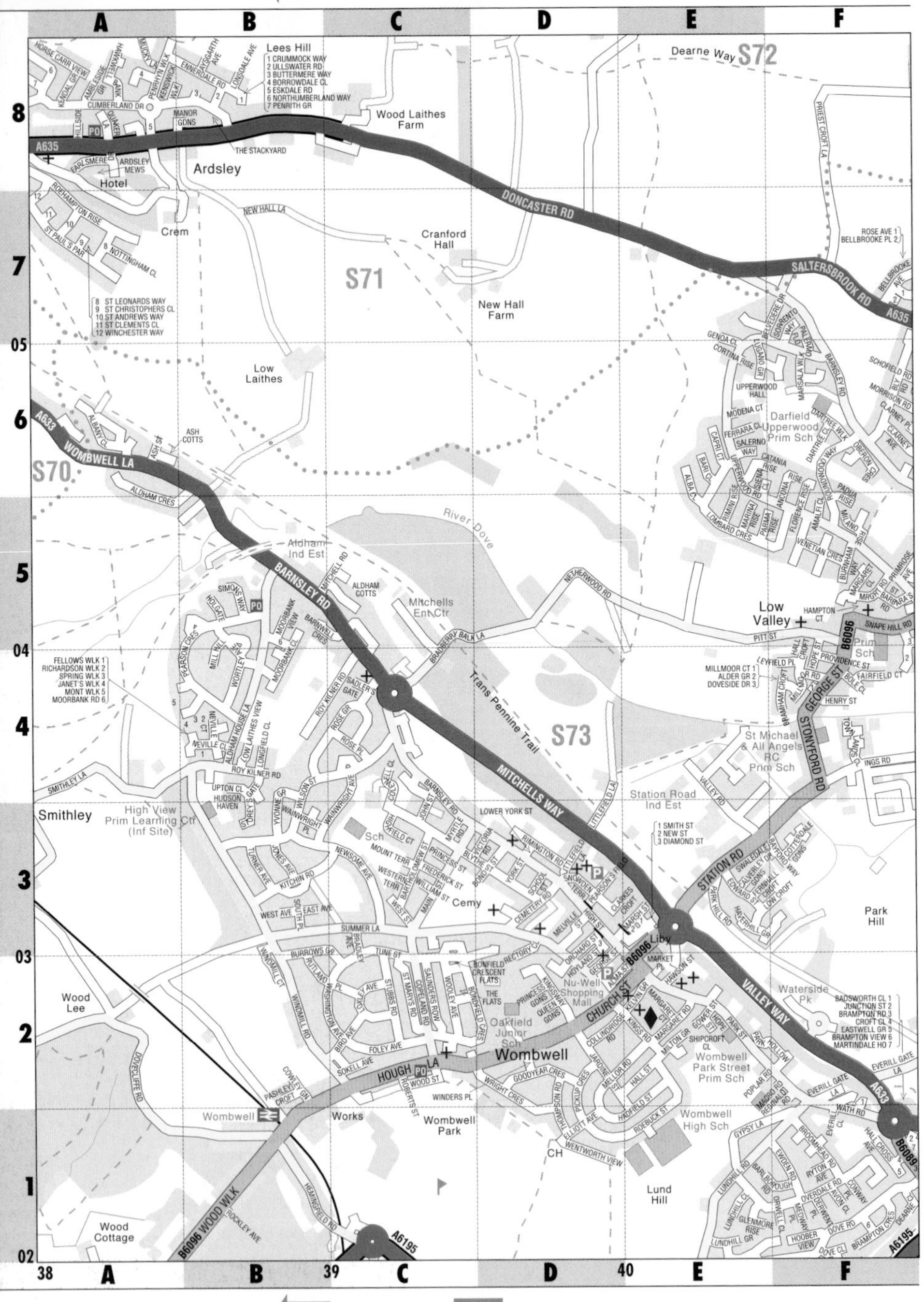
A
B
C
D
E
F
8
7
05
6
5
04
4
3
03
2
1
02
38
39
40
Lees Hill
1 CRUMMOCK WAY
2 ULLSWATER RD
3 BUTTERMERE WAY
4 BORROWDALE CL
5 ESKDALE RD
6 NORTHUMBERLAND WAY
7 PENRITH GR
Wood Laithes Farm
Dearne Way
S72
A635
Ardsley
Hotel
Crem
THE STACKYARD
DONCASTER RD
Cranford Hall
S71
New Hall Farm
SALTERSBROOK RD
8 ST LEONARDS WAY
9 ST CHRISTOPHERS CL
10 ST ANDREWS WAY
11 ST CLEMENTS CL
12 WINCHESTER WAY
Low Laithes
ROSE AVE 1
BELLBROOKE PL 2
Darfield Upperwood Prim Sch
A633
WOMBWELL LA
S70
River Dove
Aldham Ind Est
BARNSLEY RD
Mitchells Ent Ctr
Low Valley
FELLOWS WLK 1
RICHARDSON WALK 2
SPRING WLK 3
JANET'S WLK 4
MONT WLK 5
MOORBANK RD 6
MILLMOOR CT 1
ALDER GR 2
DOVESIDE DR 3
Trans Pennine Trail
S73
St Michael & All Angels RC Prim Sch
MITCHELLS WAY
Station Road Ind Est
Smithley
High View Prim Learning Ctr (Inf Site)
1 SMITH ST
2 NEW ST
3 DIAMOND ST
Cemy
Park Hill
Liby
Nu-Well Shopping Mall
Waterside Pk
Oakfield Junior Sch
Wombwell
VALLEY WAY
BADSWORTH CL 1
JUNCTION ST 2
BRAMPTON RD 3
CROFT CL 4
EASTWELL GR 5
BRAMPTON VIEW 6
MARTINDALE HO 7
Wood Lee
Wombwell
Works
Wombwell Park
Wombwell Park Street Prim Sch
Wombwell High Sch
CH
Lund Hill
B6096 WOOD WLK
Wood Cottage
A6195
B6089

55
77

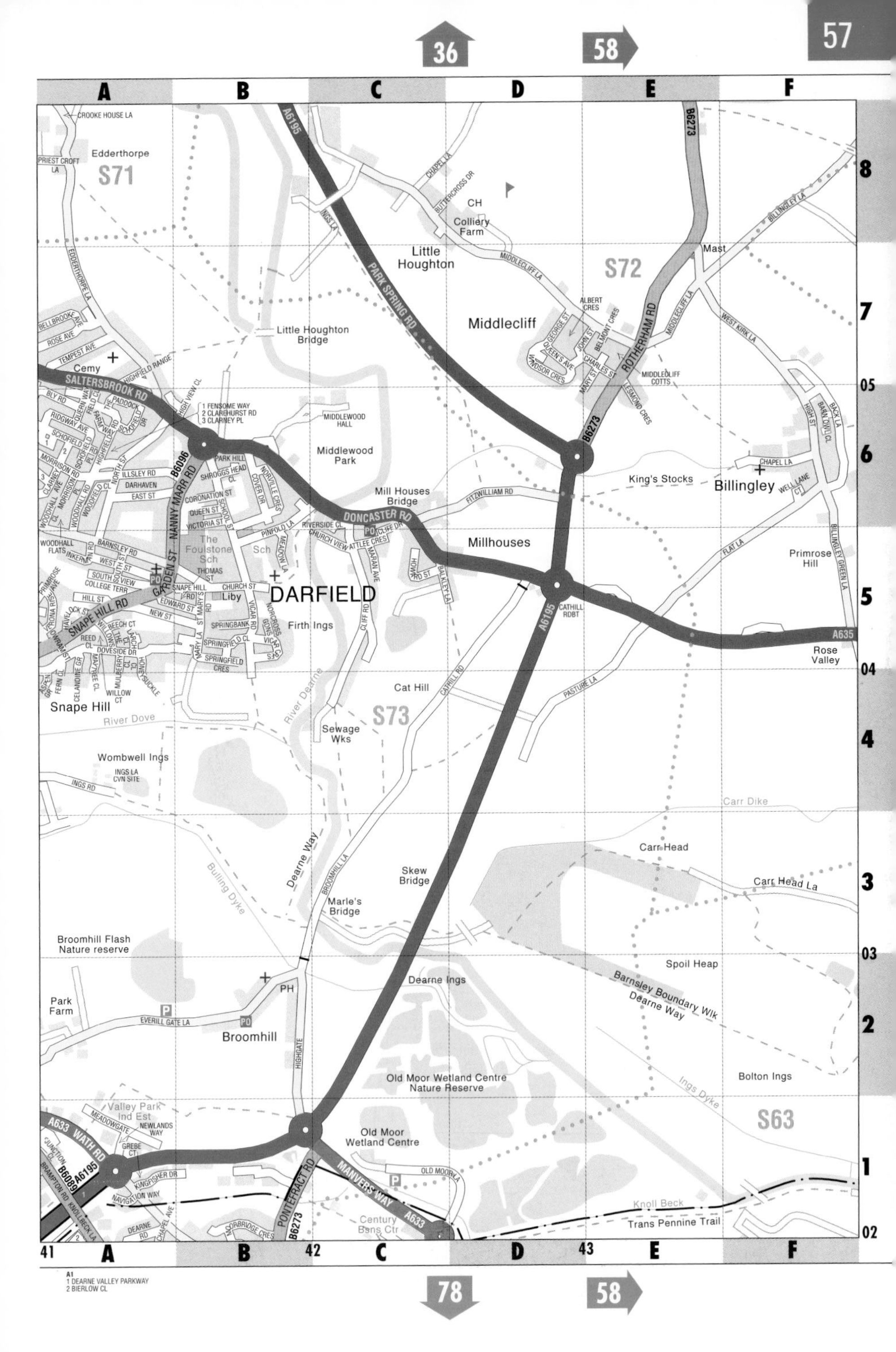

A1
1 DEARNE VALLEY PARKWAY
2 BIERLOW CL

57
37

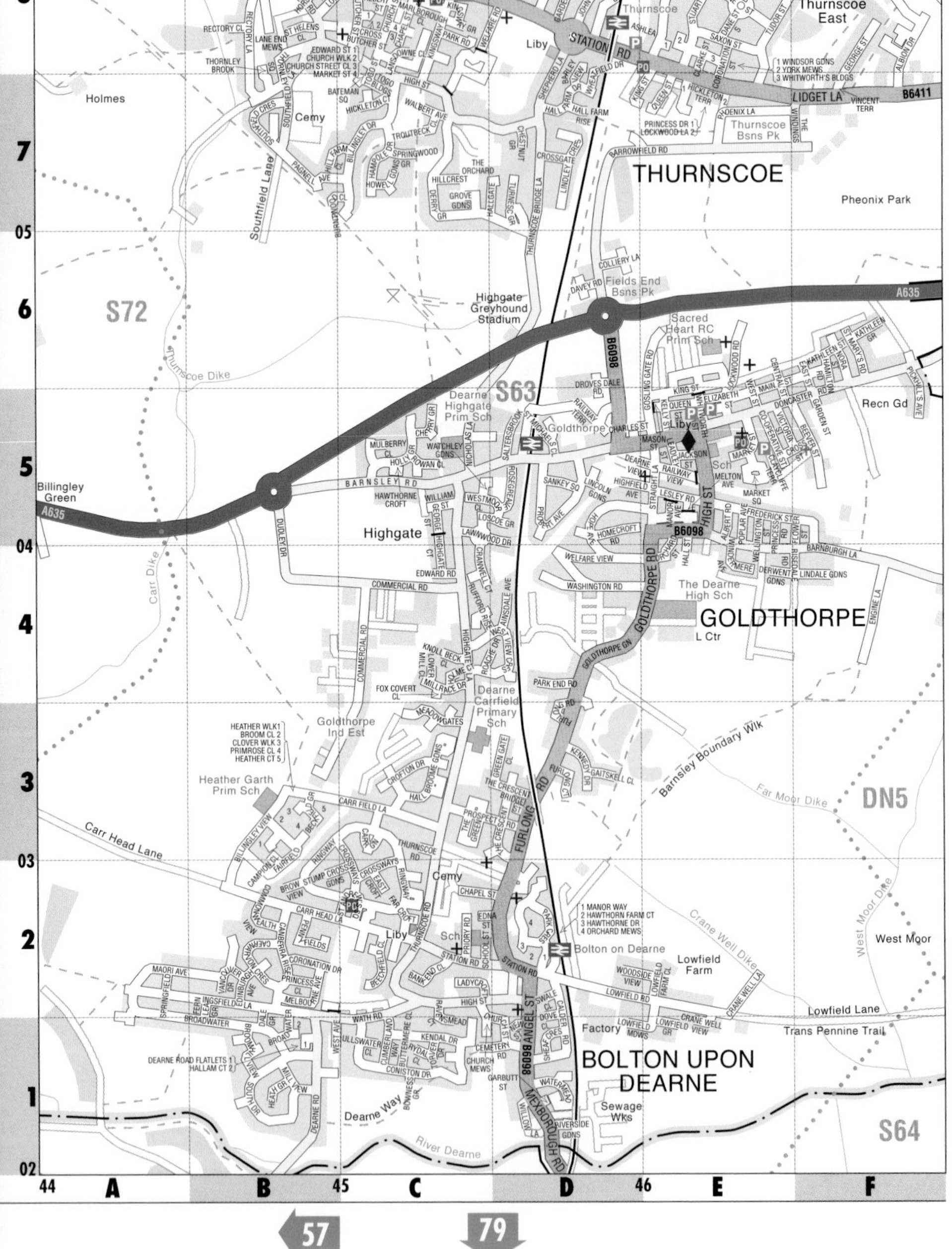
THURNSCOE
Thurnscoe East
GOLDTHORPE
BOLTON UPON DEARNE
Holmes
Billingley Green
Highgate
S72
S63
DN5
S64
HOUGHTON RD
STATION RD
LIDGET LA
B6411
A635
B6098
Highgate Greyhound Stadium
Dearne Highgate Prim Sch
The Dearne High Sch
Dearne Carrfield Primary Sch
Heather Garth Prim Sch
Goldthorpe Ind Est
Thurnscoe Bsns Pk
Fields End Bsns Pk
Sacred Heart RC Prim Sch
The Hill Prim Sch
Pheonix Park
Recn Gd
West Moor
Lowfield Farm
Lowfield Lane
Trans Pennine Trail
Carr Head Lane
Southfield Lane
Barnsley Boundary Wlk
Far Moor Dike
Crane Well Dike
West Moor Dike
Thurnscoe Dike
Carr Dike
River Dearne
Dearne Way
Sewage Wks
Factory
Bolton on Dearne
FURLONG RD
GOLDTHORPE RD
HIGH ST
MEXBOROUGH RD
ANGEL ST
A B C D E F
8 7 6 5 4 3 2 1
05 04 03 02
44 45 46

57
79

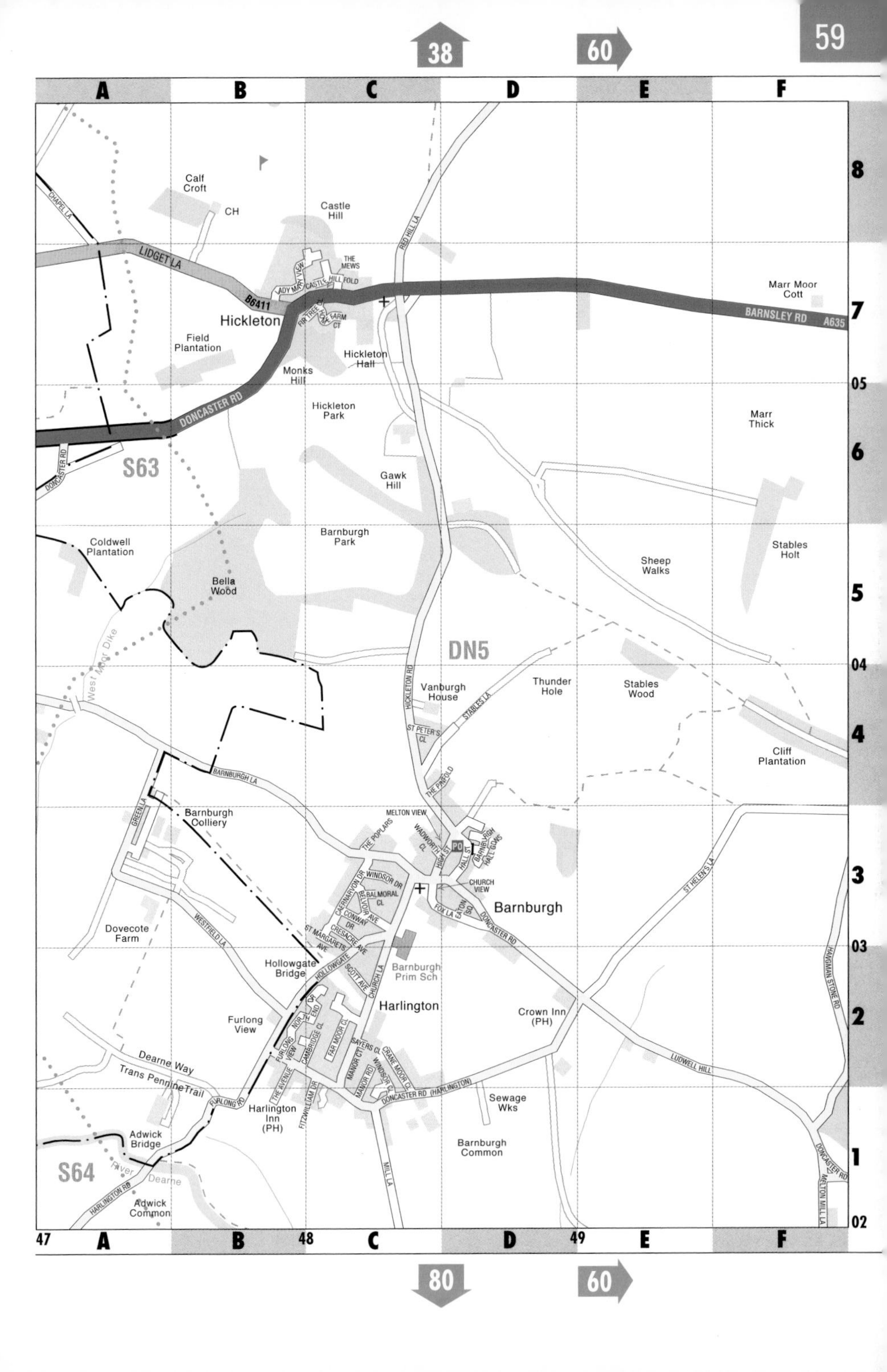

8

7

05

6

5

DN5

04

4

3

03

2

1

02

Calf
Croft

CH

Castle
Hill

THE
MEWS

HILL FOLD

LIDGET LA

B6411

ADY MRE
CASTLE

Hickleton

FIR TREE
FARM
CT

Field
Plantation

Hickleton
Hall

Monks
Hill

DONCASTER RD

Hickleton
Park

RED HILL A

Gawk
Hill

Marr Moor
Cott

BARNSLEY RD A635

Marr
Thick

Coldwell
Plantation

Barnburgh
Park

Bella
Wood

Sheep
Walks

Stables
Holt

S63

Westend Dike

HICKLETON RD

Vanburgh
House

St PETER'S
CL

STABLES LA

Thunder
Hole

Stables
Wood

Cliff
Plantation

BARNBURGH LA

THE FAIRFIELD

MELTON VIEW

THE POPLARS

WADWORTH
CL

Barnburgh
Colliery

GREENLA

WINDSOR DR

BALMORAL
CL

CHURCH
VIEW

St STEBENS LA

Barnburgh

Dovecote
Farm

WESTFIELD LA

CONWAY
CR

CRESSACRE
AVE

COX LA A

CHURCH LA

DONCASTER RD

St MARGARET'S RD

Hollowgate
Bridge

Barnburgh
Prim Sch

Crown Inn
(PH)

LUDWELL HILL

PANGEANS STONE RD

Furlong
View

FURLONG RD

POTTS CL

CAMBRIDGE CL

SAYERS CL

TEAR MOOR RD

CHERRY CROFT

Harlington

Dearne Way

Trans Pennine Trail

FURLONG RD

MANOR FM CL

DONCASTER RD (HARLINGTON)

Sewage
Wks

Barnburgh
Common

Adwick
Bridge

FITZWILLIAM LA

MELL LA

Harlington Inn
(PH)

DONCASTER RD

MELTON MILL LA

DONCASTER RD

S64

River Dearne

HARLINGTON RD

Adwick
Common

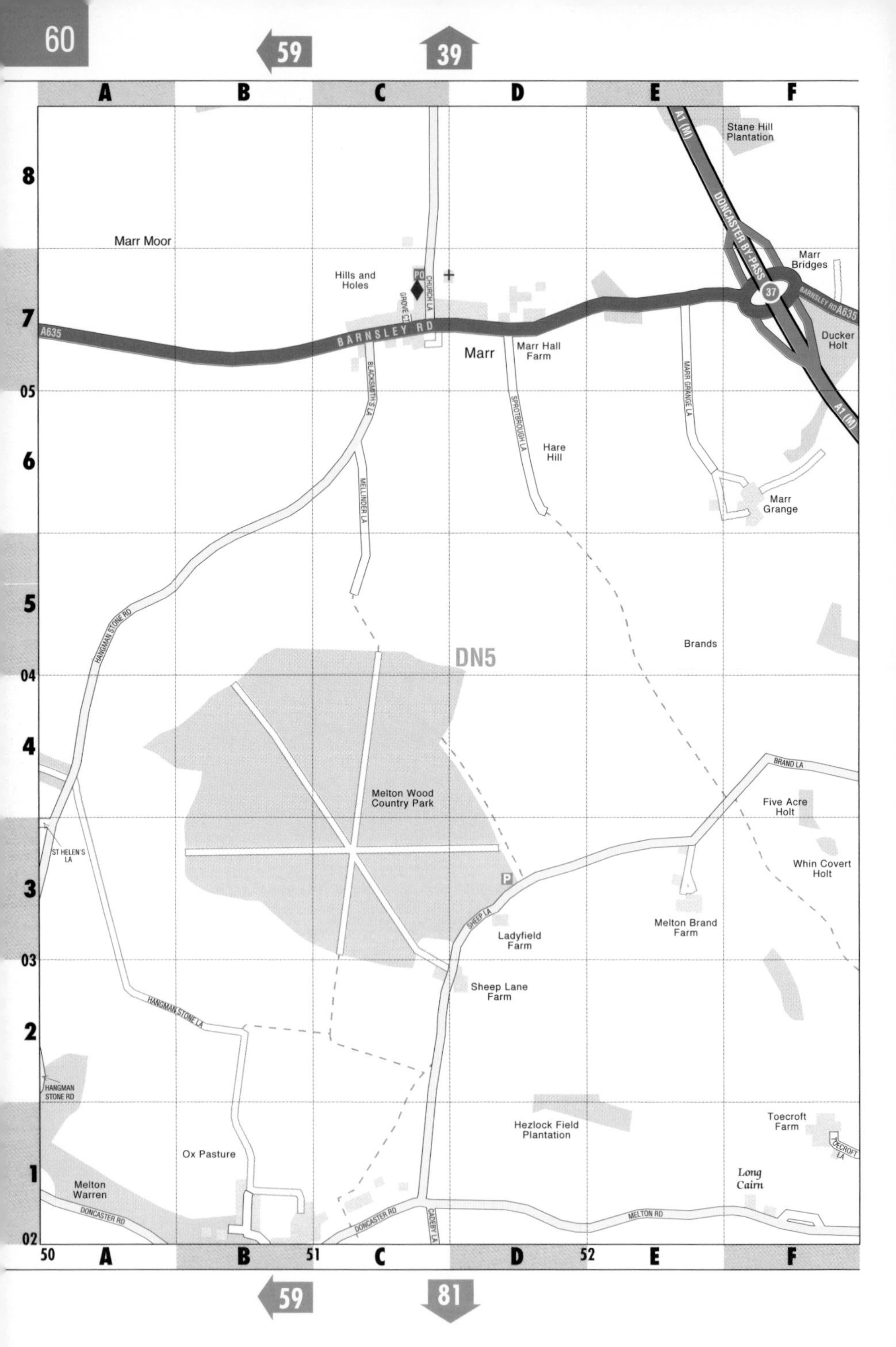
59
39
A
B
C
D
E
F
8
7
05
6
5
04
4
3
03
2
1
02
50
51
52
A1 (M)
Stane Hill Plantation
Marr Moor
DONCASTER BY-PASS
Marr Bridges
Hills and Holes
PO
CHURCH LA
GROVE CT
37
BARNSLEY RD A635
A635
BARNSLEY RD
Ducker Holt
Marr
Marr Hall Farm
BLACKSMITH'S LA
MARR GRANGE LA
SPROTBROUGH LA
A1 (M)
Hare Hill
MELLINDER LA
Marr Grange
DN5
Brands
HANGMAN STONE RD
BRAND LA
Melton Wood Country Park
Five Acre Holt
ST HELEN'S LA
Whin Covert Holt
P
SHEEP LA
Ladyfield Farm
Melton Brand Farm
Sheep Lane Farm
HANGMAN STONE LA
HANGMAN STONE RD
Hezlock Field Plantation
Toecroft Farm
TOECROFT LA
Ox Pasture
Long Cairn
Melton Warren
DONCASTER RD
DONCASTER RD
CADEBY LA
MELTON RD
59
81

40
62

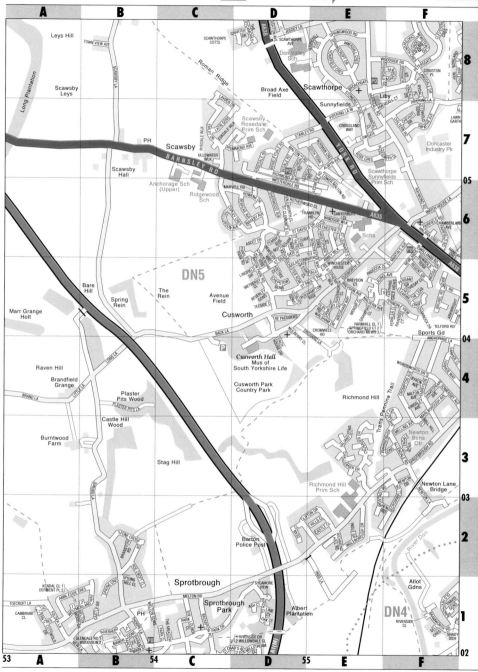

A
B
C
D
E
F
8
7
05
6
5
04
4
3
03
2
1
02
53
54
55
Leys Hill
Long Plantation
Scawsby Leys
TOWN VIEW AVE
SCAWSBY LA
Roman Ridge
SCAWTHORPE COTTS
CHARTER DR
THE SYCAMORES
ASHTON AVE
A638
JOSSEY LA
SCAWTHORPE AVE
Don Valley Sch
SPRINGWOOD RD
AMERSALL CRES
SPRINGCROFT DR
HOMEFIELD CRES
STONEHILL RISE
Broad Axe Field
Scawthorpe
BROACHGATE
STONEHILL RISE
AMERSALL RD
AMERSALL CT
Liby
PO
WOODSIDE RD
RIVERDALE RD
PETERSGATE
CONISTON PL
ESKDALE DR
RYDALL PL
LANGDALE DR
PIPERING LA E
Sunnyfields
PIPERING LA W
CROSSLAND WAY
MOSSDALE CL
LOWGATE
ROSE CRES
ROSEGARTH CL
CHILTERN RD
CHEVIOT DR
COTSWOLD GDNS
SWITHE AVE
LAWN GARTH
Doncaster Industry Pk
YORK RD
Scawthorpe Sunnyfields Prim Sch
RAYMOND RD
WATCH HOUSE LA
LAYDEN DR
LATIN GDNS
ESKDALE WLK
EMLEY DR
RYEDALE WLK
Scawsby Rosedale Prim Sch
DRUMMOND AVE
ULLSWATER WLK
STANLEY RD
NORMAN CRES
EDITH TERR
ALWYN AVE
LOWER MALTON RD
PH
Scawsby
BARNSLEY RD
Scawsby Hall
Anchorage Sch (Upper)
Ridgewood Sch
ROSEDALE RD
WENSLEYDALE RD
BEDALE RD
MALTON RD
THORNTONDALE RD
RICHMOND RD
WESTERDALE RD
FARNDALE RD
SLEDMERE RD
MARVELL RD
ROWENA DR
SHERWOOD AVE
KENILWORTH CL
ROTHERWOOD CL
FRANKLYN HO
CANTERBURY CL
WINDSOR WLK
A635
Schs
COLCHESTER CT
ST CLEMENT'S CL
BEWICKE AVE
COPLEY CRES
NASEBY AVE
ELLISON AVE
ST DAVID'S DR
ASCOT DR
PEMBROKE RISE
NOTTINGHAM WAY
ST PATRICK'S WAY
COURT CL
CHRISTOPHER'S CRES
WINCHESTER WAY
ST LEONARD'S LEA
ABBEY WLK
HAMILTON PARK RD
CHELTENHAM RISE
NEWBURY WAY
ST GILES GATE
ROCHESTER ROW
GLASTONBURY GATE
KIRKSTALL CL
WINCHESTER HOUSE
CUSWORTH LA
ST MARTIN'S AVE
FAIRFIELD RD
CHAMBERLAIN AVE
HALIFAX CRES
WILLIAMS RD
NEWBOLD TERR
NEWLANDS DR
REGENT GR
BRIDGE GR
A638
DN5
LINGFIELD DR
KEMPTON PARK RD
AINTREE AVE
CHEPSTOW GDNS
WETHERBY DR
BEVERLEY GDNS
TEESIDE CL
LEDBURY GDNS
ROEHAMPTON RISE
ST PAUL'S PAR
ST STEPHEN'S WLK
BREYDON CT
BREYDON AVE
PADDOCK CL
LAUREL AVE
FARTHING GALE MEWS
PERRAN GR
ROTHESAY CL
THE LEAS
CLEARWELL CROFT
BRUNEL RD
ARKWRIGHT RD
Bare Hill
Spring Rein
The Rein
Avenue Field
Cusworth
RAMSWORTH CL
WROXHAM WAY
MENDIP CL
GRAMPIAN CL
MALVERN AVE
FERNDALE VIEW
FERNLEA CL
RAINTREE CT
CHARNOCK DR
Marr Grange Holt
THE PADDOCKS
FILBY RD
RANBY GR
WALSHAM DR
CROMWELL HO
FARMHILL CL 1
SPRINGFIELD CT 2
ORCHARD MEWS 3
TELFORD RD
Sports Gd
ANCHORAGE LA
BACK LA
MULBERRY CL
ORCHARD LA
COACH HOUSE DR
P
Cusworth Hall
Mus of South Yorkshire Life
Cusworth Park Country Park
LONG LA
Raven Hill
Brandfield Grange
BRAND LA
LITTLE LA
Plaster Pits Wood
PLASTER PITS LA
Castle Hill Wood
Burntwood Farm
Richmond Hill
Trans Pennine Trail
WORDSWORTH DR
IVANHOE CL
IVANHOE WAY
CROMPTON AVE
BYRON AVE
TENNYSON AVE
SHAKESPEARE AVE
SOMERSBY AVE
MILTON AVE
KINGSLEY AVE
MARLBOROUGH AVE
SHELLEY GR
MELLING AVE
MILL HILL
Newton Bsns Ctr
VALIANT GDNS
CRUSADER DR
CHALLENGER DR
ASHBURNHAM GDNS
ALLENDALE RD
SPROTBROUGH RD
Stag Hill
Richmond Hill Prim Sch
NEWTON DR
Newton Lane Bridge
NEWTON LA
MONTAGU RD
CROMWELL DR
HENGIST RD
SPRING LA
CLIFTON DR
HILLS CL
CASTLE CL
DEAN CL
INGLE GR
INGLEBOROUGH DR
RICHMOND HILL RD
STONE CROSS DR
BRANSTONE RD
Barton Police Post
River Don
INGS LA
Allot Gdns
ROE CROFT CL
SPRING HILL CL
SPRING CRES
Sprotbrough
SYCAMORE VIEW
KENDAL CL 1
DERWENT PL 2
AMBLESIDE CRES
WESTMORLAND WAY
MELTON WOOD GR
CASTLE GR
MELTON RD
TOECROFT LA
CAMBRIAN CL
FERN CRES
FOLDER LA
COTSWOLD DR
PH
MELTON GDNS
THE MEADOW
PARK CL
PARK AVE
LOUNDE CL
BROMPTON RD
PARK DR
Sprotbrough Park
ASH CT
BIRCH CL
LIME CT
OAK CT
Albert Plantation
DN4
RIVERSIDE CL
OLD HEXTHORPE
TRAVIS GDNS
BRAMWORTH RD
DELL CRES
SHADY SIDE
GLENDALE RD 1
WOODVIEW 2
RIVERHEAD
MANOR GDNS
SHIRES CL
THORPE LA
PO
MAIN ST
NEW LA
1 RIVERSIDE DR
2 WILLOWDALE CL
MILLSTREAM CL
ST CHAD'S WAY
A1(M)

82
62

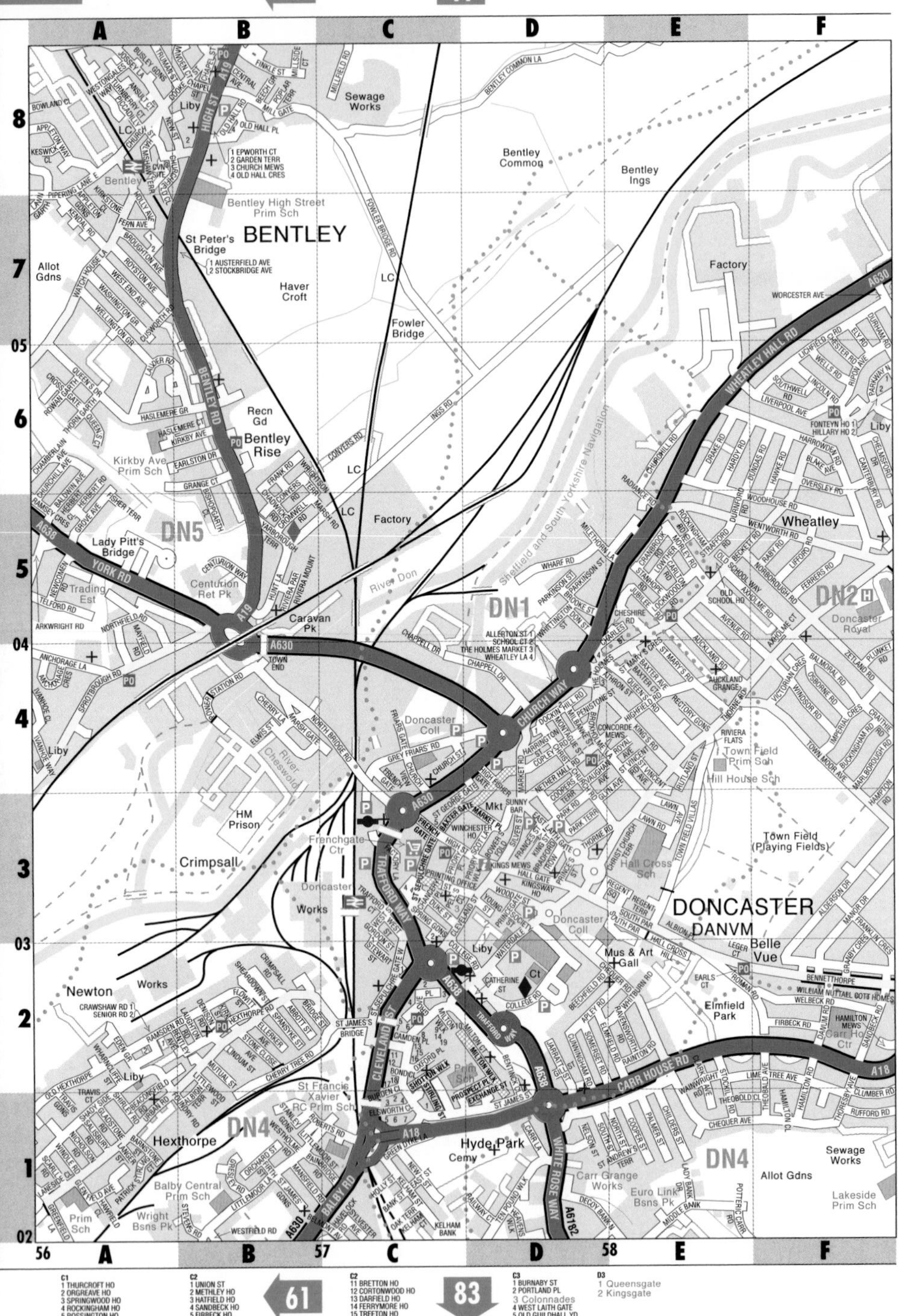

C1
1 THURCROFT HO
2 ORGREAVE HO
3 SPRINGWOOD HO
4 ROCKINGHAM HO
5 ROSSINGTON HO
6 WOOLEY HO
7 SILVERWOOD HO

C2
1 UNION ST
2 METHLEY HO
3 HATFIELD HO
4 SANDBECK HO
5 FIRBECK HO
6 SERLBY HO
7 CUSWORTH HO
8 EMLEY HO
9 WENTWORTH HO
10 ROWLAND PL

C2
11 BRETTON HO
12 CORTONWOOD HO
13 DARFIELD HO
14 FERRYMORE HO
15 TREETON HO
16 ASKERN HO
17 MALTBY HO
18 LUNDWOOD HO
19 MANTON HO

C3
1 BURNABY ST
2 PORTLAND PL
3 Colonnades
4 WEST LAITH GATE
5 OLD GUILDHALL YD

D3
1 Queensgate
2 Kingsgate

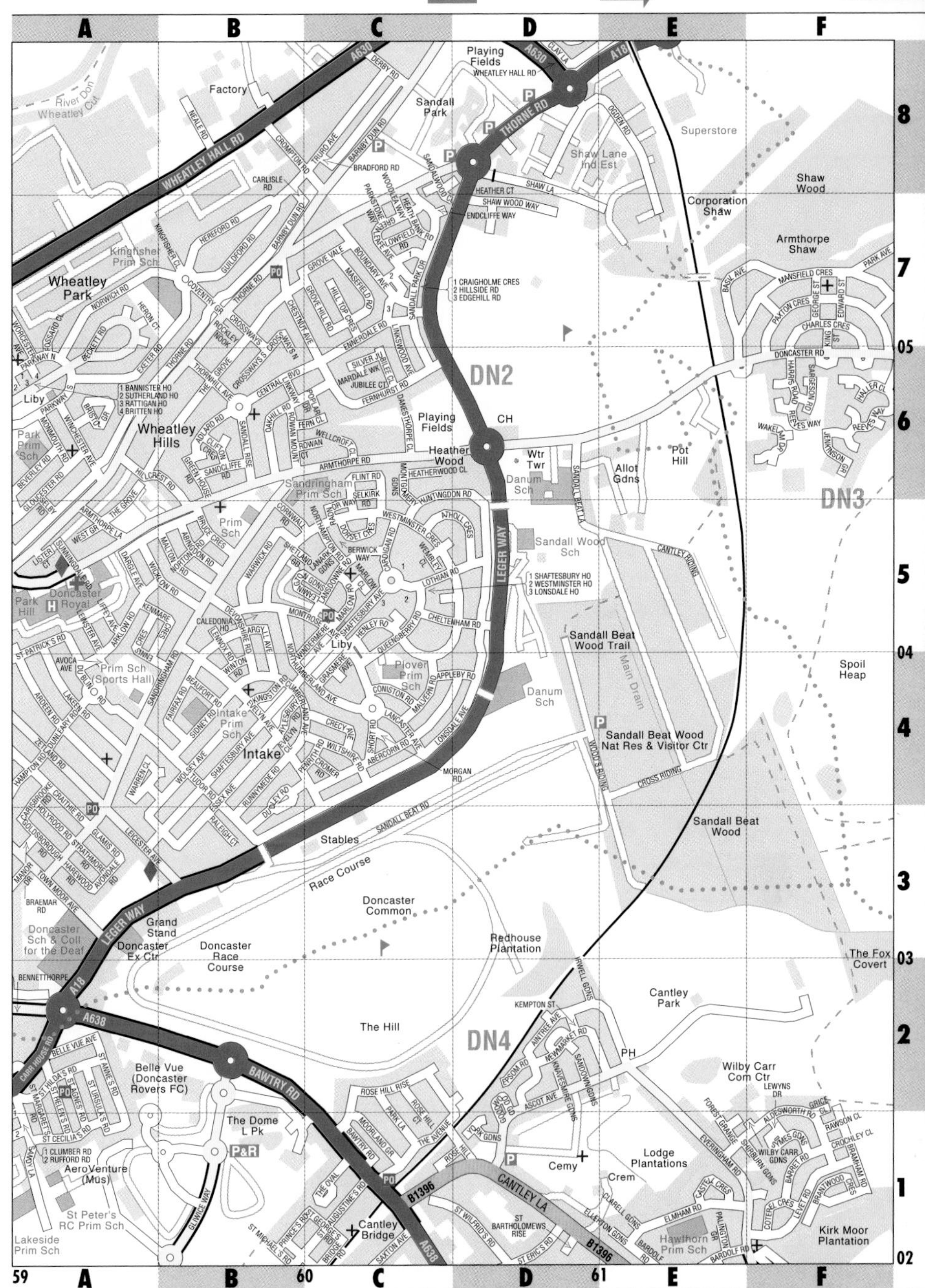

	A	B	C	D	E	F

8

7

05

6

DN2

DN3

5

04

4

3

03

2

DN4

1

02

River Don

Wheatley

Factory

Playing Fields

Wheatley Hall Rd

THORNE RD

A18

Superstore

Shaw Wood

WHEATLEY HALL RD

Sandall Park

Shaw Lane Ind Est

Corporation Shaw

Armthorpe Shaw

CARLISLE RD

BRADFORD RD

HEATHER CT

SHAW LA

SHAW WOOD WAY

ENDCLIFFE WAY

MANSFIELD CRES

CHARLES CRES

DONCASTER RD

Kingfisher Prim Sch

Wheatley Park

1 CRAIGHOLME CRES
2 HILLSIDE RD
3 EDGEHILL RD

HEREFORD RD

Liby

Park Prim Sch

1 BANNISTER HO
2 SUTHERLAND HO
3 RATTIGAN HO
4 BRITTEN HO

Wheatley Hills

Playing Fields

CH

Wtr Twr

Pot Hill

Heather Wood

HEATHERWOOD CL

Danum Sch

Allot Gdns

Sandringham Prim Sch

SELKIRK

WESTMINSTER

ATHOL CRES

Sandall Wood Sch

Prim Sch

LEGER WAY

Sandall Wood

1 SHAFTESBURY HO
2 WESTMINSTER HO
3 LONSDALE HO

CANTLEY RIDING

Doncaster Royal

Park Hill

BERWICK WAY

Liby

Sandall Beat Wood Trail

Spoil Heap

Prim Sch (Sports Hall)

Plover Prim Sch

CHELTENHAM RD

APPLEBY RD

Danum Sch

Main Drain

VICTORY RIDING

CROSSING RIDING

Intake Prim Sch

Intake

CRECY RD

ABERCORN RD

MORGAN RD

Sandall Beat Wood Nat Res & Visitor Ctr

Sandall Beat Wood

Stables

SANDALL BEAT RD

Race Course

BRAEMAR RD

Doncaster Sch & Coll for the Deaf

LEGER WAY

Grand Stand

Doncaster Ex Ctr

Doncaster Race Course

Doncaster Common

Redhouse Plantation

Cantley Park

The Fox Covert

BENNETTHORPE

A18

A638

The Hill

DN4

KEMPTON ST

PH

Wilby Carr Com Ctr

Kirk Moor Plantation

Belle Vue (Doncaster Rovers FC)

BAWTRY RD

BELLE VUE AVE

The Dome L Pk

P&R

ROSE HILL RISE

Cemy

Lodge Plantations

Crem

ST CECILIA RD

1 CLUMBER RD
2 RUFFORD RD

AeroVenture (Mus)

St Peter's RC Prim Sch

Lakeside Prim Sch

Cantley Bridge

A638

B1396

CANTLEY LA

ST BARTHOLOMEWS RISE

St Bartholomews

B1396

Hawthorn Prim Sch

A   B   C   D   E   F

63
43

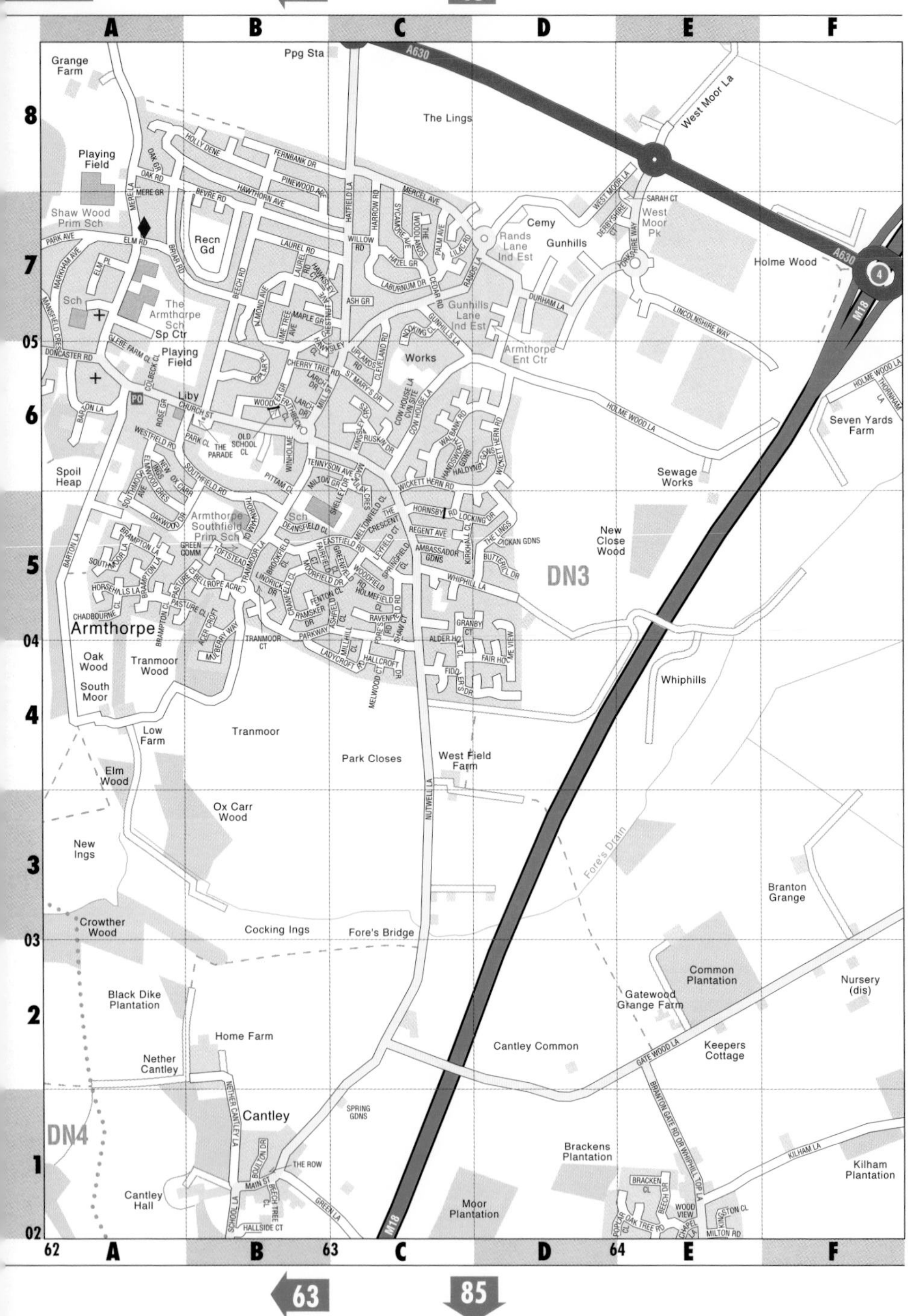
A
B
C
D
E
F
Grange Farm
Ppg Sta
A630
The Lings
West Moor La
Playing Field
Shaw Wood Prim Sch
Recn Gd
Cemy
Rands Lane Ind Est
Gunhills
West Moor Pk
Holme Wood
Sch
The Armthorpe Sch
Sp Ctr
Playing Field
Gunhills Lane Ind Est
Armthorpe Ent Ctr
Works
Liby
PO
Seven Yards Farm
Spoil Heap
Sewage Works
Armthorpe Southfield Prim Sch
New Close Wood
DN3
Armthorpe
Oak Wood
Tranmoor Wood
South Moor
Whiphills
Low Farm
Tranmoor
Park Closes
West Field Farm
Elm Wood
Ox Carr Wood
New Ings
Fore's Drain
Branton Grange
Crowther Wood
Cocking Ings
Fore's Bridge
Common Plantation
Nursery (dis)
Black Dike Plantation
Gatewood Grange Farm
Home Farm
Cantley Common
Keepers Cottage
Nether Cantley
Cantley
DN4
Brackens Plantation
Kilham Plantation
Cantley Hall
Moor Plantation
M18
NUTWELL LA
GATE WOOD LA
KILHAM LA
HOLME WOOD LA
LINCOLNSHIRE WAY
DURHAM LA
1
2
3
4
5
6
7
8
02
03
04
05
62
63
64

63
85

44

66

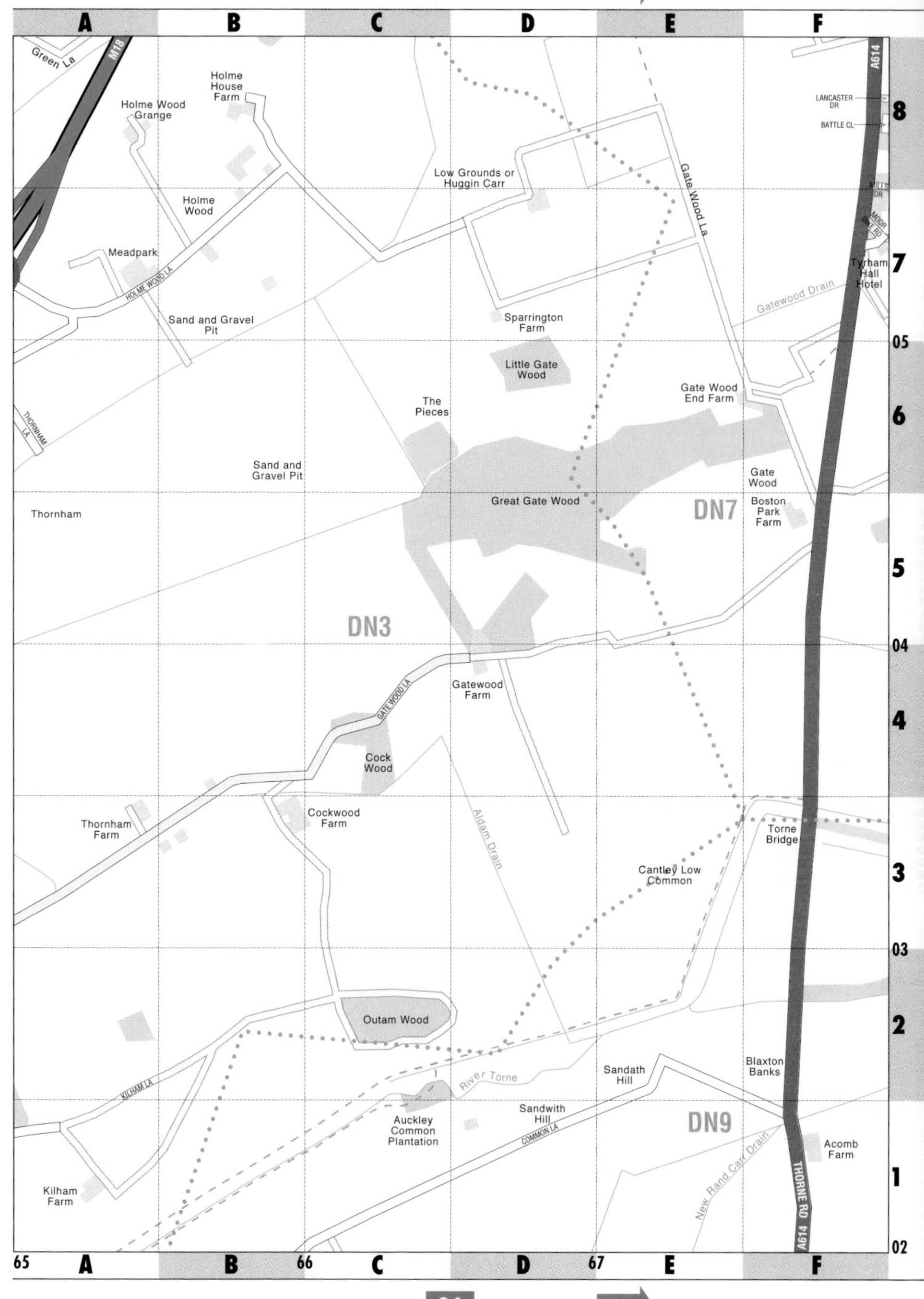

A
B
C
D
E
F
Green La
M18
Holme House Farm
Holme Wood Grange
Holme Wood
Meadpark
HOLME WOOD LA
Sand and Gravel Pit
THORNHAM LA
Sand and Gravel Pit
Thornham
Low Grounds or Huggin Carr
Gate Wood La
Sparrington Farm
Little Gate Wood
The Pieces
Great Gate Wood
Gate Wood End Farm
Gate Wood
Boston Park Farm
DN7
DN3
A614
LANCASTER DR
BATTLE CL
MILLS DR
MOOR DIKE RD
Tyrham Hall Hotel
Gatewood Drain
Gatewood Farm
GATE WOOD LA
Cock Wood
Thornham Farm
Cockwood Farm
Aldam Drain
Torne Bridge
Cantley Low Common
Outam Wood
KILHAM LA
River Torne
Sandath Hill
Blaxton Banks
Sandwith Hill
Auckley Common Plantation
COMMON LA
DN9
New Rand Carr Drain
Acomb Farm
Kilham Farm
THORNE RD
A614
8
7
05
6
5
04
4
3
03
2
1
02
65
66
67

86

66

A B C D E F

8 | HAMPDEN CRES | H M Prison | | | | |

LANCASTER DR
BLENHEIM RD
WELLINGTON RD
1 CUNNINGHAM RD
2 GIBSON RD

Playing Fields

Hatfield Moors

MILLS DR
VARSITY CL

Canberra
Cottage Farm

MOOR DIKE RD

Moor Dike Rd

DN7

7

05

Jet-Ski
Park

Sand &
Gravel Pit

6

Poor
Piece

Old Moor Drain

Ellerholme
Farm

5

04

Middle Ring Drain

North Ring Drain

MOOR LA

ACRES LA

Sewage
Wks

Chester
Cottage
Farm

Southlands
Farm

SANDS LA
LEWIS LA
SANDS LA TERR
HIGH ST

Dolwood Dr

4

South Ring Drain

Glebe
Farm

3

03

River Torne

God's Cross

Candy
Farm

DN9

Old Thatch Carr
Drain

Long Plantation

Godscross Drain

2

Long Plantation

CANDY BANK

New Thatch Carr Drain

1

02

Blaxton
Common

Sand &
Gravel Pit

NAB SAMPSON BANK

Thatch Carr
Plantation

68 A B 69 C D 70 E F

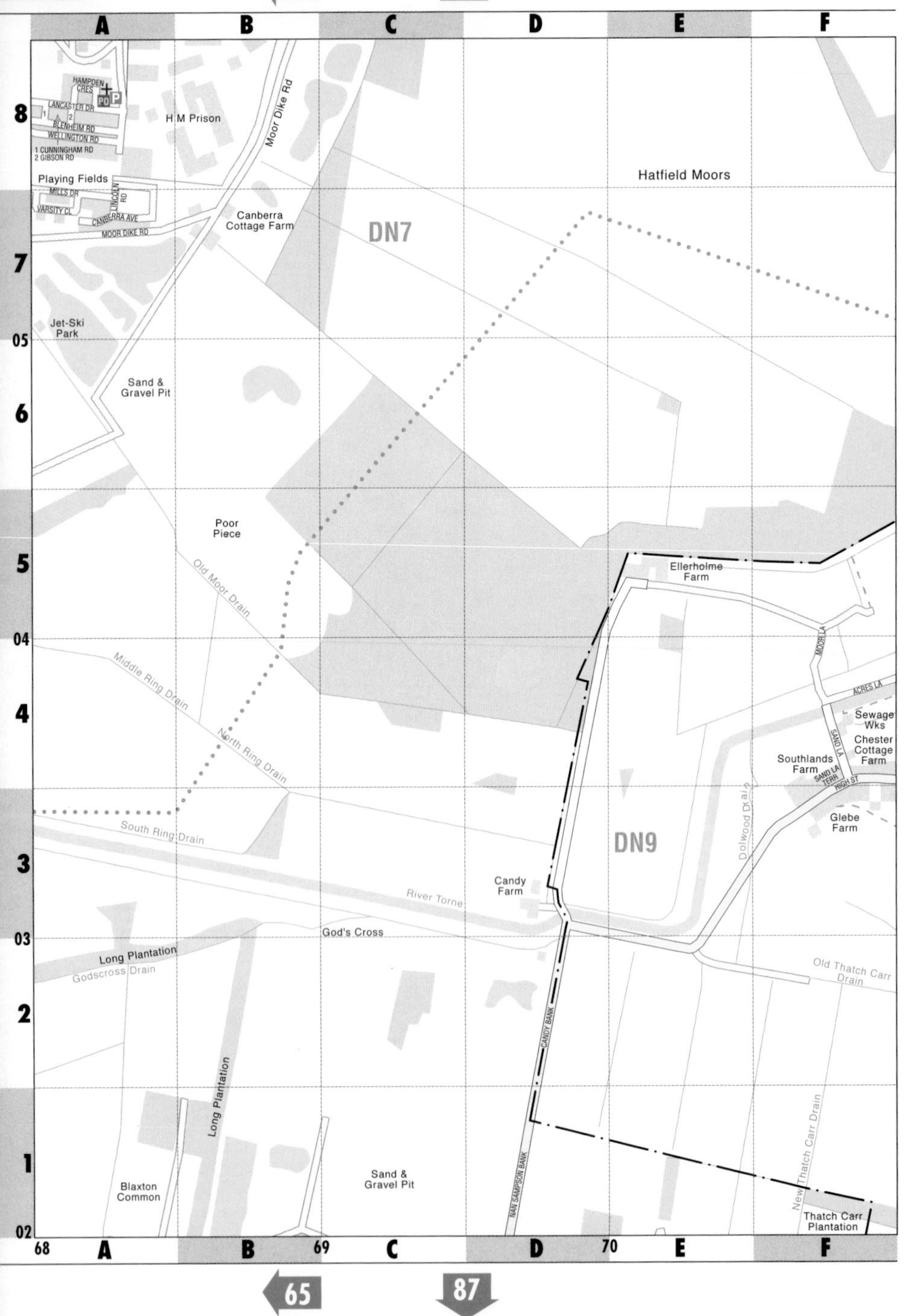

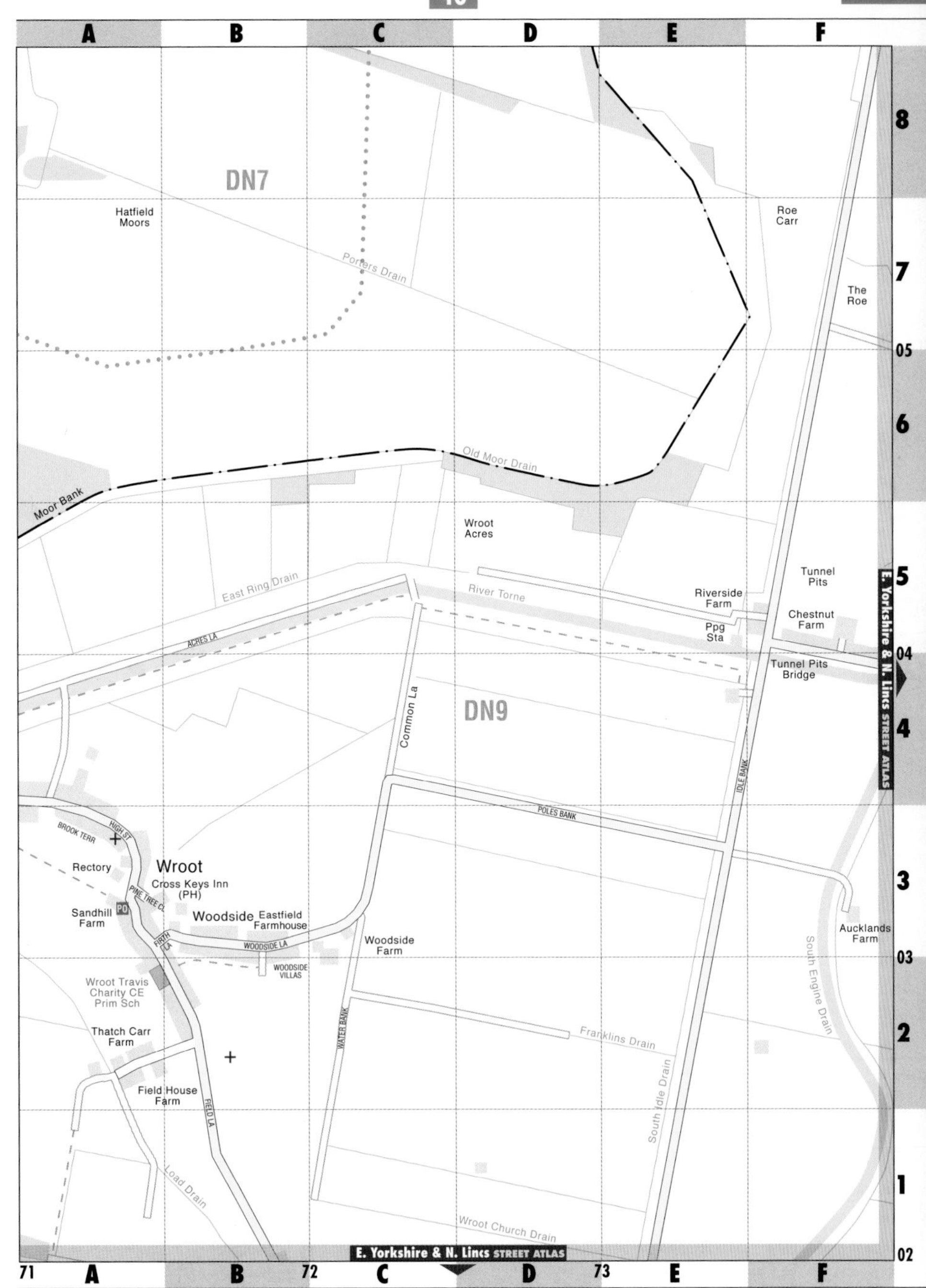

DN7

Hatfield
Moors

Porters Drain

Roe
Carr

The
Roe

Moor Bank

Old Moor Drain

Wroot
Acres

East Ring Drain

River Torne

Riverside
Farm

Tunnel
Pits

ACRES LA

Common La

DN9

Ppg
Sta

Chestnut
Farm

Tunnel Pits
Bridge

IDLE BANK

POLES BANK

Aucklands
Farm

BROOK TERR

Rectory

Wroot

Cross Keys Inn
(PH)

Woodside Eastfield
Farmhouse

Woodside
Farm

Franklins Drain

South Engine Drain

Sandhill
Farm

PINE TREE CL

FRONT LA

WOODSIDE LA

WOODSIDE
VILLAS

Wroot Travis
Charity CE
Prim Sch

Thatch Carr
Farm

Field House
Farm

FIELD LA

WATER BANK

Load Drain

South Idle Drain

Wroot Church Drain

47

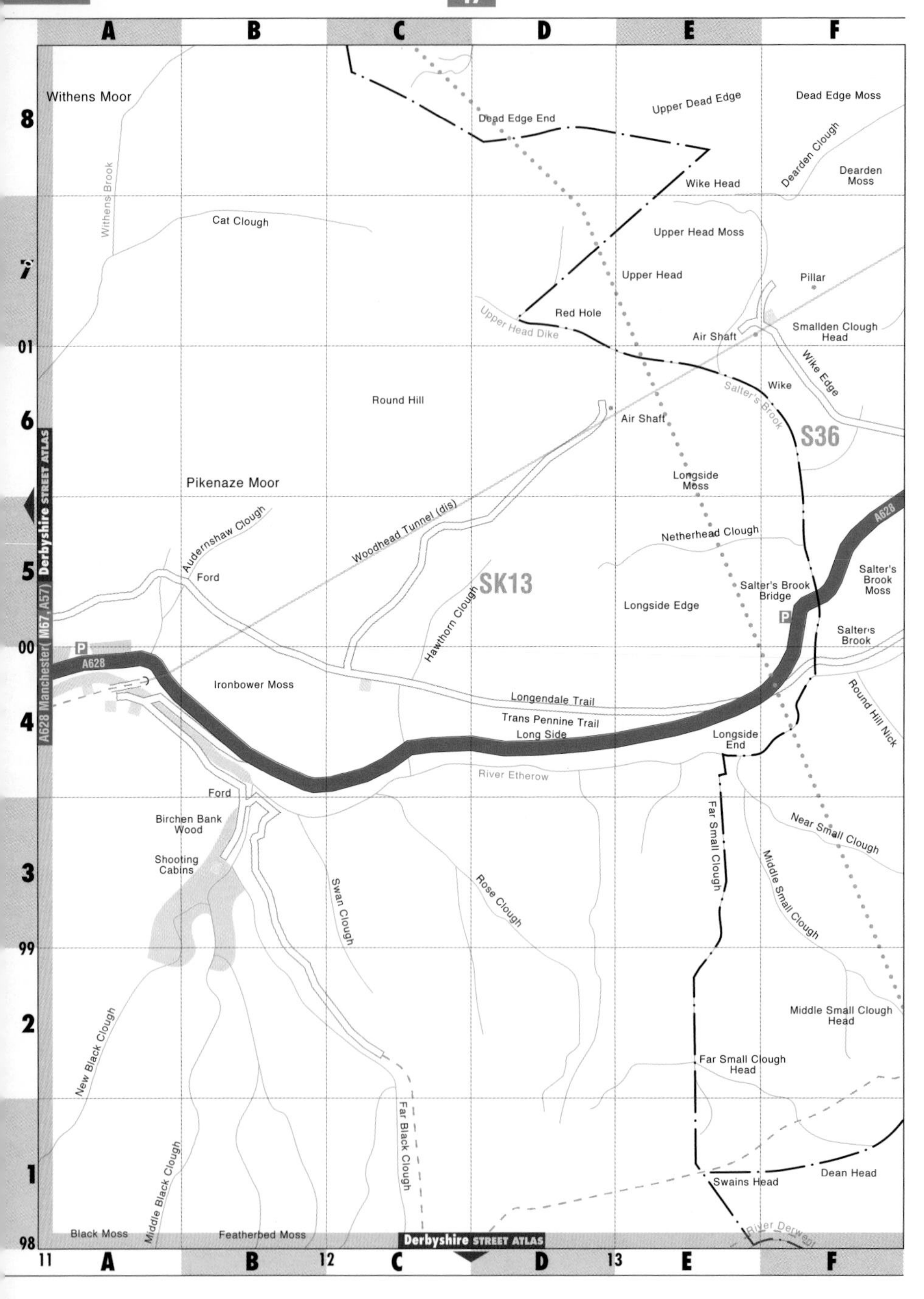
A
B
C
D
E
F
8
7
01
6
5
00
4
3
99
2
1
98
11
12
13
Withens Moor
Withens Brook
Cat Clough
Dead Edge End
Upper Dead Edge
Dead Edge Moss
Dearden Clough
Dearden Moss
Wike Head
Upper Head Moss
Upper Head
Pillar
Red Hole
Upper Head Dike
Air Shaft
Smallden Clough Head
Wike Edge
Wike
Salter's Brook
Round Hill
Air Shaft
S36
Pikenaze Moor
Longside Moss
Woodhead Tunnel (dis)
Audernshaw Clough
Netherhead Clough
A628
Ford
SK13
Hawthorn Clough
Salter's Brook Bridge
Salter's Brook Moss
Longside Edge
P
Salter's Brook
A628 Manchester (M67, A57)
Derbyshire STREET ATLAS
A628
Ironbower Moss
Longendale Trail
Trans Pennine Trail
Long Side
Longside End
Round Hill Nick
River Etherow
Ford
Birchen Bank Wood
Shooting Cabins
Swan Clough
Rose Clough
Far Small Clough
Near Small Clough
Middle Small Clough
Middle Small Clough Head
New Black Clough
Far Small Clough Head
Far Black Clough
Middle Black Clough
Swains Head
Dean Head
Black Moss
Featherbed Moss
River Derwent
Derbyshire STREET ATLAS

48

70

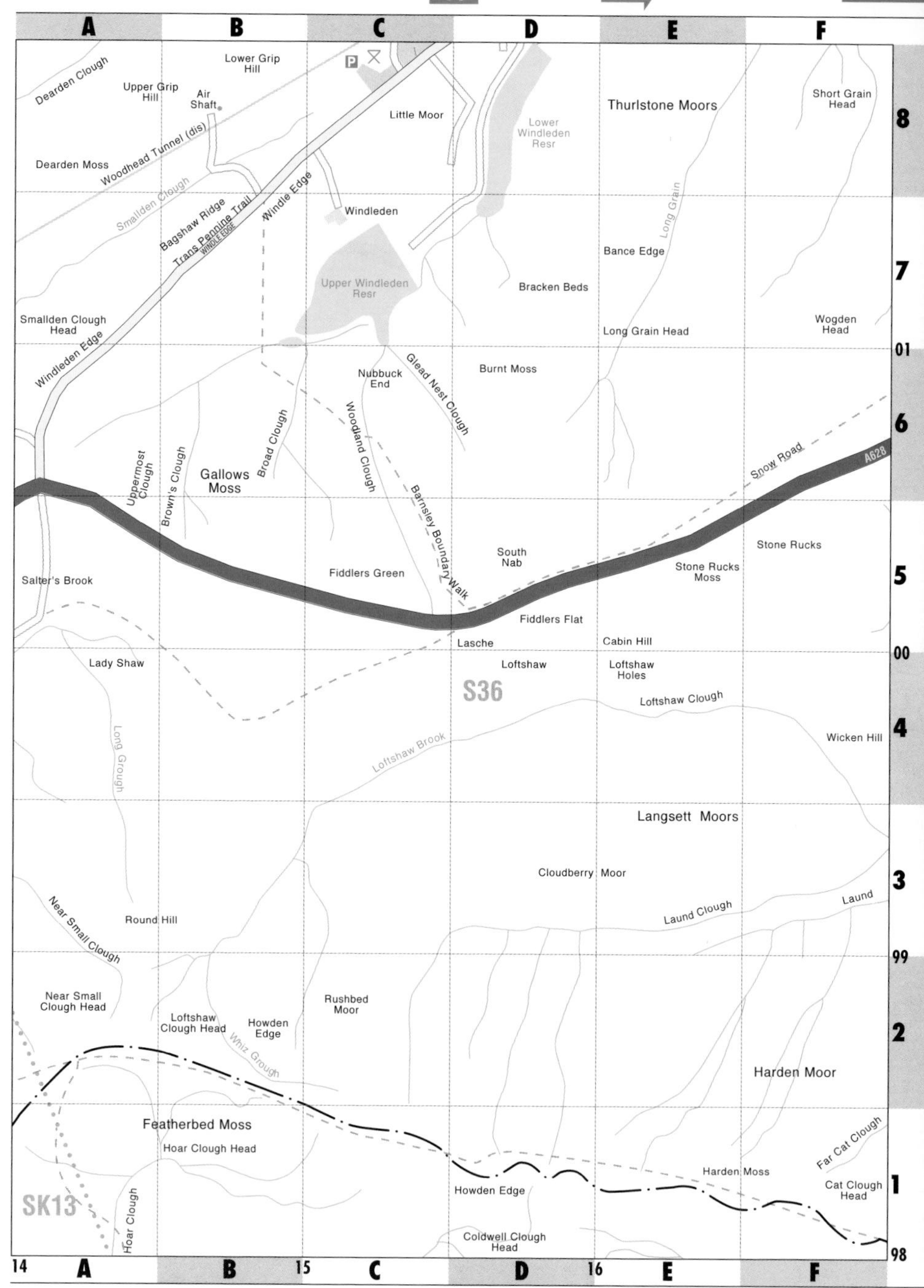

A
B
C
D
E
F
Dearden Clough
Upper Grip Hill
Lower Grip Hill
Air Shaft
Little Moor
Lower Windleden Resr
Thurlstone Moors
Short Grain Head
Woodhead Tunnel (dis)
Dearden Moss
Smallden Clough
Bagshaw Ridge
Trans Pennine Trail
WINDLE EDGE
Windle Edge
Windleden
Long Grain
Bance Edge
Upper Windleden Resr
Bracken Beds
Smallden Clough Head
Long Grain Head
Wogden Head
Windleden Edge
Nubbuck End
Glead Nest Clough
Burnt Moss
Broad Clough
Woodland Clough
Uppermost Clough
Brown's Clough
Gallows Moss
Barnsley Boundary Walk
Snow Road
A628
South Nab
Stone Rucks
Salter's Brook
Fiddlers Green
Stone Rucks Moss
Fiddlers Flat
Lasche
Cabin Hill
Lady Shaw
Loftshaw
Loftshaw Holes
S36
Loftshaw Clough
Long Grough
Loftshaw Brook
Wicken Hill
Langsett Moors
Cloudberry Moor
Near Small Clough
Round Hill
Laund Clough
Laund
Near Small Clough Head
Rushbed Moor
Loftshaw Clough Head
Howden Edge
Whiz Grough
Harden Moor
Featherbed Moss
Hoar Clough Head
Far Cat Clough
Harden Moss
Cat Clough Head
Howden Edge
SK13
Hoar Clough
Coldwell Clough Head
8
7
01
6
5
00
4
3
99
2
1
98
14
15
16
88
70

A B C D E F

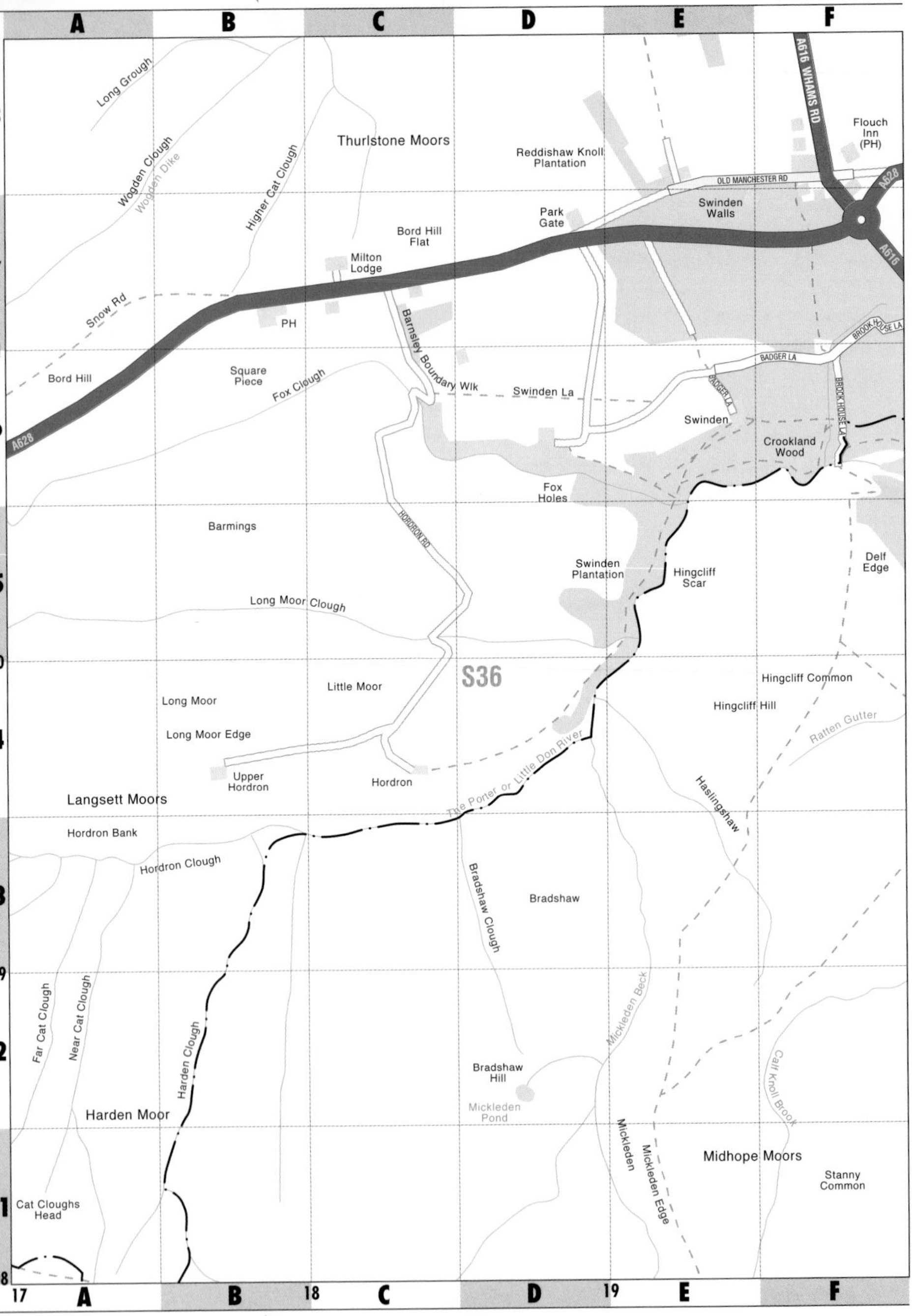

8

Long Grough

Wogden Clough
Wogden Dike

Higher Cat Clough

Thurlstone Moors

Reddishaw Knoll
Plantation

A616 WHAMS RD

Flouch Inn
(PH)

Old Manchester Rd

Swinden
Walls

A628

Park
Gate

7

Milton
Lodge

Bord Hill
Flat

Snow Rd

PH

Barnsley Boundary Wlk

A616

01

Bord Hill

Square
Piece

Fox Clough

Swinden La

Badger La

Brook House La

Brock House La

6

A628

Swinden

Crookland
Wood

Fox
Holes

Barmings

Swinden
Plantation

Hingcliff
Scar

Delf
Edge

5

Long Moor Clough

00

Little Moor

S36

Hingcliff Common

Hingcliff Hill

Ratten Gutter

Long Moor

Long Moor Edge

Upper
Hordron

Hordron

Hordron Rd

The Porter or Little Don River

Haslingshaw

4

Langsett Moors

Hordron Bank

Hordron Clough

Bradshaw Clough

Bradshaw

Mickleden Beck

Cat Knoll Brook

3

99

Far Cat Clough

Near Cat Clough

Harden Clough

Bradshaw
Hill

Mickleden
Pond

Mickleden

Mickleden Edge

Midhope Moors

Stanny
Common

2

Harden Moor

1

Cat Cloughs
Head

98

17   A   B   18   C   D   19   E   F

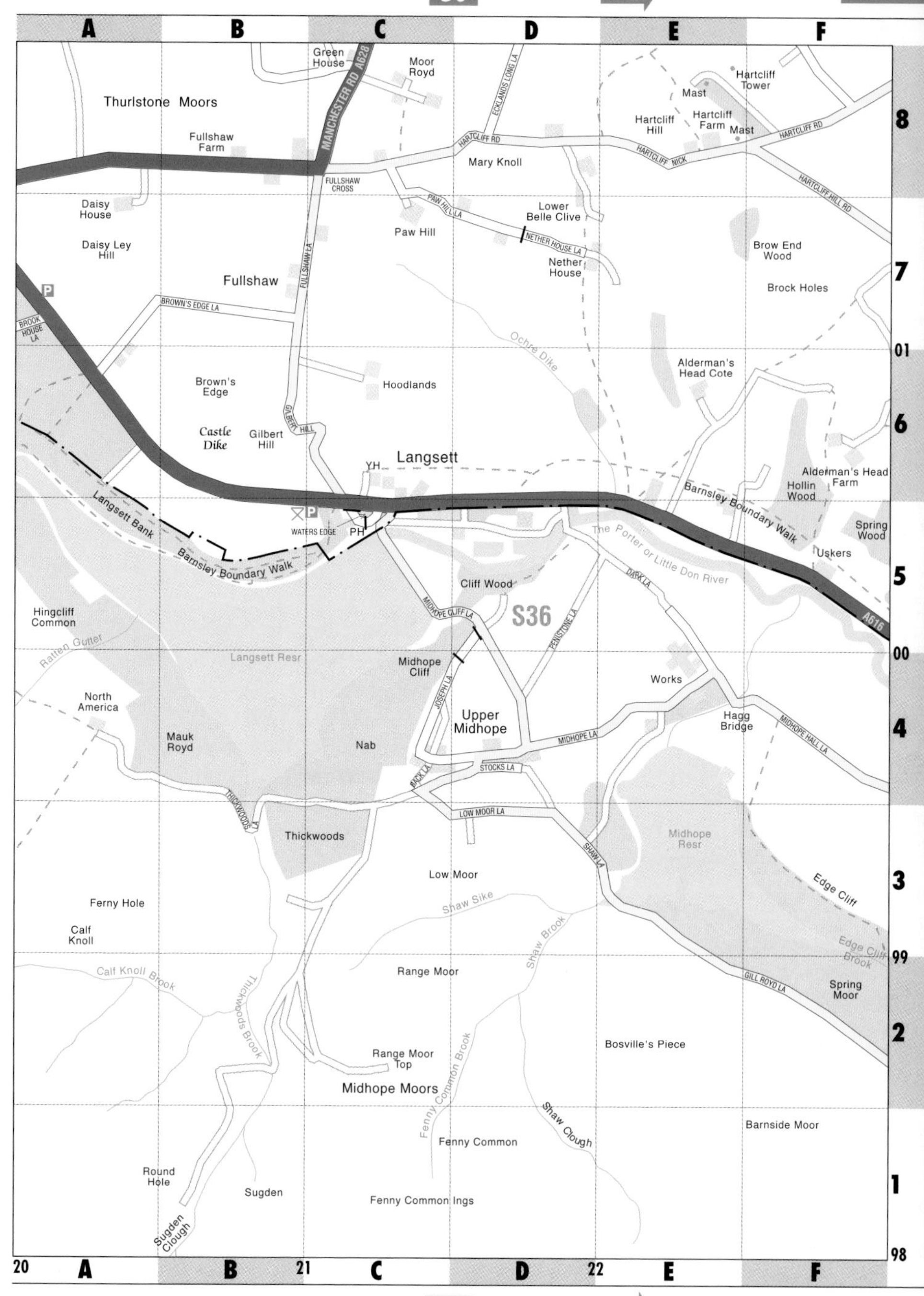

A **B** **C** **D** **E** **F**

Thurlstone Moors

Fullshaw Farm

Green House

Moor Royd

Hartcliff Tower

Mast

ECKLANDS LONG LA

HARTCLIFF RD

Hartcliff Hill

Hartcliff Farm

Mast

HARTCLIFF RD

MANCHESTER RD A628

Mary Knoll

HARTCLIFF WICK

HARTCLIFF HILL RD

FULLSHAW CROSS

Daisy House

PAW HILL LA

Lower Belle Clive

Brow End Wood

Paw Hill

NETHER HOUSE LA

FULLSHAW LA

Nether House

Brock Holes

Daisy Ley Hill

Fullshaw

BROWN'S EDGE LA

Ochre Dike

Alderman's Head Cote

P

Brown's Edge

Hoodlands

BROOK HOUSE LA

Castle Dike

Gilbert Hill

GILBERT HILL

Alderman's Head Farm

Langsett

YH

Hollin Wood

Barnsley Boundary Walk

Spring Wood

Langsett Bank

WATERS EDGE

PH

Uskers

Barnsley Boundary Walk

The Porter or Little Don River

A616

Hingcliff Common

Ratten Gutter

Cliff Wood

MIDHOPE CLIFF LA

S36

PENISTONE LA

DIRKA LA

Langsett Resr

Midhope Cliff

Works

North America

Upper Midhope

JOSEPH LA

MIDHOPE LA

Hagg Bridge

MIDHOPE HALL LA

Mauk Royd

Nab

APPLE LA

STOCKS LA

SHEPH LA

Thickwoods

THICKWOODS

LOW MOOR LA

Midhope Resr

Ferny Hole

Low Moor

Shaw Sike

Edge Cliff

Calf Knoll

Range Moor

Shaw Brook

Edge Cliff Brook

Calf Knoll Brook

Spring Moor

GILL ROYD LA

Range Moor Top

Bosville's Piece

Barnside Moor

Midhope Moors

Fenny Common Brook

Shaw Clough

Round Hole

Sugden

Fenny Common

Sugden Clough

Fenny Common Ings

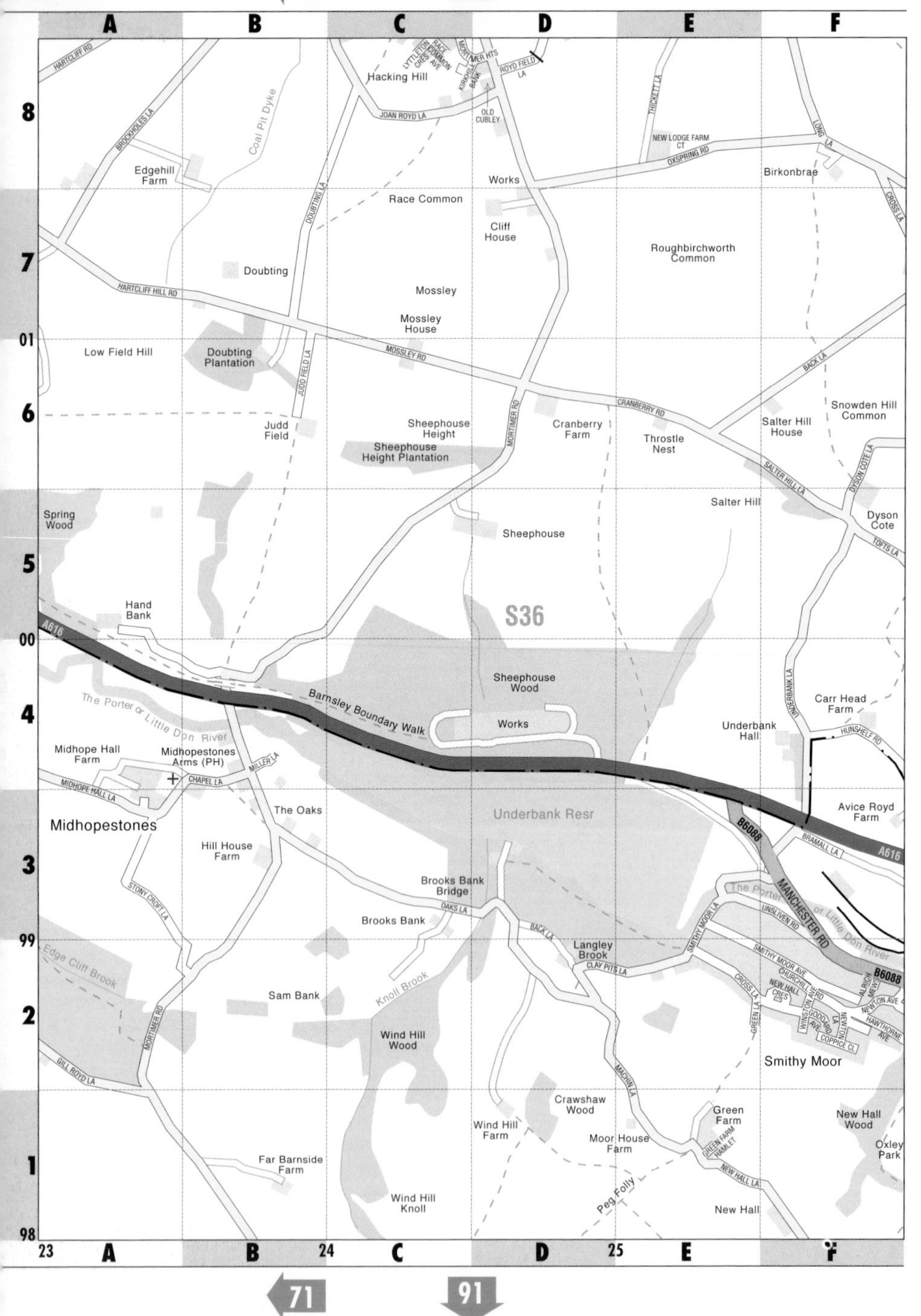

| A | B | C | D | E | F |

8

HARTCLIFF RD

Hacking Hill

JOAN ROYD LA

ROYD FIELD LA

Works

OLD CUBLEY

THICKETT LA

NEW LODGE FARM CT

OXSPRING RD

LONG LA

CROSS LA

Birkonbrae

Edgehill Farm

BROOKHOUSE LA

Coal Pit Dyke

Race Common

Cliff House

Roughbirchworth Common

7

HARTCLIFF HILL RD

Doubting

DOUBTING LA

Mossley

Mossley House

01

Low Field Hill

Doubting Plantation

JUDD FIELD LA

MOSSLEY RD

BACK LA

6

Judd Field

Sheephouse Height

Sheephouse Height Plantation

Cranberry Farm

CRANBERRY RD

Throstle Nest

Salter Hill House

Snowden Hill Common

MORTIMER RD

SALTER HILL LA

DYSON COTE LA

TOFTS LA

Spring Wood

Hand Bank

Sheephouse

Salter Hill

Dyson Cote

5

A616

S36

00

The Porter or Little Don River

Barnsley Boundary Walk

Sheephouse Wood

Carr Head Farm

HUNSHELF RD

4

Midhope Hall Farm

Midhopestones Arms (PH)

MILLER LA

CHAPEL LA

Works

Underbank Hall

V INN YARD

MIDHOPE HALL LA

Midhopestones

The Oaks

Underbank Resr

B6088

BRAMALL LA

Avice Royd Farm

A616

3

Hill House Farm

STONY CROFT LA

Brooks Bank Bridge

OAKS LA

The Porter or Little Don River

MANCHESTER RD

UNBUSLEVEN RD

NEW HALL CR

B6088

Brooks Bank

BACK LA

Langley Brook

CLAY PITS LA

SMITHY MOOR LA

SMITHY MOOR AVE

CROSS LA

NEW HALL LA

HAWTHORNE AVE

99

Edge Cliff Brook

Sam Bank

Knoll Brook

COPPICE CL

LIVINGSTONE RD

MILTON CL

2

MORTIMER RD

Wind Hill Wood

BIRCH LA

Smithy Moor

New Hall Wood

Oxley Park

GILL ROYD LA

Far Barnside Farm

Wind Hill Farm

Crawshaw Wood

Moor House Farm

Green Farm

GREEN FARM HAMLET

1

Wind Hill Knoll

Peg Folly

New Hall

NEW HALL LA

98

| 23 | A | B | 24 | C | D | 25 | E | F |

52
74

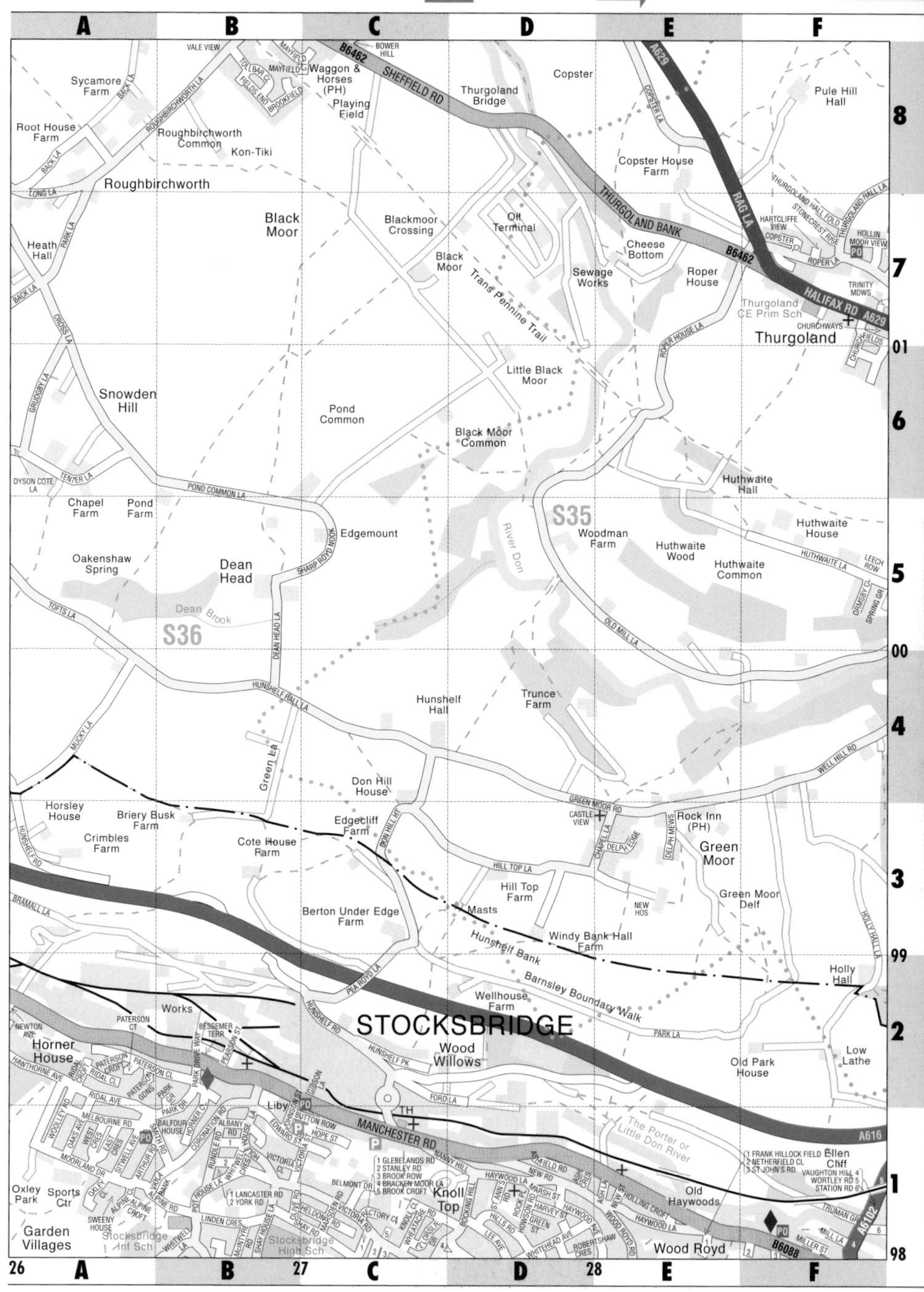
STOCKSBRIDGE
Roughbirchworth
Sycamore Farm
Root House Farm
Roughbirchworth Common
Kon-Tiki
Waggon & Horses (PH)
Playing Field
Thurgoland Bridge
Copster
Pule Hill Hall
Copster House Farm
Black Moor
Blackmoor Crossing
Oil Terminal
Cheese Bottom
Sewage Works
Roper House
Thurgoland CE Prim Sch
Thurgoland
Heath Hall
Trans Pennine Trail
Little Black Moor
Snowden Hill
Pond Common
Black Moor Common
Chapel Farm
Pond Farm
Edgemount
S35
Woodman Farm
Huthwaite Hall
Huthwaite House
Huthwaite Wood
Huthwaite Common
River Don
Oakenshaw Spring
Dean Head
Dean Brook
S36
Hunshelf Hall
Trunce Farm
Don Hill House
Horsley House
Briery Busk Farm
Crimbles Farm
Edgecliff Farm
Cote House Farm
Rock Inn (PH)
Green Moor
Hill Top Farm
Green Moor Delf
Berton Under Edge Farm
Masts
Windy Bank Hall Farm
Hunshelf Bank
Barnsley Boundary Walk
Holly Hall
Wellhouse Farm
Works
Horner House
Wood Willows
Old Park House
Low Lathe
Liby
TH
The Porter or Little Don River
Ellen Cliff
Oxley Park
Sports Ctr
Knoll Top
Old Haywoods
Garden Villages
Stocksbridge Inf Sch
Stocksbridge High Sch
Wood Royd
SHEFFIELD RD
THURGOLAND BANK
HALIFAX RD
RAG LA
MANCHESTER RD
B6462
A629
A616
B6088
A6102
1 GLEBELANDS RD
2 STANLEY RD
3 BROOK ROW
4 BRACKEN MOOR LA
5 BROOK CROFT
1 LANCASTER RD
2 YORK RD
1 FRANK HILLOCK FIELD
2 NETHERFIELD CL
3 ST JOHN'S RD
VAUGHTON HILL 4
WORTLEY RD 5
STATION RD 6
A B C D E F
8 7 01 6 5 00 4 3 99 2 1 98
26 27 28

92
74

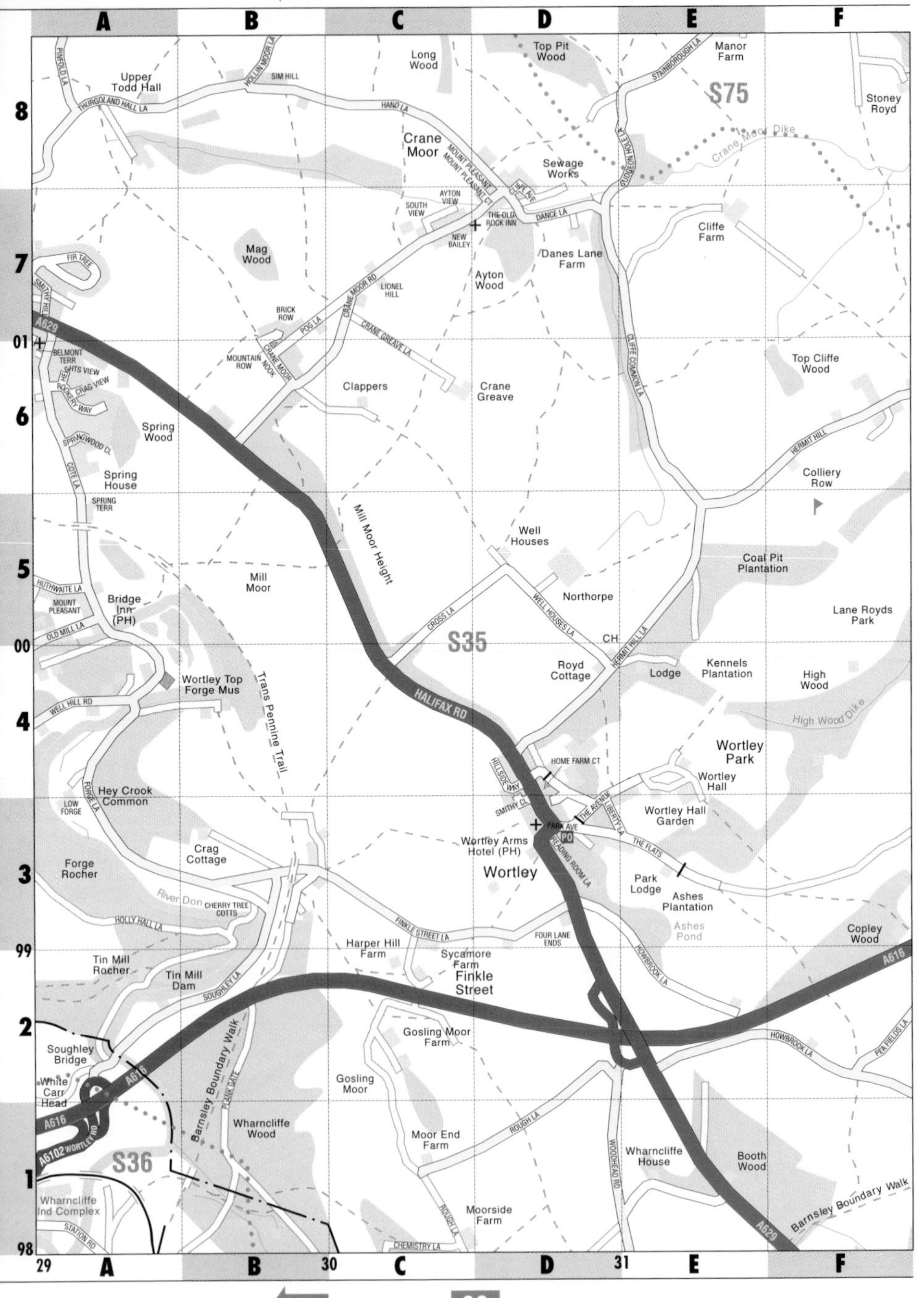
73
53
Upper Todd Hall
Long Wood
Top Pit Wood
Manor Farm
S75
Stoney Royd
Crane Moor
Sewage Works
Crane Moor Dike
Cliffe Farm
Mag Wood
Danes Lane Farm
Ayton Wood
Top Cliffe Wood
Clappers
Crane Greave
Spring Wood
Spring House
Colliery Row
Mill Moor Height
Well Houses
Coal Pit Plantation
Mill Moor
Bridge Inn (PH)
Northorpe
Lane Royds Park
S35
Royd Cottage
Lodge
Kennels Plantation
High Wood
Wortley Top Forge Mus
Trans Pennine Trail
High Wood Dike
Wortley Park
Wortley Hall
Hey Crook Common
Wortley Hall Garden
Forge Rocher
Crag Cottage
Wortley Arms Hotel (PH)
Wortley
Park Lodge
Ashes Plantation
Ashes Pond
River Don
Copley Wood
Tin Mill Rocher
Tin Mill Dam
Harper Hill Farm
Sycamore Farm
Finkle Street
Gosling Moor Farm
Soughley Bridge
White Carr Head
Gosling Moor
Wharncliffe Wood
Barnsley Boundary Walk
Moor End Farm
Wharncliffe House
Booth Wood
S36
Wharncliffe Ind Complex
Moorside Farm
HALIFAX RD
A629
A616
A6102
73
93

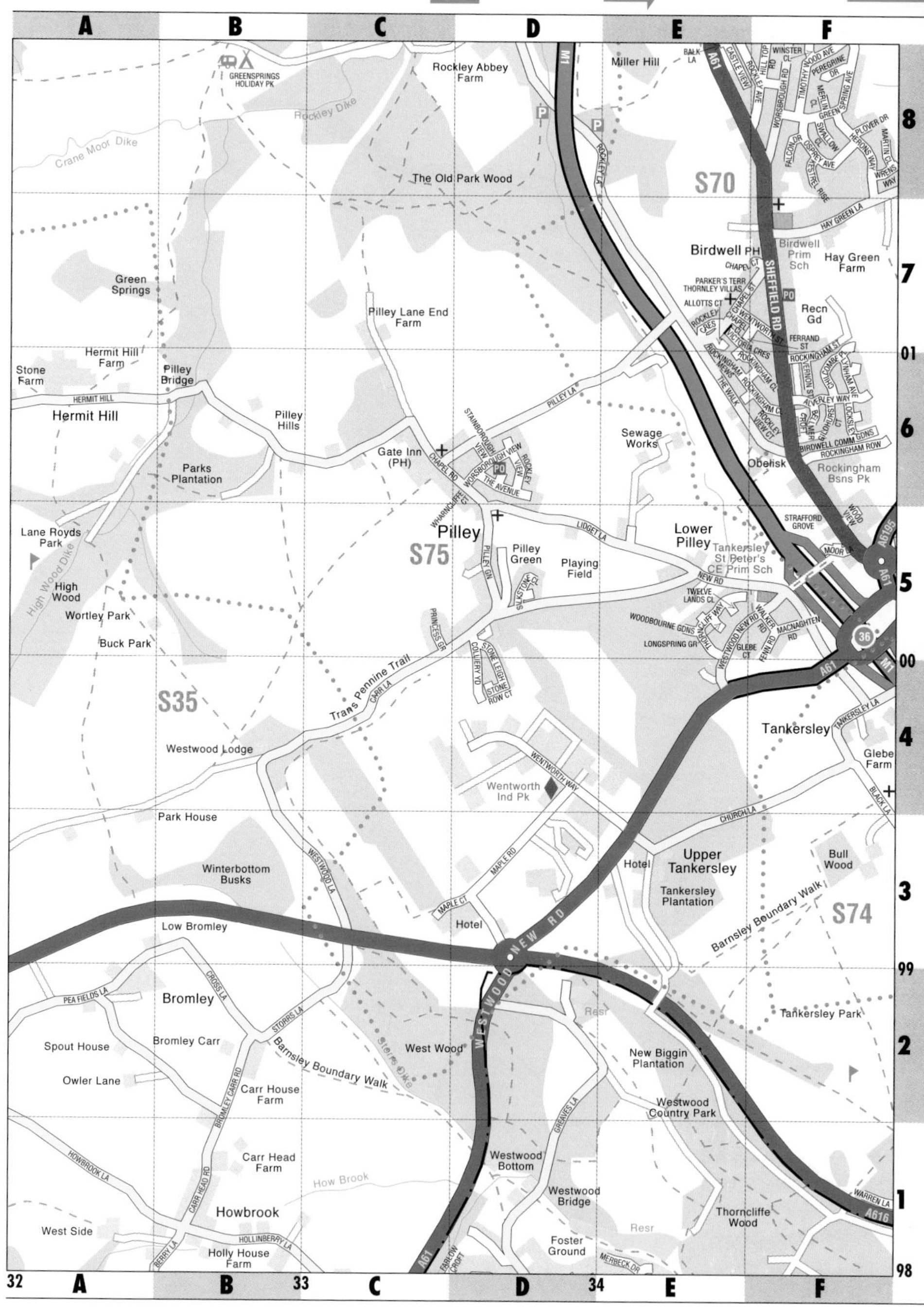

A   **B**   **C**   **D**   **E**   **F**

Crane Moor Dike

GREENSPRINGS HOLIDAY PK

Rockley Dike

Rockley Abbey Farm

Miller Hill

BALK LA

WINSTER

8

The Old Park Wood

S70

Green Springs

7

Pilley Lane End Farm

Birdwell PH

Birdwell Prim Sch

Hay Green Farm

CHAPEL

Hermit Hill Farm

Stone Farm

Pilley Bridge

HERMIT HILL

Hermit Hill

Pilley Hills

PARKER'S TERR
THORNLEY VILLAS
ALLOTTS CTS

Recn Gd

FERRAND ST
RDCKLEY
CRES

PO

01

Parks Plantation

Gate Inn (PH)

PILLEY LA

6

Sewage Works

Obelisk

ROCKINGHAM ROW

BIRDWELL COMM GDNS
Rockingham Bsns Pk

Lane Royds Park

Pilley

S75

Pilley Green

LIDGETT LA

Lower Pilley

Tankersley St Peter's CE Prim Sch

STRAFFORD GROVE

High Wood

Wortley Park

Buck Park

Playing Field

NEW RD

Woodbourne Gdns
TWELVE LANDS CL

MACNAGHTEN RD

MOOR LA

5

Trans Pennine Trail

S35

Longspring Gr

GLEBE CT

36

00

Westwood Lodge

Tankersley

Glebe Farm

4

Park House

Wentworth Ind Pk

WENTWORTH RD

CHURCH LA

Upper Tankersley

Hotel

Tankersley Plantation

Bull Wood

Barnsley Boundary Walk

S74

3

Winterbottom Busks

WESTWOOD LA

MAPLE RD

Low Bromley

MAPLE CT

Hotel

NEW RD

WESTWOOD

Bromley

Bromley Carr

CROSS LA
STORRS LA

Barnsley Boundary Walk

West Wood

Resr

New Biggin Plantation

Tankersley Park

99

Spout House

Owler Lane

Carr House Farm

PEA FIELDS LA

CARR HEAD RD

Westwood Country Park

2

Carr Head Farm

HOMEBROOK LA

How Brook

Westwood Bottom

Westwood Bridge

Thorncliffe Wood

1

West Side

Howbrook

Holly House Farm

BERRY LA

CARR HEAD LA

HOLLINBERRY LA

Resr

Foster Ground

WARREN LA

A616

32   **A**   **B**   33   **C**   **D**   34   **E**   **F**   98

75
55

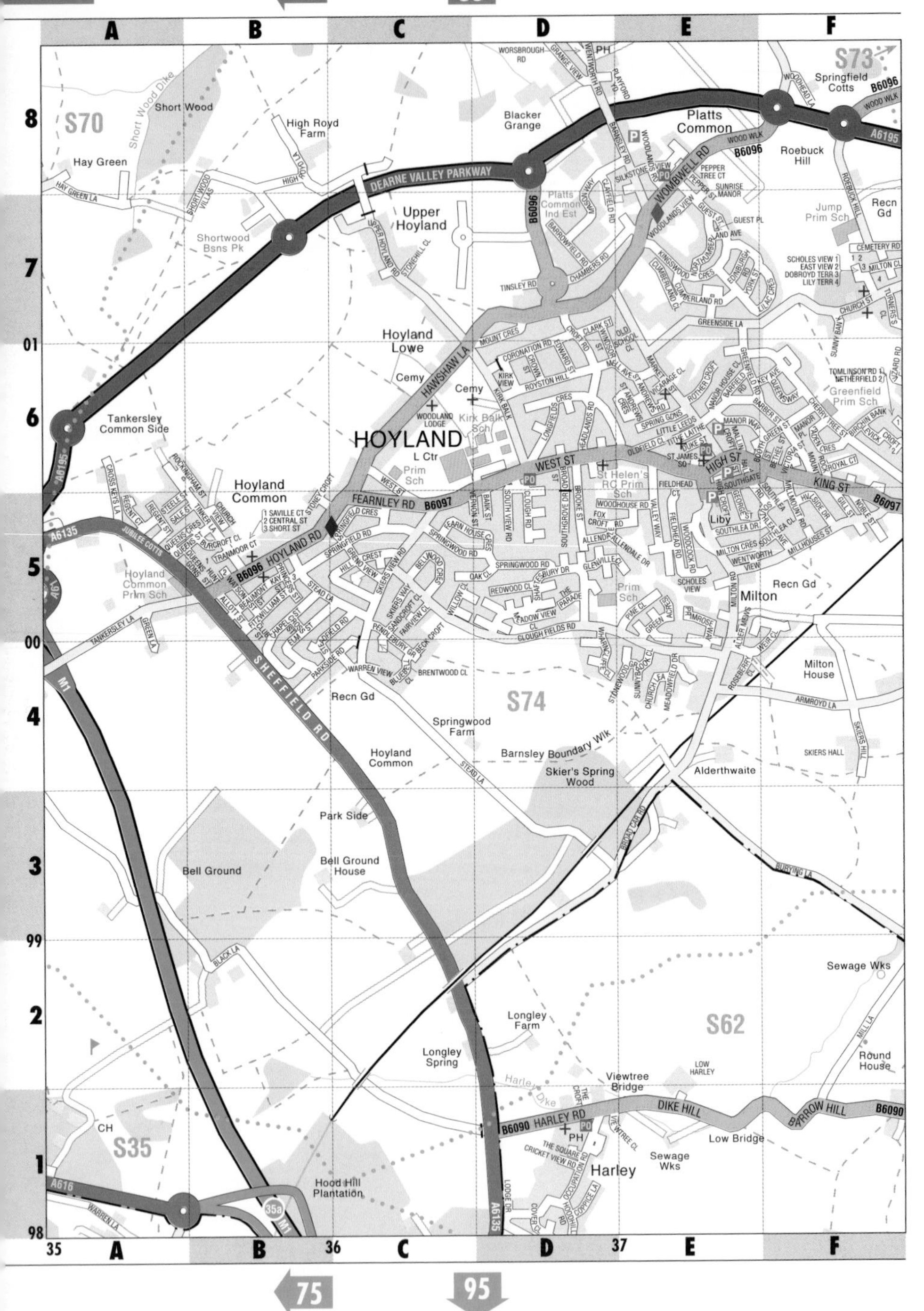
A
B
C
D
E
F
8
7
01
6
5
00
4
3
99
2
1
98
35
36
37
S70
S73
S74
S62
S35
Short Wood
Short Wood Dike
High Royd Farm
Hay Green
HAY GREEN LA
Blacker Grange
Platts Common
Springfield Cotts
Roebuck Hill
DEARNE VALLEY PARKWAY
WORSBROUGH RD
WENTWORTH RD
PH
Upper Hoyland
Shortwood Bsns Pk
Platts Common Ind Est
WOMBELL RD
B6096
A6195
Jump Prim Sch
Recn Gd
TINSLEY RD
CHAMBERS RD
CUMBERLAND RD
GREENSIDE LA
Hoyland Lowe
HAWSHAW LA
Cemy
Kirk Balk Sch
HOYLAND
L Ctr
Prim Sch
WEST ST
HIGH ST
KING ST
B6097
Tankersley Common Side
Greenfield Prim Sch
Hoyland Common
FEARNLEY RD
HOYLAND RD
1 SAVILLE CT
2 CENTRAL ST
3 SHORT ST
A6135
JUBILEE COTTS
St Helen's RC Prim Sch
Liby
Hoyland Common Prim Sch
SPRINGWOOD RD
CLOUGH FIELDS RD
Milton
TANKERSLEY LA
SHEFFIELD RD
M1
Recn Gd
Milton House
ARMROYD LA
Springwood Farm
Barnsley Boundary Wlk
Skier's Spring Wood
SKIERS HALL
Alderthwaite
STEAD LA
Park Side
Bell Ground
Bell Ground House
BURYING LA
BLACK LA
Sewage Wks
Longley Farm
Longley Spring
LOW HARLEY
Round House
Harley Dike
Viewtree Bridge
DIKE HILL
BARROW HILL
B6090
HARLEY RD
CH
Low Bridge
Sewage Wks
Harley
A616
WARREN LA
Hood Hill Plantation
35a
MILL LA

56

78

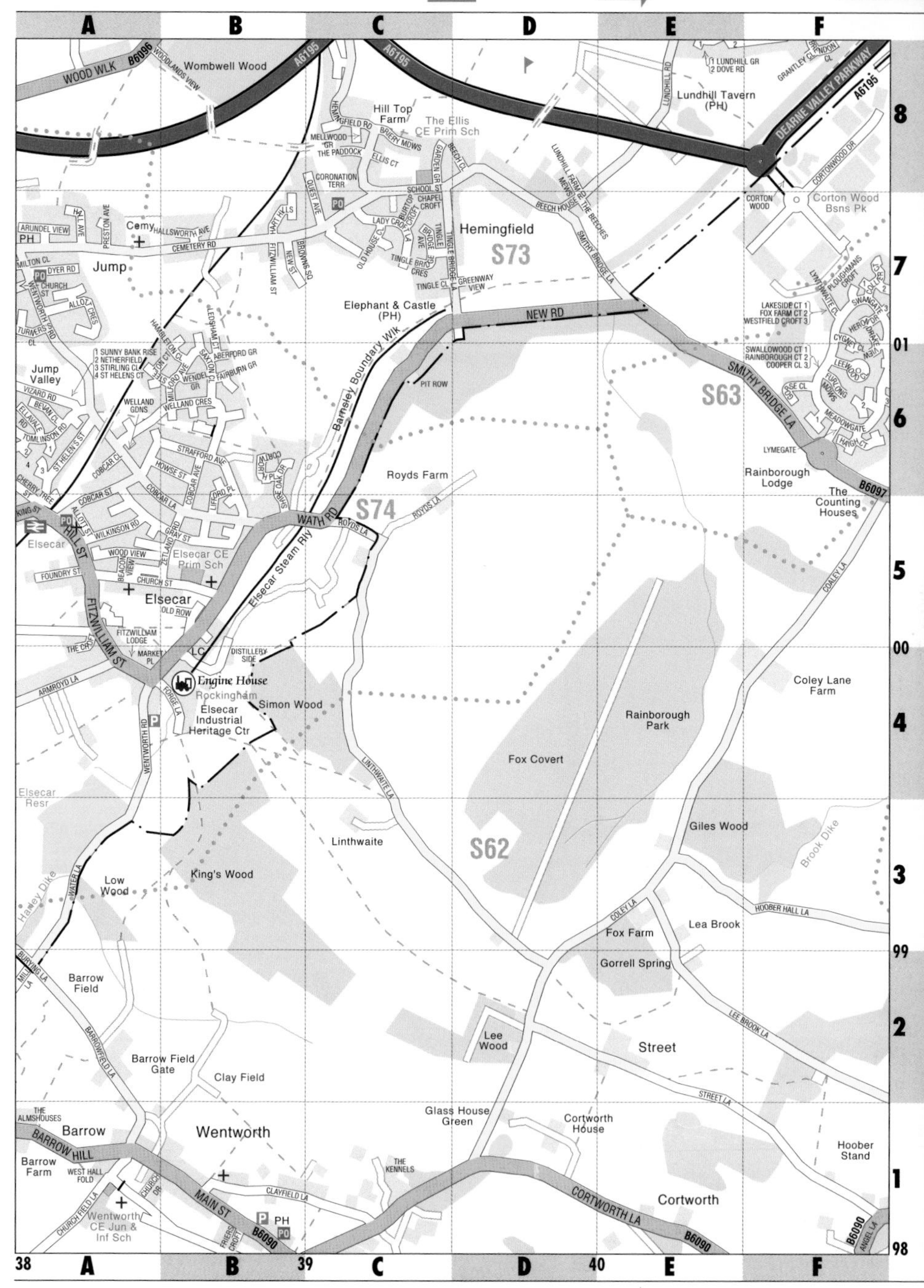
A
B
C
D
E
F
8
7
01
6
5
00
4
3
99
2
1
98
38
39
40
WOOD WLK
B6096
WOODLANDS VIEW
Wombwell Wood
A6195
Hill Top Farm
The Ellis CE Prim Sch
HEMINGFIELD RD
MELLWOOD GR
THE PADDOCK
BRIERY MDWS
ELLIS CT
CORONATION TERR
QUEST AVE
GARDEN GR
BEECH CL
SCHOOL ST
CHAPEL CROFT
LADY CROFT LA
BURTOFT CROFT
OLD HOUSE CL
TINGLE BRIDGE AVE
TINGLE BRIDGE CRES
TINGLE CL
TINGLE BRIDGE LA
GREENWAY VIEW
Hemingfield
S73
LUNDHILL RD
1 LUNDHILL GR
2 DOVE RD
GRANTLEY CL
BRENDON CL
Lundhill Tavern (PH)
LUNDHILL FARM MEWS
THE BEECHES
BEECH HOUSE
SMITHY BRIDGE LA
DEARNE VALLEY PARKWAY
A6195
CORTON WOOD
Corton Wood Bsns Pk
CORTONWOOD DR
LYNTHWAITE CL
PLOUGHMANS CROFT
SWANGATE
HERON DR
CYGNET CL
LAKESIDE CT 1
FOX FARM CT 2
WESTFIELD CROFT 3
SWALLOWOOD CT 1
RAINBOROUGH CT 2
COOPER CL 3
LEEWOOD CL
FURLONG MDWS
MEADOWGATE
HAIGH CT
LYMEGATE
Rainborough Lodge
B6097
The Counting Houses
S63
HALL AVE
PRESTON AVE
ARUNDEL VIEW
PH
Cemy
HALLSWORTH AVE
CEMETERY RD
HART HILLS
FITZWILLIAM ST
NEW ST
BROWNS SQ
MILTON CL
DYER RD
Jump
CHURCH ST
WENTWORTH RD
ALLOTT CRES
Elephant & Castle (PH)
NEW RD
1 SUNNY BANK RISE
2 NETHERFIELD
3 STIRLING CL
4 ST HELENS CT
Jump Valley
VIZARD RD
BEVAN CL
ELLAVALE RD
TOMLINSON RD
ST HELEN'S ST
HAMBLETON CL
LEDSHAM CT
SAXTON CL
ABERFORD GR
FAIRBURN GR
MILFORD AVE
WENDEL GR
WELLAND GDNS
WELLAND CRES
PIT ROW
Barnsley Boundary Wlk
SMITHY BRIDGE LA
STRAFFORD AVE
HOWSE ST
COBCAR CL
COBCAR AVE
COBCAR LA
COBCAR ST
LIFFORD PL
CHERRY TREE ST
KING ST
HILL ST
ALLOTT ST
WILKINSON RD
GRAY ST
Royds Farm
S74
WATH RD
ROYDS LA
Elsecar
WOOD VIEW
BEACON VIEW
ZETLAND RD
Elsecar CE Prim Sch
FOUNDRY ST
CHURCH ST
Elsecar
OLD ROW
Elsecar Steam Rly
FITZWILLIAM ST
FITZWILLIAM LODGE
THE CR
MARKET PL
LC
DISTILLERY SIDE
Engine House
Rockingham
ARMROYD LA
FORGE LA
Elsecar Industrial Heritage Ctr
Simon Wood
WENTWORTH RD
P
COLEY LA
Coley Lane Farm
Rainborough Park
Fox Covert
LINTHWAITE LA
Elsecar Resr
Linthwaite
S62
Giles Wood
Brook Dike
Low Wood
King's Wood
Harley Dike
WATER LA
COLEY LA
HOOBER HALL LA
Fox Farm
Lea Brook
BURYING LA
MILTON LA
Barrow Field
Gorrell Spring
BARROWFIELD LA
LEE BROOK LA
Lee Wood
Street
Barrow Field Gate
Clay Field
STREET LA
THE ALMSHOUSES
Barrow
Wentworth
Glass House Green
Cortworth House
Hoober Stand
BARROW HILL
Barrow Farm
WEST HALL FOLD
CHURCH DR
THE KENNELS
MAIN ST
CLAYFIELD LA
CORTWORTH LA
Cortworth
CHURCH FIELD LA
Wentworth CE Jun & Inf Sch
PH
PO
FRIERS CROFT
B6090
B6090
ANGEL LA

96

78

77
57

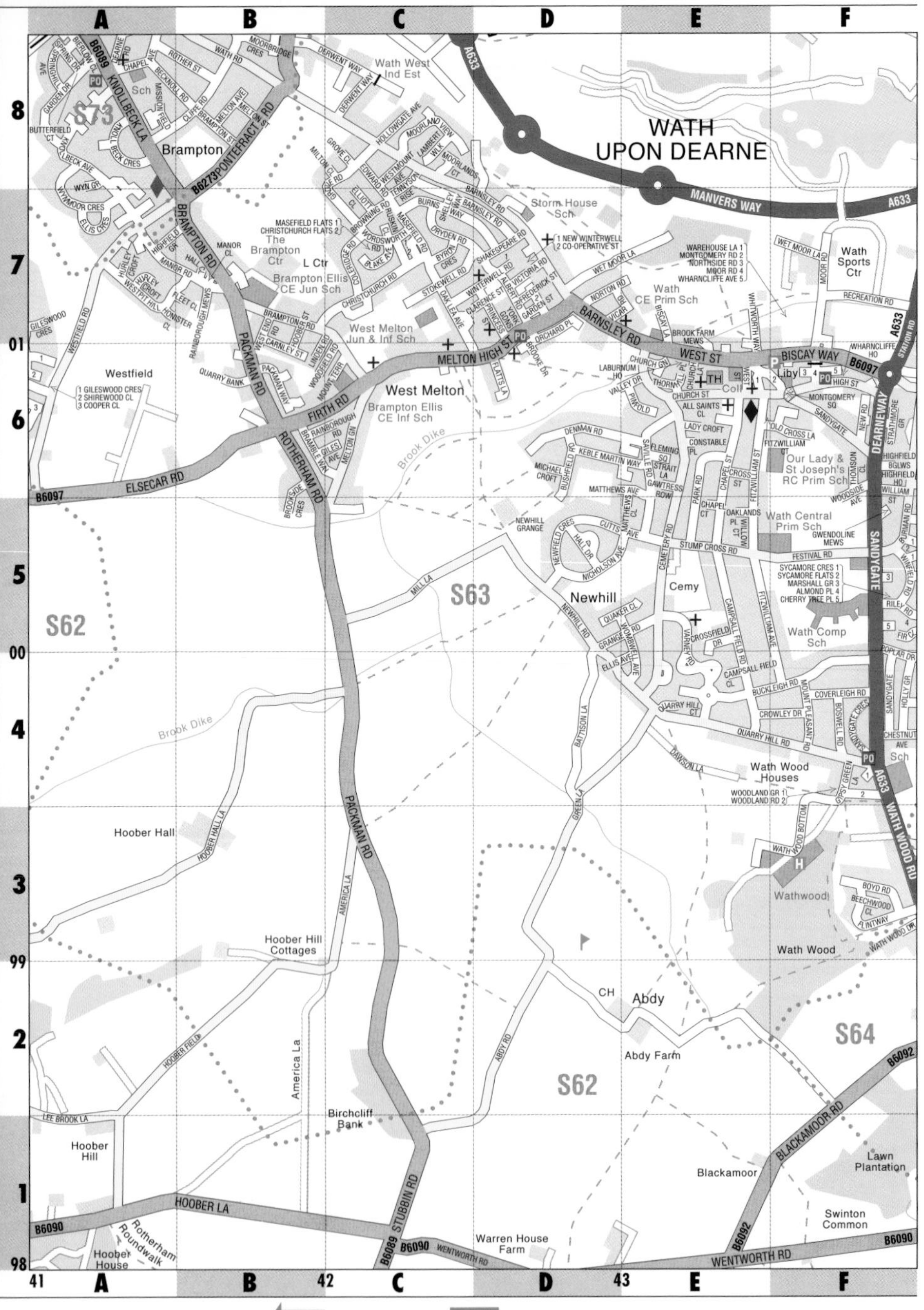
A
B
C
D
E
F
8
7
01
6
5
00
4
3
99
2
1
98
41
42
43
WATH
UPON DEARNE
Brampton
S73
Sch
Wath West
Ind Est
A633
MANVERS WAY
KNOLLBECK LA
B6089
B6273
PONTEFRACT RD
BRAMPTON RD
PACKMAN RD
ROTHERHAM RD
FIRTH RD
ELSECAR RD
B6097
MELTON HIGH ST
BARNSLEY RD
WEST ST
BISCAY WAY
DEARNEWAY
SANDYGATE
WATH WOOD RD
Storm House
Sch
The
Brampton
Ctr
L Ctr
Brampton Ellis
CE Jun Sch
West Melton
Jun & Inf Sch
West Melton
Brampton Ellis
CE Inf Sch
Westfield
Wath
CE Prim Sch
Wath
Sports
Ctr
Liby
TH
Coll
Our Lady &
St Joseph's
RC Prim Sch
Wath Central
Prim Sch
Wath Comp
Sch
Brook Dike
S63
S62
Newhill
Cemy
Wath Wood
Houses
Hoober Hall
Hoober Hill
Cottages
Wathwood
Wath Wood
CH
Abdy
Abdy Farm
S64
Birchcliff
Bank
America La
Blackamoor
Lawn
Plantation
Swinton
Common
Hoober
Hill
Hoober
House
Rotherham
Roundwalk
Warren House
Farm
HOOBER LA
B6090
STUBBIN RD
WENTWORTH RD
BLACKAMOOR RD
B6092
MILL LA
QUARRY HILL RD
STUMP CROSS RD

77
97

58

80

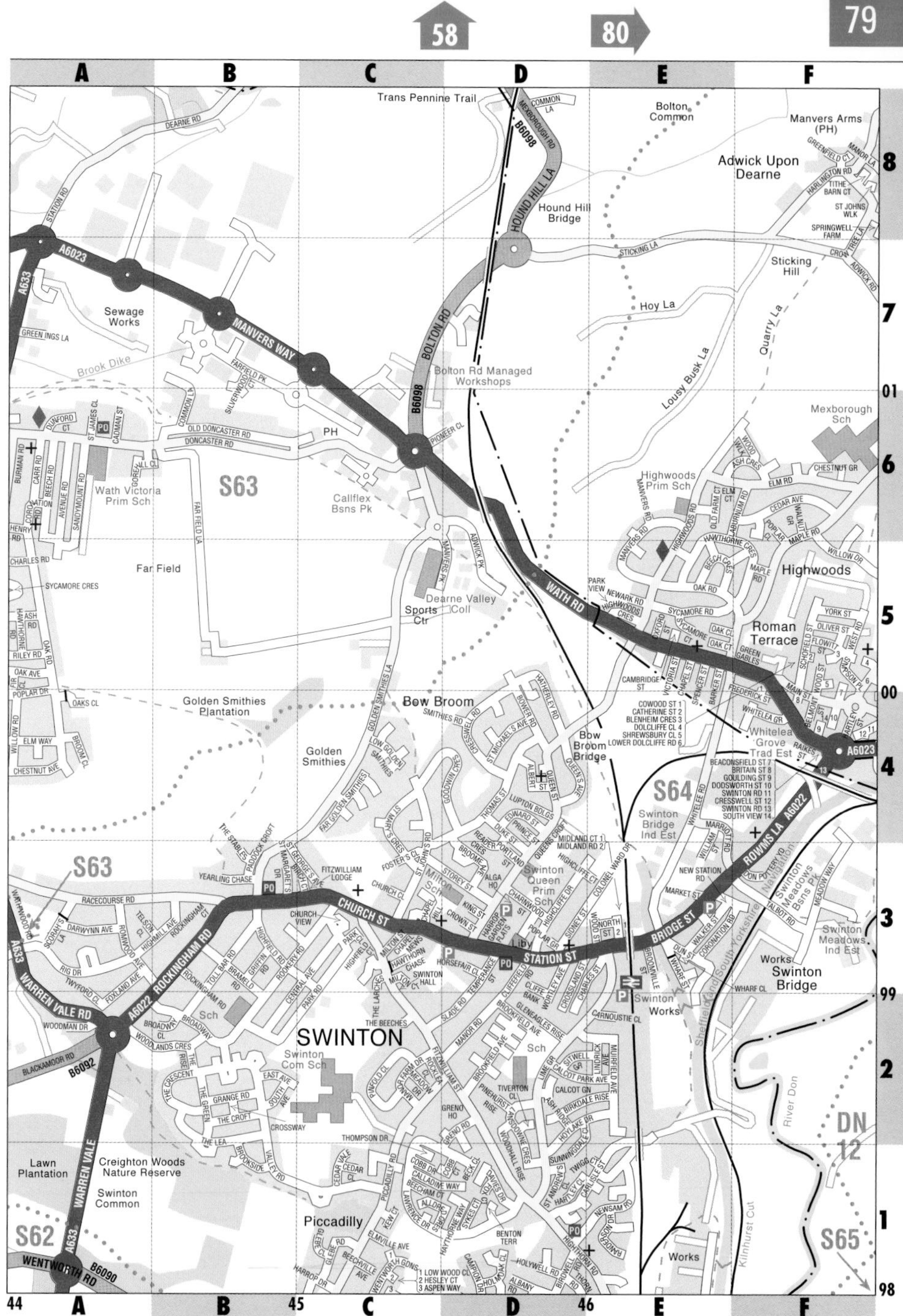

A
B
C
D
E
F
8
7
01
6
5
00
4
3
99
2
1
98
44
45
46
Trans Pennine Trail
Bolton Common
Manvers Arms (PH)
Adwick Upon Dearne
Hound Hill Bridge
Sticking Hill
Hoy La
Lousy Busk La
Quarry La
Sewage Works
Brook Dike
Bolton Rd Managed Workshops
MANVERS WAY
A6023
A633
B6098
HOUND HILL LA
BOLTON RD
STICKING LA
DEARNE RD
STATION RD
GREEN INGS LA
FARFIELD PK
SILVERWOOD CT
COMMON LA
OLD DONCASTER RD
DONCASTER RD
PIONEER CL
PH
S63
Wath Victoria Prim Sch
Callflex Bsns Pk
Mexborough Sch
Highwoods Prim Sch
Highwoods
Far Field
FAR FIELD LA
Dearne Valley Coll
Sports Ctr
WATH RD
Roman Terrace
Golden Smithies Plantation
Bow Broom
Golden Smithies
Bow Broom Bridge
Whitelea Grove Trad Est
S64
Swinton Bridge Ind Est
COWOOD ST 1
CATHERINE ST 2
BLENHEIM CRES 3
DOLCLIFFE CL 4
SHREWSBURY CL 5
LOWER DOLCLIFFE RD 6
BEACONSFIELD ST 7
BRITAIN ST 8
GOULDING ST 9
DODSWORTH ST 10
SWINTON RD 11
CRESSWELL ST 12
SWINTON RD 13
SOUTH VIEW 14
MIDLAND CT 1
MIDLAND RD 2
ROWMS LA
A6022
Swinton Meadows Bsns Pk
Swinton Meadows Ind Est
Swinton Queen Prim Sch
FITZWILLIAM LODGE
RACECOURSE RD
ROCKINGHAM RD
WARREN VALE RD
CHURCH ST
STATION ST
BRIDGE ST
Liby
Works
Swinton Bridge
Swinton Works
Sheffield and South Yorkshire Navigation
SWINTON
Swinton Com Sch
Sch
B6092
BLACKAMOOR RD
River Don
DN 12
Lawn Plantation
Creighton Woods Nature Reserve
Swinton Common
WARREN VALE
S62
WENTWORTH RD
B6090
Piccadilly
THOMPSON DR
Kilnhurst Cut
S65
1 LOW WOOD CL
2 HESLEY CT
3 ASPEN WAY

98

80

A B C D E F

8

Owler Carr

Banburgh Grange

DN5

Manor Farm

North Ings

River Dearne

Dearne Way

Trans Pennine Trail

Dearne Bridge

7

MEXBOROUGH

01

Allot Gdns

Windhill Prim Sch

1 BUTTERMERE CL
2 HOLLINGWORTH CL
3 GRASMERE CL
4 WINDMERE CL

Mexborough Low Pasture

Visitor Ctr

Sch

Cemy

Montagu

H

6

Maple Rd

Schs

Coronation Ter

Cemetery Rd

Sedgefield Way

Tennyson Ave

Bronte Gr

Windhill

Windhill Terr

Haddon Rise

S64

Victoria Rd

Albert

Grenfell Ave

Chaucer Rd

Princess Rd

Auckland Rd

Morton Rd

Addison Rd

1 CLAYFIELD CL
2 CLAYFIELD CT

Pastures Ct

5

Kirby St

Lorna Rd

Wellington

Helena St

Woodfield

Hall Ave

Byron St

Cowper Rd

Dolcliffe Common

Kelvin

Argyll St

Milton Rd

Alexandra Rd

Corden Ave

College Ct

Genoa St

Dryden Rd

1 WEST GATE
2 HENRY PL
3 GEORGE PL
4 TYAS PL

Don View Row

West View

Mexborough Bsns Ctr

College St

Herbert St

Cross Gate

Sch

Hewitt

DONCASTER RD

L Ctr

LOWFIELD WLK 1
SCHOOL WLK 2

00

Liby

P

High St

P Mkt Pl

P

Mkt Pl

New Oxford Rd

Castle Hill Row

P

LC

A6023

4

Liby

Cliff St

A6023

Market Pl

Church St

Doncaster Rd Junior Sch

Sheffield & South Yorkshire Navigation

Mexborough Power Sta

Sewage Works

LC

Denaby Main

Melton

A6023

St Chad's Sq

Lime Tree Wlk

Cliff View

Ravenfield Ct

Mexborough

Leach La

1 WADDINGTON TERR
2 STACEY HO
3 STENTONS TERR
4 GLEBE CL

River Don

CARAVAN SITE

Ferry Boat La

Denaby Lane Ind Est

Sandbeck

Shepard's Hickleton Ct

Danum St

Wheatley St

Melton

Grange Way

Stantons

Sch

3

Low Meadow

Peas Hill Plantation

Meadow La

Denaby La

The Green

Woodland

Old Denaby

Pitman Rd

Lupton Pl

Cliff

Northumberland La

Ravenscar Gdns

Sussex Gdns

Westmorland Ct

Wiltshire Ave

99

Engine House Farm

Manor Farm

TOP FOLD GOTTS

Grange Farm

Denaby Wood

Nill Top Rd

Redcares

Tadcaster Gr

Suffolk View

Devon Ct

Catterick

Lincoln Gr

DN12

WASHINGTON AVE 1
GOMERSAL AVE 2
OLDFIELD AVE 3

Denaby Ave

Pype

Conanby

2

Denaby Common

Athelstane Sch

Keighley Wlk

1

S65

98

47 A B 48 C D 49 E F

DONCASTER RD

Bath House Farm

HANGMAN STONE LA

Leylands Farm

High Melton

Crow Plantation

Melton Hall Doncaster Training Coll

Melton Park

Wetlands Wood

8

Scabba Wood

Cliff Wood

DN5

Denaby Ings Nature Reserve

PASTURE LA

7

Quarry

01

Trans Pennine Trail

CADEBY LA

6

The Ings

Old Denaby LA

BRACKENHILL

INGS RD

HOLLOW GATE

GREEN LA

1 THE PADDOCKS
2 ROSEMARY GR

PH

Cadeby Hall Farm

Cadeby

Quarry

5

00

Dearne Way

The Earth Centre

Works

Quarry (dis)

4

DONCASTER RD

Kilner's Bridge

SCHOOL WK

Liby

PO

P

Conisbrough

Conisbrough Tunnel

Conisbrough Viaduct (dis)

A630

Doncaster Road Bridge

3

Sch

St Alban's RC Prim Sch

MOLT HOUSE WK

CALDER TERR

DN12

River Don

Sewage Works

Windgate Hill

1 BELTOFT WAY
2 LINDRICK CL
3 FOLFORD WAY
4 YORK WAY
5 ERLAND WAY
6 WOODGETT WLK
7 VALLEY VIEW

SHEFFIELD RD

99

Conisbrough Balby Street Jun & Inf Sch

7 BANBURY CL
8 THRYBERGH CT

Conisbrough Station Rd Prim Sch

LOW RD

DUFTONS

WINDGATE HILL

MILNER GATE

Cemy

TICKHILL SQ 1
ALL SAINTS SQ 2
BURNASTON WLK 3
ALVESTON WLK 4
MYNDON WLK 5
CHADDESDON WLK 6

North Cliff Hill

BENTINICK ST

CRANSWICK WAY
MILNER GATE

CLIFF

DRAKE HEAD LA

CONISBROUGH

Rowena Inf Sch

Northcliffe Sch

Conisbrough Castle Visitor Ctr

DONCASTER RD

2

Morley Place Jun Sch

Liby

PO

SAXON ROW

Common Road Bridge

Conisbrough Ivanhoe Sch

A630

SHEFFIELD RD

PH

B6094

CLIFTON HILL

Conisbrough Common

1

ST PETER'S DR

1 SYCAMORE GR
2 PALM GR

98

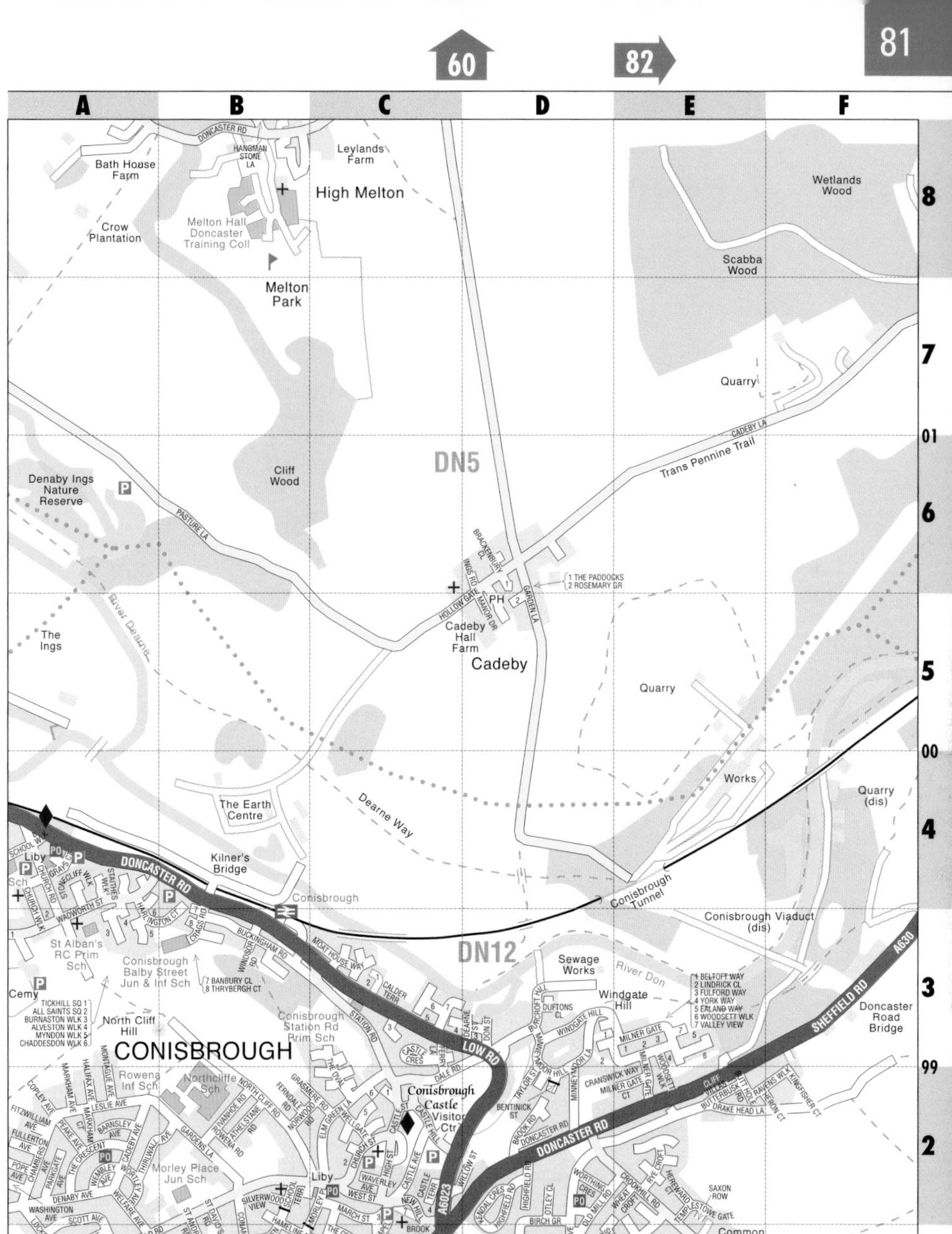

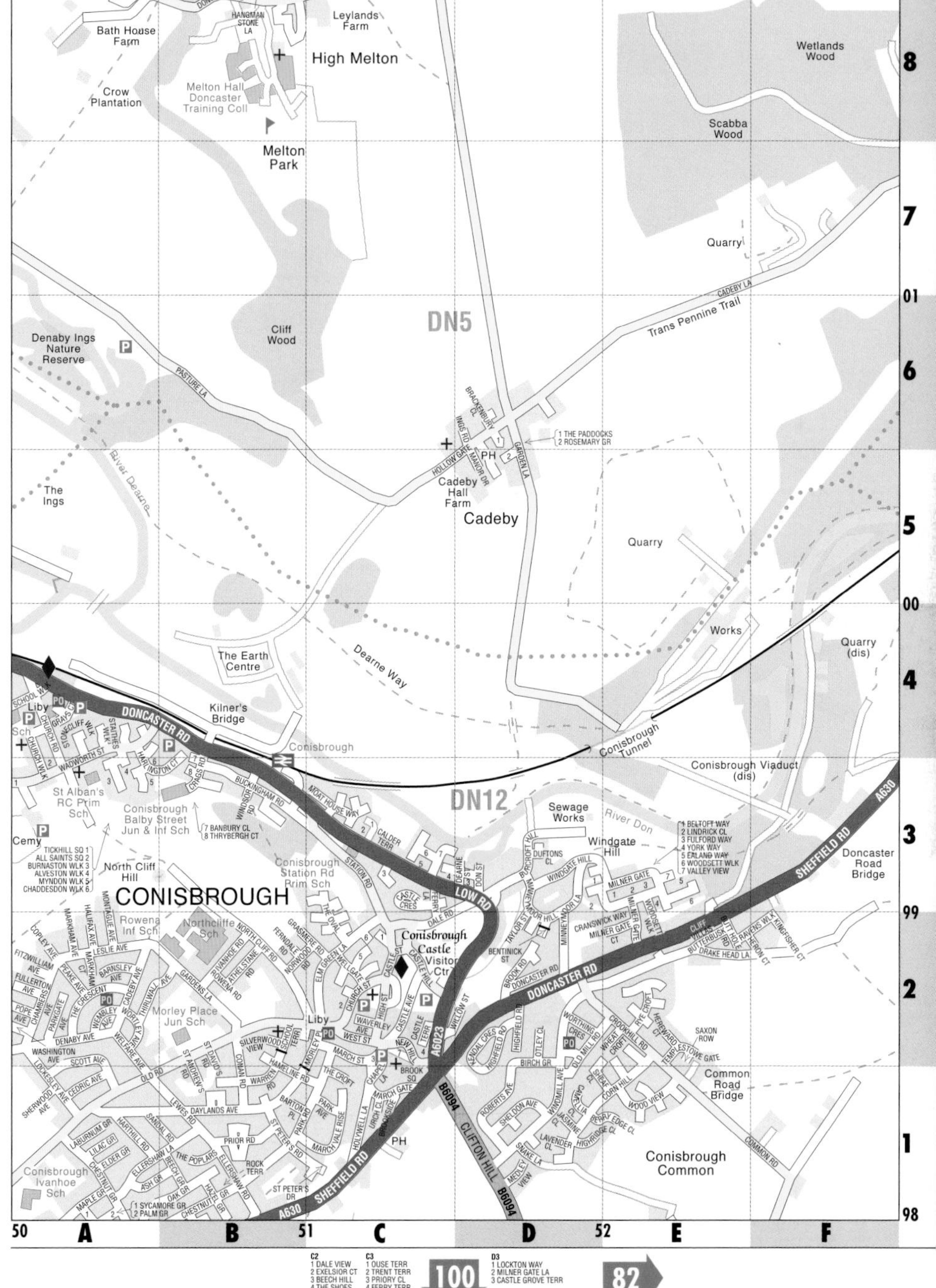

C2
1 DALE VIEW
2 EXELSIOR CT
3 BEECH HILL
4 THE SHOES
5 CASTLEWELL
6 HAMILTON CT
7 OLD HILL

C3
1 OUSE TERR
2 TRENT TERR
3 PRIORY CL
4 FERRY TERR
5 FERRY VILLAS
6 WATERSIDE VIEW
7 RIVERSIDE CL

D3
1 LOCKTON WAY
2 MILNER GATE LA
3 CASTLE GROVE TERR

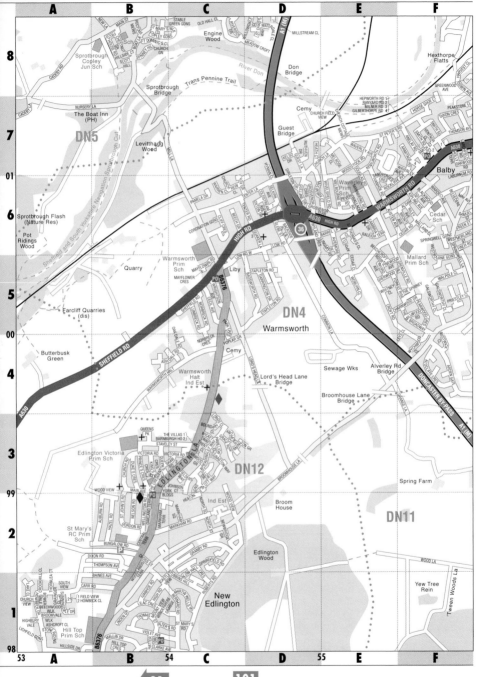

D6
1 GIFFORD DR
2 WARMSWORTH MEWS
3 WARMSWORTH CT

62
84

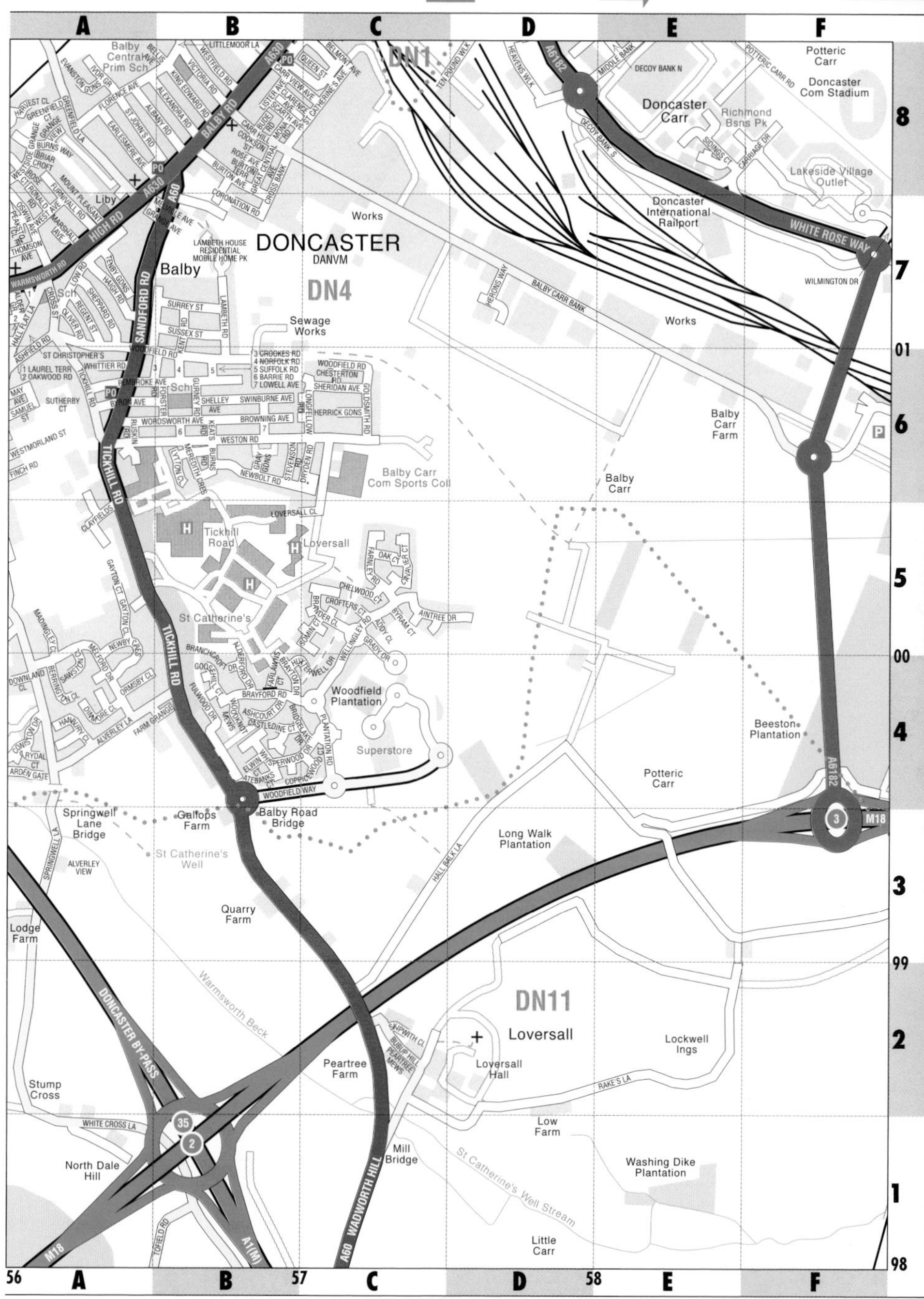
A
B
C
D
E
F
8
7
01
6
5
00
4
3
99
2
1
98
56
57
58
DONCASTER
DANVM
DN1
DN4
DN11
Balby
Balby Central Prim Sch
Liby
Sch
Works
Sewage Works
Doncaster Carr
Doncaster Com Stadium
Potteric Carr
Richmond Bsns Pk
Lakeside Village Outlet
Doncaster International Railport
WHITE ROSE WAY
WILMINGTON DR
BALBY CARR BANK
HERONS WAY
DECOY BANK N
DECOY BANK S
MIDDLE BANK
SIDINGS CT
CARRIAGE DR
POTTERIC CARR RD
HEAVENS WLK
TEN POUND WLK
A6182
A630
A60
BALBY RD
HIGH RD
WARMSWORTH RD
SANDFORD RD
TICKHILL RD
LITTLEMOOR LA
WESTFIELD RD
VICTORIA RD
KING EDWARD RD
ALEXANDRA RD
ALBANY RD
ST JOHN'S RD
EARLSMERE AVE
FLORENCE AVE
QUEEN ST
BELMONT AVE
CARR VIEW AVE
CLARENCE AVE
SCARTH AVE
ST CATHERINE'S AVE
CARR HILL
COOKSON ST
ROSE AVE
BURTON TERR
BURTON AVE
GREAT CENTRAL AVE
CROSS BANK
CORONATION RD
MELVILLE AVE
GRANGE AVE
LAMBETH HOUSE RESIDENTIAL MOBILE HOME PK
LAMBETH RD
SURREY ST
SUSSEX ST
KENT RD
WOODFIELD RD
ST CHRISTOPHER'S
WHITTIER RD
1 LAUREL TERR
2 OAKWOOD RD
3 CROOKES RD
4 NORFOLK RD
5 SUFFOLK RD
6 BARRIE RD
7 LOWELL AVE
CHESTERTON RD
SHERIDAN AVE
HERRICK GDNS
GOLDSMITH RD
LONGFELLOW RD
PEMBROKE AVE
BYRON AVE
SHELLEY AVE
SWINBURNE AVE
BROWNING AVE
WORDSWORTH AVE
WESTON RD
NEWBOLT RD
SUTHERBY CT
WESTMORLAND ST
FINCH RD
Balby Carr Com Sports Coll
Balby Carr Farm
Balby Carr
LOVERSALL CL
Tickhill Road
Loversall
St Catherine's
CLAYFIELDS
GAYTON CT
OAK CT
CAVALIER CT
CHELWOOD CT
CROFTERS CT
AINTREE DR
BYRAM CT
GRADY DR
BRANCHCROFT DR
ALDERFORD DR
BRAYFORD RD
ASHCOURT DR
CASTLEDINE CT
PLANTATION RD
Woodfield Plantation
Superstore
WOODFIELD WAY
FARM GRANGE
ALVERLEY LA
NEWBY CRES
ORMSBY CL
DOWNLAND CL
ARDEN GATE
Springwell Lane Bridge
Gallops Farm
Balby Road Bridge
St Catherine's Well
SPRINGWELL LA
ALVERLEY VIEW
Beeston Plantation
Potteric Carr
Long Walk Plantation
HALL BALK LA
M18
3
Lodge Farm
Quarry Farm
Warmsworth Beck
DONCASTER BY-PASS
Loversall
Loversall Hall
Lockwell Ings
Peartree Farm
RAKE'S LA
Stump Cross
WHITE CROSS LA
35
2
North Dale Hill
Mill Bridge
WADWORTH HILL
Low Farm
Washing Dike Plantation
St Catherine's Well Stream
Little Carr
TOFIELD RD
A1(M)
A60

102
84

83

63

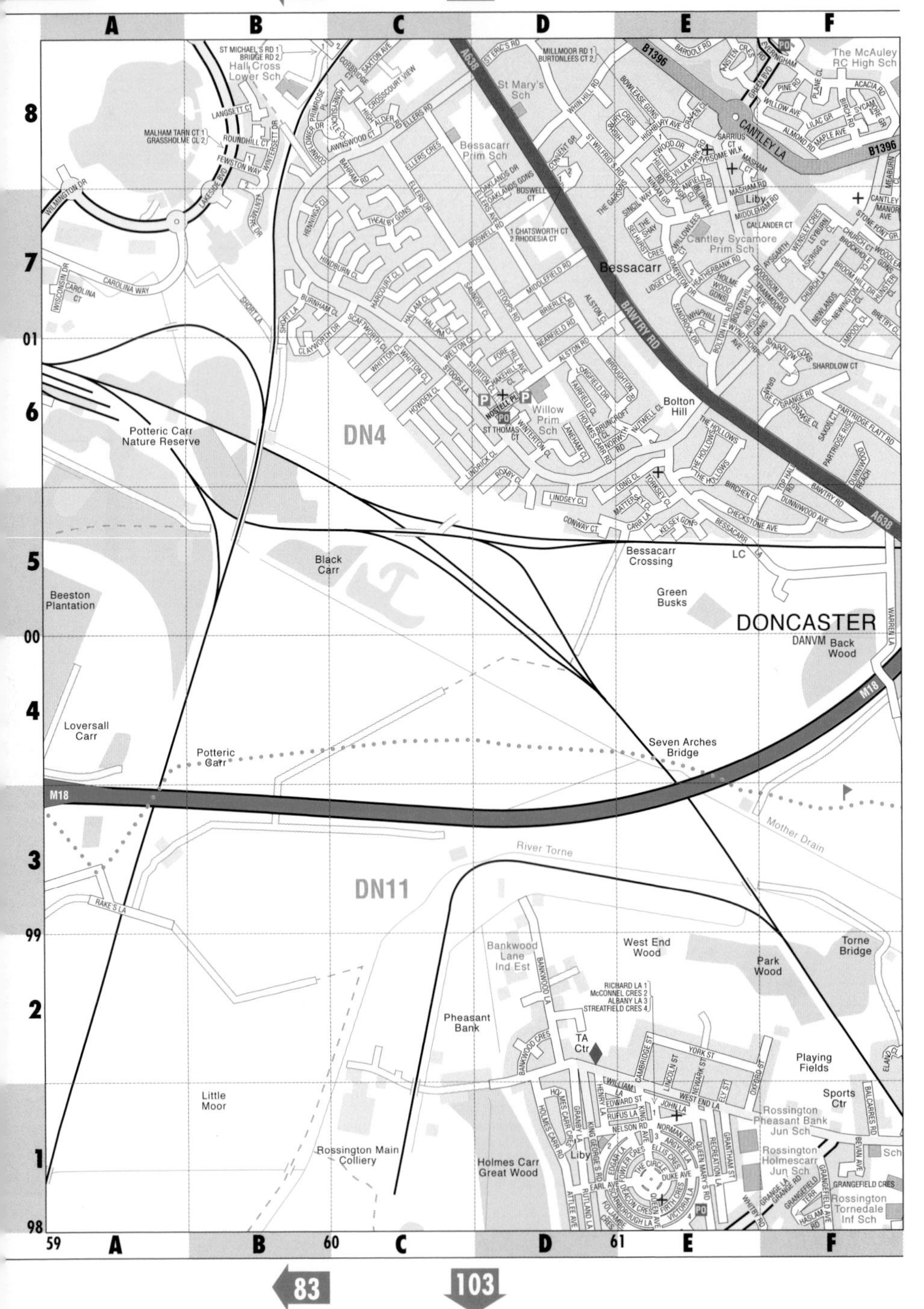

A
B
C
D
E
F
8
7
01
6
5
00
4
3
99
2
1
98
59
60
61
Hall Cross
Lower Sch
St Mary's
Sch
Bessacarr
Prim Sch
The McAuley
RC High Sch
CANTLEY LA
B1396
A638
Liby
Cantley Sycamore
Prim Sch
Bessacarr
BAWTRY RD
Willow
Prim
Sch
Bolton
Hill
DN4
Potteric Carr
Nature Reserve
Black
Carr
Bessacarr
Crossing
LC
Green
Busks
DONCASTER
DANVM
Back
Wood
Beeston
Plantation
Loversall
Carr
Potteric
Carr
Seven Arches
Bridge
M18
Mother Drain
River Torne
DN11
RAKE'S LA
West End
Wood
Bankwood
Lane
Ind Est
Park
Wood
Torne
Bridge
Pheasant
Bank
TA
Ctr
Playing
Fields
Sports
Ctr
Little
Moor
Rossington Main
Colliery
Holmes Carr
Great Wood
Rossington
Pheasant Bank
Jun Sch
Rossington
Holmescarr
Jun Sch
Rossington
Tornedale
Inf Sch
Sch
83
103

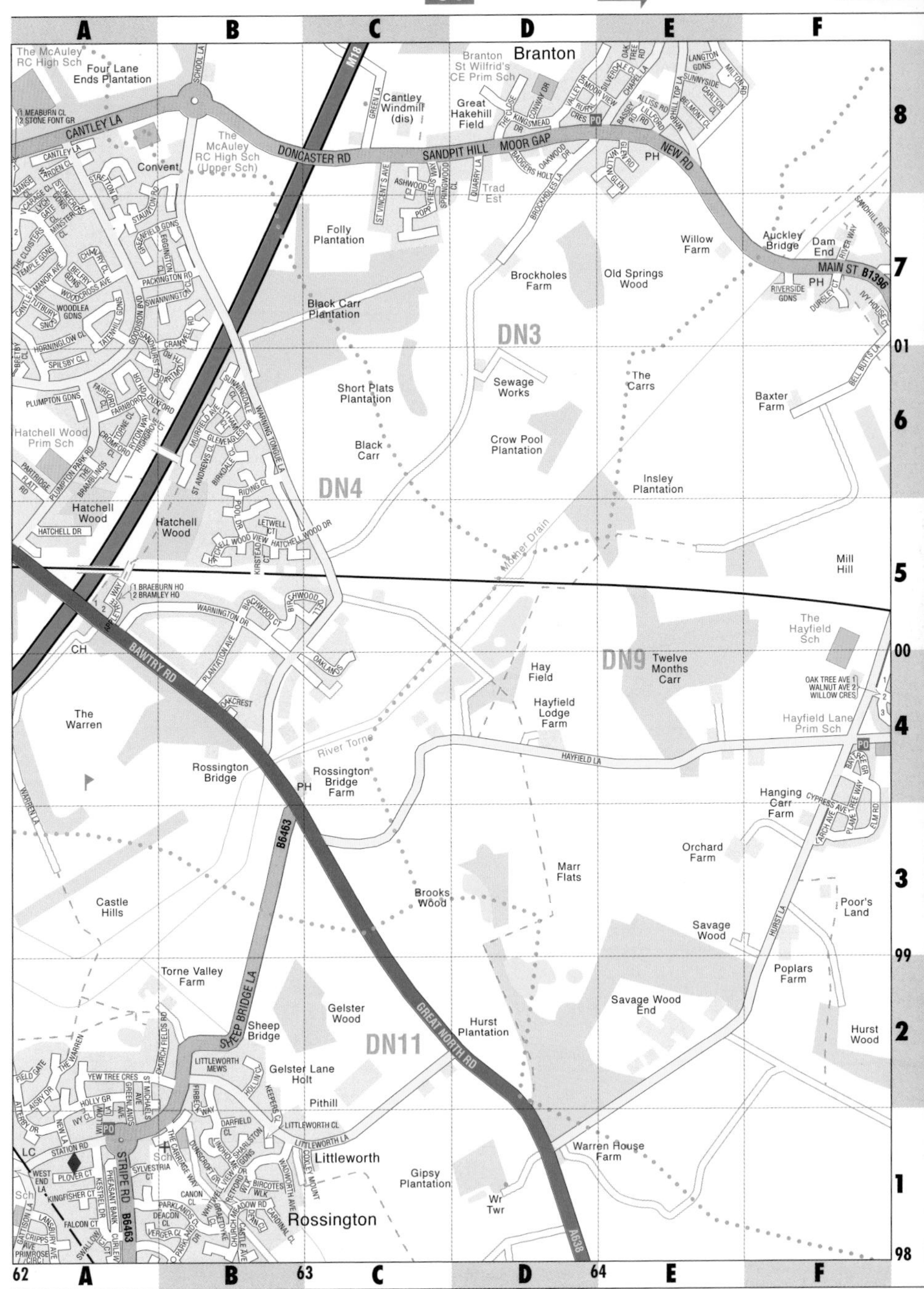

8

The McAuley RC High Sch
Four Lane Ends Plantation
CANTLEY LA
1 MEABURN CL
2 STONE FONT GR
Convent
The McAuley RC High Sch (Upper Sch)
DONCASTER RD
SANDPIT HILL
MOOR GAP
Branton
Branton St Wilfrid's CE Prim Sch
Great Hakehill Field
NEW RD
PH
Willow Farm
Auckley Bridge
Dam End
MAIN ST
B1396
PH
RIVERSIDE GDNS

7

Folly Plantation
Black Carr Plantation
Brockholes Farm
Old Springs Wood
DN3
The Carrs
Baxter Farm

01

Short Plats Plantation
Black Carr
DN4
Sewage Works
Crow Pool Plantation
Insley Plantation

6

Hatchell Wood Prim Sch
Hatchell Wood
HATCHELL DR
Hatchell Wood
LETWELL LA
Mother Drain
Mill Hill

5

1 BRAEBURN HO
2 BRAMLEY HO
WARRINGTON DR
SAWTRY RD
CH
ASHWOOD
OAKLANDS
The Hayfield Sch

00

The Warren
PLACECREST
Hay Field
Hayfield Lodge Farm
DN9
Twelve Months Carr
OAK TREE AVE 1
WALNUT AVE 2
WILLOW CRES
Hayfield Lane Prim Sch

4

Rossington Bridge
River Torne
PH
Rossington Bridge Farm
HAYFIELD LA
Hanging Carr Farm
CYPHER AVE
PARK RD

Castle Hills
Brooks Wood
Marr Flats
Orchard Farm
Savage Wood
Poor's Land

3

Torne Valley Farm
SHEEP BRIDGE LA
Sheep Bridge
Gelster Wood
GREAT NORTH RD
DN11
Savage Wood End
Poplars Farm

99

LITTLEWORTH MEWS
Gelster Lane Holt
Hurst Plantation
Hurst Wood

2

YEW TREE CRES
Pithill
STRIPE RD
B6463
LITTLEWORTH LA
Littleworth
Warren House Farm

LC
PO
Rossington
Gipsy Plantation
Wr Twr

1

98

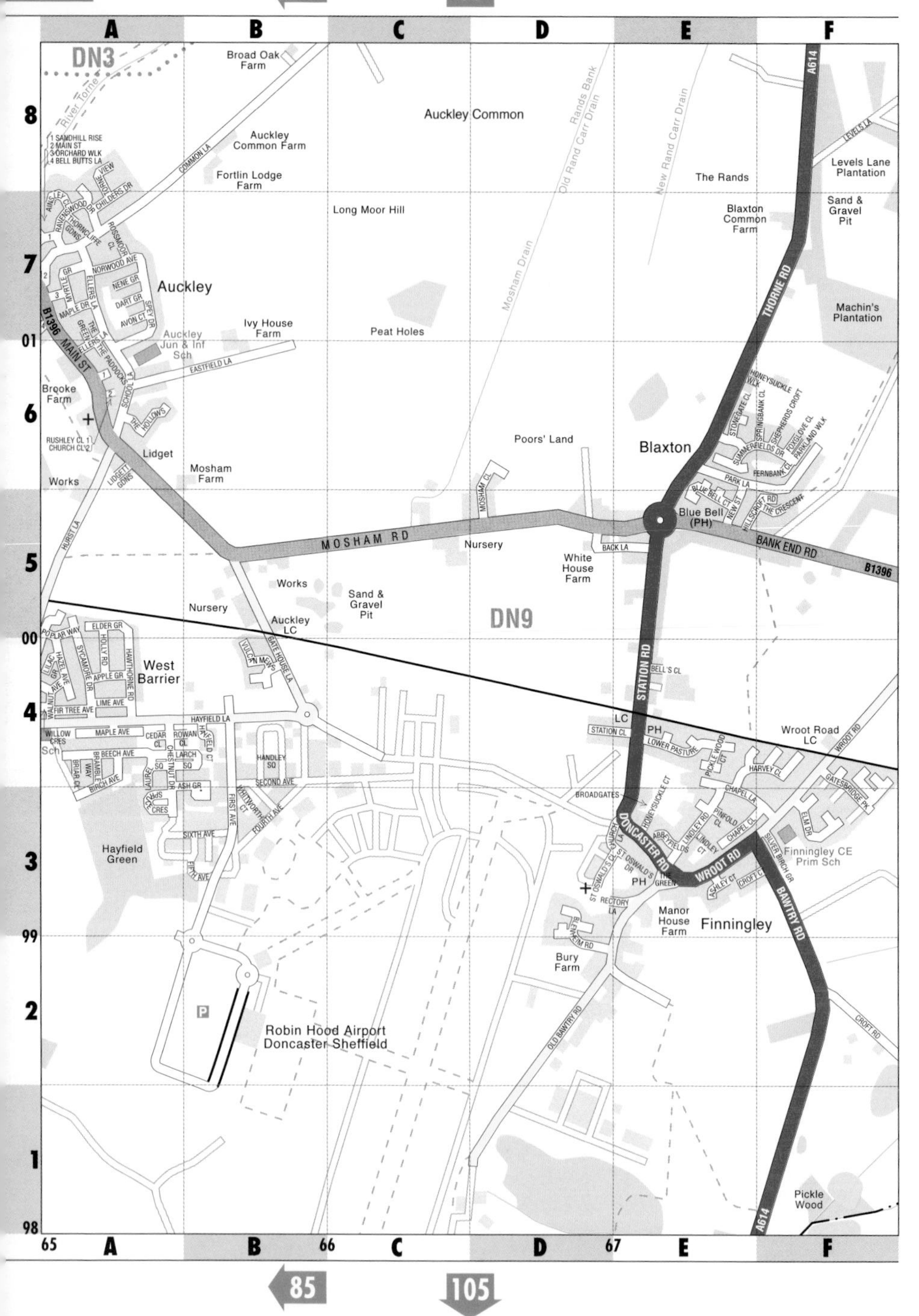

DN3

8

1 SANDHILL RISE
2 MAIN ST
3 ORCHARD WLK
4 BELL BUTTS LA

Broad Oak
Farm

Auckley Common

Auckley
Common Farm

Fortlin Lodge
Farm

Long Moor Hill

The Rands

Levels Lane
Plantation

Sand &
Gravel
Pit

Blaxton
Common
Farm

Machin's
Plantation

7

Auckley

Ivy House
Farm

Peat Holes

Auckley
Jun & Inf
Sch

EASTFIELD LA

01

Brooke
Farm

RUSHLEY CL 1
CHURCH CL 2

Lidget

Mosham
Farm

Poors' Land

Blaxton

Blue Bell
(PH)

6

Works

MOSHAM RD

Nursery

White
House
Farm

BANK END RD

BACK LA

B1396

5

Works

Nursery

Sand &
Gravel
Pit

Auckley
LC

DN9

BELL'S CL

West
Barrier

STATION RD

00

Nursery

LC
STATION CL

PH

Wroot Road
LC

4

HAYFIELD LA

LOWER PASTURE

WROOT RD

BROADGATES

DONCASTER RD

Finningley CE
Prim Sch

3

Hayfield
Green

PH

GREEN

Finningley

Manor
House
Farm

BANTRY RD

99

Bury
Farm

P

Robin Hood Airport
Doncaster Sheffield

2

A614

1

Pickle
Wood

98

66

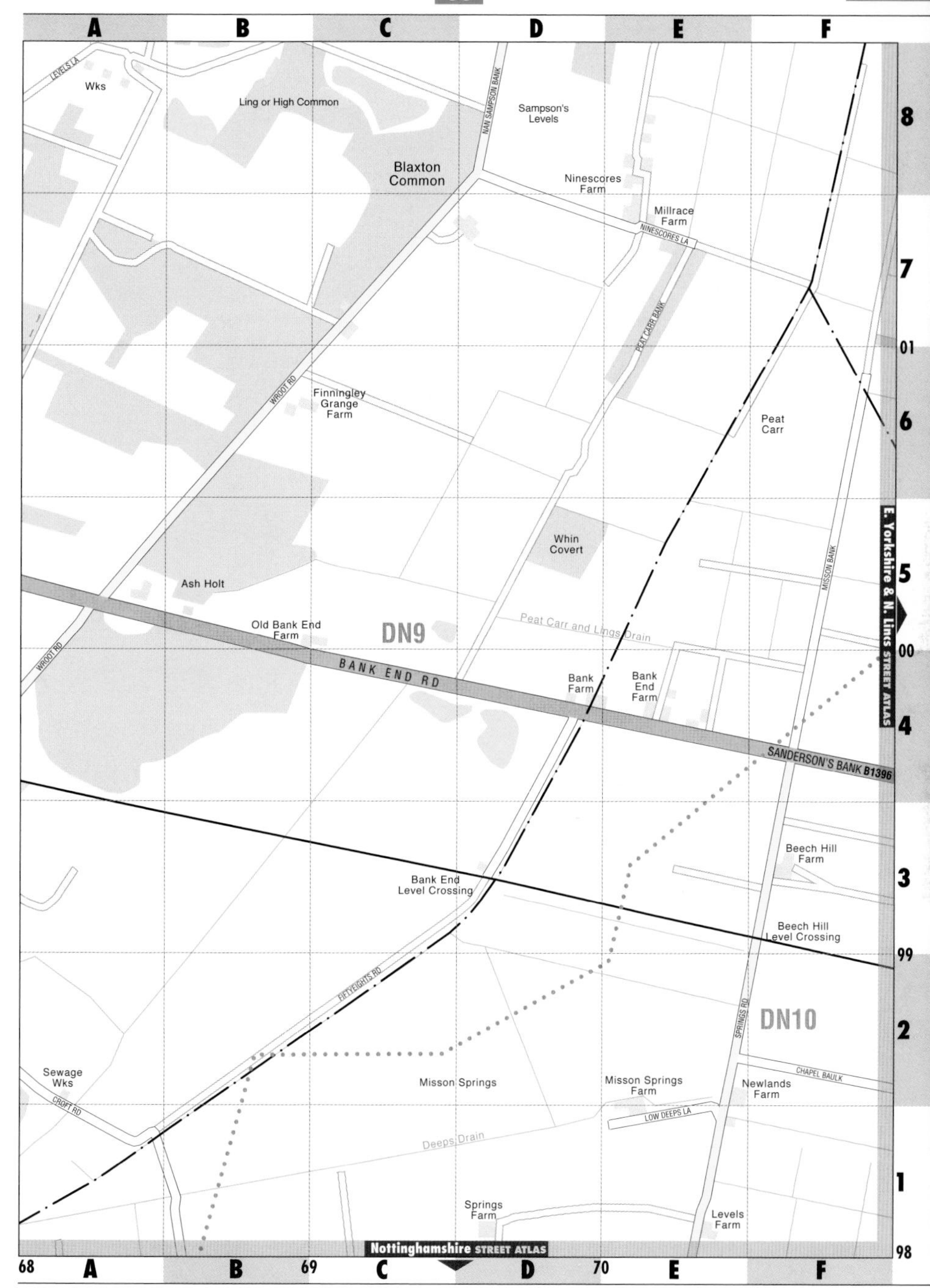

A
B
C
D
E
F
LEVELS LA
Wks
Ling or High Common
NAN SAMPSON BANK
Sampson's Levels
Blaxton Common
Ninescores Farm
Millrace Farm
NINESCORES LA
PEAT CARR BANK
WROOT RD
Finningley Grange Farm
Peat Carr
Whin Covert
MISSON BANK
Ash Holt
Old Bank End Farm
DN9
Peat Carr and Lings Drain
WROOT RD
BANK END RD
Bank Farm
Bank End Farm
SANDERSON'S BANK B1396
Beech Hill Farm
Bank End Level Crossing
Beech Hill Level Crossing
FIFTYEIGHTS RD
SPRINGS RD
DN10
Sewage Wks
CROFT RD
Misson Springs
Misson Springs Farm
Newlands Farm
CHAPEL BAULK
LOW DEEPS LA
Deeps Drain
Springs Farm
Levels Farm
8
7
01
6
5
00
4
3
99
2
1
98
68
69
70
E. Yorkshire & N. Lincs STREET ATLAS
Nottinghamshire STREET ATLAS

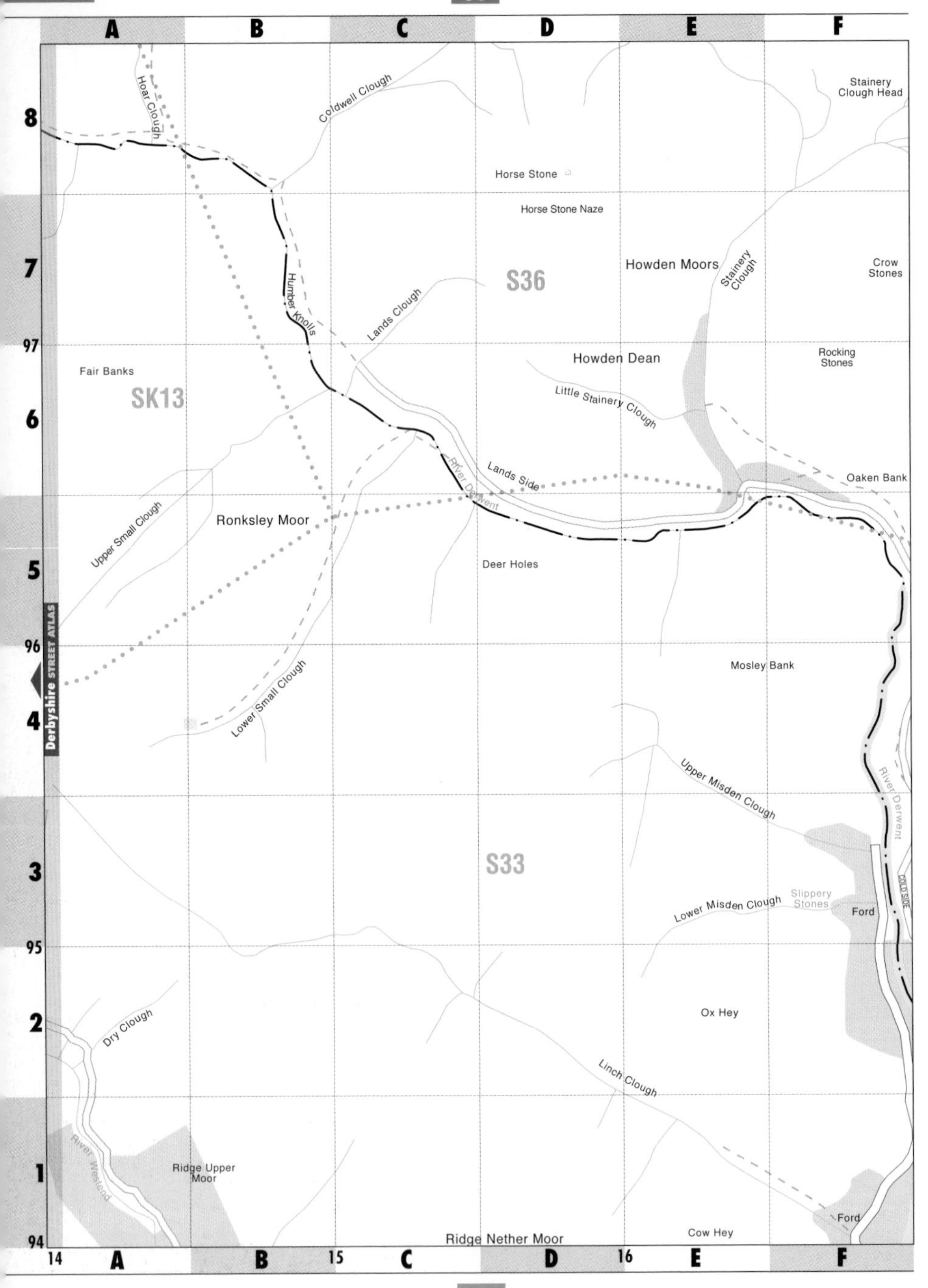

Stainery Clough Head

Hoar Clough

Coldwell Clough

8

Horse Stone

Horse Stone Naze

S36

Howden Moors

Stainery Clough

Crow Stones

7

Humber Knolls

Lands Clough

97

Fair Banks

SK13

Howden Dean

Rocking Stones

Little Stainery Clough

6

River Derwent

Lands Side

Oaken Bank

Upper Small Clough

Ronksley Moor

Deer Holes

5

96

Mosley Bank

Lower Small Clough

4

Upper Misden Clough

River Derwent

DIDS SIDE

S33

3

Lower Misden Clough

Slippery Stones

Ford

95

Dry Clough

Ox Hey

2

Linch Clough

River Westend

Ridge Upper Moor

1

Ford

94

Ridge Nether Moor

Cow Hey

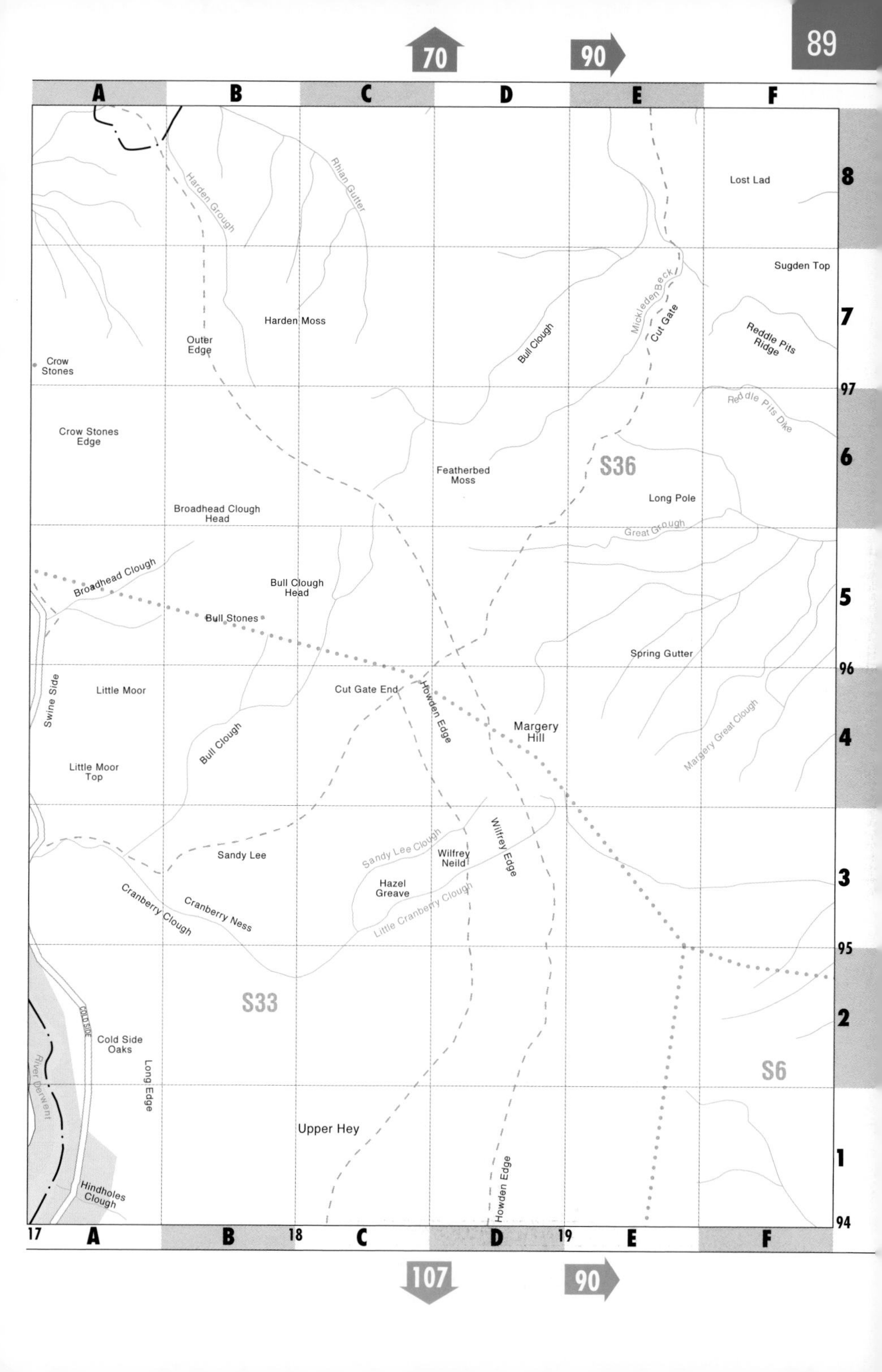

Lost Lad

Sugden Top

Harden Grough

Rhan Gutter

Harden Moss

Reddle Pits Ridge

Outer Edge

Bull Clough

Cut Gate

Mickleden Beck

Crow Stones

Reddle Pits Dike

Crow Stones Edge

Featherbed Moss

S36

Long Pole

Broadhead Clough Head

Great Grough

Broadhead Clough

Bull Clough Head

Spring Gutter

Bull Stones

Swine Side

Little Moor

Cut Gate End

Margery Hill

Margery Great Clough

Bull Clough

Howden Edge

Little Moor Top

Wilfrey Edge

Sandy Lee

Sandy Lee Clough

Wilfrey Neild

Cranberry Clough

Cranberry Ness

Hazel Greave

Little Cranberry Clough

S6

S33

Cold Side Oaks

Long Edge

River Derwent

Cold Side

Upper Hey

Howden Edge

Hindholes Clough

	A	**B**	**C**	**D**	**E**	**F**

8

Sugden Clough

Fenny Common

Pike Lowe Stones

Half Holes

7

Candlerush Edge

Pike Lowe

Earnshaw Ridge

Earnshaw

Upperwood Dike

97

Candlerush Dike

Candlerush

Great Grough

Brown Edge

Reddle Pits Dike

6

White Carr Moss

Black Dyke End

Black Dike

Spring Gutter

White Carr Ridge

Park Cote

Moor Side

5

Upper Commons

S36

White Carr

Ewden Beck

Hawthorn Clough

Washfold Flat

96

Hawthorn Flat

Gallows Rocher

Side Head Beck

4

Long Pole Ridge

Oaken Clough

Shooting Lodge

Stainery Clough

3

Brusten Croft

Broomhead Moor

95

Rushy Dike

2

Flint Hill

Middle Moss

Dukes Rd

S6

Flinthill Dike

1

Brusten Croft Ridge

Hobson Moss

Hobson Moss Dike

94

20	**A**		**B**	**21**	**C**		**D**	**22**	**E**		**F**

72

92

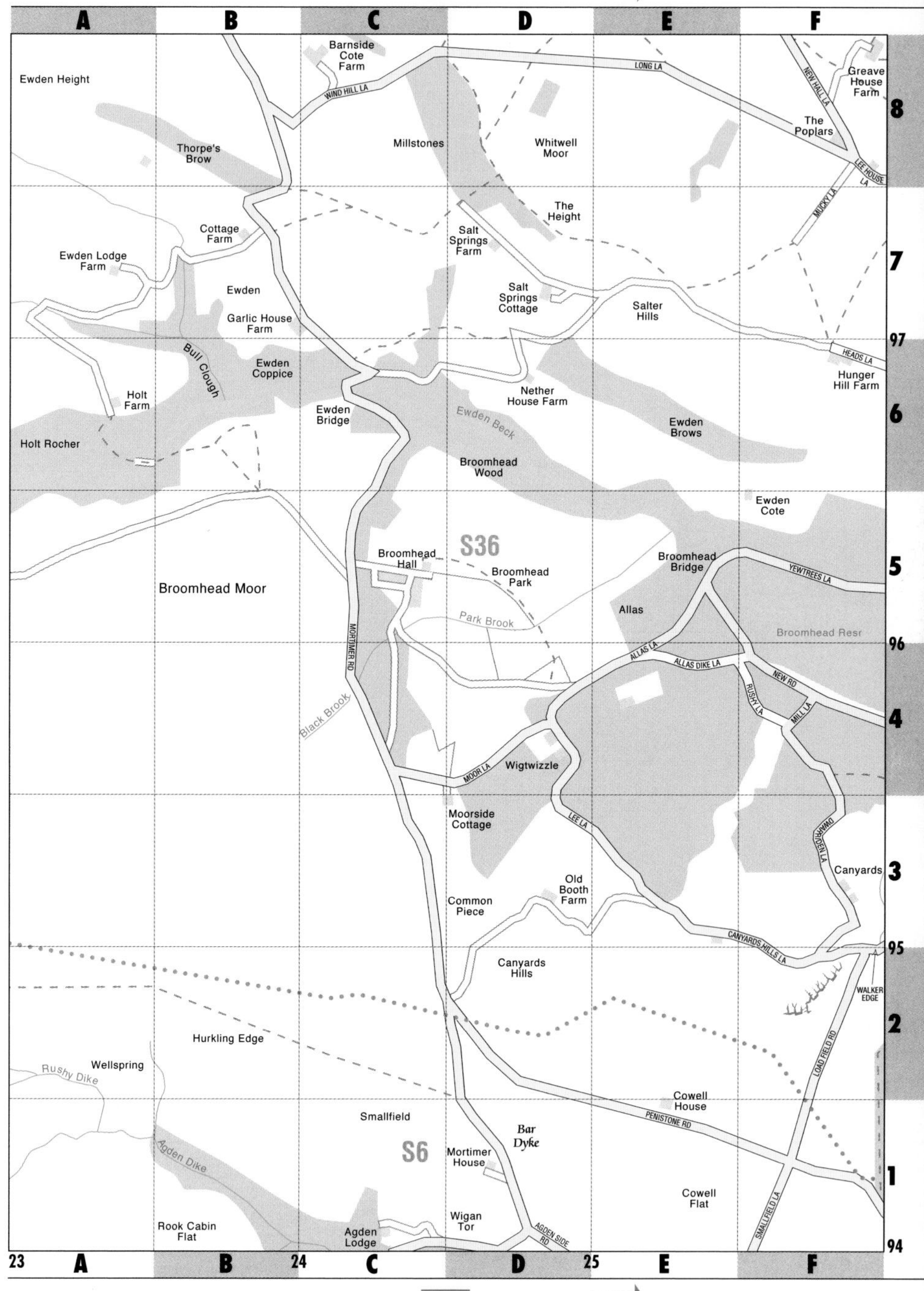

A
B
C
D
E
F
Ewden Height
Barnside Cote Farm
WIND HILL LA
LONG LA
NEW HALL LA
Greave House Farm
The Poplars
LEE HOUSE LA
Thorpe's Brow
Millstones
Whitwell Moor
The Height
MUCKY LA
Cottage Farm
Salt Springs Farm
Ewden Lodge Farm
Ewden
Salt Springs Cottage
Salter Hills
Garlic House Farm
HEADS LA
Hunger Hill Farm
Bull Clough
Ewden Coppice
Nether House Farm
Holt Farm
Ewden Bridge
Ewden Beck
Ewden Brows
Holt Rocher
Broomhead Wood
Ewden Cote
S36
Broomhead Hall
Broomhead Park
Broomhead Bridge
YEWTREES LA
Broomhead Moor
Allas
Park Brook
Broomhead Resr
MORTIMER RD
ALLAS LA
ALLAS DIKE LA
NEW RD
RUSHY LA
MILL LA
Black Brook
MOOR LA
Wigtwizzle
Moorside Cottage
LEE LA
DWARRIDEN LA
Canyards
Old Booth Farm
Common Piece
CANYARDS HILLS LA
Canyards Hills
WALKER EDGE
LOAD FIELD RD
Hurkling Edge
Wellspring
Rushy Dike
Cowell House
PENISTONE RD
Smallfield
Bar Dyke
S6
Mortimer House
Agden Dike
Cowell Flat
SMALLFIELD LA
Wigan Tor
Rook Cabin Flat
Agden Lodge
AGDEN SIDE RD
8
7
97
6
5
96
4
3
95
2
1
94
23
24
25

109

92

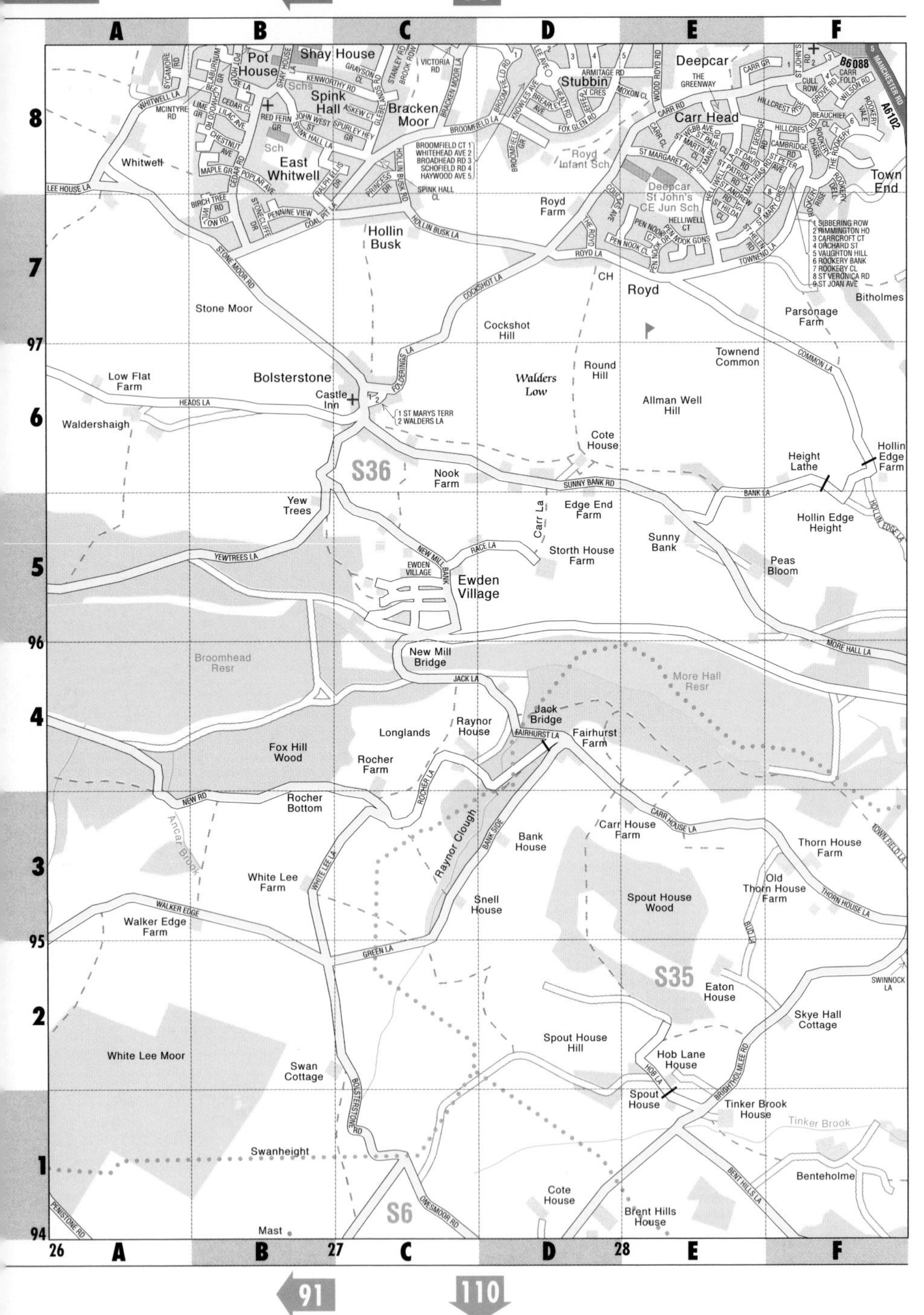
91
73
Pot House
Shay House
Spink Hall
Bracken Moor
Stubbin
Deepcar
Carr Head
Whitwell
East Whitwell
Royd Infant Sch
Deepcar St John's CE Jun Sch
Town End
Royd Farm
Hollin Busk
Royd
Bitholmes
Stone Moor
Cockshot Hill
Parsonage Farm
Townend Common
Low Flat Farm
Bolsterstone
Castle Inn
Walders Low
Round Hill
Allman Well Hill
Waldershaigh
Cote House
Hollin Edge Farm
Height Lathe
S36
Nook Farm
Yew Trees
Edge End Farm
Hollin Edge Height
Sunny Bank
Storth House Farm
Peas Bloom
Ewden Village
New Mill Bridge
Broomhead Resr
More Hall Resr
Jack Bridge
Longlands
Raynor House
Fairhurst Farm
Fox Hill Wood
Rocher Farm
Rocher Bottom
Carr House Farm
Bank House
Thorn House Farm
Raynor Clough
White Lee Farm
Old Thorn House Farm
Spout House Wood
Snell House
Walker Edge Farm
S35
Eaton House
Skye Hall Cottage
Spout House Hill
White Lee Moor
Swan Cottage
Hob Lane House
Spout House
Tinker Brook House
Tinker Brook
Swanheight
Benteholme
Cote House
Brent Hills House
S6
Mast
1 ST MARYS TERR
2 WALDERS LA
BROOMFIELD CT 1
WHITEHEAD AVE 2
BROADHEAD RD 3
SCHOFIELD RD 4
HAYWOOD AVE 5
1 SIBBERING ROW
2 RIMMINGTON HO
3 CARRCROFT CT
4 ORCHARD ST
5 VAUGHTON HILL
6 ROOKERY BANK
7 ROOKERY CL
8 ST VERONICA RD
9 ST JOAN AVE
A B C D E F
8 7 6 5 4 3 2 1
97 96 95 94
26 27 28
91
110

74
94

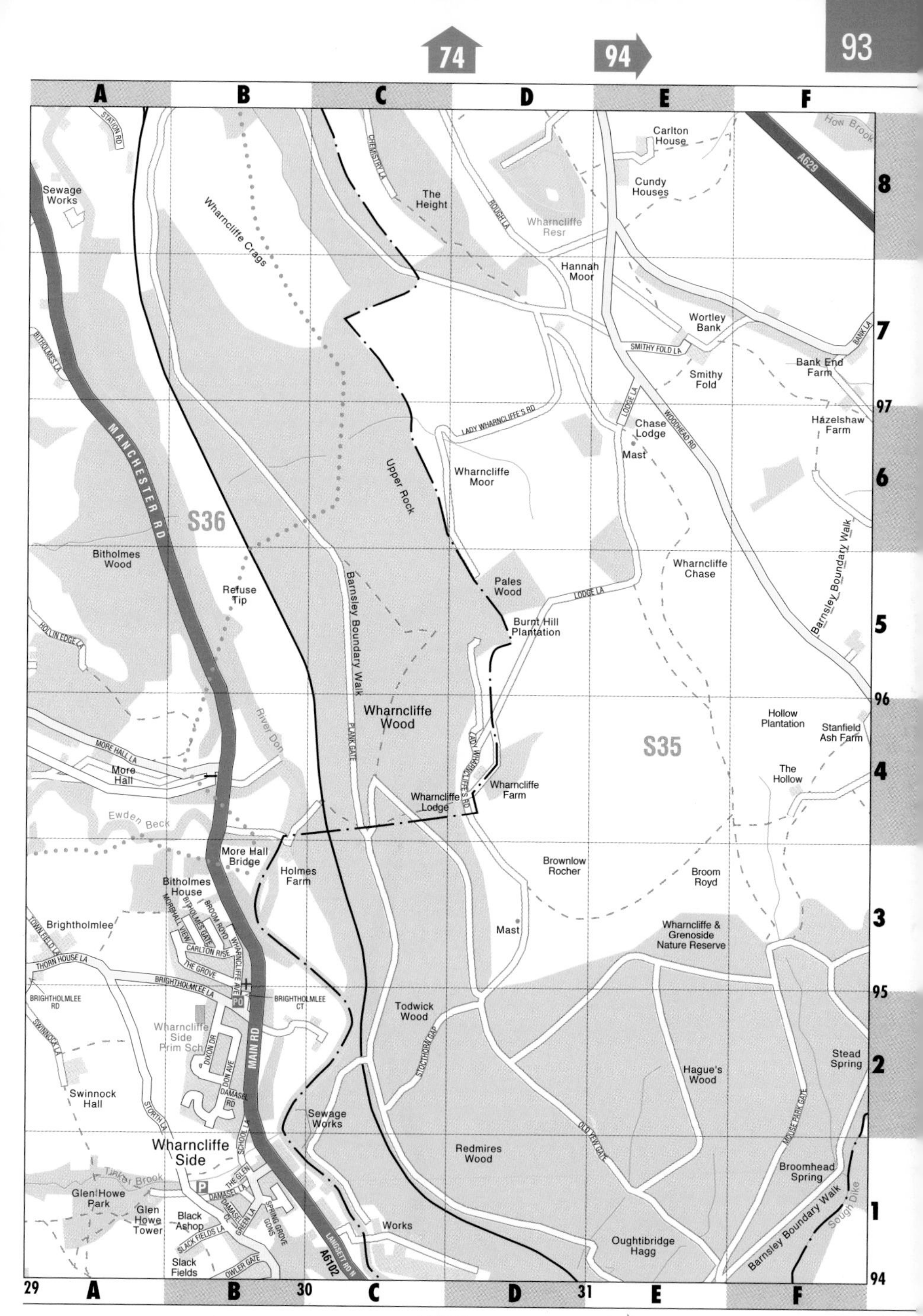
A
B
C
D
E
F
Sewage Works
Wharncliffe Crags
The Height
Wharncliffe Resr
Carlton House
Cundy Houses
Hannah Moor
Wortley Bank
Smithy Fold
Bank End Farm
Hazelshaw Farm
Chase Lodge
Mast
Wharncliffe Moor
Upper Rock
MANCHESTER RD
S36
Bitholmes Wood
Refuse Tip
Barnsley Boundary Walk
Pales Wood
Burnt Hill Plantation
Wharncliffe Chase
Wharncliffe Wood
S35
Hollow Plantation
Stanfield Ash Farm
The Hollow
More Hall
Wharncliffe Lodge
Wharncliffe Farm
Ewden Beck
River Don
More Hall Bridge
Holmes Farm
Brownlow Rocher
Broom Royd
Bitholmes House
Brightholmlee
Mast
Wharncliffe & Grenoside Nature Reserve
Todwick Wood
Wharncliffe Side Prim Sch
MAIN RD
Hague's Wood
Stead Spring
Swinnock Hall
Sewage Works
Redmires Wood
Wharncliffe Side
Tinker Brook
Broomhead Spring
Glen Howe Park
Glen Howe Tower
Black Ashop
Works
Oughtibridge Hagg
Sough Dike
Slack Fields
A6102
A629
How Brook
8
7
97
6
5
96
4
3
95
2
1
94
29
30
31

111
94

93
75

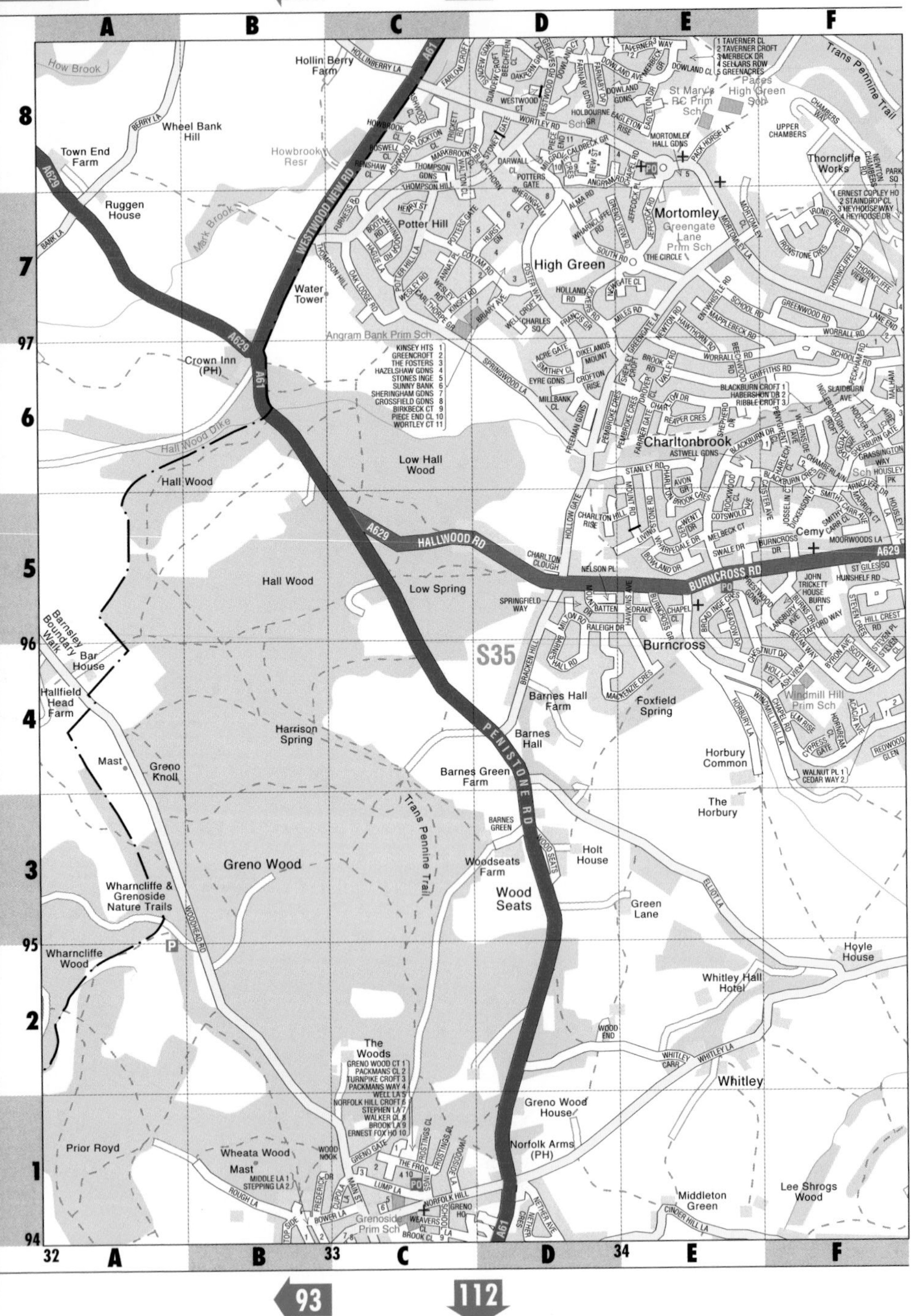
A
B
C
D
E
F
8
7
97
6
5
96
4
3
95
2
1
94
32
33
34
How Brook
Hollin Berry Farm
HOLLINBERRY LA
A61
Wheel Bank Hill
BERRY LA
Town End Farm
Howbrook Resr
A629
Ruggen House
Mark Brook
BANK LA
WESTWOOD NEW RD
THOMPSON HILL
Water Tower
Potter Hill
High Green
Mortomley
Greengate Lane Prim Sch
St Mary's RC Prim Sch
Paces High Green Sch
Trans Pennine Trail
UPPER CHAMBERS
Thorncliffe Works
1 TAVERNER CL
2 TAVERNER CROFT
3 MERBECK DR
4 SELLARS ROW
5 GREENACRES
1 ERNEST COPLEY HO
2 STAINDROP CL
3 HEYHOUSE WAY
4 HEYHOUSE DR
Angram Bank Prim Sch
KINSEY HTS 1
GREENCROFT 2
THE FOSTERS 3
HAZELSHAW GDNS 4
STONES INGE 5
SUNNY BANK 6
SHERINGHAM GDNS 7
CROSSFIELD GDNS 8
BIRKBECK CT 9
PIECE END CL 10
WORTLEY CT 11
Crown Inn (PH)
SPRINGWOOD LA
Hall Wood Dike
Low Hall Wood
Charltonbrook
BLACKBURN CROFT 1
HABERSHON DR 2
RIBBLE CROFT 3
Hall Wood
A629
HALLWOOD RD
CHARLTON CLOUGH
Cemy
MOORWOODS LA
BURNCROSS RD
PO
Low Spring
NELSON PL
SPRINGFIELD WAY
JOHN TRICKETT HOUSE
Burncross
S35
Barnsley Boundary Walk
Bar House
Hallfield Head Farm
Harrison Spring
Barnes Hall Farm
Foxfield Spring
Barnes Hall
PENISTONE RD
Windmill Hill Prim Sch
Horbury Common
WALNUT PL 1
CEDAR WAY 2
Mast
Greno Knoll
Barnes Green Farm
The Horbury
BARNES GREEN
Greno Wood
Woodseats Farm
Holt House
Wood Seats
ELLIOTT LA
Wharncliffe & Grenoside Nature Trails
WOODHEAD RD
Green Lane
Wharncliffe Wood
P
Hoyle House
Whitley Hall Hotel
WOOD END
WHITLEY CARR
WHITLEY LA
Whitley
The Woods
GRENO WOOD CT 1
PACKMANS CL 2
TURNPIKE CROFT 3
PACKMANS WAY 4
WELL LA 5
NORFOLK HILL CROFT 6
STEPHEN LA 7
WALKER CL 8
BROOK LA 9
ERNEST FOX HO 10
Greno Wood House
Prior Royd
Wheata Wood
Norfolk Arms (PH)
Mast
MIDDLE LA 1
STEPPING LA 2
NORFOLK HILL
ROUGH LA
Grenoside Prim Sch
Middleton Green
Lee Shrogs Wood
CINDER HILL LA

93
112

76
96

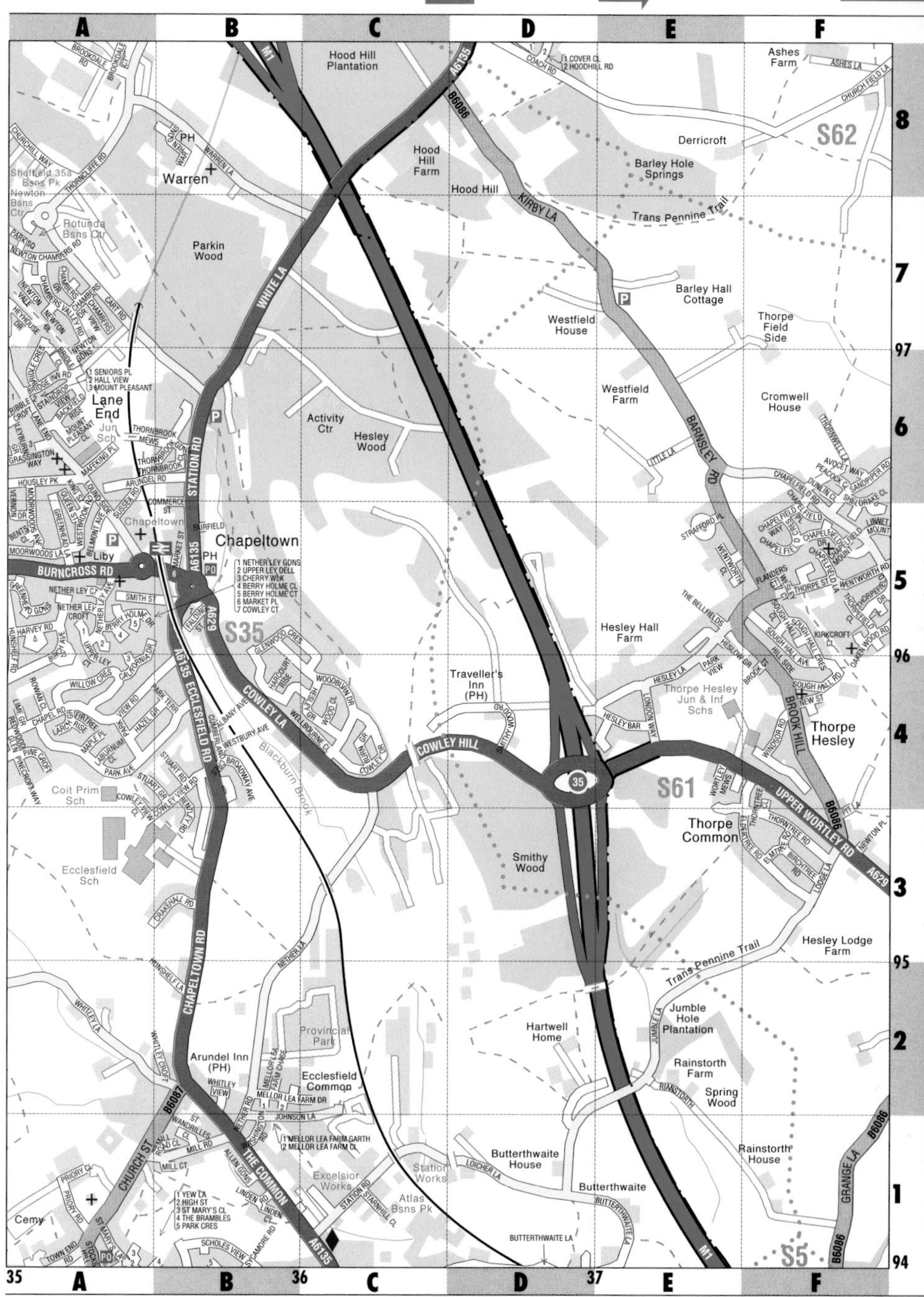
A
B
C
D
E
F
8
7
97
6
5
96
4
3
95
2
1
94
35
36
37
Hood Hill Plantation
Ashes Farm
ASHES LA
CHURCH FIELD LA
1 COVER CL
2 HOODHILL RD
COACH RD
M1
A6135
B6086
Derricroft
S62
Hood Hill Farm
Hood Hill
Barley Hole Springs
KIRBY LA
Trans Pennine Trail
Warren
WARREN LA
PH
BROOKDALE RD
BROOKDALE CT
CHURCHILL WAY
THORNCLIFFE RD
Sheffield 35a Bsns Pk
Newton Bsns Ctr
Rotunda Bsns Ctr
NEWTON CHAMBERS RD
Parkin Wood
WHITE LA
Barley Hall Cottage
Westfield House
Thorpe Field Side
CHAMBERS VALLEY RD
NEWTON VALE
HEYHOUSE DR
CART RD
1 SENIORS PL
2 HALL VIEW
3 MOUNT PLEASANT
Lane End
Jun Sch
THORNBROOK MEWS
STATION RD
Activity Ctr
Hesley Wood
Westfield Farm
Cromwell House
BARNSLEY RD
LITTLE LA
THORNWELL LA
AVOCET WAY
PEACOCK CL
DUNLIN CL
SANDPIPER RD
SHELDRAKE CL
CHAPELFIELD RD
CHAPELFIELD PL
CHAPELFIELD WAY
CHAPELFIELD DR
CHAPELFIELD MOUNT
LINNET MOUNT
HOUSLEY PK
MAFEKING PL
GRASSINGTON WAY
ARUNDEL RD
COMMERCE ST
Chapeltown
FAIRFIELD
Chapeltown
BURNCROSS RD
Liby
MOORWOODS LA
MARKET ST
A6135
PH
PO
1 NETHER LEY GDNS
2 UPPER LEY DELL
3 CHERRY WLK
4 BERRY HOLME CL
5 BERRY HOLME CT
6 MARKET PL
7 COWLEY CT
STRAFFORD PL
WENTWORTH CL
FLANDERS CT
THORPE ST
WENTWORTH RD
THE BELLFIELDS
NETHER LEY CL
SMITH ST
A629
S35
GLENWOOD CRES
HARCOURT RISE
WOODBURN DR
COWLEY LA
Hesley Hall Farm
SOUGH HALL AVE
SOUGH HALL RD
KIRKCROFT CL
OAKEN WOOD RD
HARVEY RD
UPPER LEY CT
CALIFORNIA DR
WILLOW CRES
A6135 ECCLESFIELD RD
Traveller's Inn (PH)
HESLEY LA
HESLOW GR
PARK VIEW
BROOK CT
Thorpe Hesley Jun & Inf Schs
NEW ST
BROOK HILL
Thorpe Hesley
ROWAN CL
CHAPEL RD
FIRTREE RISE
LARCH GR
MAPLE PL
LABURNUM CL
PARK AVE
HAZEL GR
PARK TERR
STUART RD
ALBANY AVE
CUMBERLAND WAY
WESTBURY AVE
BROADWAY AVE
Blackburn Brook
COWLEY HILL
SMITHY WOOD RD
HESLEY BAR
LONDON WAY
35
S61
WORTLEY MEWS
UPPER WORTLEY RD
B6086
PIT LA
NEWTON PL
Coit Prim Sch
COWLEY VIEW RD
Ecclesfield Sch
Smithy Wood
Thorpe Common
THORNTREE RD
BIRCHTREE RD
ELMTREE RD
LODGE LA
A629
Hesley Lodge Farm
CRAKEHILL RD
HUNSHELF RD
CHAPELTOWN RD
NETHER LA
Trans Pennine Trail
Jumble Hole Plantation
JUMBLE LA
WHITLEY LA
Provincial Park
Hartwell Home
Arundel Inn (PH)
WHITLEY CROFT
WHITLEY VIEW
MELLOR LEA FARM DR
Ecclesfield Common
Rainstorth Farm
RAINSTORTH
Spring Wood
B6087
JOHNSON LA
1 MELLOR LEA FARM GARTH
2 MELLOR LEA FARM CL
MILL RD
MILL CT
CHURCH ST
THE COMMON
Butterthwaite House
Rainstorth House
GRANGE LA
B6086
Excelsior Works
Station Works
LOICHER LA
Atlas Bsns Pk
STATION RD
STARNHILL CL
Butterthwaite
BUTTERTHWAITE LA
PRIORY CL
PRIORY RD
1 YEW LA
2 HIGH ST
3 ST MARY'S CL
4 THE BRAMBLES
5 PARK CRES
Cemy
ST MARY'S LA
TOWN END RD
SCHOLES VIEW
SYCAMORE RD
A6135
M1
S5
B6086

113
96

95
77

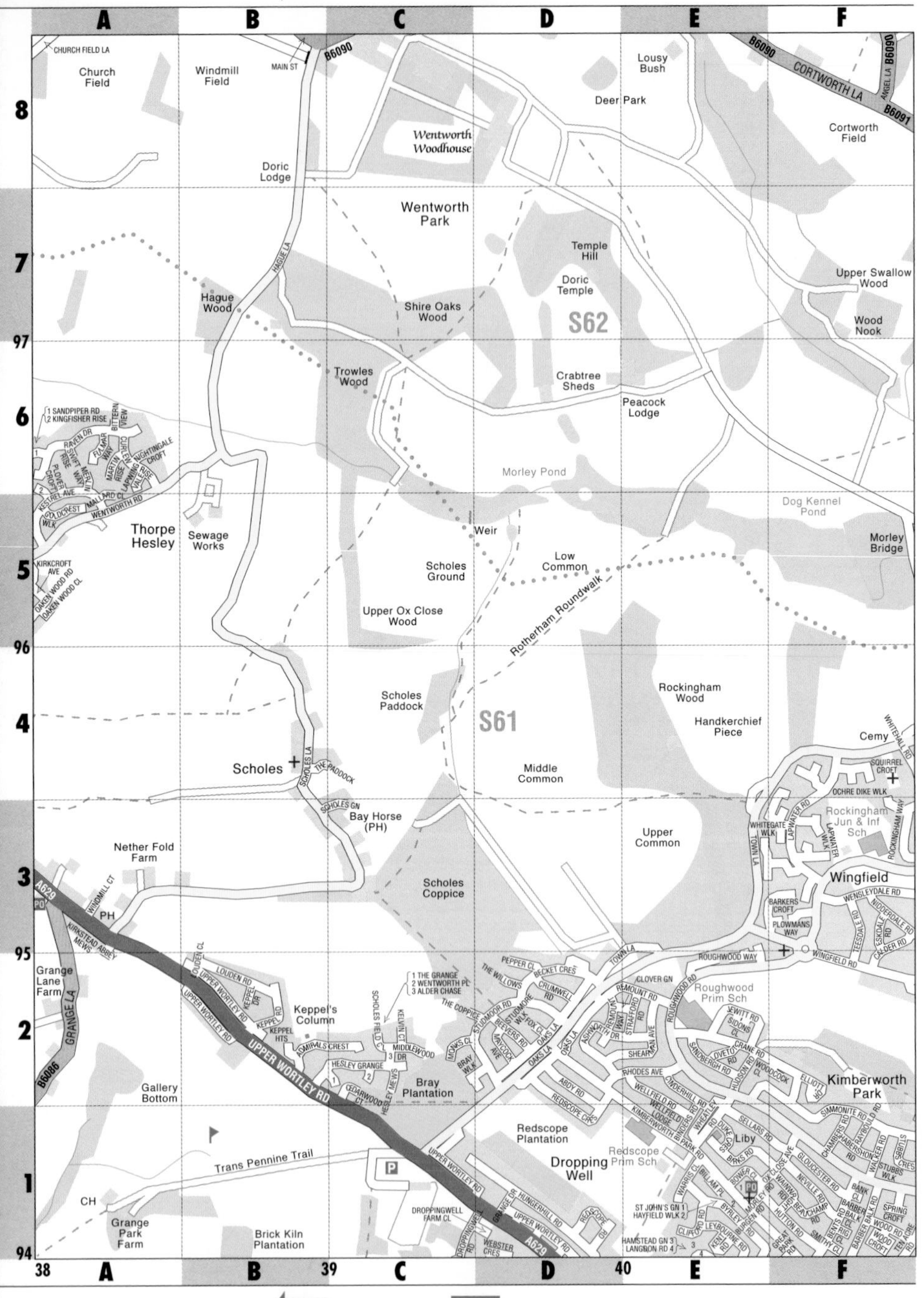
Church Field
Windmill Field
Lousy Bush
Deer Park
Cortworth Field
Wentworth Woodhouse
Doric Lodge
Wentworth Park
Temple Hill
Doric Temple
Upper Swallow Wood
Wood Nook
S62
Hague Wood
Shire Oaks Wood
Trowles Wood
Crabtree Sheds
Peacock Lodge
Morley Pond
Dog Kennel Pond
Thorpe Hesley
Sewage Works
Weir
Morley Bridge
Scholes Ground
Low Common
Upper Ox Close Wood
Rotherham Roundwalk
Rockingham Wood
Handkerchief Piece
Scholes Paddock
S61
Cemy
Scholes
Middle Common
Rockingham Jun & Inf Sch
Bay Horse (PH)
Nether Fold Farm
Upper Common
Wingfield
Scholes Coppice
Grange Lane Farm
Roughwood Prim Sch
Keppel's Column
Bray Plantation
Kimberworth Park
Gallery Bottom
Redscope Plantation
Liby
Dropping Well
Redscope Prim Sch
Trans Pennine Trail
CH
Grange Park Farm
Brick Kiln Plantation
UPPER WORTLEY RD
CORTWORTH LA
A629
B6090
B6091
B6086
GRANGE LA
HAGUE LA
SCHOLES LA
TOWN LA
WENTWORTH RD

95
114

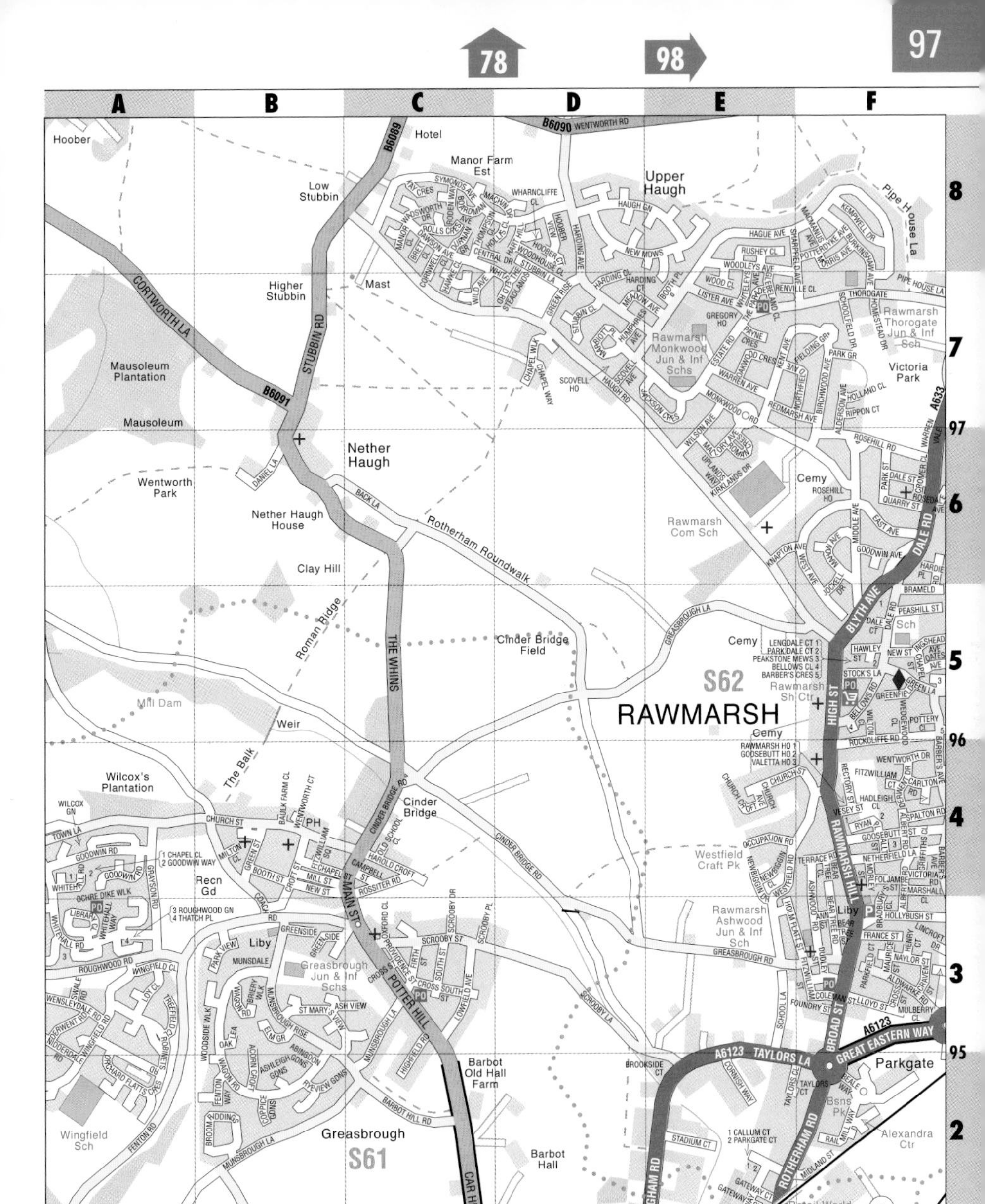
78
98
A
B
C
D
E
F
8
7
97
6
5
96
4
3
95
2
1
94
Hoober
Hotel
Manor Farm Est
Upper Haugh
Low Stubbin
Higher Stubbin
Mast
Mausoleum Plantation
Mausoleum
Nether Haugh
Wentworth Park
Nether Haugh House
Clay Hill
Rotherham Roundwalk
Roman Ridge
Cinder Bridge Field
Mill Dam
Weir
The Balk
Wilcox's Plantation
Cinder Bridge
PH
Recn Gd
Liby
Greasbrough Jun & Inf Schs
Wingfield Sch
Barbot Old Hall Farm
Greasbrough
S61
Barbot Hall
Barbot Hall Ind Est
Bassingthorpe Farm
RAWMARSH
S62
Rawmarsh Monkwood Jun & Inf Schs
Rawmarsh Thorogate Jun & Inf Sch
Victoria Park
Cemy
Rawmarsh Com Sch
Rawmarsh Sh Ctr
Westfield Craft Pk
Rawmarsh Ashwood Jun & Inf Sch
Parkgate
Bsns Pk
Alexandra Ctr
Retail World Sh Ctr & Trad Est
S60
S65
Eastwood Trad Est
41
42
43
115
98

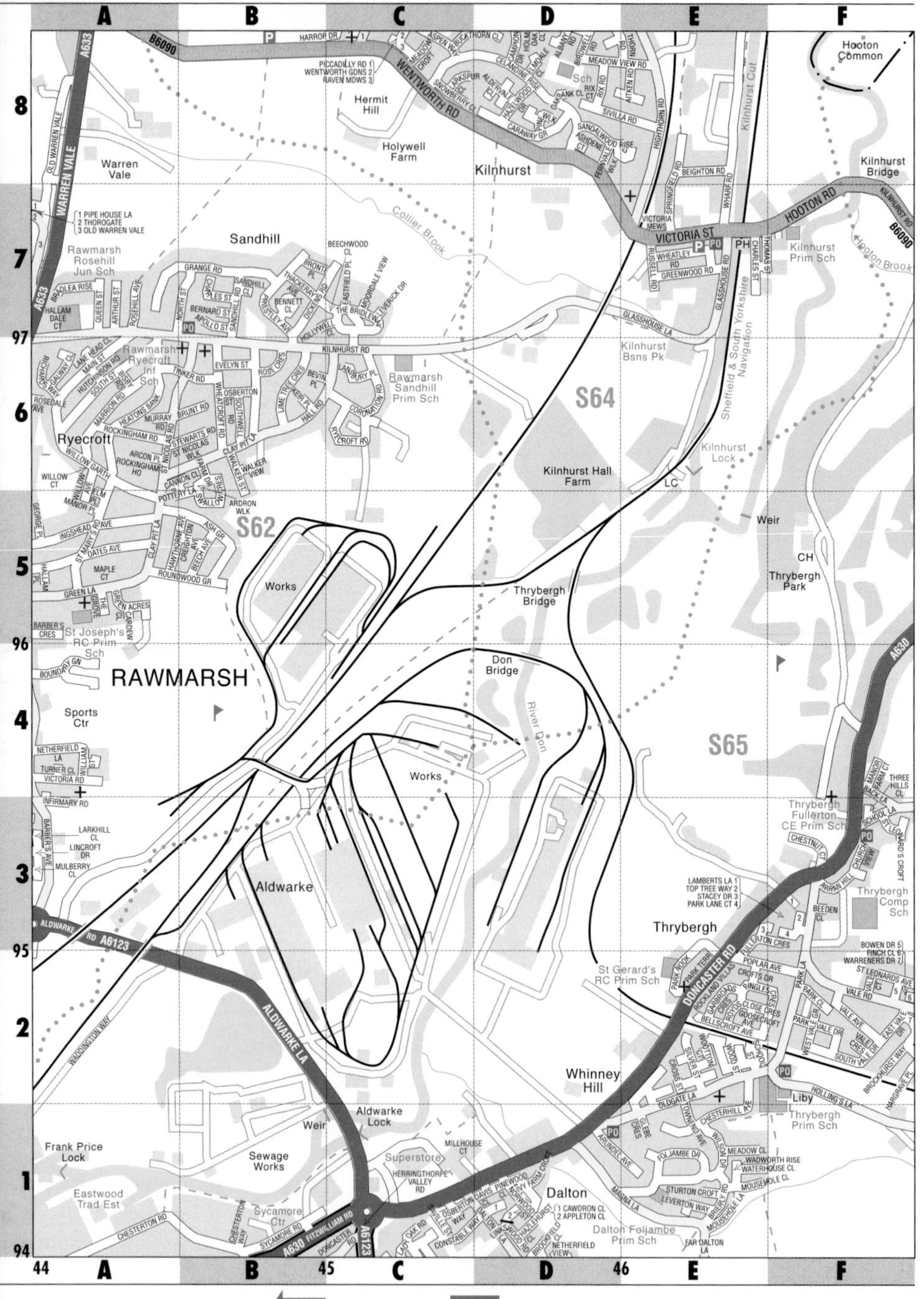

97
79

A B C D E F

8

7

97

6

5

96

4

3

95

2

1

94

44 45 46

Hooton
Common

B6090

WARREN VALE

A633

HARROP DR

PICCADILLY RD 1
WENTWORTH GDNS 2
RAVEN MOWS 3

WENTWORTH RD

Hermit
Hill

Holywell
Farm

Kilnhurst

Kilnhurst
Bridge

HOOTON RD

Hooton Brook

B6090

Kilnhurst Cut

Collier Brook

Warren
Vale

1 PIPE HOUSE LA
2 THOROGATE
3 OLD WARREN VALE

Rawmarsh
Rosehill
Jun Sch

Sandhill

BEECHWOOD
CL

GRANGE RD

Kilnhurst
Prim Sch

VICTORIA ST

Kilnhurst
Bsns Pk

S64

GLASSHOUSE LA

Sheffield & South Yorkshire Navigation

Kilnhurst
Lock

LC

Weir

CH
Thrybergh
Park

Kilnhurst Hall
Farm

RAWMARSH

Ryecroft

St Joseph's
RC Prim
Sch

BARBER'S
CRES

S62

Works

Thrybergh
Bridge

Don
Bridge

River Don

S65

THREE
HILLS

Thrybergh
Fullerton
CE Prim Sch

Sports
Ctr

NETHERFIELD
LA
TURNER CL
VICTORIA RD
INFIRMARY RD

LARKHILL
CL
LINCROFT
DR
MULBERRY
CL

Works

Aldwarke

LAMBERTS LA 1
TOP TREE WAY 2
STACEY DR 3
PARK LANE CT 4

Thrybergh

Thrybergh
Comp
Sch

BEEDEN

St Gerard's
RC Prim
Sch

BOWEN DR 5
FINCH CL 6
WARRENERS DR 7
St LEOFARDS LA

A6123

ALDWARKE RD

WADDINGTON WAY

ALDWARKE LA

Frank Price
Lock

Eastwood
Trad Est

Sewage
Works

Weir

Aldwarke
Lock

Superstore

MILEHOUSE
CT

HERRINGTHORPE
VALLEY
RD

Whinney
Hill

Liby

Thrybergh
Prim Sch

CHESTERTON RD

Sycamore
Ctr

A630 FITZWILLIAM RD

A6123

DONCASTER RD

Dalton

1 CAWDRON CL
2 APPLETON CL

NETHERFIELD
VIEW

Dalton Foljambe
Prim Sch

FAR DALTON
LA

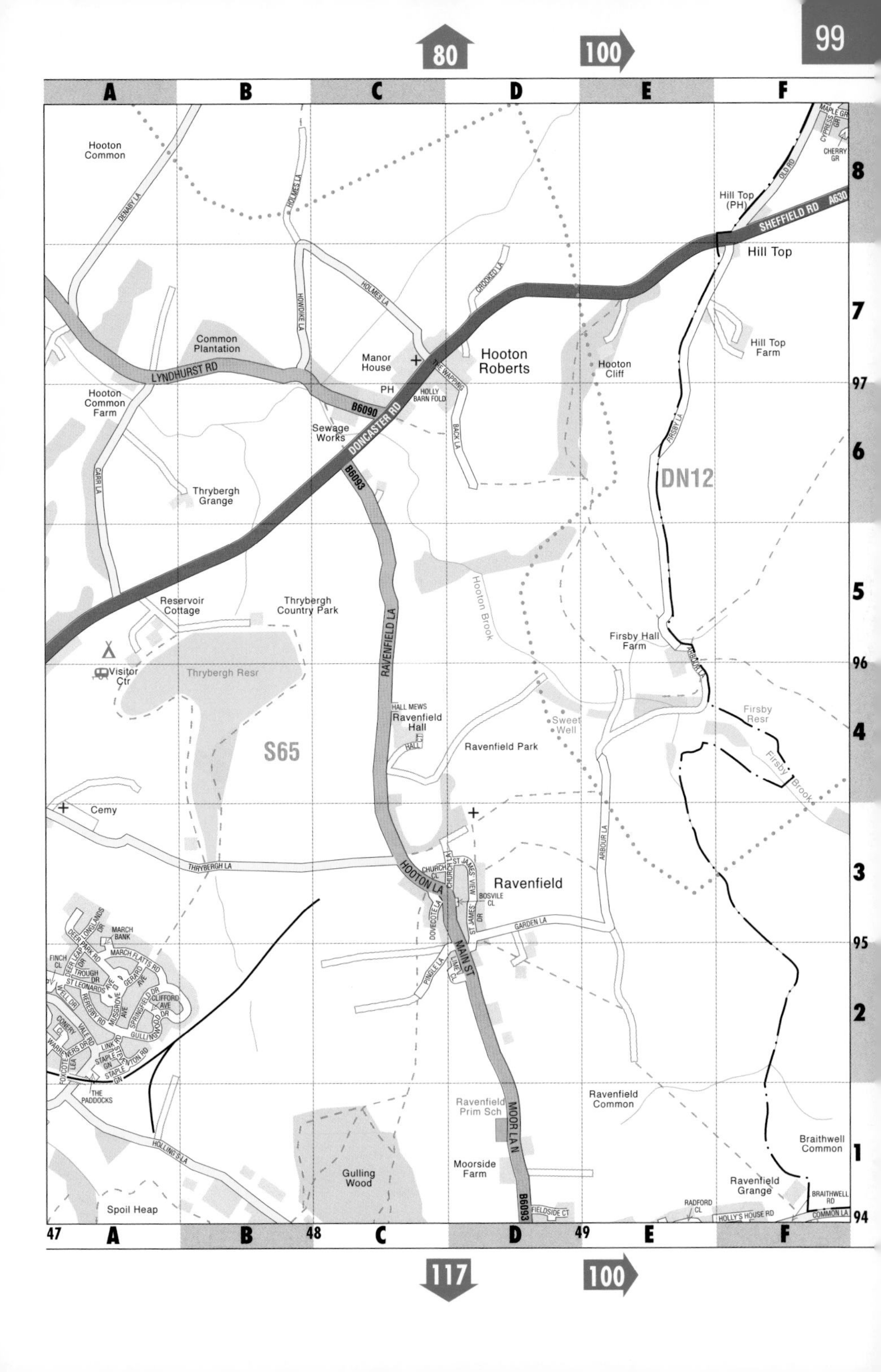
80
100
A
B
C
D
E
F
Hooton Common
DENABY LA
HOLMES LA
HOWDIKE LA
CROOKED LA
Hill Top (PH)
SHEFFIELD RD
A630
Hill Top
OLD RD
CHERRY GR
CYPRESS GR
Common Plantation
LYNDHURST RD
Manor House
Hooton Roberts
THE WAPPING
Hooton Cliff
Hill Top Farm
Hooton Common Farm
PH
HOLLY BARN FOLD
B6090
Sewage Works
DONCASTER RD
BACK LA
FIRSBY LA
DN12
CARR LA
Thrybergh Grange
B6093
Hooton Brook
Reservoir Cottage
Thrybergh Country Park
RAVENFIELD LA
Firsby Hall Farm
ARBOUR LA
Visitor Ctr
Thrybergh Resr
HALL MEWS
Ravenfield Hall
HALL CT
Sweet Well
Firsby Resr
S65
Ravenfield Park
Firsby Brook
Cemy
THRYBERGH LA
HOOTON LA
CHURCH CL
CHURCH LA
ST JAMES' VIEW
Ravenfield
BOSVILE CL
DOVECOTE LA
ST JAMES DR
GARDEN LA
MARCH BANK
LONGLANDS DR
DEER PARK RD
MARCH FLATTS RD
FINCH CL
DEER LEAP
TROUGH DR
ST LEONARDS AVE
GERARD AVE
MAIN ST
PINGLE LA
LIME CL
WELL DR
RERESBY RD
MUSGROVE AVE
SPRINGFIELD DR
CLIFFORD AVE
GULLINWOOD DR
CONERY CL
VALE RD
WARRENERS DR
LINK RD
STEVENTON RD
FOXCOTE LEA
STAPLE GN
THE PADDOCKS
Ravenfield Prim Sch
MOOR LA N
Ravenfield Common
HOLLINGS LA
Gulling Wood
Moorside Farm
Braithwell Common
Ravenfield Grange
Spoil Heap
B6093
FIELDSIDE CT
RADFORD CL
HOLLY'S HOUSE RD
BRAITHWELL RD
COMMON LA
8
7
97
6
5
96
4
3
95
2
1
94
47
48
49
117
100

99 81

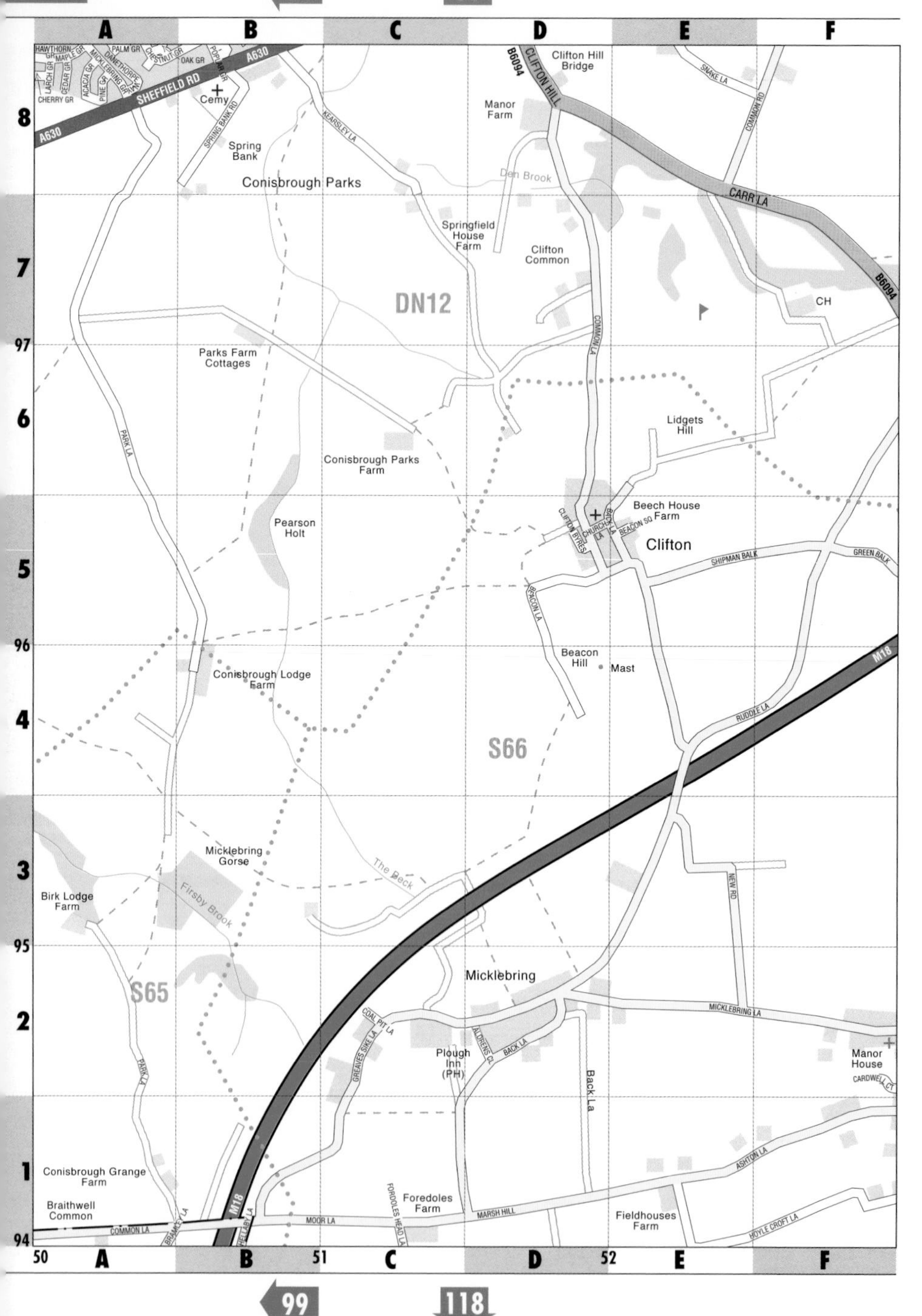

A B C D E F
8 7 97 6 5 96 4 3 95 2 1 94
SHEFFIELD RD
A630
Cemy
SPRING BANK RD
Spring Bank
Conisbrough Parks
KEARSLEY LA
B6094
CLIFTON HILL
Clifton Hill Bridge
Manor Farm
SNAKE LA
COMMON RD
Den Brook
CARR LA
Springfield House Farm
Clifton Common
DN12
CH
Parks Farm Cottages
COMMON LA
Lidgets Hill
PARK LA
Conisbrough Parks Farm
Pearson Holt
Beech House Farm
Clifton
SHIPMAN BALK
GREEN BALK
BEACON LA
Beacon Hill
Mast
Conisbrough Lodge Farm
M18
RUDDLE LA
S66
Micklebring Gorse
The Beck
Birk Lodge Farm
Firsby Brook
NEW RD
S65
Micklebring
MICKLEBRING LA
COAL PIT LA
GREAVES SIKE LA
Plough Inn (PH)
BACK LA
Back La
Manor House
CARDWELL CT
Conisbrough Grange Farm
Braithwell Common
COMMON LA
BRAMLEY LA
MOOR LA
FORDOLES HEAD LA
Foredoles Farm
MARSH HILL
ASHTON LA
Fieldhouses Farm
HOYLE CROFT LA
50 51 52

99 118

82
102

A
B
C
D
E
F
HOWBECK DR
HILLSIDE DR
B6376
MALLIN DR
HILL TOP CRES
CLARK AVE
ECCLES DR
HATTER DR
TOP VIEW CRES
ROBERTS RD
TAIT AVE
The White Greyhound (PH)
Edlington Sch
M18
Edlington Wood
EDLINGTON LA
Manor Farm
SCHOOL WLK
RECTORY GDNS
BACK LA
WOOD LA
MANOR FARM BLDGS
Old Edlington
Wadworth Wood
CARR LA
WHITE CROSS
B6094
RUDDLE LA
DN12
Peter Wood Farm
Four Acre Holt
COCKHILL LA
Cockhill House
RAKES LA
Out Moor
Paddock La
GREEN BALK
DN11
LONG GATE
B6094
LONG LEYS LA
Newland's Farm
Woodlands Farm
Out Moor Holt
STAINTON LA
COCKHILL FIELD LA
Ridgewood Farm
S66
COCKHILL LA
Lodge Farm
DONCASTER RD
BIRCHWOOD GDNS
WILLOW CRES
CHAPEL HOLE LA
TICKHILL BACK LA
MICKLEBRING LA
CHURCH GR
PO
Sewage Works
AUSTWOOD LA
LIMEKILN LA
HIGH ST
WILLOW PL
P
CARDWELL CT
Braithwell
Poggy La
The Ruddle Mill
RUDDLE MILL LA
RUDDLE MILL LA
Cedar Farm
ASHTON LA
Ruddle Dike
Holme Hall Quarries
Austwood Closes
Top La
HIRST LA
COTTAGE GR
HOLYWELL CRES
HOLYWELL LA
BROAD RIDING
Stainton Little Wood
WOOD LA
HOYLE CROFT LA
MALTBY LA
HOLME HALL LA
RAW LA
B6376
BIRKWOOD TERR
B6427
8
7
97
6
5
96
4
3
95
2
1
94
53
54
55

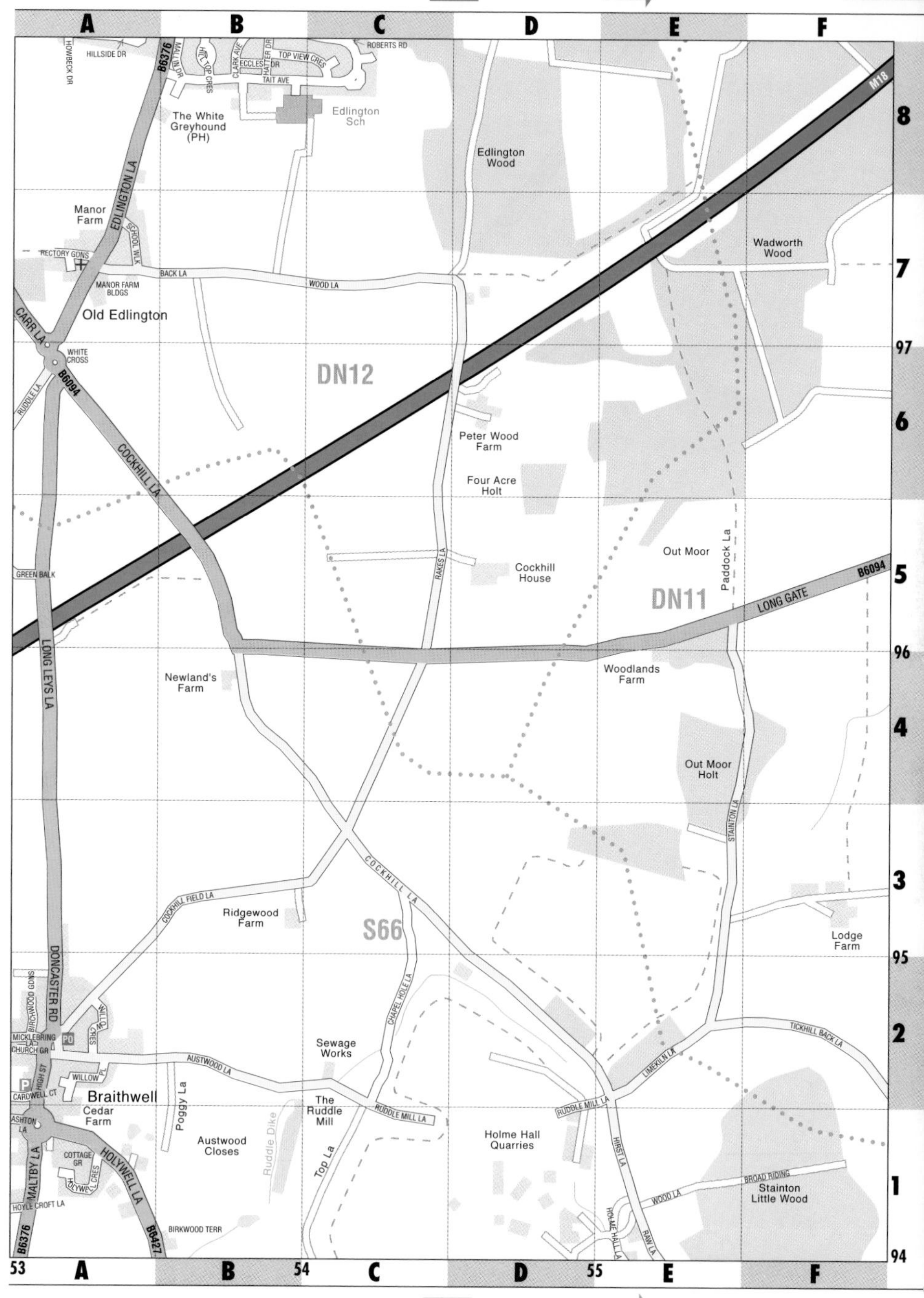

119
102

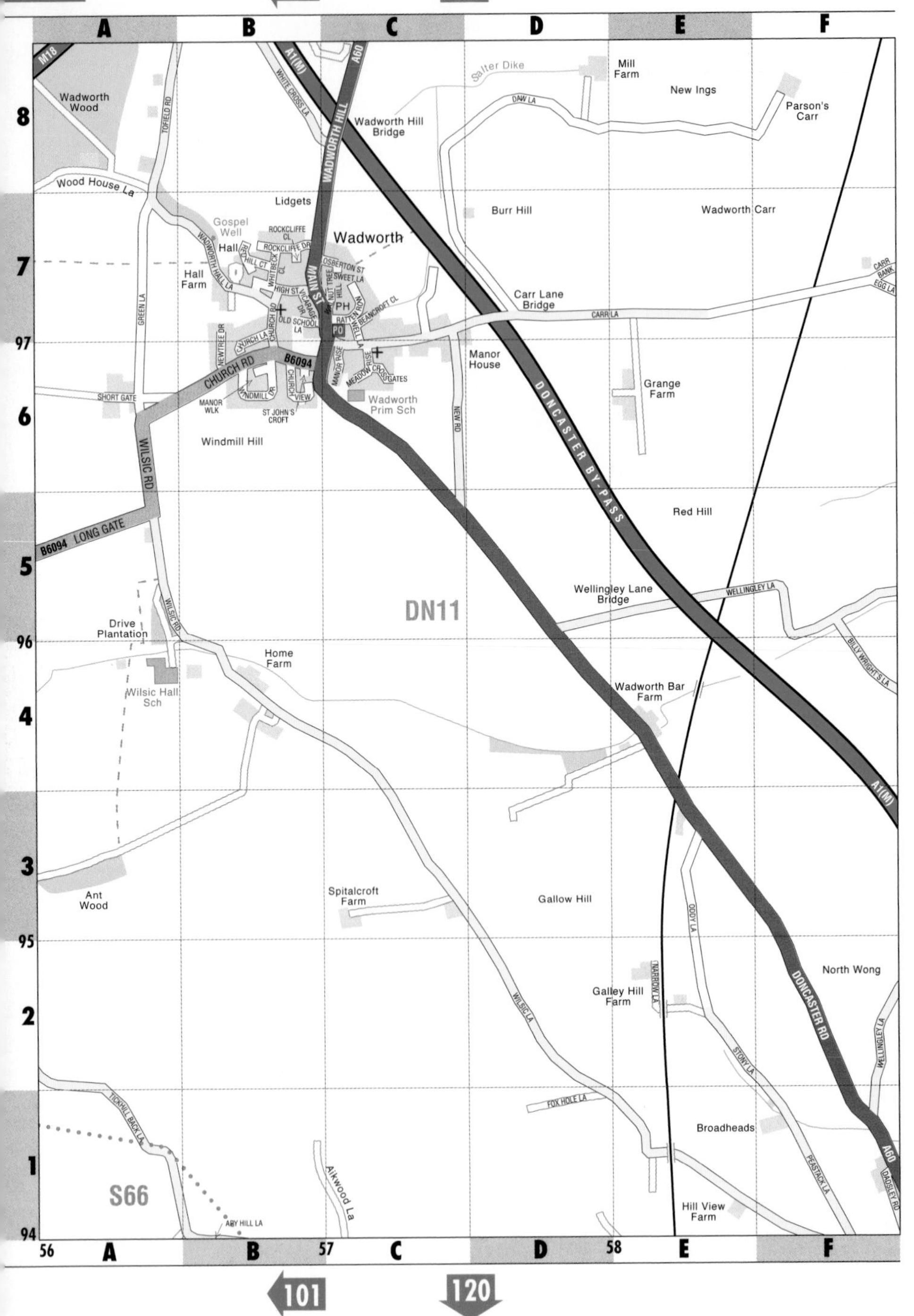

Map labels

A B C D E F

M18

Wadworth Wood

Wood House La

Salter Dike

Mill Farm

New Ings

Parson's Carr

Wadworth Hill Bridge

DAY LA

Lidgets

Gospel Well

Burr Hill

Wadworth Carr

CARR BANK

EGG LA

Wadworth

ROCKCLIFFE CL

Hall

ROCKCLIFFE DR

MILL CT

HILL CT

HIGH ST

OSBERTON ST

SWEET LA

Carr Lane Bridge

CARR LA

Hall Farm

WADWORTH LN LA

NEW PEW DR

MAIN ST

PH

BLANCROFT CL

+

97

CHURCH DR

OLD SCHOOL LA

RATS LA

PO

+

Manor House

B6094

MANOR RD

MEADOW CR

GATES

SHORT GATE

CHURCH RD

MANOR WLK

WINDMILL

HILL VIEW

ST JOHN'S CROFT

Wadworth Prim Sch

NEW RD

Grange Farm

6

Windmill Hill

WILSIC RD

DONCASTER BY-PASS

Red Hill

5

B6094 LONG GATE

Wellingley Lane Bridge

WELLINGLEY LA

BELL BRIGHT LA

Drive Plantation

WILSIC RD

96

DN11

Home Farm

Wadworth Bar Farm

A1(M)

4

Wilsic Hall Sch

3

Spitalcroft Farm

Gallow Hill

95

Ant Wood

TNAREWICK LA

LOOP LA

STONE LA

North Wong

2

Galley Hill Farm

DONCASTER RD

WELLINGLEY LA

WILSIC LA

FOX HOLE LA

Broadheads

A60

1

TICKHILL BACK LA

ALKWOOD LA

Hill View Farm

BECKSEY LA

CROSSET LA

S66

ABY HILL LA

94

56 **A** **B** 57 **C** **D** 58 **E** **F**

Parson's Carr

Refuse Tip

Wadworth Carr

Holmes Carr Great Wood

FOLJAMBE CRES 1
SKIPWITH GDNS 2
QUEEN MARY'S RD 3

Grange Lane Inf Sch

MEADOW CT 1
BOSWELL CL 2
HYPERION WAY 3

Cemy

GRANGEFIELD HESLEY
MORRISON
ABERCONWY CRES
HUNSTER GR
CLAY FLAT

WHITCOMB DR
KEPPLE

Rossington Grange Farm

Stancil

New Rossington

ELMFIELD RD 1
FARRINGDON DR 2
SEATON GDNS 3

CARR BANK

Egg La

Egg La

Little Mother Drain

River Torne

South Seats Drain

STANCIL LA

Reedy Holmes Plantation

Carr Doles

Stancil Carr

Wellingley Low Grounds

DN11

Wellingley Grange

Park Wood

Stancil

Hesley Hall Village

Hesley Hall Coll

BILLY WRIGHT'S LA

FOUR LANE ENDS

WELLINGLEY LA

Wellingley Holt

Broomhills Wood

Wellingley Farm

STANCIL LA

Nursery

Hesley Park

Goole Dike or River Torne

Dadsley Well Bridge

Bog Wood

Coneyborough Plantation

Middle Drain

B6463

STRIPE RD

Dadsley Well Stream

Limpool Farm

Eastfield Wood

Tickhill Low Common

Tickhill High Common

HIPSWELL LA

COMMON LA

Dumpling Castle Covert

Sawney Hill

Eastfield Farm House

A60 DONCASTER RD

A1 (M)

DADSLEY RD

Eastfield House

SHEEPWASH LA

Sheepwash Bridge

B6463

Dumpling Castle Farm

New Rossington

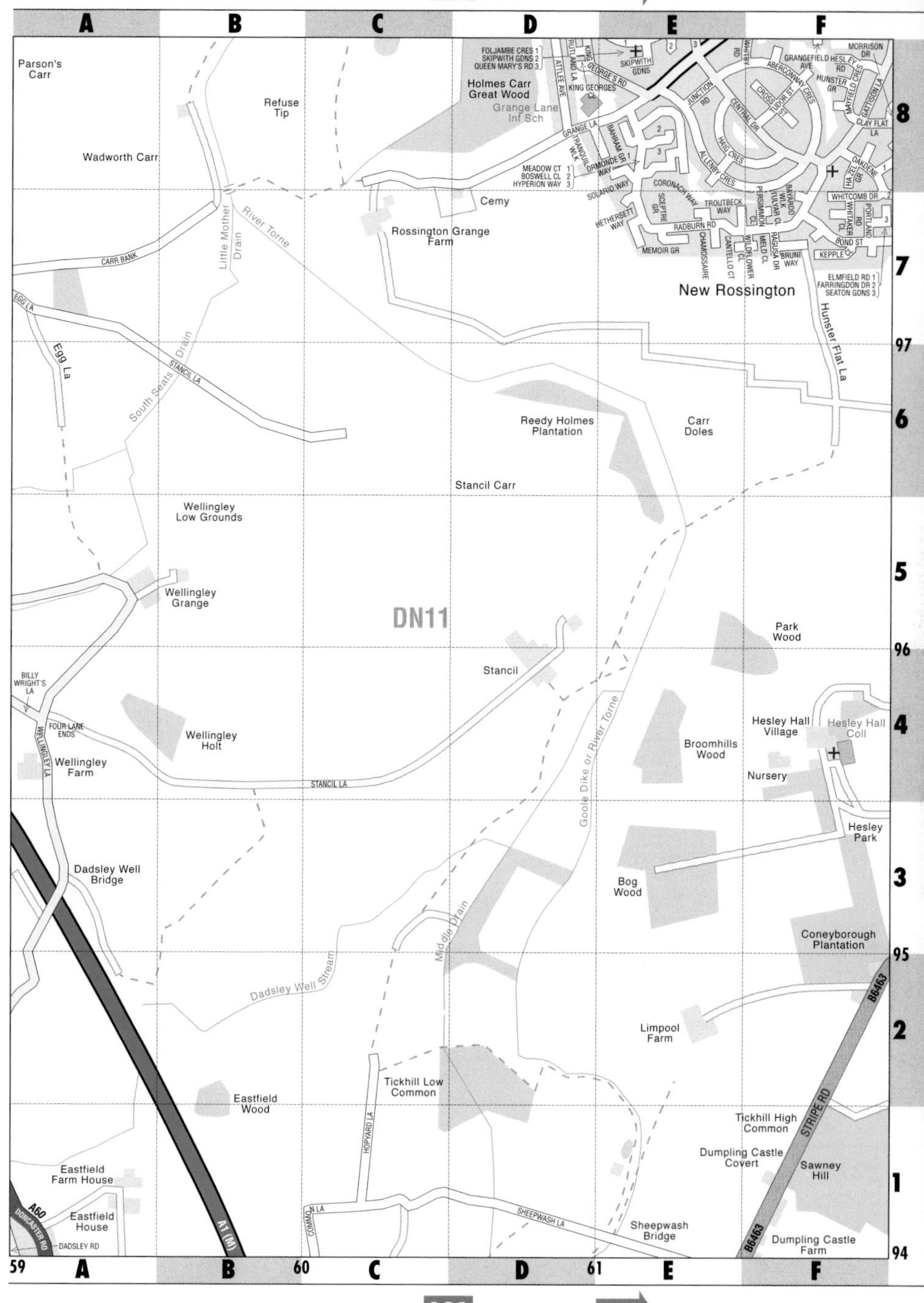

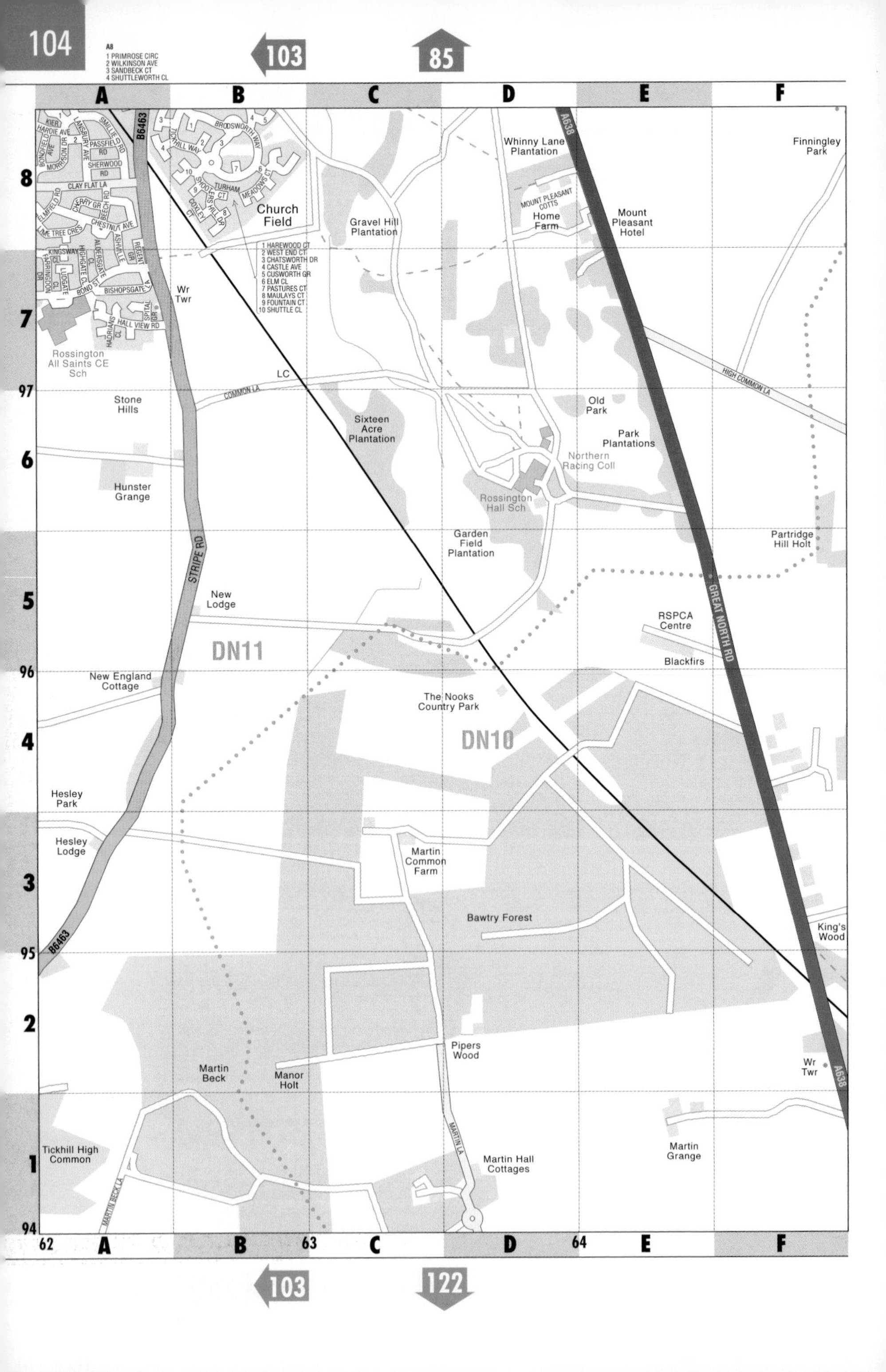

103
85

Finningley
Park

Whinny Lane
Plantation

Gravel Hill
Plantation

MOUNT PLEASANT
COTTS
Home
Farm

Mount
Pleasant
Hotel

Church
Field

1 HAREWOOD CT
2 WEST END CT
3 CHATSWORTH DR
4 CASTLE AVE
5 CUSWORTH GR
6 ELM CL
7 PASTURES CT
8 MAULAYS CT
9 FOUNTAIN CT
10 SHUTTLE CL

Wr
Twr

HIGH COMMON LA

Rossington
All Saints CE
Sch

LC

COMMON LA

Old
Park

Stone
Hills

Sixteen
Acre
Plantation

Park
Plantations

Northern
Racing Coll

Hunster
Grange

Rossington
Hall Sch

STRIPE RD

Garden
Field
Plantation

Partridge
Hill Holt

New
Lodge

RSPCA
Centre

DN11

Blackfirs

New England
Cottage

The Nooks
Country Park

DN10

GREAT NORTH RD

Hesley
Park

Hesley
Lodge

Martin
Common
Farm

Bawtry Forest

King's
Wood

Pipers
Wood

Martin
Beck

Manor
Holt

MARTIN LA

Wr
Twr

A638

Tickhill High
Common

Martin Hall
Cottages

Martin
Grange

B6463

MARTIN BECK LA

103
122

86

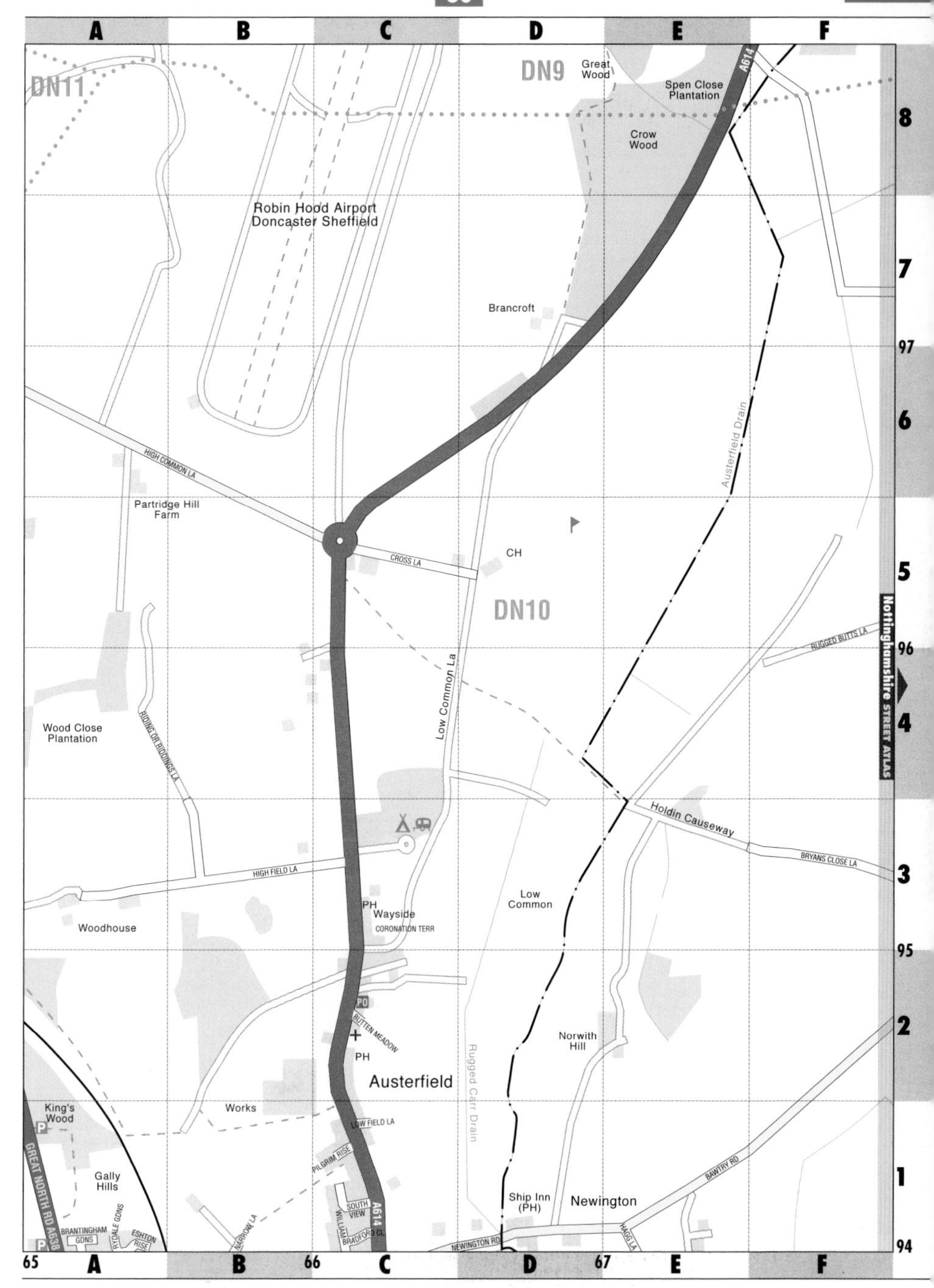
A
B
C
D
E
F
DN11
DN9
Great Wood
Spen Close Plantation
A614
8
Crow Wood
Robin Hood Airport Doncaster Sheffield
7
Brancroft
97
6
Austerfield Drain
HIGH COMMON LA
Partridge Hill Farm
CROSS LA
CH
5
DN10
RUGGED BUTTS LA
96
Nottinghamshire STREET ATLAS
Low Common La
RIDING OR RIDDINGS LA
Wood Close Plantation
4
Holdin Causeway
BRYANS CLOSE LA
HIGH FIELD LA
3
Low Common
PH
Wayside
CORONATION TERR
Woodhouse
95
PO
BUTTEN MEADOW
PH
Norwith Hill
2
Rugged Carr Drain
Austerfield
King's Wood
Works
LOW FIELD LA
GREAT NORTH RD A638
Gally Hills
PILGRIM RISE
BAWTRY RD
1
Ship Inn (PH)
Newington
SOUTH VIEW
WILLIAM
BRADFORD CL
NARROW LA
RYDALE GDNS
BRANTINGHAM GDNS
ESHTON RISE
NEWINGTON RD
HAGG LA
94
65
66
67

123

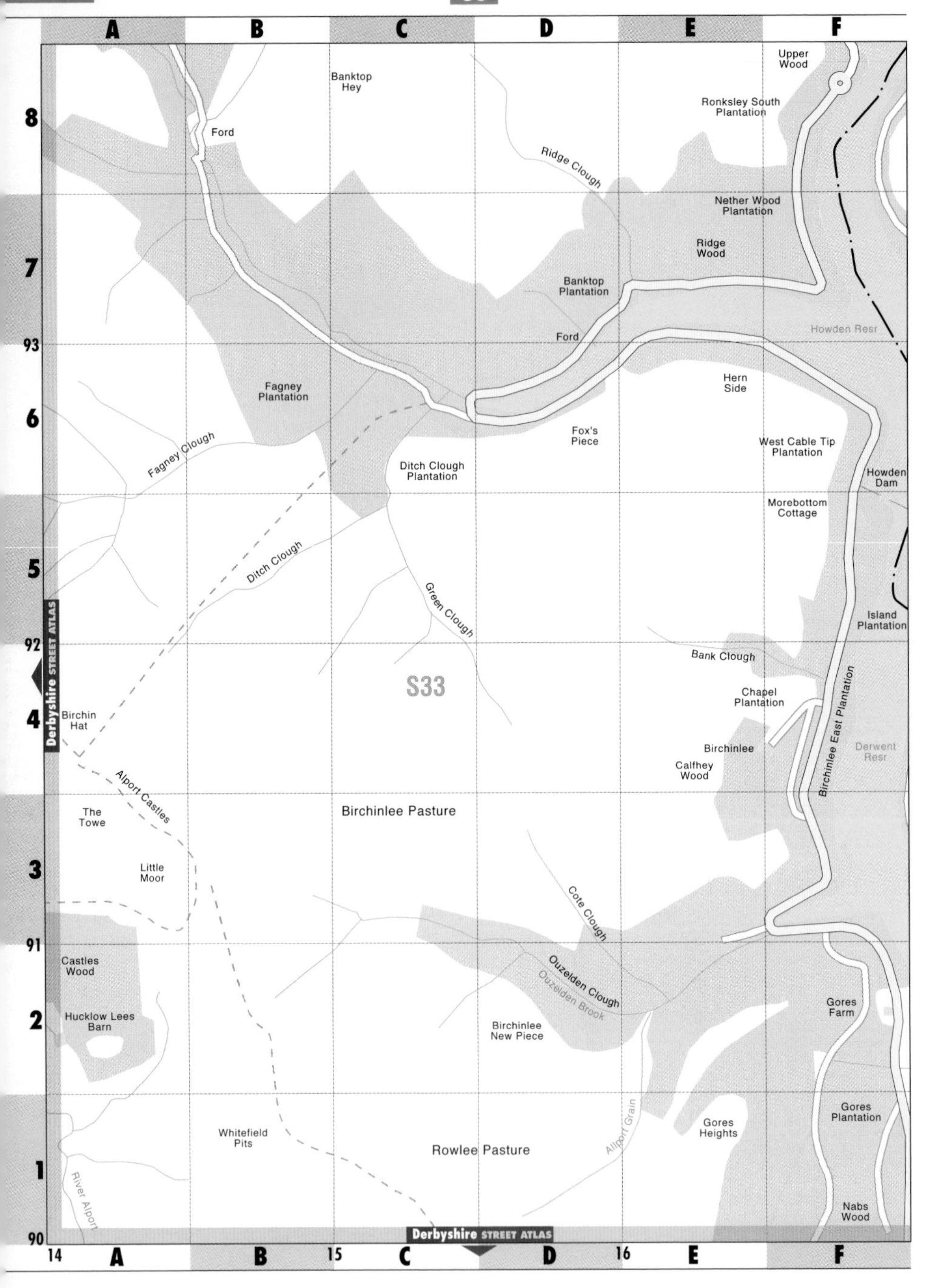

Upper Wood

Ronksley South Plantation

Banktop Hey

Ford

Ridge Clough

Nether Wood Plantation

Ridge Wood

Banktop Plantation

Ford

Howden Resr

Fagney Plantation

Hern Side

Fagney Clough

Fox's Piece

West Cable Tip Plantation

Ditch Clough Plantation

Howden Dam

Ditch Clough

Morebottom Cottage

Green Clough

Island Plantation

S33

Bank Clough

Chapel Plantation

Birchinlee East Plantation

Birchin Hat

Derwent Resr

Birchinlee

Calfhey Wood

Alport Castles

The Towe

Birchinlee Pasture

Little Moor

Cote Clough

Castles Wood

Ouzelden Clough

Ouzelden Brook

Gores Farm

Hucklow Lees Barn

Birchinlee New Piece

Gores Plantation

Whitefield Pits

Rowlee Pasture

Alport Grain

Gores Heights

River Alport

Nabs Wood

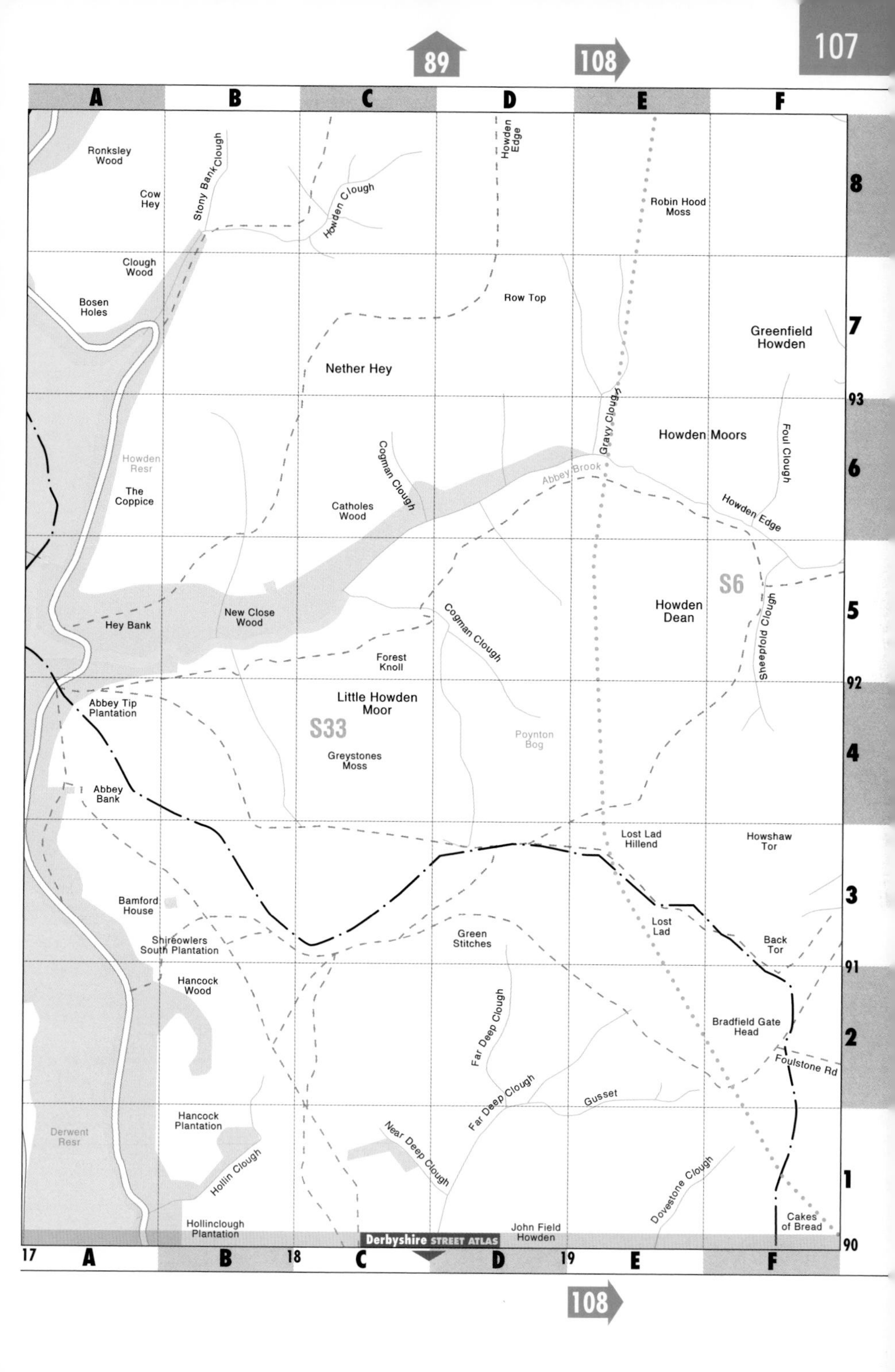
89
108
A
B
C
D
E
F
Ronksley Wood
Cow Hey
Stony Bank Clough
Howden Clough
Howden Edge
Robin Hood Moss
8
Clough Wood
Bosen Holes
Row Top
Greenfield Howden
7
Nether Hey
93
Howden Resr
The Coppice
Cogman Clough
Gravy Clough
Howden Moors
Foul Clough
6
Abbey Brook
Catholes Wood
Howden Edge
S6
New Close Wood
Hey Bank
Cogman Clough
Howden Dean
Sheepfold Clough
5
Forest Knoll
92
Abbey Tip Plantation
Little Howden Moor
S33
Poynton Bog
Greystones Moss
4
Abbey Bank
Lost Lad Hillend
Howshaw Tor
3
Bamford House
Lost Lad
Green Stitches
Back Tor
Shireowlers South Plantation
91
Hancock Wood
Far Deep Clough
Bradfield Gate Head
2
Foulstone Rd
Far Deep Clough
Gusset
Derwent Resr
Hancock Plantation
Near Deep Clough
1
Hollin Clough
Dovestone Clough
Hollinclough Plantation
John Field Howden
Cakes of Bread
90
17
18
19
108

A B C D E F

8

Round
Hill

Wet Slack

Blackhole

Hobson Moss Dike

7

Wet Slack Ridge

Cartledge Brook

93

Cartledge Flat

New Cross
(rems of)

Small
Dale

Shooting
Cabins

6

Abell Brook

Brook Crook Clough

Cartledge
Bents

Holling Dale

Thornseat
Delf

THORNSEAT
RD

Thornseat
Moor

Bents Clough

5

Cartledge Stones Ridge

Rushy Flat

S6

Holling Dale
Piece

92

Low Tor

Rushy Flat Dike

Howden
Edge

4

Brogging Moss Dike

Holling Dale
Plantation

Holling Dale Brook

Holling Dale
Cott

Bole Edge
Plantation

3

Brogging Moss
Plantation

Brogging Moss

Foulstone Dike

91

Foulstone Rd

Foulstone
Delf

Fox Hole
Carr

Strines
Bridge

MORTIMER RD

2

Foulstone Moor

PH

Strines

Brogging
End

1

Blackhole

Running Moss Dike

Strines Dike

Strines Moor Ridge

Strines
Resr

Blackhole
Moor

Broad Carr

90

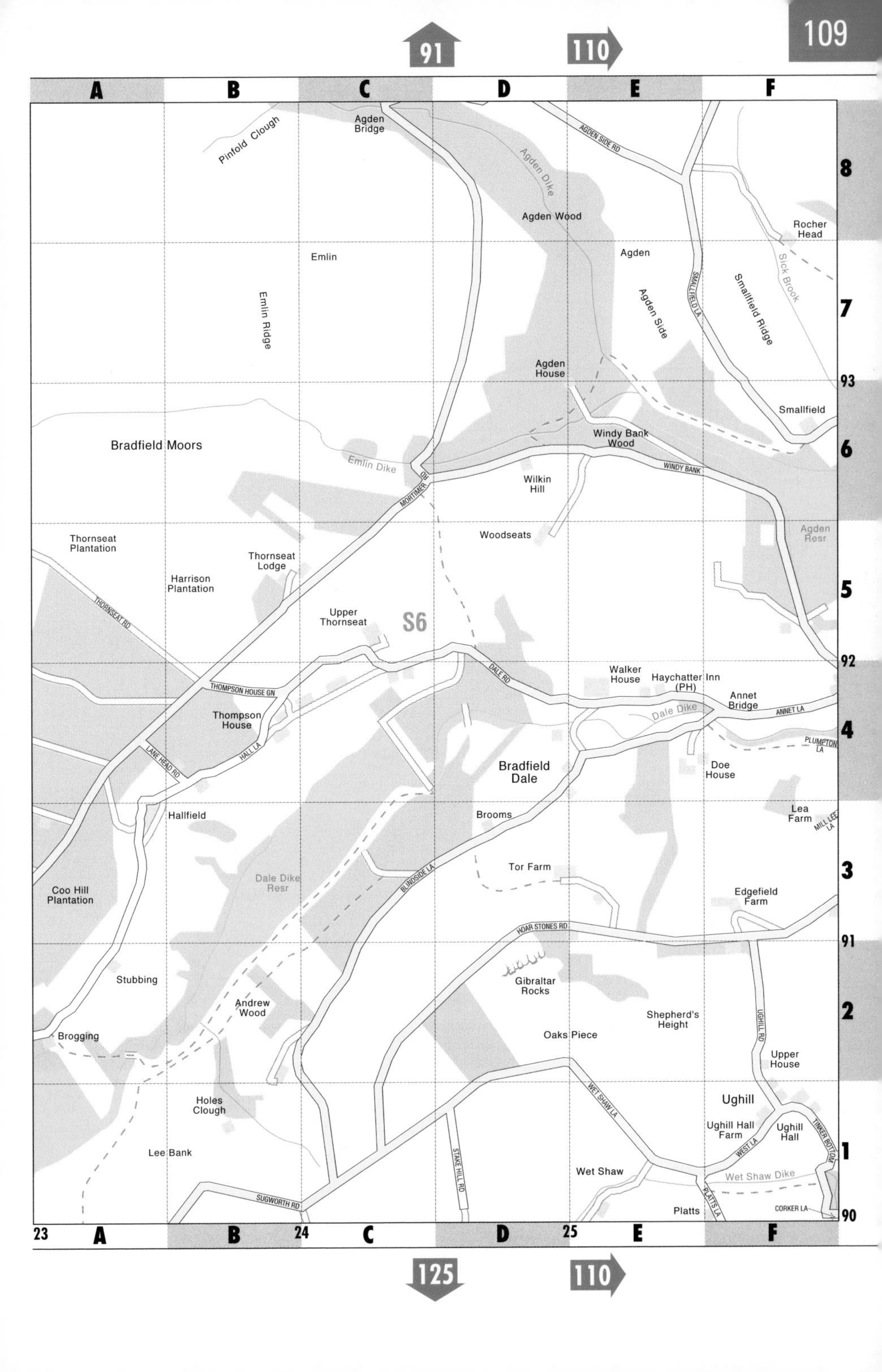
91
110
A
B
C
D
E
F
Agden Bridge
Pinfold Clough
Agden Side Rd
Agden Dike
Agden Wood
Rocher Head
Emlin
Agden
Emlin Ridge
Smallfield La
Agden Side
Smallfield Ridge
Sick Brook
Agden House
Smallfield
Bradfield Moors
Windy Bank Wood
Emlin Dike
Windy Bank
Mortimer Rd
Wilkin Hill
Thornseat Plantation
Woodseats
Agden Resr
Thornseat Lodge
Harrison Plantation
Thornseat Rd
Upper Thornseat
S6
Dale Rd
Walker House
Haychatter Inn (PH)
Annet Bridge
Thompson House Gn
Dale Dike
Annet La
Thompson House
Plumpton La
Hall La
Lane Head Rd
Bradfield Dale
Doe House
Lea Farm
Hallfield
Brooms
Mill Lee La
Tor Farm
Dale Dike Resr
Blindside La
Coo Hill Plantation
Edgefield Farm
Hoar Stones Rd
Gibraltar Rocks
Stubbing
Andrew Wood
Shepherd's Height
Brogging
Oaks Piece
Ughill Rd
Upper House
Holes Clough
Ughill
Wet Shaw La
Ughill Hall Farm
Ughill Hall
Tinker Bottom
Lee Bank
Stake Hill Rd
West La
Wet Shaw
Wet Shaw Dike
Sugworth Rd
Platts La
Platts
Corker La
8
7
93
6
5
92
4
3
91
2
1
90
23
24
25
125
110

109
92

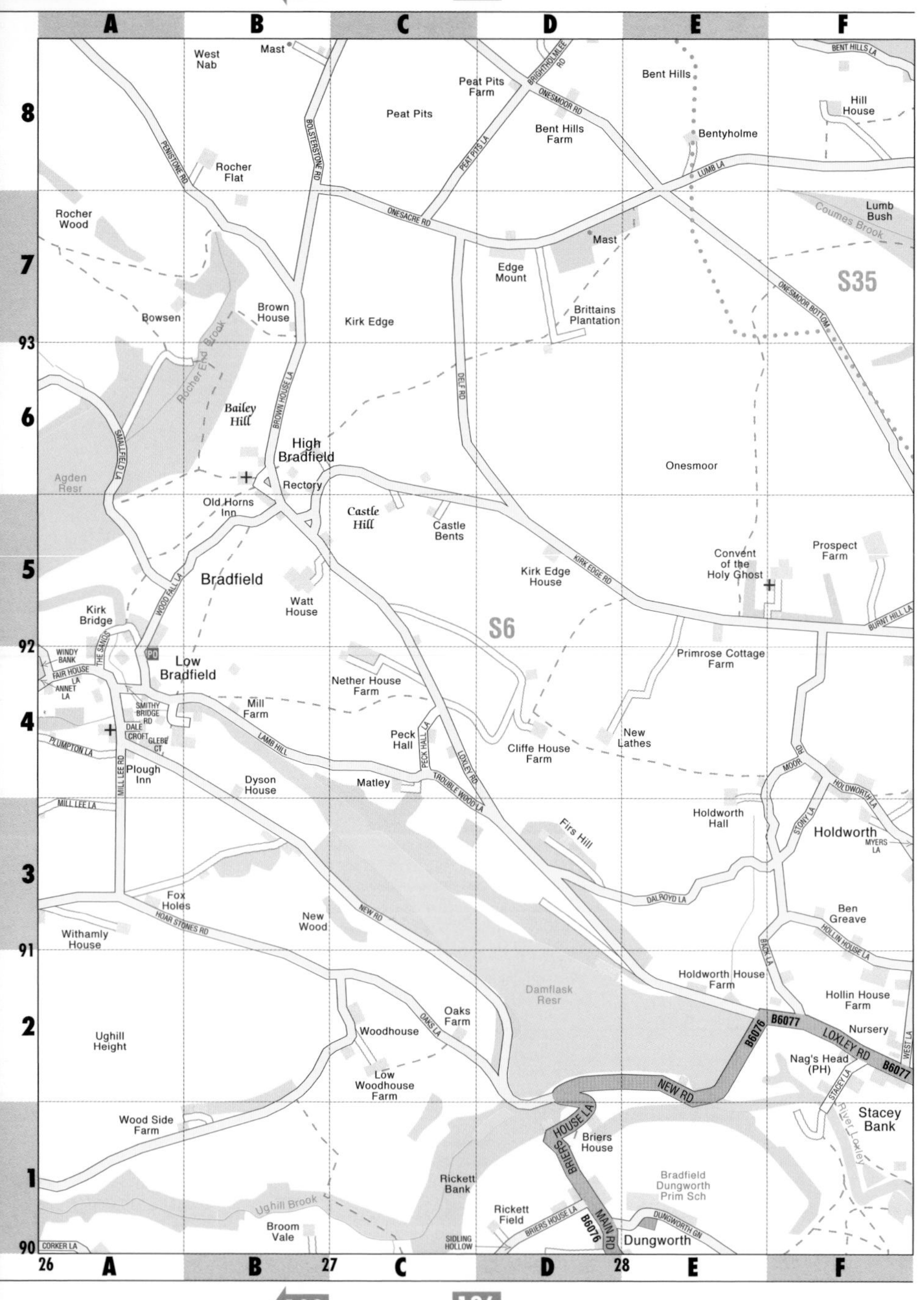
A
B
C
D
E
F
8
7
93
6
5
92
4
3
91
2
1
90
26
27
28
West Nab
Mast
Peat Pits Farm
Peat Pits
Bent Hills
Bent Hills Farm
Bentyholme
Hill House
BENT HILLS LA
BRIGHTHOLMLEE RD
ONESMOOR RD
PENISTONE RD
BOLSTERSTONE RD
PEAT PITS LA
Rocher Flat
LUMB LA
Lumb Bush
Coumes Brook
Rocher Wood
ONESACRE RD
Mast
Edge Mount
S35
Brittains Plantation
ONESMOOR BOTTOM
Bowsen
Brown House
Kirk Edge
Rocher End Brook
Bailey Hill
BROWN HOUSE LA
DELF RD
SMALLFIELD LA
High Bradfield
Onesmoor
Agden Resr
Rectory
Old Horns Inn
Castle Hill
Castle Bents
Convent of the Holy Ghost
Prospect Farm
Kirk Edge House
KIRK EDGE RD
Bradfield
WOOD FALL LA
Watt House
Kirk Bridge
S6
BURNIT HILL LA
THE SANDS
WINDY BANK
FAIR HOUSE LA
ANNET LA
PO
Low Bradfield
Primrose Cottage Farm
Nether House Farm
SMITHY BRIDGE RD
Mill Farm
DALE CROFT
GLEBE CT
Peck Hall
PECK HALL LA
LOXLEY RD
Cliffe House Farm
New Lathes
PLUMPTON LA
LAMB HILL
MOOR RD
Plough Inn
MILL LEE RD
Dyson House
Matley
TROUBLE WOOD LA
HOLDWORTH LA
MILL LEE LA
Holdworth Hall
Firs Hill
STONY LA
Holdworth
MYERS LA
DALROYD LA
Fox Holes
Ben Greave
New Wood
NEW RD
HOAR STONES RD
Withamly House
HOLLIN HOUSE LA
BACK LA
Holdworth House Farm
Damflask Resr
Hollin House Farm
B6076
B6077
LOXLEY RD
Oaks Farm
Nursery
Ughill Height
Woodhouse
OAKS LA
Nag's Head (PH)
WEST LA
Low Woodhouse Farm
NEW RD
STACEY LA
Stacey Bank
Wood Side Farm
BRIERS HOUSE LA
Briers House
River Loxley
Rickett Bank
Bradfield Dungworth Prim Sch
Ughill Brook
Rickett Field
Broom Vale
BRIERS HOUSE LA
MAIN RD
DUNGWORTH GN
SIDLING HOLLOW
CORKER LA
Dungworth

109
126

93
112

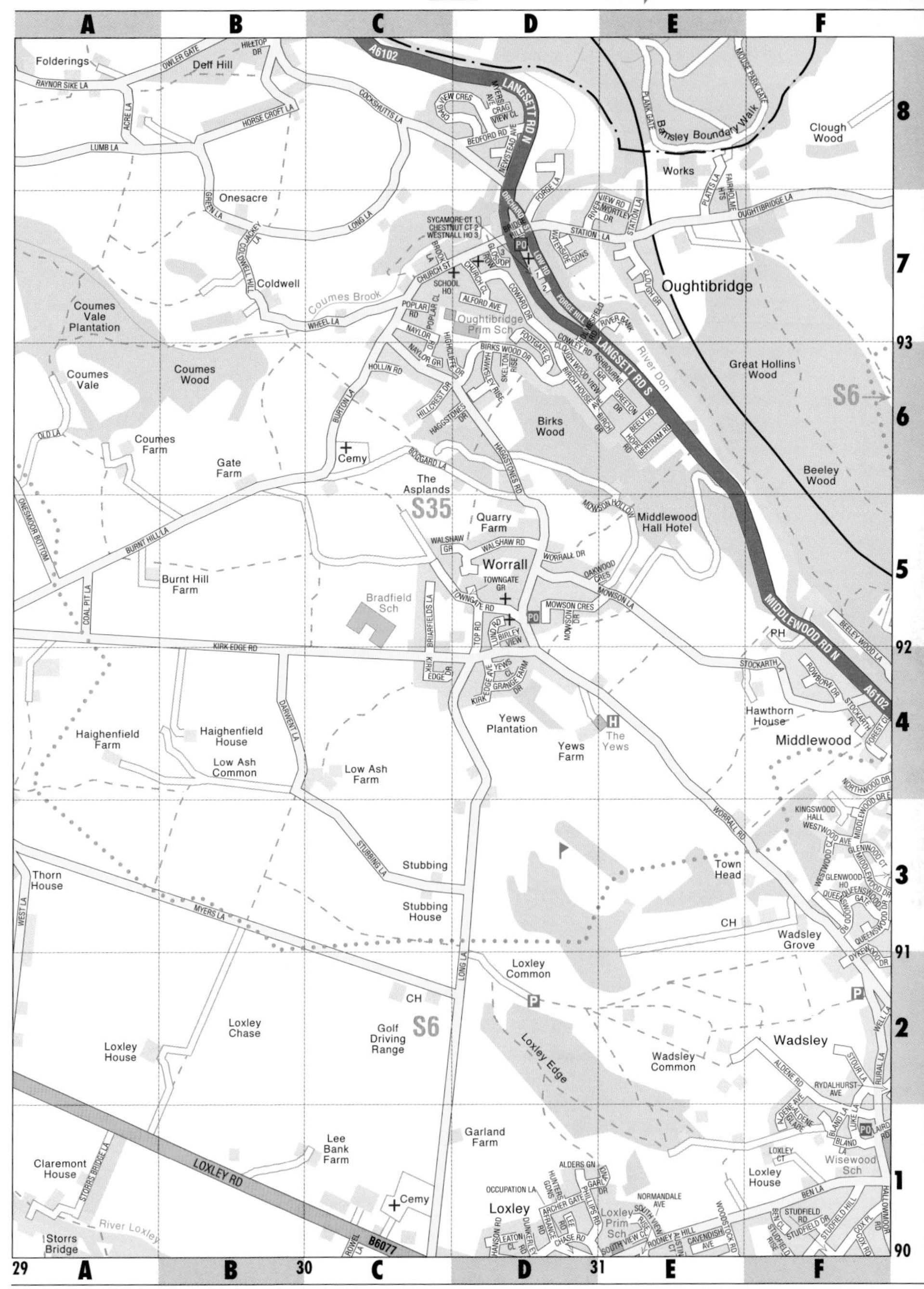
A
B
C
D
E
F
8
7
93
6
5
92
4
3
91
2
1
90
29
30
31
A6102
Folderings
Deff Hill
HILLTOP DR
OWLER GATE
RAYNOR SIKE LA
ACRE LA
HORSE CROFT LA
COCKSHUTTS LA
LUMB LA
LANGSETT RD N
CRAG VIEW CRES
MYERS AVE
CRAG VIEW CL
BEDFORD RD
NEWSTEAD AVE
MOUSE PARK GATE
PLANK GATE
Barnsley Boundary Walk
Clough Wood
Works
Onesacre
GREEN LA
LONG LA
FORGE LA
ORCHARD ST
SYCAMORE CT 1
CHESTNUT CT 2
WESTNALL HO 3
BRIDGE HILL
PO
STATION LA
RIVER VIEW RD
WORTLEY DR
STATION LA
PLATTS LA
FAIRHOLME HTS
OUGHTIBRIDGE LA
JACKEY LA
COLDWELL HILL
Coldwell
CHURCH ST
BROOK LA
SCHOOL HO
CHURCH CL
LOW RD
WATERSIDE GDNS
CLOUGH GR
Oughtibridge
Coumes Vale Plantation
Coumes Brook
WHEEL LA
POPLAR RD
POPLAR CL
ALFORD AVE
COWARD DR
FORGE HILL
RIVER BANK
Oughtibridge Prim Sch
NAYLOR RD
NAYLOR GR
HIGHCLIFFE DR
BIRKS WOOD DR
FOOTGATE CL
COWLEY RD
ASHBOURNE RD
LANGSETT RD S
River Don
Great Hollins Wood
Coumes Vale
Coumes Wood
HOLLIN RD
BURTON LA
HILLCREST DR
HAWKSLEY RISE
SKELTON RISE
CLOUGH WOOD VIEW
BIRCH HOUSE AVE
GREETON DR
BIRCH DR
BEELY RD
BERTRAM RD
HOPE RD
S6
OLD LA
Coumes Farm
HAGGSTONES DR
Birks Wood
Gate Farm
Cemy
BOGGARD LA
The Asplands
HAGGSTONES RD
Beeley Wood
ONESMOOR BOTTOM
S35
MOWSON HOLLOW
Quarry Farm
Middlewood Hall Hotel
BURNT HILL LA
WALSHAW GR
WALSHAW RD
WORRALL DR
Worrall
OAKWOOD CRES
Burnt Hill Farm
COAL PIT LA
TOWNGATE GR
Bradfield Sch
BRIARFIELDS LA
TOWNGATE RD
MOWSON CRES
MOWSON DR
MOWSON LA
MIDDLEWOOD RD N
TOP RD
LUND RD
BIRLEY VIEW
PH
BEELEY WOOD LA
KIRK EDGE RD
KIRK EDGE DR
KIRK EDGE AVE
YEWS CL
GRANGE FARM DR
STOCKARTH LA
ROWBORN DR
STOCKARTH PL
A6102
DARWENT LA
Yews Plantation
The Yews
Yews Farm
Hawthorn House
Middlewood
FOREST CL
Haighenfield Farm
Haighenfield House
Low Ash Common
Low Ash Farm
NORTHWOOD DR
WORRALL RD
KINGSWOOD HALL
WESTWOOD AVE
MIDDLEWOOD DR E
WESTWOOD CL
GLENWOOD CT
GLENWOOD HO
Thorn House
STUBBING LA
Stubbing
Town Head
QUEENSWOOD GATE
QUEENSWOOD DR
WEST LA
MYERS LA
Stubbing House
CH
Wadsley Grove
DYKES HALL RD
LONG LA
Loxley Common
CH
P
Loxley Chase
Golf Driving Range
S6
Loxley Edge
Wadsley
WELL LA
Loxley House
Wadsley Common
STOUR LA
RURAL LA
ALDENE RD
RYDALHURST AVE
ALDENE GLADE
BLAND LA
LUKE LA
LAIRD RD
PO
Lee Bank Farm
Garland Farm
LOXLEY RD
ALDERS GN
Claremont House
STORRS BRIDGE LA
OCCUPATION LA
HUNTERS GDNS
ARCHER GATE
PHILLIPS RD
NORMANDALE AVE
LOXLEY CT
Loxley House
Wisewood Sch
BEN LA
Cemy
Loxley
Loxley Prim Sch
SOUTH VIEW RD
WOODSTOCK RD
STUDFIELD RD
STUDFIELD DR
STUDFIELD HILL
COX PL
COX RD
HALLOWMOOR RD
River Loxley
Storrs Bridge
ROWEL LA
B6077
HANSON RD
LEATON CL
DUNKELD RD
FRANCE RD
LEE RD
CHASE RD
SOUTH VIEW CL
ROONEY RD
AUSTIN CL
CAVENDISH AVE
BEN CL
STUDFIELD RISE

127
112

111

94

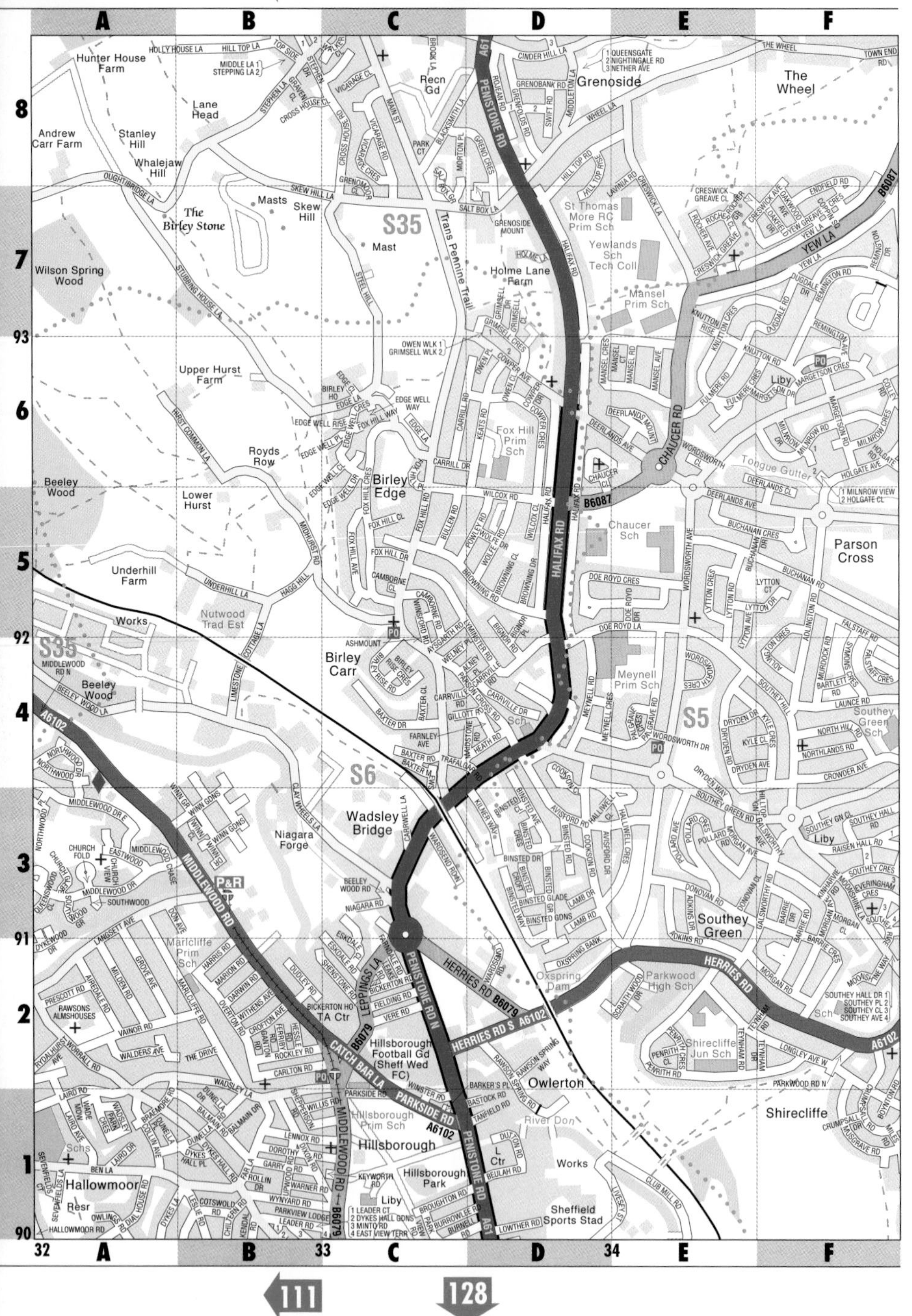

A
B
C
D
E
F
8
7
6
5
4
3
2
1
93
92
91
90
32
33
34
Hunter House Farm
Lane Head
Andrew Carr Farm
Stanley Hill
Whalejaw Hill
The Birley Stone
Masts
Skew Hill
S35
Mast
Trans Pennine Trail
Recn Gd
Grenoside
The Wheel
St Thomas More RC Prim Sch
Yewlands Sch Tech Coll
Holme Lane Farm
Mansel Prim Sch
Wilson Spring Wood
Upper Hurst Farm
Royds Row
Lower Hurst
Beeley Wood
Birley Edge
Fox Hill Prim Sch
Liby
Tongue Gutter
Chaucer Sch
Parson Cross
Underhill Farm
Nutwood Trad Est
Works
Birley Carr
Meynell Prim Sch
S5
Southey Green Sch
S6
Wadsley Bridge
Niagara Forge
Marlcliffe Prim Sch
Southey Green
Oxspring Dam
Parkwood High Sch
Shirecliffe Jun Sch
Rawsons Almshouses
TA Ctr
Hillsborough Football Gd (Sheff Wed FC)
Owlerton
Shirecliffe
Hillsborough Prim Sch
River Don
Hillsborough
Hillsborough Park
L Ctr
Works
Hallowmoor
Resr
Schs
Sheffield Sports Stad
A61
PENISTONE RD
HALIFAX RD
B6087
YEW LA
CHAUCER RD
A6102
MIDDLEWOOD RD
HERRIES RD
B6079
HERRIES RD S
PENISTONE RD N
CATCH BAR LA
PARKSIDE RD
LEPPINGS LA
P&R

111

128

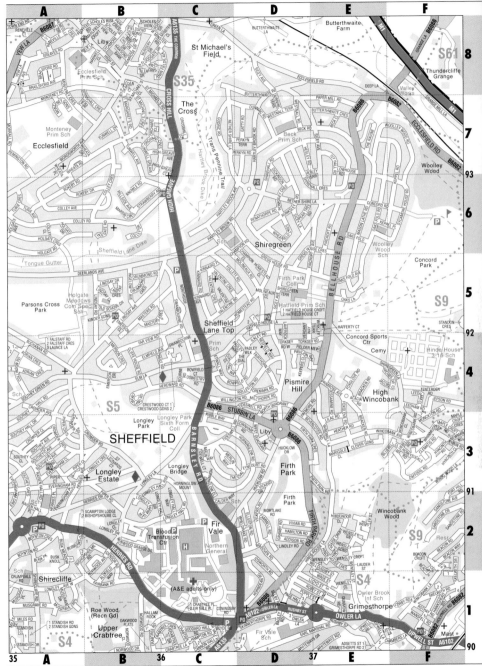

D1
1 BOLSOVER RD E
2 HEATHCOTE ST
3 BRATHAY ST
4 EARL MARSHAL CL
5 EARL MARSHAL DR
6 WHITEWAYS RD

F1
1 FARCROFT GR
2 SKELWITH CL
3 BRATHAY CL
4 BRATHAY RD
5 BIRDWELL RD
6 SOUTHWELL RD
7 CARLISLE ST E
8 WINCO RD
9 Carlisle Bsns Pk

113
96

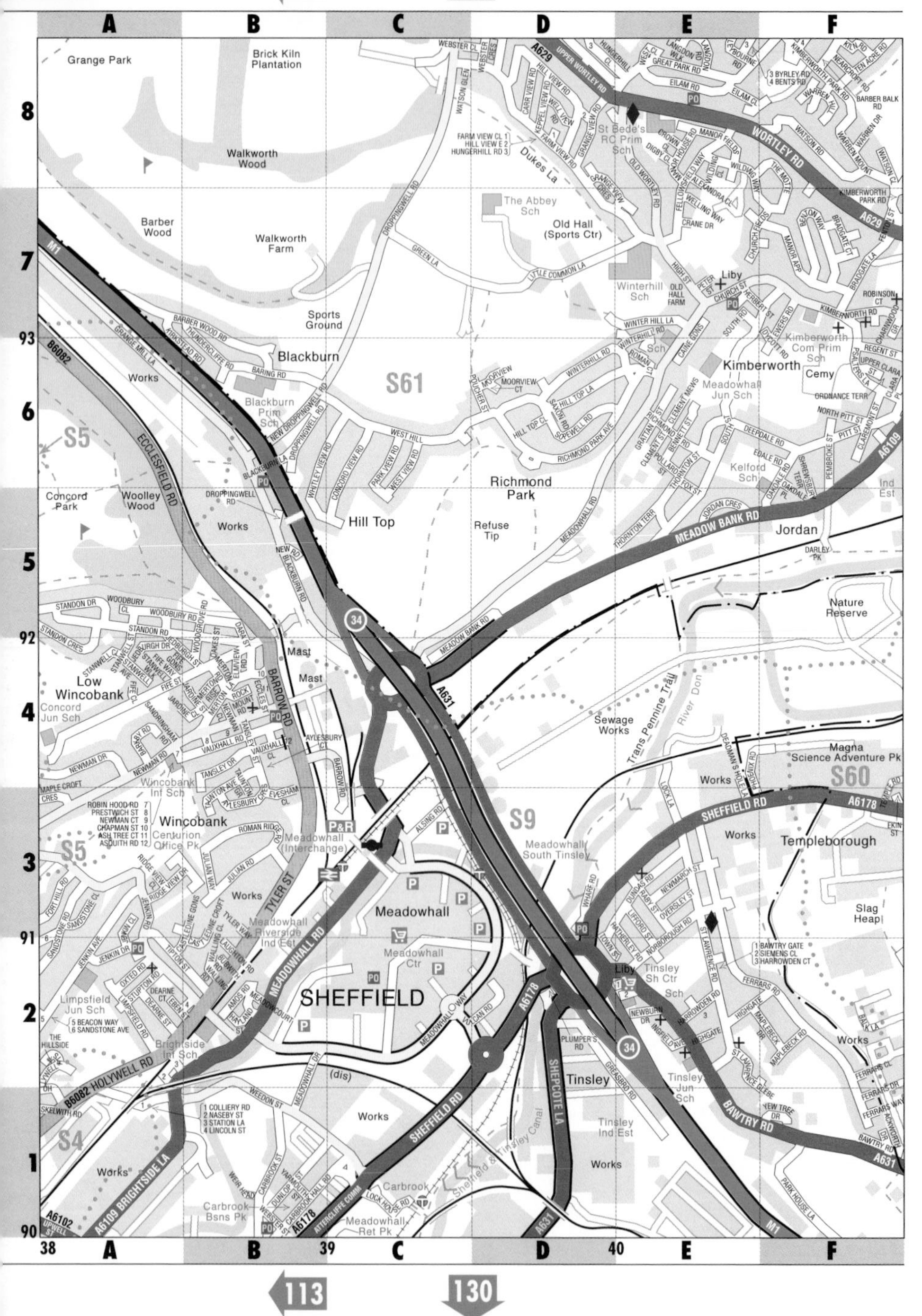
Grange Park
Brick Kiln Plantation
Walkworth Wood
Barber Wood
Walkworth Farm
The Abbey Sch
Old Hall (Sports Ctr)
St Bede's RC Prim Sch
Dukes La
Winterhill Sch
Sports Ground
Blackburn
S61
Blackburn Prim Sch
Kimberworth
Meadowhall Jun Sch
Kimberworth Com Prim Sch
Cemy
Kelford Sch
S5
Concord Park
Woolley Wood
Works
Hill Top
Richmond Park
Refuse Tip
Jordan
MEADOW BANK RD
Nature Reserve
Mast
Low Wincobank
Concord Jun Sch
Sewage Works
Trans Pennine Trail
River Don
Magna Science Adventure Pk
S60
SHEFFIELD RD
Templeborough
Wincobank Inf Sch
Wincobank
Centurion Office Pk
Meadowhall (Interchange)
S9
Meadowhall South Tinsley
Meadowhall
Meadowhall Riverside Ind Est
Meadowhall Ctr
Slag Heap
Limpsfield Jun Sch
SHEFFIELD
Tinsley Sh Ctr
Tinsley
Tinsley Jun Sch
Brightside Inf Sch
HOLYWELL RD
S4
Tinsley Ind Est
BAWTRY RD
Carbrook
Carbrook Bsns Pk
Meadowhall Ret Pk
SHEPCOTE LA
BRIGHTSIDE LA
M1
A631
A6178
A6109
A629
B6082

113
130

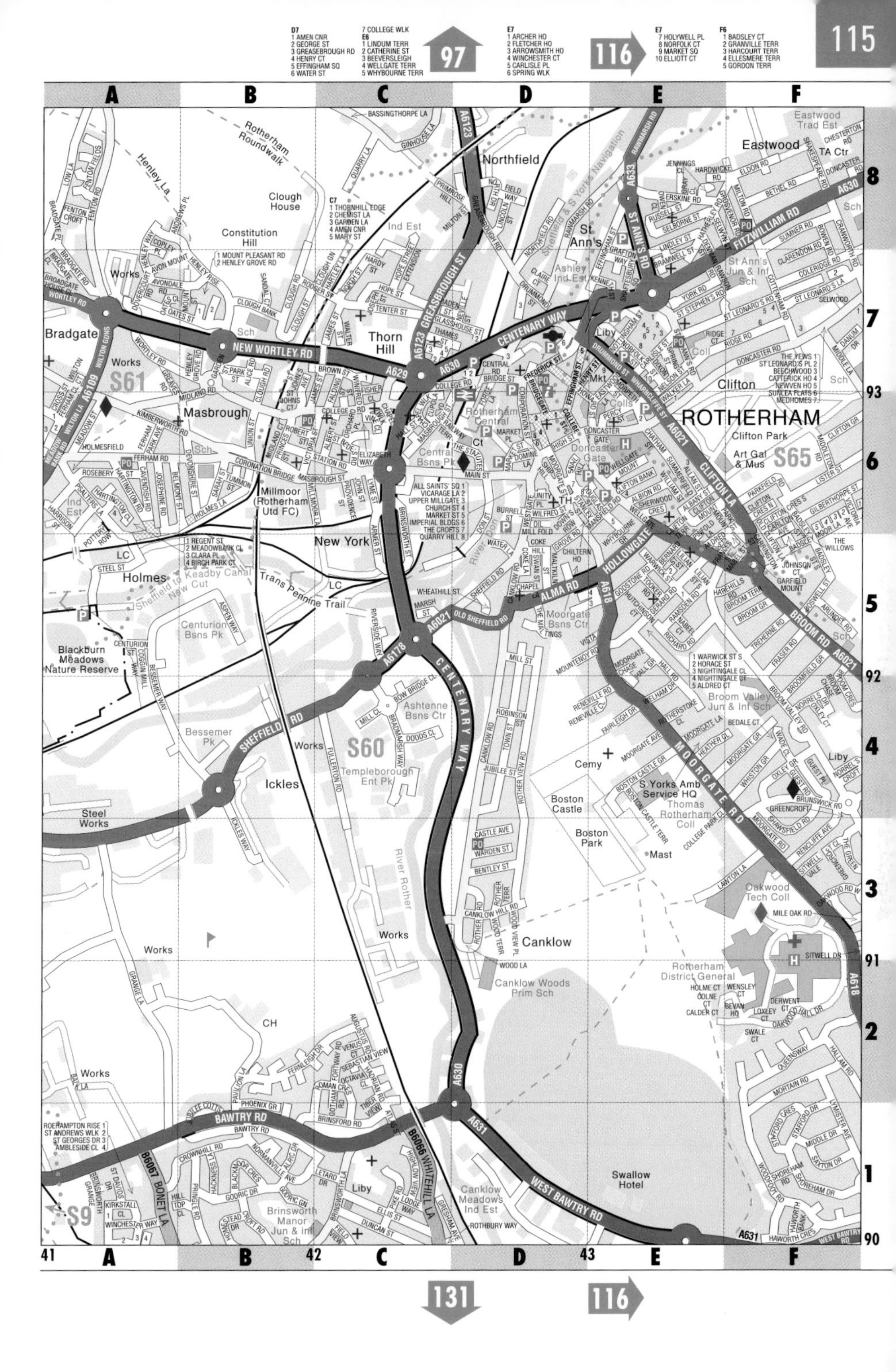
D7
1 AMEN CNR
2 GEORGE ST
3 GREASEBROUGH RD
4 HENRY CT
5 EFFINGHAM SQ
6 WATER ST
7 COLLEGE WLK
E6
1 LINDUM TERR
2 CATHERINE ST
3 BEEVERSLEIGH
4 WELLGATE TERR
5 WHYBOURNE TERR
97
E7
1 ARCHER HO
2 FLETCHER HO
3 ARROWSMITH HO
4 WINCHESTER CT
5 CARLISLE PL
6 SPRING WLK
116
E7
7 HOLYWELL PL
8 NORFOLK CT
9 MARKET SQ
10 ELLIOTT CT
F6
1 BADSLEY CT
2 GRANVILLE TERR
3 HARCOURT TERR
4 ELLESMERE TERR
5 GORDON TERR
A
B
C
D
E
F
Rotherham Roundwalk
Henley La
Clough House
Constitution Hill
Northfield
Eastwood Trad Est
Eastwood
TA Ctr
St Ann's
Ashley Ind Est
St Ann's Jun & Inf Sch
C7
1 THORNHILL EDGE
2 CHEMIST LA
3 GARDEN LA
4 AMEN CNR
5 MARY ST
1 MOUNT PLEASANT RD
2 HENLEY GROVE RD
Ind Est
Bradgate
Works
S61
Thorn Hill
NEW WORTLEY RD
CENTENARY WAY
FITZWILLIAM RD
Masbrough
Rotherham Central
Clifton
ROTHERHAM
Clifton Park
Art Gal & Mus
S65
Doncaster Gate
Mkt
Colls
Coll
Central Bsns Pk
Millmoor (Rotherham Utd FC)
ALL SAINTS' SQ 1
VICARAGE LA 2
UPPER MILLGATE 3
CHURCH ST 4
MARKET ST 5
IMPERIAL BLDGS 6
THE CROFTS 7
QUARRY HILL 8
THE YEWS 1
ST LEONARD'S PL 2
BEECHWOOD 3
CATTERICK HO 4
NEWVEN HO 5
SUNLEA FLATS 6
MEDHOMES 7
Holmes
1 REGENT ST
2 MEADOWBANK CL
3 CLARA PL
4 BIRCH PARK CT
New York
Sheffield to Keadby Canal
New Cut
Trans Pennine Trail
River Don
HOLLOWGATE
Moorgate Bsns Ctr
Centurion Bsns Pk
Blackburn Meadows Nature Reserve
1 WARWICK ST S
2 HORACE ST
3 NIGHTINGALE CL
4 NIGHTINGALE CT
5 ALDRED CT
Broom Valley Jun & Inf Sch
Ashtenne Bsns Ctr
S60
Templeborough Ent Pk
Bessemer Pk
SHEFFIELD RD
Works
Ickles
Cemy
Boston Castle
Boston Park
S Yorks Amb Service HQ
Thomas Rotherham Coll
Mast
MOORGATE RD
CENTENARY WAY
Steel Works
River Rother
Oakwood Tech Coll
Works
Canklow
Rotherham District General
Canklow Woods Prim Sch
CH
Works
BAWTRY RD
WEST BAWTRY RD
Swallow Hotel
ROEHAMPTON RISE 1
ST ANDREWS WLK 2
ST GEORGES DR 3
AMBLESIDE CL 4
S9
Liby
Brinsworth Manor Jun & Inf Sch
Canklow Meadows Ind Est
B6067 BONET LA
B6066 WHITEHILL LA
8
7
93
6
5
92
4
3
91
2
1
90
41
42
43
131
116

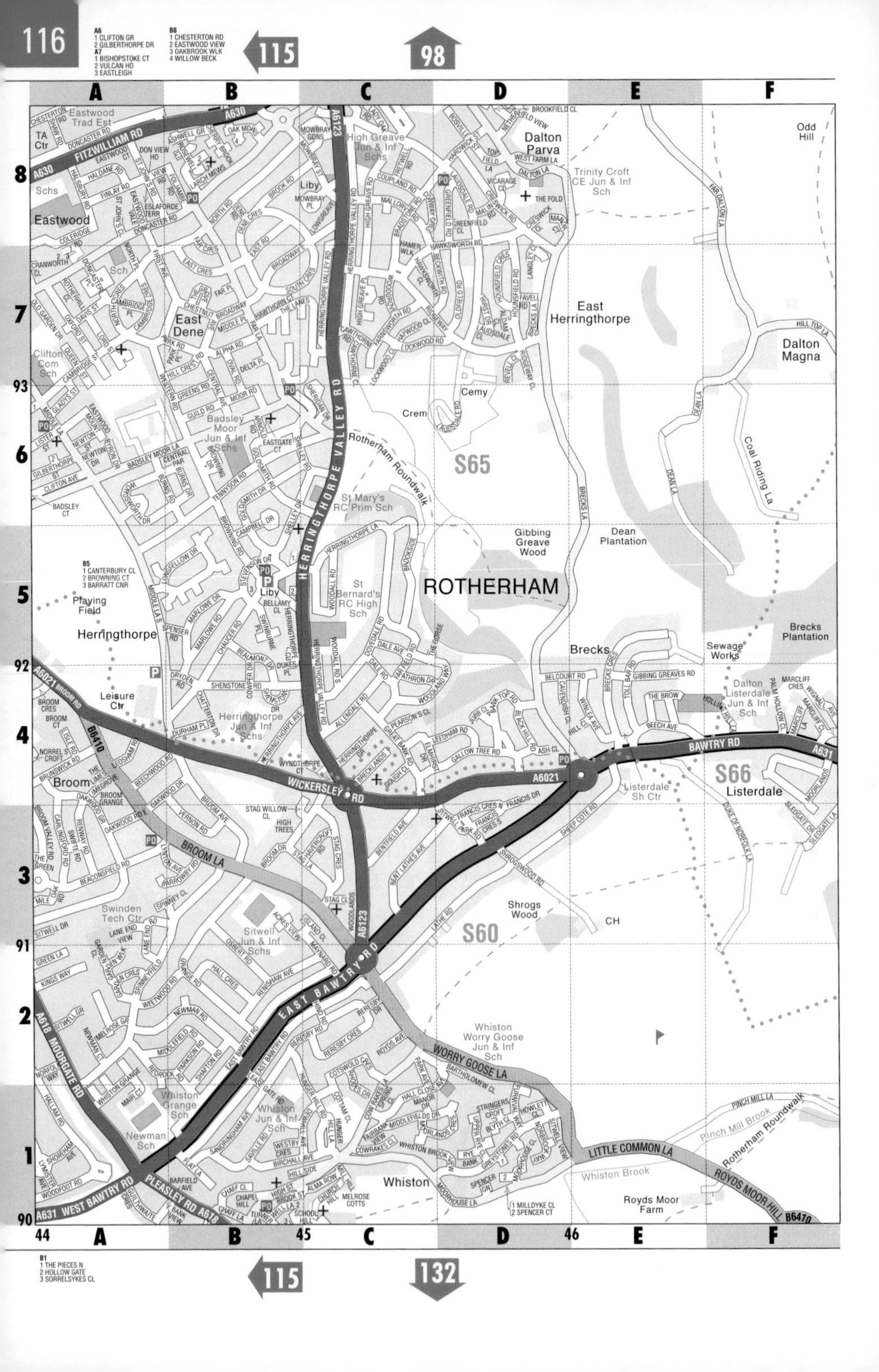

116
A6
1 CLIFTON GR
2 GILBERTHORPE DR
A7
1 BISHOPSTOKE CT
2 VULCAN HO
3 EASTLEIGH
B8
1 CHESTERTON RD
2 EASTWOOD VIEW
3 OAKBROOK WLK
4 WILLOW BECK
115
98
A B C D E F
Eastwood Trad Est
TA Ctr
FITZWILLIAM RD
A630
A6123
High Greave Jun & Inf Schs
Dalton Parva
Trinity Croft CE Jun & Inf Sch
Odd Hill
Schs
Eastwood
Liby
THE FOLD
FAR DALTON LA
Sch
East Dene
East Herringthorpe
HILL TOP LA
Dalton Magna
Clifton Com Sch
Cemy
Crem
Rotherham Roundwalk
S65
Coal Riding La
DEAN LA
HERRINGTHORPE VALLEY RD
Badsley Moor Jun & Inf Schs
St Mary's RC Prim Sch
Gibbing Greave Wood
Dean Plantation
BRECKS LA
B5
1 CANTERBURY CL
2 BROWNING CT
3 BARRATT CNR
Playing Field
Liby
St Bernard's RC High Sch
ROTHERHAM
Herringthorpe
Brecks
Sewage Works
Brecks Plantation
A6021 BROOM RD
Leisure Ctr
Herringthorpe Jun & Inf Schs
Dalton Listerdale Jun & Inf Sch
BAWTRY RD
A631
B6410
Broom
WICKERSLEY RD
A6021
Listerdale Sh Ctr
S66
Listerdale
BROOM LA
DUKE OF NORFOLK LA
Swinden Tech Ctr
Sitwell Jun & Inf Schs
Shrogs Wood
CH
S60
EAST BAWTRY RD
A618 MOORGATE RD
Whiston Worry Goose Jun & Inf Sch
WORRY GOOSE LA
Whiston Grange Sch
Whiston Jun & Inf Sch
Newman Sch
Pinch Mill Brook
Rotherham Roundwalk
LITTLE COMMON LA
Whiston Brook
A631 WEST BAWTRY RD
PLEASLEY RD A618
Whiston
1 MILLDYKE CL
2 SPENCER CT
Royds Moor Farm
ROYDS MOOR HILL
B6470
8 7 93 6 5 92 4 3 91 2 1 90
44 A B 45 C D 46 E F
B1
1 THE PIECES N
2 HOLLOW GATE
3 SORRELSYKES CL
115
132

99
118

A B C D E F

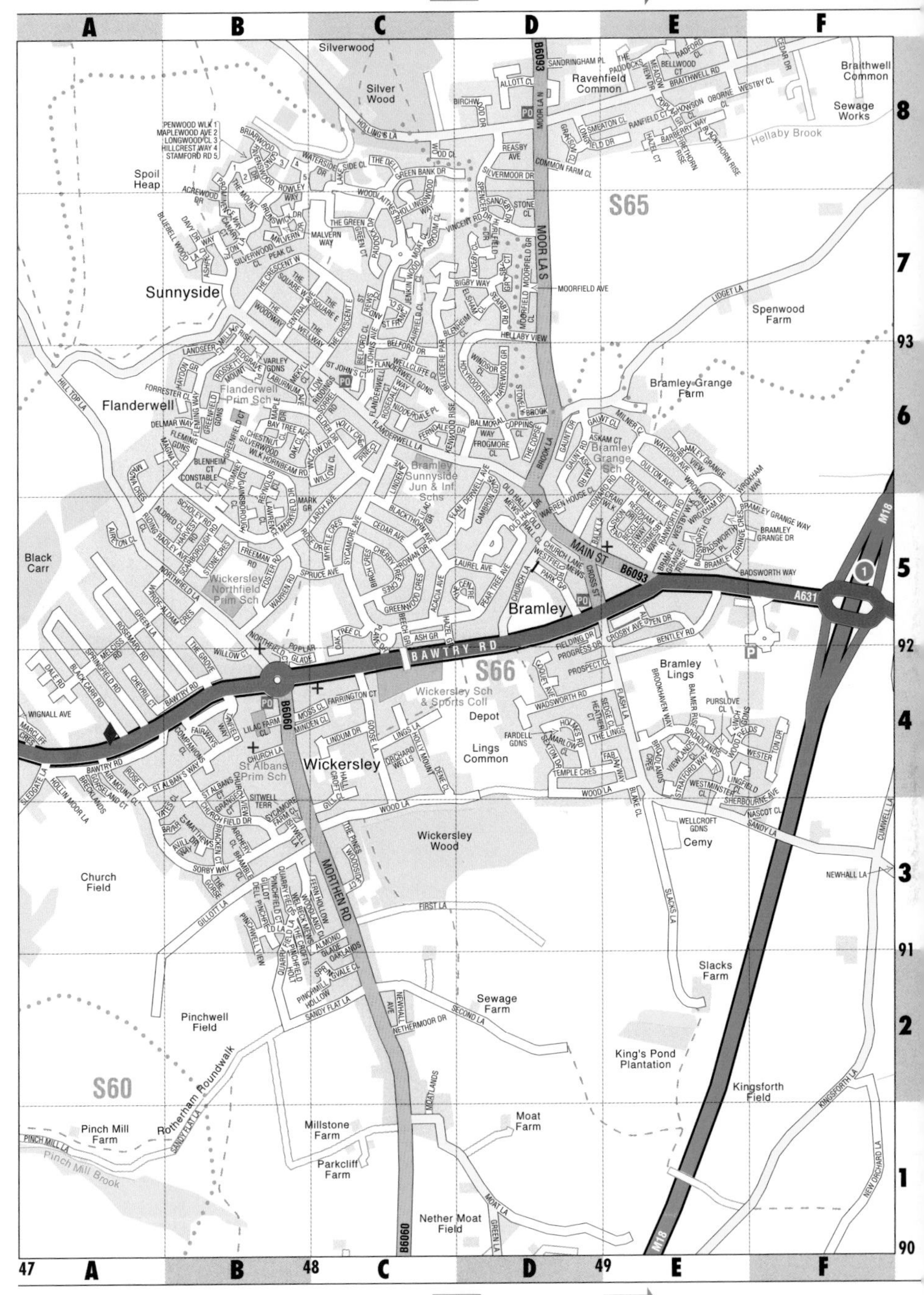
Silverwood
Silver Wood
Ravenfield Common
Braithwell Common
Sewage Works
Hellaby Brook
Spoil Heap
S65
Sunnyside
Spenwood Farm
MOOR LA S
B6093
Flanderwell
Flanderwell Prim Sch
Bramley Grange Farm
Bramley Grange Sch
Bramley Sunnyside Jun & Inf Schs
MAIN ST
Black Carr
Wickersley Northfield Prim Sch
Bramley
A631
M18
BAWTRY RD
S66
Bramley Lings
Wickersley Sch & Sports Coll
Depot
Lings Common
Wickersley
St Albans Prim Sch
B6060
Wickersley Wood
Cemy
Church Field
MORTHEN RD
Slacks Farm
Pinchwell Field
Sewage Farm
King's Pond Plantation
S60
Rotherham Roundwalk
Kingsforth Field
Pinch Mill Farm
Millstone Farm
Moat Farm
Parkcliff Farm
Pinch Mill Brook
Nether Moat Field
8
7
93
6
5
92
4
3
91
2
1
90
47
48
49

A B C D E F

133
118

117

100

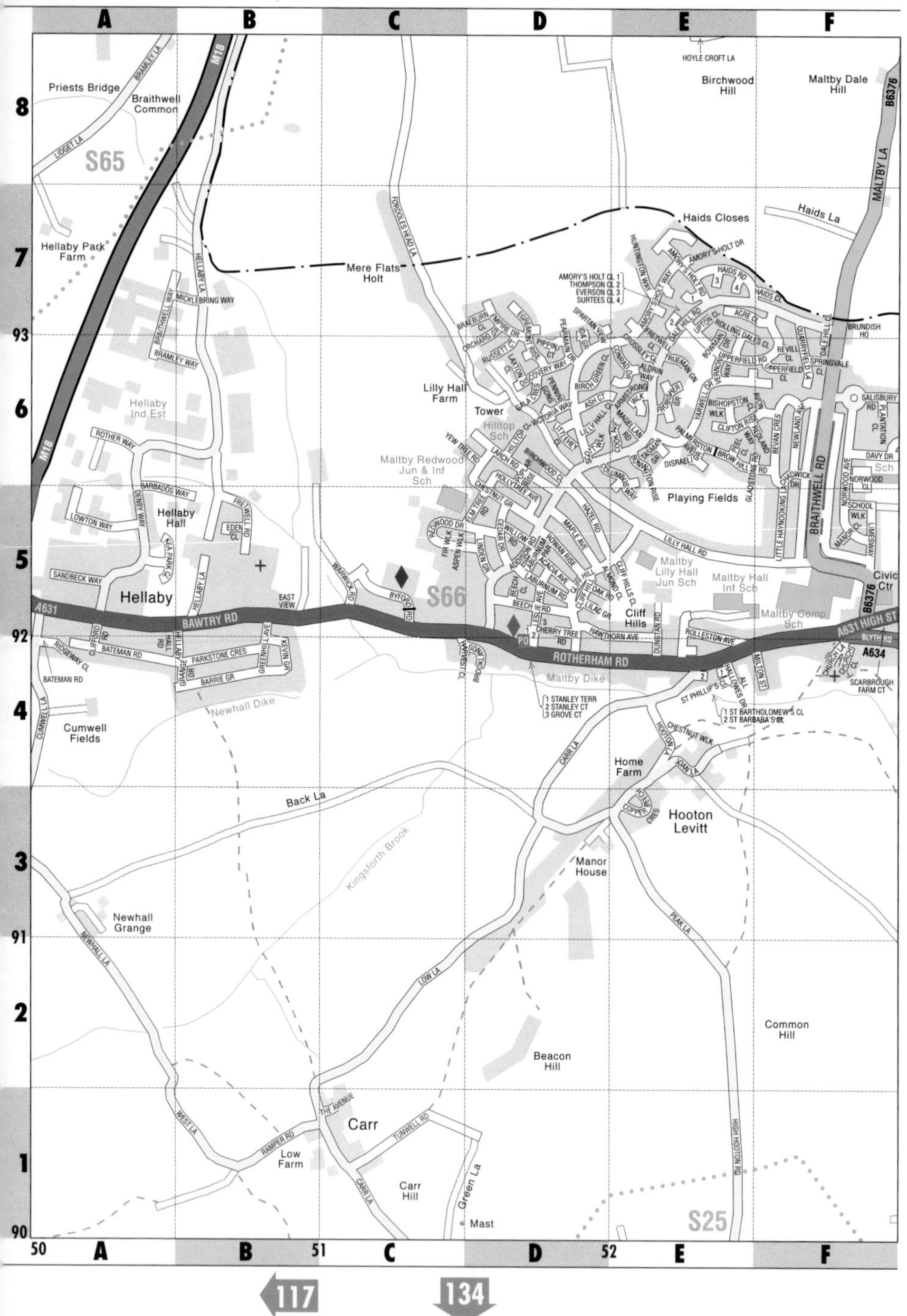

A
B
C
D
E
F
8
7
93
6
5
92
4
3
91
2
1
90
50
51
52
HOYLE CROFT LA
Priests Bridge
BRAMLEY LA
Braithwell Common
M18
Birchwood Hill
Maltby Dale Hill
B6376
LIDGET LA
S65
MALTBY LA
Haids La
Haids Closes
FORDOLES HEAD LA
Hellaby Park Farm
HELLABY LA
Mere Flats Holt
AMORY'S HOLT DR
AMORY'S HOLT CL 1
THOMPSON CL 2
EVERSON CL 3
SURTEES CL 4
HAIDS RD
HAIDS CL
MICKLEBRING WAY
BRAITHWELL WAY
BRAMLEY WAY
HUNTINGTON WAY
BRAEBURN CL
ORCHARD CR
EMPIRE DR
RUSSETT CL
PIPPIN CT
LAXTON CL
DISCOVERY WAY
PEARMAIN DR
SPARTAN VIEW
CONRAD DR
CROSSLEY CL
ALDRIN WAY
TRUEMAN GN
DALE HILL RD
UPTON CL
ACRE CL
ROLLING DALES CL
QUARRYFIELD LA
DALE HILL CL
BRUNDISH HO
UPPERFIELD RD
UPPERFIELD CL
REVILL CL
SPRINGVALE
Lilly Hall Farm
Tower
Hilltop Sch
Hellaby Ind Est
ROTHER WAY
GALA CRES
VICTORIA WAY
BIRCH GREEN CL
ASH CT
ARMSTRONG
LILLY HALL CL
MAGELLAN RD
COOK AVE
FROBISHER GR
YARWELL DR
BISHOPSTON WLK
CLIFTON RISE
SALISBURY RD
PLANTATION CL
YEW TREE RD
LARCH RD
HILLTOP CL
BIRCHWOOD CL
TASMAN GR
PALMERSTON AVE
DISRAELI GR
BROW HALL RD
BEVAN CRES
NEWLAND AVE
GLADSTONE RD
DAVY DR
Sch
Maltby Redwood Jun & Inf Sch
HOLLYTREE AVE
CHESTNUT GR
BONNINGTON RISE
COLUMBUS WAY
Playing Fields
CHADWICK DR
NORWOOD AVE
NORWOOD CL
BARBADOS WAY
LOWTON WAY
DENBY WAY
Hellaby Hall
FREYWELL RD
EDEN CL
ELM TREE RD
REDWOOD DR
FIR WLK
ASPEN WLK
CEDAR DR
WILLOW RD
MAPLE AVE
HAZEL RD
LITTLE HAYNOOKING LA
BRAITHWELL RD
SCHOOL WLK
MANOR CL
LIMESWAY
LEA PARK CL
LILLY HALL RD
5
SANDBECK WAY
Hellaby
EAST VIEW
WARWICK RD
LINDEN GR
ADDISON RD
ROWAN RISE
ACACIA AVE
LABURNUM RD
Maltby Lilly Hall Jun Sch
Maltby Hall Inf Sch
Civic Ctr
B6376
A631
BAWTRY RD
BYFORD RD
S66
BEECH CL
BEECH RD
LESLIE AVE
CLIFF HILL
OAK RD
LILAC GR
ALMOND CL
CLIFF HILLS CL
Cliff Hills
Maltby Comp Sch
A631 HIGH ST
CLIFFORD RD
HALL RD
GREENHILL AVE
KEVIN GR
CHERRY TREE RD
HAWTHORN AVE
DUNSTAN RD
ROLLESTON AVE
BLYTH RD
A634
RIDGEWAY CL
BATEMAN RD
PARKSTONE CRES
HELLABY GRANGE DR
BARRIE GR
HARVEST CL
BROOKLANDS
PO
ROTHERHAM RD
HALLOWES DR
MILTON ST
CHURCH LA
CHURCH CL
SCARBROUGH FARM CT
Maltby Dike
1 STANLEY TERR
2 STANLEY CT
3 GROVE CT
ST PHILLIP'S CL
1 ST BARTHOLOMEW'S CL
2 ST BARBARA'S CL
Newhall Dike
CUMWELL LA
Cumwell Fields
HOOTON LA
CHESTNUT WLK
CARR LA
Home Farm
JOAN LA
COPPER BEECH CRES
Hooton Levitt
Back La
Manor House
Kingsforth Brook
Newhall Grange
PEAK LA
NEWHALL LA
LOW LA
Common Hill
Beacon Hill
WEST LA
THE AVENUE
Carr
TUNWELL RD
RAMPER RD
Low Farm
HIGH HOOTON RD
Green La
CARR LA
Carr Hill
Mast
S25

117
134

101

120

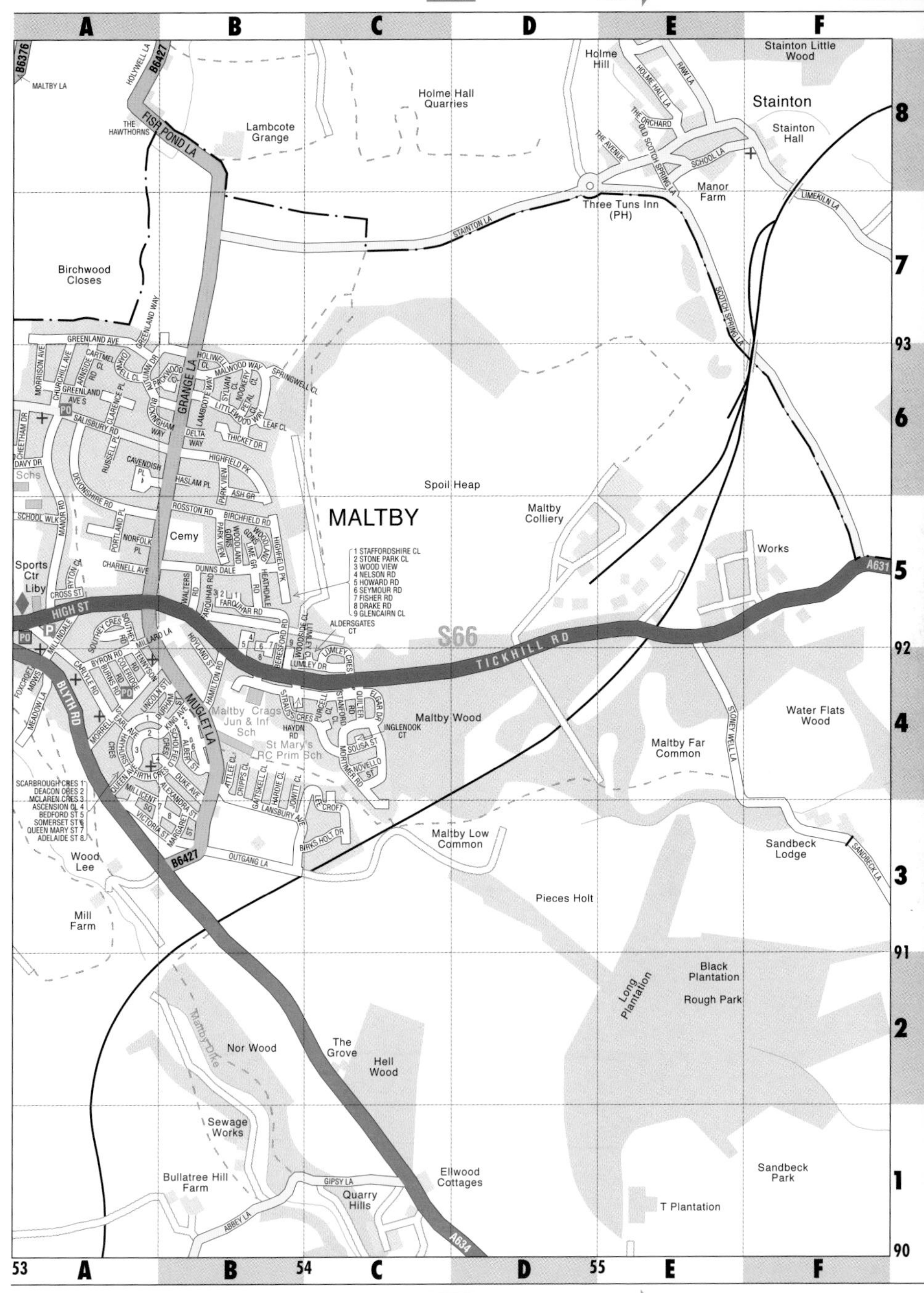

A
B
C
D
E
F
8
7
93
6
5
92
4
3
91
2
1
90
53
54
55
B6376
MALTBY LA
HOLYWELL LA
B6427
THE HAWTHORNS
FISH POND LA
Lambcote Grange
Holme Hall Quarries
Holme Hill
RAW LA
HOLME HALL LA
THE ORCHARD
OLD SCOTCH SPRING LA
THE AVENUE
SCHOOL LA
Stainton Little Wood
Stainton
Stainton Hall
Manor Farm
LIMEKILN LA
Three Tuns Inn (PH)
STAINTON LA
Birchwood Closes
SCOTCH SPRING LA
GREENLAND WAY
GREENLAND AVE
MORRISON AVE
CHURCHILL AVE
ARNSIDE RD
CARTMEL CL
GREENLAND AVE S
HOLIWELL CL
GRANGE LA
AUTUMN DR
PACKWOOD CL
MALWOOD WAY
LAMBCOTE WAY
SYLVAN CL
NOOKERY CL
PETAL CL
SPRINGWELL CL
LITTLEWOOD WAY
LEAF CL
CLARENCE PL
BUCKINGHAM WAY
DELTA WAY
THICKET DR
SALISBURY RD
CHEETHAM DR
DAVY DR
Schs
RUSSELL PL
CAVENDISH PL
HIGHFIELD PK
HASLAM PL
PARK VIEW
ASH GR
DEVONSHIRE RD
Spoil Heap
ROSSTON RD
BIRCHFIELD RD
MALTBY
Maltby Colliery
SCHOOL WLK
MANOR RD
PORTLAND PL
NORFOLK PL
Cemy
WOODLAND GDNS
PARK VIEW
LIME GR
HIGHFIELD RD
HEATHDALE
Works
1 STAFFORDSHIRE CL
2 STONE PARK CL
3 WOOD VIEW
4 NELSON RD
5 HOWARD RD
6 SEYMOUR RD
7 FISHER RD
8 DRAKE RD
9 GLENCAIRN CL
Sports Ctr
Liby
CHARNELL AVE
DUNNS DALE
RYTON CL
CROSS ST
WALTERS RD
FARQUHAR RD
A631
HIGH ST
PO
P
MILLINDALE
SOUTHEY CRES
SOUTHEY RD
MILLARD LA
HOYLAND ST
BERESFORD RD
WOODSIDE CL
LUMLEY CL
LUMLEY CRES
LUMLEY DR
ALDERSGATES CT
S66
TICKHILL RD
FOXCROFT MDWS
MEADOW LA
BLYTH RD
CARLYLE RD
BYRON RD
BURNS RD
COLERIDGE RD
TENNYSON RD
LINCOLN ST
HAMILTON RD
MUGLET LA
Maltby Crags Jun & Inf Sch
St Mary's RC Prim Sch
STRAUSS CRES
PURCELL CL
STANFORD RD
QUILTER RD
ELGAR DR
HAYDN RD
INGLENOOK CT
Maltby Wood
SOUSA ST
NOVELLO ST
MORTIMER RD
Water Flats Wood
Maltby Far Common
STONEY WELL LA
MORRELL ST
HAWKHURST CRES
QUEEN AVE
FIRTH CRES
KING AVE
SCHOFIELD CRES
ALBERT ST
DUKE AVE
ALEXANDRA ST
MILLICENT SQ
VICTORIA ST
MARGARET ST
SCARBROUGH CRES 1
DEACON CRES 2
MCLAREN CRES 3
ASCENSION CL 4
BEDFORD ST 5
SOMERSET ST 6
QUEEN MARY ST 7
ADELAIDE ST 8
TITLEE CL
CRIPPS CL
GAITSKELL CL
HARDIE CL
JOWITT CL
LANSBURY AVE
LEE CROFT
BIRKS HOLT DR
Maltby Low Common
Sandbeck Lodge
SANDBECK LA
Wood Lee
OUTGANG LA
Pieces Holt
Mill Farm
Long Plantation
Black Plantation
Rough Park
Maltby Dike
Nor Wood
The Grove
Hell Wood
Sewage Works
Bullatree Hill Farm
GIPSY LA
Quarry Hills
Ellwood Cottages
Sandbeck Park
T Plantation
ABBEY LA
A634

135

120

119
102

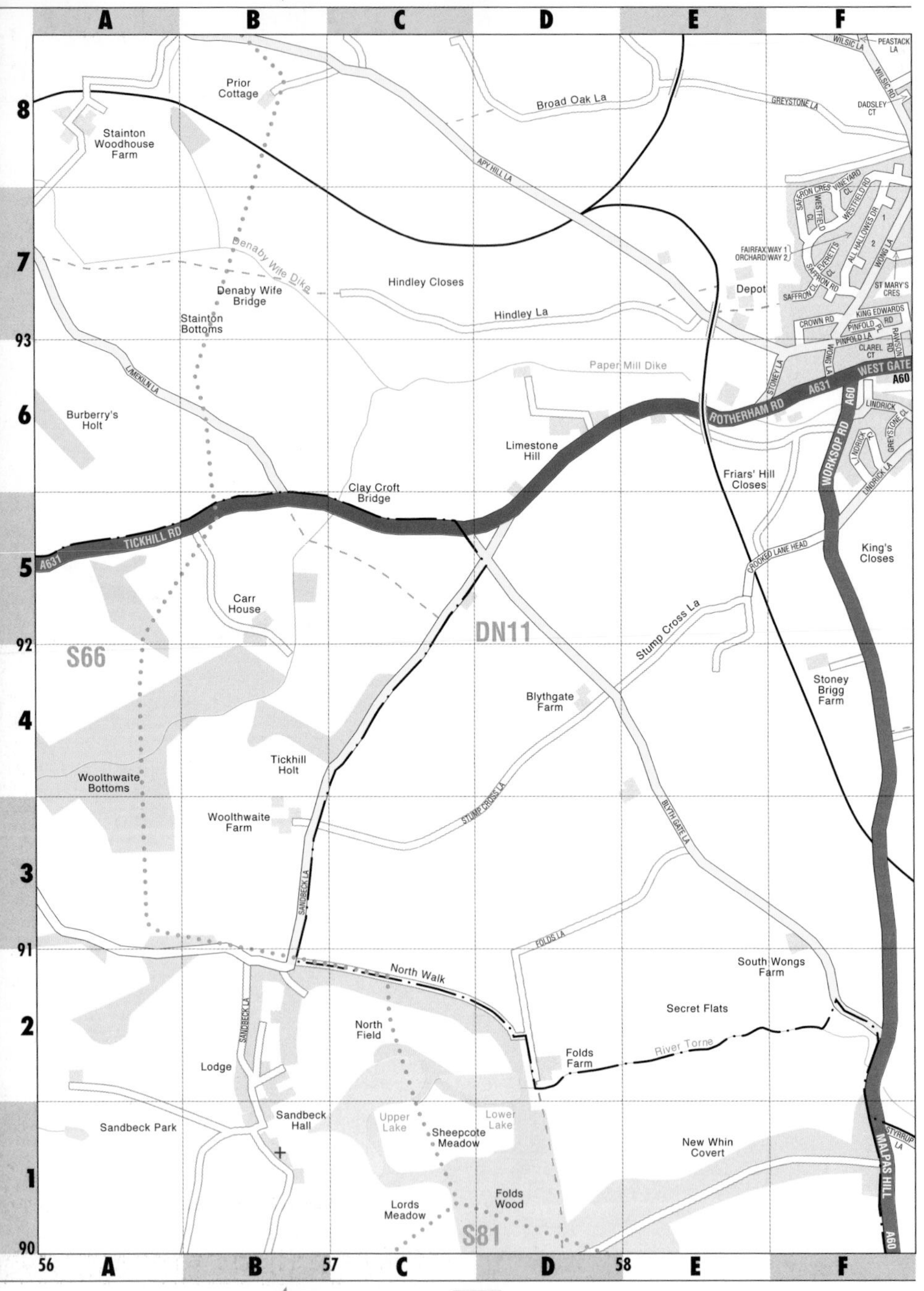
A
B
C
D
E
F
Prior Cottage
Stainton Woodhouse Farm
Broad Oak La
APY HILL LA
GREYSTONE LA
WILSIC LA
PEASTACK LA
DADSLEY CT
Denaby Wife Dike
Denaby Wife Bridge
Stainton Bottoms
Hindley Closes
Hindley La
Depot
FAIRFAX WAY 1
ORCHARD WAY 2
SAFFRON CRES
VINEYARD CL
WESTFIELD RD
ALL HALLOWS DR
ST MARY'S CRES
KING EDWARDS RD
CROWN RD
PINFOLD LA
CLAREL CT
RAWSON RD
STONEY LA
WONG LA
WEST GATE
A60
Paper Mill Dike
LIMEKILN LA
Burberry's Holt
ROTHERHAM RD
A631
Limestone Hill
LINDRICK
GREYSTONE CL
WORKSOP RD
Friars' Hill Closes
Clay Croft Bridge
TICKHILL RD
CROOKED LANE HEAD
King's Closes
Carr House
DN11
Stump Cross La
S66
Stoney Brigg Farm
Blythgate Farm
Tickhill Holt
Woolthwaite Bottoms
Woolthwaite Farm
STUMP CROSS LA
BLYTH GATE LA
SANDBECK LA
FOLDS LA
North Walk
South Wongs Farm
Secret Flats
North Field
River Torne
Folds Farm
Lodge
Sandbeck Hall
Upper Lake
Lower Lake
Sheepcote Meadow
Sandbeck Park
New Whin Covert
STYRRUP LA
MALPAS HILL
Lords Meadow
Folds Wood
S81
8
7
93
6
5
92
4
3
91
2
1
90
56
57
58

119
136

103
122

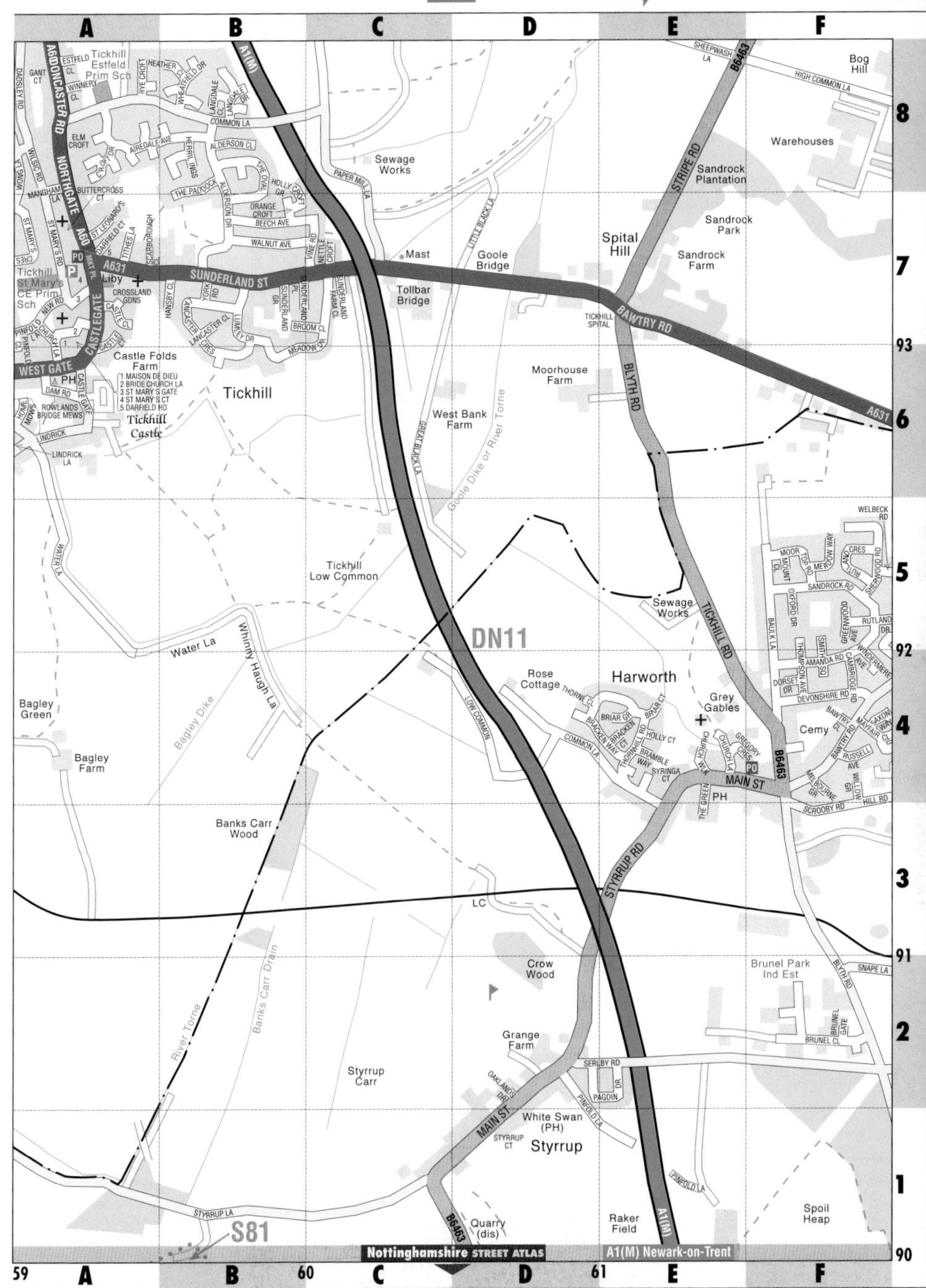
Tickhill
Tickhill Estfeld Prim Sch
Sewage Works
Warehouses
Sandrock Plantation
Sandrock Park
Sandrock Farm
Spital Hill
Goole Bridge
Tollbar Bridge
Mast
Bog Hill
SUNDERLAND ST
BAWTRY RD
STRIPE RD
HIGH COMMON LA
SHEEPWASH LA
NORTHGATE
DONCASTER RD
CASTLEGATE
WEST GATE
COMMON LA
Castle Folds Farm
1 MAISON DE DIEU
2 BRIDE CHURCH LA
3 ST MARY'S GATE
4 ST MARY'S CT
5 DARFIELD HO
Tickhill Castle
Tickhill St Mary's CE Prim Sch
Moorhouse Farm
West Bank Farm
BLYTH RD
Goole Dike or River Torne
Tickhill Low Common
Sewage Works
TICKHILL RD
DN11
Water La
Whinny Haugh La
Rose Cottage
Harworth
Grey Gables
Cemy
Bagley Green
Bagley Farm
Bagley Dike
MAIN ST
Banks Carr Wood
STYRRUP RD
LC
Crow Wood
Brunel Park Ind Est
Grange Farm
SERLBY RD
Styrrup Carr
River Torne
Banks Carr Drain
White Swan (PH)
Styrrup
STYRRUP LA
Quarry (dis)
Raker Field
Spoil Heap
S81
A1(M)
B6463
A631
A60
Nottinghamshire STREET ATLAS
A1(M) Newark-on-Trent
A B C D E F
8 7 93 6 5 92 4 3 91 2 1 90
59 60 61

122

121
104

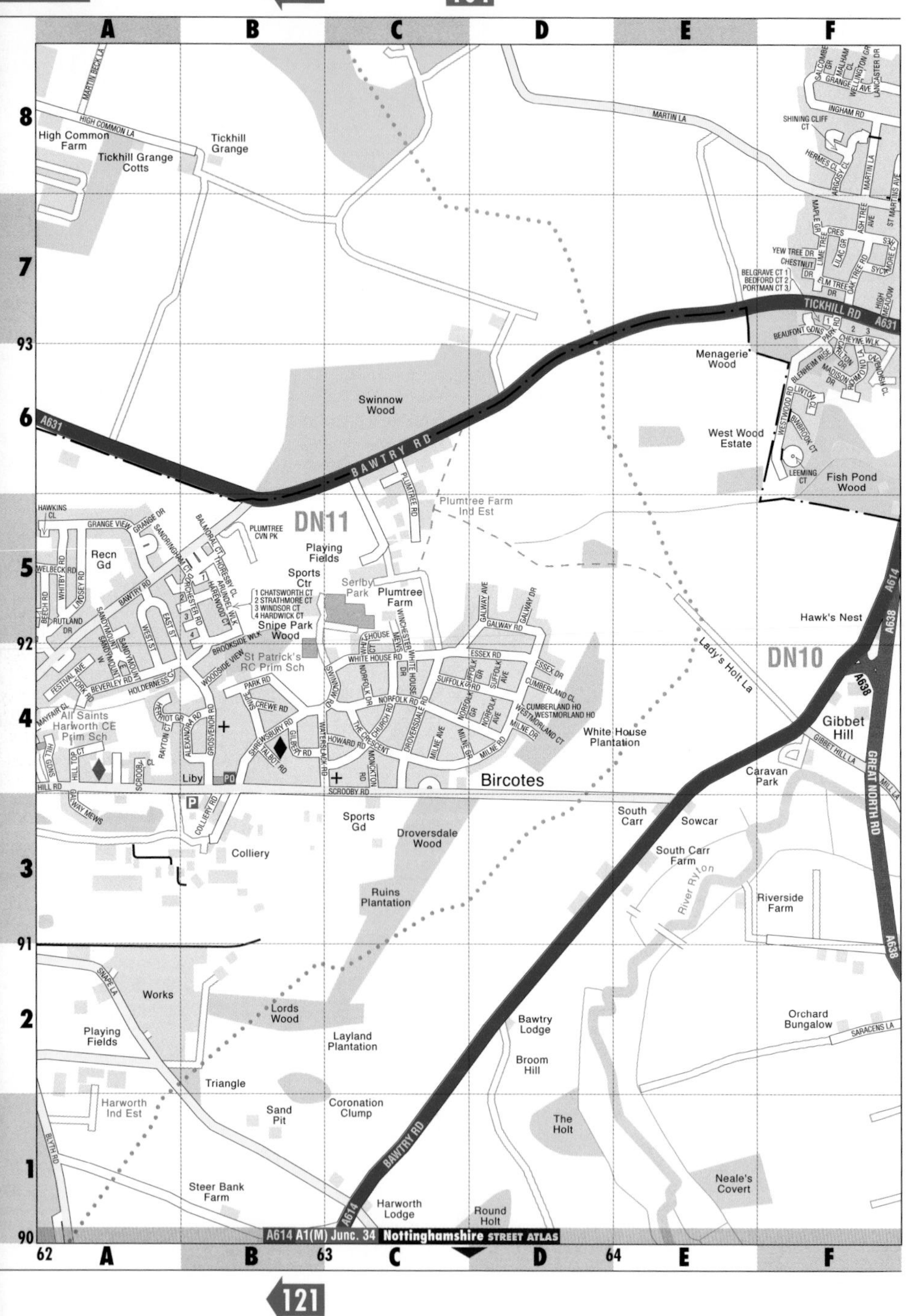
A
B
C
D
E
F
8
7
93
6
5
92
4
3
91
2
1
90
62
63
64
High Common Farm
Tickhill Grange Cotts
Tickhill Grange
HIGH COMMON LA
MARTIN BECK LA
MARTIN LA
Swinnow Wood
BAWTRY RD
A631
TICKHILL RD
Menagerie Wood
West Wood Estate
Fish Pond Wood
DN11
DN10
Playing Fields
Sports Ctr
Serlby Park
Plumtree Farm
Plumtree Farm Ind Est
PLUMTREE CVN PK
Recn Gd
Snipe Park Wood
St Patrick's RC Prim Sch
All Saints Harworth CE Prim Sch
1 CHATSWORTH CT
2 STRATHMORE CT
3 WINDSOR CT
4 HARDWICK CT
Liby
Bircotes
White House Plantation
Lady's Holt La
Hawk's Nest
Gibbet Hill
GIBBET HILL LA
Caravan Park
GREAT NORTH RD
A614
A638
South Carr
Sowcar
South Carr Farm
River Ryton
Riverside Farm
Sports Gd
Droversdale Wood
Colliery
Ruins Plantation
Works
Lords Wood
Playing Fields
Layland Plantation
Bawtry Lodge
Broom Hill
Orchard Bungalow
SARACENS LA
Triangle
Harworth Ind Est
Sand Pit
Coronation Clump
The Holt
Steer Bank Farm
Harworth Lodge
Round Holt
Neale's Covert
BLYTH RD
SNAPE LA
HILL RD
SCROOBY RD
GALWAY MEWS
COLLIERY RD
A614 A1(M) Junc. 34

121

105

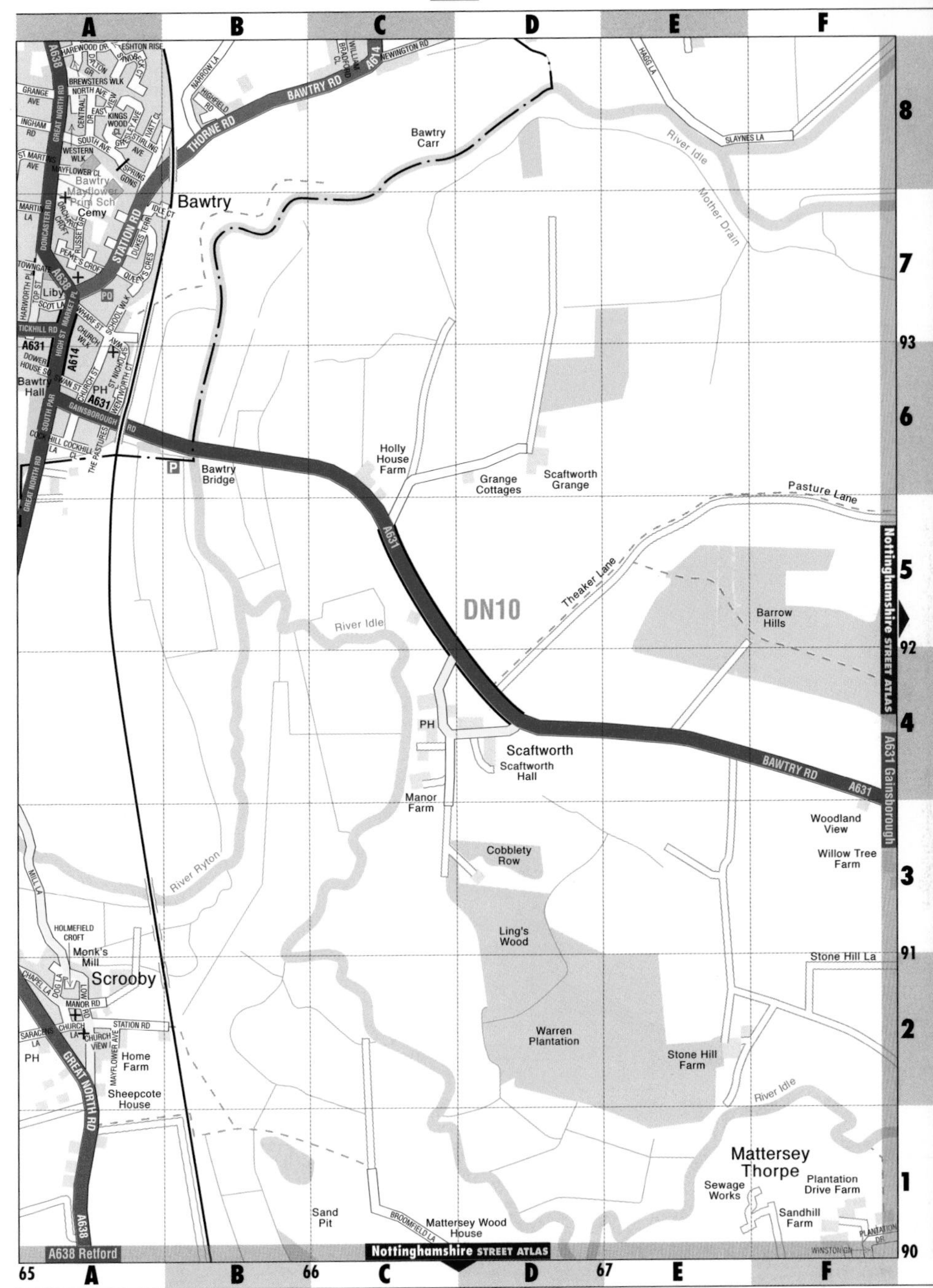

Bawtry
Bawtry Carr
Bawtry Bridge
Holly House Farm
Grange Cottages
Scaftworth Grange
Pasture Lane
Theaker Lane
DN10
River Idle
Barrow Hills
Scaftworth
Scaftworth Hall
Manor Farm
Cobblety Row
Ling's Wood
Warren Plantation
Stone Hill Farm
Stone Hill La
Woodland View
Willow Tree Farm
Mattersey Thorpe
Sewage Works
Plantation Drive Farm
Sandhill Farm
Mattersey Wood House
Sand Pit
Scrooby
Monk's Mill
Home Farm
Sheepcote House
River Ryton
Mother Drain
BAWTRY RD
THORNE RD
GREAT NORTH RD
A631
A638
A614
Nottinghamshire STREET ATLAS
A631 Gainsborough
A638 Retford

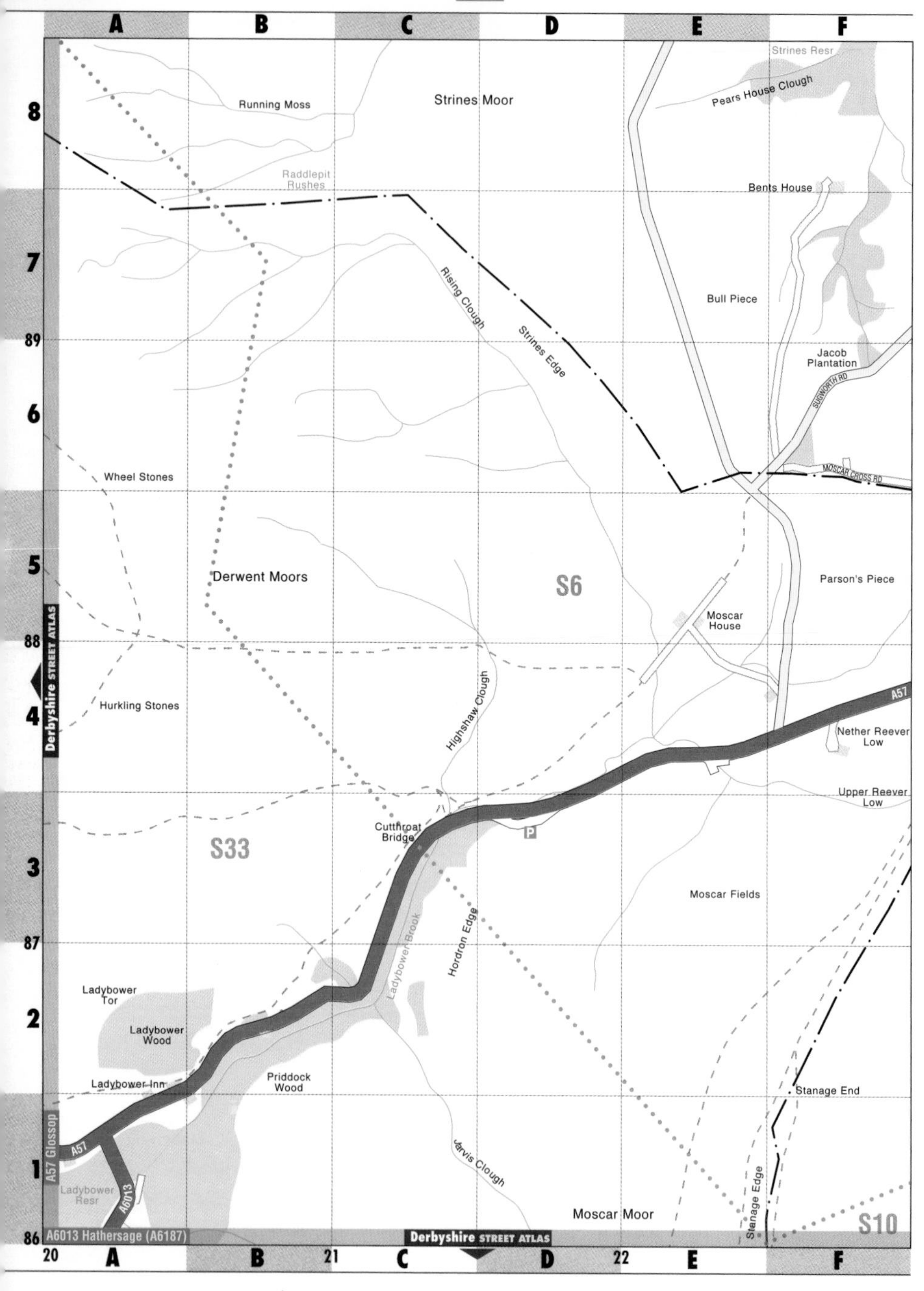

Running Moss

Strines Moor

Strines Resr

Pears House Clough

Raddlepit Rushes

Bents House

Rising Clough

Bull Piece

Strines Edge

Jacob Plantation

SLOUGH RD

Wheel Stones

MOSCAR CROSS RD

Derwent Moors

S6

Parson's Piece

Moscar House

Hurkling Stones

Highshaw Clough

A57

S33

Nether Reever Low

Cutthroat Bridge

P

Upper Reever Low

Moscar Fields

Ladybower Brook

Hordron Edge

Ladybower Tor

Ladybower Wood

Priddock Wood

Stanage End

Ladybower Inn

A57 Glossop

A57

Jarvis Clough

Stanage Edge

Ladybower Resr

A6013

Moscar Moor

S10

Derbyshire STREET ATLAS

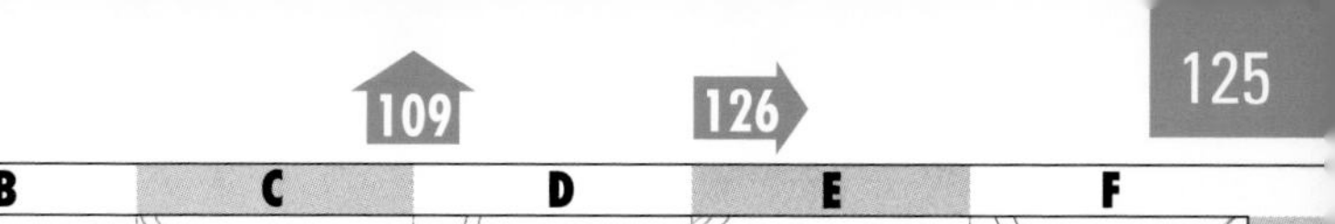
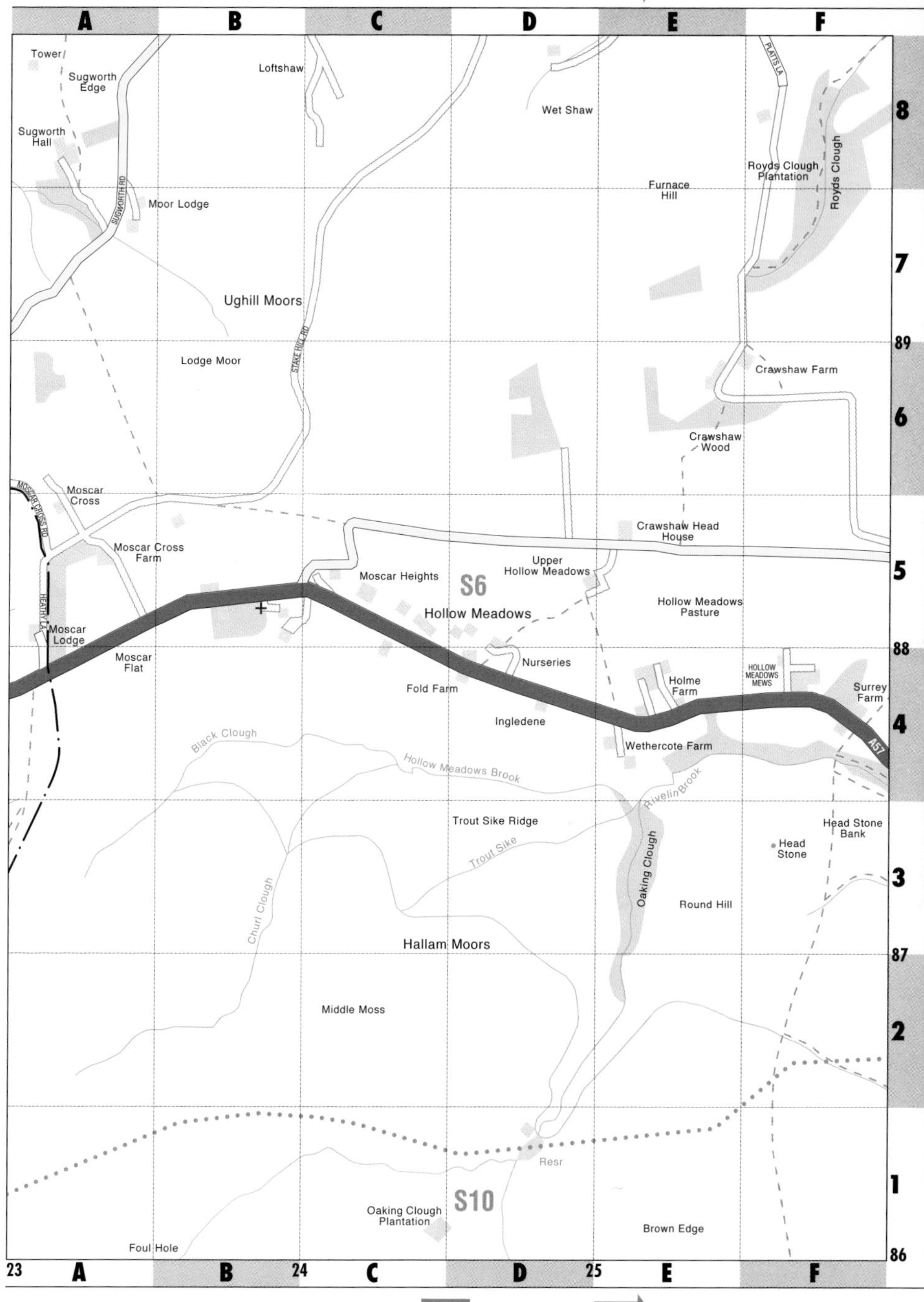

Tower
Sugworth Edge
Loftshaw
Wet Shaw
Sugworth Hall
Furnace Hill
Royds Clough Plantation
Royds Clough
Moor Lodge
SUGWORTH RD
Ughill Moors
Crawshaw Farm
Lodge Moor
STAKE HILL RD
Crawshaw Wood
Crawshaw Head House
Moscar Cross
Moscar Cross Farm
Upper Hollow Meadows
Moscar Heights
S6
Hollow Meadows
Hollow Meadows Pasture
HEATH LA
Moscar Lodge
Moscar Flat
Nurseries
Holme Farm
HOLLOW MEADOWS MEWS
Surrey Farm
Fold Farm
Ingledene
Wethercote Farm
A57
Black Clough
Hollow Meadows Brook
Rivelin Brook
Head Stone Bank
Trout Sike Ridge
Oaking Clough
Head Stone
Churt Clough
Trout Sike
Round Hill
Hallam Moors
Middle Moss
Resr
S10
Oaking Clough Plantation
Brown Edge
Foul Hole

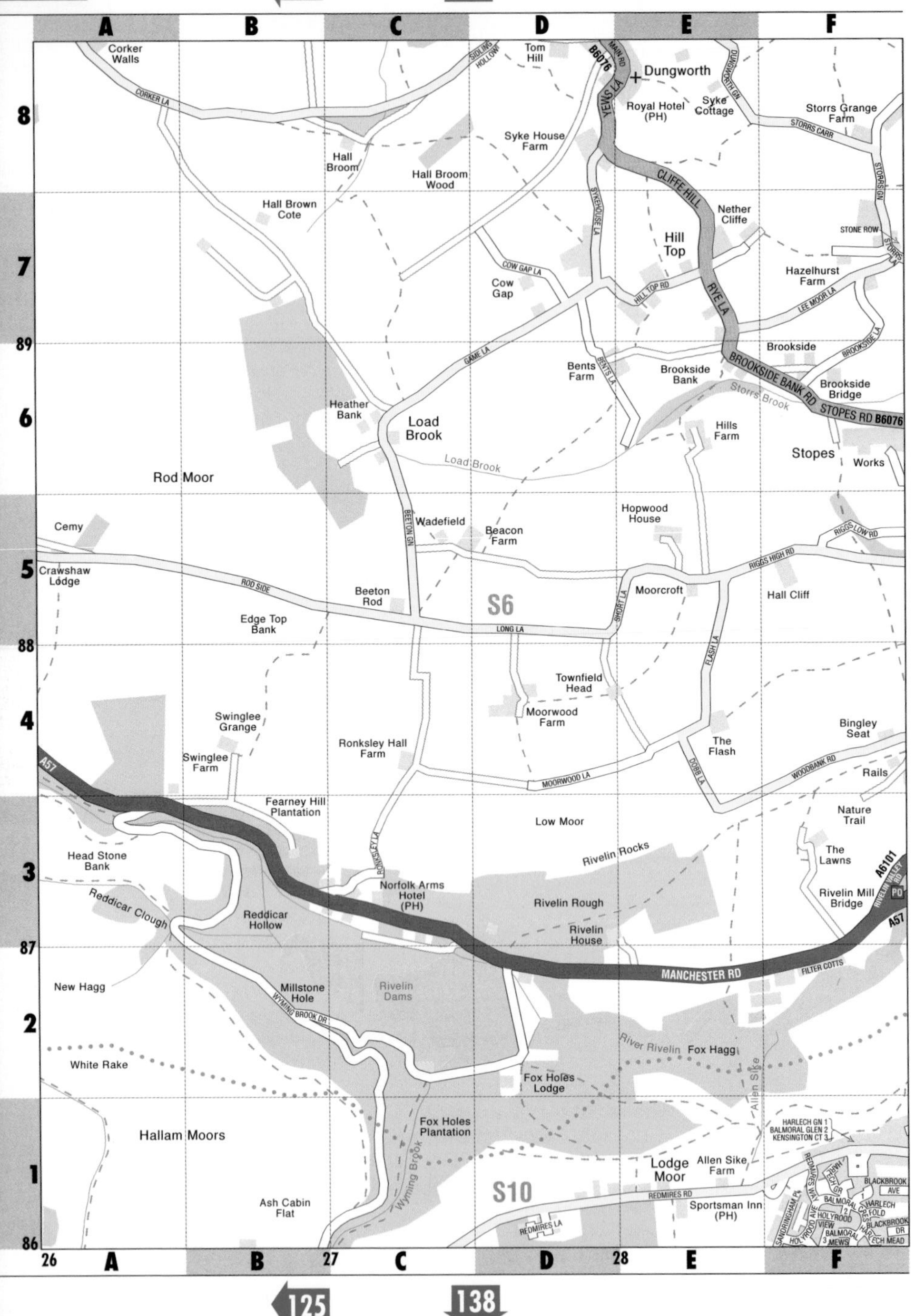

A   B   C   D   E   F

8

Corker Walls
CORKER LA
Hall Broom
Hall Brown Cote
Hall Broom Wood
SOUTH HOLLOW
Tom Hill
Syke House Farm
MAIN RD
B6076
YEWS LA
+ Dungworth
Royal Hotel (PH)
Syke Cottage
DUNGWORTH RD
Storrs Grange Farm
STORRS CARR
STORRS RD
CLIFFE HILL
Nether Cliffe
STONE ROW
Hill Top
Hazelhurst Farm
LEE MOOR LA

7

Cow Gap La
Cow Gap
HILL TOP RD
RIVE LA
Brookside
BROOKSIDE LA

89

GAME LA
Bents Farm
Brookside Bank
BROOKSIDE BANK RD
STOPES RD B6076
Brookside Bridge

6

Heather Bank
Load Brook
Hills Farm
Storrs Brook
Stopes
Works

Rod Moor
BETON DR
Load Brook
Wadefield
Beacon Farm
Hopwood House
RIGGS LOW RD

5

Cemy
Crawshaw Lodge
ROD SIDE
Beeton Rod
Edge Top Bank
S6
LONG LA
SHORT LA
Moorcroft
Hall Cliff
RIGGS HIGH RD

88

Swinglee Grange
Swinglee Farm
Ronksley Hall Farm
Townfield Head
Moorwood Farm
FLASH LA
The Flash
DOBB LA
Bingley Seat
Rails

4

A57
Fearney Hill Plantation
MOORWOOD LA
Low Moor
WOODBANK LA
Nature Trail
The Lawns
A6101

3

Head Stone Bank
Reddicar Clough
Reddicar Hollow
RONKSLEY LA
Norfolk Arms Hotel (PH)
Rivelin Rocks
Rivelin Rough
Rivelin House
Rivelin Mill Bridge
A57

87

New Hagg
Millstone Hole
WYMING BROOK DR
Rivelin Dams
MANCHESTER RD
FILTER COTTS

2

White Rake
River Rivelin
Fox Hagg
Allen Sike
Fox Holes Lodge
HARLECH GN 1
BALMORAL GLEN 2
KENSINGTON CT 3

1

Hallam Moors
Fox Holes Plantation
WYMING BROOK
S10
Lodge Moor
Allen Sike Farm
REDMIRES RD
Sportsman Inn (PH)
BLACKBROOK AVE

86

Ash Cabin Flat
REDMIRES LA

26   A   B   27   C   D   28   E   F

111

128

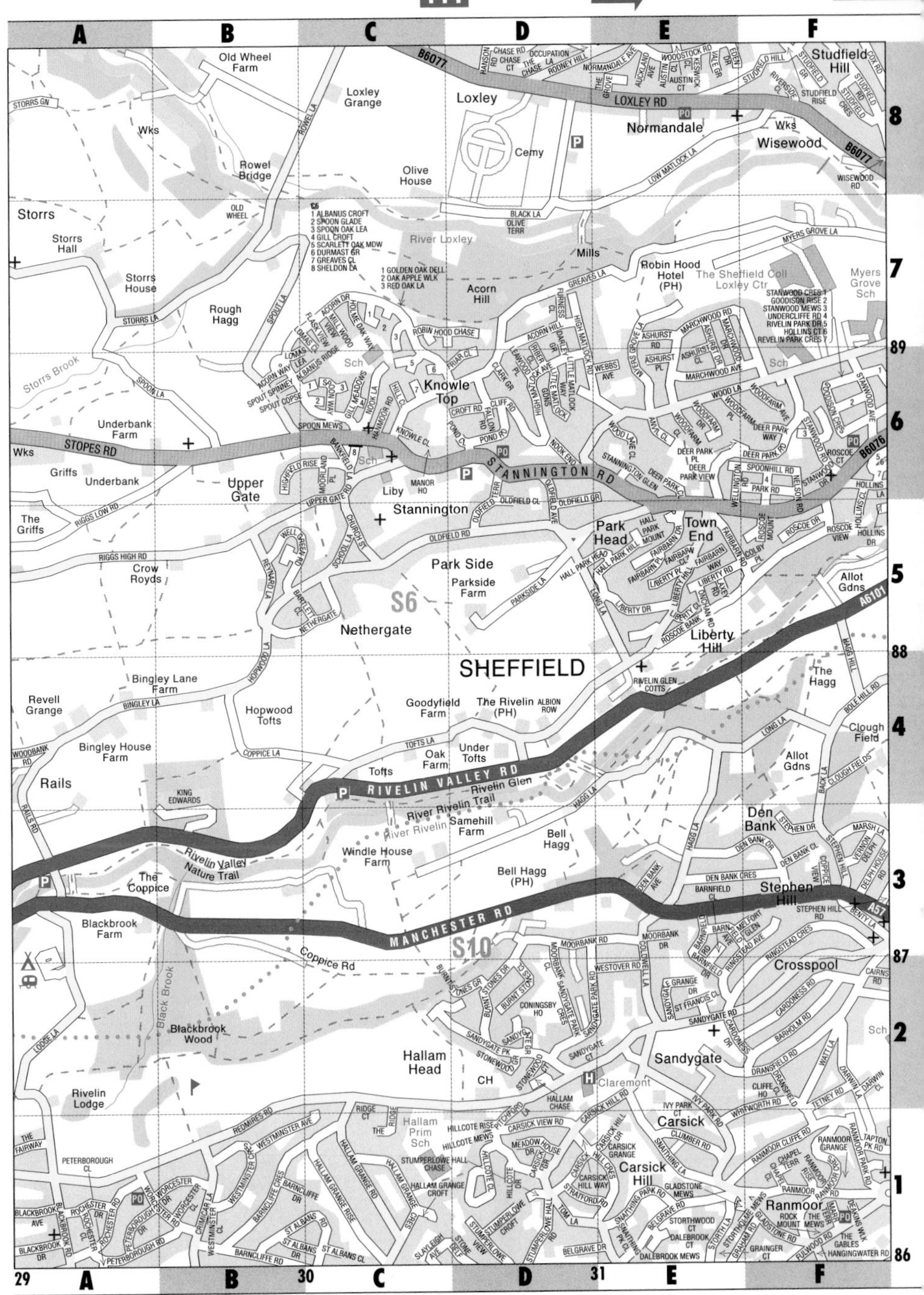

A
B
C
D
E
F
Old Wheel Farm
Loxley Grange
Loxley
Studfield Hill
Normandale
Wisewood
LOXLEY RD
B6077
Cemy
Wks
Rowel Bridge
Olive House
Storrs
Storrs Hall
Storrs House
Rough Hagg
River Loxley
Mills
Robin Hood Hotel (PH)
The Sheffield Coll Loxley Ctr
Myers Grove Sch
MYERS GROVE LA
Acorn Hill
Knowle Top
Storrs Brook
Underbank Farm
STOPES RD
Wks
Griffs
Underbank
Upper Gate
Liby
Stannington
STANNINGTON RD
Park Head
Town End
B6076
The Griffs
RIGGS LOW RD
RIGGS HIGH RD
Crow Royds
Park Side
Parkside Farm
S6
Nethergate
Allot Gdns
A6101
Liberty Hill
SHEFFIELD
The Hagg
Bingley Lane Farm
Revell Grange
Hopwood Tofts
Goodyfield Farm
The Rivelin (PH)
Clough Field
Bingley House Farm
Oak Farm
Under Tofts
Tofts
Allot Gdns
Rails
RIVELIN VALLEY RD
Rivelin Glen
River Rivelin Trail
King Edwards
River Rivelin
Samehill Farm
Bell Hagg
Den Bank
Windle House Farm
Rivelin Valley Nature Trail
The Coppice
Bell Hagg (PH)
Stephen Hill
A57
Blackbrook Farm
MANCHESTER RD
S10
Coppice Rd
Crosspool
Black Brook
Blackbrook Wood
Sandygate
Hallam Head
Claremont
Rivelin Lodge
Carsick
Hallam Prim Sch
Carsick Hill
Ranmoor
8
7
6
5
4
3
2
1
89
88
87
86
29
30
31

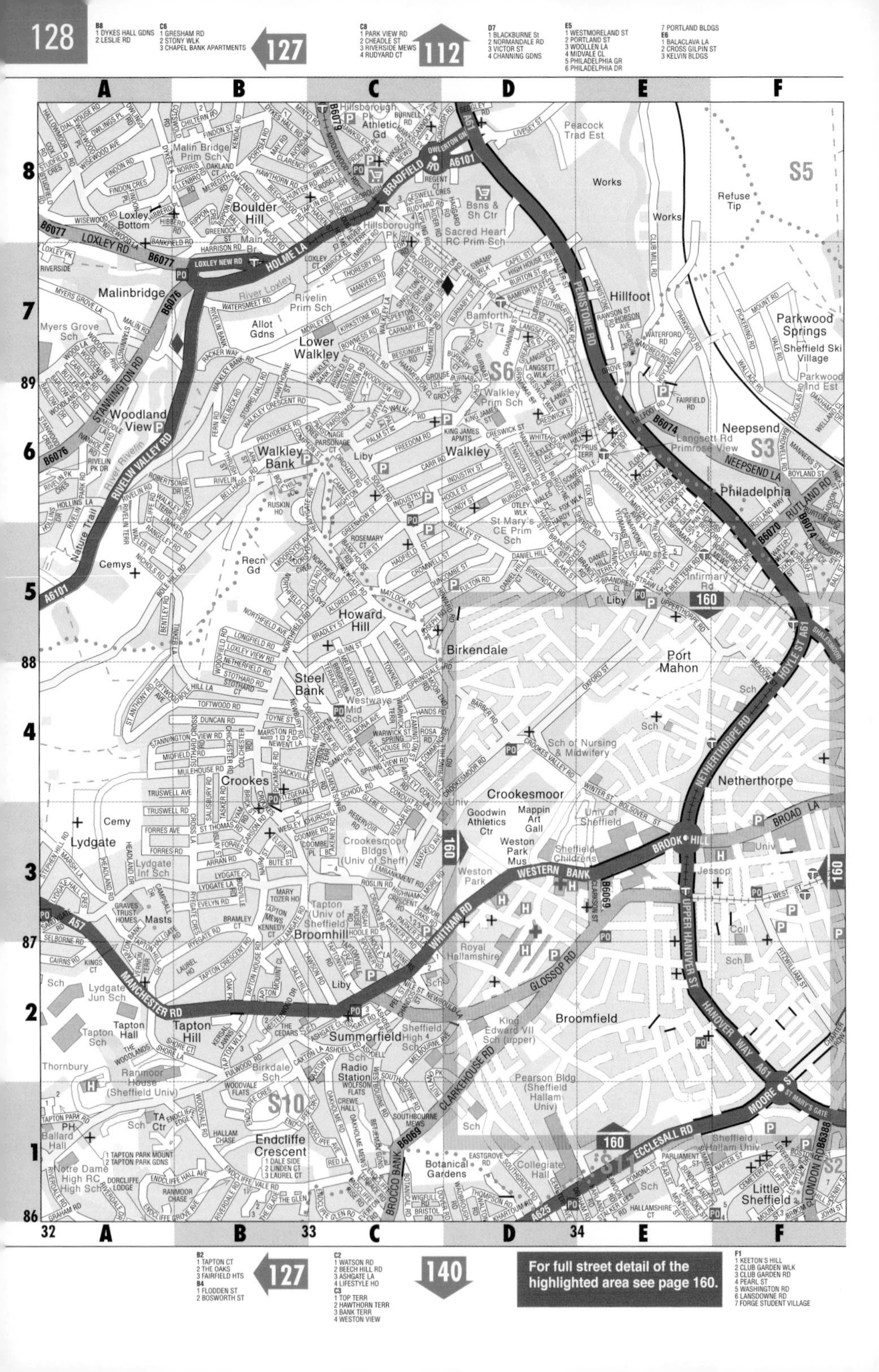
128
B8
1 DYKES HALL GDNS
2 LESLIE RD
C6
1 GRESHAM RD
2 STONY WLK
3 CHAPEL BANK APARTMENTS
127
C8
1 PARK VIEW RD
2 CHEADLE ST
3 RIVERSIDE MEWS
4 RUDYARD CT
112
D7
1 BLACKBURNE St
2 NORMANDALE RD
3 VICTOR ST
4 CHANNING GDNS
E5
1 WESTMORELAND ST
2 PORTLAND ST
3 WOOLLEN LA
4 MIDVALE CL
5 PHILADELPHIA GR
6 PHILADELPHIA DR
7 PORTLAND BLDGS
E6
1 BALACLAVA LA
2 CROSS GILPIN ST
3 KELVIN BLDGS
A
B
C
D
E
F
8
7
89
6
5
88
4
3
87
2
1
86
32
33
34
Hillsborough Pk
Athletic Gd
Peacock Trad Est
Works
S5
Refuse Tip
Malin Bridge Prim Sch
Boulder Hill
Loxley Bottom
Bsns & Sh Ctr
Sacred Heart RC Prim Sch
Hillsborough Pk
LOXLEY RD
HOLME LA
BRADFIELD RD
PENISTONE RD
Malinbridge
River Loxley
Rivelin Prim Sch
Hillfoot
Parkwood Springs
Sheffield Ski Village
Parkwood Ind Est
Myers Grove Sch
Allot Gdns
Lower Walkley
Bamforth St
S6
Walkley Prim Sch
Woodland View
STANNINGTON RD
RIVELIN VALLEY RD
River Rivelin
Walkley Bank
Liby
Walkley
Langsett Rd Primrose View
Neepsend
S3
NEEPSEND LA
Philadelphia
RUTLAND RD
Nature Trail
Ruskin Ho
St Mary's CE Prim Sch
Cemys
Recn Gd
Infirmary Rd
Howard Hill
Liby
160
Birkendale
Port Mahon
Steel Bank
Westways Mid Sch
Sch
Sch of Nursing & Midwifery
NETHERTHORPE RD
Netherthorpe
Crookes
Crookesmoor
Goodwin Athletics Ctr
Mappin Art Gall
Univ of Sheffield
BROOK HILL
BROAD LA
Cemy
Lydgate
Crookesmoor Bldgs (Univ of Sheff)
Weston Park Mus
Weston Park
Sheffield Childrens
WESTERN BANK
Jessop
Lydgate Inf Sch
Graves Trust Homes
Masts
Mary Tozer Ho
Tapton (Univ of Sheffield)
Broomhill
WHITHAM RD
UPPER HANOVER ST
Coll
Royal Hallamshire
GLOSSOP RD
Sch
Lydgate Jun Sch
MANCHESTER RD
Liby
Tapton Hall
Tapton Hill
Summerfield
Sheffield High Sch
King Edward VII Sch (upper)
Broomfield
HANOVER WAY
Thornbury
Ranmoor House (Sheffield Univ)
Birkdale Sch
Radio Station
CLARKEHOUSE RD
Pearson Bldg (Sheffield Hallam Univ)
S10
Sch
TA Ctr
Ballard Hall
Endcliffe Crescent
1 DALE SIDE
2 LINDEN CT
3 LAUREL CT
Botanical Gardens
Collegiate Hall
ECCLESALL RD
Sheffield Hallam Univ
Notre Dame High RC High Sch
Sch
S11
Little Sheffield
S2
B2
1 TAPTON CT
2 THE OAKS
3 FAIRFIELD HTS
B4
1 FLODDEN ST
2 BOSWORTH ST
127
C2
1 WATSON RD
2 BEECH HILL RD
3 ASHGATE LA
4 LIFESTYLE HO
C3
1 TOP TERR
2 HAWTHORN TERR
3 BANK TERR
4 WESTON VIEW
140
For full street detail of the highlighted area see page 160.
F1
1 KEETON'S HILL
2 CLUB GARDEN WLK
3 CLUB GARDEN RD
4 PEARL ST
5 WASHINGTON RD
6 LANSDOWNE RD
7 FORGE STUDENT VILLAGE

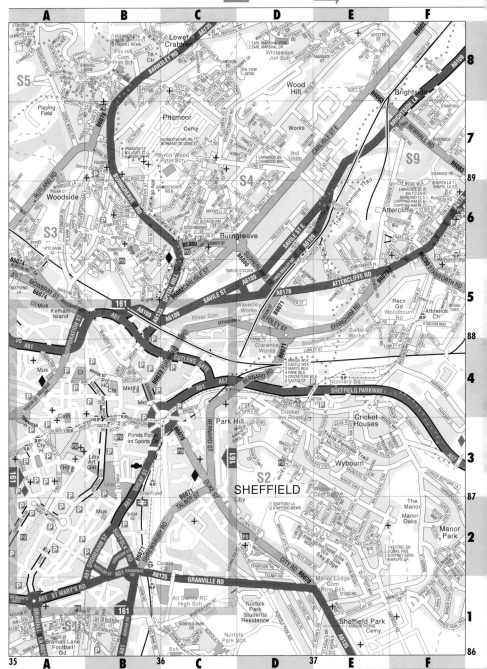

For full street detail of the highlighted area see page 161.

The A61, Inner Ring Road completion, due to open shortly after printing, has been depicted as open in this atlas

141 130

129
114

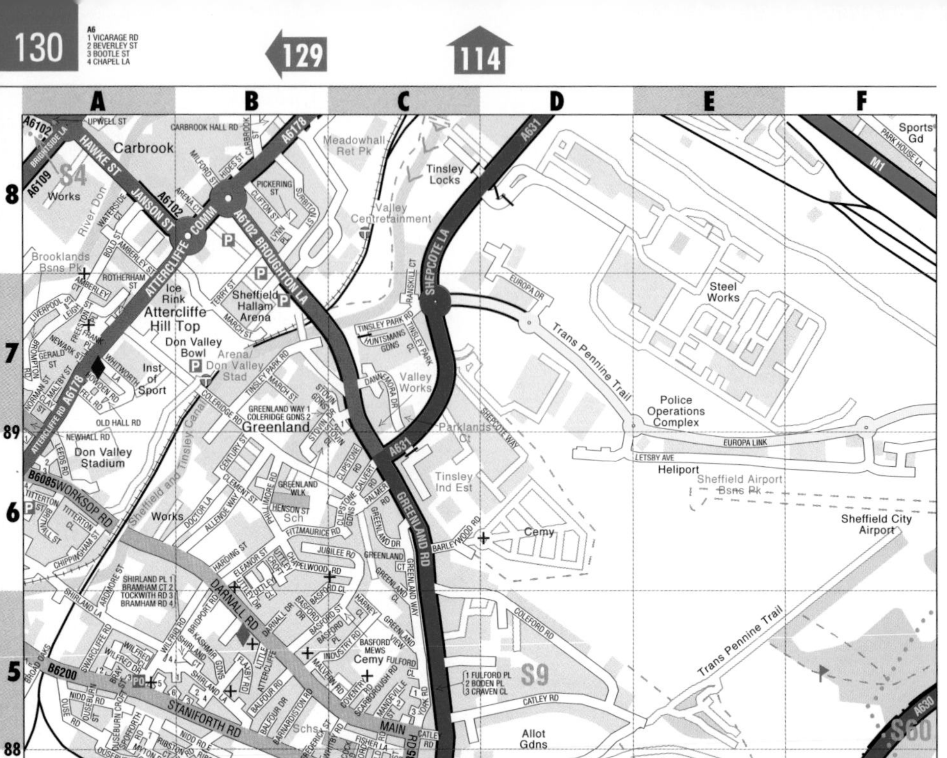

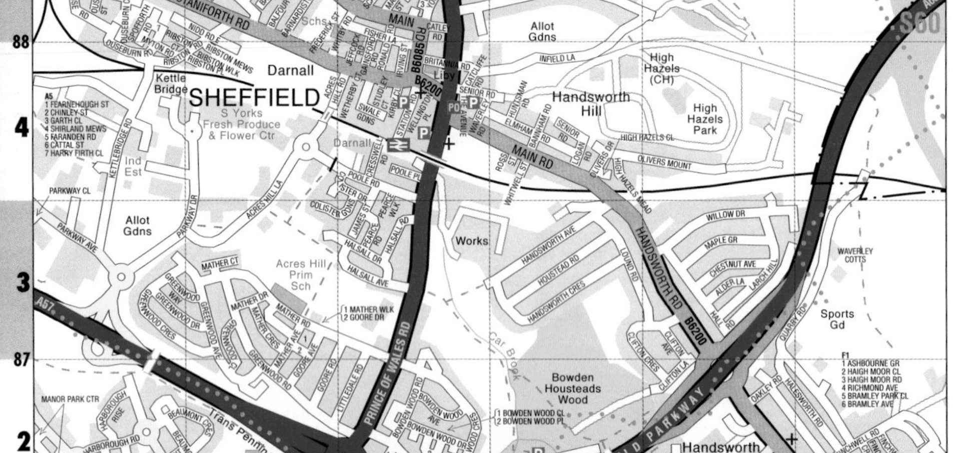

115
132

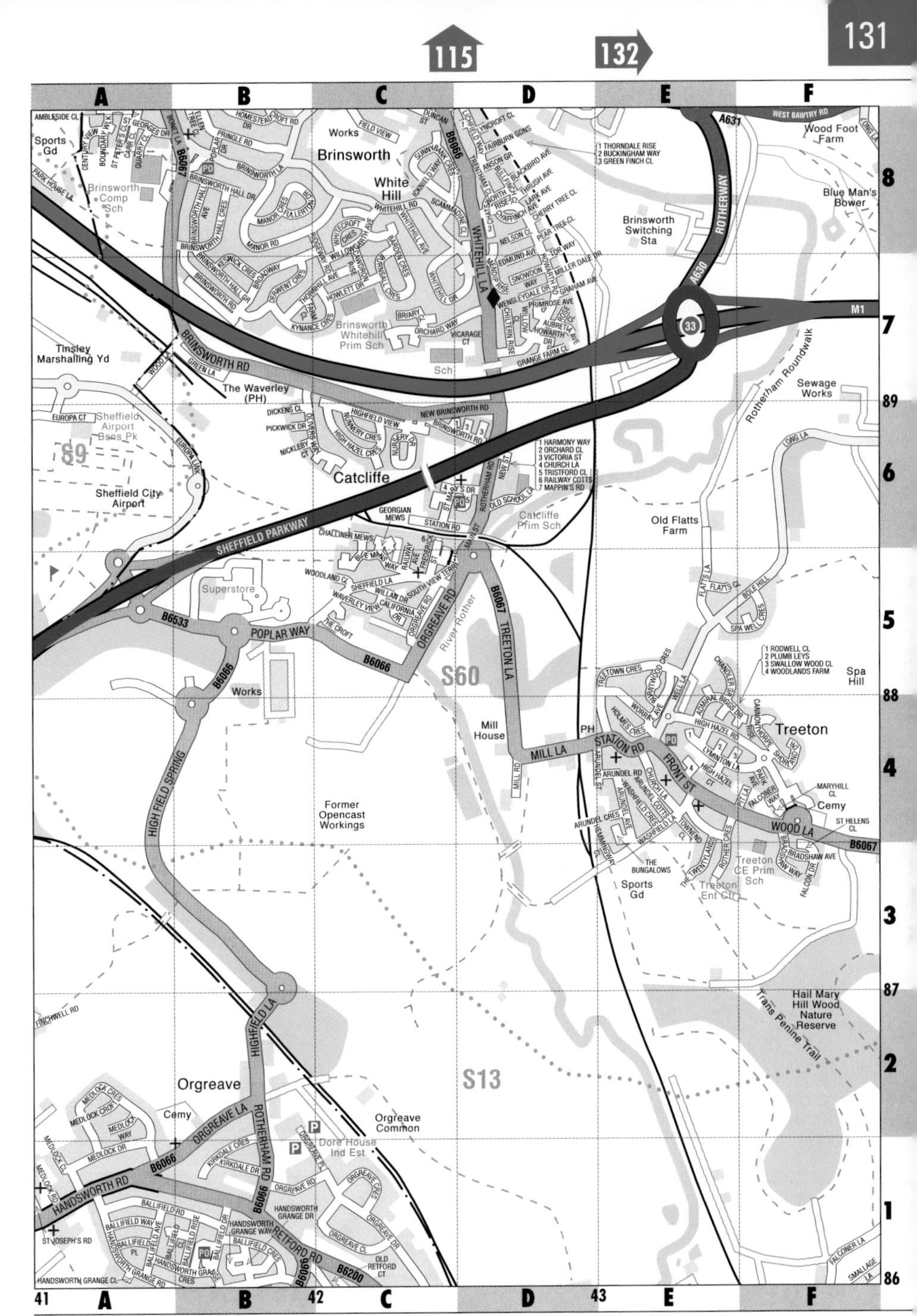
Brinsworth
White Hill
Brinsworth Comp Sch
Sports Gd
Works
Brinsworth Whitehill Prim Sch
Tinsley Marshalling Yd
The Waverley (PH)
Sheffield Airport Bsns Pk
Sheffield City Airport
Catcliffe
Catcliffe Prim Sch
Brinsworth Switching Sta
Wood Foot Farm
Blue Man's Bower
Sewage Works
Rotherham Roundwalk
Old Flatts Farm
Spa Hill
Treeton
Superstore
Works
Mill House
Former Opencast Workings
S60
S13
River Rother
Treeton CE Prim Sch
Treeton Ent Ctr
Sports Gd
Cemy
Hail Mary Hill Wood Nature Reserve
Trans Pennine Trail
Orgreave
Orgreave Common
Dore House Ind Est
SHEFFIELD PARKWAY
BRINSWORTH RD
WHITEHILL LA
ROTHERWAY
POPLAR WAY
HIGH FIELD SPRING
TREETON LA
MILL LA
STATION RD
FRONT ST
WOOD LA
HIGHFIELD LA
ROTHERHAM RD
ORGREAVE LA
HANDSWORTH RD
RETFORD RD
ORGREAVE RD
M1
A631
A630
B6066
B6067
B6533
B6200
1 THORNDALE RISE
2 BUCKINGHAM WAY
3 GREEN FINCH CL
1 HARMONY WAY
2 ORCHARD CL
3 VICTORIA ST
4 CHURCH LA
5 TRISTFORD CL
6 RAILWAY COTTS
7 MAPPIN'S RD
1 RODWELL CL
2 PLUMB LEYS
3 SWALLOW WOOD CL
4 WOODLANDS FARM
A B C D E F
8 7 6 5 4 3 2 1
89 88 87 86
41 42 43

143
132

131
116

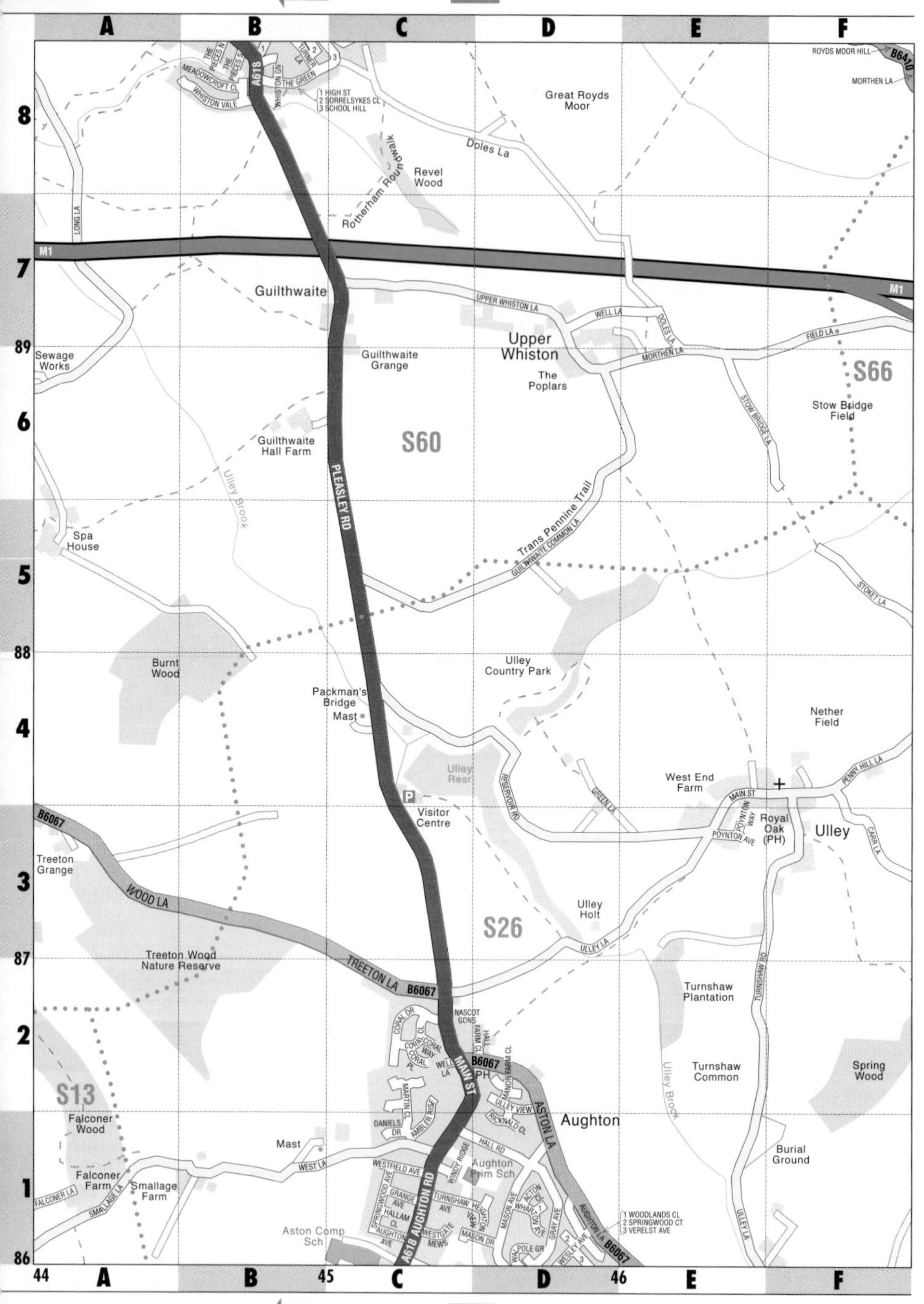
Great Royds Moor
Doles La
Revel Wood
Rotherham Roundwalk
M1
Guilthwaite
Upper Whiston
The Poplars
Guilthwaite Grange
Sewage Works
S60
S66
Stow Bridge Field
Guilthwaite Hall Farm
PLEASLEY RD
Trans Pennine Trail
Ulley Brook
Spa House
Burnt Wood
Ulley Country Park
Packman's Bridge
Mast
Nether Field
West End Farm
Ulley Resr
Visitor Centre
Royal Oak (PH)
Ulley
Treeton Grange
WOOD LA
Ulley Holt
S26
Treeton Wood Nature Reserve
TREETON LA
B6067
Turnshaw Plantation
Turnshaw Common
Spring Wood
S13
Falconer Wood
Aughton
Burial Ground
Falconer Farm
Smallage Farm
Aughton Prim Sch
Aston Comp Sch
A618 AUGHTON RD
ASTON LA
MAIN ST
1 HIGH ST
2 SORRELSYKES CL
3 SCHOOL HILL
1 WOODLANDS CL
2 SPRINGWOOD CT
3 VERELST AVE

131
144

117
134

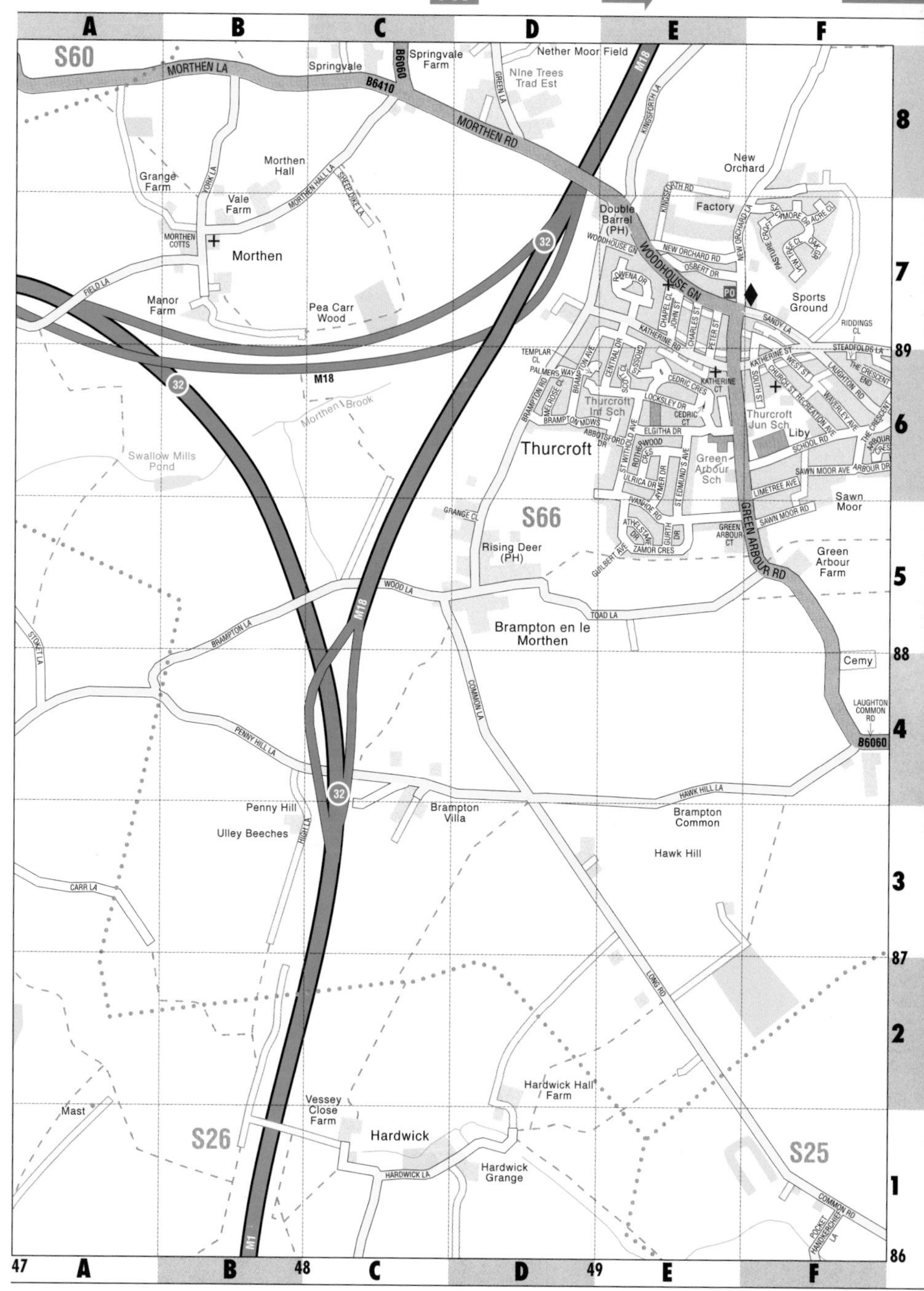
S60
MORTHEN LA
Springvale
B6060
Springvale Farm
B6410
Nether Moor Field
Nine Trees Trad Est
GREEN LA
M18
MORTHEN RD
KINGSFORTH LA
Morthen Hall
Grange Farm
YORK LA
Vale Farm
MORTHEN HALL LA
SHEEP DIKE LA
MORTHEN COTTS
Morthen
FIELD LA
Manor Farm
Pea Carr Wood
32
New Orchard
KINGSFORTH RD
Factory
Double Barrel (PH)
WOODHOUSE GN
NEW ORCHARD RD
OSBERT DR
ROWENA DR
CHAPEL CL
JOHN ST
CHARLES ST
PETER ST
PO
Sports Ground
SANDY LA
RIDDINGS CL
STEADFOLDS LA
KATHERINE RD
TEMPLAR CL
PALMERS WAY
BRAMPTON AVE
CENTRAL DR
CROSS ST
KATHERINE CT
KATHERINE ST
WEST ST
SOUTH ST
CHURCH ST
LAUGHTON RD
THE CRESCENT END
M18
BRAMPTON RD
MELROSE CL
CEDRIC CRES
Thurcroft Inf Sch
LOCKSLEY DR
CEDRIC CT
Thurcroft Jun Sch
Liby
RECREATION AVE
WAVERLEY AVE
THE CRESCENT
Morthen Brook
BRAMPTON MDWS
ABBOTSFORD DR
ELGITHA DR
ROTHER WOOD CRES
SCHOOL RD
Thurcroft
Swallow Mills Pond
ST WITHOLD AVE
ULRICA DR
RYMER DR
ST EDMUND'S AVE
Green Arbour Sch
SAWN MOOR AVE
ARBOUR DR
LIMETREE AVE
Sawn Moor
GRANGE CL
S66
IVANHOE RD
ATHELSTANE DR
GURTH DR
GREEN ARBOUR CT
SAWN MOOR RD
GREEN ARBOUR RD
Rising Deer (PH)
GUILBERT AVE
ZAMOR CRES
Green Arbour Farm
WOOD LA
M18
TOAD LA
Brampton en le Morthen
BRAMPTON LA
STONEY LA
COMMON LA
Cemy
LAUGHTON COMMON RD
B6060
PENNY HILL LA
32
HAWK HILL LA
Penny Hill
Brampton Villa
Brampton Common
Ulley Beeches
HIGH LA
Hawk Hill
CARR LA
LONG RD
Mast
Hardwick Hall Farm
Vessey Close Farm
Hardwick
S26
S25
HARDWICK LA
Hardwick Grange
COMMON RD
POCKET HANDKERCHIEF LA
M1
A
B
C
D
E
F
8
7
89
6
5
88
4
3
87
2
1
86
47
48
49

145
134

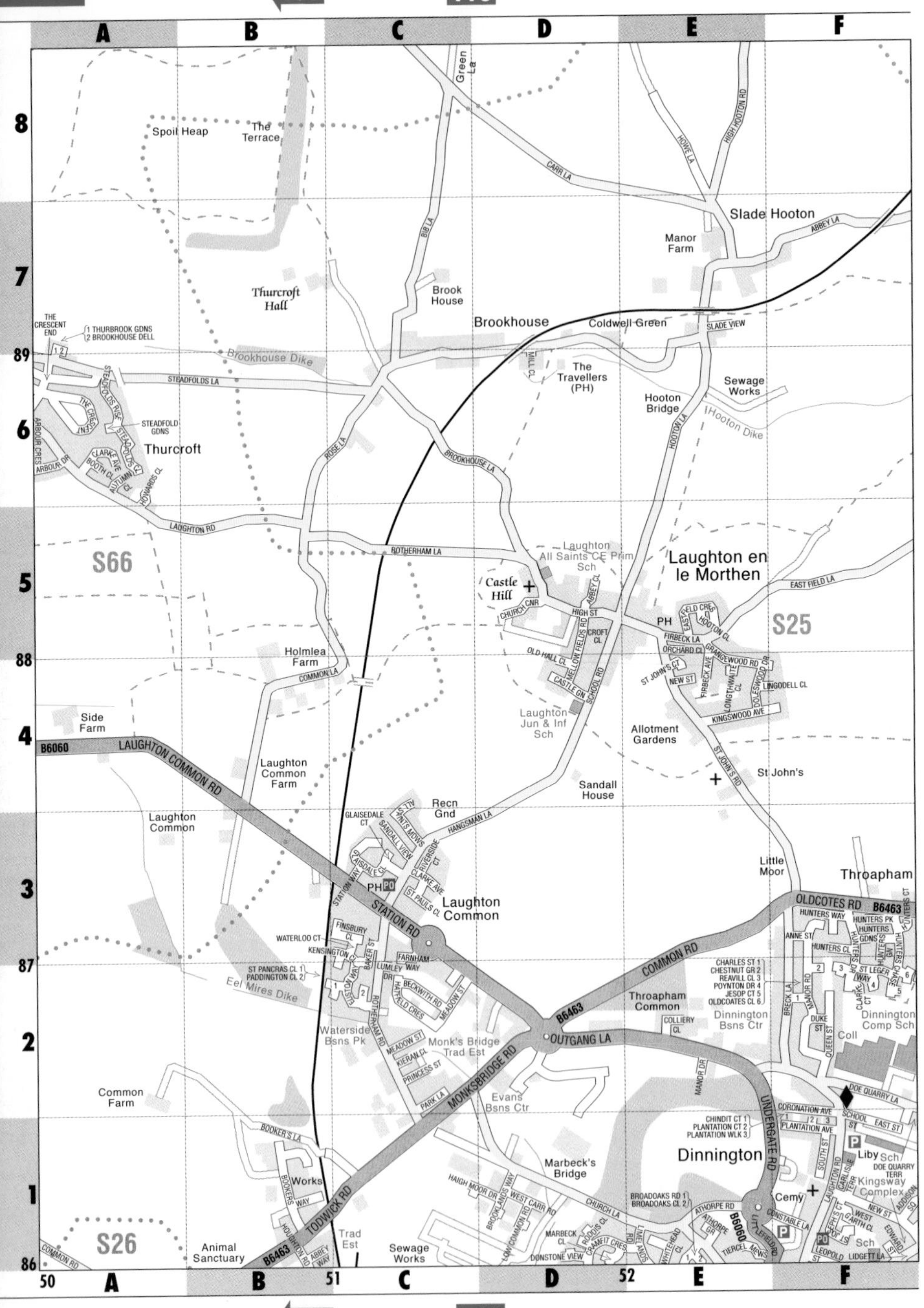
A
B
C
D
E
F
8
7
89
6
5
88
4
3
87
2
1
86
50
51
52
Spoil Heap
The Terrace
Green La
CARR LA
HOWE LA
HIGH HOOTON RD
Slade Hooton
ABBEY LA
Manor Farm
BIB LA
Thurcroft Hall
Brook House
Brookhouse
Coldwell Green
SLADE VIEW
THE CRESCENT END
1 THURBROOK GDNS
2 BROOKHOUSE DELL
Brookhouse Dike
STEADFOLDS LA
MILL CL
The Travellers (PH)
Sewage Works
Hooton Bridge
Hooton Dike
STEADFOLDS RISE
THE CRESCENT
STEADFOLD GDNS
ARBOUR CRES
ARBOUR DR
CLARKE AVE
BOOTH CL
AUTUMN CL
HOWARDS CL
Thurcroft
ROSE LA
BROOKHOUSE LA
HOOTON LA
LAUGHTON RD
S66
ROTHERHAM LA
Laughton All Saints CE Prim Sch
Laughton en le Morthen
EAST FIELD LA
Castle Hill
CHURCH CNR
HIGH ST
ABBEY CL
PH
EASTFIELD CRES
HOOTON CL
S25
FIRBECK LA
ORCHARD CL
GRANGEWOOD RD
CROFT CL
OLD HALL CL
MELLOW FIELDS RD
ST JOHN'S CT
NEW ST
FIRBECK AVE
LONGTHWAITE CL
DOLESWOOD DR
LINGODELL CL
Holmlea Farm
CASTLE GN
SCHOOL RD
KINGSWOOD AVE
COMMON LA
Laughton Jun & Inf Sch
Allotment Gardens
Side Farm
B6060
LAUGHTON COMMON RD
ST JOHN'S RD
St John's
Laughton Common Farm
Sandall House
Recn Gnd
Laughton Common
GLAISEDALE CT
ALL SAINTS MDWS
SANDALL VIEW
HANGSMAN LA
RIVERSIDE CT
Little Moor
Throapham
GLAISDALE CL
STATION WAY
PH
CLARKE AVE
ST PAULS CL
Laughton Common
STATION RD
OLDCOTES RD
B6463
HUNTERS WAY
HUNTERS PK
HUNTERS GDNS
HUNTERS CT
HUNTERS CHASE
ANNE ST
HUNTERS CL
FINSBURY CL
WATERLOO CT
KENSINGTON
BAKER ST
COMMON RD
CHARLES ST 1
CHESTNUT GR 2
REAVILL CL 3
POYNTON DR 4
JESOP CT 5
OLDCOATES CL 6
ST LEGER WAY
FARNHAM WAY
LUMLEY DR
ST PANCRAS CL 1
PADDINGTON CL 2
BECKWITH RD
HATFIELD CRES
MEADOW ST
ROTHERHAM RD
EUSTON WAY
Eel Mires Dike
Throapham Common
Dinnington Bsns Ctr
Dinnington Comp Sch
BRECK LA
MANOR RD
DUKE ST
QUEEN ST
CLARKE CT
Coll
B6463
COLLIERY CL
Waterside Bsns Pk
OUTGANG LA
MEADOW ST
KIERAN CL
PRINCESS ST
Monk's Bridge Trad Est
MONKSBRIDGE RD
MANOR DR
DOE QUARRY LA
Common Farm
PARK LA
Evans Bsns Ctr
UNDERGATE RD
CORONATION AVE
SCHOOL ST
EAST ST
CHINDIT CT 1
PLANTATION CT 2
PLANTATION WLK 3
PLANTATION AVE
BOOKER'S LA
Marbeck's Bridge
Dinnington
SOUTH ST
Liby
Sch
DOE QUARRY TERR
Kingsway Complex
Works
HAIGH MOOR DR
BROOKLANDS WAY
WEST CARR RD
CHURCH LA
BROADOAKS RD 1
BROADOAKS CL 2
Cemy
LAUGHTON RD
CARLISLE TERR
NEW ST
ADDISON SQ
BOOKERS WAY
TODWICK RD
S26
ATHORPE RD
ATHORPE GR
CONSTABLE LA
WEST GARTH CL
EDWARD ST
LOW COMMON RD
MARBECK CL
RODDIS CL
CRAMFIT CRES
LIMELANDS RD
WHITEHEAD CL
B6060
LITTLEFIELD RD
TIERCEL MEWS
Sch
COMMON RD
HOUGHTON RD
ABBEY WAY
Animal Sanctuary
B6463
Trad Est
Sewage Works
DONSTONE VIEW
LEOPOLD
LIDGETT LA

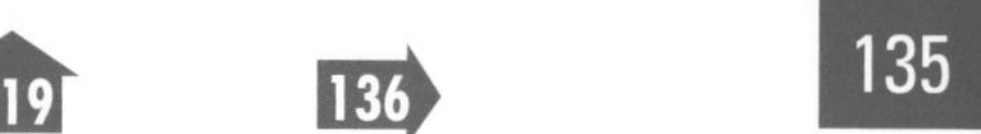

119
136

| A | B | C | D | E | F |

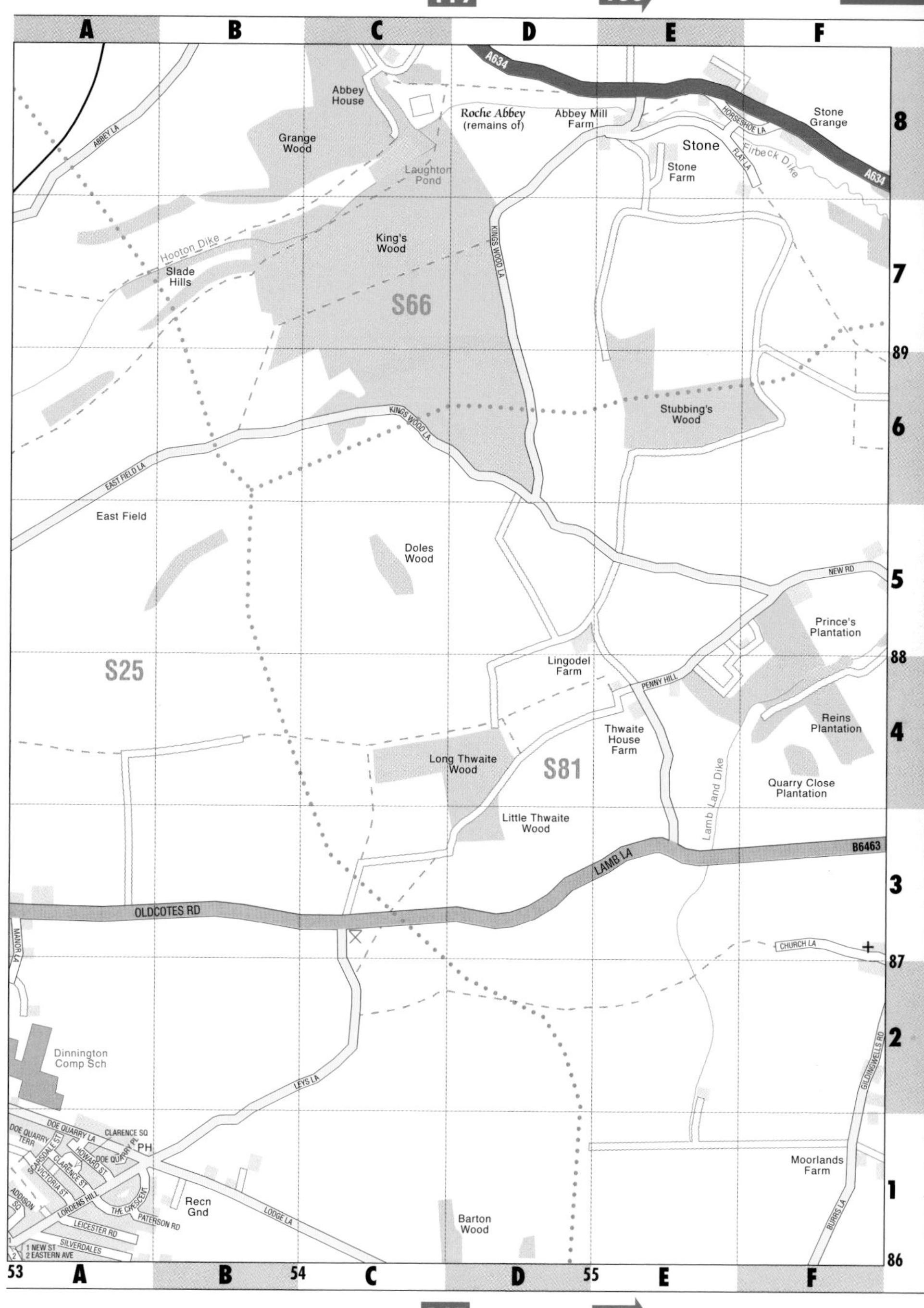

8

A634

Abbey House

Roche Abbey (remains of)

Abbey Mill Farm

ABBEY LA

Grange Wood

Laughton Pond

HORSESHOE LA

Stone Grange

Stone

Stone Farm

FLAT LA

Firbeck Dike

A634

7

King's Wood

KINGS WOOD LA

Hooton Dike

Slade Hills

S66

89

Stubbing's Wood

6

EAST FIELD LA

KINGS WOOD LA

East Field

Doles Wood

NEW RD

5

Prince's Plantation

88

S25

Lingodel Farm

PENNY HILL

Penny Hill

Reins Plantation

4

Thwaite House Farm

Long Thwaite Wood

S81

Lamb Land Dike

Quarry Close Plantation

Little Thwaite Wood

LAMB LA

B6463

3

OLDCOTES RD

CHURCH LA

GLOSSONDALE RD

87

Dinnington Comp Sch

LEYS LA

2

DOE QUARRY LA

CLARENCE SQ

PH

Moorlands Farm

Recn Gnd

LODGE LA

1

1 NEW ST 2 EASTERN AVE

SILVERDALES

Barton Wood

BIRKS LA

86

| 53 | A | 54 | B | C | D | 55 | E | F |

A   **B**   **C**   **D**   **E**   **F**

8

Sandbeck Park

Folds Wood

Old Whin Covert

DN11

New Buildings

S66

Union Wood

Thornbury Hill

Thornbury Hill LA

A60

A634

7

FOUR LANE ENDS

Firbeck Dike

Thornbury Hill Plantation

Folly Plantation

89

Home Farm

Yews Farm

A634

PH

BLYTH RD

PO

WYNEA RD

6

Firbeck Hall

MALTBY RD

Oldcotes

Burntout Wood

A634, Blyth, A1

FLAT LA

ST MARTIN'S G

OLD MDW

PH

LIME AVE

KID LA

Cow Wood

Oldcotes Dike

WEIRSIDE

MAIN ST

Nottinghamshire STREET ATLAS

Firbeck

KINGSWOOD CL

SALT HILL RD

Rough Wood

Haven Farm

B6463

Hermeston Hall

5

PARK HILL LA

LAMB LA

88

Park Hill Farm

S81

4

Ivy Lodge Plantation

CHESTNUT MEWS

CHESTNUT RD

Langold Hotel (PH)

Crow Wood

IVY LODGE LA

BURNUM RD

BIRCHWOOD CL

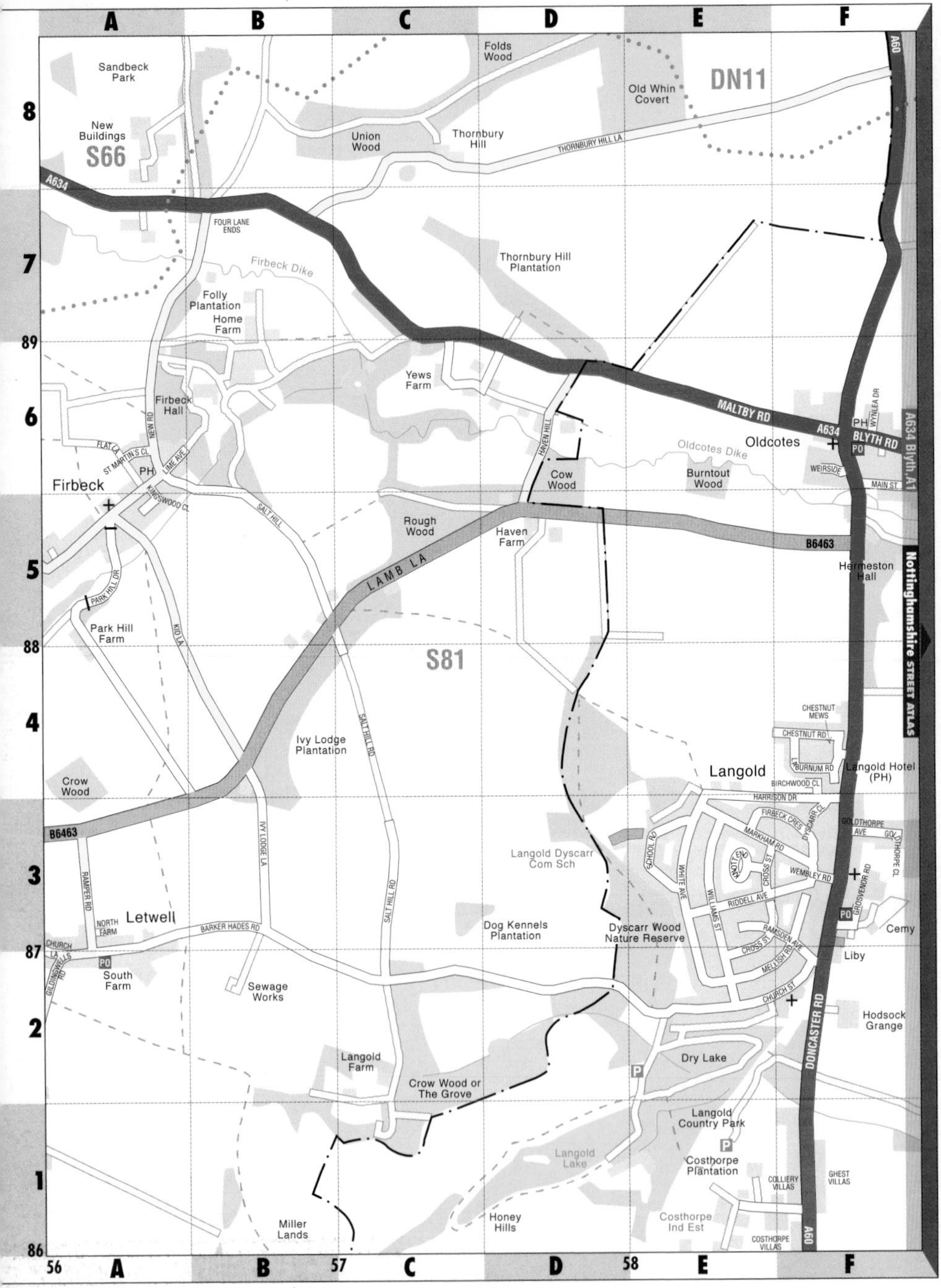

Langold

HARRISON DR

FIRBECK CRES

GOLDTHORPE AVE

PINXTON RD

COX

B6463

RAMPER RD

SALT HILL RD

Langold Dyscarr Com Sch

SCHOOL RD

MARKHAM RD

WHITE AVE

CROSS ST

WEMBLEY RD

GROSVENOR RD

PO

3

NORTH FARM

Letwell

BARKER HADES RD

Dog Kennels Plantation

Dyscarr Wood Nature Reserve

RIDDELL AVE

WALES ST

RAMSDEN AVE

MELLISH RD

Cemy

Liby

87

CHURCH LA LS

GLEDHOLT

PO

South Farm

Sewage Works

CHURCH RD

2

Langold Farm

Crow Wood or The Grove

P

Dry Lake

DONCASTER RD

Hodsock Grange

1

Langold Lake

Langold Country Park

P

Costhorpe Plantation

COLLIERY VILLAS

GHEST VILLAS

A60

86

Miller Lands

Honey Hills

Costhorpe Ind Est

Costhorpe VILLAS

56   **A**   **B**   **57**   **C**   **D**   **58**   **E**   **F**

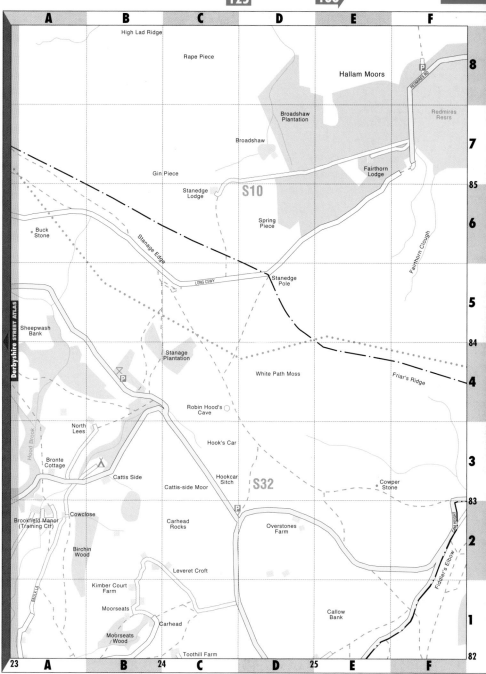

A **B** **C** **D** **E** **F**

High Lad Ridge

Rape Piece

Hallam Moors

8

REDMIRES RD

P

Broadshaw
Plantation

Redmires
Resrs

Broadshaw

7

Fairthorn
Lodge

Gin Piece

S10

Stanedge
Lodge

85

Buck
Stone

Spring
Piece

6

Stanage Edge

Fairthorn Clough

LONG CSWY

Stanedge
Pole

5

Derbyshire STREET ATLAS

Sheepwash
Bank

84

Stanage
Plantation

White Path Moss

Friar's Ridge

4

P

Robin Hood's
Cave

North
Lees

Hook's Car

3

Hood Brook

Bronte
Cottage

Hookcar
Sitch

S32

Cowper
Stone

Cattis Side

Cattis-side Moor

Brookfield Manor
(Training Ctr)

Cowclose

Carhead
Rocks

Overstones
Farm

83

P

Fiddler's Elbow

Birchin
Wood

2

Leveret Croft

Kimber Court
Farm

Moorseats

Callow
Bank

1

Carhead

Moorseats
Wood

Toothill Farm

82

23 **A** **B** 24 **C** **D** 25 **E** **F**

137
126

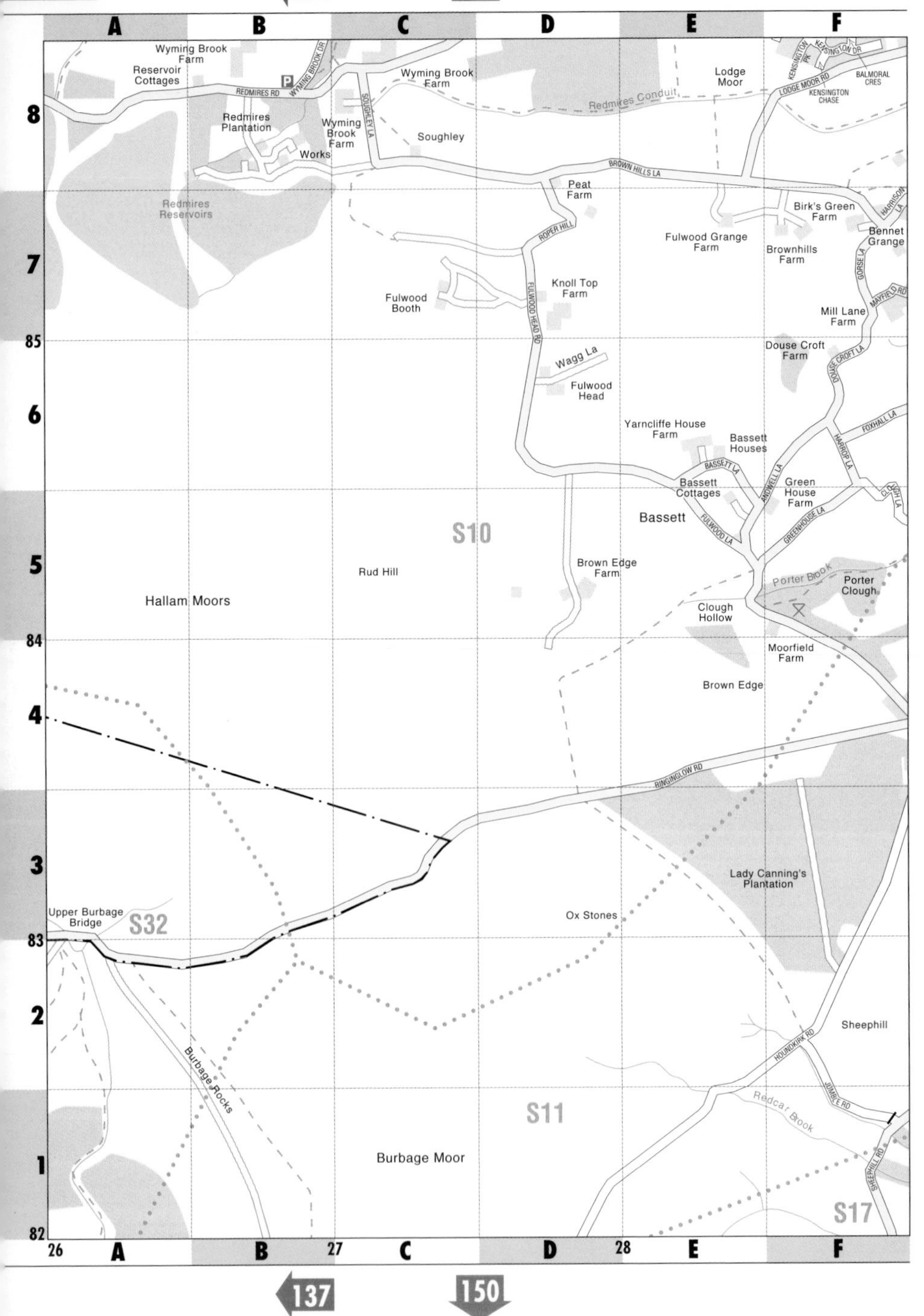
A
B
C
D
E
F
8
7
85
6
5
84
4
3
83
2
1
82
26
27
28
Wyming Brook Farm
Reservoir Cottages
REDMIRES RD
WYMING BROOK DR
Wyming Brook Farm
SOUGHLEY LA
Lodge Moor
KENSINGTON DR
KENSINGTON PK
LODGE MOOR RD
BALMORAL CRES
KENSINGTON CHASE
Redmires Conduit
Redmires Plantation
Wyming Brook Farm
Soughley
Works
BROWN HILLS LA
Peat Farm
Redmires Reservoirs
Birk's Green Farm
HARRISON LA
Bennet Grange
Fulwood Grange Farm
Brownhills Farm
ROPER HILL
GORSE LA
Knoll Top Farm
Fulwood Booth
FULWOOD HEAD RD
MAYFIELD RD
Mill Lane Farm
Douse Croft Farm
DOUSE CROFT LA
Wagg La
Fulwood Head
FOXHALL LA
Yarncliffe House Farm
Bassett Houses
BASSETT LA
HARROP LA
Bassett Cottages
ANDWELL LA
Green House Farm
CLOUGH LA
Bassett
GREENHOUSE LA
FULWOOD LA
S10
Brown Edge Farm
Rud Hill
Porter Brook
Porter Clough
Hallam Moors
Clough Hollow
Moorfield Farm
Brown Edge
BINGINGLOW RD
Lady Canning's Plantation
Upper Burbage Bridge
S32
Ox Stones
Sheephill
HOUNDKIRK RD
Burbage Rocks
JUMBLE RD
Redcar Brook
S11
SHEEPHILL RD
Burbage Moor
S17

137
150

127

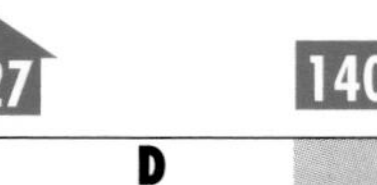

140

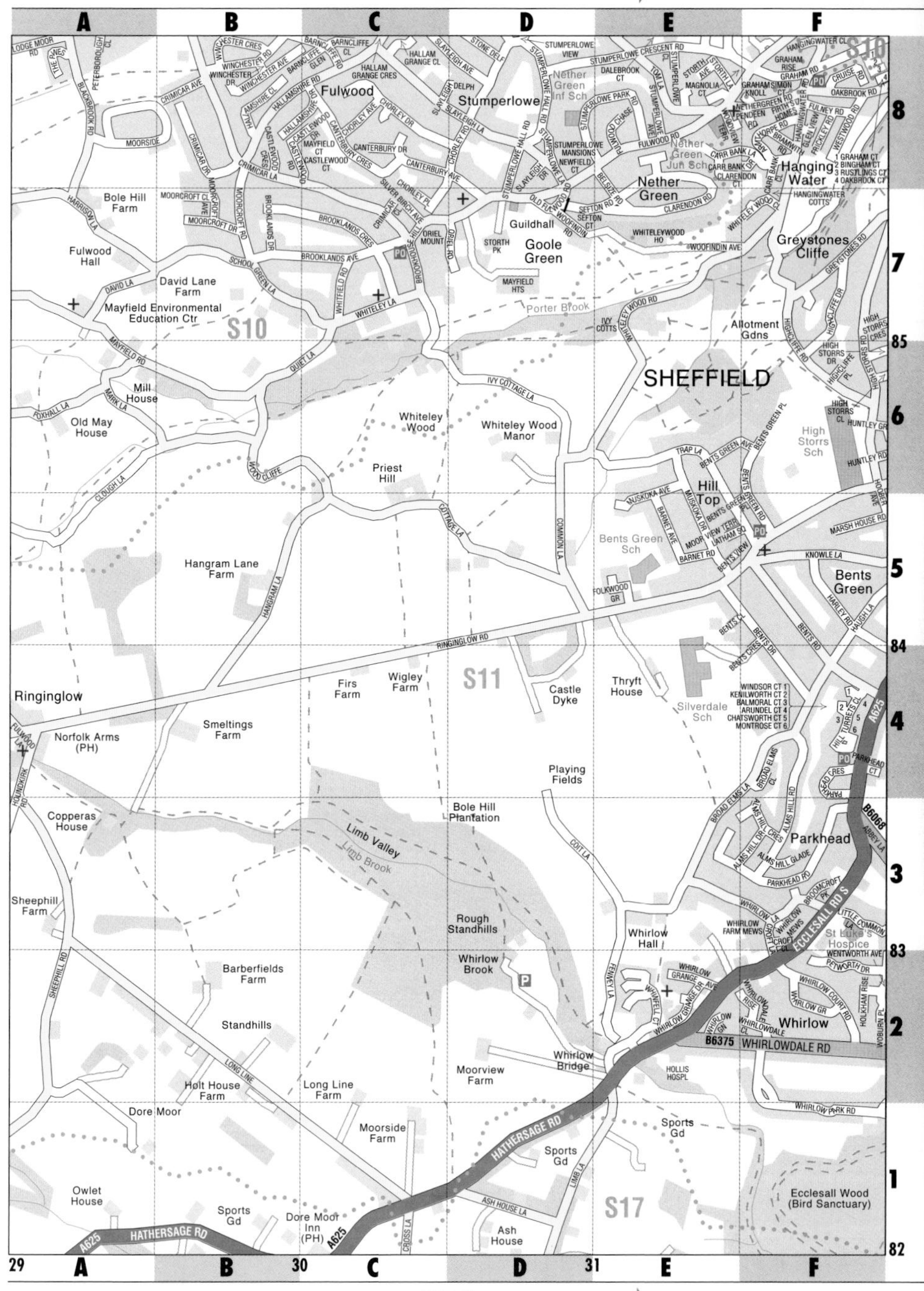

A
B
C
D
E
F
Fulwood
Stumperlowe
Nether Green Inf Sch
Nether Green Jun Sch
Nether Green
Hanging Water
Bole Hill Farm
Fulwood Hall
David Lane Farm
Mayfield Environmental Education Ctr
S10
Guildhall
Goole Green
Greystones Cliffe
Porter Brook
Allotment Gdns
SHEFFIELD
Mill House
Old May House
Whiteley Wood
Whiteley Wood Manor
Priest Hill
High Storrs Sch
Hill Top
Bents Green Sch
Hangram Lane Farm
Bents Green
RINGINGLOW RD
Ringinglow
Firs Farm
Wigley Farm
S11
Castle Dyke
Thryft House
Silverdale Sch
Norfolk Arms (PH)
Smeltings Farm
Playing Fields
Copperas House
Bole Hill Plantation
Limb Valley
Limb Brook
Parkhead
Sheephill Farm
Rough Standhills
Whirlow Hall
St Luke's Hospice
Barberfields Farm
Whirlow Brook
Standhills
Whirlow
B6375 WHIRLOWDALE RD
Holt House Farm
Long Line Farm
Moorview Farm
Whirlow Bridge
HOLLIS HOSPL
Dore Moor
Moorside Farm
Sports Gd
HATHERSAGE RD
Owlet House
Dore Moor Inn (PH)
Ash House
S17
Ecclesall Wood (Bird Sanctuary)
A625
B6068
ECCLESALL RD S
8
7
85
6
5
84
4
3
83
2
1
82
29
30
31

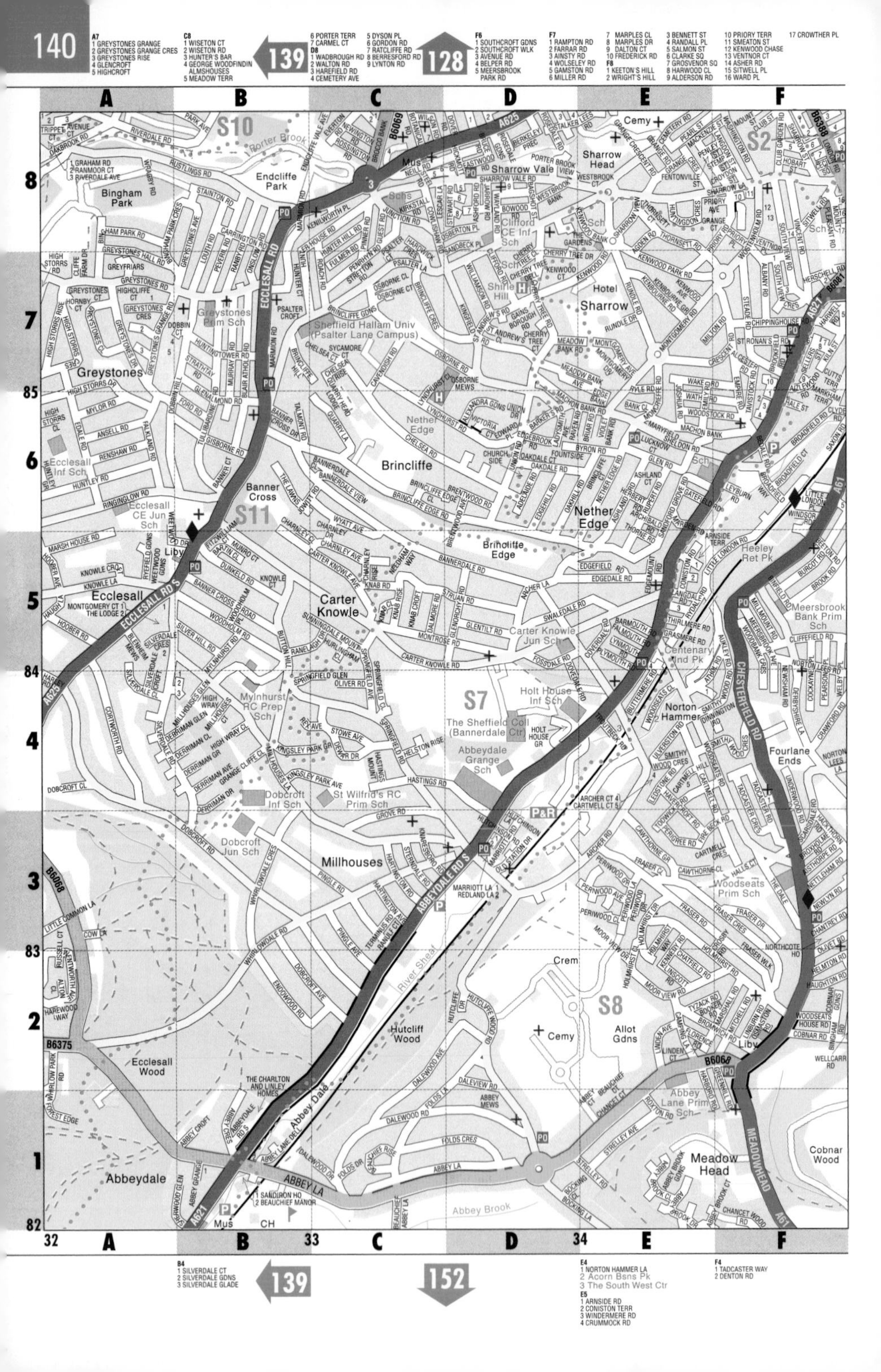
140
A7
1 GREYSTONES GRANGE
2 GREYSTONES GRANGE CRES
3 GREYSTONES RISE
4 GLENCROFT
5 HIGHCROFT
C8
1 WISETON CT
2 WISETON RD
3 HUNTER'S BAR
4 GEORGE WOODFINDIN ALMSHOUSES
5 MEADOW TERR
139
6 PORTER TERR
7 CARMEL CT
D8
1 WADBROUGH RD
2 WALTON RD
3 HAREFIELD RD
4 CEMETERY AVE
5 DYSON PL
6 GORDON RD
7 RATCLIFFE RD
8 BERRESFORD RD
9 LYNTON RD
128
F6
1 SOUTHCROFT GDNS
2 SOUTHCROFT WLK
3 AVENUE RD
4 BELPER RD
5 MEERSBROOK PARK RD
F7
1 RAMPTON RD
2 FARRAR RD
3 AINSTY RD
4 WOLSELEY RD
5 GAMSTON RD
6 MILLER RD
7 MARPLES CL
8 MARPLES DR
9 DALTON CT
10 FREDERICK RD
F8
1 KEETON'S HILL
2 WRIGHT'S HILL
3 BENNETT ST
4 RANDALL PL
5 SALMON ST
6 CLARKE SQ
7 GROSVENOR SQ
8 HARWOOD CL
9 ALDERSON RD
10 PRIORY TERR
11 SMEATON ST
12 KENWOOD CHASE
13 VENTNOR CT
14 ASHER RD
15 SITWELL PL
16 WARD PL
17 CROWTHER PL
S10
S2
S11
S7
S8
Endcliffe Park
Bingham Park
Sharrow Vale
Sharrow Head
Sharrow
Greystones
Brincliffe
Nether Edge
Banner Cross
Brincliffe Edge
Ecclesall
Carter Knowle
Heeley Ret Pk
Meersbrook Bank Prim Sch
Norton Hammer
Fourlane Ends
Millhouses
Woodseats Prim Sch
Hutcliff Wood
Ecclesall Wood
Abbeydale
Abbey Dale
Meadow Head
Cobnar Wood
Abbey Lane Prim Sch
Crem
Cemy
Allot Gdns
ECCLESALL RD
ECCLESALL RD S
ABBEYDALE RD S
CHESTERFIELD RD
MEADOWHEAD
ABBEY LA
B4
1 SILVERDALE CT
2 SILVERDALE GDNS
3 SILVERDALE GLADE
139
152
E4
1 NORTON HAMMER LA
2 Acorn Bsns Pk
3 The South West Ctr
E5
1 ARNSIDE RD
2 CONISTON TERR
3 WINDERMERE RD
4 CRUMMOCK RD
F4
1 TADCASTER WAY
2 DENTON RD

A6
1 TILLOTSON CL
2 NOWILL CT
3 NOWILL PL
4 WELLHEAD RD
5 SAXON RD
6 CHESTERFIELD RD

7 GOODWIN RD
8 PLANTATION RD
9 WHITING ST
10 SOUTHALL ST
11 MOLLOY ST
12 MOLLOY PL
13 Gordon Works

14 Meersbrook Works
A7
1 HORNER RD
2 WOLSELEY RD
3 ALDERNEY RD
4 LOWFIELD CT
5 Old Forge Bsns Pk

6 WILSON PL
A8
1 RANDALL PL
2 HARWOOD ST
3 ROWLAND RD
4 ST BARNABAS LA
5 ST BARNABAS RD

6 BELGRAVE SQ
7 CROWTHER PL
8 HOLLAND PL
9 BATT ST
10 HARRINGTON RD
11 ST WILFRID'S RD
12 ST BARNABAS HO

1 EASTCLIFFE CT
2 TOWER HO
3 QUEENS STABLES
4 QUEENS GDNS
5 QUEENS VIEW
6 QUEENS MEWS

Norfolk
Park
ST BENEDICTS

B6
1 BRADWELL ST
2 RICHARDS CT
3 STURGE CROFT
4 DENSON CL
5 FARISH PL
6 JEFFERY ST

B6
7 NICHOLSON PL
8 CARRFIELD CT
9 NICHOLSON CT
10 GREGORY CT
11 CARTER GRANGE
12 KENT GRANGE

13 CAMBRIDGE CT
14 CAMBRIDGE LODGE
15 GERARD CL

129   **142**   **141**

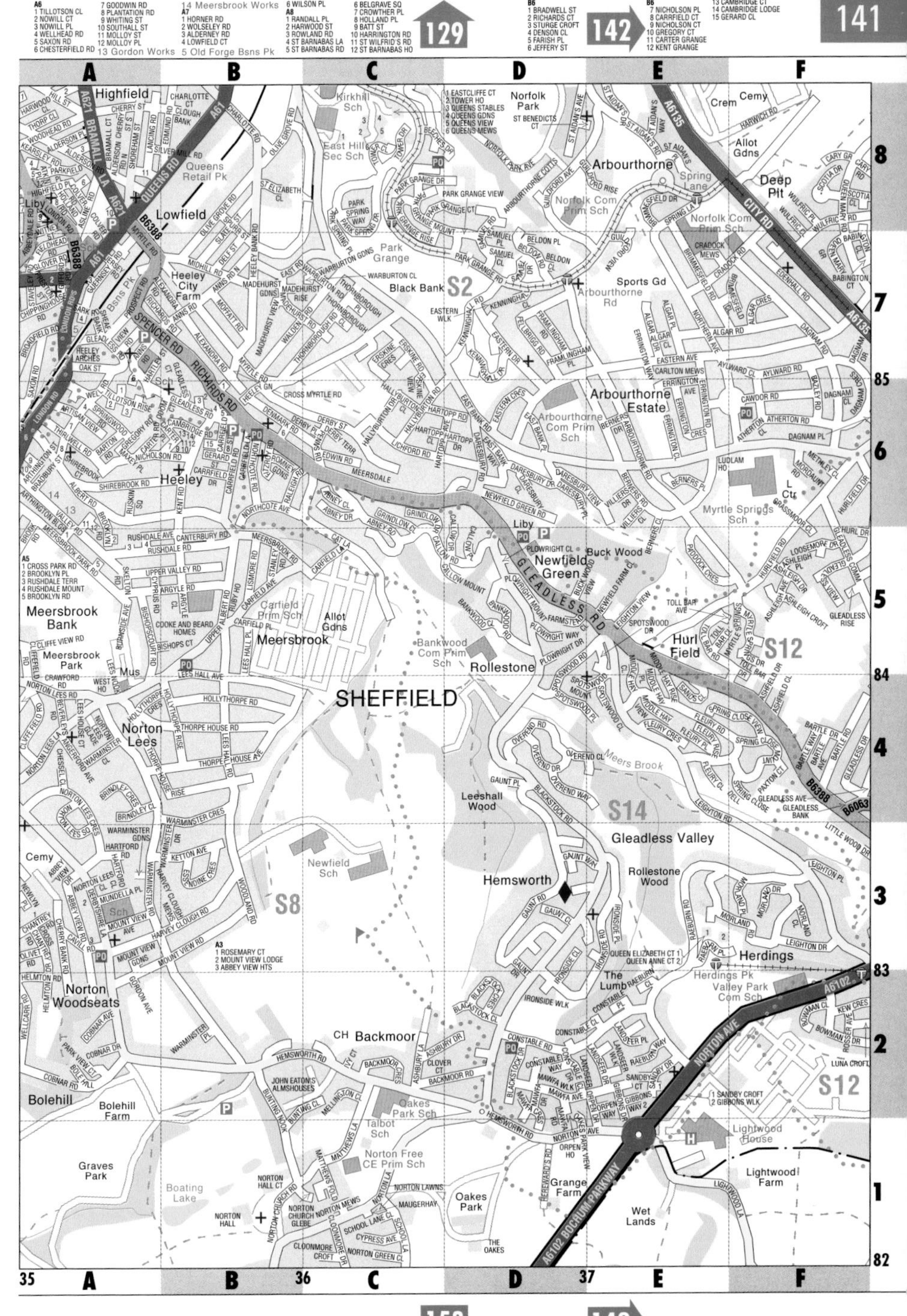

SHEFFIELD

S2

Manor
Estate

Fairleigh

PRINCE OF WALES RD

St Theresa's
RC Prim Sch

Woodthorpe
Estate

Richmond

Smelter
Wood

Teen's Painting Way

S13

Normanton
Spring

Elm Tree
Hill

MANSFIELD RD

WOODHOUSE RD

Cemy

Normanton Hill

Intake

Four Lane
Ends

Refuse
Tip

Wickfield
Plantation

RIDGEWAY RD

Common
Side

HOLLINSEND RD

Hollins
End

Gleadless
Prim Sch

Frecheville

The Sheffield
Coll
(Frecheville Ctr)

Birleyspa
Wood

Birley Spa
Com Prim Sch

Gleadless

Gleadless
Townend

GLEADLESS RD

BIRLEY MOOR RD

Birley

Spring Water
Ave

Base
Green

Birley Com
Prim Sch

S12

Birley Com
Coll

MOOR VALLEY

Charnock
Hill

WHITE LA

Whitelane
End

Charnock Hall
Prim Sch

Sunny
Bank

Birley
La

Birleywood
Farm

Birley
Moor Rd

Stoneley
Wood

Carter
Lodge
Farm

Robin Brook

Birdfield

Birley
Wood

S20

S8

HIGH LA

A4
1 GLEADLESS BANK
2 HOLLINSEND RD
3 CRISPIN RD
A3
1 GLEADLESS RISE
2 GLEADLESS VIEW

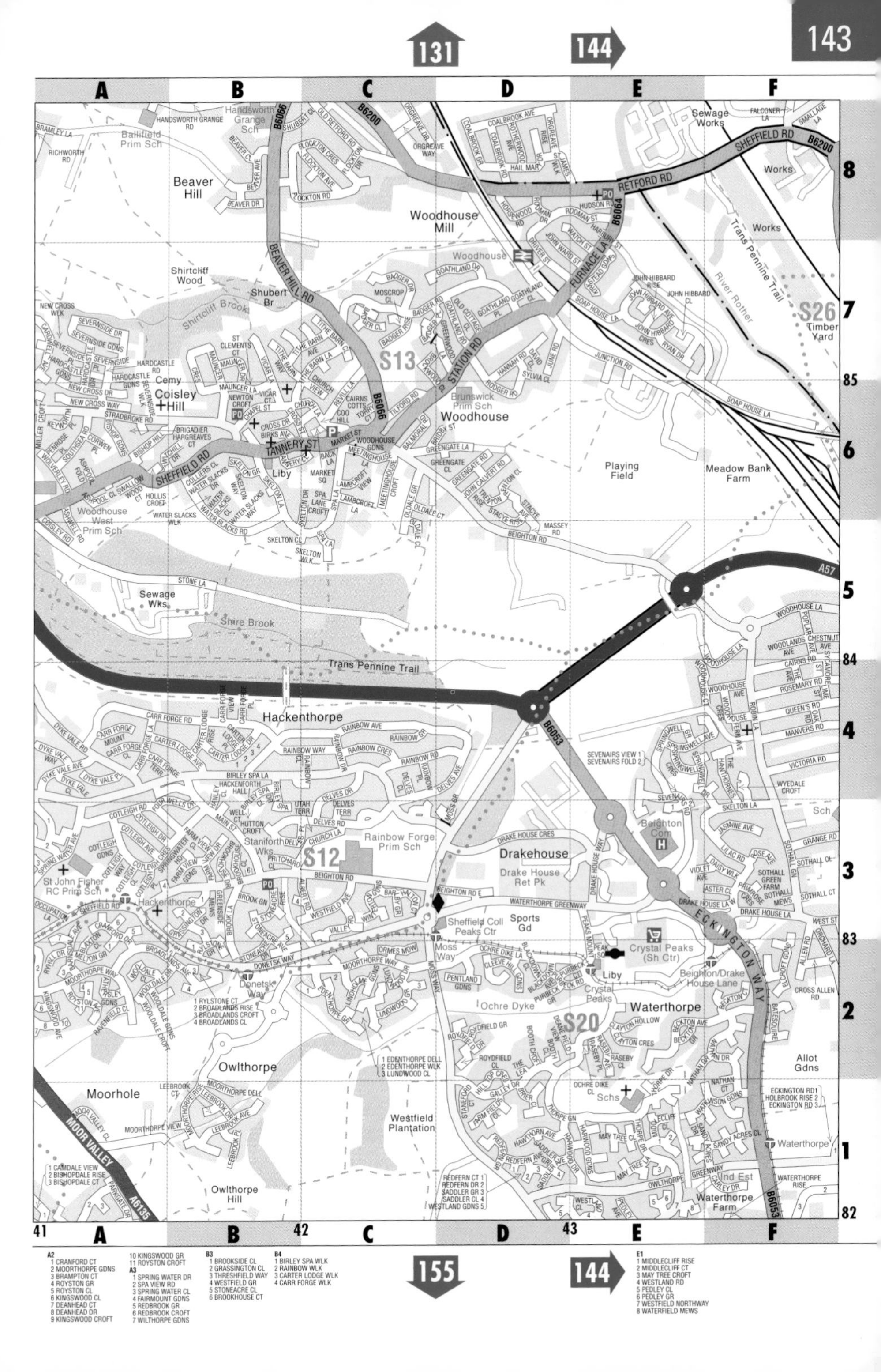

143
131
144
155
144
A B C D E F
8 7 6 5 4 3 2 1
85 84 83 82
41 42 43
Handsworth Grange Sch
HANDSWORTH GRANGE RD
Ballifield Prim Sch
Beaver Hill
Woodhouse Mill
Shirtcliff Wood
Shubert Br
Shirtcliff Brook
Cemy
Coisley Hill
Woodhouse
Brunswick Prim Sch
Liby
Woodhouse West Prim Sch
S13
S26
Sewage Works
Works
Trans Pennine Trail
River Rother
Timber Yard
Playing Field
Meadow Bank Farm
SHEFFIELD RD
RETFORD RD
STATION RD
BEAVER HILL RD
FURNACE LA
SOAP HOUSE LA
JUNCTION RD
BEIGHTON RD
STONE LA
Sewage Wks
Shire Brook
A57
Hackenthorpe
S12
Rainbow Forge Prim Sch
Staniforth Wks
Drakehouse
Drake House Ret Pk
Beighton Com
St John Fisher RC Prim Sch
Sports Gd
Sheffield Coll Peaks Ctr
Moss Way
Crystal Peaks (Sh Ctr)
Crystal Peaks
Beighton/Drake House Lane
Donetsk Way
Ochre Dyke
S20
Waterthorpe
ECKINGTON WAY
B6053
B6066
B6200
B6064
Owlthorpe
Moorhole
MOOR VALLEY
A6135
Westfield Plantation
Owlthorpe Hill
Schs
Allot Gdns
Und Est
Waterthorpe Farm
Sch
A2
1 CRANFORD CT
2 MOORTHORPE GDNS
3 BRAMPTON CT
4 ROYSTON GR
5 ROYSTON CL
6 KINGSWOOD CL
7 DEANHEAD CT
8 DEANHEAD DR
9 KINGSWOOD CROFT
10 KINGSWOOD GR
11 ROYSTON CROFT
A3
1 SPRING WATER DR
2 SPA VIEW RD
3 SPRING WATER CL
4 FAIRMOUNT GDNS
5 REDBROOK GR
6 REDBROOK CROFT
7 WILTHORPE GDNS
B3
1 BROOKSIDE CL
2 GRASSINGTON CL
3 THRESHFIELD WAY
4 WESTFIELD GR
5 STONEACRE CL
6 BROOKHOUSE CT
B4
1 BIRLEY SPA WLK
2 RAINBOW WLK
3 CARTER LODGE WLK
4 CARR FORGE WLK
E1
1 MIDDLECLIFF RISE
2 MIDDLECLIFF CT
3 MAY TREE CROFT
4 WESTLAND RD
5 PEDLEY CL
6 PEDLEY GR
7 WESTFIELD NORTHWAY
8 WATERFIELD MEWS

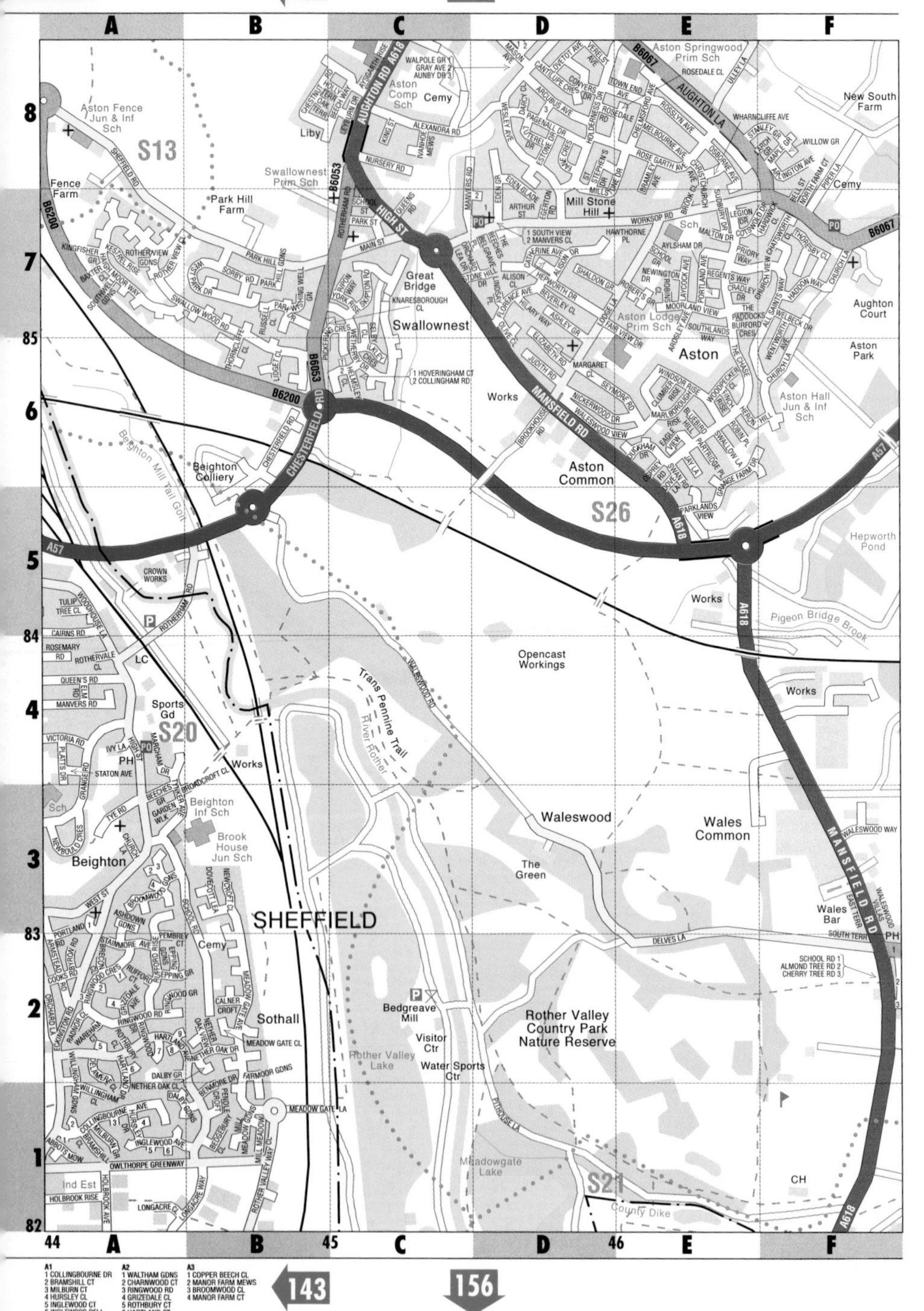

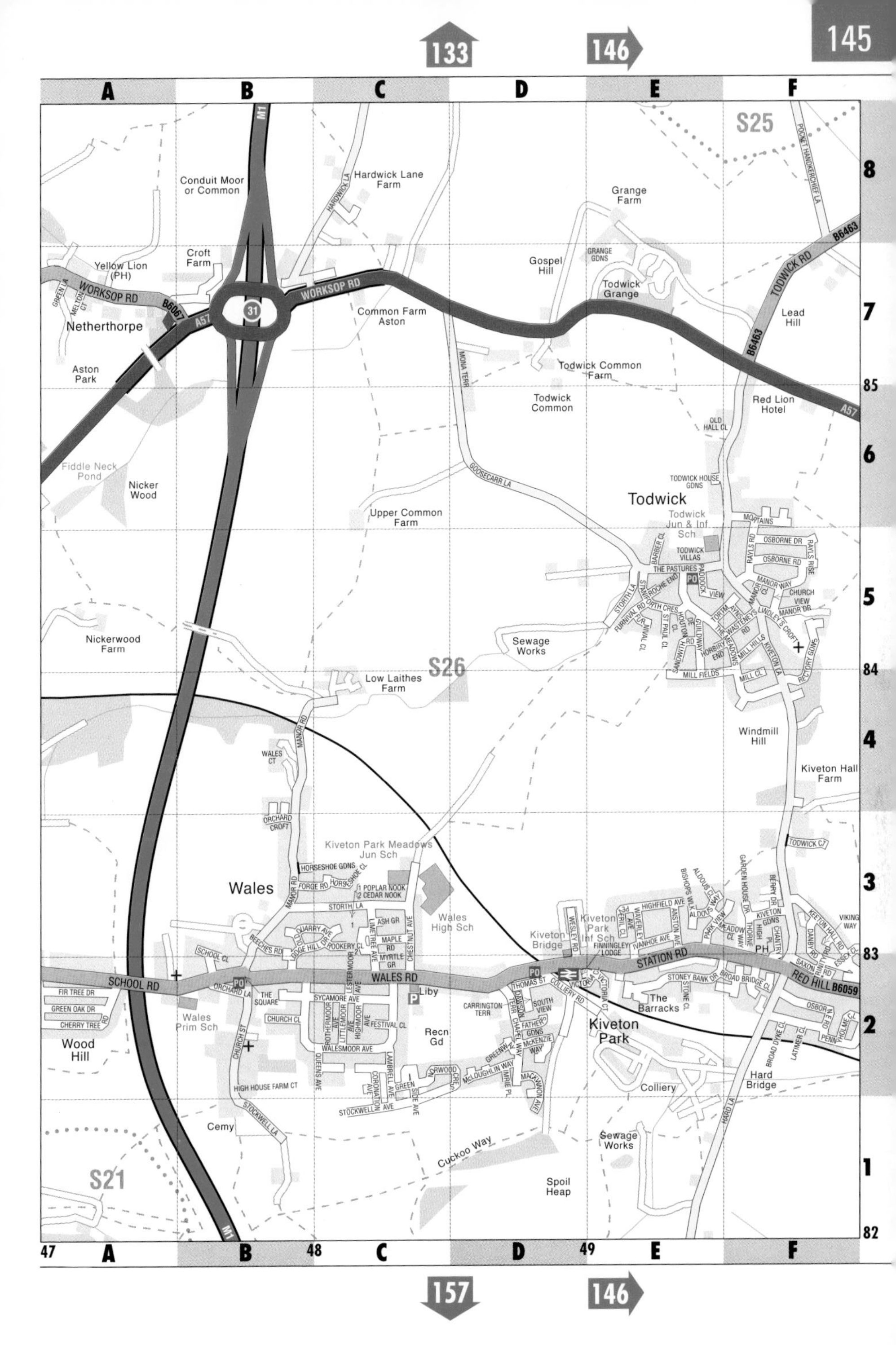

133
146
A
B
C
D
E
F
S25
8
7
6
5
4
3
2
1
85
84
83
82
47
48
49
M1
Conduit Moor
or Common
Hardwick Lane
Farm
HARDWICK LA
Grange
Farm
POCKET HANDKERCHIEF LA
B6463
TODWICK RD
Croft
Farm
Yellow Lion
(PH)
WORKSOP RD
GREEN LA
MELTON CT
B6067
A57
31
Netherthorpe
Common Farm
Aston
Gospel
Hill
GRANGE
GDNS
Todwick
Grange
Lead
Hill
Aston
Park
MONA TERR
Todwick Common
Farm
Todwick
Common
Red Lion
Hotel
OLD
HALL CL
Fiddle Neck
Pond
Nicker
Wood
GOOSECARR LA
TODWICK HOUSE
GDNS
Todwick
Todwick
Jun & Inf
Sch
Upper Common
Farm
MORTAINS
OSBORNE DR
OSBORNE RD
RAYLS RD
RAYLS RISE
BARBER CL
TODWICK
VILLAS
THE PASTURES
PADDOCK
VIEW
ROCHE END
STAINFORTH CRES
STORTH LA
FURNIVAL RD
MANOR WAY
CHURCH
VIEW
MANOR DR
LINDLEY'S CROFT
HOUTON CL
ST PAUL CL
SANDWITH RD
GUILDWAY
THE WASTENEYS
THE MEADOWS
HORBIRY END
MILL HILLS
KIVETON LA
RECTORY GDNS
MILL FIELDS
MILL CL
Nickerwood
Farm
Sewage
Works
S26
Low Laithes
Farm
Windmill
Hill
MANOR RD
WALES
CT
Kiveton Hall
Farm
ORCHARD
CROFT
Kiveton Park Meadows
Jun Sch
TODWICK CT
HORSESHOE GDNS
FORGE RD
HORSESHOE CL
1 POPLAR NOOK
2 CEDAR NOOK
Wales
STORTH LA
Wales
High Sch
ASH GR
QUARRY AVE
LODGE HILL DR
ROOKERY CL
LIMETREE AVE
MAPLE RD
MYRTLE GR
CHESTNUT AVE
BEECHES RD
SCHOOL CL
ALDOUS CL
ALDOUS WAY
BISHOPS WLK
HIGHFIELD AVE
WAVERLEY AVE
ANSTON AVE
GARDEN HOUSE DR
BERRY DR
KEETON HALL RD
VIKING WAY
Kiveton
Park
Inf Sch
Kiveton
Bridge
WESLEY RD
FINNINGLEY
LODGE
IVANHOE AVE
PARK VIEW
MEADOW CL
THORNE WAY
HIGH PL
KIVETON GDNS
CHANTRY
DANBY RD
SAXON RD
ESSEX CL
STATION RD
PH
SCHOOL RD
WALES RD
PO
THOMAS ST
COLLIERY RD
VICTORIA CT
STONEY BANK DR
BROAD BRIDGE CL
RED HILL B6059
FIR TREE DR
GREEN OAK DR
CHERRY TREE RD
ORCHARD LA
THE SQUARE
Liby
SYCAMORE AVE
LESTERMOOR AVE
DAWSON TERR
SOUTH VIEW
CARRINGTON
TERR
The
Barracks
STONE CL
OSBORNE RD
PENN
HOLME CL
Wales
Prim Sch
CHURCH CL
ROTHERMOOR AVE
LITTLEMOOR AVE
HIGHMOOR AVE
FESTIVAL CL
Recn
Gd
CHAPEL WAY
FATHER GDNS
Kiveton
Park
BROAD DYKE CL
LATIMER CL
Wood
Hill
CHURCH ST
WALESMOOR AVE
QUEENS AVE
LAMBRELL AVE
NORWOOD CRES
GREENWAY
McLOUGHLIN WAY
McKENZIE WAY
IMRIE PL
MACKINNON AVE
Hard
Bridge
Colliery
HIGH HOUSE FARM CT
CORONATION AVE
GREEN SIDE AVE
STOCKWELL AVE
STOCKWELL LA
Cemy
Sewage
Works
HARD LA
Cuckoo Way
S21
Spoil
Heap
157
146

145
134

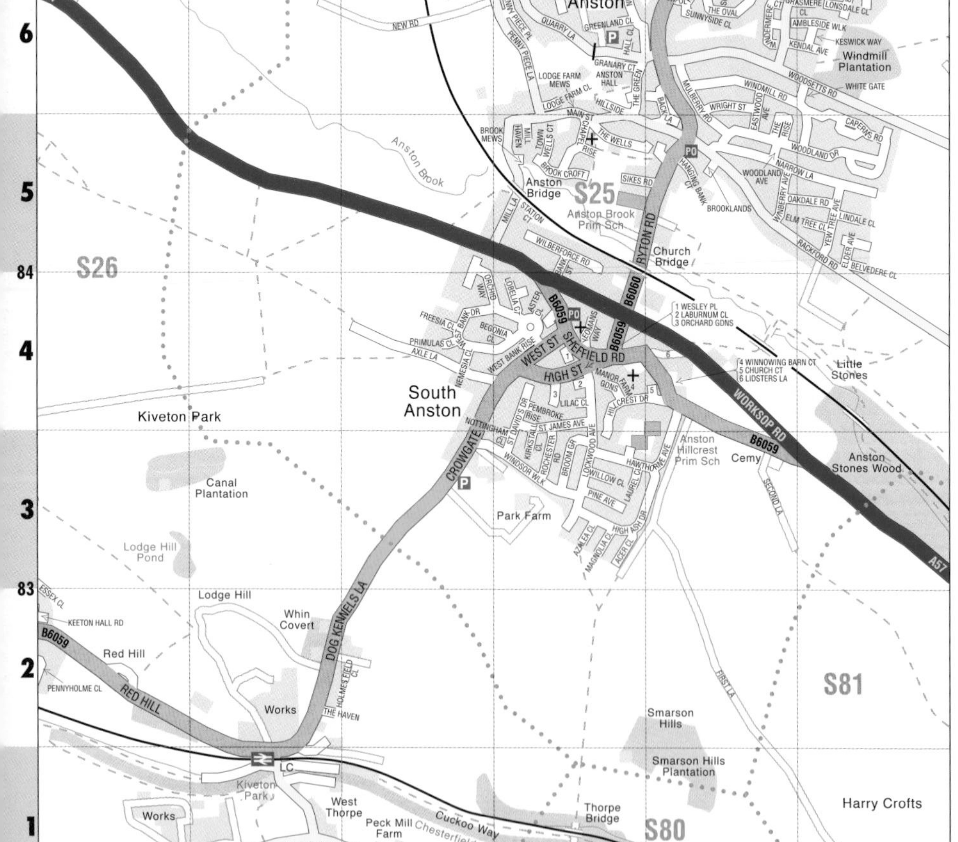
A
B
C
D
E
F
8
7
85
6
5
84
4
3
83
2
1
82
50
51
52
TODWICK RD
B6463
COMMON RD
UNIVERSAL CL
The North Anston Trad Est
HOUGHTON RD
North Anston Bsns Ctr
Sewage Works
CRAMFIT CRES
WASHINGTON CL 1
WHITEHEAD CL 2
BROADOAKS RD 3
BROADOAKS CL 4
LITTLEFIELD RD 5
LIMELANDS RD
BURGHLEY CL
MEDLOCK CT
CHURCH LA
LAUGHTON RD
LEOPOLD ST
BARLEYCROFT LA
THE CLOSE
WESTERN AVE
HALL FARM CROFT
SWINSTON HILL RD
BIRKDALE AVE
NEW RD
B6060
PARKLANDS AVE
MEADOWPARK
BLENHEIM CL
ST LEONARD'S CL
Alcove Plantation
MIDDLETON AVE
CARVER DR
FALCON WAY
TROON WLK
ST ANDREWS CL
GLENEAGLES RD
WALNUT DR
SUNNINGDALE RD
Slag Heap
Cramfit Bridge
Anston Greenlands Jun & Inf Sch
PORTLAND CL
DEVONSHIRE DR
NEWCASTLE CL
SCARBOROUGH CL
WENTWORTH WAY 1
TURNBERRY WAY 2
Cemy
LYTHAM AVE
NURSERY RD
Cramfit Brook
CRAMFIT RD
SPRINGFIELD TERR
EDINBURGH DR
NETHERTHORPE WAY
LEEDS RD
DUKERIES DR
MANVERS CL
RUTLAND AVE
WELLINGTON AVE
Anston Park Inf Sch
PARK AVE
Anston Park Jun Sch
BEECH GR
FURNESS CL
CARTMEL WLK
RYDAL RD
BORROWDALE CRES
LANGDALE WAY
Burne Farm
BUTTERMERE CL
DERWENT CL
SANCTUARY FIELDS
MARLBOROUGH CL
BEDFORD CL
ENNERDALE CL
WARWICK WAY
ULLSWATER CL
CALDBECK PL
APPLEBY WLK
LAKELAND DR
HAWKSHEAD CRES
ORCHARD AVE
THE ORCHARD
SCAFELL PL
THIRLMERE DR
CONISTON CL
PATTERDALE WAY
CRAMFIT CL
LIMEKILNS
North Anston
NURSERY CRES
ANSTON CL
PLANTATION AVE
NORFOLK DR
SUFFOLK CL
THE OVAL
SUNNYSIDE CL
WINDERMERE CT
GRASMERE CL
LONSDALE CL
AMBLESIDE WLK
KESWICK WAY
KENDAL AVE
Windmill Plantation
A57
NEW RD
PENNY PIECE PL
QUARRY LA
GREENLAND CL
HALL CL
PENNY PIECE LA
GRANARY CT
ANSTON HALL
LODGE FARM MEWS
LODGE FARM CL
THE GREEN
HILLSIDE
MAIN ST
BACK LA
MULBERRY RD
WINDMILL RD
WRIGHT ST
EASTWOOD AVE
THE RISE
WOODSETTS RD
WHITE GATE
CAPERNS RD
BROOK MEWS
MILL HAVEN
MILL TOWN
WELLS CT
CHAPEL RISE
THE WELLS
Anston Brook
BROOK CROFT
Anston Bridge
S25
SIKES RD
PO
HANGING BANK
NARROW LA
WOODLAND DR
WOODLAND AVE
WINBERRY AVE
OAKDALE RD
ELM TREE CL
YEW TREE AVE
LINDALE CL
BROOKLANDS
MILL LA
STATION CT
Anston Brook Prim Sch
RYTON RD
ELDER AVE
RACKFORD RD
BELVEDERE CL
WILBERFORCE RD
Church Bridge
S26
ORCHID WAY
LOBELIA CT
ASTER CL
BANK ST
B6059
FREESIA CL
WEST BANK DR
BEGONIA CL
YEOMANS WAY
1 WESLEY PL
2 LABURNUM CL
3 ORCHARD GDNS
PRIMULAS CL
AXLE LA
NEMESIA CL
WEST BANK RISE
WEST ST
SHEFFIELD RD
4 WINNOWING BARN CT
5 CHURCH CT
6 LIDSTERS LA
Little Stones
HIGH ST
MANOR FARM GDNS
South Anston
LILAC CL
HILLCREST DR
WORKSOP RD
Kiveton Park
NOTTINGHAM CL
PEMBROKE RISE
ST DAVID'S DR
KIRKSTALL CL
ST JAMES AVE
ROCHESTER RD
BROOM GR
LOCKWOOD AVE
HAWTHORNE AVE
Anston Hillcrest Prim Sch
Cemy
Anston Stones Wood
CROWGATE
WINDSOR WLK
WILLOW CL
LAUREL CL
SECOND LA
Canal Plantation
P
PINE AVE
Park Farm
HIGH ASH DR
AZALEA CL
MAGNOLIA CL
ACER CL
Lodge Hill Pond
ESSEX CL
Lodge Hill
KEETON HALL RD
Whin Covert
DOG KENNELS LA
Red Hill
HOLMESFIELD CL
FIRST LA
S81
PENNYHOLME CL
RED HILL
Works
THE HAVEN
Smarson Hills
LC
Smarson Hills Plantation
Kiveton Park
West Thorpe
Harry Crofts
Works
Peck Mill Farm
Cuckoo Way
Chesterfield Canal
Thorpe Bridge
S80
LADY FIELD RD
MANOR RD
PACKMAN LA
PECK MILL VIEW
Peck Mill Bottoms

145
158

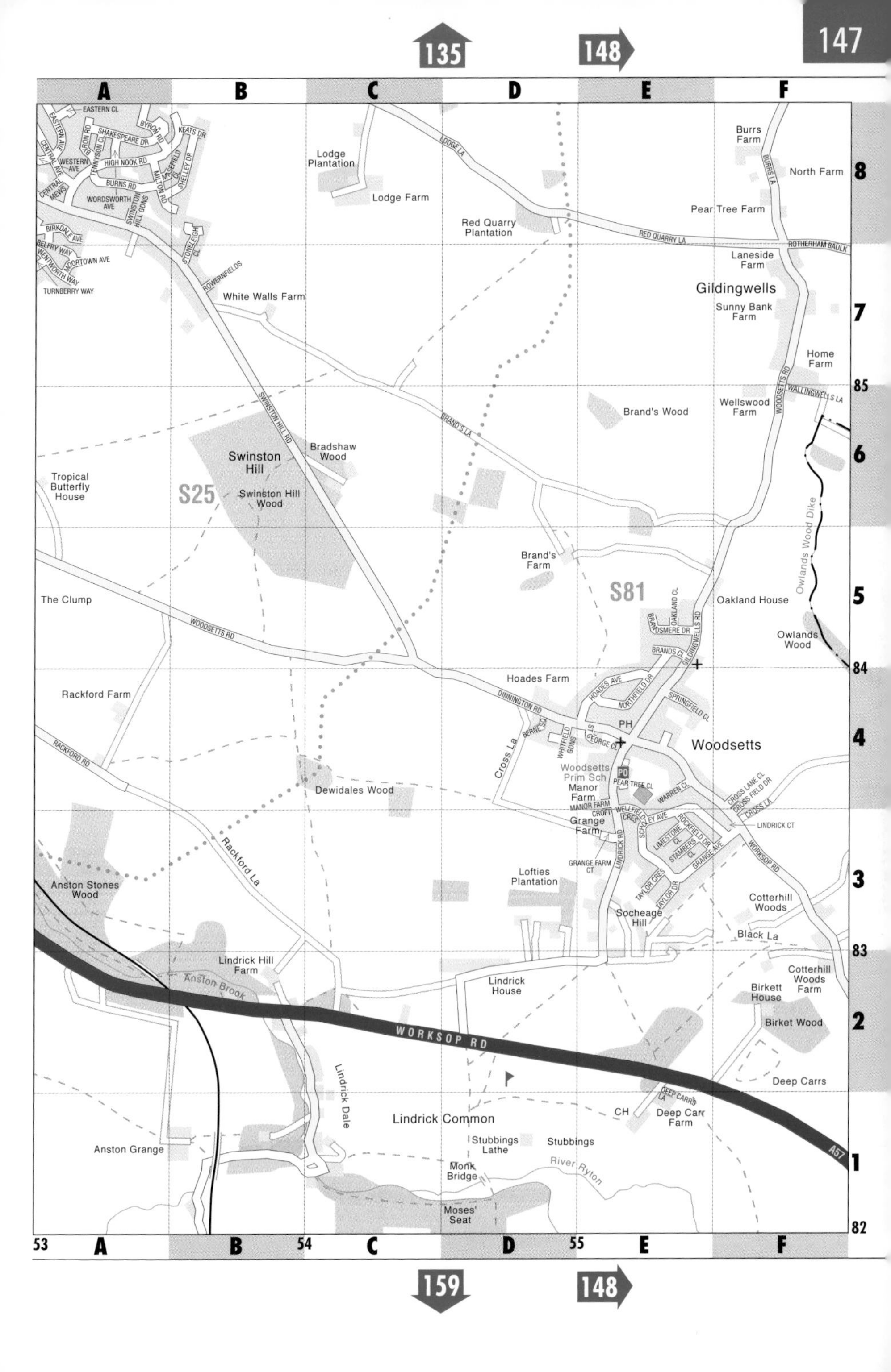

135
148
A
B
C
D
E
F
8
7
85
6
5
84
4
3
83
2
1
82
53
54
55
Lodge Plantation
Lodge Farm
Lodge La
Red Quarry Plantation
Red Quarry La
Burrs Farm
Burrs La
North Farm
Pear Tree Farm
Rotherham Baulk
Laneside Farm
Gildingwells
Sunny Bank Farm
Home Farm
Woodsetts Rd
Wallingwells La
Wellswood Farm
Brand's Wood
Brand's La
White Walls Farm
Rowernfields
Stoneleigh Cl
Eastern Cl
Byron Rd
Keats Dr
Shakespeare Dr
Tennyson Cl
High Nook Rd
Western Ave
Central Ave
Central Mews
Burns Rd
Wordsworth Ave
Swinston Hill Gdns
Milton Rd
Masefield Cl
Shelley Dr
Birkdale Ave
Belfry Way
Moortown Ave
Wentworth Way
Turnberry Way
Swinston Hill Rd
Bradshaw Wood
Swinston Hill
S25
Swinston Hill Wood
Tropical Butterfly House
The Clump
Woodsetts Rd
Brand's Farm
S81
Oakland Cl
Oakland House
Brandsmere Dr
Gildingwells Rd
Owlands Wood Dike
Owlands Wood
Brands Cl
Rackford Farm
Hoades Farm
Hoades Ave
Northfield Dr
Springfield Cl
Dinnington Rd
Berne Sq
Whitfield Gdns
St George Cl
PH
Woodsetts
Cross La
Woodsetts Prim Sch
PO
Pear Tree Cl
Manor Farm
Manor Farm Croft
Wellfield Cres
Warren Cl
Cross Lane Cl
Cross Field Dr
Cross La
Lindrick Ct
Grange Farm
Scholey Ave
Limestone Cl
Rockfield Dr
Stambers Cl
Grange Ave
Grange Farm Ct
Lindrick Rd
Worksop Rd
Rackford Rd
Dewidales Wood
Rackford La
Lofties Plantation
Taylor Cres
Taylor Dr
Socheage Hill
Cotterhill Woods
Black La
Anston Stones Wood
Lindrick Hill Farm
Anston Brook
Lindrick House
Cotterhill Woods Farm
Birkett House
Birket Wood
Worksop Rd
Lindrick Dale
Deep Carrs
Deep Carrs La
CH
Deep Carr Farm
Lindrick Common
Anston Grange
Stubbings Lathe
Stubbings
Monk Bridge
River Ryton
Moses' Seat
A57
159
148

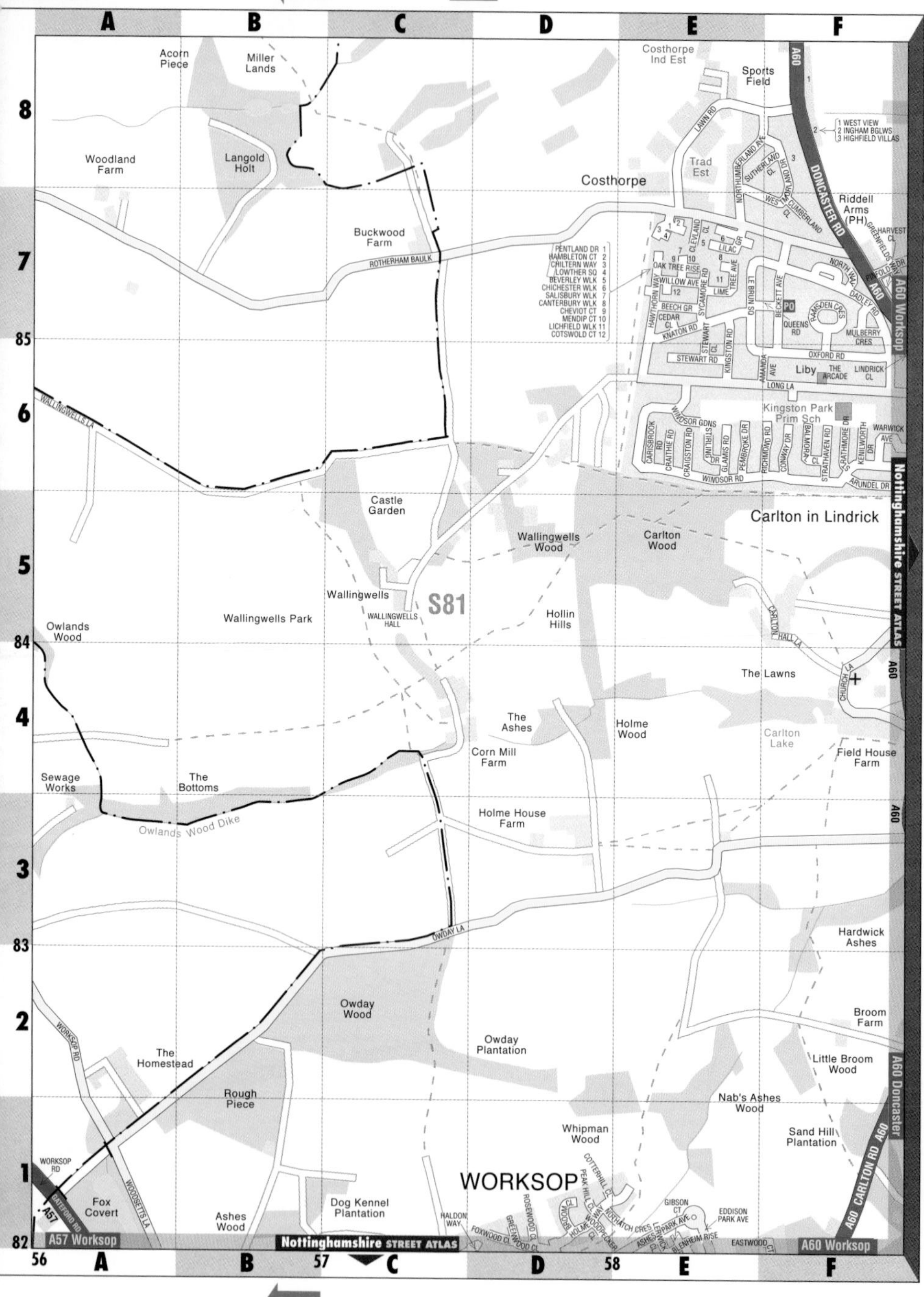

A B C D E F

8

Acorn Piece

Miller Lands

Costhorpe Ind Est

Sports Field

1 WEST VIEW
2 INGHAM BGLWS
3 HIGHFIELD VILLAS

Woodland Farm

Langold Holt

Costhorpe

Trad Est

Riddell Arms (PH)

7

Buckwood Farm

ROTHERHAM BAULK

PENTLAND DR 1
HAMBLETON CT 2
CRITERN WAY 3
LOWTHER SQ 4
BEVERLEY WLK 5
CHICHESTER WLK 6
SALISBURY WLK 7
CANTERBURY WLK 8
CHEVIOT CT 9
MENDIP CT 10
LICHFIELD WLK 11
COTSWOLD CT 12

OAK TREE RISE

WILLOW AVE

85

CEDAR
BEECH GR

KNATUR RD

PO
QUEENS RD

MULBERRY CRES

6

WOLLINGWELLS LA

OXFORD RD

STEWART RD

Liby
THE ARCADE

LINDRICK CL

LONG LA

Kingston Park Prim Sch

WARWICK AVE

WINDSOR RD

Carlton in Lindrick

Castle Garden

5

Wallingwells Wood

Carlton Wood

Wallingwells

S81

Wallingwells Park

WALLINGWELLS HALL

Hollin Hills

CARLTON HALL LA

84

Owlands Wood

The Lawns

Carlton Lake

+

4

The Ashes

Holme Wood

Field House Farm

Corn Mill Farm

Sewage Works

The Bottoms

Owlands Wood Dike

Holme House Farm

3

Hardwick Ashes

OWDAY LA

83

2

The Homestead

Owday Wood

Owday Plantation

Broom Farm

Little Broom Wood

Rough Piece

Nab's Ashes Wood

Sand Hill Plantation

Whipman Wood

1

WORKSOP RD

Fox Covert

Ashes Wood

Dog Kennel Plantation

HALDON WAY

WORKSOP

GIBSON CT

EDDISON PARK AVE

82

DONCASTER RD

A60 Worksop

Nottinghamshire STREET ATLAS

A60

A60 Doncaster

A60 CARLTON RD

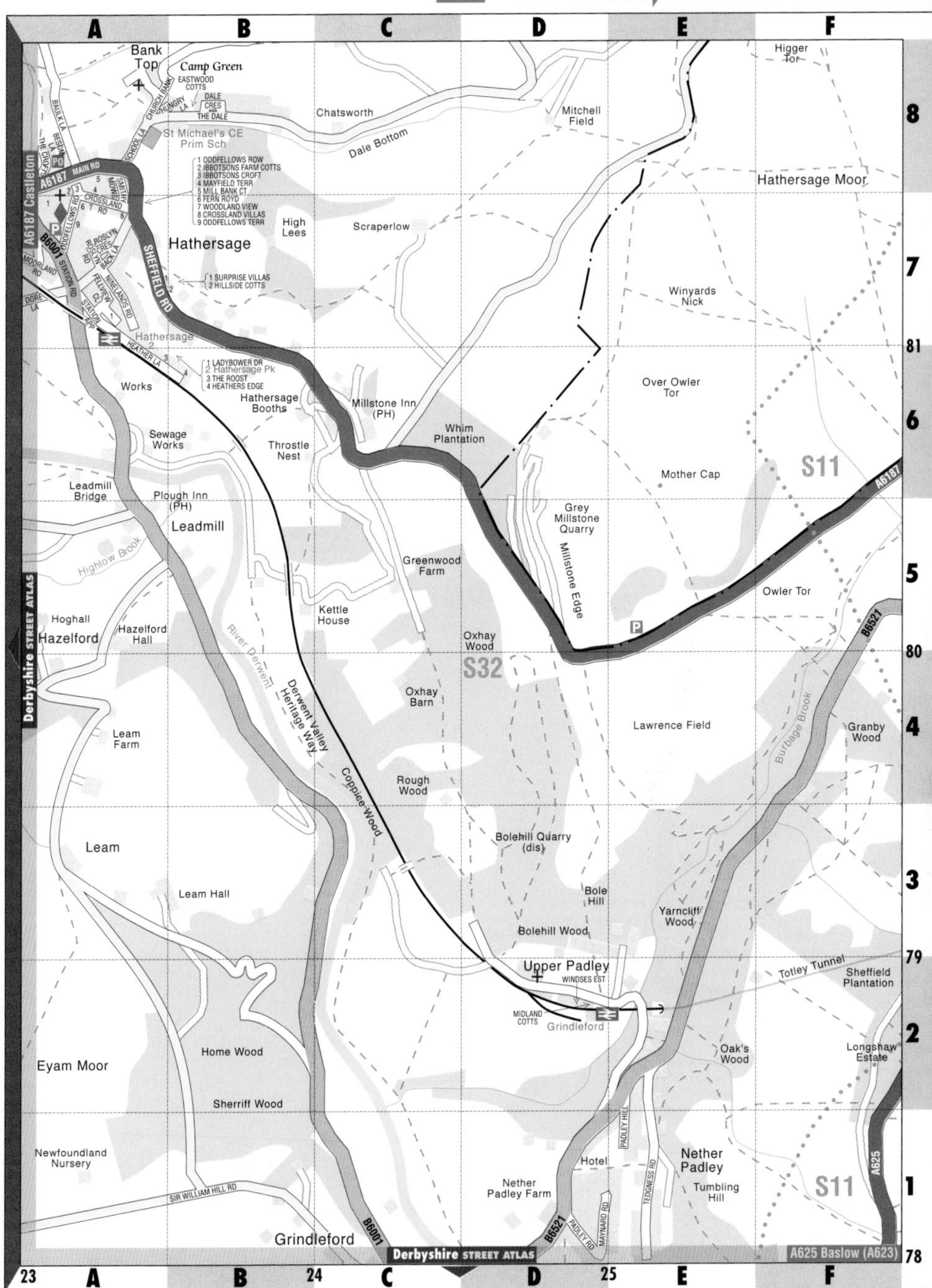

| | A | | B | | C | | D | | E | | F | |

8

Higger Tor

Bank Top

Camp Green

EASTWOOD COTTS

DALE
CRES
THE DALE

Chatsworth

Dale Bottom

Mitchell Field

St Michael's CE Prim Sch

1 ODDFELLOWS ROW
2 IBBOTSONS FARM COTTS
3 IBBOTSONS CROFT
4 MAYFIELD TERR
5 MILL BANK CT
6 FERN ROYD
7 WOODLAND VIEW
8 CROSSLAND VILLAS
9 ODDFELLOWS TERR

Hathersage Moor

7

Hathersage

1 SURPRISE VILLAS
2 HILLSIDE COTTS

High Lees

Scraperlow

Winyards Nick

81

1 LADYBOWER DR
2 Hathersage Pk
3 THE ROOST
4 HEATHERS EDGE

Works

Over Owler Tor

S11

A6187

6

Millstone Inn (PH)

Hathersage Booths

Whim Plantation

Sewage Works

Throstle Nest

Mother Cap

Leadmill Bridge

Plough Inn (PH)

Grey Millstone Quarry

5

Leadmill

Greenwood Farm

Owler Tor

Highlow Brook

Millstone Edge

Kettle House

B6521

80

Hoghall

Hazelford

Hazelford Hall

Oxhay Wood

S32

4

Leam Farm

Oxhay Barn

Lawrence Field

Granby Wood

River Derwent

Rough Wood

Burbage Brook

Leam

Coppice Wood

3

Leam Hall

Bolehill Quarry (dis)

Bole Hill

Yarncliff Wood

Derwent Valley Heritage Way

Bolehill Wood

Totley Tunnel

Sheffield Plantation

79

Eyam Moor

Home Wood

Upper Padley

WINDSES EST

MIDLAND COTTS

Grindleford

Oak's Wood

Longshaw Estate

2

S11

Sherriff Wood

A625

Newfoundland Nursery

Nether Padley

SIR WILLIAM HILL RD

Nether Padley Farm

Hotel

Tumbling Hill

PADLEY HILL

GRINDLEFORD

B6001

B6521

HAYMAN RD

TEGGNESS RD

1

78

A625 Baslow (A623)

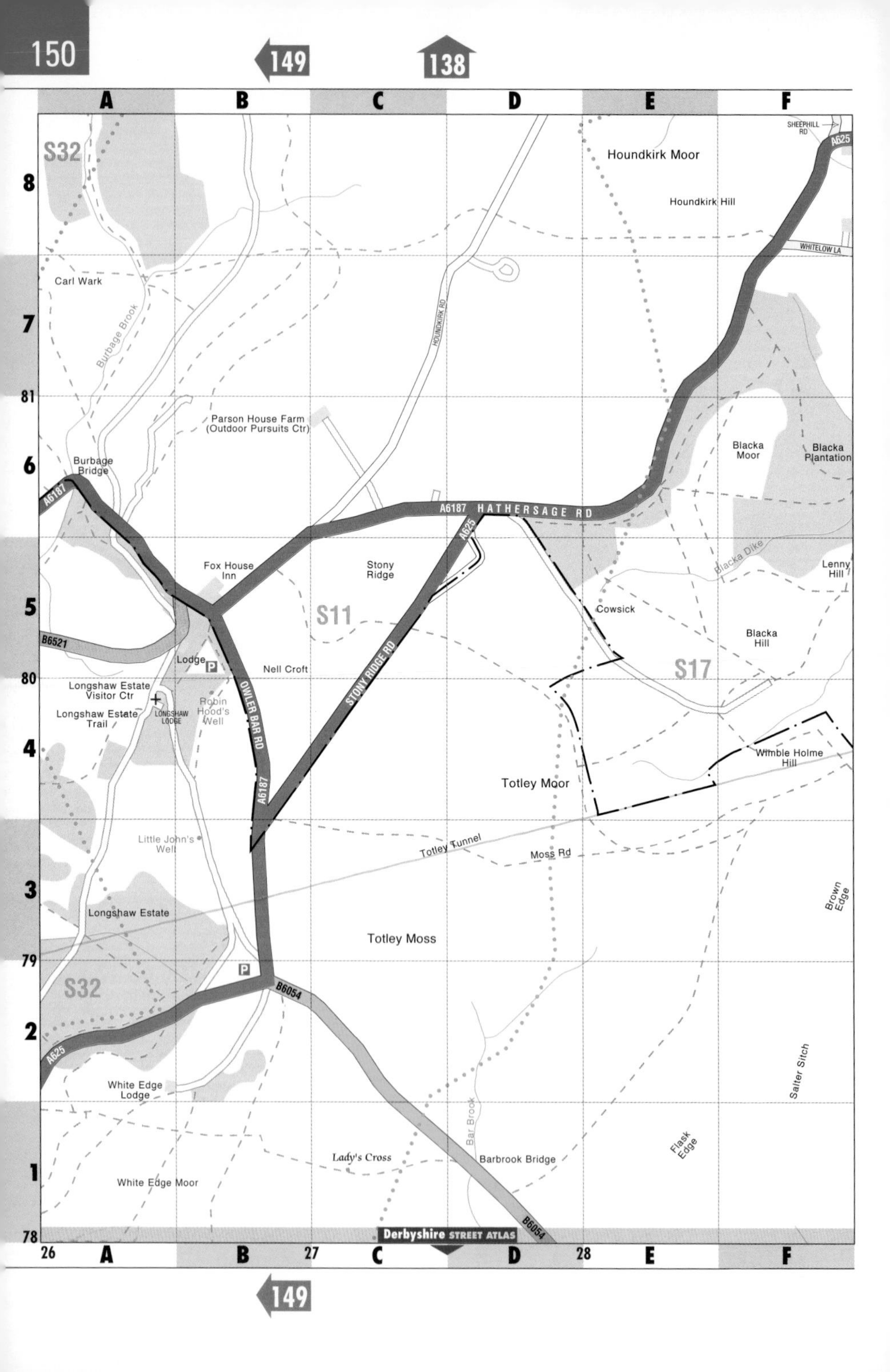

S32

A | B | C | D | E | F

8

SHEEPHILL RD

A625

Houndkirk Moor

Houndkirk Hill

WHITELOW LA

7

Carl Wark

Burbage Brook

81

Blacka Moor

Blacka Plantation

Parson House Farm
(Outdoor Pursuits Ctr)

6

Burbage Bridge

A6187

A6187 HATHERSAGE RD

A625

Blacka Dike

Lenny Hill

Fox House Inn

Stony Ridge

5

S11

Cowsick

Blacka Hill

B6521

Lodge P

Nell Croft

S17

OWLER BAR RD

80

Longshaw Estate
Visitor Ctr

Robin Hood's Well

STONY RIDGE RD

Longshaw Estate Trail

LONGSHAW LODGE

Wimble Holme Hill

4

A6187

Totley Moor

Little John's Well

Totley Tunnel

Moss Rd

Brown Edge

3

Longshaw Estate

Totley Moss

79

S32

P

B6054

2

A625

White Edge Lodge

Salter Sitch

Bar Brook

Flask Edge

1

Lady's Cross

Barbrook Bridge

White Edge Moor

78

26 | A | B | 27 | C | D | 28 | E | F

139
152

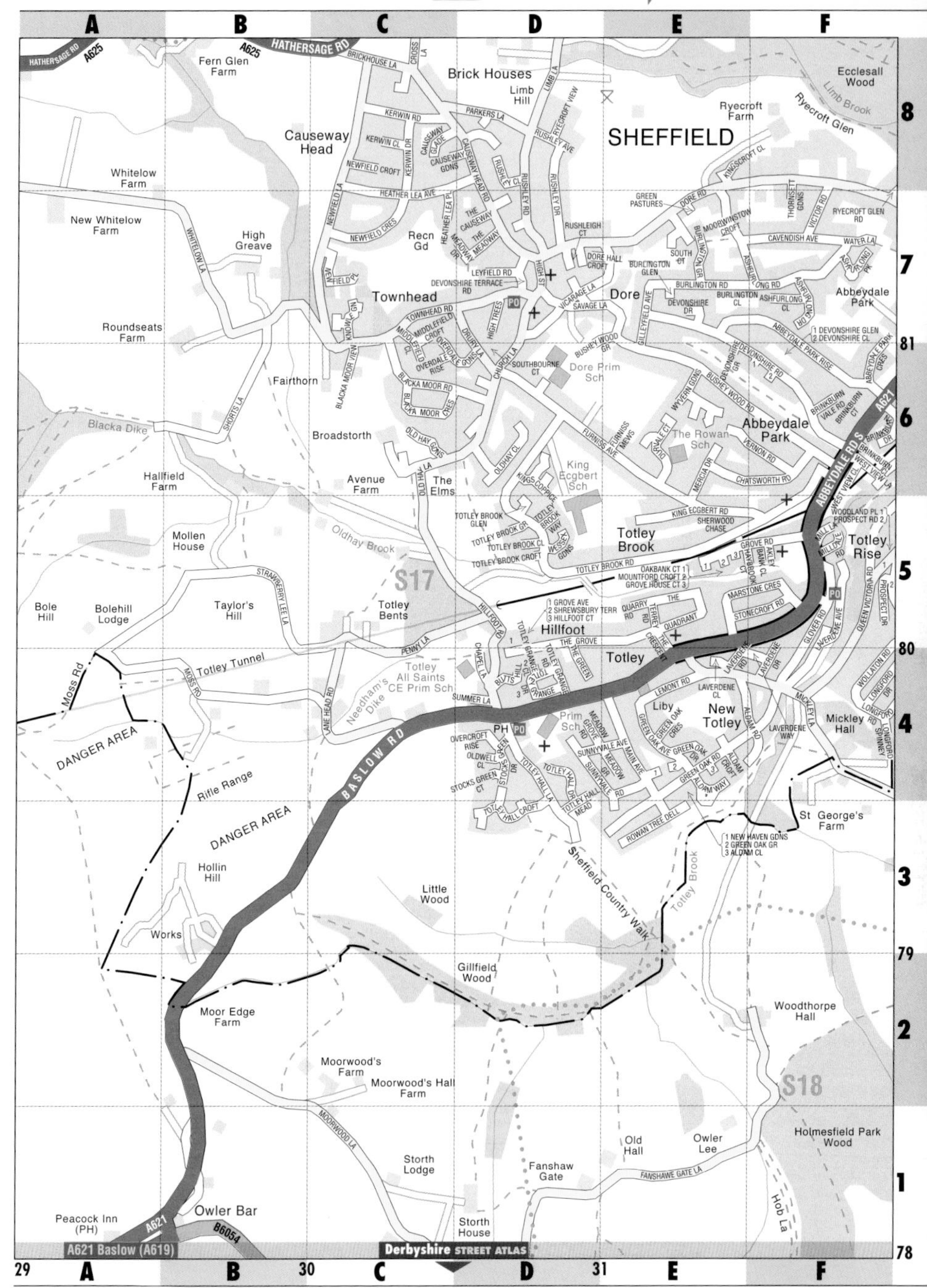
SHEFFIELD
Brick Houses
Limb Hill
Causeway Head
Whitelow Farm
New Whitelow Farm
High Greave
Fern Glen Farm
Ecclesall Wood
Ryecroft Farm
Ryecroft Glen
Limb Brook
Recn Gd
Townhead
Dore
Abbeydale Park
Roundseats Farm
Fairthorn
Broadstorth
Blacka Dike
Dore Prim Sch
The Rowan Sch
King Ecgbert Sch
Hallfield Farm
Avenue Farm
The Elms
Oldhay Brook
Mollen House
Totley Brook
Totley Rise
S17
Bole Hill
Bolehill Lodge
Taylor's Hill
Totley Bents
Hillfoot
Totley
Totley Tunnel
Totley All Saints CE Prim Sch
Needham's Dike
Moss Rd
DANGER AREA
Rifle Range
Liby
New Totley
Mickley Hall
BASLOW RD
St George's Farm
Hollin Hill
Works
Little Wood
Sheffield Country Walk
Totley Brook
Gillfield Wood
Moor Edge Farm
Woodthorpe Hall
Moorwood's Farm
Moorwood's Hall Farm
S18
Holmesfield Park Wood
Storth Lodge
Old Hall
Owler Lee
Fanshaw Gate
FANSHAWE GATE LA
Hob La
Peacock Inn (PH)
Owler Bar
Storth House
A621 Baslow (A619)
B6054
ABBEYDALE RD S
HATHERSAGE RD
A625
A621
Derbyshire STREET ATLAS

152

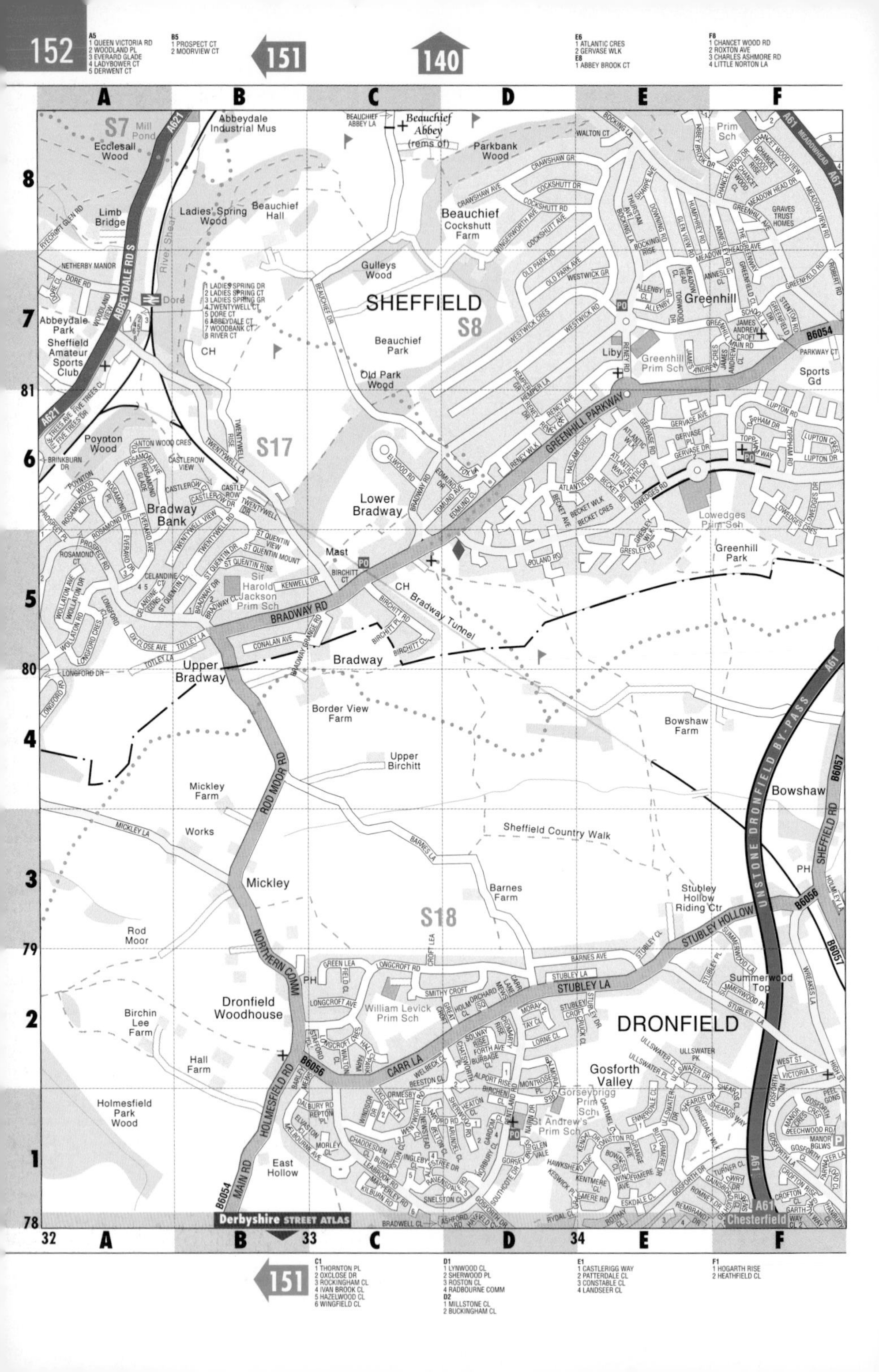
152
A5
1 QUEEN VICTORIA RD
2 WOODLAND PL
3 EVERARD GLADE
4 LADYBOWER CT
5 DERWENT CT
B5
1 PROSPECT CT
2 MOORVIEW CT
151
140
E6
1 ATLANTIC CRES
2 GERVASE WLK
E8
1 ABBEY BROOK CT
F8
1 CHANCET WOOD RD
2 ROXTON AVE
3 CHARLES ASHMORE RD
4 LITTLE NORTON LA
A
B
C
D
E
F
8
7
81
6
5
80
4
3
79
2
1
78
S7
Mill Pond
Ecclesall Wood
Abbeydale Industrial Mus
Beauchief Abbey (rems of)
Parkbank Wood
Limb Bridge
Ladies' Spring Wood
Beauchief Hall
Beauchief
Cockshutt Farm
Gulleys Wood
SHEFFIELD
S8
Greenhill
Abbeydale Park
Sheffield Amateur Sports Club
Dore
1 LADIES SPRING DR
2 LADIES SPRING CT
3 LADIES SPRING GR
4 TWENTYWELL CT
5 DORE CT
6 ABBEYDALE CT
7 WOODBANK CT
8 RIVER CT
CH
Beauchief Park
Old Park Wood
Liby
Greenhill Prim Sch
Sports Gd
Poynton Wood
S17
Lower Bradway
Bradway Bank
Lowedges Prim Sch
Greenhill Park
Mast
Sir Harold Jackson Prim Sch
Bradway Tunnel
Upper Bradway
Bradway
Border View Farm
Bowshaw Farm
Upper Birchitt
Mickley Farm
Bowshaw
Works
Sheffield Country Walk
Mickley
Barnes Farm
Stubley Hollow Riding Ctr
Rod Moor
S18
Summerwood Top
Dronfield Woodhouse
William Levick Prim Sch
DRONFIELD
Birchin Lee Farm
Hall Farm
Gosforth Valley
Gorseybrigg Prim Sch
St Andrew's Prim Sch
Holmesfield Park Wood
East Hollow
ABBEYDALE RD S
GREENHILL PARKWAY
BRADWAY RD
ROD MOOR RD
NORTHERN COMM
HOLMESFIELD RD
MAIN RD
CARR LA
STUBLEY LA
STUBLEY HOLLOW
UNSTONE DRONFIELD BY-PASS
SHEFFIELD RD
MICKLEY LA
BARNES LA
A621
A61
B6054
B6056
B6057
Derbyshire STREET ATLAS
Chesterfield
32
33
34
151
C1
1 THORNTON PL
2 OXCLOSE DR
3 ROCKINGHAM CL
4 IVAN BROOK CL
5 HAZELWOOD CL
6 WINGFIELD CL
D1
1 LYNWOOD CL
2 SHERWOOD PL
3 ROSTON CL
4 RADBOURNE COMM
D2
1 MILLSTONE CL
2 BUCKINGHAM CL
E1
1 CASTLERIGG WAY
2 PATTERDALE CL
3 CONSTABLE CL
4 LANDSEER CL
F1
1 HOGARTH RISE
2 HEATHFIELD CL

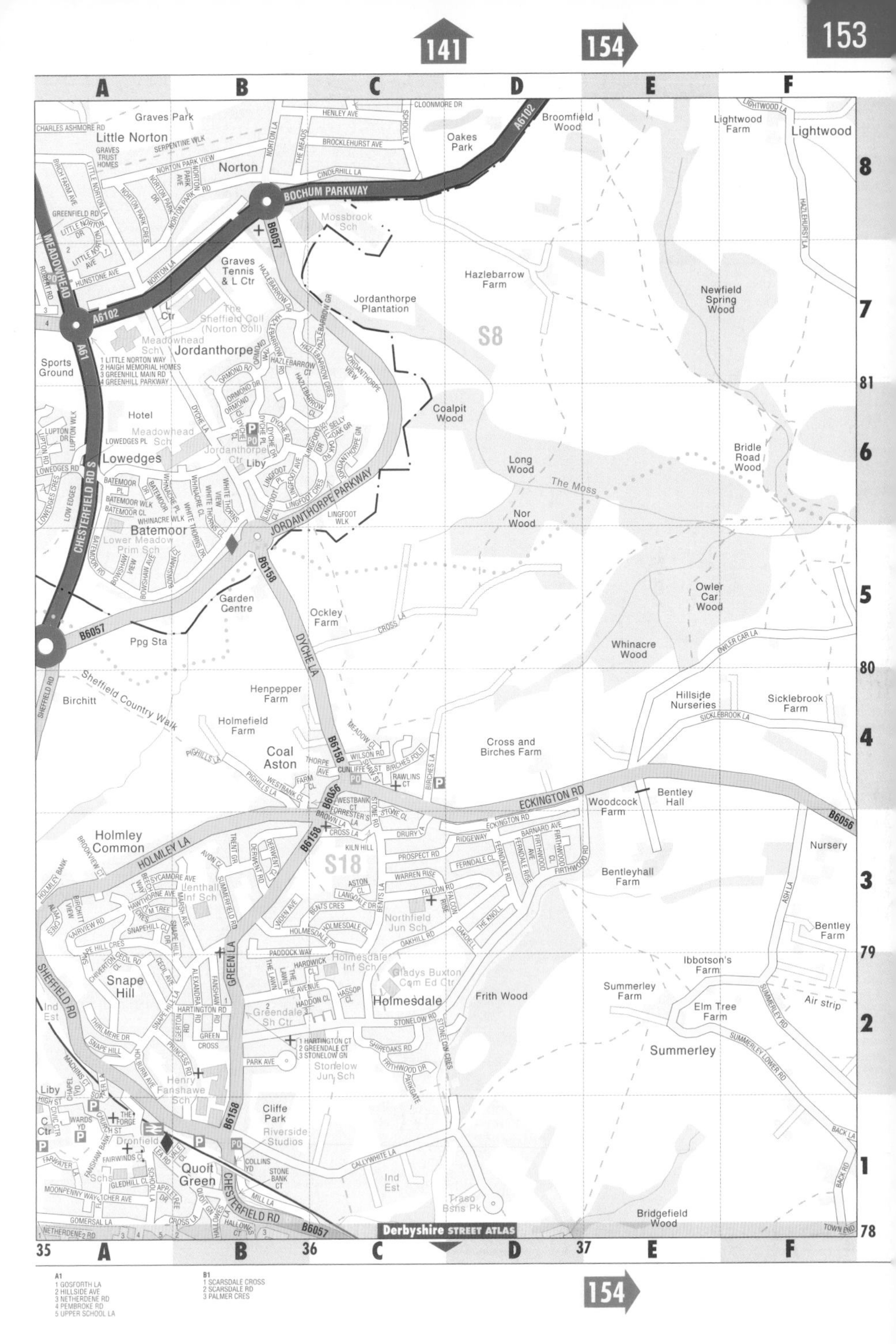

A1
1 GOSFORTH LA
2 HILLSIDE AVE
3 NETHERDENE RD
4 PEMBROKE RD
5 UPPER SCHOOL LA

B1
1 SCARSDALE CROSS
2 SCARSDALE RD
3 PALMER CRES

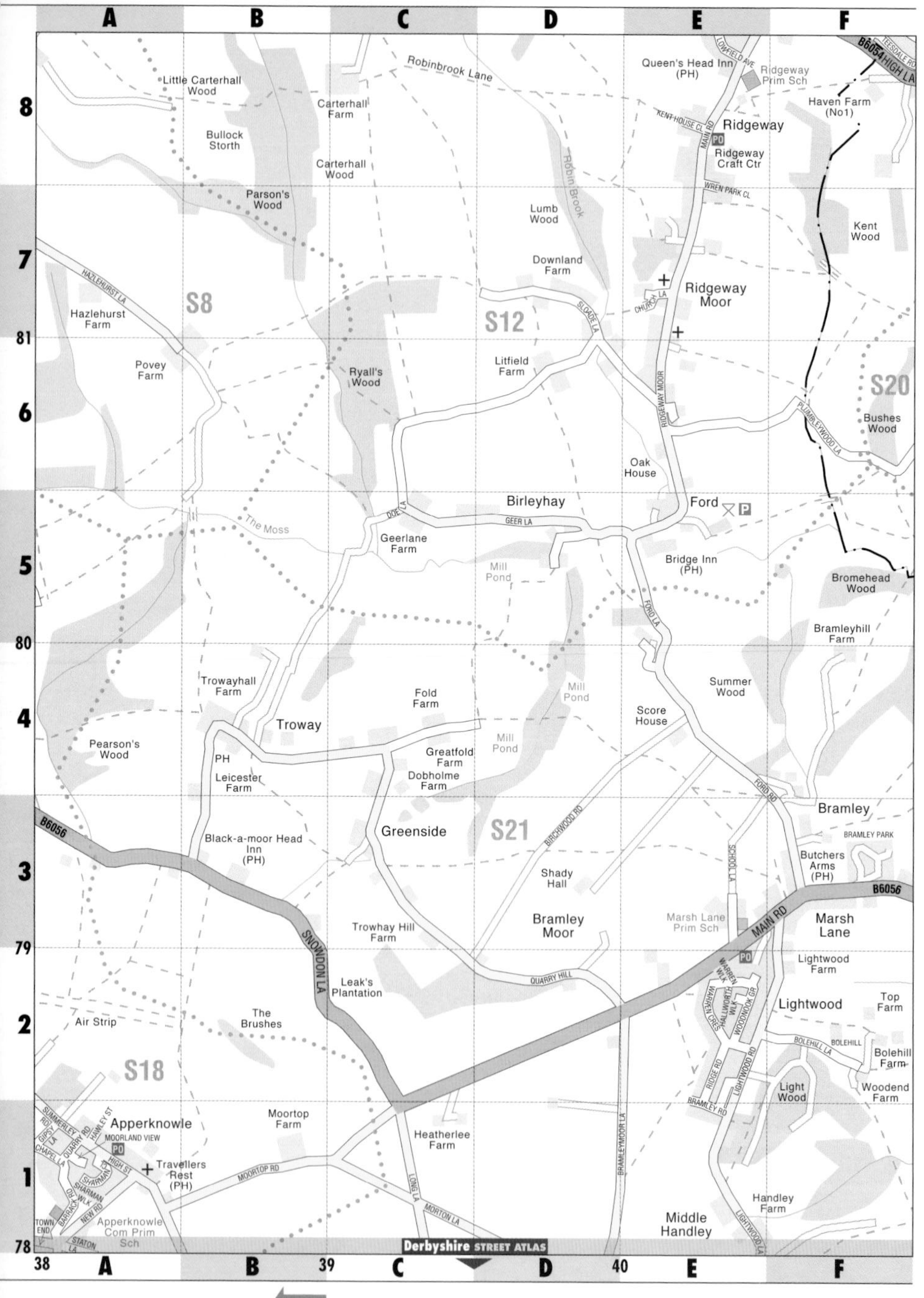

A B C D E F

8

Little Carterhall Wood

Carterhall Farm

Carterhall Wood

Robinbrook Lane

Queen's Head Inn (PH)

Ridgeway Prim Sch

Ridgeway

BB054 HIGH LA

Haven Farm (No1)

Bullock Storth

Parson's Wood

Lumb Wood

KENT HOUSE CL

PO

CHURCH LA

Ridgeway Craft Ctr

Kent Wood

7

HAZLEHURST LA

S8

Hazlehurst Farm

Downland Farm

WREN PARK CL

Ridgeway Moor

Robin Brook

81

Povey Farm

Ryall's Wood

S12

Litfield Farm

MOOR VALLEY

S20

6

DOE LA

Oak House

MARSH LANE LA

Bushes Wood

5

The Moss

Geerlane Farm

GEER LA

Birleyhay

Mill Pond

Bridge Inn (PH)

Ford

CINDER LA

Bromehead Wood

80

Bramleyhill Farm

4

Pearson's Wood

Trowayhall Farm

Troway

Fold Farm

Mill Pond

Mill Pond

Score House

TOLL RD

Summer Wood

Bramley

3

B6056

PH

Leicester Farm

Black-a-moor Head Inn (PH)

Greatfold Farm

Dobholme Farm

Greenside

S21

BIRCHWOOD RD

Shady Hall

SCHOOL LA

Butchers Arms (PH)

Bramley Park

B6056

79

SNOWDON LA

Trowhay Hill Farm

QUARRY HILL

Bramley Moor

Marsh Lane Prim Sch

MAIN RD

Marsh Lane

Lightwood Farm

2

Air Strip

S18

The Brushes

Leak's Plantation

PO

Lightwood

Light Wood

BOLEHILL LA

Top Farm

Bolehill Farm

Woodend Farm

1

Apperknowle

MOORLAND VIEW

PO

Travellers Rest (PH)

Moortop Farm

MOORTOP RD

Heatherlee Farm

LONG LA

MORTON LA

BRAMLEY WOOD LA

Handley Farm

78

Apperknowle Com Prim Sch

Middle Handley

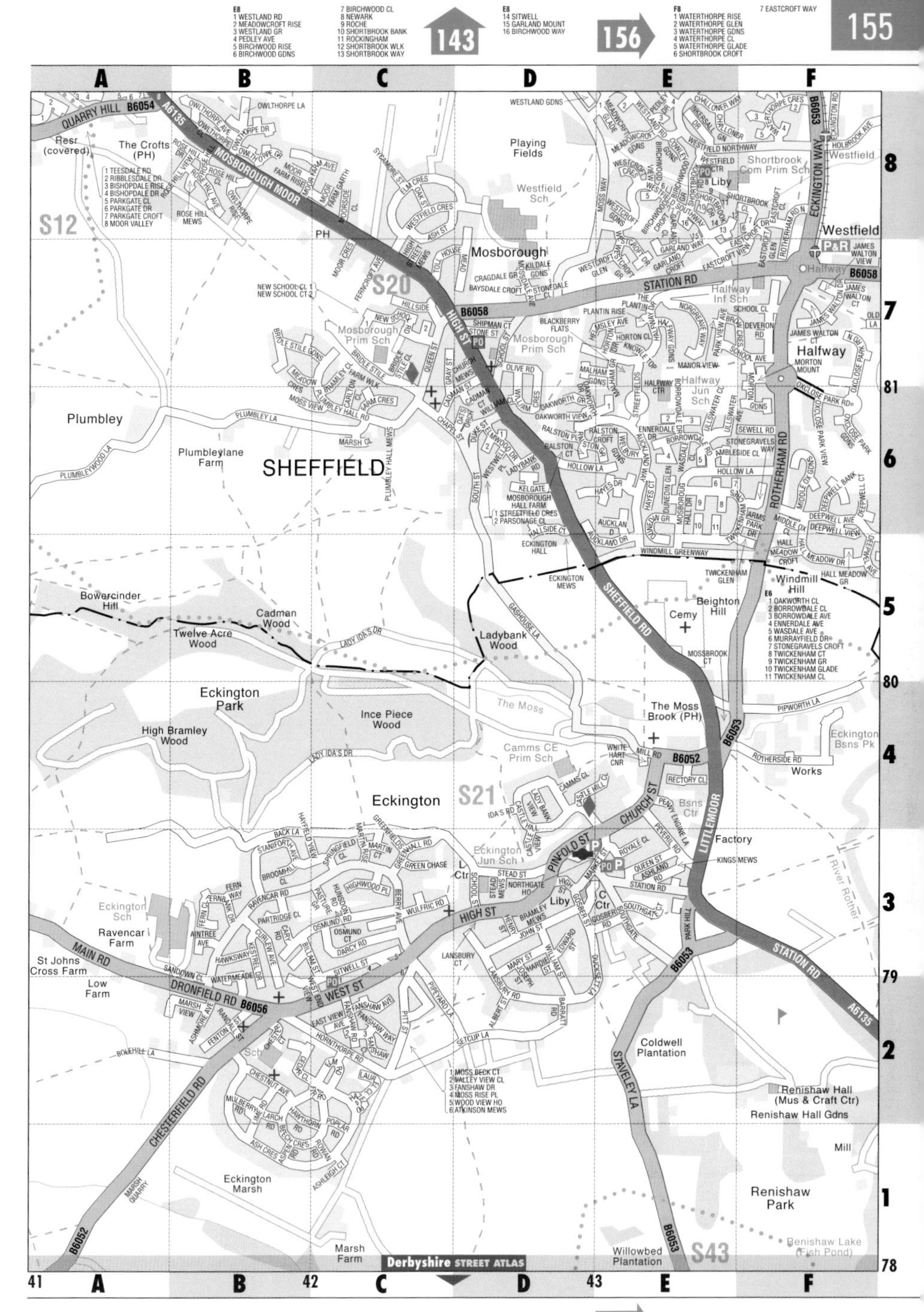
A
B
C
D
E
F
8
7
81
6
5
80
4
3
79
2
1
78
41
42
43
S12
S20
S21
S43
SHEFFIELD
Mosborough
Westfield
Halfway
Eckington
Plumbley
Plumbleylane Farm
The Crofts (PH)
Resr (covered)
Playing Fields
Westfield Sch
Shortbrook Com Prim Sch
Mosborough Prim Sch
Halfway Inf Sch
Halfway Jun Sch
Bowercinder Hill
Cadman Wood
Twelve Acre Wood
Ladybank Wood
Eckington Park
High Bramley Wood
Ince Piece Wood
The Moss
Beighton Hill
Cemy
Windmill Hill
The Moss Brook (PH)
Camms CE Prim Sch
Eckington Bsns Pk
Works
Bsns Ctr
Factory
Eckington Jun Sch
Eckington Sch
Ravencar Farm
St Johns Cross Farm
Low Farm
Coldwell Plantation
Renishaw Hall (Mus & Craft Ctr)
Renishaw Hall Gdns
Mill
Renishaw Park
Renishaw Lake (Fish Pond)
Willowbed Plantation
Eckington Marsh
Marsh Farm
River Rother
MOSBOROUGH MOOR
QUARRY HILL
HIGH ST
STATION RD
SHEFFIELD RD
LITTLEMOOR
ROTHERHAM RD
ECKINGTON WAY
CHURCH ST
WEST ST
DRONFIELD RD
MAIN RD
CHESTERFIELD RD
STAVELEY LA
PINFOLD ST
B6054
A6135
B6058
B6053
B6052
B6056
1 TEESDALE RD
2 RIBBLESDALE DR
3 BISHOPDALE RISE
4 BISHOPDALE DR
5 PARKGATE CL
6 PARKGATE DR
7 PARKGATE CROFT
8 MOOR VALLEY
NEW SCHOOL CL 1
NEW SCHOOL CT 2
1 STREETFIELD CRES
2 PARSONAGE CL
E6
1 OAKWORTH CL
2 BORROWDALE CL
3 BORROWDALE AVE
4 ENNERDALE AVE
5 WASDALE AVE
6 MURRAYFIELD DR
7 STONEGRAVELS CROFT
8 TWICKENHAM CT
9 TWICKENHAM GR
10 TWICKENHAM GLADE
11 TWICKENHAM CL
1 MOSS BECK CT
2 VALLEY VIEW CL
3 FANSHAW DR
4 MOSS RISE PL
5 WOOD VIEW HO
6 ATKINSON MEWS

155

144

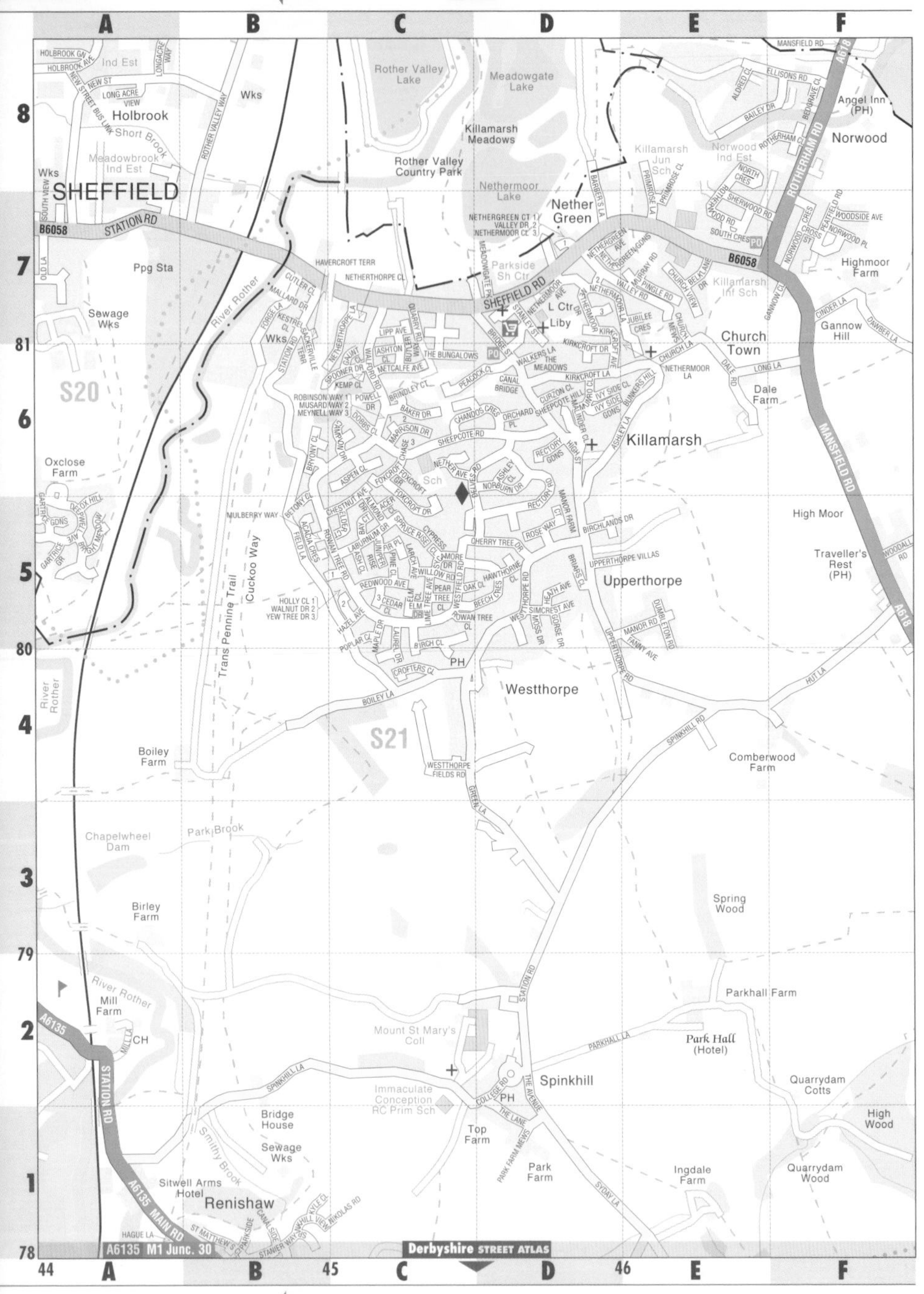

A
B
C
D
E
F
8
7
81
6
5
80
4
3
79
2
1
78
44
45
46
HOLBROOK GN
HOLBROOK AVE
Ind Est
LONGACRE WAY
NEW ST
NEW STREET BUS LINK
LONG ACRE VIEW
Holbrook
Short Brook
Meadowbrook Ind Est
Wks
SHEFFIELD
SOUTH VIEW
ROTHER VALLEY WAY
Rother Valley Lake
Meadowgate Lake
Killamarsh Meadows
Rother Valley Country Park
Nethermoor Lake
Nether Green
NETHERGREEN CT 1
VALLEY DR 2
NETHERMOOR CL 3
BARBER'S LA
Killamarsh Jun Sch
PRIMROSE LA
PRIMROSE CL
Norwood Ind Est
MANSFIELD RD
A618
ELLISONS RD
ALDRED CL
BAILEY DR
BEDGRAVE CL
ROTHERHAM CL
ROTHERHAM RD
Angel Inn (PH)
Norwood
NORTH CRES
SHERWOOD RD
ROTHERWOOD RD
SOUTH CRES
PO
WOODSIDE AVE
NORWOOD PL
PEATFIELD RD
NORWOOD CRES
CROSS ST
Highmoor Farm
B6058
STATION RD
OLD LA
Ppg Sta
Sewage Wks
River Rother
HAVERCROFT TERR
NETHERTHORPE CL
MEADOWGATE PK
Parkside Sh Ctr
SHEFFIELD RD
CUTLER CL
MALLARD GR
KESTREL CL
FORGE LA
SACKERVILLE TERR
STATION RD
Wks
NETHERTHORPE LA
LIPP AVE
QUARRY RD
GAUNT CL
ASHTON CL
BUTLER WAY
SPOONER DR
METCALFE AVE
WALFORD RD
THE BUNGALOWS
KEMP CL
STANLEY ST
BRIDGE ST
NETHERMOOR AVE
L Ctr
Liby
NETHERGREEN AVE
NETHERGREEN GDNS
MURRAY RD
VALLEY RD
PINGLE RD
CHURCH VIEW
BELK LANE DR
Killamarsh Inf Sch
GANNOW CL
NETHERMOOR LA
JUBILEE CRES
KIRKCROFT AVE
KIRKCROFT DR
CHURCH MEWS
CHURCH LA
Church Town
CINDER LA
Gannow Hill
DAWBER LA
S20
ROBINSON WAY 1
MUSARD WAY 2
MEYNELL WAY 3
POWELL DR
BRINDLEY CL
PEACOCK CL
CANAL BRIDGE
WALKERS LA
THE MEADOWS
KIRKCROFT LA
CURZON CL
SHEEPCOTE HILL
IVY SIDE CL
IVY SIDE GDNS
BUNKERS HILL
NETHERMOOR LA
DALE RD
LONG LA
Dale Farm
DOBBS CL
BAKER DR
MARRISON DR
CHANDOS CRES
ORCHARD PL
CAMPION DR
SHEEPCOTE RD
MALINDER CL
ASHLEY LA
HIGH ST
Killamarsh
MANSFIELD RD
BRYONY CL
RECTORY GDNS
ASPEN CL
FOXCROFT CHASE
FOXCROFT GR
FOXCROFT DR
Sch
NETHER AVE
ASHLEY CL
NORBURN DR
RECTORY RD
Oxclose Farm
OXCLOSE HILL
GARTRICE GDNS
GARTRICE GR
MULBERRY WAY
BETONY CL
CHESTNUT AVE
ALMOND DR
ACER CL
SPRUCE RISE
CYPRESS CL
ROSE WAY
MANOR FARM
BIRCHLANDS DR
High Moor
Trans Pennine Trail
Cuckoo Way
ACACIA CRES
FIELD LA
ROWAN TREE RD
ELDER CL
BAY CT
LABURNUM GR
JUNIPER RISE
FIR PL
PINE CL
LARCH AVE
CHERRY TREE DR
BRIARS CL
UPPERTHORPE VILLAS
WOODALL RD
Traveller's Rest (PH)
REDWOOD AVE
WILLOW RD
HAWTHORNE CL
OAK CL
BEECH CRES
WESTFIELD RD
Upperthorpe
HOLLY CL 1
WALNUT DR 2
YEW TREE DR 3
CEDAR CL
ELM CL
LIME TREE AVE
PEAR TREE CL
HAZEL AVE
ROWAN TREE CL
WESTHORPE RD
SIMCREST AVE
HEATH AVE
MOSS DR
GORSE DR
MANOR RD
DUMBLETON RD
FANNY AVE
UPPERTHORPE RD
POPLAR CL
MAPLE DR
LAUREL DR
BIRCH CL
PH
CROFTERS CL
Westthorpe
River Rother
BOILEY LA
HUT LA
S21
SPINKHILL RD
Boiley Farm
WESTTHORPE FIELDS RD
Comberwood Farm
GREEN LA
Chapelwheel Dam
Park Brook
Spring Wood
Birley Farm
STATION RD
Parkhall Farm
River Rother
Mill Farm
A6135
MILL LA
CH
Mount St Mary's Coll
PARKHALL LA
Park Hall (Hotel)
SPINKHILL LA
Immaculate Conception RC Prim Sch
COLLEGE RD
THE AVENUE
Spinkhill
PH
Quarrydam Cotts
THE LANE
Top Farm
High Wood
Bridge House
Smithy Brook
Sewage Wks
PARK FARM MEWS
Park Farm
Ingdale Farm
Quarrydam Wood
SYDAY LA
Sitwell Arms Hotel
Renishaw
KYLE CL
NIKOLAS RD
HAGUE LA
MAIN RD
ST MATTHEW'S ST
PARKSIDE
CANAL SIDE
STANIER WAY
A6135 M1 Junc. 30
Derbyshire STREET ATLAS

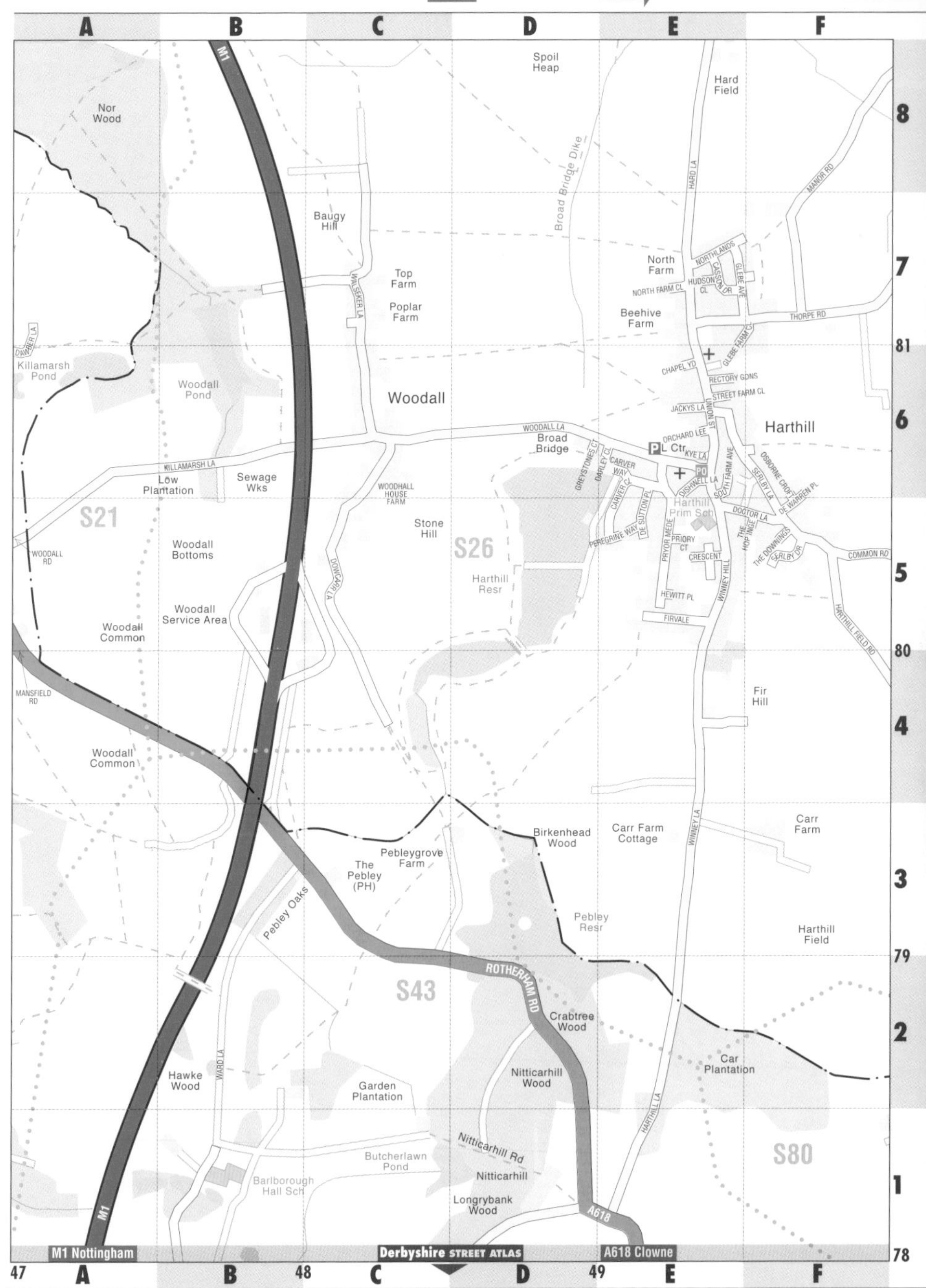

8

7

81

6

5

80

4

3

79

2

1

78

A B C D E F

Nor
Wood

M1

Baugy
Hill

Top
Farm

Poplar
Farm

Woodall

Killamarsh
Pond

Woodall
Pond

Spoil
Heap

Broad Bridge Dike

Hard
Field

North
Farm

Beehive
Farm

Harthill

CHAPEL TO

RECTORY GDNS

STREET FARM CL

JACKYS LA

ORCHARD LEE

PL Ctr

KYE LA

Harthill
Prim Sch

S21

KILLAMARSH LA

WOODALL LA

Broad
Bridge

Low
Plantation

Sewage
Wks

WOODHALL
HOUSE
FARM

Woodall
Bottoms

Stone
Hill

Woodall
RD

Woodall
Service Area

Woodall
Common

MANSFIELD
RD

Harthill
Resr

S26

DARLEY ST

CARVER
WAY

CANTLEY

PEREGRINE WAY

PHYTO MEDIE

PRIORY
CT

CRESCENT

HEWITT PL

FIRVALE

THE SUTTON LA

WINNEY HILL

DOCTOR LA

THE DRONFIELDS

SELBY CL

COMMON RD

HARTHILL FIELD RD

Fir
Hill

Woodall
Common

Pebley Oaks

WARD LA

Pebleygrove
Farm

The
Pebley
(PH)

Birkenhead
Wood

Carr Farm
Cottage

WINNEY LA

Carr
Farm

Pebley
Resr

Harthill
Field

S43

ROTHERHAM RD

Crabtree
Wood

Nitticarhill
Wood

Car
Plantation

S80

Hawke
Wood

Garden
Plantation

Butcherlawn
Pond

Nitticarhill Rd

Nitticarhill

HARTHILL LA

Longrybank
Wood

Barlborough
Hall Sch

A618

M1

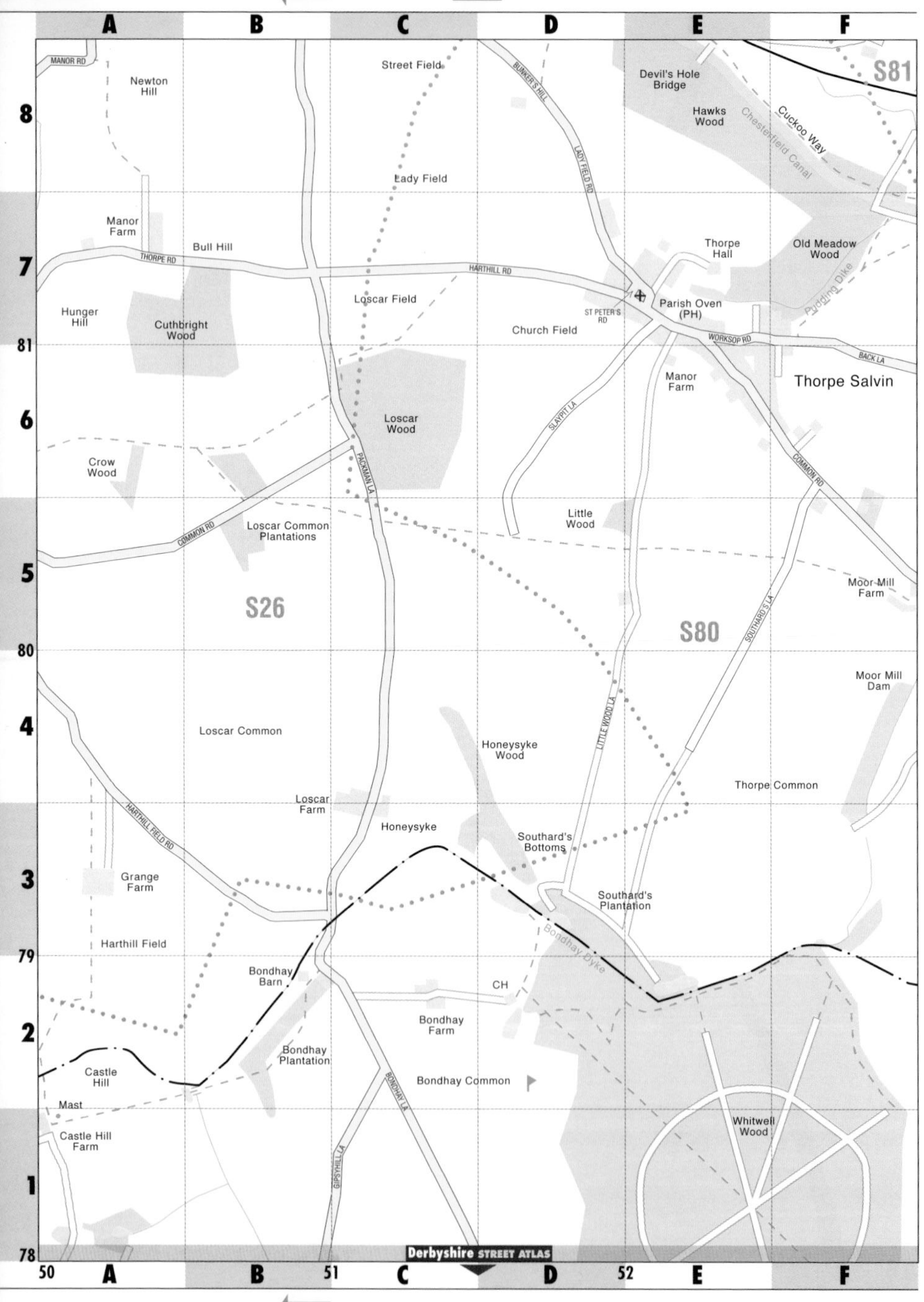

S81

MANOR RD

Newton Hill

Street Field

Devil's Hole Bridge

Hawks Wood

Cuckoo Way

Chesterfield Canal

Lady Field

Manor Farm

Bull Hill

THORPE RD

HARTHILL RD

Thorpe Hall

Old Meadow Wood

Pudding Dyke

Hunger Hill

Cuthbright Wood

Loscar Field

St PETER'S RD

Church Field

Parish Oven (PH)

Manor Farm

WORKSOP RD

BACK LA

Thorpe Salvin

Crow Wood

Loscar Wood

PACKMAN LA

SLACK LA

COMMON RD

Loscar Common Plantations

COMMON RD

Little Wood

Moor-Mill Farm

S26

S80

LITTLE WOOD LA

SOUTHGATE LA

Moor Mill Dam

Loscar Common

HARTHILL FIELD RD

Loscar Farm

Honeysyke Wood

Thorpe Common

Honeysyke

Southard's Bottoms

Grange Farm

Southard's Plantation

Bondhay Dyke

Harthill Field

Bondhay Barn

CH

BONNET LA

Bondhay Farm

Castle Hill

Bondhay Plantation

Bondhay Common

Whitwell Wood

Mast

Castle Hill Farm

PITTHILL SPUR

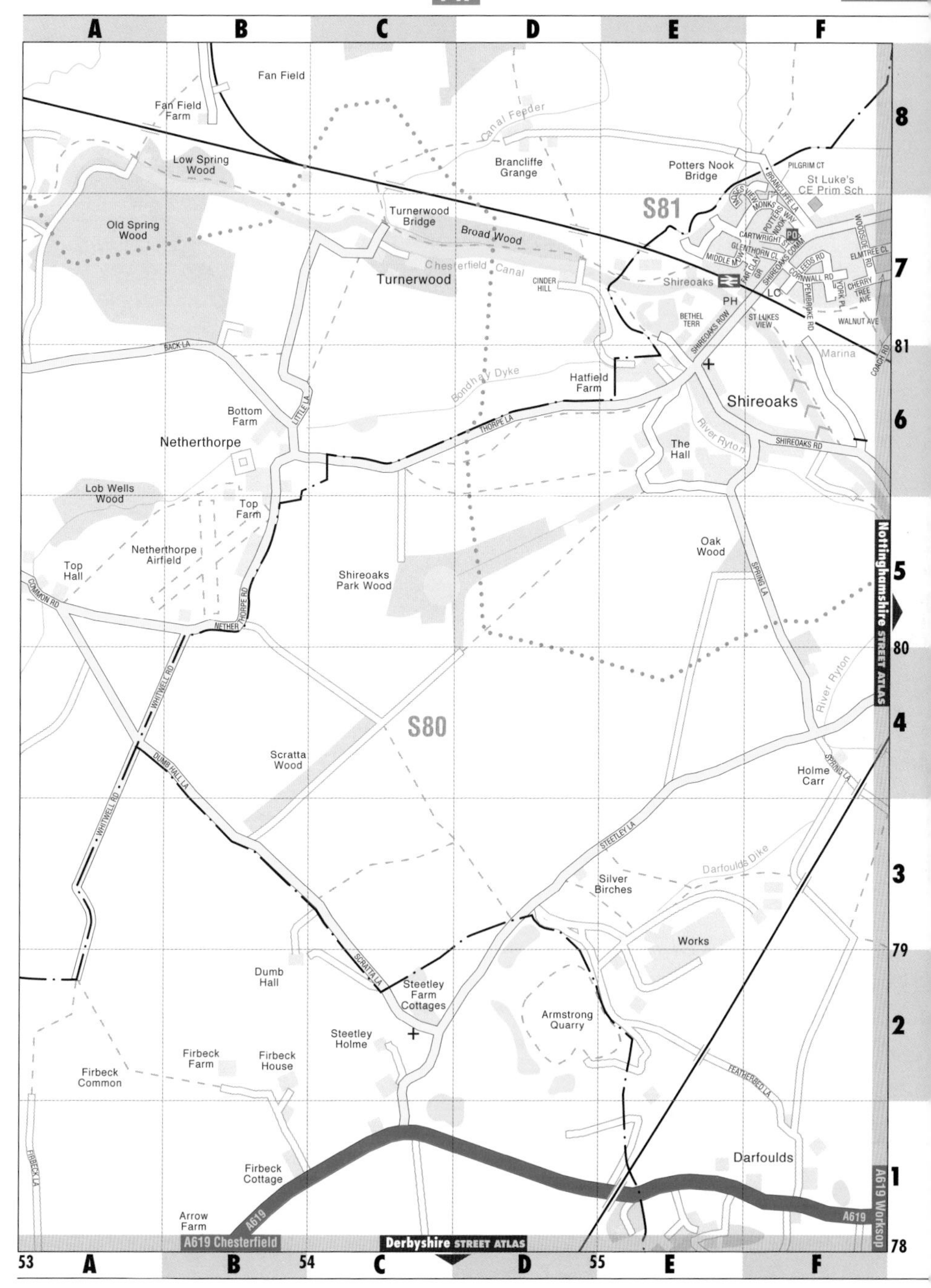

A   B   C   D   E   F

8
7
81
6
5
80
4
79
3
2
78
1

Nottinghamshire STREET ATLAS

A619 Worksop

Fan Field

Fan Field
Farm

Low Spring
Wood

Old Spring
Wood

Canal Feeder

Brancliffe
Grange

Turnerwood
Bridge

Broad Wood

Turnerwood

Chesterfield Canal

CINDER
HILL

Potters Nook
Bridge

PILGRIM CT

St Luke's
CE Prim Sch

S81

Shireoaks

PH

BETHEL
TERR

ST LUKES
VIEW

Marina

Shireoaks

BACK LA

Bondhay Dyke

Hatfield
Farm

The
Hall

River Ryton

SHIREOAKS RD

Bottom
Farm

Netherthorpe

LITTLE LA

THORPE LA

Lob Wells
Wood

Top
Farm

Netherthorpe
Airfield

Shireoaks
Park Wood

Oak
Wood

SPRING LA

River Ryton

Top
Hall

COMMON RD

NETHER

S80

Scratta
Wood

Holme
Carr

KING LA

WHITWELL RD

DUMB HALL LA

STEETLEY LA

Darfoulds Dike

Silver
Birches

Works

SCRATTA LA

Dumb
Hall

Steetley
Farm
Cottages

Armstrong
Quarry

Steetley
Holme

FIRBECK LA

Firbeck
Common

Firbeck
Farm

Firbeck
House

Darfoulds

FEATHERBED LA

Firbeck
Cottage

A619

Arrow
Farm

A619

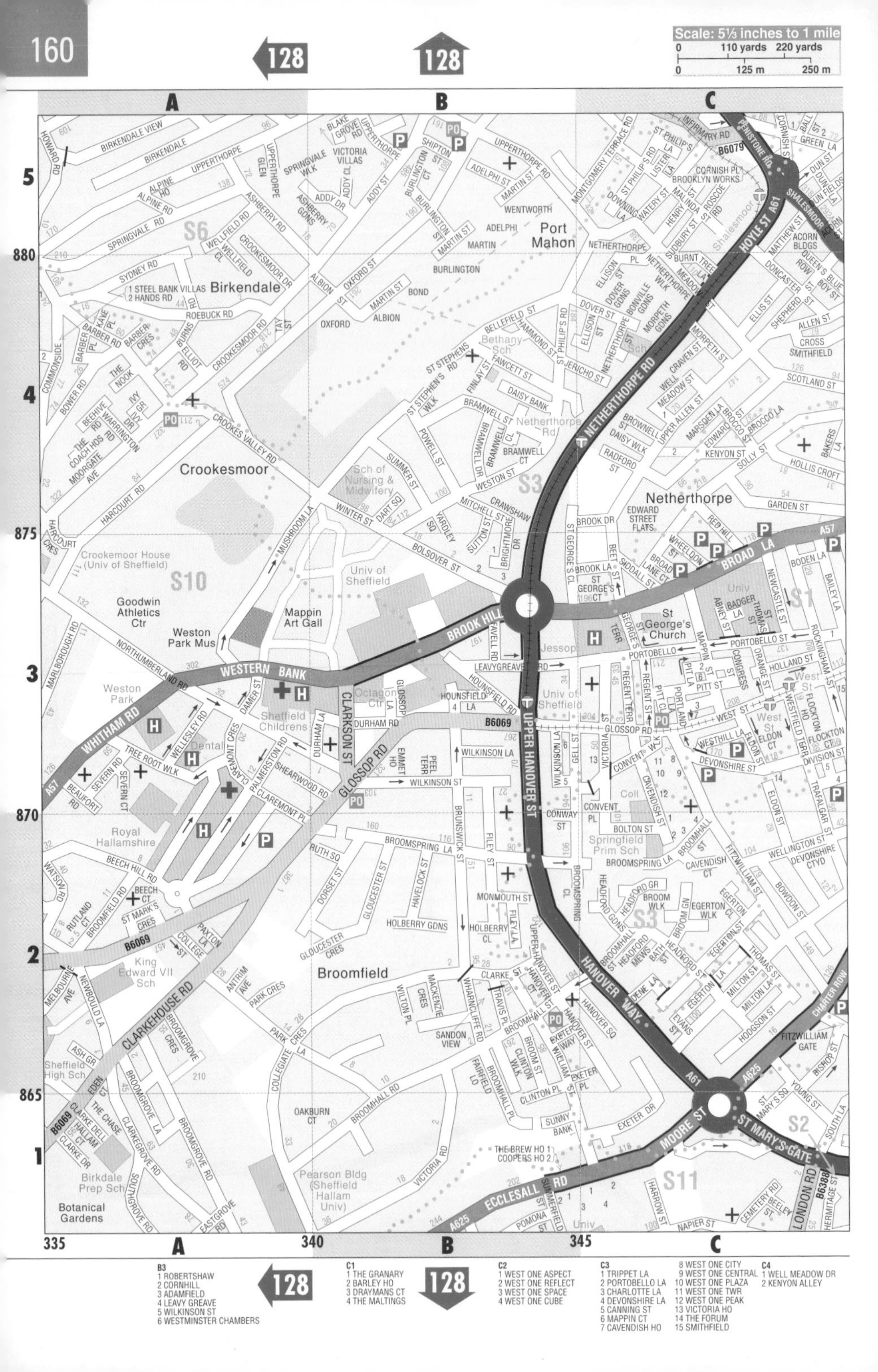

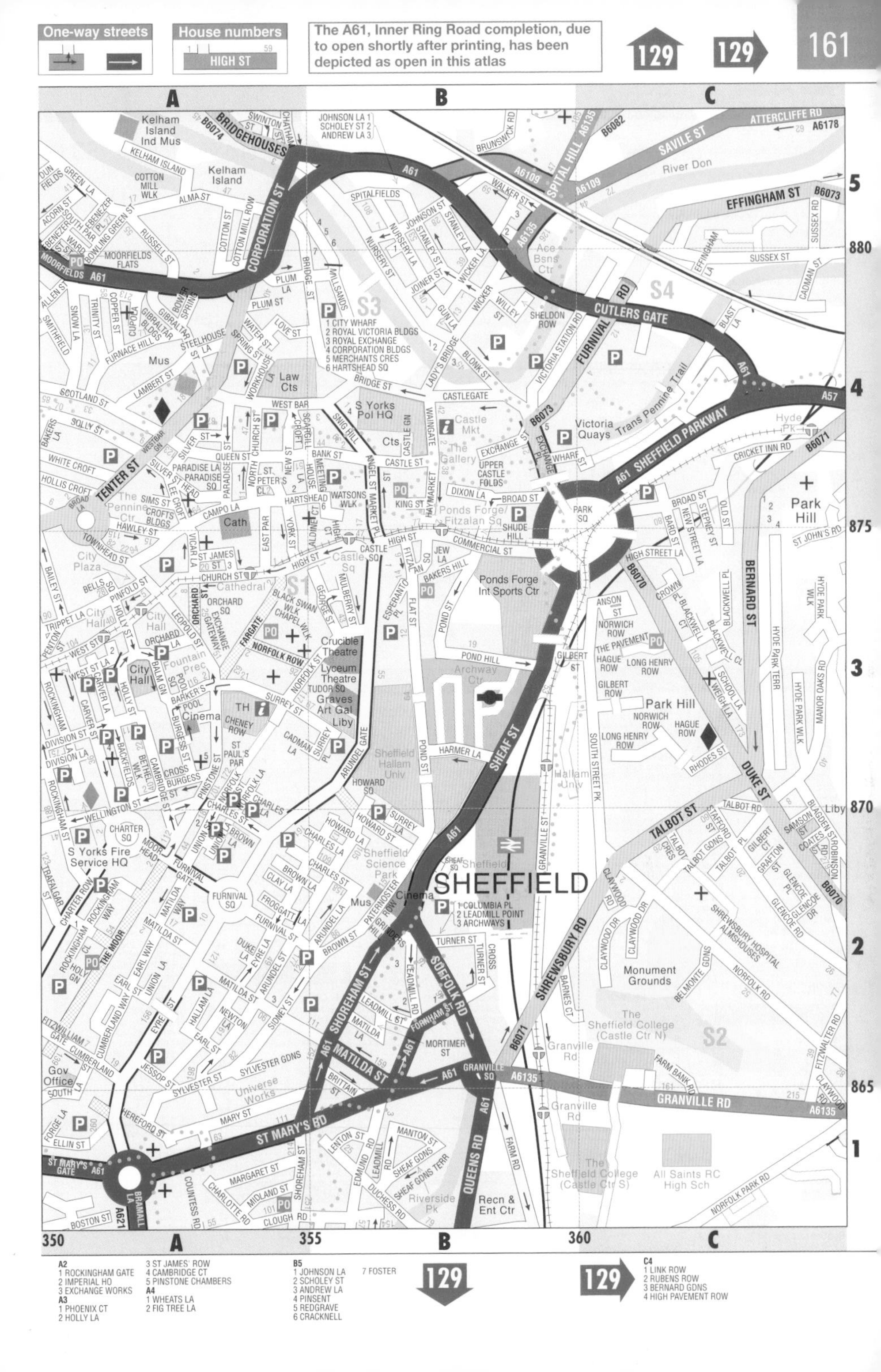

One-way streets
House numbers
HIGH ST
The A61, Inner Ring Road completion, due to open shortly after printing, has been depicted as open in this atlas
129
129
161
A
B
C
5
880
4
875
3
870
2
865
1
350
355
360
SHEFFIELD
S1
S2
S3
S4
Kelham Island Ind Mus
Kelham Island
BRIDGEHOUSES
CORPORATION ST
A61
SAVILE ST
River Don
ATTERCLIFFE RD
A6178
EFFINGHAM ST
B6073
SPITAL HILL
A6109
A6135
SUSSEX ST
CUTLERS GATE
FURNIVAL RD
VICTORIA STATION RD
Ace Bsns Ctr
SHELDON ROW
WICKER
NURSERY ST
SPITALFIELDS
JOHNSON LA 1
SCHOLEY ST 2
ANDREW LA 3
1 CITY WHARF
2 ROYAL VICTORIA BLDGS
3 ROYAL EXCHANGE
4 CORPORATION BLDGS
5 MERCHANTS CRES
6 HARTSHEAD SQ
Law Cts
S Yorks Pol HQ
Cts
Castle Mkt
The Gallery
Victoria Quays
Trans Pennine Trail
SHEFFIELD PARKWAY
A57
Hyde Pk
CRICKET INN RD
B6071
Park Hill
PARK SQ
Ponds Forge/ Fitzalan Sq
Ponds Forge Int Sports Ctr
WEST BAR
TENTER ST
MOORFIELDS
SCOTLAND ST
The Pennine Ctr
Cath
City Plaza
Cathedral
City Hall
Fountain Prec
Crucible Theatre
Lyceum Theatre
TUDOR SQ
Graves Art Gal Liby
FARGATE
NORFOLK ROW
TH
Cinema
SURREY ST
ARUNDEL GATE
Sheffield Hallam Univ
Archway Ctr
POND HILL
SHEAF ST
Hallam Univ
SOUTH STREET PK
BERNARD ST
DUKE ST
TALBOT ST
Liby
HYDE PARK TERR
MANOR OAKS RD
Sheffield Science Park
Mus
Cinema
1 COLUMBIA PL
2 LEADMILL POINT
3 ARCHWAYS
SHREWSBURY RD
Monument Grounds
SHREWSBURY HOSPITAL ALMSHOUSES
CHARTER SQ
S Yorks Fire Service HQ
FURNIVAL SQ
THE MOOR
SHOREHAM ST
SUFFOLK RD
MATILDA ST
GRANVILLE SQ
GRANVILLE RD
A6135
The Sheffield College (Castle Ctr N)
Granville Rd
The Sheffield College (Castle Ctr S)
All Saints RC High Sch
NORFOLK PARK RD
Gov Office
Universe Works
ST MARY'S RD
ST MARY'S GATE
BRAMALL LA
A621
QUEENS RD
Riverside Pk
Recn & Ent Ctr
FARM RD
A2
1 ROCKINGHAM GATE
2 IMPERIAL HO
3 EXCHANGE WORKS
A3
1 PHOENIX CT
2 HOLLY LA
3 ST JAMES' ROW
4 CAMBRIDGE CT
5 PINSTONE CHAMBERS
A4
1 WHEATS LA
2 FIG TREE LA
B5
1 JOHNSON LA
2 SCHOLEY ST
3 ANDREW LA
4 PINSENT
5 REDGRAVE
6 CRACKNELL
7 FOSTER
129
129
C4
1 LINK ROW
2 RUBENS ROW
3 BERNARD GDNS
4 HIGH PAVEMENT ROW

Index

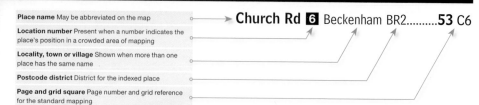

Place name May be abbreviated on the map

Location number Present when a number indicates the place's position in a crowded area of mapping

Locality, town or village Shown when more than one place has the same name

Postcode district District for the indexed place

Page and grid square Page number and grid reference for the standard mapping

Church Rd **6** Beckenham BR2.........**53** C6

Public and commercial buildings are highlighted in magenta   Places of interest are highlighted in blue with a star *

Abbreviations used in the index

Acad	**Academy**	Comm	**Common**	Gd	**Ground**	L	**Leisure**
App	**Approach**	Cott	**Cottage**	Gdn	**Garden**	La	**Lane**
Arc	**Arcade**	Cres	**Crescent**	Gn	**Green**	Liby	**Library**
Ave	**Avenue**	Cswy	**Causeway**	Gr	**Grove**	Mdw	**Meadow**
Bglw	**Bungalow**	Ct	**Court**	H	**Hall**	Meml	**Memorial**
Bldg	**Building**	Ctr	**Centre**	Ho	**House**	Mkt	**Market**
Bsns, Bus	**Business**	Ctry	**Country**	Hospl	**Hospital**	Mus	**Museum**
Bvd	**Boulevard**	Cty	**County**	HQ	**Headquarters**	Orch	**Orchard**
Cath	**Cathedral**	Dr	**Drive**	Hts	**Heights**	Pal	**Palace**
Cir	**Circus**	Dro	**Drove**	Ind	**Industrial**	Par	**Parade**
Cl	**Close**	Ed	**Education**	Inst	**Institute**	Pas	**Passage**
Cnr	**Corner**	Emb	**Embankment**	Int	**International**	Pk	**Park**
Coll	**College**	Est	**Estate**	Intc	**Interchange**	Pl	**Place**
Com	**Community**	Ex	**Exhibition**	Junc	**Junction**	Prec	**Precinct**

Prom	**Promenade**
Rd	**Road**
Recn	**Recreation**
Ret	**Retail**
Sh	**Shopping**
Sq	**Square**
St	**Street**
Sta	**Station**
Terr	**Terrace**
TH	**Town Hall**
Univ	**University**
Wk, Wlk	**Walk**
Wr	**Water**
Yd	**Yard**

Index of localities, towns and villages

A

Abbeydale 140 A1
Abbeydale Park 151 F6
Abdy 78 E2
Adwick le Street 40 A6
Adwick upon Dearne ...79 F8
Aldwarke 98 B3
Almholme 42 A5
Apperknowle 154 A1
Arbourthorne 141 E8
Arbourthorne Estate ..141 E6
Ardsley 56 B8
Arksey 41 D2
Armthorpe 64 A5
Askern 22 A7
Aston 144 E6
Athersley North 33 F8
Athersley South 34 B8
Attercliffe 129 F6
Attercliffe Hill Top 130 B7
Auckley 86 A7
Aughton 132 D1
Austerfield 105 C2

B

Backmoor 141 D2
Balby 83 B7
Bank Top 149 A8
Barnburgh 59 D3
Barnby Dun 42 F8
Barnside 49 A8
Barnsley 33 C1
Barrow 77 A1
Barugh 32 E6
Barugh Green 32 E4
Base Green 142 C3
Batemoor 153 A5
Bawtry 123 B7
Beauchief 152 D8
Beaver Hill 143 B8
Beighton 144 A3
Belle Green 35 C7
Belle Vue 62 F2
Bentley 62 B7
Bentley Rise 62 B6
Bents Green 139 F5
Bessacarr 84 E7
Billingley 57 F6
Bircotes 122 D4
Birds Edge 29 A4
Birdwell 75 E7
Birkendale 160 A4

Birley
Birley 142 F3
Birley Carr 112 C4
Birley Edge 112 C6
Birleyhay 154 D5
Blackburn 114 B6
Blacker Hill 55 D1
Blaxton 86 E6
Bloomhouse 13 F1
Bolehill 141 A2
Bolton upon Dearne ...58 D1
Boulder Hill 128 B8
Bow Broom 79 D4
Bowshaw 152 F4
Bracken Moor 92 C8
Bradfield 110 B5
Bradgate 115 A7
Bradway 152 C5
Bradway Bank 152 A6
Braithwaite 23 F5
Braithwell 101 A2
Bramley
  Dronfield 154 F3
  Rotherham 117 D5
Bramley Moor 154 D3
Brampton 78 B8
Brampton en le
  Morthen 133 D5
Branton 85 D8
Brecks 116 E5
Brick Houses 151 D8
Bridge End 51 C4
Brierley 17 A3
Brightside 129 F8
Brincliffe 140 C6
Brinsworth 131 C8
Broad Hill 51 D5
Brodsworth 39 B4
Bromley 75 B2
Brookhouse 134 D7
Broom 116 A4
Broomfield 160 B2
Broomhill
  Darfield 57 B2
  Sheffield 128 C3
Burghwallis 21 B4
Burncross 94 E4
Burngreave 129 C6

C

Cadeby 81 D5
Campsall 21 C8
Canklow 115 D3
Cantley 64 B1
Carbrook 130 A8

Carcroft
Carcroft 21 C1
Carlecotes 49 B3
Carlton 15 D1
Carlton Green 34 C8
Carlton in Lindrick ...148 F5
Carr 118 C1
Carr Head 92 E8
Carsick 127 E1
Carsick Hill 127 E1
Carter Knowle 140 C5
Castle Green 51 F2
Catliffe 131 C6
Causeway Head 151 C8
Cawthorne 31 D4
Chapeltown 95 B5
Charltonbrook 94 E1
Charnock Hill 142 B2
Church Field 104 B8
Church Town 156 E7
Clayton 37 C4
Clayton West 12 A3
Clifton
  Conisbrough 100 E5
  Rotherham 115 F7
Coal Aston 153 B4
Coisley Hill 143 B6
Common End 17 F6
Common Side 142 A5
Conanby 80 F1
Conisbrough 81 B3
Conisbrough Common ..81 E1
Cortworth 77 E1
Costhorpe 148 D8
Crane Moor 74 C8
Cricket Houses 129 E3
Crimpsall 62 B3
Crookes 128 B4
Crookesmoor 160 A4
Cross Hill 17 E6
Crosspool 127 F2
Crow Edge 49 E6
Cubley 51 D1
Cudworth 35 C6
Cudworth Common 35 D4
Cundy Cross 34 E2
Cusworth 61 D5

D

Dalton 98 D1
Dalton Magna 116 F2
Dalton Parva 116 D8
Darfield 57 B5
Darfoulds 159 F1
Darnall 130 B4
Darton 32 E8

Deepcar
Deepcar 92 E8
Deep Pit 141 F8
Denaby Main 80 E4
Den Bank 127 F3
Denby Dale 30 B6
Dinnington 134 E1
Dodworth 53 F7
Dodworth Bottom 53 F6
Dodworth Green 53 E6
Dolcliffe Common 80 A5
Doncaster 62 E3
Doncaster Carr 83 E8
Dore 151 E7
Drakehouse 143 D3
Dronfield 152 E2
Dronfield Woodhouse .152 B2
Dropping Well 96 D1
Dunford Bridge 48 D1
Dungworth 126 E8
Dunkirk 30 B5
Dunscroft 44 A6
Dunsville 43 F5

E

East Cowick 1 C7
East Dene 116 B7
Eastfield 53 B2
East Herringthorpe ...116 E7
East Whitwell 92 B8
Eastwood 115 F8
Ecclesall 140 A5
Ecclesfield 113 A7
Eckington 155 C4
Ecklands 50 D2
Edenthorpe 43 A1
Elm Tree Hill 142 A6
Elsecar 77 B5
Endcliffe Crescent ...128 B1
Eskholme 7 D8
Ewden Village 92 C5

F

Fairleigh 142 A7
Far Bank 24 F7
Felkirk 16 B6
Fenwick 6 B5
Finkle Street 74 C2
Finningley 86 E3
Firbeck 136 A6
Firth Park 113 D3
Fir Vale 113 C2
Fishlake 25 B7
Flanderwell 117 A6

Ford
Ford 154 E5
Fosterhouses 8 A2
Frecheville 142 D4
Frickley 37 F5
Fullshaw 71 B7
Fulstone 28 B7
Fulwood 139 C8

G

Garden Villages 73 A1
Gawber 33 B3
Gibbet Hill 122 F4
Gildingwells 147 F7
Gilroyd 54 A5
Gleadless 54 A5
Gleadless Townend ...142 A3
Gleadless Valley 141 E3
Goldthorpe 58 E4
Goole Green 139 D7
Gosforth Valley 152 E2
Greasbrough 97 C2
Great Houghton 36 E2
Greenhill 152 E7
Green Hill 17 D7
Greenland 130 B7
Green Moor 73 A3
Greenside 154 C3
Grenoside 112 D8
Greystones 140 A1
Greystones Cliffe 139 F7
Grimesthorpe 113 E1
Grimethorpe 36 B7
Grindleford 149 C1
Guilthwaite 132 B7

H

Hackenthorpe 143 B4
Hacking Hill 19 B3
Hade Edge 48 B7
Haigh 13 B5
Halfway 155 F7
Hallam Head 127 C2
Hallam Moors 138 A5
Hallowmoor 112 A1
Hallowmoor 20 B1
Hampole 28 A4
Handsworth 130 E2
Handsworth Hill 130 D4
Hanging Water 139 F8
Hangsman Hill 8 E1
Hardwick 133 C1
Harley 76 D1
Harlington 59 C2
Harthill 135 F7

Harworth 121 E4
Hatfield 44 C8
Hatfield Woodhouse .. 44 E6
Hathersage 149 B7
Havercroft 16 B8
Hay Green 25 B8
Haywood 22 E6
Hazelford 149 A5
Hazlehead 49 F2
Heeley 141 B6
Hellaby 118 A5
Hemingfield 77 D7
Hemsworth
  Sheffield 141 D3
  South Kirkby 17 C8
Herdings 141 F3
Hermit Hill 75 A6
Herringthorpe 116 A5
Hexthorpe 62 A1
Hickleton 59 B7
Higham 32 E3
High Bradfield 110 B6
Highfield
  Hemsworth 17 D6
  Sheffield 141 A8
Highfields 40 B2
Highgate 58 C5
High Green 94 D7
High Hoyland 12 C1
High Melton 81 C8
High Wincobank 113 E4
Highwoods 79 F5
Hillfoot
  Dronfield 151 D5
  Sheffield 128 E7
Hillsborough 112 C1
Hill Top
  Oughtibridge 139 E5
  Rotherham 114 C5
  Sheffield 126 E7
Holbrook 156 A8
Holdworth 110 F3
Hollin Busk 92 C7
Hollins End 142 C5
Hollow Meadows .. 125 D5
Holme
  Askern 22 B2
  Holmfirth 47 A8
Holmes 115 A5
Holmesdale 153 C2
Holmley Common ... 153 A3
Honeywell 33 F3
Hood Green 53 E2
Hooton Levitt 118 E3
Hooton Pagnell 38 C5
Hooton Roberts 99 D7
Horner House 73 A2
Howard Hill 128 C5
Howbrook 75 B1
Hoyland 76 C6
Hoyland Common 76 B5
Hoyland Lowe 76 C7
Hoylandswaine 52 A6
Hoyle Mill 34 C1
Hurl Field 141 E5
Hyde Park 62 D1

I

Ickles 115 B4
Ingbirchworth 29 E1
Instoneville 21 F7
Intake
  Doncaster 63 B4
  Sheffield 142 B5

J

Jordan 114 F7
Jordanthorpe 153 B7
Jump 77 A7

K

Kendray 55 C7
Kexbrough 32 C7
Killamarsh 156 E6
Kilnhurst 98 D8
Kimberworth 114 E6
Kimberworth Park ... 96 F7
Kingstone 54 D7
Kirk Bramwith 24 A4
Kirk Sandall 42 E3
Kirk Smeaton 3 D5
Kitchenroyd 30 B8
Kiveton Park 145 E2
Knoll Top 73 D1
Knowle Top 127 C6

L

Lane End 95 A6
Lane Head 28 E6
Langold 136 E4
Langsett 71 C6
Laughton Common .. 134 C3
Laughton en le Morthen 134 E5
Leadmill 149 B5
Letwell 136 A3
Liberty Hill 127 E5
Lightwood
  Eckington 154 F2
  Sheffield 153 F8
Listerdale 116 F4

Little Hemsworth 17 F6
Little Houghton 57 C7
Little London 1 A7
Little Norton 153 A8
Little Sheffield 128 F1
Little Smeaton 3 E6
Littleworth 85 C1
Load Brook 126 C6
Lodge Moor 126 E1
Longley Estate 113 B3
Long Sandall 42 C2
Loversall 83 D2
Low Barugh 32 F6
Low Bradfield 110 A4
Lowedges 153 A6
Lower Bradway 152 C6
Lower Crabtree ... 129 C8
Lower Cumberworth .. 29 E8
Lower Denby 30 B4
Lower Lewden 55 D4
Lower Pilley 75 E5
Lower Walkley 128 C7
Lockfield 141 B8
Low Field 17 F7
Low Valley 56 F5
Low Wincobank 114 A4
Loxley 111 D1
Lundwood 34 E3
Lydgate 128 A3

M

Malinbridge 128 A7
Maltby 119 C5
Manor Estate 142 B8
Manor Park 129 F2
Mapplewell 14 C1
Marr 60 D7
Marsh Lane 154 F3
Masbrough 115 B6
Mattersey Thorpe .. 123 F1
Meadowhall 114 C3
Meadow Head 140 E1
Measborough Dike .. 55 B8
Meersbrook 141 B5
Meersbrook Bank .. 141 A5
Mexborough 80 B7
Micklebring 100 D2
Mickley 152 B3
Middlecliff 57 D7
Middle Handley ... 154 E1
Middlewood 111 F4
Midhopestones 72 A3
Millhouse Green ... 50 E3
Millhouses
  Darfield 57 D5
  Sheffield 140 C3
Milton 76 E5
Minsthorpe 19 A5
Monk Bretton 34 B4
Moor End 53 B5
Moorends 9 D4
Moorhole 143 A1
Moorthorpe 18 B7
Morthen 133 B7
Mortomley 94 E7
Mosborough 155 D7
Moss 6 B1

N

Neepsend 128 F6
Nether Edge 140 E6
Nether End 30 D4
Nethergate 127 C5
Nether Green
  Killamarsh 156 D7
  Sheffield 139 E8
Nether Haugh 97 C6
Nether Padley 149 E1
Netherthorpe
  Aston 145 A7
  Sheffield 160 C4
  Worksop 159 B6
New Edlington 82 C1
Newfield Green 141 D5
Newhill 78 D5
Newington 105 D1
New Lodge 33 E7
New Rossington ... 103 E7
Newton 62 A2
New Totley 151 E4
New Village 41 B2
New York 115 C5
Normandale 127 E8
Normanton Spring .. 142 F6
North Anston 146 D6
North Elmsall 19 B6
Northfield 115 D8
Norton
  Doncaster 4 C3
  Sheffield 153 B8
Norton Lees 141 A4
Norton Woodseats .. 141 A2
Norwood 156 F8
Notton 14 F6

O

Oldcotes 136 F6
Old Denaby 80 C3
Old Edlington 101 A7
Old Mill 34 A3
Old Town 33 C3
Orgreave 131 B2

Oughtibridge 111 E7
Owler Bar 151 B1
Owlerton 112 D2
Owlthorpe 143 B2
Owston 21 E3
Oxspring 52 B1

P

Parkgate 97 F2
Parkhead 139 F3
Park Head 127 E5
Park Hill 161 C3
Park Mill 12 A4
Park Side 127 D5
Parkwood Springs .. 128 F7
Parson Cross 112 F5
Penistone 51 C3
Philadelphia 128 F6
Piccadilly 79 C1
Pickburn 39 D4
Pilley 75 D5
Pincheon Green 8 B7
Pismire Hill 113 D4
Pitsmoor 129 C7
Platts Common 76 E8
Plumbley 155 A6
Pogmoor 33 B2
Port Mahon 160 B5
Pot House 92 B8

Q

Quoit Green 153 B1

R

Rails 127 A4
Ranmoor 127 F1
Ravenfield 99 D3
Rawcliffe 2 A8
Rawcliffe Bridge 2 D7
Rawmarsh 97 C5
Redbrook 33 A4
Renishaw 156 B1
Richmond 142 E7
Richmond Hill 61 E4
Richmond Park ... 114 D6
Ridgeway 154 D7
Ridgeway Moor ... 154 E7
Rollestone 141 D5
Roman Terrace 79 F5
Rossington 85 C1
Rostholme 41 A2
Rotherham 115 F6
Roughbirchworth ... 73 A8
Royd 92 E7
Royston 13 E3
Ryecroft 98 A6
Ryhill 16 A8

S

St Ann's 115 D8
St Helen's 34 C5
St Michael's Field ... 113 C8
Sandhill
  Great Houghton ... 36 F1
  Rawmarsh 98 B7
Sandygate 127 E2
Scaftworth 123 D4
Scawsby 61 C7
Scawthorpe 61 E8
Scholes 96 B4
Scrooby 123 A2
Shaftholme 41 D5
Shafton 16 B3
Shafton Two Gates .. 16 C2
Sharrow 140 E7
Shaw Lands 33 C1
Shay House 92 B8
Sheffield 161 B2
Sheffield Lane Top .. 113 C5
Sheffield Park 129 E1
Shepley 28 F8
Shirecliffe 113 A1
Shiregreen 113 D6
Shireoaks 159 F6
Silkstone 52 F8
Silkstone Common .. 53 A5
Skelbrooke 20 C5
Skellow 20 F1
Slade Hooton 134 E7
Smithies 34 A5
Smithley 56 A3
Smithy Green 33 F5
Smithy Moor 72 F2
Snape Hill
  Darfield 57 A4
  Dronfield 153 A2
Snowden Hill 73 A6
Sothall 144 B2
South Anston 146 C4
South Bramwith ... 23 A3
South Elmsall 19 A1
South End 5 E8
Southey Green 112 E3
South Hiendley ... 16 D6
South Kirkby 18 C1
Spink Hall 92 B8
Spinkhill 156 D2
Spital Hill 121 E7
Spring Vale 51 F3
Sprotbrough 61 C1

Sprotbrough Park 61 C1
Stacey Bank 110 F1
Staincross 14 B2
Stainforth 23 F3
Stainton 119 F8
Stairfoot 55 F8
Stannington 127 C5
Steel Bank 128 B4
Stephen Hill 127 F3
Stockbridge 41 C2
Stocksbridge 73 C2
Stone 135 E8
Stopes 126 F6
Storrs 127 A7
Street 77 E2
Stubbin 92 D8
Studfield Hill 127 F8
Stumperlowe 139 D8
Styrrup 121 D1
Summerfield 128 C2
Summerley 153 E2
Sunnyside
  Doncaster 42 E3
  Rotherham 117 B7
Sutton 21 E5
Swaithe 55 E5
Swallownest 144 C7
Swinton 79 C2
Swinton Bridge 79 F3
Sykehouse 7 C6

T

Tankersley 75 F4
Tapton Hill 128 B2
Templeborough ... 114 F3
The Cross 113 C7
The Green 51 D2
The Parks 43 F8
The Wheel 112 F8
Thorne 26 C7
Thorn Hill 115 C7
Thorpe Common 95 B3
Thorpe Hesley 95 F4
Thorpe in Balne 23 B2
Thorpe Salvin ... 158 F6
Throapham 134 F3
Thrybergh 98 E3
Thurcroft 133 D6
Thurgoland 73 F7
Thurlstone 51 A4
Thurnscoe 58 E7
Thurnscoe East 58 F8
Tickhill 121 B6
Tilts 33 C4
Tinsley 114 D2
Todwick 145 E6
Toll Bar 41 A5
Topham 7 A7
Top o' th' Town 51 A4
Totley 151 E4
Totley Brook 151 E5
Totley Rise 151 F5
Town End
  Sheffield 127 E5
  Stocksbridge 92 F8
Townhead
  Penistone 48 F2
  Sheffield 151 C7
Treeton 131 F4
Trister Hill 30 E7
Troway 154 B4
Turnerwood 159 C7

U

Ughill 109 F1
Ulley 132 F3
Upper Bradway 152 B4
Upper Crabtree ... 113 B1
Upper Cudworth 35 C8
Upper Cumberworth .. 29 B6
Upper Denby 29 F3
Upper Gate 127 B6
Upper Haugh 97 E8
Upper Hoyland 76 C7
Upper Midhope 71 D4
Upper Padley 149 D2
Upper Tankersley ... 75 E3
Upperthorpe 136 D5
Upper Whiston ... 132 D7
Upton 19 A8

V

Victoria 49 B7

W

Wadsley 111 F2
Wadsley Bridge ... 112 C3
Wadworth 102 C7
Walden Stubbs 4 E6
Wales 145 B3
Wales Common 144 E3
Waleswood 144 D3
Walkley 128 D6
Walkley Bank 128 B6
Ward Green 54 E6
Warmsworth 82 D5
Warren 95 B8
Waterthorpe 143 E2
Wath upon Dearne ... 78 E8
Wentworth 77 B1

West Barrier 86 A4
West Bretton 12 F8
West Cowick 1 A7
West End 44 D5
Westfield 155 F8
West Green 34 F6
West Melton 78 C6
Westthorpe 156 D4
Wharncliffe Side ... 93 B1
Wheatley 62 F5
Wheatley Hills 63 B6
Wheatley Park 63 A7
Whin Moor 52 D7
Whinney Hill 98 D2
Whirlow 139 F2
Whiston 116 C1
White Hill 131 C8
Whitley 94 E2
Whitley Common ... 49 E7
Wickersley 117 C4
Wike Well End 26 D5
Wilthorpe 33 C4
Wincobank 114 B3
Windhill 80 C6
Wingfield 96 F3
Wisewood 127 F8
Wombwell 56 D2
Woodall 157 C6
Wood Hill
  Sheffield 129 D8
  Wales 145 A2
Woodhouse 143 D6
Woodhouse Mill ... 143 D8
Woodlands 40 B4
Woodlands East 40 C4
Woodland View 128 A6
Wood Royd 73 E1
Wood Seats 94 D3
Woodseats 147 F4
Woodside 129 A6
Woodthorpe Estate .. 142 C7
Wood Willows 73 D2
Woolley 13 F7
Worksop 148 D1
Wormley Hill 8 D5
Worrall 111 D5
Worsbrough 55 B3
Worsbrough Bridge .. 55 A4
Worsbrough Common .. 54 E6
Worsbrough Dale ... 55 C4
Wortley 74 D3
Wrangbrook 19 F7
Wroot 67 B3
Wybourn 129 E3

Index of streets, hospitals, industrial estates, railway stations, schools, shopping centres, universities and places of interest

A

Aaron Wilkinson Ct WF9 18 A2
Abbe's Cl The DN6 21 B5
Abbe's Wlk The DN6 21 D4
Abbey's Walk Mobile Home Pk DN7 25 B1
Abbey Brook Cl S8 140 E1
Abbey Brook Ct S8 140 E1
Abbey Brook Dr S8 152 E8
Abbey Brook Gdns S8 140 E1
Abbey Cl
Holmfirth HD9 48 B7
Laughton en le M S25 134 D5
Abbey Cres S7 140 B1
Abbey Croft S7 140 B1
Abbey Ct
Holmfirth HD9 48 B7
Sheffield S8 140 E1
Abbeydale Ct S17 152 A7
Abbeydale Grange Sch S7 140 D4
Abbeydale Industrial Mus* S7 152 B8
Abbeydale Park Cres S17 151 F6
Abbeydale Park Rise S17 151 F6
Abbeydale Prim Sch S7 140 E6
Abbeydale Rd S7 140 E5
Abbeydale Rd S S7 140 B1
Abbey Dr DN7 44 A8
Abbey Farm Dr HD8 28 F8
Abbey Farm View S72 35 C5
Abbeyfield Rd
Dunscroft DN7 43 F8
Sheffield S4 129 B8
Abbeyfields DN9 86 E3
Abbey Gdns DN7 44 A7
Abbey Gn
Dodworth S75 54 A6
Hatfield DN7 44 A8
Abbey Gr
Barnsley S71 34 E3
Hatfield DN7 44 A8
Abbey Grange S7 140 B1
Abbey La
Barnsley S71 34 E2
Laughton en le M S66 135 A8
Sheffield S7, S8, S11 140 B1
Abbey Lane Dell S8 140 B1
Abbey Lane Prim Sch S8 140 E2
Abbey Mews S8 140 D1
Abbey Rd DN7 44 A8
Abbey Rd S HD8 28 E8
Abbey Sch The S61 114 D7
Abbey View Dr S8 141 A3
Abbey View Hts 3 S8 141 A3
Abbey View Rd S8 141 A3
Abbey Way
Hatfield DN7 25 A1
North Anston S25 134 B1
Abbey Wlk DN5 61 E6
Abbot La WF4 14 B6
Abbots Cl S72 35 C5
Abbotsford Dr S66 133 E6
Abbots Mdw S20 144 A1
Abbots Rd S71 34 F3
Abbott St DN4 62 B2
Abdy Rd
Rotherham S61 96 D2
Wath u D S62 78 D2
Aberconway Cres DN11 103 F8
Abercorn Rd DN2 63 C4
Aberford Gr S74 77 B6
Abingdon Gdns S61 97 B2
Abingdon Rd DN2 63 B5
Abney Cl S14 141 C6
Abney Dr S14 141 C6
Abney Rd S14 141 C6
Abney St S1 160 C3
Acacia Ave
Chapeltown S35 94 F4
Maltby S66 118 D5
Rotherham S66 117 C5
South Elmsall WF9 19 A4
Acacia Cres S21 156 B5
Acacia Ct DN5 41 A2
Acacia Gr
Conisbrough DN12 100 A8
Shafton S72 16 C2
Acacia Rd
Adwick le S DN6 21 A2
Doncaster DN4 84 F8
Sheffield S5 113 E4
Ace Bsns Ctr S3 161 B4
Acer Cl
Killamarsh S21 156 C5
South Anston S25 146 D3
Acer Croft DN3 64 B5
Ackworth Dr S9 114 F1
Acomb Common Rd DN7 44 F8
Acorn Bldgs S3 160 C5
Acorn Bsns Pk 2 S8 140 E4
Acorn Croft S61 97 B2
Acorn Ctr The S72 36 A6
Acorn Dr S6 127 C7
Acorn Hill S6 127 D7
Acorn St S3 161 A5
Acorn Way
Grimethorpe S72 35 F6
Grimethorpe S72 36 A6
Sheffield S6 127 B6
Acre Cl
Kirk Sandall DN3 42 F2
Maltby S66 118 E7
Thurcroft S66 133 F7
Acre Gate S35 94 D6
Acre La
Penistone S36 51 D6
Shepley HD9 28 B6
Wharncliffe Side S35 111 A8
Acre Rd S72 35 C4
Acres Hill La S9 130 B4
Acres Hill Prim Sch S9 130 B3
Acres Hill Rd S9 130 C4
Acres La DN9 67 B5
Acres View S65 116 B3
Acrewood Dr S66 117 B7
Acton Cl S26 132 D1
Adamfield 3 S3 160 B3
Adam La S75 32 A2
Adastral Ave S12 142 A2
Addison Rd
Maltby S66 118 D5
Mexborough S64 80 C5
Sheffield S5 113 D2
Addison Sq S25 135 A1
Addy Cl
Doncaster DN4 83 C5
Sheffield S6 160 B5
Addy Cres WF9 18 F3
Addy Dr S6 160 B5
Addy St S6 160 B5
Adelaide La S3 128 F5
Adelaide Rd
Norton DN6 4 D3
Sheffield S7 140 D6
Adelaide St S66 119 B3
Adelphi S6 160 B5
Adelphi St S6 160 B5
Adkin Royd S75 52 F8
Adkins Dr S5 112 E3
Adkins Rd S5 112 E3
Adlard Rd DN2 63 B6
Adlington Cres S5 112 F4
Adlington Rd S5 112 F5
Admiral Biggs Dr S60 131 E4
Admirals Crest S61 96 B2
Adrian Cres S5 113 A4
Adsetts St S4 113 E1
Adwick Ave DN5 40 F5
Adwick Ct S64 80 B4
Adwick La
Adwick le S DN5 40 E6
Bentley DN5 40 E6
Adwick Park Jun Sch DN6 40 B5
Adwick Pk S64 79 D5
Adwick Rd S64 80 B6
Adwick Sta DN6 40 C6
Adwick Washington Inf Sch DN6 40 C4
AeroVenture/S Yorks Aircraft Mus* DN4 63 A1
Agden Rd S7 140 E8
Agden Side Rd S6 109 E8
Agnes Rd
Barnsley S70 54 E8
Kexbrough S75 32 E8
Agnes Terr 6 S70 54 E8
Ainsdale Ave S63 58 D4
Ainsdale Cl S71 15 B5
Ainsdale Ct S71 34 D6
Ainsdale Rd S71 15 B5
Ainsley Cl DN9 86 A7
Ainsley Rd S10 128 C4
Ainsty Rd 3 S7 140 F7
Aintree Ave
Doncaster DN4 63 D2
Eckington S21 155 B3
Aintree Cl DN5 61 D5
Aintree Dr
Doncaster DN4 83 C5
Mexborough S64 80 B6
Aire Cl S35 94 F6
Airedale Ave DN11 121 A8
Airedale Rd
Kexbrough S75 32 D8
Sheffield S6 112 A2
Aireton Cl S66 117 A5
Aireton Rd 7 S70 33 E2
Airey La DN6 23 A2
Air Mount Cl S66 117 A4
Airstone Rd DN6 21 F7
Aisby Dr DN11 85 A2
Aisthorpe Rd S8 140 F3
Aitken Rd S62 98 E8
Aizlewood Rd S8 140 F7
Akley Bank Cl S17 151 F5
Alan Rd S75 32 E8
Alba Cl S73 56 E6
Albanus Croft 1 S6 127 C6
Albanus Ridge S6 127 C6
Albany Ave S35 95 B4
Albany Cl S73 56 A6
Albany Cres WF9 18 F2
Albany La DN11 84 E1
Albany Pl 5 WF9 18 F2
Albany Rd
Doncaster DN4 83 B8
Sheffield S7 140 F7
Stocksbridge S36 73 B1
Swinton S64 79 D1
Albany St
Rotherham S65 115 E6
4 South Elmsall WF9 18 F2
Albert Cres S72 57 D7
Albert Rd
Goldthorpe S63 58 E5
Mexborough S64 80 A5
Rawmarsh S62 97 F4
Sheffield, Hackenthorpe S12 143 C3
Sheffield, Heeley S8 141 A6
Wath u D S63 78 D7
Albert St E 9 S70 33 F1
Albert St
Barnsley S70 33 F1
Cudworth S72 16 C1
Eckington S21 155 D2
Maltby S66 119 B4
Rotherham S60 115 C6
Swinton S64 79 D4
Thorne DN8 26 C8
Thurnscoe S63 58 C8
Albert Terrace Rd S6 128 E5
Albion S6 160 B4
Albion Dr S63 58 F8
Albion Ho 10 S70 54 F8
Albion Pl
Doncaster DN1 62 E3
South Elmsall WF9 19 A3
Albion Rd
Rotherham S60 115 E6
Royston S71 34 C8
Albion Row S6 127 D4
Albion St S6 160 B4
Albion Terr
12 Barnsley S70 55 A8
Doncaster DN4 62 B1
Alcester Rd S7 140 F7
Aldam Cl
Rotherham S65 116 D7
Sheffield S17 151 E4
Aldam Croft S17 151 E4
Aldam Rd
Doncaster DN4 82 F6
Sheffield S17 151 F4
Aldam Way S17 151 E4
Aldbeck Croft S75 32 E7
Aldbury Cl S71 34 B6
Aldcliffe Cres DN4 82 F4
Aldene Ave S6 111 F1
Aldene Glade S6 111 F1
Aldene Rd S6 111 F2
Alder Chase S61 96 C2
Alder Cl S75 14 A1
Alderford Dr DN4 83 B4
Alder Gr
Darfield S73 56 F4
Doncaster DN4 83 A7
Thorne DN8 9 C3
Alder Holt Cl DN3 64 C4
Alder La S9 130 E3
Alder Mews S74 76 E5
Alderney Rd 3 S8 141 A7
Aldersgate Cl DN11 104 A7
Aldersgate Ct S66 119 C4
Alders Gn S6 111 D1
Alderson Ave S62 97 F7
Alderson Cl DN11 121 B8
Alderson Dr
Barnsley S71 34 A6
Doncaster DN2 62 F3
Tickhill DN11 121 B7
Alderson Pl S2 141 A8
Alderson Rd S2 141 A8
Alderson Rd N S2 141 A8
Aldervale Cl S64 98 D8
Aldesworth Rd DN4 63 F2
Aldfield Way S5 113 B2
Aldham Cotts S73 56 C5
Aldham Cres S73 56 A5
Aldham House La S73 56 B4
Aldham Ind Est S73 56 B5
Aldine Ct S1 161 B4
Aldous Cl S26 145 E3
Aldous Way S26 145 E3
Aldred Cl
Killamarsh S21 156 E8
Rotherham S66 117 B5
Aldred Ct S60 115 E5
Aldred Rd S10 128 C5
Aldred St S60 115 E5
Aldrens Cl S66 100 D2
Aldrin Way S66 118 E6
Aldwarke La S62, S65 98 B2
Aldwarke Rd S62 97 F3
Alexander Gdns S75 31 E4
Alexander St DN5 41 C1
Alexandra Cl S61 114 E8
Alexandra Ctr S62 97 F2
Alexandra Gdns S11 140 D6
Alexandra Rd
Adwick le S DN6 40 D6
Aston S26 144 C8
Bentley DN5 41 B1
Bircotes DN11 122 B4
Doncaster DN4 83 B8
Alexandra Rd *continued*
Dronfield S18 153 B2
Mexborough S64 80 B5
Sheffield S2 141 B7
Thorne DN8 9 D4
Alexandra St
Maltby S66 119 B3
Thorne DN8 9 B1
Alexandra Terr S71 55 F8
Alford Ave S35 111 D7
Alford Cl S75 33 B4
Alfred Rd
Askern DN6 21 F7
Sheffield S9 129 F7
Alfred St S71 15 E4
Alga Ho S64 79 D3
Algar Cl S2 141 E7
Algar Cres S2 141 F7
Algar Dr S2 141 E7
Algar Pl S2 141 E7
Algar Rd S2 141 E7
Alhambra Sh Ctr 20 S70 33 F1
Alice Rd S61 115 B7
Alison Cl S26 144 D7
Alison Cres S2 130 B1
Alison Dr S26 144 D7
Allan St S65 115 E6
Allas Dike La S36 91 E4
Allas La S36 91 E4
Allatt Cl S70 54 F8
Alldred Cres S64 79 C1
Allenby Cl S8 152 E7
Allenby Cres DN11 103 E8
Allenby Dr S8 152 E7
Allendale S70 55 C5
Allendale Ct S70 55 C5
Allendale Dr S74 76 D5
Allendale Gdns DN5 61 F3
Allendale Rd
Barnsley S75 33 E3
Bentley DN5 61 F3
Hoyland S74 76 D5
Kexbrough S75 32 D8
Rotherham S65 116 C4
Allende Way S9 130 B6
Allen Gdns S35 95 B1
Allen Rd S20 143 F2
Allen St S3 160 C4
Allerton St DN1 62 D4
Allestree Dr S18 152 C1
All Hallows Dr
Maltby S66 118 E4
Tickhill DN11 120 F7
Alliance St S4 129 D7
Alliss Rd DN3 85 E8
Allott Cl
Rotherham S65 117 D8
South Elmsall WF9 18 F3
Allott Cres S74 77 A7
Allotts Ct S70 75 E7
Allott St
Hoyland, Elsecar S74 77 A5
Hoyland S74 76 B5
All Saints' Sq S60 115 D6
All Saints Cl
Silkstone S75 32 A1
Wath u D S63 78 E6
All Saints Harworth CE Prim Sch DN11 122 A4
All Saints Mdws S25 134 C3
All Saints RC High Sch S2 161 C1
All Saints Sq DN12 81 A3
All Saints Way S26 144 F7
Allsopps Yd S74 55 D1
Allt St S62 97 F4
Alma Cres S18 153 A3
Alma Rd
Chapeltown S35 94 D7
Rotherham S60 115 D5
Alma Row S60 116 C1
Alma St
Barnsley S70 33 D1
Sheffield S3 161 A5
Wombwell S73 56 E2
Almholme La DN5 41 E4
Almond Ave
Armthorpe DN3 64 B7
Cudworth S72 35 B7
Almond Cl
Maltby S66 118 D5
South Elmsall WF9 19 A5
Almond Dr S21 156 C5
Almond Glade S66 117 C3
Almond Pl S63 78 F5
Almond Rd DN4 84 F8
Almond Tree Rd S26 144 F2
Alms Hill Cres S11 139 F3
Alms Hill Dr S11 139 F3
Alms Hill Glade S11 139 F3
Alms Hill Rd S11 139 F3
Almshouses DN5 41 D2
Almshouses The S62 77 A1
Alney Pl S6 112 D4
Alnwick Dr S12 142 C5
Alnwick Rd S12 142 B5
Alperton Cl S71 34 F5
Alpha Ct DN8 25 F8
Alpha Rd S65 116 B7
Alpha St DN5 40 F5
Alpine Cl S36 73 A1
Alpine Croft S36 73 A1
Alpine Ct WF9 17 D8
Alpine Ho S6 160 A5
Alpine Rd
Sheffield S6 160 A5
Stocksbridge S36 73 B1
Alpine View WF9 17 D8
Alport Ave S12 142 E5
Alport Dr S12 142 E5
Alport Gr S12 142 E5
Alport Pl S12 142 E4
Alport Rd S12 142 E5
Alport Rise S18 152 D2
Alric Dr
Barnsley S71 34 E1
Brinsworth S60 115 B1
Alrich Mews S36 72 F2
Alsing Rd S9 114 C3
Alston Cl
Doncaster DN4 84 D7
Silkstone S75 52 F8
Alston Rd DN4 84 D6
Alton Cl S11 140 A2
Alton Way S75 14 A1
Alvaston Wlk DN12 81 A3
Alverley La DN4 83 A4
Alverley View DN11 83 A3
Alverley Way S70 75 F6
Alwyn Ave DN5 61 E7
Alwyn Rd DN8 26 C7
Amalfi Cl S73 56 F5
Amanda Ave S81 148 E6
Amanda Dr DN7 44 C7
Amanda Rd DN11 121 F4
Ambassador Gdns DN3 64 C5
Amberley Ct S9 130 A7
Amberley Rise DN6 20 F2
Amberley St S9 130 A8
Ambler Rise S26 132 C1
Ambleside Cl
Brinsworth S60 131 A8
Sheffield S20 155 E6
Ambleside Cres DN5 61 A1
Ambleside Gr S71 56 A8
Ambleside Wlk S25 146 F6
Ambrose Ave DN7 44 C8
Amen Cnr
1 Rotherham S60 115 D7
4 Rotherham, Thorn Hill S60 115 C7
America La S73 78 C3
Amersall Cres DN5 61 E8
Amersall Ct DN5 61 E7
Amersall Rd DN5 61 E7
Amory's Holt Cl S66 118 E7
Amory's Holt Dr S66 118 E7
Amory's Holt Rd S66 118 E7
Amory's Holt Way S66 118 E7
Amos Rd S9 114 B2
Amwell Gn DN7 44 A6
Amy Rd DN5 41 C3
Anchorage Cres DN5 62 A4
Anchorage La DN5 61 F4
Anchorage Sch (Lower) The DN5 61 E6
Anchorage Sch (Upper) The DN5 61 C7
Anchor Cl DN8 26 B7
Ancient La DN7 44 E5
Ancona Rise S73 56 F6
Ancote Cl S75 33 A1
Andover Dr S3 129 A6
Andover St
Sheffield S3 129 B6
Sheffield, Woodside S3 129 A6
Andrew La S3 161 B5
Andrews Pl S61 115 A8
Andwell La S10 138 F6
Anelay Rd DN4 82 F7
Anfield Rd DN4 84 E8
Angel St
Bolton u D S63 58 D1
Sheffield S3 161 B4
Angerford Ave S8 141 A4
Angleton Ave S2 142 C8
Angleton Cl S2 142 C8
Angleton Gdns S2 142 C8
Angleton Gn S2 142 C8
Angleton Mews S2 142 C8
Angram Bank Prim Sch S35 94 C7
Angram Rd S35 94 D8
Annan Cl S75 32 F5
Anna Rd DN6 21 F7
Annat Pl S35 94 C7
Annat Royd La S36 50 C8
Anne Cres S72 16 E5
Annesley Cl S8 152 F7
Annesley Rd S8 152 F7
Anne St S25 134 F3
Annet La S6 109 F4
Anns Grove Prim Sch S2 141 A7
Anns Rd S2 141 A7
Anns Rd N S2 141 B7
Ann St S62 97 F3
Ansdell Rd DN5 41 B2
Ansell Rd S11 140 A6
Anson Gr S60 131 D8
Anson St S2 161 C3
Ansten Cres DN4 84 E8
Anston Ave S26 145 E3

Anston Brook Prim Sch S25 146 D5
Anston Cl S25 146 D6
Anston Dr WF9 19 A5
Anston Greenlands Jun & Inf Sch S25 146 E7
Anston Hall S25 146 D6
Anston Hillcrest Prim Sch S25 146 D3
Anston Park Inf Sch S25 146 E7
Anston Park Jun Sch S25 146 F7
Ansult Ct DN5 62 A8
Antrim Ave S10 160 A2
Anvil Cl S6 127 E6
Anvil Cotts S75 32 E7
Anvil Cres S35 113 B8
Apley Rd DN1 62 D2
Apollo St S62 98 B7
Apostle Cl DN4 82 E6
Apperknowle Com Prim Sch S18 154 A1
Appleby Cl S75 13 F1
Appleby Pl DN6 20 F2
Appleby Rd DN2 63 D4
Appleby Wlk S25 146 F7
Applegarth Cl S12 142 A6
Applegarth Dr S12 142 A6
Apple Gr DN9 86 A4
Applehaigh Ct WF4 15 A5
Applehaigh Dr DN3 42 E5
Applehaigh Gr S71 15 A4
Applehaigh La WF4 15 A6
Applehaigh View S71 15 A4
Applehurst Bank S70 55 B8
Applehurst La DN6 23 A1
Appleton Cl S65 98 D1
Appleton Gdns DN5 62 A8
Appleton Way
Bentley DN5 62 A8
Worsbrough S70 55 A5
Appletree Dr S18 153 A1
Appletree Way DN4 85 A5
April Cl S71 34 D4
April Dr S71 34 D4
Apy Hill La DN11 120 D8
Aqueduct St S71 33 F3
Arbour Cres S66 133 F6
Arbour Dr S66 133 F6
Arbour La S65 99 E3
Arbourthorne S2 129 E1
Arbourthorne Com Prim Sch S2 141 D6
Arbourthorne Cotts S2 141 D8
Arbourthorne Rd S2 141 E6
Arcade The
Barnsley S70 33 F1
Carlton in L S81 148 F6
Archbishop Holgate Hospl WF9 17 A6
Archdale Cl S2 142 B8
Archdale Rd S2 142 A8
Archer Ct S8 140 E4
Archer Gate S6 111 D1
Archer Ho 1 S65 115 E7
Archer La S7 140 D5
Archer Rd S8 140 E3
Archery Cl S66 117 B3
Archibald Rd S7 140 E6
Archway Ctr S1 161 B3
Archways S2 161 B2
Arcon Pl S62 98 A6
Arcubus Ave S26 144 D8
Ardeen Rd DN2 63 A4
Arden Gate DN4 82 F4
Ardmore St S9 130 A5
Ardron Wlk S62 98 B6
Ardsley Ave S26 144 E7
Ardsley Cl S20 142 F2
Ardsley Dr S20 142 F2
Ardsley Gr S20 142 F2
Ardsley Mews S71 56 A8
Ardsley Rd S70 55 D5
Arena Ct S9 130 B8
Argosy Cl DN10 122 F8
Argyle Cl S8 141 B5
Argyle La DN11 84 E1
Argyle Rd S8 141 B5
Argyle St S64 80 A5
Argyll Ave DN2 63 B5
Arklow Rd DN2 63 A5
Arksey Common La DN2, DN3, DN5 42 A3
Arksey La DN5 41 C1
Arksey Prim Sch DN5 41 D2
Arkwright Rd DN5 61 F5
Arley St S2 129 A1
Arlington Ave S26 144 F8
Arlott Way DN12 82 C3
Armer St S60 115 C5
Armitage Bldgs S36 51 C3
Armitage Rd
Doncaster DN4 82 F7
Stocksbridge S36 92 D8
Armroyd La S74 76 F4
Arms Park Dr S20 155 F6
Armstead Rd S20 144 A2
Armstrong Wlk S66 118 E6
Armthorpe Ent Ctr DN3 64 D7
Armthorpe La
Doncaster, Wheatley Hills DN2, DN3 63 A5
Kirk Sandall DN3 43 B4
Armthorpe Rd
Doncaster DN2 63 C6
Sheffield S11 139 F8
Armthorpe Sch The DN3 64 A7
Armthorpe Southfield Prim Sch DN3 64 B5
Armthorpe Tranmoor Prim Sch DN3 64 B5
Armyne Gr S71 34 E1
Army Row S71 15 D4
Armytage Wlk WF9 18 C3
Arncliffe Dr
Barnsley S70 54 B8
Chapeltown S35 94 F6
Arnold Ave
Barnsley S71 33 F7
Sheffield S12 142 B1
Arnold Cres S64 80 A6
Arnold Rd S65 116 B6
Arnold St S6 128 C6
Arnside Rd
Maltby S66 119 A6
1 Sheffield S8 140 E5
Arnside Terr S8 140 E5
Arran Hill S65 98 F3
Arran Rd S10 128 B3
Arras St S9 129 F5
Arren Cl DN3 42 F8
Arrowsmith Ho 3 S65 115 E7
Arthington Blgs S2 141 A6
Arthington St S8 141 A6
Arthur Ave DN5 41 B2
Arthur Pl DN5 41 C2
Arthur Rd S36 73 A1
Arthur St
Aston S26 144 D7
Bentley DN5 41 C2
Rawmarsh S62 98 A7
Worsbrough S70 55 A5
Artisan View S8 141 A6
Arundel Ave
Rotherham S65 98 D1
Treeton S60 131 E4
Arundel Cl S18 152 D1
Arundel Cotts S60 131 E4
Arundel Cres S60 131 E4
Arundel Ct S11 139 F4
Arundel Dr S81 148 F6
Arundel Gate S1 161 B3
Arundel Gdns
Bentley DN5 61 F8
Royston S71 15 C4
Arundel La S1 161 B2
Arundell Dr S71 34 F5
Arundel Rd
Chapeltown S35 95 A6
Norton DN6 4 D3
Rotherham S60, S65 115 F5
Treeton S60 131 E4
Arundel St
Sheffield S1 161 A2
Stainforth DN7 24 E3
Treeton S60 131 E4
Arundel View S74 77 A7
Arundel Wlk DN11 122 B5
Ascension Cl S66 119 B4
Ascot Ave DN4 63 D2
Ascot Cl S64 80 B6
Ascot Dr DN5 61 D6
Ascot St S1 129 A1
Ashberry Cl S63 58 D8
Ashberry Gdns S6 160 A5
Ashberry Rd S6 160 A5
Ashbourne Gr
Oughtibridge S35 111 E6
1 Sheffield S13 130 F1
Ashbourne Rd
Barnsley S71 34 A7
Sheffield S13 130 F1
Ashburnham Cl DN6 4 E3
Ashburnham Gdns DN5 61 F3
Ashburnham Rd DN8 26 A7
Ashburnham Wlk DN6 4 E3
Ashburton Cl DN6 40 A6
Ashbury Dr S8 141 C2
Ashbury La S8 141 C2
Ashby Ct S70 54 D8
Ash Cl
Killamarsh S21 156 C5
Rotherham S65 116 D4
Ash Cotts S73 56 A6
Ashcourt Dr DN4 83 B4
Ash Cres
Eckington S21 155 B1
Mexborough S64 79 F6
Stocksbridge S36 73 D1
Ashcroft Cl DN12 82 A1
Ash Ct
Maltby S66 118 D6
Sprotbrough DN5 61 D1
Ashdale Cl DN3 42 F1
Ash Dale Rd DN4 82 C4
Ashdell S10 128 C2
Ashdell La S10 128 C2
Ashdell Prep Sch S10 128 B2
Ashdell Rd S10 128 C2
Ashdene Ct S62 98 D8
Ashdown Gdns S20 144 A3
Ashdown Pl DN5 61 F8
Ash Dyke Cl S75 32 D7
Asher Rd 14 S7 140 F8
Ashes La S62 95 F8
Ashes Park Ave S81 148 E1
Ashfield Ave DN8 26 A6
Ashfield Cl
Armthorpe DN3 64 C5
Barnsley S75 33 C3
Sheffield S12 141 F4
Ashfield Ct S70 55 D8
Ashfield Dr S12 141 F4
Ashfield Gr DN7 24 F4
Ashfield Ho WF9 17 D6
Ashfield Rd
Doncaster DN4 83 A6
Dunscroft DN7 43 F7
Hemsworth WF9 17 D5
Stocksbridge S36 73 D1
Thorne DN8 25 E5
Ash Fields Rd DN5 42 B8
Ashfield Way S66 117 B7
Ashford Rd
Dronfield S18 152 D1
Sheffield S11 140 D8
Ashfurlong Cl S17 151 F7
Ashfurlong Dr S17 151 F7
Ashfurlong Pk S17 151 F7
Ashfurlong Rd S17 151 F7
Ashgate Cl S10 128 C2
Ashgate La 3 S10 128 C2
Ashgate Rd S10 128 C2
Ash Gr
Armthorpe DN3 64 C7
Barnsley S70 55 D7
Conisbrough DN12 81 A1
Finningley DN9 86 B4
Maltby S66 119 B6
Rawmarsh S62 98 B5
Rotherham S66 117 C5
Sheffield S10 160 A2
South Elmsall WF9 19 A4
Wales S26 145 C3
Ash Grove Jun & Inf Sch WF9 19 A4
Ash Hill Cres DN7 44 B7
Ash Hill Rd
Hatfield DN7 44 B7
Sykehouse DN14 7 A5
Ash House La S17 139 D1
Ash La
Stocksbridge S36 73 E1
Unstone S18 153 F3
Ashland Ct S7 140 E6
Ashland Rd
Eckington S21 155 E3
Sheffield S7 140 E6
Ashlea S63 58 E8
Ashleigh S72 17 A3
Ashleigh Ave S12 141 F5
Ashleigh Croft S12 141 F5
Ashleigh Ct S21 155 C1
Ashleigh Dr S12 141 F5
Ashleigh Gdns S61 97 B2
Ashleigh Pl S12 141 F5
Ashleigh Vale S70 55 C8
Ashley Cl S21 156 D6
Ashley Croft 2 S71 15 B4
Ashley Ct
Finningley DN9 86 E3
South Kirkby WF9 17 F1
Ashley Gr S26 144 D7
Ashley Ind Est S60 115 D7
Ashley La S21 156 D6
Ashmore Ave S21 155 B2
Ashmount S6 112 C4
Ash Mount S72 16 C3
Ashover Cl 5 S70 55 A4
Ashpool Cl S13 143 A6
Ashpool Fold S13 143 A6
Ashrams Ct 2 S70 33 D1
Ash Rd
Adwick le S DN6 21 B2
Shafton S72 16 D2
Thorpe in B DN3 42 C8
Wath u D S63 79 A5
Ash Ridge S64 79 D2
Ash St
Barnsley S73 56 A6
Sheffield, Mosborough S20 155 C8
Sheffield S6 128 E6
Ashtenne Bsns Ctr S60 115 C4
Ashton Ave DN5 61 D8
Ashton Cl S21 156 C6
Ashton Dr DN3 42 E4
Ashton La S66 100 E1
Ash Tree Ave DN10 122 F7
Ash Tree Ct S9 114 B4
Ash Tree Rd DN8 26 C6
Ashurst Cl S6 127 E6
Ashurst Dr S6 127 E7
Ashurst Pl S6 127 E6
Ashurst Rd S6 127 E7
Ash View
Chapeltown S35 94 F4
Rotherham S61 97 B3
Ashville DN11 104 A8
Ashwell Cl S72 16 C3
Ashwell Gr S65 116 B8
Ashwell Rd S13 143 A6
Ashwood Cl
Branton DN3 85 C8
Chapeltown S35 94 C8
Worsbrough S70 55 B4
Ashwood Gr S72 36 D3
Ashwood Rd
Chapeltown S35 94 C8
Rawmarsh S62 97 F3
Ashworth Dr S61 96 D2
Askam Ct S66 117 D6
Askam Rd S66 117 D6
Askern Ct DN5 41 A1
Askern Grange La DN6 22 C8
Askern Ho 16 DN1 62 C2
Askern Ind Est DN6 22 C8
Askern Littlemoor Inf Sch DN6 21 E7
Askern Moss Road Inf Sch DN6 22 B8
Askern Rd
Adwick le S DN5, DN6 21 E1
Askern Rd *continued*
Bentley DN5 41 A3
Askern Spa Jun Sch DN6 21 F6
Askew Ct S36 92 C8
Askham Gr WF9 19 E7
Askrigg Cl DN4 84 F7
Asline Rd S2 141 A8
Aspen Cl
Edenthorpe DN3 42 F1
Killamarsh S21 156 C6
Aspen Gr S73 57 A4
Aspen Rd S21 155 B1
Aspen Way
Rotherham S60 115 B5
Swinton S64 98 C8
Aspen Wlk S66 118 C5
Asquith Rd
Bentley DN5 41 B1
Sheffield S9 114 B4
Astcote Ct DN3 42 E4
Aster Cl
Sheffield S20 143 F3
South Anston S25 146 D4
Aston CE Jun & Inf Sch S26 144 E7
Aston Chase WF9 17 D6
Aston Cl S18 153 C3
Aston Comp Sch S26 144 C8
Aston Dr S71 34 A6
Aston Fence Jun & Inf Sch S13 144 A8
Aston Gn DN7 44 A6
Aston Hall Jun & Inf Sch S26 144 F6
Aston La S26 132 D1
Aston Lodge Prim Sch S26 144 D6
Aston Springwood Prim Sch S26 144 E8
Aston St S2 129 D4
Astwell Gdns S35 94 E6
Atebanks Ct DN4 83 B4
Athelstan Cl S13 130 E1
Athelstane Cres DN3 42 F2
Athelstane Dr S66 133 E5
Athelstane Rd DN12 81 B2
Athelstane Sch DN12 80 F1
Athelstan Prim Sch S13 130 E1
Athelstan Rd S13 130 E1
Athersley Cres S71 34 B6
Athersley Gdns S20 143 A2
Athersley North Prim Sch S71 33 E8
Athersley Rd S71 34 B6
Athersley South Prim Sch S71 33 F7
Atherton Cl S2 141 F6
Atherton Rd S2 141 F6
Atholl Cres DN2 63 D5
Athol Rd S8 140 E4
Athorpe Gr S25 134 E1
Athorpe Rd S25 134 E1
Athron Dr S65 116 C4
Athron St DN1 62 D4
Atkin Pl S2 141 A8
Atkinson Mews S21 155 C3
Atlantic Cres 1 S8 152 E6
Atlantic Dr S8 152 E6
Atlantic Way S8 152 E6
Atlantic Wlk S8 152 E6
Atlas Bsns Pk S35 95 C1
Atlas St
Brinsworth S60 115 C1
Sheffield S4 129 D6
Atlas Way S4 129 E7
Atterby Dr DN11 85 A1
Attercliffe Comm S9 130 A8
Attercliffe Rd S4, S9 129 E5
Attlee Ave DN11 84 D1
Attlee Cl S66 119 B4
Attlee Cres S73 57 C5
Aubretia Ave S60 131 D7
Auburn Rd DN12 82 B2
Auckland Ave S6 127 E8
Auckland Dr S20 155 E5
Auckland Gr DN8 9 E3
Auckland Grange DN2 62 E4
Auckland Rd
Doncaster DN2 62 E4
Mexborough S64 80 B5
Auckland Rise S20 155 E6
Auckland Way S20 155 E6
Auckley Jun & Inf Sch DN9 86 A6
Audrey Rd S13 142 C7
Aughton Ave S26 132 C1
Aughton Cl S13 142 D7
Aughton Cres S13 142 D7
Aughton Dr S13 142 C8
Aughton La S26 144 E8
Aughton Prim Sch S26 132 D1
Aughton Rd S26 144 C8
Augustus Rd S60 115 C2
Aukley Rd S8 140 F5
Aunby Dr S26 144 D8
Austen Ave DN4 82 E6
Austen Dr S66 117 E5
Austerfield Ave DN5 62 A7
Austin Cl S6 127 E8
Austin Ct S6 127 E8
Austwick Cl
Darton S75 14 A2
Doncaster DN4 82 F4
Austwick Wlk 5 S70 33 D2
Austwood La S66 101 B2
Autumn Cl S66 134 A6
Autumn Dr S66 119 A6
Avalon Rise WF9 19 A2
Avenue Ct S11 140 A8
Avenue Rd
Askern DN6 21 F7
Doncaster DN2 62 E5
3 Sheffield S7 140 F6
Wath u D S63 79 A6
Avenue The
Askern DN6 21 F7
Barnburgh DN5 59 B2
Bentley DN5 41 C2
Carr S66 118 C1
Doncaster DN4 63 C1
Dronfield S18 153 B2
Norton DN6 4 C1
Pilley S75 75 D6
Royston S71 15 E4
Sheffield, Beighton S20 143 F4
Sheffield, Darnall S9 130 C4
Spinkhill S21 156 D2
Stainton S66 119 E8
Thorne DN8 9 C4
Wortley S35 74 D3
Aviemore Rd DN4 82 E6
Avill Way S66 117 B3
Avisford Dr S5 112 D3
Avisford Rd S5 112 D3
Avoca Ave DN2 63 A4
Avocet Way S61 95 F6
Avon Cl
Barnsley S75 32 E3
Dronfield S18 153 B3
Maltby S66 118 F6
Wombwell S73 56 F1
Avon Ct DN9 86 A7
Avondale Dr S71 15 C1
Avondale Rd
Doncaster DN2 63 A3
Rotherham S61 115 A7
Sheffield S6 128 B8
Avon Gr S35 94 E6
Avon Mount S61 115 A7
Avon St S71 34 A1
Axholme Ct DN2 62 F5
Axholme Gn DN8 26 C6
Axholme Rd DN2 62 F5
Axle La S25 146 C4
Aylesbury Cres S9 114 B3
Aylesbury Ct S9 114 B4
Aylesbury Rd DN2 63 B4
Aylesford Cl S71 33 F3
Aylsham Dr S26 144 E7
Aylward Cl S2 141 F7
Aylward Rd S2 141 F7
Aymer Dr S66 133 E6
Ayots Gn DN7 44 A6
Ayrsome Wlk DN4 84 E8
Aysgarth Ave S71 56 B8
Aysgarth Cl DN4 84 F7
Aysgarth Rd S6 112 C5
Aysgarth Rise S26 144 C8
Ayton View S35 74 C7
Ayton Wlk DN5 41 A2
Azalea Cl S25 146 D3

B

Babington Cl S2 141 F7
Babington Ct S2 141 F7
Babur Rd S4 129 D6
Back Field La DN7 44 D7
Backfield Rise S35 95 A6
Backfields S1 161 A3
Backhouse La WF4 13 F7
Back La
Barnsley S71 34 C5
Bentley DN5 61 C5
Blaxton DN9 86 E5
Braithwell S66 100 D2
Clayton DN5 37 C4
Clayton West HD8 12 A3
Clifton S66 100 D5
East Cowick DN14 1 C7
Eckington S21 155 B3
Great Houghton S72 57 F6
Hathersage S32 149 A7
Hooton Pagnell DN5 38 D5
Hooton Roberts S65 99 D6
Ingbirchworth S36 50 F8
Midhopestones S36 71 C4
New Edlington DN12 101 B7
North Anston S25 146 E6
Norton, Campsall DN6 21 C8
Norton DN6 4 C4
Oxspring S36 52 A1
Oxspring, Snowden Hill S36 72 F6
Penistone S36 51 D3
Rawmarsh S62 97 C6
Rotherham S65 98 F4
Sheffield, Den Bank S10 127 F4
Sheffield S13 143 C6
Sheffield, Stacey Bank S6 110 E2
South Elmsall WF9 19 A6
Stainforth DN7 24 E4
Stocksbridge S36 72 D3
Thorpe Salvin S80 159 B6
Unstone S18 153 F1
Woolley WF4 14 A6
Back Lane W S71 15 A4
Backmoor Cres S8 141 C2
Backmoor Rd S8 141 D2
Back Poplar Terr S71 15 E4
Back Rd S18 153 F1
Backside La DN4 82 D6
Bacon La S9 129 E5

Baden St
Rotherham S60 115 C7
Worsbrough S70 55 B4
Badger Cl S13 143 C7
Badger Dr S13 143 C7
Badger La
Langsett S36 70 F6
Sheffield S1 160 C3
Walden Stubbs DN6 5 B7
Badger Pl S13 143 D7
Badger Rd S13 143 C7
Badger Rise S13 143 C7
Badgers Holt DN3 85 D8
Badsley Ct 1 S65 115 F6
Badsley Moor Jun & Inf Schs
S65 116 B6
Badsley Moor La S65 116 A6
Badsley St S S65 115 F5
Badsley St S65 115 F6
Badsworth Cl
Rotherham S66 117 E5
Wombwell S73 56 F2
Badsworth Pl S66 117 E5
Badsworth Rd DN4 82 D5
Badsworth View WF9 19 A8
Badsworth Way S66 117 E5
Bagden La
Denby Dale HD8 30 D8
Denby Dale, Trister Hill HD8 30 E7
Bagger Wood Hill S75 53 D3
Bagger Wood Rd S35, S75 53 D2
Bagley Rd S4 113 D1
Bagshaw's Rd S12 142 B6
Bagshot St S11 140 D8
Bahram Gr DN11 103 E8
Bahram Rd DN4 84 C8
Bailey Cres WF9 19 A4
Bailey Dr S21 156 E8
Bailey La
Hatfield DN8 25 D4
Sheffield S1 160 C3
Bailey Mews DN5 40 E1
Bailey St S1 161 A3
Bainbridge Rd DN4 62 C1
Baines Ave DN12 82 B1
Bainton Dr S70 54 D7
Bakehouse La S75 33 A3
Baker Dr S21 156 C6
Bakers Hill S1 161 B3
Bakers La S1 160 C4
Baker St
Laughton en le M S25 134 C3
Sheffield S9 129 F6
Bakewell Rd S71 34 A6
Balaclava La 1 S6 128 E6
Balaclava Rd S6 128 E6
Bala St S71 33 F1
Balby Carr Bank DN4 83 D7
Balby Carr Com Sports Coll
DN4 83 C6
Balby Central Prim Sch
DN4 62 B1
Balby Rd DN4 83 B8
Balcarres Rd DN11 84 F1
Baldwin Ave DN5 62 A5
Baldwin St S9 129 E5
Balfour Dr S9 130 B5
Balfour Ho S36 73 B1
Balfour Rd
Bentley DN5 41 C1
Sheffield S9 130 B5
Balk Farm Ct S70 54 E1
Balk La
Barnsley S70 54 E1
Brinsworth S60 115 A2
Denby Dale HD8 29 C6
Rotherham S66 117 D5
South Elmsall WF9 19 D4
Balkley La S73 57 C5
Balk The
Bentley DN5 41 E6
Darton S75 14 C2
Ballam Ave DN5 40 E1
Ballard Hall (Sheffield
Hallam Univ) S10 128 A1
Ballfield Ave S75 32 C8
Ballfield La S75 32 C8
Ballifield Ave S13 131 A1
Ballifield Cl S13 131 B1
Ballifield Cres S13 131 B1
Ballifield Dr S13 131 B1
Ballifield Pl S13 131 A1
Ballifield Prim Sch S13 143 A8
Ballifield Rd S13 131 A1
Ballifield Rise S13 131 B1
Ballifield Way S13 131 A1
Ball Rd S6 128 B8
Ball St S3 128 F5
Balmain Dr S6 112 B1
Balmain Rd S6 112 B1
Balmer Rise S66 117 E4
Balm Gn S1 161 A3
Balmoral Cl
Barnburgh DN5 59 C3
Carlton in L S81 148 F6
Penistone S36 51 A4
Balmoral Cres
Dronfield S18 152 D2
Sheffield S10 126 F1
Balmoral Ct
Harworth DN11 122 B5
Sheffield S11 139 F4
Balmoral Glen S10 126 F1
Balmoral Mews S10 126 F1
Balmoral Rd
Doncaster DN2 62 F4
Hatfield DN7 44 A8
Sheffield S13 143 C6
Balmoral Way S66 117 D6
Baltic La S9 129 F6
Baltic Rd S9 129 F6
Baltic Works S9 129 E5
Bamford Ave S71 34 A6
Bamford Cl S75 53 E7
Bamforth St S6 128 D7
Banbury Cl DN12 81 B3
Bank Cl
Rotherham S61 96 F1
Sheffield S7 140 E6
Bank End Ave S70 55 C5
Bank End Cl S63 58 C2
Bank End La
Clayton West HD8 12 A1
High Hoyland HD8 12 A1
Bank End Rd
Blaxton DN9 86 F5
Finningley DN9 87 C4
Worsbrough S70 55 C5
Bankfield La S6 127 C6
Bankfield Rd S6 128 B8
Bank Hall Gr HD8 28 F8
Bank House Rd S6 128 C5
Bank La
Denby Dale HD8 29 F4
Stocksbridge S36 92 E5
Wortley S35 94 A7
Bank Side S35 92 D3
Bank St
Barnsley S70 54 F7
Barnsley, Stairfoot S71 55 E8
Cudworth S72 35 B7
Doncaster DN1 62 C1
Hemsworth WF9 17 D7
Hoyland S74 76 D5
Mexborough S64 80 A4
Sheffield S1 161 B4
South Anston S25 146 D5
Bank Terr 3 S10 128 C3
Bank Top Rd S65 116 D4
Bank View S60 116 B1
Bankwood Cl S14 141 D5
Bankwood Com Prim Sch
S14 141 D5
Bankwood Cres DN11 84 D2
Bankwood La DN11 84 D2
Bankwood Lane Ind Est
DN11 84 D2
Bankwood Rd S14 141 D5
Banner Cross Dr S11 140 B6
Banner Cross Rd S11 140 B5
Banner Ct S11 140 B6
Bannerdale Cl S11 140 C6
Bannerdale Rd S7, S11 140 D5
Bannerdale View S11 140 C6
Bannham Rd S9 130 D4
Bannister Ho DN2 63 A6
Bannister La DN6 20 C5
Bar Ave S75 33 D8
Barbados Way S66 118 A5
Barber's Ave S62 98 A3
Barber's Cres S62 98 A5
Barber's La S21 156 D7
Barber Balk Cl S61 96 F1
Barber Balk Rd S61 96 F1
Barber Cl S26 145 E5
Barber Cres S10 160 A4
Barber Pl S10 160 A4
Barber Rd S10 160 A4
Barberry Ct S70 55 B8
Barberry Way S65 117 E8
Barber St S74 76 F6
Barber Wood Rd S61 114 B7
Barbot Hall Ind Est S61 97 D1
Barbot Hill Rd S61 97 C2
Barcroft Flatt S75 33 A4
Bar Croft La DN5 22 F6
Barden Cres S60 131 C7
Barden Dr S75 33 B3
Bardolf Rd DN4 84 E8
Bardon Rd DN3 42 F3
Bard St S2 161 C3
Bardwell Rd S3 128 F6
Bare Bones Rd HD9 48 B5
Barewell Hill S72, WF9 17 B5
Barfield Ave S60 116 A1
Barfield Rd S74 76 E6
Barholm Rd S10 127 F2
Bari Cl S73 56 E6
Baring Rd S61 114 B6
Barkby Rd S9 114 A4
Barker's Pl S6 112 C1
Barker's Pool S1 161 A3
Barker's Rd S7 140 D6
Barker Hades Rd S81 136 B3
Barkers Croft S61 96 F3
Barker St S64 79 E5
Bark House La S75 31 C4
Bark Mdws S75 54 A7
Barkston Rd S71 34 C6
Bar La S75 33 D8
Barlborough Hall Sch
S43 157 B1
Barlborough Rd S73 56 F1
Barlby Gr S12 143 C3
Barley Cl S70 55 A4
Barleycroft La S25 146 F8
Barley Ho 2 S11 160 C1
Barley Mews S18 152 B2
Barley View S63 58 D7
Barleywood Rd S9 130 C6
Barlow Dr S6 128 A6
Barlow Rd S6 128 A6
Barmouth Rd S7 140 E5
Barnabas Wlk S71 33 F3
Barnard Ave S18 153 D3
Barnardiston Rd S9 130 B5
Barnburgh Hall Gdns
DN5 59 D3
Barnburgh Ho DN12 82 C3
Barnburgh La DN5 59 B4
Barnburgh Prim Sch DN5 59 C2
Barnby Dun Prim Sch
DN3 42 F7
Barnby Dun Rd DN2 63 C8
Barncliffe Cl S10 139 C8
Barncliffe Cres S10 127 B1
Barncliffe Dr S10 127 B1
Barncliffe Glen S10 139 C8
Barncliffe Rd S10 127 B1
Barnes Ave S18 152 E2
Barnes Ct S2 161 B2
Barnes Gn S35 94 D3
Barnes Hall Rd S35 94 D4
Barnes La S18 152 C3
Barnet Ave S11 139 E5
Barnet Gn DN7 44 A6
Barnet Rd S11 139 E5
Barnfield Ave S10 127 E3
Barnfield Cl S10 127 E3
Barnfield Dr S10 127 E2
Barnfield Rd S10 127 E3
Barnfold Pl S72 16 C2
Barn Owl Cl S72 57 F6
Barnsdale Ave S20 143 A2
Barnsdale Bar DN6 20 C8
Barnsdale Mews DN6 21 C8
Barnsdale View DN6 4 C3
Barnsdale Way WF9 19 E7
Barnside Cl S36 51 D2
Barnside La HD9 28 A1
Barnsley Ave DN12 81 A2
Barnsley Bsns & Innov Ctr
S75 33 B4
Barnsley Coll S70 33 E2
Barnsley Coll (Annexe)
S75 33 E3
Barnsley Hospl S75 33 C3
Barnsley Rd
Bentley DN5 61 C7
Brierley S72 17 A4
Cudworth S72 35 B6
Darfield S73 56 F6
Denby Dale HD8 29 C5
Dodworth S75 53 F8
Goldthorpe S63 58 C5
Hemsworth WF9 17 C6
Hoyland S74 76 E8
Kexbrough S75 32 E7
Marr DN5 60 C7
Penistone, Broad Hill S36 51 E5
Penistone S36 52 A6
Sheffield S5 113 C4
Silkstone S75 53 A8
Silkstone, Whin Moor S36,
S75 52 C7
South Elmsall WF9 18 E3
Thorne DN8 9 E3
Wath u D S63 78 D7
Wentworth S61 95 E6
Wombwell S73 56 B5
Wombwell S73 56 C3
Woolley WF4 14 C6
Barnsley Sta S70 33 F2
Barnstone St DN4 62 A1
Barnwell Cres S73 56 B5
Baron St S1 129 A1
Barrack La S6 128 E6
Barrack Rd S18 154 A1
Barrat Cnr 3 S65 116 B5
Barratt Rd S21 155 D2
Barrel La DN4 82 E6
Barret Rd DN4 63 F1
Barretta St 3 S4 113 D1
Barrie Cres S5 112 F2
Barrie Dr S5 112 F3
Barrie Gr S66 118 B4
Barrier Bank DN14 1 D3
Barrie Rd
Doncaster DN4 83 B6
Sheffield S5 112 F3
Barrowby Rd S60 116 B3
Barrowfield La S62 77 A2
Barrowfield Rd
Hoyland S74 76 D7
Thurnscoe S63 58 E7
Barrow Hill S62 76 F1
Barrow Rd
Sheffield S9 114 B4
Sheffield S9 114 C4
Bartholomew Cl S60 116 D2
Bartholomew St S73 56 C3
Bartin Cl S11 140 B5
Bartle Ave S12 141 F4
Bartle Dr S12 141 F4
Bartle Rd S12 141 F4
Bartlett Cl S6 127 C5
Bartlett Rd S5 112 F4
Bartle Way S12 141 F4
Barton La DN3 64 A5
Barton Pl DN12 81 B1
Barton Rd S8 141 A6
Barton Way WF9 19 A5
Barugh Green Prim Sch
S75 32 D4
Barugh Green Rd S75 32 F4
Barugh La S75 32 E5
Basegreen Ave S12 142 B3
Basegreen Cl S12 142 C3
Basegreen Cres S12 142 B3
Basegreen Dr S12 142 C3
Basegreen Pl S12 142 B3
Basegreen Rd S12 142 C3
Basegreen Way S12 142 C3
Basford Cl S9 130 C6
Basford Dr S9 130 B5
Basford Mews S9 130 C5
Basford Pl S9 130 B5
Basford St S9 130 B4
Basil Ave DN3 63 E7
Basildon Rd S63 37 C1
Basil Griffith Ct S4 129 B8
Baslow Cres S75 53 E7
Baslow Rd
Barnsley S71 34 B7
Sheffield S17 151 C4
Bassett La S10 138 E6
Bassett Pl S2 129 D2
Bassett Rd S2 129 E2
Bassey Rd DN3 85 E8
Bassingthorpe La S61 97 B1
Bassledene Ct S2 142 A8
Bassledene Rd S2 142 A8
Bastock Rd S6 112 D1
Bate La DN14 7 A6
Bateman Cl S72 16 B2
Bateman Rd S66 118 A4
Bateman Sq S63 58 C7
Batemoor Cl S8 153 A6
Batemoor Dr S8 153 A6
Batemoor Pl S8 153 A6
Batemoor Rd S8 153 A5
Batemoor Wlk S8 153 A6
Batesquire S20 143 F2
Bates St S10 128 C5
Bath St S3 160 C2
Battison La S63 78 D4
Battle Cl DN7 65 F8
Batt St 9 S8 141 A8
Batty Ave S72 35 A6
Batworth Dr S5 129 A8
Batworth Rd S5 129 A8
Baulk Farm Cl S61 97 B4
Baulk La
Harworth DN11 121 F5
Hathersage S32 149 A8
Bawtry Cl DN11 121 F4
Bawtry Gate S9 114 E2
Bawtry Mayflower Prim Sch
DN10 123 A8
Bawtry Rd
Austerfield DN10 123 C8
Bawtry DN10 123 F4
Brinsworth S60 115 B1
Doncaster DN4 84 E7
Finningley DN9 86 F3
Harworth DN11 122 A5
Hatfield DN7 44 F5
Hellaby S66 118 B5
Misson DN10 105 E1
Rossington DN4 85 B4
Rotherham S66 117 C4
Styrrup DN11 122 C1
Tickhill DN11 121 E7
Baxter Ave DN1 62 E4
Baxter Cl
Sheffield, Birley Carr S6 112 C4
Sheffield S26 144 A7
Baxter Ct DN1 62 E4
Baxter Dr S6 112 C4
Baxter Gate DN1 62 C3
Baxter Mews S6 112 C4
Baxter Rd S6 112 C4
Bayardo Wlk DN11 103 F7
Baycliff Cl S71 34 D6
Bay Ct S21 156 C5
Bayfield Cl HD9 48 B8
Bayford Way S73 56 F3
Baylee St 3 WF9 17 E6
Baysdale Croft S20 155 D7
Bay Tree Ave S66 117 B6
Baytree Gr DN9 85 F4
Bazley Rd S2 141 F6
Beacon Cl
Sheffield S9 113 F1
Silkstone S75 53 A6
Beacon Croft S9 113 F2
Beacon Ct S75 53 A6
Beacon Dr WF9 19 A8
Beaconfield Rd WF9 19 A8
Beacon Hill
Silkstone S75 53 A6
Upton WF9 19 A8
Beacon Ho WF9 19 A8
Beacon La S66 100 D5
Beacon Rd S9 113 F2
Beaconsfield Rd
Doncaster DN4 62 A1
Rotherham S60 116 A3
Beaconsfield St
1 Barnsley S70 54 E8
Mexborough S64 79 F4
Beacon Sq S66 100 E5
Beacon View
Hoyland S74 77 A5
South Kirkby WF9 18 C3
Upton WF9 19 A8
Beacon Way S9 113 F2
Beale Way S62 97 F2
Beamshaw WF9 18 B1
Beancroft Cl DN11 102 C7
Bear Tree Cl S62 97 F4
Bear Tree Rd S62 97 F3
Bear Tree St S62 97 F3
Beauchamp Rd S61 96 F1
Beauchief Abbey La S8 140 C1
Beauchief Abbey (rems of)*
S8 152 C8
Beauchief Cl S36 92 F8
Beauchief Ct S8 140 E1
Beauchief Dr S17 152 C7
Beauchief Manor S7 140 B1
Beauchief Rise S8 140 C1
Beaufont Gdns DN10 122 F7
Beaufort Rd
Doncaster DN2 63 B4
Sheffield S10 160 A3
Beaulieu Cl S75 33 C8
Beaulieu View S75 33 C8
Beaumont Ave
Adwick le S DN6 39 F6
Barnsley S70 33 B1
Sheffield S2 130 B2
South Elmsall WF9 18 F3
Beaumont Cl S2 130 B2
Beaumont Cres S2 130 B2
Beaumont Dr
Rotherham S65 116 B5
West Bretton WF4 12 E7
Beaumont Mews S2 130 B1
Beaumont Rd S75 32 C8
Beaumont Rd N S2 130 B1
Beaumont St S74 76 B5
Beaumont Way S2 130 A2
Beaver Ave S13 143 B8
Beaver Cl S13 143 B8
Beaver Dr S13 143 B8
Beaver Hill Rd S13 143 B7
Beccles Way S66 117 E5
Beck Cl
Sheffield S5 113 E7
Swinton S64 79 D1
Beck Croft S74 76 C4
Becket Ave S8 152 D6
Becket Cres
Rotherham S61 96 D2
Sheffield S8 152 E6
Becket Rd S8 152 E6
Beckett Ave S81 148 F7
Beckett Hospl Terr 15
S70 54 F8
Beckett Rd DN2 62 F5
Beckett St S71 33 F2
Becket Wlk S8 152 E6
Beckfield Gr S63 58 B3
Becknoll Rd S73 78 A8
Beck Prim Sch S5 113 D7
Beck Rd S5 113 D7
Beck Rise WF9 17 D7
Beckside S75 31 E4
Beckton Ave S20 143 E2
Beckton Ct S20 143 F2
Beckton Gr S20 143 E2
Beck View WF4 15 A6
Beckwith Rd
Dinnington S25 134 C2
Rotherham S65 116 D7
Bedale Ct S60 115 F4
Bedale Rd
Bentley DN5 61 D7
Sheffield S8 140 F6
Bedale Wlk S72 16 C3
Bedding Edge Rd HD9 49 A7
Bedford Cl S25 146 D7
Bedford Ct DN10 122 F7
Bedford Rd S35 111 D8
Bedford St
Barnsley S70 54 F7
Grimethorpe S72 36 A5
Maltby S66 119 B4
Sheffield S6 128 F5
Bedford Terr S71 34 A5
Bedgebury Cl S20 144 B1
Bedgrave Cl S21 156 F8
Beecham Ct S64 79 C1
Beech Ave
Cudworth S72 35 B8
Finningley DN9 86 A4
Rawmarsh S62 98 B5
Rotherham S65 116 E4
Silkstone S75 53 A5
Tickhill DN11 121 B7
Beech Cl
Brierley S72 17 A3
Hoyland S73 77 D8
Maltby S66 118 D5
South Kirkby WF9 18 B2
Beech Cres
Eckington S21 155 B1
Killamarsh S21 156 D5
Mexborough S64 79 E5
Stainforth DN7 24 F4
Beechcroft Rd DN4 82 E5
Beech Ct
Darfield S73 57 A5
Sheffield S10 160 A2
Beech Dr DN3 64 E1
Beeches Dr S2 141 C8
Beeches Gr S20 144 A3
Beeches Rd S26 145 B3
Beeches The
Aston S26 144 D7
Hoyland S73 77 D7
Kirk Sandall DN3 42 F4
Swinton S64 79 C2
Beechfern Cl S35 94 D8
Beechfield Cl S63 58 C2
Beechfield Rd
Doncaster DN1 62 D2
Dunscroft DN7 43 F7
Beech Gr
Barnsley S70 54 D7
Bentley DN5 62 B8
Carlton in L S81 148 E7
Conisbrough DN12 81 B1
Dinnington S25 146 F7
Rotherham S66 117 C5

Beech Gr *continued*
Warmsworth DN4 . . . . 82 C6
Beech Hill 3 DN12 . . . . 81 C2
Beech Hill Rd
2 Sheffield S10 . . . . 128 C2
Sheffield S10 . . . . 160 A2
Beech House Rd S73 . . . . . 77 D7
Beechlea S63 . . . . 37 C1
Beech Rd
Adwick le S DN6 . . . . 21 A1
Armthorpe DN3 . . . . 64 B7
Harworth DN11 . . . . 122 A5
Maltby S66 . . . . 118 D5
Norton DN6 . . . . 4 D1
Rossington DN11 . . . . 104 A8
Shafton S72 . . . . 16 D2
Upton WF9 . . . . 19 B7
Wath u D S63 . . . . 79 A6
Beech St
Barnsley S70 . . . . 54 F8
South Elmsall WF9 . . . . 18 E1
Beech Tree Ave DN8 . . . . . . 26 C6
Beech Tree Cl DN3 . . . . 64 B1
Beechville Ave S64 . . . . 79 C1
Beech Way
Aston S26 . . . . 144 C8
Dronfield S18 . . . . 153 A3
Beechwood S65 . . . . 115 F7
Beechwood Cl
Edenthorpe DN3 . . . . 43 A1
Rawmarsh S62 . . . . 98 C7
Swinton S63 . . . . 78 F3
Beechwood Cres WF9 . . . . . 17 C6
Beechwood Ct DN7 . . . . 44 B6
Beechwood Mount WF9 . . . 17 D6
Beechwood Rd
Chapeltown S35 . . . . 94 E6
Dronfield S18 . . . . 152 F1
Rotherham S60 . . . . 116 A4
Sheffield S6 . . . . 128 B8
Stocksbridge S36 . . . . 92 B8
Beechwood Wlk DN12 . . . . 82 A1
Beeden Cl S65 . . . . 98 F3
Beehive Rd S10 . . . . 160 A4
Beeley St S11 . . . . 160 C1
Beeley Wood La S35, S6 . 112 A4
Beeley Wood Rd S6 . . . . . 112 C3
Beely Rd S35 . . . . 111 E6
Beeston Cl S18 . . . . 152 C2
Beeston Sq S71 . . . . 33 F8
Beeton Gn S6 . . . . 126 C5
Beeton Rd S8 . . . . 140 F5
Beet St S3 . . . . 160 C3
Beever Cl S75 . . . . 33 A3
Beever La S75 . . . . 33 A3
Beeversleigh 3 S65 . . . . . 115 E6
Beevers Rd S61 . . . . 96 D2
Beever St S63 . . . . 58 F5
Beevor Ct S71 . . . . 34 A1
Beevor St S71 . . . . 34 B1
Begonia Cl S25 . . . . 146 D4
Beighton Com Hospl
S20 . . . . 143 E3
Beighton Inf Sch S20 . . . 144 A5
Beighton Rd
Sheffield, Hackenthorpe
S12 . . . . 143 C3
Sheffield, Woodhouse S13 . 143 D5
Swinton S62 . . . . 98 E8
Beighton Rd E S20 . . . . . . 143 D3
Belcourt Rd S65 . . . . 116 D4
Beldon Cl S2 . . . . 141 D7
Beldon Pl S2 . . . . 141 D7
Beldon Rd S2 . . . . 141 D7
Belford Cl S66 . . . . 117 C6
Belford Dr S66 . . . . 117 C6
Belfry Gdns DN4 . . . . 85 A7
Belfry Way S25 . . . . 147 A7
Belgrave Ct DN10 . . . . 122 F7
Belgrave Dr S10 . . . . 127 D1
Belgrave Pl S26 . . . . 144 D7
Belgrave Rd
Barnsley S71 . . . . 34 A1
Sheffield S10 . . . . 127 E1
Belgrave Sq 6 S2 . . . . . . 141 A8
Belklane Dr S21 . . . . 156 E7
Bell's Cl DN9 . . . . 86 E4
Bellamy Cl S65 . . . . 116 B5
Bell Bank View S70 . . . . 54 F5
Bellbank Way S71 . . . . 33 F8
Bellbrooke Pl S73 . . . . 56 F7
Bell Butts La DN9 . . . . 85 F6
Bell Croft La DN6 . . . . 23 A1
Bellefield St S3 . . . . 160 B4
Belle Green Cl S72 . . . . 35 C7
Belle Green Gdns S72 . . . . 35 C7
Belle Green La S72 . . . . 35 C7
Bellerby Pl DN6 . . . . 20 F2
Bellerby Rd DN6 . . . . 20 F2
Belle Vue Ave DN4 . . . . 63 A2
Belle Vue Rd 2 S64 . . . . 80 A5
Belle Vue Terr DN8 . . . . 26 B7
Bellfields The S61 . . . . 95 E5
Bell Gn DN14 . . . . 7 D4
Bellhagg Rd S6 . . . . 128 B6
Bellhouse Rd S5 . . . . 113 E5
Bellis Ave DN4 . . . . 83 B8
Bellmer Cl S71 . . . . 34 A5
Bellmer Croft S70 . . . . 75 F6
Bellmont Cres WF9 . . . . 17 E6
Bellows Cl S62 . . . . 97 F5
Bellows Rd S62 . . . . 97 F5
Bellrope Acre DN3 . . . . 64 B5
Bellscroft Ave S65 . . . . 98 E2
Bells Sq S1 . . . . 161 A3
Bell St
Aston S26 . . . . 144 F7
Upton WF9 . . . . 19 E8
Bell View Mews DN8 . . . . . . 26 B7
Bellwood Cres
Hoyland S74 . . . . 76 C5
Thorne DN8 . . . . 26 A8
Bellwood Ct S65 . . . . 117 E8
Belmont S72 . . . . 35 C4
Belmont Ave
Barnsley S71 . . . . 34 B5
Chapeltown S35 . . . . 95 A5
Doncaster DN4 . . . . 83 C8
Belmont Cl DN3 . . . . 85 E8
Belmont Cres S72 . . . . 57 E7
Belmont Dr S36 . . . . 73 C1
Belmonte Gdns S2 . . . . . . 161 C2
Belmont St
Mexborough S64 . . . . 79 F4
Rotherham S61 . . . . 115 A6
Belmont Terr
Thorne DN8 . . . . 26 B7
Thurgoland S35 . . . . 74 A6
Belmont Way WF9 . . . . 19 B3
Belper Rd 4 S7 . . . . 140 F6
Belridge Cl S75 . . . . 33 B4
Belsize Rd S10 . . . . 139 E7
Beltoft Way DN12 . . . . 81 E3
Belton Cl S18 . . . . 152 C1
Belvedere DN4 . . . . 82 F6
Belvedere Cl
Askern DN6 . . . . 22 B8
North Anston S25 . . . . 146 F5
Shafton S72 . . . . 16 C2
Belvedere Dr
Darfield S73 . . . . 56 F7
Thorne DN8 . . . . 9 C3
Belvedere Par S66 . . . . . . 117 C6
Belvoir Ave DN5 . . . . 59 C3
Ben Bank Rd S75 . . . . 53 C6
Bence Cl S75 . . . . 32 E7
Bence La S75 . . . . 32 D7
Ben Cl S6 . . . . 111 F1
Benita Ave S64 . . . . 80 C4
Ben La S6 . . . . 112 A1
Benmore Dr S20 . . . . 144 B1
Bennett Cl S62 . . . . 98 B7
Bennetthorpe DN2 . . . . 62 F2
Bennett St
Rotherham S61 . . . . 114 E6
3 Sheffield S2 . . . . 140 F8
Benson Rd S2 . . . . 129 E2
Bentfield Ave S60 . . . . 116 C3
Bentham Dr S71 . . . . 34 D4
Bentham Way S75 . . . . 14 A2
Bent Hills La S35 . . . . 92 E1
Bentinck Cl DN1 . . . . 62 D2
Bentinick St DN12 . . . . 81 D2
Bent La HD9 . . . . 48 B8
Bent Lathes Ave S60 . . . . 116 C3
Bentley Ave DN4 . . . . 62 B2
Bentley Cl S71 . . . . 34 E5
Bentley Common La DN5 . . 62 D8
Bentley High Street Prim Sch
DN5 . . . . 62 B7
Bentley Moor La DN6 . . . . . 40 E7
Bentley New Village Prim
Sch DN5 . . . . 41 B2
Bentley Rd
Bentley DN5 . . . . 62 B6
Chapeltown S35 . . . . 95 B3
Rotherham S66 . . . . 117 E5
Sheffield S6 . . . . 128 A5
Bentley St S60 . . . . 115 D3
Bentley Sta DN5 . . . . 62 A8
Benton Terr S64 . . . . 79 D1
Benton Way S61 . . . . 114 F7
Bent Rd HD9 . . . . 48 D7
Bents Cl
Chapeltown S35 . . . . 95 A5
Sheffield S11 . . . . 139 E5
Bents Cres
Dronfield S18 . . . . 153 C3
Sheffield S11 . . . . 139 F5
Bents Dr S11 . . . . 139 F5
Bents Green Ave S11 . . . . 139 E6
Bents Green Pl S11 . . . . . . 139 E5
Bents Green Rd S11 . . . . . 139 F5
Bents Green Sch S11 . . . . . 139 E5
Bents La
Dronfield S18 . . . . 153 C3
Sheffield S6 . . . . 126 D6
Bents Rd
Carlecotes S36 . . . . 49 D4
Rotherham S61 . . . . 96 F1
Sheffield S11 . . . . 139 F5
Bent St S36 . . . . 51 C4
Bents View S11 . . . . 139 E5
Benty La S10 . . . . 127 F3
Beresford Rd S66 . . . . 119 B4
Beresford St DN5 . . . . 41 C1
Berkeley Croft S71 . . . . 15 B4
Berkeley Prec S11 . . . . 140 D8
Berkley Cl S70 . . . . 54 F5
Bernard Gdns 3 S2 . . . . . 161 C4
Bernard Rd
New Edlington DN12 . . . . 82 C1
Sheffield S2, S4 . . . . 129 D4
Bernard St
Rawmarsh S62 . . . . 98 B7
Rotherham S60 . . . . 115 E5
Sheffield S2 . . . . 161 C3
Berners Cl S2 . . . . 141 E6
Berners Dr S2 . . . . 141 E6
Berners Pl S2 . . . . 141 E6
Berners Rd S2 . . . . 141 E6
Berneslai Cl S70 . . . . 33 E2
Berneslai Ct 2 S70 . . . . . . 33 E2
Berne Sq S81 . . . . 147 D4
Bernshall Cres S5 . . . . 113 B7
Berresford Rd 8 S11 . . . . 140 D8
Berrington Cl DN4 . . . . 83 A4
Berry Ave S21 . . . . 155 C3
Berrydale S70 . . . . 55 B5
Berry Dr S26 . . . . 145 F3
Berry Edge Cl DN12 . . . . . . 81 D1
Berry Holme Cl S35 . . . . 95 A5
Berry Holme Ct S35 . . . . 95 A5
Berry Holme Dr S35 . . . . . . 95 A5
Berry La S35 . . . . 94 A8
Berry Moor Cotts S75 . . . . . 53 A3
Berrywell Ave S36 . . . . 51 E2
Bertram Rd S35 . . . . 111 E6
Berwick Way DN2 . . . . 63 C5
Besom La S32 . . . . 149 A8
Bessacarr La DN4 . . . . 84 E5
Bessacarr Prim Sch DN4 . . 84 C8
Bessemer Pk S60 . . . . 115 B4
Bessemer Pl S9 . . . . 129 E5
Bessemer Rd S9 . . . . 129 E6
Bessemer Terr S36 . . . . 73 B2
Bessemer Way S60 . . . . . 115 A4
Bessingby Rd S6 . . . . 128 C7
Bethany Sch S3 . . . . 160 B4
Bethel Rd S65 . . . . 115 F8
Bethel St S74 . . . . 76 F6
Bethel Terr S81 . . . . 159 E7
Bethel Wlk S1 . . . . 161 A3
Betjeman Gdns S10 . . . . . 128 C1
Betony Cl S21 . . . . 156 B5
Between Rivers La DN14 . . . 1 C4
Beulah Rd S6 . . . . 112 D1
Bevan Ave DN11 . . . . 84 F1
Bevan Cl S74 . . . . 77 A6
Bevan Cres S66 . . . . 118 F6
Bevan Ho S60 . . . . 115 F2
Bevan Way S35 . . . . 94 F4
Bevercotes Rd S5 . . . . 113 E3
Beverley Ave S70 . . . . 54 F5
Beverley Cl
Aston S26 . . . . 144 D7
Barnsley S71 . . . . 33 E7
Beverley Gdns DN5 . . . . 61 D5
Beverley Rd
Doncaster DN2 . . . . 63 A6
Harworth DN11 . . . . 122 A4
Beverleys Rd S8 . . . . 141 A4
Beverley St 2 S9 . . . . 130 A6
Beverley Wlk S81 . . . . 148 E7
Bevin Pl S62 . . . . 98 B6
Bevre Rd DN3 . . . . 64 B7
Bewdley Ct S71 . . . . 15 D4
Bewicke Ave DN5 . . . . 61 D6
Bhatia Cl 1 S64 . . . . 80 A5
Bib La S25, S66 . . . . 134 C7
Bickerton Ho S6 . . . . 112 C2
Bickerton Rd S6 . . . . 112 C2
Bierlow Cl S73 . . . . 78 A8
Bigby Way S66 . . . . 117 D7
Bignor Pl S6 . . . . 112 D5
Bignor Rd S6 . . . . 112 D4
Bilham La DN5 . . . . 38 D2
Bilham Rd HD8 . . . . 12 A2
Bilham Row DN5 . . . . 38 F3
Billam Pl S61 . . . . 96 E1
Billam St S21 . . . . 155 B3
Billingley Dr S63 . . . . 58 C7
Billingley Green La S72 . . . 57 F5
Billingley La S72 . . . . 57 F8
Billingley View S63 . . . . 58 B3
Billy Wright's La DN11 . . . 102 F4
Bilston St S6 . . . . 128 D7
Binbrook Ct DN10 . . . . 122 F6
Binders Rd S61 . . . . 96 E1
Binfield Rd S8 . . . . 140 F5
Bingham Ct S11 . . . . 139 F8
Bingham Park Cres S11 . 140 A8
Bingham Park Rd S11 . . . 140 A8
Bingham Rd S8 . . . . 140 F2
Bingley Ct 12 S70 . . . . 33 D2
Bingley La S6 . . . . 127 A4
Bingley St S75 . . . . 33 D2
Binsted Ave S5 . . . . 112 D3
Binsted Cl S5 . . . . 112 D3
Binsted Cres S5 . . . . 112 D3
Binsted Croft S5 . . . . 112 D3
Binsted Dr S5 . . . . 112 D3
Binsted Gdns S5 . . . . 112 D3
Binsted Glade S5 . . . . 112 D3
Binsted Gr S5 . . . . 112 D3
Binsted Rd S5 . . . . 112 D3
Binsted Way S5 . . . . 112 D3
Birchall Ave S60 . . . . 116 B1
Birch Ave
Adwick le S DN6 . . . . 21 A1
Chapeltown S35 . . . . 95 A5
Finningley DN9 . . . . 86 A4
Birch Cl
Havercroft WF4 . . . . 16 B8
Killamarsh S21 . . . . 156 C5
Sprotbrough DN5 . . . . 61 D1
Birch Cres S66 . . . . 117 C5
Birch Ct S64 . . . . 79 C3
Birchdale Cl DN3 . . . . 42 F1
Birchen Cl
Doncaster DN4 . . . . 84 E5
Dronfield S18 . . . . 152 D1
Birches Fold S18 . . . . 153 C4
Birches La S18 . . . . 153 C4
Birch Farm Ave S8 . . . . . . 153 A8
Birchfield Cres S75 . . . . 54 A8
Birchfield Rd S66 . . . . 119 B5
Birchfield Wlk S75 . . . . 33 B2
Birch Gr
Conisbrough DN12 . . . . 81 D2
Oughtibridge S35 . . . . 111 E6
Birch Green Cl S66 . . . . . . 118 D6
Birch House Ave S35 . . . . 111 D6
Birchin Bank S74 . . . . 76 F6
Birchitt Cl S17 . . . . 152 C5
Birchitt Ct S17 . . . . 152 C5
Birchitt Pl S17 . . . . 152 C5
Birchitt Rd S17 . . . . 152 C5
Birchitt View S18 . . . . 153 A3
Birchlands Dr S21 . . . . 156 D5
Birch Park Ct S61 . . . . 115 A6
Birch Rd
Barnsley S70 . . . . 55 D7
Doncaster DN4 . . . . 84 F8
Sheffield S9 . . . . 129 E6
Birch Tree Cl DN3 . . . . 43 A7
Birchtree Rd S61 . . . . 95 F3
Birch Tree Rd S36 . . . . 92 B7
Birchvale Rd S12 . . . . 142 D3
Birchwood Ave S62 . . . . 97 F7
Birchwood Cl
Langold S81 . . . . 136 F4
Maltby S66 . . . . 118 D6
7 Sheffield S20 . . . . 155 E8
Thorne DN8 . . . . 9 B1
Birchwood Croft S20 . . . . 155 E8
Birchwood Ct DN4 . . . . 85 B5
Birchwood Dell DN4 . . . . . . 85 C5
Birchwood Dr S65 . . . . 117 D8
Birchwood Gdns
Braithwell S66 . . . . 101 A2
6 Sheffield S20 . . . . 155 E8
Birchwood Gr S20 . . . . 155 E8
Birchwood Rd S21 . . . . . . 154 D3
Birchwood Rise 5 S20 . . . 155 E8
Birchwood View S20 . . . . . 155 E8
Birchwood Way 16 S20 . . . 155 E8
Bircotes Wlk DN11 . . . . 85 B1
Bird Ave S73 . . . . 56 C2
Bird La S36 . . . . 52 E2
Birdsedge Farm Mews
HD8 . . . . 29 A4
Birdsedge First Sch HD8 . . 29 A4
Birds Edge La HD8 . . . . 28 F4
Birdsnest La HD8 . . . . 28 D2
Birdwell Comm S70 . . . . 75 F6
Birdwell Prim Sch S70 . . . . 75 F7
Birdwell Rd
Dodworth S75 . . . . 54 B6
5 Sheffield S4 . . . . 113 F1
Swinton S64 . . . . 79 D1
Birk Ave S70 . . . . 55 C7
Birkbeck Ct S35 . . . . 94 D8
Birk Cres S70 . . . . 55 C7
Birkdale Ave S25 . . . . 147 A8
Birkdale Cl
Cudworth S72 . . . . 35 C8
Doncaster DN4 . . . . 85 B6
Birkdale Prep Sch S10 . . . 160 A1
Birkdale Rd S71 . . . . 15 B5
Birkdale Rise S64 . . . . 79 D2
Birkdale Sch S10 . . . . 128 C2
Birkendale S6 . . . . 160 A5
Birkendale Rd S6 . . . . 128 D5
Birkendale View S6 . . . . . . 160 A5
Birk Gn S70 . . . . 55 D7
Birk Hill Inf Sch S21 . . . . . 155 B2
Birk House La
Barnsley S70 . . . . 55 D7
Shepley HD8 . . . . 29 B8
Birklands Ave S13 . . . . . . 130 E1
Birklands Cl S13 . . . . 130 E1
Birklands Dr S13 . . . . 130 E1
Birk Rd S70 . . . . 55 C7
Birks Ave
Penistone S36 . . . . 50 E3
Sheffield S13 . . . . 143 B6
Birks Cotts S36 . . . . 50 E3
Birks Holt Dr S66 . . . . 119 C3
Birks La S36 . . . . 50 E3
Birks Rd S61 . . . . 96 E1
Birks Wood Dr S35 . . . . . . 111 D6
Birk Terr S70 . . . . 55 C7
Birkwood Ave S72 . . . . 35 C4
Birkwood Prim Sch S72 . . . 35 C5
Birkwood Terr S66 . . . . . . 101 B1
Birley Com Coll S12 . . . . . 142 D2
Birley Com Prim Sch
S12 . . . . 142 D3
Birley Ho S6 . . . . 112 C6
Birley La S12 . . . . 142 D2
Birley Moor Ave S12 . . . . . 142 E3
Birley Moor Cl S12 . . . . . . 142 E3
Birley Moor Cres S12 . . . . 142 E2
Birley Moor Dr S12 . . . . . . 142 E2
Birley Moor Pl S12 . . . . . . 142 E2
Birley Moor Rd S12 . . . . . . 142 E4
Birley Moor Way S12 . . . . 142 E2
Birley Rise Cres S6 . . . . . 112 C4
Birley Rise Rd S6 . . . . 112 C4
Birley School Mews S13 . 142 E5
Birley Spa Cl S12 . . . . 143 B4
Birley Spa Com Prim Sch
S12 . . . . 142 F4
Birley Spa Dr S12 . . . . 143 B4
Birley Spa La S12 . . . . 143 B4
Birley Spa Wlk 1 S12 . . . 143 B4
Birley Vale Ave S12 . . . . . 142 C5
Birley Vale Cl S12 . . . . 142 C4
Birley View S35 . . . . 111 D5
Birthwaite Rd S75 . . . . 13 B1
Bisby Rd S62 . . . . 98 A6
Biscay La S63 . . . . 78 E7
Biscay Way S63 . . . . 78 F6
Bishopdale Ct S20 . . . . . . 143 A1
Bishopdale Dr S20 . . . . . . 155 A8
Bishopdale Rise S20 . . . . 143 A1
Bishopgarth Cl DN5 . . . . . . 62 B5
Bishop Gdns S13 . . . . 143 A6
Bishop Hill S13 . . . . 143 A6
Bishopscourt Rd S8 . . . . . 141 A5
Bishops Ct S8 . . . . 141 B5
Bishopsgate La DN11 . . . . 104 A7
Bishopsholme Cl S5 . . . . . 113 A2
Bishopsholme Rd S5 . . . . . 113 B2
Bishops House Mus* S8 141 A4
Bishop St S3 . . . . 160 C2
Bishopstoke Ct 1 S65 . . . 116 A7
Bishopston Wlk S66 . . . . . 118 E6
Bishops Way S71 . . . . 34 C3
Bishops Wlk S26 . . . . 145 E3
Bisley Cl S71 . . . . 15 E4
Bismarck St S70 . . . . 54 F7
Bitholmes Gate S35 . . . . . . 93 B3
Bitholmes La S36 . . . . 93 A7
Bittern View S61 . . . . 96 A6
Blacka Moor Cres S17 . . . 151 C6
Blackamoor Rd S64 . . . . . . 78 F1
Blacka Moor Rd S17 . . . . . 151 C6
Blacka Moor View S17 . . . 151 C6
Blackberry Flats S20 . . . . 155 E7
Blackbird Ave S60 . . . . 131 D8
Blackbrook Ave S10 . . . . . 127 A1
Blackbrook Dr S10 . . . . . . 127 A1
Blackbrook Rd S10 . . . . . . 139 A8
Blackburn Cres S35 . . . . . . 94 F6
Blackburn Croft S35 . . . . . . 94 F6
Blackburn Dr S35 . . . . 94 E6
Blackburne St 1 S6 . . . . . 128 D7
Blackburn La
Barnsley S75 . . . . 33 D2
Rotherham S61 . . . . 114 B6
Worsbrough S70 . . . . 55 A5
Blackburn Prim Sch S61 . 114 B6
Blackburn Rd S61 . . . . 114 B5
Blackburn St S70 . . . . 55 A5
Black Carr Rd S66 . . . . . . 117 A4
Blackdown Ave S20 . . . . . 143 D2
Blackdown Cl S20 . . . . 143 D2
Blackergreen La S36, S75 . . 52 E5
Blacker Green La DN5 . . . . 22 D4
Blacker La
Shafton S72 . . . . 16 C3
Worsbrough S70 . . . . 55 B2
Blacker Rd S75 . . . . 33 C8
Blackheath Cl S71 . . . . 34 B7
Blackheath Rd S71 . . . . 34 B7
Blackheath Wlk S71 . . . . . . 34 B7
Black Hill Rd S65 . . . . 116 D4
Black Horse Cl S75 . . . . 53 A5
Black Horse Dr S75 . . . . 53 A5
Black La
Hoyland S74 . . . . 76 B2
Sheffield S6 . . . . 127 D7
Blackmoor Cres S60 . . . . . 115 B1
Blackmore St S4 . . . . 129 D5
Blacksmith's La DN5 . . . . . . 60 C7
Blacksmith La S35 . . . . . . 112 C8
Blackstock Cl S14 . . . . 141 D2
Blackstock Cres S14 . . . . . 141 D2
Blackstock Dr S14 . . . . 141 D2
Blackstock Rd S14 . . . . 141 D4
Black Swan Wlk S1 . . . . . . 161 A3
Black Syke La DN14 . . . . 8 C4
Blackthorn Ave S66 . . . . . 117 C5
Blackthorn Cl S35 . . . . 94 D8
Blackthorn Rise S65 . . . . . 117 E8
Blackwell Cl S2 . . . . 161 C3
Blackwell Ct S2 . . . . 161 C3
Blackwell Pl S2 . . . . 161 C3
Blackwood Ave DN4 . . . . 82 F6
Blagden St S2 . . . . 161 C2
Blair Athol Rd S11 . . . . . . 140 B7
Blake Ave
Doncaster DN2 . . . . 62 F6
Wath u D S63 . . . . 78 C7
Blake Cl S66 . . . . 117 E4
Blake Grove Rd S6 . . . . . . 160 B5
Blakeley Cl S71 . . . . 34 B7
Blakeney Rd S10 . . . . 128 C3
Blake St S6 . . . . 128 D5
Bland La S6 . . . . 111 F1
Bland St S4 . . . . 129 E8
Blaxton Cl S20 . . . . 143 A2
Blayton Rd S4 . . . . 129 C8
Bleachcroft Way S70 . . . . . . 55 E7
Bleak Ave S72 . . . . 16 C2
Bleakley Ave WF4 . . . . 15 B6
Bleakley Cl S72 . . . . 16 C2
Bleakley La WF4 . . . . 15 B6
Bleakley Terr WF4 . . . . 15 B6
Bleasdale Gr S71 . . . . 34 A4
Blenheim Ave S70 . . . . 54 E8
Blenheim Cl
Dinnington S25 . . . . 146 E8
Hatfield DN7 . . . . 44 A6
Rotherham S66 . . . . 117 C7
Blenheim Cres S64 . . . . 79 F5
Blenheim Ct S66 . . . . 117 B6
Blenheim Gr S70 . . . . 54 D8
Blenheim Mews S11 . . . . . 140 A5
Blenheim Rd
Barnsley S70 . . . . 54 E8
Finningley DN9 . . . . 86 D3
Hatfield DN7 . . . . 66 A8
Blenheim Rise
Bawtry DN10 . . . . 122 F6
Worksop S81 . . . . 148 E1
Blindside La S6 . . . . 109 C3
Bloemfontein St S72 . . . . . . 35 B6
Blonk St S1 . . . . 161 B4
Bloomfield Rd S75 . . . . 13 F1
Bloomfield Rise S75 . . . . . . 13 F1
Bloomhill Cl DN8 . . . . 9 D4
Bloomhill Ct DN8 . . . . 9 C4
Bloom Hill Gr DN8 . . . . 9 C3
Bloomhouse La S75 . . . . 13 F1

Blossom Ave DN6 22 B7
Blossom Cres S12 142 B3
Blossoms The 11 S70 33 D2
Blow Hall Cres DN12 82 C2
Blucher St S70 33 E1
Bluebell Ave S36 51 C2
Bluebell Cl
Hoyland S74 76 C4
Sheffield S5 113 F3
Blue Bell Ct DN9 86 E5
Bluebell Rd
Darton S75 13 E3
Sheffield S5 113 F3
Bluebell Way WF9 18 F7
Bluebell Wood La S66 117 B7
Bluebird Hill S26 144 E6
Blue Boy St S3 160 C4
Bluehills La HD8 29 E6
Blue Mans Way S60 131 C5
Blundell Cl DN4 84 E7
Blundell Ct S71 34 D5
Blundell St WF9 18 E3
Blyde Rd S5 113 C1
Bly Rd S73 56 F6
Blyth Ave S62 97 F5
Blyth Cl S60 116 D1
Blythe St S73 56 D3
Blyth Gate La DN11 120 E3
Blyth Rd
Maltby S66 119 A4
Oldcotes S81 136 F6
Styrrup DN11 121 F2
Tickhill DN11 121 E6
Boardman Ave S62 97 C8
Boating Dyke Way DN8 26 A7
Boat La DN5 82 B8
Bochum Parkway S8 153 C8
Bocking Cl S8 140 D1
Bocking Hill S36 73 D1
Bocking La
Sheffield, Greenhill S8 152 E8
Sheffield S8 140 D1
Bocking Rise S8 152 E8
Boden La S1 160 C3
Boden Pl S9 130 C5
Bodmin Ct S71 34 B3
Bodmin St S9 129 F6
Boggard La
Oughtibridge S35 111 C6
Penistone S36 51 C2
Boiley La S21 156 C4
Boland Rd S8 152 D5
Bold St S9 130 A8
Bole Cl S73 56 F4
BoleHill S21 154 F2
Bole Hill
Sheffield S8 141 A2
Treeton S60 131 F5
Bole Hill Cl S6 128 B6
Bolehill La
Eckington S21 154 F2
Sheffield S10 128 B4
Bole Hill Rd S6 128 A5
Bolsover Rd S5 113 D2
Bolsover Rd E 1 S5 113 D1
Bolsover St S3 160 B3
Bolsterstone Rd S36 92 C1
Bolton Hill Rd DN4 84 E7
Bolton on Dearne Sta
S63 58 C2
Bolton Rd S63 79 C7
Bolton Rd Managed
Workshops S63 79 D7
Bolton St
Conisbrough DN12 80 F3
Sheffield S3 160 C2
Bond S6 160 B4
Bond Cl DN1 62 C2
Bondfield Ave DN11 104 A8
Bondfield Cres S73 56 D2
Bondhay La S80 158 C2
Bond Rd S75 33 D3
Bond St
Rossington DN11 104 A7
Wombwell S73 56 D3
Bone La DN6 21 C8
Bonet La S60 115 A1
Bonfield Crescent Flats
S73 56 C2
Bonington Rise S66 118 E6
Bonville Gdns S3 160 C4
Booker's La S25 134 B1
Booker Rd S8 140 E2
Bookers Way S25 134 B1
Bootham Cl DN7 44 B8
Bootham Cres DN7 24 F3
Bootham La DN7 25 A2
Bootham Lane Ind Est
DN7 25 B1
Bootham Rd DN7 24 F3
Booth Cl
Sheffield S20 143 D2
Thurcroft S66 134 A6
Booth Croft S20 143 D2
Booth Pl S62 97 E7
Booth Rd S35 94 C7
Booth St
Hoyland S74 76 E6
Rotherham S61 97 B4
Bootle St 3 S9 130 A6
Borough Mews S6 128 F5
Borough Rd S6 128 D8
Borrowdale Ave 3 S20 155 E6
Borrowdale Cl
Adwick le S DN6 21 C1

Borrowdale Cl *continued*
Barnsley S71 56 A8
2 Sheffield S20 155 E6
Borrowdale Cres S25 146 F7
Borrowdale Dr S20 155 E6
Borrowdale Rd S20 155 E6
Boshaw HD9 48 B8
Boston Castle Gr S60 115 E4
Boston Castle Terr S60 115 E4
Boston St S2 129 A1
Bosvile Cl S65 99 D3
Bosville Rd S10 128 B3
Bosville St
Penistone S36 51 E2
Rotherham S65 116 D8
Boswell Cl
Chapeltown S35 94 C8
Rossington DN11 103 E8
4 Royston S71 15 B4
Boswell Ct DN4 84 D7
Boswell Rd
Doncaster DN4 84 D7
Wath u D S63 78 F4
Boswell St S65 115 F5
Bosworth Cl DN7 44 A5
Bosworth Rd DN6 40 A6
Bosworth St 2 S10 128 B4
Botanical Rd S11 128 C1
Botany Bay La DN7 43 C7
Bot Gdns (Sheffield)*
S11 128 D1
Botham St S4 129 E8
Botsford St S3 129 A6
Boulder Bridge La S71 15 F1
Boulevard The DN3 42 E2
Boulton Dr DN3 64 B1
Boundary Ave DN2 63 C7
Boundary Cl DN12 82 C3
Boundary Dr S72 17 A3
Boundary Gn S62 98 A4
Boundary Rd S2 129 E2
Boundary St 7 S70 55 B8
Boundary Wlk S60 131 A8
Bourne Ct S75 14 C2
Bourne Rd
Sheffield S5 113 C4
Worsbrough S70 55 A4
Bourne Wlk S75 14 C2
Bow Bridge Cl S60 115 C4
Bowden Gr S75 53 F7
Bowden Wood Ave S9 130 C2
Bowden Wood Cl S9 130 C2
Bowden Wood Cres S9 130 C2
Bowden Wood Dr S9 130 C2
Bowden Wood Pl S9 130 C2
Bowden Wood Rd S9 130 C2
Bowdon St S1 160 C2
Bowen Dr S65 98 F2
Bowen Rd S65 115 F8
Bower's Fold DN1 62 D3
Bower Cl S61 96 E1
Bower Hill S36 52 C1
Bower La S35 94 B1
Bower Rd
Sheffield S10 160 A4
Swinton S64 79 D4
Bower Spring S3 161 A4
Bower St S3 161 A4
Bower Vale DN12 82 A1
Bowes Rd DN3 42 E1
Bowfell View S71 34 A4
Bowfield Ct S5 113 C4
Bowfield Rd S5 113 D4
Bowland Cl DN5 61 F8
Bowland Cres S70 54 F4
Bowland Dr S35 94 E5
Bowlease Gdns DN4 84 E8
Bowling Green St S3 161 A5
Bowman Cl S12 141 F2
Bowman Dr S66 118 E6
Bowness Cl S18 152 E1
Bowness Dr DN6 22 C8
Bowness Gr S63 58 C1
Bowness Rd S6 128 C7
Bowood Rd S11 140 D8
Bowshaw S18 152 F4
Bowshaw Ave S8 153 A5
Bowshaw Cl S8 153 A5
Bowshaw View S8 153 A5
Bow St S72 35 B7
Boyce St S6 128 D5
Boycott Way WF9 19 A4
Boyd Rd S63 78 F3
Boyland St S3 128 F6
Boynton Cres S5 113 A2
Boynton Rd S5 113 A2
Brabbs Ave DN7 44 C8
Brackenbury Cl DN5 81 D6
Bracken Cl DN3 64 E1
Bracken Ct
Harworth DN11 121 E4
Rotherham S66 117 B3
Brackenfield Gr S12 142 D3
Bracken Heen Cl DN7 44 B8
Bracken Hill
Chapeltown S35 94 D4
South Kirkby WF9 18 D4
Bracken Moor La S36 92 C8
Bracken Rd S5 113 E3
Bracken Way DN11 121 E4
Brackley St S3 129 B6
Bradberry Balk La S73 56 C5
Bradbury's Cl S62 97 F3
Bradbury St
Barnsley S70 33 D1
Sheffield S8 141 A6
Bradfield Dungworth Prim
Sch S6 110 E1

Bradfield Rd S6 128 C8
Bradfield Sch S35 111 C5
Bradford Rd DN2 63 C8
Bradford Row DN1 62 D3
Bradgate Cl S61 115 A7
Bradgate Ct S61 114 F7
Bradgate La S61 114 F7
Bradgate Pl S61 115 A8
Bradgate Rd S61 115 A7
Bradlea Rise S62 98 A7
Bradley Ave S73 56 C3
Bradley Carr Terr WF9 37 E8
Bradley St S10 128 C5
Bradmarsh Way S60 115 C4
Bradshaw Ave S60 131 F3
Bradshaw Cl S75 33 A2
Bradshaw Way S60 131 F3
Bradstone Rd S65 116 C8
Bradway Cl S17 152 B5
Bradway Dr S17 152 B5
Bradway Grange Rd S17 152 C5
Bradway Rd
Sheffield, Bradway S17 152 B5
Sheffield, Lower Bradway
S17 152 C6
Bradwell Ave S75 54 A6
Bradwell Cl S18 152 C1
Bradwell St 1 S2 141 B6
Braeburn Cl S66 118 D7
Braeburn Ho DN4 85 A5
Braemar Croft S72 16 D7
Braemar Rd DN2 63 A3
Braemar Rise S72 16 D7
Braemore Rd S6 112 A1
Brailesford Cl S5 113 A8
Brailsford Ave S5 113 A8
Brailsford Rd S5 113 A8
Braithwaite Ct WF9 17 E8
Braithwaite La DN7 23 F7
Braithwaite St S75 14 C1
Braithwell Cl DN5 41 A3
Braithwell Rd
Bentley DN5 41 A3
Maltby S66 118 F5
Rotherham S65 117 E8
Braithwell Way S66 118 A7
Braithwell Wlk DN12 80 F4
Bramah St S71 15 C1
Bramall Ct S2 141 A8
Bramall La
Sheffield S2 141 A8
Stocksbridge S36 72 F3
Bramall Lane Football Gd
S2 129 A1
Bramar Rd DN7 44 A8
Bramble Cl S66 117 B3
Bramble Rd S72 16 E6
Brambles The
Royston S71 15 A4
Sheffield S35 95 B1
Bramble Way
Finningley DN9 86 A4
Harworth DN11 121 E4
Wath u D S63 78 B6
Bramblings The DN4 85 A6
Bramcote Ave S71 33 E8
Brameld Rd
Rawmarsh S62 97 F5
Swinton S64 79 B3
Bramham Croft S73 56 F4
Bramham Ct S9 130 B5
Bramham Rd
Doncaster DN4 63 F1
Sheffield S9 130 B5
Bramley Ave
Aston S26 144 E8
Sheffield S13 142 F8
Bramley Carr S70 54 B7
Bramley Cl S20 155 C7
Bramley Ct
4 Conisbrough DN12 80 F3
Sheffield S10 128 B3
Bramley Dr S13 130 F1
Bramley Grange Cres
S66 117 E5
Bramley Grange Dr S66 117 E5
Bramley Grange Prim Sch
S66 117 E6
Bramley Grange Rise
S66 117 E5
Bramley Grange View
S66 117 E6
Bramley Grange Way
S66 117 F5
Bramley Hall Rd S13 142 F8
Bramley Ho DN4 85 A5
Bramley La
Rotherham S65 118 A8
Sheffield S13 142 F8
West Bretton WF4 13 B8
Bramley Mews S21 155 D3
Bramleymoor La S21 154 E1
Bramley Park Cl S13 142 F8
Bramley Park Rd S13 130 F1
Bramley Pk S21 154 F3
Bramley Rd S21 154 E1
Bramley Sunnyside Jun & Inf
Schs S66 117 C6
Bramley Way S66 118 B6
Brampton Ave S66 133 D6
Brampton Cl DN3 64 A5
Brampton Cortonwood Inf
Sch S73 78 A8
Brampton Cres S73 56 F1
Brampton Ct
3 Sheffield S20 143 A2
South Elmsall WF9 19 A5
Brampton Ctr The S63 78 B7

Brampton Ellis CE Inf Sch
S63 78 C6
Brampton Ellis CE Jun Sch
S63 78 B7
Brampton La
Armthorpe DN3 64 A5
Ulley S66 133 B5
Brampton Mdws S66 133 D6
Brampton Rd
Thurcroft S66 133 D6
Wath u D S63 78 B7
Wombwell S73 57 A1
Brampton St S73 78 B8
Brampton View S73 56 F1
Bramshill Cl S20 144 A1
Bramshill Ct 2 S20 144 A1
Bramwell Cl S3 160 B4
Bramwell Ct S3 160 B4
Bramwell Dr S3 160 B4
Bramwell St
Rotherham S65 115 E7
Sheffield S3 160 B4
Bramwith La
Barnby Dun DN3 42 E8
Kirk Bramwith DN3 23 F2
Bramwith Rd S11 139 F8
Bramworth Rd DN4 61 F1
Branchcroft Dr DN4 83 B4
Brancliffe La S81 159 F8
Brand's La S25, S81 147 D6
Brander Cl DN4 83 C5
Brandeth Rd S6 128 E5
Brand La DN5 60 F4
Brandon St S3 129 B7
Brandreth Cl S6 128 E5
Brands Cl S81 147 E5
Brandsmere Dr S81 147 E5
Branksome Ave S70 33 C1
Bransby St S6 128 D5
Branstone Rd DN5 61 B2
Brantingham Gdns DN10 105 A1
Branton Gate Rd or Whiphill
Top La DN3 64 E1
Branton St Wilfrid's CE Prim
Sch DN3 85 D8
Brantwood Cres DN4 63 F1
Brantwood Sch S7 140 E8
Brathay Cl 3 S4 113 F1
Brathay Rd 4 S4 113 F1
Brayford Rd DN4 83 B4
Bray St S9 130 A5
Brayton Dr DN4 83 B4
Brayton Gdns DN6 21 C8
Bray Wlk S61 96 C2
Brearley Ave S36 92 D8
Breck La S25 134 F2
Brecklands
Rotherham S65 116 C4
Rotherham, Wickersley
S66 117 A4
Brecks Cres S65 116 E4
Brecks La
Kirk Sandall DN3 43 A4
Rotherham, Brecks S65 116 E6
Brecon Cl S20 144 A2
Bredon Cl WF9 17 F7
Breeze Mount Ct DN7 24 F4
Brendon Cl S73 77 F8
Brentwood Ave S11 140 D6
Brentwood Cl S74 76 C4
Brentwood Rd S11 140 D6
Bressingham Cl S4 129 C6
Bressingham Rd S4 129 C6
Bretby Cl DN4 85 A6
Brettas Pk S71 34 A4
Brett Cl S62 97 C8
Brettegate WF9 17 C7
Bretton Cl
Brierley S72 16 F2
Hatfield DN7 44 A6
Kexbrough S75 32 C8
Bretton Ctry Pk* WF4 12 F7
Bretton Ctry Pk Visitor Ctr*
S75 13 A6
Bretton Gr S12 142 D3
Bretton Hall Coll WF4 12 E6
Bretton Ho 11 DN1 62 C2
Bretton La WF4 12 F8
Bretton Rd S75 32 D8
Bretton View S72 35 A5
Brew Ho The S11 160 B1
Brewsters Wlk DN10 123 A8
Breydon Ave DN5 61 E5
Breydon Ct DN5 61 E5
Briar Cl DN9 86 A4
Briar Croft DN4 83 A8
Briar Ct
Harworth DN11 121 E4
Rotherham S66 117 B3
Briarfield HD8 30 A6
Briarfield Ave S12 142 A3
Briarfield Cres S12 142 A2
Briarfield Rd S12 142 A3
Briarfields La S35 111 C5
Briar Gr
Brierley S72 17 A3
Harworth DN11 121 E4
Penistone S36 51 D2
Briar Rd
Adwick le S DN6 21 A1
Armthorpe DN3 64 A7
Sheffield S7 140 E6
Briar Rise S70 55 A4
Briars Cl S21 156 D5
Briars La DN7 24 F5
Briarwood Gdns S66 117 B8
Briary Ave S35 94 D7
Briary Cl S60 131 C7

Brickhouse La S17 151 C8
Brick Kiln La DN6 23 B8
Brick Row S35 74 B7
Brick St S10 128 B3
Brickyard The S72 16 C1
Bridby St S13 143 C6
Bride Church La DN11 121 A7
Bridgegate S60 115 D7
Bridge Gdns S71 33 F3
Bridge Gr DN5 61 F5
Bridge Hill
Oughtibridge S35 111 D7
Stainforth DN7 24 E4
Bridgehouses S3 161 A5
Bridge Inn Rd S35 95 A6
Bridge La DN14 2 C7
Bridgelake Dr DN4 83 C4
Bridge Rd DN4 63 C1
Bridge St
Barnsley S71 33 F2
Bolton u D S63 58 D3
Darton S75 13 E1
Doncaster DN4 62 B2
Killamarsh S21 156 D6
Penistone S36 51 C4
Rotherham S60 115 D7
Sheffield S3 161 B4
Swinton S64 79 E3
Thorne DN8 26 B7
Bridge Terr DN14 2 D7
Bridgewater Park Dr DN6 20 F2
Bridle Cl S35 95 A6
Bridle Cres S35 95 A6
Bridle Stile S20 155 C7
Bridle Stile Cl S20 155 C7
Bridle Stile Gdns S20 155 B7
Bridleway The S62 98 C7
Bridport Rd S9 130 B5
Brier Cl S20 143 D1
Brierey Cl S75 33 A8
Brierfield Cl S75 33 C2
Brierholme Carr Rd DN7 25 F1
Brierholme Cl DN7 25 E1
Brierholme Ings Rd DN7 44 F8
Brier La WF4 16 C8
Brierley CE Prim Sch S72 17 A3
Brierley Cres WF9 18 C3
Brierley Rd
Brierley S72 17 A1
Doncaster DN4 84 D7
Grimethorpe S72 36 A8
Shafton S72 16 D2
Shafton S72 16 E2
South Hiendley S72 16 E5
Brierly Rd S65 98 E1
Briers House La S6 110 D1
Brier St S6 128 C8
Briery Mdws S73 77 C8
Briery Wlk S61 97 B3
Brigadier Hargreaves Ct
S13 143 A6
Briggs St S71 15 C1
Brightholmlee Ct S35 93 B2
Brightholmlee La S35 93 B3
Brightholmlee Rd S35 92 E2
Bright Mdw S20 156 A5
Brightmore Dr S3 160 B3
Brighton St S72 36 A7
Brighton Terrace Rd
S10 128 C4
Brightside Inf Sch S9 114 B2
Brightside La S9 129 F7
Brightside Way S9 129 F8
Brimham Cl 2 DN3 42 E4
Brimmesfield Cl S2 141 F7
Brimmesfield Dr S2 141 E8
Brimmesfield Rd S2 141 E7
Brinckman St S70 55 A8
Brincliffe Cres S11 140 C7
Brincliffe Ct S7 140 E6
Brincliffe Edge Cl S11 140 C6
Brincliffe Edge Rd S7,
S11 140 C6
Brincliffe Gdns S11 140 C7
Brincliffe Hill S11 140 B7
Brindley Cl S8 141 A4
Brindley Cres S8 141 A4
Brindley Ct S21 156 C6
Brinkburn Cl S17 151 F6
Brinkburn Ct S17 151 F6
Brinkburn Dr S17 151 F6
Brinkburn Vale Rd S17 151 F6
Brinsford Rd S60 115 C1
Brinsworth Comp Sch
S60 131 A8
Brinsworth Grange S60 115 A1
Brinsworth Hall Ave S60 131 B8
Brinsworth Hall Cres
S60 131 B8
Brinsworth Hall Dr S60 131 B8
Brinsworth Hall Gr S60 131 B7
Brinsworth Howarth Prim
Sch S60 131 C7
Brinsworth La S60 131 B8
Brinsworth Manor Jun & Inf
Sch S60 115 C1
Brinsworth Rd
Catliffe S60 131 B7
Catliffe S60 131 C6
Brinsworth St
Rotherham S60 115 C6
Sheffield S9 129 F6
Brinsworth Whitehill Prim
Sch S60 131 C7
Bristol Gr DN2 63 A6
Bristol Rd S11 128 C1
Britain St S64 79 F4
Britannia Cl S70 54 F8

Britannia Ho 11 S70 ... 54 F8
Britannia Rd S9 ... 130 C4
Britland Cl S75 ... 33 A2
Britnall St S9 ... 130 A6
Briton Sq S63 ... 37 E1
Briton St S63 ... 37 E1
Brittain St S2 ... 161 B2
Britten Ho DN2 ... 63 A6
Broachgate DN5 ... 61 E8
Broad Balk DN5 ... 38 E6
Broadbent Gate Rd DN8 ... 9 D1
Broad Bridge Cl S26 ... 145 F2
Broad Car Rd S74 ... 76 E3
Broad Carr La HD9 ... 28 A2
Broadcroft Cl S20 ... 144 B3
Broad Dyke Cl S26 ... 145 F2
Broad Elms Cl S11 ... 139 F4
Broad Elms La S11 ... 139 E3
Broadfield Ct S8 ... 140 F6
Broadfield Rd S8 ... 140 F6
Broadfield Way S8 ... 140 F6
Broadgate House Cl S61 ... 115 A7
Broadgates DN9 ... 86 E3
Broad Gates S75 ... 52 F8
Broadhead Rd S36 ... 92 D8
Broad Inge Cres S35 ... 94 E5
Broad Ings La DN3 ... 23 D1
Broad La
Sheffield S1 ... 161 A4
South Elmsall WF9 ... 18 E1
South Kirkby WF9 ... 37 C8
Sykehouse DN14 ... 7 B6
Broadlands S66 ... 117 E4
Broadlands Ave S20 ... 143 B2
Broadlands Cl
Hatfield DN7 ... 44 A7
Sheffield S20 ... 143 B2
Broadlands Cres S66 ... 117 E4
Broadlands Croft S20 ... 143 B2
Broadlands Rise S20 ... 143 B2
Broad Lane Bsns Ctr WF9 ... 18 F1
Broad Lane Ct S1 ... 160 C3
Broadley Rd S13 ... 142 C7
Broad Oak La S36 ... 30 D2
Broad Oaks S9 ... 129 F5
Broadoaks Cl S25 ... 134 E1
Broadoaks Rd S25 ... 134 E1
Broad Riding S66 ... 101 F1
Broad St
Hoyland S74 ... 76 D6
Rawmarsh S62 ... 97 F3
Sheffield, Park Hill S2 ... 161 C4
Sheffield S2 ... 161 B4
Broadstone Rd HD8 ... 28 F3
Broadwater S63 ... 58 B1
Broadwater Dr DN7 ... 44 A6
Broadway
Barnsley S70 ... 54 C8
Brinsworth S60 ... 131 B7
Darton S75 ... 14 B1
Dunscroft DN7 ... 43 F7
Rotherham S65 ... 116 B7
South Elmsall WF9 ... 18 E1
Swinton S64 ... 79 B2
Broadway Ave S35 ... 95 B4
Broadway Cl S64 ... 79 B2
Broadway Ct 2 S70 ... 33 B1
Broadway E S65 ... 116 B7
Broadway Nook DN7 ... 43 F6
Broadway Terr WF9 ... 18 E1
Broadway The DN4 ... 82 F5
Brocco Bank S11 ... 128 C1
Brocco La S1, S3 ... 160 C4
Brocco St S1, S3 ... 160 C4
Brockenhurst Rd DN7 ... 44 C7
Brockfield Cl 6 S70 ... 55 A5
Brockhole Cl DN4 ... 84 F7
Brockholes Farm* DN3 ... 85 D7
Brockholes La
Branton DN3 ... 85 D7
Penistone S36 ... 72 A8
Brockhurst Way S65 ... 98 F2
Brocklehurst Ave
Barnsley S70 ... 55 D6
Sheffield S8 ... 153 C8
Brockwood Cl S13 ... 143 C7
Broc-O-Bank DN6 ... 4 C3
Brodsworth Hall* DN5 ... 39 B3
Brodsworth Way DN11 ... 104 B8
Bromcliffe Pk S71 ... 34 E5
Bromfield Ct S71 ... 15 D4
Bromley Bank HD8 ... 29 E6
Bromley Carr Rd S35 ... 75 B2
Brompton Rd
Sheffield S9 ... 130 A7
Sprotbrough DN5 ... 61 C1
Bromwich Rd S8 ... 140 F2
Bronte Ave DN4 ... 82 F6
Bronte Cl S71 ... 34 B3
Bronte Gr
Hemsworth WF9 ... 17 C6
Mexborough S64 ... 80 B6
Bronte Pl S62 ... 98 B7
Brook Cl
Aston S26 ... 144 E7
Sheffield S35 ... 94 C1
Brook Croft
North Anston S25 ... 146 D5
Stocksbridge S36 ... 73 C1
Brook Ct S61 ... 95 F4
Brookdale Ct S35 ... 95 A8
Brookdale Hts S75 ... 54 A6
Brookdale Rd S35 ... 95 A8
Brook Dr S3 ... 160 C4
Brooke Dr S43 ... 78 D6
Brooke St
Doncaster DN1 ... 62 D5
Hoyland S74 ... 76 D5

Brooke St *continued*
Thorne DN8 ... 26 A8
Brook Farm Mews S63 ... 78 E6
Brookfield S36 ... 73 B8
Brookfield Ave S64 ... 79 D2
Brookfield Cl
Armthorpe DN3 ... 64 B5
Rotherham S65 ... 98 D1
Thorne DN8 ... 26 A8
Brookfield Mews DN5 ... 41 E2
Brookfield Rd S7 ... 140 F7
Brookfield Terr S71 ... 34 C8
Brook Gn S12 ... 143 B3
Brookhaven Way S66 ... 117 E4
Brook Hill
Rotherham S61 ... 95 F4
Sheffield S3 ... 160 B3
Brook Hill La
Carlecotes S36 ... 49 B3
Dunford Bridge S36 ... 48 F2
Brookhill Rd S75 ... 32 B8
Brook Hos S75 ... 31 E4
Brookhouse Cl S12 ... 143 B3
Brookhouse Ct 6 S12 ... 143 B3
Brookhouse Dell S66 ... 134 A7
Brookhouse Dr S12 ... 143 B3
Brookhouse Hill S10 ... 139 C7
Brook House Jun Sch S20 ... 144 B3
Brookhouse La S25 ... 134 C6
Brook House La S36 ... 70 F7
Brookhouse Rd S26 ... 144 D6
Brook La
Oughtibridge S35 ... 111 C7
Rotherham S66 ... 117 D6
Sheffield, Grenoside S35 ... 94 C1
Sheffield, Hackenthorpe S12 ... 143 B3
Sheffield S3 ... 160 C3
Brooklands
Maltby S66 ... 118 D4
North Anston S25 ... 146 E5
Brooklands Ave S10 ... 139 C7
Brooklands Bsns Pk S9 ... 130 A7
Brooklands Cres S10 ... 139 C7
Brooklands Dr S10 ... 139 B7
Brooklands Rd DN6 ... 40 D7
Brooklands Way S25 ... 134 D1
Brooklyn Pl 2 S8 ... 141 A5
Brooklyn Rd 5 S8 ... 141 A5
Brooklyn Works S3 ... 160 C5
Brook Mews S25 ... 146 D5
Brook Rd
Chapeltown S35 ... 94 E6
Conisbrough DN12 ... 81 D2
Rotherham S65 ... 116 B8
Sheffield S8 ... 140 F5
Brook Row S36 ... 73 C1
Brooksfield WF9 ... 18 D4
Brookside
Conisbrough DN12 ... 81 C1
Denby Dale HD8 ... 29 F6
Hemsworth WF9 ... 17 E7
Rotherham S65 ... 116 C5
Swinton S64 ... 79 B1
Brookside Bank Rd S6 ... 126 F6
Brookside Cl 1 S12 ... 143 B3
Brookside Cres S63 ... 78 B6
Brookside Ct S61 ... 97 E2
Brookside Dr S70 ... 55 D6
Brookside La S6 ... 126 F6
Brookside St WF9 ... 18 F3
Brookside Terr WF9 ... 18 F3
Brookside Wlk DN11 ... 122 B4
Brook Sq DN12 ... 81 C1
Brook St S60 ... 116 B1
Brook Terr DN9 ... 67 A3
Brookvale S71 ... 34 D3
Brookview Ct S18 ... 153 A3
Brook Way DN5 ... 41 D1
Broom Ave S60 ... 116 B3
Broombank HD8 ... 29 F5
Broom Chase S60 ... 115 F4
Broom Cl
Barnsley S70 ... 55 D6
Bolton u D S63 ... 58 B3
Darton S75 ... 14 A1
Rotherham S66 ... 117 C7
Sheffield S11 ... 128 F1
Tickhill DN11 ... 121 C7
Wath u D S63 ... 79 A4
Worksop S81 ... 148 D1
Broomcliffe Gdns S72 ... 16 C2
Broom Cres S60 ... 115 F4
Broomcroft S75 ... 54 B6
Broomcroft Pk S11 ... 139 F3
Broom Ct
Hatfield DN7 ... 44 A7
Rotherham S60 ... 116 A4
Broom Dr S60 ... 116 B3
Broome Ave S64 ... 79 D3
Broomfield Cl S70 ... 54 B8
Broomfield Ct S36 ... 92 D8
Broomfield Gr
Rotherham S60 ... 115 F5
Stocksbridge S36 ... 92 D8
Broomfield La
Mattersey Thorpe DN10 ... 123 C1
Stocksbridge S36 ... 92 C8
Broomfield Rd
Sheffield S10 ... 160 A2
Stocksbridge S36 ... 92 D8
Broomfield Wlk S36 ... 51 C2
Broom Gn S3 ... 160 C2
Broom Gr
Rotherham S60 ... 115 F5
South Anston S25 ... 146 D3
Broom Grange S60 ... 116 A4

Broomgrove Cres S10 ... 160 A2
Broomgrove La S10 ... 160 A1
Broomgrove Rd S10 ... 160 A1
Broomhall Pl S10 ... 160 B1
Broomhall Rd S10 ... 160 B1
Broomhall St
Sheffield, Broomfield S3 ... 160 B2
Sheffield S3 ... 160 C2
Broomhead Ct S75 ... 33 B8
Broomhead Rd S73 ... 56 F1
Broomhill DN12 ... 80 F3
Broomhill Cl S21 ... 155 B3
Broom Hill Dr DN4 ... 84 F7
Broomhill Flash Nature reserve* S73 ... 57 A3
Broomhill Inf Sch S10 ... 128 C2
Broomhill La S73 ... 57 C3
Broomhill View S63 ... 58 B1
Broomhouse Cl HD8 ... 30 A5
Broomhouse La DN12, DN4 ... 82 D3
BroomhouseLane Ind Est DN12 ... 82 C2
Broom La S60 ... 116 B3
Broom Rd S60 ... 115 F5
Broom Riddings S61 ... 97 B2
Broomroyd S70 ... 55 B4
Broom Royd S35 ... 93 B3
Broomspring Cl S3 ... 160 B2
Broomspring La S10 ... 160 C2
Broom St S10 ... 160 B2
Broom Terr S60 ... 115 F5
Broomvale Wlk DN12 ... 82 A1
Broom Valley Jun & Inf Schs S60 ... 115 F4
Broom Valley Rd S60 ... 116 A3
Broomville St S64 ... 79 E3
Broom Wlk S3 ... 160 C2
Broomwood Cl 3 S20 ... 144 A3
Broomwood Gdns S20 ... 144 A3
Brosley Ave DN3 ... 43 A7
Brotherton St S3 ... 129 B6
Brough Gn S75 ... 54 A6
Broughton Ave DN5 ... 62 A7
Broughton La S9 ... 130 B8
Broughton Rd
Doncaster DN4 ... 84 E6
Sheffield S6 ... 112 C1
Brow Cl S70 ... 54 F6
Brow Cres S20 ... 155 F7
Brow Hill Rd S66 ... 118 E6
Brow La HD8 ... 30 D6
Brown's Edge La S36 ... 71 B7
Brown's Edge Rd S36 ... 49 E8
Brownell St S3 ... 160 C4
Brownhill La HD9 ... 47 B8
Brown Hills La S10 ... 138 E8
Brown House La S6 ... 110 B6
Browning Ave DN4 ... 83 B6
Browning Cl
Barnsley S71 ... 34 B5
Sheffield S6 ... 112 D5
Browning Ct 2 S65 ... 116 B5
Browning Dr
Rotherham S65 ... 116 B6
Sheffield S6 ... 112 D5
Browning Rd
Barnby Dun DN3 ... 42 F8
Mexborough S64 ... 80 A6
Rotherham S65 ... 116 B5
Sheffield S6 ... 112 D5
Wath u D S63 ... 78 C7
Brown La
Dronfield S18 ... 153 C3
Sheffield S1 ... 161 A2
Brownroyd Ave S71 ... 15 C2
Browns La DN8 ... 26 A7
Browns Sq S73 ... 77 B7
Brown St
Rotherham S60 ... 115 C7
Sheffield S1 ... 161 B2
Brow The S65 ... 116 E4
Brow View S63 ... 58 B2
Broxbourne Gdns DN5 ... 41 B1
Broxholme La DN1 ... 62 D4
Broxholme Rd S8 ... 140 F3
Bruce Ave S70 ... 54 F7
Bruce Cres DN2 ... 63 B5
Bruce Rd S11 ... 140 D8
Bruncroft Cl DN4 ... 84 D6
Brundish Ho S66 ... 118 F7
Brunel Cl DN11 ... 121 F2
Brunel Gate DN11 ... 121 F2
Brunel Park Ind Est DN11 ... 121 F2
Brunel Rd DN5 ... 61 F5
Bruni Way DN11 ... 103 F7
Brunswick Cl S71 ... 34 A6
Brunswick Dr S66 ... 117 B7
Brunswick Prim Sch S13 ... 143 D6
Brunswick Rd
Rotherham S60 ... 115 F4
Sheffield S3 ... 129 B5
Brunswick Sq DN7 ... 24 E3
Brunswick St
Sheffield S10 ... 160 B2
Thurnscoe S63 ... 37 F1
Brunt Rd S62 ... 98 B6
Brushfield Gr S12 ... 142 D4
Bryans Close La DN10 ... 105 F3
Bryony Cl S21 ... 156 B6
Bryson Cl DN8 ... 9 C1
Bubup Hill DN11 ... 83 C2
Bubwith Rd S9 ... 114 B2
Buchanan Cres S5 ... 112 E5
Buchanan Dr S5 ... 112 E5
Buchanan Rd S5 ... 112 F5

Buckden Rd 7 S70 ... 33 D2
Buckenham Dr S4 ... 129 C6
Buckenham St S4 ... 129 C6
Buckingham Cl 2 S18 ... 152 D2
Buckingham Ct 1 S71 ... 15 B4
Buckingham Rd
Conisbrough DN12 ... 81 B3
Doncaster DN2 ... 62 F4
Buckingham Way
Brinsworth S60 ... 131 D8
Maltby S66 ... 119 A6
Royston S71 ... 15 B4
Buckleigh Rd S63 ... 78 F4
Buckley Ct S70 ... 54 F8
Buckley Ho 13 S70 ... 54 F8
Buckthorn Cl S64 ... 98 C8
Buck Wood View S14 ... 141 D5
Bude Ct S71 ... 34 C3
Bude Rd DN4 ... 83 B8
Bud La S35 ... 92 E3
Bullcroft Cl DN6 ... 40 C8
Bullen Rd S6 ... 112 C5
Bullenshaw Rd WF9 ... 17 D6
Bullfinch Cl S60 ... 131 D8
Bull Haw La S75 ... 52 F8
Bullhouse La S36 ... 50 C2
Bullivant Rd DN7 ... 44 C8
Bull La WF9 ... 18 C2
Bull Moor Rd DN7 ... 45 B7
Bungalow Rd DN12 ... 82 B2
Bungalows The
Killamarsh S21 ... 156 C6
Treeton S60 ... 131 E4
Bunker's Hill S80 ... 158 D8
Bunkers Hill S21 ... 156 E6
Bunting Cl S8 ... 141 B2
Bunting Nook S8 ... 141 B1
Burbage Cl S18 ... 152 D2
Burbage Gr S12 ... 142 D5
Burcot Rd S8 ... 140 F5
Burcroft Cl S74 ... 76 B5
Burcroft Hill DN12 ... 81 D3
Burden Cl DN1 ... 62 C2
Burford Ave DN4 ... 82 E5
Burford Cres S26 ... 144 E7
Burgar Rd DN8 ... 26 B5
Burgen Rd S61 ... 96 E1
Burgess Rd S9 ... 129 F6
Burgess St S1 ... 161 A3
Burghley Cl S25 ... 146 E8
Burghwallis La DN6 ... 21 C6
Burghwallis Rd DN6 ... 21 B6
Burgoyne Cl S6 ... 128 D6
Burgoyne Rd S6 ... 128 D6
Burkinshaw Ave S62 ... 97 F8
Burleigh Ct 12 S70 ... 33 F1
Burleigh St 3 S70 ... 54 F8
Burlington S6 ... 160 B4
Burlington Arc 2 S70 ... 33 F1
Burlington Cl S17 ... 151 E7
Burlington Ct S6 ... 160 B5
Burlington Glen S17 ... 151 E7
Burlington Gr S17 ... 151 E7
Burlington Rd S17 ... 151 E7
Burlington St S6 ... 160 B5
Burman Rd S63 ... 78 F5
Burnaby Cres S6 ... 128 D7
Burnaby Ct S6 ... 128 D7
Burnaby Gn S6 ... 128 D7
Burnaby St
1 Doncaster DN1 ... 62 C3
Sheffield S6 ... 128 D7
Burnaston Cl S18 ... 152 C1
Burnaston Wlk DN12 ... 81 A3
Burncross Dr S35 ... 94 F5
Burncross Gr S35 ... 94 E5
Burncross Rd S35 ... 94 E5
Burnell Rd S6 ... 112 C1
Burnett Cl S36 ... 51 E2
Burn Gr S35 ... 95 C4
Burngreave Bank S4 ... 129 B6
Burngreave Rd S3 ... 129 B6
Burngreave St S3 ... 129 B6
Burngrove Pl S3 ... 129 B7
Burnham Ave S75 ... 14 B1
Burnham Cl DN4 ... 84 B7
Burnham Gr DN5 ... 61 F8
Burnham Way S73 ... 56 F5
Burn Pl S71 ... 33 E7
Burnsall Cres S60 ... 131 C7
Burnsall Gr S70 ... 55 D6
Burns Ave WF9 ... 17 F1
Burns Ct S35 ... 94 F5
Burns Dr
Chapeltown S35 ... 94 F5
Rotherham S65 ... 116 B6
Burnside S63 ... 37 C1
Burnside Ave S8 ... 141 A5
Burns Rd
Barnby Dun DN3 ... 42 F8
Dinnington S25 ... 147 A8
Doncaster DN4 ... 83 B6
Maltby S66 ... 119 A4
Rotherham S65 ... 116 B6
Sheffield S6 ... 160 A4
Burns St DN5 ... 41 C1
Burn's Villas DN7 ... 24 F4
Burns Way
Doncaster DN4 ... 83 A8
Wath u D S63 ... 78 C7
Burnt Hill La S35 ... 111 A5
Burnt Stones Cl S10 ... 127 D2
Burnt Stones Dr S10 ... 127 D2
Burnt Stones Gr S10 ... 127 D2
Burnt Tree La S3 ... 160 C5
Burntwood Ave WF9 ... 18 C2
Burntwood Bank WF9 ... 17 D5
Burntwood Cl S63 ... 58 B7

Burntwood Cres S60 ... 131 E5
Burnt Wood Cres WF9 ... 18 C2
Burntwood Dr WF9 ... 18 C1
Burntwood Gr WF9 ... 18 C1
Burntwood Jun & Inf Sch WF9 ... 18 C2
Burnt Wood La
Grimethorpe S72 ... 36 E8
South Kirkby S72 ... 17 E1
Burntwood Rd S72 ... 36 B6
Burntwood Sports & L Ctr S72 ... 17 C2
Burrell St S60 ... 115 D6
Burrowlee Rd S6 ... 112 C1
Burrows Dr S5 ... 113 A2
Burrows Gr S73 ... 56 B3
Burrs La S81 ... 147 F8
Burton Ave
Barnsley S71 ... 34 D4
Doncaster DN4 ... 83 B8
Burton Bank Rd S71 ... 34 B4
Burton Cres S71 ... 34 E5
Burton La S35 ... 111 C6
Burtonlees Ct DN4 ... 84 E7
Burton Rd
Barnsley, Monk Bretton S71 ... 34 D5
Barnsley S71 ... 34 B3
Sheffield S3 ... 128 F6
Burton Road Bsns Pk S71 ... 34 E5
Burton Road Prim Sch S71 ... 34 A3
Burton St
Barnsley S71 ... 33 E3
Sheffield S6 ... 128 D7
South Elmsall WF9 ... 18 F2
Burton Terr
3 Barnsley S70 ... 55 B8
Doncaster DN4 ... 83 B8
Burtop Croft S73 ... 77 C7
Burying La S62, S74 ... 76 F3
Bushey Wood Gr S17 ... 151 D7
Bushey Wood Rd S17 ... 151 E6
Bushfield Rd S63 ... 78 D6
Bush St WF9 ... 17 E6
Busk Knoll S5 ... 113 A2
Busk Mdw S5 ... 113 A2
Busk Meadow Inf Sch S5 ... 113 A1
Busk Pk S5 ... 113 A2
Busley Gdns DN5 ... 62 A8
Butcher Hill WF9 ... 17 E8
Butcher St S63 ... 58 C8
Butchill Ave S5 ... 113 A8
Bute St S10 ... 128 B3
Butler Rd S6 ... 128 A6
Butler Way S21 ... 156 C6
Butten Mdw DN10 ... 105 C2
Butterbusk DN12 ... 81 E2
Buttercross DN6 ... 21 A1
Buttercross Cl DN6 ... 21 A2
Buttercross Ct DN11 ... 121 A7
Buttercross Dr S72 ... 57 C8
Buttercup Cl WF9 ... 18 F7
Butterfield Cl DN14 ... 1 C7
Butterfield Ct S73 ... 78 A8
Butterill Dr DN3 ... 64 D5
Butterley Dr S70 ... 55 D6
Butterleys S75 ... 54 A7
Buttermere Cl
Adwick le S DN6 ... 21 C1
Bolton u D S63 ... 58 C1
Mexborough S64 ... 80 C6
North Anston S25 ... 146 E7
Buttermere Dr S18 ... 152 E1
Buttermere Rd S7 ... 140 E4
Buttermere Way S71 ... 56 B8
Butterthwaite Cres S5 ... 113 E7
Butterthwaite La S35 ... 95 D1
Butterthwaite Rd S5 ... 113 D8
Butterton Cl S75 ... 14 C1
Butt Hole Rd DN12 ... 81 E2
Butt La DN5 ... 38 E4
Button Hill S11 ... 140 B5
Button Row S36 ... 73 C1
Butts Hill S17 ... 151 D4
Buxton Rd S71 ... 34 A7
Byford Rd S66 ... 118 C5
Byland Way S71 ... 34 D2
Byram Ct DN4 ... 83 C5
Byrley Rd S61 ... 96 E1
Byrne Cl S75 ... 32 E4
Byron Ave
Bentley DN5 ... 61 F4
Chapeltown S35 ... 94 F4
Doncaster DN4 ... 83 A6
Norton DN6 ... 4 C1
Byron Cres S63 ... 78 C7
Byron Dr
Barnsley S71 ... 34 B4
Rotherham S65 ... 116 A6
Byron Rd
Dinnington S25 ... 147 A8
Maltby S66 ... 119 A4
Mexborough S64 ... 80 C5
Sheffield, Beighton S20 ... 144 A2
Sheffield, Nether Edge S7 ... 140 E6
Byron St S72 ... 36 E1
Byron Wood Prim Sch S4 ... 129 C7

C

Caddon Ave WF9 ... 19 B2

Cadeby Ave DN12 81 A2
Cadeby La DN5 81 E7
Cadeby Rd DN5 82 A8
Cadman Ct S20 155 D6
Cadman La S1 161 B3
Cadman Rd S12 142 C6
Cadman St
Sheffield, Park Hill S4 161 C4
Sheffield S20 155 D6
Wath u D S63 79 A6
Cadwell Cl S72 35 C8
Caernarvon Cres S63 58 B2
Caernarvon Dr DN5 59 C3
Caine Gdns S61 114 E6
Cairns Cotts S13 143 C6
Cairns Rd
Sheffield, Beighton S20 143 F4
Sheffield S10 128 A2
Caister Ave S35 94 F5
Caistor Ave S70 54 C7
Calabria Gr S70 55 B8
Calcot Gn S64 79 D2
Calcot Park Ave S64 79 D2
Caldbeck Gr S35 94 D8
Caldbeck Pl S25 146 F7
Calder Ave S71 15 E3
Calder Cl S71 15 E3
Calder Cres S70 55 D7
Calder Ct S60 115 E2
Calder Rd
Bolton u D S63 58 D1
Rotherham S61 96 F3
Calder Terr DN12 81 C3
Caldervale S71 15 E4
Calder Way S5 113 C2
Caledonia Ho DN2 63 B5
Calf Hey La S36 49 D7
California Cres S70 54 F7
California Dr
Catliffe S60 131 C5
Chapeltown S35 95 A4
California Gdns 18 S70 54 F8
California St S70 54 E7
California Terr S70 54 E7
Calladine Way S64 79 C1
Callander Ct DN4 84 E7
Callflex Bsns Pk S63 79 C6
Callis La S36 51 E1
Callis Way S36 51 D2
Callow Dr S14 141 D5
Callow Mount S14 141 D5
Callow Pl S14 141 D5
Callow Rd S14 141 C5
Callum Ct S62 97 E2
Callywhite La S18 153 C1
Calner Croft S20 144 B2
Calver Cl S75 54 A5
Calverley Gdns S73 56 E3
Calvert Rd S9 130 C6
Calvey Orch S72 35 C7
Camborne Cl S6 112 C5
Camborne Rd S6 112 C5
Camborne Way S71 34 B3
Cambourne Cl DN6 40 B6
Cambria Dr DN4 82 E6
Cambrian Cl DN5 61 A1
Cambridge Cl DN5 59 C2
Cambridge Cres S65 116 A7
Cambridge Ct
13 Sheffield, Heeley S8 141 B6
4 Sheffield S1 161 A3
Cambridge Lodge 14 S8 141 B6
Cambridge Pl S65 116 A7
Cambridge Rd
Harworth DN11 121 F4
Sheffield S8 141 B6
Stocksbridge S36 92 F8
Cambridge St
Mexborough S64 79 E5
Rossington DN11 84 E2
Rotherham S65 116 A7
Sheffield S1 161 A3
South Elmsall WF9 18 E3
Cambron Gdns S66 117 D6
Camdale Rise S12 142 F1
Camdale View S12 143 A1
Camden Pl DN1 62 C2
Camellia Cl DN12 81 D1
Camellia Dr DN3 42 F3
Camelot Way WF9 19 A2
Cam Height S32 137 F2
Cammell Rd S5 113 D2
Camms CE Prim Sch
S21 155 D4
Camms Cl S21 155 D4
Camm St S6 128 C6
Campbell Dr S65 116 B6
Campbell St S61 97 C4
Camping La S8 140 E2
Campion Cl S63 58 B3
Campion Dr
Killamarsh S21 156 C6
Swinton S64 98 D8
Campo La S1 161 A4
Camp Rd WF9 17 F1
Campsall Balk DN6 4 D2
Campsall Ctry Pk* DN6 21 D8
Campsall Dr S10 128 A3
Campsall Field Cl S63 78 E4
Campsall Field Rd S63 78 E5
Campsall Hall Rd DN6 4 D1
Campsall Park Rd DN6 4 D1
Campsall Rd DN6 21 F8
Campsmount Dr DN6 21 C8
Campsmount Tech Coll
DN6 4 B2
Canada St
Barnsley S70 54 E7
Sheffield S4 129 D7
Canal Bridge S21 156 D6
Canalside
Renishaw S21 156 B1
Thorne DN8 26 B6
Canal St
Barnsley S71 33 F3
Sheffield S4 129 D4
Canal View DN8 26 B6
Canal Way S71 33 F3
Canary Ct S66 117 B7
Canberra Ave DN7 66 A7
Canberra Rise S63 58 B2
Candy Bank DN9 66 D2
Canklow Hill Rd S60 115 D3
Canklow Meadows Ind Est
S60 115 D1
Canklow Rd S60 115 D4
Canklow Woods Prim Sch
S60 115 D2
Canning St 5 S1 160 C3
Cannock St S6 128 C8
Cannon Cl S62 98 B6
Cannon Hall Ctry Pk*
S75 31 D5
Cannon Hall House & Mus*
S75 31 C5
Cannon Hall Rd S5 113 C1
Cannonthorpe Rise S60 131 F4
Cannon Way S75 32 F5
Canon Cl DN11 85 B1
Canon Popham CE Prim Sch
DN3 42 F3
Canons Way S71 34 C3
Cantello Ct DN11 103 E7
Canterbury Ave S10 139 C8
Canterbury Cl
Bentley DN5 61 E6
1 Rotherham S65 116 B5
Canterbury Cres S10 139 C8
Canterbury Dr S10 139 C8
Canterbury Rd
Doncaster DN2 62 F6
Hatfield DN7 44 A8
Sheffield S8 141 B5
Canterbury Wlk S81 148 E7
Cantilupe Cres S26 144 D8
Cantley La DN4 84 E8
Cantley Manor Ave DN4 85 A7
Cantley Riding DN2 63 E5
Cantley Sycamore Prim Sch
DN4 84 E7
Canyards Hills La S36 91 F3
Capel St S6 128 D7
Caperns Rd S25 146 F5
Capitol Pk DN8 25 F8
Capri Ct S73 56 E6
Capstan Way DN8 26 A7
Caraway Gr S64 98 D8
Carbis Cl S71 34 B3
Carbrook Bsns Pk S9 114 B1
Carbrook Hall Rd S9 114 B1
Carbrook St S9 114 B1
Carcroft Ent Pk DN6 40 C8
Carcroft Prim Sch DN6 21 C1
Cardew Cl S62 98 A5
Cardigan Rd DN2 63 C5
Cardinal Cl DN11 85 B1
Cardoness Dr S10 127 E2
Cardoness Rd S10 127 F2
Cardwell Ave S13 143 A7
Cardwell Ct S66 100 F2
Cardwell Dr S13 142 F7
Carey Ave S71 34 A2
Carfield Ave S8 141 B5
Carfield La S8 141 C5
Carfield Pl S8 141 B5
Carfield Prim Sch S8 141 B5
Car Hill S61 97 C2
Carisbrooke Rd DN2 63 A4
Carisbrook Rd S81 148 E6
Carlby Rd S6 128 A7
Carley Dr S20 143 F1
Carlingford Rd S60 116 A3
Carlin St S13 142 E6
Carlisle Bsns Pk S9 113 F1
Carlisle Pl 5 S65 115 E7
Carlisle Rd
Doncaster DN2 63 B7
Sheffield S4 129 E8
Carlisle St E S4 129 E7
Carlisle St
Rotherham S65 115 E7
Sheffield S4 129 C5
Swinton S64 79 E1
Carlisle Terr S25 134 F1
Carlthorpe Gr S35 94 C7
Carlton Ave S65 115 F5
Carlton Cl
Branton DN3 85 E8
Hemsworth WF9 17 C5
Sheffield S20 155 C6
Carlton Dr DN10 122 F6
Carlton Gdns WF9 18 F3
Carlton Gn S71 15 C1
Carlton Hall La S81 148 F4
Carlton Ind Est S71 34 C7
Carlton Jun & Inf Sch
WF9 18 F2
Carlton Marsh Nature
Reserve* S71 15 F1
Carlton Mews S2 141 E7
Carlton Prim Sch S71 34 D8
Carlton Rd
Barnsley S71 34 B7
Carlton in L S81 148 F1
Doncaster DN1 62 E5
Rawmarsh S62 97 F4
Royston S71 34 B7
Sheffield S6 112 B2
South Elmsall WF9 18 F3
Carlton Rise S35 93 B3
Carlton St
Barnsley S71 33 F4
Cudworth S72 35 B7
Grimethorpe S72 36 A6
Carlyle Rd S66 119 A4
Carlyle St S64 80 A5
Carmel Ct 7 S11 140 C8
Carnaby Rd S6 128 C7
Carnarvon St S6 128 E5
Carnforth Rd S71 34 D5
Carnley St S63 78 B6
Carnoustie Cl S64 79 E2
Carolina Ct DN4 84 A7
Carolina Way DN4 84 A7
Carpenter Croft S12 142 C6
Carpenter Gdns S12 142 C6
Carpenter Mews S12 142 C6
Carr Bank DN11 103 A7
Carr Bank Cl S11 139 F8
Carr Bank Dr S11 139 F8
Carr Bank La S11 139 E8
Carr Cl
Brinsworth S60 131 A8
Stocksbridge S36 92 E8
Carrcroft Ct S36 92 F8
Carrfield Cl S75 32 D7
Carrfield Ct 8 S8 141 B6
Carrfield Dr S8 141 B6
Carrfield La S8 141 B6
Carr Field La S63 58 C3
Carrfield Rd S8 141 B6
Carrfield St S8 141 B6
Carr Fold S36 92 F8
Carr Forge Cl S12 143 A4
Carr Forge La S12 143 A4
Carr Forge Mount S12 143 A4
Carr Forge Pl S12 143 B4
Carr Forge Rd S12 143 B4
Carr Forge Terr S12 143 A4
Carr Forge View S12 143 B4
Carr Forge Wlk 4 S12 143 B4
Carr Furlong S71 14 F1
Carr Gn S63 58 C3
Carr Gr S36 92 E8
Carr Grange Works DN4 62 D1
Carr Green La S75 33 C8
Carr Head La
Bolton u D S63 58 B2
Penistone S36 51 B7
Carr Head Rd S35 75 B1
Carr Hill DN4 83 B8
Carr Hill Rd HD8 29 A6
Carr House Ctr DN4 62 F2
Carr House La S35 92 E3
Carr House Rd DN1, DN4 62 E2
Carriage Dr DN4 83 F8
Carriage Way The DN11 85 B1
Carrill Dr S6 112 C6
Carrill Rd S6 112 C6
Carrington Ave S75 33 E3
Carrington Rd S11 140 B8
Carrington St
Barnsley S75 33 D3
Rotherham S65 115 F5
Carrington Terr S26 145 D2
Carr La
Clifton DN12 100 E7
Doncaster, Bessacarr DN4 84 E5
Doncaster, Hyde Park DN4 62 D1
Dronfield S18 152 C2
Hooton Roberts S65 99 A6
Ingbirchworth S36 30 B8
Laughton en le M S25, S66 134 D8
Maltby S66 118 D4
Pilley S75 75 C4
Shepley HD8 28 F6
South Kirkby WF9 18 D4
Ulley S26, S66 133 A3
Wadworth DN11 102 D7
Carr Lane Mews S18 152 D2
Carr Mount HD8 29 A6
Carroll Ct WF9 18 E3
Carron Dr S75 33 C7
Carr Rd
New Edlington DN12 82 B1
Sheffield S6 128 C6
Stocksbridge S36 92 E8
Wath u D S63 79 A6
Carr Side La DN7 44 C5
Carrs La S72 35 B4
Carr St S71 34 D5
Carr View WF9 18 C3
Carr View Ave DN4 83 B8
Carr View Rd S61 114 D8
Carrville Dr S6 112 D4
Carrville Rd S6 112 D4
Carrville Rd W S6 112 C4
Carrwell La S6 112 C3
Carrwood Rd S71 34 E1
Carsick Gr S10 127 D1
Carsick Grange S10 127 E1
Carsick Hill Cres S10 127 E1
Carsick Hill Dr S10 127 E1
Carsick Hill Rd S10 127 E2
Carsick Hill Way S10 127 D1
Carsick View Rd S10 127 D1
Carson Mount S12 142 B3
Carson Rd S10 128 B3
Carter Grange 11 S8 141 B6
Carterhall La S12 142 C2
Carterhall Rd S12 142 B2
Carter Knowle Ave S11 140 C5
Carter Knowle Jun Sch
S7 140 D5
Carter Knowle Rd S7,
S11 140 C5
Carter Lodge Ave S12 143 B4
Carter Lodge Dr S12 143 B4
Carter Lodge Pl S12 143 B4
Carter Lodge Rise S12 143 B4
Carter Lodge Wlk 3
S12 143 B4
Carter Pl S8 141 B6
Carter Rd S8 141 A6
Cartmel Cl
Dronfield S18 152 E1
Maltby S66 119 A6
Cartmel Ct S71 34 D7
Cartmell Cres S8 140 F3
Cartmell Ct S8 140 E4
Cartmell Hill S8 140 E4
Cartmell Rd S8 140 E4
Cartmel Wlk S25 146 F7
Cart Rd S35 95 A7
Cartworth Moor Rd HD9 47 E8
Cartwright St S81 159 F7
Car Vale Dr S13 142 C8
Car Vale View S13 142 C8
Carver Cl S26 157 E6
Carver Dr S25 146 E8
Carver La S1 161 A3
Carver St S1 161 A3
Carver Way S26 157 E6
Carwood Cl S4 129 D7
Carwood Gn S4 129 D7
Carwood Gr S4 129 D7
Carwood Park Ind Units
S4 129 D7
Carwood Rd S4 129 D7
Carwood Way S4 129 D7
Cary Gr S2 141 F8
Cary Rd
Eckington S21 155 B3
Sheffield S2 142 A8
Casson's Rd DN8 26 A8
Casson Dr S26 157 E7
Castell Cres DN4 63 E1
Castle Ave
Conisbrough DN12 81 C2
Rossington DN11 104 B8
Rotherham S60 115 D3
Castlebeck Ave S2 130 C1
Castlebeck Croft S2 130 C1
Castlebeck Ct S2 130 C1
Castlebeck Dr S2 142 C8
Castle Cl
Barnsley S71 34 B3
Bentley DN5 61 E2
Dodworth S75 54 A6
Penistone S36 51 E2
Tickhill DN11 121 A7
Castle Cres DN12 81 C3
Castle Ct
Sheffield S2 129 D4
Tickhill DN11 121 A7
Castledale Croft S2 142 B8
Castledale Gr S2 142 C8
Castledale Pl S2 142 B8
Castledine Croft S9 114 B2
Castledine Ct DN4 83 B4
Castledine Gdns S9 114 B2
Castle Dr S75 53 E2
Castlegate
Sheffield S3 161 B4
Tickhill DN11 121 A7
Castle Gn
Laughton en le M S25 134 D4
Sheffield S3 161 B4
Castle Gr DN5 61 B1
Castle Grove Terr 3
DN12 81 D3
Castle Hill
Conisbrough DN12 81 C2
Eckington S21 155 D4
Castle Hill Ave S64 80 D4
Castle Hill Cl S21 155 D4
Castle Hill Fold DN5 59 C7
Castle Hills First & Middle
Schs DN5 40 F1
Castle Hills Rd DN5 40 E1
Castle La S36 51 E2
Castle Mews DN5 40 F1
Castle Mkt S3 161 B4
Castlereagh St 9 S70 33 E1
Castlerigg Way 1 S18 152 E1
Castle Row S17 152 B6
Castlerow Cl S17 152 B6
Castlerow Dr S17 152 B6
Castlerow View S17 152 B6
Castle Sq S1 161 B3
Castle St
Barnsley S70 54 E8
Conisbrough DN12 81 C2
Penistone S36 51 E2
Sheffield S3 161 B4
Castle Terr DN12 81 C2
Castle View
Barnsley S70 75 E8
Dodworth S75 53 F8
Eckington S21 155 D3
Hood Green S75 53 E2
New Edlington DN12 82 B1
Stocksbridge S35 73 D3
Castlewell 5 DN12 81 C2
Castle Wlk S2 129 D4
Castlewood Cres S10 139 B8
Castlewood Ct S10 139 C8
Castlewood Dr S10 139 B8
Castlewood Rd S10 139 B8
Castor Rd S9 129 F7
Catania Rise S73 56 E6
Catch Bar La S6 112 C2
Catcliffe Prim Sch S60 131 D6
Catcliffe Rd S9 130 C4
Cathedral Ct DN7 43 E4
Catherine Ave S26 144 D7
Catherine Rd S4 129 C6
Catherine St
Doncaster DN1 62 D2
Mexborough S64 79 F5
2 Rotherham S65 115 E6
Sheffield S3 129 B6
Cat Hill La S36 51 D8
Cathill Rd S73 57 D4
Cathill Rdbt S73 57 D5
Cat La S2, S8 141 C5
Catley Rd
Sheffield, Darnall S9 130 C5
Sheffield S9 130 D5
Catling La DN3 42 F7
Catshaw La S36 50 B3
Cattal St 6 S9 130 A5
Catterick Cl DN12 80 F2
Catterick Ho S65 115 F7
Caulk La S70 55 F5
Causeway Gdns S17 151 D8
Causeway Glade S17 151 C8
Causeway Head Rd S17 151 D8
Causeway The S17 151 D7
Cavalier Ct DN4 83 C5
Cavendish Ave
Sheffield, Abbeydale Park
S17 151 F7
Sheffield, Loxley S6 111 E1
Cavendish Cl
Bawtry DN10 122 F6
Rotherham S65 116 D4
Cavendish Ct
Barnsley S75 33 E3
Sheffield S3 160 C2
Cavendish Ho 7 S1 160 C3
Cavendish Pl S66 119 A6
Cavendish Rd
Barnsley S75 33 E3
Bentley DN5 41 A4
Rotherham S61 115 A6
Sheffield S11 140 C7
Cavendish St S3 160 C3
Cavendish Terr DN5 41 A5
Cave St S9 129 F5
Cavill Rd S8 141 A3
Cawdor Rd S2 141 F6
Cawdor St DN5 41 B1
Cawdron Cl S65 98 D1
Cawdron Rise S60 131 C7
Cawley Pl S71 34 A4
Cawston Rd S4 129 C8
Cawthorne CE Prim Sch
S75 31 E4
Cawthorne Cl
Dodworth S75 54 A6
Rotherham S65 116 C7
Sheffield S8 140 E3
Cawthorne Gr S8 140 E3
Cawthorne La S75 32 B6
Cawthorne Mus* S75 31 E5
Cawthorne Rd
Barnsley S75 32 D5
Rotherham S65 116 C7
Cawthorne View S36 51 F6
Caxton La S10 128 C2
Caxton Rd
Adwick le S DN6 40 B5
Sheffield S10 128 C2
Caxton St S70 33 E2
Caythorpe Cl S71 35 A5
Cayton Cl S71 33 E7
Cecil Ave
Dronfield S18 153 A2
Warmsworth DN4 82 C5
Cecil Rd S18 153 A2
Cecil Sq S2 140 F8
Cedar Ave
Mexborough S64 79 F6
Rotherham S66 117 C5
Cedar Cl
Carlton in L S81 148 E7
Doncaster DN4 82 E5
Eckington S21 155 B2
Finningley DN9 86 A4
Killamarsh S21 156 C5
Royston S71 15 A4
Stocksbridge S36 92 B8
Swinton S64 79 C1
Cedar Cres S70 55 B7
Cedar Dr
Maltby S66 118 D5
Rotherham S65 117 F8
Cedar Gr
Conisbrough DN12 100 A8
Stainforth DN7 25 A4
Cedar Nook S26 145 C3
Cedar Rd
Armthorpe DN3 64 C7
Doncaster DN4 82 F6
Stocksbridge S36 92 B8
Thorne DN8 9 C1
Cedar Sch DN4 82 F6
Cedars The S10 128 B2
Cedar Vale S64 79 C1
Cedar Way S35 94 F4
Cedar Wlk DN6 21 C8
Cedarwood Ct S61 96 C2
Cedric Ave DN12 81 A1
Cedric Cres S66 133 E6

Cedric Ct S66 133 E6
Cedric Rd DN3 43 A1
Celandine Ct S17 152 A5
Celandine Gdns S17 152 A5
Celandine Gr S73 57 A5
Celandine Rise S64 98 D8
Cemetery Ave S11 128 D1
Cemetery Rd
Adwick le S DN6 40 B4
Barnsley S70 55 A8
Bolton u D S63 58 D1
Grimethorpe S72 36 B6
Hatfield DN7 44 E7
Hemsworth WF9 17 C8
Hoyland S73 77 B7
Mexborough S64 80 A5
Sheffield S11 128 F1
Sheffield S11 160 C1
Wath u D S63 78 E5
Wombwell S73 56 D3
Centenary Ind Pk S8 140 E5
Centenary Market Hall S65 115 E7
Centenary Way S60 115 D4
Central Ave
Adwick le S DN6 40 A4
Bentley DN5 62 B8
Dinnington S25 147 A8
Grimethorpe S72 36 A8
Rotherham, East Dene S65 116 B6
Rotherham, Sunnyside S66 117 B7
South Elmsall WF9 18 F2
Swinton S64 79 C3
Central Bsns Pk S60 115 C6
Central Bvd DN2 63 B6
Central Dr
Bawtry DN10 123 A8
Rawmarsh S62 97 C8
Rossington DN11 103 E8
Royston S71 15 C3
Thurcroft S66 133 E6
Central Mews S25 147 A8
Central Par S65 116 B6
Central Rd S60 115 D7
Central St
Goldthorpe S63 58 E6
Hoyland S74 76 B5
Central Terr DN12 82 B2
Centre St
Hemsworth WF9 17 D8
South Elmsall WF9 19 A3
Centre The S66 117 D5
Centurion Bsns Pk S60 115 B5
Centurion Office Pk S9 114 B3
Centurion Ret Pk DN5 62 B5
Centurion St S60 115 A5
Centurion Way DN5 62 B5
Century Bsns Ctr S63 57 C1
Century Cl DN3 42 D2
Century Ct DN12 82 C3
Century Gdns DN5 41 C1
Century St S9 130 B6
Century View S60 131 A8
Chadbourne Cl DN3 64 A5
Chaddesden Cl S18 152 C1
Chaddesdon Wlk DN12 81 A3
Chadwick Dr S66 118 F6
Chadwick Gdns DN5 41 E2
Chadwick Rd
Adwick le S DN6 40 A4
Bentley DN5 62 B5
Sheffield S13 142 C7
Thorne DN8 9 D4
Chaff Cl S60 116 B1
Chaffinch Ave S60 131 D8
Chaff La S60 116 B1
Chalbury Cl S75 33 B4
Challenger Cres S63 37 D1
Challenger Dr DN5 61 E3
Challiner Mews S60 131 C6
Challoner Gn S20 155 E8
Challoner Way S20 155 E8
Chalmers Dr DN2 42 D1
Chaloner Hts S74 55 D1
Chamberlain Ave DN5 62 A6
Chamberlain Ct S35 94 F6
Chambers Ave DN12 81 A2
Chambers Dr S35 95 A7
Chambers Gr S35 95 A7
Chambers La S4 113 F1
Chambers Rd
Hoyland S74 76 D7
Rotherham S61 96 F1
Chambers Valley Rd S35 95 A7
Chambers View S35 95 A7
Chambers Way S35 94 F8
Chamossaire DN11 103 E7
Champion Cl S5 113 D6
Champion Rd S5 113 D6
Chancel Way S71 34 C3
Chancery Pl DN1 62 C3
Chancet Ct S8 140 E1
Chancet Wood Cl S8 152 F8
Chancet Wood Dr S8 152 F8
Chancet Wood Rd S8 140 F1
Chancet Wood Rise S8 152 F8
Chancet Wood View S8 152 F8
Chandler Gr S60 131 E5
Chandos Cres S21 156 D6
Chandos St S10 128 C2
Channing Gdns 4 S6 128 D7
Channing St S6 128 D7
Chantrey Rd S8 140 F3
Chantry Cl DN4 85 A7
Chantry Gr S71 15 C3
Chantry Pl S26 145 F3
Chapel Ave
Barnsley S71 15 C1
Chapel Ave *continued*
Wath u D S73 78 A8
Chapel Bank Apartments 3 S6 128 C6
Chapel Baulk DN10 87 F2
Chapel Cl
Barnsley S70 75 E7
Chapeltown S35 94 E5
Finningley DN9 86 E3
Rotherham S61 97 A4
Shafton S72 16 C3
Sheffield S10 127 F1
Thurcroft S66 133 E7
Chapel Croft S73 77 C7
Chapel Ct
Barnsley, Birdwell S70 75 F7
Barnsley S71 55 F8
Denby Dale HD8 29 F6
Wath u D S63 78 E5
Chapelfield Cres S61 95 F5
Chapelfield Dr S61 95 F5
Chapelfield La S61 95 F5
Chapel Field La S36 51 C2
Chapelfield Mount S61 95 F5
Chapelfield Pl S61 95 F5
Chapelfield Rd S61 95 F6
Chapelfields WF9 18 B1
Chapelfield Way S61 95 F5
Chapel Field Wlk S36 51 C2
Chapel Hill
Askern DN6 22 A8
Clayton DN5 37 C4
Hoyland S74 55 D1
Rotherham S60 116 B1
Swinton S64 79 C3
Chapel Hole La S66 101 C2
Chapel La
Apperknowle S18 154 A1
Barnsley S71 34 C8
Branton DN3 85 E8
Conisbrough DN12 81 C1
Finningley DN9 86 E3
Great Houghton, Billingley S72 57 F6
Great Houghton S72 36 D1
Kirk Smeaton WF8 3 E6
Midhopestones S36 72 B4
Penistone S36 51 C2
Rotherham S60 115 D5
Scrooby DN10 123 A2
Sheffield, Hillfoot S17 151 D4
4 Sheffield S9 130 A6
South Elmsall WF9 19 B3
Stocksbridge S35 73 E3
Sykehouse DN14 7 B7
Thorne DN8 26 B7
Thurnscoe S63 37 F1
Chapel Mews
Darton S75 14 C1
Swinton S64 79 C3
Chapel Pl S71 55 F8
Chapel Rd
Chapeltown, Mortomley S35 94 E8
Chapeltown S35 94 F4
Pilley S75 75 C6
Chapel Rise S25 146 D5
Chapelsfield La DN5 37 C4
Chapel St
Adwick le S DN6 40 B8
Barnsley, Birdwell S70 75 E7
Barnsley S71 55 F8
Bentley DN5 62 B8
Bolton u D S63 58 C2
Grimethorpe S72 36 A6
Hoyland S74 76 B5
Mexborough S64 79 E5
Rawmarsh S62 97 F5
Rotherham S61 97 B4
Shafton S72 16 C3
Sheffield, Coisley Hill S13 143 B6
Sheffield S20 155 C6
Thurnscoe S63 58 C8
Wath u D S63 78 E6
Chapel Terr S10 127 F1
Chapeltown Rd S35 95 B2
Chapeltown Sta S35 95 B5
Chapel View DN3 63 F7
Chapel Way
Kiveton Park S26 145 D2
Rawmarsh S62 97 D7
Chapel Wlk
2 Mexborough S64 80 A4
Rawmarsh S62 97 D7
Rotherham S60 115 C6
Sheffield S1 161 B3
Chapelwood Rd S9 130 B6
Chapel Yd
Dronfield S18 153 A2
Harthill S26 157 E6
Chapman St S9 114 B4
Chappell Cl S36 51 F6
Chappell Dr DN1 62 D4
Chappell Rd S36 51 F6
Chapter Way
Barnsley S71 34 C3
Silkstone S75 32 A1
Charity St S71 34 F6
Charles Ashmore Rd S8 153 A8
Charles Clifford Dental Hospl The S10 160 A3
Charles Cres DN3 63 F7
Charles Ct DN8 9 C1
Charles La S1 161 B2
Charles Rd S63 79 A5
Charles Sq S35 94 D7
Charles St
Adwick le S DN6 21 B1
Charles St *continued*
Barnsley, Shaw Lands S70 54 E8
Cudworth S72 35 C8
Dinnington S25 134 F2
Doncaster DN1 62 E5
Goldthorpe S63 58 E5
Great Houghton S72 57 E7
Grimethorpe S72 36 A6
Rawmarsh S62 98 B7
Sheffield S1 161 A3
Sheffield S1 161 B2
South Hiendley S72 16 E5
Swinton, Kilnhurst S62 98 E7
Swinton S64 79 D3
Thurcroft S66 133 E7
6 Worsbrough S70 55 A4
Charleville WF9 18 E4
Charlotte Ct S2 141 B8
Charlotte La 3 S1 160 C3
Charlotte Rd S1, S2 129 B1
Charlton Brook Cres S35 94 E5
Charlton Clough S35 94 D5
Charlton Dr S35 94 E6
Charlton Hill Rise S35 94 D5
Charlton & Linley Homes The S7 140 B1
Charnell Ave S66 119 A5
Charnley Ave S11 140 C5
Charnley Cl S11 140 B5
Charnley Dr S11 140 C5
Charnley Rise S11 140 C5
Charnock Ave S12 142 B2
Charnock Cres S12 142 A3
Charnock Dale Rd S12 142 B2
Charnock Dr
Bentley DN5 61 F5
Sheffield S12 142 B3
Charnock Gr S12 142 B2
Charnock Hall Prim Sch S12 142 B2
Charnock Hall Rd S12 142 A2
Charnock View Rd S12 142 B2
Charnock Wood Rd S12 142 B1
Charnwood Ct 2 S20 144 A2
Charnwood Dr DN4 82 F5
Charnwood Gr S61 114 F7
Charnwood St S64 79 D3
Charter Arc 8 S70 33 F1
Charter Dr DN5 61 D8
Charter Row S1 161 A2
Charter Sq S1 161 A2
Chase Ct S6 127 D8
Chase Rd S6 111 D1
Chase Sch DN7 44 B7
Chase The
Aston S26 144 E6
Sheffield, Loxley S6 127 D8
Sheffield S10 160 A1
Chatfield Rd S8 140 E2
Chatham St
Rotherham S65 115 E6
Sheffield S3 161 A5
Chatsworth Ave S64 80 D5
Chatsworth Cl S26 144 F7
Chatsworth Cres DN5 61 F8
Chatsworth Ct
Doncaster DN4 84 D8
Harworth DN11 122 B5
Sheffield S11 139 F4
Chatsworth Dr DN11 104 B8
Chatsworth Park Ave S12 142 A5
Chatsworth Park Dr S12 142 A5
Chatsworth Park Gr S12 142 A5
Chatsworth Park Rd S12 142 A5
Chatsworth Park Rise S12 142 A5
Chatsworth Pl S18 152 D2
Chatsworth Rd
Barnsley S71 34 A7
Sheffield S17 151 F6
Chatsworth Rise
Brinsworth S60 131 D8
Dodworth S75 53 F6
Chatterton Dr S65 116 B4
Chaucer Cl S5 112 D6
Chaucer Rd
Mexborough S64 80 C5
Rotherham S65 116 B5
Sheffield S5 112 E6
Chaucer Sch S5 112 E5
Cheadle St 2 S6 128 C8
Cheapside S70 33 F1
Checkstone Ave DN4 84 E5
Chedworth Cl S75 32 E7
Cheese Gate Nab Side HD8, HD9 28 A2
Cheetham Dr S66 119 A6
Chelmsford Ave S26 144 E8
Chelmsford Dr DN2 62 F6
Chelsea Ct S11 140 C7
Chelsea Rd S11 140 C6
Chelsea Rise S11 140 C7
Cheltenham Rd DN2 63 D5
Cheltenham Rise DN5 61 D5
Chelwood Ct DN4 83 C5
Chemist La 2 S60 115 C7
Chemistry La S35 93 C8
Cheney Row S1 161 A3
Chepstow Dr S64 80 B6
Chepstow Gdns DN5 61 D5
Chequer Ave DN4 62 E1
Chequer La DN7 23 F3
Chequer Rd DN1 62 E2
Cheriton Ave DN6 40 A5
Cherry Bank Rd S8 141 A3
Cherry Brook S65 116 B8
Cherry Cl
Cudworth S72 35 B8
Royston S71 15 A4
Cherry Garth
Bentley DN5 41 B3
Hemsworth WF9 17 C6
Norton DN6 21 C8
Cherry Gr
Conisbrough DN12 100 A8
Goldthorpe S63 58 C5
Rossington DN11 104 A8
Cherry Hills S75 14 A1
Cherry La DN5 62 B4
Cherry St S S2 141 A8
Cherrys Rd S71 34 D2
Cherry St S2 141 A8
Cherry Tree Ave S81 159 F7
Cherry Tree Cl
Brinsworth S60 131 D8
Darton S75 14 C1
Sheffield S11 140 D7
Cherry Tree Cotts S35 74 B3
Cherry Tree Cres S66 117 C5
Cherry Tree Ct S11 140 D7
Cherry Tree Dell S11 140 D7
Cherry Tree Dr
Hatfield DN7 25 A1
Killamarsh S21 156 D5
Sheffield S11 140 D7
Thorne DN8 9 B1
Cherry Tree Gr DN7 25 A1
Cherry Tree Pl S63 78 F5
Cherry Tree Rd
Armthorpe DN3 64 B6
Doncaster DN4 62 B2
Maltby S66 118 D5
Sheffield S11 140 D7
Wales S26 145 A2
Cherry Tree St S74 76 F6
Cherry Wlk S35 95 A4
Chesham Rd S70 33 D1
Cheshire Rd DN1 62 E5
Chessel Cl S8 141 A4
Chester Ct S21 155 B2
Chesterfield Rd
Aston S26 144 B6
Dronfield S18 153 B1
Eckington S21 155 B2
Sheffield S8 140 F4
Chesterfield Rd S S8 153 A6
Chesterhill Ave S65 98 E1
Chester Rd DN2 62 F6
Chesterton Rd
Doncaster DN4 83 C6
Rotherham S65 98 A1
Chesterton Way S65 98 B1
Chesterwood Dr S10 128 B2
Chestnut Ave
Adwick le S DN6 21 B1
Armthorpe DN3 64 B7
Brierley S72 16 F2
Doncaster DN2 63 B7
Eckington S21 155 B2
Killamarsh S21 156 C5
Rossington DN11 104 A8
Rotherham S65 116 B7
Sheffield, Beighton S20 143 F5
Sheffield, Handsworth Hill S9 130 E3
Stainforth DN7 25 A4
Stocksbridge S36 92 B8
Thorne DN8 26 C6
Wales S26 145 C3
Wath u D S63 79 A4
Chestnut Cl S66 117 B6
Chestnut Cres S70 55 B7
Chestnut Ct
4 Barnsley S70 54 F7
Bentley DN5 41 A2
Oughtibridge S35 111 D7
Rotherham S65 98 F3
Chestnut Dr
Bawtry DN10 122 F7
Chapeltown S35 94 F4
Finningley DN9 86 A4
South Hiendley S72 16 D5
Chestnut Gr
Conisbrough DN12 81 A1
Dinnington S25 134 F2
Hemsworth WF9 17 F6
Maltby S66 118 D5
Mexborough S64 79 F6
Sprotbrough DN5 82 B8
Thurnscoe S63 58 D7
Chestnut Mews
Langold S81 136 F4
South Hiendley S72 16 D5
Chestnut Rd
Aston S26 144 B8
Langold S81 136 F4
Chestnut St
Grimethorpe S72 36 B5
South Elmsall WF9 18 F1
Chestnut Wlk S66 118 E4
Chevet La WF4 15 B8
Chevet Rise S71 15 B4
Chevet View S71 15 A4
Cheviot Cl
Hemsworth WF9 17 F7
Thorne DN8 26 A6
Cheviot Ct S81 148 E7
Cheviot Dr DN5 61 F7
Cheviot Wlk 3 S75 33 B2
Chevril Ct S66 117 A4
Cheyne Wlk DN10 122 F7
Chichester Rd S10 128 B4
Chichester Wlk S81 148 E7
Chilcombe Pl S70 75 F6
Childers Dr DN9 86 A7
Childers St DN4 62 E1
Chiltern Cres DN5 61 A1
Chiltern Ct WF9 17 F7
Chiltern Ho S60 115 D6
Chiltern Rd
Bentley DN5 61 F7
Sheffield S6 128 B8
Chiltern Rise S60 131 D7
Chiltern Way S81 148 E7
Chiltern Wlk 2 S75 33 B2
Chilton St S70 55 A8
Chilwell Cl S71 14 F1
Chilwell Gdns S71 14 F1
Chilwell Mews S71 14 F1
Chindit Ct S25 134 F1
Chinley St 2 S9 130 A5
Chippingham Pl S9 129 F6
Chippingham St S9 130 A6
Chippinghouse Rd S7, S8 140 F7
Chiverton Cl S18 153 A2
Chorley Ave S10 139 C8
Chorley Dr S10 139 C8
Chorley Pl S10 139 C7
Chorley Rd S10 139 D8
Christchurch Ave S26 144 E8
Christchurch Flats S63 78 C7
Christchurch Rd S63 78 C7
Christ Church Rd
Doncaster DN1 62 D4
Sheffield S3 129 B7
Church Ave
Rawmarsh S62 97 E4
South Kirkby WF9 18 C2
Church Balk
Kirk Sandall DN3 42 F2
Thorne DN8 26 C7
Church Balk Gdns DN3 42 F3
Church Balk La DN3 42 F2
Church Bank S32 149 A8
Church Cl
Auckley DN9 86 A6
Darton S75 13 E1
Hemsworth WF9 17 D7
Maltby S66 118 F4
Oughtibridge S35 111 D7
Ravenfield S65 99 C3
Shepley HD8 28 E8
Swinton S64 79 C3
Thorne DN8 26 C7
Wales S26 145 B2
Church Cnr S25 134 D5
Church Cottage Mews DN4 82 E7
Church Croft
Kirk Sandall DN3 42 E3
Rawmarsh S62 97 E4
Church Ct
Doncaster DN4 84 F7
South Anston S25 146 E4
Churchdale Mews S12 142 D4
Churchdale Rd S12 142 D4
Church Dr
Brierley S72 16 F3
South Kirkby WF9 18 C2
Wentworth S62 77 A1
Churchfield S70 33 E2
Churchfield Ave
Cudworth S72 35 B6
Kexbrough S75 32 C8
Churchfield Cl
Bentley DN5 62 A8
Kexbrough S75 32 B8
Churchfield Cres S72 35 B6
Churchfield Ct
9 Barnsley S70 33 E2
Kexbrough S75 32 D8
Church Field Dr S66 117 B3
Churchfield Gdns S71 15 D1
Churchfield La
Kexbrough S75 32 C8
Kirk Smeaton WF8 3 F7
Womersley DN6 4 A8
Church Field La S62 77 A1
Church Field Rd
Askern DN6 21 E8
Clayton DN5 37 E4
Norton DN6 4 D1
Churchfields S35 73 F7
Church Fields S61 114 E7
Churchfields Cl 8 S70 33 E2
Churchfields Cvn Site DN5 62 A8
Church Fields Rd DN11 85 B2
Churchfield Terr S72 35 B6
Church Field View DN4 82 E7
Church Fold S6 112 A3
Church Glebe S6 112 A3
Church Gn
Sprotbrough DN5 82 B8
Wath u D S63 78 E6
Church Gr
Barnsley S71 34 C4
Braithwell S66 101 A2
South Kirkby WF9 18 C2
Church Hill
Rotherham S60 116 C1
Royston S71 15 D3
Church Hts S36 51 F7
Churchill Ave
Bentley DN5 62 A6
Hatfield DN7 44 E7
Maltby S66 119 A6
Churchill Rd
Doncaster DN1 62 E6

Churchill Rd *continued*
Sheffield S10 . . . 128 C3
Stocksbridge S36 . . . 72 F2
Church La
Adwick le S DN6 . . . 40 C6
Aston S26 . . . 144 F6
Barnburgh DN5 . . . 59 C2
Barnby Dun DN3 . . . 42 E8
3 Barnsley S70 . . . 33 E2
Carlton in L S81 . . . 148 F4
Catliffe S60 . . . 131 C6
Cawthorne S75 . . . 31 F4
Chapeltown S75 . . . 75 E3
Clifton S66 . . . 100 D5
Dinnington S25 . . . 134 D1
Doncaster, Bessacarr DN4 . . 84 F7
Doncaster DN4 . . . 82 D7
Eckington S12 . . . 154 E7
Finningley DN9 . . . 86 E3
Fishlake DN7 . . . 25 B7
Harworth DN11 . . . 121 E4
High Hoyland S75 . . . 12 C1
Killamarsh S21 . . . 156 E6
Letwell S81 . . . 135 F3
Maltby S66 . . . 118 F4
Marr DN5 . . . 60 C7
Penistone S36 . . . 51 F7
Ravenfield S65 . . . 99 D3
Rotherham, Bramley S66 . . 117 D5
Rotherham, Wickersley S66 . . . 117 B4
Ryhill, Felkirk WF4 . . . 16 A6
Ryhill S71 . . . 15 F7
Scrooby DN10 . . . 123 A2
Sheffield, Beighton S20 . . . 144 A3
Sheffield S9 . . . 129 F6
Sheffield, Townhead S17 . . 151 D6
Sheffield, Woodhouse S13 . 143 C6
Shepley HD8 . . . 28 E8
Tickhill DN11 . . . 121 A7
Treeton S60 . . . 131 E4
Wadworth DN11 . . . 102 B7
Wath u D S63 . . . 78 E6
Worsbrough S70 . . . 55 A2
Church Lane Mews S66 . 117 D5
Church Lea S74 . . . 76 E4
Church Mdws S25 . . . 146 E8
Church Meadow Rd DN11 . 85 B1
Church Mews
Bentley DN5 . . . 62 A8
Bolton u D S63 . . . 58 C1
Killamarsh S21 . . . 156 E7
Mexborough S64 . . . 80 C4
Sheffield S20 . . . 155 D7
Church Mount WF9 . . . 18 C2
Church Rd
Barnby Dun DN3 . . . 42 F8
Bircotes DN11 . . . 122 C4
Cawthorne S75 . . . 31 E4
Conisbrough DN12 . . . 81 A4
Kirk Sandall DN3 . . . 42 F4
New Edlington DN12 . . . 82 B3
Stainforth DN7 . . . 24 E3
Wadworth DN11 . . . 102 B6
Church Rein Cl DN4 . . . 82 C6
Church Side S7 . . . 140 D6
Church St
Armthorpe DN3 . . . 64 B6
Barnsley, Carlton S71 . . . 15 D1
Barnsley, Gawber S75 . . . 33 A3
Barnsley S70 . . . 33 E2
Bawtry DN10 . . . 123 A6
Bentley DN5 . . . 62 A8
Bolton u D S63 . . . 58 D1
Brierley S72 . . . 17 A2
Cawthorne S75 . . . 31 F4
Conisbrough DN12 . . . 81 C2
Cudworth S72 . . . 35 B6
Darfield S73 . . . 57 B5
Darton S75 . . . 13 E1
Doncaster DN1 . . . 62 C4
Dronfield S18 . . . 153 A1
Eckington S21 . . . 155 E4
Fishlake DN7 . . . 25 B7
Great Houghton S72 . . . 36 E2
Hoyland, Elsecar S74 . . . 77 A5
Hoyland, Jump S74 . . . 76 F7
Langold S81 . . . 136 F2
Mapplewell S75 . . . 14 C1
Mexborough S64 . . . 80 C4
Oughtibridge S35 . . . 111 C7
Penistone S36 . . . 51 D3
Rawmarsh S62 . . . 97 E4
Rotherham, Kimberworth S61 . . . 114 E7
Rotherham S60 . . . 115 D6
Rotherham, Wingfield S61 . . . 97 B4
Royston S71 . . . 15 C3
Sheffield, Ecclesfield S35 . . . 95 A1
Sheffield S1 . . . 161 A3
Sheffield, Stannington S6 . 127 C5
South Elmsall WF9 . . . 19 A2
Swinton S64 . . . 79 C3
Thorne DN8 . . . 26 B7
Thurcroft S66 . . . 133 F6
Thurnscoe S63 . . . 58 C8
Wales S26 . . . 145 B2
Wath u D S63 . . . 78 E6
Wombwell S73 . . . 56 D2
Woolley WF4 . . . 13 F7
Church Street Cl S63 . . . 58 C8
Church Top WF9 . . . 18 C2
Church View
Aston S26 . . . 144 F7
Barnburgh DN5 . . . 59 C3
Church View *continued*
Barnsley S75 . . . 33 D3
Cudworth S72 . . . 35 B6
Darfield S73 . . . 57 C5
Doncaster DN1 . . . 62 C4
Hoyland S74 . . . 76 B5
Killamarsh S21 . . . 156 E7
New Edlington DN12 . . . 82 A1
Norton DN6 . . . 4 C1
Rotherham, Thrybergh S65 . . 98 F3
Rotherham, Wickersley S66 . . . 117 B3
Scrooby DN10 . . . 123 A2
Sheffield S6 . . . 112 A3
Sheffield, Woodhouse S13 . 143 C6
South Kirkby WF9 . . . 18 C2
Swinton S64 . . . 79 C3
Todwick S26 . . . 145 F5
Wadworth DN11 . . . 102 B6
Church View Cres S36 . . . 51 D3
Church View Rd S36 . . . 51 D3
Church Villas WF9 . . . 18 C2
Church Way DN1 . . . 62 D4
Churchways S35 . . . 73 F7
Church Wlk
Bawtry DN10 . . . 123 A7
Conisbrough DN12 . . . 81 A4
Harworth DN11 . . . 121 E4
Hatfield DN7 . . . 44 C8
Thurnscoe S63 . . . 58 C8
Churcroft S75 . . . 33 A4
Cinder Bridge Rd S62 . . . 97 D4
Cinder Hill S81 . . . 159 D7
Cinderhill La S8 . . . 153 C8
Cinder Hill La S35 . . . 94 E1
Cinderhill Rd S61 . . . 96 E2
Cinder Hills Way S75 . . . 54 A7
Cinder La S21 . . . 156 F7
Circle Cl S2 . . . 130 B1
Circle The
Chapeltown S35 . . . 94 E7
Rossington DN11 . . . 84 E1
Sheffield S2 . . . 130 A1
Thorne DN8 . . . 9 D3
Circuit The DN6 . . . 39 F5
City Plaza S1 . . . 161 A3
City Rd S12, S2 . . . 141 F8
City Sch The S13 . . . 142 F6
City Wharf S3 . . . 161 B4
Civic Ctr S18 . . . 153 A1
Claire Ct S60 . . . 115 D7
Clanricarde St S71 . . . 33 F4
Claphouse Fold S75 . . . 13 A5
Clara Pl S61 . . . 114 F6
Clarehurst Rd S73 . . . 57 A6
Clarel Cl S36 . . . 51 C2
Clarel Ct DN11 . . . 120 F6
Clarell Gdns DN4 . . . 63 E1
Clarel St S36 . . . 51 C2
Claremont Cres S10 . . . 160 A3
Claremont Gdns S71 . . . 34 F4
Claremont Hospl S10 . . . 127 D2
Claremont Pl S10 . . . 160 A3
Claremont St S61 . . . 114 F6
Clarence Ave DN4 . . . 83 B8
Clarence Pl S66 . . . 119 A6
Clarence Rd
Barnsley S71 . . . 34 B4
Sheffield S6 . . . 128 B8
Clarence Sq S25 . . . 135 A1
Clarence St
Dinnington S25 . . . 135 A1
Wath u D S63 . . . 78 D7
Clarence Works S4 . . . 129 D5
Clarendon Ct S10 . . . 139 E8
Clarendon Rd
Rotherham S65 . . . 115 F7
Sheffield S10 . . . 139 E7
Clarendon St S70 . . . 54 D8
Clark Ave DN4 . . . 62 E2
Clarke Ave
Laughton en le M S25 . . . 134 C3
New Edlington DN12 . . . 82 B1
Thurcroft S66 . . . 134 A6
Clarke Ct S25 . . . 134 F2
Clarke Dell S10 . . . 160 A1
Clarke Dr S10 . . . 160 A1
Clarkegrove Rd S10 . . . 160 A1
Clarkehouse Rd S10 . . . 160 A2
Clarkes Croft S73 . . . 56 D3
Clarke Sq 6 S11 . . . 140 F8
Clarke St
Barnsley S75 . . . 33 D3
Sheffield S10 . . . 160 B2
Thurnscoe S63 . . . 58 E8
Clark Gr S6 . . . 127 D6
Clarks Ct DN6 . . . 40 B6
Clarkson St
Sheffield S10 . . . 160 B3
Worsbrough S70 . . . 55 C5
Clark St S74 . . . 76 D7
Clarney Ave S73 . . . 56 F6
Clarney Pl S73 . . . 57 A6
Clay Bank DN6 . . . 23 A5
Clay Bank Rd DN8 . . . 26 F4
Claycliffe Ave S75 . . . 32 F4
Claycliffe Bsns Pk S75 . . . 32 F5
Claycliffe Office Pk S75 . . . 33 A4
Claycliffe Rd S75 . . . 32 F5
Claycliffe Terr
Barnsley S70 . . . 54 D8
Goldthorpe S63 . . . 58 E5
Clayfield Ave S64 . . . 80 D6
Clayfield Cl S64 . . . 80 D5
Clayfield Ct S64 . . . 80 D5
Clayfield La S62 . . . 77 B1
Clayfield Rd
Hoyland S74 . . . 76 D8
Clayfield Rd *continued*
Mexborough S64 . . . 80 D5
Clayfields DN4 . . . 83 A5
Clayfield View S64 . . . 80 D5
Clay Flat La DN11 . . . 104 A8
Clay La
Doncaster DN2 . . . 42 D1
Doncaster, Long Sandall DN2 . . . 42 C2
Sheffield S1 . . . 161 A2
Clay La W DN2 . . . 42 C1
Clay Pit La S62 . . . 98 B6
Clay Pits La S36 . . . 72 D2
Clayroyd S70 . . . 55 A5
Clay St S9 . . . 130 A7
Clayton Ave
Thurnscoe S63 . . . 37 B1
Upton WF9 . . . 19 E8
Clayton Cres S20 . . . 143 E2
Clayton Dr S63 . . . 58 B8
Clayton Hollow S20 . . . 143 E2
Clayton Holt WF9 . . . 18 B1
Clayton La
Hooton Pagnell DN5 . . . 38 C5
Thurnscoe S63 . . . 37 B2
Clayton View WF9 . . . 18 B1
Clay Wheels La S6 . . . 112 B3
Claywood Dr S2 . . . 161 C2
Claywood Rd
Sheffield S2 . . . 161 C1
Sheffield S2 . . . 161 C2
Clayworth Dr DN4 . . . 84 B6
Clear View S72 . . . 36 A8
Clearwell Croft DN5 . . . 61 F5
Cleeve Hill Gdns S20 . . . 143 D2
Clematis Rd S5 . . . 113 F3
Clement Mews S61 . . . 114 E6
Clementson Rd S10 . . . 128 C4
Clement St
Rotherham S61 . . . 114 E6
Sheffield S9 . . . 130 B6
Clevedon Cres DN5 . . . 61 F8
Clevedon Way S71 . . . 15 B4
Cleveland Rd DN3 . . . 64 C6
Cleveland St
Doncaster DN1 . . . 62 C2
Sheffield S6 . . . 128 E5
Cleveland Way DN7 . . . 44 B8
Clevland Cl S81 . . . 148 E7
Cliff Cres DN4 . . . 82 C6
Cliff Ct DN12 . . . 80 F3
Cliff Dr S73 . . . 57 C5
Cliffe Ave
Thurgoland S35 . . . 74 D7
Worsbrough S70 . . . 55 B5
Cliffe Bank S64 . . . 79 D3
Cliffe Cl S72 . . . 16 F3
Cliffe Common La S35 . . . 74 E6
Cliffe Cres S75 . . . 53 E7
Cliffe Ct S71 . . . 34 C3
Cliffedale Cres S70 . . . 55 B6
Cliffe Farm Dr S11 . . . 140 A7
Cliffefield Rd
Sheffield S8 . . . 141 A5
Swinton S64 . . . 79 D3
Cliffe Field Rd S8 . . . 141 A4
Cliffe Hill
Cawthorne S75 . . . 31 E5
Sheffield S6 . . . 126 E8
Cliffe Ho S10 . . . 127 F2
Cliffe House Rd S5 . . . 113 B4
Cliffe La S71 . . . 34 C3
Cliffe Pk HD8 . . . 28 E8
Cliffe Rd
Sheffield S6 . . . 128 A6
Shepley HD8 . . . 28 E8
Wath u D S73 . . . 78 B8
Cliffe Side HD8 . . . 28 E8
Cliffe View Rd S8 . . . 141 A5
Cliff Hill S66 . . . 118 D5
Cliff Hill Rd DN6 . . . 4 B3
Cliff Hills Cl S66 . . . 118 E5
Cliff La S72 . . . 16 F2
Clifford Ave S65 . . . 99 A2
Clifford CE Inf Sch S11 . 140 D8
Clifford Rd
Hellaby S66 . . . 118 A5
Rotherham S61 . . . 96 E1
Sheffield S11 . . . 140 D7
South Kirkby WF9 . . . 18 B2
Clifford St
Cudworth S72 . . . 16 C1
South Elmsall WF9 . . . 18 F2
Clifford Wlk DN12 . . . 80 E3
Cliff Rd
Darfield S73 . . . 57 C5
Sheffield S6 . . . 127 D6
Cliff St
Mexborough S64 . . . 80 A4
Sheffield S11 . . . 128 F1
Cliff Terr S71 . . . 34 A1
Cliff View DN12 . . . 80 F4
Clifton Ave
Barnsley S71 . . . 33 E8
Rotherham S65 . . . 116 A6
Sheffield S9 . . . 130 E3
Clifton Bank S60 . . . 115 E6
Clifton Byres S66 . . . 100 D5
Clifton Cl S71 . . . 33 E8
Clifton Com Arts Sch S65 . . . 116 A7
Clifton Comp Upper Sch S65 . . . 116 A8
Clifton Cres
Barnsley S71 . . . 14 E1
Doncaster DN2 . . . 63 B6
Sheffield S9 . . . 130 D3
Clifton Cres N S65 . . . 115 F6
Clifton Cres S S65 . . . 115 F6
Clifton Ct DN8 . . . 26 A8
Clifton Dr DN5 . . . 61 E2
Clifton Gdns S72 . . . 16 E3
Clifton Gr S65 . . . 115 F6
Clifton Hill DN12 . . . 81 D1
Clifton La
Rotherham S65 . . . 115 E6
Sheffield S9 . . . 130 E2
Clifton Mount S65 . . . 115 E6
Clifton Park Mus* S65 . . . 115 F6
Clifton Rd S72 . . . 36 A7
Clifton Rise S66 . . . 118 E6
Clifton St
6 Barnsley S70 . . . 55 A8
Hemsworth WF9 . . . 17 C6
Sheffield S9 . . . 130 B8
Clifton Terr S65 . . . 115 E6
Clinton Pl S10 . . . 160 B2
Clinton Wlk S10 . . . 160 B2
Clipstone Ave S71 . . . 34 A8
Clipstone Gdns S9 . . . 130 C6
Clipstone Rd S9 . . . 130 C6
Clock Row Ave WF9 . . . 18 D3
Clock Row Gr WF9 . . . 18 D3
Clock Row Mount WF9 . . . 18 D3
Cloisters The
Barnsley S70 . . . 54 F2
Doncaster DN4 . . . 85 A7
Cloisters Way S71 . . . 34 D3
Cloonmore Croft S8 . . . 141 C1
Cloonmore Dr S8 . . . 141 C1
Close St WF9 . . . 17 C7
Close The
Barnsley, Lundwood S71 . . . 34 E3
Barnsley S71 . . . 15 C1
Branton DN3 . . . 85 D8
Clayton DN5 . . . 37 C4
Dinnington S25 . . . 146 F8
Norton DN6 . . . 4 D3
Cloudberry Way S75 . . . 33 D8
Clough Bank
Rotherham S61 . . . 115 B7
Sheffield S2 . . . 141 B8
Clough Fields S10 . . . 127 F4
Clough Fields Rd S74 . . . 76 D5
Clough Foot La HD9 . . . 48 A7
Clough Gn S61 . . . 115 C7
Clough Gr S35 . . . 111 E7
Clough Head S36 . . . 51 D1
Clough House La HD8 . . . 30 C6
Clough La
Norton DN6 . . . 5 C2
Sheffield S10 . . . 139 A6
Clough Rd
Hoyland S74 . . . 76 D5
Rotherham S61 . . . 115 B7
Sheffield S1, S2 . . . 129 A1
Clough St S61 . . . 115 B7
Clough Wood View S35 . 111 D6
Clovelly Rd DN3 . . . 42 F2
Clover Ct S8 . . . 141 C2
Clover Gdns S5 . . . 113 E3
Clover Gn S61 . . . 96 E2
Cloverlands Dr S75 . . . 33 D8
Clover Wlk
Bolton u D S63 . . . 58 B3
Upton WF9 . . . 19 A7
Club Garden Rd S11 . . . 140 F8
Club Garden Wlk 2 S11 . 128 F1
Club Mill Rd S6 . . . 128 E7
Club St
Barnsley S71 . . . 34 C4
Hoyland S74 . . . 76 B5
Sheffield S11 . . . 140 F8
Clumber Rd
Doncaster DN4 . . . 62 F1
Sheffield S10 . . . 127 E1
Clumber Rise S26 . . . 144 E6
Clumber St S75 . . . 33 C2
Clun Rd S4 . . . 129 C6
Clun St S4 . . . 129 C6
Clyde Rd S8 . . . 140 F6
Clyde St S71 . . . 34 A1
Coach Gate La S36 . . . 30 D3
Coach House Dr DN5 . . . 61 D4
Coach House La S70 . . . 55 A6
Coach Houses The S10 . . 160 A4
Coach Rd
Rotherham, Greasbrough S61 . . . 97 B3
Rotherham S62 . . . 95 D8
Shireoaks S81 . . . 159 F6
Coalbrook Ave S13 . . . 143 D8
Coalbrook Gr S13 . . . 143 D8
Coalbrook Rd S13 . . . 143 D8
Coalby Wlk S70 . . . 33 E2
Coaley La S62 . . . 77 F5
Coalpit La HD8 . . . 29 F3
Coal Pit La
Braithwell S66 . . . 100 C2
Cudworth S72 . . . 35 C5
Denby Dale HD8 . . . 29 D8
Kirk Smeaton WF8 . . . 3 A3
Oughtibridge S35 . . . 111 A5
South Elmsall WF9 . . . 19 E4
Stocksbridge S36 . . . 92 B7
Coalpit Rd DN12 . . . 80 E3
Coates La S36, S75 . . . 52 E2
Coates St S2 . . . 161 C2
Cobb Ct S64 . . . 79 D1
Cobb Dr S64 . . . 79 C1
Cobbler Hall WF4 . . . 12 F8
Cobcar Ave S74 . . . 77 B6
Cobcar Cl S74 . . . 77 A6
Cobcar La S74 . . . 77 B5
Cobcar St S74 . . . 77 A5
Cobden Ave S64 . . . 80 B5
Cobden Pl S10 . . . 128 C4
Cobden Terr S10 . . . 128 C4
Cobden View Rd S10 . . . 128 C4
Cobnar Ave S8 . . . 141 A2
Cobnar Dr S8 . . . 141 A2
Cobnar Gdns S8 . . . 140 F2
Cobnar Rd S8 . . . 140 F2
Cockayne Pl S8 . . . 140 F4
Cockerham Ave S75 . . . 33 E3
Cockerham La S75 . . . 33 E3
Cockhill Cl DN10 . . . 123 A6
Cockhill Field La S66 . . . 101 B3
Cockhill La DN12 . . . 101 C3
Cock Hill La DN10 . . . 123 A6
Cockshot La S36 . . . 92 D7
Cockshutt Ave S8 . . . 152 D8
Cockshutt Dr S8 . . . 152 D8
Cockshutt Rd S8 . . . 152 D8
Cockshutts La
Oughtibridge S35 . . . 111 C8
Wharncliffe Side S35 . . . 111 C8
Coggin Mill Way S60 . . . 115 A5
Coisley Hill S13 . . . 142 F6
Coisley Rd S13 . . . 143 A5
Coit La S11 . . . 139 D3
Coit Prim Sch S35 . . . 95 A4
Coke Hill S60 . . . 115 D5
Coke La S60 . . . 115 D5
Colbeck Cl DN3 . . . 64 A6
Colby Pl S6 . . . 127 F5
Colchester Ct DN5 . . . 61 E6
Colchester Rd S10 . . . 128 B4
Cold Hiendley Common La WF4, S71 . . . 15 D8
Cold Side S33 . . . 89 A2
Coldstream Ave DN4 . . . 82 D6
Coldwell Hill S35 . . . 111 B7
Coldwell La S10 . . . 127 E2
Coldwells Fold S36 . . . 51 A4
Coleford Rd S9 . . . 130 D5
Coleman St S62 . . . 97 F3
Coleridge Ave S71 . . . 34 B4
Coleridge Gdns S9 . . . 130 C7
Coleridge Prim Sch S65 . 116 A8
Coleridge Rd
Barnby Dun DN3 . . . 42 F8
Maltby S66 . . . 119 A4
Rotherham S65 . . . 115 F7
Sheffield S9 . . . 130 B7
Wath u D S63 . . . 78 C7
Colewell Cl S73 . . . 56 C4
Coley La S62 . . . 77 E3
Colister Dr S9 . . . 130 C4
Colister Gdns S9 . . . 130 C3
College Cl S4 . . . 129 C8
College Ct
Mexborough S64 . . . 80 B5
Sheffield S4 . . . 129 C8
College Park Cl S60 . . . 115 E4
College Rd
Doncaster DN1 . . . 62 D2
Mexborough S64 . . . 80 B5
Rotherham, Masbrough S60 . . . 115 C6
Rotherham S60 . . . 115 C7
Spinkhill S21 . . . 156 D2
College St
Rotherham S60 . . . 115 D6
Sheffield S10 . . . 160 A2
College Terr S73 . . . 57 A5
College Wlk 7 S60 . . . 115 D7
Collegiate Cres S10 . . . 160 A2
Collegiate Hall (Sheffield Hallam Univ) S10 . . . 128 D1
Colley Ave
Barnsley S70 . . . 55 C6
Sheffield S5 . . . 113 A6
Colley Cl S5 . . . 113 A6
Colley Cres
Barnsley S70 . . . 55 C6
Sheffield S5 . . . 113 B6
Colley Dr S5 . . . 113 B6
Colley Pl S70 . . . 55 C7
Colley Rd S5 . . . 113 A6
Collier Ct S63 . . . 77 F7
Collier Rd S72 . . . 16 D1
Colliers Cl S13 . . . 143 B6
Colliery Cl S25 . . . 134 E2
Colliery La S63 . . . 58 D6
Colliery Rd
Bircotes DN11 . . . 122 B3
Kiveton Park S26 . . . 145 D2
Sheffield S9 . . . 114 A1
Colliery Villas S81 . . . 136 F1
Colliery Yd S75 . . . 75 D4
Collin Ave S6 . . . 112 A1
Collindridge Rd S73 . . . 56 D2
Collingbourne Ave S20 . . 144 A1
Collingbourne Dr 1 S20 . . . 144 A1
Collingham Rd S26 . . . 144 C6
Collins Cl S75 . . . 53 E7
Collinson Rd S5 . . . 113 A4
Collins Yd S18 . . . 153 B1
Colne Ct S60 . . . 115 E2
Colonel Ward Dr S64 . . . 79 E3
Colonnades 3 DN1 . . . 62 C3
Colster Cl S75 . . . 33 A2
Coltfield S70 . . . 54 F1
Coltishall Ave S66 . . . 117 E6
Columbia Pl S1 . . . 161 B2
Columbia St S70 . . . 54 E7
Columbus Way S66 . . . 118 E6
Colver Rd S2 . . . 141 A8
Colvin Cl DN5 . . . 41 E1
Colwall St S9 . . . 129 F6
Commerce St S35 . . . 95 B5
Commercial Rd S63 . . . 58 C4

Commercial St
Barnsley S70 55 A8
Sheffield S1 161 B3
Common Farm Cl S65 117 D8
Common La
Auckley DN9 65 D1
Barnby Dun DN7 43 C7
Bentley DN5 42 A4
Clayton DN5 37 C5
Clifton DN12, S66 100 D7
Denby Dale HD8 30 B6
Doncaster DN4 82 E5
Harworth DN11 121 D4
Laughton en le M S66 134 B4
Mexborough S63 79 D8
Norton DN6 4 D3
Rossington DN11 104 B6
Rotherham S65 100 A1
Royston S71 15 C5
Sheffield S11 139 D5
Stocksbridge S36 92 F6
Thurcroft S66 133 D4
Tickhill DN11 121 B8
Walden Stubbs DN6 5 B6
Wath u D S63 79 B6
Woolley WF4 13 D8
Woolley WF4 13 F8
Common Rd
Brierley S72 17 B2
Conisbrough DN12 81 F1
Dinnington S25 134 E3
Harthill S26 158 B5
North Anston S25, S26 146 B8
South Kirkby S72, WF9 17 E1
Thorpe Salvin S80 158 F6
Thurnscoe S63 58 B8
Common Road Ave WF9 18 A1
Common Road Inf Sch WF9 18 A1
Commonside S10 160 A4
Common The S35 95 B1
Commonwealth View S63 58 B2
Companions Cl S66 117 B4
Compton St S6 128 C6
Conalan Ave S17 152 B5
Conan Rd DN12 81 B1
Concorde Mews DN1 62 D4
Concord Jun Sch S9 114 A4
Concord Rd S5 113 E6
Concord Sports Ctr S5 113 E4
Concord View Rd S61 114 C6
Conduit La S10 128 C4
Conduit Rd S10 128 C4
Cone La S75 53 A6
Conery Cl S65 99 A2
Coney Rd DN5 41 A4
Congress St S1 160 C3
Coningsburgh Rd DN3 42 F1
Coningsby Ho S10 127 D2
Coningsby Rd S5 113 C1
Conisborough Way WF9 17 E8
Conisbrough Balby Street Jun & Inf Sch DN12 81 B3
Conisbrough Castle* DN12 81 C2
Conisbrough Castle Visitor Ctr* DN12 81 C2
Conisbrough Ivanhoe Jun & Inf Sch DN12 81 A1
Conisbrough Sta DN12 81 B3
Conisbrough Station Road Prim Sch DN12 81 C3
Coniston Ave S75 14 A2
Coniston Cl
North Anston S25 146 F6
Penistone S36 51 D4
Coniston Ct S64 80 C6
Coniston Dr
Bolton u D S63 58 C1
Doncaster DN4 83 A4
Coniston Pl DN5 61 F8
Coniston Rd
Askern DN6 22 C8
Barnsley S71 34 A1
Doncaster, Intake DN2 63 C4
Dronfield S18 152 E1
3 Kirk Sandall DN3 42 F4
Mexborough S64 80 C6
Sheffield S8 140 E5
Coniston Terr 2 S8 140 E5
Connaught Dr 1 DN3 42 F4
Conrad Dr S66 118 E6
Constable Cl
3 Dronfield S18 152 E1
Rotherham S66 117 B5
Sheffield S14 141 E2
Constable Dr S14 141 D2
Constable La S25 134 F1
Constable Pl
Sheffield S14 141 E2
Wath u D S63 78 E6
Constable Rd S14 141 D2
Constable Way
Rotherham S65 98 C1
Sheffield S14 141 D2
Convent Ave WF9 18 C2
Convent Gr DN4 84 D8
Convent Pl S3 160 C3
Convent Wlk S3 160 C3
Conway Cres S65 116 C8
Conway Ct DN4 84 D5
Conway Dr
Barnburgh DN5 59 C3
Branton DN3 85 D8
Carlton in L S81 148 F6
Conway Pl S73 56 F1
Conway St
Barnsley S70 55 D8
Conway St *continued*
Sheffield S3 160 B3
Conway Terr S64 80 A6
Conyers Dr S26 144 D8
Conyers Rd DN5 62 B5
Coo Hill S13 143 C6
Cook Ave S66 118 E6
Cooke & Beard Homes S8 141 B5
Cooke St DN5 62 B8
Cookridge Dr DN7 44 B7
Cookson Cl S5 112 D4
Cookson Rd S5 112 D3
Cookson St DN4 83 B8
Cooks Rd S20 144 A2
Cooks Wood Rd S3 129 A7
Coombe Pl S10 128 C3
Coombe Rd S10 128 C3
Cooper Art Gall S70 33 E2
Co-operative Cotts S72 16 F3
Co-Operative St
Cudworth S72 35 B6
Goldthorpe S63 58 E5
Wath u D S63 78 D7
Cooper Cl S63 78 A6
Cooper Ho 3 WF9 17 D6
Cooper La S36 52 B8
Cooper Rd S75 32 C8
Coopers Ho S11 160 B1
Coopers Mill Bsns Pk DN2 42 C1
Cooper St DN4 62 E1
Coopers Terr DN1 62 D4
Copeland Rd S73 56 C2
Cope St S70 54 F7
Copley Ave DN12 81 A2
Copley Cres DN5 61 D6
Copley Gdns DN5 82 B8
Copley La HD8 29 B8
Copley Pl S61 115 A7
Copley Rd DN1 62 D4
Copperas Cl S36 50 E3
Copper Beech Cl 1 S20 144 A3
Copper Beech Cres S66 118 E3
Copper Cl S70 54 F8
Copper St S3 161 A4
Coppice Ave
Barnsley S75 33 B4
Hatfield DN7 44 A6
Coppice Cl S36 72 F2
Coppice Gdns S61 97 B2
Coppice Gr DN7 44 B7
Coppice La
Harley S62 76 D1
Hatfield DN7 44 B6
Sheffield S6 127 B4
Coppice Rd DN6 40 C2
Coppice The S61 96 D2
Coppice View S10 127 F3
Coppicewood Ct DN4 83 C4
Coppins Cl S66 117 D6
Coppin Sq S5 112 F7
Copse The S66 117 D6
Copster Cl S35 73 F7
Copster La S35, S36 52 D1
Copthurst Rd HD9 47 E7
Coquet Ave S66 117 D4
Coral Cl S26 132 C2
Coral Dr S26 132 C2
Coral Pl S26 132 C2
Coral Way S26 132 C2
Corbridge Ct DN4 84 C8
Corby Rd S4 113 F1
Corker Bottoms La S2 129 F3
Corker La S6 126 A8
Corker Rd S12 142 A6
Cornfall Pl 1 S70 33 D1
Cornflower Dr DN4 84 B8
Cornhill 2 S3 160 B3
Corn Hill DN12 81 E1
Cornish Pl S3 160 C5
Cornish St S3 128 F5
Cornish Way S62 97 E2
Cornwall Cl S71 34 B4
Cornwall Rd
Doncaster DN2 63 B5
Shireoaks S81 159 F7
Cornwell Cl S62 97 C8
Coronach Way DN11 103 E8
Corona Dr DN8 9 B1
Coronation Ave
Dinnington S25 134 F1
Grimethorpe S72 36 A6
Royston S71 15 E4
Shafton S72 16 B3
Wales S26 145 C2
Coronation Bridge S60, S61 115 B6
Coronation Cotts DN3 42 E8
Coronation Cres S70 54 F1
Coronation Ct S64 80 A6
Coronation Dr
Barnsley S70 54 F1
Bolton u D S63 58 B2
Coronation Flats DN7 24 F4
Coronation Gdns DN4 82 C6
Coronation Rd
Barnsley S75 32 D4
Doncaster DN4 83 B7
Hoyland S74 76 D6
Rawmarsh S62 98 C6
Stainforth DN7 24 F4
Stocksbridge S36 73 B1
Swinton S64 79 E3
Wath u D S63 79 A6
Coronation St
Barnsley S71 34 C4
Darfield S73 57 B6
Coronation St *continued*
Thurnscoe S63 58 E8
Coronation Terr
Austerfield DN10 105 C3
Barnsley S71 55 F8
Hoyland S73 77 C8
Corporation Bldgs S3 161 B4
Corporation St
Barnsley S70 55 A8
Rotherham S60 115 D6
Sheffield S3 161 A4
Cortina Rise S73 56 E6
Corton Wood S63 77 F8
Corton Wood Bsns Pk S63 77 F7
Cortonwood Dr S73 77 F8
Cortonwood Ho 12 DN1 62 C2
Cortworth La S62 77 E1
Cortworth Pl S74 77 B6
Cortworth Rd S11 140 A4
Corwen Pl S13 143 A6
Cosgrove Ct 2 DN3 43 A2
Cossey Rd S4 129 D6
Costhorpe Ind Est S81 136 E1
Costhorpe Villas S81 136 F1
Cote La
Holmfirth HD9 48 A8
Thurgoland S35 74 A6
Coterel Cres DN4 63 F1
Cotleigh Ave S12 143 A3
Cotleigh Cl S12 143 A3
Cotleigh Cres S12 143 A3
Cotleigh Dr S12 143 A3
Cotleigh Gdns S12 143 A3
Cotleigh Pl S12 143 A3
Cotleigh Rd S12 143 A3
Cotleigh Way S12 143 A3
Cotswold Ave S35 94 E5
Cotswold Cl
Barnsley S75 33 B2
Hemsworth WF9 17 F7
Cotswold Cres S60 116 C2
Cotswold Ct S81 148 E7
Cotswold Dr
Aston S26 144 E7
Sprotbrough DN5 61 A1
Cotswold Gdns DN5 61 F7
Cotswold Rd
Sheffield S6 128 B8
Thorne DN8 26 A6
Cottage Gr S66 101 A1
Cottage La S11 139 D5
Cottage Mdws DN14 7 B6
Cottam Cl S60 116 C1
Cottam Croft WF9 17 E7
Cottam Rd S35 94 D7
Cottenham Rd S65 115 F7
Cotterdale Gdns S73 56 F3
Cotterhill Cl S81 148 D1
Cottesmore Cl S75 33 C3
Cottingham St S9 129 F4
Cotton Mill Row S3 161 A5
Cotton Mill Wlk S3 161 A5
Cotton St S3 161 A5
Coulman Rd DN8 26 D8
Coulman Road Ind Est DN8 26 D8
Coulman St DN8 26 D8
Coultas Ave S36 92 D7
Countess Rd S1 129 A1
County Way S70 33 F2
Coupe Rd S3 129 B6
Coupland Rd S65 116 C8
Court Cl DN5 61 D6
Courtyard The
Barnsley S75 33 A1
Conisbrough DN12 80 C3
Court Yard The WF4 14 A7
Coventry Gr DN2 63 B7
Coventry Rd
Sheffield S9 130 C5
Thorne DN8 26 C7
Cover Cl S62 76 D1
Coverdale Rd S7 140 E5
Cover Dr S73 57 B6
Coverleigh Rd S63 78 F4
Coward Dr S35 111 D7
Cowcliff Hill Rd HD9 48 D8
Cow Gap La S6 126 D7
Cow House La DN3 64 C6
Cow House La Cvn Site DN3 64 C6
Cowick CE Prim Sch DN14 1 C8
Cowick Rd DN14 8 E4
Cow La
Havercroft WF4 16 B8
Sheffield S11 140 A3
Cowley Ct S35 95 B5
Cowley Dr S35 95 C4
Cowley Gdns S20 155 E8
Cowley Gn S73 56 B2
Cowley Hill S35, S61 95 D4
Cowley La S35 95 B4
Cowley Pl DN3 42 F4
Cowley Rd S35 111 D6
Cowley View Cl S35 95 A4
Cowley View Rd S35 95 B4
Cowlishaw Rd S11 140 C8
Cowood St S64 79 F5
Cowper Ave S6 112 D6
Cowper Cres S6 112 D6
Cowper Dr
Rotherham S65 116 B4
Sheffield S6 112 D6
Cowper Rd S64 80 C5
Cowrakes Cl S60 116 C1
Cow Rakes La S60 116 C1
Coxley Ct DN11 104 B8
Coxley Mount DN11 85 C1
Cox Pl S6 127 F1
Cox Rd S6 127 F8
Crabgate Dr DN6 20 E2
Crabgate La DN6 20 E2
Crabtree Ave S5 113 C1
Crabtree Cl S5 113 C1
Crabtree Cres S5 113 B1
Crabtree Dr
Great Houghton S72 36 D3
Sheffield S5 113 C1
Crabtree La S5 113 C1
Crab Tree La WF8 3 B3
Crabtree Pl S5 113 C1
Crabtree Rd
Hatfield DN7 24 F1
Sheffield S5 113 B1
Cracknell 6 S3 161 B5
Cradley Dr S26 144 E7
Cradock Mews S2 141 E7
Cradock Rd S2 141 F7
Craganour Pl 7 DN12 80 F3
Cragdale Gr S20 155 D7
Crags Rd DN12 81 B3
Crag View S35 74 A6
Crag View Cl S35 111 D8
Crag View Cres S35 111 C8
Craigholme Cres DN2 63 C7
Craigston Rd S81 148 E6
Craig Wlk S66 117 E5
Craithie Rd
Carlton in L S81 148 E6
Doncaster DN2 63 A4
Crakehall Rd S35 95 B3
Cramfit Cl S25 146 D6
Cramfit Cres S25 146 E8
Cramfit Rd S25 146 C7
Cramlands S75 54 A7
Cranberry Rd S36 72 E6
Cranborne Dr S75 13 F1
Cranbrook Rd DN1 62 E5
Cranbrook St S70 54 D8
Crane Dr S61 114 E7
Crane Greave La S35 74 C6
Crane Moor Cl DN5 59 C2
Crane Moor Nook S35 74 B6
Crane Moor Rd S35 74 C7
Crane Rd S61 96 E2
Crane Well La S63 58 E2
Crane Well View S63 58 E1
Cranfield Cl DN3 64 B5
Cranfield Dr DN6 21 A2
Cranford Ct 1 S20 143 A2
Cranford Dr S20 143 A3
Cranford Gdns S71 15 B4
Cranleigh Gdns DN6 40 A5
Cranston Cl S71 34 D4
Cranswick Way DN12 81 E2
Cranwell Rd DN4 85 B7
Cranworth Cl S65 116 A7
Cranworth Pl S3 129 B6
Cranworth Rd
Rotherham S65 115 F8
Sheffield S3 129 B6
Craven Cl
Doncaster DN4 84 E8
Royston S71 15 B4
Sheffield S9 130 C5
Craven Rd
Dunscroft DN7 43 F8
Hemsworth WF9 17 D6
Craven St
Rawmarsh S62 97 F3
Sheffield S3 160 C4
Craven Wood Cl S75 33 A3
Crawford Rd S8 140 F4
Crawley Ave WF9 18 D3
Crawshaw S3 160 B4
Crawshaw Ave S8 152 D8
Crawshaw Gr S8 152 D8
Crawshaw Rd DN4 62 A2
Cream St S2 129 B1
Crecy Ave DN2 63 C4
Creighton Ave S62 98 B5
Creighton Woods Nature Reserve* S64 79 B1
Cresacre Ave DN5 59 C3
Crescent S26 157 E5
Crescent End The S66 134 A6
Crescent E The S66 117 C7
Crescent Rd S7 140 F7
Crescent The
Adwick le S DN6 40 A4
Armthorpe DN3 64 C5
Barnsley S75 33 B4
Bircotes DN11 122 C4
Blaxton DN9 86 F5
Bolton u D S63 58 D3
Conisbrough DN12 81 A2
Dinnington S25 135 A1
Edenthorpe DN3 43 A2
Hatfield DN7 25 A1
Hood Green S75 53 E2
New Edlington DN12 82 B3
Sheffield S17 151 E5
Swinton S64 79 B2
Thurcroft S66 134 A6
Crescent W The S66 117 B7
Cresswell Rd
Sheffield S9 130 C4
Swinton S64 79 D4
Cresswell St
Barnsley S75 33 C2
Mexborough S64 79 F4
Crest Rd S5 113 C4
Crestwood Ct S5 113 C4
Crestwood Gdns S5 113 C4
Creswick Ave S5 112 F7
Creswick Cl S65 116 D8
Creswick Greave S35 112 E7
Creswick Greave Cl S35 112 E7
Creswick La S35 112 E7
Creswick Rd S65 116 D8
Creswick St S6 128 D6
Creswick Way S6 128 D6
Crewe Hall S10 128 C1
Crewe Rd DN11 122 B4
Crich Ave S71 34 A7
Cricketers Wlk S2 129 D4
Cricket Inn Cres S2 129 E3
Cricket Inn Rd S2 129 D4
Cricket View Rd S62 76 D1
Cridling Gdns DN6 4 E3
Crimicar Ave S10 139 B8
Crimicar Cl S10 139 C7
Crimicar Dr S10 139 B8
Crimicar La S10 139 B8
Crimpsall Rd DN4 62 B2
Cripps Ave DN11 85 A1
Cripps Cl S66 119 B4
Crispin Cl S12 142 A4
Crispin Dr S12 142 A4
Crispin Gdns S12 142 A4
Crispin Rd 3 S12 142 A4
Croasdale Gdns DN6 21 C1
Crochley Cl DN4 63 F1
Croft Ave S71 15 B3
Croft Cl
5 Darton S75 14 A1
Laughton en le M S25 134 D5
Sheffield S11 139 F3
Wombwell S73 56 F1
Croft Ct
Dunsville DN7 43 F5
Finningley DN9 86 E3
Kirk Sandall DN3 43 A3
Croft Dr
Darton S75 14 B1
Penistone S36 50 E3
Tickhill DN11 121 A8
Crofters Cl S21 156 C4
Crofters Ct DN4 83 C5
Croft La S11 139 F3
Croft Lea S18 152 C2
Crofton Ave S6 112 B2
Crofton Cl S18 152 F1
Crofton Dr S63 58 C3
Crofton Rise
Chapeltown S35 94 D6
Dronfield S18 152 F1
Croft Rd
Barnsley S70 55 C7
Brinsworth S60 115 B1
Doncaster DN4 82 E5
Finningley DN9 87 A1
Hoyland S74 76 D7
Sheffield, Intake S12 142 B5
Sheffield S6 127 D6
Crofts Bldgs S1 161 A4
Crofts Dr S65 98 E2
Crofts La DN7 24 D4
Croft St
Rotherham S61 97 B4
Worsbrough S70 55 A5
Crofts The
Hathersage S32 149 A8
Rotherham S60 115 D6
Rotherham, Wickersley S66 117 B3
Croft The
Barnsley S75 32 E5
Bentley DN5 41 E3
Catliffe S60 131 C5
Conisbrough DN12 81 C1
Denby Dale HD8 29 B6
Harley S62 76 D1
Hoyland S74 77 A5
Penistone S36 51 F6
Swinton S64 79 B2
Thorne DN8 26 C5
West Bretton WF4 12 F8
Cromarty Rise S18 152 D2
Cromer Cl S62 97 F6
Cromer Rd DN2 63 C4
Cromer St S72 36 A7
Cromford Ave S71 34 B6
Cromford Cl DN4 85 A6
Cromford St S2 129 B1
Crompton Ave
Barnsley S70 54 D8
Bentley DN5 61 F4
Crompton Rd DN2 63 B8
Cromwell Ct DN6 20 F1
Cromwell Dr DN5 61 F2
Cromwell Gr DN6 21 A2
Cromwell Ho DN5 61 E5
Cromwell Mount S70 54 E6
Cromwell Rd
Bentley DN5 62 B5
Mexborough S64 80 A4
Cromwell St
Sheffield S6 128 C5
Thurnscoe S63 37 E1
Cronkhill La S71 15 D1
Crooked La S65 99 D8
Crooked Lane Head DN11 120 F5
Crooke House La S71 36 A1
Crookes S10 128 B3
Crookes Broom Ave DN7 44 B7
Crookes Broom La DN7 44 A7
Crookes La S71 15 C1

Crookesmoorbldgs (Univ of Sheff) S10 128 C3
Crookesmoor Bldgs (Univ of Sheffield) S10 128 C3
Crookesmoor Dr S6 160 A4
Crookesmoor House (Univ of Sheffield) S10 160 A3
Crookesmoor Rd S10, S6 160 A4
Crookes Rd
Doncaster DN4 83 B6
Sheffield S10 128 C3
Crookes St S70 33 D1
Crookes Valley Rd S3, S10 160 A4
Crookhill Cl DN12 82 A1
Crookhill Rd DN12 81 E2
Crook Tree La DN7 25 E2
Cropton Rd S71 15 B3
Crosby Ave S66 117 E5
Crosby Ct S71 34 D5
Crosby Rd S8 140 F3
Crosby St S72 35 B8
Cross Allen Rd S20 143 F2
Cross Bank DN4 83 B8
Cross Bedford St S6 128 F5
Cross Burgess St S1 161 A3
Cross Butcher St S63 58 C8
Cross Chantrey Rd S8 141 A3
Crosscourt View DN4 84 C8
Cross Dr S13 143 B6
Crossfield Dr
Adwick le S DN6 21 A2
Wath u D S63 78 E5
Cross Field Dr S81 147 F4
Crossfield Gdns S35 94 D7
Crossfield House Cl DN6 21 A2
Crossfield La DN6 21 A2
Crossgate
Darton S75 14 B1
Thurnscoe S63 58 D7
Cross Gate
Bentley DN5 62 A6
Mexborough S64 80 C4
Crossgates DN11 102 C6
Cross Gilpin St 2 S6 128 E6
Cross Hill
Adwick le S DN6 20 F1
Brierley S72 16 F3
Hemsworth WF9 17 D7
Sheffield S35 113 C7
Crosshill Cl S35 113 C7
Cross Hill Ct DN6 20 F2
Cross House Cl S35 112 B8
Cross House Rd S35 112 C8
Cross Keys La S74 76 A6
Cross La
Austerfield DN10 105 C5
Dronfield, Coal Aston S18 153 C3
Dronfield, Quoit Green S18 153 B1
Dronfield S18 153 C5
Oxspring S36 73 A7
Penistone, Hoylandswaine S36 51 F8
Penistone S36 51 A1
Royston S71 15 E3
Sheffield, Brick Houses S17 139 C1
Sheffield S10 128 B3
Shepley HD8 28 E6
Stocksbridge S36 72 E2
Woodsetts S81 147 F4
Wortley, Bromley S35 75 B2
Wortley S35 74 C5
Crossland Dr S12 142 A3
Crossland Gdns DN11 121 A7
Crossland Pl S12 142 A4
Crossland Rd S32 149 A7
Crossland St S64 79 D3
Crossland Villas S32 149 A7
Crossland Way DN5 61 E7
Cross Lane Cl S81 147 F4
Crossley Cl S66 118 E6
Cross Myrtle Rd S2 141 B7
Cross Park Rd 1 S8 141 A5
Cross Rd DN7 45 C7
Cross Riding DN2 63 E4
Cross Smithfield S3 160 C4
Cross South St S61 97 C3
Cross St
Barnsley, Barugh Green S75 32 D4
Barnsley, Monk Bretton S71 34 C4
Barnsley S75 33 D3
Bentley DN5 41 B1
Doncaster DN4 83 A7
Goldthorpe S63 58 F5
Great Houghton S72 36 E1
Grimethorpe S72 36 B6
Hemsworth WF9 17 C7
Hoyland S74 76 B5
Killamarsh S21 156 F7
Langold S81 136 E3
Maltby S66 119 A5
New Edlington DN12 82 B2
Rawmarsh S62 97 F3
Rossington DN11 103 F8
Rotherham, Bradgate S61 115 A6
Rotherham, Bramley S66 117 D5
Rotherham, Greasbrough S61 97 C3
Rotherham, Whinney Hill S65 98 E2
Sheffield S13 143 B6
Thurcroft S66 133 E6
Upton WF9 19 D8
Cross St *continued*
Wath u D S63 78 E6
Worsbrough S70 55 B6
Cross Turner St S2 161 B2
Crossway S64 79 B2
Crossways
Bolton u D S63 58 C2
Doncaster DN2 63 B7
Stainforth DN7 24 F4
Crossways N DN2 63 B7
Crossways S DN2 63 B6
Crossways The S2 130 B1
Crowden Wlk S75 33 A1
Crowder Ave S5 113 A4
Crowder Cl S5 113 A3
Crowder Cres S5 113 A3
Crowder Rd S5 113 B3
Crowgate S25 146 C3
Crowland Rd S5 113 B4
Crowley Dr S63 78 F4
Crown Ave
Barnsley S70 55 A7
Cudworth S72 35 C4
Crown Cl
Barnsley S70 55 A7
Rotherham S61 114 E8
Crownhill Rd S60 115 B1
Crown Hill Rd S70 33 A1
Crown Pl S2 161 C3
Crown Rd DN11 120 F7
Crown St
Barnsley S70 55 A7
Hoyland S74 76 D6
Swinton S64 79 D3
Crown Well Ct S71 55 F8
Crown Well Hill S71 55 F8
Crown Works S20 144 A5
Crown Yd WF9 18 D3
Crowther Pl 7 S7 141 A8
Crow Tree Bank DN8 46 B8
Crow Tree La S64 79 F7
Croydon St S11 140 F8
Crucible Theatre* S1 161 B3
Cruck Cl S18 152 E2
Cruise Rd S11 139 F8
Crummock Rd 4 S7 140 E5
Crummock Way S71 56 B8
Crumpsall Dr S5 112 F1
Crumpsall Rd S5 112 F1
Crumwell Rd S61 96 D2
Crusader Dr DN5 61 E3
Crystal Peaks (Sh Ctr) S20 143 E2
Cubley Brook Ct S36 51 C2
Cubley Rise Rd S36 51 C1
Cuckoo La DN7 25 C2
Cuckstool Rd HD8 30 A6
Cudworth Churchfield Prim Sch S72 35 B7
Cudworth View S72 36 A6
Cullabine Ct S2 142 A7
Cullabine Rd S2 142 A7
Cull Row S36 92 F8
Cumberland Ave DN2 63 B4
Cumberland Cl
Bircotes DN11 122 D4
Carlton in L S81 148 F7
Hoyland S74 76 E7
Worsbrough S70 54 F5
Cumberland Cres S35 95 B4
Cumberland Dr S71 56 A8
Cumberland Ho DN11 122 D4
Cumberland Pl 5 DN12 80 F3
Cumberland Rd S74 76 E7
Cumberland St S1 161 A2
Cumberland Way
Bolton u D S63 58 C1
Sheffield S1 161 A2
Cumberworth CE Fst Sch HD8 29 B6
Cumberworth La
Denby Dale, Lower Cumberworth HD8 29 E7
Shepley HD8 28 F6
Cumbrian Wlk 1 S75 33 B2
Cundy St S6 128 D6
Cunliffe St S18 153 C4
Cunningham Rd
Doncaster DN1 62 D2
Hatfield DN7 66 A8
Cupola S3 161 A4
Cupola La S35 94 C1
Cupola Yd S60 115 C6
Curlew Ave S21 155 B3
Curlew Ct DN11 85 A1
Curlew Ridge S2 129 D2
Curlew Rise S61 96 A6
Curzen Cres DN3 43 A4
Curzon Cl S21 156 D6
Cusworth Gr DN11 104 B8
Cusworth Ho 7 DN1 62 C2
Cusworth La DN5 61 E5
Cusworth Park Ctry Pk* DN5 61 D4
Cusworth Rd DN5 62 A7
Cuthbert Bank Rd S6 128 D7
Cuthbert Rd S6 128 D7
Cutler Cl S21 156 B7
Cutlers Ave S70 54 D8
Cutlers Gate S3, S4 161 C4
Cuttlehurst HD8 30 D8
Cutts Ave S63 78 D5
Cutts Field View S71 15 B5
Cutts Terr S8 140 F7
Cutty La S75 33 D3
Cyclops St S4 129 E8
Cygnet Cl S63 77 F7
Cypress Ave
Finningley DN9 85 F3
Sheffield S8 141 C1
Cypress Cl S21 156 C5
Cypress Gate S35 94 F4
Cypress Gr DN12 99 F8
Cypress Rd S70 55 B7
Cyprus Rd S8 141 A5
Cyprus Terr S6 128 D6

D

Dadley Rd S81 148 F7
Dadsley Ct DN11 120 F8
Dadsley Rd DN11 121 A8
Daffodil Rd S5 113 F3
Dagnam Cl S2 141 F6
Dagnam Cres S2 141 F6
Dagnam Dr S2 141 F7
Dagnam Pl S2 141 F6
Dagnam Rd S2 141 F7
Daisy Bank S3 160 B4
Daisy Fold WF9 18 F7
Daisy Lee La HD9 48 C7
Daisy Wlk
Sheffield, Beighton S20 143 F3
Sheffield, Netherthorpe S3 160 C4
Dalbury Rd S18 152 C1
Dalby Croft S36 51 E3
Dalby Gdns S20 144 A1
Dalby Gr S20 144 A2
Dale Ave S65 116 C5
Dalebrook Ct S10 127 E1
Dalebrook Mews S10 127 E1
Dale Cl
Barnsley S71 34 A7
Denby Dale HD8 29 F5
Dale Cres S32 149 B8
Dale Croft S6 110 A4
Dalecroft Rd DN6 40 B8
Dale Ct S62 97 F5
Dale Gr S63 58 B1
Dale Green Rd S70 54 F4
Dale Hill Cl S66 118 F7
Dale Hill Rd S66 118 E7
Dale La WF9 19 B5
Dale Lane Ind Est WF9 19 B5
Dale Pit Rd DN7 44 F5
Dale Rd
Bradfield S6 109 D4
Conisbrough DN12 81 C2
Killamarsh S21 156 E6
Rawmarsh S62 97 F6
Rotherham, Brecks S65 116 C4
Rotherham, Wickersley S66 117 A4
Dale Side S10 128 B1
Dale St S62 97 F6
Daleswood Ave S70 33 B1
Daleswood Dr S70 55 D5
Dale The
Hathersage S32 149 B8
Sheffield S8 140 F3
Dale View
1 Conisbrough DN12 81 C2
Hemsworth WF9 17 F6
Daleview Rd S8 140 D2
Dalewood Ave S8 140 C2
Dalewood Dr S8 140 C1
Dalewood Rd S8 140 C1
Dalmore Rd S7 140 C5
Dalroyd La S6 110 E3
Dalton Ct
3 Conisbrough DN12 80 F3
9 Sheffield S8 140 F7
Dalton Foljambe Prim Sch S65 98 E1
Dalton Gr DN10 123 A8
Dalton La S65 116 D8
Dalton Listerdale Jun & Inf Sch S65 116 F4
Dalton Terr 10 S70 55 A8
Dalton Wlk DN6 21 B5
Damasel Cl S35 93 B1
Damasel La S35 93 B1
Damasel Rd S35 93 B2
Damer St S10 160 A3
Dam Rd DN11 121 A6
Damsteads S75 54 A7
Danby Rd S26 145 F2
Dance La S35 74 D7
Danebrook Cl S2 130 C1
Danebrook Ct S2 130 C1
Danebrook Dr S2 130 C1
Dane St N S63 58 E8
Dane St S S63 58 E8
Dane St S63 58 E8
Danesthorpe Cl DN2 63 C6
Danesway DN5 40 F1
Danethorpe Way DN12 100 A8
Danewood Ave S2 130 C1
Danewood Croft S2 130 C1
Danewood Gdns S2 130 C1
Danewood Gr S2 130 C1
Daniel Hill S6 128 E5
Daniel Hill Ct S6 128 D5
Daniel Hill St S6 128 D5
Daniel Hill Terr S6 128 E5
Daniel La S62 97 B6
Daniels Dr S26 132 C1
Dannemora Dr S9 130 C7
Danum Cl DN8 26 C7
Danum Ct DN12 80 F3
Danum Dr S65 115 F7
Danum Rd
Doncaster DN4 62 F2
Hatfield DN7 44 B6
Danum Sch
Doncaster, Intake DN2 63 D4
Doncaster, Intake DN2 63 D6
Dara St S61 114 B5
Darcy Cl S26 144 D8
Darcy Rd S21 155 C3
Daresbury Cl S2 141 D6
Daresbury Dr S2 141 D6
Daresbury Pl S2 141 D6
Daresbury Rd S2 141 D6
Daresbury View S2 141 D6
Darfield All Saints CE Prim Sch S73 57 B5
Darfield Ave S20 142 F2
Darfield Cl
Rossington DN11 85 B1
Sheffield S20 142 F2
Darfield Ct DN11 121 A7
Darfield Ho
13 Doncaster DN1 62 C2
Tickhill DN11 121 A7
Darfield Rd S72 35 D4
Darfield Upperwood Prim Sch S73 56 F6
Darfield Valley Prim Sch S73 56 F5
Dargle Ave DN2 63 A5
Darhaven S73 57 A6
Dark La
Barnsley S70 54 B7
Cawthorne S75 31 E5
Midhopestones S36 71 E5
Worsbrough S70 55 B3
Darley S70 55 C5
Darley Ave
Barnsley S71 34 A7
Worsbrough S70 54 F6
Darley Cl
Barnsley S71 34 A7
Harthill S26 157 E6
Darley Cliff Cotts S70 55 B5
Darley Gr S6 127 D6
Darley Pk S61 114 F5
Darley Terr S75 33 D2
Darley Yd S70 55 B5
Darlington Gr DN8 9 C4
Darlington Wlk DN8 9 C4
Darnall Dr S9 130 B5
Darnall Rd S9 130 B5
Darnall Sta S9 130 C4
Darnley Dr S2 142 A8
Darrington Dr DN4 82 D5
Darrington Pl S71 34 E3
Dart Gr DN9 86 A7
Dartmouth Rd DN4 85 B6
Darton Bsns Pk S75 32 E8
Darton Hall Cl S75 13 F1
Darton Hall Dr S75 13 F1
Darton High Sch S75 32 B8
Darton La S75 33 A8
Darton Prim Sch S75 13 F1
Darton Rd S75 31 F5
Darton St S70 55 D7
Darton Sta S75 13 E1
Dartree Cl S73 56 F6
Dartree Wlk S73 56 F6
Dart Sq S3 160 B4
Darwall Cl S35 94 D8
Darwent La S35 111 B4
Darwin Cl S10 127 F2
Darwin La S10 127 F2
Darwin Rd S6 112 B2
Darwynn Ave S64 79 A3
Davey Rd S63 58 D6
David Cl S13 143 D7
David La S10 139 A7
Davies Dr S64 79 D1
Davis Cl S65 98 D1
Davis Rd DN6 21 E7
Davis St S65 116 A7
Davy Dr
Maltby S66 118 F6
Rotherham S66 117 B7
Davy Rd DN12 80 E3
Dawber La S21 156 F7
Dawcroft Ave S70 55 A5
Daw La
Bentley DN5 41 B2
Wadworth DN11 102 D8
Dawlands Cl S2 130 B1
Dawlands Dr S2 130 B1
Dawson Ave S62 97 C8
Dawson La S63 78 E4
Dawson Terr S26 145 D2
Daw Wood DN5 41 C3
Dayhouse Ct S75 33 B4
Dayhouse Way S75 33 B4
Daykin Cl S75 32 D8
Daylands Ave DN12 81 B1
Day St S70 54 E8
Deacon Cl DN11 85 B1
Deacon Cres
Maltby S66 119 A4
Rossington DN11 84 E1
Deacons Way S71 34 C3
Deadman's Hole La S9 114 E3
Deakins Wlk S10 127 F1
Dean Cl
Bentley DN5 61 D2
Rossington DN11 85 B1
Deane Field View S20 143 D2
Deanhead Ct 7 S20 143 A2
Deanhead Dr 8 S20 143 A2
Dean Head La S36 73 B5
Dean La
Holmfirth HD9 48 D8
Rotherham S65 116 E6
Deansfield Cl DN3 64 B5
Dean St S70 33 D1
Deans Way S71 34 C4
Dearden Ct S35 113 B8
Dearne Carrfield Prim Sch S63 58 C3
Dearne Cl S73 56 F1
Dearne Ct S9 114 A2
Dearne Dike La HD8 28 E5
Dearne Goldthorpe Prim Sch S63 58 E5
Dearne Hall Fold S75 32 F6
Dearne Hall Rd S75 32 F6
Dearne Highgate Prim Sch S63 58 C5
Dearne High Sch The S63 58 E4
Dearne Rd
Bolton u D S63 58 B1
Wath u D S63 79 B8
Wombwell S73 57 A1
Dearne Road Flatlets S63 58 B1
Dearneside Rd HD8 29 F5
Dearne St
Conisbrough DN12 81 D3
Darton S75 13 F1
Great Houghton S72 36 E1
Sheffield S9 114 A2
South Elmsall WF9 18 F3
Dearne Valley Coll S63 79 C5
Dearne Valley Coll (Rockingham Ctr) S63 78 E6
Dearne Valley Parkway
Hoyland S74 76 C8
Wombwell S73 77 F8
Dearne View S63 58 E5
Dearneway S63 78 F6
Dearnfield HD8 29 C6
Dearnley View S75 33 D4
Decoy Bank N DN4 62 D1
Decoy Bank S DN4 83 E7
Deepcar La S72 35 E3
Deep Carrs La S81 147 E2
Deepcar St John's CE Jun Sch S36 92 E8
Deepdale Croft S75 32 F5
Deepdale Rd S61 114 F6
Deep La S5 113 F8
Deepwell Ave S20 155 F6
Deepwell Bank S20 155 F6
Deepwell Ct S20 155 F6
Deepwell View S20 155 F6
Deerlands Ave
Sheffield S5 112 E6
Sheffield S5 113 B6
Deerlands Cl S5 112 F6
Deerlands Mount S5 112 E6
Deer Leap Dr S65 99 A2
Deer Park Cl S6 127 E6
Deer Park Pl S6 127 E6
Deer Park Rd
Rotherham S65 99 A2
Sheffield S6 127 F6
Deer Park View S6 127 E6
Deer Park Way S6 127 F6
Deershaw La HD8 28 C5
Deershaw Sike La HD8 28 C5
De Houton Cl S26 145 E5
Deightonby St S63 37 E1
De Lacy Dr S70 55 A5
Delamere Cl S20 144 A2
De La Salle Dr S4 129 C7
Delf Rd S6 110 C6
Delf St S2 141 B7
Della Ave S70 54 D8
Dell Ave S72 36 A8
Dell Cres DN4 61 F1
Dell The S66 117 C8
Delmar Way S66 117 B6
Delph Cl S75 32 A1
Delph Edge S35 73 E3
Delph House Rd S10 127 F3
Delph Mews S35 73 E3
Delta Pl S65 116 B7
Delta Way S66 119 B6
Delves Ave S12 143 D4
Delves Cl S12 143 C4
Delves Dr S12 143 C4
Delves La S26 144 E2
Delves Pl S12 143 B3
Delves Rd
Killamarsh S21 156 C6
Sheffield S12 143 C3
Delves Terr S12 143 C3
Denaby Ave DN12 81 A2
Denaby Ings Nature Reserve* DN5 81 A6
Denaby Ings Visitor Ctr* DN5 80 F6
Denaby La
Conisbrough DN12 80 C3
Hooton Roberts S65 99 A8
Denaby Lane Ind Est DN12 80 E3
Denaby Main Prim Sch DN12 81 A4
Den Bank Ave S10 127 E3
Den Bank Cl S10 127 F3
Den Bank Cres S10 127 E3
Den Bank Dr S10 127 F3
Denby CE Fst Sch HD8 29 F3
Denby Dale Ind Est HD8 29 F6
Denby Dale Rd WF4 12 C8
Denby Dale Sta HD8 29 E6
Denby Hall La HD8 30 D4
Denby La
Denby Dale, Lower Denby HD8 30 C4
Denby Dale, Upper Denby HD8 29 F3

Denby Rd S71 33 F7
Denby St
Bentley DN5 41 B1
Sheffield S2 129 A1
Denby Way S66 118 A5
Dene Cl S66 117 C4
Dene Cres S65 116 B8
Denehall Rd DN3 43 A3
Dene La S3 160 C2
Dene Rd S65 116 B8
Denham Rd S11 128 E1
Denholme Cl S3 129 B5
Denholme Mdw WF9 18 F4
Denison Ct 9 S70 54 F8
Denison Rd DN4 62 B2
Denman Rd S63 78 D6
Denman St S65 115 E8
Denmark Rd S2 141 B6
Denson Cl 4 S2 141 B6
Dent La S12 142 F2
Denton Rd 2 S8 140 F4
Dentons Green La DN3 42 F4
Denton St S71 33 F2
Denver Rd DN6 4 E3
Derby Pl S2 141 C6
Derby Rd DN2 63 C8
Derbyshire Ct DN3 64 E7
Derbyshire La S8 141 A3
Derby St
Barnsley S70 33 D1
Sheffield S2 141 C6
Derby Terr S2 141 C6
Derriman Ave S11 140 B4
Derriman Cl S11 140 B4
Derriman Dr S11 140 B4
Derriman Glen S11 140 A4
Derriman Gr S11 140 B4
Derry Gr S63 58 C7
Derwent Cl
Barnsley S71 34 B7
Dronfield S18 153 B3
North Anston S25 146 F7
Derwent Cres
Barnsley S71 34 B7
Brinsworth S60 131 B7
Derwent Ct
Rotherham S60 115 F2
5 Sheffield S17 152 A5
Derwent Dr
Chapeltown S35 94 E5
Kirk Sandall DN3 42 F3
Mexborough S64 80 C6
Rawmarsh S62 97 F4
Derwent Gdns S63 58 E4
Derwent Pl
Sprotbrough DN5 61 B1
Wombwell S73 56 F1
Derwent Rd
Barnsley S71 34 B7
Dronfield S18 153 B3
Mexborough S64 80 C6
Rotherham S61 97 A3
Derwent St S2 129 D4
Derwent Terr S64 80 A6
Derwent Way S63 78 C8
De Sutton Pl S26 157 E5
Deveron Rd S20 155 F7
Devon Ct DN12 80 F2
Devon Rd S4 129 C8
Devonshire Cl S17 151 F6
Devonshire Ctyd S1 160 C2
Devonshire Dr
Barnsley S75 33 D4
North Anston S25 146 E7
Sheffield S17 151 E7
Devonshire Glen S17 151 F6
Devonshire Gr S17 151 E6
Devonshire La 4 S1 160 C3
Devonshire Rd
Doncaster DN2 63 B5
Harworth DN11 121 F4
Maltby S66 119 A6
Sheffield S17 151 F6
Devonshire St
Rotherham S61 115 B6
Sheffield S3 160 C3
Devonshire Terrace Rd
S17 151 D7
Dewar Dr S7 140 C4
De Warren Pl S26 157 F5
Dewhill Ave S60 116 B1
Dial Cl S5 113 C4
Dial House Rd S6 112 A1
Dial The S5 113 D5
Dial Way S5 113 C4
Diamond Ave WF9 18 E3
Diamond St S73 56 D3
Dickan Gdns DN3 64 D5
Dick Edge La HD8 28 B2
Dickens Cl S60 131 B6
Dickenson Ct S35 94 F5
Dickens Rd S62 98 B7
Dickinson Pl 13 S70 54 F7
Dickinson Rd
12 Barnsley S70 54 F7
Sheffield S5 113 D7
Digby Cl S61 114 E8
Dike Hill S62 76 E1
Dikelands Mount S35 94 D6
Dillington Rd S70 54 F7
Dillington Sq S70 54 F7
Dillington Terr 5 S70 54 F7
Dinmore Cl DN4 83 A4
Dinnington Bsns Ctr S25 134 E2
Dinnington Com Prim Sch
S25 134 F2
Dinnington Comp Sch
S25 135 A2
Dinnington Rd
Sheffield S8 140 F4
Woodsetts S81 147 D4
Dirleton Dr DN4 82 D6
Dirty La DN7 25 A7
Discovery Way S66 118 D6
Dishwell La S26 157 E6
Disraeli Gr S66 118 E6
Distillery Side S74 77 B4
Ditchingham St S4 129 C6
Division La S1 161 A3
Division St S1 161 A3
Dixon Cres DN4 82 F7
Dixon Dr S35 93 B2
Dixon La S1 161 B4
Dixon Rd
New Edlington DN12 82 B2
Sheffield S6 112 B1
Dixon St
Rotherham S65 115 E7
Sheffield S3 128 F5
Dobbin Ct S11 140 B7
Dobbin Hill S11 140 B6
Dobb La S6 126 E4
Dobbs Cl S21 156 C6
Dobcroft Ave S7 140 B2
Dobcroft Cl S11 140 A4
Dobcroft Inf Sch S7 140 B4
Dobcroft Jun Sch S7 140 B3
Dobcroft Rd S7, S11 140 B3
Dobeller La DN14 2 D8
Dobie St S70 54 F8
Dob Royd HD8 28 D7
Dobroyd Terr S74 76 F7
Dobsyke Cl S70 55 D5
Dockin Hill Rd DN1 62 D4
Doctor La
Harthill S26 157 F5
Sheffield S9 130 B6
Dodds Cl S60 115 C4
Dodd St S6 128 C7
Dodson Dr S13 130 F2
Dodsworth St S64 79 F4
Dodworth Bsns Pk S75 53 D8
Dodworth Green Rd S75 53 E6
Dodworth Rd S70 33 C1
Dodworth St John the
Baptist Prim Sch S75 53 F7
Dodworth Sta S75 53 E7
Doe La
Barnsley S70 54 F3
Eckington S12 154 C5
Doe Quarry La S25 135 A1
Doe Quarry Pl S25 135 A1
Doe Quarry Terr S25 135 A1
Doe Royd Cres S5 112 D5
Doe Royd Dr S5 112 E5
Doe Royd La S5 112 E5
Dog Croft La DN2 42 A2
Dog Hill S72 16 C3
Dog Hill Dr S72 16 C3
Dog Kennel Hill S75 31 E3
Dog Kennels La S26 146 B2
Dog La DN10 123 A2
Dolcliffe Cl S64 79 F5
Dolcliffe Rd S64 80 A4
Dole Rd DN17 11 D1
Doles Ave S71 15 B3
Doles Cres S71 15 B3
Doles La S60 132 E7
Doleswood Dr S25 134 E4
Dome L Pk The* DN4 63 B1
Domine La S60 115 D6
Dominoe Gr S12 142 D5
Don Ave
Sheffield S6 112 A3
Wharncliffe Side S35 93 B2
Doncaster By-Pass
Brodsworth DN5, DN6 39 D4
Doncaster DN4 82 F4
Doncaster Coll (Church
View) DN1 62 C4
Doncaster Coll (Waterdale)
DN1 62 D3
Doncaster Com Stad DN4 83 F8
Doncaster Ex Ctr* DN2 63 A3
Doncaster Gate S65 115 E6
Doncaster Gate Hospl
S65 115 E6
Doncaster Industry Pk
DN5 61 F7
Doncaster International
Railport DN4 83 E7
Doncaster La
Adwick le S DN6 40 C4
Hampole DN6 20 C3
Doncaster Mus & Art Gall*
DN1 62 D2
Doncaster Pl S65 116 A7
Doncaster Race Course*
DN2 63 B3
Doncaster Rd
Adwick le S DN5 41 A8
Adwick le S, Highfields DN6 40 C2
Adwick le S, Owston DN6 21 F4
Armthorpe DN3 63 F6
Barnburgh DN5 59 D3
Barnsley S71 56 C8
Bawtry DN10 123 A7
Braithwell S66 101 A2
Brodsworth DN5 39 D3
Conisbrough, Conisbrough
Common DN12 81 D2
Conisbrough DN12 81 A4
Darfield S73 57 C6
Doncaster, Bessacarr DN3 85 C8
Finningley DN9 86 E3
Goldthorpe S63 58 F5
Doncaster Rd *continued*
Hampole DN6, WF9 19 D5
Hatfield DN7 44 B6
Hickleton DN5 59 B6
High Melton DN5 81 B8
Hooton Roberts S65 99 C6
Kirk Sandall DN3 42 F4
Kirk Smeaton WF8 3 A1
Langold S81 136 F2
Mexborough S64 80 D5
Rotherham, Eastwood S65 116 A8
Rotherham S65 98 C1
South Elmsall DN6, WF9 19 A2
Stainforth DN7 24 C3
Tickhill DN11 102 F2
Upton WF9 18 E7
Wath u D S63 79 B6
Doncaster Rd Harlington
DN5 59 C1
Doncaster Road Jun Sch
S64 80 C4
Doncaster Road Prim Sch
S70 55 A8
Doncaster Royal Infmy
DN2 63 A5
Doncaster Sch & Coll for the
Deaf DN2 63 A3
Doncaster St S3 160 C4
Doncaster Sta DN1 62 C3
Don Dr S70 55 D7
Donetsk Way S12, S20 143 B2
Don Hill Height S35 73 C3
Donnington Rd
Mexborough S64 80 D6
Sheffield S2 129 D1
Donovan Cl S5 112 E3
Donovan Rd S5 112 E3
Don Pottery Yd S64 79 F3
Don Rd S9 129 F7
Don St
Conisbrough DN12 81 D3
Doncaster DN1 62 D5
Penistone S36 51 F2
Rotherham S60 115 D6
Donstone View S25 134 D1
Don Terr S36 51 B4
Don Valley Bowl S9 130 B7
Don Valley Sch & Performing
Arts Coll DN5 61 D8
Don Valley Stad S9 130 A6
Don View S36 48 D1
Don View Ho S65 116 A8
Don View Row S64 80 D5
Dorchester Pl S70 54 F5
Dorchester Rd DN11 122 B5
Dorcliffe Lodge S10 128 A1
Dore Cl S17 152 A7
Dore Ct S17 152 A7
Dore Hall Croft S17 151 D7
Dore House Ind Est S13 131 C1
Dore La S32 149 A7
Dore Prim Sch S17 151 D6
Dore Rd S17 151 E8
Dore Sta S17 152 A7
Dorking St S4 129 C5
Dorman Ave WF9 19 D8
Dorothy Ave DN8 25 F8
Dorothy Hyman Sports Ctr &
Stad S72 35 B6
Dorothy Rd S6 112 B1
Dorset Cl WF9 17 D8
Dorset Cres DN2 63 C5
Dorset Dr DN11 121 F4
Dorset St S10 160 B2
Double Bridges Rd DN8 26 D4
Double Lidget DN3 24 B2
Doubting La S36 72 B7
Douglas Rd
Doncaster DN4 82 E7
Sheffield S3 128 F7
Douglas St S60 115 E6
Douse Croft La S10 138 F6
Dovebush Way S75 32 F5
Dove Cl
Bolton u D S63 58 D2
Wombwell S73 56 F1
Dovecliffe Rd S73 55 F3
Dovecote La S65 99 C3
Dovecote Mews S71 34 C4
Dovecott Lea S20 144 B3
Dovedale S70 55 B4
Dovedale Rd
Rotherham S65 116 C5
Sheffield S7 140 D5
Dove Hill S71 15 D4
Dove La S26 144 E6
Dovercourt Rd
Rotherham S61 115 A7
Sheffield S2 129 E1
Dove Rd S73 56 F1
Dover Gdns S3 160 C4
Dover Rd S11 128 D1
Dover St S3 160 C4
Doveside Dr S73 57 A5
Dowcarr La S26 157 C5
Dower House Sq DN10 123 A6
Dowland Ave S35 94 E8
Dowland Cl S35 94 E8
Dowland Ct S35 94 D8
Dowland Gdns S35 94 E8
Down's Row S60 115 D6
Downe Cl DN14 1 C7
Downes Cres S75 33 B3
Downgate Dr S4 129 F8
Downham Rd S5 113 D3
Downing La S3 160 C5
Downing Rd S8 152 E8
Downing Sq S36 51 D2
Downings The S26 157 F5
Downland Cl DN4 83 A4
Dowsons La DN14 1 C7
Drake Cl S35 94 E5
Drake Head La DN12 81 E2
Drake House Cres S20 143 D3
Drake House La S20 143 F3
Drake House La W S20 143 F3
Drake House Ret Pk S20 143 D3
Drake House Way S20 143 E3
Drake Rd
Doncaster DN2 62 E6
Maltby S66 119 B4
Drake View S63 77 F6
Dr Anderson Ave DN7 24 F4
Dransfield Ave S36 51 D2
Dransfield Cl S10 127 F2
Dransfield Rd S10 127 F2
Draycott Wlk DN6 40 B8
Draymans Ct 3 S11 160 C1
Drive Colley S5 113 B6
Driver St S13 143 D7
Drive The
Edenthorpe DN3 43 A2
Sheffield S6 112 B2
Dronfield Inf Sch S18 153 A1
Dronfield Jun Sch S18 153 A1
Dronfield Rd S21 155 B2
Dronfield Sta S18 153 A1
Droppingwell Farm Cl
S61 96 D1
Droppingwell Rd
Rotherham S61 114 C7
Sheffield S61 114 B5
Drover Cl S35 94 E6
Droversdale Rd DN11 122 C4
Droves Dale Rd S63 58 D6
Drummond Ave DN5 61 D7
Drummond Cres S5 113 B5
Drummond Rd S5 113 B5
Drummond St
Rotherham S65 115 E7
Rotherham, St Ann's S60 115 D7
Drury Farm Ct S75 33 A1
Drury La
Dronfield S18 153 C3
Sheffield S17 151 D7
Dryden Ave S5 112 E4
Dryden Dr S5 112 E4
Dryden Rd
Barnsley S71 34 A2
Doncaster DN4 83 C6
Mexborough S64 80 C5
Rotherham S65 116 B4
Sheffield S5 112 E4
Wath u D S63 78 C7
Dryden Way S5 112 E3
Dry Hill La HD8 30 B5
Dryhurst Cl DN6 4 E3
Dublin Rd DN2 63 A4
Duchess Rd S2 161 B1
Duckham Dr S26 144 E6
Ducksett La S21 155 E2
Dudley Dr S63 58 B5
Dudley Rd
Doncaster DN2 63 B4
Sheffield S6 112 B2
Dudley St S62 97 F3
Duftons Cl DN12 81 D3
Dugdale Dr S5 112 F7
Dugdale Rd S5 112 F7
Duke's Cres DN12 82 B3
Duke Ave
Maltby S66 119 B4
Rossington DN11 84 E1
Duke Cres
Barnsley S70 54 F8
Rotherham S61 96 E1
Duke La S1 161 A2
Duke Of Norfolk La S60 116 F3
Dukeries Dr S25 146 E7
Dukes Pl S65 116 B5
Duke St
Barnsley S70 54 F8
Dinnington S25 134 F2
Doncaster DN1 62 C3
Grimethorpe S72 36 A6
Hoyland S74 76 E6
Sheffield, Park Hill S2 161 C3
Sheffield S20 155 D6
Stainforth DN7 24 E3
Swinton S64 79 D4
Dukes Terr DN10 123 A7
Dumb Hall La S80 159 B4
Dumbleton Rd S21 156 E5
Duncan Rd S10 128 B4
Duncan St S60 115 C1
Duncombe St S6 128 D5
Dundas Rd
Doncaster DN2 62 F6
Sheffield S9 114 E3
Dunedin Glen S20 155 E6
Dunedin Gr S20 155 E6
Dunella Dr S6 112 B1
Dunella Pl S6 112 A1
Dunella Rd S6 112 B1
Dunelm Cres DN8 9 D3
Dun Fields S3 160 C5
Dunford Ct S63 79 A6
Dunford Rd
Dunford Bridge HD9 48 D3
Holmfirth, Hade Edge HD9 48 B7
Holmfirth HD9 48 B8
Dungworth Gn S6 110 E1
Dunkeld Rd S11 140 B5
Dunkerley Rd S6 111 D1
Dun La S3 160 C5
Dunleary Rd DN2 63 A4
Dunlin Cl S61 95 F6
Dunlop St S9 114 B1
Dunmere Cl S71 34 A5
Dunmow Rd S4 113 E1
Dunninc Rd S5 113 D7
Dunninc Terr S5 113 D7
Dunniwood Ave DN4 84 F5
Dunniwood Reach DN4 84 F6
Dunns Dale S66 119 B5
Dunscroft Gr DN11 85 B1
Dunsil Villas WF9 18 F1
Dunsley Terr WF9 18 A2
Dun St
Sheffield S3 160 C5
Swinton S64 79 E3
Dunstan Dr DN8 26 A7
Dunstan Rd S66 118 E4
Dunsville Prim Sch DN7 44 A5
Durham Ave DN8 26 A8
Durham La
Armthorpe DN3 64 D7
Sheffield S10 160 B3
Durham Pl S65 116 B4
Durham Rd
Doncaster DN2 62 F7
Hatfield DN7 44 A8
Sheffield S10 160 B3
Durham St S66 119 B4
Durlstone Cl S12 142 A5
Durlstone Cres S12 142 A5
Durlstone Dr S12 142 A5
Durlstone Gr S12 142 A5
Durmast Gr 6 S6 127 C6
Durnan Gr S62 97 C8
Durnford Rd DN2 62 E5
Dursley Ct DN9 85 F7
Durvale Ct S17 151 E6
Dustan Wlk DN8 26 A7
Dutton Rd S6 112 D1
Duxford Ct DN4 85 A6
Dwarriden La S36 91 F3
Dyche Cl S8 153 B6
Dyche Dr S8 153 B6
Dyche La S8, S18 153 B5
Dyche Pl S8 153 B6
Dyche Rd S8 153 B6
Dycott Rd S61 114 F7
Dyer Rd S74 77 A7
Dyke Bottom HD8 28 F8
Dykes Hall Gdns 1 S6 128 B8
Dykes Hall Pl S6 112 B1
Dykes Hall Rd S6 128 B8
Dykes La S6 128 A8
Dyke Vale Ave S12 143 A4
Dyke Vale Cl S12 143 A4
Dyke Vale Pl S12 143 A4
Dyke Vale Rd S12 142 F5
Dyke Vale Way S12 143 A4
Dykewood Dr S6 111 F2
Dyscarr Cl S81 136 F3
Dyscarr Wood Nature
Reserve* S81 136 E3
Dyson Cote La S36 72 F6
Dyson Pl 5 S11 140 D8
Dyson St S70 54 D7

E

Eaden Cres S74 76 F6
Eagleton Dr S35 94 E8
Eagleton Rise S35 94 E8
Eagle View S26 144 E6
Ealand Way DN12 81 E3
Eaming View S71 34 A3
Earl Ave
Maltby S66 119 A4
Rossington DN11 84 D1
Earldom Cl S4 129 C6
Earldom Dr S4 129 C6
Earldom Rd S4 129 C7
Earldom St S4 129 C6
Earlesmere Ave DN4 83 A8
Earl Marshal Cl 4 S4 113 D1
Earl Marshal Dr 5 S4 113 D1
Earl Marshal Rd S4 113 D1
Earl Marshal View S4 129 D8
Earls Ct DN1 62 E2
Earlsmere Dr S71 56 A8
Earl St S1 161 A2
Earlston Dr DN5 62 B6
Earl Way S1 161 A2
Earnshaw Terr S75 33 E3
Earsham St S4 129 D6
East Ave
Adwick le S DN6 40 A5
Rawmarsh S62 97 F6
South Elmsall WF9 19 B4
Stainforth DN7 24 F2
Swinton S64 79 B2
Upton WF9 19 A7
Wombwell S73 56 B3
East Bank DN7 24 E5
East Bank Pl S2 141 D6
East Bank Rd S2 141 D6
East Bank Way S2 141 D6
East Bawtry Rd S60 116 C2
East Cl S36 52 A1
Eastcliffe Ct S2 141 C8
East Coast Rd S9 129 E6
East Cres
Rotherham S65 116 B7
Stocksbridge S36 73 A1
East Croft S63 58 C2
Eastcroft Cl S20 155 F8

Eastcroft Dr S20 .... 155 F8
Eastcroft Glen S20 .... 155 F8
Eastcroft View S20 .... 155 F7
Eastcroft Way 7 S20 .... 155 F8
East Dale Cl WF9 .... 17 F7
East Dene JMI Sch S65 . 116 A7
East End DN7 .... 24 F4
East End Cres S71 .... 15 E3
Eastern Ave
Dinnington S25 .... 147 A8
Sheffield S2 .... 141 E7
Eastern Cl S25 .... 147 A8
Eastern Cres S2 .... 141 D6
Eastern Dr S2 .... 141 D7
Eastern Wlk S2 .... 141 D7
Eastfield HD8 .... 28 F8
Eastfield Ave S36 .... 51 D3
Eastfield Cl S75 .... 33 D8
Eastfield Cres
Laughton en le M S25 .... 134 E5
Mapplewell S75 .... 33 D8
Eastfield Dr DN6 .... 22 B8
Eastfield La
Auckley DN9 .... 86 B6
Thurgoland S35, S75 .... 53 B2
East Field La S25 .... 135 A6
Eastfield Pl S62 .... 98 C7
Eastfield Rd
Armthorpe DN3 .... 64 C5
Sheffield S10 .... 128 C5
East Field Rd DN7 .... 25 A8
Eastfields S70 .... 55 B4
Eastgate
Barnsley S70 .... 33 E2
Hemsworth WF9 .... 17 E6
East Gate DN8 .... 9 C3
Eastgate Ct S65 .... 116 B6
East Gate Wlk DN8 .... 9 C4
East Glade Ave S12 .... 142 E3
East Glade Cl S12 .... 142 E3
East Glade Cres S12 .... 142 E4
East Glade Dell S12 .... 142 E4
East Glade Pl S12 .... 142 E3
East Glade Rd S12 .... 142 E3
East Glade Sq S12 .... 142 E3
East Glade Way S12 .... 142 E4
East Green Villas DN8 .... 9 D4
Eastgrove Rd S10 .... 160 A1
East Hill Sec Sch S2 .... 141 C8
East La DN7 .... 24 F3
East Laith Gate DN1 .... 62 D3
Eastleigh 3 S65 .... 116 A7
Eastmoor Gr S71 .... 15 C1
East Mount WF4 .... 16 B8
East Par S1 .... 161 A3
East Pinfold S71 .... 15 C2
East Rd
Oxspring S36 .... 52 A1
Rotherham S65 .... 116 B8
Sheffield S2 .... 141 B7
East Service Rd DN3 .... 42 D8
East St
Darfield S73 .... 57 A6
Dinnington S25 .... 134 F1
Doncaster DN1 .... 62 C1
Goldthorpe S63 .... 58 F6
Harworth DN11 .... 122 A5
South Elmsall WF9 .... 19 B4
South Hiendley S72 .... 16 E5
Worsbrough S70 .... 55 C4
East Terr S26 .... 144 F3
East Vale Dr S65 .... 98 F2
East View
Bawtry DN10 .... 123 A8
Cudworth S72 .... 35 B7
Hellaby S66 .... 118 B5
Hoyland S74 .... 76 F7
Norton DN6 .... 4 D1
East View Ave S21 .... 155 C2
East View Terr S6 .... 112 C1
Eastwell Gr S73 .... 56 F1
Eastwood S6 .... 112 A3
Eastwood Ave S25 .... 146 E6
Eastwood Cotts S32 .... 149 B8
Eastwood Ct
Rotherham S65 .... 116 A8
Worksop S81 .... 148 F1
Eastwood La S65 .... 115 E7
Eastwood Mount S65 .... 116 A6
Eastwood Rd S11 .... 140 D8
Eastwood Trad Est S65 .... 98 A1
Eastwood Vale S65 .... 116 A8
Eastwood View 2 S65 .... 116 B8
Eaton Pl
Hemsworth WF9 .... 17 E7
Sheffield S2 .... 129 D3
Eaton Sq DN5 .... 59 D3
Eaton Wlk WF9 .... 19 A5
Ebberton Cl WF9 .... 17 E8
Ebenezer Pl S3 .... 161 A5
Ebenezer St
Great Houghton S72 .... 36 F1
Sheffield S3 .... 161 A5
Eben St S9 .... 114 A2
Ebson House La HD9 .... 28 B6
Ecclesall CE Jun Sch
S11 .... 140 A6
Ecclesall Inf Sch S11 .... 140 A6
Ecclesall Rd S11 .... 140 B7
Ecclesall Rd S S11 .... 139 F3
Eccles Dr DN12 .... 101 B8
Ecclesfield Prim Sch S5 113 A8
Ecclesfield Rd
Chapeltown S35 .... 95 B4
Sheffield S5 .... 113 E8
Ecclesfield Sch S35 .... 95 A3
Eccles St S9 .... 114 B4
Eccleston Rd DN3 .... 43 A5
Eckington Bsns Pk S21 .. 155 F4
Eckington Hall S20 .... 155 D5
Eckington Jun Sch S21 . 155 D3
Eckington Mews S20 .... 155 D5
Eckington Rd
Dronfield S18 .... 153 D4
Sheffield S20 .... 144 A2
Eckington Sch S21 .... 155 A3
Eckington Way S20 .... 143 F3
Ecklands Long La S36 .... 71 D8
Ecton Dr DN3 .... 42 E5
Edale Rd
Rotherham S61 .... 114 F6
Sheffield S11 .... 140 A6
Edale Rise S75 .... 53 E7
Edderthorpe La S73 .... 57 A7
Eddison Park Ave S81 .... 148 E1
Eddyfield Rd S36 .... 52 A2
Eden Cl
Barnsley S75 .... 32 E5
Hellaby S66 .... 118 B5
Edencroft Dr DN3 .... 43 A3
Eden Ct S10 .... 160 A2
Eden Dr
Askern DN6 .... 22 C8
Sheffield S6 .... 127 E8
Edenfield Cl S71 .... 34 D6
Eden Field Rd DN3 .... 43 A3
Eden Glade S26 .... 144 D8
Eden Gr
Aston S26 .... 144 D8
Doncaster DN4 .... 62 A2
Eden Grove Rd DN3 .... 43 A2
Edenhall Rd S2 .... 141 F7
Edensor Rd S5 .... 113 B2
Eden Terr S64 .... 80 A6
Edenthorpe Dell S20 .... 143 C2
Edenthorpe Gr S20 .... 143 C2
Edenthorpe Hall Prim Sch
DN3 .... 43 A2
Edenthorpe Wlk S20 .... 143 C2
Edgar La DN11 .... 84 D1
Edgbaston Way DN12 .... 82 C3
Edge Bank S7 .... 140 E6
Edgebrook Rd S7 .... 140 D6
Edge Cl S6 .... 112 C6
Edgecliffe Pl S71 .... 34 A5
Edgedale Rd S7 .... 140 E5
Edgefield Rd S7 .... 140 E5
Edge Gn DN3 .... 43 A4
Edgehill Rd
Darton S75 .... 14 B2
Doncaster DN2 .... 63 C7
Sheffield S7 .... 140 D6
Edge La S6 .... 112 C6
Edgelands Rise S72 .... 35 B5
Edgemount Rd S7 .... 140 E5
Edge Well Cl S6 .... 112 C6
Edge Well Cres S6 .... 112 C6
Edge Well Dr S6 .... 112 C6
Edge Well Pl S6 .... 112 C6
Edge Well Rise S6 .... 112 C6
Edge Well Way S6 .... 112 C6
Edinburgh Ave S63 .... 58 B2
Edinburgh Cl S71 .... 34 B4
Edinburgh Dr S25 .... 146 D7
Edinburgh Rd S74 .... 76 E7
Edith Terr DN5 .... 61 E7
Edlington La DN12, DN4 .... 82 C3
Edlington Sch DN12 .... 101 B8
Edlington Victoria Prim Sch
DN12 .... 82 B3
Edmonton Cl S75 .... 33 B2
Edmund Ave
Brinsworth S60 .... 131 D7
Sheffield S17 .... 152 D6
Edmund Cl S17 .... 152 D6
Edmund Dr S17 .... 152 D6
Edmund Rd S2 .... 161 B1
Edmunds Prim Sch The
S70 .... 55 B5
Edmunds Rd S70 .... 55 C4
Edmund St 4 S70 .... 55 A4
Edna St
Bolton u D S63 .... 58 C2
South Elmsall WF9 .... 19 A3
Edward Cl S70 .... 55 C7
Edward Ct DN8 .... 9 C1
Edward Pl S11 .... 140 D6
Edward Rd
Adwick le S DN6 .... 40 D6
Adwick le S, Skellow DN6 .... 21 B2
Goldthorpe S63 .... 58 C4
Wath u D S63 .... 78 C8
Edward Sheerien Sec Sch
S71 .... 34 C7
Edward St
Armthorpe DN3 .... 63 F7
Bentley DN5 .... 41 B1
Darfield S73 .... 57 B5
Dinnington S25 .... 134 F1
Eckington S21 .... 155 D3
Great Houghton S72 .... 36 E1
Hoyland S74 .... 76 D6
Mapplewell S75 .... 33 C8
Rossington DN11 .... 84 E1
Sheffield S3 .... 160 C4
Stocksbridge S36 .... 73 B1
Swinton S64 .... 79 D4
Thurnscoe S63 .... 58 C8
Wombwell S73 .... 56 E3
Edward Street Flats S3 . 160 C4
Edwin Rd
Adwick le S DN6 .... 40 A4
Sheffield S2 .... 141 C6
Edwins Cl S71 .... 34 A7
Effingham La S4 .... 161 C4
Effingham Rd S4, S9 .... 129 D5
Effingham Sq 5 S65 .... 115 D7
Effingham St
Rotherham S65 .... 115 D7
Rotherham, St Ann's S65 .... 115 E8
Sheffield S4 .... 161 C5
Egerton Cl S3 .... 160 C2
Egerton La S3 .... 160 C2
Egerton Rd
Aston S26 .... 144 D7
Dronfield S18 .... 153 B2
Egerton St S1 .... 160 C2
Egerton Wlk S3 .... 160 C2
Eggington Cl DN4 .... 85 B7
Egg La DN11 .... 102 F7
Eglins Rd DN8 .... 9 D1
Egmanton Rd S71 .... 14 F1
Egremont Rise S66 .... 118 D6
Eilam Cl S61 .... 114 E8
Eilam Rd S61 .... 114 E8
Ekin St S9 .... 114 F3
Eland Cl DN11 .... 84 F2
Eland Rd DN12 .... 80 E3
Elcroft Gdns S20 .... 143 F2
Elder Ave
North Anston S25 .... 146 F5
Upton WF9 .... 19 C8
Elder Ct S21 .... 156 C5
Elder Dr
Rotherham S66 .... 117 C6
Upton WF9 .... 19 C8
Elder Gr
Conisbrough DN12 .... 81 A1
Finningley DN9 .... 86 A5
Eldertree Rd S61 .... 95 F3
Elder Way S72 .... 16 E6
Eldon Arc 1 S70 .... 33 F1
Eldon Ct S1 .... 160 C3
Eldon Gr DN8 .... 9 E3
Eldon Rd S65 .... 115 F8
Eldon St N S71 .... 33 F2
Eldon St
Barnsley S70 .... 33 F1
Sheffield S1 .... 160 C3
Eleanor Ct DN3 .... 42 E1
Eleanor St S9 .... 130 B6
Elgar Dr S66 .... 119 C4
Elgin St S10 .... 128 B3
Elgitha Dr S66 .... 133 E6
Elizabeth Ave
Kirk Sandall DN3 .... 43 A3
South Hiendley S72 .... 16 E5
Elizabeth Ct WF9 .... 17 F6
Elizabeth Rd S26 .... 144 D6
Elizabeth St
Goldthorpe S63 .... 58 E5
Grimethorpe S72 .... 36 A6
Elizabeth Way S60 .... 115 C6
Elland Cl S71 .... 33 E7
Ella Rd S4 .... 129 C7
Ellavale Rd S74 .... 77 A6
Ellenbro Rd S6 .... 128 B8
Ellen Tree Cl S60 .... 131 B8
Ellerker Ave DN4 .... 62 B2
Ellers Ave DN4 .... 84 D7
Ellers Cres DN4 .... 84 C8
Ellers Dr DN4 .... 84 C7
Ellershaw La DN12 .... 81 A1
Ellershaw Rd DN12 .... 81 B1
Ellers La DN9 .... 86 A7
Ellers Rd DN4 .... 84 C8
Ellerton Gdns DN4 .... 63 E1
Ellerton Rd S5 .... 113 D2
Ellesmere Gr DN7 .... 25 B4
Ellesmere Rd S4 .... 129 C6
Ellesmere Rd N S4 .... 129 C7
Ellesmere Terr 4 S65 .... 115 F6
Ellesmere Wlk S4 .... 129 C6
Ellington Ct S70 .... 54 C7
Ellin St S1 .... 161 A1
Elliot La S35 .... 94 E3
Elliot Rd S6 .... 160 A4
Elliott Ave S73 .... 56 D1
Elliott Cl S63 .... 78 C7
Elliott Ct 10 S65 .... 115 E7
Elliott Dr S61 .... 96 F2
Elliott La S35 .... 94 D4
Elliottville St S6 .... 128 C6
Ellis Ave S63 .... 78 E4
Ellis CE Prim Sch The
S73 .... 77 C8
Ellis Cres
Rossington DN11 .... 84 E1
Wath u D S73 .... 78 A7
Ellis Ct S73 .... 77 C8
Ellisons Rd S21 .... 156 F8
Ellison St
Sheffield S3 .... 160 C4
Thorne DN8 .... 26 B6
Ellis St
Brinsworth S60 .... 115 C1
Sheffield S3 .... 160 C4
Elliston Ave S75 .... 14 C1
Ellorslie Dr S36 .... 73 C1
Ellwood S71 .... 34 E4
Elmbridge Cl S71 .... 15 E3
Elm Cl
Barnby Dun DN3 .... 42 F7
Killamarsh S21 .... 156 C5
Rossington DN11 .... 104 B8
Elm Cotts S72 .... 36 E2
Elm Cres
Bentley DN5 .... 41 C2
Sheffield S20 .... 155 C8
Elm Croft DN11 .... 121 A8
Elm Ct
Mexborough S64 .... 79 E6
Worsbrough S70 .... 55 B4
Elmdale Cl S64 .... 98 D8
Elmdale Dr DN3 .... 42 F1
Elm Dr
Finningley DN9 .... 86 F3
Killamarsh S21 .... 156 C5
Elmfield Ave S5 .... 113 B4
Elmfield Rd
Doncaster DN1 .... 62 E2
Rossington DN11 .... 104 A8
Elm Gr
Rotherham S61 .... 97 B3
South Elmsall WF9 .... 18 F3
Elm Green La DN12 .... 81 C2
Elmham Rd
Doncaster DN4 .... 63 E1
Sheffield S9 .... 130 D4
Elmhirst Dr S65 .... 116 C4
Elmhirst La S75 .... 32 D1
Elmhirst Pk S75 .... 53 D8
Elmhirst Rd DN8 .... 26 C7
Elmhirst Sch The S70 .... 55 D5
Elm La S5 .... 113 B4
Elmore Rd S10 .... 128 C3
Elm Pl
Armthorpe DN3 .... 64 A7
Barnsley S71 .... 34 D5
Rawmarsh S62 .... 98 A5
Elm Rd
Adwick le S DN6 .... 21 B2
Armthorpe DN3 .... 64 A7
Eckington S21 .... 155 C2
Finningley DN9 .... 85 F3
Hemsworth WF9 .... 17 E7
Mexborough S64 .... 79 F6
Sheffield S20 .... 144 A4
Elm Rise S35 .... 94 F4
Elm Row S71 .... 34 B1
Elmsall Dr WF9 .... 19 C5
Elmsall La DN5, DN6 .... 38 C7
Elmsall Way WF9 .... 19 C5
Elmsdale S70 .... 55 B4
Elmsdale Cl WF9 .... 19 B2
Elmsham Fold WF9 .... 17 E7
Elm St S74 .... 76 B5
Elmtree Cl S81 .... 159 F7
Elm Tree Cl S25 .... 146 F5
Elm Tree Cres S18 .... 153 A3
Elm Tree Dr DN10 .... 122 F7
Elm Tree Gr DN8 .... 26 B6
Elm Tree Ho S12 .... 142 A6
Elmtree Rd S61 .... 95 F3
Elm Tree Rd S66 .... 118 D5
Elmview Rd S9 .... 114 B4
Elmville Ave S64 .... 79 C1
Elm Way S63 .... 79 A4
Elmwood Ave DN6 .... 39 F6
Elmwood Cres DN3 .... 64 A6
Elmwood Dr S20 .... 155 D6
Elsecar CE Prim Sch S74 .. 77 B5
Elsecar Industrial Heritage
Ctr* S74 .... 77 B4
Elsecar Rd S63 .... 78 A6
Elsecar Sta S74 .... 77 A5
Elsecar Steam Rly* S74 .. 77 B5
Elsham Cl S66 .... 117 D7
Elstead Cl S75 .... 32 E5
Elstree Dr S12 .... 142 B4
Elstree Rd S12 .... 142 B4
Elsworth Cl DN1 .... 62 C1
Elton La S66 .... 117 B7
Elvaston Cl S18 .... 152 B1
Elwin Ct DN4 .... 83 B4
Elwis St DN5 .... 62 B4
Elwood Rd S17 .... 152 C6
Ely Rd DN2 .... 62 F7
Ely St DN11 .... 84 E1
Embankment Rd S10 .... 128 C3
Emerson Ave DN7 .... 24 F3
Emerson Cl S5 .... 113 B5
Emerson Cres S5 .... 113 B4
Emerson Dr S5 .... 113 B4
Emily Cl S71 .... 34 D2
Emily Rd S7 .... 140 E6
Emily St WF9 .... 18 D3
Emley Dr DN5 .... 61 C7
Emley Ho 8 DN1 .... 62 C2
Emmanuel Jun Sch S20 .. 143 E1
Emmet Ho S10 .... 160 B3
Empire Dr S66 .... 118 D7
Empire Ho WF9 .... 18 F3
Empire Rd S7 .... 140 F6
Empire Terr S71 .... 15 D4
Emsley Ave S72 .... 35 C4
Endcliffe Ave S10 .... 128 C1
Endcliffe Cres S10 .... 128 B1
Endcliffe Edge S10 .... 128 B1
Endcliffe Glen Rd S11 .... 128 C1
Endcliffe Grove Ave S10 . 128 B1
Endcliffe Hall Ave S10 .... 128 B1
Endcliffe Rise Rd S11 .... 128 C1
Endcliffe Terrace Rd
S11 .... 128 C1
Endcliffe Vale Ave S11 .... 140 C8
Endcliffe Vale Rd S10 .... 128 B1
Endcliffe Way DN2 .... 63 C7
Endfield Rd S5 .... 112 F7
Endowood Rd S7 .... 140 B2
Enfield Pl S13 .... 130 F2
Engine La
Goldthorpe S63 .... 58 F4
Grimethorpe S72 .... 35 E7
Engine Lane Cl S72 .... 16 D1
Ennerdale Ave 4 S20 .... 155 E6
Ennerdale Cl
Dronfield S18 .... 152 E1
Ennerdale Cl *continued*
Mexborough S64 .... 80 C6
North Anston S25 .... 146 E7
Ennerdale Dr S20 .... 155 E6
Ennerdale Rd
Barnsley S71 .... 56 B8
Doncaster DN2 .... 63 C7
Ennis Cres DN2 .... 63 A5
Entwhistle Rd S35 .... 94 E7
Epping Gdns S20 .... 144 A2
Epping Gr S20 .... 144 A2
Epsom Cl S64 .... 80 B6
Epsom Rd DN4 .... 63 D2
Epworth Cl DN5 .... 62 B8
Epworth Rd DN7 .... 44 E7
Eric St WF9 .... 19 A3
Ernest Copley Ho S35 .... 94 F6
Ernest Fox Ho S35 .... 94 C1
Errington Ave S2 .... 141 E6
Errington Cl S2 .... 141 E6
Errington Cres S2 .... 141 E6
Errington Rd S2 .... 141 E6
Errington Way S2 .... 141 E7
Erskine Cres S2 .... 141 C7
Erskine Rd
Rotherham S65 .... 115 E8
Sheffield S2 .... 141 C7
Erskine View S2 .... 141 C7
Eshton Ct S75 .... 14 A2
Eshton Rise
Austerfield DN10 .... 105 A1
Bawtry DN10 .... 123 A8
Eshton Wlk 4 S70 .... 33 D1
Eskdale Cl
Dronfield S18 .... 152 E1
Sheffield S6 .... 112 C2
Eskdale Dr DN5 .... 61 F8
Eskdale Rd
Barnsley S71 .... 56 A8
Rotherham S61 .... 96 F3
Sheffield S6 .... 112 C2
Eskdale Wlk DN5 .... 61 C7
Eskholme La DN14 .... 7 D8
Eslaforde Terr S65 .... 116 A8
Esperanto Pl S1 .... 161 B3
Essendine Cres S8 .... 141 B3
Essex Ave DN2 .... 63 B4
Essex Cl S26 .... 145 F3
Essex Dr DN11 .... 122 D4
Essex Rd
1 Barnsley S70 .... 54 F7
Bircotes DN11 .... 122 D4
Sheffield S2 .... 129 D1
Estate Rd S62 .... 97 E7
Estfeld Cl DN11 .... 121 A8
Estone Dr S26 .... 144 D8
Etwall Way S5 .... 113 C4
Eunice La HD8 .... 29 C6
Euro Link Bsns Pk DN4 .. 62 E1
Europa Ct S9 .... 131 A6
Europa Dr S9 .... 130 D7
Europa Link S9 .... 130 E6
Euston Way S25 .... 134 C2
Evans Bsns Ctr S25 .... 134 D2
Evans St S3 .... 160 C2
Evanston Gdns DN4 .... 83 A8
Eva Ratcliffe Ho 1 S5 .. 113 A8
Eveline St S72 .... 35 B6
Evelyn Ave DN2 .... 63 B4
Evelyn Cl DN2 .... 63 B4
Evelyn Rd S10 .... 128 B3
Evelyn St S62 .... 98 B6
Evelyn Terr 2 S70 .... 55 B8
Everard Ave S17 .... 152 A5
Everard Dr S17 .... 152 A5
Everard Glade 3 S17 .... 152 A5
Everdale Mount
Hemsworth WF9 .... 17 C6
South Elmsall WF9 .... 18 E3
Everetts Cl DN11 .... 120 F7
Everill Cl S73 .... 56 F1
Everill Gate La S73 .... 57 A2
Everingham Cl S5 .... 113 A3
Everingham Cres S5 .... 113 A3
Everingham Pl S5 .... 113 A3
Everingham Rd
Doncaster DN4 .... 63 E1
Sheffield S5 .... 113 A3
Everson Cl S66 .... 118 E7
Everton Rd S11 .... 140 C8
Evesham Cl S9 .... 114 B3
Ewden Rd S73 .... 56 F1
Ewden Village S36 .... 92 C5
Ewden Way S75 .... 33 A1
Ewers Rd S61 .... 114 F7
Ewood Dr DN4 .... 84 E8
Excalibur Dr WF9 .... 19 A2
Excelsior Ct 2 DN12 .... 81 C2
Excelsior Works S35 .... 95 C1
Exchange Gateway S1 .. 161 A3
Exchange Pl S2 .... 161 B4
Exchange St
Doncaster DN1 .... 62 D1
Sheffield S2 .... 161 B4
South Elmsall WF9 .... 18 F3
Exchange Works 3 S1 .. 161 A2
Exeter Dr S3 .... 160 C1
Exeter Pl S3 .... 160 B2
Exeter Rd DN2 .... 63 A6
Exeter Way S3 .... 160 B2
Exley Ave S6 .... 128 D6
Eyam Cl S75 .... 53 E7
Eyam Rd S10 .... 128 B3
Eyncourt Rd S5 .... 113 D3
Eyre Gdns S35 .... 94 D6
Eyre La S1 .... 161 A2
Eyre St S1 .... 161 A2

F

Fabian Way S66 117 E4
Factory La DN1 62 C3
Fairbank Rd S5 113 B1
Fairbank View S60 116 C1
Fairbarn Cl S6 127 E5
Fairbarn Dr S6 127 E5
Fairbarn Pl S6 127 E5
Fairbarn Rd S6 127 E5
Fairbarn Way S6 127 E5
Fairburn Gdns S60 131 D8
Fairburn Gr S74 77 B6
Fairfax Dr S2 142 B8
Fairfax Rd
Doncaster DN2 63 B4
Sheffield S2 142 B8
Fairfax Rise S2 142 B8
Fairfax Way DN11 120 F7
Fairfield
Bolton u D S63 58 B2
Chapeltown S35 95 B5
Rawcliffe Bridge DN14 2 D7
Fair Field S70 54 F1
Fairfield Cl
Doncaster DN4 84 D6
Rotherham S66 117 C7
Fairfield Cotts S71 15 F1
Fairfield Ct
Armthorpe DN3 64 B5
Darfield S73 56 F4
Fairfield Hts 3 S10 128 B2
Fairfield Lo S10 160 B2
Fairfield Rd
Bentley DN5 61 F6
Sheffield S6 128 E6
Fairfields HD8 29 F3
Fairford Cl DN4 85 A6
Fairholme Hts S35 111 E7
Fair Holme View DN3 64 D4
Fair House La S6 110 A4
Fairhurst La S35 92 D4
Fairleigh S2 142 A8
Fairleigh Dr S60 115 E4
Fairmount Gdns 4 S12 143 A3
Fairthorn Rd S5 113 D4
Fairtree Wlk DN8 26 B7
Fair View Ave DN6 39 F5
Fairview Cl S74 76 C5
Fairview Ct DN3 42 F6
Fair View Dr S26 144 E7
Fairview Rd S18 153 A3
Fairview Terr DN3 42 F6
Fairview Villas DN3 42 F6
Fairway S75 54 A6
Fairway Ave S75 14 C2
Fairways S66 117 B4
Fairway The
Sheffield S10 127 A1
Thorne DN8 9 D4
Fairwinds Cl S18 153 A1
Faith St
Barnsley S71 34 F6
South Kirkby WF9 18 D4
Falcon Cl DN6 40 B6
Falcon Ct DN11 85 A1
Falcon Dr
Barnsley S70 75 F8
Treeton S60 131 F3
Falconer Cl S75 13 D1
Falconer La S13 131 F1
Falconer Way S60 131 F4
Falcon Knowl Ing S75 13 D1
Falcon Rd S18 153 C3
Falcon Rise S18 153 D3
Falcon St S70 33 E2
Falcon Way S25 146 E8
Falding St
Chapeltown S35 95 B5
Rotherham S60 115 C6
Falkland Rd S11 140 A6
Fall Bank Cres S75 53 D7
Fall Bank Ind Est S75 53 D8
Falledge La HD8 29 E2
Fall Head La S75 32 B1
Fallon Rd S6 127 D6
Fall View S75 53 A8
Falmouth Cl S71 34 B3
Falmouth Rd S7 140 E5
Falstaff Cres S5 112 F4
Falstaff Rd S5 112 F5
Falthwaite Green La S75 53 D3
Fane Cres S26 144 D8
Fanny Ave S21 156 E5
Fanshaw Ave S21 155 C2
Fanshaw Bank S18 153 A1
Fanshaw Cl S21 155 C2
Fanshaw Dr S21 155 C2
Fanshawe Gate La S17, S18 151 E1
Fanshaw Rd
Dronfield S18 153 B2
Eckington S21 155 C2
Fanshaw Way S21 155 C2
Faraday Rd S9 129 E6
Faranden Rd 5 S9 130 A5
Far Bank La DN7 24 F7
Far Clay Gr S81 159 F7
Farcliff DN5 61 B1
Far Common Rd DN7 45 B7
Far Cres S65 116 B7
Far Croft S63 58 C2
Farcroft Gr 1 S4 113 F1
Far Dalton La S65 116 F8
Fardell Gdns S66 117 D4
Far Field Cl DN3 43 A3
Far Field La
Barnsley S71 34 E6
Wath u D S63 79 B6
Farfield Pk S63 79 B7
Far Field Rd
Kirk Sandall DN3 43 A3
Rotherham S65 116 C5
Fargate S1 161 A3
Far Golden Smithies S64 79 C4
Farish Pl 5 S2 141 B6
Far La
Holmfirth HD9 48 E8
Rotherham S65 116 B7
Sheffield S6 112 B1
Far Lawns S71 15 D1
Farlawns Ct DN4 83 B4
Farlow Croft S35 94 C8
Farm Bank Rd S2 161 C2
Farm Cl
Barnsley S71 34 C4
Brinsworth S60 131 B7
Dronfield S18 153 B4
Edenthorpe DN3 43 A1
Sheffield S12 142 A2
Farm Cres S20 155 C6
Farm Ct DN6 40 C6
Farm Dr S62 98 B6
Farm Fields Cl S20 143 D1
Farm Grange DN4 83 B4
Farmhill Cl DN5 61 E5
Farm House La S75 33 A2
Far Moor Cl DN5 59 C2
Farmoor Gdns S20 144 B2
Farm Rd
Barnsley S70 55 C6
Sheffield S2 161 B1
Farmstead Cl S14 141 D5
Farm View Cl
Rotherham S61 114 D8
Sheffield S12 143 B3
Farm View Dr S12 143 B3
Farm View Gdns S12 143 B3
Farm View Rd S61 114 D8
Farm Way S73 57 A6
Farm Wlk S20 155 C7
Farnaby Dr S35 94 D8
Farnaby Gdns S35 94 D8
Farnborough Dr DN4 85 A6
Farndale Rd
Bentley DN5 61 D7
Sheffield S6 112 C2
Farnham Way S25 134 C3
Farnley Ave S6 112 D4
Farnley Rd DN4 83 C5
Farnsworth Rd S65 116 C7
Far Pl S65 116 B7
Farquhar Rd S66 119 B5
Farrar Rd 2 S7 140 F7
Farrar St S70 33 D1
Farrier Gate S35 94 E6
Farriers Ct DN8 26 B7
Farringdon Dr DN11 104 A7
Farrington Ct S66 117 C4
Farrow Cl S75 54 A7
Farthing Gale Mews DN5 61 F5
Far Townend S75 54 A7
Far View Rd S5 113 B4
Farview Terr S70 54 E7
Farwater La S18 152 F1
Far Well La HD9 28 B8
Fathers Gdns S26 145 D2
Favell Rd
Rotherham S65 116 D7
Sheffield S3 160 B3
Fawcett St S3 160 B4
Fearnehough St 1 S9 130 A5
Fearn House Cres S74 76 C5
Fearnley Rd S74 76 C5
Fearn's Bldgs S36 51 C3
Fearnville Gr S71 15 C3
Featherbed La S80 159 F2
Felkirk Dr WF4 16 A8
Felkirk View S72 16 B3
Fellbrigg Rd S2 141 D7
Fellowsfield Way S61 114 E8
Fellows Wlk S73 56 B4
Fell Rd S9 130 A7
Fell St S9 129 F8
Fellview Cl S32 149 A7
Fen Ct 1 DN3 43 A2
Fenland Rd DN8 26 C6
Fenney La S11 139 E2
Fenn Rd S75 75 F5
Fensome Way S73 57 A6
Fenton Cl
Armthorpe DN3 64 B5
South Kirkby WF9 18 B1
Fenton Croft S61 115 A8
Fenton Fields S61 115 A8
Fenton Rd S61 97 A2
Fenton St
4 Barnsley S70 33 E1
Eckington S21 155 B2
Rotherham S61 114 F7
Fentonville St S11 140 E8
Fenton Way S61 97 B2
Fenwick Common La
Fenwick DN6 6 A4
Moss DN6 5 F2
Fenwick La DN6 5 E2
Feoffees Rd S35 113 B8
Ferguson St S9 129 F6
Ferham Cl S61 115 A6
Ferham Park Ave S61 115 A6
Ferham Prim Sch S61 115 B6
Ferham Rd S61 115 A6
Fern Ave
Bentley DN5 62 A7
Fern Ave *continued*
Sheffield S20 143 F4
Fern Bank DN6 40 B6
Fernbank Cl DN9 86 F6
Fernbank Dr
Armthorpe DN3 64 B8
Eckington S21 155 B3
Fernbank Sch DN6 40 C6
Fern Cl
Darfield S73 57 A5
Doncaster DN2 63 C6
Eckington S21 155 B3
Ferncroft Ave S20 155 C7
Ferndale Cl S18 153 D3
Ferndale Dr
Rotherham S66 117 C6
Thorne DN8 9 C2
Ferndale Pl WF9 17 D6
Ferndale Rd
Conisbrough DN12 81 B2
Dronfield S18 153 D3
Ferndale Rise S18 153 D3
Ferndale View DN5 61 F5
Fernhall Cl DN3 43 A3
Fernhall Croft S73 56 E3
Fern Hollow S66 117 C3
Fernhurst Rd DN2 63 C6
Fernlea Cl DN5 61 F5
Fernlea Gr S35 113 B8
Fern Lea Gr S63 58 B2
Fernleigh Dr S60 115 B2
Fern Rd S6 128 B6
Fern Royd S32 149 A7
Fernvale Wlk S62 98 D8
Fern Way S21 155 B3
Ferrand St S70 75 F7
Ferrara Cl S73 56 E6
Ferrars Cl S9 114 F2
Ferrars Dr S9 114 F1
Ferrars Rd S9 114 F2
Ferrars Way S9 114 F1
Ferrers Rd DN2 62 F5
Ferriby Rd S6 112 B2
Ferry Boat La S64 80 C3
Ferry La DN12 81 C3
Ferry Moor La S72 35 D6
Ferrymoor Way S72 35 E6
Ferrymore Ho 14 DN1 62 C2
Ferry Rd DN7 8 E2
Ferry Terr 4 DN12 81 C3
Ferry Villas 5 DN12 81 C3
Fersfield St S4 129 D5
Festival Ave DN11 122 A4
Festival Cl S26 145 C2
Festival Rd S63 78 F5
Fewston Way DN4 84 B8
Fiddler's Dr DN3 64 C4
Field Cl
Darfield S73 57 A6
Dronfield S18 152 C2
Field Cres 2 WF9 18 F2
Field Dr S72 35 C5
Fielder Mews S5 113 E4
Fielders Way DN12 82 C3
Field Gate DN11 85 A2
Fieldhead Ct S74 76 E6
Field Head Manor S75 53 C8
Fieldhead Rd
Hoyland S74 76 E5
Sheffield S8 141 A7
Field House Rd DN5 82 B8
Fieldhouse Way S4 129 D7
Fielding Dr S66 117 D5
Fielding Gr S62 97 F7
Fielding Rd S6 112 C2
Field La
Barnsley S70 55 E7
Killamarsh S21 156 B5
Penistone S36 50 D1
Rotherham S66 133 A7
South Elmsall WF9 19 C4
Upper Whiston S60, S66 132 F7
Upton WF9 19 A8
Wroot DN9 67 B1
Field Rd
Stainforth DN7 24 E4
Thorne DN8 26 B8
Fields End S36 73 B8
Fields End Bsns Pk S63 58 D6
Fieldsend Ct WF9 19 A7
Fieldsend Gdns S35 113 B8
Fieldside DN3 42 F1
Field Side DN8 26 A8
Fieldside Ct S65 99 D1
Field Station Rd DN6 42 A8
Field View
Brinsworth S60 131 C8
New Edlington DN12 82 A1
Field Way
Rotherham S60 115 D8
Shepley HD8 28 E8
Fife Cl S9 114 A4
Fife Gdns S9 114 A4
Fife St
Barnsley S70 54 D8
Sheffield S9 114 A4
Fife Way S9 114 A4
Fifth Ave
Adwick le S DN6 40 C3
Finningley DN9 86 B3
Fifth Sq DN7 24 E4
Fiftyeights Rd DN9 87 C2
Fig Tree La 2 S1 161 A4
Filby Rd DN5 61 E5
Filey Ave S71 15 D4
Filey La S3 160 B2
Filey St S10 160 B2
Filter Cotts S6 126 F2
Finch Cl S65 99 A2
Finch Gdns S66 117 E4
Finch Rd DN4 82 F6
Finch Rise S26 144 E6
Finchwell Cl S13 130 F2
Finchwell Cres S13 130 F2
Finchwell Rd S13 130 F2
Findon Cres S6 128 A8
Findon Pl S6 128 A8
Findon Rd S6 128 A8
Findon St S6 128 B8
Finghall Rd DN6 20 F2
Finkle Cl WF4 13 F7
Finkle Ct DN8 26 B7
Finkle St
Bentley DN5 62 B8
Stainforth DN7 24 E5
Thorne DN8 26 B7
Woolley WF4 13 F7
Finkle Street La S35 74 C3
Finlay Rd S65 116 A8
Finlay St S3 160 B4
Finningley CE Prim Sch DN9 86 F3
Finningley Lodge S26 145 D2
Finnley's La DN14 1 A7
Finsbury Cl S25 134 C3
Firbeck Ave S25 134 E4
Firbeck Cres S81 136 F3
Firbeck Ho 5 DN1 62 C2
Firbeck La
Laughton en le M S25 134 E5
Whitwell S80 159 A1
Firbeck Rd DN4 62 F2
Firbeck Way DN11 85 B1
Fir Cl S63 79 A5
Fircroft Ave S5 113 D5
Fircroft Rd S5 113 E6
Firebeck Rd S8 140 E3
Firethorn Rise S65 117 E8
Firham Cl S71 15 A4
Fir Pl S21 156 C5
Fir Rd S21 155 C2
Firsby La DN12 99 E6
Firshill Ave S4 129 B8
Firshill Cl S4 129 B8
Firs Hill Com Prim Sch S3 129 B8
Firshill Cres S4 129 A8
Firshill Croft S4 129 A8
Firshill Gdns S4 129 A8
Firshill Glade S4 129 A8
Firshill Mews S4 129 B8
Firshill Rd S4 129 B8
Firshill Rise S4 129 B8
Firshill Way S4 129 A8
Firshill Wlk S4 129 A8
Firs La S36 51 D7
Fir St S6 128 C5
First Ave
Adwick le S DN6 40 C4
Finningley DN9 86 B3
Rotherham S65 116 A7
Royston S71 15 D4
South Kirkby WF9 17 F1
Upton WF9 19 A7
Firs The
Barnsley S70 55 C6
Royston S71 15 A4
First La
Rotherham S66 117 C3
South Anston S25 146 E2
First Sq DN7 24 E4
Firth Ave S72 35 A6
Firth Cres
Maltby S66 119 A4
Rossington DN11 84 E1
Firth Dr S4 129 D6
Firth Field Rd DN7 44 E8
Firth La DN9 67 A3
Firth Park Ave S5 113 E3
Firth Park Com Arts Coll S5 113 D5
Firth Park Cres S5 113 D3
Firth Park Rd S5 113 E2
Firth Rd S63 78 C6
Firth's Homes S11 139 F8
Firth St
4 Barnsley S71 33 F2
Doncaster DN4 62 B1
Rotherham S61 97 C3
Shepley HD8 28 E8
Firthwood Ave S18 153 D3
Firthwood Cl S18 153 D3
Firthwood Rd S18 153 D3
Fir Tree S35 74 A7
Fir Tree Ave DN9 86 A4
Fir Tree Cl DN5 59 C7
Fir Tree Dr
Norton DN6 4 C3
Wales S26 145 A2
Firtree Rise S35 95 A4
Firvale S26 157 E5
Fir Vale Pl S5 113 C1
Fir Vale Rd S5 113 C1
Fir Vale Sch S4 113 D1
Fir View Gdns S4 129 D8
Fir Wlk S66 118 C5
Fish Dam La
Barnsley S71 34 D7
Royston S71 34 D7
Fisher Cl S60 115 C7
Fisher La S9 130 C5
Fisher Rd S66 119 B5
Fisher St DN5 41 B2
Fisher Terr DN5 62 A5
Fishlake Nab DN7 24 E6
Fish Pond La S66 119 B8
Fishponds Rd S13 142 C7
Fishponds Rd W S13 142 C7
Fitzalan Rd S13 130 F1
Fitzalan Sq S1 161 B3
Fitzgerald Rd S10 128 B4
Fitzhubert Rd
Sheffield S2 142 A7
Sheffield S2 142 A8
Fitzmaurice Rd S9 130 B6
Fitzroy Rd S2 141 B6
Fitzwalter Rd S2 129 D2
Fitzwilliam Ave
Conisbrough DN12 81 A2
Wath u D S63 78 E5
Fitzwilliam Ct
Rawmarsh S62 97 F4
Sheffield S11 140 B5
Wath u D S63 78 E6
Fitzwilliam Dr DN5 59 C1
Fitzwilliam Gate S1 161 A2
Fitzwilliam Lodge
Hoyland S74 77 A4
Swinton S64 79 C3
Fitzwilliam Prim Sch S64 79 B2
Fitzwilliam Rd
Darfield S73 57 D6
Rotherham S65 116 A8
Fitzwilliam Sq S61 97 B4
Fitzwilliam St
Barnsley S70 33 E1
Hoyland, Elsecar S74 77 A5
Hoyland, Hemingfield S73 77 B7
Hoyland S74 76 B5
Rawmarsh S62 97 F3
Sheffield S1 160 C2
Swinton S64 79 D2
Wath u D S63 78 E6
Five Acres S75 31 F5
Five Lane Ends DN6 20 E1
Five Oaks DN5 41 E3
Five Trees Ave S17 152 A6
Five Trees Cl S17 152 A6
Five Trees Dr S17 152 A6
Five Weirs Wlk S9 129 F6
Flanders Ct S61 95 F5
Flanderwell Ave S66 117 D5
Flanderwell Ct S66 117 C6
Flanderwell Gdns S66 117 C6
Flanderwell La S66 117 C6
Flanderwell Prim Sch S66 117 B6
Flash La
Rotherham S66 117 E4
Sheffield S6 126 E4
Flashley Carr La DN6 6 F2
Flask View S6 127 C7
Flat La
Firbeck S81 136 A6
Firbeck, Stone S66 135 E8
Great Houghton S72 57 F5
Rotherham S60 116 B1
Flat St S1 161 B3
Flats The
Wombwell S73 56 C2
Wortley S35 74 E3
Flatts Cl S60 131 E5
Flatts La
Treeton S60 131 E5
Wath u D S63 78 D6
Flavell Cl WF9 18 B1
Flaxby Rd S9 130 B5
Flax Lea S70 55 A5
Fleet Cl S63 78 B7
Fleet Hill Cres S71 34 A5
Fleet La DN7 24 E5
Fleets Cl DN7 24 E5
Fleet St S9 129 F7
Fleetwood Ave S71 34 C5
Fleming Gdns S66 117 B6
Fleming Pl 5 S70 54 E8
Fleming Sq S63 78 E6
Fleming Way S66 117 B6
Fletcher Ave S18 153 A1
Fletcher Ho 2 S65 115 E7
Fleury Cl S14 141 E4
Fleury Cres S14 141 E4
Fleury Pl S14 141 E4
Fleury Rd S14 141 E4
Fleury Rise S14 141 E4
Flight Hill HD9 48 C5
Flint La HD9 49 A5
Flint Rd DN2 63 C6
Flintway S63 78 F3
Flockton Ave S13 143 C8
Flockton Cres S13 143 C8
Flockton Ct S1 160 C3
Flockton Dr S13 143 C8
Flockton Ho S1 160 C3
Flockton Rd S13 143 C8
Flodden St 1 S10 128 B4
Floodgate Dr S35 113 B8
Flora St S6 128 E6
Florence Ave
Aston S26 144 D7
Doncaster DN4 83 A8
Florence Rd S8 140 E2
Florence Rise S73 56 F5
Flour Mills Mus* S70 54 F3
Flower St S63 58 F5
Flowitt St
Doncaster DN4 62 B2
Mexborough S64 79 F5
Folderings La S36 92 C6
Folder La DN5 61 A1
Folds Cres S8 140 D1

Folds Dr S8 140 C1
Folds La
Sheffield S8 140 C1
Tickhill DN11 120 D3
Fold The S65 116 D8
Foley Ave S73 56 C2
Foley St S4 129 D5
Foljambe Cres DN11 84 E1
Foljambe Dr S65 98 E1
Foljambe Rd S65 116 B8
Foljambe St S62 97 F4
Folkwood Gr S11 139 E5
Follett Rd S5 113 C5
Folly La S36 50 F5
Fonteyn Ho DN2 62 F6
Fontwell Dr S64 80 B6
Footgate Cl S35 111 D6
Forbes Rd S6 128 C8
Ford Cl S18 152 F1
Ford La
Eckington S12, S21 154 E5
Stocksbridge S36 73 C2
Fordoles Head La
Braithwell S66 100 C1
Maltby S66 118 C7
Ford Rd
Eckington S21 154 E4
Sheffield S11 140 B6
Fordstead La DN3 42 D7
Fore's Rd DN3 64 C5
Fore Hill Ave DN4 84 D6
Foremark Rd S5 113 D4
Forest Cl S35 111 F4
Forest Edge S7 140 A1
Forest Grange DN4 63 E1
Forest Rd S71 33 F8
Forest Rise DN4 82 F5
Forge Hill S35 111 D7
Forge La
Hoyland S74 77 B4
Killamarsh S21 156 B7
Oughtibridge S35 111 D8
Rotherham S60 115 D6
Sheffield S1 161 A1
Wortley S35 74 A3
Forge Rd S26 145 C3
Forge Student Village 7
S2 128 F1
Forge The
Barnsley S71 34 A5
Dronfield S18 153 A1
Formby Ct S71 34 D6
Forncett St S4 129 D6
Fornham St S2 161 B2
Forres Ave S10 128 A3
Forres Rd S10 128 B3
Forrester's Cl DN6 4 C3
Forrester's La S18 153 C4
Forrester Cl S66 117 B6
Forster Rd DN4 83 B6
Forth Ave S18 152 D2
Fort Hill Rd S9 114 A3
Fortway Rd S60 115 C2
Forum The 14 S1 160 C3
Fossard Cl DN2 63 A7
Fossard Way DN5 40 F1
Fossdale Rd S7 140 D5
Foster's Cl S64 79 C3
Foster 7 S3 161 B5
Foster Place La HD9 28 A2
Foster Rd
Rotherham S66 117 B5
Thorne DN8 26 A8
Foster St S70 55 D8
Fosters The S35 94 D7
Foster Way S35 94 D7
Fothergill Dr DN3 43 B3
Foulstone Sch The S73 57 B5
Foundry Ct S3 129 B7
Foundry La DN8 26 A7
Foundry Rd DN4 62 B1
Foundry St
2 Barnsley S70 54 E8
Hoyland S74 77 A5
Rawmarsh S62 97 F3
Fountain Cl S75 13 E1
Fountain Ct
Barnsley S71 14 E1
Rossington DN11 104 B8
Fountain Par S75 14 C1
Fountain Prec S1 161 A3
Fountains Cl 4 DN3 42 E4
Fountain Sq S75 13 E1
Fountains Way S71 34 D3
Fountside S7 140 D6
Four Lands Cl S75 32 E5
Four Lane End S36 52 D2
Four Lane Ends
Maltby S81 136 B7
Wadworth DN11 103 A4
Wortley S35 74 D3
Fourth Ave
Adwick le S DN6 40 C3
Finningley DN9 86 B3
Fourth Sq DN7 24 E4
Four Wells Dr S12 143 B4
Fowler Bridge Rd DN5 62 C7
Fowler Cres DN11 84 E1
Fox Cl S61 96 D2
Foxcote Lea S65 99 A2
Fox Covert Cl S63 58 C4
Fox Covert Rd or Whin
Covert La WF8 3 E2
Fox Croft S74 76 D5
Foxcroft Chase S21 156 C6
Foxcroft Dr S21 156 C5
Foxcroft Gr S21 156 C6
Foxcroft Mdws S66 119 A4
Fox Ct S64 79 D1
Foxdale Ave S12 142 B5
Foxen Croft S71 34 E4
Fox Farm Ct S63 77 F7
Fox Fields S36 52 A1
Foxfield Wlk S70 55 D6
Fox Glen Rd S36 92 D8
Foxglove Cl DN9 86 F6
Foxglove Rd S5 113 E4
Fox Gr DN4 82 C6
Foxhall La S10 139 A6
Fox Hill S3 129 A6
Fox Hill Ave S6 112 C5
Fox Hill Cl S6 112 C5
Fox Hill Cres S6 112 C5
Fox Hill Dr S6 112 C5
Fox Hill Pl S6 112 C6
Fox Hill Prim Sch S6 112 D6
Foxhill Rd DN8 26 C6
Fox Hill Rd S6 112 C5
Fox Hill Way S6 112 C6
Fox Hole La DN11 102 D1
Fox Holes Gr S36 49 D5
Foxhunters Way WF9 18 F1
Fox La
Barnburgh DN5 59 D3
Sheffield, Base Green S12 142 C3
Sheffield, Lower Bradway
S17 152 D6
Foxland Ave S64 79 A3
Fox Lane Ct S12 142 C4
Fox Lane View S12 142 C4
Fox Rd S6 128 E6
Fox Royd HD8 28 E8
Foxroyd Cl S71 55 F8
Fox St
Rotherham S61 114 E6
Sheffield S3 129 B6
Fox Wlk S6 128 D6
Foxwood Ave S12 142 B6
Foxwood Cl S81 148 D1
Foxwood Dr S12 142 B6
Foxwood Gr S12 142 B5
Foxwood Rd S12 142 B6
Framlingham Pl S2 141 D7
Framlingham Rd S2 141 D7
France Rd S6 111 D1
Frances St
Doncaster DN1 62 D3
Rotherham S60 115 E5
France St S62 97 F3
Francis Cres N S60 116 D3
Francis Cres S S60 116 D3
Francis Dr S60 116 D4
Francis Gr S35 94 D7
Francus Royd S71 15 C1
Frank Hillock Field S36 73 E1
Franklin Cres DN2 62 F3
Franklyn Ho DN5 61 E6
Frank Pl S9 130 A7
Frank Rd DN5 62 B6
Fraser Cl S8 140 E3
Fraser Cres S8 140 F3
Fraser Dr S8 140 F3
Fraser Rd
Rotherham S60 115 F5
Sheffield S8 140 E3
Fraser Wlk S8 140 F2
Frederick Ave S70 54 D8
Frederick Dr S35 94 B1
Frederick Rd 10 S7 140 F7
Frederick St
Catliffe S60 131 C5
Goldthorpe S63 58 E5
Mexborough S64 79 F5
Rotherham S60 115 D7
Sheffield S9 130 B4
Wath u D S63 78 D7
Wombwell S73 56 C3
Frederic Pl 8 S70 54 F7
Fred Mulley Rd S4 129 D6
Freedom Ct S6 128 D7
Freedom Rd S6 128 C6
Freeman Gdns S35 94 D6
Freeman Rd S66 117 B5
Freeman St S70 54 F8
Freemans Yd S70 33 F1
Freesia Cl S25 146 C4
Freeston Pl S9 130 A7
French Gate DN1 62 C3
Frenchgate Ctr DN1 62 C3
French St
Adwick le S DN6 21 A1
Bentley DN5 41 B2
Fretson Cl S2 142 A8
Fretson Gn S2 142 A8
Fretson Rd S2 142 A8
Fretson Rd S S2 142 A8
Fretwell Cl S66 118 E6
Fretwell Rd
Hellaby S66 118 B5
Rotherham S65 116 C8
Friar's Rd S71 34 F3
Friar Cl S6 127 D6
Friars Croft S62 77 B1
Friars Gate DN1 62 C4
Frickley Bridge La S72 16 F4
Frickley La DN5, DN6, WF9 38 A8
Frickley Rd S11 139 F8
Frithbeck Cl DN3 64 B6
Frith Cl S12 142 B5
Frith Rd S12 142 B5
Frithwood Dr S18 153 C2
Frobisher Gr S66 118 E6
Froggatt La S1 161 A2
Frogmore Cl S66 117 D6
Frontier Works DN8 9 C1
Front St S60 131 E4
Frostings Cl S35 94 C1
Frostings The S35 94 C1
Fulford Cl
Darton S75 14 A1
Sheffield S9 130 C5
Fulford Pl S9 130 C5
Fulford Way DN12 81 E3
Fullerton Ave DN12 81 A2
Fullerton Cl DN6 20 F2
Fullerton Cres S65 98 E3
Fullerton Dr S60 131 B8
Fullerton House Sch
DN12 80 F3
Fullerton Rd S60 115 C4
Fullshaw Cross S36 71 C8
Fullshaw La S36 71 B7
Fulmar Way S61 96 A6
Fulmer Cl S71 34 B6
Fulmere Cres S5 112 E6
Fulmere Rd S5 112 E6
Fulmer Rd S11 140 C7
Fulney Rd S11 139 F8
Fulstone HD9 28 B7
Fulstone Hall La HD9 28 A7
Fulstone Rd HD4 28 B8
Fulton Rd S6 128 D5
Fulwood Chase S10 139 E8
Fulwood Dr DN4 83 B4
Fulwood Head Rd S10 138 D7
Fulwood La S10, S11 138 E5
Fulwood Rd S10 128 B2
Furlong Ct S63 58 D3
Furlong Mdws S63 77 F6
Furlong Rd
Barnburgh DN5 59 B1
Bolton u D S63 58 D3
Furlong View DN5 59 B2
Furnace Cotts S36 49 D6
Furnace Hill S3 161 A4
Furnace La S13 143 E7
Furness Cl
Dinnington S25 146 F7
Sheffield S6 127 D7
Furness Dene S71 34 D5
Furness Rd S35 94 C7
Furniss Ave S17 151 D6
Furniss Mews S17 151 E6
Furnival Cl S26 145 E5
Furnival Gate S1 161 A2
Furnivall Rd DN4 83 A7
Furnival Rd
Sheffield S4 161 C4
Todwick S26 145 E5
Furnival Sq S1 161 A2
Furnival St S1 161 A2
Furnival Way S60 116 D1
Fylde Cl S71 34 D6

G

Gables The S10 127 F1
Gadding Moor Rd S75 30 F1
Gainford Rd DN8 9 D4
Gainford Sq DN8 9 D4
Gainsborough Cl S66 117 B5
Gainsborough Rd
Bawtry DN10 123 A6
Dronfield S18 152 E1
Sheffield S11 140 D7
Gainsborough Way S71 34 B4
Gainsford Rd S9 130 C4
Gaitskell Cl
Goldthorpe S63 58 D3
Maltby S66 119 B4
Gala Cres S66 118 D6
Galahad Way WF9 19 A2
Gallery The S3 161 B4
Galley Dr S20 143 D1
Gallon Croft WF9 18 E3
Gallows La WF4 13 F8
Gallow Tree Rd S65 116 D4
Galpharm Way S75 53 E8
Galsworthy Ave S5 112 F3
Galsworthy Cl DN4 82 F5
Galsworthy Rd S5 112 F3
Galway Ave DN11 122 D5
Galway Cl
Rawmarsh S62 98 A6
Royston S71 15 C4
Galway Dr DN11 122 D5
Galway Mews DN11 122 A3
Galway Rd DN11 122 D5
Game La S6 126 D6
Gamston Rd 5 S8 140 F7
Gannow Cl S21 156 F7
Gant Ct DN11 121 A8
Ganton Pl S71 33 E7
Ganton Rd S6 112 B2
Garbroads Cres S65 98 E2
Garbutt St S63 58 D1
Garden Cl S60 116 A2
Garden Cres S60 116 A2
Garden Ct S70 33 B1
Garden Dr S73 78 A8
Garden Gr S73 77 C8
Garden House Cl S71 34 C5
Garden House Dr S26 145 F3
Gardenia Rd DN3 42 E3
Garden La
Cadeby DN5 81 D5
Ravenfield S65 99 D3
3 Rotherham S60 115 C7
Garden Rd DN8 9 D4
Gardens La DN12 81 B2
Garden St
16 Barnsley S70 54 F8
Darfield S73 57 A5
Goldthorpe S63 58 F5
Mexborough S64 80 A4
Rotherham S61 115 B7
Sheffield S1 160 C4
Thurnscoe S63 58 D8
Wath u D S63 78 D7
Gardens The
Doncaster DN4 84 E7
Sheffield S11 140 E8
Garden Terr
Bentley DN5 62 B8
Denby Dale HD8 29 F5
Garden Wlk
Rotherham S60 116 A2
Sheffield S20 144 A3
Gardom Cl S18 152 D1
Garfield Mount S65 115 F5
Gargrave Cl DN6 22 C8
Gargrave Cres WF9 17 C6
Gargrave Pl WF9 17 C6
Garland Cl S20 155 E7
Garland Croft S20 155 E7
Garland Dr S6 111 E1
Garland Mount 15 S20 155 E8
Garland Way S20 155 E7
Garraby Cl S72 36 E2
Garry Rd S6 112 B1
Garside Bldgs S36 51 C3
Garter St S4 129 D7
Garth Cl 3 S9 130 A5
Garth Way S18 152 F1
Garth Way Cl S18 152 F1
Gartrice Gdns S20 156 A5
Gartrice Gr S20 156 A5
Gashouse La
Eckington S20, S21 155 D5
Sheffield S20, S21 155 D5
Gate Cres S75 53 F8
Gatefield Rd S7 140 E6
Gate Foot La HD8, HD9 28 C5
Gateford Rd S81 148 A1
Gate Head La HD9 49 A8
Gatehouse Ct S75 53 F8
Gate House La DN9 86 B5
Gatesbridge Pk DN9 86 F4
Gateway Cl S62 97 E2
Gateway Ct S62 97 E2
Gateway The S62 97 E2
Gatewood La DN7 44 D4
Gate Wood La DN3 64 E2
Gateworth Gr DN6 22 B8
Gattison La DN11 103 F8
Gatty Rd S5 113 D7
Gaunt Cl
Killamarsh S21 156 C6
Rotherham S66 117 E6
Sheffield S14 141 D3
Gaunt Dr
Rotherham S66 117 D6
Sheffield S14 141 D3
Gaunt Pl S14 141 D4
Gaunt Rd
Rotherham S66 117 D6
Sheffield S14 141 D3
Gaunt Way S14 141 D3
Gawber Prim Sch S75 33 A3
Gawber Rd S75 33 C3
Gawtress Row S63 78 E6
Gayle Ct 6 S70 33 D2
Gayton Cl DN4 83 A5
Gayton Ct DN4 83 A5
Gayton Rd S4 129 C8
Geer La S12 154 D5
Geeseness La DN7 8 B3
Gell St S3 160 B3
Geneva Sq DN8 9 D3
Genn La S70 54 E5
Genoa Cl S73 56 E6
Genoa St S64 80 B5
George Buckley Ct WF9 18 A2
George La WF4 14 E6
George Pl
Mexborough S64 80 C5
Rawmarsh S62 98 A5
George Sq S70 33 E1
George St
Adwick le S DN6 21 B1
Armthorpe DN3 63 F7
Barnsley S70 33 E1
Bentley DN5 41 B2
Cudworth S72 35 C8
Darfield S73 56 F4
Darton S75 14 B1
Goldthorpe S63 58 C5
Great Houghton S72 57 D7
Hoyland S74 76 E5
2 Rotherham S60 115 D7
Sheffield S1 161 B3
South Hiendley S72 16 D6
Thurnscoe S63 58 F8
Wombwell S73 56 D2
Worsbrough S70 55 A4
Worsbrough, Worsbrough Dale
S70 55 C4
George Woodfindin
Almshouses 4 S11 140 C8
George Yd S70 33 E1
Georgian Mews S60 131 C6
Gerald Cl S70 55 C7
Gerald Cres S70 55 D8
Gerald Pl S70 55 C7
Gerald Rd S70 55 C7
Gerald St S9 130 A7
Gerald Wlk S70 55 C7
Gerard Ave S65 99 A2
Gerard Cl 15 S8 141 B6
Gerard Rd S60 115 E5
Gerard St S8 141 B6
Gervase Ave S8 152 E6
Gervase Dr S8 152 E6
Gervase Pl S8 152 E6
Gervase Rd S8 152 E6
Gervase Wlk 2 S8 152 E6
Ghest Villas S81 136 F1
Gibbet Hill La DN10 122 F4
Gibbing Greaves Rd S65 116 E4
Gibbon La DN7, DN8 25 E4
Gibbons Dr S14 141 E2
Gibbons Way S14 141 E2
Gibbons Wlk S14 141 E2
Gibraltar Bldgs S3 161 A4
Gibraltar St S3 161 A4
Gibson Ct S81 148 E1
Gibson La S36 73 C2
Gibson Rd DN7 66 A8
Gifford Dr 1 DN4 82 D6
Gifford Rd S8 141 A7
Gilbert Ct S2 161 C2
Gilbert Gr S70 55 D8
Gilbert Hill S36 71 B6
Gilberthorpe Dr 2 S65 116 A6
Gilberthorpe Rd DN4 82 F7
Gilberthorpe St S65 115 F6
Gilbert Rd DN11 122 B4
Gilbert Row S2 161 C3
Gilbert St S1 161 B3
Gilder Way S72 16 C2
Gildhurst Ct S70 75 F6
Gildingwells Rd
Letwell S81 135 F2
Woodsetts S81 147 E5
Giles Ave S63 78 C6
Gileswood Cres S63 78 A7
Gill Cl S66 117 C3
Gill Croft 4 S6 127 C6
Gilleyfield Ave S17 151 E7
Gill Mdws S6 127 C6
Gillot Dell S66 117 B3
Gillot Ind Est S70 33 D2
Gillott La S66 117 B3
Gillott Rd S6 112 D4
Gill Royd La S36 71 F2
Gill St
Doncaster DN1 62 D2
Hoyland S74 76 F5
Gilpin La S6 128 E6
Gilpin St S6 128 E6
Gilroyd La S75 54 B5
Gilthwaites Cres HD8 30 A7
Gilthwaites Fst Sch HD8 30 A7
Gilthwaites Gr HD8 30 A6
Gilthwaites La HD8 30 A7
Gilthwaites Top HD8 30 A7
Ginhouse La S61 115 C8
Gipsy Green La S63 78 F4
Gipsyhill La S80 158 C1
Gipsy La
Apperknowle S18 154 A1
Maltby S66 119 C1
Woolley WF4 13 F6
Gisborne Rd S11 140 B6
Glade Croft S12 142 A4
Glade Lea S12 142 A4
Glade The S10 128 B1
Glade View DN3 42 F4
Gladstone Mews S10 127 E1
Gladstone Rd
Doncaster DN4 62 A1
Maltby S66 118 E6
Sheffield S10 127 F1
Gladys Buxton Com Ed Ctr
S18 153 C2
Gladys St S65 116 A6
Glaisdale Cl S25 134 C3
Glaisedale Ct S25 134 C3
Glamis Rd
Carlton in L S81 148 E6
Doncaster DN2 63 A3
Glasshouse La S64 98 E7
Glasshouse Rd S64 98 E7
Glasshouse St S60 115 D7
Glastonbury Gate DN5 61 D5
Gleadless Ave S12 142 A4
Gleadless Bank S12 141 F4
Gleadless Comm S12 142 A5
Gleadless Ct S2 141 B6
Gleadless Dr S12 141 F4
Gleadless Mount S12 142 A3
Gleadless Prim Sch S12 142 B5
Gleadless Rd S12, S14,
S2 141 D5
Gleadless Rise
1 Sheffield, Gleadless
Townend S12 142 A3
Sheffield S12 141 F5
Gleadless View
2 Sheffield, Gleadless
Townend S12 142 A3
Sheffield S12 141 F5
Glebe Ave S26 157 E7
Glebe Cl
Mexborough S64 80 B4
Swinton S64 79 C1
Glebe Cres S65 98 E1
Glebe Ct
Bradfield S6 110 A4
Pilley S75 75 E5
Glebe Farm Cl
Armthorpe DN3 64 A7
Harthill S26 157 E7
Glebeland Cl S62 97 E7
Glebelands Rd S36 92 C8

Glebe Rd
Norton DN6 ... 4 D1
Sheffield S10 ... 128 C3
Swinton S64 ... 79 C1
Thorne DN8 ... 26 C7
Glebe St DN4 ... 82 D6
Gledhill Ave S36 ... 51 C1
Gledhill Cl S18 ... 153 A1
Gledhill Ct S36 ... 51 C1
Glenalmond Rd S11 ... 140 B6
Glencairn Cl S66 ... 119 B4
Glencoe Cl DN7 ... 44 A8
Glencoe Dr S2 ... 161 C2
Glencoe Pl S2 ... 161 C2
Glencoe Rd S2 ... 161 C2
Glencroft 4 S11 ... 140 A7
Glendale Cl S75 ... 33 B2
Glendale Rd DN5 ... 61 B1
Gleneagles Dr DN4 ... 85 B6
Gleneagles Rd S25 ... 146 F8
Gleneagles Rise S64 ... 79 D2
Glen Field Ave DN4 ... 62 A1
Glenholme Dr S13 ... 142 E7
Glenholme Pl S13 ... 142 F7
Glenholme Rd S13 ... 142 F7
Glenholme Way S13 ... 142 E7
Glenmoor Ave S70 ... 54 B8
Glenmore Croft S12 ... 142 C6
Glenmore Rise S73 ... 56 E1
Glenorchy Rd S7 ... 140 D5
Glen Rd
Branton DN3 ... 85 E8
Sheffield S7 ... 140 E6
Glen The
Sheffield S10 ... 128 B1
Wharncliffe Side S35 ... 93 B1
Glenthorn Cl S81 ... 159 F7
Glentilt Rd S7 ... 140 D5
Glen Vale S18 ... 152 D1
Glen View S11 ... 139 F8
Glen View Rd S8 ... 152 E8
Glenville Cl S74 ... 76 D5
Glenwood Cres S35 ... 95 B5
Glenwood Ct S6 ... 111 F3
Glenwood Ho S6 ... 111 F3
Gliwice Way DN4 ... 63 B2
Glossop La S10 ... 160 B3
Glossop Rd S10 ... 160 B3
Glossop Row S35 ... 111 D7
Gloucester Cres S10 ... 160 B2
Gloucester Rd
Doncaster DN2 ... 63 A6
Rotherham S61 ... 96 F1
Gloucester St S10 ... 160 B2
Glover Rd
Sheffield, Highfield S8 ... 141 A7
Sheffield, Totley Rise S17 ... 151 F5
Glyn Ave DN1 ... 62 E4
Goathead La DN14 ... 1 D7
Goathland Cl S13 ... 143 D7
Goathland Dr S13 ... 143 D7
Goathland Pl S13 ... 143 D7
Goathland Rd S13 ... 143 D7
Goddard Ave S36 ... 72 F2
Goddard Hall Rd S5 ... 113 C1
Godfrey's Cotts DN8 ... 9 B8
Godfrey Rd DN8 ... 26 A7
Godley Cl S71 ... 15 D4
Godley St S71 ... 15 D4
Godric Dr S60 ... 115 B1
Godric Gn S60 ... 115 B1
Godric Rd S5 ... 113 C7
Godstone Rd S60 ... 115 E5
Goldcrest Wlk S61 ... 96 A5
Gold Croft 5 S70 ... 55 A8
Golden Oak Dell S6 ... 127 C7
Golden Smithies La S63, S64 ... 79 C4
Goldsborough Rd DN2 ... 63 A3
Goldsmith Dr S65 ... 116 B6
Goldsmith Rd
Doncaster DN4 ... 83 C6
Rotherham S65 ... 116 B6
Gold St S70 ... 55 A8
Goldthorpe Ave S81 ... 136 F3
Goldthorpe Cl S81 ... 136 F3
Goldthorpe Gn S63 ... 58 D4
Goldthorpe Ind Est S63 ... 58 C3
Goldthorpe Rd S63 ... 58 E4
Goldthorpe Sta S63 ... 58 D5
Gomersal La S18 ... 153 A1
Gomersall Ave DN12 ... 80 F2
Gooder Ave S71 ... 15 C3
Goodison Bvd DN4 ... 85 A7
Goodison Cres S6 ... 127 F6
Goodison Rise S6 ... 127 F6
Goodwin Athletics Ctr (Univ of Sheffield) The S10 ... 160 A3
Goodwin Ave S62 ... 97 F6
Goodwin Cres S64 ... 79 D4
Goodwin Rd
Rotherham S61 ... 97 A4
7 Sheffield S8 ... 141 A6
Goodwin Way S61 ... 97 A4
Goodwood Gdns DN4 ... 63 D2
Goodyear Cres S73 ... 56 D2
Goore Ave S9 ... 130 B2
Goore Dr S9 ... 130 B3
Goore Rd S9 ... 130 B2
Gooseacre Ave S63 ... 37 C1
Gooseacre Prim Sch S63 ... 37 C1
Goosebutt Ho S62 ... 97 F4
Goosebutt St S62 ... 97 F4
Goosecarr La S26 ... 145 D6
Goosecroft Ave S65 ... 98 E2
Goosehill Ct DN4 ... 83 B4
Goosehole La WF9 ... 19 B1
Goose La S66 ... 117 C4
Gordon Ave S8 ... 141 A2
Gordon Pl WF9 ... 18 F2
Gordon Rd
New Edlington DN12 ... 82 B2
6 Sheffield S11 ... 140 D8
Gordon Sq DN7 ... 24 E3
Gordon St
Barnsley S70 ... 55 E8
Doncaster DN1 ... 62 C3
Gordon Terr 5 S65 ... 115 F6
Gordon Works S2 ... 141 A6
Gorehill Cl S63 ... 79 A6
Gorse Cl
Dunsville DN7 ... 43 F5
Wath u D S63 ... 77 F6
Gorse Dr S21 ... 156 D5
Gorse La S10 ... 138 F7
Gorseland Ct S66 ... 117 A4
Gorse The
Rotherham, Herringthorpe S65 ... 116 C5
Rotherham, Wickersley S66 ... 117 B3
Gorsey Brigg S18 ... 152 D1
Gorseybrigg Cty Jun Sch S18 ... 152 D1
Gorseybrigg Inf Sch S18 ... 152 D1
Gosber Rd S21 ... 155 E3
Gosber St S21 ... 155 D3
Gosforth Cl S18 ... 152 F1
Gosforth Cres S18 ... 152 F1
Gosforth Dr
Dronfield, Dronfield Woodhouse S18 ... 152 D1
Dronfield, Gosforth Valley S18 ... 152 E1
Gosforth Gn S18 ... 152 F1
Gosforth La S18 ... 152 F1
Gosling Gate Rd S63 ... 58 E6
Gossips Wood Rd DN14 ... 2 D7
Gotham Rd S60 ... 115 C2
Gough Cl S65 ... 116 C4
Goulding St S64 ... 79 F4
Gowdall Gn DN5 ... 41 A3
Gower St
Sheffield S4 ... 129 C6
Wombwell S73 ... 56 E2
Grace Rd DN12 ... 82 C3
Grace St S71 ... 34 F6
Grady Dr DN4 ... 83 C5
Graftdyke Cl DN11 ... 85 B1
Grafton St
Barnsley S70 ... 33 D1
Sheffield S2 ... 161 C2
Grafton Way S65 ... 115 E7
Graham's Orch S70 ... 33 E1
Graham Ave
Brinsworth S60 ... 131 D7
Upton WF9 ... 19 D8
Graham Ct S11 ... 139 F8
Graham Ho 2 DN3 ... 42 F4
Graham Knoll S11 ... 139 F8
Graham Rd
Kirk Sandall DN3 ... 42 F3
Sheffield S10 ... 139 F8
Graham Rise S11 ... 139 F8
Grainger Cl DN12 ... 82 A1
Grainger Ct S10 ... 127 E1
Grammar St S6 ... 128 D7
Grampian Cl
Barnsley S75 ... 33 B2
Bentley DN5 ... 61 E5
Grampian Way DN8 ... 26 A5
Granary Ct S25 ... 146 D6
Granary The 1 S11 ... 160 C1
Granby Cres DN2 ... 62 F2
Granby Ct
Armthorpe DN3 ... 64 C5
South Elmsall WF9 ... 19 A5
Granby La DN11 ... 84 D1
Granby Rd
New Edlington DN12 ... 82 C2
Sheffield S5 ... 113 D2
Grange Ave
Aston S26 ... 132 C1
Bawtry DN10 ... 122 F8
Doncaster DN4 ... 83 A7
Dronfield S18 ... 152 E1
Hatfield DN7 ... 44 C8
South Elmsall WF9 ... 19 A3
Woodsetts S81 ... 147 E3
Grange Cl
Askern DN6 ... 22 C8
Brierley S72 ... 16 F3
Doncaster DN4 ... 84 F6
Hatfield DN7 ... 44 B8
Thurcroft S66 ... 133 D5
Grange Cliffe Cl S11 ... 140 B4
Grange Cres
Barnsley S71 ... 34 E2
Sheffield S11 ... 140 E8
Thurnscoe S63 ... 58 E8
Grange Crescent Rd S11 ... 140 E8
Grange Ct
Bentley DN5 ... 62 B6
Doncaster DN4 ... 84 F6
Rotherham S66 ... 117 B4
Sheffield S11 ... 140 E8
Grange Dr
Harworth DN11 ... 122 A5
Hellaby S66 ... 118 B4
Rotherham S61 ... 96 D1
Grange Farm Cl S60 ... 131 D7
Grange Farm Ct S81 ... 147 E3
Grange Farm Dr
Aston S26 ... 144 E6
Oughtibridge S35 ... 111 D4
Grangefield Ave DN11 ... 84 F1
Grangefield Cres DN11 ... 84 F1
Grangefield Terr DN11 ... 84 F1
Grange Gdns S26 ... 145 E7
Grange Gr DN8 ... 9 D4
Grange Ho S72 ... 16 F3
Grange La
Barnsley S71 ... 34 E1
Brinsworth S60 ... 115 A2
Burghwallis DN6 ... 21 A4
Doncaster DN4 ... 82 F4
Maltby S66 ... 119 B6
Rossington DN11 ... 103 D8
Rotherham S5, S61 ... 95 F1
Grange Lane Ind Est S71 ... 55 E8
Grange Lane Inf Sch DN11 ... 103 D8
Grange Mill La S61 ... 114 A6
Grange Pk DN3 ... 43 A4
Grange Rd
Adwick le S DN6 ... 40 C3
Bentley DN5 ... 41 A4
Brierley S72 ... 16 F2
Doncaster DN4 ... 84 F6
Norton DN6 ... 4 D1
Rawmarsh S62 ... 98 B7
Rossington DN11 ... 84 F1
Rotherham S60 ... 116 B2
Royston S71 ... 15 B3
Sheffield, Beighton S20 ... 144 A4
Sheffield, Sharrow S11 ... 140 E8
Swinton S64 ... 79 B2
Thorne DN8 ... 9 D4
Wath u D S63 ... 78 E5
West Cowick DN14 ... 1 A8
Grange Rise WF9 ... 17 D7
Grange Sq DN8 ... 9 D4
Grange St S63 ... 58 E8
Grange The
Adwick le S DN6 ... 21 A2
Rotherham S61 ... 96 C2
Grange View
Doncaster DN4 ... 83 A8
Harworth DN11 ... 122 A5
Hemsworth WF9 ... 17 D6
Hoyland S74 ... 76 D8
Grange View Cres S61 ... 114 D8
Grange View Rd S61 ... 114 D8
Grangeway WF9 ... 17 D7
Grange Way DN12 ... 80 F3
Grangewood Rd S25 ... 134 E4
Granham Acre S72 ... 16 C2
Grantham St DN11 ... 84 E1
Grantley Cl S73 ... 77 F8
Granville Cres DN7 ... 24 F3
Granville Rd S2 ... 161 C1
Granville Sq S2 ... 161 B2
Granville St
Barnsley S75 ... 33 D3
Sheffield S2 ... 161 B2
Granville Terr 2 S65 ... 115 F6
Grasby Ct S66 ... 117 D7
Grasmere Ave DN2 ... 63 C4
Grasmere Cl
Mexborough S64 ... 80 D6
North Anston S25 ... 146 F6
Penistone S36 ... 51 D4
Grasmere Cres S75 ... 14 A3
Grasmere Rd
Adwick le S DN6 ... 21 C1
Barnsley S71 ... 34 A1
Conisbrough DN12 ... 81 C2
Dronfield S18 ... 152 D1
Sheffield S8 ... 140 E5
Grassdale View S12 ... 142 F3
Grassholme Cl DN4 ... 84 B8
Grassington Cl 2 S12 ... 143 B3
Grassington Dr S12 ... 143 B3
Grassington Way S35 ... 94 F6
Grassmoor Cl S12 ... 141 F5
Grassthorpe Rd S12 ... 142 B4
Grattan St S61 ... 114 E6
Graven Cl S35 ... 112 B8
Graves Art Gal* S1 ... 161 B3
Graves Tennis & L Ctr S8 ... 153 B7
Graves Trust Homes
Sheffield, Common Side S12 ... 142 A5
Sheffield, Greenhill S8 ... 152 F8
Sheffield, Little Norton S8 ... 153 A8
Sheffield S10 ... 128 A3
Gray's Rd S71 ... 15 C1
Gray Ave S26 ... 132 D1
Gray Cl S65 ... 115 E8
Gray Gdns DN4 ... 83 B6
Grays Ct DN12 ... 81 A4
Grayson Cl
Rotherham S65 ... 117 D8
Stocksbridge S36 ... 92 C8
Grayson Rd S61 ... 97 A4
Gray St
Hoyland S74 ... 77 B5
Sheffield, Mosborough S20 ... 155 C7
Sheffield S3 ... 129 B6
Greasbro Rd S9 ... 114 D2
Greasbrough Jun & Inf Sch S61 ... 97 B3
Greasbrough La S62 ... 97 E5
Greasbrough Rd S62 ... 97 E3
Greasbrough St S60 ... 115 C7
Greasebrough Rd
Rotherham, Northfield S60, S61 ... 115 D8
3 Rotherham S60 ... 115 D7
Great Bank Rd S65 ... 116 C4
Great Black La DN11 ... 121 C6
Great Broad Ing S75 ... 33 B4
Great Central Ave DN4 ... 83 B8
Great Cliffe Rd S75 ... 53 E8
Great Croft S18 ... 152 D2
Great Eastern Way S62 ... 97 F3
Great North Rd
Adwick le S DN6 ... 40 B3
Rossington DN11 ... 104 F5
Scrooby DN10 ... 123 A2
Great Park Rd S61 ... 114 E8
Greave Rd HD9 ... 48 A8
Greaves Cl 7 S6 ... 127 C6
Greaves Fold 4 S75 ... 33 B2
Greaves La
Chapeltown S35 ... 75 D2
Sheffield S6 ... 127 D7
Greaves Rd
Rotherham S61 ... 115 A7
Sheffield S5 ... 113 A8
Greaves Sike La S66 ... 100 C2
Greaves St S6 ... 128 D7
Grebe Ct S73 ... 57 A1
Green's Rd DN7 ... 43 F5
Green Abbey HD9 ... 48 B7
Greenacre Cl DN7 ... 43 F4
Greenacre Dr HD8 ... 29 E3
Greenacre Rd WF9 ... 19 C8
Greenacres S35 ... 94 E8
Green Acres
Grimethorpe S72 ... 36 A7
Hoyland S74 ... 76 E5
Penistone S36 ... 51 E3
Rawmarsh S62 ... 98 A5
Greenacre Sch S70 ... 54 C7
Green Arbour Ct S66 ... 133 E5
Green Arbour Rd S66 ... 133 F5
Green Arbour Sch S66 ... 133 E6
Green Balk S66 ... 100 F5
Greenbank S71 ... 14 F1
Green Bank DN8 ... 27 B3
Green Bank Dr S66 ... 117 C8
Greenbank Wlk S72 ... 35 F7
Green Brook Pl S36 ... 51 D2
Green Bvd DN4 ... 84 E8
Green Chase S21 ... 155 C3
Green Comm DN3 ... 64 B5
Greencroft
Chapeltown S35 ... 94 D7
Rotherham S60 ... 115 F4
Greencroft Cl S60 ... 115 F3
Green Cross S18 ... 153 B2
Green Ct S66 ... 117 C7
Greendale Ct S18 ... 153 B2
Greendale Sh Ctr S18 ... 153 B2
Green Dyke La DN1 ... 62 C1
Green Farm Hamlet S36 ... 72 E1
Greenfield S62 ... 97 F5
Greenfield Cl
Armthorpe DN3 ... 64 C5
Barnby Dun DN3 ... 43 A6
Denby Dale HD8 ... 29 F3
Rotherham S65 ... 116 D8
Sheffield S8 ... 152 F7
Greenfield Cotts S71 ... 34 C8
Greenfield Ct
Doncaster DN4 ... 83 A8
Mexborough S64 ... 79 F8
Rotherham S66 ... 117 B6
Greenfield Dr S8 ... 152 F7
Greenfield Gdns
Barnsley S71 ... 14 E1
Doncaster DN4 ... 85 A7
Rotherham S66 ... 117 B6
Greenfield La DN4 ... 83 A8
Greenfield Prim Sch S74 ... 76 F6
Greenfield Rd
Hemsworth WF9 ... 17 D5
Hoyland S74 ... 76 E6
Rotherham S65 ... 116 D8
Sheffield S8 ... 152 F7
Greenfields S21 ... 155 C3
Greenfields Way S81 ... 148 F7
Green Finch Cl S60 ... 131 D8
Greenfoot Cl S75 ... 33 D3
Greenfoot La S75 ... 33 D3
Green Gables S64 ... 79 F5
Greengate Cl S13 ... 143 D6
Green Gate Cl S63 ... 58 D3
Greengate La
Chapeltown S35 ... 94 E7
Sheffield S13 ... 143 D6
Greengate Lane Prim Sch S35 ... 94 E7
Greengate Rd
Norton WF8 ... 3 F3
Sheffield S13 ... 143 D6
Greenhall Rd S21 ... 155 C3
Greenhead Gdns S35 ... 95 A5
Greenhead La S35 ... 95 A5
Greenhill Ave
Barnsley S71 ... 33 F3
Hellaby S66 ... 118 B4
Sheffield S8 ... 152 F8
Green Hill Gr S36 ... 52 A6
Greenhill Main Rd S8 ... 152 F7
Greenhill Parkway S8 ... 152 D6
Greenhill Prim Sch S8 ... 152 E7
Greenhill Rd S8 ... 140 F2
Greenhouse La S10 ... 138 F5
Green House Rd DN2 ... 63 B6
Greenhow St S6 ... 128 C5
Green Ings La S63 ... 79 A7
Green La
Adwick le S DN6 ... 40 A4
Adwick le S, Skellow DN6 ... 20 E3
Askern DN6 ... 21 F7
Aston S26 ... 145 A7
Barnburgh DN5 ... 59 A3
Barnsley S75 ... 54 C5
Green La continued
Bentley DN5 ... 40 B1
Bradfield S36 ... 92 C2
Branton DN3 ... 64 B1
Catliffe S60 ... 131 B7
Denby Dale HD8 ... 29 B2
Dodworth S75 ... 54 A6
Dronfield S18 ... 153 B2
Hatfield DN7 ... 44 C2
Hoyland S74 ... 76 A5
Killamarsh S21 ... 156 C3
Notton WF4 ... 15 A5
Oughtibridge S35 ... 111 B7
Penistone S75 ... 52 C7
Rawmarsh S62 ... 98 A5
Rotherham, Broom S60 ... 116 A2
Rotherham, Dropping Well S61 ... 114 C7
Rotherham, Listerdale S66 ... 117 A5
Rotherham S66 ... 133 D8
Sheffield S3 ... 161 A5
Sheffield, St Michael's Field S35 ... 113 C8
South Kirkby WF9 ... 18 B2
Stocksbridge S36 ... 72 E2
Ulley S26 ... 132 D4
Upton WF9 ... 19 C8
Wadworth DN11 ... 102 A7
Wath u D S63 ... 78 D3
Wharncliffe Side S35 ... 93 B1
Greenland S75 ... 31 B8
Greenland Ave S66 ... 119 A7
Greenland Ave S S66 ... 119 A6
Greenland Cl
North Anston S25 ... 146 D6
Sheffield S9 ... 130 C5
Greenland Ct S9 ... 130 C6
Greenland Dr S9 ... 130 C6
Greenland La
East Cowick DN14 ... 1 E5
Rawcliffe DN14 ... 2 B4
Greenland Rd S9 ... 130 C6
Greenlands Ave DN11 ... 85 A2
Greenlands Jun & Inf Schs S9 ... 130 C5
Greenland View
Sheffield S9 ... 130 C5
Worsbrough S70 ... 54 F4
Greenland Way
Maltby S66 ... 119 A7
Sheffield, Greenland S9 ... 130 C7
Sheffield S9 ... 130 C6
Greenland Wlk S9 ... 130 B6
Green Lea S18 ... 152 C2
Greenleafe Ave DN2 ... 63 C7
Green Moor Rd S35 ... 73 E3
Green Oak Ave S17 ... 151 E4
Green Oak Cres S17 ... 151 E4
Green Oak Dr
Sheffield S17 ... 151 E4
Wales S26 ... 145 A2
Green Oak Gr S17 ... 151 E4
Green Oak Rd S17 ... 151 E4
Greenock St S6 ... 128 B8
Green Pastures S17 ... 151 E7
Green Rd S36 ... 51 D2
Green Rise S62 ... 97 D7
Green Royd DN7 ... 25 A7
Greenset View S71 ... 14 E1
Greenside
Darton S75 ... 14 C1
Denby Dale HD8 ... 30 A7
Havercroft WF4 ... 16 B8
Penistone S36 ... 52 A6
Rotherham S61 ... 97 B3
Shafton S72 ... 16 B4
Skelmanthorpe HD8 ... 29 E8
Greenside Ave
Darton S75 ... 14 C1
Wales S26 ... 145 C2
Greenside Gdns S36 ... 52 A6
Greenside La S74 ... 76 E7
Greenside Mews S12 ... 143 B3
Greenside Pl S75 ... 14 C1
Green Spring Ave S70 ... 75 F8
Greensprings Holiday Pk S75 ... 75 B8
Greens Rd S65 ... 116 B6
Green St
Doncaster DN4 ... 82 F6
Hoyland S74 ... 76 F6
Rotherham S61 ... 97 B4
Stocksbridge S36 ... 73 D1
Worsbrough S70 ... 55 C5
Green The
Bolton u D S63 ... 58 C3
Branton DN9 ... 86 A7
Conisbrough DN12 ... 80 C3
Finningley DN9 ... 86 E3
Harworth DN11 ... 121 E3
Moorends DN8 ... 9 D4
North Anston S25 ... 146 D6
Penistone S36 ... 51 D2
Penistone, Thurlstone S36 ... 51 A4
Rotherham, Broom S60 ... 115 F3
Rotherham S66 ... 117 C7
Rotherham, Whiston S60 ... 132 B8
Royston S71 ... 15 C3
Sheffield S17 ... 151 D4
South Kirkby WF9 ... 18 C3
Swinton S64 ... 79 B2
Thorne DN8 ... 26 B7
Woolley WF4 ... 14 A7
Green View The S72 ... 16 C4
Greenway S26 ... 145 D2

Greenway The
Sheffield S6 . . . . .152 F8
Stocksbridge S36. . . . . .92 E8
Greenway View S73 . . . . . . .77 D7
Greenwood Ave
Doncaster DN4 . . . . .82 F8
Harworth DN11 . . . . .121 F5
Sheffield S9 . . . . .130 B3
Upton WF9. . . . . .19 C8
Worsbrough S70 . . . . .55 B5
Greenwood Cl
Sheffield S9 . . . . .130 B3
Upton WF9. . . . . .19 C8
Worksop S81. . . . . .148 D1
Greenwood Cres
Rotherham S66 . . . . .117 C5
Royston S71. . . . . .15 B4
Sheffield S9 . . . . .130 B3
Greenwood Dr S9 . . . . .130 A3
Greenwood La S13. . . . . . . .143 D7
Greenwood Rd
Chapeltown S35. . . . . .94 F7
Sheffield S9 . . . . .130 B2
Swinton S62. . . . . .98 E7
Greenwood Terr S70 . . . . . . .33 E2
Greenwood Way S71. . . . . . .130 A3
Greenwood Wlk DN6. . . . . . .22 C8
Greeton Dr S35. . . . . .111 E6
Gregg House Cres S5 . . . . . .113 D6
Gregg House Rd S5. . . . . . . .113 D5
Greggs Ct S70. . . . . .55 D8
Gregory's Bldgs S72 . . . . . . .36 D2
Gregory Cres DN11 . . . . . . .121 E4
Gregory Ct [10] S8 . . . . .141 B6
Gregory Ho S62 . . . . .97 E7
Gregory Rd S8. . . . . .141 A6
Grenfell Ave S64. . . . . .80 B5
Grenfolds Rd S35. . . . . .112 D8
Grenobank Rd S35. . . . . . . .112 D8
Greno Cres S35. . . . . .112 D8
Greno Gate S35. . . . . .94 C1
Greno Ho
Sheffield S35. . . . . .94 C1
Swinton S64. . . . . .79 D2
Grenomoor Cl S35. . . . . . . .112 C7
Greno Rd S64 . . . . .79 D2
Grenoside Com Prim Sch
S35. . . . . .94 C1
Grenoside Mount S6. . . . . . .112 D7
Greno View
Hood Green S75 . . . . .53 D2
Hoyland S74. . . . . .79 E6
Greno View Rd S35 . . . . .94 E7
Greno Wood Ct S35. . . . . . . .94 C1
Grenville Pl S75 . . . . .33 C3
Grenville Rd S4 . . . . .82 F5
Gresham Ave S60. . . . . .131 D8
Gresham Rd [1] S6. . . . . .128 C6
Gresley Ave DN10. . . . . .123 A8
Gresley Rd
Doncaster DN4 . . . . .62 B1
Sheffield S8. . . . . .152 E5
Gresley Wlk S8 . . . . .152 E5
Grey Friars' Rd DN1. . . . . . . .62 C4
Greyfriars S11 . . . . .140 A7
Greystock St S4 . . . . .129 E6
Greystone Cl DN11. . . . . . . .120 F6
Greystone La DN11 . . . . . . .120 F8
Greystones
Sheffield S11 . . . . .140 B8
Worsbrough S70 . . . . .54 F4
Greystones Cl S11 . . . . .140 A7
Greystones Cres S11. . . . . . .140 A7
Greystones Ct
Harthill S26 . . . . .157 D6
Sheffield S11 . . . . .140 A7
Greystones Dr S11. . . . . . . .140 A7
Greystones Grange [1]
. . . . .140 A7
Greystones Grange Cres [2]
S11. . . . . .140 A7
Greystones Grange Rd
S11. . . . . .140 A7
Greystones Hall Rd S11. . . . .140 A7
Greystones Prim Sch
S11. . . . . .140 B7
Greystones Rd
Rotherham S60 . . . . .116 D1
Sheffield S11 . . . . .140 A7
Greystones Rise [3] S11 . . . . .140 A7
Grice Cl DN4 . . . . .63 F2
Griffin Rd S64 . . . . .79 B3
Griffiths Cl S62. . . . . .97 F4
Griffiths Rd S35 . . . . .94 B6
Grime La HD9 . . . . .49 D8
Grimesthorpe Rd
Sheffield S4. . . . . .129 C6
Sheffield, Wood Hill S4 . . . . .129 D8
Grimesthorpe Rd S S4 . . . . .129 C6
Grimethorpe St [1] WF9. . . . . .18 F2
Grimsell Cl S6 . . . . .112 D7
Grimsell Cres S6 . . . . .112 D7
Grimsell Dr S6 . . . . .112 D7
Grimsell Wlk S6 . . . . .112 D6
Grinders Hill S2. . . . . .161 B2
Grindleford Sta S32. . . . . . . .149 D2
Grindlow Cl S14 . . . . .141 C6
Grindlow Dr S14. . . . . .141 C6
Grisedale Wlk S18. . . . . .152 E1
Grizedale Ave S20 . . . . .144 A2
Grizedale Cl [4] S20. . . . . . . .144 A2
Grosvenor Ave WF9 . . . . .19 A7
Grosvenor Cres
Bentley DN5. . . . . .41 D2
Doncaster DN4 . . . . .82 D6

Grosvenor Ct DN7 . . . . .25 B7
Grosvenor Dr S70. . . . . .33 C1
Grosvenor Rd
Adwick le S DN6 . . . . .40 B5
Bircotes DN11 . . . . .122 B4
Langold S81. . . . . .136 F3
Rotherham S65 . . . . .115 F8
Grosvenor Sq [7] S2. . . . . . .140 F8
Grosvenor Terr DN4 . . . . . . .82 D6
Grouse Croft S6 . . . . .128 D6
Grouse St S6 . . . . .128 C7
Grove Ave
Bentley DN5. . . . . .62 A5
Hemsworth WF9 . . . . .17 E6
Sheffield, Hillfoot S17 . . . . . .151 D5
Sheffield S6 . . . . .112 A2
South Kirkby WF9 . . . . .18 C2
Grove Cl
Penistone S36 . . . . .51 D1
Wath u D S63. . . . . .78 C8
Grove Ct
Maltby S66. . . . . .118 D5
Marr DN5. . . . . .60 C7
Grove Dr WF9 . . . . .18 B2
Grove Hall Cl DN3 . . . . .43 A2
Grove Head WF9. . . . . .18 B2
Grove Hill Rd DN2 . . . . .62 F3
Grove House Ct S17 . . . . . . .151 E5
Grove La
Hemsworth WF9 . . . . .17 E6
South Kirkby WF9 . . . . .18 B2
Grove Lea Cl WF9 . . . . .17 E6
Grove Lea Prim Sch WF9. . . . .17 E7
Grove Mount WF9 . . . . .145 B2
Grove Pl
Doncaster DN1 . . . . .62 C2
Hemsworth WF9 . . . . .17 E6
Grove Rd
Darton S75 . . . . .14 A1
Fishlake DN7 . . . . .25 B7
Rotherham S60 . . . . .115 D5
Sheffield, Millhouses S7 . . . .140 C3
Sheffield, Totley Brook S17 .151 F5
Stocksbridge S36. . . . . .92 F8
Wath u D S63. . . . . .78 C8
Grove Sq S6. . . . . .128 E7
Grove St
Barnsley S71 . . . . .34 A1
South Kirkby WF9 . . . . .18 B2
Worsbrough S70 . . . . .55 C5
Grove Street Prim Sch
S71. . . . . .34 A1
Grove Terr WF9 . . . . .17 E6
Grove The
Barnby Dun DN3 . . . . .42 E8
Cudworth S72 . . . . .16 B1
Doncaster DN2 . . . . .63 B6
Rawmarsh S62 . . . . .98 A5
Rotherham, East Dene S65 .116 B7
Rotherham, Wickersley
S66. . . . . .117 B4
Sheffield, Hillfoot S17 . . . . . .151 D5
Sheffield S6 . . . . .127 E8
South Elmsall WF9. . . . . .18 F4
Wharncliffe Side S35. . . . . . . .93 B3
Grove Vale DN2. . . . . .63 C7
Grove Way WF9. . . . . .18 B2
Grudgby La S18 . . . . .73 A6
Gudgeon Hole La S75. . . . . . .74 E8
Guernsey Rd S2 . . . . .141 A7
Guest La
Doncaster DN4 . . . . .82 D7
Silkstone S75. . . . . .32 A1
Guest Pl
Hoyland S74. . . . . .76 E7
Rotherham S60 . . . . .115 F4
Guest Rd
Barnsley S75 . . . . .33 D3
Rotherham S60 . . . . .115 F4
Sheffield S11 . . . . .140 C8
Guest St S74 . . . . .76 E7
Guilbert Ave S66. . . . . .133 E5
Guildford Ave S2 . . . . .141 D8
Guildford Rd
Doncaster DN2 . . . . .63 B7
Royston S71. . . . . .15 B5
Guildford Rise S2. . . . . .141 E8
Guildford View S2 . . . . .141 E7
Guildhall Ind Est DN3 . . . . . .42 E3
Guild Rd S65 . . . . .116 B6
Guildway S26. . . . . .145 E8
Guilthwaite Common La S26,
S60. . . . . .132 D5
Guilthwaite Cres S60 . . . . . .116 A1
Guinevere Dr WF9 . . . . .19 A2
Gullane Dr DN4. . . . . .82 D6
Gullingwood Dr S65 . . . . .99 A2
Gully The HD8 . . . . .28 C5
Gunhills Lane Ind Est
DN3 . . . . .64 C7
Gun La S33. . . . . .161 B4
Gunthwaite La S36 . . . . .30 B2
Gunthwaite Top HD8 . . . . . . .29 F3
Gurney Rd DN4 . . . . .83 B6
Gurth Ave DN3 . . . . .43 A2
Gurth Avenue Cvn Site
DN3 . . . . .43 A2
Gurth Dr S66 . . . . .132 D5
Gwendoline Mews S63. . . . . . .78 F5
Gyme Cnr DN14. . . . . .1 E8
Gypsy La S73 . . . . .56 E1

H

Habershon Dr S35 . . . . .94 F6
Habershon Rd S61. . . . . .96 F1

Hackenforth Hall S12 . . . .143 B3
Hacking La S9 . . . . .19 B3
Hackings Ave S36. . . . . .51 C1
Hackness La S4 . . . . .115 B1
Hackthorn Rd S8 . . . . .140 F3
Haddingley La HD8 . . . . . . .28 C4
Haddon Cl
Dodworth S75 . . . . .53 E7
Dronfield S18. . . . . .153 B2
South Elmsall WF9. . . . . .19 A5
Haddon Rd S71. . . . . .34 B6
Haddon St S64 . . . . .80 D6
Haddon St S3 . . . . .128 F6
Haddon Way S26 . . . . .144 F7
Hadds La DN8 . . . . .8 F6
Hadds Nook Rd DN8 . . . . .9 A6
Hade Edge Jun & Inf Sch
HD9 . . . . .48 B8
Haden St S6. . . . . .128 C8
Hadfield St
Sheffield S6. . . . . .128 C5
Wombwell S73. . . . . .56 E1
Hadleigh Cl S62 . . . . .97 F4
Hadrian Rd S60. . . . . .115 C2
Hadrians Cl DN11 . . . . .104 A7
Hafferty Ct S5 . . . . .113 E5
Haggard Rd S6 . . . . .128 D8
Hagg Hill
Sheffield, Birley Carr S6 . . . .112 B5
Sheffield S10 . . . . .127 F4
Hagg La
Austerfield DN10 . . . . .123 E8
Sheffield S10. . . . . .127 E3
Haggs La DN6 . . . . .6 B3
Haggstones Dr S35 . . . . . . .111 D6
Haggstones Rd S35. . . . . . . .111 D6
Hague Ave S62 . . . . .97 E8
Hague Cres WF9 . . . . .17 E5
Hague La
Chapeltown S35. . . . . .94 C7
Renishaw S21 . . . . .156 A1
Wentworth S61, S62 . . . . . . .96 B7
Hague Park Cl WF9 . . . . .18 B3
Hague Park Coppice WF9 .18 B3
Hague Park Gdns WF9 . . . . .18 B3
Hague Park La WF9 . . . . .18 B3
Hague Park Wlk WF9 . . . . . .18 B3
Hague Row S21 . . . . .161 C3
Hague Terr WF9 . . . . .17 E6
Haids Cl S66 . . . . .118 F7
Haids Rd S66 . . . . .118 E7
Haig Cres
Rossington DN11. . . . . .103 E8
Stairfoot DN7. . . . . .24 F3
Haigh Cl S36 . . . . .51 F6
Haigh Croft S71. . . . . .15 B4
Haigh Ct S63 . . . . .77 F6
Haigh Head Rd S36 . . . . .51 F7
Haigh Hill S75 . . . . .13 C6
Haigh La
Penistone S36 . . . . .52 A7
Woolley S75, WF4 . . . . .13 C5
Haigh Meml Homes S8 . . . . .137 E3
Haigh Mews S75 . . . . .13 C5
Haigh Moor Cl [2] S13 . . . . . .130 F1
Haigh Moor Dr S25. . . . . . . .134 D1
Haigh Moor Rd S13. . . . . . . .142 F8
Haigh Moor Way S26 . . . . . .144 A2
Haigh Moor Wlk S13. . . . . . .142 F8
Haigh Rd DN4 . . . . .83 A7
Haigh St S6 . . . . .9 D4
Haig Mary Dr S13 . . . . .143 D8
Hail Mary Hill Wood Nature
Reserve* S60. . . . . .131 F2
Haise Mount S75 . . . . .14 A1
Hakehill Cl DN4. . . . . .84 D6
Halcyon Cl S12 . . . . .142 F3
Haldane Cl S72 . . . . .16 F3
Haldane Rd S65 . . . . .116 A8
Haldene S70. . . . . .54 C4
Haldon Way S81 . . . . .148 D1
Haldynby Gdns DN3 . . . . .64 D6
Hale Hill La DN7. . . . . .44 E5
Hale St S8 . . . . .140 F6
Halesworth Rd S13 . . . . .130 F2
Halfway Ctr S20 . . . . .155 E7
Halfway Dr S20. . . . . .155 E7
Halfway Gdns S20 . . . . .155 E7
Halfway Jun & Inf Sch
S20. . . . . .155 E7
Halfway Jun Sch S20 . . . . . . .155 E6
Halifax Ave DN12 . . . . .81 A2
Halifax Cres DN5 . . . . .61 F6
Halifax Rd
Penistone S36 . . . . .51 D6
Sheffield S6 . . . . .112 D5
Wortley S35. . . . . .74 C4
Halifax St S71 . . . . .33 E4
Halham Chase
Sheffield, Hallam Head
S10 . . . . .127 D2
Sheffield S10. . . . . .128 B1
Hallam Cl
Aston S26 . . . . .132 C1
Doncaster DN4 . . . . .84 C7
Hallam Ct
Bolton u D S63. . . . . .58 B1
Sheffield S10. . . . . .160 A1
Hallam Dale Ct S61. . . . . . . .98 A7
Hallamgate Rd S10 . . . . . . .128 B3
Hallam Grange Cl S10 . . . . .128 C2
Hallam Grange Cres S10 127 C1
Hallam Grange Croft
S10. . . . . .127 C1
Hallam Grange Rise S10. . . .127 C1
Hallam La S11. . . . . .161 A2
Hallam Pl S62 . . . . .98 A5

Hallam Prim Sch S10 . . . . .127 C1
Hallam Rd S60 . . . . .116 A1
Hallam Rock S5 . . . . .113 B1
Hallamshire Cl S10 . . . . . . .139 B8
Hallamshire Ct S11 . . . . . . .128 E1
Hallamshire Dr S10 . . . . . . .139 C8
Hallamshire Rd S10. . . . . . .139 B8
Hallam Way S35 . . . . .113 B8
Hall Ave
Hoyland S74. . . . . .77 A7
Mexborough S64 . . . . .80 B5
Hall Balk La
Barnsley S75 . . . . .33 D3
Doncaster DN11 . . . . .83 C3
Hall Bank S75 . . . . .33 D4
Hall Brig DN5. . . . . .37 C4
Hall Broome Gdns S63. . . . . .58 C3
Hallcar St S4 . . . . .129 C5
Hall Cl
Dronfield S18. . . . . .152 C2
Hemsworth WF9 . . . . .17 D7
North Anston S25 . . . . .146 D6
Wath u D S63. . . . . .78 B7
Worsbrough S70 . . . . .55 A2
Hall Close Ave S60. . . . . . . .116 C1
Hall Cres S60 . . . . .116 B2
Hall Croft
Darfield S73. . . . . .56 F4
Rotherham S66 . . . . .117 C4
Hallcroft Dr S61. . . . . .64 C4
Hallcroft Gdns S72. . . . . . . .36 E2
Hallcroft Rise S71 . . . . .15 B3
Hall Cross Ave S73. . . . . . . .56 F1
Hall Cross Hill DN1 . . . . . . .62 C2
Hall Cross Lower Sch
DN4 . . . . .84 B8
Hall Cross Sch DN1 . . . . .62 E3
Hall Ct S65 . . . . .99 C4
Hall Dr S63 . . . . .78 D5
Haller Cl DN3. . . . . .63 F6
Hall Farm Cl S26 . . . . .132 D2
Hall Farm Croft S25 . . . . . . .146 F8
Hall Farm Dr S63 . . . . .58 D7
Hall Farm Gr S36 . . . . .52 A6
Hall Farm Rise S63 . . . . .58 D7
Hall Field La WF4. . . . . .36 A1
Hall Flat La DN4 . . . . .83 A7
Hallgate S63 . . . . .58 D7
Hall Gate
Doncaster DN1 . . . . .62 D3
Mexborough S64 . . . . .80 C5
Penistone S36 . . . . .51 D4
Hallgate Rd S10 . . . . .128 A3
Hall Gr
Darton S75 . . . . .14 C1
Rotherham S60 . . . . .115 E5
Halliwell Cl S5 . . . . .112 E3
Halliwell Cres S5 . . . . .112 E3
Hall La
Bradfield S6. . . . . .109 B4
Kirk Bramwith DN7 . . . . .24 B3
Norton DN6 . . . . .4 D4
South Elmsall WF9 . . . . .18 E4
Hall Meadow Croft S20. . . . .155 F5
Hall Meadow Dr S20 . . . . . .155 F5
Hall Meadow Gr S20 . . . . . .155 F5
Hall Mews S65 . . . . .99 C4
Hallowes Ct S18 . . . . .153 B1
Hallowes La S18. . . . . .153 B1
Hallowmoor Rd S6 . . . . .128 A8
Hall Park Head S6 . . . . .127 E5
Hall Park Mount S6 . . . . . . .127 E5
Hall Pl S71 . . . . .34 C4
Hall Rd
Aston S26 . . . . .132 D1
Rawmarsh S62 . . . . .98 B6
Rotherham S60 . . . . .115 C5
Sheffield, Handsworth S13 .130 F2
Sheffield S9 . . . . .130 E3
Hall Royd La S75 . . . . .53 B6
Hall Royd Wlk S75 . . . . .53 A5
Halls Ct S8 . . . . .140 F3
Hallside Ct
Branton DN3 . . . . .64 B1
Sheffield S20. . . . . .155 D6
Hall St
Barnburgh DN5 . . . . .59 D3
Goldthorpe S63 . . . . .58 F7
Hoyland S74. . . . . .76 E6
Rotherham S60 . . . . .115 C6
Wombwell S73. . . . . .56 E2
Hallsworth Ave S73 . . . . .77 B7
Hall Syke HD8 . . . . .28 D8
Hall View S35. . . . . .95 A6
Hall View Rd DN11 . . . . .104 A7
Hall Villa La DN5. . . . . .61 B3
Hallwood Rd S35 . . . . .94 C5
Hallworth Wlk S21. . . . . .154 E2
Hallyburton Cl S2 . . . . .141 C6
Hallyburton Cl S2 . . . . .141 C6
Hallyburton Rd S2 . . . . .141 C6
Halmshaw Terr DN5. . . . . . . .62 A8
Halsall Ave S9 . . . . .130 C3
Halsall Dr S9 . . . . .130 C3
Halsall Rd S9 . . . . .130 C3
Halsbury Rd S65. . . . . .116 A8
Halstead Gr S75 . . . . .14 A2
Halton Ct S12 . . . . .143 C3
Hamble Ct S8 . . . . .33 C8
Hambleton Cl
Barnsley S75 . . . . .33 B2
Hoyland S74. . . . . .77 B6
Hambleton Ct S81. . . . . .148 E7
Hameline Rd DN12. . . . . .81 B1
Hamel Rise WF9 . . . . .17 D6
Hamer Wlk S65. . . . . .116 C4

Hamilton Cl
Doncaster DN4 . . . . .62 F1
Rawmarsh S64 . . . . .80 C6
Hamilton Ct [6] DN2. . . . . . . .81 C2
Hamilton Mews DN4 . . . . . . .62 F1
Hamilton Park Rd DN5 . . . . . .61 D6
Hamilton Rd
Doncaster DN4 . . . . .62 F2
Goldthorpe S63 . . . . .58 F6
Maltby S66. . . . . .119 B4
Sheffield S5 . . . . .113 D2
Hammerton Cl S6 . . . . .128 C7
Hammerton Rd S6. . . . . . . .128 C7
Hammond St S3 . . . . .160 B4
Hampden Cres DN7 . . . . .66 A8
Hampden Rd S64 . . . . .80 B4
Hamper La S36 . . . . .51 F6
Hampole Balk La DN6. . . . . . .20 E1
Hampole Dr S63 . . . . .58 C7
Hampole Field La DN6 . . . . . .19 F1
Hampson Gdns DN3 . . . . .43 A3
Hampton Ct S73 . . . . .56 F5
Hampton Rd
Doncaster DN2 . . . . .62 F4
Dunscroft DN7. . . . . .43 F8
Sheffield S5 . . . . .113 C1
Hamstead Gn S61. . . . . .96 E1
Hanbury Cl
Barnsley S71 . . . . .34 D4
Doncaster DN4 . . . . .83 A4
Dronfield S18. . . . . .152 F1
Hand La S35. . . . . .74 C8
Handley Sq DN9 . . . . .86 B4
Handley St S3 . . . . .129 B5
Hands Rd S10 . . . . .128 C4
Handsworth Ave S9 . . . . . . .130 D3
Handsworth Cres S9 . . . . . .130 D3
Handsworth Gdns DN3 . . . . .64 C6
Handsworth Grange Cl
S13. . . . . .131 A1
Handsworth Grange Cres
S13. . . . . .131 B1
Handsworth Grange Dr
S13. . . . . .131 B1
Handsworth Grange Rd
S13. . . . . .131 A1
Handsworth Grange Way
S13. . . . . .131 B1
Handsworth Rd S13, S9. . . . .130 F2
Hanging Bank Ct S25 . . . . . .146 E5
Hangingwater Cl S10 . . . . . .139 F8
Hangingwater Cotts S11 . . .139 F7
Hangingwater Rd S11. . . . . .139 F8
Hangman Stone La DN5. . . . .60 B2
Hangman Stone Rd
Barnburgh DN5. . . . . .59 F2
Marr DN5. . . . . .60 B5
Hangram La S11. . . . . .139 B5
Hangsman La S35 . . . . .134 C3
Hangthwaite La DN6. . . . . . . .40 D3
Hangthwaite Rd DN6. . . . . . .40 F7
Hanley Cl S12 . . . . .142 B3
Hanmoor Rd S6 . . . . .127 C6
Hannah Rd S13 . . . . .143 D7
Hannas Royd S73 . . . . .54 A7
Hanover Ct
Sheffield S3 . . . . .160 B2
[4] Worsbrough S70. . . . . . . .55 A5
Hanover Sq
Sheffield S3 . . . . .160 C2
Thurnscoe S63. . . . . .58 E3
Hanover St
Sheffield S3 . . . . .160 C2
Thurnscoe S63. . . . . .37 E1
Hanover Way S3 . . . . .160 C2
Hansby Cl DN11 . . . . .121 B7
Hanslope View DN3 . . . . .42 E5
Hanson Rd S6 . . . . .127 D8
Hanson St S74 . . . . .76 E5
Hanwell Cl S35. . . . . .113 B8
Harbord Rd S8 . . . . .140 E2
Harborough Ave S2 . . . . . . .130 A1
Harborough Cl S2 . . . . .130 A2
Harborough Dr S2 . . . . .130 A2
Harborough Hill Rd S70,
S71. . . . . .33 F2
Harborough Rd S2 . . . . .130 A2
Harborough Rise S2 . . . . . . .130 A2
Harborough Way S2 . . . . . . .130 A1
Harbury St S13 . . . . .143 E8
Harcourt Cl DN4. . . . . .84 C7
Harcourt Cres S10. . . . . . . .160 A3
Harcourt Rd S10 . . . . .160 A3
Harcourt Rise S35 . . . . .95 B4
Harcourt Terr [3] S65. . . . . . .115 F6
Hardcastle Dr S12 . . . . .143 A7
Hardcastle Gdns S13. . . . . . .143 A7
Hardcastle Rd S13. . . . . . . .143 A7
Harden Cl
Barnsley S75 . . . . .33 A2
Penistone S75 . . . . .51 D2
Hardie Cl S66 . . . . .119 B4
Hardie Pl S62 . . . . .97 F6
Hardie St S21 . . . . .155 D3
Harding Ave S62 . . . . .97 D8
Harding Cl S62 . . . . .97 D7
Harding St S9 . . . . .130 B6
Hard La S26 . . . . .145 F1
Hardwick Cl
Aston S26 . . . . .144 F7
Dronfield S18. . . . . .153 C2
Ryhill WF4 . . . .
[7] Worsbrough S70. . . . . . . .55 A4
Hardwick Cres
Barnsley S71 . . . . .34 B7

Hardwick Cres continued
Sheffield S11. . . . . .140 C8
Hardwick Ct DN11. . . . . .122 B5
Hardwicke Rd S65 . . . . .115 E8
Hardwick Gr S75 . . . . .53 F6
Hardwick La S26 . . . . .145 C8
Hardwick St S65. . . . . .116 D8
Hardy Pl S6 . . . . .128 D5
Hardy Rd DN2 . . . . .62 E6
Hardy St S60 . . . . .115 C7
Haredon Cl S75. . . . . .14 A2
Harefield Rd ⬛ S11. . . . . . .140 D8
Harehills Rd S60. . . . . .115 E5
Harewood Ave
Adwick le S DN6 . . . . .39 F5
Barnsley S70 . . . . .33 B1
Kirk Sandall DN3 . . . . .43 A4
Harewood Ct
Harworth DN11. . . . . .122 B5
Rossington DN11. . . . . .104 B8
Harewood Dr DN10 . . . . . . .123 A8
Harewood Gr S66. . . . . .117 D6
Harewood La WF9 . . . . .19 D8
Harewood Rd DN2 . . . . .63 A3
Harewood Way S11 . . . . . . .140 A2
Hargrave Pl S65 . . . . .98 F2
Harland Rd S11. . . . . .128 E1
Harlech Cl S35 . . . . .94 F6
Harlech Fold S10. . . . . .126 F1
Harlech Gn S10. . . . . .126 F1
Harlech Gr S10 . . . . .126 F1
Harlech Mead S10 . . . . .126 F1
Harleston St S4 . . . . .129 D6
Harley Rd
Harley S62. . . . . .76 D1
Sheffield S11 . . . . .139 F5
Harlington Cl DN12. . . . . . .81 A3
Harlington Rd
Mexborough, Adwick Upon
Dearne S64. . . . . .79 F8
Mexborough S64 . . . . .80 B6
Harmby Cl DN6. . . . . .20 F2
Harmer La S1 . . . . .161 B3
Harmony Way S60 . . . . .131 C6
Harney Cl S19 . . . . .130 C5
Harold Ave
Adwick le S DN6 . . . . .40 A5
Barnsley S71 . . . . .34 E4
Harold Croft S61 . . . . .97 C4
Harold St S6 . . . . .128 D6
Harpenden Cl DN7. . . . . . . .44 A6
Harpendon Dr DN7 . . . . .44 A6
Harriers Ct WF9 . . . . .18 F1
Harriet Cl S70. . . . . .55 A7
Harrington Cl S71 . . . . .34 C4
Harrington Rd ⬛ S2 . . . . . .141 A8
Harrington St DN1. . . . . . . .62 D4
Harrison Dr S81. . . . . .136 F3
Harrison La S10 . . . . .139 A7
Harrison Rd S64. . . . . .128 B7
Harrison St S61 . . . . .115 A6
Harris Rd
Armthorpe DN3. . . . . .63 F6
Sheffield S6 . . . . .112 B2
Harrogate Dr DN12 . . . . . . .80 E2
Harrogate Rd S26. . . . . . . .144 C6
Harrop Dr S64. . . . . .79 C1
Harrop Garden Flats S64. . .79 D3
Harrop La S10 . . . . .138 F6
Harrowden Ct S9 . . . . .114 E2
Harrowden Rd
Doncaster DN2 . . . . .62 F6
Sheffield S9 . . . . .114 E2
Harrow Rd S11. . . . . .64 C7
Harrow St
Sheffield S11 . . . . .160 C1
South Elmsall WF9 . . . . .18 E1
Harry Firth Cl ⬛ S9 . . . . .130 A5
Harry Rd S75. . . . . .33 B3
Hartcliff Ave S36. . . . . .50 L1
Hartcliffe La S36 . . . . .50 L1
Hartcliffe View S35. . . . . . .73 A7
Hartcliff Hill Rd S36. . . . . .72 A7
Hartcliff Nick S36 . . . . .71 E8
Hartcliff Rd
Penistone, Ecklands S36 . . . .71 D8
Penistone S36. . . . . .51 B1
Hartford Cl S18. . . . . .141 A3
Hartford Rd S8 . . . . .141 A3
Hart Hill S62 . . . . .97 D8
Harthill Field Rd S26 . . . . .158 A3
Harthill La S43 . . . . .157 E1
Harthill Prim Sch S26 . . . . .157 E5

Harthill Rd
Conisbrough DN12. . . . . . . .81 A1
Sheffield S13 . . . . .142 B7
Thorpe Salvin S80. . . . . . . .158 D7
Hart Hills S73 . . . . .77 B7
Hartington Ave S7 . . . . . . .140 C3
Hartington Cl S61 . . . . .115 A6
Hartington Ct S18 . . . . . . .153 B2
Hartington Dr S71 . . . . .33 F4
Hartington Rd
Dronfield S18. . . . . .153 B2
Rotherham S61 . . . . .115 A6
Sheffield S7 . . . . .140 C3
Hartland Ave S19 . . . . .144 A2
Hartland Cres DN3. . . . . . . .42 F2
Hartland Ct ⬛ S20 . . . . . . .144 A2
Hartland Dr S20 . . . . .144 A2
Hartley Brook Ave S5 . . . . .113 C6
Hartley Brook Prim Sch
S5. . . . . .113 C6
Hartley Brook Rd S5 . . . . . .113 C6
Hartley Cl
South Elmsall WF9. . . . . . . .19 A4
Swinton S64 . . . . .79 D1
Hartley La S61. . . . . .115 C7

Hartley St
Mexborough S64 . . . . .79 F4
Sheffield S2 . . . . .141 A7
Hartopp Ave S2. . . . . .141 C6
Hartopp Cl S2 . . . . .141 C6
Hartopp Dr S2 . . . . .141 D6
Hartopp Rd S2 . . . . .141 D6
Harts Head S1. . . . . .161 B4
Hartshead Sq S3 . . . . .161 B4

Harvest Cl
Carlton in L S81. . . . . .148 F7
Doncaster DN4 . . . . .82 F8
Kirk Sandall DN3 . . . . .43 A3
Maltby S66. . . . . .118 C4
Worsbrough S70 . . . . .55 A4
Harvest La S3 . . . . .129 A5
Harvest Rd S66. . . . . .117 B5
Harvest Way DN14 . . . . .2 D7
Harvey Cl DN9. . . . . .86 F4
Harvey Clough Mews S8 . . .141 B3
Harvey Clough Rd S8 . . . . .141 B3
Harvey Rd S35. . . . . .95 A5
Harvey St
Barnsley S70 . . . . .54 D8
Stocksbridge S36. . . . . .73 D1
Harwell Rd S8. . . . . .140 F7
Harwich Rd S2 . . . . .129 F1
Harwood Cl S2 . . . . .141 A8
Harwood Dr S20 . . . . .143 E1
Harwood Gdns S20. . . . . . .143 E1
Harwood St ⬛ S2 . . . . .141 A8
Harwood Terr S71 . . . . .34 C2
Harworth Ind Est DN11. . . .122 A1
Harworth Rd DN10 . . . . . . .123 A7
Haslam Cres S8 . . . . .152 E6
Haslam Pl S66. . . . . .119 B6
Haslam Rd DN11. . . . . .84 F1
Haslehurst Rd S2 . . . . .129 C2
Haslemere Ct DN5. . . . . . . .62 A6
Haslemere Gr DN5. . . . . . . .62 B6
Hassop Cl S18 . . . . .153 C2
Hastilar Cl S2 . . . . .142 B8
Hastilar Rd S2 . . . . .142 B8
Hastilar Rd S S13. . . . . . . .142 C7
Hastings Mount S7 . . . . . . .140 C4
Hastings Rd S7 . . . . .140 C4
Hastings St S72 . . . . .36 A7
Hatchell Dr DN4. . . . . .85 A5
Hatchell Wood Dr DN4. . . . .85 B5
Hatchell Wood Prim Sch
DN4. . . . . .85 A6
Hatchell Wood View DN4. . .85 B5
Hatfield Cl S71 . . . . .33 E7
Hatfield Cres S35 . . . . .14 B4
*Hatfield Crookesbroom Prim
Sch* DN7. . . . . .44 A8
Hatfield Gdns S71 . . . . .15 B4
Hatfield High Sch DN7. . . . .44 B7
Hatfield Ho ⬛ DN1 . . . . . . .62 C2
Hatfield House Croft S5. . .113 D5
Hatfield House Ct S5. . . . . .113 D5
Hatfield House La S5 . . . . .113 D5
Hatfield La
Armthorpe DN3. . . . . .64 C7
Barnby Dun DN3 . . . . .43 B6
Edenthorpe DN3. . . . . .43 C1
Hatfield Manor CE Jun Sch
DN7 . . . . .44 C8
Hatfield Prim Sch S65 . . . .113 D5
Hatfield Rd DN7, DN8. . . . . .44 B7
*Hatfield Sheep Dip Lane
Prim Sch* DN7. . . . . .44 A7
Hatfield & Stainforth Sta
DN7. . . . . .24 F2
Hatfield Travis CE Inf Sch
DN7. . . . . .44 C8
*Hatfield Water Park & Visitor
Ctr* * DN7 . . . . .25 D1
Hatfield Woodouse Prim Sch
DN7 . . . . .45 A6
Hatherley Rd
Rotherham S65 . . . . .115 E8
Sheffield S9 . . . . .114 E2
Swinton S64 . . . . .79 D4
Hathersage Pk S32 . . . . . . .149 A7
Hathersage Rd S11, S17 . . .150 D6
Hathersage Sta S32 . . . . . .149 D4
Hatter Dr DN12. . . . . .101 B8
Hatton Rd S6. . . . . .128 B7
Haugh Gn S62 . . . . .97 D8
Haugh La S11 . . . . .139 F5
Haugh Rd S62. . . . . .97 D7
Haughton Rd S8 . . . . .140 F2
Hauxwell Cl DN6. . . . . .20 F2
Havelock Rd DN4 . . . . .62 C1
Havelock St
Barnsley S70 . . . . .54 D8
Darfield S73. . . . . .57 A5
Sheffield S10 . . . . .160 B2
Swinton S64. . . . . .131 B6
Haven The S26 . . . . .146 B2
Havercroft Jun & Inf Sch
WF4 . . . . .16 B8
Havercroft Rd
Rotherham S60 . . . . .116 C3
Sheffield S8 . . . . .140 E3
Havercroft Rise S72. . . . . . .16 E6
Havercroft Terr S72. . . . . . .156 B7
Haverdale Rise S75 . . . . . . .33 D3
Haverhill Gr S73. . . . . .56 E3
Haverlands La S70. . . . . . . .54 E4
Haverlands Ridge S70 . . . . .54 F4
Haverlands The WF9 . . . . . .17 E6
Haw Ct S75. . . . . .52 F8
Hawes Cl S64. . . . . .80 C6
Hawfield Cl DN4 . . . . .62 A1
Hawke Cl
Norton DN6 . . . . .4 E3

Hawke Cl continued
Rawmarsh S62 . . . . .97 C7
Hawke Rd DN2 . . . . .62 F6
Hawke St S9 . . . . .130 A8
Hawk Hill La S66 . . . . .133 E4
Hawkhouse Green La
DN3 . . . . .23 D7
Hawkins Ave S35. . . . . .94 E5
Hawkins Cl DN11 . . . . .122 A6
Hawkshead Ave S18 . . . . . .152 E1
Hawkshead Cres S25 . . . . .146 F6
Hawkshead Rd S4 . . . . .113 F1
Hawksley Ave S6 . . . . .128 C8
Hawksley Cl DN3 . . . . .64 B6
Hawksley Dr DN3 . . . . .64 B7
Hawksley Mews S6 . . . . . . .128 C8
Hawksley Rd S6 . . . . .128 C8
Hawksley Rise S35. . . . . . . .116 D1
Hawksway S21. . . . . .155 B3
Hawksworth Cl S65. . . . . . .116 C7
Hawksworth Rd
Rotherham S65 . . . . .116 D8
Sheffield S6 . . . . .128 C8
Hawkwell Bank S71. . . . . . .56 A8
Hawley St
Apperknowle S18. . . . . .154 A1
Rawmarsh S62 . . . . .97 F5
Sheffield S1 . . . . .161 A4
Haworth Bank S60. . . . . . . .113 F1
Haworth Cl S71. . . . . .34 B3
Haworth Cres S60 . . . . .115 F1
Hawshaw La S74 . . . . .76 C6
Hawson St S73 . . . . .56 E2
Hawthorn Ave
Armthorpe DN3. . . . . .64 B7
Maltby S66. . . . . .118 E5
Hawthorn Ct S65 . . . . .116 B7
Hawthorne Ave
Dronfield S18. . . . . .153 A3
Dunsville DN7 . . . . .43 E4
Hemsworth WF9 . . . . .17 D6
Norton DN6. . . . . .4 F3
Rawmarsh S62 . . . . .98 A5
South Anston S25 . . . . .146 E3
Thorne DN8 . . . . .9 B1
Hawthorne Chase S64 . . . . .79 C3
Hawthorne Cl S63 . . . . .56 D5
Hawthorne Cres
Adwick le S DN6 . . . . .21 A1
Dodworth S75 . . . . .53 E8
Hemsworth WF9 . . . . .17 C6
Mexborough S64 . . . . .79 C2
Hawthorne Croft S63 . . . . . .58 C5
Hawthorne Dr S63 . . . . .32 B8
Hawthorne Dr S63. . . . . . . .58 D2
Hawthorne Flats S63. . . . . .37 D1
Hawthorne Gr
Bentley DN5. . . . . .41 B2
Thorne DN8 . . . . .9 B1
Wath u D S63. . . . . .79 A5
Hawthorne Pl S26 . . . . .144 E7
Hawthorne St
Barnsley S70 . . . . .54 E8
Shafton S72 . . . . .16 C3
Sheffield S6 . . . . .128 C8
Hawthornes The S20. . . . . .143 F4
Hawthorne Way S81. . . . . . .148 E2
Hawthorn Gr
Conisbrough DN12. . . . . . . .100 A8
Silkstone S75 . . . . .31 F1
Hawthorn Prim Sch DN4. . .63 E1
Hawthorn Rd
Chapeltown S35. . . . . .94 E7
Eckington S21 . . . . .155 B2
Sheffield S6 . . . . .128 B8
Hawthorns The S20. . . . . . .119 A8
Hawthorn Terr ⬛ S10. . . . .128 C3
Hawthorn Way S81 . . . . . . .148 E2
Hawtop La WF4. . . . . .13 F5
Haxby Cl S13. . . . . .142 E6
Haxby Pl S13 . . . . .142 E6
Haxby St S13. . . . . .142 E6
Haybrook Cl S17 . . . . .151 E5
Haydn Rd S66 . . . . .119 B4
Haydock Cl S64. . . . . .80 A6
Haydon Gr S66. . . . . .117 B6
Hayes Croft ⬛ S70 . . . . . . .33 F7
Hayes Cl S20 . . . . .155 E6
Hayes Dr S20. . . . . .155 E6
Hayes La DN7 . . . . .8 B2
Hayfield Cl
Barnby Dun DN3 . . . . .43 A7
Dodworth S75 . . . . .53 E7
Dronfield S18 . . . . .152 E8
Hayfield Cres S12. . . . . . . .142 D3
Hayfield Dr DN9 . . . . .86 B4
Hayfield Dr S12. . . . . .142 D3
Hayfield La DN9 . . . . .86 B4
Hayfield Lane Prim Sch
DN9 . . . . .85 F4
Hayfield Pl S12 . . . . .142 D3
Hayfield Sch The DN9. . . . . .85 F5
Hayfield View S21. . . . . . . .155 A6
Hayfield Wlk S61 . . . . .96 E1
Hay Green La S70 . . . . .54 A4
Hayhurst Cres S66. . . . . . . .119 A4
Hayland St S9 . . . . .114 A2
Haylock Cl S75 . . . . .32 E3
Haymarket S1. . . . . .161 B4
Haynes Cl DN8 . . . . .26 C7
Haynes Gdns DN8. . . . . . . .26 C7
Haynes Gn DN8. . . . . .26 C6

Haynes Gr DN8 . . . . .26 C6
Haynes Rd DN8. . . . . .26 C7
Haythorne Way S64. . . . . . .79 D1
Haywagon Park Homes
DN6. . . . . .24 A2
Haywood Ave S36. . . . . .73 D1
Haywood Cl S65 . . . . .116 C7
Haywood La
Askern DN5, DN6. . . . . .22 C5
Stocksbridge, Knoll Top S36 .73 D1
Stocksbridge, Wood Royd
S36 . . . . .72 D6
Haywood Pl ⬛ DN6. . . . . . . .22 B8
Hazel Ave
Finningley DN9 . . . . .86 A4
Killamarsh S21 . . . . .156 C5
Hazelbadge Cres S12 . . . . .142 E3
Hazel Ct S65 . . . . .117 E8
Hazel Gr
Armthorpe DN3 . . . . .64 C7
Chapeltown S35. . . . . .95 A4
Conisbrough DN12. . . . . . . .81 B1
Rossington DN11 . . . . .103 F8
Rotherham S66 . . . . .117 C5
Hazel La DN6. . . . . .20 A2
Hazel Rd
Eckington S21 . . . . .155 C2
Hatfield DN7 . . . . .24 F1
Maltby S66. . . . . .118 D5
New Edlington DN12 . . . . . .82 B2
Hazelshaw S75. . . . . .54 A6
Hazelshaw Gdns S35. . . . . .94 D7
Hazelwood S71. . . . . .34 A5
Hazelwood Cl ⬛ S18 . . . . .152 C1
Hazelwood Dr S64. . . . . . . .98 D8
Hazelwood Gdns ⬛ WF9 . . .17 E6
Hazlebarrow Cl S8 . . . . . . .153 C6
Hazlebarrow Cres S8 . . . . .153 B7
Hazlebarrow Ct S8. . . . . . . .153 B7
Hazlebarrow Dr S8 . . . . . . .153 B7
Hazlebarrow Gr S8 . . . . . . .153 C7
Hazlebarrow Rd S8 . . . . . . .153 B7
Hazledene Cres S72 . . . . . .16 D1
Hazledene Rd S72 . . . . .16 D1
Hazlehurst Cl S65 . . . . .98 D1
Hazlehurst La S8 . . . . .153 F8
Headford Gdns S3. . . . . . . .160 C2
Headford Mews S3. . . . . . . .160 C2
Headford St S3. . . . . .160 C2
Headingley Cl DN3. . . . . . . .42 F5
Headingley Rd DN6. . . . . . . .4 D3
Headingley Way DN12. . . . .82 C3
Headland Dr S10 . . . . .128 A3
Headland Rd S10 . . . . .128 A3
Headlands Rd S74 . . . . .76 C6
Heads La S36. . . . . .92 B6
Heath Ave S21. . . . . .156 D5
Heath Bank Rd DN2. . . . . . .63 C7
Heathcote St ⬛ S4 . . . . . . .113 D1
Heath Ct DN4. . . . . .82 D7
Heatherbank Rd DN4 . . . . . .84 E7
Heather Garth Prim Sch
S63. . . . . .58 D2
Heather Knowle S75. . . . . . .54 A7
Heather La S32 . . . . .149 A6
Heather Lea Ave S17. . . . . .151 C7
Heather Lea Pl S17 . . . . . . .151 C7
Heather Rd S75 . . . . .113 E3
Heathers Edge S32 . . . . . . .149 A6
Heather Wlk S63 . . . . .58 B3
Heatherwood Cl DN3 . . . . . .63 C6
Heathfield Cl
Barnby Dun DN3 . . . . .43 A6
⬛ Dronfield S18 . . . . .152 F1
Heathfield Rd S12 . . . . .142 D4
Heathfields S70 . . . . .55 B8
Heath Gr S63 . . . . .58 B1
Heath Rd
Sheffield S6 . . . . .112 D4
Stocksbridge S36 . . . . .92 D8
Heathy La S66 . . . . .121 B6
Heaton Gdns DN12. . . . . . . .82 C3
Heatons Bank S62. . . . . . . .98 A6
Heator La HD8. . . . . .29 A7
Heavens Wlk DN4 . . . . .62 D1
Heavygate Ave S10 . . . . . . .128 B6
Heavygate Rd S10 . . . . .128 C5
Hebble Oval WF9. . . . . .19 B2
Hebble Way WF9 . . . . .19 B1
Hedge Hill Rd S36. . . . . . . .51 A3
Hedge La S75 . . . . .32 D8
Heeley Arches S2. . . . . .141 A7
Heeley Bank Rd S2 . . . . . . .141 A7
Heeley City Farm * S2. . . . .141 A7
Heeley Gn S2 . . . . .141 B6
Heeley Ret Pk S8 . . . . .140 F5
Heelis St S70 . . . . .54 F8
Heighton View S21 . . . . . . .132 D1
Heights View S35. . . . . .74 A6
Helena Cl S70 . . . . .55 A5
Helena St S64 . . . . .80 A5
Helensburgh Cl S75. . . . . . .32 E8
Hellaby Hall Rd S66 . . . . . .118 A6
Hellaby La S66 . . . . .118 B6
Hellaby View S65 . . . . .117 D7
Helliwell Ct S36 . . . . .92 E7

Har–Hes **181**

Helliwell La S36. . . . . .92 E8
Helmsley Ave S20. . . . . . . .155 E7
Helmsley Cl S26 . . . . .144 C6
Helmton Dr S8 . . . . .141 A2
Helmton Rd S8. . . . . .140 F2
Helston Cres S71. . . . . .34 B3
Helston Rise S7 . . . . .140 C4
Hemingfield Rd S73 . . . . . . .77 C8
Heming's Way WF9 . . . . . . .19 B3
Hemmingway Cl S60. . . . . . .131 E3
Hemper Gr S8. . . . . .152 D7
Hemper La S8. . . . . .152 D7
Hemp Pits Rd DN5 . . . . .41 D1
Hemsworth Arts & Com Coll
WF9 . . . . .17 E7
Hemsworth Rd
Sheffield S8, S14 . . . . .141 C2
South Kirkby WF9 . . . . .17 F4
Henderson Glen S71 . . . . . .15 A3
Hendon St S13 . . . . .130 F1
Hengist Dr DN5 . . . . .61 F2
Henley Ave S8 . . . . .153 C8
Henley Grove Rd S61 . . . . .115 B3
Henley Rd DN2 . . . . .63 C5
Henley Rise S61 . . . . .115 B7
Henley St DN11 . . . . .84 F8
Henry Ave WF4 . . . . .16 C4
Henry Cl S72 . . . . .16 C3
Henry Ct
Rawmarsh S62 . . . . .97 F3
⬛ Rotherham S60 . . . . .115 D7
Thorne DN8 . . . . .9 C1
Henry Fanshawe Sch
S18. . . . . .153 B2
Henry La DN11 . . . . .84 D1
Henry Pl S64 . . . . .80 C5
Henry Rd S63. . . . . .79 A6
Henry St
Chapeltown S35. . . . . .94 C7
Darfield S73. . . . . .56 F4
Eckington S21 . . . . .155 D3
Sheffield S3 . . . . .160 C5
⬛ Worsbrough S70. . . . . . . .55 A5
Henshall St ⬛ S70. . . . . . . .55 A8
Henson St S9. . . . . .130 B6
Heppenstall La S9 . . . . .129 F6
Heptinstall St S70 . . . . .55 B5
Hepworth Dr S26 . . . . .144 D7
Hepworth Rd DN4. . . . . .82 F7
Herald Rd DN2 . . . . .42 E1
Herbert Cl DN5 . . . . .62 A5
Herbert Rd
Bentley DN5. . . . . .62 A5
Sheffield S7 . . . . .140 E6
Herbert St
Mexborough S64 . . . . .80 C5
Rotherham S61 . . . . .114 E7
Herdings Ct S12. . . . . .142 A3
Herdings Rd S12 . . . . .142 A3
Herdings View S12 . . . . . . .142 A3
Hereford Cl WF9 . . . . .17 D8
Hereford Rd DN2 . . . . .63 B7
Hereward Ct DN12 . . . . .81 E2
Hereward Rd S5. . . . . .113 C4
Hereward's Rd S14 . . . . . . .141 D1
Hermes Cl DN10 . . . . .122 E8
Hermitage St S2. . . . . .160 C1
Hermitage The DN8 . . . . .9 D3
Hermit Hill S35. . . . . .74 F6
Hermit Hill La S35 . . . . .74 E4
Hermit La S75 . . . . .32 F3
Heron Ct
Conisbrough DN12. . . . . . . .81 F2
Doncaster DN2 . . . . .63 A7
Heron Dr S63 . . . . .77 F7
Heron Hill S26. . . . . .144 E6
Heron Mount S2 . . . . .129 E2
Herons Way
Barnsley S70 . . . . .75 F8
Doncaster DN4 . . . . .83 D7
Herrick Gdns DN4 . . . . .83 C6
Herrick Rd DN3. . . . . .42 F8
Herries Ave S5 . . . . .113 B3
Herries Dr S5 . . . . .113 B2
Herries Pl S5. . . . . .113 A2
Herries Rd S5, S6. . . . . . . .112 D2
Herries Rd S S5 . . . . .113 A2
Herril Ings DN11. . . . . .121 B8
Herringthorpe Ave S65. . . . .116 B4
Herringthorpe Cl S65. . . . . .116 B5
Herringthorpe Gr S65. . . . . .116 C4
Herringthorpe Jun & Inf Sch
S65. . . . . .116 B4
Herringthorpe La S65. . . . . .116 B4
Herringthorpe Valley Rd S60,
S65. . . . . .116 C6
Herriot Gr DN11 . . . . .122 A4
Herschell Rd S7. . . . . .140 F7
Hesketh Dr DN3. . . . . .43 A4
Hesley Bar S61. . . . . .95 E4
Hesley Ct S5. . . . . .99 C1
Hesley Gr S35. . . . . .95 C4
Hesley Grange S61 . . . . .96 C2
Hesley Hall Coll DN11. . . . .103 F4
Hesley Mews S61. . . . . .96 C2
Hesley Rd
Rossington DN11. . . . . .103 F8
Sheffield S5 . . . . .113 D7
Hesley Terr S5. . . . . .113 E7

Heslow Gr S61 95 E5
Hessey St S13 142 F6
Hessle Rd S6 112 B2
Hethersett Way DN11 103 E7
Hewitt Pl S26 157 E5
Hewitt St S64 80 C5
Hexthorpe Prim Sch DN4 62 A1
Hexthorpe Rd DN4 62 B2
Heyhouse Dr S35 94 F7
Heyhouse Way S35 94 F7
Heysham Gn S71 34 D6
Hey Slack La HD8 28 C2
Heywood Bottom HD8 30 A6
Heyworth La DN6 22 E8
Hibberd Pl S6 128 A8
Hibberd Rd S6 128 B8
Hibbert Terr 3 S70 54 F7
Hickleton Ct S63 58 C7
Hickleton Rd DN5 59 C4
Hickleton St DN12 80 F3
Hickleton Terr S63 58 E7
Hickmott Rd S11 140 D8
Hickson Dr S71 34 E4
Hicks St S3 129 A6
Hides St S9 130 B8
High Alder Rd DN4 84 C8
Higham Common Rd S75 32 B3
Higham Ct S75 32 E2
Higham La S75 32 E1
Higham View S75 32 D7
High Ash Ave HD8 12 A2
High Ash Cl WF4 14 F7
High Ash Dr S25 146 D3
High Balk S75 33 D4
High Bank S36 51 A3
High Bank La S36 50 E4
High Bridge Rd DN8 26 F5
Highbury Ave DN4 84 E8
Highbury Cres DN4 84 E8
Highbury Vale DN12 82 A1
High Cl S75 13 D1
Highcliffe Ct
Sheffield S11 140 A7
Swinton S64 79 E3
Highcliffe Dr
Oughtibridge S35 111 D6
Sheffield S11 139 F7
Swinton S64 79 D3
Highcliffe Pl S11 139 F6
Highcliffe Rd S11 139 F6
High Common La
Austerfield DN10 105 B6
Tickhill DN11 121 F8
Highcroft 5 S11 140 A7
High Croft S74 76 E5
High Croft Dr S71 33 F8
High Ct S1 161 B3
Highfield Ave
Barnsley S71 34 A6
Denby Dale HD8 29 A4
Goldthorpe S63 58 D5
Kiveton Park S26 145 E3
Worsbrough S70 54 F6
Highfield Bglws S63 78 F6
Highfield Cl
Barnby Dun DN3 43 A7
Hatfield DN7 25 B1
Highfield Cotts S75 32 A1
Highfield Ct
Shepley HD8 28 E6
Swinton S64 79 C3
Wombwell S73 56 C3
Highfield Ctr WF9 17 D6
Highfield Gr S63 78 A7
Highfield Ho S63 78 F6
Highfield La
Thorpe in B DN6 23 B4
Treeton S13, S60 131 C3
High Field La DN10 105 B3
Highfield Pk S66 119 B6
Highfield Pl
Hemsworth WF9 17 C6
Sheffield S2 141 A8
Highfield Range S73 57 A7
Highfield Rd
Askern DN6 22 B8
Bawtry DN10 123 B8
Conisbrough DN12 81 D2
Darfield S73 57 A6
Doncaster DN1 62 E4
Hemsworth WF9 17 D6
Rotherham S61 97 C3
Swinton S64 79 B3
Highfield Rise S6 127 C6
Highfields S36 51 F6
Highfields Country Pk* DN6 40 B3
Highfields Prim Sch DN6 40 B2
High Field Spring S60 131 A4
Highfields Rd S75 32 B8
Highfield View S60 131 C6
Highfield Villas S81 148 F8
High Fisher Gate DN1 62 D4
Highgate
Sheffield S9 114 E2
Wombwell S73 57 B2
Highgate Cl DN11 104 A7
Highgate Ct S63 58 C4
Highgate Greyhound Stad S63 58 D6
Highgate La S63 58 C4
High Gate Way S72 16 C2
High Greave S5 113 C6
High Greave Ave S5 113 C7
High Greave Ct S5 113 C6
High Greave Jun & Inf Schs S65 116 C8
High Greave Pl S65 116 C7
High Greave Rd S65 116 C8
High Green Prim Sch S35 94 D8
Highgrove Ct DN4 85 A6
High Hazel Cres S60 131 C6
High Hazel Ct S60 131 E4
High Hazel Rd
Thorne DN8 9 D3
Treeton S60 131 E4
High Hazels Cl S9 130 D4
High Hazels Mead S9 130 D4
High Hooton Rd S66 118 E1
High House Farm Ct S26 145 B2
High House Terr S6 128 D7
High Hoyland La S75 31 B8
High La
Eckington S12 142 E1
Ingbirchworth S36 50 E7
Sheffield S12 154 F8
Ulley S66 133 C3
High Lee La S36 52 A4
High Levels Bank DN8 27 C1
Highlow View S60 115 C1
High Matlock Ave S6 127 D6
High Matlock Rd S6 127 D6
High Mdw DN10 122 F7
Highmill Ave S64 79 B3
Highmoor Ave S26 145 C2
Highnam Crescent Rd S10 128 C3
High Nook Rd S25 147 A8
High Pavement Row 4 S2 161 C4
High Rd
Doncaster, Balby DN4 83 A7
New Edlington DN12 82 B1
Warmsworth DN4 82 C6
High Ridge S70 54 F5
Highridge Cl DN12 81 D1
High Royd Ave S72 35 B6
High Royd Cotts S36 52 A5
High Royd La
Barnsley S74 76 B8
Penistone S36 52 A5
Highroyds S70 54 F6
High St
Adwick le S DN6 40 C8
Apperknowle S18 154 A1
Askern DN6 22 A7
Aston S26 144 C7
Barnburgh DN5 59 D3
Barnby Dun DN3 42 F7
Barnsley S71 34 C4
Bawtry DN10 123 A6
Bentley, Arksey DN5 41 D2
Bentley DN5 62 B8
Bolton u D S63 58 C2
Braithwell S66 101 A2
Clayton West HD8 12 A1
Conisbrough DN12 81 C2
Darton S75 14 A2
Dodworth S75 53 F7
Doncaster DN1 62 D3
Dronfield S18 153 A1
Dunsville DN7 43 E4
East Cowick DN14 1 C7
Eckington S21 155 D3
Goldthorpe S63 58 E5
Great Houghton, Billingley S72 57 F6
Great Houghton S72 36 D2
Grimethorpe S72 36 A6
Hatfield DN7 44 D8
Hoyland S74 76 E6
Killamarsh S21 156 D6
Laughton en le M S25 134 D5
Maltby S66 119 A5
Mexborough S64 80 A4
Norton, Campsall DN6 21 C8
Norton DN6 4 D3
Penistone S36 51 D2
Rawmarsh S62 97 F5
Rotherham, Kimberworth S61 114 E7
Rotherham S60 115 D6
Rotherham, Whiston S60 116 B1
Royston S71 15 B3
Shafton S72 16 C2
Sheffield, Beighton S20 144 A4
Sheffield, Dore S17 151 D7
Sheffield, Ecclesfield S35 113 B8
Sheffield, Mosborough S20 155 D7
Sheffield S3 161 B3
Silkstone S75 53 A8
South Anston S25 146 D4
South Elmsall WF9 19 A3
South Hiendley S72 16 E5
Thurnscoe S63 58 C7
Upton WF9 19 B7
Wadworth DN11 102 B7
Wath u D S63 78 F6
West Cowick DN14 1 A7
Wombwell S73 56 D3
Woolley WF4 14 A7
Worsbrough S70 55 B5
Wroot DN9 67 A3
Highstone Ave S70 54 F7
Highstone Cnr S70 54 F6
Highstone Cres S70 54 E7
Highstone Ct S70 54 F7
Highstone La S70 54 F6
Highstone Rd S70 54 F7
Highstone Vale S70 54 E7
High Storrs Cl S11 140 A6
High Storrs Cres S11 140 A7
High Storrs Dr S11 140 A7
High Storrs Rd S11 139 F6
High Storrs Rise S11 140 A7
High Storrs Sch S11 139 F6
High Street La S2 161 C3
High Street Mews S20 155 C7
High Thorne Way S26 145 F3
Highthorn Rd S62 98 E8
High Thorns S75 52 F8
Highton St S6 128 C6
High Trees
Rotherham S60 116 B3
Sheffield S17 151 D7
High View
Royston S71 15 B3
Sheffield S5 129 A8
High View Cl S73 57 B6
High View Prim Learning Ctr S73 56 C3
High View Prim Learning Ctr (Infant Site) S73 56 B3
High Well Hill La S72 16 C6
Highwood Cl S75 32 C8
Highwood Pl S21 155 C3
Highwoods Cres S64 79 E5
Highwoods Prim Sch S64 79 E6
Highwoods Rd S64 79 E6
High Wray S11 140 B4
High Wray Cl S11 140 B4
Hilary Way S26 144 D7
Hild Ave S72 35 D4
Hillary Ho DN2 62 F6
Hill Cl
Rotherham S65 116 E4
Sheffield S6 127 C6
Hillcote Cl S10 127 D1
Hillcote Dr S10 127 D1
Hillcote Mews S10 127 D1
Hillcote Rise S10 127 D1
Hillcrest S63 58 C7
Hill Crest
Adwick le S DN6 20 E1
Hoyland S74 76 C5
Hillcrest Dr
Oughtibridge S35 111 C6
South Anston S25 146 D4
Hillcrest Rd
Doncaster DN2 63 A6
Stocksbridge S36 92 F8
Hill Crest Rd
Chapeltown S35 94 F5
Rotherham S65 116 B7
Hillcrest Rise S36 92 F8
Hillcrest Way S66 117 B8
Hill End Rd S75 33 C7
Hill Est WF9 19 B7
Hill Farm Cl S63 58 B7
Hillfold WF9 19 B3
Hillfoot Ct S17 151 D4
Hillfoot Rd
Sheffield, Hillfoot S17 151 D5
Sheffield S3 128 E6
Hill Gdns DN11 122 A4
Hill House Sch DN1 62 E4
Hill Primary Sch The S63 37 F1
Hill Rd DN11 121 F4
Hillsborough Barracks Bsns & Sh Ctr S6 128 D8
Hillsborough Ctr Sh Arc S6 128 C8
Hillsborough Football Ground S6 112 C2
Hillsborough Pl S6 128 C8
Hillsborough Prim Sch S6 112 C2
Hillsborough Rd
Doncaster DN4 84 E8
Sheffield S6 128 C8
Hills Cl
Bentley DN5 61 E2
4 Mexborough S64 80 A5
Hillscroft Rd DN9 86 E5
Hillside
Barnsley S71 56 A8
Denby Dale HD8 30 A6
North Anston S25 146 D6
Sheffield S20 155 C7
Hill Side
Rotherham S60 116 C1
Rotherham, Thorpe Hesley S61 95 F4
Hillside Ave
2 Dronfield S18 153 A1
Sheffield S5 113 B6
Hillside Cl S36 51 F6
Hillside Cotts S32 149 B7
Hillside Cres S72 17 A2
Hillside Ct
Rotherham S61 97 D1
South Elmsall WF9 19 A4
Sprotbrough DN5 82 B8
Hillside Dr
Hoyland S74 76 F5
New Edlington DN12 82 A1
Hillside Gr S72 17 A2
Hill Side La S36 50 F2
Hillside Mount S72 17 A2
Hillside Rd DN2 63 C7
Hillside The S4 114 A2
Hillside Way S35 74 D4
Hills Rd S36 73 D1
Hill St
Barnsley S71 55 E8
Darfield S73 57 A5
Hoyland S74 77 A5
Sheffield S2 129 A1
Hilltop S72 16 F3
Hill Top S75 31 E5
Hill Top Ave S71 14 E1
Hilltop Cl S66 118 D6
Hill Top Cl
Brinsworth S60 115 B1
Notton WF4 15 B6
Rotherham S61 114 D6
Hill Top Cres
Doncaster DN2 63 C7
New Edlington DN12 101 B8
Sheffield S20 143 D2
Hill Top Ct DN11 122 A4
Hilltop Dr S35 111 B8
Hill Top Est WF9 17 F1
Hilltop Gdns DN12 80 F2
Hilltop Gn S5 112 F3
Hill Top La
Barnsley S75 33 B3
Rotherham, Flanderwell S65, S66 117 A6
Rotherham, Richmond Park S61 114 D6
Sheffield S35 112 B8
Stocksbridge S35 73 D3
Hill Top Prim Sch DN12 82 A1
Hill Top Rd
Barnsley S70 75 F8
Conisbrough DN12 80 E2
Sheffield, Grenoside S35 112 D8
Sheffield, Hill Top S6 126 E7
Hill Top Rise S35 112 D8
Hilltop Sch S66 118 D6
Hill Top Smihies S71 33 F6
Hill Top View HD9 48 B8
Hill Turrets Cl S11 139 F4
Hill View E S61 114 D8
Hill View Rd S61 114 D8
Hilmian Way WF9 17 F5
Hilton Dr S35 113 B8
Hilton St
Askern DN6 22 A8
Barnsley S75 33 D2
Hindburn Cl DN4 84 C7
Hinde House 3-16 Sch S5 113 F4
Hinde House Cres S4 113 E2
Hinde House Croft S4 113 E2
Hinde House La S4 113 E2
Hinde St S4 113 E1
Hindewood Cl S4 113 E2
Hindle St S70 33 D1
Hind Rd S60 116 C2
Hinds Cres WF9 18 F3
Hirst Common La S6 112 B6
Hirst Dr S65 116 D7
Hirst Gate S64 80 C5
Hirst La
Shepley HD8 28 B5
Stainton S66 101 E1
HM Young Offenders Inst DN7 25 F1
Hoades Ave S81 147 E4
Hoar Stones Rd S6 109 D3
Hobart St S11 140 F8
Hobcroft Terr DN6 21 B1
Hob La S35 92 E2
Hobson Ave S6 128 E7
Hobson Pl S6 128 E7
Hodder Ct S35 94 F6
Hoddesdon Cres DN7 44 A5
Hodge La WF8 3 E6
Hodgkinson Ave S36 51 D3
Hodgson St S3 160 C2
Hodroyd Cl S72 16 D1
Hodroyd Cotts S72 16 F2
Hodroyd La S72 16 D1
Hodster La S72 36 D4
Hogarth Rise 1 S18 152 F1
Hog Close La HD9 49 C8
Holberry Cl S10 160 B2
Holberry Gdns S10 160 B2
Holbourne Gr S35 94 D8
Holbrook Ave S20 156 A8
Holbrook Dr S13 142 B6
Holbrook Gn S20 156 A8
Holbrook Rd S13 142 B7
Holbrook Rise S20 144 A1
Holburn Ave S18 153 A2
Holden Ct 14 S70 33 E1
Holderness Cl DN11 122 A4
Holderness Dr S26 144 D8
Holdings Rd S2 129 D1
Holdroyd's Yd S75 53 F6
Holdworth La S6 110 F4
Hole House La S36 73 B1
Holgate S73 56 B5
Holgate Ave S5 112 F6
Holgate Cl S5 112 F6
Holgate Cres
Hemsworth WF9 17 C7
Sheffield S5 113 A6
Holgate Dr S5 113 A6
Holgate Gdns WF9 17 C7
Holgate Meadows Com Specl Sch S5 113 B5
Holgate Mount S70 54 F6
Holgate Rd S5 113 A6
Holgate Sch S70 33 D1
Holgate View S72 17 B3
Holiwell Cl S66 119 B6
Holkham Rise S11 139 F2
Holland Cl S62 97 F7
Holland Pl 8 S2 141 A8
Holland Rd
Chapeltown S35 94 D7
Sheffield S2 141 A8
Holland St S1 160 C3
Hollinberry La S35 75 B1
Hollin Bridge La DN7 45 B5
Hollin Bridge Rd DN7 45 A6
Hollin Busk La S36 92 C7
Hollin Busk Rd S36 92 C8
Hollin Cl DN11 85 B2
Hollin Croft S75 54 A8
Hollindale Dr S12 142 C5
Hollin Edge HD8 30 A6
Hollin Edge La S36 92 F5
Holling's La S65 117 C8
Holling Croft S36 73 E1
Holling Hill La S66 116 F4
Hollingswood Way S66 117 C7
Hollingworth Cl S64 80 D6
Hollin House La
Clayton West HD8 31 A8
Sheffield S6 110 F3
Shepley HD9 28 A5
Hollin La S36 50 A4
Hollin Moor La
Rotherham S66 117 A4
Thurgoland S35 53 B1
Hollin Moor View S35 73 F7
Hollin Rd S35 111 C6
Hollins Cl S6 127 F5
Hollins Ct S6 127 F6
Hollins Dr S6 128 A5
Hollinsend Ave S12 142 C5
Hollinsend Pl S12 142 C5
Hollinsend Rd S12 142 B5
Hollins La S6 128 A6
Hollins Mount WF9 17 C7
Hollins The S75 54 A6
Hollins Wood Gr S72 35 D4
Hollis Cl S62 97 D8
Hollis Croft
Sheffield, Coisley Hill S13 143 A6
Sheffield, Netherthorpe S1 160 C4
Hollis Hospl S11 139 E2
Hollowdene S75 33 C3
Hollowgate
Barnburgh DN5 59 C2
Rotherham S60 115 E5
Hollow Gate
Cadeby DN5 81 C5
Chapeltown S35 94 D5
2 Rotherham S60 116 B1
Hollowgate Ave S63 78 C8
Hollow La
Sheffield, Mosborough S20 155 D6
Sheffield S20 155 E6
Hollow Meadows Mews S6 125 F4
Hollows The
Auckley DN9 86 A6
Doncaster DN4 84 E6
Holly's House Rd S65 99 F1
Holly Ave DN5 62 A7
Hollybank S12 142 B6
Hollybank Ave
Denby Dale HD8 29 C6
Sheffield S12 142 C6
Hollybank Cl S12 142 D6
Hollybank Cres S12 142 C6
Hollybank Dr S12 142 D6
Hollybank Rd S12 142 C6
Hollybank Way S12 142 D6
Holly Barn Fold S65 99 C6
Holly Bush Dr S63 58 D8
Hollybush St S62 97 F3
Holly Cl
Chapeltown S35 94 F4
Killamarsh S21 156 C5
South Elmsall WF9 18 F2
Holly Cres S66 117 C6
Hollycroft Ave S71 15 B3
Holly Croft Gr DN11 121 B7
Holly Ct
15 Barnsley S70 54 F7
Harworth DN11 121 E4
Holly Dene DN3 64 B8
Holly Dr DN5 41 B2
Holly Farm S72 16 C3
Hollygarth Ct WF9 17 D7
Hollygate S70 55 B5
Holly Gdns S12 142 C6
Holly Gr
Brierley S72 17 A3
Goldthorpe S63 58 C5
Rossington DN11 85 A2
Sheffield S12 142 C6
Wath u D S63 78 F4
Holly Hall La S35 73 F3
Holly House La S35 112 B8
Holly La 2 S1 161 A3
Holly Mount S66 117 C4
Holly Rd
Finningley DN9 86 A4
Thorne DN8 9 C2
Holly St
Doncaster DN1 62 C1
Hemsworth WF9 17 D7
Sheffield S1 161 A3
Holly Terr
Aston S26 144 C8
Doncaster DN4 82 F7
Hollythorpe Cres S8 141 A4
Hollythorpe Rd S8 141 B4
Hollythorpe Rise S8 141 B4
Hollytree Ave S66 118 D6
Hollywell Cl S62 98 B7
Hollywell Hts S4, S9 114 A2
Holly Wlk DN8 9 C2
Holm Cl S18 152 D2
Holme Cl S6 128 C8
Holme Ct
Goldthorpe S63 58 C4

Holme Ct *continued*
Rotherham S60 . . . . 115 E2
Holmefield Cl DN3 . . . . 64 C5
Holmefield Croft DN10 . . 123 A2
Holme Fleet La DN3 . . . . . . 23 D2
Holme Gdns DN7 . . . . 24 F5
Holme Hall La S66 . . . . 119 E8
Holme La
Askern DN5 . . . . 22 B2
Sheffield, Grenoside S35 . . 112 D7
Holme Oak Way S6 . . . . . 127 C7
Holme Rise WF9 . . . . 19 A2
Holmeroyd Rd DN6 . . . . 40 E7
Holmes Carr Cres DN11 . . . 84 D1
Holmes Carr Rd
Doncaster DN4 . . . . 84 D6
Rossington DN11 . . . . 84 D1
Holmes Cres S60 . . . . 131 E4
Holmesdale Cl S18 . . . . . 153 C3
Holmesdale Inf Sch S18. 153 C2
Holmesdale Rd S18 . . . . . 153 C3
Holmesfield S60 . . . . 115 A6
Holmes Field Cl S26 . . . . 146 C2
Holmesfield Rd
Dronfield S18 . . . . 152 B1
Oughtibridge S35 . . . . 111 D7
Holmes La
Hooton Roberts S65 . . . . 99 C7
Rotherham S61 . . . . 115 B6
Holmes Market The DN1 . . 62 D4
Holmes Rd S66 . . . . 117 D4
Holmes The DN1 . . . . 62 D4
Holme Styes La HD9 . . . . . . 48 A8
Holme View Rd S75 . . . . 32 B8
Holme Way S81 . . . . 148 D1
Holme Wood Ct 4 DN3 . . . 43 A2
Holme Wood Gdns DN4 . . . 84 E7
Holme Wood La DN3 . . . . . . 64 E6
Holmfirth Rd HD8 . . . . 28 E6
Holm Flatt St S62 . . . . 97 E3
Holmhirst Cl S8 . . . . 140 E2
Holmhirst Dr S8 . . . . 140 E3
Holmhirst Rd S8 . . . . 140 F2
Holmhirst Way S8 . . . . . . 140 E3
Holmley Bank S18 . . . . . . 153 A3
Holmley La S18 . . . . 153 A3
Holmoak Cl S64 . . . . 79 D1
Holmshaw Cl DN3 . . . . 43 A3
Holmshaw Dr S13 . . . . 142 E8
Holmshaw Gr S13 . . . . 142 E8
Holmsley Ave WF9 . . . . 18 A2
Holmsley Gr WF9 . . . . 18 A2
Holmsley La S72, WF9 . . . . 17 E2
Holmsley Mount WF9 . . . . . 18 A2
Holt House Gr S7 . . . . 140 D4
Holt House Inf Sch S7 . . 140 D4
Holtwood Rd S4 . . . . 129 B7
Holwick Cl S75 . . . . 52 F8
Holwick Ct 2 S70 . . . . 33 E1
Holy Cross Deanery CE Prim Sch S71 . . . . 34 B6
Holy Family RC Prim Sch DN7 . . . . 24 F5
Holy Gn S1 . . . . 161 A2
Holyoake Ave S13 . . . . 142 E8
Holyrood Ave S10 . . . . 126 F1
Holy Rood RC Prim Sch S70 . . . . 33 D1
Holyrood Rd DN2 . . . . 63 A3
Holyrood Rise S66 . . . . . . 117 D6
Holyrood View S10 . . . . . . 126 F1
Holywell Cres S66 . . . . . . 101 A1
Holywell La
Braithwell S66 . . . . 101 A1
Conisbrough DN12 . . . . 81 C1
Holywell Pl 7 S65 . . . . 115 E7
Holywell Rd
Sheffield S4, S9 . . . . 114 A2
Swinton S64 . . . . 79 D1
Homecroft Rd S63 . . . . 58 D5
Home Farm Ct
Hickleton DN5 . . . . 59 C7
Hooton Pagnell DN5 . . . . 38 D5
West Bretton WF4 . . . . 12 F7
Wortley S35 . . . . 74 D4
Homefield Cres DN5 . . . . . . 61 E8
Home Mdws DN11 . . . . 121 A6
Homestead Cl S5 . . . . 113 D5
Homestead Dr
Brinsworth S60 . . . . 115 B1
Rawmarsh S62 . . . . 97 F7
Homestead Garth DN7 . . . . 44 B8
Homestead Rd S5 . . . . 113 D5
Homestead The DN5 . . . . . . 41 B1
Honey Lands La DN5 . . . . . . 22 D2
Honeysuckle Cl
Darfield S73 . . . . 57 A5
Doncaster DN4 . . . . 84 C8
Honeysuckle Ct DN9 . . . . . . 86 E3
Honeysuckle Rd S5 . . . . . . 113 F3
Honeysuckle Wlk DN9 . . . . 86 E6
Honeywell Cl S71 . . . . 33 F3
Honeywell Gr S71 . . . . 33 F4
Honeywell La S71, S75 . . . . 33 E3
Honeywell Pl S71 . . . . 33 F3
Honeywell St S71 . . . . 33 F3
Honister Cl S63 . . . . 78 A7
Hoober Ave S11 . . . . 140 A5
Hoober Ct S62 . . . . 97 D8
Hoober Field S62, S63 . . . . 78 B2
Hoober Hall La S62 . . . . . . 78 B3
Hoober La S62 . . . . 78 B1
Hoober Rd S11 . . . . 140 A5
Hoober St S63 . . . . 78 B7
Hoober Stand* S62 . . . . 77 F1
Hoober View
Rawmarsh S62 . . . . 97 D8
Wombwell S73 . . . . 56 F1
Hood Green Rd S75 . . . . 53 E2
Hoodhill Rd
Harley S62 . . . . 76 D1
Rotherham S62 . . . . 95 D8
Hood St WF9 . . . . 18 E1
Hoole La S10 . . . . 128 C2
Hoole Rd S10 . . . . 128 C3
Hoole St S6 . . . . 128 D6
Hooton Cl S25 . . . . 134 E5
Hooton La
Laughton en le M S25 . . . . . 134 E6
Maltby S66 . . . . 118 E4
Ravenfield S65 . . . . 99 C3
Hooton Pagnell All Saints CE Prim Sch DN5 . . . . 38 C5
Hooton Rd
Brodsworth DN5 . . . . 38 F4
Swinton S64 . . . . 98 F7
Hope Ave S63 . . . . 58 D5
Hopedale Rd S12 . . . . 142 D4
Hopefield Ave S12 . . . . . . 142 D4
Hopefield Ct HD9 . . . . 48 B7
Hope Rd S35 . . . . 111 E6
Hope St
Barnsley S75 . . . . 33 D2
Barnsley, West Green S71 . . . 34 F6
Darfield S73 . . . . 56 F4
Havercroft WF4 . . . . 16 C8
Mapplewell S75 . . . . 33 C8
5 Mexborough S64 . . . . 80 A4
Rotherham S60 . . . . 115 C7
Stocksbridge S36 . . . . 73 C1
Wombwell S73 . . . . 56 E2
Hope Street Extension
S60 . . . . 115 C7
Hopewell St S70 . . . . 55 D8
Hop Hills DN7 . . . . 25 A1
Hop Hills La DN7 . . . . 25 A1
Hop Inge The S26 . . . . 157 F5
Hopping La S35 . . . . 52 F1
Hopwood La S6 . . . . 127 B4
Hopwood St S70 . . . . 33 E2
Hopyard La DN11 . . . . 103 C1
Horace St S60 . . . . 115 E5
Horbiry End S26 . . . . 145 E5
Horbury La S35 . . . . 94 E4
Horbury Rd S72 . . . . 35 B8
Hordron Rd S36 . . . . 70 C5
Hores Shoe Ct DN4 . . . . 82 F7
Hornbeam Cl S35 . . . . 94 F4
Hornbeam Rd S66 . . . . 117 B6
Hornby Ct S11 . . . . 140 A7
Hornby St S70 . . . . 55 A7
Horn Cote La HD9 . . . . 28 A6
Horncroft S75 . . . . 31 F5
Horndean Rd S5 . . . . 113 D1
Horner Cl S36 . . . . 73 B2
Horner Rd 1 S7 . . . . 141 A7
Hornes La S75 . . . . 14 C1
Horninglow Cl
Doncaster DN4 . . . . 85 A7
Sheffield S5 . . . . 113 C3
Horninglow Mount S5 . . . 113 C3
Horninglow Rd S5 . . . . 113 D3
Horn La
Ingbirchworth S36 . . . . 29 B1
Shepley HD9 . . . . 28 A6
Hornsby Rd DN3 . . . . 64 C5
Hornthorpe Rd S21 . . . . . . 155 C2
Hornthwaite Cl S36 . . . . 51 B3
Hornthwaite Hill Rd S36 . . 51 A3
Horse Carr View S71 . . . . . . 56 A8
Horse Croft La S35 . . . . . . 111 B8
Horsefair Cl S64 . . . . 79 D3
Horse Fair Gn DN8 . . . . 26 B7
Horsehills La DN3 . . . . 64 A5
Horsemoor Rd S63 . . . . 58 B8
Horseshoe Cl S26 . . . . 145 C3
Horseshoe Gdns S26 . . . . 145 B3
Horseshoe La S66 . . . . 135 E8
Horsewood Cl S70 . . . . 54 B8
Horsewood Rd S13 . . . . . . 143 D8
Horton Cl S20 . . . . 155 E7
Horton Dr S20 . . . . 155 E7
Horton View DN3 . . . . 42 E5
Hough La S73 . . . . 56 C2
Houghton Rd
North Anston S25 . . . . 146 B8
Thurnscoe S63 . . . . 58 B8
Hound Hill La
Barnsley S70 . . . . 54 D5
Mexborough S63 . . . . 79 D8
Houndkirk Rd S11 . . . . 138 F2
Hounsfield Cres S65 . . . . . 116 D7
Hounsfield La S10 . . . . 160 B3
Hounsfield Rd
Rotherham S65 . . . . 116 D7
Sheffield S3 . . . . 160 B3
Houps Rd DN8 . . . . 26 C7
House Carr La S75 . . . . 53 C4
Housley La S35 . . . . 94 F5
Housley Pk S35 . . . . 95 A6
Houstead Rd S9 . . . . 130 D3
Hoveringham Ct S26 . . . . . 144 C6
Howard La S2 . . . . 161 B2
Howard Rd
Bircotes DN11 . . . . 122 C4
Maltby S66 . . . . 119 B5
Rotherham S66 . . . . 117 E6
Sheffield S6 . . . . 160 A5
Howards Cl S66 . . . . 134 A6
Howard Sq S1 . . . . 161 B3
Howard St
7 Barnsley S70 . . . . 54 F7
Darfield S73 . . . . 57 C5
Dinnington S25 . . . . 135 A1
Rotherham S65 . . . . 115 E6
Sheffield S1 . . . . 161 B2
Howarth Dr S60 . . . . 131 D7
Howarth Rd S60 . . . . 131 D7
Howbeck Cl DN12 . . . . 82 A1
Howbeck Dr DN12 . . . . 82 A1
Howbrook Cl S35 . . . . 94 C8
Howden Ave DN6 . . . . 20 E1
Howden Cl
Darton S75 . . . . 13 F1
Doncaster DN4 . . . . 84 C6
Howden Rd S9 . . . . 130 A7
Howdike La S65 . . . . 99 B7
Howe La S25 . . . . 134 E8
Howell Gdns S63 . . . . 58 C7
Howell La S72, DN5 . . . . 36 F5
Howell Wood Ctry Pk* S72, WF9, DN5 . . . . 36 F7
Howlett Cl S60 . . . . 116 D1
Howlett Dr S60 . . . . 131 C7
Howse St S74 . . . . 77 B6
Howson Cl S65 . . . . 117 E8
Howson Rd S36 . . . . 73 D1
Howville Ave DN7 . . . . 44 E6
Howville Rd DN7 . . . . 44 E6
Hoylake Dr S64 . . . . 79 D2
Hoyland Cl S36 . . . . 50 D3
Hoyland Common Prim Sch S74 . . . . 76 A5
Hoyland Rd
Hoyland S74 . . . . 76 B5
Sheffield S3 . . . . 128 E7
Hoyland St
Maltby S66 . . . . 119 B4
Wombwell S73 . . . . 56 D2
Hoylandswaine Prim Sch S36 . . . . 52 A7
Hoyland Terr WF9 . . . . 18 A2
Hoyle Croft La S66 . . . . . . 100 F1
Hoyle Mill Rd S70 . . . . 55 D8
Hoyle St S3 . . . . 160 C5
Hucklow Dr S5 . . . . 113 D3
Hucklow Prim Sch S5 . . . 113 C2
Hucklow Rd S5 . . . . 113 D3
Huddersfield Rd
Barnsley S70, S75 . . . . 33 D3
Ingbirchworth S36 . . . . 50 F8
Penistone S36 . . . . 51 C5
West Bretton S75, WF4 . . . . . 13 A6
Hudson Ave WF4 . . . . 15 B6
Hudson Cl S26 . . . . 157 E7
Hudson Haven S73 . . . . 56 B3
Hudson Rd
Rotherham S61 . . . . 96 E2
Sheffield S13 . . . . 143 E8
Huggin Carr Rd DN7 . . . . . . 44 F1
Hugh Hill La DN7 . . . . 25 B4
Humber Cl DN6 . . . . 21 A1
Humber Ct DN6 . . . . 21 A1
Humberside Way S71 . . . . . 34 D6
Humphrey Rd S8 . . . . 152 E8
Humphries Ave S62 . . . . 97 D7
Hund Oak Dr DN7 . . . . 44 B8
Hungerhill Cl S61 . . . . 114 D8
Hungerhill La DN3 . . . . 42 E2
Hunger Hill La S60 . . . . . . 116 C1
Hungerhill Rd S61 . . . . 96 D1
Hunger Hill Rd S60 . . . . . . 116 C1
Hungerhill Sch DN3 . . . . 42 E2
Hungry La S32 . . . . 149 B8
Hunningley Cl S70 . . . . 55 E7
Hunningley La S70 . . . . 55 D7
Hunningley Prim Sch S70 55 D7
Hunsdon Rd S21 . . . . 155 C3
Hunshelf Hall La S36 . . . . . 73 B4
Hunshelf La S35 . . . . 95 B2
Hunshelf Pk S36 . . . . 73 C2
Hunshelf Rd
Chapeltown S35 . . . . 95 A5
Stocksbridge S36 . . . . 73 A3
Stocksbridge, Wood Willows S36 . . . . 73 C2
Hunsley St S4 . . . . 129 E8
Hunster Cl DN4 . . . . 84 F7
Hunster Gr DN11 . . . . 103 F8
Hunstone Ave S8 . . . . 153 A7
Hunt Cl S71 . . . . 34 C4
Hunter's Ave S70 . . . . 54 A8
Hunter's Bar 3 S11 . . . . . . 140 C8
Hunter's Bar Jun & Inf Schs S11 . . . . 140 C8
Hunter's La S13 . . . . 142 C6
Hunter Ct S11 . . . . 140 B7
Hunter Hill Rd S11 . . . . . . 140 C8
Hunter House Rd S11 . . . . 140 C8
Hunter Rd S6 . . . . 128 B8
Hunters Chase S25 . . . . . . 134 F3
Hunters Cl S25 . . . . 134 F3
Hunters Ct S25 . . . . 134 F3
Hunters Dr S25 . . . . 134 F3
Hunters Gdns
Dinnington S25 . . . . 134 F3
Sheffield S6 . . . . 111 D1
Hunters Gn S25 . . . . 134 F3
Hunters Pk S25 . . . . 134 F3
Hunters Rise S75 . . . . 33 B1
Hunters Way S25 . . . . 134 F3
Huntingdon Cres S11 . . . . 140 E8
Huntingdon Rd DN2 . . . . . . 63 C6
Huntington St DN5 . . . . 41 B2
Huntington Way S66 . . . . . 118 E7
Huntingtower Rd S11 . . . . 140 B7
Hunt La DN5 . . . . 62 B5
Huntley Gr S11 . . . . 139 F6
Huntley Rd S11 . . . . 140 A6
Huntsman Rd S9 . . . . 130 D4
Huntsmans Gdns S9 . . . . . 130 C7
Hunt St S74 . . . . 76 B5
Hurl Dr S12 . . . . 141 F5
Hurley Croft S63 . . . . 78 A7
Hurlfield Ct S12 . . . . 142 A6
Hurlfield Dr
Rotherham S65 . . . . 117 D7
Sheffield S12 . . . . 141 F6
Hurlfield Rd S12 . . . . 141 F5
Hurlingham Cl S11 . . . . . . 140 C5
Hurlstone Cl DN3 . . . . 43 A3
Hursley Cl 4 S20 . . . . 144 A1
Hursley Dr S20 . . . . 144 A1
Hurst Gn S35 . . . . 94 D7
Hurst La
Auckley DN9 . . . . 86 A5
Finningley DN9 . . . . 85 F3
Hushells La DN7 . . . . 7 F3
Huskar Cl S75 . . . . 52 F8
Hutchinson Ct S60 . . . . . . 115 E5
Hutchinson La S7 . . . . 140 D3
Hutchinson Rd
Rawmarsh S62 . . . . 98 A6
Sheffield S7 . . . . 140 D3
Hutcliffe Dr S8 . . . . 140 D2
Hutcliffe Wood Rd S8 . . . 140 D2
Huthwaite La S35 . . . . 73 F5
Hut La S21 . . . . 156 F4
Hutton Croft S12 . . . . 143 B3
Hutton Dr WF9 . . . . 19 A4
Hutton Rd S61 . . . . 96 F1
Huxterwell Dr DN4 . . . . 83 B4
Hyacinth Cl S5 . . . . 113 F3
Hyacinth Rd S5 . . . . 113 F3
Hyde Park Terr S2 . . . . . . 161 C3
Hyde Park Wlk S2 . . . . 161 C3
Hyland Cres DN4 . . . . 82 D6
Hyman Cl DN4 . . . . 82 D7
Hyman Wlk WF9 . . . . 19 A4
Hyperion Way DN11 . . . . . 103 E8

I

Ibberson Ave S75 . . . . 33 B8
Ibbotson Rd S6 . . . . 128 C6
Ibbotsons Croft S32 . . . . . 149 A8
Ibbotsons Farm Cotts
S32 . . . . 149 A8
Ibsen Cres DN3 . . . . 42 F8
Ickles Way S60 . . . . 115 B3
Icknield Way S60 . . . . 131 C8
Ida's Rd S21 . . . . 155 D4
Ida Gr S66 . . . . 118 D6
Idle Bank DN9 . . . . 67 E4
Idle Ct DN10 . . . . 123 A7
Idsworth Rd S5 . . . . 113 D2
Ilkley Cres S26 . . . . 144 C6
Ilkley Rd S5 . . . . 113 D4
Illsley Rd S73 . . . . 57 A6
Imperial Bldgs S60 . . . . . . 115 D6
Imperial Cres DN2 . . . . 62 F4
Imperial Ho 2 S1 . . . . 161 A2
Imrie Pl S26 . . . . 145 D2
Industry Rd
Royston S71 . . . . 34 C7
Sheffield S9 . . . . 130 C5
Industry St S6 . . . . 128 C6
Infield La S9 . . . . 130 D4
Infirmary Rd
Rawmarsh S62 . . . . 98 A3
Sheffield S6 . . . . 128 E5
Ingbirchworth La S36 . . . . . 50 E7
Ingbirchworth Rd S36 . . . . 51 A4
Ingelow Ave S5 . . . . 113 B5
Ingfield Ave S9 . . . . 114 E2
Ingham Bglws S81 . . . . . . 148 F8
Ingham Rd DN10 . . . . 122 F8
Ingleborough Croft S35 . . . 94 F6
Ingleborough Dr DN5 . . . . . 61 E2
Ingleby Cl S18 . . . . 152 C1
Ingledene Mews DN3 . . . . . 42 F7
Ingle Gr DN5 . . . . 61 E2
Inglenook Ct S66 . . . . 119 C4
Inglenook Dr DN8 . . . . 26 C8
Ingleton Wlk 4 S70 . . . . . . 33 D2
Inglewood S75 . . . . 14 A1
Inglewood Ave S20 . . . . . . 144 A1
Inglewood Ct 5 S20 . . . . . 144 A1
Inglewood Dell 6 S20 . . . 144 A1
Ingram Cres DN7 . . . . 43 F7
Ingram Ct S2 . . . . 129 D2
Ingram Gr DN7 . . . . 43 F7
Ingram Rd
Dunscroft DN7 . . . . 43 F6
Sheffield S2 . . . . 129 D2
Ings Cl WF9 . . . . 18 D3
Ingsfield La S63 . . . . 58 B2
Ingshead Ave S62 . . . . 98 A5
Ings Holt WF9 . . . . 18 D4
Ings La
Adwick le S DN6 . . . . 40 A8
Bentley, Arksey DN5 . . . . 41 E2
Bentley DN5 . . . . 42 A2
Bentley, Richmond Hill DN5 . . 61 E1
Great Houghton S72 . . . . 57 C8
Kirk Bramwith DN7 . . . . 24 E6
Ings La Cvn Site S73 . . . . . . 57 A4
Ings Rd
Bentley DN5 . . . . 62 C6
Cadeby DN5 . . . . 81 D6
Darfield S73 . . . . 57 B3
Ings Way
Bentley DN5 . . . . 41 D2
Ingbirchworth S36 . . . . 29 D1
Ingswell Ave WF4 . . . . 15 A7
Ingswell Dr WF4 . . . . 14 F7
Ings Wlk WF9 . . . . 18 D3
Inkerman Ct HD8 . . . . 30 A5
Inkerman Rd S73 . . . . 57 A5
Inkerman Way HD8 . . . . 29 F5
Inkersall Dr S20 . . . . 155 E8
Innovation Way S75 . . . . . . 33 C4
Insley Gdns DN4 . . . . 84 E7
Instone Terr DN6 . . . . 21 F6
Intake Cres S75 . . . . 53 F5
Intake Gdns S75 . . . . 33 B2
Intake La
Barnsley S75 . . . . 33 B2
Cudworth S72 . . . . 35 B8
Shepley HD8 . . . . 28 B4
Woolley WF4 . . . . 13 E8
Intake Prim Sch
Doncaster DN2 . . . . 63 B4
Sheffield S12 . . . . 142 C6
Intake Prim Sch (Sports Hall) DN2 . . . . 63 A4
Interchange Way 6 S71 . . 33 F2
Inverness Rd DN7 . . . . 44 A8
Ironside Cl S14 . . . . 141 D3
Ironside Pl S14 . . . . 141 E3
Ironside Rd S14 . . . . 141 E3
Ironside Wlk S14 . . . . 141 D2
Ironstone Cres S35 . . . . 94 F7
Ironstone Dr S35 . . . . 94 F7
Irving St S9 . . . . 130 C4
Irwell Gdns DN4 . . . . 63 D2
Island Cl S65 . . . . 116 C3
Islay St S10 . . . . 128 B3
Issott St S71 . . . . 33 F3
Ivan Brook Cl 4 S18 . . . . . 152 C1
Ivanhoe Ave S26 . . . . 145 E3
Ivanhoe Cl DN5 . . . . 61 F4
Ivanhoe Mews S26 . . . . . . 144 C8
Ivanhoe Rd
Conisbrough DN12 . . . . 81 B2
Doncaster DN4 . . . . 82 E6
Edenthorpe DN3 . . . . 42 F1
New Edlington DN12 . . . . . . 82 B1
Sheffield S6 . . . . 128 A6
Thurcroft S66 . . . . 133 E5
Ivanhoe Way DN5 . . . . 61 F4
Ivatt Cl DN10 . . . . 123 A8
Ivor Gr DN4 . . . . 83 A8
Ivy Cl
Hatfield DN7 . . . . 44 C8
Rossington DN11 . . . . 85 A2
South Elmsall WF9 . . . . 18 F2
Ivy Cottage La S10, S11 . . 139 D6
Ivy Cotts
Royston S71 . . . . 15 D4
Sheffield S11 . . . . 139 E7
Ivy Ct
Cudworth S72 . . . . 35 B6
Sheffield S8 . . . . 141 C2
Ivy Dr S10 . . . . 160 A4
Ivy Farm Cl S71 . . . . 15 D1
Ivy Farm Croft S65 . . . . 98 D1
Ivy Gr S10 . . . . 160 A4
Ivy Hall Rd S5 . . . . 113 E7
Ivy House Ct DN9 . . . . 85 F7
Ivy La
Sheffield S20 . . . . 144 A4
West Cowick DN14 . . . . 1 A7
Ivy Lodge La S81 . . . . 136 B3
Ivy Park Ct S10 . . . . 127 E2
Ivy Park Rd S10 . . . . 127 E1
Ivy Rd DN8 . . . . 9 B2
Ivy Rose Ct DN7 . . . . 24 E2
Ivy Side Cl S21 . . . . 156 D6
Ivy Side Gdns S21 . . . . . . 156 D6
Ivy Terr
4 Barnsley S70 . . . . 55 A8
South Elmsall WF9 . . . . 19 A3

J

Jack Close Orch S71 . . . . . 15 C4
Jackey La S35 . . . . 111 B7
Jack La S36 . . . . 92 C4
Jack Row La DN7 . . . . 24 C7
Jackson Cres S62 . . . . 97 E7
Jackson Ho 2 WF9 . . . . 17 D6
Jackson St
Cudworth S72 . . . . 35 A6
Goldthorpe S63 . . . . 58 E5
Jacks Way WF9 . . . . 19 C8
Jackys La S26 . . . . 157 E6
Jacobs Cl S5 . . . . 113 E4
Jacobs Dr S5 . . . . 113 F4
Jacobs Hall Ct S75 . . . . 32 C8
Jacques Pl S71 . . . . 34 D2
Jamaica St S4 . . . . 129 C7
James Andrew Cl S8 . . . . 152 F7
James Andrew Cres S8 . . 152 E7
James Andrew Croft S8 . . 152 F7
James Ct DN8 . . . . 9 C1
James Rd DN6 . . . . 40 D7
James St
Barnsley S71 . . . . 33 F2
Mexborough S64 . . . . 80 D5
Rotherham S60 . . . . 115 C7
Sheffield S9 . . . . 130 C3
South Hiendley S72 . . . . 16 F6
Worsbrough S70 . . . . 55 C5
James Walton Ct S20 . . . . 155 F7
James Walton Dr S20 . . . . 155 F7
James Walton Pl S20 . . . . 155 F7
James Walton View S20 . . 155 F7
Janet's Wlk S73 . . . . 56 B4
Janson St S9 . . . . 130 A8
Jardine Cl S9 . . . . 114 B4
Jardine St
Sheffield S9 . . . . 114 B4
Wombwell S73 . . . . 56 D2
Jarratt St DN1 . . . . 62 D2

Jarrow Rd S11 140 D8
Jasmine Ave S20 143 F3
Jasmine Cl DN12 81 D1
Jaunty Ave S12 142 C4
Jaunty Cl S12 142 B3
Jaunty Cres S12 142 C4
Jaunty Dr S12 142 B3
Jaunty La S12 142 B4
Jaunty Mount S12 142 C3
Jaunty Pl S12 142 B3
Jaunty Rd S12 142 C3
Jaunty View S12 142 C3
Jaunty Way S12 142 B4
Jay La S26 144 E6
Jebb La
Cawthorne S75 12 E3
High Hoyland S75 12 F3
Jedburgh Dr S9 114 A4
Jedburgh St S9 114 B4
Jeffcock Pl S35 94 E7
Jeffcock Rd
Chapeltown S35 94 E7
Sheffield S9 130 C4
Jefferson Ave DN2 42 D1
Jeffery Cres S36 92 D8
Jeffery St 6 S2 141 B6
Jenkin Ave S9 114 A2
Jenkin Cl S9 114 A3
Jenkin Dr S9 114 A2
Jenkin Rd S5, S9 114 A3
Jenkinson Gr DN3 63 F6
Jenkin Wood Cl S66 117 C7
Jenkyn La HD8 28 D8
Jennings Cl S65 115 E8
Jepson Rd S5 113 F4
Jericho St S3 160 C4
Jermyn Ave S12 142 F4
Jermyn Cl S12 142 F3
Jermyn Cres S12 142 F4
Jermyn Croft S75 53 F7
Jermyn Dr S12 142 F3
Jermyn Way S12 142 F3
Jersey Rd S2 141 A7
Jesmond Ave S71 15 C3
Jesop Ct S25 134 F2
Jessamine Rd S5 113 E4
Jessell St S9 129 F5
Jessop Hospl S3 160 A3
Jessop St S1 161 A2
Jewitt Rd S61 96 E2
Jew La S1 161 B3
Joan Croft La DN5, DN6 22 E1
Joan La S66 118 E4
Joan Royd La S36 72 C8
Jockell Dr S62 97 F5
Jockey Rd S36 52 C2
John Calvert Rd S13 143 D6
John Eaton's Almshouses
S8 141 B2
John Hibbard Ave S13 143 E7
John Hibbard Cl S13 143 E7
John Hibbard Cres S13 143 E7
John Hibbard Rise S13 143 E7
John La DN11 84 E1
Johnny Moor Long La
DN14 2 C4
Johnson Ct
New Edlington DN12 82 C3
Rotherham S65 115 F5
Johnson La
Sheffield, Ecclesfield S35 95 B1
Sheffield S3 161 B5
Johnson St
Barnsley S75 33 D2
Sheffield S3 161 B5
Stocksbridge S36 73 B1
John St
Barnsley S70 54 F8
Eckington S21 155 D3
Great Houghton, Middlecliff
S72 57 E7
Great Houghton S72 36 F1
Mexborough S64 80 A4
Rotherham S60 115 C6
Sheffield S2 129 A1
South Elmsall WF9 18 F2
Thurcroft S66 133 E7
Thurnscoe S63 58 D8
Wombwell S73 56 C3
3 Worsbrough S70 55 A4
Johnston's Rd DN7, DN8 25 C5
John Trickett Ho S35 94 F5
John Ward St S13 143 D7
John West St S36 92 B8
Joiner St S3 161 B4
Jones Ave S73 56 B3
Jons Ave WF9 18 A2
Jordan Cres S61 114 E5
Jordanthorpe Ctr S8 153 B6
Jordanthorpe Gn S8 153 C6
Jordanthorpe Parkway
S8 153 C6
Jordanthorpe View S8 153 C7
Joseph Ct 12 S70 54 F8
Josephine Rd S61 115 A6
Joseph La S36 71 C4
Joseph Rd S6 128 C5
Joseph St
Barnsley S70 54 F8
Eckington S21 155 D3
Grimethorpe S72 36 A6
Rotherham S60 115 C7
Joshua Rd S7 140 E6
Jos La HD8 28 E8
Josselin Ct S35 94 F5
Jossey La DN5 40 E1
Jos Way HD8 28 E8
Jowett House La S75 31 B4
Jowitt Cl S66 119 B4
Jowitt Rd S11 140 C6
Jubb Cl S65 116 D4
Jubilee Cl WF9 17 F6
Jubilee Cotts
Brinsworth S60 115 B1
Havercroft WF4 16 B8
Hoyland S74 76 A5
Jubilee Cres S21 156 E7
Jubilee Ct DN2 63 C6
Jubilee Gdns S71 15 D4
Jubilee Rd
Doncaster DN1 62 E5
Sheffield S9 130 C6
Jubilee St S60 115 D4
Jubilee Terr 1 S70 55 B8
Judd Field La S36 72 B6
Judith Rd S26 144 D6
Judy Row S71 34 C4
Juggernaut Trade Ctr
S71 34 A4
Julian Rd S9 114 B3
Julian Way S9 114 B3
Jumble La S35 95 E2
Jumble Rd S11 138 F1
Jump Prim Sch S74 76 F7
Junction Cl S73 57 A1
Junction Rd
Rossington DN11 103 E8
Sheffield S11 140 C8
Sheffield, Woodhouse S13 143 E7
Stainforth DN7 24 E4
Junction St
Barnsley S70 55 B8
Wombwell S73 56 F1
Junction Terr 4 S70 55 B8
June Rd S13 143 D7
Juniper Rise S21 156 C5

K

Kashmir Gdns S9 130 B5
Katherine Ct S66 133 E6
Katherine Rd S66 133 E7
Katherine St S66 133 F6
Kathleen Gr S63 58 F6
Kathleen St S63 58 F6
Kay's Terr S70 55 E7
Kay Cres S62 97 C8
Kaye Pl S10 160 A4
Kaye St 1 S71 33 F2
Kay St S74 76 B5
Kea Park Cl S66 118 A5
Kearsley La DN12 100 C8
Kearsley Rd S2 141 A8
Keats Dr S25 147 B8
Keats Gr S36 51 D4
Keats Rd
Doncaster DN4 83 B6
Sheffield S6 112 D6
Keble Martin Way S63 78 D6
Keenan Ave WF9 18 E1
Keeper La WF4 14 D5
Keepers Cl
Rossington DN11 85 B1
Sheffield S5 113 D4
Keeton's Hill 1 S2 140 F8
Keeton Hall Rd S26 145 F3
Keighley Wlk DN12 80 F1
Keir Pl S62 98 B6
Keir St S70 33 D2
Keir Terr S70 33 D2
Kelby Croft S75 32 F5
Kelford Sch S61 114 F6
Kelgate S20 155 D6
Kelham Bank DN1 62 C1
Kelham Ct DN1 62 C1
Kelham Island S3 161 A5
Kelham Island Ind Mus*
S3 161 A5
Kelham St DN1 62 C1
Kelly St S63 58 E5
Kelsey Gdns DN4 84 E5
Kelsey Terr 2 S70 54 F7
Kelso Dr DN4 82 D7
Kelvin Bdgs 3 S6 128 E6
Kelvin Ct S61 96 C2
Kelvin Gr S73 56 E2
Kelvin St S64 80 A5
Kemp Cl S21 156 C6
Kempton Dr DN7 43 E4
Kempton Gdns S64 80 C6
Kempton Park Rd DN5 61 D5
Kempton St DN4 63 D2
Kempwell Dr S62 97 F8
Kenbourne Gr S7 140 E7
Kenbourne Rd S7 140 E7
Kendal Ave S25 146 F6
Kendal Cl DN5 61 A1
Kendal Cres
Conisbrough DN12 81 D2
Worsbrough S70 55 A3
Kendal Dr
Bolton u D S63 58 C1
Dronfield S18 152 E1
Kendal Gn S70 54 E4
Kendal Gr S71 56 A8
Kendal Green Rd S70 54 E4
Kendal Rd
Bentley DN5 62 A7
Sheffield S6 128 B8
Kendal Vale S70 55 A3
Kendon Gdns DN8 26 C8
Kendray Bsns Ctr S70 55 C7
Kendray Hospl S70 55 C8
Kendray Prim Sch S70 55 C7
Kendray St S70, SK71 33 F1
Kenilworth Cl DN5 61 D6
Kenilworth Ct S11 139 F4
Kenilworth Dr S81 148 F6
Kenilworth Pl S11 140 C8
Kenilworth Rd DN4 82 E7
Kenmare Cres DN2 63 B5
Kennedy Cl S36 50 E3
Kennedy Ct S10 128 B3
Kennedy Dr S63 58 D3
Kennedy Rd S8 140 E2
Kennels The S62 77 C1
Kenneth Ave
Dunsville DN7 43 F4
Stainforth DN7 24 F4
Kenneth St S65 115 E7
Kenninghall Cl S2 141 D7
Kenninghall Dr S2 141 D7
Kenninghall Rd S2 141 D7
Kennington Ave DN6 39 F5
Kennington Gr DN12 82 C3
Kenrock Cl DN5 41 E1
Kensington Ave S36 51 A4
Kensington Chase S10 138 F8
Kensington Cl S25 134 C3
Kensington Ct S10 126 F1
Kensington Dr S10 138 F8
Kensington Pk S10 138 F8
Kensington Rd S75 33 D3
Kent Ave S62 97 E7
Kent Cl S71 15 C4
Kent Grange 12 S8 141 B6
Kent House Cl S12 154 E8
Kentmere Cl S18 152 E1
Kentmere Dr DN4 84 B7
Kent Rd
Doncaster DN4 83 B7
Rotherham S61 96 E1
Sheffield S8 141 B6
Kents Gdns DN8 9 D3
Kenwell Dr S17 152 B5
Kenwood Ave S7 140 E7
Kenwood Bank S7 140 E8
Kenwood Chase 12 S7 140 F8
Kenwood Cl S70 55 D8
Kenwood Ct S11 140 D7
Kenwood Park Rd S7 140 E7
Kenwood Rd S7 140 E7
Kenwood Rise S66 117 C6
Kenworthy Rd
Barnsley S70 54 F7
Stocksbridge S36 92 B8
Kenyon Alley 2 S3 160 C4
Kenyon Bank HD8 29 F5
Kenyon Cl DN8 26 B8
Kenyon St
Sheffield S3 160 C4
South Elmsall WF9 19 A3
Keppel Dr S61 96 B2
Keppel Hts S61 96 B2
Keppel Pl S5 113 E6
Keppel Rd
Rotherham S61 96 B2
Sheffield S5 113 F7
Keppel View Rd S61 114 D8
Kepple Cl DN11 103 F7
Keresforth Cl S70 54 C8
Keresforth Ct S70 54 C8
Keresforth Hall Rd S70 54 D7
Keresforth Hill Rd S70 54 C7
Keresforth Prim Sch S75 54 A6
Keresforth Rd S75 54 A6
Kersal Lawns S10 128 B2
Kerwin Cl S17 151 C8
Kerwin Dr S17 151 C8
Kerwin Rd S17 151 C8
Kestrel Ave S61 96 A5
Kestrel Cl S21 156 B7
Kestrel Dr
Adwick le S DN6 40 B6
Eckington S21 155 B3
Rossington DN11 85 A1
Kestrel Gn S2 129 E2
Kestrel Rise
Barnsley S70 75 F8
Sheffield S26 144 A7
Keswick Cl
Bentley DN5 62 A8
Sheffield S6 127 E8
Keswick Cres S60 131 B7
Keswick Pl S18 152 D1
Keswick Rd S75 14 A3
Keswick Way S25 146 F6
Keswick Wlk S71 56 A8
Kettlebridge Rd S9 130 A4
Ketton Ave S8 141 B3
Ketton Wlk S75 33 C3
Kevin Gr S66 118 B4
Kew Cres S12 142 A2
Kew Ct S64 79 C1
Kexborough Prim Sch
S75 32 B8
Kexbrough Dr S75 32 D8
Key Ave S74 76 F6
Key Hill La S72 16 F3
Keyworth Cl DN6 22 B8
Keyworth Pl S13 143 A6
Keyworth Rd S6 112 C1
Khartoum Rd S11 128 D1
Kibroyd Dr S75 32 D7
Kid La S81 136 A5
Kieran Cl S25 134 C2
Kier Hardie Ave DN11 104 A8
Kilburn Rd S18 152 C1
Kildale Gdns S20 155 D7
Kildonan Gr S12 142 C3
Kilham La DN3 64 F1
Killamarsh Inf Sch S21 156 E7
Killamarsh Jun Sch S21 156 E7
Killamarsh La S21, S26 157 B6
Kiln Bent Rd HD9 47 A6
Kilner Way S6 112 D3
Kiln Hill S18 153 C3
Kilnhurst Bsns Pk S64 98 E6
Kilnhurst Prim Sch S64 98 F7
Kilnhurst Rd S62 98 C6
Kilnhurst St Thomas CE Prim
Sch S64 98 D8
Kiln La HD8 12 A4
Kiln Rd S61 114 F8
Kilnsea Wlk 1 S70 33 E1
Kiln St S8 140 F7
Kilton Hill S3 129 B6
Kilton Pl S3 129 B6
Kilvington Ave S13 142 B7
Kilvington Cres S13 142 B7
Kilvington Rd S13 142 B7
Kimberley St S9 129 F6
Kimberworth Com Prim Sch
S61 114 F7
Kimberworth Park Rd
S61 96 E1
Kimberworth Rd S61 115 A6
Kinder Gdns S5 113 B5
Kine Moor La S75 52 D6
King's Cl DN7 44 B8
King's Cres DN12 82 B3
King's Rd
Askern DN6 22 B8
Cudworth S72 16 C1
Doncaster DN1 62 E4
Mexborough S64 80 B5
King's St S72 36 A6
King's Terr DN6 22 B8
King's Wood* DN10 105 A1
King Ave
Maltby S66 119 B4
Rossington DN11 84 E1
King Ecgbert Rd S17 151 E5
King Ecgbert Sch S17 151 D6
King Edward's Gdns 9
S70 54 E8
King Edward Cres DN8 9 B1
King Edward Rd DN4 83 B8
King Edwards S6 127 B4
King Edwards Rd DN11 120 F7
King Edward St
Barnsley S71 34 D6
Hemsworth WF9 17 E6
King Edward VII Sch
Sheffield S10 160 A2
Sheffield, Tapton Hill S10 128 A2
Kingfield Rd S11 140 D7
Kingfisher Cl DN2 63 B7
Kingfisher Ct
Conisbrough DN12 81 F2
Rossington DN11 85 A1
Kingfisher Dr S73 57 A1
Kingfisher Gr S26 144 A7
Kingfisher Prim Sch DN2 63 B7
Kingfisher Rd DN6 40 B6
Kingfisher Rise S61 96 A6
King George's Rd DN11 84 D1
King Georges Cl DN11 103 D8
King Georges Ct DN7 24 E2
King George Sq DN3 42 F5
King George Terr 5 S70 55 B8
King James Apartments
S6 128 D6
King James St S6 128 D6
Kings Coppice S17 151 D6
Kings Court Rd DN8 9 C1
Kings Croft
South Kirkby WF9 18 B3
Worsbrough S70 55 C5
Kingscroft Cl S17 151 E8
Kings Ct S10 128 A2
Kingsforth La S66 117 F2
Kingsforth Rd S66 133 E8
Kingsgate 2 DN1 62 D3
Kingsland Ct S71 15 D4
Kingsley Ave DN5 61 F4
Kingsley Cl S71 34 A6
Kingsley Cres DN3 64 C6
Kingsley Park Ave S7 140 B4
Kingsley Park Gr S11 140 B4
Kingsley Rd DN6 40 A5
Kingsmead DN8 9 C3
Kingsmead Dr DN3 85 D8
Kings Mews
Doncaster DN1 62 D3
Eckington S21 155 E3
Kings Rd S73 56 E2
King St
Armthorpe DN3 63 F7
Aston S26 144 C8
Barnsley S70 54 F8
Chapeltown S35 95 A6
Doncaster DN1 62 D3
Goldthorpe S63 58 E5
Hoyland S74 76 F6
Sheffield S3 161 B4
Swinton S64 79 D3
Thorne DN8 26 B7
Thurnscoe S63 58 E7
Kingston Cl DN3 64 E1
Kingstone Pl S70 54 D7
Kingstone Sch The S70 54 C8
Kingston Park Prim Sch
S81 148 F6
Kingston Rd
Carlton in L S81 148 E6
Doncaster DN2 63 B4
Kingston St S4 129 D7
Kingsway
Darton S75 14 A1
Stainforth DN7 24 E3
Thurnscoe S63 58 C8
Wombwell S73 56 D2
Kings Way S60 116 A2
Kingsway Cl DN11 104 A7
Kingsway Complex S25 134 F1
Kingsway Gr S63 58 C8
Kingsway Ho DN1 62 D3
Kingswood Ave
Laughton en le M S25 134 E4
Sheffield S20 143 A2
Kingswood Cl
Firbeck S81 136 A6
6 Sheffield S20 143 A2
Kings Wood Cl DN10 123 A8
Kingswood Cres S74 76 E7
Kingswood Croft 9 S20 143 A2
Kingswood Gr 10 S20 143 A2
Kingswood Hall S6 111 F3
Kings Wood La S66, S81 135 C6
Kingwell Cres S70 54 F6
Kingwell Croft S70 55 A5
Kingwell Mews 1 S70 55 A5
Kingwell Rd S70 55 A5
Kinharvie Rd S5 112 F3
Kinnaird Ave S5 113 C5
Kinnaird Pl S5 113 C5
Kinnaird Rd S5 113 C5
Kinsbourne Gn DN7 44 A7
Kinsey Hts S35 94 D7
Kinsey Rd S35 94 C7
Kiplin Dr DN6 4 C3
Kipling Ave DN4 82 F6
Kipling Rd
Barnby Dun DN3 42 F8
Sheffield S6 128 C8
Kirby Cl S9 130 C4
Kirby La S35 95 D7
Kirby St S64 80 A5
Kirk Balk S74 76 D6
Kirk Balk Sch S74 76 D6
Kirkbridge Way WF9 18 F3
Kirkby Ave
Barnsley S71 34 A8
Bentley DN5 62 B6
Sheffield S12 142 A4
Kirkby Avenue Prim Sch
DN5 62 A6
Kirkby Cl WF9 18 C3
Kirkby Dr S12 142 A4
Kirkbygate WF9 17 E5
Kirkby Rd
Hemsworth WF9 17 E6
Sheffield S12 142 A4
Kirkby View S12 142 A4
Kirkby Way S12 142 A3
Kirkcroft Ave
Killamarsh S21 156 D7
Rotherham S61 96 A5
Kirkcroft Cl S61 95 F5
Kirkcroft Dr S21 156 D6
Kirkcroft La S21 156 D6
Kirk Cross Cres S71 15 C2
Kirkdale Cres S13 131 B1
Kirkdale Dr S13 131 B1
Kirk Edge Ave S35 111 D4
Kirk Edge Dr S35 111 C4
Kirk Edge Rd
Bradfield S6 110 D5
Oughtibridge S35 111 B5
Kirkfield Cl S75 31 F4
Kirkfield Way S71 15 C2
Kirkgate La S72 16 C6
Kirkhall Cl DN3 64 C5
Kirkham Cl S71 34 C3
Kirkham Pl S71 34 D7
Kirkhill Bank S36 72 C8
Kirkhill Sch S2 141 C8
Kirkhouse Green Rd DN7 24 A8
Kirk La DN14 7 E6
Kirkland Gdns S71 34 A5
Kirklands Dr S62 97 E6
Kirk Sandall Ind Est DN3 42 E4
Kirk Sandall Jun & Inf Schs
DN3 42 F3
Kirk Sandall Sta DN3 42 E4
Kirk Smeaton CE Prim Sch
WF8 3 D6
Kirk St
Doncaster DN4 62 B2
Sheffield S4 129 C6
Kirkstall Cl
Bentley DN5 61 D5
Brinsworth S60 115 A1
South Anston S25 146 D3
Kirkstall Rd
Barnsley S71 33 E7
Sheffield S11 140 C8
Kirkstead Abbey Mews
S61 96 A3
Kirkstead Gdns S13 143 E7
Kirkstead Rd S61 114 A6
Kirkstone Cl DN5 62 A7
Kirkstone Rd S6 128 C7
Kirk View S74 76 D6
Kirk Way S71 34 D3
Kirkwood Cl S36 52 A2
Kirstead Ct DN4 85 B5
Kirton La DN8 25 D4
Kirton Rd S4 129 C8
Kitchin Rd S73 56 B3
Kitson Dr S71 34 D3
Kiveton Bridge Sta S26 145 D2
Kiveton Gdns S26 145 F3
Kiveton La S26 145 F5

Kiveton Park Inf Sch S26 145 D3
Kiveton Park Meadows Jun Sch S26 145 C3
Kiveton Park Sta S26 146 B1
Knabbs La S75 52 F5
Knab Cl S7 140 C5
Knab Croft S7 140 C5
Knab Rd S7 140 C5
Knab Rise S7 140 C5
Knapton Ave S62 97 E6
Knaresboro Rd S7 140 C3
Knaresborough Cl S26 144 C7
Knaresborough Rd DN12 80 F1
Knaton Rd S81 148 E7
Knavesmire Gdns DN4 63 D2
Knightscroft Par WF9 19 A2
Knollbeck Ave S73 78 A8
Knoll Beck Cl S63 58 C4
Knollbeck Cres S73 78 A8
Knollbeck La S73 78 A8
Knoll Cl S36 73 C1
Knoll The S18 153 D3
Knott End S81 136 E3
Knowle Cl S6 127 C6
Knowle Croft S11 140 A5
Knowle Ct S11 140 B5
Knowle Gn S17 151 C7
Knowle La S11 139 F5
Knowle Park Ave HD8 28 F8
Knowle Rd
Sheffield S5 113 B6
Worsbrough S70 55 B6
Knowles Ave S36 92 D8
Knowles St S36 51 F2
Knowles Wlk WF9 19 A4
Knowle The HD8 28 F8
Knowle Top S20 155 E7
Knowsley St 5 S70 33 D1
Knutton Cres S5 112 E7
Knutton Rd S5 112 F6
Knutton Rise S5 112 E7
Krapacz Ct DN6 40 C2
Kye La S26 157 E6
Kyle Cl
Renishaw S21 156 B1
Sheffield S5 112 F4
Kyle Cres S5 112 F4
Kynance Cres S60 131 C7

L

Laburnam Gr S70 55 C4
Laburnum Ave
Rotherham S66 117 B6
Thorne DN8 9 C3
Laburnum Cl
Chapeltown S35 95 A4
South Anston S25 146 D4
Laburnum Dr DN3 64 C7
Laburnum Gr
Conisbrough DN12 81 A1
Killamarsh S21 156 C5
Stocksbridge S36 92 B8
Laburnum Ho S63 78 E6
Laburnum Par S66 118 D5
Laburnum Pl DN5 41 B2
Laburnum Rd
Doncaster DN4 82 F7
Langold S81 136 F4
Maltby S66 118 D5
Mexborough S64 79 F6
Laceby Cl S66 117 D7
Laceby Ct S70 54 C7
Lacewood Prim Sch S63 58 C2
Lacy St WF9 17 C7
Ladies Spring Ct S17 152 A7
Ladies Spring Dr S17 152 A7
Ladies Spring Gr S17 152 A7
Ladock Cl S71 34 B3
Lady's Bridge S3 161 B4
Lady Bank Dr DN4 62 E1
Ladybank Rd S20 155 D6
Lady Bank View S21 155 D4
Ladybower Ct 4 S17 152 A5
Ladybower Dr S32 149 A7
Ladycroft S63 58 C2
Lady Croft S63 78 E6
Lady Croft La S73 77 C7
Ladycroft Rd DN3 64 C4
Lady Field Rd S80 158 D8
Lady Gap La DN6 21 D5
Lady Ida's Dr
Eckington S21 155 C4
Sheffield S21 155 C5
Lady Mary View DN5 59 B7
Ladymead S71 34 B4
Lady Oak Rd S65 116 C8
Ladyroyd S75 52 F5
Ladyroyd Croft S72 35 A6
Ladysmith Ave S7 140 D6
Lady Wharncliffe's Rd
Stocksbridge S35 93 D4
Wortley S35 93 D6
Ladywood Prim Sch S72 36 B6
Ladywood Rd S72 36 B6
Laird Ave S6 112 A1
Laird Dr S6 112 A1
Laird Rd S6 112 A1
Lairds Way S36 51 E3
Laithe Croft S75 53 F7
Laithes Cl S71 34 B7
Laithes Cres S71 33 F7
Laithes La S71 34 A7
Laithes Sh Ctr S71 33 F7
Lake Cl DN12 82 A1
Lake Ct DN6 40 C4
Lakeen Rd DN2 63 A4
Lakeland Cl S72 35 C5
Lakeland Dr S25 146 F7
Lake Rd DN6 40 C3
Lakeside Bvd DN4 84 B8
Lakeside Cl S66 117 C8
Lakeside Ct S63 77 F7
Lakeside Prim Sch DN4 63 A1
Lakeside View S36 51 A7
Lakeside Village Outlet DN4 83 F8
Lambcote Way S66 119 B6
Lambcroft La S13 143 C6
Lambcroft View S13 143 C6
Lamb Dr S5 112 D3
Lambecroft S71 15 C1
Lambe Flatt S75 32 C8
Lambert Fold S75 54 A7
Lambert Rd S70 55 C7
Lamberts La S65 98 F3
Lambert St S3 161 A4
Lambert Wlk
Barnsley S70 55 C8
Wath u D S63 78 C8
Lambeth House Residential Mobile Home Pk DN4 83 B7
Lambeth Rd DN4 83 B7
Lamb Hill S6 110 B4
Lamb Hill Cl S13 142 D7
Lamb La
Barnsley S71 34 C5
Firbeck S81 136 C5
Lambra Rd S70 33 F1
Lamb Rd S5 112 D3
Lambrell Ave S26 145 C2
Lanark Dr S64 80 C6
Lanark Gdns DN2 63 C5
Lancar Ct S71 34 A4
Lancaster Ave
Doncaster, Intake DN2 63 C4
Kirk Sandall DN3 42 F4
Lancaster Cl DN11 121 B7
Lancaster Cres DN11 121 B7
Lancaster Ct 11 S70 33 D1
Lancaster Dr
Bawtry DN10 122 F8
Hatfield DN7 66 A8
Lancaster Gate 6 S70 33 E2
Lancaster Rd S36 73 B1
Lancaster St
Barnsley S70 33 D1
Sheffield S3 128 F5
Thurnscoe S63 37 E1
Lancelot Ct WF9 19 A2
Lancing Rd
Sheffield, Highfield S2 141 A8
Sheffield S2 129 B1
Land Ends Rd DN8 8 F2
Landsdown Ave WF9 18 A1
Landseer Cl
4 Dronfield S18 152 E1
Sheffield S14 141 D2
Landseer Ct S66 117 B6
Landseer Dr S14 141 E2
Landseer Pl S14 141 E2
Landseer Wlk S14 141 E2
Lane Cotts S71 15 C3
Lane End S35 95 A6
Lane End Mews S63 58 B8
Lane End Rd S60 116 A3
Lane End View S60 116 A3
Lane Hackings HD8 29 E7
Lane Hackings Gn HD8 29 E7
Laneham Cl DN4 84 D6
Lane Head Cl
Darton S75 14 A2
Rawmarsh S62 98 A6
Lane Head Rd
Bradfield S6 109 A4
Cawthorne S75 31 D3
Sheffield S17 151 C4
Shepley HD8 28 E7
Lane Head Rise S75 14 A2
Laneside Cl DN4 62 A1
Lanes The S65 116 B7
Lane The
Royston S71 15 C4
Spinkhill S21 156 D1
Langar Cl DN5 41 A4
Lang Ave S71 34 E2
Langcliff Cl S75 14 A2
Lang Cres S71 34 E2
Langdale Cl DN11 121 B8
Langdale Ct 10 S70 33 F1
Langdale Dr
Bentley DN5 61 F8
Dronfield S18 153 C3
Tickhill DN11 121 B8
Langdale Rd
Adwick le S DN6 21 C1
Barnsley, Barugh S75 32 E5
Barnsley S71 34 A1
Sheffield S8 140 E5
Langdale Way S25 146 F7
Langdon Rd S61 114 E8
Langdon St S11 140 F8
Langdon Wlk
1 Barnsley S70 33 D2
Rotherham S61 114 E8
Langer St DN4 62 A1
Langley Cl S65 116 D7
Langleys Rd DN6 4 D1
Langold Ctry Pk* S81 136 E1
Langold Dr DN6 4 D3
Langold Dyscarr Com Sch S81 136 D3
Langsett Ave S6 112 A3
Langsett Cl S6 128 D7
Langsett Cres S6 128 D7
Langsett Ct
Barnsley S71 33 E7
Doncaster DN4 84 B8
Langsett Gr S6 128 D6
Langsett Rd
Barnsley S71 33 E7
Sheffield S6 128 D7
Langsett Rd N
Oughtibridge S35 111 D8
Wharncliffe Side S35 111 D8
Langsett Rd S S35 111 E6
Langsett Rise S6 128 D7
Langsett Wlk S6 128 D7
Langthwaite Grange Ind Est WF9 18 D2
Langthwaite La
Bentley DN5 40 E2
South Elmsall WF9 18 E2
Langthwaite Rd
Bentley DN5 40 E1
South Kirkby WF9 18 D2
Langton Gdns DN3 85 E8
Lansbury Ave
Chapeltown S35 94 F5
Maltby S66 119 B3
Rossington DN11 104 A8
Lansbury Ct S21 155 D3
Lansbury Pl S62 98 C6
Lansbury Rd S21 155 D2
Lansdowne Cl S63 58 C8
Lansdowne Cres
Kexbrough S75 32 D7
Swinton S64 79 D2
Lansdowne Rd
Doncaster DN2 63 C5
6 Sheffield S11 128 F1
Lanyon Way S71 34 B3
Lapwater Rd S61 96 F3
Lapwater Wlk S61 96 F3
Lapwing Vale S61 96 A6
Larch Ave
Finningley DN9 85 F3
Killamarsh S21 156 C5
Rotherham S66 117 C5
Larch Cl S73 57 A5
Larch Dr DN3 64 B6
Larches The S64 79 C3
Larchfield Pl S71 34 D5
Larchfield Rd DN4 82 F7
Larch Gr
Aston S26 144 F8
Chapeltown S35 95 A4
Conisbrough DN12 100 A8
Larch Hill S9 130 E3
Larch Mews S65 116 B8
Larch Pl S70 55 C6
Larch Rd
Eckington S21 155 B2
Maltby S66 118 D6
Larch Sq DN9 86 B4
Large Sq DN7 24 E4
Lark Ave S60 131 D8
Larkhill Cl S62 98 A3
Larkspur Cl
Edenthorpe DN3 42 F1
Swinton S64 98 C8
Lark St S6 128 B6
Larwood Gr DN12 82 C3
Latchmoor Cl S75 33 D4
Latham Sq
Kirk Sandall DN3 42 F5
Sheffield S11 139 E5
Lathe Rd S60 116 D3
Lathkill Cl S13 142 C7
Lathkill Rd S13 142 C7
Latimer Cl S26 145 F2
Latin Gdns DN5 61 C7
Lauder Rd DN5 62 A6
Lauder St S4 113 E2
Laudsdale Cl S65 116 D7
Laudsdale Rd S65 116 D8
Laughton All Saints CE Prim Sch S25 134 D5
Laughton Common Rd S66 134 B4
Laughton Jun & Inf Sch S25 134 D4
Laughton Rd
Dinnington S25 134 F1
Doncaster DN4 62 B2
Sheffield S9 114 B2
Thurcroft S66 134 A5
Launce Rd S5 112 F4
Laurel Ave
Barnsley S70 55 D7
Bentley DN5 61 E5
Rotherham S66 117 D5
Thorne DN8 9 C3
Laurel Cl
Eckington S21 155 C2
South Anston S25 146 D3
Laurel Ct S10 128 B1
Laurel Dr S21 156 C5
Laurel Ho S10 128 B2
Laurel Rd DN3 64 B7
Laurel Sq DN9 86 A4
Laurel Terr
Adwick le S DN6 21 B1
Doncaster DN4 83 A7
Laurold Ave DN7 45 A6
Lavender Cl DN12 81 D1
Lavender Ct WF9 17 D6
Lavender Way WF9 17 D6
Lavenham Pl DN6 20 E2
Laverack St S13 130 F1
Laverdene Ave S17 151 F5
Laverdene Cl S17 151 E4
Laverdene Dr S17 151 F4
Laverdene Rd S17 151 E4
Laverdene Way S17 151 F4
Laverock Way S5 113 D5
Lavinia Rd S35 112 E8
Law Common Rd HD9 48 E5
Lawn Ave
Adwick le S DN6 39 F6
Doncaster DN1 62 E3
Lawndale DN6 20 F2
Lawndale Fold S75 13 F1
Lawn Garth DN5 62 A7
Lawn La DN6 6 C5
Lawn Rd
Carlton in L S81 148 E8
Doncaster DN1 62 E3
Lawns The S11 140 B6
Lawnswood Ct DN4 84 C8
Lawn The S18 153 B2
Lawnwood Dr S63 58 C5
Lawrence Cl
Barnsley S75 32 E3
Rotherham S66 117 B5
Lawrence Dr S64 79 C1
Lawrence St S9 129 F6
Law Slack Rd HD9 48 D6
Lawson Rd S10 128 C2
Lawton La S60 115 F3
Laxey Rd S6 127 E5
Laxton Cl S66 118 D6
Laxton Rd S71 33 F8
Laycock Ave S26 144 E7
Layden Dr DN5 61 C7
Leabrook Rd S18 152 C1
Leach La S64 80 B4
Leadbeater Dr S12 142 A5
Leadbeater Rd S12 142 A4
Leader Ct S6 112 B1
Leader Rd S6 112 B1
Leadley St S63 58 E5
Leadmill Point S1 161 B2
Leadmill Rd
Sheffield, Highfield S2 161 B1
Sheffield S1, S2 161 B2
Leadmill St S1 161 B2
Lea Dr HD8 28 F8
Leaf Cl S66 119 B6
Lea Head HD8 28 E8
Leake Rd S6 112 C2
Leak Hall Cres HD8 29 F6
Leak Hall La HD8 30 A6
Lea La S36 50 B3
Leamington Gdns DN2 63 B5
Leamington St S10 128 C4
Leapings La S36 50 F3
Lea Rd
Barnsley S71 34 B7
Dronfield S18 153 A1
Lease Gate Rd S60 116 B2
Leas The DN5 61 F5
Lea The
Sheffield S20 143 D2
Swinton S64 79 B2
Leaton Cl S6 111 D1
Leavy Greave 4 S10 160 B3
Leavygreave Rd S3 160 B3
Leawood Pl S6 127 D6
Le Brun Sq S81 148 E7
Ledbury Gdns DN5 61 D5
Ledbury Rd S71 33 F6
Ledsham Ct S74 77 B6
Ledsham Rd S60 116 A4
Ledstone Rd S8 140 E4
Lee Ave S36 73 D1
Leebrook Ave S20 143 B1
Leebrook Ct S20 143 B1
Leebrook Dr S20 143 B1
Lee Brook La S62 77 F2
Leebrook Pl S20 143 B1
Leech Row S35 73 F5
Lee Croft
Maltby S66 119 C4
Sheffield S1 161 A4
Leedham Cl S5 113 F4
Leedham Rd
Rotherham S65 116 D4
Sheffield S5 113 F4
Leeds Ave S25 146 E7
Leeds Rd
Sheffield S9 130 A6
Shireoaks S81 159 F7
Lee House La S36 92 A8
Lee La
Bradfield S36 91 D3
Darton S71 14 E2
Leeming Ct DN10 122 F6
Lee Moor La S6 126 F7
Lee Rd S6 111 D1
Lees Ave S36 51 D3
Lees Hall Ave S8 141 B5
Lees Hall Pl S8 141 B5
Lees Hall Rd S8 141 B4
Lees House Ct S8 141 A4
Lees Nook S8 141 A4
Leewood Cl S63 77 F6
Leger Ct DN1 62 E2
Leger Way DN2 63 C4
Legion Dr S26 144 E7
Leicester Ave DN2 63 A3
Leicester Rd S25 135 A1
Leigh St S9 130 A7
Leighton Cl S71 33 F3
Leighton Dr S14 141 F3
Leighton Pl S14 141 F3
Leighton Rd S14 141 E4
Leighton View S14 141 E5
Leinster Ave DN2 63 A5
Lemont Rd S17 151 E4
Lengdale Ct S62 97 F5
Lennox Rd
Doncaster DN2 63 B5
Sheffield S6 112 B1
Lenny Balk DN5, DN6 38 E7
Lenthall Inf Sch S18 153 B3
Lenton St S2 161 B1
Leonard Cl S2 142 A7
Leopold Ave S25 146 F8
Leopold St
Barnsley S70 54 D8
Dinnington S25 146 F8
Sheffield S1 161 A3
Leppings La S6 112 C2
Lepton Gdns S70 55 D6
Lerwick Cl S81 148 E1
Lescar La S11 140 C8
Lesley Rd S63 58 E5
Leslie Ave
Conisbrough DN12 81 A2
Maltby S66 118 D5
Leslie Rd
Barnsley S70 55 D7
Sheffield S6 112 B1
Lesmond Cres S72 57 E6
Lestermoor Ave S26 145 C2
Letard Dr S60 115 C1
Letsby Ave S9 130 E6
Letwell Ct DN4 85 B5
Levels La DN9 86 F8
Leverick Dr S62 98 C7
Leverstock Gn DN7 44 A7
Leverton Dr S11 128 F1
Leverton Gdns S11 128 F1
Leverton Way S65 98 E1
Leveson St S4 129 D5
Levet Rd DN4 63 F1
Levick Croft S74 76 F6
Lewdendale S70 55 A4
Lewden Farm La S70 55 D4
Lewes Rd DN12 81 B1
Lewis Rd
Barnsley S71 34 E4
Sheffield S13 142 C7
Lewyns Dr DN4 63 F1
Leybourne Rd S61 96 E1
Leybrook Croft WF9 17 E7
Leyburn Cl DN4 84 F7
Leyburn Dr S26 144 C8
Leyburn Gr S35 95 A6
Leyburn Rd
Adwick le S DN6 20 F2
Sheffield S8 140 F6
Ley End S70 54 F4
Leyfield Ct DN3 64 C5
Leyfield Pl S73 56 F4
Leyfield Rd S17 151 D7
Leyland Ave DN7 44 C7
Leylands The S75 33 B4
Leyland Wlk S75 33 B4
Leys Cl DN4 82 F5
Leys La
Dinnington S25 135 C2
Hampole DN6 20 C2
Kirk Smeaton WF8 3 C7
Leys The WF9 18 A1
Liberty Cl S6 127 E5
Liberty Dr S6 127 E5
Liberty Hill S6 127 E5
Liberty La S35 74 D3
Liberty Pl S6 127 E5
Liberty Rd S6 127 E5
Library Cl S61 97 A3
Lichen Cl DN3 42 F1
Lichfield Gdns DN12 82 A1
Lichfield Rd
Doncaster DN2 62 F6
Hatfield DN7 44 A8
Lichfield Way S60 131 D8
Lichfield Wlk S81 148 E7
Lichford Rd S2 141 C6
Lidgate DN14 1 C8
Lidgate Cres WF9 18 E2
Lidgate La S72 16 B3
Lidget Cl
Aston S26 144 B6
Doncaster DN4 84 E7
Lidget La
Hickleton DN5 59 A7
Pilley S75 75 D5
Rotherham S65 117 E7
Thurnscoe S63 58 F7
Lidgett Gdns DN9 86 A6
Lidgett La S25 146 F8
Lidgett Way S71 15 C5
Lifestyle Ho 4 S10 128 C2
Liffey Ave DN2 63 A5
Lifford Pl S74 77 B5
Lifford Rd DN2 62 F5
Lifford St S9 114 E3
Lightwood House Hospl S8 141 E1
Lightwood La
Eckington, Middle Handley S21 154 E1
Eckington S8 141 F1
Lightwood Rd S21 154 E2
Lignum Terr 1 DN6 22 B8
Lilac Ave S36 92 B8
Lilac Cl S25 146 D4
Lilac Cres
Hoyland S74 76 F7
New Edlington DN12 82 B1
Lilac Farm Cl S66 117 B4

Lilac Gr
Bawtry DN10 122 F7
Carlton in L S81 148 E7
Conisbrough DN12 81 A1
Doncaster DN4 84 F8
Finningley DN9 86 A4
Maltby S66 118 D5
Rotherham S66 117 C5
Lilac Rd
Armthorpe DN3 64 C7
Sheffield, Beighton S20 143 F3
Sheffield, High Wincobank S5 113 E3
Lilacs The S71 15 E4
Liley La S36 50 D1
Lilian St S S60 115 E5
Lilian St S60 115 E5
Lilley St WF9 17 D6
Lilley Terr WF9 18 B2
Lillford Rd DN3 85 E8
Lilly Hall Cl S66 118 D6
Lilly Hall Rd S66 118 E5
Lily Terr S74 76 F7
Limb La S17 139 D1
Limbreck Ct DN5 41 A1
Limbrick Cl S6 128 C7
Limbrick Rd S6 128 C7
Lime Ave
Finningley DN9 86 A4
Firbeck S81 136 A6
Lime Cl S65 99 D2
Lime Cres WF9 18 E1
Lime Ct DN5 61 D1
Limedale View DN3 43 A6
Lime Gr
Barnsley S71 15 C1
Chapeltown S35 95 A4
Maltby S66 119 B5
South Elmsall WF9 18 E1
Stocksbridge S36 92 B8
Swinton S64 79 D2
Limegrove S60 116 A4
Limekiln La
Stainton DN11, S66 101 E2
Tickhill S66 120 A6
Limekilns S25 146 D6
Limelands Rd S25 146 E8
Lime Rd S21 155 B2
Limes Ave
Barnsley S75 33 B3
Darton S75 14 C2
Limes Cl S75 14 C2
Lime St
Sheffield, Beighton S20 143 F4
Sheffield S6 128 E6
Limes The S60 116 A4
Limestone Cl S81 147 E3
Limestone Cottage La S6 112 B4
Limesway
Barnsley S75 33 B3
Maltby S66 118 F5
Limetree Ave
Thurcroft S66 133 F6
Wales S26 145 C3
Lime Tree Ave
Armthorpe DN3 64 B7
Carlton in L S81 148 E7
Doncaster DN4 62 F2
Killamarsh S21 156 C5
Lime Tree Cl S72 35 B7
Lime Tree Cres
Bawtry DN10 122 F7
Rawmarsh S62 98 B6
Rossington DN11 104 A8
Lime Tree Ct
Doncaster DN4 62 F1
Hemsworth WF9 17 C6
Lime Tree Gr DN8 26 B8
Lime Tree Wlk DN12 80 F4
Limpool Cl DN4 84 F7
Limpsfield Jun Sch S9 114 A2
Limpsfield Rd S9 114 A2
Linaker Rd S6 128 B5
Linburn Cl S71 15 A4
Linburn Rd S8 140 F2
Linby Rd S71 33 F8
Lincoln Cl DN12 80 F2
Lincoln Cres WF9 19 A4
Lincoln Gdns S63 58 D5
Lincoln Rd
Doncaster DN2 62 F6
Hatfield DN7 66 A7
Lincolnshire Way DN3 64 E7
Lincoln St
Maltby S66 119 B4
Rossington DN11 84 E2
Rotherham S60 115 D8
Sheffield S9 114 B2
Lincroft Dr S62 98 A3
Lindale Cl S25 146 F5
Lindale Croft WF9 17 E5
Lindale Gdns S63 58 F4
Lindales The [3] S75 33 C2
Linden Ave
Dronfield S18 153 B3
Rotherham S66 117 C6
Sheffield S8 140 E2
Linden Cl DN7 44 B8
Linden Cres S36 73 B1
Linden Ct
Sheffield, Ecclesfield S35 95 B1
Sheffield, Meadow Head S8 140 E2
Sheffield S10 128 B1
Linden Gr
Maltby S66 118 D5
New Edlington DN12 82 B1
Linden Rd
Sheffield S35 95 B1
Wath u D S63 78 B6
Linden Wlk DN5 41 A4
Lindholme Bank Rd DN7 45 D2
Lindholme Dr DN11 85 B1
Lindholme Gdns S20 143 C2
Lindhurst Rd S71 33 F8
Lindley's Croft S26 145 F5
Lindley Cres S63 58 D7
Lindley Ct DN9 86 E3
Lindley Rd
Finningley DN9 86 E3
Sheffield S5 113 D2
Lindley St S65 115 E8
Lindrick DN11 121 A6
Lindrick Ave S64 79 E2
Lindrick Cl
Carlton in L S81 148 F6
Conisbrough DN12 81 E3
Cudworth S72 16 C1
Doncaster DN4 84 D6
Tickhill DN11 120 F6
Lindrick Ct S81 147 F3
Lindrick Dr DN3 64 B5
Lindrick La DN11 120 F6
Lindrick Rd
Hatfield DN7 44 F6
Woodsetts S81 147 E3
Lindsay Ave S5 113 B5
Lindsay Cl S5 113 B5
Lindsay Cres S5 113 B5
Lindsay Dr S5 113 B5
Lindsay Pl S26 144 D7
Lindsay Rd S5 113 B5
Lindsey Cl DN4 84 D5
Lindsey Rd DN11 122 A5
Lindum Dr S66 117 C4
Lindum St DN4 62 B2
Lindum Terr [1] S65 115 E6
Lingamore Leys S63 37 D1
Lingard Ct S75 33 D2
Lingard St S75 33 D2
Lingfield Cl S66 117 E4
Lingfield Dr DN5 61 D5
Ling Field Rd DN5 39 B3
Lingfield Wlk S64 80 C6
Lingfoot Ave S8 153 B6
Lingfoot Cl S8 153 B6
Lingfoot Cres S8 153 C6
Lingfoot Dr S8 153 C6
Lingfoot Pl S8 153 B6
Lingfoot Wlk S8 153 C6
Ling House La DN7 24 C2
Lingmoor Cl DN4 82 E6
Lingodell Cl S25 134 E4
Lings La
Hatfield DN7 44 B5
Rotherham S66 117 C4
Upton DN6 20 A8
Lings The
Armthorpe DN3 64 D5
Rotherham S66 117 E4
Lingthwaite S75 54 A7
Link Rd S65 99 A2
Link Row [1] S2 161 C4
Links View S75 14 B2
Linkswood Ave DN2 63 C6
Linkswood Rd S65 98 D1
Link The S75 54 A6
Linkway
Doncaster DN2 63 B6
Hatfield DN7 44 F6
Norton DN6 4 D3
Linley La S12, S13 142 E5
Linnet Mount S61 95 F5
Linscott Rd S8 140 E2
Linshaws Rd HD9 47 E5
Linthwaite La S62, S74 77 C4
Linton Cl
Barnsley S70 54 B8
Bawtry DN10 122 F6
Lion Cott S75 31 E4
Lionel Hill S35 74 C7
Lipp Ave S21 156 C7
Liskeard Pl DN6 40 A5
Lisle Rd S60 116 A4
Lismore Rd S8 141 B5
Lister Ave
Doncaster DN4 83 B8
Rawmarsh S62 97 E7
Sheffield S12 142 B3
Lister Cl S12 142 B3
Lister Cres S12 142 B3
Lister Ct DN2 63 A5
Listerdale Sh Ctr S65 116 E4
Lister Dr S12 142 B3
Lister La S3 160 C5
Lister Pl S12 142 B3
Lister Rd S6 128 C7
Lister Row S72 36 D3
Lister St S65 115 F6
Lister Way S12 142 B3
Litherop La HD8 12 C5
Litherop Rd S75 12 D3
Little Attercliffe S9 130 B5
Little Black La DN11 121 D7
Little Common La
Rotherham, Kimberworth S61 114 D7
Rotherham, Whiston S60 116 E1
Sheffield S11 139 F3
Littledale Rd S9 130 C2
Littlefield La S73 56 D3
Littlefield Rd S25 134 E1
Little Haynooking La S66 118 F5
Little Hemsworth WF9 17 E6
Littlehey Cl S66 118 D6
Little La
Doncaster DN2 42 C1
Kirk Smeaton WF8 4 A7
Sheffield, Grimesthorpe S4 113 F1
Sheffield, Woodthorpe Estate S12 142 B6
South Elmsall, Moorthorpe WF9 18 F3
South Elmsall WF9 19 B3
Sprotbrough DN5 61 A4
Thorpe Salvin S80 159 B6
Upton WF9 19 B7
Wentworth S61 95 E6
Little Leeds S74 76 E6
Little London La DN14 1 A7
Little London Pl S8 140 F6
Little London Rd S8 140 F5
Little Matlock Gdns S6 127 D6
Little Matlock Way S6 127 D6
Littlemoor S21 155 E4
Littlemoor Ave S26 145 C2
Littlemoor Bsns Ctr S21 155 E4
Littlemoor La DN4 62 B1
Littlemoor St DN4 62 B1
Little New Cl S75 33 B3
Little Norton Ave S8 153 A8
Little Norton Dr S8 153 A8
Little Norton La S8 153 A8
Little Norton Way S8 153 A7
Little Westfields S71 15 A4
Little Wood Dr S12 142 A3
Little Wood La S26, S80 158 D4
Littlewood Rd DN8 26 C7
Little Wood Rd S12 142 A3
Littlewood St DN4 62 B2
Littlewood Way S66 119 B6
Littleworth Cl DN11 85 B1
Littleworth Grange Prim Learning Ctr S71 34 D3
Littleworth La
Barnsley S71 34 D3
Rossington DN11 85 C1
Littleworth Mews DN11 85 B2
Litton Wlk
[2] Barnsley S70 33 D2
Shafton S72 16 C3
Liverpool Ave DN2 62 F6
Liverpool St S9 130 A7
Livingstone Ave DN2 42 D1
Livingstone Cres S71 34 B5
Livingstone Rd S35 94 E5
Livingstone Terr [4] S70 54 E8
Livingston Rd S9 129 E6
Llewelyn Cres DN6 21 F7
Lloyd St
Rawmarsh S62 97 F3
Sheffield S4 113 E1
Lloyds Terr DN7 24 F1
Load Field Rd S6, S36 91 F2
Loakfield Dr S5 112 F7
Lobelia Cres DN3 42 F3
Lobelia Ct S25 146 D4
Lobwood S70 55 B5
Lobwood La S70 55 B5
Locarno Rd DN8 9 D3
Lockeaflash Cres S70 55 D7
Locke Ave
Barnsley, Shaw Lands S70 54 E8
Worsbrough S70 54 F6
Locke Rd S75 54 A6
Lockesley Ave DN12 81 A1
Locke St S70 54 D7
Lockgate Rd DN14 5 F8
Lock Hill DN8 26 A7
Lock House Rd S9 114 C1
Locking Dr DN3 64 D5
Lock La
Sheffield S9 114 E3
Thorne DN8 26 A7
Locksley Ave DN3 42 F2
Locksley Dr S66 133 E6
Locksley Gdns
Barnsley S70 75 F6
Norton DN6 4 C1
Lock St S6 128 E6
Lockton Cl S35 94 C8
Lockton Way [1] DN12 81 D3
Lockwood Ave S25 146 D3
Lockwood Cl
Rotherham S65 116 C7
Thorne DN8 26 D7
Lockwood Gdns S36 52 A6
Lockwood La
[11] Barnsley S70 54 F7
Thurnscoe S63 58 E7
Lockwood Rd
Doncaster DN1 62 E5
Goldthorpe S63 58 E6
Rotherham S65 116 C7
Lodge Ct DN7 44 B7
Lodge Dr S62 76 D1
Lodge Farm Cl S25 146 D6
Lodge Farm Mews S25 146 D6
Lodge Hill Dr S26 145 B3
Lodge La
Aston S26 144 D7
Dinnington S25 135 B1
Kirk Bramwith DN7 24 B6
Rotherham S61 95 F3
Sheffield S10, S6 127 A2
West Cowick DN14 1 A8
Wortley S35 93 D5
Lodge Moor Rd S10 138 F8
Lodge Rd DN6 21 C2
Lodge St WF9 17 D8
Lodge The S11 140 A5
Lodge Way S60 115 C1
Logan Rd S9 130 D4
Loicher La S35 95 D1
Lomas Cl S6 127 C7
Lomas Lea S6 127 B6
Lombard Cl S75 33 E3
Lombard Cres S73 56 E5
London La DN6 6 B1
London Rd S2 140 F8
London Rd S S2 141 A7
London Way S61 95 E4
Long Acre S71 15 B1
Longacre Cl S20 144 A1
Long Acre View S20 156 A8
Longacre Way S20 144 B1
Longcar La S70 54 D8
Longcar Prim Sch S70 54 D8
Long Cl DN4 84 E6
Long Cliffe Cl S72 16 C2
Long Close La
Shepley HD8 28 C7
South Elmsall WF9 19 C6
Long Croft S75 14 B1
Longcroft Ave S18 152 C2
Longcroft Cres S18 152 C2
Longcroft Rd S18 152 C2
Long Cswy
Barnsley S71 34 D3
Hathersage S10, S32 137 C5
Longdale Croft S71 34 B4
Longdale Dr WF9 18 E4
Long Edge La DN5 40 E1
Longfellow Dr S65 116 B5
Longfellow Rd DN4 83 C6
Longfield Cl S73 56 B4
Longfield Dr
Darton S75 14 B1
Doncaster DN4 84 D6
Rotherham S65 117 D8
Long Field Dr DN3 43 B3
Longfield Rd S10 128 B5
Long Field Rd DN3 43 A3
Longfields Cres S74 76 D6
Longfields Rd S71 34 B8
Longford Cl S17 152 A5
Longford Cres S17 152 A5
Longford Dr S17 151 F4
Longford Rd S17 152 A4
Longford Spinney S17 151 F4
Long Gate DN11 101 F5
Long Gr DN7 24 E4
Long Henry Row S2 161 C3
Long Ing Rd HD9 48 A7
Long La
Apperknowle S21 154 C1
Carlton in L S81 148 F6
Killamarsh S21 156 F6
Kirk Smeaton WF8 3 D3
Oughtibridge S35 111 C7
Oxspring S36 72 F8
Rotherham S60 132 A7
Sheffield, Loxley S6, S35 111 D2
Sheffield S10 127 F4
Sheffield, Stopes S6 126 D5
Shepley HD8 28 E8
Sprotbrough DN5 61 B4
Stocksbridge S36 91 E8
Longlands Dr
Mapplewell S75 33 B8
Rotherham S65 99 A3
Long Lands La DN5, DN6 39 E5
Longley Ave W S5 112 F2
Longley Cl
Barnsley S75 32 E4
Sheffield S5 113 B2
Longley Cres S5 113 B3
Longley Dr S5 113 B2
Longley Edge Rd HD9 48 B8
Longley Farm View S5 113 B2
Longley Hall Gr S5 113 C2
Longley Hall Rd S5 113 C2
Longley Hall Rise S5 113 B3
Longley Hall Way S5 113 C2
Longley Ings S36 52 A2
Longley La
Holmfirth HD9 48 A8
Sheffield S5 113 B3
Longley Park Sixth Form Coll S5 113 C3
Longley Prim Sch S5 113 A2
Long Leys La S66 101 A5
Longley St S75 32 E4
Long Line S11 139 B2
Longman Rd S70 33 E2
Long Rd S26, S66 133 E2
Longridge Rd S71 34 D6
Long Royd La HD8 29 B8
Longshaw Est* S32 149 F2
Longshaw Estate Trail* S11 150 A4
Longshaw Estate Visitor Ctr* S11 150 A4
Longshaw Lodge S11 150 A4
Longside Way S75 33 A1
Longsight Rd S75 14 A1
Longspring Gr S75 75 E5
Longstone Cres S12 142 D4
Longthwaite Cl S25 134 E4
Long Toft Prim Sch DN7 24 E4
Longton Rd DN3 43 A4
Longwood Cl S66 117 B8
Longworth Rd WF9 17 D6
Lonsbrough Way WF9 19 A4
Lonsdale Ave
Barnsley S71 56 B8
Doncaster DN2 63 D4
Lonsdale Cl S25 146 F6
Lonsdale Ho DN2 63 C5
Lonsdale Rd S6 128 C7
Loosemore Dr S12 141 F5
Lopham Cl S4 129 D6
Lopham St S3 129 B5
Lord's Head La DN4 82 D4
Lordens Hill S25 135 A1
Lords Cl DN12 82 C3
Lord St
Barnsley S71 34 C2
Rotherham S65 116 A7
Stainforth DN7 24 E3
Lorna Rd S64 80 A5
Lorne Cl S18 152 D2
Lorne Rd S63 58 C8
Loscoe Gr S63 58 C5
Lotherton Rd WF9 17 E7
Lothian Rd DN2 63 C5
Louden Cl S61 96 B2
Louden Rd S61 96 B2
Lounde Cl DN5 61 C1
Lound Inf Sch S35 94 F6
Lound Jun Sch S35 95 A6
Lound La DN5 38 F5
Lound Rd S9 130 D3
Lound Side S35 95 A5
Louth Rd S11 140 B8
Lovell St S4 129 D5
Loversall Cl DN4 83 C5
Loversall Hospl DN4 83 C5
Love St S3 161 A4
Lovetot Ave S26 144 D8
Lovetot Rd
Rotherham S61 96 E2
Sheffield S9 129 E5
Lowburn Rd S13 142 C7
Low Common Rd S25 134 D1
Low Croft
Royston S71 15 D3
Wombwell S73 56 E3
Low Cudworth S72 35 B5
Low Cudworth Gn S72 35 B5
Low Deeps La DN10 87 E1
Low Edges S8 153 A6
Lowedges Cres S8 152 F6
Lowedges Dr S8 152 F6
Lowedges Pl S8 153 A6
Lowedges Prim Sch S8 152 E6
Lowedges Rd S8 152 E6
Lowe La S75 53 F3
Lowell Ave DN4 83 B6
Lower Boundary Rd DN6 42 B7
Lower Castlereagh St [6] S70 33 E1
Lower Collier Fold S75 31 F5
Lower Common La HD8 30 D8
Lower Denby La HD8 30 B4
Lower Dolcliffe Rd S64 79 F5
Lower Haigh Head S36 51 F7
Lower High Royds S75 33 A8
Lower Kenyon St DN8 26 B8
Lower Limes S70 55 B4
Lower Malton Rd DN5 61 E6
Lower Maythorn La HD9 49 D8
Lower Meadow Prim Sch S8 153 A5
Lower Mill Cl S63 58 C4
Lower Northcroft WF9 19 A3
Lower Northfield La WF9 18 C3
Lower Pasture DN9 86 E4
Lower Putting Mill HD8 30 B7
Lower Thomas St [3] S70 54 E8
Lower Unwin St S36 51 D2
Lower York St S73 56 D3
Low Farm Gdns WF9 19 B7
Lowfield Ave
Eckington S12 154 E8
Rotherham S61 97 C3
Lowfield Cl DN3 43 A6
Lowfield Com Prim Sch S2 141 A7
Lowfield Cres WF9 17 E7
Lowfield Ct [4] S2 141 A7
Lowfield Farm Cl S63 58 E2
Lowfield Gr S63 58 E1
Low Field La DN10 105 C1
Lowfield Mdws S63 58 D1
Lowfield Rd
Bolton u D S63 58 D2
Doncaster DN2 63 C7
Hemsworth WF9 17 F7
Lowfield Wlk DN12 80 F4
Low Fold HD8 29 E7
Low Fold Ct HD8 29 F3
Low Forge S35 74 A3
Lowgate
Balne DN14 6 A8
Bentley DN5 61 E7
Low Gate WF9 19 A3
Low Golden Smithies S64 79 C4
Low Grange Sq S63 58 C8
Lowgreave S65 116 C8
Low Harley S62 76 E2
Lowhill DN8 8 F1
Lowhouse Rd S5 113 E7
Low La
Carr S66 118 C2
Kirk Bramwith DN7 23 F4
Rotherham S61 115 A8
Low Laithes View S73 56 B4
Lowlands Cl
Barnsley S71 34 D5
Bentley DN5 41 B3
Lowlands Wlk DN6 22 B8
Low Levels Bank DN8 46 C6
Low Matlock La S6 127 E8
Low Moor La S36 71 D3

Low Pasture Cl S75 .... 54 A7
Low Rd
Conisbrough DN12 .... 81 D3
Doncaster DN4 .... 83 A7
Oughtibridge S35 .... 111 D7
Scrooby DN10 .... 123 A2
Sheffield S6 .... 128 A6
Thurgoland S36 .... 52 D1
Low Rd E DN4 .... 82 D6
Low Rd W DN4 .... 82 C6
Low Riddings S66 ...... 117 C6
Low Row S75 .... 13 E3
Lowry Dr S18 .... 152 F1
Low St S75 .... 54 B6
Lowther Rd
Doncaster DN1 .... 62 E5
Sheffield S6 .... 112 D1
Lowther Sq S81 .... 148 E7
Lowton Way S66 .... 118 A5
Low View S75 .... 53 F7
Low Wood Cl S64 .... 79 C1
Loxdale Gdns S70 .... 33 D2
Loxley Ave S73 .... 56 C2
Loxley Ct
Rotherham S60 .... 115 F2
Sheffield, Loxley S6 .... 111 F1
Sheffield S6 .... 128 C7
Loxley Mount DN6 .... 4 C1
Loxley New Rd S6 .... 128 B7
Loxley Pk S6 .... 128 A7
Loxley Prim Sch S6 ...... 111 E1
Loxley Rd
Barnsley S71 .... 34 F3
Bradfield S6 .... 110 C4
Sheffield S6 .... 127 E8
Loxley View Rd S10 ...... 128 B5
Loy Cl S61 .... 97 A3
Lucas St S4 .... 129 C7
Lucknow Ct S7 .... 140 E6
Ludgate Cl DN11 .... 104 A7
Ludlam Ho S2 .... 141 E6
Ludwell Hill DN5 .... 59 E2
Lugano Gr S73 .... 56 E6
Luke La S6 .... 111 F1
Lulworth Cl 6 S70 .... 55 B8
Lumb La S6 .... 110 E8
Lumley Cl S66 .... 119 C4
Lumley Cres S66 .... 119 C4
Lumley Dr
Dinnington S25 .... 134 C2
Maltby S66 .... 119 C4
Tickhill DN11 .... 121 B7
Lumley St
Sheffield S4, S9 .... 129 D4
Sheffield S9 .... 129 F4
Lump La S35 .... 94 C1
Luna Croft S12 .... 141 F2
Lunbreck Rd DN4 .... 82 C5
Lund Ave S71 .... 34 F3
Lund Cl S71 .... 34 F3
Lund Cres S71 .... 34 F3
Lundhill Cl S73 .... 56 E1
Lundhill Farm Mews S73 .. 77 D8
Lundhill Gr S73 .... 56 E1
Lund Hill La S71 .... 15 F5
Lundhill Rd S73 .... 56 E1
Lund La S71 .... 34 F3
Lund Rd S35 .... 111 D5
Lundwood Cl S20 .... 143 C2
Lundwood Dr S20 .... 143 C2
Lundwood Gr S20 .... 143 C2
Lundwood Ho 18 DN1 ..... 62 C2
Lunn Rd S72 .... 35 B6
Lupton Bdlgs S64 .... 79 D4
Lupton Cres S8 .... 152 F6
Lupton Dr S8 .... 152 F6
Lupton Rd S8 .... 152 F6
Lupton Wlk S8 .... 153 A6
Luterel Dr S26 .... 144 D8
Lutterworth Dr DN6 .... 40 A6
Lyceum Theatre★ S1 ..... 161 B3
Lych Gate Cl DN4 .... 85 A7
Lydgate Ct S10 .... 128 B3
Lydgate Hall Cres S10 .. 128 A3
Lydgate Inf Sch S10 .... 128 A3
Lydgate Jun Sch S10 .... 128 A2
Lydgate La S10 .... 128 B3
Lydgate Rd HD8 .... 28 F8
Lymegate S63 .... 77 F6
Lyme St S60 .... 115 C6
Lyme Terr DN6 .... 20 E1
Lyminster Rd S6 .... 112 D4
Lyminton La S60 .... 131 E4
Lymister Ave S60 .... 115 F1
Lyncroft Cl S60 .... 131 D8
Lyndale Ave DN3 .... 42 F1
Lynden Ave DN6 .... 40 A6
Lyndhurst Bank S36 ...... 51 D2
Lyndhurst Cl
Norton DN6 .... 4 E3
Sheffield S11 .... 140 C6
Thorne DN8 .... 25 F8
Lyndhurst Cres DN3 ...... 42 E3
Lyndhurst Ct DN6 .... 4 E3
Lyndhurst Dr DN6 .... 4 E3
Lyndhurst Rd
Hooton Roberts S65 .... 99 B7
Sheffield S11 .... 140 D6
Lyndhurst Rise DN6 .... 4 E3
Lyndhurst Villas DN6 ...... 4 E3
Lynham Ave S70 .... 75 F6
Lynmouth Rd S7 .... 140 E5
Lynn Pl S9 .... 130 B8
Lynthwaite Cl S63 .... 77 F7
Lynton Ave S60 .... 116 B3
Lynton Dr DN3 .... 42 E2
Lynton Pl S75 .... 32 D8
Lynton Rd 9 S11 .... 140 D8
Lynwood Cl 1 S18 ..... 152 D1
Lynwood Dr
Barnsley S71 .... 15 C1
Mexborough S64 .... 80 A6
Lyons Rd S4 .... 129 C7
Lyons St S4 .... 129 D7
Lytham Ave
Barnsley S71 .... 34 D5
Dinnington S25 .... 146 F7
Lytham Cl DN4 .... 85 B6
Lyttleton Cres S36 .... 51 C1
Lytton Ave S5 .... 112 E5
Lytton Cl DN4 .... 83 B6
Lytton Cres S5 .... 112 E5
Lytton Ct S5 .... 112 F5
Lytton Dr S5 .... 112 F5
Lytton Rd S5 .... 112 E5

M

Mabel St S60 .... 115 F5
MacAulay Cres DN3 .... 64 C6
McAuley RC High Sch The DN4 .... 85 A8
McConnel Cres DN11 ..... 84 D1
Machin Dr S62 .... 97 D8
Machin La S36 .... 72 E2
Machins Ct S18 .... 153 A2
Machon Bank S7 .... 140 E6
Machon Bank Rd S7 ..... 140 E6
McIntyre Rd S36 .... 73 B1
Mackenzie Cres
Chapeltown S35 .... 94 E4
Sheffield S10 .... 160 B2
Mackenzie St S11 .... 140 E8
McKenzie Way S26 ...... 145 D2
Mackey Cres S72 .... 16 F3
MacKinnon Ave S26 ..... 145 D2
McLaren Ave WF9 .... 19 D8
McLaren Cres S66 ...... 119 A4
McLintock Way S70 .... 33 D1
McLoughlin Way S26 ... 145 D2
Macmanus Ave S62 .... 97 F8
Macnaghten Rd S75 ...... 75 F5
Macro Rd S73 .... 56 F2
Madam La DN3 .... 42 E8
Madehurst Gdns S2 ...... 141 B7
Madehurst Rd S2 .... 141 B7
Madehurst Rise S2 ...... 141 B7
Madehurst View S2 ...... 141 B7
Madingley Cl DN4 .... 83 A5
Madison Dr DN10 .... 122 F6
Mafeking Pl S35 .... 95 A6
Magellan Rd S66 .... 118 E6
Maggot La S75 .... 52 D2
Magna Cl S66 .... 117 B6
Magna Cres S66 .... 117 A6
Magna La S65 .... 98 E1
Magna Science Adventure Pk★ S60 .... 114 F4
Magnet Ct DN5 .... 41 A3
Magnolia Cl
Kirk Sandall DN3 .... 42 F3
Shafton S72 .... 16 D2
South Anston S25 .... 146 D3
Magnolia Ct S10 .... 139 E8
Magpie Gr S2 .... 129 E2
Mahon Ave S62 .... 97 F6
Maidstone Rd S6 .... 112 D4
Maidwell Way DN3 .... 42 E5
Main Ave
New Edlington DN12 .... 82 B3
Sheffield S17 .... 151 E4
Main Rd
Dronfield S18 .... 152 B1
Eckington, Lightwood S21 .. 154 F3
Eckington, Ridgeway S12 .. 154 E8
Hathersage S32 .... 149 A8
Renishaw S21 .... 156 A1
Sheffield, Darnall S9 ..... 130 C4
Sheffield, Dungworth S6 .. 110 D1
Sheffield, Handsworth Hill S9 .... 130 D4
Wharncliffe Side S35 .... 93 B2
Main St
Aston, Aughton S26 ...... 132 C2
Aston, Swallownest S26 .. 144 C7
Auckley DN9 .... 86 A6
Branton DN3 .... 64 B1
Catliffe S60 .... 131 D6
Fishlake DN7 .... 25 A7
Goldthorpe S63 .... 58 E6
Hampole DN6 .... 20 B1
Harworth DN11 .... 121 E4
Hatfield DN7 .... 44 F6
Kirk Smeaton WF8 .... 3 D6
Mexborough S64 .... 79 F4
North Anston S25 .... 146 D6
Oldcotes S81 .... 136 F6
Ravenfield S65 .... 99 D2
Rawmarsh S62 .... 98 A6
Rotherham, Bramley S66 .. 117 D5
Rotherham, Greasbrough S61 .... 97 C3
Rotherham S60 .... 115 D6
Sheffield, Grenoside S35 .. 112 C8
Sheffield, Hackenthorpe S12 .... 143 B3
Sheffield S35 .... 94 C1
South Hiendley S72 .... 16 D6
Sprotbrough DN5 .... 82 B8
Styrrup DN11 .... 121 D1
Ulley S26 .... 132 E4
Upton WF9 .... 19 D8
Wadworth DN11 .... 102 B7
Wentworth S62 .... 77 B1
Wombwell S73 .... 56 C3
Main View DN7 .... 25 B4
Mair Ct S60 .... 116 A1
Maison De Dieu DN11 ... 121 A7
Makin St S64 .... 80 C4
Malcolm Cl S70 .... 55 D8
Malham Cl
Bawtry DN10 .... 122 F8
Shafton S72 .... 16 C3
Malham Ct 3 S70 .... 33 D2
Malham Gdns S20 ...... 155 D7
Malham Gr S20 .... 155 E7
Malham Pl S35 .... 94 F6
Malham Tarn Ct DN4 ...... 84 B8
Malin Bridge Prim Sch S6 .... 128 B8
Malincroft S75 .... 33 B8
Malinda St S3 .... 160 C5
Malinder Cl S21 .... 156 D6
Malin Rd
Rotherham S65 .... 116 D8
Sheffield S6 .... 128 A7
Mallard Ave DN3 .... 42 F6
Mallard Cl
Doncaster DN4 .... 82 F6
Rotherham S61 .... 96 A5
Mallard Dr S21 .... 156 B7
Mallard Prim Sch DN4 .... 82 F6
Mallin Croft S74 .... 76 E6
Mallin Dr DN12 .... 82 B1
Mallory Ave S62 .... 97 E6
Mallory Dr S64 .... 80 D6
Mallory Rd S65 .... 116 C8
Mallory Way S72 .... 35 C7
Malpas Hill DN11 .... 120 F1
Maltas Ct S70 .... 55 C5
Maltby Comp Sch S66 ... 118 F5
Maltby Crags Jun & Inf Sch S66 .... 119 B4
Maltby Hall Inf Sch S66 .. 118 E5
Maltby Ho 17 DN1 .... 62 C2
Maltby La S66 .... 118 F8
Maltby Lilly Hall Jun Sch S66 .... 118 E5
Maltby Manor Jun & Inf Schs S66 .... 119 A6
Maltby Rd S81 .... 136 E6
Maltby Redwood Jun & Inf Sch S66 .... 118 C5
Maltby St S9 .... 130 A7
Malthouse Rd 18 S70 ..... 33 F1
Maltings Ct DN3 .... 42 F5
Maltings The
Rotherham S60 .... 115 D5
4 Sheffield S11 .... 160 C1
Maltkiln Dr WF4 .... 12 F8
Maltkiln St S60 .... 115 D5
Maltkin Cotts DN3 .... 42 F5
Malton Dr S26 .... 144 E7
Malton Pl S71 .... 33 E7
Malton Rd
Bentley DN5 .... 61 D7
Doncaster DN2 .... 63 B5
Upton WF9 .... 19 D8
Malton St S4 .... 129 C7
Maltravers Cl S2 .... 129 E2
Maltravers Cres S2 ...... 129 E3
Maltravers Pl S2 .... 129 E3
Maltravers Rd S2 .... 129 E3
Maltravers Terr S2 ...... 129 E2
Maltravers Way S2 ...... 129 E3
Malvern Ave DN5 .... 61 E5
Malvern Cl
Barnsley S75 .... 33 B2
Thorne DN8 .... 26 A6
Malvern Dr S66 .... 117 B7
Malvern Rd
Doncaster DN2 .... 63 C4
Sheffield S9 .... 130 B5
Malvern Way S66 .... 117 B7
Malwood Way S66 .... 119 B6
Manchester Ho DN6 .... 40 C8
Manchester Rd
Penistone S36 .... 50 D3
Sheffield S10, S6 .... 127 D3
Stocksbridge S36 .... 73 C1
Mandale Rd DN3 .... 42 F8
Mandeville St S9 .... 130 C5
Mangham La DN11 .... 121 A8
Mangham Rd S61, S62 ..... 97 E2
Mangham Way S61 .... 97 D1
Mannering Rd DN4 .... 82 E6
Manners St S3 .... 128 F6
Manor App S61 .... 114 F7
Manor Ave S63 .... 58 E5
Manor Bglws S18 .... 152 F1
Manor Cl
Barnby Dun DN3 .... 42 E7
Kirk Smeaton WF8 .... 3 D5
Maltby S66 .... 118 F5
Norton DN6 .... 4 C3
Notton WF4 .... 14 F7
Rawmarsh S62 .... 97 C8
Todwick S26 .... 145 F5
Wath u D S63 .... 78 B7
Manor Cres
Brinsworth S60 .... 131 B8
Dronfield S18 .... 152 F1
Grimethorpe S72 .... 36 A8
Manor Croft S72 .... 16 D6
Manor Ct
Barnburgh DN5 .... 59 C2
Conisbrough DN12 .... 80 E3
Rotherham S65 .... 116 D8
Royston S71 .... 15 A3
Manor Dev Ctr S9 .... 130 B1
Manor Dr
Cadeby DN5 .... 81 D5
Dinnington S25 .... 134 E2
Manor Dr *continued*
Doncaster DN2 .... 62 F3
Rotherham S60 .... 116 C1
Royston S71 .... 15 B3
South Hiendley S72 .... 16 D6
Todwick S26 .... 145 F5
Manor End S70 .... 54 F5
Manor Est DN5 .... 40 F4
Manor Farm Bldgs DN12 101 A7
Manor Farm Cl
Adwick le S DN6 .... 40 B6
Askern DN6 .... 21 E5
Aston S26 .... 132 D2
Royston S71 .... 34 D8
Manor Farm Croft S81 ... 147 E4
Manor Farm Ct
Cudworth S72 .... 35 B6
Killamarsh S21 .... 156 D5
Rotherham S65 .... 98 F4
4 Sheffield S20 .... 144 A3
Manor Farm Dr S64 .... 79 C2
Manor Farm Est WF9 ...... 19 A3
Manor Farm Gdns S25 .. 146 D4
Manor Farm La DN14 .... 7 A5
Manor Farm Mews 2 S20 .... 144 A3
Manor Fields
Great Houghton S72 .... 36 E2
Rotherham S61 .... 114 E8
Manor Garth DN6 .... 4 E3
Manor Gdns
Barnsley S71 .... 56 B8
Hatfield DN7 .... 44 C7
Sprotbrough DN5 .... 61 B1
Manor Gr
Grimethorpe S72 .... 35 F8
Royston S71 .... 15 B3
South Kirkby WF9 .... 18 A1
Manor Grange HD8 .... 28 D8
Manor Ho S6 .... 127 C6
Manor House Cl S74 ...... 76 E6
Manor House Ct DN5 ...... 40 F1
Manor House Rd S61 .... 114 E8
Manor La
Dinnington S25 .... 135 A3
Mexborough S64 .... 80 A7
Oxspring S36 .... 52 C1
Sheffield S2 .... 129 F2
Manor Laith Rd S2 ..... 129 D2
Manor Lodge Com Prim Sch S2 .... 129 E1
Manor Oaks Cl S2 .... 129 E3
Manor Oaks Ct S2 .... 129 D3
Manor Oaks Dr S2 .... 129 D3
Manor Oaks Gdns S2 .... 129 D3
Manor Oaks Pl S2 .... 129 E2
Manor Oaks Rd S2 .... 129 D3
Manor Occupation Rd S71 .... 15 B4
Manor Park Ave S2 ...... 129 F1
Manor Park Cl S2 .... 129 F1
Manor Park Cres S2 ..... 129 F1
Manor Park Ct S2 .... 129 F1
Manor Park Ctr S2 ...... 129 F2
Manor Park Dr S2 .... 129 F1
Manor Park Pl S2 .... 129 F2
Manor Park Rd S2 .... 129 F2
Manor Park Rise S2 ..... 129 F2
Manor Park Way S2 ..... 129 F1
Manor Pk S75 .... 52 F8
Manor Pl
Hoyland S74 .... 76 F6
Rawmarsh S62 .... 98 A5
Manor Rd
Askern DN6 .... 21 F7
Barnburgh DN5 .... 59 C2
Barnby Dun DN3 .... 42 F8
Bentley DN5 .... 41 A4
Brinsworth S60 .... 131 B8
Clayton West HD8 .... 12 A4
Cudworth S72 .... 35 A6
Dinnington S25 .... 134 F2
Harthill S26 .... 157 F8
Hatfield DN7 .... 44 C7
Killamarsh S21 .... 156 E5
Maltby S66 .... 119 A5
Scrooby DN10 .... 123 A2
Stainforth DN7 .... 24 E5
Swinton S64 .... 79 D2
Thurnscoe S63 .... 58 C8
Wales S26 .... 145 B3
Wath u D S63 .... 78 B7
Manor Rise DN11 .... 102 C6
Manor Sq S63 .... 58 C8
Manor St S71 .... 34 D8
Manor View
Shafton S72 .... 16 C2
Sheffield S20 .... 155 E7
Upton WF9 .... 19 A8
Manor Way
Askern DN6 .... 21 F6
Bolton u D S63 .... 58 D2
Hoyland S74 .... 76 E6
Sheffield S2 .... 129 F3
Todwick S26 .... 145 F5
Manor Wlk DN11 .... 102 B6
Manse Cl DN4 .... 85 A8
Manse Farm Mews S72 ... 35 C7
Mansel Ave S5 .... 112 E6
Mansel Cres S5 .... 112 D6
Mansel Ct S5 .... 112 E6
Mansel Prim Sch S5 ..... 112 E7
Mansel Rd S5 .... 112 E6
Mansfield Cres
Adwick le S DN6 .... 21 B2
Armthorpe DN3 .... 63 F7
Mansfield Dr S12 .... 142 C6
Mansfield Rd
Aston S26 .... 144 F3
Barnsley S71 .... 33 F8
Doncaster DN4 .... 62 B1
Killamarsh S21 .... 156 F6
Rotherham S60 .... 115 E6
Sheffield S12 .... 142 B6
Wales S26 .... 144 F3
Mansfield View S12 ..... 142 B6
Mansion Court Gdns DN8 .26 C8
Manton Ho 19 DN1 .... 62 C2
Manton St S2 .... 161 B1
Manvers Cl
Aston S26 .... 144 D7
North Anston S25 .... 146 E7
Manvers Pk S63 .... 79 D5
Manvers Rd
Aston S26 .... 144 C7
Mexborough S64 .... 79 E5
Sheffield, Beighton S20 ... 143 F4
Sheffield S6 .... 128 C7
Manvers Way S63 .... 79 B7
Maori Ave S63 .... 58 A2
Maple Ave
Doncaster DN4 .... 84 F8
Finningley DN9 .... 86 A4
Maltby S66 .... 118 D5
Maplebeck Dr S9 .... 114 F2
Maplebeck Rd S9 .... 114 F2
Maple Cl S70 .... 55 B7
Maple Croft Cres S9 .... 114 A3
Maple Croft Rd S9 .... 113 F3
Maple Ct
Pilley S75 .... 75 D3
Rawmarsh S62 .... 98 A5
Maple Dr
Auckley DN9 .... 86 A7
Killamarsh S21 .... 156 C5
Rotherham S66 .... 117 B6
Maple Est S75 .... 33 C1
Maple Gr
Armthorpe DN3 .... 64 B7
Aston S26 .... 144 F8
Bawtry DN10 .... 122 F7
Conisbrough DN12 .... 100 A8
Sheffield S9 .... 130 E3
Stocksbridge S36 .... 92 B8
Maple Pl S35 .... 95 A4
Maple Rd
Darton S75 .... 14 A1
Mexborough S64 .... 79 F6
Pilley S75 .... 75 D3
Thorne DN8 .... 9 C1
Wales S26 .... 145 C3
Maplewood Ave S66 ..... 117 B8
Mapperley Rd S18 ...... 152 C1
Mappin's Rd S60 .... 131 D5
Mappin Art Gall★ S10 ... 160 A3
Mappin Ct 6 S1 .... 160 C3
Mappin St S1 .... 160 C3
Mapplebeck Rd S35 .... 94 E7
Mapplewell Bsns Pk S75 .. 33 C8
Mapplewell Dr S75 .... 33 C8
Mapplewell Prim Sch S75 14 C1
Maran Ave S73 .... 57 C5
Marbeck Cl S25 .... 134 D1
Marcham Dr S20 .... 144 A4
March Bank S65 .... 99 A3
March Flatts Rd S65 ...... 99 A2
March Gate DN12 .... 81 C1
March St
Conisbrough DN12 .... 81 C2
Sheffield S9 .... 130 B7
March Vale Rise DN12 ..... 81 C1
Marchwood Ave S6 ...... 127 E6
Marchwood Dr S6 .... 127 E7
Marchwood Rd S6 .... 127 E7
Marcliff Cl S66 .... 116 F4
Marcliff Cres S66 .... 116 F4
Marcliff La S66 .... 116 F4
Mardale Wlk DN2 .... 63 C6
Marden Rd S7 .... 140 E6
Margaret Cl
Aston S26 .... 144 D6
Darfield S73 .... 56 F5
Margaret Ct S73 .... 56 E2
Margaret Rd
Darfield S73 .... 56 F5
Wombwell S73 .... 56 E2
Margaret St
Maltby S66 .... 119 B3
Sheffield S1 .... 161 A1
Margate Dr S4 .... 129 D8
Margate St
Grimethorpe S72 .... 36 A7
Sheffield S4 .... 129 E8
Margetson Cres S5 ...... 112 F6
Margetson Dr S5 .... 112 F6
Margetson Rd S5 .... 112 F6
Marguerite Gdns WF9 ..... 19 D8
Marian Cres DN6 .... 21 E8
Marian Rd DN3 .... 42 E2
Marigold Cl S5 .... 113 E3
Marina Rise S73 .... 56 E5
Marina View DN8 .... 26 B5
Marion Cl WF9 .... 18 C2
Marion Rd S6 .... 112 B2
Markbrook Dr S35 .... 94 C8
Market Cl S71 .... 34 A1
Market Hill 3 S70 .... 33 E1
Market Par 6 S70 .... 33 F1
Market Pl
Askern DN6 .... 22 A8
Bawtry DN10 .... 123 A7
Chapeltown S35 .... 95 B5

Market Pl *continued*
Cudworth S72 . . . 35 B7
Doncaster DN1 . . . 62 D3
Hoyland S74 . . . 77 A4
Penistone S36 . . . 51 D3
Rotherham S60 . . . 115 D6
Sheffield S1 . . . 161 B4
Thorne DN8 . . . 26 B7
Tickhill DN11 . . . 121 A7
Wombwell S73 . . . 56 E2
Market Rd DN1 . . . 62 D4
Market Sq
Goldthorpe S63 . . . 58 E5
[9] Rotherham S65 . . . 115 E7
Sheffield S13 . . . 143 C6
Market St
Adwick le S DN6 . . . 40 B2
Barnsley S70 . . . 33 E1
Chapeltown S35 . . . 95 B5
Cudworth S72 . . . 35 B7
Eckington S21 . . . 155 E3
Goldthorpe S63 . . . 58 E5
Hemsworth WF9 . . . 17 D7
Hoyland S74 . . . 76 E6
[1] Mexborough S64 . . . 80 A4
Mexborough S64 . . . 80 B4
Penistone S36 . . . 51 D3
Rotherham S60 . . . 115 D6
Sheffield S13 . . . 143 C6
Swinton S64 . . . 79 E3
Thurnscoe S63 . . . 58 C8
Markfield Dr S66 . . . 117 B5
Mark Gr S66 . . . 117 B5
Markham Ave
Adwick le S DN6 . . . 21 C1
Armthorpe DN3 . . . 64 A7
Conisbrough DN12 . . . 81 A2
Markham Ct DN12 . . . 81 A2
Markham Rd
Langold S81 . . . 136 E3
New Edlington DN12 . . . 82 C2
Markham Sq DN12 . . . 82 C2
Markham Terr
New Edlington DN12 . . . 82 B2
Sheffield S8 . . . 140 F6
Mark La S10 . . . 139 A6
Mark St [8] S70 . . . 33 E1
Marlborough Ave DN5 . . . 61 F4
Marlborough Cl
North Anston S25 . . . 146 D7
Thurnscoe S63 . . . 58 C8
Marlborough Cres DN6 . . . 22 B7
Marlborough Croft WF9 . . . 18 F4
Marlborough Rd
Askern DN6 . . . 22 B8
Doncaster DN2 . . . 62 F4
Sheffield S10 . . . 160 A3
Thorne DN8 . . . 26 C8
Marlborough Rise S26 . . . 144 E6
Marlborough Terr [8] S70 . . 54 E8
Marlcliffe Com Prim Sch
S6 . . . 112 B2
Marlcliffe Rd S6 . . . 112 B2
Marlfield Croft S35 . . . 113 B8
Marlow Cl
Doncaster DN2 . . . 63 C5
Rotherham S66 . . . 117 D4
Marlowe Dr S65 . . . 116 B5
Marlowe Rd
Barnby Dun DN3 . . . 42 F8
Rotherham S65 . . . 116 B5
Marlow Rd DN2 . . . 63 C5
Marmion Rd S11 . . . 140 B8
Marples Cl [7] S8 . . . 140 F7
Marples Dr [8] S8 . . . 140 F7
Marquis Gdns DN3 . . . 42 F7
Marr Grange La DN5 . . . 60 E7
Marrick Ct S35 . . . 94 F5
Marrion Rd S62 . . . 98 A6
Marriott La S7 . . . 140 D3
Marriott Pl S62 . . . 97 D7
Marriott Rd
Sheffield S7 . . . 140 D3
Swinton S64 . . . 79 E4
Marrison Dr S21 . . . 156 C6
Marr Terr S10 . . . 127 F1
Marrtree Bsns Pk S36 . . . 51 F2
Marsala Wlk S73 . . . 56 F6
Marsden Gdns [6] DN3 . . . 42 E4
Marsden Gr DN8 . . . 26 A8
Marsden La S3 . . . 160 C4
Marsden Rd S36 . . . 73 C1
Marshall Ave DN4 . . . 83 A7
Marshall Cl S62 . . . 97 F4
Marshall Dr WF9 . . . 18 F3
Marshall Gr S63 . . . 78 F5
Marshall Rd S8 . . . 140 F2
Marsh Ave S18 . . . 153 B3
Marsh Cl S20 . . . 155 C6
Marshfield S70 . . . 54 F1
Marsh Gate DN5 . . . 62 B4
Marsh Hill S66 . . . 100 D1
Marsh Hill La DN14 . . . 7 F7
Marsh House Rd S11 . . . 140 A5
Marsh La
Bentley DN5 . . . 41 C4
Sheffield S10 . . . 128 A3
Shepley HD8 . . . 28 D7
Thorne DN8 . . . 9 A4
Thorpe in B, Almholme DN3 . 42 C6
Thorpe in B DN3 . . . 23 C1
Marshland Rd DN8 . . . 9 C3
Marsh Lane Prim Sch
S21 . . . 154 E3
Marsh Lea Gr WF9 . . . 17 F7
Marsh Quarry S21 . . . 155 A1
Marsh Rd
Bentley DN5 . . . 62 B5
Thorpe in B DN6 . . . 23 D4
Marsh St
Rotherham S60 . . . 115 C5
Stocksbridge S36 . . . 73 D1
Wombwell S73 . . . 56 E3
Marsh View S21 . . . 155 B2
Marsh Wlk S2 . . . 129 D4
Marson Ave DN6 . . . 39 F5
Marston Cres S71 . . . 33 F6
Marstone Cres S17 . . . 151 F5
Marston Rd S10 . . . 128 B4
Martin's Rd S71 . . . 34 F3
Martin S6 . . . 160 B5
Martin Beck La DN11 . . . 104 A1
Martin Cl
Aston S26 . . . 132 C2
Barnsley S70 . . . 75 F8
Martin Cres S5 . . . 113 B6
Martin Croft S75 . . . 52 F8
Martin Ct S21 . . . 155 C3
Martindale Ho S73 . . . 56 F1
Martindale Wlk DN6 . . . 40 C8
Martin La
Bawtry DN10 . . . 122 E8
Hoyland S74 . . . 55 D1
Martin Rise
Eckington S21 . . . 155 C3
Rotherham S61 . . . 96 A6
Martin St S6 . . . 160 B5
Martin Wells Rd DN12 . . . 82 C1
Marton Ave WF9 . . . 17 C6
Marton Gr DN7 . . . 44 B7
Marton Rd DN5 . . . 40 F5
Marvell Rd DN5 . . . 61 D6
Mary's Pl [2] S75 . . . 33 C2
Mary Ann Cl S71 . . . 34 D2
Maryfield S7 . . . 140 E6
Maryhill Cl S60 . . . 131 F4
Mary La S73 . . . 57 B5
Mary Rd DN6 . . . 21 F7
Mary St
Barnsley S75 . . . 32 D4
Eckington S21 . . . 155 D3
Great Houghton S72 . . . 57 E7
[5] Rotherham S60 . . . 115 C7
Sheffield S1 . . . 161 A1
Marys Wlk S2 . . . 129 D4
Mary Tozer Ho S10 . . . 128 B3
Masbrough St S60 . . . 115 C6
Masefield Cl S25 . . . 147 A8
Masefield Flats S63 . . . 78 C7
Masefield Rd
Doncaster DN2 . . . 63 C7
Sheffield S13 . . . 142 C6
Wath u D S63 . . . 78 C7
Masham Ct DN4 . . . 84 E8
Masham Rd DN4 . . . 84 E7
Mason Ave S26 . . . 132 D1
Mason Cres S13 . . . 142 D6
Mason Dr S26 . . . 132 D1
Mason Gr S13 . . . 142 D7
Mason Lathe Rd S5 . . . 113 E6
Mason St S63 . . . 58 E5
Masons Way S70 . . . 55 C6
Mason Way S74 . . . 76 D7
Massey Rd S13 . . . 143 D5
Mastall La DN5 . . . 41 F2
Masters Cres S5 . . . 113 B5
Masters Rd S5 . . . 113 B5
Mather Ave S9 . . . 130 B3
Mather Cres S9 . . . 130 B3
Mather Ct S9 . . . 130 B3
Mather Dr S9 . . . 130 B3
Mather Rd S9 . . . 130 B3
Mather Wlk S9 . . . 130 B3
Matilda La S1 . . . 161 B2
Matilda St S1 . . . 161 A2
Matilda Way S1 . . . 161 A2
Matlock Rd
Barnsley S71 . . . 34 B6
Sheffield S6 . . . 128 C5
Mattersey Cl DN4 . . . 84 E5
Matthew Gap S36 . . . 51 A4
Matthews Ave S63 . . . 78 E6
Matthews Cl S63 . . . 78 E5
Matthews Dr S66 . . . 117 B3
Matthews Fold S8 . . . 141 C1
Matthews La S8 . . . 141 C1
Matthew St S3 . . . 160 C5
Mauds Terr S71 . . . 34 C4
Maugerhay S8 . . . 141 C1
Maulays Ct DN11 . . . 104 B8
Mauncer Cres S13 . . . 143 B7
Mauncer Dr S13 . . . 143 B7
Mauncer La S13 . . . 143 B6
Maun Way S5 . . . 113 C3
Maurice St S62 . . . 97 F3
Mawfa Ave S14 . . . 141 D2
Mawfa Cres S14 . . . 141 D2
Mawfa Dr S14 . . . 141 D2
Mawfa Rd S14 . . . 141 D2
Mawfa Wlk S14 . . . 141 D2
Mawfield Rd S75 . . . 33 A4
Mawson Green La DN14 . . . 7 F6
Maxey Pl S8 . . . 141 A6
Maxfield Ave S10 . . . 128 C3
Maxwell St S4 . . . 129 C6
Maxwell Way S4 . . . 129 C6
May Ave DN4 . . . 83 A6
Mayberry Dr S75 . . . 31 F1
Maycock Ave S61 . . . 96 D2
May Day Gn [3] S70 . . . 33 F1
May Day Green Arc [7]
S70 . . . 33 F1
Mayfair Cl DN11 . . . 121 F4
Mayfair Pl WF9 . . . 17 D7
Mayfield
Askern DN6 . . . 22 A8
Barnsley S71 . . . 34 B4
Oxspring S36 . . . 73 B8
Mayfield Ave DN7 . . . 25 B4
Mayfield Cres
Rossington DN11 . . . 103 F8
Worsbrough S70 . . . 54 E6
Mayfield Ct
Oxspring S36 . . . 73 C8
Sheffield S10 . . . 139 C8
Mayfield Hts S10 . . . 139 D7
Mayfield Rd
Bentley DN5 . . . 62 A4
Sheffield S10 . . . 139 A6
Mayfields DN5 . . . 40 D1
Mayfields Way WF9 . . . 18 B1
Mayfield Terr
Askern DN6 . . . 22 A8
Hathersage S32 . . . 149 A8
Mayflower Ave DN10 . . . 123 A2
Mayflower Cl DN10 . . . 123 A8
Mayflower Cres DN4 . . . 82 C5
Mayflower Ct S12 . . . 142 B6
Mayflower Rd DN4 . . . 82 C5
Maynard Rd
Grindleford S32 . . . 149 D1
Rotherham S60 . . . 116 C2
May Rd S6 . . . 128 B8
May Terr S70 . . . 33 C1
Maythorne Cl S75 . . . 33 C8
Maytree Cl S73 . . . 57 A5
May Tree Cl S20 . . . 143 E1
May Tree Croft [3] S20 . . . 143 E1
May Tree La S20 . . . 143 E1
Meaburn Cl DN4 . . . 84 F8
Meadow Ave
Cudworth S72 . . . 35 D4
Rawmarsh S62 . . . 97 D7
Meadow Bank Ave S7 . . . 140 D7
Meadowbank Cl S61 . . . 115 A6
Meadow Bank Rd
Rotherham S61 . . . 114 E5
Sheffield S11 . . . 140 D7
Meadowbrook Ind Est
S20 . . . 156 A8
Meadow Cl
Dronfield S18 . . . 153 C4
Hemsworth WF9 . . . 17 C6
Kiveton Park S26 . . . 145 F3
Rotherham S65 . . . 98 E1
Meadowcourt S9 . . . 114 B2
Meadow Cres
Royston S71 . . . 15 D3
Sheffield S20 . . . 155 B7
Meadow Croft
Hemsworth WF9 . . . 17 E5
Kirk Sandall DN3 . . . 43 A2
Shafton S72 . . . 16 C3
Sprotbrough DN5 . . . 82 D8
Swinton S64 . . . 98 C8
Meadowcroft Cl S60 . . . 132 B8
Meadowcroft Gdns S20 . . 155 E8
Meadowcroft Glade S20 . 155 E8
Meadowcroft Rise [2]
S20 . . . 155 E8
Meadow Ct
Adwick le S DN6 . . . 40 C5
Rossington DN11 . . . 103 E8
Royston S71 . . . 15 D3
South Elmsall WF9 . . . 19 B3
Meadow Dr
Barnsley S71 . . . 34 D4
Chapeltown S35 . . . 94 E5
Swinton S64 . . . 79 C2
Tickhill DN11 . . . 121 B6
Meadowfield Dr S74 . . . 76 E4
Meadow Field Rd DN3 . . . 43 A6
Meadowgate
Wath u D S63 . . . 77 F6
Wombwell S73 . . . 57 A1
Meadow Gate Ave S20 . . . 144 B2
Meadow Gate Cl S20 . . . 144 B2
Meadow Gate La S20 . . . 144 B1
Meadowgate Pk S21 . . . 156 D7
Meadowgates S63 . . . 58 C3
Meadow Gr S17 . . . 151 E4
Meadow Grove Rd S17 . . 151 D4
Meadowhall Ctr S9 . . . 114 C2
Meadowhall Dr S9 . . . 114 B2
Meadowhall (Interchange)
Sta S9 . . . 114 C3
Meadowhall Jun Sch
S61 . . . 114 E6
Meadowhall Rd
Rotherham S61 . . . 114 D5
Sheffield S9 . . . 114 B2
Meadowhall Ret Pk S9 . . 130 C8
Meadowhall Riverside Ind
Est S9 . . . 114 B3
Meadowhall Way S9 . . . 114 C2
Meadowhead S8 . . . 152 F8
Meadow Head Ave S8 . . . 152 F8
Meadow Head Cl S8 . . . 152 E7
Meadow Head Dr S8 . . . 152 F8
Meadowhead Sch S8 . . . 153 A7
Meadow House Dr S10 . . 127 D1
Meadow La
Conisbrough DN12 . . . 80 B3
Darfield S73 . . . 57 B5
Kexbrough S75 . . . 32 E7
Maltby S66 . . . 119 A4
Meadowland Rise S72 . . . 35 C5
Meadowpark Croft S25 . . 146 E8
Meadow Rd S71 . . . 15 D3
Meadow Rise
Barnby Dun DN3 . . . 43 A7
Meadow Rise *continued*
Hemsworth WF9 . . . 17 C7
Wadworth DN11 . . . 102 C6
Meadows Ct DN11 . . . 104 B8
Meadow St
Barnsley S71 . . . 33 F2
Dinnington S25 . . . 134 C2
Rotherham S61 . . . 115 A6
Sheffield S3 . . . 160 C4
Meadows The
Denby Dale HD8 . . . 29 F5
Killamarsh S21 . . . 156 D6
Silkstone S75 . . . 52 F5
Todwick S26 . . . 145 F5
Meadow Terr [5] S11 . . . 140 C8
Meadow The DN5 . . . 61 C1
Meadow View
Askern DN6 . . . 22 C7
Penistone S36 . . . 51 F6
Worsbrough S70 . . . 55 A5
Meadow View Cl S74 . . . 76 D5
Meadow View Dr S65 . . . 117 E8
Meadow View Rd
Sheffield S8 . . . 152 F8
Swinton S64 . . . 98 D8
Meadow Way
Harworth DN11 . . . 121 F5
Swinton S64 . . . 79 F3
Meadow Wlk DN3 . . . 43 A3
Meadstead Dr S71 . . . 15 B3
Meadstead Fold S71 . . . 15 B3
Meads The S8 . . . 153 B8
Meadway Dr S17 . . . 151 D7
Meadway The S17 . . . 151 D7
Meal Hill La HD9 . . . 28 A3
Mears Cl S36 . . . 51 E3
Measham Dr DN7 . . . 25 B5
Mede The DN6 . . . 39 F5
Medhomes S65 . . . 115 F7
Medina Way S75 . . . 32 F5
Medlar Croft [10] S70 . . . 33 D2
Medley View DN12 . . . 81 D1
Medlock Cl S13 . . . 131 A1
Medlock Cres S13 . . . 131 A2
Medlock Croft S13 . . . 131 A2
Medlock Ct S25 . . . 146 F8
Medlock Dr S13 . . . 131 A1
Medlock Rd S13 . . . 131 A1
Medlock Way S13 . . . 131 A2
Medway Cl S75 . . . 32 F5
Medway Pl S73 . . . 56 F1
Meersbrook Ave S8 . . . 140 F5
Meersbrook Bank Prim Sch
S8 . . . 140 F5
Meersbrook Park Rd S8 141 A5
Meersbrook Rd S8 . . . 141 B5
Meersbrook Works S2 . . 141 A6
Meersdale S2 . . . 141 C6
Meetinghouse Croft S13 143 C6
Meetinghouse La
Sheffield S1 . . . 161 B4
Sheffield, Woodhouse S13 . 143 C6
Mekyll Cl S66 . . . 117 B6
Melbeck Ct S35 . . . 94 E5
Melbourne Ave
Aston S26 . . . 144 E8
Bolton u D S63 . . . 58 B2
Dronfield S18 . . . 152 B1
Sheffield S10 . . . 128 C2
Melbourne Gr DN11 . . . 121 F4
Melbourne Rd
Doncaster DN4 . . . 82 E6
Stocksbridge S36 . . . 73 A1
Melbourne Villas WF9 . . . 17 C6
Melbourn Rd S10 . . . 128 C4
Melciss Rd S66 . . . 117 A4
Meld Cl DN11 . . . 103 F7
Melford Cl S75 . . . 14 B1
Melford Dr DN4 . . . 83 A5
Melfort Glen S10 . . . 127 E3
Mell Ave S74 . . . 76 E6
Mellinder La DN5 . . . 60 C6
Melling Ave DN5 . . . 61 F3
Mellington Cl S8 . . . 141 C2
Mellish Rd S81 . . . 136 F2
Mellor Lea Farm Chase
S35 . . . 95 B2
Mellor Lea Farm Cl S35 . . 95 B2
Mellor Lea Farm Dr S35 . . 95 B2
Mellor Lea Farm Garth
S35 . . . 95 B2
Mellor Rd S73 . . . 56 D2
Mellow Fields Rd S25 . . . 134 D5
Mellwood Gr S73 . . . 77 C8
Mellwood La WF9 . . . 18 F3
Melrose Cl
Doncaster DN4 . . . 82 E7
Thurcroft S66 . . . 133 D6
Melrose Cotts S60 . . . 116 C1
Melrose Gr S60 . . . 116 A2
Melrose Rd S3 . . . 129 B7
Melrose Way S71 . . . 34 D2
Melton Ave
Goldthorpe S63 . . . 58 E5
Wath u D S73 . . . 78 B8
Melton Cl WF9 . . . 19 A5
Melton Ct
Aston S26 . . . 145 A7
Conisbrough DN12 . . . 80 F4
Meltonfield Cl DN3 . . . 64 C5
Melton Gdns DN5 . . . 61 B1
Melton Gn S63 . . . 78 C6
Melton Gr S20 . . . 143 A2
Melton Hall Doncaster
Training Coll DN5 . . . 81 B8
Melton High St S63 . . . 78 D6
Melton Mill La DN5 . . . 80 F8
Melton Rd
High Melton DN5 . . . 60 E1
Sprotbrough DN5 . . . 61 C1
Melton St
[2] Mexborough S64 . . . 80 C4
Wath u D S73 . . . 78 B8
Melton Terr S70 . . . 55 C5
Melton View DN5 . . . 59 C3
Melton Way S71 . . . 15 C5
Melton Wood Country Pk*
DN5 . . . 60 C4
Melton Wood Gr DN5 . . . 61 B1
Melville Ave DN4 . . . 83 B7
Melville Dr S2 . . . 142 A8
Melville St S73 . . . 56 D3
Melvinia Cres S75 . . . 33 D4
Melwood Ct DN3 . . . 64 C4
Memoir Gr DN11 . . . 103 E7
Mendip Cl
Barnsley S75 . . . 33 B2
Bentley DN5 . . . 61 E5
Mendip Ct S81 . . . 148 E7
Mendip Rise S60 . . . 131 D7
Menson Dr DN7 . . . 44 B8
Merbeck Dr S35 . . . 75 E1
Merbeck Gr S35 . . . 94 E8
Mercel Ave DN3 . . . 64 C7
Merchants Cres S3 . . . 161 B4
Merchants Way DN2 . . . 42 C1
Mercia Dr S17 . . . 151 E6
Meredith Cres DN4 . . . 83 B6
Meredith Rd S6 . . . 128 B8
Mere Gr DN3 . . . 64 A7
Mere La DN3 . . . 64 A7
Merlin Cl
Adwick le S DN6 . . . 40 B6
Barnsley S70 . . . 75 F8
South Elmsall WF9 . . . 19 A2
Merlin Way
Rotherham S61 . . . 96 A6
Sheffield S5 . . . 113 C3
Merrill Rd S63 . . . 37 C1
Merton La S9 . . . 114 B4
Merton Rd S9 . . . 114 B4
Merton Rise S9 . . . 114 B4
Metcalfe Ave S21 . . . 156 C6
Methley Cl S12 . . . 141 F6
Methley Ho [2] DN1 . . . 62 C2
Methley St S72 . . . 35 B6
Metro Trad Ctr S75 . . . 32 E5
Mews The
Hickleton DN5 . . . 59 C7
Sheffield S10 . . . 127 F1
Mexborough Bsns Ctr
S64 . . . 80 B5
Mexborough Montagu Jun
Sch S64 . . . 80 A6
Mexborough Park Road Inf
Sch S64 . . . 80 A6
Mexborough Pitt Street Inf
Sch S64 . . . 80 C4
Mexborough Rd S63 . . . 58 D1
Mexborough St John The
Baptist CE Prim Sch
S64 . . . 80 B6
Mexborough Sch S64 . . . 79 F6
Mexborough Sta S64 . . . 80 A4
Meynell Com Prim Sch
S5 . . . 112 E4
Meynell Cres S5 . . . 112 D4
Meynell Rd S5 . . . 112 D4
Meynell Way S21 . . . 156 C6
Meyrick Dr S75 . . . 32 D7
Michael's Est S72 . . . 36 A7
Michael Croft S63 . . . 78 D6
Michael Rd S71 . . . 34 F2
Mickelden Way S75 . . . 33 A1
Micklebring Gr DN12 . . . 100 A8
Micklebring La S66 . . . 100 E2
Micklebring Way S66 . . . 118 B7
Micklethwaite Gr DN8 . . . 9 C4
Micklethwaite Rd DN8 . . . 9 C4
Mickley La S17, S18 . . . 151 F4
Middle Ave S62 . . . 97 F6
Middle Bank DN4 . . . 62 E1
Middlebrook La DN8 . . . 26 B7
Middleburn Cl S70 . . . 55 A7
Middle Cl S75 . . . 13 C1
Middlecliff Cl S20 . . . 143 E1
Middlecliff Cotts S72 . . . 57 E7
Middlecliff Ct [2] S20 . . . 143 E1
Middlecliffe Dr S36 . . . 49 D5
Middlecliff La S72 . . . 57 D7
Middlecliff Rise [1] S20 . . 143 E1
Middle Dr S60 . . . 115 F1
Middlefield Cl S17 . . . 151 C7
Middlefield Croft S17 . . . 151 C7
Middlefield La WF8 . . . 3 B4
Middle Field La WF4 . . . 13 F6
Middlefield Rd
Doncaster DN4 . . . 84 D7
Rotherham S60 . . . 116 B2
Middle Field Rd S75 . . . 53 D8
Middlefields Dr S60 . . . 116 C1
Middlegate DN5 . . . 40 E1
Middleham Rd DN4 . . . 84 E7
Middle Hay Cl S14 . . . 141 E4
Middle Hay Pl S14 . . . 141 E4
Middle Hay Rise S14 . . . 141 E4
Middle Hay View S14 . . . 141 E4
Middle La
Askern DN5 . . . 22 D2
Rotherham S65 . . . 116 A6
Sheffield, Grenoside S35 . . . 94 B1
Sheffield S6 . . . 128 A6
Middle La S S65 . . . 116 A5
Middle Mdw S81 . . . 159 E7
Middle Ox Cl S20 . . . 155 F6

Middle Ox Gdns S20 . . . . . 155 F6
Middle Pl S65 . . . . . 116 B7
Middlesex St S70 . . . . . 54 F7
Middleton Ave S25 . . . . . 146 E8
Middleton La S35 . . . . . 112 D8
Middleton Rd S65 . . . . . 115 F6
Middlewood Chase S6 . . 112 A3
Middlewood Dr
Rotherham S61 . . . . . 96 C2
Sheffield S6 . . . . . 112 A3
Middlewood Dr E S6 . . . . 112 A3
Middlewood Hall S73 . . . . . 57 C6
Middlewood Rd S6 . . . . . 112 B3
Middlewood Rd N
Oughtibridge S35 . . . . . 111 F5
Sheffield S35 . . . . . 111 F5
Middlewoods S75 . . . . . 54 A7
Middlewoods Way S71 . . . . 34 B8
Midfield Rd S10 . . . . . 128 B4
Midhill Rd S2 . . . . . 141 B7
Midhope Cliff La S36 . . . . 71 C5
Midhope Hall La S36 . . . . . 71 F4
Midhope La S36 . . . . . 71 D4
Midhope Way S75 . . . . . 33 A1
Midhurst Gr S75 . . . . . 32 E5
Midhurst Rd S6 . . . . . 112 B5
Midland Cotts
Grindleford S32 . . . . . 149 D2
Ryhill S71 . . . . . 15 D7
Midland Ct
Rotherham S60 . . . . . 115 B6
Swinton S64 . . . . . 79 E3
Midland Rd
Rotherham S61 . . . . . 115 B6
Royston S71 . . . . . 15 D4
Swinton S64 . . . . . 79 E3
Midland St
Barnsley S70 . . . . . 33 F1
Rotherham S62 . . . . . 97 F2
Sheffield S1 . . . . . 161 A1
Midland Sta S1 . . . . . 161 B2
Midvale Ave S6 . . . . . 128 E6
Midvale Cl 4 S6 . . . . . 128 E5
Milano Rise S73 . . . . . 56 F5
Milbanke St DN1 . . . . . 62 D4
Milburn Ct 3 S20 . . . . . 144 A1
Milburn Gr S20 . . . . . 144 A1
Milcroft Cres DN7 . . . . . 44 B8
Milden Pl S70 . . . . . 55 A7
Milden Rd S6 . . . . . 112 A2
Mile End Ave DN7 . . . . . 44 A5
Milefield Ct S72 . . . . . 35 F7
Milefield La S72 . . . . . 35 F7
Milefield Prim Sch S72 . . . 35 F7
Milefield View S72 . . . . . 35 F7
Mile Oak Rd S60 . . . . . 116 A3
Miles Cl S5 . . . . . 113 A1
Miles Rd
Chapeltown S35 . . . . . 94 E7
Sheffield S5 . . . . . 113 A1
Mileswood Cl S72 . . . . . 36 D3
Milethorn La DN1 . . . . . 62 D5
Milford Ave S74 . . . . . 77 B6
Milford St S9 . . . . . 130 B8
Milgate St S71 . . . . . 15 D4
Milgrove Cres S35 . . . . . 94 D8
Millais Rise S66 . . . . . 117 B7
Millard Ave DN7 . . . . . 44 B8
Millard La S66 . . . . . 119 A5
Millard Nook DN7 . . . . . 44 B7
Millars Wlk WF9 . . . . . 18 A1
Millbank Cl S35 . . . . . 94 D6
Mill Bank Ct S32 . . . . . 149 A8
Mill Cl
Laughton en le M S25 . . . . 134 D6
Rotherham S60 . . . . . 115 C4
South Kirkby WF9 . . . . . 18 A1
Todwick S26 . . . . . 145 F4
Mill Croft DN7 . . . . . 24 E3
Mill Ct
Sheffield S35 . . . . . 95 B1
3 Worsbrough S70 . . . . . 55 A5
Milldale Rd S17 . . . . . 151 F5
Milldyke Cl S60 . . . . . 116 D1
Miller Cl DN8 . . . . . 26 C6
Miller Croft S13 . . . . . 143 A6
Miller Dale Dr S60 . . . . . 131 D7
Miller Hill HD8 . . . . . 30 A5
Miller Hill Bank HD8 . . . . . 30 A5
Miller La
Midhopestones S36 . . . . . 72 B4
Thorne DN8 . . . . . 26 C6
Miller Rd 6 S8 . . . . . 140 F7
Millers Croft S71 . . . . . 15 C4
Millers Dale S70 . . . . . 55 A4
Miller St S36 . . . . . 73 F1
Mill Field Ct DN3 . . . . . 43 A6
Millfield Rd
Bentley DN5 . . . . . 62 C8
Thorne DN8 . . . . . 26 B8
Mill Field Rd DN7 . . . . . 7 F1
Mill Fields S26 . . . . . 145 E4
Mill Gate DN5 . . . . . 62 B8
Mill Haven S25 . . . . . 146 D5
Mill Hill
Rotherham S60 . . . . . 116 C1
Wombwell S73 . . . . . 56 B4
Millhill Cl DN3 . . . . . 64 C4
Mill Hill Cl DN5 . . . . . 61 F3
Mill Hill Rd DN7 . . . . . 44 C6
Mill Hills S26 . . . . . 145 F5
Millhouse Ct S65 . . . . . 98 C1
Mill House Cvn Pk DN6 . . . 22 C8
Millhouse La S36 . . . . . 50 D3
Millhouse Prim Sch S36 . . 50 D3
Millhouses Ct S11 . . . . . 140 B4
Millhouses Glen S11 . . . . . 140 B4
Millhouses La S7, S11 . . . . 140 B4
Millhouses St S74 . . . . . 76 F5
Millicent Sq S66 . . . . . 119 A3
Millindale S66 . . . . . 119 A5
Mill La
Adwick le S DN6 . . . . . 40 C6
Adwick le S, Skellow DN6 . . . 20 F2
Barnburgh DN5 . . . . . 59 C1
Bradfield S36 . . . . . 91 F4
Darton S75 . . . . . 13 E1
Doncaster DN4, DN5 . . . . . 82 C7
Dronfield S18 . . . . . 153 B1
Harley S62 . . . . . 76 F2
Havercroft WF4 . . . . . 16 B8
Ingbirchworth S36 . . . . . 50 E8
North Anston S25 . . . . . 146 D5
Notton WF4 . . . . . 14 D8
Penistone S36 . . . . . 50 F3
Rawcliffe DN14 . . . . . 2 A8
Renishaw S21 . . . . . 156 A2
Scrooby DN10 . . . . . 123 A3
Sheffield S17 . . . . . 151 F5
South Anston S25 . . . . . 146 D5
South Elmsall WF9 . . . . . 19 B4
South Kirkby WF9 . . . . . 18 A2
Stocksbridge S36 . . . . . 73 F1
Treeton S60 . . . . . 131 D4
Wath u D S63 . . . . . 78 C5
Mill Lee La S6 . . . . . 110 A3
Mill Lee Rd S6 . . . . . 110 A4
Mill Meadow Cl S20 . . . . . 144 B1
Mill Meadow Gdns S20 . . 144 B1
Millmoor Ct S73 . . . . . 56 F4
Millmoor La S60 . . . . . 115 B6
Millmoor Rd
Darfield S73 . . . . . 56 F4
Doncaster DN4 . . . . . 84 E8
Millmoor (Rotherham Utd FC) S60 . . . . . 115 B6
Millmount Rd
Hoyland S74 . . . . . 76 F5
Sheffield S8 . . . . . 140 F5
Millrace Dr S63 . . . . . 58 C4
Mill Rd
Eckington S21 . . . . . 155 E4
Sheffield S35 . . . . . 95 B1
Treeton S60 . . . . . 131 D4
Mill Road Cl S35 . . . . . 95 B1
Millsands S3 . . . . . 161 B4
Mills Dr DN7 . . . . . 66 A7
Mill Shaw La HD8, HD9 . . . . 28 B1
Millside S72 . . . . . 16 C3
Millside Ct DN5 . . . . . 62 B8
Millside Wlk S72 . . . . . 16 C3
Mill St
Armthorpe DN3 . . . . . 64 B6
Rotherham, Greasbrough S61 . . . . . 97 B4
Rotherham S60 . . . . . 115 D5
South Kirkby WF9 . . . . . 18 A2
Millstone Cl 1 S18 . . . . . 152 D2
Millstone Dr S26 . . . . . 144 D7
Millstones S36 . . . . . 52 C1
Millstream Cl DN5 . . . . . 61 D1
Millthorpe Rd S5 . . . . . 113 D4
Mill View
Bolton u D S63 . . . . . 58 B1
Hemsworth WF9 . . . . . 17 C6
Stainforth DN7 . . . . . 24 E3
Millwood Rd DN4 . . . . . 82 F5
Mill Wood View S6 . . . . . 127 C7
Milne Ave DN11 . . . . . 122 C4
Milne Dr DN11 . . . . . 122 D4
Milne Gr DN11 . . . . . 122 C4
Milner Ave S36 . . . . . 51 B4
Milner Cl S66 . . . . . 117 E6
Milne Rd DN11 . . . . . 122 D4
Milner Gate DN12 . . . . . 81 E3
Milner Gate Ct DN12 . . . . . 81 E2
Milner Gate La 2 DN12 . . . 81 D3
Milner Rd DN4 . . . . . 82 F7
Milnes St 9 S70 . . . . . 55 A8
Milne St S75 . . . . . 32 E4
Milnrow Cres S5 . . . . . 112 F6
Milnrow Dr S5 . . . . . 112 F6
Milnrow Rd S5 . . . . . 112 F6
Milnrow View S5 . . . . . 112 F6
Milton Ave DN5 . . . . . 61 F4
Milton Cl
Hoyland S74 . . . . . 76 F7
Rotherham S61 . . . . . 97 B4
Wath u D S63 . . . . . 78 C8
Milton Cres S74 . . . . . 76 E5
Milton Ct
Doncaster DN1 . . . . . 62 D2
Swinton S64 . . . . . 79 C3
Milton Gr
Armthorpe DN3 . . . . . 64 C6
Kirk Sandall DN3 . . . . . 42 F2
Wombwell S73 . . . . . 56 E2
Milton La S1 . . . . . 160 C2
Milton Rd
Adwick le S DN6 . . . . . 21 C1
Branton DN3 . . . . . 85 E8
Chapeltown S35 . . . . . 94 D5
Dinnington S25 . . . . . 147 A8
Hoyland S74 . . . . . 76 E5
Mexborough S64 . . . . . 80 A5
Rotherham S65 . . . . . 115 F8
Sheffield S7 . . . . . 140 F7
Milton Sch S64 . . . . . 79 D3
Milton St
Great Houghton S72 . . . . . 36 D2
Maltby S66 . . . . . 118 F4
Rotherham S60 . . . . . 115 D8
Sheffield S1, S3 . . . . . 160 C2
Swinton S64 . . . . . 79 C3
Milton Wlk DN1 . . . . . 62 D2
Minden Cl S66 . . . . . 117 B4
Minden Ct DN5 . . . . . 62 B8
Minna Rd S3 . . . . . 129 B7
Minneymoor Hill DN12 . . . . 81 D3
Minneymoor La DN12 . . . . . 81 D2
Minster Cl
Doncaster DN4 . . . . . 85 A7
Sheffield S35 . . . . . 113 C8
Minster Rd S35 . . . . . 113 B8
Minster Way S71 . . . . . 34 D3
Minsthorpe Com Coll WF9 . . . . . 19 A5
Minsthorpe La WF9 . . . . . 18 E4
Minsthorpe Vale WF9 . . . . . 18 F4
Minto Rd S6 . . . . . 128 B8
Mission Field S73 . . . . . 78 A8
Misson Bank DN9 . . . . . 87 F5
Mitchell's St S70 . . . . . 55 E5
Mitchell Cl
Hatfield DN7 . . . . . 25 A1
Worsbrough S70 . . . . . 55 D5
Mitchell Rd
Sheffield S8 . . . . . 140 F2
Wombwell S73 . . . . . 56 C5
Mitchells Ent Ctr S73 . . . . . 56 C5
Mitchell St S3 . . . . . 160 B4
Mitchells Way S73 . . . . . 56 D4
Mitchelson Ave S75 . . . . . 53 E7
Moat Cl S66 . . . . . 117 C7
Moat Croft DN5 . . . . . 40 F1
Moat Hills Ct DN5 . . . . . 41 B1
Moat House Way DN12 . . . . 81 C3
Moat La S66 . . . . . 117 D1
Moatlands S66 . . . . . 117 C2
Modena Ct S73 . . . . . 56 E6
Moffat Gdns DN2 . . . . . 42 D1
Moffatt Rd S2 . . . . . 141 B7
Moira Cl DN7 . . . . . 25 B5
Molineaux Cl S5 . . . . . 113 D5
Molineaux Rd S5 . . . . . 113 D5
Molloy Pl 12 S8 . . . . . 141 A6
Molloy St 11 S8 . . . . . 141 A6
Molly Hurst La WF4 . . . . . 13 F7
Mona Ave S10 . . . . . 128 C4
Mona Rd
Doncaster DN4 . . . . . 83 B8
Sheffield S10 . . . . . 128 C4
Mona St S75 . . . . . 33 D2
Mona Terr S26 . . . . . 145 D7
Monckton Rd
Bircotes DN11 . . . . . 122 C4
Sheffield S5 . . . . . 113 F3
Moncrieffe Rd S7 . . . . . 140 E6
Monk Bretton Priory* S71 . . . . . 34 E2
Monksbridge Rd S25 . . . . 134 D2
Monk's Bridge Trad Est S25 . . . . . 134 C2
Monks Cl
Hatfield DN7 . . . . . 25 A1
Rotherham S61 . . . . . 96 C2
Monkspring S70 . . . . . 55 C5
Monks Way
Barnsley S71 . . . . . 34 D3
Shireoaks S81 . . . . . 159 F7
Monk Terr S71 . . . . . 34 E5
Monkton Way S71 . . . . . 15 C5
Monkwood Rd S62 . . . . . 97 E7
Monmouth Rd DN2 . . . . . 63 A6
Monmouth St S3 . . . . . 160 B2
Monsal Cres S71 . . . . . 34 A7
Monsal St S63 . . . . . 58 C8
Montague Ave DN12 . . . . . 81 A2
Montague St
Cudworth S72 . . . . . 35 C8
Doncaster DN1 . . . . . 62 D4
Sheffield S11 . . . . . 128 E1
Montagu Hospl S64 . . . . . 80 A6
Montagu Rd DN5 . . . . . 61 E3
Montagu St 5 S64 . . . . . 80 C4
Monteney Cres S5 . . . . . 113 A8
Monteney Gdns S5 . . . . . 113 A7
Monteney Prim Sch S5 . 113 A7
Monteney Rd S5 . . . . . 113 A8
Montfort Dr S3 . . . . . 129 B6
Montgomery Ave S7 . . . . . 140 E7
Montgomery Ct S11 . . . . . 140 A5
Montgomery Dr S7 . . . . . 140 E7
Montgomery Gdns DN2 . . . 63 C6
Montgomery Rd
Sheffield S7 . . . . . 140 E7
Wath u D S63 . . . . . 78 F6
Montgomery Sq S63 . . . . . 78 F6
Montgomery Terrace Rd S6 . . . . . 160 C5
Montrose Ave
Darton S75 . . . . . 13 F1
Doncaster DN2 . . . . . 63 C5
Montrose Ct S11 . . . . . 139 F4
Montrose Pl S18 . . . . . 152 D2
Montrose Rd S7 . . . . . 140 C5
Mont Wlk S73 . . . . . 56 A4
Monument Dr S72 . . . . . 16 F2
Moonpenny Way S18 . . . . 153 A1
Moonshine La S5 . . . . . 112 F3
Moonshine Way S5 . . . . . 112 F2
Moorbank Cl
Barnsley S75 . . . . . 33 C4
Sheffield S10 . . . . . 127 D2
Wombwell S73 . . . . . 56 B4
Moorbank Dr S10 . . . . . 127 E3
Moorbank Rd
Sheffield S10 . . . . . 127 D3
Wombwell S73 . . . . . 56 B5
Moorbank View S73 . . . . . 56 B5
Moorbridge Cres S73 . . . . . 57 B1
Moor Cres S20 . . . . . 155 C7
Moorcrest Rise S75 . . . . . 14 B2
Moorcroft Ave S10 . . . . . 139 B7
Moorcroft Cl S10 . . . . . 139 B7
Moorcroft Dr S10 . . . . . 139 B7
Moorcroft Rd S10 . . . . . 139 B7
Moordale View S62 . . . . . 98 C7
Moor Dike Rd
Hatfield DN7 . . . . . 66 A7
Hatfield, Hatfield Woodhouse DN7 . . . . . 45 B4
Moor Edges Rd DN8 . . . . . 26 E7
Moor End Hos S75 . . . . . 53 B5
Moorend La S75 . . . . . 53 A5
Moor End Rd S10 . . . . . 128 C4
Moorends Rd DN8 . . . . . 9 C7
Moore St S3 . . . . . 160 C1
Moor Farm Ave S20 . . . . . 155 B8
Moor Farm Garth S20 . . . 155 C8
Moor Farm Rise S20 . . . . . 155 B8
Moorfield Ave S65 . . . . . 117 D7
Moorfield Cl S65 . . . . . 117 D7
Moorfield Cres WF9 . . . . . 17 C6
Moorfield Dr DN3 . . . . . 64 B5
Moorfield Gr S65 . . . . . 117 D7
Moorfield Pl WF9 . . . . . 17 C6
Moorfields S3 . . . . . 161 A4
Moorfields Flats S3 . . . . . 161 A4
Moor Gap DN3 . . . . . 85 D8
Moorgate Ave
Rotherham S60 . . . . . 115 E4
Sheffield S10 . . . . . 160 A4
Moorgate Bsns Ctr S60 . 115 D5
Moorgate Chase S60 . . . . . 115 E5
Moorgate Gr S60 . . . . . 115 F4
Moorgate La S60 . . . . . 115 E4
Moorgate Rd S60 . . . . . 115 E4
Moorgate St S60 . . . . . 115 D6
Moor G reen Cl S75 . . . . . 33 A1
Moor Head S1 . . . . . 161 A2
Moorhouse Cl S60 . . . . . 116 D1
Moorhouse Ct WF9 . . . . . 19 A1
Moorhouse Ct Mews WF9 . 19 A1
Moorhouse Gap DN6 . . . . . 19 F1
Moorhouse La
Hooton Pagnell WF9 . . . . . 19 D1
Rotherham S60 . . . . . 116 D1
Woolley S75 . . . . . 13 C5
Moorhouse View WF9 . . . . . 19 B2
Moor La
Barnsley S70 . . . . . 75 F5
Bradfield S36 . . . . . 91 D4
Braithwell S66 . . . . . 100 C1
Great Houghton S72 . . . . . 36 E4
Hatfield DN8 . . . . . 46 A6
Kirk Sandall DN3 . . . . . 42 E5
Sykehouse DN14 . . . . . 7 B7
Thorne DN8 . . . . . 9 D2
Wroot DN9 . . . . . 66 F4
Moor La N S65 . . . . . 99 D1
Moorland Ave
Barnsley S70 . . . . . 54 B8
Darton S75 . . . . . 14 B2
Moorland Cres S75 . . . . . 14 B2
Moorland Dr S36 . . . . . 73 A1
Moorland Gr DN4 . . . . . 63 C1
Moorland Pl
Sheffield S6 . . . . . 127 C6
Silkstone S75 . . . . . 53 A5
Moorland Rd S32 . . . . . 149 A7
Moorlands S66 . . . . . 116 F4
Moorlands Cres S60 . . . . . 116 D1
Moorlands Ct S63 . . . . . 78 C8
Moorland Terr S72 . . . . . 35 C5
Moorland View
Apperknowle S18 . . . . . 154 A1
Aston S26 . . . . . 144 E7
Clayton West HD8 . . . . . 12 A2
Sheffield S12 . . . . . 142 A2
Wath u D S63 . . . . . 78 C8
Moor La S S65 . . . . . 117 D7
Moor Ley S70 . . . . . 54 F1
Moor Oaks Rd S10 . . . . . 128 C3
Moor Owners Rd DN8 . . . . . 27 B7
Moor Rd
Rawcliffe Bridge DN14 . . . . . 2 E5
Rotherham S65 . . . . . 116 B6
Sheffield S6 . . . . . 110 F4
Thorne DN8 . . . . . 26 E5
Wath u D S63 . . . . . 78 F7
Moorshutt Rd WF9 . . . . . 17 C6
Moorside S10 . . . . . 139 A8
Moorside Ave S36 . . . . . 51 D1
Moorside Cl
Mapplewell S75 . . . . . 33 B8
Sheffield S20 . . . . . 155 C8
Moorside Ct DN8 . . . . . 9 C3
Moorsyde Ave S10 . . . . . 128 B5
Moorsyde Cres S10 . . . . . 128 B5
Moor The S1 . . . . . 161 A2
Moorthorpe Dell S20 . . . . 143 B1
Moorthorpe Gdns 2 S20 . . . . . 143 A2
Moorthorpe Gn S20 . . . . . 142 F2
Moorthorpe Prim sch WF9 . . . . . 18 E3
Moorthorpe Rise S20 . . . . 143 B1
Moorthorpe Sta WF9 . . . . . 18 E3
Moorthorpe View S20 . . . . 143 B1
Moorthorpe Way
Sheffield, Birley S20 . . . . . 143 A2
Sheffield S20 . . . . . 143 C2
Moor Top Dr WF9 . . . . . 17 D5
Moortop Rd S18, S21 . . . . 154 B1
Moor Top Rd DN11 . . . . . 121 F5
Moortown Ave S25 . . . . . 147 A7
Moor Valley S20 . . . . . 143 A1
Moor Valley Cl S20 . . . . . 143 A1
Moorview S61 . . . . . 114 D6
Moor View DN3 . . . . . 85 E8
Moorview Ct
Rotherham S61 . . . . . 114 D6
2 Sheffield S17 . . . . . 152 B5
Moor View Dr S8 . . . . . 140 E2
Moor View Rd S8 . . . . . 140 E2
Moor View Terr S11 . . . . . 139 E5
Moorwinstow Croft S17 . . 151 E7
Moorwood La
Holmesfield S17 . . . . . 151 C1
Sheffield S6 . . . . . 126 D4
Moorwoods Ave S35 . . . . . 95 A5
Moorwoods La S35 . . . . . 95 A5
Moray Pl S18 . . . . . 152 D2
Mordaunt Rd S2 . . . . . 141 F6
More Hall La S36 . . . . . 93 A4
Morehall View S35 . . . . . 93 B3
Morgan Ave S5 . . . . . 112 E3
Morgan Cl S5 . . . . . 112 F3
Morgan Rd
Doncaster DN2 . . . . . 63 C4
Sheffield S5 . . . . . 112 F2
Morland Cl S14 . . . . . 141 F3
Morland Dr S14 . . . . . 141 F3
Morland Pl S14 . . . . . 141 F3
Morland Rd S14 . . . . . 141 F3
Morley Cl S18 . . . . . 152 C1
Morley Fold HD8 . . . . . 29 F5
Morley Pl DN12 . . . . . 81 C2
Morley Place Jun Sch DN12 . . . . . 81 B2
Morley Rd
Doncaster DN1 . . . . . 62 E5
Rotherham S61 . . . . . 96 E1
Morley St
Rawmarsh S62 . . . . . 97 F4
Sheffield S6 . . . . . 128 C7
Morpeth Gdns S3 . . . . . 160 C4
Morpeth St
Rotherham S65 . . . . . 115 E6
Sheffield S3 . . . . . 160 C4
Morrall Rd S5 . . . . . 113 A7
Morrell St S66 . . . . . 119 A4
Morris Ave S62 . . . . . 97 F8
Morrison Ave S66 . . . . . 119 A6
Morrison Dr DN11 . . . . . 104 A8
Morrison Pl S73 . . . . . 57 A6
Morrison Rd S73 . . . . . 57 A6
Mortain Rd S60 . . . . . 115 F2
Mortains S26 . . . . . 145 F6
Morthen Cotts S66 . . . . . 133 B7
Morthen Hall La S66 . . . . 133 C8
Morthen La
Rotherham S60, S66 . . . . . 133 B8
Upper Whiston S60 . . . . . 132 E6
Morthen Rd
Rotherham S66 . . . . . 117 C3
Thurcroft S66 . . . . . 133 D8
Mortimer Dr S36 . . . . . 51 C1
Mortimer Hts S36 . . . . . 72 C8
Mortimer Rd
Bradfield S36 . . . . . 91 C4
Langsett S36 . . . . . 72 D6
Maltby S66 . . . . . 119 C4
Midhopestones S36 . . . . . 72 A2
Penistone S36 . . . . . 51 C1
Mortimer St S1 . . . . . 161 B2
Mortlake Rd S5 . . . . . 113 D2
Mortomley Cl S35 . . . . . 94 E7
Mortomley Hall Gdns S35 . 94 E8
Mortomley La S35 . . . . . 94 E7
Morton Cl S71 . . . . . 34 D5
Morton Gdns S20 . . . . . 155 F6
Morton La S18, S21 . . . . . 154 C1
Morton Mount S20 . . . . . 155 F7
Morton Pl S35 . . . . . 112 C8
Morton Rd S64 . . . . . 80 C5
Morvern Mdws WF9 . . . . . 17 F7
Mosborough Hall Dr S20 155 E6
Mosborough Hall Farm S20 . . . . . 155 D6
Mosborough Moor S20 . . . 155 B8
Mosborough Prim Sch
Sheffield S20 . . . . . 155 C7
Sheffield S20 . . . . . 155 D7
Mosborough Rd S13 . . . . . 142 B7
Moscar Cross Rd S6 . . . . . 125 A5
Moscrop Cl S13 . . . . . 143 C7
Moses View S81 . . . . . 159 F7
Mosham Cl DN9 . . . . . 86 D5
Mosham Rd DN9 . . . . . 86 C5
Moss Beck Ct S21 . . . . . 155 C2
Mossbrook Ct S21 . . . . . 155 E4
Mossbrook Sch S8 . . . . . 153 C8
Moss Cl S66 . . . . . 117 B4
Mosscroft La DN7 . . . . . 44 D5
Mossdale Ave S20 . . . . . 155 D7
Mossdale Cl DN5 . . . . . 61 E7
Moss Dr S21 . . . . . 156 D5
Moss Edge Rd HD9 . . . . . 47 C8
Moss Gr S12 . . . . . 143 D3
Moss Haven DN6 . . . . . 6 B1
Moss La DN6 . . . . . 23 C5
Mossley Rd S36 . . . . . 72 C6
Moss Rd
Askern DN6 . . . . . 22 C8
Moss DN6 . . . . . 6 C1
Sheffield S17 . . . . . 151 B4
Moss Rise Pl S21 . . . . . 155 C3
Moss Terr DN8 . . . . . 9 C5
Moss View S20 . . . . . 155 C6
Moss Way S20 . . . . . 143 C2
Motehall Dr S2 . . . . . 130 A1
Motehall Pl S2 . . . . . 130 B1
Motehall Rd S2 . . . . . 130 B1
Motehall Way S2 . . . . . 130 A1

Motehall Wlk 2 S2 130 B1
Motte The S61 114 F8
Mottram St S71 33 F2
Moulton Chase WF9 17 E7
Mountain Row S35 74 B6
Mount Ave
Great Houghton S72 36 E1
Grimethorpe S72 36 A8
Hemsworth WF9 17 D7
Mountbatten Dr S35 94 D5
Mount Cl
10 Barnsley S70 54 F7
Harworth DN11 121 F5
Mount Cres S74 76 D7
Mountenoy Rd S60 115 E5
Mountfields Wlk WF9 18 B1
Mountford Croft S17 151 E5
Mount Osborne Ind Pk S71 34 B1
Mount Pleasant
Chapeltown S35 95 A6
Doncaster DN4 83 A7
Grimethorpe S72 36 A8
Kirk Smeaton WF8 3 F6
Oxspring S36 52 B2
Thorne DN8 9 C3
Thurgoland, Crane Moor S35 74 C8
Thurgoland S35 74 A5
Worsbrough S70 55 B4
Mount Pleasant Cl S35 95 A6
Mount Pleasant Cotts DN11 104 D8
Mount Pleasant Ct S35 74 D7
Mount Pleasant Rd
Rotherham S61 115 B7
Sheffield S11 140 F8
Thorne DN8 9 B3
Wath u D S63 78 F4
Mount Rd
Chapeltown S35 94 E5
Grimethorpe S72 36 A8
Sheffield S3 128 F7
Mount St Mary's RC Coll S21 156 C2
Mount St
Barnsley S71 55 F8
Barnsley, Shaw Lands S70 54 E8
Rotherham S61 115 B7
Sheffield S11 128 F1
Mount Terr
Wath u D S63 78 C6
Wombwell S73 56 C3
Mount The
Edenthorpe DN3 43 A1
Rotherham S66 117 B7
Mount Vernon Ave S70 54 F7
Mount Vernon Cres S70 55 A6
Mount Vernon Hospl S70 54 F6
Mount Vernon Rd S70 55 A6
Mount View DN12 82 B1
Mount View Ave S8 141 A3
Mount View Gdns S8 141 A3
Mount View Lodge 2 S8 141 A3
Mount View Rd S8 141 B3
Mousehole Cl S65 98 E1
Mousehole La S65 98 E1
Mouse Park Gate S35 93 F2
Mowbray Gdns S65 116 C8
Mowbray Pl S65 116 C8
Mowbray Rd DN8 26 C6
Mowbray St
Rotherham S65 116 C8
Sheffield S3 129 A5
Mowson Cres S35 111 D5
Mowson Dr S35 111 D5
Mowson Hollow S35 111 E5
Mowson La S35 111 E5
Moxon Cl S36 92 E8
Mucky La
Barnsley S71 35 A1
Stocksbridge S36 91 F7
Stocksbridge, Snowden Hill S36 73 A4
Muglet La S66 119 B4
Muirfield Ave
Doncaster DN4 85 B6
Swinton S64 79 E2
Muirfield Cl S72 16 C1
Muirfields The S75 14 A1
Mulberry Ave DN8 9 C2
Mulberry Cl
Bentley DN5 61 D5
Darfield S73 57 A5
Goldthorpe S63 58 C5
Rawmarsh S62 98 A3
Mulberry Cres S81 148 F7
Mulberry Ct DN4 82 D6
Mulberry Rd
Eckington S21 155 B2
North Anston S25 146 E6
Mulberry St S1 161 B3
Mulberry Way
Armthorpe DN3 64 B5
Killamarsh S21 156 B5
Mulehouse Rd S10 128 B4
Mundella Pl S8 141 A3
Mundella Prim Sch S8 141 A3
Munro Cl S21 156 D6
Munro Ct S11 140 B5
Munsbrough La S61 97 B2
Munsbrough Rise S61 97 B3
Munsdale S61 97 B3
Murdoch Pl S71 33 E7
Murdock Rd S5 112 F4
Murrayfield Dr 6 S20 155 E6
Murray Rd
Killamarsh S21 156 E7
Rawmarsh S62 98 A6
Sheffield S11 140 B7
Musard Way S21 156 C6
Museum of South Yorkshire Life* DN5 61 D4
Musgrave Cres S5 113 A1
Musgrave Dr S5 113 A1
Musgrave Pl S5 113 A1
Musgrave Rd S5 112 F1
Musgrove Ave S65 99 A2
Mushroom La S3, S10 160 A4
Muskoka Ave S11 139 E5
Muskoka Dr S11 139 E5
Mutual St DN4 62 B2
Myers Ave S35 111 D8
Myers Grove La S6 127 E7
Myers Grove Sch S6 127 F7
Myers La S35 111 B3
Mylnhurst RC Prep Sch S11 140 B4
Mylnhurst Rd S11 140 B5
Mylor Ct S71 34 C3
Mylor Rd S11 140 A6
Myndon Wlk DN12 81 A3
Myrtle Cres S66 117 C5
Myrtle Gr
Auckley DN9 86 A7
Wales S26 145 C2
Myrtle Rd
Dunscroft DN7 43 F8
Sheffield S2 141 B7
Wombwell S73 56 C3
Myrtle Springs S12 141 F5
Myrtle Springs Dr S12 141 F5
Myrtle Springs Sch S2 141 F6
Myrtle St S75 33 C2
Mysten Croft S75 33 D4
Myton Rd S9 130 A4

N

Nabeel Ct S60 115 E5
Nab La DN7 24 F7
Naigh Moor Way S71 15 C5
Nairn Dr S18 152 D1
Nairn St S10 128 B3
Nancy Cres S72 36 B6
Nancy Rd S72 36 B6
Nanny Hill S36 73 C1
Nanny Marr Rd S73 57 B6
Nan Sampson Bank DN9 87 D8
Napier Mount S70 54 F6
Napier St S11 128 F1
Narrow Balk DN5 38 E5
Narrow La
Askern DN5 22 D4
Bawtry DN10 123 B8
North Anston S25 146 E5
Tickhill DN11 102 E2
Nascot Cl S66 117 F3
Nascot Gdns S26 132 C2
Naseby Ave DN5 61 D6
Naseby Cl DN7 44 A5
Naseby St S9 114 A2
Nathan Ct S20 143 F1
Nathan Dr S20 143 F2
Nathan Gr S20 143 E2
National Arts Education Archive (Trust) Mus* WF4 12 E6
National Centre for Popular Music* S1 161 B2
Navan Rd S2 142 A7
Navigation Way S73 57 A1
Navvy La S71 15 D7
Naylor Gr
Dodworth S75 53 F7
Oughtibridge S35 111 C6
Naylor Rd S35 111 C7
Naylor St S62 97 F3
Neale Rd DN2 63 B8
Nearcroft Rd S61 114 F8
Nearfield Rd DN4 84 D7
Needham Way S7 140 C5
Needlewood S75 53 F6
Neepsend La S3 128 F6
Neill Rd S11 140 C8
Nelson Ave S71 34 B4
Nelson Cl S60 131 D8
Nelson Mandela Wlk 3 S2 130 B1
Nelson Pl S35 94 D5
Nelson Rd
Maltby S66 119 B5
New Edlington DN12 82 B2
Rossington DN11 84 E1
Sheffield S6 127 F6
Nelson Sq DN7 24 E3
Nelson St
5 Barnsley S70 33 E1
Doncaster DN4 62 D1
Rotherham S65 115 E7
South Hiendley S72 16 E5
Nemesia Cl S25 146 C4
Nene Gr DN9 86 A7
Nesfield Way S5 113 D4
Nether Ave
Killamarsh S21 156 C6
Sheffield S35 94 D1
Netherby Manor S17 152 A7
Nether Cantley La DN3 64 B1
Nether Cres S35 94 D1
Nethercroft S75 32 E5
Netherdale Ct HD8 30 D4
Netherdene Rd S18 153 A1
Nether Edge Hospl S11 140 C6
Nether Edge Rd S7 140 E6
Netherfield S74 77 A6
Netherfield Cl S36 73 F1
Netherfield Croft S72 16 C2
Netherfield La S62 97 F4
Netherfield Rd S10 128 B4
Netherfield View S65 116 D8
Nethergate S6 127 C5
Nethergreen Ave S21 156 D7
Nethergreen Ct S21 156 D7
Nethergreen Gdns S21 156 D7
Nether Green Inf Sch S10 139 D8
Nether Green Jun Sch S10 139 E8
Nethergreen Rd S11 139 F8
Nether Hall Rd DN1 62 D4
Nether House La S36 71 D7
Nether La S35 95 B3
Nether Ley Ave S35 95 A5
Nether Ley Croft S35 95 A5
Nether Ley Ct S35 95 A5
Nether Ley Gdns S35 95 A5
Nethermoor Ave S21 156 D7
Nethermoor Cl S21 156 D7
Nethermoor Dr
Killamarsh S21 156 D7
Rotherham S66 117 C2
Nethermoor La S21 156 D7
Nether Oak Cl S20 144 B2
Nether Oak Dr S20 144 B2
Nether Oak View S20 144 B2
Nether Rd
Sheffield S35 95 B1
Silkstone S75 32 A1
Nether Royd View S75 53 A5
Nether Shire La S5 113 D6
Netherthorpe Airfield S80 159 B5
Netherthorpe Cl S21 156 C7
Netherthorpe La S21 156 C7
Netherthorpe Pl S3 160 C4
Netherthorpe Prim Sch S3 160 C4
Netherthorpe Rd S3 160 C4
Nether Thorpe Rd S80 159 B5
Netherthorpe St S3 160 C4
Netherthorpe Way S25 146 E7
Netherthorpe Wlk S3 160 C4
Nether Wheel Row S13 142 F5
Netherwood Rd S73 56 D5
Nettle Croft DN11 121 C7
Nettleham Rd S8 140 F3
Nettlehome DN7 44 B8
Nettleton Ho 1 WF9 17 D6
Network Ctr S75 33 A5
Neville Ave S70 55 C7
Neville Cl
Barnsley S70 55 D7
Sheffield S3 129 B5
South Kirkby WF9 18 C3
Wombwell S73 56 B4
Neville Cres S70 55 D7
Neville Ct S73 56 B4
Neville Dr S3 129 B6
Neville La DN7 24 A8
Neville Pits La DN14 5 C8
Neville Rd S61 96 F1
Neville St S60 115 D7
Newark 8 S20 155 E8
Newark Cl S75 14 B2
Newark Rd S64 79 E5
Newark St
Rossington DN11 84 E1
Sheffield S9 130 A7
New Bailey S35 74 C7
Newbiggin Cl S62 97 E4
Newbiggin Dr S62 97 E4
Newbold Terr DN5 61 F5
Newbolt Rd DN4 83 B6
Newbould Cres S20 144 A3
Newbould La S10 160 A2
Newbridge Gr
Barnsley S71 34 B3
New Edlington DN12 82 C2
New Brighton HD8 29 B3
New Brinsworth Rd S60 131 D6
Newburn Dr S9 114 E2
Newbury Dr WF9 19 A5
Newbury Rd S10 128 B4
Newbury Way DN5 61 D6
Newby Cres DN4 83 A5
Newby Ct WF9 17 E7
Newcastle Cl S25 146 E7
Newcastle St S1 160 C3
New Chapel Ave S36 51 C1
New Cl S75 52 F8
New Close La DN6 20 E7
Newcomen Rd DN5 62 A5
New Cotts DN14 2 E6
Newcroft Cl S20 144 B3
New Cross Dr S13 143 A6
New Cross Way S13 143 A6
New Cross Wlk S13 143 A7
Newdale Ave S72 35 A5
New Droppingwell Rd S61 114 B6
Newent La S10 128 B4
Newfield Ave S71 34 D4
Newfield Cl DN3 43 B7
Newfield Cres
Sheffield S17 151 C7
Wath u D S63 78 D5
Newfield Croft S17 151 C8
Newfield Ct S10 139 D8
Newfield Farm Cl S14 141 E5
Newfield Green Rd S2 141 D6
Newfield La S17 151 C7
Newfield Pl S17 151 C7
Newfields Ave DN8 9 D2
Newfield Sch S8 141 C3
Newfields Cl DN8 9 C2
Newfields Dr DN8 9 C2
Newgate Cl S35 94 E7
New Gn DN7 24 E4
Newhall Ave S66 117 C2
New Hall Cres S36 72 F2
Newhall La S66 118 A2
New Hall La
Barnsley S71 56 B7
Stocksbridge S36 72 E1
Newhall Rd
Kirk Sandall DN3 43 A3
Sheffield S9 129 F7
New Haven Gdns S17 151 E4
Newhill WF9 18 B1
New Hill DN12 81 C2
Newhill Grange S63 78 D5
Newhill Rd
Barnsley S71 34 A4
Wath u D S63 78 D5
Newholme Dr DN8 9 C3
New Hos S35 73 E3
New Ings DN3 64 A6
New Ings La DN6 23 D2
Newington Ave S72 35 B8
Newington Cl DN4 84 F7
Newington Dr S26 144 E7
Newington Rd
Austerfield DN10 123 C8
Sheffield S11 140 C8
New Inn La DN7 24 E5
New La
Rawcliffe DN14 2 A8
Rossington DN11 85 A1
Sprotbrough DN5 61 B1
Upton WF9 19 A7
Newland Ave
Cudworth S72 35 A5
Maltby S66 118 F6
Newland Rd S71 33 F7
Newlands Ave
Adwick le S DN6 20 F2
Sheffield S12 142 A6
Newlands Cl DN4 84 F7
Newlands Dr
Bentley DN5 61 F6
Sheffield S12 142 A6
Newlands Gr S12 142 B6
Newlands Rd S12 142 A6
Newlands Way S73 57 A1
New Lane Cres WF9 19 A7
New Lodge Cres S71 33 E7
New Lodge Farm Ct S36 72 E8
Newlyn Dr S71 34 B3
Newlyn Pl S8 141 A3
Newlyn Rd S8 140 F3
Newman Ave S71 15 C1
Newman Cl S9 114 B4
Newman Ct
Rotherham S60 116 A2
Sheffield S9 114 B4
Newman Dr S9 114 A4
Newman Rd
Rotherham S60 116 B2
Sheffield S9 114 A4
Newman Sch S60 116 A1
Newmarche Dr DN6 22 C8
Newmarch St S9 114 E3
Newmarket Rd DN4 63 D2
New Mdws S62 97 D8
New Mill Bank S36 92 C5
New Mill Field Rd DN7 44 D7
New Orchard La S66 133 E7
New Orchard Rd S66 133 E7
New Oxford Rd S64 80 B4
New Park Est DN7 25 A5
New Rd
Apperknowle S18 154 A1
Bradfield, Low Bradfield S6 110 C3
Bradfield S36 92 B3
Braithwell S66 100 E3
Branton DN3 85 E8
Cawthorne S75 31 B5
Darton S75 14 B1
Dinnington S25 146 F8
Firbeck S81 136 A6
Hoyland S73 77 D7
North Anston S25 146 C6
Norton, Campsall DN6 21 B8
Norton DN6 4 F3
Penistone S36 30 E1
Pilley S75 75 E5
Sheffield, Hill Top S61 114 B5
Sheffield S6 110 E2
Stocksbridge S36 73 D1
Swinefleet DN14 11 E7
Tickhill DN11 121 A7
Wadworth DN11 102 C6
Wath u D S63 78 F6
Woolley WF4 14 B6
New Row La S36 50 E8
New Royd S36 50 E3
Newsam Rd S64 79 E1
New School Cl S20 155 C7
New School Ct S20 155 C7
New School Rd S20 155 C7
Newsham Rd S8 140 F4
New Smithy Ave S36 51 A4
New Smithy Dr S36 51 A4
Newsome Ave S73 56 C3
New St
Adwick le S DN6 21 D1
Barnsley S70 33 F1
Barnsley, Shaw Lands S70 54 E8
Barnsley, Stairfoot S71 55 E8
Bentley DN5 62 B8
Blaxton DN9 86 E5
Bolton u D S63 58 D1
Catliffe S60 131 D6
Chapeltown S35 94 D8
Darfield S73 57 A5
Darton S75 14 B1
Dinnington S25 134 F1
Dodworth S75 53 F6
Doncaster DN1 62 C1
Great Houghton S72 36 E1
Grimethorpe S72 36 A7
Hoyland S73 77 B7
Laughton en le M S25 134 E4
Mexborough S64 80 D5
Rawmarsh S62 97 F5
Rotherham, Greasbrough S61 97 B4
Rotherham, Thorpe Hesley S61 95 F4
Royston S71 15 C3
Sheffield, Holbrook S20 156 A8
Sheffield S1 161 A4
South Elmsall WF9 18 E3
South Hiendley S72 16 D6
Stocksbridge S36 73 E1
Wombwell S73 56 E3
Worsbrough S70 55 A4
Worsbrough, Worsbrough Dale S70 55 C4
New Station Rd S64 79 E3
Newstead Ave
Oughtibridge S35 111 D8
Sheffield S12 142 E3
Newstead Cl
Dronfield S18 152 C1
Sheffield S12 142 E3
Newstead Dr S12 142 E2
Newstead Gr S12 142 E3
Newstead Pl S12 142 E2
Newstead Rd
Barnsley S71 33 E8
Bentley DN5 61 F8
Sheffield S12 142 F3
Newstead Rise S12 142 F2
Newstead Way S12 142 E2
New Street Bus Link S20 156 A8
New Street La S2 161 C4
Newthorpe Rd DN6 4 C3
Newton Ave S36 72 F2
Newton Bsns Ctr
Bentley DN5 61 F3
Chapeltown S35 95 A7
Newton Chambers Rd S35 95 A7
Newton Cl S35 95 A7
Newton Croft S13 143 B6
Newton Ct 9 S70 33 D2
Newton Dr
Bentley DN5 61 F3
Rotherham S65 116 A6
Newton Gdns S35 95 A7
Newton La
Bentley DN5 61 F3
Sheffield S1 161 A2
Stocksbridge S36 72 F2
Newton Pl S61 95 F3
Newton Rd S35 94 E7
Newton St
Barnsley S70 33 D2
Rotherham S65 116 A6
Newton Vale S35 95 A7
Newtown Ave
Cudworth S72 35 B5
Royston S71 15 B4
Newtown Gn S72 35 B5
Newtree Dr DN11 102 B6
Newven Ho S65 115 F7
New Winterwell S63 78 D7
New Wortley Rd S60, S61 115 B7
Niagara Rd S6 112 C3
Nicholas La S63 58 C5
Nicholas St S70 33 D1
Nichol La HD9 28 A2
Nicholson Ave
Barnsley S75 32 E4
Wath u D S63 78 D5
Nicholson Ct 9 S8 141 B6
Nicholson Pl 7 S8 141 B6
Nicholson Rd
Doncaster DN4 62 A1
Sheffield S8 141 A6
Nichols Rd S6 128 A5
Nickerwood Dr S26 144 D6
Nickleby Ct S60 131 B6
Nidderdale Pl S66 117 C6
Nidderdale Rd S61 96 F3
Nidd Rd S9 130 A5
Nidd Rd E S9 130 B5
Nightingale Cl S60 115 E5
Nightingale Croft S61 96 A6
Nightingale Ct S60 115 E5
Nightingale Rd S35 112 D8
Nikolas Rd S21 156 B1
Nile St S10 128 C2
Ninelands Rd S32 149 A7
Ninescores La DN9 87 E7
Nine Trees Trad Est S66 133 D8
Ninian Gr DN4 84 E7
Noble St S74 76 F5
Nodder Rd S13 142 C7
Noehill Pl S2 130 B1

Noehill Rd S2 . . . . .130 B1
Nook End S6 . . . . 127 D6
Nookery Cl S66 . . . . .119 B6
Nooking Cl DN3 . . . . .64 C7
Nook La
  Penistone S36 . . . . .51 E1
  Sheffield S6 . . . . 127 C6
Nook Lane Jun Sch S6. . . 127 C6
Nooks Country Park The*
  DN10 . . . . 104 D4
Nooks The HD8 . . . . 28 E8
Nook The
  Penistone S36 . . . . .52 A6
  Sheffield S10 . . . . 160 A4
Nora St S63 . . . . .58 F6
Norborough Rd
  Doncaster DN2 . . . . .62 F5
  Sheffield S9 . . . . 114 E3
Norbreck Cres DN4 . . . . . .82 C4
Norbreck Rd
  Askern DN6 . . . . .22 C7
  Warmsworth DN4 . . . . . . .82 C5
Norbrook Way S60 . . . . . 116 D1
Norburn Dr S21 . . . . 156 D6
Norbury Cl S18 . . . . 152 D1
Norcroft S70 . . . . .54 F6
Norcroft La S75 . . . . .31 F3
Norcross Gdns S73 . . . . . .57 B5
Norfolk Ave DN11 . . . . . . 122 D4
Norfolk Cl S71. . . . . .34 B4
Norfolk Com Prim Sch
  Sheffield S2 . . . . 141 D8
  Sheffield S2 . . . . 141 E7
Norfolk Ct 8 S65. . . . . . .115 E7
Norfolk Dr
  Bircotes DN11 . . . . 122 C4
  North Anston S25 . . . . . . 146 E6
Norfolk Gr DN11 . . . . 122 C4
Norfolk Hill S35 . . . . .94 C1
Norfolk Hill Croft S35. . . .94 C1
Norfolk La S1 . . . . 161 A3
Norfolk Park Ave S2 . . . . 141 D8
Norfolk Park Dr S2 . . . . . 129 C1
Norfolk Park Rd S2 . . . . . 161 C1
Norfolk Park Sch S2 . . . . 129 C1
Norfolk Park Students
  Residence 129 D1
Norfolk Pl S66. . . . . 119 A5
Norfolk Rd
  Bircotes DN11 . . . . 122 C4
  Doncaster DN4 . . . . .83 B6
  Great Houghton S72 . . . . .36 F1
  Sheffield S2 . . . . 161 C2
Norfolk Row S1 . . . . 161 A3
Norfolk St
  Rotherham S65 . . . . .115 E7
  Sheffield S1 . . . . 161 B3
Norfolk Way S60. . . . . . . 116 A2
Norgreave Way S20. . . . . 155 E7
Norman Cl
  Barnsley S71 . . . . .34 C4
  Worsbrough S70 . . . . .55 A5
Norman Cres
  Bentley DN5 . . . . .61 E7
  Rossington DN11. . . . . . . .84 E1
Normancroft Cres S2 . . . 130 C1
Normancroft Ct S2 . . . . . 130 C1
Normancroft Dr S2 . . . . . 130 B1
Normancroft Way S2 . . . 130 C1
Normandale Ave S6. . . . . 127 E8
Normandale Rd
  Great Houghton S72 . . . . .36 E2
  2 Sheffield S6 . . . . 128 D7
Norman Dr DN7 . . . . .44 B6
Norman Rd
  Denby Dale HD8 . . . . .29 F5
  Hatfield DN7 . . . . .44 B6
Norman St
  Sheffield S3 . . . . 130 A7
  Thurnscoe S63. . . . . .58 E8
Normanton Gdns S4 . . . . 129 C7
Normanton Gr S13. . . . . . 142 F6
Normanton Hill S13. . . . . 142 D6
Normanton Spring Ct
  S13. . . . . 142 F6
Normanton Spring Rd
  S13. . . . . 142 F5
Normanville Ave S4 . . . . 129 C7
Norrel's Croft S60 . . . . . .115 F4
Norrels Dr S60 . . . . .115 F4
Norris Rd S6 . . . . 128 B8
Norroy St S4 . . . . 129 D6
Norstead Cres S66. . . . . .117 F5
Northampton Rd DN2 . . . .63 C5
North Anston Bsns Ctr
  S25. . . . . 146 C8
North Anston Trad Est The
  S25. . . . . 146 B8
North Ave
  Bawtry DN10 . . . . 123 A8
  South Elmsall WF9 . . . . . .18 F2
North Bridge Rd DN5 . . . .62 C4
North Church St S1. . . . . 161 A4
North Cl S71 . . . . .15 C3
Northcliffe Rd DN12. . . . . .81 B2
North Cliff Rd DN12. . . . . .81 B2
North Common Rd DN8 . . .9 B4
Northcote Ave S2. . . . . . . 141 B6
Northcote Ho S8 . . . . 140 F3
Northcote Terr 4 S75. . . .33 C2
North Cres
  Killamarsh S21 . . . . 156 E8
  Rotherham S65 . . . . .116 A7
  South Elmsall WF9 . . . . . .19 A3
Northcroft
  Shafton S72. . . . . .16 C2
  South Elmsall WF9 . . . . . .19 A3

Northcroft Ave WF9. . . . . .19 A4
Northern Doncaster Technology
  Coll DN6. . . . . .40 B5
North Dr S60 . . . . .115 D8
North Eastern Rd DN8 . . .26 A8
North End Dr DN5 . . . . . . .59 C2
Northern Ave S2. . . . . 141 E7
Northern Coll Wentworth
  Castle S75 . . . . .53 F3
Northern Comm S18. . . . . 152 B2
Northern General Hospl
  S5. . . . . 113 C2
Northern Racing Coll
  DN11. . . . . 104 D6
North Farm S81 . . . . 136 A3
North Farm Cl S26. . . . . . 157 E7
North Farm Ct S26. . . . . . 144 F7
North Field
  Doncaster DN4 . . . . .53 F8
  Silkstone S75. . . . . .52 F8
Northfield Ave
  Rawmarsh S62 . . . . .97 F7
  Sheffield S10 . . . . 128 B5
  South Kirkby WF9 . . . . . . .18 C3
Northfield Cl S10 . . . . . . 128 C5
Northfield Ct
  Rotherham S66 . . . . .117 B4
  Sheffield S10 . . . . 128 B5
  South Kirkby WF9 . . . . . . .18 C3
Northfield Dr
  South Kirkby WF9 . . . . . . .18 C3
  Woodsetts S81 . . . . 147 E4
Northfield Grange WF9 . . .18 C3
Northfield La
  Rotherham S66 . . . . .117 B5
  South Kirkby WF9 . . . . . . .18 C3
North Field La DN3 . . . . . .23 E1
Northfield Prim Sch WF9. .18 C3
Northfield Rd
  Bentley DN5. . . . . .62 A5
  Rotherham S60 . . . . .115 D8
  Sheffield S10 . . . . 128 B5
North Field Rd DN5, DN6 . .38 D7
Northfield St WF9 . . . . . . .18 B3
Northgate
  Barnsley S75 . . . . .33 C3
  South Hiendley S72 . . . . . .16 E6
  Thorne DN8 . . . . .9 C4
  Tickhill DN11 . . . . 121 A8
North Gate S64 . . . . .80 C5
Northgate Ho S21 . . . . . . 155 D3
North Hill Rd S5 . . . . .112 F4
North Ings Rd DN7. . . . . . .44 D8
North La
  Cawthorne S75 . . . . .31 A2
  Sykehouse DN14 . . . . .7 E7
  Sykehouse, Eskholme DN14 . 7 E8
Northlands
  Adwick le S DN6 . . . . .40 A6
  Harthill S26 . . . . 157 E7
  Royston S71. . . . . .15 C4
Northlands Rd S5. . . . . . . .112 F4
Northmoor Rd DN17 . . . . . .11 F2
Northorpe S70. . . . . .54 B6
North Park La DN6 . . . . . . .21 C3
North Pitt St S61 . . . . .114 F6
North Pl
  Barnsley S75 . . . . .33 B3
  Mexborough S64 . . . . 116 A7
North Quadrant S5 . . . . . 113 D4
North Rd
  Barnsley S75 . . . . .116 B8
  Royston S71. . . . . .15 D4
  Thorpe in B DN3 . . . . .42 C8
North Row HD8 . . . . .28 D8
North Royds Wood S71 . . .14 F1
Northside S5 . . . . 113 C5
Northside Rd S63. . . . . . . .78 F6
North Sq DN12 . . . . .82 C2
North St
  Darfield S73. . . . . .57 A6
  Doncaster DN4 . . . . .62 E1
  New Edlington DN12 . . . . . .82 C2
  Rawmarsh S62 . . . . .98 B7
  Rotherham S60 . . . . .115 C7
  South Kirkby WF9 . . . . . . .18 B3
  Swinton S64 . . . . .79 C3
North Swaithe Cl DN5. . . .41 A2
Northumberland Ave
  Carlton in L S81. . . . . 148 E8
  Doncaster DN2 . . . . .63 C4
  Hoyland S74. . . . . .76 E7
Northumberland La DN12 .80 F3
Northumberland Rd S10 . 160 A3
Northumberland Way S71 .56 A8
North View S72. . . . . .35 F6
North Way S81 . . . . 148 F7
North Wlk WF9 . . . . .17 D8
Northwood S5 . . . . 112 A4
Northwood Dr S6 . . . . 112 A4
Northwood Pl S6. . . . . 112 A3
Norton Ave S14. . . . . 141 E2
Norton Church Glebe
  S8. . . . . 141 C1
Norton Church Rd S8 . . . . 141 B1
Norton Common La DN6 . . .4 C4
Norton Common Rd DN6 . . .5 A2
Norton Free CE Prim Sch
  S8. . . . . 141 C1
Norton Green Cl S8. . . . . . 141 C1
Norton Hall S8 . . . . 141 B1
Norton Hall Ct S8 . . . . 141 B1
Norton Hammer La 1
  S8. . . . . 140 E4
Norton Inf Sch DN6 . . . . . .4 C3
Norton Jun Sch DN6 . . . . . .4 D3

Norton & Kirk Smeaton Rd
  WF8. . . . . .3 E4
Norton La S8. . . . . 141 C1
Norton Lawns S8. . . . . 141 C1
Norton Lees Cl S8 . . . . . . 141 A3
Norton Lees Cres S8. . . . . 141 A3
Norton Lees Glade S8 . . . 141 A4
Norton Lees La S8. . . . . . . 141 A4
Norton Lees Rd S8 . . . . . . 141 A4
Norton Lees Sq S8. . . . . . 141 A3
Norton Mews S8 . . . . 141 C1
Norton Mill La DN6. . . . . . .4 C4
Norton Park Ave S8. . . . . . 153 A8
Norton Park Cres S8. . . . . 153 A8
Norton Park Dr S8. . . . . . . 153 A8
Norton Park Rd S8 . . . . . . 153 A8
Norton Park View S8. . . . . 153 B8
Norton Rd
  Doncaster DN2 . . . . .63 B5
  Wath o S63. . . . . .78 D7
Norville Cres S73 . . . . .57 B6
Norwich Rd DN2. . . . . .63 A7
Norwich Row S2. . . . . 161 C3
Norwith Rd DN4 . . . . .84 D6
Norwood Ave
  Auckley DN9 . . . . .86 A7
  Sheffield S66. . . . . .118 F6
  Sheffield S5 . . . . 113 B2
Norwood Cl
  Maltby S66. . . . . .118 F6
  Sheffield S5 . . . . 113 B1
Norwood Cres
  Killamarsh S21 . . . . 156 F7
  Kiveton Park S26. . . . . . . 145 D2
Norwood Dr
  Barnsley S75 . . . . .32 E5
  Bentley DN5. . . . . .41 B3
  Brierley S72. . . . . .17 A3
  Sheffield S5 . . . . 113 B1
Norwood Grange Dr S5. . . 113 B2
Norwood Ind Est S21 . . . . 156 E8
Norwood La S36 . . . . .50 F6
Norwood Pl S21 . . . . 156 F7
Norwood Rd
  Conisbrough DN12. . . . . . .81 B2
  Hatfield DN7 . . . . .24 F1
  Hemsworth WF9 . . . . .17 D5
  Sheffield S5 . . . . 113 B1
Norwood St S65. . . . . .98 D1
Nostell Fold S75 . . . . .53 F6
Nostell Pl DN4. . . . . .84 D6
Notre Dame High RC High
  Sch S10. . . . . 128 A1
Nottingham Cl
  Barnsley S71 . . . . .56 A7
  Bentley DN5. . . . . .61 D6
  South Anston S25 . . . . . . 146 D3
Nottingham Cliff S12 . . . . 129 B6
Nottingham St
  Rotherham S65 . . . . .115 E7
  Sheffield S3 . . . . 129 B6
Notton La WF4 . . . . .15 B6
Novara Cl S70 . . . . .55 B8
Novello St S66 . . . . 119 C4
Nowill Cl 2 S8. . . . . 141 A4
Nowill Pl 3 S8 . . . . 141 A6
Nunnery Cres S60 . . . . . . 131 C6
Nunnery Dr S2 . . . . 129 F3
Nunnery Terr S2 . . . . 129 F3
Nunnington Way 3 DN3 . .62 E4
Nunthorpe Cl DN7 . . . . . . .44 B7
Nursery Cres S25 . . . . 146 D6
Nursery Rd
  Catliffe S60 . . . . 131 C6
  Sheffield S35. . . . . .113 B8
Nursery Gdns S70 . . . . . . .55 E7
Nursery Gr S35 . . . . .113 B8
Nursery La
  Sheffield S3 . . . . 161 B5
  Sprotbrough DN5. . . . . . . .82 A7
Nursery Rd
  Aston S26 . . . . 144 C8
  North Anston S25 . . . . . . 146 E7
Nursery St
  Barnsley S70 . . . . .54 E8
  Sheffield S3 . . . . 161 B5
Nutfields Gr DN7 . . . . .24 F4
Nuthatch Cres S81. . . . . . 148 D1
Nuttall Pl S2 . . . . 129 D3
Nutwell Cl DN4 . . . . .84 E6
Nutwell La
  Armthorpe DN3 . . . . .64 C3
  Branton DN3 . . . . .64 C3
Nutwood Trad Est S6. . . . .112 B5
Nu-Well Shopping Mall
  S73. . . . . .56 D2

O

Oak Apple Wlk S6 . . . . . . 127 C7
Oak Ave S63. . . . . .79 A5
Oakbank Cl S64 . . . . .98 D8
Oakbank Ct S17 . . . . 151 E5
Oakbrook Ct S11 . . . . 139 F8
Oakbrook Rd S11 . . . . 139 F8
Oakbrook Wlk 3 S65 . . . . 116 B8
Oakburn Ct S10 . . . . 160 A1
Oak Cl
  Hoyland S74. . . . . .76 D5
  Killamarsh S21 . . . . 156 C5
  Mexborough S64 . . . . .79 E5
  Rotherham S66 . . . . .117 B6
Oak Cres
  Havercroft WF4 . . . . .16 B8
  Thorne DN8 . . . . .9 B1
Oakcrest DN4. . . . . .85 B4

Oak Ct
  Doncaster DN4 . . . . .83 C5
  Mexborough S64 . . . . .79 E5
  Sprotbrough DN5. . . . . . . .61 D1
Oak St S60 . . . . .55 B4
Oakdale Cl
  Edenthorpe DN3 . . . . .42 F1
  Worsbrough S70 . . . . .55 B4
Oakdale Ct S7 . . . . 140 D6
Oakdale Pl S61 . . . . .114 F6
Oakdale Rd
  North Anston S25 . . . . . . 146 F5
  Rotherham S61 . . . . .114 F6
  Sheffield S7 . . . . 140 D6
Oakdale Terr S71 . . . . .34 A1
Oakdene S9. . . . . .129 A5
Oak Dale Rd DN4 . . . . .82 C4
Oakdell S18 . . . . 153 D3
Oakdene DN11. . . . . .103 F8
Oaken Wood Cl S61. . . . . . .96 A5
Oaken Wood Rd S61. . . . . . 95 F5
Oakes Gn S9 . . . . 129 F6
Oakes Cres DN8 . . . . 141 C2
Oakes Park View S14. . . . . 141 D1
Oakes St S9 . . . . .114 B4
Oakes The S8. . . . . 141 D1
Oakfern Gr S35. . . . . .94 D8
Oakfield Ct S25 . . . . .14 A1
Oakfield Jun Sch S73 . . . .56 D2
Oakfield Wlk S75 . . . . .33 B2
Oak Gr
  Armthorpe DN3 . . . . .64 A8
  Conisbrough DN12. . . . . . .81 B1
  Thurcroft S66. . . . . .133 F7
Oak Grove Gn S17 . . . . . . 151 E4
Oakham Dr S3. . . . . 128 F6
Oakham Pl S73 . . . . .33 C3
Oak Haven Ave S72 . . . . . .36 E1
Oakhill Rd
  Doncaster DN2 . . . . .63 B6
  Dronfield S18. . . . . .153 C3
  Sheffield S7 . . . . 140 D6
Oakholme Mews S10 . . . . 128 C1
Oakholme Rd S10 . . . . 128 C1
Oakland Ave DN7 . . . . .44 A7
Oakland Ct S81. . . . . 147 E5
Oakland Gr S66 . . . . 128 B8
Oakland Rd S6 . . . . 128 B8
Oaklands
  Rossington DN11. . . . . . . .85 C4
  Rotherham S66 . . . . .117 C3
Oaklands Ave S71 . . . . . . .34 D4
Oaklands Dr
  Doncaster DN4 . . . . .84 D8
  Styrrup DN11. . . . . 121 D2
Oaklands Gdns DN4. . . . . .84 D7
Oaklands Pl S63 . . . . .78 E5
Oakland Terr DN12. . . . . . .82 B2
Oaklea S70 . . . . .55 C4
Oak Lea S61. . . . . .97 B3
Oak Lea Ave S63. . . . . .78 C7
Oaklea Ct S15 . . . . .14 B2
Oak Leigh S75. . . . . .31 E4
Oakley Rd S13 . . . . 130 E2
Oak Lodge Rd S35 . . . . . . .94 C7
Oakmead Gr S35. . . . . 116 B8
Oakmoor Gr DN8 . . . . .9 D4
Oakmoor Rd DN8 . . . . .9 D5
Oak Park Rise S70 . . . . . . .55 A7
Oak Pk S10. . . . . 128 B2
Oak Rd
  Armthorpe DN3 . . . . .64 A8
  Maltby S66. . . . . .118 D5
  Mexborough S64 . . . . .79 E5
  Shafton S72. . . . . .16 D2
  Sheffield, Beighton S20. . . 143 F4
  Sheffield, Gleadless Townend
    S12 . . . . 142 A2
Oakroyd Cres S72. . . . . . . .36 A6
Oaks Ave S36 . . . . .73 A1
Oaks Bsns Pk S70 . . . . . . .34 D1
Oaks Cl S63 . . . . .79 A4
Oaks Cres S70 . . . . .55 C8
Oaks Farm Cl S75 . . . . . . .13 F1
Oaks Farm Dr S75 . . . . . . .13 F1
Oaks Fold S5 . . . . .113 E6
Oaks Fold Ave S5. . . . . . . .113 E6
Oaks Fold Rd S5. . . . . .113 E6
Oaks La
  Barnsley, Hoyle Mill S71 . . .34 D1
  Barnsley S70 . . . . .55 C8
  Bradfield S6. . . . . .110 C2
  Midhopestones S36. . . . . .72 C3
  Rotherham S61 . . . . .96 D2
  Sheffield S5 . . . . 113 E6
Oak St
  Barnsley S70 . . . . .33 D1
  Grimethorpe S72 . . . . .36 B5
  Sheffield, Heeley S8 . . . . . 141 A7
  Sheffield S20 . . . . 143 F4
  Sheffield S74 . . . . .18 F1
Oaks The 2 S10. . . . . 128 B2
Oaks Wood Dr S75. . . . . . .14 A8
Oak Terr
  Aston S26 . . . . 144 B8
  Doncaster DN1 . . . . .62 D3
Oak Tree Ave
  Cudworth S72 . . . . .35 D4
  Finningley DN9 . . . . .85 F4
Oak Tree Cl
  Kexbrough S75 . . . . .32 D8
  Rotherham S66 . . . . .117 C5
Oak Tree Gr WF9 . . . . .17 F6
Oak Tree Rd
  Bawtry DN10 . . . . 122 F7

Oak Tree Rd continued
  Branton DN3 . . . . .64 E1
Oaktree Rise S81 . . . . 148 E7
Oakwell (Barnsley FC)
  S71. . . . . .34 A1
Oakwell Bsns & Youth Ent
  Ctr S71 . . . . .34 B1
Oakwell Cl S66 . . . . .119 A6
Oakwell Dr DN6 . . . . .22 C8
Oakwell La S71. . . . . .34 A1
Oak Well La S70 . . . . .55 A8
Oakwell Terr S71. . . . . .34 A1
Oakwell View S70 . . . . .55 A8
Oakwood Ave
  Royston S71. . . . . .15 C4
  Sheffield S5 . . . . .112 F7
Oakwood Cl S10 . . . . .55 C4
Oakwood Cres
  Oughtibridge S35. . . . . . . 111 D5
  Rawmarsh S62 . . . . .97 E7
  Royston S71. . . . . .15 B4
Oakwood Dr
  Armthorpe DN3 . . . . .64 A5
  Branton DN3 . . . . .85 D8
  Hemsworth WF9 . . . . .17 E6
  Rotherham S60 . . . . 116 A4
Oakwood Flats S5 . . . . . . .113 B1
Oakwood Gr S60. . . . . 116 A3
Oakwood Hall Dr S60 . . . .115 F2
Oakwood Rd
  Doncaster DN4 . . . . .82 F7
  Royston S71. . . . . .15 B4
Oakwood Rd E S60 . . . . . . 116 A3
Oakwood Rd W S60. . . . . .115 F3
Oakwood Sq S60 . . . . .32 B8
Oakwood Tech Coll S60 . . .115 F3
Oakworth Cl
  Barnsley S75 . . . . .33 B3
  1 Sheffield S20 . . . . 155 E6
Oakworth Dr S20 . . . . 155 D6
Oakworth Gr S20 . . . . 155 D6
Oakworth View S20 . . . . . 155 D6
Oates Ave S62 . . . . .98 A5
Oates Cl S61 . . . . .115 A7
Oates St S61 . . . . .115 A7
Oats Orch S20 . . . . 155 D6
Oberon Cres S73 . . . . .56 F6
Oborne Cl S65. . . . . .117 E8
Occupation La
  Sheffield, Birley S12 . . . . . 142 F3
  Sheffield, Loxley S6. . . . . . 111 D1
Occupation Rd
  Harley S62. . . . . .76 D1
  Rawmarsh S62 . . . . .97 E4
Ochre Dike Cl S20 . . . . . . 143 E2
Ochre Dike La S20 . . . . . . 143 D2
Ochre Dike Wlk S61 . . . . . .97 A4
Octagon Ctr* S10 . . . . . . 160 B3
Octavia Cl S60 . . . . 115 C2
Oddfellows Rd S32 . . . . . 149 A7
Oddfellows Row S32. . . . . 149 A7
Oddfellows Terr S32 . . . . . 149 A7
Oddy La DN11 . . . . 102 E3
Odom Ct S2 . . . . 141 B6
Ogden Rd DN2. . . . . .63 E8
Oil Mill Fold S60 . . . . .115 C6
Oldale Cl S13 . . . . 143 C5
Oldale Ct S13 . . . . 143 C5
Oldale Gr S13 . . . . 143 C5
Old Anna Lane or Long La
  S36. . . . . .51 B4
Old Bar La HD9 . . . . .49 B8
Old Bawtry Rd DN9 . . . . . .86 D2
Old Carpenter's Yd DN7 . .24 D4
Old Clifton La S65 . . . . . . .97 D8
Oldcoates Cl S25 . . . . 134 F2
Oldcotes Rd S25 . . . . 135 B3
Old Cottage Cl S13 . . . . . 143 D7
Old Cross La S63 . . . . .78 F6
Old Cubley S36 . . . . .72 D8
Old Doncaster Rd S63 . . . .79 B6
Old Epworth Rd E DN7 . . .44 E7
Old Epworth Rd W DN7 . . .44 D7
Old Farm Ct S64 . . . . .79 E6
Old Farm Way WF9 . . . . . .19 B7
Oldfield Ave
  Conisbrough DN12. . . . . . .80 F2
  Sheffield S6 . . . . 127 D6
Oldfield Cl
  Barnby Dun DN3 . . . . .43 B6
  Hoyland S74. . . . . .76 E6
Oldfield Cres DN7 . . . . . . .24 D3
Oldfield Gr S6. . . . . 127 D6
Oldfield La DN7. . . . . .24 D3
Old Field La DN7 . . . . .24 D3
Oldfield Lane Flats DN7 . .24 D3
Oldfield Rd
  Rotherham S65 . . . . .116 D7
  Sheffield S6 . . . . 127 D5
  Thorne DN8 . . . . .26 C6
Oldfield Terr S6 . . . . 127 D5
Old Forge Bsns Pk 5
  S2. . . . . 141 A7
Old Fulwood Rd S10 . . . . . 139 D7
Old Garden Dr S65. . . . . . 116 A7
Oldgate La S65 . . . . .79 A4
Old Guildhall Yd 5 DN1. . .62 C3
Old Hall Cl
  Laughton en le M S25. . . . 134 D4
  Rotherham S66 . . . . .117 D5
  Sprotbrough DN5. . . . . . . .82 C8
  Todwick S26. . . . . 145 E6
Old Hall Cres DN5 . . . . . . .62 B8

Old Hall Dr S66 . . . . 117 D5
Old Hall Farm S61 . . . . 114 E7
Old Hall Fm DN6 . . . . 4 D6
Old Hall Mews S66 . . . . . . 117 D5
Old Hall Pl DN5 . . . . 62 B8
Old Hall Rd
 Adwick le S DN6 . . . . 20 F2
 Bentley DN5 . . . . 62 B8
 Sheffield S9 . . . . 130 A7
Old Hall Wlk S72 . . . . 36 E1
Oldhay Cl S17 . . . . 151 C6
Old Hay Gdns S17 . . . . . . 151 C6
Old Hay La S17 . . . . 151 C6
Old Hexthorpe DN4 . . . . . . 62 A2
Old Hill **7** DN12 . . . . 81 C2
Old House Cl S73 . . . . 77 C7
Old La
 Oughtibridge S20 . . . . . . 111 A6
 Sheffield S35 . . . . 156 A7
Old Manchester Rd S36 . . 70 E8
Old Manor Dr S36 . . . . 52 B1
Old Mill Cl WF7 . . . . 17 C7
Old Mill La
 Barnsley S70, S71 . . . . . . 33 F2
 Thurgoland S35 . . . . 73 E5
Old Mill Rd DN12 . . . . 81 D2
Old Moor La S63, S73 . . . 57 C1
Old Moor Wetland Centre
 Nature Reserve* S63 . . . 57 C1
Old Moor Wetland Ctr*
 S63 . . . . 57 C1
Old Oaks View S70 . . . . . . 55 C8
Old Orchard The WF9 . . . . 17 D7
Old Park Ave S8 . . . . 152 D7
Old Park Rd S8 . . . . 152 D7
Old Quarry Ave S26 . . . . 145 B3
Old Rd
 Barnsley S71 . . . . 34 A5
 Conisbrough DN12 . . . . . . 81 A1
Old Retford Ct S13 . . . . . 131 C1
Old Retford Rd S13 . . . . . 143 C8
Old Rock Inn The S35 . . . 74 D7
Old Row S74 . . . . 77 B5
Oldroyd Ave S72 . . . . 36 A6
Oldroyd Row S75 . . . . 53 F6
Old School Cl
 Armthorpe DN3 . . . . 64 B6
 Hoyland S74 . . . . 76 E7
 Rotherham S61 . . . . 97 C4
 Sykehouse DN14 . . . . 7 C7
Old School Ct S75 . . . . 32 E5
Old School Dr S5 . . . . 113 B5
Old School Ho DN2 . . . . . . 62 E5
Old School La
 Catliffe S60 . . . . 131 D6
 Wadworth DN11 . . . . 102 B7
Old School Way DN2 . . . . . 62 E5
Old Scotch Spring La
 S66 . . . . 119 E8
Old Sheffield Rd S60 . . . 115 D5
Old St
 Hampole DN6 . . . . 19 F7
 Hooton Pagnell DN5 . . . . 38 F7
 Sheffield S2 . . . . 161 C4
Old Station Dr S7 . . . . . . 140 D3
Old Thorne Rd DN7 . . . . . . 44 D8
Old Village St DN6 . . . . . . 21 A4
Old Warren Vale S62 . . . . 98 A8
Oldwell Cl S17 . . . . 151 D4
Old Wheel S6 . . . . 127 B7
Old Wortley Rd S61 . . . . 114 E8
Old Yew Gate S35 . . . . 93 E1
Olive Cl S26 . . . . 144 D7
Olive Cres S12 . . . . 142 A2
Olive Grove Rd S2 . . . . . . 141 B8
Olive Rd
 Sheffield S20 . . . . 155 D7
 Stocksbridge S36 . . . . . . 73 B1
Oliver Rd
 Doncaster DN4 . . . . 83 A7
 Sheffield S7 . . . . 140 C4
Olivers Dr S9 . . . . 130 D4
Olivers Mount S9 . . . . . . 130 E4
Olivers St S64 . . . . 79 F5
Olivers Way S60 . . . . 131 B6
Olive Terr S60 . . . . 127 D7
Olivet Rd S8 . . . . 140 F3
Ollerton Rd S71 . . . . 33 F8
Omega Bvd DN6 . . . . 25 F8
Onchan Rd S6 . . . . 127 E5
Onesacre Rd S6 . . . . 127 E5
Onesmoor Bottom S35 . . 110 F7
Onesmoor Rd S6 . . . . 110 D8
Onslow Rd S13 . . . . 140 B7
Onward Way WF9 . . . . 18 D1
Open Coll of the Arts S75 33 B5
Orange Croft DN11 . . . . . 121 B7
Orange St S11 . . . . 160 C3
Orchard Ave S25 . . . . 146 E7
Orchard Cft S75 . . . . 32 E8
Orchard Cl
 Barnsley S71 . . . . 34 C5
 Catliffe S60 . . . . 131 D6
 Darton S75 . . . . 14 B1
 Dunsville DN7 . . . . 43 F5
 5 Kirk Sandall DN3 . . . . 42 E4
 Laughton en le M S25 . . 134 E5
 Mexborough S64 . . . . 80 A5
 Norton DN6 . . . . 4 D1
 Sheffield S5 . . . . 113 B7
Orchard Cres S5 . . . . 113 B7
Orchard Croft
 Bawtry DN10 . . . . 123 A7

Orchard Croft *continued*
 Dodworth S75 . . . . 54 A6
 Wales S26 . . . . 145 B3
Orchard Ct S75 . . . . 33 E3
Orchard Dr
 Dunsville DN7 . . . . 43 F5
 Norton DN6 . . . . 4 D3
 South Hiendley S72 . . . . 16 D6
Orchard Flatts Cres S61 . . 97 A2
Orchard Gdns S25 . . . . . 146 D4
Orchard Gr
 Hatfield DN7 . . . . 25 A1
 Maltby S66 . . . . 118 D7
Orchard La
 Bentley DN5 . . . . 61 E5
 Sheffield, Beighton S20 . . 143 F2
 Sheffield S1 . . . . 161 A3
 Thorne DN8 . . . . 9 D3
Orchard Lea Dr S26 . . . . 144 D7
Orchard Lea Dr S26 . . . . 157 E6
Orchard Mews
 Barnsley S75 . . . . 33 E3
 Bentley DN5 . . . . 61 E5
 Bolton u D S63 . . . . 58 D2
Orchard Pl
 Cudworth S72 . . . . 35 C5
 Killamarsh S21 . . . . 156 D6
 Rotherham S60 . . . . 115 C6
 Wath u D S63 . . . . 78 D7
Orchard Rd Sq 128 C6
Orchard Sq
 Dronfield S18 . . . . 152 D2
 Sheffield S1 . . . . 161 A3
Orchard St
 Doncaster DN4 . . . . 62 B1
 Goldthorpe S63 . . . . 58 E4
 Oughtibridge S35 . . . . . 111 D7
 Sheffield S1 . . . . 161 A3
 Stocksbridge S36 . . . . . . 92 F8
 Thorne DN8 . . . . 26 B7
 Wombwell S73 . . . . 56 D3
Orchard Terr S75 . . . . 31 F4
Orchard The
 North Anston S25 . . . . . 146 E6
 Norton DN6 . . . . 21 C8
 Stanton S60 . . . . 119 E8
 Thurnscoe S63 . . . . 58 C7
Orchard Way
 Brinsworth S60 . . . . 131 C7
 Thurnscoe S60 . . . . 58 D8
 Tickhill DN11 . . . . 120 F7
Orchard Wells S66 . . . . . 117 C4
Orchard Wlk
 Auckley DN9 . . . . 86 A7
 Barnsley S71 . . . . 33 F3
Orchid Crest WF9 . . . . . . 19 A8
Orchid Way S25 . . . . 146 C4
Ordnance Terr S61 . . . . . 114 F6
Oregrave Cl S13 . . . . 131 C1
Oregreave Cres S13 . . . 131 C1
Oregreave Dr S13 . . . . . 131 C1
Oregreave Ho **2** S13 . . . 131 B1
Oregreave La S13 . . . . . . 62 C1
Oregreave Pl S13 . . . . . . 131 B1
Orgreave Rd
 Catliffe S60 . . . . 131 C5
 Orgreave S13 . . . . 131 B1
Orgreave Rise S13 . . . . . 143 D8
Oriel Mount S10 . . . . 139 C7
Oriel Rd S10 . . . . 139 D7
Oriel Way S71 . . . . 34 D3
Ormesby Cl S18 . . . . 152 C1
Ormesby Cres DN5 . . . . . 61 E5
Ormesby Way S66 . . . . . 117 E5
Ormes Mdw S20 . . . . 143 C2
Ormond Cl S8 . . . . 153 B6
Ormond Dr S8 . . . . 153 B6
Ormonde Way DN11 . . . . 103 E8
Ormond Rd S8 . . . . 153 B7
Ormond Way S8 . . . . 153 B7
Ormsby Cl
 Doncaster DN4 . . . . 83 A4
 Thurgoland S35 . . . . 73 F5
Orpen Dr S14 . . . . 141 E2
Orpen Ho S8 . . . . 141 D2
Orpen Way S14 . . . . 141 E2
Orphanage Rd S3 . . . . . . 129 B8
Orwell Cl S73 . . . . 56 F1
Osbert Dr S66 . . . . 133 E7
Osberton Pl S11 . . . . 140 D8
Osberton St
 Rawmarsh S62 . . . . 98 B6
 Wadworth DN11 . . . . . . 102 C7
Osberton Way S65 . . . . . . 98 C1
Osbert Rd S60 . . . . 116 B2
Osborne Ave
 Adwick le S DN6 . . . . 39 F5
 Aston S26 . . . . 144 E8
Osborne Cl
 Barnsley S71 . . . . 34 D4
 Sheffield S11 . . . . 140 C7
Osborne Croft S26 . . . . . 157 F6
Osborne Ct
 Barnsley S71 . . . . 34 D4
 Sheffield S11 . . . . 140 C7
Osborne Mews
 Barnsley S70 . . . . 55 A8
 Sheffield S11 . . . . 140 D7
Osborne Rd
 Doncaster DN2 . . . . 62 F4
 Kiveton Park S26 . . . . . 145 F2
 Sheffield S11 . . . . 140 D7
 Todwick S26 . . . . 145 A8
Osgathorpe Cres S4 . . . 129 C8
Osgathorpe Dr S4 . . . . . 129 D8
Osgathorpe Rd S4 . . . . . 129 C8
Osmaston Rd S8 . . . . 140 F2

Osmond Dr S70 . . . . 55 A5
Osmond Pl S70 . . . . 55 A5
Osmond Way S70 . . . . 55 A5
Osmund Ct S21 . . . . 155 C3
Osmund Rd S21 . . . . 155 C3
Osprey Ave S70 . . . . 75 F8
Osprey Cl DN6 . . . . 40 B6
Osprey Gdns S2 . . . . 129 E2
Osprey Rd S66 . . . . 144 E6
Oswestry Rd S5 . . . . 113 C4
Oswin Ave DN4 . . . . 83 A7
Otley Cl DN12 . . . . 81 D2
Otley Wlk S6 . . . . 128 D6
Otter St S9 . . . . 129 F6
Oughton Way S4 . . . . 129 D7
Oulton Ave S66 . . . . 117 E6
Oulton Dr S72 . . . . 35 C7
Our Lady of Mt Carmel Sch
 Prim Sch DN2 . . . . 63 A3
Our Lady of Perpetual Help
 RC Prim Sch DN5 . . . . . . 41 B1
Our Lady of Sorrows RC Prim
 Sch DN3 . . . . 64 A7
Our Lady's & St Joseph's RC
 Prim Sch S63 . . . . 78 F6
Ouseburn Croft S9 . . . . 130 A5
Ouseburn Rd S9 . . . . . . 130 A4
Ouseburn St S9 . . . . 130 A5
Ouse Rd S9 . . . . 130 A5
Ouse Terr **1** DN12 . . . . . . 81 C3
Ouslethwaite Ct S70 . . . 54 E6
Ouslethwaite Hall S70 . . 54 E6
Ouson Gdns S71 . . . . 15 C1
Outgang La
 Dinnington S25 . . . . . . 134 D2
 Maltby S66 . . . . 119 B3
Outram Rd S2 . . . . 129 E2
Outram Rd S65 . . . . 116 B7
Oval Rd S65 . . . . 116 B7
Oval The
 Adwick le S DN6 . . . . 39 F6
 Conisbrough DN12 . . . . . 81 C2
 Doncaster DN4 . . . . 63 C1
 Hatfield DN7 . . . . 24 F1
 North Anston S25 . . . . . 146 E6
 Notton WF4 . . . . 15 B6
 Sheffield S5 . . . . 113 D3
 Tickhill DN11 . . . . 121 B8
Overcroft Rise S17 . . . . 151 D4
Overdale Ave S70 . . . . . . 54 D5
Overdale Gdns S17 . . . . 151 D6
Overdale Rd S73 . . . . 56 F1
Overdale Rise S17 . . . . . 151 C6
Overend Cl S14 . . . . 141 D4
Overend Dr S14 . . . . 141 D4
Overend Rd S14 . . . . 141 D4
Overend Way S14 . . . . . 141 D4
Oversley Rd DN2 . . . . 62 F6
Oversley St S9 . . . . 114 E3
Overton Rd S6 . . . . 112 B2
Owday La
 Carlton in L S81 . . . . . . 148 C3
 Worksop S81 . . . . 148 C3
Owen Cl
 Rotherham S65 . . . . 115 E8
 Sheffield S6 . . . . 112 D6
Owen Pl S6 . . . . 112 D6
Owen Wlk S6 . . . . 112 D7
Owler Bar Rd S11 . . . . . . 150 B4
Owler Car La S18 . . . . . . 153 F5
Owler Gate S35 . . . . 111 B8
Owler La S4 . . . . 113 D1
Owlerton Gn S6 . . . . 128 D8
Owlings Pl S6 . . . . 112 A6
Owlings Rd S6 . . . . 112 A1
Owlthorpe Ave S20 . . . . 155 B8
Owlthorpe Cl S20 . . . . . . 155 B8
Owlthorpe Gr S20 . . . . . 155 B8
Owlthorpe Greenway
 Sheffield S20 . . . . 143 E1
 Sheffield, Waterthorpe
 S20 . . . . 143 E1
Owlthorpe La S20 . . . . . 155 B8
Owlthorpe Rise S20 . . . 155 B8
Owram St S73 . . . . 57 A5
Owston La DN5, DN6 . . . . 21 E2
Owston Park Prim Sch
 DN6 . . . . 21 B2
Owston Rd DN6 . . . . 21 C1
Ox Carr DN3 . . . . 64 A6
Ox Close Ave
 Rotherham S61 . . . . 96 F1
 Sheffield S17 . . . . 152 A5
Oxclose Dr **2** S18 . . . . 152 C1
Oxclose La S18 . . . . 152 C1
Oxclose Park Gdns S20 . . 155 F6
Oxclose Park Rd N S20 . . 155 F7
Oxclose Park Rd S20 . . . 155 F6
Oxclose Park View S20 . . 155 F7
Oxford **1** S6 . . . . 160 B4
Oxford Cl S61 . . . . 97 C3
Oxford Dr DN11 . . . . 121 F5
Oxford St
 Barnsley S70 . . . . 55 A1
 Barnsley, Stairfoot S71 . . 55 E8
 Mexborough S64 . . . . 79 E5
 Rossington DN11 . . . . . . 84 E2

Oxford St *continued*
 Rotherham S65 . . . . 116 A7
 Sheffield, Port Mahon S6 . . 160 B4
 South Elmsall WF9 . . . . . 18 F2
Ox Hill S20 . . . . 156 A5
Ox Lee La HD9 . . . . 48 E8
Oxley Cl S36 . . . . 73 A1
Oxley Ct S60 . . . . 115 F4
Oxley Gr S60 . . . . 115 F4
Oxspring Bank S5 . . . . . 112 D2
Oxspring La S36 . . . . 52 B2
Oxspring Prim Sch S36 . . 52 B1
Oxspring Rd S36 . . . . 72 E8
Oxted Rd S9 . . . . 114 A2
Oxton Dr DN4 . . . . 82 D6
Oxton Rd S71 . . . . 34 A8

P

Paces High Green Sch
 S35 . . . . 94 E8
Pack Horse Cl HD8 . . . . . 12 A4
Pack Horse Gn S75 . . . . . 52 F8
Pack Horse La S35 . . . . . 94 E8
Packington Rd DN4 . . . . . 85 B7
Packman La S26, S80 . . . 158 C6
Packman Rd
 Wath u D, Brampton S63 . . 78 B6
 Wath u D S63 . . . . 78 C3
Packmans Cl S13 . . . . . . 94 C1
Packmans Way S63 . . . . . 94 C1
Packwood Cl S66 . . . . . . 119 B6
Paddington Cl S25 . . . . . 134 C2
Paddock Cl
 Bentley DN5 . . . . 61 E5
 Darton S75 . . . . 14 C1
Paddock Cres S2 . . . . . . 141 E5
Paddock Croft S64 . . . . . 79 B3
Paddock Dr S66 . . . . 117 C7
Paddock Gr S72 . . . . 35 C7
Paddock Rd S63 . . . . 78 B5
Paddocks The
 Aston S26 . . . . 144 E7
 Auckley DN9 . . . . 86 A6
 Bentley DN5 . . . . 61 D5
 Cadeby DN5 . . . . 81 D6
 Rotherham S65 . . . . 117 B8
 Rotherham, Thrybergh S65 . . 99 A2
Paddock The
 Adwick le S DN6 . . . . 40 C6
 Barnby Dun DN3 . . . . . . 42 E8
 Darfield S73 . . . . 57 A6
 Hoyland S73 . . . . 77 C8
 Rotherham S64 . . . . 96 B4
 Tickhill DN11 . . . . 121 B8
 Woolley WF4 . . . . 14 A7
Paddock View S26 . . . . . 145 E5
Paddock Way S18 . . . . . 153 B3
Padley Cl S75 . . . . 53 E7
Padley Hill S32 . . . . 149 E1
Padley Rd S32 . . . . 149 D1
Padley Way S13 . . . . 114 D4
Padley Wlk S13 . . . . 114 D4
Padua Rise S73 . . . . 56 F5
Pagdin Dr DN11 . . . . 121 E2
Page Hall Rd S4 . . . . 114 A1
Pagenall Dr S26 . . . . 144 D8
Paget St S9 . . . . 129 F7
Pagnell Ave S63 . . . . 58 B7
Palermo Fold S73 . . . . . . 56 F6
Palgrave Cres S5 . . . . . . 112 E4
Palgrave Rd S5 . . . . 112 E4
Palington Gr DN4 . . . . . . 63 E1
Pall Mall S70 . . . . 33 F1
Palm Ave DN4 . . . . 62 C7
Palmer's Ave WF9 . . . . . . 19 B2
Palmer Cl S36 . . . . 51 C1
Palmer Cres **3** S18 . . . 153 B1
Palmer La DN6 . . . . 23 F6
Palmer Rd S9 . . . . 130 C6
Palmer St
 Doncaster DN4 . . . . 62 C1
 Sheffield S9 . . . . 129 F5
Palmerston Ave S66 . . . 118 E6
Palmerston Rd S10 . . . . 160 A3
Palmers Way S64 . . . . . . 133 D6
Palm Gr DN12 . . . . 81 A1
Palm Grove Ct DN6 . . . . . . 9 C1
Palm Hollow Cl S66 . . . 116 F4
Palm La S6 . . . . 128 C6
Palm St
 Barnsley S75 . . . . 33 D3
 Sheffield S6 . . . . 128 C6
Pamela Dr DN4 . . . . 82 C6
Pangbourne Rd S63 . . . . . 37 C1
Pantry Gn S70 . . . . 55 C5
Pantry Hill S70 . . . . 55 C5
Pantry Well S70 . . . . 55 C4
Paper Mill La DN11 . . . . 121 C8
Paper Mill Rd
 Rawcliffe Bridge DN14 . . 2 D7
 Sheffield S5 . . . . 113 C4
Parade The
 Armthorpe DN3 . . . . 64 B6
 3 Askern DN6 . . . . 22 B8
 Hoyland S74 . . . . 76 D5
 Rawmarsh S62 . . . . 79 A4
Paradise La S1 . . . . 161 A4
Paradise Sq S1 . . . . 161 A4
Paradise St S1 . . . . 161 A4
Parish Way S11 . . . . 34 D1
Park Ave
 Adwick le S DN6 . . . . 40 C8
 Armthorpe DN3 . . . . 64 A7
 Barnsley S70 . . . . 33 F7
 Barnsley, Shaw Lands S70 . . 54 E8

Park Ave *continued*
 Brierley S72 . . . . 17 B3
 Chapeltown S35 . . . . 95 A4
 Conisbrough DN12 . . . . . 81 C1
 Cudworth S72 . . . . 35 B8
 Dronfield S18 . . . . 153 B2
 Grimethorpe S72 . . . . . . 36 A8
 Mexborough S64 . . . . 80 A5
 North Anston S25 . . . . . 146 E7
 Penistone S36 . . . . 51 C3
 Rotherham S60 . . . . 116 C2
 Royston S71 . . . . 15 D3
 Sheffield S10 . . . . 140 B8
 South Kirkby WF9 . . . . . 18 B2
 Sprotbrough DN5 . . . . . . 61 C1
 Treeton S60 . . . . 131 F4
 West Cowick DN14 . . . . . 1 A7
 Wortley S35 . . . . 74 D3
Park Ave Ct S70 . . . . 54 E8
Park Cl
 Maplewell DN3 . . . . 64 B6
 Mapplewell S75 . . . . 33 C8
 Rotherham S65 . . . . 98 F2
 Sprotbrough DN5 . . . . . . 61 C1
 Swinton S64 . . . . 79 C3
Park Cres
 Bolton u D S63 . . . . 58 D2
 Royston S71 . . . . 15 D3
Park Crest WF9 . . . . 17 D7
Park Ct
 Sheffield S35 . . . . 112 C8
 Thurnscoe S63 . . . . 58 D8
Park Dale S62 . . . . 97 F5
Park Dr
 Aston S26 . . . . 144 B7
 Norton DN6 . . . . 4 D1
 Sprotbrough DN5 . . . . . . 61 C1
 Stocksbridge S36 . . . . . . 73 B1
Parkdrive S73 . . . . 54 B4
Park Drive Way S36 . . . . 73 B2
Park End Rd S63 . . . . 58 D4
Parker's La S10 . . . . 128 C3
Parker's Rd S10 . . . . 128 C3
Parkers La S17 . . . . 151 D8
Parker St S70 . . . . 33 D1
Parker's Terr S70 . . . . 75 E7
Park Est WF9 . . . . 18 C2
Park Farm S18 . . . . 152 C2
Park Farm Gdns WF9 . . . 18 C3
Park Farm Mews S21 . . . 156 D1
Parkfield Cl S62 . . . . 97 F3
Parkfield Pl S2 . . . . 141 A8
Parkfield Rd S65 . . . . . . 115 F6
Parkgate
 Dronfield S18 . . . . 153 C2
 South Kirkby WF9 . . . . . 18 B1
Parkgate Ave S20 . . . . . 155 A8
Parkgate Cl S20 . . . . 155 A8
Parkgate Croft S20 . . . . 155 A8
Parkgate Ct S62 . . . . 97 E2
Parkgate Dr S20 . . . . 143 A1
Park Gr
 Barnsley S70 . . . . 54 E8
 Rawmarsh S62 . . . . 97 F7
 Rotherham S66 . . . . 117 D5
 Stocksbridge S36 . . . . . . 73 B2
Park Grange Croft S2 . . . 129 C1
Park Grange Ct S2 . . . . . 141 C8
Park Grange Dr S2 . . . . . 141 C8
Park Grange Mount S2 . . 141 C8
Park Grange Rd S2 . . . . . 141 C8
Park Grange Rise S2 . . . 141 C8
Park Grange View S2 . . . 141 B8
Parkhall La S21 . . . . 156 D2
Parkhead HD8 . . . . 28 F5
Parkhead Cl S71 . . . . 15 A4
Parkhead Cres S11 . . . . 139 C4
Parkhead Ct S11 . . . . . . 139 F4
Park Head La HD8 . . . . . . 28 F5
Parkhead Rd S11 . . . . . . 139 F3
Park Hill
 Aston S26 . . . . 144 B7
 Darfield S73 . . . . 57 B6
 Eckington S21 . . . . 155 C3
 Kexbrough S75 . . . . 13 B2
Parkhill Cres DN3 . . . . . . 43 A7
Park Hill Dr S61 . . . . 136 A5
Park Hill Gdns S26 . . . . 144 B7
Park Hill Gr S75 . . . . 152 F8
Parkhill Rd DN3 . . . . 43 A7
Park Hill Rd S73 . . . . 56 E3
Park Hollow S73 . . . . 56 F2
Park House La S9 . . . . . . 130 F8
Parkin House La S36 . . . 50 D2
Parkinson St DN1 . . . . . . 62 D5
Park La
 Blaxton DN9 . . . . 86 F5
 Conisbrough DN12 . . . . 100 A6
 Denby Dale HD8 . . . . 29 B5
 Dinnington S25 . . . . . . 134 C2
 Donningtonn S25 . . . . . . 12 D8
 Great Houghton S72 . . . 36 D2
 Oxspring S36 . . . . 73 A7
 Penistone S36 . . . . 51 D3
 Rotherham S65 . . . . 98 E8
 Sheffield, Broomfield S10 . . 160 A2
 Stocksbridge S36 . . . . . . 73 E2
 West Bretton WF4 . . . . . 12 F7
Parklands DN3 . . . . 42 E1
Parklands S11 . . . . 85 E1
Parklands Ave S25 . . . . 146 E8
Parklands Cl DN11 . . . . . 85 B1

Parklands Ct S9 130 C7
Parklands View S26 144 E5
Parkland View S71 34 F5
Parkland Wlk DN9 86 F6
Park Lane Cl DN7 43 F4
Park Lane Ct S65 98 F3
Park Lane Rd DN7 43 E4
Park Mount S65 115 E6
Park Nook S65 98 E2
Park Pl S65 116 B7
Park Prim Sch DN2 63 A6
Park Rd
Askern DN6 21 F7
Barnsley, Shaw Lands S70 54 E7
Bawtry DN10 122 F7
Bentley DN5 41 A1
Brierley S72 17 B3
Conisbrough DN12 81 B1
Doncaster DN1 62 D3
Grimethorpe S72 36 A8
Mexborough S64 80 A5
Rotherham S65 116 B7
Sheffield S6 127 F6
Swinton S64 79 C2
Thorne DN8 9 D3
Thurnscoe S63 58 C8
Wath u D S63 78 E6
Worsbrough S70 55 A4
Parkside
Barnsley S71 15 D1
Renishaw S21 156 B1
Parkside La S6 127 D5
Parkside Mews S70 55 B5
Parkside Rd
Hoyland S74 76 B4
Sheffield S6 112 C1
Parkside Sh Ctr S21 156 D7
Parkson Rd S60 116 B2
Park Spring Dr S2 141 C8
Park Spring Pl S2 141 C8
Park Spring Rd
Great Houghton S72 57 C7
Grimethorpe S72 36 B2
Park Spring Way S2 141 C8
Park Sq
Chapeltown S35 95 A7
Sheffield S2 161 C4
Parks Rd DN7 43 F8
Park St
Aston S26 144 C7
Barnsley S70 54 E8
Rawmarsh S62 97 F6
Rotherham S61 115 B7
Wombwell S73 56 E2
Parkstone Cres S66 118 B4
Parkstone Delph S12 142 A2
Parkstone Gr DN7 44 B8
Parkstone Way DN2 63 C7
Park Terr
Chapeltown S35 95 B4
Doncaster DN1 62 D3
Rotherham S65 98 E2
South Elmsall WF9 19 A2
Park The
Adwick le S DN6 40 A3
Cawthorne S75 31 E4
Park Vale Dr S65 98 F2
Parkview S70 55 B5
Park View
Adwick le S DN6 40 C5
Barnsley S70 54 C7
Brierley S72 17 B3
Brodsworth DN5 39 C3
Dodworth S75 53 F7
Kiveton Park S26 145 E3
Maltby S66 119 B5
Mexborough S64 79 E5
Rotherham, Greasbrough S61 97 B3
Rotherham, Thorpe Hesley S61 95 E4
Royston S71 15 D3
Shafton S72 16 D2
South Kirkby WF9 18 D3
Thorne DN8 26 B6
Park View Ave S20 155 E7
Park View Ct S8 141 A2
Parkview Lodge S6 112 B1
Park View Rd
Chapeltown S35 95 A4
Darton S75 14 D1
Rotherham S61 114 C6
Sheffield S6 112 C1
Parkway DN3 64 B5
Park Way DN6 40 B6
Parkway Ave S9 129 F4
Parkway Cl S9 129 F4
Parkway Ct S8 152 F7
Parkway Dr S9 130 B3
Parkway N DN2 63 A6
Parkways DN7 44 C7
Parkway S DN2 63 A6
Park Wlk S2 129 D4
Parkwood High Sch S5, S6 112 E2
Parkwood Ind Est S3 128 F6
Parkwood Rd S3 128 E7
Parkwood Rd N S5 112 F2
Parkwood Rise DN3 43 A5
Parliament St S11 128 E1
Parma Rise S73 56 E5
Parsley Hay Cl S13 130 F1
Parsley Hay Dr S13 130 F1
Parsley Hay Gdns S13 130 F1
Parsley Hay Rd S13 130 F1
Parsonage Cl S20 155 D6
Parsonage Cres S6 128 C6
Parsonage Ct S6 128 C6
Parsonage St S6 128 C6
Parson Cross CE Prim Sch S6 112 D4
Parson Cross Rd S6 112 D4
Parson La WF4 14 A8
Partridge Cl S21 155 B3
Partridge Dale S75 53 B3
Partridge Flatt Rd DN4 84 F6
Partridge Pl S26 144 E6
Partridge Rd DN3 42 F7
Partridge Rise DN4 84 F6
Partridge View S2 129 E2
Pashley Croft S73 56 B2
Pashley Rd DN8 26 C6
Passfield Rd DN11 104 A8
Passhouses Rd S4 129 B8
Pasture Acre DN3 64 A5
Pasture Cl DN3 64 A5
Pasture Croft S66 133 F7
Pasture Gdns DN6 4 E3
Pasture Gr S21 155 C3
Pasture La
Cadeby DN5 81 B6
Darfield S73 57 D4
Pastures Ct
Mexborough S64 80 D5
Rossington DN11 104 B8
Pastures Rd S64 80 F5
Pastures The
Bawtry DN10 123 A6
Mexborough S64 80 D5
Todwick S26 145 E5
Paternoster Row S1 161 B2
Paterson Cl S36 73 A2
Paterson Croft S36 73 A2
Paterson Ct S36 73 A2
Paterson Gdns S36 73 A2
Paterson Rd S25 135 A1
Patmore Rd S5 113 D4
Patrick Stirling Ct DN4 62 A1
Patterdale Cl
Adwick le S DN6 21 C1
2 Dronfield S18 152 E1
Patterdale Way S25 146 F6
Pavement The S2 161 C3
Pavilion Cl S72 17 A3
Pavilion La S60 115 B2
Pavilion Way S5 113 D4
Pavillion Cl DN12 82 C3
Paw Hill La S36 71 C7
Paxton Ave DN6 21 D1
Paxton Cres DN3 63 F7
Paxton Ct S14 141 F4
Paxton La S10 160 A2
Payler Cl S2 142 A8
Payne Cres S62 97 E7
Peacehaven DN3 42 F7
Peacock Cl
Killamarsh S21 156 D6
Rotherham S61 95 F6
Peacock Trad Est S6 128 D8
Pea Fields La S35 75 A2
Peak Chase S72 16 F2
Peak Cl S66 117 B7
Peakdale Cres S12 142 E5
Peake's Croft DN10 123 A7
Peake Ave DN12 81 A2
Peak Hill Cl S81 148 D1
Peak La S66 118 E3
Peak Rd S71 34 A7
Peaks Mount S20 143 E3
Peak Sq S20 143 E2
Peakstone Cl DN4 83 A7
Peakstone Mews S62 97 F5
Pearce Rd S9 130 C3
Pearce Wlk S9 130 C4
Pearl St S11 140 E8
Pearmain Dr S66 118 D6
Pea Royd La S36 73 C2
Pearson's Cl S65 116 C4
Pearson's Field S73 56 D3
Pearson Bldg (Sheffield Hallam Univ) S10 160 A1
Pearson Cres S73 56 B4
Pearson Pl S8 140 F4
Pearson St S36 73 B2
Pear St S11 128 E1
Peartree Ave S63 58 C8
Pear Tree Ave S66 117 D5
Pear Tree Cl
Brinsworth S60 131 D8
Great Houghton S72 36 D2
Killamarsh S21 156 C5
Kirk Bramwith DN7 23 F5
Woodsetts S81 147 E4
Pear Tree Ct S63 58 C8
Pear Tree La
Hemsworth WF9 17 D7
Kirk Bramwith DN7 24 A7
Peartree Mews DN11 83 C2
Peartree Orch S71 15 D5
Pear Tree Rd S5 113 D6
Pearwood Cres DN4 82 F5
Peasehill Cl S70 54 E8
Peashill St S62 97 F5
Peastack La DN11 102 F1
Peat Carr Bank DN9 87 E7
Peatfield Rd S21 156 F7
Peat Pits La S6 110 C8
Peck Hall La S6 110 C4
Peckham Rd S35 94 F6
Peck Mill View S26 146 B1
Pedley Ave 4 S20 155 E8
Pedley Cl 5 S20 143 E1
Pedley Dr S20 155 E8
Pedley Gr 6 S20 143 E1
Peel Castle Rd DN8 26 C6
Peel Cl S66 118 E6
Peel Gdns S18 152 F1
Peel Hill Rd DN8 26 C6
Peel Par S70 33 E1
Peel Pl S71 34 A3
Peel St Arc S70 33 E1
Peel Sq S70 33 E1
Peel St
Barnsley S70 33 E1
Barnsley, Worsbrough Common S70 54 F7
Sheffield S10 128 C2
Peel Terr S10 160 B3
Pell's Cl DN1 62 C3
Pembrey Ct S20 144 A2
Pembridge Ct S71 15 C4
Pembroke Ave DN4 83 B6
Pembroke Cres S35 94 E6
Pembroke Dr S81 148 E6
Pembroke Rd
4 Dronfield S18 153 A1
Shireoaks S81 159 F7
Pembroke Rise
Bentley DN5 61 D6
South Anston S25 146 D4
Pembroke St
Rotherham S61 114 F6
Sheffield S11 128 E1
Penarth Ave WF9 19 A7
Penarth Terr WF9 18 F7
Pendeen Rd S11 139 F8
Pendennis Ave WF9 18 F4
Pendlebury Gr S74 76 C5
Pendle Croft S20 144 B1
Pendon Ho S36 51 D3
Pendragon Pl WF9 19 A2
Pengeston Rd S36 51 C2
Penistone Ct S36 51 E3
Penistone Gram Sch S36 51 C5
Penistone La S36 71 D5
Penistone Rd
Bradfield S6 91 E1
Chapeltown S35 94 D4
Denby Dale HD7, HD8, S36 29 C3
Holmfirth, Hade Edge HD9 48 D7
Sheffield S3, S6 128 E7
Shepley HD8, HD9 28 C6
Penistone Rd N S6 112 C2
Penistone St DN1 62 D4
Penistone Sta S36 51 E3
Penley St S11 140 F8
Penlington Cl WF9 17 D5
Pennine Cl S75 14 A2
Pennine Ctr The S1 161 A4
Pennine Edge S36 49 D6
Pennine Gdns S66 118 D6
Pennine Rd DN8 26 A6
Pennine View
Darton S75 14 A2
Stocksbridge S36 92 B7
Upton WF9 19 A8
Pennine Way
Barnsley S75 33 B2
Hemsworth WF9 17 F7
Pen Nook Cl S36 92 E7
Pen Nook Ct S36 92 E7
Pen Nook Dr S36 92 E7
Pen Nook Gdns S36 92 E7
Penns Rd S2 141 C6
Penny Engine La S21 155 E4
Pennyfields S63 58 B2
Penny Hill S81 135 E4
Penny Hill La S26, S66 133 B4
Pennyholme Cl S26 145 F2
Penny La S17 151 C5
Penny Piece La S25 146 D6
Penny Piece Pl S25 146 D6
Penrhyn Rd S11 140 C7
Penrhyn Wlk S71 56 A8
Penrith Cl S5 112 E2
Penrith Cres S5 112 E2
Penrith Gr S71 56 A8
Penrith Rd
Doncaster DN2 63 C4
Sheffield S5 112 E2
Penrose Pl S13 143 A6
Penthorpe Cl S12 142 B6
Pentland Dr S81 148 E7
Pentland Gdns S20 143 D2
Pentland Rd S18 152 D1
Penton St S1 161 A3
Penwood Wlk S66 117 B8
Penyghent Cl S35 94 F6
Pepper Cl S61 96 D2
Pepper St S74 76 E8
Pepper Tree Ct S74 76 E8
Percy St
Rotherham S65 115 E6
Sheffield S3 128 F5
Peregrine Dr S70 75 F8
Peregrine Way S26 157 E5
Perigree Rd S8 140 E3
Periwood Ave S8 140 E3
Periwood Cl S8 140 E3
Periwood Dr S8 140 E3
Periwood Gr S8 140 E3
Periwood La S8 140 E3
Perkyn Rd S5 113 D7
Perkyn Terr S5 113 D7
Perran Gr DN5 61 F5
Perseverance St S70 33 D1
Persimmon Cl DN11 103 F7
Perth Cl S64 80 C6
Petal Cl S66 119 B6
Peter's Rd DN12 82 B1
Peterborough Cl S10 139 A8
Peterborough Dr S10 127 A1
Peterborough Rd S10 127 A1
Peterfoot Way S71 15 C1
Petersgate DN5 61 F8
Peter St
Rotherham S61 114 E7
Thurcroft S66 133 E7
Petre Dr S4 129 E8
Petre St S4 129 D8
Petunia Rd DN3 42 F3
Petworth Croft 3 S71 15 B4
Petworth Dr S11 139 F2
Peveril Cl S26 145 E3
Peveril Cres S71 34 A7
Peveril Rd
Doncaster DN4 82 E6
Eckington S21 155 E3
Sheffield S11 140 B7
Pexton Rd S4 129 C8
Pheasant Bank DN11 85 A1
Philadelphia Dr 6 S6 128 E5
Philadelphia Gdns S6 128 E5
Philadelphia Gr 5 S6 128 E5
Philip Rd S70 55 D7
Phillimore Com Prim Sch S9 130 B6
Phillimore Rd S9 130 B6
Phillips Rd S6 111 D1
Phoenix Ct
Eckington S12 142 E1
1 Sheffield S1 161 A3
Phoenix Gr S60 115 B1
Phoenix La S63 58 E7
Phoenix Rd
Eckington S12 142 E1
Rotherham S9 114 E4
Piccadilly DN5 62 A8
Piccadilly Rd S64 79 C1
Pickard Cres S13 142 D8
Pickard Dr S13 142 D8
Pickburn La DN5 39 D3
Pickering Cres S26 144 C7
Pickering Gr DN8 26 B6
Pickering Rd
Bentley DN5 41 B3
Sheffield S3 128 F7
Pickering St S9 130 B8
Pickhill's Ave S63 58 F5
Pickle Wood Ct DN9 86 E4
Pickmere Rd S10 128 B4
Pickup Cres S73 56 D2
Pickwick Dr S60 131 B6
Piece End S35 94 D8
Piece End Cl S35 94 D8
Pieces N The S60 132 B8
Pieces S The S60 132 B8
Pighills La S18 153 B4
Pike Lowe Gr S75 33 D8
Pike Rd S60 115 C1
Pilgrim Ct S81 159 F7
Pilgrim Rise DN10 105 C1
Pilgrim St S3 129 B7
Pilley Gn S75 75 D5
Pilley La S70, S75 75 D6
Pincheon Green La DN14 8 B7
Pinchfield Ct S66 117 B3
Pinchfield Holt S66 117 B3
Pinchfield La S66 117 B3
Pinchmill Hollow S66 117 C2
Pinch Mill La S60 116 F1
Pinchwell View S66 117 B3
Pindar Oaks St S70 55 A8
Pindar St S70 55 B8
Pinder Ct DN7 25 B7
Pine Ave S25 146 D3
Pine Cl
Barnsley S70 55 C6
Hoyland S74 76 E5
Killamarsh S21 156 C5
Rotherham S66 117 C6
Pine Croft S35 95 A4
Pinecroft Way S35 95 A4
Pinefield Ave DN3 43 A6
Pinefield Rd DN3 43 A6
Pine Gr DN12 100 A8
Pinehall Dr S71 34 D4
Pine Hall Rd DN3 42 F6
Pinehurst Rise S64 79 D2
Pine Rd DN4 84 F8
Pine St WF9 18 E1
Pines The
Rotherham S66 117 C3
Sheffield S10 139 A8
Pine Tree Cl DN9 67 A3
Pine Wlk S64 98 D8
Pinewood Ave
Armthorpe DN3 64 B8
Doncaster DN4 82 E5
Pinewood Cl
Great Houghton S72 36 D3
Rotherham S65 98 D1
Pinfield Cl S72 36 E2
Pinfold S63 78 E6
Pinfold Cl
Barnsley S71 55 E8
Finningley DN9 86 E3
Swinton S64 79 C2
Tickhill DN11 121 A7
Pinfold Cotts S72 35 C6
Pinfold Cross WF8 3 D5
Pinfold Ct DN3 42 F6
Pinfold Dr S81 148 F7
Pinfold Gdns
Cudworth S72 35 C5
Fishlake DN7 25 A8
Pinfold Hill S70 55 A6
Pinfold La
Darfield S73 57 B6
Fishlake DN7 25 A8
Kirk Smeaton WF8 3 D5
Moss DN6 6 B1
Pinfold La *continued*
Norton DN6 4 D3
Rotherham S60 115 E5
Royston S71 15 C2
Sheffield S3 129 B7
Styrrup DN11 121 D1
Thorne DN8 26 A8
Thurgoland S75 53 A2
Tickhill DN11 120 F7
Pinfold Lands S64 80 B4
Pinfold Pl DN11 120 F7
Pinfold St
Eckington S21 155 D3
Sheffield S1 161 A3
Pinfold The DN5 59 C4
Pingle Ave S7 140 C3
Pingle La S65 99 C2
Pingle Rd
Killamarsh S21 156 E7
Sheffield S7 140 C3
Pingle Rise HD8 30 A7
Pingles Cres S65 98 F2
Pinner Rd S11 140 C8
Pinsent 4 S3 161 B5
Pinstone Chambers 5 S1 161 A3
Pinstone St S1 161 A3
Pioneer Cl S63 79 C6
Pipe House La S62 97 F7
Piper Cl S5 113 A3
Piper Cres S5 113 A3
Piper Ct S5 113 A3
Pipering La E DN5 61 F8
Pipering La W DN5 61 E7
Piper La S26 144 F8
Piper Rd S5 113 B2
Piper Well La HD8 28 E6
Pipeyard La S21 155 C2
Pippin Ct S66 118 D6
Pipworth Gr S2 130 C1
Pipworth Jun & Inf Schs S2 130 B1
Pipworth La S21 155 F4
Pipworth Rd S2 130 B1
Pisgah House Rd S10 128 C3
Pitchford La S10 127 D1
Pithouse La S26 144 D1
Pit La
Rotherham S61 95 F3
Sheffield S12 142 A6
Treeton S60 131 F4
Pitman Rd DN12 80 E3
Pit Row S73 77 C6
Pitsmoor Rd
Sheffield S3 129 B8
Sheffield, Woodside S3 129 A6
Pittam Cl DN3 64 B6
Pitt Cl S1 160 C3
Pitt La S1 160 C3
Pitt St W 10 S70 33 E1
Pitt St
Barnsley S70 33 E1
Darfield S73 56 E5
Eckington S21 155 C2
Mexborough S64 80 C5
Rotherham S61 114 F6
Sheffield S1 160 C3
Place The 6 S70 33 D1
Plains La DN8 46 E6
Plane Cl DN4 84 F8
Plane Dr S66 117 C4
Planet Rd DN6 40 C7
Plane Tree Way DN9 85 F3
Plank Gate
Oughtibridge S35 111 E8
Wharncliffe Side S35, S36 93 C4
Wortley S35 74 B2
Plantation Ave
Dinnington S25 134 F1
North Anston S25 146 E6
Rossington DN4 85 B4
Royston S71 15 D3
Plantation Cl
Askern DN6 22 C7
Maltby S66 118 F6
Plantation Ct S25 134 F1
Plantation Dr DN10 123 F1
Plantation Rd
Doncaster DN4 83 C4
8 Sheffield S8 141 A6
Thorne DN8 26 B7
Thorpe in B DN6 42 B7
Plantation Wlk S25 134 F1
Plantin Rise S20 155 E7
Plantin The S20 155 E7
Plaster Pits La DN5 61 B4
Platts Common Ind Est S74 76 D7
Platts Dr S20 144 A4
Platts La
Bradfield S6 109 F1
Oughtibridge S35 111 E8
Platt St S3 129 A6
Playford Yd S74 76 D8
Pleasant Ave S72 36 E2
Pleasant Cl S12 142 B6
Pleasant Rd S12 142 B6
Pleasant View S72 35 C4
Pleasley Rd S60 132 C6
Plimsoll St WF9 17 D7
Ploughmans Croft S63 77 F7
Plover Croft S61 96 A6
Plover Ct
Rossington DN11 85 A1
Sheffield S2 129 E2

Plover Dr S70 75 F8
Plover Prim Sch DN2 63 C4
Plowmans Way S61 96 F3
Plowright Cl S14 141 D5
Plowright Dr S14 141 D5
Plowright Mount S14 141 D5
Plowright Way S14 141 D5
Plumber St 8 S70 33 D1
Plumbley Hall Mews S20 155 C6
Plumbley Hall Rd S20 155 C6
Plumbley La S20 155 B6
Plumb Leys S60 131 E4
Plumbleywood La S12, S20 154 F6
Plum La S3 161 A4
Plumper's Rd S9 114 D2
Plumpton Ave S64 80 C6
Plumpton Gdns DN4 85 A6
Plumpton La S6 110 A4
Plumpton Park Rd DN4 85 A6
Plumpton Pk S72 16 C2
Plum St S3 161 A4
Plumtree Cvn Pk DN11 122 B5
Plumtree Farm Ind Est DN11 122 C5
Plumtree Hill Rd DN7 24 E6
Plumtree Rd DN11 122 C5
Plunket Rd DN2 62 F4
Plymouth Rd S7 140 E5
Pocket Handkerchief La
- Thurcroft S25 133 F1
- Todwick S25, S26 145 F8

Poffinder Wood Rd DN8 25 D5
Pog La S35 74 B7
Pogmoor La S75 33 A1
Pogmoor Rd S75 33 B2
Pog Well La S75 32 E3
Poles Bank DN9 67 D3
Polka Ct S3 129 A6
Pollard Ave S5 112 E3
Pollard Cres S5 112 E3
Pollard Rd S5 112 E3
Pollard St S61 114 E6
Pollitt St S75 33 D3
Pollyfox Way S75 53 F7
Polton Cl DN7 25 A5
Polton Toft DN7 25 A5
Pomona St S11 128 E1
Pond Cl S6 127 D6
Pond Common La S36 73 B6
Pond Hill S1 161 B3
Pondon Cl WF9 17 E7
Pond Rd S6 127 D6
Ponds Forge International Sports Ctr S1 161 B3
Pond St
- Barnsley S70 54 E8
- Sheffield S1 161 B3

Ponker La HD8 29 E8
Pontefract Rd
- Barnsley S71 34 D2
- Cudworth S72 16 C1
- Wath u D S73 78 B8

Pontefract Road Prim Sch S72 35 B8
Pontefract Terr 4 WF9 17 E6
Pool Ave DN6 22 A8
Pool Dr DN4 85 B5
Poole Pl S9 130 C4
Poole Rd S9 130 C4
Pool Hill La HD8 30 D6
Pools La S71 15 E3
Pool Sq S1 161 A3
Pope Ave DN12 81 A2
Pope Pius X RC High Sch S63 78 F4
Poplar Ave
- Goldthorpe S63 58 E5
- Rotherham S65 98 E2
- Shafton S72 16 C2
- Sheffield S20 143 F5
- Stocksbridge S36 92 B8

Poplar Cl
- Branton DN3 64 E1
- Killamarsh S21 156 C5
- Mexborough S64 79 F6
- Oughtibridge S35 111 C7

Poplar Dr
- Brinsworth S60 131 B8
- Doncaster DN2 63 C6
- Wath u D S63 79 A4

Poplar Glade S66 117 B4
Poplar Gr
- Askern DN6 22 A8
- Barnsley S71 34 E4
- Conisbrough DN12 100 B8
- Rotherham S65 117 E8
- Swinton S64 79 D3
- Warmsworth DN4 82 C4

Poplar Nook S26 145 C3
Poplar Pl DN3 64 B6
Poplar Rd
- Adwick le S DN6 21 B1
- Dunscroft DN7 43 F8
- Eckington S21 155 C2
- Oughtibridge S35 111 C7
- Wombwell S73 56 E2

Poplar Rise S66 118 D6
Poplars Rd S70 55 B7
Poplar St S72 36 B6
Poplars The
- Barnburgh DN5 59 C3
- Conisbrough DN12 81 B1

Poplar Terr
- Bentley DN5 62 B8
- Royston S71 15 D4
- South Elmsall WF9 19 A2

Poplar Way
- Catliffe S60 131 B5
- Finningley DN9 86 A5

Popple St S4 113 D1
Poppyfields Way DN3 85 C8
Porter Ave 1 S75 33 C2
Porter Brook View S11 140 D8
Porter Croft CE Prim Sch S11 128 E1
Porter Terr
- 5 Barnsley S75 33 B2
- 6 Sheffield S11 140 C8

Portland Ave S26 144 E7
Portland Bdgs 7 S6 128 E5
Portland Bsns Pk S13 130 E2
Portland Cl S25 146 E8
Portland Ct S6 128 E6
Portland La S1 160 C3
Portland Pl
- 2 Doncaster DN1 62 C3
- Maltby S66 119 A5
- Upton WF9 19 A7

Portland Rd
- Rossington DN11 103 F7
- Sheffield S20 144 A3

Portland St
- Barnsley S70 55 B8
- Rawcliffe Bridge DN14 2 C7
- 2 Sheffield S6 128 E5
- Swinton S64 79 D3

Portman Ct DN10 122 F7
Portobello S1 160 C3
Portobello La 2 S1 160 C3
Portobello St S1 160 C3
Portsea Rd S6 128 B8
Pot House La S36 73 B1
Potterdyke Ave S62 97 F8
Potter Hill S61 97 C3
Potter Hill La S35 94 C7
Potteric Carr Nature Reserve* DN4 84 A6
Potteric Carr Rd DN4 62 E1
Potters Gate
- Chapeltown S35 94 C7
- Shepley HD8 28 E1

Potters Nook S81 159 F7
Pottery Cl S62 97 F5
Pottery La S62 98 B5
Pottery Row S61 115 A6
Potts Cres S72 36 E2
Poucher St S61 114 D6
Poulton St S71 34 D6
Powder Mill La S70 55 C3
Powell Dr S21 156 C6
Powell St
- Sheffield S3 160 B4
- South Kirkby WF9 18 D3
- Worsbrough S70 55 B4

Power Station Rd DN5 62 B4
Powley Rd S6 112 D5
Poxton Gr WF9 18 E1
Poynton Ave S26 132 E3
Poynton Dr S25 134 F2
Poynton Way S26 132 E3
Poynton Wood Cres S17 152 A6
Poynton Wood Glade S17 152 A6
Prescott Gr DN7 44 A8
Prescott Rd S6 112 A2
President Way S4 129 D6
Preston Ave S74 77 A7
Preston St S8 141 A7
Preston Way S71 34 D6
Prestwich St S9 114 B4
Prestwood Gdns S35 94 E5
Priest Croft La S73 56 F8
Priestley Ave
- Kexbrough S75 32 C8
- Rawmarsh S62 98 B7

Priestley Cl DN4 82 F5
Priestley St S2 129 B1
Priest Royd 4 S75 14 A1
Primrose Ave
- Brinsworth S60 131 D7
- Darfield S73 56 F5
- Sheffield S5 113 E4

Primrose Circ 1 DN11 104 A8
Primrose Cl
- Bolton u D S63 58 B3
- Killamarsh S21 156 E7

Primrose Cres S20 143 F3
Primrose Dr S35 113 B8
Primrose Hill
- Rotherham S60 115 D8
- Sheffield S6 128 D6

Primrose La S21 156 F7
Primrose Way S74 76 E5
Primulas Cl S25 146 C4
Prince's Cres DN12 82 B3
Prince's Rd DN4 63 B1
Prince's Sq DN3 42 F4
Prince's St DN1 62 D3
Prince Arthur St S75 33 D2
Prince Edward Prim Sch S12 142 A7
Princegate DN1 62 D3
Prince Of Wales Rd S2, S9 130 C2
Princess Ave
- South Elmsall WF9 18 F2
- Stainforth DN7 24 E4

Princess Cl S63 58 B2
Princess Ct S2 142 B8
Princess Dr
- Stocksbridge S36 92 C8
- Thurnscoe S63 58 E7

Princess Gdns S73 56 D2
Princess Gr S75 75 C5
Princess Rd
- Dronfield S18 153 B2
- Goldthorpe S63 58 E5
- Mexborough S64 80 B5

Princess St
- Adwick le S DN6 40 B4
- Barnsley S70 54 E8
- Cudworth S72 16 C1
- Darton S75 14 A1
- Dinnington S25 134 C2
- Grimethorpe S72 36 A6
- Hoyland S74 76 B5
- Sheffield S4 129 D6
- Wath u D S63 78 D7
- Wombwell S73 56 C3

Princes St S60 115 B6
Prince St S64 79 D4
Pringle Rd S60 131 B8
Printing Office St DN1 62 C3
Prior Rd DN12 81 B1
Priory Ave S7 140 F8
Priory Cl
- Barnsley S70 54 F2
- 3 Conisbrough DN12 81 C3
- 3 Mexborough S64 80 C4
- Sheffield S35 95 A1

Priory Cres S71 34 E3
Priory Ct S26 157 E5
Priory Est WF9 19 B3
Priory Pl
- Barnsley S71 34 E4
- Doncaster DN1 62 C3
- Sheffield S7 140 F8

Priory Rd
- Barnsley S71 34 E4
- Bolton u D S63 58 C2
- Norton DN6 4 D4
- Sheffield, Ecclesfield S35 95 A1
- Sheffield, Sharrow Head S7 140 F8

Priory Sch & Sports Coll S71 34 D3
Priory Terr 10 S7 140 F8
Priory Way S26 144 E7
Priory Wlk DN1 62 D3
Pritchard Cl S12 143 B3
Probert Ave S63 58 D5
Proctor Pl S6 128 C8
Progress Dr S66 117 D5
Prominence Way S66 117 B7
Prospect S36 51 A3
Prospect Cl S66 117 D4
Prospect Cotts WF9 18 E3
Prospect Ct 1 S17 152 B5
Prospect Dr S17 151 F5
Prospect Pl
- Doncaster DN1 62 D2
- Sheffield S17 152 A5

Prospect Rd
- Bentley DN5 41 A4
- Bolton u D S63 58 C3
- Cudworth S72 35 B6
- Dronfield S18 153 C3
- Rawcliffe Bridge DN14 2 D8
- Sheffield, Bradway Bank S17 152 A5
- Sheffield, Lowfield S2 141 A7

Prospect St
- Barnsley S70 33 D2
- Cudworth S72 35 B7
- Norton DN6 4 C3

Prospect Terr WF9 18 B2
Providence Ct S70 54 F8
Providence Rd S6 128 B6
Providence St
- Darfield S73 56 F4
- Rotherham, Greasbrough S61 97 C3
- Rotherham, New York S60 115 C6

Provincial Pk S35 95 C2
Pryor Mede S26 157 E5
Psalter Croft S11 140 B7
Psalter Ct S11 140 C7
Psalter La S11 140 C7
Psalters Dr S36 52 B1
Psalters La
- Rotherham, Holmes S61 115 A6
- Rotherham, Kimberworth S61 114 F6

Pudding & Dip La DN7 44 B8
Pump St HD8 29 B3
Purbeck Ct S20 143 D2
Purbeck Gr S20 143 D2
Purbeck Rd S20 143 D2
Purcell Cl S66 119 C4
Purslove Cl S66 117 E4
Putting Mill Wlk HD8 30 B6
Pye Ave S75 33 B8
Pye Bank CE Prim Sch S3 129 B6
Pye Bank Cl S3 129 A6
Pye Bank Dr S3 129 A6
Pye Bank Rd S3 129 A6
Pym Rd S64 80 A5

Q

Quadrant The S17 151 E5
Quail Rise S2 129 E2
Quaker Bottom HD8 29 C3
Quaker Cl S63 78 D5
Quaker La
- Barnsley S71 56 A8
- Barnsley, Stairfoot S71 55 F8
- Warmsworth DN4 82 D6

Quantock Cl DN8 26 A5
Quarry Bank S63 78 B6
Quarry Bank Cl S72 35 B5
Quarry Cl
- Brinsworth S60 131 A8
- Kexbrough S75 32 D8

Quarryfield La S66 118 F6
Quarry Field La S66 117 B3
Quarry Fields S66 117 B3
Quarry Head Lodge S11 140 C7
Quarry Hill
- Eckington S21 154 D2
- Rotherham S60 115 D6
- Sheffield S20 155 A8

Quarry Hill Ct S63 78 E4
Quarry Hill Rd S63 78 E4
Quarry La
- Adwick le S DN6 40 A4
- Branton DN3 85 D8
- North Anston S25 146 D6
- Rotherham S61 115 C8
- Sheffield S11 140 C6
- Upton WF9 19 A8

Quarry Pl S25 135 A1
Quarry Rd
- Apperknowle S18 154 A1
- Hoyland S74 55 D1
- Killamarsh S21 156 C7
- Norton DN6 4 F3
- Sheffield, Handsworth S13 130 E3
- Sheffield, Totley Brook S17 151 E5

Quarry St
- 4 Barnsley S70 54 F8
- Barnsley, Smithies S71 34 A5
- Cudworth S72 35 B7
- Mexborough S64 80 B4
- Rawmarsh S62 97 F6

Quarry Vale S72 35 B5
Quarry Vale Gr S12 142 C4
Quarry Vale Rd S12 142 C4
Quay Rd DN8 8 F1
Quayside DN8 8 E1
Queen's Ave
- Barnsley S75 33 D2
- Great Houghton S72 57 D7
- Swinton S64 79 D4

Queen's Cres
- Bawtry DN10 123 A7
- New Edlington DN12 82 B3
- Stainforth DN7 24 E3

Queen's Ct
- Bentley DN5 62 A6
- Thorne DN8 26 A7

Queen's Dr
- Bentley DN5 62 A6
- Cudworth S72 16 C1
- Dodworth S75 54 A7
- Shafton S72 16 B3

Queen's Rd
- Adwick le S DN6 40 C8
- Askern DN6 22 B8
- Barnsley S71 34 A1
- Cudworth S72 16 C1
- Doncaster DN1 62 E4
- Sheffield S20 143 F4

Queen's Row S3 160 C4
Queen's Terr S64 80 B5
Queen Anne Ct S14 141 E3
Queen Ave
- Maltby S66 119 A4
- Rossington DN11 84 E1

Queen Elizabeth Ct
- Sheffield S14 141 E3
- Thorne DN8 26 B7

Queen Gdns S73 56 D2
Queen Mary's Rd DN11 84 E1
Queen Mary Cl S2 142 A7
Queen Mary Cres
- Kirk Sandall DN3 42 F4
- Sheffield S2 142 A8

Queen Mary Ct S2 142 A8
Queen Mary Gr S2 141 F7
Queen Mary Mews S2 142 A7
Queen Mary Rd S2 142 B8
Queen Mary St S66 119 A3
Queen St S 5 S70 33 F1
Queens Ave S26 145 C2
Queensberry Rd DN2 63 C5
Queens Cres S74 76 A5
Queens Croft S64 79 D4
Queens Dr S75 33 C3
Queensgate
- 1 Doncaster DN1 62 D3
- Sheffield S35 112 D8

Queens Gdns
- Barnsley S75 33 C3
- Hoyland S74 76 B5
- Sheffield S2 141 C8

Queens Mews S2 141 C8
Queens Pk DN12 82 B3
Queens Rd
- Aston S26 144 C7
- Carlton in L S81 148 F7
- Grimethorpe S72 36 B6
- Sheffield, Lowfield S2 141 B8
- Sheffield S2 161 B1

Queens Ret Pk S2 141 B8
Queens St S74 76 B5
Queens Stables S2 141 C8
Queen St
- 4 Barnsley S70 33 F1
- Chapeltown S35 95 A5
- Darfield S73 57 B6

Queen St *continued*
- Dinnington S25 134 F2
- Doncaster DN4 83 C8
- Eckington S21 155 E3
- Goldthorpe S63 58 E5
- Penistone S36 51 E3
- Rawmarsh S62 98 A7
- Rotherham S65 116 A7
- Sheffield, Mosborough S20 155 C7
- Sheffield S1 161 A4
- South Elmsall WF9 18 F2
- Swinton S64 79 D4
- Thorne DN8 26 A7
- Thurnscoe S63 58 E7

Queens View S2 141 C8
Queensway
- Barnsley, Old Town S75 33 C3
- Grimethorpe S72 36 A6
- Hoyland S74 76 F6
- Rotherham S60 115 F2
- Royston S71 15 C4
- Worsbrough S70 55 B5

Queenswood Cl S6 112 A3
Queenswood Dr S6 111 F3
Queenswood Gate S6 111 F3
Queenswood Rd S6 111 F3
Queen Victoria Rd S17 151 F5
Quern Way S73 57 A6
Quest Ave S73 77 C7
Quiet La S10 139 C6
Quilter Rd S66 119 C4
Quintec Ct S61 97 E1
Quoit Gn S18 153 B1

R

Raby Rd DN2 62 F5
Raby St S9 114 E3
Race Common Ave S36 72 C8
Racecommon La S70 54 E7
Racecommon Rd S70 54 D8
Racecourse Rd S64 79 A3
Race La S36 92 D5
Race St S70 33 E1
Racker Way S6 128 B7
Rackford Rd S25 146 F5
Radbourne Comm 4 S18 152 D1
Radburn Rd DN11 103 E7
Radcliffe Cl DN5 40 E1
Radcliffe La DN5 40 E1
Radcliffe Mount DN5 41 A2
Radcliffe Rd
- Barnsley S71 34 A8
- Bentley DN5 41 A2

Radford Cl S65 117 E8
Radford Park Ave WF9 18 B1
Radford St S3 160 C4
Radiance Rd DN1 62 E5
Radley Ave S66 117 B5
Radnor Cl S20 144 A2
Radnor Way DN2 63 C5
Raeburn Cl S14 141 E2
Raeburn Pl S14 141 E3
Raeburn Rd S14 141 E3
Raeburn Way S14 141 E2
Rag La S35 73 F7
Ragusa Dr DN11 103 F7
Raikes St S64 79 F4
Rail Mill Way S62 97 F2
Rails Rd S6 127 A3
Railway Ave S60 131 C5
Railway Cotts
- Catliffe S60 131 C6
- Dodworth S75 53 E7
- Dunford Bridge S36 48 F2
- South Elmsall WF9 19 E7

Railway Ct DN4 62 D1
Railway Terr
- Goldthorpe S63 58 D5
- Rotherham S60 115 C6

Railway View S63 58 E5
Rainborough Ct S63 77 F6
Rainborough Mews S63 78 B7
Rainborough Rd S63 78 B6
Rainbow Ave S12 143 C4
Rainbow Cl S12 143 C4
Rainbow Cres S12 143 C4
Rainbow Dr S12 143 C4
Rainbow Forge Prim Sch S12 143 C3
Rainbow Gr S12 143 C4
Rainbow Pl S12 143 C4
Rainbow Rd S12 143 C4
Rainbow Way S12 143 C4
Rainbow Wlk 2 S12 143 B4
Rainford Dr S71 34 D6
Rainford Sq DN3 42 F5
Rainsbutt Rd DN17 11 F1
Rainton Gr S75 33 B4
Rainton Rd DN1 62 E2
Raintree Ct DN5 61 F5
Raisen Hall Pl S5 113 A2
Raisen Hall Rd S5 113 A3
Rake's La DN11 83 E2
Rake Bridge Bank DN7 44 B3
Rakes La DN12 101 C5
Raleigh Ct DN2 63 B3
Raleigh Dr S35 94 D5
Raleigh Rd S2 141 B6
Raleigh Terr DN4 82 E6
Raley St S70 54 D8
Ralph Ellis Dr S36 92 B8
Ralston Croft S20 155 E6
Ralston Ct S20 155 D6
Ralston Gr S20 155 D6

Ralston Pl S20 155 D6
Ramper Rd
Carr S66 118 B1
Letwell S81 136 A3
Rampton Rd 1 S7 140 F7
Ramsden Ave S81 136 F3
Ramsden Cres S81 148 F7
Ramsden La HD9 47 B7
Ramsden Rd
Doncaster DN4 62 B2
Holme HD9 47 C7
Rotherham S60 115 E5
Ramsey Cres DN5 62 A5
Ramsey Rd S10 128 C4
Ramsker Dr DN3 64 B5
Ramskir La DN7 24 F5
Ramskir View DN7 24 F4
Ramsworth Cl DN5 61 E5
Ranby Rd S11 140 B7
Randall Pl 4 S2 140 F8
Randall St
Eckington S21 155 B2
Sheffield S2 129 A1
Randerson Dr S64 79 E1
Rands La DN3 64 D7
Rands Lane Ind Est DN3 64 D7
Ranelagh Dr S11 140 B5
Ranfield Ct S65 117 E8
Rangeley Rd S6 128 A5
Ranmoor Chase S10 128 B1
Ranmoor Cliffe Rd S10 127 F1
Ranmoor Cres S10 127 F1
Ranmoor Ct 2 S10 140 A8
Ranmoor Grange S10 127 F1
Ranmoor House (Sheffield Univ) S10 128 A2
Ranmoor Park Rd S10 127 F1
Ranmoor Rd S10 127 F1
Ranmoor Rise S10 127 F1
Ranskill Ct S9 130 C7
Ranulf Ct S7 140 C3
Ranworth Rd S66 117 E5
Ranyard Rd DN4 82 F7
Raseby Ave S20 143 E2
Raseby Cl S20 143 E2
Raseby Pl S20 143 E2
Rasen Cl S64 80 C6
Ratcliffe Rd 7 S11 140 D8
Ratten Row
Dodworth S75 53 E6
Wadworth DN11 102 C7
Rattigan Ho DN2 63 A6
Ravencar Rd S21 155 B3
Ravencarr Pl S2 130 A1
Ravencarr Rd S2 130 A1
Raven Dr S61 96 A6
Ravenfield Cl S20 143 A2
Ravenfield Dr S71 34 A5
Ravenfield La S65 99 C5
Ravenfield Prim Sch S65 99 D1
Ravenfield Rd DN3 64 C5
Ravenfield St DN12 80 F4
Ravenholt S70 55 A4
Raven La S72 16 A6
Raven Mdws S64 98 C8
Ravenna Cl S70 55 B8
Raven Rd S7 140 D6
Raven Royd S71 14 F1
Ravenscar Cl DN12 80 F3
Ravens Cl S75 33 B8
Ravenscourt S70 55 B4
Ravenscroft Ave S13 142 E8
Ravenscroft Cl S13 142 E8
Ravenscroft Cres S13 142 E8
Ravenscroft Ct S13 142 E8
Ravenscroft Dr S13 142 E7
Ravenscroft Oval S13 142 E8
Ravenscroft Pl S13 142 E8
Ravenscroft Rd S13 142 E7
Ravenscroft Way S13 142 E8
Ravensdale Rd S18 152 D1
Ravenshaw Cl S75 33 B3
Ravensmead Ct S63 58 C1
Ravens Wlk DN12 81 E2
Ravenswood Dr
Auckley DN9 86 A7
Rotherham S66 117 B8
Ravensworth Rd DN1 62 E2
Ravine The S5 113 E7
Rawcliffe Bridge Prim Sch DN14 2 D7
Rawcliffe Sta DN14 2 B8
Raw La S66 119 E8
Rawlins Ct S18 153 C4
Rawmarsh Ashwood Jun & Inf Sch S62 97 F3
Rawmarsh Com Sch S62 97 E6
Rawmarsh Hill S62 97 F4
Rawmarsh Ho S62 97 F4
Rawmarsh Monkwood Jun & Inf Schs S62 97 E7
Rawmarsh Rd S60 115 D8
Rawmarsh Rosehill Jun Sch S62 98 A7
Rawmarsh Ryecroft Inf Sch S62 98 A6
Rawmarsh St Mary's CE Prim Sch S62 97 F5
Rawmarsh Sandhill Prim Sch S62 98 C6
Rawmarsh Sh Ctr S62 97 F5
Rawmarsh Thorogate Jun & Inf Sch S62 97 F7
Rawson Cl DN4 63 F1
Rawson Rd
Rotherham S65 115 E7
Tickhill DN11 120 F6
Rawsons Almshouses S6 112 A2
Rawsons Bank S35 113 B8
Rawson Spring Rd S6 112 D2
Rawson Spring Way S6 112 D2
Rawson St S6 128 E7
Raybould Rd S61 96 F1
Rayls Rd S26 145 F5
Rayls Rise S26 145 F5
Raymond Ave S72 36 A6
Raymond Rd
Barnsley S70 55 D8
Bentley DN5 61 F6
Raynald Rd S2 130 A1
Raynor Sike La S35 111 A8
Rayton Ct DN11 122 A4
Reader Cres S64 79 D3
Reading Gate DN14 11 F7
Reading Room La S35 74 D3
Reaper Cres S35 94 E6
Reasbeck Terr S71 33 F5
Reasby Ave S65 117 D8
Reavill Cl S25 134 F2
Rebecca Mews S70 54 F8
Rebecca Row S70 54 F8
Recreation Ave S66 133 F6
Recreation La DN11 84 E1
Recreation Rd
Adwick le S DN6 40 B4
Wath u D S63 78 F7
Rectory Cl
Barnsley S71 15 D1
Eckington S21 155 E4
Stocksbridge S36 73 C1
Thurnscoe S63 58 B8
Wombwell S73 56 D3
Rectory Ct WF8 3 D6
Rectory Garth WF9 17 D7
Rectory Gdns
Doncaster DN1 62 E4
Harthill S26 157 E6
Killamarsh S21 156 D6
New Edlington DN12 101 A7
Todwick S26 145 F5
Rectory La
Finningley DN9 86 E3
Thurnscoe S63 58 B8
Rectory Mews DN5 82 B8
Rectory Rd S21 156 D5
Rectory St S62 97 F4
Rectory Way S71 34 D3
Redbourne Rd DN5 41 B1
Redbrook Bsns Pk S75 33 B4
Redbrook Croft 6 S20 143 A3
Redbrook Ct S75 33 C4
Redbrook Gr 5 S20 143 A3
Redbrook Rd S75 33 B3
Redbrook View S75 33 C4
Redbrook Wlk S75 33 C4
Redcar Cl DN12 80 E2
Redcar Rd S10 128 C3
Redcliffe Cl S75 33 B4
Redfearn St 2 S71 33 F2
Redfern Ave S20 143 D1
Redfern Ct S20 143 D1
Redfern Dr S20 143 D1
Redfern Gr S20 143 D1
Red Fern Gr S36 92 B8
Redgrave 5 S3 161 B5
Redgrave Pl S66 117 B6
Redhall Cl DN3 43 A4
Red Hill
Kiveton Park S26 146 A2
Sheffield S1 160 C3
Redhill Ave S70 55 C8
Redhill Ct DN11 102 B7
Red Hill La DN5 59 C8
Redhouse Cvn Pk DN7 44 F2
Red House La
Adwick le S DN6 40 A7
Brodsworth DN5, DN6 39 D6
Red La S10 128 C1
Redland Cres DN8 9 C1
Redland Gr S75 14 B2
Redland La S7 140 D3
Redland Way S66 118 E6
Redmarsh Ave S62 97 E7
Redmires La S10 126 D1
Redmires Rd
Hallam Moors S10 138 B8
Sheffield S10 127 B1
Redmires Way S10 126 F1
Red Oak La S6 127 C7
Red Quarry La S81 147 E8
Redrock Rd S60 116 A2
Redscope Cres S61 96 D1
Redscope Prim Sch S61 96 E1
Redscope Rd S61 96 D1
Redthorne Way S72 16 C3
Redthorn Rd S13 142 F8
Redthorpe Crest S75 33 A4
Redwood Ave
Killamarsh S21 156 C5
Royston S71 15 C3
Redwood Cl S74 76 D5
Redwood Dr S66 118 C5
Redwood Glen S35 94 F4
Reed Cl S73 57 A5
Reedham Dr S66 117 E5
Reedholme La DN8 8 E8
Reeves Way DN3 63 F6
Regent Ave DN3 64 C5
Regent Cres
Barnsley S71 33 F7
South Hiendley S72 16 E5
Regent Ct
Hoyland S74 76 A5
Sheffield S6 128 C8
Regent Gdns S70 33 E3
Regent Gr
Bentley DN5 61 F5
Rossington DN11 104 A7
Regent St S 5 S70 33 F2
Regent Sq DN1 62 E3
Regent St
Barnsley S70 33 F2
Doncaster DN4 83 A7
Hemsworth WF9 17 C7
Hoyland S74 76 A5
Rotherham S61 114 F6
Sheffield S1 160 C3
South Elmsall WF9 18 E3
South Hiendley S72 16 E5
Regents Way S26 144 E7
Regent Terr
Doncaster DN1 62 E3
Sheffield S3 160 C3
Regina Cres
Brierley S72 16 E2
Havercroft WF4 16 C8
Reginald Rd
Barnsley S70 55 D7
Wombwell S73 56 F2
Reignhead Prim Sch S20 144 A3
Rembrandt Dr S18 152 E1
Remington Ave S5 112 F7
Remington Dr S5 112 F7
Remington Rd S5 112 F7
Remount Rd S61 96 E2
Remount Way S61 96 D2
Remple Ave DN7 45 A6
Remple Common Rd DN7 44 F5
Remple La DN7 45 A6
Renald La S36 51 E7
Renathorpe Rd S5 113 D6
Rencliffe Ave S60 115 F3
Reneville Cl S60 115 E4
Reneville Cres S5 113 A8
Reneville Ct S5 113 A8
Reneville Dr S5 113 A8
Reneville Rd S60 115 E4
Reney Ave S8 152 D6
Reney Cres S8 152 D6
Reney Dr S8 152 D6
Reney Rd S8 152 E7
Reney Wlk S8 152 D6
Renishaw Ave S60 116 B2
Renishaw Hall Gdns* S21 155 F2
Renishaw Hall (Mus & Craft Ctr)* S21 155 F2
Renshaw Cl S35 94 C8
Renshaw Rd S11 140 A6
Renville Cl S62 97 E7
Renway Rd S60 116 A3
Repton Pl S18 152 C1
Repton Rd DN6 40 B8
Reresby Cres S60 116 C2
Reresby Dr S60 116 C2
Reresby Rd
Rotherham, Thrybergh S65 99 A2
Rotherham, Whiston S60 116 C2
Reresby Wlk DN12 80 F4
Reservoir Rd
Sheffield S10 128 C3
Ulley S26 132 D4
Retail World Sh Ctr & Trad Est S60 97 F1
Retford Rd
Aston S13 143 E8
Orgreave S13 131 B1
Sheffield, Woodhouse Mill S13 143 E8
Retford Wlk DN11 85 B1
Revel Garth HD8 30 A5
Revell Cl S65 116 D7
Revill Cl S66 118 F6
Revill La S13 143 C6
Rex Ave S7 140 C4
Reynard La S6 127 B5
Reynolds Cl S66 117 B6
Rhodes Ave S61 96 E2
Rhodes Dr S60 116 C2
Rhodes Fair Acres Caravan Site DN7 24 E2
Rhodesia Ct DN4 84 D8
Rhodes St S2 161 C3
Rhodes Terr 7 S70 55 A8
Rianstorth S35 95 E2
Ribble Croft S35 95 A6
Ribblesdale Dr S12 142 F1
Ribble Way S5 113 C3
Riber Ave S71 34 A7
Riber Cl S6 127 D6
Ribston Ct S9 130 B4
Ribston Mews S9 130 B4
Ribston Pl S9 130 B4
Ribston Rd S9 130 B4
Ribston Wlk S9 130 B4
Richard Ave S71 34 A6
Richard La DN11 84 E1
Richard Newman Prim Sch S71 33 F7
Richard Rd
Barnsley S71 34 A6
Kexbrough S75 32 E8
Rotherham S60 115 E5
Richards Ct 2 S2 141 B6
Richardson Wlk S73 56 B4
Richards Rd S2 141 B6
Richard St 9 S70 33 D1
Richards Way S62 98 A6
Rich Farm Cl DN5 41 D3
Richmond Ave
Kexbrough S75 32 D7
Sheffield S13 142 F8
Richmond Bsns Pk DN4 83 E8
Richmond Ct S13 142 D7
Richmond Dr DN6 22 C8
Richmond Farm Mews S13 142 D7
Richmond Gr S13 142 E8
Richmond Hall Ave S13 142 D8
Richmond Hall Cres S13 142 D7
Richmond Hall Dr S13 142 D8
Richmond Hall Rd S13 142 D8
Richmond Hall Way S13 142 D7
Richmond Hill Ho S13 142 D7
Richmond Hill Prim Sch DN5 61 E3
Richmond Hill Rd
Bentley DN5 61 E2
Sheffield S13 142 D7
Richmond La DN10 122 F6
Richmond Park Ave
Rotherham S61 114 D6
Sheffield S13 130 E2
Richmond Park Cl S13 130 E1
Richmond Park Cres S13 130 E2
Richmond Park Croft S13 130 E2
Richmond Park Dr S13 130 E1
Richmond Park Gr S13 130 E1
Richmond Park Rd S13 130 E1
Richmond Park Rise S9 130 D2
Richmond Park View S13 130 E1
Richmond Park Way S13 130 E1
Richmond Pl S13 142 D7
Richmond Rd
Bentley DN5 61 D7
Carlton in L S81 148 F6
Rotherham S61 114 E6
Sheffield S13 142 D7
Thorne DN8 9 D4
Thurnscoe S63 58 C8
Upton WF9 19 A7
Richmond St
7 Barnsley S70 33 D1
Sheffield S3 129 B6
Richworth Rd S13 142 F8
Ricknald Cl S26 132 D1
Ridal Ave S36 73 A2
Ridal Cl S36 73 A2
Ridal Croft S36 73 A2
Riddell Ave S81 136 E3
Riddings Cl
Hemsworth WF9 17 D5
Sheffield S2 142 A7
Thurcroft S66 133 F6
Riddings La DN10 105 A4
Rider Rd S6 128 C8
Ridge Balk La DN6 39 F5
Ridge Ct
Rotherham S65 115 E7
Sheffield S10 127 C2
Ridgehill Ave S12 142 B5
Ridgehill Gr S12 142 B5
Ridge Rd
Adwick le S DN6 40 B2
Eckington S21 154 E2
Rotherham S65 115 F7
Ridgestone Ave WF9 17 E7
Ridge The
Adwick le S DN6 39 F4
Sheffield S10 127 C1
Ridge View Cl S9 114 A3
Ridge View Dr S9 114 A3
Ridgewalk Way S70 54 F6
Ridgeway
Dronfield S18 153 D3
Rotherham S65 116 D7
Ridgeway Cl
Hellaby S66 118 A4
Rotherham S65 116 D7
Ridgeway Craft Ctr* S12 154 E8
Ridgeway Cres
Barnsley S71 15 C1
Sheffield S12 142 A6
Ridgeway Dr S12 142 A6
Ridgeway Moor S12 154 E6
Ridgeway Prim Sch S12 154 E8
Ridgeway Rd
Brinsworth S60 131 C8
Sheffield S12 142 A5
Ridgewood Ave DN3 42 F1
Ridgewood Sch DN5 61 C6
Ridgill Ave DN6 21 A1
Ridgway Ave S73 57 A6
Riding Cl
Doncaster DN4 85 B6
Rotherham S66 117 A5
Riding or Riddings La DN10 105 A4
Ridings Ave S71 34 B5
Ridings The S71 34 C5
Rig Cl S61 96 F1
Rig Dr S64 79 A3
Riggs High Rd S6 126 F5
Riggs Low Rd S6 127 A5
Riley Ave DN4 82 F6
Rill Ct WF9 17 D7
Rimington Rd S73 56 D3
Rimini Rise S73 56 E5
Rimmington Ho S36 92 F8
Ringinglow Rd S11 139 D5
Ringstead Ave S10 127 E3
Ringstead Cres S10 127 F3
Ringstone Gr S72 17 B3
Ringway S63 58 B3
Ringwood Cres S20 144 A2
Ringwood Dr S20 144 A2
Ringwood Gr S20 144 A2
Ringwood Rd 3 S20 144 A2
Ringwood Way WF9 17 F7
Ripley Gr S75 33 B4
Ripley St S6 128 C7
Ripon Ave DN2 62 F6
Ripon St S9 129 F5
Ripon Way S26 144 C7
Rippon Cres S6 128 B8
Rippon Ct S62 97 F7
Rippon Rd S6 128 B8
Risedale Rd S63 58 F4
Rise The
Brierley S72 17 A2
North Anston S25 146 E5
Swinton S64 79 B2
Rising St S3 129 B6
Rivelin Bank S6 128 B7
Rivelin Glen Cotts S6 127 E4
Rivelin Park Cres S6 128 A6
Rivelin Park Dr S6 128 A6
Rivelin Park Rd S6 128 A6
Rivelin Prim Sch S6 128 C7
Rivelin Rd S6 128 A6
Rivelin St S6 128 B6
Rivelin Terr S6 128 A6
Rivelin Valley Nature Trail* S6 127 B3
Rivelin Valley Rd S6 127 C4
River Bank S35 111 E7
River Ct S17 152 A7
Riverdale Ave 3 S10 140 A8
Riverdale Dr S10 128 A1
Riverdale Rd
Bentley DN5 61 E8
Sheffield S10 140 A8
Riverhead DN5 61 B1
River La DN7 25 B7
River Rivelin Trail* S6 127 D4
Riverside S6 128 A7
Riverside Cl
7 Conisbrough DN12 81 C3
Darfield S73 57 C6
Doncaster DN4 61 F1
Sheffield S6 127 F8
Riverside Ct
Denby Dale HD8 30 A6
Laughton en le M S25 134 C3
4 Mexborough S64 80 C4
Sheffield S9 129 F7
Riverside Dr DN5 82 C8
Riverside Gdns
Auckley DN9 85 F7
Bolton u D S63 58 D1
Riverside Mews 3 S6 128 C8
Riverside Pk
Sheffield S2 161 B1
Stainforth DN7 24 A8
Riverside Studios S18 153 B1
Riverside Way S60 115 C5
River Terr S6 128 C8
River Valley View HD8 30 A6
River View Rd S35 111 E7
River Way DN9 85 F7
Riviera Flats DN1 62 E4
Riviera Mount DN5 62 B5
Riviera Par DN5 62 B5
Rix Ct S64 98 D8
Rix Rd S62 98 D8
Roache Dr S63 58 C4
Roach Rd S11 140 C7
Robert Ave S71 34 D2
Robert Ogden Sch The S63 37 B1
Robert Rd S8 153 A7
Roberts Ave DN12 81 D1
Roberts Gr S26 144 E7
Robertshaw 1 S3 160 B3
Robertshaw Cres S36 73 D1
Robertson Dr S6 128 A6
Robertson Rd S6 128 B6
Robertson Sq DN7 24 E4
Roberts Rd
Doncaster DN4 62 B1
New Edlington DN12 82 C1
Roberts St
Cudworth S72 35 B7
Wombwell S73 56 C2
Robert St S60 115 B6
Robey St S4 113 E1
Robinets Rd S61 97 A3
Robin Hood Airport Doncaster Sheffield DN9 86 B2
Robin Hood Ave S71 15 D4
Robin Hood Chase S6 127 C7
Robin Hood Cres DN3 43 A1
Robin Hood Rd
Edenthorpe DN3 43 A1
Sheffield S9 114 A4
Robin La
Hemsworth WF9 17 A5
Royston S71 15 D4
Sheffield S20 143 F4
Robin Pl S26 144 E6
Robins Cl S26 144 E7
Robinson Ct S61 114 F7
Robinson Rd S2 161 C2
Robinson St S60 115 D4
Robinson Way S21 156 C6
Rob Royd S75 53 F6
Rob Roy La S70 54 D6

Roche 9 S20 155 E8
Roche Abbey* S66 135 C8
Roche Cl S71 34 B3
Roche End S26 145 E5
Rocher Ave S35 112 E7
Rocher Cl S35 112 E7
Rocher Gr S35 112 E7
Rocher La S36 92 C4
Rochester Cl S10 127 A1
Rochester Dr S10 127 A1
Rochester Rd
Barnsley S71 34 B4
Sheffield S10 127 A1
South Anston S25 146 D3
Rochester Row DN5 61 D5
Rockcliffe Cl DN11 102 B7
Rockcliffe Dr DN11 102 B7
Rockcliffe Rd S62 97 F5
Rockfield Dr S81 147 E3
Rockingham 11 S20 155 E8
Rockingham Bsns Pk S70 75 F6
Rockingham Cl
Barnsley S70 75 F6
3 Dronfield S18 152 C1
Sheffield S1 161 A2
Rockingham Ct
Barnsley S71 34 A1
Swinton S64 79 B3
Rockingham Gate 1 S1 161 A2
Rockingham Ho
4 Doncaster DN1 62 C1
Rawmarsh S62 98 A6
Rockingham Jun & Inf Sch S61 96 F3
Rockingham La S1 161 A3
Rockingham Mews S70 75 E6
Rockingham Rd
Dodworth S75 54 A6
Doncaster DN2 62 E5
Rawmarsh S62 98 A6
Swinton S64 79 B3
Rockingham Row S70 75 F6
Rockingham St
Barnsley, Birdwell S70 75 F6
Barnsley S71 33 E4
Grimethorpe S72 36 A7
Hoyland S74 76 B6
Sheffield S1 160 C3
Rockingham Sta* S74 77 B4
Rockingham Way
Rotherham S61 96 F3
Sheffield S1 161 A2
Rockland Villas S65 98 E2
Rocklea Cl S64 79 C2
Rockley Ave
Barnsley S70 75 F8
Hoyland S71 56 B1
Rockley Cres S70 75 E7
Rockley La
Askern DN5, DN6 22 B3
Barnsley S70, S75 75 D8
Hood Green S75 54 C2
Rockley Mdws S70 54 C7
Rockley Nook DN2 63 B7
Rockley Old Hall S70 54 E2
Rockley Rd S6 112 B2
Rockleys S75 54 A6
Rockley View S75 75 D6
Rockley View Ct S70 75 F6
Rockliffe Ave DN4 82 E6
Rock Mount
Hoyland S74 76 F6
Sheffield S10 127 F1
Rock Mount Rd S9 114 B4
Rock Pl S36 73 D1
Rockside Rd S36 51 A3
Rock St
Barnsley S70 33 E2
Sheffield S3 129 B6
Rock Terr DN12 81 B1
Rockwood Cl
Chapeltown S35 94 E5
Darton S75 13 F1
Rockwood Rise HD8 30 A7
Roddis Cl S25 134 D1
Roden Way S62 97 C8
Rodes Ave S72 36 E1
Rodger Rd S13 143 D6
Rodger St S61 115 C7
Rodman Dr S13 143 D8
Rodman St S13 143 E8
Rod Moor Rd S17, S18 152 B4
Rodney Hill S6 111 E1
Rod Side S6 126 B5
Rodwell Cl S60 131 E4
Roebuck Hill S74 76 F8
Roebuck Rd S6 160 A4
Roebuck St S73 56 E1
Roeburn Cl S75 14 A2
Roe Croft Cl DN5 61 B2
Roehampton Rise
Barnsley S71 56 A7
Bentley DN5 61 E5
Brinsworth S60 115 A1
Roe La S3 129 B8
Roewood Ct S3 129 B8
Roger Rd S71 34 E2
Rojean Rd S35 112 D8
Rokeby Dr S5 113 B6
Rokeby Rd S5 113 A6
Rolleston Ave S66 118 E5
Rolleston Rd
Adwick le S DN6 40 B8
Sheffield S5 113 D4
Rollin Dr S6 112 B1
Rolling Dales Cl S66 118 E6
Rolls Cres S62 97 C8
Roman Cres
Brinsworth S60 115 C2
Rawmarsh S62 97 E6
Roman Ct S61 114 E6
Romandale Gdns S2 130 C1
Roman Rd
Doncaster DN4 62 E2
Kexbrough S75 32 D8
Roman Ridge DN5 40 A4
Roman Ridge Rd S9 114 B3
Roman St S63 37 E1
Romney Cl S66 117 B6
Romney Dr S18 152 E1
Romney Gdns S2 141 B6
Romsdal Rd S10 128 C4
Romwood Ave S64 79 A3
Ronald Rd
Doncaster DN4 83 A7
Sheffield S9 130 C4
Ronksley Cres S5 113 D6
Ronksley La S6 126 C3
Ronksley Rd S5 113 D6
Rookdale Cl S75 33 B4
Rookery Bank S36 92 F8
Rookery Chase S36 92 F8
Rookery Cl
Stocksbridge S36 92 F8
Wales S26 145 C3
Rookery Dell S36 92 F8
Rookery Rd S64 79 B3
Rookery Rise S36 92 F7
Rookery The S36 92 F8
Rookery Vale S36 92 F8
Rookery Way S35 74 A6
Rook Hill S70 55 C5
Roost The S32 149 A6
Roper Hill S10 138 D7
Roper House La S35 73 E7
Roper La S35 73 F7
Rope Wlk DN8 26 A7
Rosamond Ave S17 152 A6
Rosamond Cl S17 152 A6
Rosamond Ct S17 152 A5
Rosamond Dr S17 152 A6
Rosamond Glade S17 152 A6
Rosamond Pl S17 152 A6
Rosa Rd S10 128 C4
Roscoe Bank S6 127 E5
Roscoe Ct S6 127 F6
Roscoe Dr S6 127 F5
Roscoe Mount S6 127 F5
Roscoe Rd S3 160 C5
Roscoe View S6 127 F5
Rose Ave
Darfield S73 57 A7
Doncaster DN4 83 B8
Sheffield S20 143 F3
Upton WF9 19 A7
Roseberry Ave DN7 44 B7
Roseberry Cl S74 76 E4
Rosebery St
Barnsley S70 55 D8
Rotherham S61 115 A6
Rosebery Terr 2 S70 55 A8
Rose Cl
Brinsworth S60 131 D7
Upton WF9 19 A7
Rose Cres
Bentley DN5 61 E7
Rawmarsh S62 98 B6
Rose Ct
Doncaster DN4 83 A8
Rotherham S66 117 A4
Rosedale Ave S62 97 F6
Rosedale Cl
Aston S26 144 E8
Upton WF9 19 B7
Rosedale Gdns
Barnsley S70 33 C1
Sheffield S11 140 D8
Rosedale Rd
Aston S26 144 E8
Bentley DN5 41 A2
Bentley, Scawsby DN5 61 D7
Sheffield S11 140 D8
Rosedale Way S66 117 C6
Rose Dr S66 117 C5
Rose Garth Ave S26 144 E8
Rosegarth Cl DN5 61 E7
Rose Gr
Armthorpe DN3 64 A6
Upton WF9 19 A7
Wombwell S73 56 C4
Rosegreave S63 58 D5
Rosehill DN14 2 C7
Rose Hill
Doncaster DN4 63 D1
Sheffield S20 155 B8
Rosehill Ave
Hemsworth WF9 17 C6
Rawmarsh S62 98 A7
Rose Hill Ave S20 155 B8
Rose Hill Cl
Penistone S36 51 D2
Sheffield S20 155 B8
Rosehill Ct S70 33 E2
Rose Hill Ct DN4 63 C2
Rose Hill Dr
Dodworth S75 53 F7
Sheffield S20 155 B8
Rosehill Ho S62 97 F6
Rose Hill Mews S20 155 B8
Rosehill Rd S62 97 F6
Rose Hill Rise DN4 63 C2
Rosehill Terr DN14 2 D7
Rose Hill View S20 155 B8
Rose La
Askern DN6 21 F5
Laughton en le M S25 134 C6
Roselle St S6 128 C8
Rosemary Ct
1 Sheffield, Norton Woodseats S8 141 A3
Sheffield S6 128 C5
Rosemary Gr DN5 81 D5
Rosemary Rd
Rotherham S66 117 A5
Sheffield S20 143 F4
Rose Pl S73 56 C4
Rose Tree Ave S72 35 B7
Rose Tree Ct S72 35 B7
Rose Way S21 156 D5
Rosewell Ct S65 116 B8
Rosewood Cl S81 148 D1
Rosewood Dr DN3 42 E8
Roslin Rd S10 128 C3
Roslyn Cres S32 149 A7
Roslyn Rd S32 149 A7
Rosser Ave S12 141 F2
Rossetti Mount S66 117 B6
Rossington All Saints CE Sch DN11 104 A7
Rossington Hall Sch DN11 104 D6
Rossington Ho 5 DN1 62 C1
Rossington Holmescarr Jun Sch DN11 84 E1
Rossington Pheasant Bank Jun Sch DN11 84 E1
Rossington Rd S11 140 C8
Rossington St Michael's CE Prim Sch DN11 85 B1
Rossington St DN12 80 F4
Rossington Tornedale Inf Sch DN11 84 F1
Rossiter Rd S61 97 C4
Rosslyn Ave S26 144 E8
Rosslyn Cres DN5 41 B2
Rossmoor Cl DN9 86 A7
Ross St S9 130 D4
Rosston Rd S66 119 B5
Rostholme Sq DN5 41 B2
Roston Cl 3 S18 152 D1
Rothay Cl S18 152 E1
Rothay Rd S4 113 F1
Rothbury Cl S20 144 A2
Rothbury Ct 5 S20 144 A2
Rothbury Way S60 115 C1
Rother Cres S60 131 E4
Rother Croft S74 76 E6
Rother Garth WF9 19 B2
Rotherham Baulk
Carlton in L S81 148 C7
Gildingwells S81 148 C7
Rotherham Central Sta S60 115 D6
Rotherham Cl S21 156 F8
Rotherham Coll S25 134 F2
Rotherham Coll of Arts & Tech S65 115 E7
Rotherham District General Hospl S60 115 F2
Rotherham La S25 134 C5
Rotherham Rd
Aston S26 144 C7
Barnsley S71, S72 34 B4
Catliffe S60 131 D6
Dinnington S25 134 C2
Eckington S20, S21 155 F6
Great Houghton S72 57 E7
Killamarsh S21 156 F8
Maltby S66 118 D4
Orgreave S13 131 B1
Rotherham S62 97 E2
Sheffield, Beighton S20 144 A5
Sheffield S20, S21 155 F6
Spinkhill S43 157 D2
Tickhill DN11 120 E6
Wath u D S63 78 B6
Rotherham Rd N S20 155 F8
Rotherham St S9 130 A7
Rotherhill Cl S65 116 A7
Rother Mews WF9 19 B2
Rothermoor Ave S26 145 C2
Rother Rd S60 115 D3
Rotherside Rd S21 155 F4
Rother St S73 78 B8
Rotherstoke Cl S60 115 E4
Rother Terr S60 115 D3
Rothervale Cl S20 144 A4
Rother Valley Country Park Visitor Ctr* S26 144 C2
Rother Valley Ctry Pk Nature Reserve* S26, S21 144 D2
Rother Valley Water Sports Ctr* S26 144 C2
Rother Valley Way S20 156 B8
Rother View Cl S26 144 A7
Rother View Gdns S26 144 A7
Rother View Rd S60 115 D4
Rotherway S60 131 E8
Rother Way S66 118 A6
Rotherwood Ave S13 143 D8
Rotherwood Cl DN5 61 D6
Rotherwood Cres S66 133 E6
Rotherwood Rd S21 156 E7
Rothesay Cl DN5 61 F5
Rotunda Bsns Ctr S35 95 A7
Roughbirchworth La S36 52 B1
Rough La
Sheffield S35 94 B1
Wortley S35 74 D1
Roughwood Gn S61 97 A3
Roughwood Prim Sch S61 96 E2
Roughwood Rd S61 96 E2
Roughwood Way S61 96 E2
Round Close Rd HD9 48 B6
Roundel St S9 129 F5
Round Green La S75 54 C3
Round Hill S75 14 A1
Roundhill Ct DN4 84 B8
Roundwood Ct 2 S70 55 A4
Roundwood Gr S62 98 B5
Roundwood Way S73 56 F6
Rowan Cl
Barnsley S70 54 F7
Chapeltown S35 95 A4
Finningley DN9 86 A4
Goldthorpe S63 58 C5
Thorne DN8 9 C3
Rowan Ct DN2 63 C6
Rowan Dr
Barnsley S75 33 B3
Rotherham S66 117 C5
Rowan Garth DN5 62 A6
Rowan La S72 16 E6
Rowan Mount DN2 63 B6
Rowan Rd S21 155 C1
Rowan Rise S66 118 D5
Rowan Sch The S17 151 E6
Rowan Tree Cl S21 156 C5
Rowan Tree Dell S17 151 E3
Rowan Tree Rd S21 156 C5
Rowborn Dr S35 111 F4
Rowdale Cres S12 142 D5
Rowe Cl WF9 19 A4
Rowel La S6 127 C8
Rowena Ave DN3 42 F1
Rowena Dr
Bentley DN5 61 D6
Thurcroft S66 133 E7
Rowena Inf Sch DN12 81 B2
Rowena Rd DN12 81 B2
Rowernfields S25 147 B7
Rowgate HD8 29 B6
Row Gate HD8 28 D6
Rowland Pl 10 DN1 62 C2
Rowland Rd
Barnsley S75 33 C3
3 Sheffield S2 141 A8
Rowlands Ave WF9 19 A7
Rowlands Bridge Mews DN11 121 A6
Rowland St
Royston S71 15 D4
Sheffield S3 129 A5
Rowley Croft WF9 19 A2
Rowley Ct WF9 19 A2
Rowley La WF9 19 A2
Rowley Way S66 117 B8
Rowms La S64 79 F3
Rowsley St S2 129 B1
Row The DN3 64 B1
Roxby Cl DN4 84 D6
Roxton Ave 2 S8 152 F8
Roxton Rd S8 140 E1
Royal Ave DN1 62 E4
Royal Ct
Barnsley S75 32 E6
Hoyland S74 76 F6
Royal Dr DN14 2 B8
Royale Cl S21 155 E3
Royal Exchange S3 161 B4
Royal Hallamshire Hospl S10 160 A2
Royal St S70 33 E2
Royal Victoria Bldgs S3 161 B4
Royd Ave
Cudworth S72 35 B6
Darton S75 14 B1
Penistone S36 50 D3
Royd Cl S70 54 F4
Roydfield Cl S20 143 D2
Roydfield Dr S20 143 D2
Roydfield Gr S20 143 D2
Royd Field La S36 72 D8
Royd Inf Sch S36 92 E8
Royd La
Barnsley S75 32 D3
Cawthorne S75 32 C3
Penistone S36 50 D4
Stocksbridge S36 92 D7
Royd Moor Ct S36 51 A4
Royd Moor Hall Farm S36 50 E5
Royd Moor La WF9 18 B8
Royd Moor Rd S36 50 E5
Royds Ave S60 116 C2
Royds Close Cres S65 98 E2
Royds La
Hoyland S74 77 C5
Sheffield S4 129 E6
Royds Moor Hill S60 116 F1
Royds Pk HD8 30 A6
Royds The HD8 12 A3
Royd The S36 92 D7
Roy Kilner Rd
Wombwell S73 56 B4
Wombwell S73 56 C4
Royles Cl WF9 18 C2
Royston Ave
Bentley DN5 62 A7
Sheffield S20 143 A2
Royston Cl 5 S20 143 A2
Royston Croft 11 S20 143 A2
Royston Gr 4 S20 143 A2
Royston High Sch S71 15 C4
Royston Hill S74 76 D6
Royston La S71 15 C2
Royston Meadstead Prim Sch S71 15 B3
Royston Parkside Prim Sch S71 15 C3
Royston Rd S72 16 B1
Royston St John the Baptist CE Prim Sch S71 15 C3
Royston Summer Fields Prim Sch S71 15 A4
Rubens Cl S18 152 F1
Rubens Row 2 S2 161 C4
Ruby Ho S8 141 B5
Rud Broom La S36 51 C3
Rudd Broom Cl S36 51 C2
Ruddle La S66 100 E4
Ruddle Mill La S66 101 C1
Rudgate La DN14 8 C6
Rudston Prep Sch S60 115 F5
Rudyard Ct 4 S6 128 C8
Rudyard Rd S6 128 C8
Rufford Ave S71 34 A8
Rufford Cl WF4 16 A8
Rufford Ct S20 144 A2
Rufford Rd DN4 62 F1
Rufford Rise
Goldthorpe S63 58 C4
Sheffield S20 144 A2
Rufus La DN11 84 E1
Rugby St S3 129 A6
Rugged Butts La DN10 105 F5
Rundle Dr S7 140 E7
Rundle Rd
Sheffield S7 140 E7
Stocksbridge S36 73 B1
Runnymede Rd DN2 63 B4
Rupert Rd S7 140 E6
Rural Cres DN3 85 D8
Rural La S6 111 F2
Ruscombe Pl S71 15 C1
Rushby St S4 113 D1
Rushdale Ave S8 141 B5
Rushdale Mount 4 S8 141 A5
Rushdale Rd S8 141 B5
Rushdale Terr 3 S8 141 A5
Rushey Cl S62 97 E8
Rushleigh Ct S17 151 D7
Rushley Ave S17 151 D8
Rushley Cl
Auckley DN9 86 A6
Sheffield S17 151 D8
Rushley Dr S17 151 D7
Rushley Rd S17 151 D7
Rushworth Cl S75 32 C8
Rushy La S36 91 F4
Rushy Moor Ave DN6 22 B7
Rushy Moor La DN6 22 B7
Rushy Moor Rd DN5 22 D6
Ruskin Ave S64 80 B6
Ruskin Cl S63 78 C7
Ruskin Dr DN3 64 C6
Ruskin Ho S6 128 B6
Ruskin Rd DN4 83 A6
Ruskin Sq S8 141 A6
Russell Ave DN11 121 F4
Russell Cl
Aston S26 144 B7
Barnsley S71 34 B5
Russell Ct S11 140 A2
Russell Pl S66 119 A6
Russell Rd S62 98 E7
Russell St
Rotherham S65 115 E8
Sheffield S3 161 A5
Russet Gr DN10 123 A7
Russett Ct S66 118 D6
Rustlings Ct S11 139 F8
Rustlings Rd S11 140 B8
Ruston Dr S71 15 C4
Ruthin St S4 129 E8
Ruth Sq S10 160 B2
Ruthven Dr DN4 82 D7
Rutland Ave S25 146 D7
Rutland Cres DN11 121 F5
Rutland Ct S10 160 A2
Rutland Dr DN11 121 F5
Rutland La DN11 84 D1
Rutland Pk S10 128 C2
Rutland Pl S73 56 B2
Rutland Rd S3 129 A6
Rutland St DN1 62 E4
Rutland Way
Barnsley S75 33 C3
Sheffield S3 128 F5
Ryan Dr S13 143 E7
Ryan Pl S62 97 F4
Rydal Cl
Bolton u D S63 58 C1
Dinnington S25 146 F7
Dronfield S18 152 D1
Penistone S36 51 D4
Rydal Ct DN4 83 A4
Rydale Gdns DN10 105 A1
Rydalhurst Ave S6 112 A2
Rydall Pl DN5 61 F8
Rydal Rd
Adwick le S DN6 21 C1
Dinnington S25 146 F7
Sheffield S8 140 E5
Rydal Terr S71 34 A1
Rydal Way S64 80 C6
Rye Bank S60 116 D1
Rye Croft
Barnsley S71 34 A6
Conisbrough DN12 81 E2
Tickhill DN11 121 A8
Ryecroft Ave DN6 4 C3
Ryecroft Farm Cl S72 16 D7
Ryecroft Glen Rd S17 152 A8
Ryecroft Rd
Norton DN6 4 C2

Ryecroft Rd *continued*
Rawmarsh S62 ... 98 C6
Ryecroft View S17 ... 151 D8
Ryedale Wlk DN5 ... 61 C7
Ryefield Gdns S11 ... 140 A5
Ryegate Cres S10 ... 128 B3
Ryegate Rd S10 ... 128 B3
Rye La S6 ... 126 E7
Ryeview Gdns S61 ... 97 B2
Ryhill Dr S20 ... 143 A2
Ryhill Pits La WF4 ... 15 F8
Ryle Rd S7 ... 140 E7
Rylstone Ct S12 ... 143 B2
Rylstone Gr S12 ... 143 B2
Rylstone Wlk S70 ... 55 D6
Ryton Ave S73 ... 56 F1
Ryton Cl S66 ... 119 A5
Ryton Rd S25 ... 146 D5
Ryton Way DN4 ... 85 A6

S

Sackerville Terr S21 ... 156 B7
Sackup La S75 ... 13 F1
Sackville Rd S10 ... 128 B4
Sackville St S70 ... 33 E2
Sacred Heart RC Prim Sch
Goldthorpe S63 ... 58 E6
Hemsworth WF9 ... 17 D6
Sheffield S6 ... 128 C7
Saddler Ave S20 ... 143 D1
Saddler Cl S20 ... 143 D1
Saddler Gn S20 ... 143 D1
Saddler Gr S20 ... 143 D1
Sadler's Gate S73 ... 56 C4
Sadler Gate 5 S70 ... 33 E2
Saffron Cl DN11 ... 120 F7
Saffron Cres DN11 ... 120 F7
Saffron Rd DN11 ... 120 F7
St Agnes' Rd DN4 ... 63 A2
St Aidan's Ave S2 ... 141 D8
St Aidan's Dr S2 ... 141 E8
St Aidan's Pl S2 ... 141 E8
St Aidan's Rd S2 ... 141 E8
St Aidan's Way S2 ... 141 E8
St Aidans CE Prim Sch
DN2 ... 42 D1
St Alban's RC Prim Sch
DN12 ... 81 A3
St Alban's Way S66 ... 117 B4
St Albans CE Prim Sch
S66 ... 117 B4
St Albans Cl S10 ... 127 C1
St Albans Ct S66 ... 117 B4
St Albans Dr S10 ... 127 B1
St Albans Rd S10 ... 127 C1
St Andrew's Cl
Sheffield S11 ... 140 D7
Swinton S64 ... 79 D1
St Andrew's Prim Sch
S18 ... 152 D1
St Andrew's Rd
Conisbrough DN12 ... 81 B1
Sheffield S11 ... 140 D7
St Andrew's Sq S63 ... 58 C2
St Andrew's Terr DN4 ... 62 E1
St Andrew's Way DN3 ... 43 A6
St Andrew Rd S36 ... 92 E8
St Andrews Cl
Dinnington S25 ... 146 F8
Doncaster DN4 ... 85 B6
Rotherham S66 ... 117 C7
St Andrews Cres S74 ... 76 E6
St Andrews Dr S75 ... 14 A1
St Andrews Gr DN7 ... 44 B7
St Andrews Rd S74 ... 76 E6
St Andrews Way S71 ... 56 A7
St Andrews Wlk S60 ... 115 A1
St Ann's Jun & Inf Sch
S65 ... 115 F7
St Ann's RC Prim Sch S36 92 B8
St Ann's Rd
Rotherham S65 ... 115 E7
Stocksbridge S36 ... 73 D1
St Anne's Dr S71 ... 34 D6
St Anne's Rd DN4 ... 63 A2
St Anthony Rd S10 ... 128 A4
St Augustine's Rd DN4 ... 63 C1
St Austell Dr S75 ... 32 E4
St Barbara's Cl S66 ... 118 E4
St Barbara's Rd S73 ... 56 F5
St Barnabas Ho 12 S2 ... 141 A8
St Barnabas La 4 S2 ... 141 A8
St Barnabas Rd 5 S2 ... 141 A8
St Bart's Terr 14 S70 ... 54 F8
St Bartholomew's Cl S66 118 E4
St Bartholomews Rise
DN2 ... 63 D1
St Bede's RC Prim Sch
S61 ... 114 E8
St Bede's Rd S60 ... 115 C6
St Benedicts Ct S2 ... 141 D8
St Bernard's RC High Sch
S65 ... 116 C5
St Catherine's Ave DN4 ... 83 C8
St Catherine's Dr DN7 ... 43 E4
St Catherine's Hospl DN4 . 83 B5
St Catherine's RC Prim Sch
S4 ... 129 B8
St Catherines Way S75 ... 33 B1
St Cecilia's Rd DN4 ... 63 A1
St Chad's Sq DN12 ... 80 F4
St Chad's Way DN5 ... 61 D1
St Charles St S9 ... 129 E6
St Christopher's DN4 ... 83 A7
St Christopher's Cres DN5 61 E6
St Christophers Cl S71 ... 56 A7
St Clement's Cl DN5 ... 61 D6
St Clements Cl S71 ... 56 A7
St Clements Ct S13 ... 143 B6
St David's Dr
Barnsley S71 ... 55 F8
Bentley DN5 ... 61 D6
South Anston S25 ... 146 D4
St David's Rd DN12 ... 81 B2
St David Rd S36 ... 92 E8
St Davids Dr S60 ... 115 A1
St Dominic's Cl DN5 ... 82 B8
St Dominic's RC Prim Sch
S71 ... 34 C7
St Edmund's Ave S66 ... 133 E6
St Edwards Ave S70 ... 54 D8
St Edwin Reach DN7 ... 24 F1
St Edwins Cl DN7 ... 44 A8
St Edwins Dr DN7 ... 44 A7
St Elizabeth Cl S2 ... 141 B8
St Eric's Rd DN4 ... 63 D1
St Francis Bvd S71 ... 34 D7
St Francis Cl
Rotherham S66 ... 117 C7
Sheffield S10 ... 127 E2
St Francis Xavier RC Prim
Sch DN4 ... 62 C1
St George's Ave
Dunsville DN7 ... 43 F5
Swinton S64 ... 79 C3
St George's Church S1 ... 160 C3
St George's Cl S3 ... 160 B3
St George's Rd
Barnsley S70 ... 54 E8
Doncaster DN4 ... 63 C1
St George's Terr S1 ... 160 C3
St George Cl S81 ... 147 E4
St George Gate DN1 ... 62 C3
St George Rd S36 ... 92 E8
St Georges Cl DN8 ... 26 D5
St George's Ct S1 ... 160 C3
St Georges Dr S60 ... 131 A8
St Georges Rd DN8 ... 26 D5
St Gerard's RC Prim Sch
S65 ... 98 E2
St Giles CE Prim Sch
S21 ... 156 C6
St Giles Gate DN5 ... 61 D6
St Giles Sq S35 ... 94 F5
St Helen's Ave
Barnsley S71 ... 34 B5
Hemsworth WF9 ... 17 C7
St Helen's Bvd S71 ... 34 B6
St Helen's La DN5 ... 59 E3
St Helen's Prim Sch S71 ... 34 D5
St Helen's Rd DN4 ... 63 A2
St Helen's Sq DN3 ... 42 F4
St Helen's St S74 ... 77 A6
St Helen Rd S36 ... 92 E7
St Helens CE Jun & Inf Sch
WF9 ... 17 C6
St Helens Cl
Thurnscoe S63 ... 58 B8
Treeton S60 ... 131 F3
St Helens Ct S74 ... 77 A6
St Helen's RC Prim Sch
S74 ... 76 D6
St Helens Way S71 ... 34 D5
St Helier Dr S75 ... 33 B2
St Hilda's Rd DN4 ... 63 A2
St Hilda Ave S70 ... 33 C1
St Hilda Cl S36 ... 92 E7
St Hildas Cl S63 ... 37 E1
St James' Dr S65 ... 99 D3
St James' Gdns DN4 ... 62 B1
St James' Row 3 S1 ... 161 A3
St James's Bridge DN4 ... 62 C2
St James' St S1 ... 161 A3
St James' View S65 ... 99 D3
St James Ave
Dunsville DN7 ... 43 F5
South Anston S25 ... 146 D4
St James Cl
Kirk Sandall DN3 ... 42 F4
Wath u D S63 ... 79 A6
St James' Cl S70 ... 55 A4
St James Sq S74 ... 76 E6
St James St DN1 ... 62 D1
St James Wlk S13 ... 143 D8
St Joan Ave S36 ... 92 E7
St John's Ave
Barnsley S75 ... 32 E4
Rotherham S60 ... 115 B7
St John's Cl
Dodworth S75 ... 53 E6
Penistone S36 ... 51 C2
Rotherham S65 ... 116 A8
St John's Ct
Laughton en le M S25 ... 134 E4
Rotherham S66 ... 117 C6
St John's Gn S61 ... 96 E1
St John's Rd
Barnsley S70 ... 54 E8
Cudworth S72 ... 35 B6
Doncaster DN4 ... 83 A8
Laughton en le M S25 ... 134 E4
New Edlington DN12 ... 82 B2
Rotherham S65 ... 116 A8
Sheffield S2 ... 129 D4
Stocksbridge S36 ... 92 F8
Swinton S64 ... 79 C3
St John's Wlk S71 ... 15 D4
St John Fisher RC Prim Sch
S12 ... 143 A3
St Johns S36 ... 51 F6
St Johns Ave S66 ... 117 C6
St John's Croft DN11 ... 102 B6
St Johns Ct S60 ... 115 B6
St Johns Wlk S64 ... 79 F8
St John the Baptist CE Inf
Sch S36 ... 51 C2
St John the Baptist CE Jun
Sch S36 ... 51 C2
St Joseph's Ct S25 ... 134 F1
St Joseph's RC Prim Sch
Dinnington S25 ... 134 F1
Rawmarsh S62 ... 98 A5
Rossington DN11 ... 84 F1
Sheffield S13 ... 130 F1
St Joseph's Rd S13 ... 130 F1
St Joseph & St Teresa's RC
Prim Sch DN6 ... 40 C4
St Josephs Gdns S70 ... 55 B8
St Josephs RC Prim Sch
WF9 ... 18 E3
St Julien's Mount S75 ... 31 E4
St Julien's Way S75 ... 31 E4
St Lawrence's Terr DN6 ... 40 C6
St Lawrence Ct DN6 ... 40 A6
St Lawrence Glebe S9 ... 114 E2
St Lawrence Rd
Dunscroft DN7 ... 43 F7
Sheffield S9 ... 114 E2
St Leger Way S25 ... 134 F2
St Leonard's DN11 ... 121 A7
St Leonard's Cl S25 ... 146 F8
St Leonard's Croft S65 ... 98 F3
St Leonard's La S65 ... 115 F7
St Leonard's Lea DN5 ... 61 E6
St Leonard's Pl S65 ... 115 F7
St Leonard's Rd S65 ... 115 F7
St Leonards Ave S65 ... 99 A2
St Leonards Cl S5 ... 113 B3
St Leonards Way S71 ... 56 A7
St Luke's CE Prim Sch
S81 ... 159 F7
St Luke's Cl DN7 ... 43 E4
St Luke's Hospice S11 ... 139 F3
St Lukes View S81 ... 159 F7
St Lukes Way S71 ... 34 C3
St Margaret's Ct WF9 ... 19 B6
St Margaret's Dr S64 ... 79 B3
St Margaret's Rd
Doncaster DN4 ... 63 A1
Sheffield S35 ... 113 B7
St Margaret Ave S36 ... 92 E8
St Margarets Ave DN5 ... 59 C3
St Maries RC Prim Sch
S10 ... 128 A1
St Mark's Cres S10 ... 160 A2
St Mark Rd S36 ... 92 E8
St Marks Ct HD8 ... 28 E6
St Martin's Ave DN5 ... 61 F6
St Martin's Cl S81 ... 136 A6
St Martin Cl S36 ... 92 E8
St Martins Ave DN10 ... 123 A8
St Martins Cl S75 ... 33 B1
St Mary's CE Prim Sch
Barnsley S75 ... 33 C2
Worsbrough S70 ... 54 F1
St Mary's Cl
Sheffield S35 ... 95 A1
South Elmsall WF9 ... 19 A2
St Mary's Cres
Doncaster DN1 ... 62 E4
Swinton S64 ... 79 C4
Tickhill DN11 ... 121 A7
St Mary's Ct DN11 ... 121 A7
St Mary's Dr
Armthorpe DN3 ... 64 C6
Catliffe S60 ... 131 C6
Dunsville DN7 ... 43 E4
St Mary's Gate
4 Barnsley S70 ... 33 E2
Sheffield S2, S3 ... 160 C1
Tickhill DN11 ... 121 A7
St Mary's Gdn S70 ... 55 A2
St Mary's La S35 ... 95 A1
St Mary's Pl S70 ... 33 E2
St Mary's RC Prim Sch
S65 ... 116 C6
St Mary's RC Prim Sch High
Gn S35 ... 94 E8
St Mary's Rd
Darfield S73 ... 57 B5
Doncaster DN1 ... 62 E4
Dunsville DN7 ... 43 E4
Goldthorpe S63 ... 58 F6
New Edlington DN12 ... 82 C1
Rawmarsh S62 ... 98 A5
Sheffield S1, S2 ... 161 B1
Tickhill DN11 ... 121 A7
St Mary's Sch DN4 ... 84 D8
St Mary's Sq S2 ... 160 C1
St Mary's St S36 ... 51 D3
St Mary's View S61 ... 97 B3
St Mary Cres S36 ... 92 F7
St Mary's CE Prim Sch
S6 ... 128 D6
St Marys Cl S72 ... 35 B6
St Mary's RC Prim Sch
Maltby S66 ... 119 B4
New Edlington DN12 ... 82 B2
St Marys Rd S73 ... 56 C2
St Marys Terr S36 ... 92 C6
St Mary's Wlk DN5 ... 82 B8
St Matthew's Cl S21 ... 156 B1
St Matthews Way S71 ... 34 C3
St Matthias Rd S36 ... 92 E8
St Michael's Ave
Barnsley S71 ... 34 D6
Swinton S64 ... 79 D4
St Michael's CE Prim Sch
S32 ... 149 A8
St Michael's Cl
Sheffield S35 ... 113 B8
Thorne DN8 ... 26 D6
St Michael's Cres S35 ... 113 B7
St Michael's Dr DN8 ... 26 D6
St Michael's RC & CE High
Sch S71 ... 34 B7
St Michael's Rd
Doncaster DN4 ... 63 B1
Sheffield S35 ... 113 B7
St Michael & All Angels RC
Prim Sch S73 ... 56 F4
St Michaels Ave DN11 ... 85 A2
St Michaels Cl S63 ... 58 D5
St Nicholas Cl DN3 ... 42 E2
St Nicholas Rd DN8 ... 26 B7
St Nicholas Way DN10 ... 123 A6
St Nicolas Rd S62 ... 98 A6
St Nicolas Wlk S62 ... 98 B6
St Oswald's Cl DN9 ... 86 D3
St Oswald's Dr
Finningley DN9 ... 86 E3
Kirk Sandall DN3 ... 42 F2
St Oswald Ct 2 WF9 ... 17 E6
St Owens Dr S75 ... 33 B2
St Pancras Cl S25 ... 134 C2
St Patrick's RC Prim Sch
S5 ... 113 C4
St Patrick's Rd DN2 ... 63 A5
St Patrick's Way DN5 ... 61 D6
St Patrick Rd S36 ... 92 E8
St Patrick's RC Prim Sch
DN11 ... 122 B4
St Paul's Cl WF9 ... 19 D8
St Paul's Par
Barnsley S71 ... 56 A7
Bentley DN5 ... 61 E5
Sheffield S1 ... 161 A3
St Paul Cl
Stocksbridge S36 ... 92 E8
Todwick S26 ... 145 E5
St Pauls Cl S25 ... 134 C3
St Pauls Rd S75 ... 33 C3
St Peter's Cl
Barnburgh DN5 ... 59 C4
Brinsworth S60 ... 131 A8
Sheffield S1 ... 161 A4
St Peter's Dr DN12 ... 81 C1
St Peter's Gate S63 ... 37 C1
St Peter's RC Prim Sch
DN4 ... 63 A1
St Peter's Rd
Conisbrough DN12 ... 81 B1
Doncaster DN4 ... 82 E7
Thorpe Salvin S80 ... 158 E7
St Peter's Terr 1 S70 ... 55 A8
St Peter Ave S36 ... 92 F8
St Peter's Cl DN3 ... 42 E8
St Peter's Terr DN6 ... 22 A8
St Philip's La S3 ... 160 C5
St Philip's Rd S3 ... 160 B4
St Phillip's Cl S66 ... 118 E4
St Quentin Cl S17 ... 152 B5
St Quentin Dr S17 ... 152 B5
St Quentin Mount S17 ... 152 B5
St Quentin Rise S17 ... 152 B5
St Quentin View S17 ... 152 B5
St Ronan's Rd S7 ... 140 F7
St Sepulchre Gate DN1 ... 62 C3
St Sepulchre Gate W DN1,
DN4 ... 62 C2
St Stephen's Dr S26 ... 144 D8
St Stephen's Rd S65 ... 115 E7
St Stephen's Wlk S3 ... 160 B4
St Stephens Rd S3 ... 160 B4
St Stephens Wlk DN5 ... 61 E5
St Theresa's RC Prim Sch
S2 ... 142 B7
St Thomas's Cl DN4 ... 82 E6
St Thomas's Rd S75 ... 33 A4
St Thomas Ct DN4 ... 84 D6
St Thomas More RC Prim
Sch S35 ... 112 E7
St Thomas of Canterbury RC
Prim Sch S8 ... 152 F8
St Thomas Rd S10 ... 128 B3
St Thomas St S1 ... 160 C3
St Ursula's Rd DN4 ... 63 A2
St Veronica Rd S36 ... 92 F7
St Vincent's Ave DN3 ... 85 C8
St Vincent Ave
Adwick le S DN6 ... 39 F6
Doncaster DN1 ... 62 E4
St Vincent Rd DN1 ... 62 E4
St Wandrilles Cl S35 ... 95 B1
St Wilfrid's RC Prim Sch
S7 ... 140 C4
St Wilfrid's Rd
Doncaster DN4 ... 84 D8
11 Sheffield S2 ... 141 A8
St Withold Ave S66 ... 133 E6
Salcombe Cl S75 ... 33 C8
Salcombe Gr DN10 ... 122 F8
Sale Hill S10 ... 128 B2
Salerno Way S73 ... 56 E6
Sales La DN14 ... 7 D5
Sale St S74 ... 76 A5
Salisbury Rd
Doncaster DN4 ... 62 A1
Maltby S66 ... 119 A6
Sheffield S10 ... 128 B4
Salisbury St S75 ... 33 D3
Salisbury Wlk S81 ... 148 E7
Salmon St 5 S11 ... 140 F8
Salt Box Gr S35 ... 112 C7
Salt Box La S35 ... 112 D7
Salter's Way S36 ... 51 D2
Salter Hill La S36 ... 72 F6
Salter Oak Croft S71 ... 15 C1
Saltersbrook S63 ... 58 D5
Saltersbrook Rd S73 ... 57 A7
Salt Hill S81 ... 136 B5
Salt Hill Rd S81 ... 136 C4
Samson St S2 ... 161 C2
Samuel Cl S2 ... 141 D7
Samuel Dr S2 ... 141 D7
Samuel Pl S2 ... 141 D7
Samuel Rd
Barnsley S75 ... 33 B3
Sheffield S2 ... 141 D8
Samuel Sq S75 ... 33 B3
Samuel St DN4 ... 83 A6
Sanctuary Fields S25 ... 146 D7
Sandal Ct S61 ... 115 B7
Sandall Beat La DN2 ... 63 D5
Sandall Beat Rd DN2 ... 63 C3
Sandall Beat Wood Nat Res
& Visitor Ctr* DN2, DN3,
DN4 ... 63 E4
Sandall Beat Wood Trail*
DN2 ... 63 E5
Sandall Carr Rd DN3 ... 42 E3
Sandall La DN3 ... 42 E4
Sandall Park Dr DN2 ... 63 C7
Sandall Rise DN2 ... 63 B6
Sandall Stones Rd DN3 ... 42 D3
Sandall View S25 ... 134 C3
Sandall Wood Sch DN2 ... 63 D5
Sandal Rd DN12 ... 81 B1
Sandalwood Cl DN2 ... 63 C8
Sandalwood Rise S62 ... 98 D8
Sandbeck Cl S71 ... 33 F3
Sandbeck Ct
Bawtry DN10 ... 123 A8
Conisbrough DN12 ... 80 F3
3 Rossington DN11 ... 104 A8
Sandbeck Ho 4 DN1 ... 62 C2
Sandbeck La S66 ... 120 B2
Sandbeck Pl S11 ... 140 D8
Sandbeck Rd DN4 ... 62 F2
Sandbeck Way S66 ... 118 A5
Sandbed Rd S3 ... 128 E7
Sandbergh Rd S61 ... 96 E2
Sandby Croft S14 ... 141 E2
Sandby Ct S14 ... 141 E2
Sandby Dr S14 ... 141 E2
Sandcliffe Rd DN2 ... 63 B6
Sandcroft Cl S74 ... 76 C5
Sandeby Dr S65 ... 117 D7
Sanderson's Bank DN10 ... 87 F4
Sanderson St S9 ... 129 F7
Sandford Ct
14 Barnsley S70 ... 33 D1
Barnsley S70 ... 54 D8
Sandford Grove Rd S7 ... 140 E6
Sandford Rd
Doncaster DN4 ... 83 A7
South Elmsall WF9 ... 19 A5
Sandhill Cl S62 ... 98 B7
Sandhill Ct S72 ... 36 F1
Sandhill Gr S72 ... 17 A1
Sandhill Prim Sch S72 ... 36 E1
Sandhill Rd S62 ... 98 B7
Sandhill Rise DN9 ... 86 A7
Sandhurst Pl S10 ... 128 C4
Sandhurst Rd DN4 ... 85 A6
Sandiron Ho S7 ... 140 B1
Sand La DN9 ... 66 F4
Sand La Terr DN9 ... 66 F4
Sandon View S10 ... 160 B2
Sandown Cl S21 ... 155 B2
Sandown Gdns DN4 ... 63 D2
Sandown Rd S64 ... 80 B6
Sandpiper Rd S61 ... 95 F6
Sandpit Hill DN3 ... 85 D8
Sandringham Ave S60 ... 116 B1
Sandringham Cl S36 ... 51 A4
Sandringham Ct DN11 ... 122 B5
Sandringham Pl
Rotherham S65 ... 117 D8
Sheffield S10 ... 126 F1
Sandringham Prim Sch
DN2 ... 63 B6
Sandringham Rd
Doncaster DN2 ... 63 B4
Sheffield S9 ... 114 A4
Sandrock Dr DN4 ... 84 E7
Sandrock Rd DN11 ... 121 F5
Sands Cl S14 ... 141 E4
Sands The S6 ... 110 A4
Sandstone Ave S9 ... 113 F2
Sandstone Cl S9 ... 114 A3
Sandstone Dr S9 ... 113 F2
Sandstone Rd S9 ... 114 A3
Sandtoft Rd DN7 ... 45 C8
Sandwith Rd S26 ... 145 E5
Sandy Acres Cl S20 ... 143 F1
Sandy Acres Dr S20 ... 143 F1
Sandybridge La S72 ... 16 B4
Sandybridge Lane Ind Est
S72 ... 16 B3
Sandycroft Cres DN4 ... 82 E6
Sandyfields View DN6 ... 21 B1
Sandy Flat La S66 ... 117 B2
Sandygate S63 ... 78 F5
Sandygate Cres S63 ... 78 F4
Sandygate Ct S10 ... 127 D2
Sandygate Gr S10 ... 127 D2
Sandygate Grange Dr
S10 ... 127 E2
Sandygate La WF9 ... 17 C7
Sandygate Park Cres
S10 ... 127 D2
Sandygate Park Rd S10 ... 127 D2
Sandygate Pk S10 ... 127 D2
Sandygate Rd S10 ... 127 E2

Sandy La
Doncaster DN4 ... 63 A1
Hoyland S74 ... 55 F2
Rotherham S66 ... 117 F3
Thurcroft S66 ... 133 F7
Sandymount DN11 ... 122 A5
Sandymount E DN11 ... 122 A4
Sandymount Rd S63 ... 79 A6
Sandymount W DN11 ... 122 A4
Sankey Sq S63 ... 58 D5
Saracens La DN10 ... 122 F2
Sarah Ct DN3 ... 64 E7
Sarah St
4 Mexborough S64 ... 80 A4
Rotherham S61 ... 115 B6
Sargeson Rd DN3 ... 63 F6
Sark Rd S2 ... 141 A7
Sarrius Ct DN4 ... 84 E8
Saundby Cl DN4 ... 84 C7
Saunderson Rd S36 ... 51 B4
Saunders Pl S2 ... 129 E3
Saunders Rd S2 ... 129 E3
Saunders Row S73 ... 56 C2
Savage La S17 ... 151 D7
Savile St E S4 ... 129 D6
Savile St S4 ... 161 C5
Savile Wlk S72 ... 17 B3
Saville Ct S74 ... 76 F7
Saville Hall La S75 ... 53 F6
Saville La S36 ... 51 A3
Saville Rd
Dodworth S75 ... 54 A6
Rotherham S60 ... 116 B1
Wath u D S63 ... 78 E6
Saville St
Cudworth S72 ... 35 B7
Rotherham S65 ... 98 C1
Saville Terr 7 S70 ... 54 E8
Sawdon Rd S11 ... 128 E1
Sawn Moor Ave S66 ... 133 F6
Sawn Moor Rd S66 ... 133 F5
Sawston Cl DN4 ... 83 A4
Saxon Ave WF9 ... 17 F2
Saxon Cl WF9 ... 19 E7
Saxon Cres S70 ... 55 A5
Saxon Ct DN4 ... 84 F6
Saxon Gr WF9 ... 18 A1
Saxonlea Ave S2 ... 130 C1
Saxonlea Cres S2 ... 130 C1
Saxonlea Ct S2 ... 130 C1
Saxonlea Dr 4 S2 ... 130 B1
Saxon Mount WF9 ... 17 F1
Saxon Rd
Kiveton Park S26 ... 145 F2
Rotherham S61 ... 114 D6
Sheffield S2 ... 141 A6
Saxon Row DN12 ... 81 E2
Saxon St
Cudworth S72 ... 35 B6
Thurnscoe S63 ... 58 E8
Saxon Way DN11 ... 121 F4
Saxton Ave DN4 ... 63 C1
Saxton Cl S74 ... 77 B6
Saxton Dr S60 ... 115 F1
Sayers Cl DN5 ... 59 C2
Scafell Pl S25 ... 146 F6
Scaftworth Cl DN4 ... 84 C7
Scaly Gate
Shepley, Barnside HD9 ... 28 A2
Shepley HD9 ... 28 A5
Scammadine Cl S60 ... 131 D8
Scampton Lodge S5 ... 113 B2
Scarborough Cl
North Anston S25 ... 146 E7
Tickhill DN11 ... 121 A7
Scarborough La DN11 ... 84 E1
Scarborough Rd
Rotherham S66 ... 117 B5
Sheffield S9 ... 130 C5
Scarbrough Cres S66 ... 119 A4
Scarbrough Farm Ct S66 118 F5
Scarfield Cl S71 ... 55 F8
Scar Hole La HD8, HD9 ... 28 A3
Scar La S71 ... 55 F8
Scarlett Oak Mdw 5 S6 127 C6
Scarll Rd DN4 ... 62 A1
Scarsdale Cross 1 S18 .. 153 B1
Scarsdale Rd
2 Dronfield S18 ... 153 B1
Sheffield S8 ... 140 F3
Scarsdale St S25 ... 135 A1
Scarth Ave DN4 ... 83 B8
Scawsby La DN5 ... 61 B8
Scawsby Rosedale Prim Sch DN5 ... 61 D7
Scawsby Saltersgate Inf & Jun Sch DN5 ... 61 E6
Scawthorpe Ave DN5 ... 40 D1
Scawthorpe Cotts DN5 ... 61 C8
Scawthorpe Sunnyfields Prim Sch DN5 ... 61 E7
Sceptone Gr S72 ... 16 C3
Sceptre Gr DN11 ... 103 E7
Schofield Dr S73 ... 57 A6
Schofield Pl S73 ... 57 A6
Schofield Rd
Darfield S73 ... 57 A6
Stocksbridge S36 ... 92 D8
Schofield St S64 ... 79 F5
Sch of Nursing & Midwifery S3 ... 160 B4
Schole Ave S36 ... 51 C3
Schole Hill La S36 ... 51 B2
Scholes Field Cl S61 ... 96 C2
Scholes Gn S61 ... 96 C3
Scholes La S61 ... 96 B4
Scholes Moor Rd HD9 ... 48 B8
Scholes Rise S35 ... 113 B8
Scholes View
Hoyland, Jump S74 ... 76 F7
Hoyland, Milton S74 ... 76 E5
Sheffield S35 ... 95 B1
Scholey Ave S81 ... 147 E3
Scholey Rd S66 ... 117 B5
Scholey St S3 ... 161 B5
Scholfield Cres S66 ... 119 B4
School Ave S20 ... 155 F7
School Cl
Sheffield S20 ... 155 F7
Wales S26 ... 145 B2
School Ct DN1 ... 62 D4
Schoolfield Dr S62 ... 97 F7
School Gr S26 ... 144 E7
School Green La S10 ... 139 B7
School Hill
Cudworth S72 ... 35 B7
Rotherham S60 ... 116 B1
School Ho S35 ... 111 C7
School La
Auckley DN9 ... 86 A6
Denby Dale HD8 ... 30 A6
Doncaster DN3 ... 85 B8
Dronfield S18 ... 153 A1
Eckington S21 ... 154 E3
Hathersage S32 ... 149 A8
Rawmarsh S62 ... 97 E3
Rotherham S65 ... 98 F3
Sheffield, Greenhill S8 ... 152 F7
Sheffield, Grenoside S35 ... 94 C1
Sheffield, Park Hill S2 ... 161 C3
Sheffield S8 ... 141 C1
Sheffield, Stannington S6 . 127 C5
Stainton S66 ... 119 E8
Wharncliffe Side S35 ... 93 B1
School Lane Cl S8 ... 141 C1
School Rd
Chapeltown S35 ... 94 F6
Langold S81 ... 136 E3
Laughton en le M S25 ... 134 D4
Sheffield S10 ... 128 C4
Sheffield, Sothall S20 ... 144 B3
Thurcroft S66 ... 133 F6
Wales S26 ... 145 A2
School St
Aston S26 ... 144 C7
Barnsley S75 ... 33 D3
Barnsley, Stairfoot S70 ... 55 E8
Bolton u D S63 ... 58 C2
Cudworth S72 ... 35 B8
Darfield S73 ... 57 B6
Darton S75 ... 13 E1
Dinnington S25 ... 134 F1
Eckington S21 ... 155 D3
Great Houghton S72 ... 36 E2
Hoyland S73 ... 77 C8
, Mapplewell S75 ... 14 C1
Rotherham S65 ... 98 E2
Sheffield S20 ... 155 D7
Thurnscoe S63 ... 58 D8
Upton WF9 ... 19 D8
Wombwell S73 ... 56 D3
School Terr DN12 ... 81 B2
School Wlk
Bawtry DN10 ... 123 A7
Conisbrough DN12 ... 81 A4
Maltby S66 ... 119 A5
New Edlington DN12 ... 101 A7
Scorah's La S64 ... 79 A3
Scorcher Hills La DN6 ... 20 E5
Scotch Spring La S66 ... 119 E7
Scotia Cl S2 ... 141 F8
Scotia Dr S2 ... 141 F8
Scot La
Bawtry DN10 ... 123 A7
Doncaster DN1 ... 62 D3
Scotland St S3 ... 161 A4
Scott Ave
Barnburgh DN5 ... 59 C2
Conisbrough DN12 ... 81 A2
Scott Cl S66 ... 133 E6
Scott Cres DN3 ... 42 E3
Scott Hill DN5 ... 82 B8
Scott Rd S4 ... 129 C8
Scott St S4 ... 129 E8
Scott Way S35 ... 94 F4
Scott Wlk S66 ... 118 D6
Scovell Ave S62 ... 97 D7
Scovell Ho S62 ... 97 D7
Scowerdons Cl S12 ... 142 F5
Scowerdons Dr S12 ... 142 F5
Scraith Wood Dr S5 ... 112 E2
Scratta La S80 ... 159 C2
Scrooby Cl DN11 ... 122 A4
Scrooby Dr S61 ... 97 C3
Scrooby La S62 ... 97 D3
Scrooby Pl S61 ... 97 C3
Scrooby Rd
Bircotes DN11 ... 122 C4
Harworth DN11 ... 121 F3
Scrooby St S61 ... 97 C3
Sea Breeze Terr S13 ... 142 D8
Seabrook Rd S2 ... 129 D2
Seagrave Ave S12 ... 142 B4
Seagrave Cres S12 ... 142 B4
Seagrave Dr S12 ... 142 B4
Seagrave Rd S12 ... 142 B4
Searby Rd S66 ... 117 D7
Seaton Cl S2 ... 129 F2
Seaton Cres S2 ... 129 F2
Seaton Gdns DN11 ... 103 F7
Seaton Pl S2 ... 129 F2
Seaton Way S2 ... 129 F2
Sebastian View S60 ... 115 C2
Seckar La WF4 ... 14 B8
Second Ave
Adwick le S DN6 ... 40 C4
Finningley DN9 ... 86 B4
South Kirkby WF9 ... 17 F1
Upton WF9 ... 19 A8
Second La
Rotherham S66 ... 117 D2
South Anston S25 ... 146 E3
Second Sq DN7 ... 24 E4
Sedan St S4 ... 129 C7
Sedge Cl S66 ... 117 E4
Sedgefield Way S64 ... 80 B6
Sedgley Rd S6 ... 128 D8
Sefton Ct S10 ... 139 D7
Sefton Rd S10 ... 139 E7
Selborne Rd S10 ... 128 A3
Selborne St S65 ... 115 E8
Selbourne Cl S75 ... 32 E5
Selby Cl S26 ... 144 C7
Selby Rd
Barnsley S71 ... 33 F7
Doncaster DN2 ... 63 A5
Moorends DN8 ... 8 E5
Sheffield S4 ... 113 D1
Walden Stubbs DN6 ... 5 A4
Selhurst Cres DN4 ... 84 E7
Selig Par S12 ... 142 C2
Selkirk Ave DN4 ... 82 D6
Selkirk Rd DN2 ... 63 C6
Sellars Rd S61 ... 96 E1
Sellars Row S35 ... 94 E8
Sellers St S8 ... 140 F7
Selly Oak Gr S8 ... 153 C6
Selly Oak Rd S8 ... 153 C6
Selwood S65 ... 115 F7
Selwyn St S65 ... 115 E8
Senior Rd
Doncaster DN4 ... 62 A2
Sheffield S9 ... 130 C4
Seniors Pl S35 ... 95 A6
Sennen Croft S71 ... 34 B3
Serlby Dr S26 ... 157 F5
Serlby Ho 6 DN1 ... 62 C2
Serlby La S26 ... 157 F6
Serlby Park Bsns & Ent Learning Com DN11 ... 122 C5
Serlby Rd DN11 ... 121 E2
Serpentine Wlk S8 ... 153 B8
Setcup La S21 ... 155 D2
Seth Terr S70 ... 55 A8
Sevenairs Fold S20 ... 143 E3
Sevenairs Rd S20 ... 143 E3
Sevenairs View S20 ... 143 E3
Sevenfields Ct S6 ... 112 A1
Sevenfields La S6 ... 112 A1
Severn Ct S10 ... 160 A3
Severn Rd S10 ... 160 A3
Severnside Dr S13 ... 143 A7
Severnside Gdns S13 ... 143 A7
Severnside Pl S13 ... 143 A7
Severnside Wlk S13 ... 143 A6
Sewell Rd S20 ... 155 F6
Sexton Dr S66 ... 117 D4
Seymore Rd S26 ... 144 E6
Seymour Rd S66 ... 119 B5
Shackleton Rd DN2 ... 42 D1
Shackleton View S36 ... 51 D2
Shady Side DN4 ... 62 A1
Shaftesbury Ave DN2 ... 63 B4
Shaftesbury Dr S74 ... 76 D5
Shaftesbury Ho DN2 ... 63 C5
Shaftesbury St S70 ... 55 E8
Shaftholme La DN5 ... 41 C6
Shaftholme Rd DN5 ... 41 D4
Shafton Hall Dr S72 ... 16 B3
Shafton Prim Sch S72 ... 16 C2
Shafton Rd S60 ... 116 B2
Shaftsbury Ave DN6 ... 39 F5
Shaftsbury Sq S65 ... 115 E7
Shakespeare Ave
Bentley DN5 ... 61 F4
Norton DN6 ... 4 C1
Shakespeare Dr S25 ... 147 A8
Shakespeare Rd
Bentley DN5 ... 41 B1
Rotherham S65 ... 115 F8
Wath u D S63 ... 78 D7
Shaldon Gr S26 ... 144 D7
Shalesmoor S3 ... 160 C5
Shambles St S70 ... 33 E1
Shardlow Ct DN4 ... 84 F6
Shardlow Gdns DN4 ... 84 F6
Sharlston Gdns DN11 ... 85 B1
Sharman Cl S18 ... 154 A1
Sharman Wlk S18 ... 154 A1
Sharpe Ave S8 ... 152 E8
Sharpfield Ave S62 ... 97 F8
Sharp Royd Nook S36 ... 73 C5
Sharrard Cl S12 ... 142 B5
Sharrard Dr S12 ... 142 B5
Sharrard Gr S12 ... 142 B6
Sharrard Rd S12 ... 142 B5
Sharrow Inf Sch S7 ... 140 F8
Sharrow Jun Sch S7 ... 140 F8
Sharrow La S11 ... 140 F8
Sharrow St S11 ... 140 F8
Sharrow Vale Rd S11 ... 140 D8
Sharrow View S7 ... 140 E8
Shaw Cl WF9 ... 19 A4
Shaw Ct DN3 ... 64 C5
Shawfield Cl DN3 ... 43 A6
Shawfield Rd S71 ... 34 C6
Shaw La
Barnsley, Carlton S71 ... 15 E1
Barnsley S70 ... 33 D1
Darton S75 ... 14 C2
Doncaster DN2 ... 63 D8
Shaw La *continued*
Fenwick DN6 ... 6 A4
Midhopestones S36 ... 71 D3
Shawlands Prim Sch S70 .. 54 D8
Shaw Lane Ind Est DN2 ... 63 D8
Shaw Rd
New Edlington DN12 ... 82 C3
Rotherham S65 ... 116 A8
Shawsfield Rd S60 ... 115 F3
Shaw St
Barnsley S70 ... 54 D8
Dronfield S18 ... 153 C4
Shaw Wood Prim Sch DN3 ... 64 A7
Shaw Wood Way DN2 ... 63 D7
Shay House La S36 ... 92 B8
Shay Rd S36 ... 73 C1
Shay The DN4 ... 84 E7
Sheaf Bank S2 ... 141 A7
Sheaf Bank Bsns Pk S2 . 141 A7
Sheaf Cl DN12 ... 81 D1
Sheaf Cres S63 ... 58 D1
Sheaf Ct S70 ... 55 D7
Sheaf Gardens Terr S2 ... 161 B1
Sheaf Gdns S2 ... 161 B1
Sheaf Sq S1 ... 161 B2
Sheaf St S1 ... 161 B3
Sheardown St DN4 ... 62 B2
Sheards Cl S18 ... 152 F1
Sheards Dr S18 ... 152 E1
Sheards Way S18 ... 152 F1
Shearman Ave S61 ... 96 E2
Shearwood Rd S10 ... 160 B3
Sheep Bridge La DN11 ... 85 B2
Sheepcote Hill S21 ... 156 D6
Sheep Cote La DN7 ... 44 C4
Sheepcote Rd S21 ... 156 C6
Sheep Cote Rd S60 ... 116 E3
Sheep Dike La S66 ... 133 C7
Sheep Dip La DN7 ... 44 A7
Sheephill Rd S11 ... 139 A2
Sheep La DN5 ... 60 D3
Sheepwalk La WF9 ... 19 E8
Sheepwash La DN11 ... 103 D1
Sheerien Cl S71 ... 33 E8
Sheffield 35a Bsns Pk S35 ... 95 A8
Sheffield Airport Bsns Pk S9, S60 ... 130 E6
Sheffield Cath★ S1 ... 161 A4
Sheffield Childrens Hospl S10 ... 160 A3
Sheffield City Airport S60 ... 131 A6
Sheffield Coll (Bannerdale Ctr) The S7 ... 140 D4
Sheffield Coll Loxley Ctr The S6 ... 127 F7
Sheffield Coll (Norton Coll) The S8 ... 153 B7
Sheffield Coll Peaks Ctr S20 ... 143 D3
Sheffield Coll The (Castle Ctr N) S2 ... 161 C2
Sheffield Coll The (Castle Ctr S) S2 ... 161 C1
Sheffield Coll The (Frecheville Ctr) S12 .. 142 C4
Sheffield Fire & Police Mus★ S1 ... 161 A4
Sheffield Hallam Arena S9 ... 130 B7
Sheffield Hallam Univ
Sheffield, Little Sheffield S11 ... 128 F1
Sheffield S1 ... 161 B3
Sheffield Hallam Univ (Psalter Lane Campus) S11 ... 140 C7
Sheffield High Sch S10 . 128 C2
Sheffield La S60 ... 131 C5
Sheffield Parkway
Catliffe S60 ... 131 B6
Sheffield S9 ... 130 D2
Sheffield Rd
Aston S13 ... 144 A8
Barnsley S70 ... 75 F7
Conisbrough, Conisbrough Common DN12 ... 81 F3
Conisbrough DN12 ... 81 C1
Doncaster DN12 ... 82 B4
Dronfield S18 ... 152 F3
Eckington S20, S21 ... 155 E5
Hathersage S32 ... 149 A7
Holmfirth HD9 ... 49 B8
Hoyland S62, S74 ... 76 B4
Killamarsh S21 ... 156 D7
Oxspring S36 ... 52 B1
Rotherham S60 ... 115 B4
Sheffield, Coisley Hill S13 .. 143 B6
Sheffield, Hackenthorpe S12, S20 ... 143 A3
Sheffield, Meadowhall S9 . 114 C1
Sheffield S20, S21 ... 155 E5
Sheffield, Templeborough S9, S60 ... 114 E3
South Anston S25 ... 146 D4
Sheffield Science Pk S2 . 161 B2
Sheffield Ski Village★ S3 ... 128 F7
Sheffield Sta S1 ... 161 B2
Sheldon Ave DN12 ... 81 D1
Sheldon La 8 S6 ... 127 C6
Sheldon Rd
Sheffield S7 ... 140 E6
Stocksbridge S36 ... 73 C1
Sheldon Row S3 ... 161 B4
Sheldon St S2 ... 129 A1
Sheldrake Cl S61 ... 95 F5
Shelley Ave DN4 ... 83 B6
Shelley Cl S36 ... 51 D4
Shelley Dr
Armthorpe DN3 ... 64 C6
Barnsley S71 ... 34 B3
Dinnington S25 ... 147 B8
Rotherham S65 ... 116 B6
Shelley Gr DN5 ... 61 F4
Shelley Rd S65 ... 116 C6
Shelley Rise DN6 ... 40 A5
Shelley Way S63 ... 78 C7
Shelley Woodhouse La HD8 ... 29 E8
Shenley Cl DN7 ... 44 A6
Shenstone Dr S65 ... 116 B4
Shenstone Rd
Rotherham S65 ... 116 B4
Sheffield S6 ... 112 C2
Shepcote La S9 ... 130 C8
Shepcote Way S9 ... 130 D7
Shephard's Cl DN12 ... 80 F3
Shepherd Dr S35 ... 94 E6
Shepherd La S63 ... 58 D7
Shepherds Croft DN9 ... 86 F6
Shepherd St S3 ... 160 C4
Shepley Croft S35 ... 94 E6
Shepley Fst Sch HD8 ... 28 E8
Sheppard Rd DN4 ... 83 A7
Shepperson Rd S6 ... 112 B1
Sherbourne Ave S66 ... 117 E3
Sherburn Cl DN6 ... 20 E2
Sherburn Gate S35 ... 94 F6
Sherburn Rd S71 ... 33 E7
Sherde Rd S6 ... 128 E5
Sheridan Ave DN4 ... 83 C6
Sheridan Ct S71 ... 34 B3
Sheridan Dr S65 ... 116 C6
Sheridan Rd DN3 ... 42 F8
Sheringham Cl S35 ... 94 D7
Sheringham Gdns S35 ... 94 D7
Sherwood Ave
Askern DN6 ... 21 E7
Bentley DN5 ... 61 D6
Conisbrough DN12 ... 81 A1
Kirk Sandall DN3 ... 42 F2
Sherwood Chase S17 ... 151 E5
Sherwood Cl DN6 ... 21 C8
Sherwood Cres S60 ... 115 E6
Sherwood Dr
Adwick le S DN6 ... 20 E2
Doncaster DN4 ... 82 E5
Sherwood Glen S7 ... 140 B1
Sherwood Pl 2 S18 ... 152 D1
Sherwood Rd
Dronfield S18 ... 152 D1
Harworth DN11 ... 121 F5
Killamarsh S21 ... 156 E7
Rossington DN11 ... 104 A8
Sherwood St 15 S71 ... 33 F1
Sherwood Way S72 ... 16 A1
Shetland Gdns DN2 ... 63 B5
Shield Ave S70 ... 55 A5
Shildon Gr DN8 ... 9 E3
Shining Cliff Ct DN10 ... 122 F8
Shinwell Dr WF9 ... 19 D8
Shipcroft Cl S73 ... 56 E2
Ship Hill S60 ... 115 D6
Shipman Balk S66 ... 100 E5
Shipman Ct S20 ... 155 D7
Shipton St S6 ... 160 B5
Shirburn Gdns DN4 ... 63 F1
Shirebrook Ct S2 ... 141 A6
Shirebrook Rd S8 ... 141 A6
Shirecliffe Cl S3 ... 129 B7
Shirecliffe Jun Sch S5 ... 112 E2
Shirecliffe La S3 ... 129 A7
Shirecliffe Rd S5 ... 113 A1
Shiregreen La S5 ... 113 F4
Shiregreen Terr S5 ... 113 D5
Shirehall Cres S5 ... 113 E6
Shirehall Rd S5 ... 113 D7
Shire Oak Dr S74 ... 77 B6
Shireoaks Comm S81 ... 159 F7
Shireoaks Rd
Dronfield S18 ... 153 C2
Shireoaks S81 ... 159 F6
Shireoaks Row S81 ... 159 E7
Shireoaks Sta S81 ... 159 E7
Shireoaks Way S72 ... 36 A8
Shires Cl DN5 ... 61 B1
Shirewood Cl S63 ... 78 A6
Shirland Ave S71 ... 34 A6
Shirland Ct S9 ... 130 B5
Shirland La S9 ... 130 A5
Shirland Mews 4 S9 ... 130 A5
Shirland Pl S9 ... 130 B5
Shirle Hill Hospl & Sch S11 ... 140 D7
Shirley La DN5 ... 22 C5
Shirley Rd
Doncaster DN4 ... 62 A1
Sheffield S3 ... 129 B7
Shoes The 4 DN12 ... 81 C2
Shooter's Grove Prim Sch S6 ... 127 F6
Shooters Hill Dr DN11 ... 104 B8
Shore Ct S10 ... 128 B2
Shore Hall La S36 ... 50 E2
Shoreham Ave S60 ... 116 A1
Shoreham Dr S60 ... 115 F1
Shoreham Rd S60 ... 115 F1
Shoreham St S1 ... 161 B2
Shore La S10 ... 128 A2
Shorland Dr S60 ... 131 F4
Shortbrook Bank 10 S20 . 155 E8
Shortbrook Cl S20 ... 155 F8

Shortbrook Com Prim Sch S20 155 E8
Shortbrook Croft 6 S20 155 F8
Shortbrook Dr S20 155 E8
Shortbrook Rd S20 155 E8
Shortbrook Way 13 S20 155 E8
Shortbrook Wlk 12 S20 155 E8
Shortfield Ct S71 33 E8
Short Gate DN11 102 A6
Short La
- Doncaster DN4 84 B7
- Sheffield S6 126 E5
Short Rd DN2 63 C4
Shortridge St S9 129 F6
Shorts La S17 151 B6
Short St S74 76 B5
Shortwood Bsns Pk S74 76 B7
Short Wood Cl S70 54 F1
Shortwood La DN5 37 B4
Short Wood Villas S74 76 B8
Shotton Wlk DN1 62 C2
Shrewsbury Cl
- Mexborough S64 79 F5
- Penistone S36 51 D3
Shrewsbury Hospl Almshouses S2 161 C2
Shrewsbury Rd
- Bircotes DN11 122 B4
- Penistone S36 51 D3
- Sheffield S2 161 B2
Shrewsbury Terr
- Rotherham S61 114 F5
- Sheffield S17 151 D4
Shroggs Head Cl S73 57 B6
Shrogswood Rd S60 116 D3
Shubert Cl S13 143 B8
Shude Hill S1 161 B3
Shuttle Cl DN11 104 B8
Shuttleworth Cl 4 DN11 104 A8
Sibbering Row S36 92 F8
Sicey Ave S5 113 D5
Sicey La S5 113 D6
Sicklebrook La S18 153 F4
Sidcop Rd S72 35 B8
Siddall St S1 160 C3
Sidings Ct DN4 83 E8
Sidling Hollow S6 126 D8
Sidney Rd DN2 63 B4
Sidney St
- Sheffield S1 161 A2
- Swinton S64 79 D3
Sidons Cl S61 96 E2
Siemens Cl S9 114 E2
Siena Cl S73 56 E6
Sike Cl S75 13 D1
Sike La S36 51 B1
Sikes Rd S25 146 D5
Silkstone Cl
- Pilley S75 75 D5
- Sheffield S12 142 E4
Silkstone Common Jun & Inf Sch S75 53 A5
Silkstone Common Sta S75 53 A5
Silkstone Cres S12 142 E4
Silkstone Cross S75 52 F7
Silkstone Dr S12 142 D4
Silkstone La
- Cawthorne S75 31 F3
- Silkstone S75 32 A1
Silkstone Oval DN8 9 D3
Silkstone Pl S12 142 E4
Silkstone Prim Sch S75 52 F7
Silkstone Rd S12 142 E4
Silkstone View S74 76 E8
Silver Birch Ave S10 139 C7
Silver Birch Gr DN9 86 F3
Silverdale Cl
- Branton DN3 85 E8
- Sheffield S11 140 A4
Silverdale Cres S11 140 A5
Silverdale Croft S11 140 A4
Silverdale Ct 1 S11 140 B4
Silverdale Dr S71 34 D5
Silverdale Gdns 2 S11 140 B4
Silverdale Glade 3 S11 140 B4
Silverdale Rd S11 140 A4
Silverdales S25 135 A1
Silverdale Sch S11 139 E4
Silver Hill Rd S11 140 B5
Silver Jubilee Cl DN2 63 C6
Silver Mill Rd S2 141 A8
Silvermoor Dr S65 117 D8
Silver St
- Barnsley S70 54 E8
- Dodworth S75 53 F6
- Doncaster DN1 62 D3
- Rotherham S65 98 E2
- Sheffield S1 161 A4
- Stainforth DN7 24 E4
- Thorne DN8 26 B7
Silverstone Ave S72 35 C7
Silver Street Head S1 161 A4
Silverwood Cl S66 117 B7
Silverwood Ct S63 79 B7
Silverwood Ho 7 DN1 62 C1
Silverwood View DN12 81 B2
Silverwood Wlk S66 117 B6
Simcrest Ave S21 156 D5
Sim Hill S35 74 B8
Simmonite Rd S61 96 F1
Simon Ct S11 139 F8
Simons Way S73 56 B5
Simpson Pl S64 79 F5
Simpson Rd WF9 19 B4
Sim Royd La HD8 30 D4
Sims St S1 161 A4
Sincil Way DN4 84 E7
Singleton Cres S6 128 C7
Singleton Gr S6 128 C7
Singleton Rd S6 128 C7
Sir Frederick Mappin Bldg (Univ of Sheffield) S1 160 C3
Sir Harold Jackson Prim Sch S17 152 B5
Sir William Hill Rd S32 149 B1
Sitka Cl S71 15 B2
Sitwell 14 S20 155 E8
Sitwell Ave S36 73 A1
Sitwell Dr S60 116 A3
Sitwell Gr
- Rotherham S60 116 A2
- Swinton S64 79 D2
Sitwell Jun & Inf Schs S60 116 B3
Sitwell La S66 117 B3
Sitwell Park Rd S60 116 D3
Sitwell Pl 15 S7 140 F8
Sitwell Rd S7 140 F8
Sitwell St S21 155 C3
Sitwell Terr S66 117 B3
Sitwell Vale S60 115 F3
Sitwell View S60 116 D1
Sivilla Rd S62 98 D8
Sixrood La DN6 21 A5
Sixth Ave DN9 86 B3
Skellow Cross DN6 21 B2
Skellow Hall Gdns DN6 20 F1
Skellow Rd DN6 21 A1
Skelton Ave S75 14 B1
Skelton Cl S13 143 C5
Skelton Dr S13 143 C6
Skelton Gr S13 143 B6
Skelton La
- Sheffield, Beighton S20 143 F3
- Sheffield, Coisley Hill S13 143 B6
Skelton Rd S8 141 A5
Skelton Rise S35 111 D6
Skelton Way S13 143 B6
Skelton Wlk S13 143 C5
Skelwith Cl 2 S4 113 F1
Skelwith Dr S4 113 F1
Skelwith Rd S4 113 F1
Skew Hill La S35 112 B7
Skiers Hall S74 76 F4
Skiers Hill S74 76 F4
Skiers View Rd S74 76 C5
Skiers Way S74 76 C5
Skinnerthorpe Rd S4 113 D1
Skinpit La S36 52 A6
Skipton Cl DN12 80 E3
Skipton Rd
- Aston S26 144 C7
- Sheffield S4 129 C8
Skipwith Cl DN11 83 C2
Skipwith Gdns DN11 103 E8
Skye Croft S71 15 C5
Skye Edge Ave S2 129 E2
Skye Edge Rd S2 129 D2
Slack Fields La S35 93 B1
Slack La S72 16 B5
Slacks La S66 117 E3
Slack Top La HD8, HD9 28 C1
Slade Rd S64 79 D2
Slade View S25 134 E7
Slaidburn Ave S35 94 F6
Slant Gate S36 50 E4
Slate St S2 141 B8
Slayleigh Ave S10 139 D8
Slayleigh Delph S10 139 C8
Slayleigh Dr S10 139 D8
Slayleigh La S10 139 D8
Slaynes La DN10 123 E8
Slay Pit Cl DN7 44 E6
Slaypit La S80 158 D6
Slay Pit La DN7 44 F7
Sleaford St S9 129 F6
Sledbrook Cres S36 49 C6
Sledgate Dr S66 116 F3
Sledgate La S66 117 A4
Sledmere Rd DN5 61 E6
Sleep Hill La
- Hampole DN6 20 B6
- South Elmsall DN6 19 F7
Slinn St S10 128 C5
Slitting Mill La S9 129 F6
Sloade La S12 154 D7
Smallage La S13 131 F1
Smalldale Rd S12 142 D4
Smallfield La S6 109 E7
Small Gr DN7 24 E4
Small La S36 52 B8
Smawell La WF4 15 B7
Smeatley's La WF8 3 E7
Smeaton Cl S65 117 E8
Smeaton Rd WF9 19 E8
Smeaton St 11 S7 140 F8
Smelter Wood Ave S13 142 E7
Smelter Wood Cl S13 142 E7
Smelter Wood Cres S13 142 F7
Smelter Wood Ct S13 142 E7
Smelter Wood Dr S13 142 E7
Smelter Wood La S13 142 E7
Smelter Wood Pl S13 142 F7
Smelter Wood Rd S13 142 E7
Smelter Wood Rise S13 142 F7
Smelter Wood Way S13 142 E7
Smillie Rd DN11 104 A8
Smithey Cl S35 94 D6
Smithfield
- Sheffield, Netherthorpe S3 161 A4
- 15 Sheffield S1 160 C3
Smithfield Rd S12 142 A3
Smithies La S71, S75 33 F4
Smithies Lane Cvn Site S71 33 F5
Smithies Rd S64 79 D4
Smithies St S71 33 E4
Smithley La
- Hoyland S73 55 F3
- Wombwell S73 56 A4
Smith Rd S36 73 B1
Smith Sq
- Doncaster DN4 82 F7
- Harworth DN11 121 F4
Smith St
- Chapeltown S35 95 A5
- Doncaster DN4 82 F7
- Wombwell S73 56 E3
Smith Wlk WF9 19 A4
Smithy Bridge La S63 77 F6
Smithy Bridge Rd S6 110 A4
Smithy Carr Ave S35 94 F5
Smithy Carr Cl S35 94 F5
Smithy Cl
- Rotherham S61 96 F1
- Wortley S35 74 D3
Smithy Croft S18 152 D2
Smithy Fold La S35 93 E7
Smithy Hill
- Denby Dale HD8 29 F3
- Thurgoland S35 74 A7
Smithy Mdws S32 149 A8
Smithy Moor Ave S36 72 F2
Smithy Moor La S36 72 E3
Smithy Wood Cres
- Sheffield S8 140 E4
- Sheffield S8 140 F4
Smithy Wood La S75 53 F6
Smithy Wood Rd
- Chapeltown S61 95 D4
- Sheffield S8 140 F4
Snail Hill S60 115 D6
Snailsden Way S75 33 D8
Snaithing La S10 127 E1
Snaithing Park Cl S10 127 E1
Snaithing Park Rd S10 127 E1
Snaith Rd DN14 1 C8
Snake La
- Conisbrough DN12 100 E8
- Thorne DN8 26 A6
Snape Hill S18 153 A2
Snapehill Cl S18 153 A3
Snape Hill Cres S18 153 A3
Snape Hill Dr S18 153 B3
Snape Hill La S18 153 A2
Snape Hill Rd S73 57 A5
Snape La DN11 122 A2
Snatchells La DN14 7 E4
Snelston Cl S18 152 D1
Snetterton Cl S72 35 C7
Snig Hill S3 161 B4
Snipe Park Rd DN11 122 B4
Snittle Rd HD9 48 B6
Snowberry Cl S64 98 C8
Snowden Terr S73 56 D3
Snowdon La S21 154 B2
Snowdon Way S60 131 D7
Snow Hill S75 53 F6
Snow La S3 161 A4
Snug La HD9 28 A1
Snydale Rd S72 35 B6
Soaper La S18 153 A2
Soap House La S13 143 F6
Society St DN1 62 D3
Sokell Ave S73 56 C2
Solario Way DN11 103 E7
Solly St S1 160 C4
Solway Rise S18 152 D2
Somercotes Rd S12 142 D5
Somersby Ave DN5 61 F4
Somerset Rd
- Doncaster DN1 62 D2
- Sheffield S3 129 B6
Somerset St
- 8 Barnsley S70 33 D2
- Cudworth S72 35 B6
- Maltby S66 119 B4
- Sheffield S3 129 B6
Somerton Dr
- Doncaster DN4 84 E7
- Hatfield DN7 44 F6
Somerville Terr S6 128 E6
Somin Ct DN4 83 C5
Sopewell Rd S61 114 D6
Sorby Rd S26 144 B7
Sorby St S4 129 C5
Sorby Way S66 117 B3
Sorrell La DN7 8 B2
Sorrel Rd S66 117 C6
Sorrelsykes Cl S60 132 B8
Sorrento Way S73 56 F7
Sothall Cl S20 143 F3
Sothall Ct S20 143 F3
Sothall Gn S20 143 F3
Sothall Green Farm S20 143 F3
Sothall Mews S20 143 F3
Sough Hall Ave S61 95 F5
Sough Hall Cl S61 95 F5
Sough Hall Cres S61 95 F5
Sough Hall Rd S61 95 F4
Soughley La
- Sheffield S10 138 C8
- Wortley S35 74 B2
Sour La DN7, DN8 25 C8
Sousa St S66 119 C4
Southall St 10 S8 141 A6
Southard's La S80 158 E5
South Ave
- Bawtry DN10 123 A8
- South Elmsall WF9 18 F2
- Swinton S64 79 B2
South Bank DN7 24 E5
Southbourne Ct S17 151 D6
Southbourne Mews S10 128 C1
Southbourne Rd S10 128 C1
South Cl S71 15 C2
Southcote Dr S18 152 D1
South Cres
- Dodworth S75 53 F7
- Killamarsh S21 156 E7
- Rotherham S65 116 C7
- South Elmsall WF9 19 B4
South Croft
- Denby Dale HD8 29 F3
- Shafton S72 16 C3
Southcroft Gdns 1 S7 140 F6
Southcroft Wlk 2 S7 140 F6
South Ct S17 151 E7
South Dr
- Bolton u D S63 58 B1
- Royston S71 15 C2
South Elmsall Sta WF9 19 A3
South End
- Hatfield DN7 24 F1
- Thorne DN8 26 C5
South End La DN14 5 E8
Southend Pl S2 129 E2
Southend Rd S2 129 E2
Southey Ave S5 113 A3
Southey Cl S5 112 F3
Southey Cres
- Maltby S66 119 A5
- Sheffield S5 113 A3
Southey Dr S5 113 A3
Southey Green Cl S5 112 F3
Southey Green Com Prim Sch S5 112 F4
Southey Green Rd S5 112 E3
Southey Hall Dr S5 113 A3
Southey Hall Rd S5 113 A4
Southey Hill S5 112 F4
Southey Pl S5 112 F3
Southey Rd S66 119 A5
Southey Rise S5 112 F3
South Farm Ave S26 157 E6
South Farm Dr DN6 21 A1
Southfield Cl DN8 26 C5
Southfield Cres S63 58 B7
Southfield La S63 58 B7
Southfield Rd
- Armthorpe DN3 64 B6
- Cudworth S72 35 D4
- Thorne DN8 26 C6
Southgate
- Barnsley S75 33 C3
- Eckington S21 155 E3
- Hoyland S74 76 E6
- Penistone S36 51 E2
- Shafton S72 16 D2
- South Hiendley S72 16 E6
Southgate Ct S21 155 E3
Southgrove Dr S74 76 D5
Southgrove Rd S10 160 A1
South Hiendley Jun & Inf Sch S72 16 D6
South La
- Cawthorne S75 31 C1
- Sheffield S1 161 A1
Southlands Way S26 144 E7
Southlea Ave S74 76 F5
Southlea Cl S74 76 F5
Southlea Dr S74 76 E5
Southlea Rd S74 76 E5
Southmoor Ave DN3 64 A6
Southmoor La DN3 64 A5
Southmoor Rd S72, WF9 17 D3
South Par
- Bawtry DN10 123 A6
- Doncaster DN1 62 E3
- Sheffield S3 161 A5
- Thorne DN8 26 B6
South Pl
- Barnsley S75 33 B3
- Wombwell S73 56 B3
South Precipitator Rd DN3 42 D8
South Rd
- Chapeltown S35 94 D7
- Dodworth S75 53 F8
- Rotherham S61 114 E7
- Sheffield S6 128 C6
- Thorne DN8 9 D3
- Thorpe in B DN3 42 C8
Southsea Rd S13 143 A6
South St
- Adwick le S DN6 40 C2
- Barnsley S70 33 D1
- Darfield S73 57 A5
- Dinnington S25 134 F1
- Dodworth S75 53 F6
- Doncaster DN4 62 D1
- Hemsworth WF9 17 E6
- Rawmarsh S62 98 A6
- Rotherham, Greasbrough S61 97 C3
- Rotherham, Kimberworth S61 114 E6
- Sheffield S20 155 D6
- Thurcroft S66 133 F6
South Street Pk S2 161 C3
South Terr S26 144 F2
South Vale Dr S65 98 F2
South View
- Aston S26 144 D7
- Austerfield DN10 105 C1
- Darfield S73 57 A5
- Kiveton Park S26 145 D2
- Mexborough S64 79 F4
- Rawcliffe Bridge DN14 2 D7
South View *continued*
- Sheffield S20 156 A7
- Thurgoland S35 74 C7
South View Cl S6 111 E1
South View Cres S7 140 F7
South View Fold S36 50 E8
South View Rd
- Hoyland S74 76 D5
- Sheffield S7 140 F8
South View Rise S6 111 E1
South View Terr S60 131 C5
Southwell Gdns S26 144 A7
Southwell Rd
- Doncaster DN2 62 F6
- Rawmarsh S62 98 B6
- 6 Sheffield S4 113 F1
Southwell Rise S64 80 B6
Southwell St 13 S75 33 D2
South West Ctr The 3 S8 140 E4
Southwood S6 112 A3
South Wood Dr DN8 26 B5
Southwood Gr S6 112 A3
South Yorkshire Bldgs S75 53 B5
South Yorkshire Fresh Produce & Flower Ctr S9 130 B4
South Yorkshire (Redbrook) Ind Est S75 32 F5
Sovereign Ind Est HD8 28 F6
Spa Brook Cl S12 142 F4
Spa Brook Dr S12 142 F5
Spa La S13 143 C6
Spa Lane Croft S13 143 C6
Spalton Rd S62 97 F4
Spansyke St DN4 62 B2
Sparkfields S75 33 B8
Spark La S75 33 B8
Spartan View S66 118 D7
Spa Terr DN6 22 A8
Spa View Ave S12 142 F3
Spa View Dr S12 142 F3
Spa View Pl S12 142 F3
Spa View Rd S12 142 F3
Spa View Terr S12 142 F3
Spa View Way S12 142 F3
Spa Well Cres S60 131 F5
Spa Well Gr S72 17 A3
Speeton Rd S6 128 C7
Spencer Croft S75 31 F5
Spencer Ct S60 116 D1
Spencer Dr S65 117 D7
Spencer Gn S60 116 D1
Spencer Rd S2 141 A7
Spencer St
- Barnsley S70 54 E8
- Mexborough S64 79 E5
Spennithorne Rd DN6 20 F2
Spenser Rd S65 116 B5
Spey Cl S75 33 C7
Spey Dr DN9 86 A7
Spicer House La S36 50 B7
Spilsby Cl DN4 85 A6
Spink Hall Cl S36 92 C8
Spink Hall La S36 92 B8
Spinkhill Ave S13 142 C8
Spinkhill Dr S13 142 D8
Spinkhill Immaculate Conception Prim Sch S21 156 C2
Spinkhill La S21 156 B2
Spinkhill Rd
- Killamarsh S21 156 E4
- Sheffield S13 142 D8
Spinkhill View S21 156 B1
Spinney Cl S60 116 B3
Spinneyfield S60 116 A2
Spinney Hill DN5 82 B8
Spinney The
- Barnby Dun DN3 43 A6
- Doncaster DN4 82 F5
Spinney Wlk DN8 26 D7
Spitalfields S3 161 B5
Spital Gr DN11 104 A7
Spital Hill S4 129 C5
Spital La S3 129 C5
Spital St S3 129 B5
Spittlerush La DN6 4 A4
Spofforth Rd S9 130 A5
Spooner Dr S21 156 C6
Spooner Rd S10 128 C2
Spoon Glade 2 S6 127 C6
Spoonhill Rd S6 127 F6
Spoon La S6 127 A6
Spoon Mews S6 127 C6
Spoon Oak Lea 3 S6 127 C6
Spoon Way S6 127 C6
Spotswood Cl S14 141 E4
Spotswood Dr S14 141 E5
Spotswood Mount S14 141 E4
Spotswood Pl S14 141 D4
Spotswood Rd S14 141 D5
Spout Copse S6 127 B6
Spout La S6 127 B7
Spout Spinney S6 127 B6
Springbank S73 57 B5
Springbank Cl
- Blaxton DN9 86 F6
- Royston S71 34 C8
Spring Bank Rd DN12 100 B8
Spring Cl S60 116 C1
Spring Close Dell S14 141 F4
Spring Close Mount S14 141 F4
Spring Close View S14 141 F4

Spring Cres DN5 61 B1
Spring Croft S61 96 F1
Springcroft Dr DN5 61 E8
Spring Dr S73 78 A8
Spring Farm WF4 15 A6
Springfield S63 58 A2
Springfield Ave
Hatfield DN7 44 C7
Hemsworth WF9 17 E6
Sheffield S7 140 C5
Springfield Cl
Armthorpe DN3 64 C5
Darfield S73 57 B5
Eckington S21 155 C3
Rotherham S61 97 D1
Sheffield S7 140 C4
Woodsetts S81 147 E4
Springfield Cres
Darfield S73 57 B5
Hoyland S74 76 C5
Norton WF8 3 E5
Springfield Ct DN5 61 E5
Springfield Dr
Denby Dale HD8 29 A4
Rotherham S65 99 A2
Springfield Glen S7 140 B4
Springfield Mills HD8 29 F5
Springfield Mount WF9 18 E1
Springfield Pl S70 33 D1
Springfield Prim Sch S3 160 C2
Springfield Rd
Grimethorpe S72 35 F7
Hoyland S74 76 C5
New Edlington DN12 82 C2
Rotherham S66 117 A4
Sheffield S7 140 C4
Swinton S62 98 E7
Springfields S75 33 A4
Springfield St S70 33 D1
Springfield Terr S25 146 C7
Springfield Way S35 94 D5
Spring Gdns
Barnsley S71 34 C4
Bawtry DN10 123 A8
Branton DN3 64 C1
Doncaster DN1 62 C3
Hoyland S74 76 E6
Spring Gr
Barnsley S71 15 D1
Thurgoland S35 73 F5
Spring Grove Gdns S35 93 B1
Spring Hill S10 128 C4
Springhill Ave S73 78 A8
Spring Hill Cl DN5 61 B1
Spring Hill Rd S10 128 C4
Spring House Rd S10 128 C4
Springhouses HD8 29 F5
Spring La
Barnsley S71 15 D1
Sheffield S2 141 E8
Shireoaks S80, S81 159 F5
Sprotbrough DN5 61 B3
Spring Ram Bsns Pk S75 13 D1
Springs Rd DN10 87 E2
Spring St
Barnsley S70 54 E8
Rotherham S65 115 E7
Sheffield S3 161 A4
Springstone Ave WF9 17 E7
Spring Terr
South Elmsall WF9 18 F2
Thurgoland S35 74 A5
Spring Vale Ave S70 54 F4
Springvale Cl
Maltby S66 118 F6
Rotherham S66 117 C2
Springvale Gr S36 51 E3
Springvale Prim Sch S36 51 F3
Springvale Rd
Great Houghton S72 36 E2
Grimethorpe S72 35 F6
Sheffield S10 128 C4
Spring Vale Rd WF9 18 C3
Springvale Rise WF9 17 D8
Springvale Wlk S6 160 B5
Spring View Rd S10 128 C4
Springville Gdns WF9 19 B7
Spring Water Ave S12 143 A3
Spring Water Cl 3 S12 143 A3
Spring Water Dr 1 S12 143 A3
Springwater Ho S12 143 B3
Springwell Ave S20 143 E4
Springwell Cl S66 119 B6
Springwell Cres S20 143 E4
Springwell Ct WF9 17 E6
Springwell Ctr S71 34 B6
Springwell Dr S20 143 E4
Springwell Farm S64 79 F8
Springwell Gdns DN4 82 F6
Springwell Gr S20 143 E4
Springwell La DN4 83 A3
Spring Wlk
6 Rotherham S65 115 E7
Wombwell S73 56 B4
Springwood Ave S26 132 C1
Springwood Cl
Branton DN3 85 C8
Thurgoland S35 74 A6
Springwood Ct S26 132 D1
Springwood Gr S63 58 C7
Springwood Ho 3 DN1 62 C1
Springwood La S35 94 D6
Springwood Prim Sch S74 76 D5
Springwood Rd
Bentley DN5 61 E8
Hoyland S74 76 C5
Sheffield S8 141 A6
Springwood View S36 51 F3
Sprotbrough Copley Jun Sch DN5 82 B8
Sprotbrough Flash (Nature Res)* DN5 82 A6
Sprotbrough La DN5 60 D6
Sprotbrough Orchard Inf Sch DN5 82 B8
Sprotbrough Rd DN5 62 A4
Spruce Ave
Rotherham S66 117 C5
Royston S71 15 B3
Spruce Cres DN9 86 A3
Spruce Rise S21 156 C5
Spry La S63 37 B3
Spurley Hey Gr S36 92 C8
Spurr St S2 141 B8
Square E The S66 117 C7
Square The
Barnsley S70 54 D8
Grimethorpe S72 36 B6
Harley S62 76 D1
Shepley HD8 28 E8
Wales S26 145 B2
Square W The S66 117 B7
Squirrel Croft S61 96 F4
Stable Green Gdns DN5 82 C8
Stables La DN5 59 D4
Stables The S64 79 B3
Stable Yard Cotts DN6 21 D3
Stacey Cres S72 35 F7
Stacey Dr S65 98 E3
Stacey Ho S64 80 B4
Stacey La S6 110 F2
Stackyard The S71 56 B8
Stacye Ave S13 143 D6
Stacye Rise S13 143 D5
Stadium Ct S62 97 E2
Stadium Way
Rotherham S60 97 F1
Sheffield S9 129 F5
South Elmsall WF9 19 B5
Stafford Cl S18 152 C2
Stafford Cres S60 115 F1
Stafford Dr S60 115 F1
Stafford La S2 129 D2
Stafford Mews S2 129 D2
Stafford Pl 6 DN12 80 F3
Stafford Rd
Adwick le S DN6 40 C4
Sheffield S2 129 D2
Staffordshire Cl S66 119 B5
Stafford St S2 161 C2
Stafford Way S35 94 F5
Stag Cl S60 116 C3
Stag Cres S60 116 C3
Stag La S60 116 B3
Stag Willow Cl S60 116 B3
Stainborough Cl S75 53 F6
Stainborough La S75 53 F1
Stainborough Rd S75 53 F6
Stainborough View
Pilley S75 75 D6
Worsbrough S70 54 F5
Staincross Comm S75 14 B2
Staindrop Cl S35 94 F7
Staindrop View S35 95 A6
Stainforth Kirton Lane Prim Sch DN7 25 A5
Stainforth Moor Rd DN7, DN8 45 D5
Stainforth Rd DN3 43 B8
Stainley Cl S75 33 B4
Stainmore Ave S20 144 A2
Stainmore Cl S75 52 F8
Stainton Cl S71 33 E6
Stainton La
Stainton S66 119 D7
Wadworth DN11 101 E3
Stainton Rd S11 140 B8
Stainton St DN12 80 F3
Stairfoot Bsns Pk S70 55 E7
Stairfoot Way S70 55 E7
Stair Rd S4 129 C8
Staithes Wlk DN12 81 A4
Stake Hill Rd S6 125 B6
Stalker Lees Rd S11 140 D8
Stambers Cl S81 147 E3
Stamford Rd S66 117 B8
Stamford St S9 129 F7
Stamford Way S75 14 B2
Stampers Hill S75 54 D2
Stanage Rise S12 142 E5
Stanbury Cl S75 33 B4
Stancil La
Wadworth DN11 103 B6
Wadworth DN11 103 C4
Standhill Cres S71 33 E7
Standish Ave S5 129 A8
Standish Bank S5 129 A8
Standish Cl S5 113 A1
Standish Cres WF9 18 C4
Standish Dr S5 113 A1
Standish Gdns S5 129 A8
Standish Rd S5 113 A1
Standish Way S5 129 A8
Standon Cres S9 114 A5
Standon Dr S9 114 A5
Standon Rd S9 114 A5
Staneford Ct S20 143 D1
Stanford Cl S66 119 C4
Stanford Rd S18 152 C1
Stanhope Ave S75 31 F5
Stanhope Gdns S75 33 C3
Stanhope Rd
Doncaster DN1 62 E5
Sheffield S12 142 C5
Stanhope St 3 S70 33 D1
Stanhurst La DN7 26 A1
Stanier Way S21 156 B1
Staniforth Ave S21 155 B3
Staniforth Cres S26 145 E5
Staniforth Rd S9 130 B5
Staniforth Wks S12 143 B3
Stanley Ct S66 118 D5
Stanley Gdns
Doncaster DN4 62 B1
Stainforth DN7 24 E3
Stanley Gr
Aston S26 144 F8
Hatfield DN7 25 A1
Stanley La S3 161 B5
Stanley Rd
Barnsley S70 55 E7
Bentley DN5 61 D7
Chapeltown S35 94 E6
Sheffield S8 141 B5
Stainforth DN7 24 E3
Stocksbridge S36 73 C1
Stanley Sq DN3 42 F4
Stanley St
Barnsley S70 33 D1
Cudworth S72 35 C4
Killamarsh S21 156 D7
Rotherham S60 115 D6
Sheffield S3 161 B5
Stanley Terr S66 118 D5
Stannington Glen S6 127 E6
Stannington Inf Sch S6 127 C6
Stannington Rd S6 127 D6
Stannington Rise S6 128 A7
Stannington View Rd S10 128 B4
Stanton Cres S12 142 D4
Stan Valley WF8 3 E6
Stanwell Ave S9 114 A4
Stanwell Cl S9 114 A4
Stanwell St S9 114 A4
Stanwell Wlk S9 114 A4
Stanwood Ave S6 127 F6
Stanwood Cres S6 128 A6
Stanwood Dr S6 127 F6
Stanwood Mews S6 127 F6
Stanwood Rd S6 127 F6
Staple Gn S65 99 A2
Stapleton Rd DN4 82 D5
Starkbridge La DN14 7 B6
Star La S70 33 E1
Starling Ho 4 WF9 17 D6
Starling Mead S2 129 E2
Starnhill Cl S35 95 C1
Station App S32 149 A7
Station Cl DN9 86 E4
Station Ct
Hatfield DN7 44 B8
South Anston S25 146 D5
Station La
Oughtibridge S35 111 D7
Sheffield S9 114 A2
Station Rd
Adwick le S DN6 40 D7
Askern DN6 22 A8
Barnby Dun DN3 42 F6
Barnsley S70 33 D2
Barnsley, West Green S71 34 F5
Bawtry DN10 123 A7
Bentley DN5 41 D2
Bolton u D S63 58 C2
Catliffe S60 131 C6
Chapeltown S35 95 B6
Conisbrough DN12 81 C3
Darfield S73 56 E3
Darton S75 13 E1
Dodworth S75 53 E7
Finningley DN9 86 E4
Hatfield DN7 44 B8
Hatfield, Stainforth DN7 24 F1
Hathersage S32 149 A7
Hemsworth WF9 17 E7
Killamarsh S21 156 B6
Kiveton Park S26 145 E2
Laughton en le M S25 134 C3
Mexborough S64 80 A4
Norton DN6 4 E3
Rawcliffe DN14 2 B8
Renishaw S21 156 A2
Rossington DN11 85 A1
Rotherham S60 115 C6
Royston S71 15 B4
Scrooby DN10 123 A2
Sheffield, Darnall S9 130 C4
Sheffield, Ecclesfield S35 95 C1
Sheffield S20 155 E7
Sheffield, Woodhouse S13 143 D7
Shepley HD8 28 E8
South Elmsall WF9 19 A3
Spinkhill S21 156 D2
Stocksbridge S36 74 A1
Thurnscoe S63 58 D8
Treeton S60 131 E4
Wath u D S63 79 A8
Worsbrough S70 55 D4
Station Road Ind Est S73 56 E4
Station St S64 79 D3
Station Terr S71 15 E4
Station Way S25 134 C3
Station Works S35 95 C1
Staton Ave S20 144 A4
Staton La S18 154 A1
Statutes The S60 115 D6
Staunton Rd DN4 85 A7
Staveley La S21 155 E2
Staveley Rd S8 141 A7
Staveley St DN12 82 B3
Steade Rd S7 140 F7
Steadfield Rd S74 76 C5
Steadfolds Gdns S66 134 A6
Steadfolds Cl S66 134 A6
Steadfolds La S66 134 B6
Steadfolds Rise S66 134 A6
Stead La S74 76 C4
Steadlands The S62 97 D7
Stead Mews S21 155 D3
Stead St S21 155 D3
Steed Court Bsns Pk WF9 19 C8
Steel Bank Villas S6 160 A4
Steele St S74 76 A5
Steel Hill S6, S35 112 C7
Steelhouse La S3 161 A4
Steel Rd S11 140 C8
Steel St S61 115 A5
Steep La S36 52 A4
Steetley La
Whitwell S80 159 E3
Worksop S80 159 E3
Steeton Ct S74 77 A6
Stemp St S11 140 F8
Stenton Rd S8 152 F7
Stentons Terr S64 80 B4
Stephen Dr
Sheffield, Grenoside S35 112 B8
Sheffield S10 127 F3
Stephen Hill S10 127 F3
Stephen Hill Rd S10 128 A3
Stephen La S35 112 B8
Stepney St S2 161 C4
Stepping La S35 94 B1
Sterndale Rd S7 140 C3
Steven Cl S35 94 F4
Steven Cres S35 94 F5
Steven Pl S35 94 F4
Stevenson Dr
Barnsley S75 32 E4
Rotherham S65 116 B5
Stevenson Rd
Doncaster DN4 83 B6
Sheffield S9 129 E6
Stevenson Way S9 129 F6
Stevens Rd DN4 62 B1
Steventon Rd S65 99 A2
Stewart Cl S81 148 E6
Stewart Rd
Carlton in L S81 148 E6
Sheffield S11 140 D8
Stewarts Rd S62 98 B6
Stewart St DN1 62 C2
Sticking La S63, S64 79 E7
Stirling Ave DN10 123 A8
Stirling Cl S74 77 A6
Stirling Dr S81 148 E6
Stirling Prim Sch DN1 62 C2
Stirling St DN1 62 C1
Stirling Way S2 142 A8
Stock's La
Barnsley S75 33 D2
Rawmarsh S62 97 F5
Stockarth La S35 111 F4
Stockarth Pl S35 111 F4
Stockbridge Ave DN5 62 A7
Stockbridge Cvn Pk DN5 41 C1
Stockbridge La DN6 21 E3
Stockil Rd DN4 62 E2
Stockingate WF9 18 B2
Stockingate Mill Jun Sch WF9 18 A1
Stock Rd S2 129 E1
Stocksbridge High Sch S36 73 B1
Stocksbridge Inf Sch S36 73 B1
Stocksbridge Jun Sch S36 92 B8
Stocksbridge La DN5 41 C2
Stocks Dr
Rawcliffe Bridge DN14 2 C7
Shepley HD8 28 E8
Stocks Green Ct S17 151 D4
Stocks Green Dr S17 151 D4
Stocks Hill S35 95 A1
Stocks Hill Cl S71 15 C1
Stocks La S36 71 D4
Stocks Way HD8 28 D8
Stockton Cl S3 129 B5
Stockwell Ave S26 145 C1
Stockwell Gn S71 34 B5
Stockwell La S26 145 B1
Stocthorn Gap S35 93 C2
Stoke St S9 129 E5
Stoket La S60 132 F5
Stokewell Rd S63 78 C7
Stoneacre Ave S12 143 B3
Stoneacre Cl 5 S12 143 B3
Stoneacre Dr S12 143 B2
Stoneacre Rise S12 143 B3
Stone Bank Ct S18 153 B1
Stonebridge La S72 36 F2
Stone Cl
Dronfield S18 153 C3
Kiveton Park S26 145 E2
Rotherham S65 117 D7
Stonecliffe Dr S36 92 B7
Stonecliffe Pl S2 130 A1
Stonecliffe Rd S2 130 A1
Stonecliffe Wlk 1 S2 130 B1
Stonecliff Wlk DN12 81 A4
Stone Close Ave DN4 62 B2
Stone Cres S66 117 B5
Stonecrest Rise S35 73 F7
Stonecroft Ct S75 52 F5
Stonecroft Gdns HD8 28 F8
Stonecroft Rd S17 151 F5
Stone Cross Dr DN5 61 B2
Stonecross Gdns DN4 85 A7
Stone Ct S72 16 E5
Stonedale Cl S20 155 D7
Stone Delf S10 127 D1
Stone Font Gr DN4 85 A7
Stonegarth Cl S72 35 B6
Stonegate DN8 26 B7
Stonegate Cl DN9 86 E6
Stonegravels Croft 7 S20 155 E6
Stonegravels Way S20 155 F6
Stonehill Cl S74 76 C7
Stone Hill Dr S26 144 D7
Stone Hill Rd DN7 44 F7
Stonehill Rise
Bentley DN5 61 E7
Cudworth S72 35 B6
Penistone S36 51 C1
Stone La S13 143 B5
Stonelea Cl S75 52 F8
Stone Lea Gr WF9 19 A2
Stone Leigh S75 75 D4
Stoneleigh Cl S25 147 B7
Stoneleigh Croft 9 S70 54 F7
Stoneley Cl S12 142 B1
Stoneley Cres S12 142 B1
Stoneley Dell S12 142 B1
Stoneley Dr S12 142 B1
Stonelow Cres S18 153 C2
Stonelow Gn S18 153 B2
Stonelow Jun Sch S18 153 C2
Stonelow Rd S18 153 C2
Stonely Brook S65 117 D6
Stone Moor Rd S36 92 B7
Stone Park Cl S66 119 B5
Stone Rd S18 153 C3
Stone Riding DN12 82 A1
Stone Row S6 126 F7
Stone Row Ct S75 75 D4
Stonerow Way S60 97 F1
Stones Inge S35 94 D7
Stone St
Barnsley S71 33 E4
Sheffield S20 155 D7
Stonewood Ct S10 127 D2
Stonewood Gr
Hoyland S74 76 E4
Sheffield S10 127 D2
Stoney Bank Dr S26 145 E2
Stoneybrook Cl WF4 12 F8
Stoney Croft S74 76 B5
Stoney Gate S35 94 D8
Stoney La DN11 120 F6
Stoneyleigh Ct S70 33 E2
Stoney Royd S71 14 F1
Stoney Well La S66 119 E4
Stony Cl DN7 24 F5
Stony Croft La
Burghwallis DN6 21 A3
Midhopestones S36 72 A3
Stonyford Rd S73 56 F4
Stony La
Sheffield S6 110 F3
Tickhill DN11 102 E2
Stony Ridge Rd S11 150 C5
Stony Wlk 2 S6 128 C6
Stoops La DN4 84 C6
Stoops Rd DN4 84 D7
Stopes Rd S6 127 A6
Store St S2 129 B1
Storey's Gate S73 56 B4
Storey St S64 79 D3
Storm House Sch S63 78 D7
Storrs Bridge La S6 111 A1
Storrs Carr S6 126 F8
Storrs Gn S6 126 F8
Storrs Hall Rd S6 128 B6
Storrs La
Askern DN5 22 C4
Oxspring S36 52 C4
Sheffield S6 127 A7
Wortley S35 75 B2
Storrs Mill S72 35 D3
Storrs Mill La S72 35 E2
Storrs Wood View S72 35 D4
Storth Ave S10 139 E8
Storth La
Sheffield, Ranmoor S10 127 E1
Sheffield S10 139 E8
Todwick S26 145 E5
Wales S26 145 C3
Wharncliffe Side S35 93 A2
Stortholme Mews S10 127 E1
Storth Pk S10 139 D7
Storthwood Ct S10 127 E1
Stotfold Dr S63 58 C8
Stotfold Rd DN5 37 E3
Stothard Ct S10 128 B4
Stothard Rd S10 128 B4
Stottercliffe Rd S36 51 C3
Stour La S6 111 F2
Stovin Cl S9 130 C7
Stovin Dr S9 130 B7
Stovin Gdns S9 130 C7
Stow Bridge La S60 132 E6
Stowe Ave S7 140 C4
Stradbroke Ave S13 142 D7
Stradbroke Cl S13 142 E7
Stradbroke Cres S13 142 E7
Stradbroke Dr S13 142 E7
Stradbroke Pl S13 142 E7
Stradbroke Prim Sch S13 142 D7
Stradbroke Rd S13 142 E6
Stradbroke Way S13 142 E7
Stradbroke Wlk S13 142 D7

Strafford Ave
Hoyland S74 77 B6
Worsbrough S70 54 F6
Strafford Gr S70 75 F5
Strafford Ind Pk S75 54 A5
Strafford Pl S61 95 E5
Strafford Rd
Doncaster DN2 62 E5
Rotherham S61 96 E2
Strafford St S75 32 C8
Strafford Wlk S75 53 F6
Strafforth Ho 1 DN12 80 F3
Straight La
Goldthorpe S63 58 E5
Hampole DN6 20 B4
Strait La S63 78 E6
Stratford Rd S10 127 D1
Stratford Way S66 117 E4
Strathaven Rd S81 148 F6
Strathmore Ct DN11 122 B5
Strathmore Dr S81 148 F6
Strathmore Gdns WF9 19 B4
Strathmore Gr S63 78 F6
Strathmore Rd DN2 63 A3
Strathtay Rd S11 140 B7
Strauss Cres S66 119 B4
Strawberry Ave S5 113 B6
Strawberry Gdns S71 15 D4
Strawberry Lee La S17 151 B5
Straw La S6 128 E5
Streatfield Cres DN11 84 E1
Street Farm Cl S26 157 E6
Streetfield Cres S20 155 D6
Streetfields S20 155 E6
Street La
Hooton Pagnell DN5 38 F3
Wentworth S62 77 E2
Strelley Ave S8 140 E1
Strelley Rd
Barnsley S71 33 E8
Sheffield S8 140 E1
Stretton Cl DN4 85 A8
Stretton Rd
Barnsley S71 34 A5
Sheffield S11 140 C7
Strickland Rd WF9 19 D8
Strines Moor Rd HD9 48 C8
Stringers Croft S60 116 D1
Stripe Rd
Rossington DN11 104 B5
Tickhill DN11 103 F1
Struan Rd S7 140 D5
Strutt Rd S3 129 A7
Stuart Gr S35 95 B4
Stuart Rd S35 95 B4
Stuart St S63 58 E8
Stubbin Cl S62 97 D7
Stubbing House La S6, S35 112 B7
Stubbing La S35 111 C3
Stubbin La
Denby Dale HD8 30 B6
Rawmarsh S62 97 D8
Sheffield S5 113 D4
Stubbin Rd S62 97 B7
Stubbins Hill DN12 82 C1
Stubbs Cres S61 96 F1
Stubbs La DN6 4 D4
Stubbs Rd
Kirk Smeaton WF8 4 A5
Wombwell S73 56 C2
Stubbs Wlk S61 96 F1
Stubley Cl S18 152 E2
Stubley Croft S18 152 D2
Stubley Dr S18 152 E2
Stubley Hollow S18 152 F3
Stubley La S18 152 D2
Stubley Pl S18 152 E2
Studfield Cres S6 127 F8
Studfield Dr S6 111 F1
Studfield Gr S6 127 F8
Studfield Hill S6 127 F8
Studfield Rd S6 127 F8
Studfield Rise S6 127 F8
Studley Ct S9 130 C4
Studley Gdns 1 DN3 42 E4
Studmoor Rd S61 96 D2
Studmoor Wlk S61 96 D2
Stump Cross Gdns S63 58 B2
Stump Cross La DN11 120 D3
Stump Cross Rd S63 78 E5
Stumperlowe Ave S10 139 E8
Stumperlowe Cl S10 139 E8
Stumperlowe Crescent Rd S10 139 E8
Stumperlowe Croft S10 127 D1
Stumperlowe Hall Chase S10 127 D1
Stumperlowe Hall Rd S10 139 D8
Stumperlowe La S10 139 D8
Stumperlowe Mans S10 139 D8
Stumperlowe Park Rd S10 139 E8
Stumperlowe View S10 127 D1
Stupton Rd S9 114 A2
Sturge Croft 3 S2 141 B6
Sturton Cl DN4 84 D6
Sturton Croft S65 98 E1
Sturton Rd S4 129 C8
Stygate La DN6 4 C2
Styrrup Ct DN11 121 D1
Styrrup La DN11 121 B1
Styrrup Rd DN11 121 E3
Sudbury Dr S26 144 E7
Sudbury St S3 160 C5
Suffolk Ave DN11 122 D4
Suffolk Cl S25 146 E6
Suffolk Gr DN11 122 D4
Suffolk Rd
Bircotes DN11 122 D4
Doncaster DN4 83 B6
Sheffield S2 161 B2
Suffolk View DN12 80 F2
Sugworth Rd S6 125 A7
Sulby Gr S70 55 D6
Sullivan Gr WF9 18 B1
Summerdale Rd S72 35 A5
Summerfield S65 115 E6
Summerfield Rd S18 153 B3
Summerfields Dr DN9 86 E6
Summerfield St S11 128 E1
Summer Ford Croft S36 29 D1
Summer La
Barnsley S70, S75 33 D2
Royston S71 15 B4
Sheffield S17 151 D4
Wombwell S73 56 C3
Summer Lane Prim Sch S75 33 C2
Summerley Lower Rd S18 153 F2
Summerley Rd S18 153 F2
Summer Rd S71 15 B4
Summer St
Barnsley S70 33 D2
Sheffield S3 160 B4
Summer View S71 15 B3
Summerwood La S18 152 F3
Summerwood Pl S18 152 F2
Sumner Rd S65 115 F8
Sunderland Farm Cl DN11 121 C7
Sunderland Gr DN11 121 B7
Sunderland Pl DN11 121 B7
Sunderland St
Sheffield S11 128 E1
Tickhill DN11 121 B7
Sunderland Terr S70 55 A8
Sundew Croft S35 94 D8
Sundew Gdns S35 94 D8
Sundown Pl S13 142 F8
Sundown Rd S13 142 F8
Sunlea Flats S65 115 F7
Sunningdale Ave S75 14 A1
Sunningdale Cl
Doncaster DN4 85 B6
Swinton S64 79 D2
Sunningdale Dr
Cudworth S72 16 C1
New Edlington DN12 82 A1
Sunningdale Mount S11 140 C5
Sunningdale Rd
Dinnington S25 146 F8
Doncaster DN2 63 A5
Hatfield DN7 44 F6
Sunny Ave
South Elmsall WF9 19 B2
Upton WF9 19 A7
Sunnybank
Denby Dale HD8 29 F5
Edenthorpe DN3 43 A1
Sunny Bank
Chapeltown S35 94 D7
Hoyland S74 76 F7
Sheffield S10 160 B1
Sunnybank Cres S60 131 C8
Sunny Bank Dr S72 35 C5
Sunny Bank Rd
Silkstone S75 52 F8
Stocksbridge S36 92 D6
Sunny Bank Rise S74 77 A6
Sunny Bar DN1 62 D3
Sunnybrook Cl S74 76 E4
Sunnymede Ave DN6 22 B8
Sunnymede Cres 5 DN6 22 B8
Sunnymede Terr DN6 22 B8
Sunnymede View DN6 22 B8
Sunnyside
Branton DN3 85 E8
Kirk Sandall DN3 42 E2
Stainforth DN7 24 D4
Sunnyside Cl S25 146 E6
Sunnyvale Ave S17 151 E4
Sunnyvale Mount WF9 18 E3
Sunnyvale Rd S17 151 D4
Sunrise Manor S74 76 E8
Sun Side HD8 28 F5
Surbiton St S9 130 B8
Surprise Villas S32 149 A7
Surrey Cl S70 54 F7
Surrey La S1 161 B2
Surrey Pl S1 161 B3
Surrey St
Doncaster DN4 83 B7
Sheffield S1 161 A3
Surtees Cl S66 118 E7
Sussex Cl WF9 17 D8
Sussex Gdns DN12 80 F3
Sussex Rd
Chapeltown S35 95 A5
Sheffield S4 161 C5
Sussex St
Doncaster DN4 83 B7
Sheffield S4 161 C4
Suthard Cross Rd S10 128 B4
Sutherby Ct DN4 83 A6
Sutherland Cl S81 148 F8
Sutherland Ho DN2 63 A6
Sutherland Rd S4 129 C6
Sutherland St S4 129 D5
Sutton Ave S71 33 F8
Suttonfield Rd DN6 21 D6
Sutton Rd
Askern DN6 21 E5
Kirk Sandall DN3 43 A5
Sutton Rd *continued*
Norton DN6 21 C8
Sutton St S3 160 B3
Suzanne Cres WF9 18 E3
Swaithe Ave DN5 61 F7
Swaithedale S70 55 C5
Swaithe View S70 55 D5
Swale Cl S63 58 D2
Swale Ct S60 115 F2
Swaledale Dr S73 56 E3
Swaledale Rd S7 140 D5
Swale Dr S35 94 E5
Swale Gdns S9 130 C4
Swale Rd S61 97 A3
Swallow Cl
Barnsley S70 75 F8
Kexbrough S75 32 D8
Swallow Cres S62 98 B5
Swallow Ct DN11 85 A1
Swallow Hill Rd S75 33 B7
Swallow La S26 144 E6
Swallownest Prim Sch S26 144 C7
Swallowood Ct S63 77 F6
Swallow Wood Cl S60 131 E4
Swallow Wood Ct S13 143 A6
Swallow Wood Rd S26 144 B7
Swamp Wlk S6 128 D7
Swanbourne Pl S5 113 C4
Swanbourne Rd S5 113 C5
Swanee Rd S70 55 C7
Swangate S63 77 F7
Swanland Cl DN8 26 D5
Swanland Ct DN8 26 C5
Swannington Cl DN4 85 B7
Swan Rd S26 144 E6
Swan St
Bawtry DN10 123 A6
Bentley DN5 41 B1
Rotherham S60 115 D5
Swan Syke Dr DN6 4 E3
Swarcliffe Rd S9 130 A5
Sweeny Ho S36 73 A1
Sweet La DN11 102 C7
Sweyn Croft S70 55 A5
Swifte Rd S60 116 A3
Swift Rd S35 112 D8
Swift Rise S61 96 A6
Swift St S75 33 D2
Swift Way S2 129 E1
Swinburne Ave
Adwick le S DN6 40 A5
Doncaster DN4 83 B6
Swinburne Cl DN3 42 F8
Swinburne Pl S65 116 B5
Swinden Tech Ctr S60 116 A3
Swinnock La S35 93 A2
Swinnow Rd DN11 122 C4
Swinston Hill Gdns S25 147 A8
Swinston Hill Rd S25, S81 147 B6
Swinton Bridge Ind Est S64 79 E4
Swinton Brookfield Prim Sch S64 79 D2
Swinton Com Sch S64 79 C2
Swinton Hall S64 79 C3
Swinton Meadows Bsns Pk S64 79 F3
Swinton Meadows Ind Est S64 79 F3
Swinton Queen Prim Sch S64 79 D3
Swinton Rd S64 79 F4
Swinton St S3 161 A5
Swinton Sta S64 79 E3
Swithen Hill S75 13 B3
Sycamore Ave
Armthorpe DN3 64 C7
Cudworth S72 35 B7
Dronfield S18 153 A3
Grimethorpe S72 36 B5
Rotherham S66 117 C5
Wales S26 145 C2
Sycamore Cres
Bawtry DN10 122 F7
Wath u D S63 78 F5
Sycamore Ct
Mexborough S64 79 E5
Oughtibridge S35 111 D7
Sheffield S11 140 C7
Sycamore Ctr S65 98 B1
Sycamore Dr
Finningley DN9 86 A4
Killamarsh S21 156 C5
Royston S71 15 A3
Thurcroft S66 133 F7
Sycamore Farm Cl S66 117 B3
Sycamore Flats S63 78 F5
Sycamore Gn HD8 29 E7
Sycamore Gr
Conisbrough DN12 81 A1
Doncaster DN4 84 F8
Sycamore Hall Prep Sch DN4 83 A7
Sycamore House Rd S5 113 F6
Sycamore La WF4 12 F8
Sycamore Rd
Barnby Dun DN3 42 F7
Carlton in L S81 148 E7
Hemsworth WF9 17 C6
Mexborough S64 79 E5
Rotherham S65 98 B1
Sheffield S35 113 B8
Stocksbridge S36 92 A8
Sycamore St
Barnsley S75 33 C2
Sheffield, Beighton S20 143 F4
Sycamore St *continued*
Sheffield S20 155 C8
Sycamores The
Bentley DN5 61 D8
Sheffield S13 142 C6
Sycamore View DN5 61 D1
Sycamore Wlk
Penistone S36 51 D3
Thurnscoe S63 37 D1
Syday La S21 156 D1
Sydney Rd S6 160 A4
Sykehouse La S6 126 D7
Sykehouse Rd DN14 7 E7
Sykes Ave S75 33 D2
Sykes Ct S64 79 D1
Sykes St S70 54 D7
Sylvan Cl S66 119 B6
Sylvester Ave DN4 62 C1
Sylvester Gdns S1 161 A2
Sylvester St S1 161 A2
Sylvestria Ct DN11 85 A1
Sylvia Cl S13 143 D7
Symes Gdns DN4 63 F1
Symonds Ave S62 97 C8
Symons Cres S5 112 F4
Syringa Ct DN11 121 E4

T

Tadcaster Cl DN12 80 F2
Tadcaster Cres S8 140 F4
Tadcaster Rd S8 140 F4
Tadcaster Way 1 S8 140 F4
Tait Ave DN12 101 B8
Talbot Ave DN3 42 F7
Talbot Circ DN3 43 A7
Talbot Cres S2 161 C2
Talbot Gdns S2 161 C2
Talbot Pl S2 161 C2
Talbot Rd
Bircotes DN11 122 B4
Penistone S36 51 C3
Sheffield S2 161 C3
Swinton S64 79 F3
Talbot Sch S8 141 C2
Talbot St S2 161 C2
Talmont Rd S11 140 B6
Tamar Cl S75 32 E3
Tanfield Cl S71 15 A4
Tanfield Rd S6 112 D1
Tanfield Way S66 117 B4
Tankersley La S74 76 A5
Tankersley St Peter's CE Prim Sch S75 75 F5
Tank Row S71 34 D1
Tannery Cl S13 143 B6
Tannery St S13 143 B6
Tan Pit Cl DN5 37 D4
Tanpit La DN6 4 D5
Tan Pit La DN5 37 D4
Tansley Dr S9 114 B4
Tansley St S9 114 B4
Tanyard Croft S72 17 A3
Taplin Rd S6 128 B8
Tapton Bank S10 128 A2
Tapton Crescent Rd S10 128 B2
Tapton Ct 1 S10 128 B2
Tapton Hill Rd S10 128 A2
Tapton House Rd S10 128 B2
Tapton Mews S10 128 B3
Tapton Mount Cl S10 128 B2
Tapton Park Gdns S10 128 A1
Tapton Park Rd S10 128 A1
Tapton Sch S10 128 A2
Tapton (Univ of Sheffield) S10 128 C3
Taptonville Cres S10 128 C2
Taptonville Rd S10 128 C2
Tapton Wlk S10 128 B2
Tarleton Cl DN3 43 A4
Tasker Rd S10 128 B4
Tasman Gr S66 118 E6
Tatenhill Gdns DN4 85 A7
Taunton Ave S9 114 B3
Taunton Gdns S64 80 C6
Taunton Gr S9 114 B4
Taverner Cl S35 94 D8
Taverner Croft S35 94 E8
Taverner Way S35 94 E8
Tavistock Rd S7 140 F7
Tavy Cl S75 32 E5
Tay Cl
Dronfield S18 152 D2
Mapplewell S75 33 C7
Taylor Cres
Grimethorpe S72 36 B6
Woodsetts S81 147 E3
Taylor Dr S81 147 E3
Taylor Hill S75 31 E4
Taylor Row 5 S70 54 F8
Taylors Cl S62 97 E2
Taylors Ct S62 97 F2
Taylors La S62 97 F2
Taylor St DN12 81 D2
Tay St S6 160 A4
Teapot Cnr DN5 37 D4
Tedgness Rd S32 149 E1
Teesdale Rd
Rotherham S61 96 F3
Sheffield S12 154 F8
Teeside Cl DN5 61 D5
Telford Rd DN5 62 A5
Telson Cl S64 79 A3
Temperance St S64 79 D3
Tempest Ave S73 57 A7
Tempest Rd WF9 18 C4
Templar Cl S66 133 D6
Templeborough Ent Pk S60 115 C4
Temple Cres S66 117 D4
Temple Gdns DN4 85 A7
Temple Rd S9 114 F3
Templestowe Gate DN12 81 E2
Temple Way S71 34 D3
Ten Acre Rd S61 114 F8
Tenby Gdns DN4 83 A7
Ten Lands La WF4 16 A7
Tennyson Ave
Armthorpe DN3 64 C6
Bentley DN5 61 F4
Mexborough S64 80 B6
Norton DN6 4 C1
Thorne DN8 26 C7
Tennyson Cl
Dinnington S25 147 A8
Penistone S36 51 D4
Tennyson Rd
Barnsley S71 34 B3
Bentley DN5 41 B1
Maltby S66 119 A4
Rotherham S65 116 B6
Sheffield S6 128 D6
Tennyson Rise S63 78 C8
Ten Pound Wlk DN4 62 D1
Ten Row HD8 29 A4
Tenter Balk La DN6 40 B5
Tenterden Rd S5 113 F4
Tenter Hill S36 51 A4
Tenter House Ct HD8 30 B5
Tenter La
Oxspring S36 73 A6
Warmsworth DN4 82 D6
Tenter Rd DN4 82 D6
Tenters Gn S70 54 F4
Tenter St
Rotherham S60 115 C7
Sheffield S1 161 A4
Terminus Rd S7 140 C3
Terrace Rd S62 97 F4
Terrey Rd S17 151 E5
Terry St S9 130 B7
Tetney Rd S10 127 F2
Tewitt Rd DN5 41 A4
Teynham Dr S5 112 F2
Teynham Rd S5 112 E2
Thackeray Ave S62 98 B7
Thames St S60 115 C7
Thatch Pl S61 97 A3
Thealby Gdns DN4 84 C7
Thellusson Ave DN5 61 C6
Theobald Ave DN4 62 F2
Theobald Cl DN4 62 E1
Theodore Rd DN6 21 E7
Thicket Dr S66 119 B6
Thicket La S70 55 C4
Thickett La S36 72 E8
Thickwoods La S36 71 B3
Third Ave
Adwick le S DN6 40 C4
Upton WF9 19 A8
Third Sq DN7 24 E4
Thirlmere Ct S64 80 D6
Thirlmere Dr
Dronfield S18 153 A2
North Anston S25 146 F6
Thirlmere Gdns DN3 42 F3
Thirlmere Rd
Barnsley S71 34 A1
Sheffield S8 140 E5
Thirlwall Ave DN12 81 A2
Thirlwell Rd S8 141 A6
Thirsk Cl DN12 80 E2
Thistle Dr WF9 18 F7
Thistley Ct S72 35 F8
Thomas Rd DN7 24 F3
Thomas Rotherham Coll S60 115 E4
Thomas St
2 Barnsley S70 54 F8
Darfield S73 57 B5
Hemsworth WF9 17 E6
Kiveton Park S26 145 D2
New Edlington DN12 82 B1
Sheffield S1 160 C2
Swinton, Bow Broom S64 79 D4
Swinton, Kilnhurst S62 98 E7
Worsbrough S70 55 A5
Thomas Way WF9 19 A4
Thompson Ave
Harworth DN11 121 F4
New Edlington DN12 82 B2
Thompson Cl
Maltby S66 118 E7
Rawmarsh S62 97 C8
Thompson Dr
Hatfield DN7 44 B7
Swinton S64 79 C1
Thompson Gdns S35 94 C8
Thompson Hill S35 94 C7
Thompson House Gn S6 109 B4
Thompson Nook DN7 44 B8
Thompson Rd
Sheffield S11 128 D1
Wombwell S73 56 D2
Thompson Terr DN6 22 A8
Thomson Ave DN4 82 F7
Thomson Cl S63 78 F6
Thoresby Ave
Barnsley S71 34 C3
Doncaster DN4 62 F1
Thoresby Cl
Aston S26 144 F7

Thoresby Cl *continued*
Harworth DN11 122 B5
Thoresby Rd S6 128 C7
Thornborough Cl S2 141 C7
Thornborough Pl S2 141 C7
Thornborough Rd S2 141 C7
Thornbridge Ave S12 142 D3
Thornbridge Cl S12 142 D3
Thornbridge Cres S12 142 E3
Thornbridge Dr S12 142 D3
Thornbridge Gr S12 142 D3
Thornbridge La S12 142 E3
Thornbridge Pl S12 142 D3
Thornbridge Rd S12 142 D3
Thornbridge Rise S12 142 E3
Thornbridge Way S12 142 E3
Thornbrook Cl S35 95 B6
Thornbrook Gdns S35 95 B6
Thornbrook Mews S35 95 B6
Thornbury Hill La S81 136 D8
Thornbury Hospl S10 128 A1
Thorncliffe Cl S26 144 B6
Thorncliffe Gdns DN9 86 A7
Thorncliffe La S35 94 F7
Thorncliffe Rd S35 95 A8
Thorncliffe View S35 94 F7
Thorncliff Way S75 75 E5
Thorndale Rise S60 131 D8
Thorne Brooke Prim Sch DN8 26 D6
Thorne Cl
Barnsley S71 33 E7
Harworth DN11 121 D4
Thorne & Dikesmarsh Rd DN8 9 A3
Thorne End Rd S75 14 B2
Thorne Green Top Prim Sch DN8 26 B6
Thorne King Edward Prim Sch DN8 26 C8
Thornely Ave S75 53 F8
Thorne Moorends Marshlands Prim Sch DN8 9 D3
Thorne Moorends West Road Prim Sch DN8 9 D3
Thorne North Sta DN8 26 A8
Thorne Rd
Bawtry DN10 123 B8
Blaxton DN9 86 F7
Doncaster DN1 62 D3
Hatfield DN7 25 E2
Sheffield S7 140 E5
Stainforth DN7 24 F4
Thorne South Sta DN8 26 C5
Thorne Waste Drain Rd DN8 27 D7
Thorn Garth DN5 62 A6
Thornham Cl DN3 64 B5
Thornham La DN3 64 F6
Thornhill Ave
Brinsworth S60 131 C7
Doncaster DN2 63 B6
Thornhill Edge 1 S60 115 C7
Thornhill Pl S63 78 E6
Thornhill Prim Sch S61 115 B7
Thornhill Rd DN11 121 E4
Thorn House La S35 92 F3
Thorn La DN3 42 D2
Thornlea Ct DN12 82 A1
Thornley Brook S63 58 B8
Thornley Sq S63 58 B8
Thornley Villas S70 75 E7
Thorn Rd S62 98 D8
Thornseat Rd S6 109 A5
Thornsett Ct S7 140 E8
Thornsett Gdns S17 151 F8
Thornsett Rd S7 140 E8
Thornton Cl WF9 17 D5
Thornton Ct WF9 19 D8
Thorntondale Rd DN5 61 D7
Thornton Pl 1 S18 152 C1
Thornton Rd S70 55 C7
Thornton St S61 114 E5
Thornton Terr
Barnsley S70 55 C7
Rotherham S61 114 E6
Thorntree Cl S61 95 F4
Thorntree La S75 33 D3
Thorntree Rd S61 95 F3
Thornwell Gr S72 35 A6
Thornwell La S61 95 F6
Thornwood Cl S63 37 C1
Thornwood Ct S63 37 D1
Thorogate S62 97 F7
Thorold Pl DN3 43 A5
Thorp Cl S2 141 A8
Thorpe Ave S18 153 C4
Thorpe Bank DN3 23 D1
Thorpe Dr S20 143 E1
Thorpefield Cl S61 95 F5
Thorpefield Dr S61 95 F5
Thorpe Gn S20 143 D1
Thorpe Grange La DN5 22 E4
Thorpehall Rd DN3 43 A3
Thorpe Hesley Inf Sch S61 95 E4
Thorpe Hesley Jun Sch S61 95 F4
Thorpe House Ave S8 141 B4
Thorpe House Rd S8 141 B4
Thorpe House Rise S8 141 B4
Thorpe La
Shireoaks S80, S81 159 D6
Sprotbrough DN5 61 B1
Thorpe La *continued*
Thorpe in B DN6 23 B2
Thorpe Marsh Nature Reserve* DN6 41 F8
Thorpe Marsh Nature Trail* DN3 42 C7
Thorpe Mere Rd DN6 42 A7
Thorpe Mere View DN6 42 A8
Thorpe Rd S26 158 A7
Thorpes Ave HD8 30 A7
Thorpe St S61 95 F5
Three Hills Cl S65 98 F3
Three Nooks La S72 16 B1
Threshfield Way 3 S12 143 B3
Thrislington Sq DN8 9 D4
Thrush Ave S60 131 D8
Thrush St S6 128 B6
Thruxton Cl S72 35 C8
Thrybergh Comp Sch S65 98 F3
Thrybergh Ct DN12 81 B3
Thrybergh Ctry Pk & Visitor Ctr* S65 99 C5
Thrybergh Fullerton CE Prim Sch S65 98 F3
Thrybergh La S65 99 B3
Thrybergh Prim Sch S65 98 E2
Thundercliffe Rd S61 114 B6
Thurbrook Gdns S66 134 A7
Thurcroft Ho 1 DN1 62 C1
Thurcroft Inf Sch S66 133 E6
Thurcroft Jun Sch S66 133 F6
Thurgoland Bank S35 73 E7
Thurgoland CE Prim Sch S35 73 F7
Thurgoland Hall Fold S35 73 F7
Thurgoland Hall La S35 74 A8
Thurlstone Prim Sch S36 51 A4
Thurlstone Rd S36 51 B4
Thurnscoe Bridge La S63 58 D7
Thurnscoe Bsns Pk S63 58 E7
Thurnscoe La S72 36 F1
Thurnscoe Rd S63 58 C2
Thurnscoe Sta S63 58 D8
Thurstan Ave S8 152 E8
Tiber View S60 115 C2
Tickhill Back La DN11 101 F2
Tickhill Estfeld Prim Sch DN11 121 A8
Tickhill Rd
Bawtry DN10 122 F7
Doncaster DN4 83 B4
Harworth DN11 121 E5
Maltby S66 119 D4
Tickhill Road Hospl DN4 83 B5
Tickhill St Mary's CE Prim Sch DN11 121 A7
Tickhill Spital DN11 121 E7
Tickhill Sq DN12 80 F3
Tickhill St DN12 80 F4
Tickhill Way DN11 104 B8
Tideswell Rd S5 113 C3
Tidewell Ct S5 113 C3
Tideworth Hague La DN14 7 E6
Tiercel Mews S25 134 E1
Tilford Rd S13 143 C6
Tillotson Cl 1 S8 141 A6
Tillotson Rise S8 141 A6
Tilt Farm Cvn Site DN5 41 B7
Tiltshills La DN5 41 A7
Tilts La
Bentley DN5 41 C7
Bentley, Shaftholme DN5 41 D6
Timothy Wood Ave S70 75 F8
Tingle Bridge Ave S73 77 C7
Tingle Bridge Cres S73 77 C7
Tingle Bridge La S73 77 C7
Tingle Cl S73 77 C7
Tinker Bottom S6 109 F1
Tinker La
Hoyland S74 76 B5
Sheffield S10, S6 128 B5
Tinker Rd S62 98 B6
Tinsley Ind Est
Sheffield, Greenland S9 130 C6
Sheffield, Tinsley S9 114 D1
Tinsley Inf Sch S9 114 E2
Tinsley Jun Sch S9 114 E2
Tinsley Park Cl S9 130 C7
Tinsley Park Rd S9 130 B7
Tinsley Rd S74 76 D7
Tinsley Sh Ctr S9 114 E2
Tippit La S72 35 C6
Tipsey Ct S75 14 D1
Tipton St S9 114 A2
Tithe Barn Ave S13 143 C7
Tithe Barn Cl S13 143 C7
Tithe Barn Ct S64 79 F8
Tithe Barn La
Sheffield S13 143 C7
Thorne DN8 26 C7
Tithe Barn Way S13 143 B7
Tithe Laithe S74 76 E6
Tithes La DN11 121 A7
Titterton Cl S9 130 A6
Titterton St S9 130 A6
Tiverton Cl S64 79 D2
Tivy Dale S75 31 E4
Tivy Dale Cl S75 31 E4
Tivydale Dr S75 32 E7
Tivy Dale Dr S75 31 E4
Toad La S66 133 E5
Toby Wood La HD8 29 D5
Tockwith Rd S9 130 B5
Todmorden Cl DN12 80 E3
Todwick Ct S26 145 F3
Todwick House Gdns S26 145 E6
Todwick Jun & Inf Sch S26 145 E5
Todwick Rd
Sheffield S8 140 E3
Todwick S26 146 A8
Todwick Villas S26 145 E5
Toecroft La DN5 61 A1
Tofield Rd DN11 102 A8
Tofts La
Oxspring S36 73 A5
Sheffield S6 127 C4
Toftstead DN3 64 B5
Toftwood Ave S10 128 A4
Toftwood Rd S10 128 B4
Toga Bldgs S63 58 C7
Togo Bldgs S63 58 C7
Togo St S63 58 C7
Toll Bar Ave S12 141 E5
Tollbar Cl S36 73 B8
Toll Bar Cl S12 141 E5
Toll Bar Dr S12 141 F5
Toll Bar Prim Sch DN5 41 A5
Toll Bar Rd
Rotherham S65 116 E4
Sheffield S12 141 E5
Swinton S64 79 B3
Tollesby La DN7 44 B7
Tollgate Cl S72 16 D1
Tollgate Ct S3 129 B7
Toll House Mead S20 155 C7
Tolson Ct S36 51 C4
Tomlinson Rd S74 77 A6
Tom Wood Ash La WF9 19 E7
Tooker Rd S60 115 E5
Topcliffe Rd S71 34 A5
Top Field La S65 116 D8
Top Fold Cotts DN12 80 B2
Top Hall Rd DN4 84 F6
Top House Ct WF8 3 D6
Top La
Clayton DN5 37 B5
Kirk Bramwith DN7 24 A5
Toppham Dr S8 152 F6
Toppham Rd S8 152 F6
Toppham Way S8 152 F6
Top Rd
Barnby Dun DN3 42 F7
Denby Dale HD8 29 E7
Oughtibridge S35 111 D5
Top Row S75 13 E3
Top Side S35 112 B8
Top St
Bawtry DN10 123 A7
Hemsworth WF9 17 C7
Top Terr 1 S10 128 C3
Top Tree Way S65 98 F3
Top View Cres DN12 101 B8
Torbay Rd S4 129 D7
Tor Cl S71 34 B5
Torksey Cl DN4 84 E5
Torksey Rd S5 113 D4
Torksey Rd W S5 113 D4
Torne Cl DN4 85 A6
Torne View DN9 86 A8
Tornville Cres DN14 2 D8
Torry Ct S13 143 C6
Tortmayns S26 145 F5
Torver Dr S63 58 C1
Tor Way S60 131 D8
Torwood Dr S8 152 E7
Totley All Saints CE Prim Sch S17 151 D4
Totley Brook Cl S17 151 D5
Totley Brook Croft S17 151 D5
Totley Brook Glen S17 151 D5
Totley Brook Gr S17 151 D5
Totley Brook Rd S17 151 E5
Totley Brook Way S17 151 D5
Totley Cl S71 34 B7
Totley Grange Cl S17 151 D4
Totley Grange Dr S17 151 D4
Totley Grange Rd S17 151 D4
Totley Hall Croft S17 151 D3
Totley Hall Dr S17 151 D4
Totley Hall La S17 151 D4
Totley Hall Mead S17 151 D3
Totley La S17 152 A5
Totley Prim Sch S17 151 D4
Towcester Way S64 80 C6
Tower Ave WF9 19 A8
Tower Cl
Bentley DN5 40 D1
Sheffield S2 141 C8
Tower Dr S2 141 C8
Tower Ho S2 141 C8
Tower St S70 54 E7
Town End
Apperknowle S18 154 A1
Doncaster DN5 62 B4
Townend Ave S65 98 E1
Town End Ave S26 144 E8
Townend Cl S60 131 E4
Townend La S36 92 E7
Town End Rd S35 113 A8
Townend St S10 128 C4
Town Field La S35 93 A3
Town Field Prim Sch DN1 62 E4
Town Fields Ave S35 113 C8
Town Field Villas DN1 62 E3
Towngate
Bawtry DN10 123 A7
Darton S75 14 B1
Penistone S36 51 A4
Silkstone S75 52 F8
Towngate Gr S35 111 D5
Towngate Mews 1 S75 14 B1
Towngate Rd S35 111 D5
Townhead Rd S17 151 C7
Townhead St S1 161 A3
Town La S61 96 E3
Town Lands Cl S73 56 F4
Town Moor Ave DN2 62 F4
Town St
Hemsworth WF9 17 C7
Rotherham S60 115 D4
Sheffield S9 114 D2
Town View Ave DN5 61 B8
Town Wells Ct S25 146 D5
Toyne St S10 128 B4
Traditional Heritage Mus* S11 140 C8
Trafalgar Ho DN6 21 C1
Trafalgar Rd S6 112 C4
Trafalgar St
Adwick le S DN6 21 C1
Sheffield S1 160 C2
Trafalgar Way DN6 21 C1
Trafford Ct DN1 62 C3
Trafford Rd DN6 4 D3
Trafford Way DN1 62 C2
Tranmoor Ave DN4 84 F7
Tranmoor Ct
Armthorpe DN3 64 B5
Hoyland S74 76 B5
Tranmoor La DN3 64 B5
Tranquil Wlk DN11 103 D8
Trap La S11 139 E6
Traso Bsns Pk S18 153 D1
Travey Rd S2 142 A7
Travis Ave DN8 26 C7
Travis Cl
Hatfield DN7 44 C8
Thorne DN8 26 C7
Travis Ct DN4 62 A1
Travis Gdns
Doncaster, Hexthorpe DN4 61 F1
Doncaster, Hexthorpe DN4 62 A1
Travis Gr DN8 26 D7
Travis Pl S10 160 B2
Tredis Cl S71 34 B3
Treecrest Rise S75 33 E4
Treefield Cl S61 97 A3
Treelands S75 33 B3
Tree Root Wlk S10 160 A3
Treeton CE Prim Sch S60 131 F3
Treeton Ent Ctr S60 131 E3
Treeton Ho 15 DN1 62 C2
Treeton La
Aston S26 132 C2
Catliffe S60 131 D5
Treeton Wood Nature Reserve* S26 132 A2
Treetown Cres S60 131 E5
Treherne Rd S60 115 F5
Trelawney Wlk S70 54 F5
Trent Cl DN12 82 C3
Trent Gdns DN3 42 F5
Trent Gr S18 153 B3
Trentham Cl S60 131 D8
Trenton Cl S13 143 D6
Trenton Rise S13 143 D6
Trent St S9 129 E6
Trent Terr 2 DN12 81 C3
Treswell Cres S6 128 C8
Trewan Ct S71 34 B3
Trickett Rd
Chapeltown S35 94 C8
Sheffield S6 128 C7
Trinity Acad DN8 26 C8
Trinity Croft CE Jun & Inf Sch S65 116 D8
Trinity Ct WF9 19 A3
Trinity Dr HD8 29 F5
Trinity Mdws S35 73 F7
Trinity Mews S70 54 D8
Trinity Rd S26 145 F2
Trinity St S3 161 A4
Trinity Wlk WF9 19 A4
Trippet Ct S10 140 A8
Trippet La S1 161 A3
Tristford Cl S60 131 D6
Troon Rd DN7 44 C7
Troon Wlk S25 146 F8
Tropical Butterfly Ho* S25 147 A6
Trouble Wood La S6 110 C4
Trough Dr S65 99 A2
Trough La WF9 19 C3
Troutbeck Cl S63 58 C7
Troutbeck Rd S7 140 E4
Troutbeck Way DN11 103 E7
Trowell Way S71 33 F8
Trueman Gn S66 118 E6
Trueman Terr S71 34 E2
Trueman Way WF9 19 A4
Truman Gr S36 73 F1
Truman St DN5 62 A8
Trumfleet La DN6 23 C7
Trundle La DN7 24 F8
Truro Ave DN2 63 C8
Truro Ct S71 34 B3
Truswell Ave S10 128 B4
Truswell Rd S10 128 A3
Tudor Ct
Grimethorpe S72 36 A6
South Elmsall WF9 18 F3
Tudor Rd
Adwick le S DN6 40 C3
Doncaster DN2 63 B4
Tudor Sq S1 161 B3
Tudor St
Rossington DN11 103 F8
Thurnscoe S63 58 E8
Tudor Way S70 55 A5
Tudworth Field Rd DN8 26 C2
Tudworth Rd
Hatfield DN8 26 B3
Thorne DN8 26 B3
Tuffolds Cl S2 142 A7
Tulip Tree Cl S20 144 A5
Tullibardine Rd S11 140 B6
Tulyar Cl DN11 103 F7
Tumbling La S71 34 F5
Tummon Rd S2 129 E2
Tummon St S61 115 B6
Tune St
Barnsley S70 55 A8
Wombwell S73 56 C3
Tun La S72 16 D7
Tunwell Ave S5 113 B7
Tunwell Dr S5 113 B7
Tunwell Greave S5 113 B7
Tunwell Rd S66 118 C1
Tup La WF4 16 C8
Turf Moor Rd DN7 45 B5
Turham Ct DN11 104 B8
Turie Ave S5 113 A6
Turie Cres S5 113 A6
Turnberry Ct DN5 62 A8
Turnberry Gr S72 16 C1
Turnberry Way S25 146 F7
Turner Ave S73 56 B3
Turner Bsns Pk S13 130 E2
Turner Cl
Dronfield S18 152 F1
Rawmarsh S62 98 A4
Turner La S60 132 B8
Turners's Cl S74 76 F7
Turners La S10 128 C2
Turner St
Great Houghton S72 36 E1
Sheffield S2 161 B2
Turnesc Gr S63 58 D7
Turnpike Croft S35 94 C1
Turnshaw Ave S26 132 C1
Turnshaw Rd S26 132 E2
Tuscany Gdns S70 55 B8
Tuscany Villas 8 S70 55 B8
Tutbury Gdns DN4 85 A7
Tuxford Cres S71 34 D2
Twelve Lands Cl S75 75 E5
Twentylands The S60 131 E3
Twentywell Ct S17 152 A7
Twentywell Dr S17 152 B6
Twentywell La S17 152 B6
Twentywell Rd S17 152 B5
Twentywell Rise S17 152 B6
Twentywell View S17 152 B6
Twibell St S71 34 A3
Twickenham Cl 11 S20 155 E6
Twickenham Cres S20 155 F6
Twickenham Ct 8 S20 155 E6
Twickenham Glade 10 S20 155 E6
Twickenham Glen S20 155 F5
Twickenham Gr 9 S20 155 E6
Twigg Ct S64 79 E1
Twitchill Dr S13 143 A6
Two Gates Way S72 16 C2
Twyford Cl S64 79 A2
Tyas Pl S64 80 C5
Tyas Rd S5 113 B7
Tye Rd S20 144 A3
Tyler St S9 114 B3
Tyler Way S9 114 B3
Tylney Rd S2 129 D2
Tynedale Ct DN3 43 A4
Tynker Ave S20 144 A3
Tyzack Rd S8 140 E2

U

Ughill Rd S6 109 F2
Uldale Wlk DN6 21 C1
Ulley Cres S13 142 B7
Ulley Ctry Pk* S26 132 D4
Ulley Ctry Pk Visitor Ctr* S26 132 C4
Ulley La
Aston S26 144 E8
Ulley S26 132 D3
Ulley Rd S13 142 B7
Ulley View S26 132 D2
Ullswater Ave S20 155 E6
Ullswater Cl
Bolton u D S63 58 C1
Dronfield S18 152 E2
North Anston S25 146 E7
Sheffield S20 155 E6
Ullswater Dr S18 152 E2
Ullswater Pk S18 152 E2
Ullswater Pl S18 152 E2
Ullswater Rd
Barnsley S71 56 B8
Mexborough S64 80 D6
Ullswater Wlk DN5 61 C7
Ulrica Dr S66 133 E6
Ulverston Ave DN6 22 C8
Ulverston Rd S8 140 E4
Underbank La S36 72 F4
Undercliffe Rd S6 127 F6
Undergate Rd S25 134 E1
Underhill S70 55 B4
Underhill La S6 112 B5
Underwood Ave S70 55 C6
Underwood Rd S8 140 F4
Union Ct S70 54 F8
Union Dr S11 140 D6
Union La S1 161 A2
Union Rd
Sheffield S11 140 D6

Union Rd continued
Thorne DN8 26 A7
Union St
Barnsley S70 54 F8
1 Doncaster DN1 62 C2
Harthill S26 157 E6
Hemsworth WF9 17 E6
Rotherham S61 115 B6
Sheffield S1 161 A2
Unity Pl S60 115 D6
Universal Cl S25 146 B8
Universe Works S1 161 A1
Univ of Sheffield S10 160 B3
Unsliven Rd S36 72 F3
Unstone Dronfield By-Pass S18 152 F3
Unstone St S1 129 A1
Unwin Cres S36 51 D2
Unwin St S36 51 D2
Uplands Ave S75 32 C8
Uplands Rd DN3 64 C6
Uplands Way S62 97 E6
Upper Albert Rd S8 141 B5
Upper Allen St S3 160 C4
Upper Ash Gr WF9 19 B3
Upper Castle Folds S3 161 B4
Upper Chambers S35 94 F8
Upper Clara St S61 114 F6
Upper Cliffe Rd S75 53 E8
Upper Common La
Clayton West HD8 12 A1
Clayton West HD8 30 F8
Upperfield Cl S66 118 F6
Upper Field La
High Hoyland S75 12 E1
Kexbrough S75 12 E1
Upperfield Rd S66 118 E6
Upper Folderings S75 53 F7
Upper Forest Rd S71 33 F8
Upper Gate Rd S6 127 C6
Upper Hanover St S3 160 B3
Upper High Royds S75 33 A8
Upper House Fold HD8 29 F3
Upper House Rd HD9 48 C8
Upper Hoyland Rd S74 76 C7
Upper Kenyon St DN8 26 B8
Upper Ley Ct S35 95 A5
Upper Ley Dell S35 95 A5
Upper Lunns Cl S71 15 E3
Upper Maythorne La HD9 49 D8
Upper Millgate S60 115 D6
Upper New St 1 S70 54 F8
Upper Norcroft S75 31 F3
Upper Rye Cl S60 116 D1
Upper School La 5 S18 153 A1
Upper Sheffield Rd S70 55 A6
Upperthorpe S6 160 A5
Upperthorpe Glen S6 160 A5
Upperthorpe Rd
Killamarsh S21 156 D4
Sheffield S6 160 B5
Upperthorpe Villas S21 156 D5
Upper Valley Rd S8 141 B5
Upper Whiston La S60 132 D7
Upperwood Hall S73 56 E6
Upperwood Rd S73 56 E6
Upper Wortley Rd S61 96 B2
Upton Cl
Maltby S66 118 E7
Wombwell S73 56 B4
Upton Prim Sch WF9 19 C8
Upwell Hill S4 113 E1
Upwell La S4 113 E1
Upwell St S4 113 F1
Upwood Rd S6 112 B1
Urban Rd DN4 62 A1
Urch Cl DN12 81 C1
Utah Terr S12 143 C3
Uttley Cl S9 130 B6
Uttley Croft S9 130 B6
Uttley Dr S9 130 B6
Uttoxeter Ave S64 80 C6

V

Vaal St S70 55 B8
Vainor Rd S6 112 A2
Vale Ave S65 98 F2
Vale Cl S18 153 B1
Vale Cres S65 98 F2
Vale Ct S65 98 F2
Vale Gr S6 127 E8
Valentine Cl S5 113 C5
Valentine Cres S5 113 C5
Valentine Rd S5 113 C5
Vale Rd
Rotherham S65 99 A2
Sheffield S3 128 F7
Valestone Ave WF9 17 E7
Valetta Ho S62 97 F4
Vale View S36 73 B8
Valiant Gdns DN5 61 E3
Valley Ave WF9 19 B3
Valley Dr
Branton DN3 85 D8
Killamarsh S21 156 D7
Wath u D S63 78 E6
Valley Gr S71 34 F5
Valley Park Com Sch S14 141 F2
Valley Park Ind Est S73 57 A1
Valley Rd
Chapeltown S35 94 E6
Darfield S73 56 E4
Darton S75 14 A1
Killamarsh S21 156 D7
Valley Rd continued
Sheffield, Hackenthorpe S12 143 C3
Sheffield, Heeley S8 141 A6
Swinton S64 79 B1
Valley St WF9 18 F2
Valley View
Conisbrough DN12 81 E3
South Elmsall WF9 19 B3
Valley View Cl S21 155 C2
Valley Way
Hoyland S74 76 E5
Wombwell S73 56 E2
Valley Works
Sheffield, Greenland S9 130 C7
Sheffield S5 113 F8
Vancouver Dr S63 58 B2
Varley Gdns S66 117 B6
Varney Rd S63 78 E4
Varsity Cl DN7 66 A7
Vaughan Ave
Doncaster DN1 62 D4
Norton DN6 4 D1
Vaughan Rd S75 33 B3
Vaughan Terr S72 36 E2
Vaughton Hill S36 73 F1
Vauxhall Cl S9 114 B4
Vauxhall Rd S9 114 B4
Velvet Wood Cl S75 33 A3
Venetian Cres S73 56 F5
Ventnor Cl DN4 82 F7
Ventnor Ct 13 S7 140 F8
Ventnor Pl S7 140 F8
Venus Ct S60 115 C2
Verdant Way S5 113 D5
Verdon St S3 129 B5
Verelst Ave S26 144 D8
Vere Rd S6 112 C2
Verger Cl DN11 85 B1
Vermuyden Rd DN8 9 D3
Vernon Cl S70 54 F7
Vernon Cres S70 54 F5
Vernon Delph S10 127 F3
Vernon Dr S35 95 A5
Vernon Rd
Rotherham S60 116 B3
Sheffield S17 151 F6
Worsbrough S70 55 A4
Vernon St N 3 S71 33 F2
Vernon St
Barnsley, Birdwell S70 75 F6
Barnsley S71 33 F2
Hoyland S74 76 C5
Vernon Terr S10 128 A2
Vernon Way
Barnsley S75 33 B3
Maltby S66 118 E6
Verona Rise S73 57 A5
Vesey St S62 97 F4
Vicarage Cl
Doncaster DN4 85 A7
Hoyland S74 76 E6
Mexborough S64 80 C4
Rotherham S65 116 D8
Sheffield S35 112 C8
South Kirkby WF9 18 C3
Vicarage Cres S35 112 C8
Vicarage Ct S60 131 D7
Vicarage Dr DN11 102 B7
Vicarage Farm Ct S75 53 A8
Vicarage La
Rotherham S60 115 D6
Royston S71 15 C3
Sheffield S17 151 D7
Vicarage Rd
Sheffield, Grenoside S35 112 C8
Sheffield S9 129 F6
Vicarage Way DN5 41 E2
Vicarage Wlk S36 51 D3
Vicar Cres S73 57 B5
Vicar Ct S13 143 B6
Vicar La
Sheffield, Coisley Hill S13 143 B7
Sheffield S1 161 A3
Vicar Rd
Darfield S73 57 B5
Wath u D S63 78 D7
Vickers Ave WF9 18 E1
Vickers Dr S5 113 D3
Vickers Rd
Chapeltown S35 94 D7
Sheffield S5 113 D2
Victoria Ave
1 Barnsley S70 33 E2
Hatfield DN7 44 C8
Rotherham S65 115 F6
Victoria Cl
Kiveton Park S26 145 E2
Stainforth DN7 24 F2
Stocksbridge S36 73 B1
Thorne DN8 26 C5
Victoria Cres
Barnsley, Birdwell S70 75 E7
Barnsley S70, S75 33 D2
Victoria Cres W S75 33 D2
Victoria Ct
Bentley DN5 41 B3
Kiveton Park S26 145 E2
Sheffield S11 140 D6
Upton WF9 19 A7
Victoria Ho 13 S3 160 C3
Victoria La DN11 84 E1
Victoria Mews S64 98 E7
Victorian Cres DN2 62 F4
Victoria Rd
Adwick le S DN6 40 D6
Askern DN6 21 F6
Victoria Rd continued
Barnsley S70 33 E2
Bentley DN5 41 B3
Doncaster DN4 83 B8
Mexborough S64 80 A5
New Edlington DN12 82 B3
Norton DN6 4 C3
Rawmarsh S62 98 A4
Royston S71 15 D4
Sheffield, Beighton S20 143 F4
Sheffield, Broomfield S10 160 B1
Stocksbridge S36 73 C1
Wath u D S63 78 D7
Wombwell S73 56 D3
Victoria St
Barnsley S70 33 E2
Barnsley, Stairfoot S70 55 D8
Catliffe S60 131 D6
Cudworth S72 35 B7
Darfield S73 57 B6
Dinnington S25 135 A1
Dronfield S18 152 F2
Goldthorpe S63 58 E5
Hemsworth WF9 17 E6
Hoyland S74 76 F6
Maltby S66 119 A3
Mexborough S64 79 E5
Penistone S36 51 D3
Rotherham S60 115 B6
Sheffield S3 160 C3
Stocksbridge S36 73 C1
Swinton S62 98 E7
Victoria Station Rd S4 161 C4
Victoria Terr 11 S70 55 A8
Victoria Villas S6 160 B5
Victoria Way S66 118 D6
Victor Rd
Sheffield S17 151 F7
South Kirkby WF9 18 C2
Victor St
Adwick le S DN6 40 B8
3 Sheffield S6 128 D7
South Elmsall WF9 18 F2
Victor Terr 3 S70 55 A8
Viewland Cl S72 35 C5
Viewlands S75 53 A5
Viewlands Cl
Penistone S36 51 D5
Rotherham S66 117 E4
View Rd
Rotherham S65 116 A8
Sheffield S2 141 A7
Views The S75 14 B1
Viewtree Cl S62 76 D1
Vikinglea Cl S2 142 B8
Vikinglea Dr S2 142 B8
Vikinglea Glade S2 130 B1
Vikinglea Rd S2 130 B1
Viking Way S26 145 F3
Villa Gdns DN5 41 A5
Village Ct S72 35 C7
Village St DN6 40 C6
Villa Park Rd DN4 84 E8
Villa Rd DN6 40 B5
Villas The DN12 82 C3
Villiers Cl S2 141 E6
Villiers Dr S2 141 E6
Vincent Rd
Barnsley S71 34 F3
Rotherham S65 117 D7
Sheffield S7 140 F8
Vincent Terr S63 58 F7
Vine Cl
Barnsley S71 34 C4
Rotherham S60 115 C6
Vine Rd DN11 121 C7
Vineyard Cl DN11 120 F8
Viola Bank S36 73 B1
Violet Ave
New Edlington DN12 82 B1
Sheffield S20 143 F3
Violet Bank Rd S7 140 E6
Vissett Cl WF9 17 B6
Vissitt La WF9 17 B6
Vista S60 115 E5
Vivian Rd S5 113 D2
Vizard Rd S74 77 A6
Vulcan Ho 2 S65 116 A7
Vulcan Mews DN9 86 B4
Vulcan Rd S9 114 D2
Vulcan Way DN7 45 A1

W

Wadbrough Rd S11 128 D1
Waddington Rd S75 33 B2
Waddington Terr S64 80 B4
Waddington Way S65 98 A2
Wade Cl S60 115 F4
Wade Mdw S6 112 A1
Wade St
Barnsley S75 33 B2
Sheffield S4 113 E1
Wadsley La S6 112 B2
Wadsley Park Cres S6 112 A1
Wadsworth Ave S12 142 D5
Wadsworth Cl S12 142 D5
Wadsworth Dr
Rawmarsh S62 97 C8
Sheffield S12 142 D5
Wadsworth Rd
Rotherham S66 117 D4
Sheffield S12 142 C5
Wadworth Ave DN11 85 B1
Wadworth Cl DN5 59 C3
Wadworth Hall La DN11 102 B7
Wadworth Hill DN11 102 C8
Wadworth Prim Sch DN11 102 C6
Wadworth Rise S65 98 E1
Wadworth St DN12 81 A3
Waggon La WF9 19 C8
Waggons Way DN7 24 F2
Wagon Rd S61 97 B2
Waingate S3 161 B4
Wainscot Pl DN6 21 A2
Wainscott Cl S71 34 C5
Wainwright Ave
Sheffield S13 142 D8
Wombwell S73 56 C3
Wainwright Cres S13 142 D8
Wainwright Pl S73 56 B3
Wainwright Rd
Doncaster DN4 62 E2
Rotherham S61 96 F1
Wakefield Rd
Barnsley, Athersley North S71, S75 33 E7
Barnsley S71 34 A4
Darton S75 14 C2
Denby Dale HD8 30 B7
Emley HD8 12 B5
Hemsworth WF9 17 D8
Wakelam Dr DN3 63 F6
Wake Rd S7 140 E7
Walbank Rd DN3 64 C6
Walbert Ave S63 58 C7
Walbrook S70 55 B4
Walden Ave DN5 40 E1
Walden Rd S2 141 B7
Walden Stubbs Rd DN6 4 D4
Walders Ave S6 112 A2
Walders La S36 92 C6
Wales Ct S26 145 B4
Wales High Sch S26 145 C3
Walesmoor Ave S26 145 C2
Wales Pl S6 128 D6
Wales Prim Sch S26 145 B2
Wales Rd S26 145 C2
Waleswood Rd S20, S26 144 C4
Waleswood View S26 144 D6
Waleswood Villas S26 144 F3
Waleswood Way S26 144 F3
Walford Rd S21 156 C6
Walker Cl S35 112 C8
Walker Edge S36 92 A3
Walker La S65 115 E7
Walker Rd
Pilley S75 75 F5
Rotherham S61 96 F1
Walkers La S21 156 D6
Walker St
Rawmarsh S62 98 B6
Sheffield S3 161 B5
Swinton S64 79 E3
Walkers Terr S71 34 C5
Walker View S62 98 B6
Walkley Bank Cl S6 128 C7
Walkley Bank Rd S6 128 B7
Walkley Crescent Rd S6 128 B6
Walkley La S6 128 C7
Walkley Prim Sch S6 128 D6
Walkley Rd S6 128 C6
Walkley St S6 128 D5
Walkley Terr S6 128 A6
Walk The S70 75 E6
Wallace Rd
Doncaster DN4 82 E6
Sheffield S3 128 F7
Walled Gdn The WF4 14 A7
Waller Rd S6 128 A5
Walling Cl S9 114 B2
Walling Rd S9 114 B2
Wallingwells Hall S81 148 C5
Wallingwells La S81 147 F6
Wall Nook HD8 28 D6
Wall Nook La HD8 28 D6
Wallroyds HD8 29 F5
Wall St S70 54 E8
Walmsley Dr WF9 19 B7
Walney Fold S71 34 D6
Walnut Ave
Finningley DN9 86 A4
Shireoaks S81 159 F7
Tickhill DN11 121 B7
Walnut Cl S70 54 F7
Walnut Dr
Dinnington S25 146 F8
Killamarsh S21 156 C5
Walnut Gr S64 79 F6
Walnut Pl S35 94 F4
Walnut Rd DN8 9 B1
Walnut St WF9 18 F1
Walnut Tree Hill DN11 102 C7
Walpole Cl DN4 82 F5
Walpole Gr S26 132 D1
Walseker La S26 157 C7
Walsham Dr DN5 61 E5
Walshaw Gr S35 111 C5
Walshaw Rd S35 111 D5
Walters Rd S66 119 B5
Walter St
Rotherham S60 115 C7
Sheffield S6 128 D7
Waltham Dr DN6 20 E2
Waltham Gdns 1 S20 144 A2
Waltham St 7 S70 54 F8
Waltheof Rd S2 142 A8
Waltheof Sch S2 130 B2
Walton Cl
Chapeltown S35 94 C8
Dronfield S18 152 C2
Walton Ct S8 152 E8
Walton Rd
Sheffield S11 128 D1
Walton Rd continued
Upton WF9 19 D8
Walton St N S75 33 C3
Walton St S75 33 C3
Wannop St S62 97 F3
Wansfell Rd S4 113 F1
Wansfell Terr S71 34 A1
Wapping The S65 99 D7
Warburton Cl S2 141 C7
Warburton Gdns S2 141 C7
Warburton Rd S2 141 C7
Ward Cl S36 51 D2
Warde-Aldam Cres S66 117 A5
Warde Ave DN4 82 F6
Warden Cl DN4 85 A8
Warden St S60 115 D3
Ward Green Prim Sch S70 54 F5
Ward La S43 157 B2
Wardlow Rd S12 142 D5
Ward Pl 16 S7 140 F8
Wardsend Rd S6 112 D2
Wardsend Rd N S6 112 C3
Ward St
Penistone S36 51 D2
Sheffield S3 161 A5
Wards Yd S18 153 A1
Wareham Ct S20 144 A2
Wareham Gr S75 54 A8
Warehouse La S63 78 E6
Warley Rd S2 129 E1
Warminster Cl S8 141 A4
Warminster Cres S8 141 B4
Warminster Dr S8 141 B3
Warminster Gdns S8 141 A3
Warminster Pl S8 141 B2
Warminster Rd S8 141 A3
Warmsworth Ct 3 DN4 82 D6
Warmsworth Halt DN12 82 B4
Warmsworth Halt Ind Est DN12 82 C4
Warmsworth Mews 2 DN4 82 D6
Warmsworth Prim Sch DN4 82 C6
Warmsworth Rd DN4 82 E6
Warner Ave S75 33 B2
Warner Pl S75 33 C2
Warner Rd
Barnsley S75 33 B2
Sheffield S6 112 B1
Warnington Dr DN4 85 B5
Warning Tongue La DN4 85 B6
Warren Ave S62 97 E7
Warren Cl
Doncaster, Intake DN2 63 A4
Royston S71 15 D5
Warmsworth DN4 82 C6
Woodsetts S81 147 E4
Warren Cres
Barnsley S70 54 F7
Eckington S21 154 E2
Warren Dr S61 114 F8
Warreners Dr S65 99 A2
Warren Gdns S35 95 B8
Warren Hill S61 114 F8
Warren House Cl S66 117 D5
Warren La
Chapeltown S35 76 A1
Chapeltown, Warren S35 95 B8
Darton S75 14 B4
Doncaster DN4 84 F5
Rossington DN11 85 A3
Warren Mount S61 114 F8
Warrenne Cl DN7 44 A7
Warrenne Rd DN7 44 A8
Warren Pl 14 S70 54 F7
Warren Quarry La S70 54 F7
Warren Rd
Conisbrough DN12 81 B1
Rotherham S66 117 B5
Thorne DN8 26 C6
Warren Rise S18 153 C3
Warren St
Sheffield S4 129 D5
Sheffield S4 129 E5
Warren The DN11 85 A2
Warren Vale
Rawmarsh S62 98 A7
Swinton S64 79 A1
Warren Vale Rd S64 79 A2
Warren View
Barnsley S70 54 F7
Hoyland S74 76 C4
Warren Wlk
Eckington S21 154 E2
Royston S71 15 D5
Warrington Rd S10 160 A4
Warris Cl S61 96 E1
Warris Pl S2 129 D3
Warsop Rd S71 14 E1
Warwick Ave S81 148 F6
Warwick Cl DN7 45 A6
Warwick Rd
Barnsley S71 34 B4
Doncaster DN2 63 B5
Maltby S66 118 C5
Warwick St S S60 115 E5
Warwick St
Rotherham S60 115 E5
Sheffield S10 128 C4
Warwick Terr S10 128 C4
Warwick Way S25 146 E7
Wasdale Ave 5 S20 155 E6
Wasdale Cl S20 155 E6

Washfield Cres S60 131 E4
Washfield La S60 131 E4
Washford Rd S9 129 E5
Washington Ave
Conisbrough DN12 81 A2
Wombwell S73 56 B2
Washington Cl S25 146 E8
Washington Gr DN5 62 A7
Washington Rd
Adwick le S DN6 40 C5
Goldthorpe S63 58 D4
Sheffield, Ecclesfield S35 95 B1
Sheffield, Sharrow Head S11 140 F8
Washington St S64 80 B5
Wasteneys Rd S26 145 F5
Watch House La DN5 62 A7
Watchley Gdns S63 58 C5
Watchley La DN5 38 B3
Watch St S13 143 E8
Water Bank DN9 67 C2
Waterdale DN1 62 D3
Waterdale Cl DN5 82 D8
Waterdale Rd S70 54 F4
Waterfield Mews 8 S20 143 E1
Waterfield Pl S70 55 E8
Waterford Rd S3 128 E7
Waterhall La S36 51 D4
Water Hall View S36 51 D4
Waterhouse Cl S65 98 E1
Watering Place Rd S36 51 A3
Water La
Hoyland S74 77 A3
Kirk Smeaton WF8 3 E6
Rotherham S60 115 D5
Sheffield S17 151 F7
South Kirkby WF9 17 F4
Stainforth DN7 24 E5
Tickhill DN11 121 A5
Woolley WF4 14 A8
Waterloo Ct S25 134 C3
Waterloo Rd 12 S70 33 D1
Waterloo Wlk S3 128 F5
Watermead S63 58 D1
Watermeade S21 155 B2
Watermead Inf Sch S5 112 F2
Water Royd Dr S75 54 A7
Waters Edge S36 71 C5
Waterside DN8 25 E8
Waterside Bsns Pk S25 134 C2
Waterside Ct S9 130 A8
Waterside Dr S66 117 C8
Waterside Gdns S35 111 D7
Waterside Pk S73 56 F2
Waterside View 6 DN12 81 C3
Waterslack Rd DN11 122 B4
Water Slacks Cl S13 143 B6
Water Slacks Dr S13 143 B6
Water Slacks Rd S13 143 B5
Water Slacks Way S13 143 B6
Water Slacks Wlk S13 143 B6
Watersmeet Rd S6 128 B7
Water St
6 Rotherham S65 115 D7
Sheffield S3 161 A4
Waterthorpe Cl 4 S20 155 F8
Waterthorpe Cres S20 155 F8
Waterthorpe Gdns 3 S20 155 F8
Waterthorpe Glade 5 S20 155 F8
Waterthorpe Glen 2 S20 155 F8
Waterthorpe Greenway S20 143 D3
Waterthorpe Inf Sch S20 143 E1
Waterthorpe Rise 1 S20 155 F8
Waterton Cl WF9 18 D3
Waterton La DN7 44 C3
Watery St S3 160 C5
Wath Central Prim Sch S63 78 F5
Wath CE Prim Sch S63 78 E7
Wath Comp Sch S63 78 F5
Wath Rd
Bolton u D S63 58 C1
Hoyland S74 77 C5
Sheffield S7 140 E6
Wath u D S63, S64 79 D5
Wombwell S73 57 A1
Wath Victoria Prim Sch S63 79 A6
Wath West Ind Est S63 78 C8
Wath Wood Bottom S63 78 F3
Wath Wood Dr S64 78 F3
Wathwood Hospl S63 78 F3
Wath Wood Rd S63 78 F3
Watkinson Gdns S20 143 F1
Watnall Rd S71 33 F8
Watson Cl S61 114 F8
Watson Glen S61 114 C8
Watson Rd
Rotherham S61 114 F8
Sheffield S10 160 A2
Watson's Croft DN7 25 B4
Watson St S74 76 B5
Watsons Wlk S3 161 B4
Watt La S10 127 F2
Waulkmill Cl WF9 19 A7
Waveney Dr S75 32 E3
Waverley Ave
Conisbrough DN12 81 C2
Doncaster DN4 82 E7
Waverley Ave *continued*
Kiveton Park S26 145 E3
Thurcroft S66 133 F6
Waverley Cotts S13 130 F3
Waverley Ct DN5 41 A4
Waverley Prim Sch DN4 82 E6
Waverley Rd S9 130 C4
Waverley View S60 131 C5
Waverley Works S4 129 D5
Waycliffe S71 34 C3
Wayford Ave S66 117 E6
Wayland Ave S70 54 F5
Wayland Rd S11 140 D8
Weakland Cl S12 142 F3
Weakland Cres S12 142 F3
Weakland Dr S12 142 F3
Weakland Way S12 142 F3
Weatherall Pl DN6 20 F2
Weather Hill La HD9 47 E8
Weaver Cl S75 32 E3
Weavers Cl S35 94 C1
Weavers Ct S36 51 D2
Weavers Wlk HD8 30 B7
Webb Ave S36 92 E8
Webbs Ave S6 127 E6
Webster Cl S61 114 D8
Webster Cres S61 114 D8
Webster St S9 114 B1
Wedgewood Cl S62 97 F5
Weedon St S9 114 B1
Weetshaw Cl S72 16 C1
Weetshaw La S72 16 B1
Weetwood Dr S11 140 B5
Weetwood Gdns S11 140 A5
Weetwood Rd S60 116 A2
Weigh La S2 161 C3
Weir Cl S74 76 F4
Weir Head S9 114 B1
Weirside S81 136 F6
Welbeck Cl S18 152 C2
Welbeck Dr S26 144 F7
Welbeck Mews S66 117 B3
Welbeck Rd
Doncaster DN4 62 F2
Harworth DN11 122 A5
Sheffield S6 128 B6
Welbeck St S75 33 D2
Welbury Gdns S20 155 E6
Welby Pl S8 140 F5
Welfare Ave DN12 81 A2
Welfare Rd
Adwick le S DN6 40 C4
Thurnscoe S63 58 D8
Welfare View
Dodworth S75 53 F8
Goldthorpe S63 58 D4
Welham Dr S60 115 E4
Welland Cl S3 128 F6
Welland Cres S74 77 B6
Welland Ct S75 32 E3
Welland Gdns S74 77 A6
Wellbourne Cl S35 95 C4
Wellcarr Rd S8 141 A2
Wellcliffe Cl S66 117 C6
Well Croft S35 94 D7
Wellcroft Cl DN2 63 C6
Wellcroft Gdns S66 117 E4
Wellcroft Ho S71 15 C3
Well Ct S12 143 B3
Well Dr S65 99 A2
Wellesley Rd S10 160 A3
Wellfield Cl
Eckington S12 142 E1
Sheffield S6 160 A5
Wellfield Cres S81 147 E3
Wellfield Gdns S71 15 D5
Wellfield Gr S36 51 D5
Wellfield Lodge S61 96 E1
Wellfield Rd
Barnsley S75 33 D3
Rotherham S61 96 E2
Sheffield S6 160 A5
Wellgate
Conisbrough DN12 81 C2
Darton S75 14 B1
Rotherham S60 115 E6
Wellgate Mount S60 115 E6
Wellgate Prim Sch S75 14 B1
Wellgate Terr 4 S60 115 E6
Well Green Rd S6 127 B5
Wellhead Rd 4 S8 141 A6
Well Hill Gr S71 15 C4
Well Hill Rd S35 73 F4
Well House La S36 51 D5
Well Houses La S35 74 D5
Wellhouse Way S36 51 D5
Wellingley La
Tickhill DN11 102 F2
Wadworth DN11 102 E5
Wellingley Rd DN4 83 C5
Wellington Ave S25 146 D7
Wellington Cl S71 34 B4
Wellington Cres S70 55 C5
Wellington Gr
Bawtry DN10 122 F8
Bentley DN5 62 A7
Wellingtonia Dr DN6 4 C1
Wellington Pl
13 Barnsley S70 33 D1
Sheffield S9 130 C4
Wellington Rd
Hatfield DN7 66 A8
New Edlington DN12 82 B2
Sheffield S6 127 E6
Wellington St
Barnsley S70 33 E1
Goldthorpe S63 58 E5
Mexborough S64 80 A5
Wellington St *continued*
Sheffield S1 160 C2
Stainforth DN7 24 F4
Welling Way S61 114 E7
Well La
Aston S26 132 C2
Barnsley S71 34 C5
Burghwallis DN6 21 A4
Rotherham S60 116 B1
Sheffield S35 113 B8
Sheffield, Wadsley S6 111 F2
Treeton S60 131 E5
Upper Whiston S60 132 D7
Wadworth DN11 102 C7
Well Lane Ct S72 57 F6
Well Meadow Dr 1 S3 160 C4
Well Meadow St S3 160 C4
Well Rd S8 141 A6
Wells Ct S75 33 C8
Wells Mount HD8 29 A6
Wells Rd DN2 62 F6
Wells St
Cudworth S72 35 B6
Kexbrough S75 32 E8
Well St 10 S70 33 D1
Wells The S25 146 D5
Wellsyke Rd DN6 40 D7
Wellthorne Ave S36 29 E1
Wellthorne La S36 29 D1
Well View Rd S61 114 D8
Wellway The S66 117 C7
Welney Pl S6 112 C4
Welton Cl DN4 84 C6
Welwyn Cl S12 142 B4
Welwyn Ct S12 142 B4
Welwyn Rd S12 142 B4
Wembley Ave DN12 81 A2
Wembley Cl DN2 63 C5
Wembley Rd
Langold S81 136 F3
Thorne DN8 9 D3
Wenchirst La DN7 8 A2
Wendan Rd DN8 26 B5
Wendel Gr S74 77 B6
Wenlock St S13 130 F1
Wensley Cl S4 113 E1
Wensley Cres DN4 84 F7
Wensley Croft S4 113 E2
Wensley Ct
Barnsley S71 33 E7
Rotherham S60 115 F2
Sheffield S4 113 E2
Wensleydale Dr S60 131 D7
Wensleydale Rd
Bentley DN5 61 D7
Rotherham S61 96 F3
Wensley Gdns S4 113 E2
Wensley Gn S4 113 E2
Wensley Rd S71 33 E7
Wensley St
Sheffield S4 113 E2
Thurnscoe S63 58 B8
Wentdale WF8 3 E6
Went Edge Rd WF8 3 B6
Wentworth S6 160 B5
Wentworth Ave
Aston S26 144 F7
Sheffield S11 140 A2
Wentworth CE Jun & Inf Sch S62 77 A1
Wentworth Cl
Rotherham S61 95 E5
Woolley WF4 13 F7
Wentworth Cres
Mapplewell S75 33 D8
Penistone S36 51 D3
Wentworth Ct
Bawtry DN10 123 A6
Rotherham S61 97 B4
Wentworth Dr
Mapplewell S75 33 D8
Rawmarsh S62 97 F4
South Kirkby WF9 18 C3
Wentworth Gdns S64 79 C1
Wentworth Ho 9 DN1 62 C2
Wentworth Ind Pk S75 75 D4
Wentworth Mdws S36 51 D4
Wentworth Mews
Barnsley S70 33 C1
Penistone S36 51 D3
Wentworth Pl S61 96 C2
Wentworth Rd
Doncaster DN2 62 F5
Dronfield S18 152 C1
Hoyland, Elsecar S74 77 A4
Hoyland, Jump S74 77 A7
Hoyland S74 55 D2
Kexbrough S75 32 D8
Mapplewell S75 33 C8
Penistone S36 51 D4
Rawmarsh S62 97 D8
Rotherham S61 96 A5
Swinton S64 98 C8
Wentworth St
Barnsley, Birdwell S70 75 F7
Barnsley S71 33 E3
Wentworth View
Hoyland S74 76 E5
Wombwell S73 56 D1
Wentworth Way
Dodworth S75 53 F6
North Anston S25 147 A7
Pilley S75 75 D4
Wescoe Ave S72 36 F1
Wesley Ave S26 144 D8
Wesley Ct S61 95 F5
Wesley La S10 128 B3
Wesley Pl S25 146 D4
Wesley Rd
Chapeltown S35 94 C7
Kiveton Park S26 145 D3
Wesley St
Barnsley S70 33 F1
South Elmsall WF9 18 E2
Wesley Terr HD8 29 F6
Wessenden Cl S75 33 A1
Wessex Gdns S17 151 D5
Westacre S36 51 E3
West Ave
Adwick le S DN6 39 F4
Bolton u D S63 58 B1
Doncaster DN4 83 A7
Rawmarsh S62 97 F6
Royston S71 15 D4
South Elmsall WF9 19 B4
Stainforth DN7 24 F4
Wombwell S73 56 B3
West Bank DN7 24 D5
Westbank Cl S18 153 B4
Westbank Ct S18 153 C4
West Bank Dr S25 146 C4
West Bank Rise S25 146 D4
West Bar S3 161 A4
Westbar Gn S1 161 A4
West Bawtry Rd S60 115 D1
Westbourne Gdns DN4 82 F5
Westbourne Gr S75 33 D3
Westbourne Rd S10 128 C2
Westbourne Sch S10 128 C2
Westbourne Terr S70 33 C1
West Bretton Jun & Inf Sch WF4 12 F8
Westbrook Bank S11 140 D8
Westbrook Ct S11 140 E8
Westbrook Rd S35 95 A5
Westbury Ave S35 95 B4
Westbury Cl S75 33 B4
Westbury St S9 129 F5
Westby Cl S65 117 E8
Westby Cres S60 116 B1
Westby Wlk S66 117 E5
West Carr Rd S25 134 D1
West Circuit DN3 42 C8
West Cl S61 114 E8
West Cres
Oxspring S36 52 A2
Stocksbridge S36 73 A1
Westcroft Cres S20 155 E8
Westcroft Dr S20 155 E7
Westcroft Gdns S20 155 E8
Westcroft Glen S20 155 E7
Westcroft Gr S20 155 E7
Westcroft Rd WF9 17 D7
West Ct DN8 26 B6
West Don St S6 128 E6
West End Ave
Bentley DN5 62 A7
Penistone S36 50 D3
Royston S71 15 A3
West End Cres S71 15 A3
West End Ct DN11 104 B8
West End La DN11 84 E1
West End Prim Sch WF9 17 C7
West End Rd
Norton DN6 4 C3
Wath u D S63 78 B7
West End View S21 155 C2
Westerdale Rd DN5 61 D6
Western Ave S25 146 F8
Western Bank S10 160 A3
Western Cl S25 146 F8
Western Rd
Rotherham S65 116 B6
Sheffield S10 128 C4
Western St S70 33 E2
Western Terr S73 56 C3
Western Wlk DN10 123 A8
Westerton Dr S66 117 F4
West Farm La S65 116 D8
Westfield Ave
Aston S26 132 C1
Penistone S36 51 A4
Sheffield S12 143 C3
Westfield Bglws
3 South Elmsall WF9 18 F2
South Elmsall WF9 19 A2
Westfield Cl DN11 120 F7
Westfield Craft Pk S62 97 E4
Westfield Cres
Askern DN6 22 B8
Sheffield S20 155 C8
Thurnscoe S63 37 C1
Westfield Croft S63 77 F7
Westfield Ctr S20 155 E8
Westfield Gr
Ingbirchworth S36 29 D1
4 Sheffield S12 143 B3
Westfield La
Barnburgh DN5 59 B3
Fishlake DN7 7 C1
Norton WF8 3 F3
Penistone S36 51 A4
South Elmsall WF9 18 F2
Westfield Northway S20 155 E8
Westfield Rd
Armthorpe DN3 64 A6
Doncaster DN4 83 B8
Fishlake DN7 24 D8
Hatfield DN7 44 C8
Hemsworth WF9 17 D7
Killamarsh S21 156 C5
Rawmarsh S62 97 E4
Rotherham S66 117 D5
Tickhill DN11 120 F7
Wath u D S63 78 A7
Westfields
Royston S71 15 A4
Worsbrough S70 55 A4
Westfield Sch S20 155 D8
Westfield Southway S20 155 E8
Westfield St S70 33 D1
Westfield Sta S20 155 F8
Westfield Terr S1 160 C3
Westfield Villas DN7 44 C8
West Garth Cl S25 134 F1
Westgate
Barnsley, Monk Bretton S71 34 B4
Barnsley S70 33 E1
Hemsworth WF9 17 C6
Penistone S36 51 E2
Rotherham S60 115 D6
West Gate
Holme HD9 47 F8
Mexborough S64 80 C5
Tickhill DN11 120 F6
Westgate Mews S26 132 C1
West Gr
Doncaster DN2 63 A5
Royston S71 15 A4
West Green Dr DN3 42 E4
West Hall Fold S62 77 A1
Westhaven S72 35 C5
West Hill S61 114 C6
Westhill La S3 160 C3
West Ho S8 141 A4
Westholme Rd DN4 62 B1
West Kirk La S72 57 F7
West La
Aston S26 132 B1
Bradfield S6 109 F1
Carr S66 118 B1
Sheffield S6 111 A2
Sykehouse DN14 6 F4
West Laith Gate 4 DN1 62 C3
Westland Cl S20 143 E1
Westland Gdns S20 143 D1
Westland Gr 3 S20 155 E8
Westland Rd 1 S20 155 E8
West Meadows Prim Sch S74 76 C6
West Melton Jun & Inf Sch S63 78 C7
Westminster Ave S10 127 B1
Westminster Chambers 6 S3 160 B3
Westminster Cl
Rotherham S66 117 E4
Sheffield S10 127 B1
Westminster Cres
Doncaster DN2 63 C5
Sheffield S10 127 B1
Westminster Dr DN7 43 E4
Westminster Ho DN2 63 C5
Westmoor Cl S63 58 C5
West Moor Cres S75 33 A1
West Moor La DN3 64 D8
West Moor Pk DN3 64 E7
Westmoreland St 1 S6 128 E5
Westmorland Ct DN11 122 D4
Westmorland Dr S81 148 F8
Westmorland Ho DN11 122 D4
Westmorland La DN12 80 F3
Westmorland St DN4 82 F6
Westmorland Way DN5 61 B1
Westmount Ave S63 78 C8
Westnall Ho S35 111 D7
Westnall Rd S5 113 D7
Westnall Terr S5 113 D7
Westoff La S72 16 D7
West One Aspect 1 S3 160 C2
West One Central 9 S1 160 C3
West One City 8 S1 160 C3
West One Cube 4 S3 160 C2
West One Peak 12 S1 160 C3
West One Plaza 10 S1 160 C3
West One Reflect 2 S3 160 C2
West One Space 3 S3 160 C2
West One Twr 11 S1 160 C3
Westongales Way DN5 62 A8
Weston Park Hospl S10 160 A3
Weston Park Mus* S10 160 A3
Weston Rd DN4 83 B6
Weston St S3 160 B4
Weston View 4 S10 128 C3
Westover Rd S10 127 E2
West Park Dr S26 144 B7
West Pinfold S71 15 C2
Westpit Hill S63 78 A7
West Pl DN5 41 B1
West Quadrant S5 113 D3
West Rd
Barnsley S75 33 C2
Mexborough S64 79 F5
Thorne DN8 9 D3
West Service Rd DN3 42 C8
Westside Grange DN4 83 A8
West St
Conisbrough DN12 81 C2
Darfield S73 57 A5
Doncaster DN1 62 C3
Dronfield S18 152 F2
Eckington S21 155 C2
Goldthorpe S63 58 E5
Harworth DN11 122 A5
Hemsworth WF9 17 C7
Hoyland S74 76 D6
Mexborough S64 80 A4
Royston S71 15 D4
Sheffield, Beighton S20 144 A3
Sheffield S1 160 C3
South Anston S25 146 D4
South Elmsall WF9 19 B4

West St *continued*
South Hiendley S72 16 E5
South Kirkby WF9 18 A2
Thorne DN8 26 B6
Thurcroft S66 133 F6
Wath u D S63 78 E6
Wombwell S73 56 C3
Worsbrough S70 55 B4
West Street La S1 161 A3
Westthorpe Fields Rd S21 156 C4
Westthorpe Rd S21 156 D5
West Vale Gr S65 98 F2
West View
Barnsley S70 54 E7
Carlton in L S81 148 F8
Cudworth S72 35 C5
Silkstone S75 53 A6
West View Cl S17 151 F6
West View Cres S63 58 D4
West View La S17 151 F6
West View Rd
Mexborough S64 80 A4
Rotherham S61 114 C6
Westville Rd S75 33 D3
West Way S70 33 E1
Westways Middle Sch S10 128 C4
Westwell Pl S20 155 D6
Westwick Cres S8 152 D7
Westwick Gr S8 152 E7
Westwick Rd S8 152 E7
Westwood Ave S6 111 F3
Westwood Cl S6 111 F3
Westwood Ct
Barnsley S70 33 E2
Chapeltown S35 94 D8
Westwood Ctry Pk* S35 75 E2
Westwood La S35, S75 75 C3
Westwood New Rd
Chapeltown S35 94 C7
Pilley, Tankersley S75 75 E5
Pilley, Upper Tankersley S35, S75 75 D3
Westwood Rd
Bawtry DN10 122 F6
Chapeltown S35 94 D8
Sheffield S11 139 F8
Wetherby Cl DN5 61 D5
Wetherby Ct S9 130 C4
Wetherby Dr
Aston S26 144 C6
Mexborough S64 80 B6
Wet Moor La
Wath u D S63 78 F7
Wath u D, West Melton S63 78 D7
Wet Shaw La S6 109 E1
Whaley Rd S75 33 A5
Whams Rd S36 49 F2
Wharf Cl S64 79 E3
Wharfedale Dr S35 94 E5
Wharfedale Rd S75 33 B2
Wharf Rd
Doncaster DN1 62 D5
Sheffield S9 114 D3
Swinton S62 98 E7
Wharf St
Barnsley S71 34 A3
Bawtry DN10 123 A7
Sheffield S2 161 B4
Swinton S64 79 E3
Wharncliffe S75 54 A6
Wharncliffe Ave
Aston S26 144 E8
Wath u D S63 78 F6
Wharncliffe Side S35 93 B3
Wharncliffe Bsns Pk S71 34 B8
Wharncliffe Cl
Hoyland S74 76 D4
Rawmarsh S62 97 D8
Wharncliffe Ct S75 75 D6
Wharncliffe & Grenoside Nature Reserve* S35 93 E3
Wharncliffe & Grenoside Nature Trails* S35 94 A3
Wharncliffe Ho S63 78 F6
Wharncliffe Ind Complex S36 74 A1
Wharncliffe Rd
Chapeltown S35 94 D7
Sheffield S10 160 B2
Wharncliffe Side Prim Sch S35 93 B2
Wharncliffe St
Barnsley S70 33 D1
Doncaster DN4 62 A2
Rotherham S65 115 E6
Royston S71 34 D8
Wharton Ave S26 132 D1
Wheatacre Rd S36 73 C1
Wheata Dr S5 113 B7
Wheata Pl S5 113 A7
Wheata Rd S5 113 A7
Wheat Croft DN12 81 E2
Wheatcroft Rd S62 98 B6
Wheatcrofts S70 33 D1
Wheatfield Cl DN3 43 A6
Wheatfield Cres S5 113 D6
Wheatfield Dr
Thurnscoe S63 58 D7
Tickhill DN11 121 B8
Wheatfields DN8 26 B7
Wheathill St S60 115 D5
Wheat Holme La DN5 41 D8
Wheatley Cl S71 33 F4
Wheatley Gr S13 130 E1
Wheatley Hall Rd DN2 62 F6
Wheatley Hill La HD8 30 E8
Wheatley La DN1 62 D4
Wheatley Pl [8] DN12 80 F3
Wheatley Rd
Barnsley S70 55 E7
Bentley DN5 41 A2
Rotherham S61 96 E1
Swinton S62 98 E7
Wheatley Rise S75 14 B2
Wheatley St DN12 80 F3
Wheats La [1] S1 161 A4
Wheeldon St S1 160 C3
Wheel La
Oughtibridge S35 111 C7
Sheffield S35 112 D8
Wheel The S35 112 F8
Wheldrake Rd S5 113 D2
Whernside Ave S35 94 F6
Whih Moor La S75 52 C7
Whinacre Cl S8 153 B6
Whinacre Pl S8 153 A6
Whinacre Wlk S8 153 A6
Whinby Croft S75 53 F7
Whinby Rd S75 53 E8
Whin Cl WF9 17 D5
Whinfell Cl DN6 40 B6
Whinfell Ct S11 139 E2
Whin Gdns S63 37 D1
Whin Hill Rd DN4 84 D8
Whinmoor Cl S75 31 F1
Whinmoor Ct S75 31 F1
Whinmoor Dr
Clayton West HD8 12 A4
Silkstone S75 31 F1
Whinmoor Rd
Chapeltown S35 94 C7
Sheffield S5 113 F3
Whinmoor View S75 31 F1
Whinmoor Way S75 31 F1
Whinside Cres S63 37 C1
Whins The S61, S62 97 C5
Whiphill Cl DN4 84 E7
Whiphill La DN3 64 C5
Whirlow Court Rd S11 139 F2
Whirlowdale Cl S11 139 F2
Whirlowdale Cres S7 140 B3
Whirlowdale Rd S7, S11 140 B3
Whirlowdale Rise S11 139 F2
Whirlow Farm Mews S11 139 F2
Whirlow Gn S11 139 E2
Whirlow Gr S11 139 F2
Whirlow Grange Ave S11 139 E2
Whirlow Grange Dr S11 139 E2
Whirlow La S11 139 F3
Whirlow Mews S11 139 F3
Whirlow Park Rd S11 139 F1
Whispering Mdws DN14 7 C7
Whisperwood Dr DN4 83 C4
Whiston Brook View S60 116 D1
Whiston Gn S60 132 B8
Whiston Gr S60 115 F4
Whiston Grange S60 116 A1
Whiston Grange Sch S60 116 B1
Whiston Jun & Inf Sch S60 116 B1
Whiston Vale S60 132 B8
Whiston Worry Goose Jun & Inf Sch S60 116 D1
Whitaker Cl DN11 103 F7
Whitbeck Cl DN11 102 B7
Whitbourne Cl S71 33 F5
Whitburn Rd DN1 62 E2
Whitby Rd
Harworth DN11 122 A5
Rossington DN11 103 F8
Sheffield S9 130 C5
Whitcomb Dr DN11 103 F7
White's La S2 129 D3
White Apron St WF9 18 B2
White Ave S81 136 E3
White Croft S1 161 A4
Whitecroft Cres S60 131 C8
White Cross DN12 101 A6
White Cross Ave S72 35 B5
White Cross Ct S72 35 C5
White Cross Gdns S72 16 D6
White Cross La
Doncaster DN11 83 B1
Wadworth DN11 102 B8
Worsbrough S70 55 D5
White Cross Mount S72 35 C5
White Cross Rd S72 35 B5
White Cross Rise S70 55 D5
White Gate S25 146 F6
White Gate Rd HD9 47 D7
Whitegate Wlk S61 96 F3
Whitehall Rd S61 97 A3
Whitehall Way S61 97 A3
White Hart Cnr S21 155 E4
White Hart Fold WF9 19 B6
Whitehead Ave S36 73 D1
Whitehead Cl S25 134 E1
Whitehill Ave S60 131 C8
White Hill Ave S70 33 B1
Whitehill Dr S60 131 C7
White Hill Gr [5] S70 33 B1
Whitehill La S60 131 D7
Whitehill Rd S60 131 C8
White Hill Terr [4] S70 33 B1
White House Cl
Hatfield DN7 44 A7
Stainforth DN7 24 E5
Whitehouse Ct DN11 122 C4
White House Dr DN11 122 C4
Whitehouse La S6 128 D6
Whitehouse Rd S6 128 D6
White House Rd DN11 122 C4
White House View DN3 42 E8
White La
Chapeltown S35 95 B7
Eckington S12 142 C2
Hooton Pagnell DN5 38 E4
Thorne DN8 26 A7
Whitelea Gr S64 79 F4
Whitelea Grove Trad Est S64 79 F4
White Lee La S36 92 B3
Whitelee Rd S64 79 E4
White Ley Bank HD9 28 A7
Whiteley La S10 139 C7
White Ley Rd WF8 3 E1
Whiteleys Ave S62 97 E7
Whiteley Wood Cl S11 139 F7
Whiteleywood Ho S11 139 E7
Whiteley Wood Rd S11 139 E7
Whitelow La S17 151 B7
White Rose Ct DN5 41 C1
White Rose Way DN4 83 F7
White Thorns Cl S8 153 B5
White Thorns Dr S8 153 B5
White Thorns View S8 153 B6
Whiteways Cl S4 129 D8
Whiteways Dr S4 129 D8
Whiteways Gr S4 129 D8
Whiteways Jun Sch S4 129 D8
Whiteways Rd S4 129 D8
Whitewood Cl S71 15 B3
Whitfield Gdns S81 147 D4
Whitfield Rd
Rawmarsh S62 97 D7
Sheffield S10 139 C7
Whitham Rd S10 160 A3
Whiting St [9] S8 141 A6
Whitley Carr S35 94 E2
Whitley Croft S35 95 B2
Whitley La S35 94 E2
Whitley Rd S36 49 E7
Whitley View S35 95 B2
Whitley View Rd S61 114 B6
Whitney Cl DN4 82 E5
Whittier Rd DN4 83 A6
Whittington St DN1 62 D5
Whitton Cl DN4 84 C6
Whitwell Cres S36 73 B1
Whitwell La S36 92 A8
Whitwell Rd S80 159 A4
Whitwell St S9 130 D4
Whitwell View DN11 85 B1
Whitworth Ct DN9 86 B3
Whitworth La S9 130 A7
Whitworth Rd S10 127 F2
Whitworth's Bldgs S63 58 E8
Whitworth St S63 58 E5
Whitworth Way S63 78 E7
Whybourne Gr S60 115 E5
Whybourne Terr [5] S60 115 E6
Whyn View S63 58 C8
Wicker S3 161 B4
Wicker La S3 161 B4
Wickersley Northfield Prim Sch S66 117 B5
Wickersley Rd S60 116 C4
Wickersley Sch & Sports Coll S66 117 C4
Wickett Hern Rd DN3 64 C6
Wicket Way DN12 82 C3
Wickfield Cl S12 142 F5
Wickfield Dr S12 142 F5
Wickfield Gr S12 142 E4
Wickfield Pl S12 142 F5
Wickfield Rd S12 142 F5
Wicklow Rd DN2 63 B5
Widdop Cl S13 142 D8
Widdop Croft S13 142 D8
Widford Gn DN7 44 A6
Wigfield Dr S70 54 F5
Wigfield Farm* S70 54 F4
Wigfull Rd S11 128 C1
Wignall Ave S66 116 F4
Wike Gate Cl DN8 26 D6
Wike Gate Gr DN8 26 D6
Wike Gate Rd DN8 26 D6
Wike Rd S71 34 E2
Wilberforce Rd
Doncaster DN2 42 D1
South Anston S25 146 D5
Wilbrook Rise S75 33 A4
Wilby Carr Gdns DN4 63 F1
Wilby La S70 55 A8
Wilcox Cl S6 112 D5
Wilcox Gn S61 97 A4
Wilcox Rd S6 112 D5
Wild Ave S62 97 C7
Wildene Dr S64 80 A6
Wildflower Cl DN11 103 F7
Wilding Cl S61 114 E8
Wilding Way S61 114 E8
Wilford Rd S71 14 E1
Wilfred Cl S9 130 A5
Wilfred Dr S9 130 A5
Wilfred St S60 115 D6
Wilfrid Rd S9 130 A5
Wilkinson Ave
[2] Rossington DN11 104 A8
Thorne DN8 9 C2
Wilkinson La S10 160 B3
Wilkinson Rd S74 77 A5
Wilkinson St
[17] Barnsley S70 54 F8
[5] Sheffield S10 160 B3
Willan Dr S60 131 C5
Willbury Dr S12 142 A6
Willey St S3 161 B4
William Bradford Cl DN10 105 C1
William Cl S20 155 D6
William Cres S20 155 D6
William La DN11 84 E1
William Levick Prim Sch S18 152 C2
William Nuttall Cott Homes DN2 62 F2
Williamson Rd S11 140 D7
Williams Rd DN5 61 F6
Williams St S81 136 E3
William St
Eckington S21 155 D3
Goldthorpe S63 58 C5
Rawmarsh S62 98 A4
Rotherham S60 115 E6
Sheffield S10 160 B2
Swinton S64 79 E3
Wath u D S63 78 F6
Wombwell S73 56 C3
Worsbrough S70 55 A5
Willingham Cl S20 144 A1
Willingham Gdns S20 144 A2
Willington Rd
Adwick le S DN6 21 B1
Sheffield S5 113 C4
Willis Rd S6 112 B1
Willman Rd S71 34 F3
Willoughby St S4 113 E2
Willow Ave
Carlton in L S81 148 E7
Doncaster DN4 84 F8
Rawmarsh S62 98 A6
Thorne DN8 9 B2
Willow Bank S71, S75 33 E4
Willow Beck
Notton WF4 15 A6
[4] Rotherham S65 116 B8
Willow Bridge La DN6 23 E6
Willowbridge Rd WF8 4 A6
Willowbrook DN6 20 F2
Willow Brook Cl S75 33 A8
Willow Cl
Brinsworth S60 131 D7
Cudworth S72 35 B7
Hoyland S74 76 C5
Rotherham S66 117 C6
South Anston S25 146 D3
Willow Cotts DN7 24 E8
Willow Cres
Braithwell S66 101 A2
Chapeltown S35 95 A4
Finningley DN9 85 F4
Thorne DN8 9 C1
Willow Ct
Darfield S73 57 A5
Rawmarsh S62 98 A6
Rotherham S66 117 B4
Wath u D S63 78 E5
Willowdale Cl DN5 82 D8
Willow Dene Rd S72 36 A7
Willow Dr
Havercroft WF4 16 B8
Hemsworth WF9 17 D5
Mexborough S64 79 F5
New Edlington DN12 82 C3
Rotherham S66 117 C6
Sheffield S9 130 E3
Willow Garth
Rawmarsh S62 98 A6
South Elmsall WF9 19 B2
Willowgarth Ave S60 131 C8
Willowgarth Cl WF4 16 A8
Willowgarth High Sch S72 17 A1
Willow Garth La DN6 5 C1
Willow Glen DN3 85 E8
Willow Gr
Aston S26 144 F8
Harworth DN11 121 F4
Thorne DN8 9 C1
Willow La
Bolton u D S63 58 D1
Rossington DN11 85 A2
Willowlees Ct DN4 84 E7
Willow Pl S66 101 A2
Willow Prim Sch DN4 84 D6
Willow Rd
Armthorpe DN3 64 C7
Killamarsh S21 156 C5
Maltby S66 118 D5
Norton DN6 4 D1
Stocksbridge S36 92 B7
Thorne DN8 9 B1
Thurnscoe S63 37 D1
Wath u D S63 79 A4
Willow St
Barnsley S70 54 D8
Conisbrough DN12 81 C2
Willows The
Darfield S73 57 A5
Oxspring S36 52 B1
Rotherham, Dropping Well S61 96 D2
Rotherham S65 115 F5
Willow Wlk DN5 41 A3
Wilmington Dr DN4 84 A7
Wilsden Gr S75 33 B4
Wilsic Hall Sch DN11 102 A4
Wilsic La DN11 102 D2
Wilsic Rd
Tickhill DN11 121 A8
Wadworth DN11 102 A5
Wilson Ave
Penistone S36 51 D2
Rawmarsh S62 97 E6
Wilson Carlile College of Evangilsm S3 160 C3
Wilson Dr S65 98 E1
Wilson Gr S71 34 F4
Wilson Pl [6] S8 141 A7
Wilson Rd
Dronfield S18 153 C4
Sheffield S11 140 C8
Stocksbridge S36 92 F8
Wilson St
Sheffield S3 129 A6
Wombwell S73 56 B4
Wilson Wlk S75 54 A6
Wilthorpe Ave S75 33 C4
Wilthorpe Cres S75 33 C4
Wilthorpe Farm Rd S75 33 C4
Wilthorpe Gdns [7] S20 143 A3
Wilthorpe Gn S75 33 C4
Wilthorpe Inf Sch S75 33 D4
Wilthorpe Jun Sch S75 33 D4
Wilthorpe La S75 33 B4
Wilthorpe Rd S75 33 B4
Wilton Cl S62 97 F5
Wilton Ct S61 115 A7
Wilton Gdns S61 115 A7
Wilton La S61 115 A6
Wilton Pl S10 160 B2
Wiltshire Ave DN12 80 F3
Wiltshire Rd DN2 63 C4
Winberry Ave S25 146 E7
Wincanton Cl S64 80 B6
Winchester Ave
Doncaster DN2 63 A6
Sheffield S10 139 B8
Winchester Cres S10 139 B8
Winchester Ct [4] S65 115 E7
Winchester Dr S10 139 B8
Winchester Flats DN7 44 A8
Winchester Ho
Bentley DN5 61 E6
Doncaster DN1 62 D3
Winchester Mews DN11 122 C4
Winchester Rd
Hatfield DN7 44 A8
Sheffield S10 139 B8
Winchester Way
Barnsley S71 56 A7
Bentley DN5 61 E6
Brinsworth S60 115 A1
South Elmsall WF9 19 A4
Wincobank Ave S5 113 F3
Wincobank Cl S5 113 F3
Wincobank Inf Sch S9 114 A4
Wincobank La S4 113 F1
Wincobank Rd S5 113 F3
Winco Rd [8] S4 113 F1
Winco Wood La S5 113 F3
Windam Dr DN3 42 F8
Windermere Ave
Doncaster DN2 63 C5
Dronfield S18 152 E1
Goldthorpe S63 58 E4
Harworth DN11 121 F4
Windermere Cl
Adwick le S DN6 21 A1
Mexborough S64 80 D6
Windermere Cres DN3 42 F3
Windermere Ct S25 146 E6
Windermere Grange DN12 82 B1
Windermere Rd
Barnsley S71 34 A1
Penistone S36 51 D4
[3] Sheffield S8 140 E5
Winders Pl S73 56 D2
Windgate Hill DN12 81 D3
Windham Cl S71 33 F3
Windhill Ave
Darton S75 14 A3
Mexborough S64 80 C5
Windhill Cres
Darton S75 14 A3
Mexborough S64 80 C6
Windhill Dr S75 14 A3
Windhill La S75 14 A3
Wind Hill La S36 91 C8
Windhill Mount S75 14 A3
Windhill Prim Sch S64 80 C6
Windhill Terr S64 80 C6
Windings The S63 58 F7
Windlass Cl DN8 26 A7
Windle Edge S36 69 B7
Windle Rd DN4 62 A1
Windle Sq DN3 42 F4
Windlestone Sq DN8 9 D3
Windmill Ave
Conisbrough DN12 81 D1
Grimethorpe S72 36 A8
Windmill Balk La DN6 40 B5
Windmill Cotts DN6 4 B2
Windmill Ct
Rotherham S61 96 A3
Wombwell S73 56 B2
Windmill Dr DN11 102 B6
Windmill Greenway S20 155 E5
Windmill Hill La S35 94 F4
Windmill Hill Prim Sch S35 94 F4
Windmill La
Norton DN6 4 C2
Sheffield S5 113 E3
Shepley HD8 28 D3
Wind Mill La S36 51 A3
Windmill Mdw DN6 4 C3

Windmill Rd
North Anston S25 146 E6
Wombwell S73 56 B2
Windses Est S32 149 D2
Windsor Ave
Kexbrough S75 32 C8
Penistone S36 51 A4
Windsor Cl
Askern DN6 22 C8
Barnburgh DN5 59 C2
Rotherham S66 117 D6
Windsor Cres
Barnsley S71 34 B3
Great Houghton S72 57 D7
Windsor Ct
Dunsville DN7 43 E4
Harworth DN11 122 B5
Sheffield S11 139 F4
Windsor Dr
Barnburgh DN5 59 C3
Dodworth S75 53 F7
Dronfield S18 152 C1
Mexborough S64 80 C6
Windsor Gdns
Carlton in L S81 148 E6
Thurnscoe S63 58 E8
Windsor Rd
Carlton in L S81 148 E6
Conisbrough DN12 81 B3
Doncaster DN2 62 F4
Hemsworth WF9 17 F6
Rotherham S61 95 F4
Sheffield S8 140 F6
Stainforth DN7 24 E3
Windsor Rise S26 144 E6
Windsor Sq
Stainforth DN7 24 E3
Thurnscoe S63 58 E8
Windsor St
Hoyland S74 76 D6
Sheffield S4 129 D6
Sheffield S4 129 E5
South Elmsall WF9 19 A2
Thurnscoe S63 58 E8
Windsor Wlk
Bentley DN5 61 E6
South Anston S25 146 D3
Windy Bank S6 109 E6
Windy House La S2 142 A8
Windy Ridge S26 132 C1
Winfield Rd S63 78 F5
Wingerworth Ave S8 152 D8
Wingfield Cl
6 Dronfield S18 152 C1
Rotherham S61 97 A3
Wingfield Cres S12 142 C5
Wingfield Rd
Barnsley S71 34 A7
Rotherham S61 96 F2
Wingfield Sch S61 97 A2
Winholme DN3 64 B6
Winifred St S60 115 C7
Winkley Terr S5 113 E5
Winlea Ave S65 116 E4
Winmarith Ct S71 15 B3
Winn Cl S6 112 B3
Winn Dr S6 112 B3
Winnery Cl DN11 121 A8
Winney Hill S26 157 E5
Winney La S26 157 E3
Winn Gdns S6 112 B3
Winn Gr S6 112 B3
Winnipeg Rd DN5 41 B1
Winnowing Barn Ct S25 146 D4
Winsford Rd S6 112 C5
Winster Cl S70 54 F1
Winster Rd S6 112 C1
Winston Ave S36 72 F2
Winston Gn DN10 123 F1
Winter Ave
Barnsley S75 33 C2
Royston S71 15 C5
Winter Hill La S61 114 E7
Winterhill Rd S61 114 D6
Winterhill Sch S61 114 E7
Winter Rd S75 33 C2
Wintersett Dr DN4 84 B8
Winter St S3 160 B4
Winter Terr S75 33 C2
Winterton Cl DN4 84 D6
Winterton Gdns S12 143 C3
Winterwell Rd S63 78 D7
Winton Cl S70 55 A7
Winton Rd DN2 63 B4
Wisconsin Dr DN4 84 A7
Wiseley Croft S72 36 A8
Wiseton Ct 1 S11 140 C8
Wiseton Rd 2 S11 140 C8
Wisewood Ave S6 128 A8
Wisewood La S6 128 A8
Wisewood Pl S6 128 A8
Wisewood Prim Sch S6 112 A1
Wisewood Rd S6 128 A8
Wisewood Sch & Com Sports Coll S6 112 A1
Wishing Well Gn S26 144 B7
Witham Ct S75 32 E3
Withens Ave S6 112 B2
Withens Ct S75 14 A1
Withyside HD8 30 A6
Witmore St WF9 19 A3
Witney St S8 141 A8
Wittsend Park Cvn Site DN5 41 E3
Wivelsfield Rd DN4 82 E6
Woburn Cl DN4 82 E5
Woburn Pl
Dodworth S75 53 F6
Sheffield S11 139 F2
Wolfe Dr S6 112 D5
Wolfe Rd S6 112 D5
Wolfson Flats S10 128 C1
Wollaton Ave S17 152 A5
Wollaton Cl S71 33 E8
Wollaton Dr S17 152 A5
Wollaton Rd S17 152 A5
Wolseley Rd 2 S8 141 A7
Wolsey Ave DN2 63 B4
Wolverley Rd S13 143 A6
Wombwell Ave S63 78 E5
Wombwell High Sch S73 56 E1
Wombwell John Street Inf Sch S73 56 C3
Wombwell La
Barnsley S70 55 F7
Hoyland S74 55 E2
Wombwell Park Street Prim Sch S73 56 E2
Wombwell Rd S74 76 E7
Wombwell Sta S73 56 B1
Wong La DN11 120 F7
Wood's Riding DN2 63 D4
Wood Acres S75 33 A4
Woodall La S26 157 D6
Woodall Rd
Killamarsh S21 156 F5
Rotherham S65 116 C5
Woodall Rd S S65 116 C4
Woodbank Cres S8 140 F5
Woodbank Ct S17 152 A7
Woodbank Rd S6 126 F4
Woodbine Rd S9 129 F7
Woodbourne Gdns S75 75 E5
Woodbourn Hill S9 129 F5
Woodbourn Rd S9 129 F4
Woodburn Dr S35 95 C4
Woodbury Cl S9 114 A5
Woodbury Rd S9 114 A5
Wood Cl
Chapeltown S35 95 C4
Rawmarsh S62 97 E7
Rotherham S65 117 C8
Wood Cliffe S10, S11 139 B6
Woodcock Cl S61 96 F2
Woodcock Pl S2 129 D3
Woodcock Rd S74 76 E5
Woodcock Way
Adwick le S DN6 40 B7
South Elmsall WF9 19 A4
Wood Cotts S36 52 B1
Wood Croft S61 96 F1
Woodcross Ave DN4 85 A7
Wood End
Sheffield S35 94 D2
Shepley HD8 28 C8
Wood End Ave S36 51 C1
Woodend Cl S6 128 A7
Woodend Dr S6 128 A7
Wood End La HD8 28 C7
Woodfall La S6 110 A5
Wood Fall La S6 110 A5
Woodfarm Ave S6 127 F6
Woodfarm Cl S6 127 E6
Woodfarm Dr S6 127 E6
Woodfarm Pl S6 127 E6
Woodfield Ave S64 80 B5
Woodfield Cl S73 57 A6
Woodfield Prim Sch DN4 83 B6
Woodfield Rd
Armthorpe DN3 64 C5
Doncaster, Balby DN4 83 A6
Doncaster, Balby DN4 83 C6
Norton DN6 20 E8
Sheffield S10 128 B5
Wath u D S63 78 C6
Wood Fields S66 117 E4
Woodfield Way DN4 83 B4
Wood Fold S3 129 A7
Woodfoot Rd S60 115 F1
Woodford Rd DN3 42 F8
Woodgarth Ct DN6 21 C8
Woodgrove Rd
Rotherham S65 116 C7
Sheffield S9 114 B4
Woodhall Cl S73 57 A6
Woodhall Flats S73 57 A6
Woodhall House Farm S26 157 C6
Woodhall Rd S73 57 A6
Woodhall Rise S64 79 D2
Woodhead Dr S74 55 D1
Woodhead La S74 55 E1
Woodhead Rd
Sheffield, Highfield S2 141 A8
Sheffield S35 94 B3
Wortley S35 93 E6
Woodholm Pl S11 140 B5
Woodholm Rd S11 140 B5
Woodhouse Ave S20 143 F4
Woodhouse Cl S62 97 D8
Woodhouse Cres S20 143 F4
Woodhouse Ct S20 143 F4
Woodhouse Gdns S13 143 C6
Woodhouse Gn S66 133 E7
Woodhouse Green Rd DN7 24 D7
Woodhouse La
Emley HD8 12 A7
Hatfield DN7 44 B4
Sheffield S20 143 F5
Woolley WF4, S75 14 B5
Woodhouse Rd
Doncaster DN2 62 F5
Woodhouse Rd *continued*
Hoyland S74 76 E5
Sheffield S12 142 B6
Woodhouse Sta S13 143 D7
Woodhouse West Prim Sch S13 143 A6
Woodkirk Cl S36 51 F2
Woodknot Mews DN4 83 B4
Wood La
Barnsley S71 15 C1
Catliffe S60 131 A7
Darton S71 14 E2
Denby Dale HD8 29 E6
Doncaster DN11 82 F2
Fishlake, Hay Green DN7 25 B8
New Edlington DN12 101 C7
Rotherham, Canklow S60 115 D3
Rotherham, Wickersley S66 117 C3
Sheffield S6 127 E6
Stainton S66 101 E1
Thorne DN7 8 E2
Thurcroft S66 133 C5
Treeton S60 132 A3
Woodlaithes Rd S66 117 C7
Woodland Ave S25 146 E5
Woodland Cl
Catliffe S60 131 C5
Rotherham S66 117 C3
Woodland Dr
Barnsley S70 54 B8
North Anston S25 146 F5
Sheffield S12 142 B2
Woodland Gdns S66 119 B5
Woodland Gr S63 78 F4
Woodland Lodge S74 76 C6
Woodland Pl S17 151 F5
Woodland Rd
Sheffield S8 141 B3
Wath u D S63 78 F4
Woodland Rise S75 53 A5
Woodlands S60 116 C3
Woodlands Ave S20 143 F5
Woodlands Cl
Aston S26 132 D1
Denby Dale HD8 30 A6
Woodlands Cres
Hemsworth WF9 17 E8
Swinton S64 79 B2
Woodlands Farm S60 131 E4
Woodlands Prim Schs DN6 40 A4
Woodlands Rd
Adwick le S DN6 40 B4
Hoyland S74 76 E8
Woodlands Rise DN6 4 C1
Woodlands Terr DN12 82 B2
Woodlands The
Armthorpe DN3 64 C7
Sheffield S10 128 A2
Woodlands View
Adwick le S DN6 40 A4
Great Houghton S72 36 E2
Hoyland, Jump S73 77 A8
Hoyland S74 76 E7
Woodlands Way DN12 80 F3
Woodland Terr S72 36 B5
Woodland View
Cudworth S72 35 B5
Hathersage S32 149 A7
1 Mexborough S64 80 C4
Sheffield, Abbeydale Park S17 152 A7
Sheffield, Charnock Hill S12 142 B2
Silkstone S75 53 A5
Woodland View Rd S6 128 A6
Woodland Way S65 116 D4
Wood Lane Cl S6 127 E6
Woodlea 6 WF9 18 F2
Woodlea Gdns DN4 85 A7
Woodlea Gr DN3 64 B6
Woodlea Way DN2 63 C7
Woodleys Ave S62 97 E8
Woodman Dr S64 79 A2
Woodmoor Ct S71 34 B7
Wood Moor Rd WF9 17 F7
Woodmoor St S71 34 D8
Wood Nook
Denby Dale HD8 29 F6
Sheffield S35 94 C1
Woodnook Gr S21 154 E2
Wood Park View S71 14 F1
Woodpecker Cl
Aston S26 144 E6
Worksop S81 148 D1
Wood Rd
Rotherham S61 96 F1
Sheffield S6 128 B8
Woodrove Ave S13 142 B7
Woodrove Cl S13 142 B7
Woodroyd Ave S71 15 C1
Woodroyd Cl S71 15 C1
Wood Royd Hill La HD9 49 B8
Wood Royd Rd S36 92 E8
Wood Seats S35 94 D3
Woodseats Cl S8 140 E4
Woodseats House Rd S8 140 F2
Woodseats Prim Sch S8 140 F3
Woodseats Rd S8 140 F4
Woodsetts La S81 148 A1
Woodsetts Prim Sch S81 147 E4
Woodsetts Rd
Gildingwells S81 147 F6
North Anston S25, S81 147 B5
Woodsett Wlk DN12 81 E3
Woodside HD8 30 A6
Woodside Ave
Killamarsh S21 156 F7
Wath u D S63 78 F6
Woodside Cl S66 119 B4
Woodside Ct
Adwick le S DN6 40 A4
Rotherham S66 117 C3
Woodside La
Sheffield, Grenoside S35 94 C1
Sheffield S3 129 A6
Wroot DN9 67 B3
Woodside Rd
Adwick le S DN6 40 A4
Bentley DN5 61 F8
Shireoaks S81 159 F7
Woodside View
Bircotes DN11 122 B4
Bolton u D S63 58 D2
Woodside Villas DN9 67 B2
Woodside Wlk S61 97 B3
Wood Spring Ct S4 129 E8
Wood St
Barnsley S70 54 F8
Doncaster DN1 62 D3
Mexborough S64 79 F5
Rotherham S65 98 E2
Sheffield S6 128 E6
South Hiendley S72 16 F6
Swinton S64 79 E3
Wombwell S73 56 C2
Woodstock Gdns S75 33 D4
Woodstock Rd
Barnsley S75 33 D4
Doncaster DN4 82 E7
Sheffield, Normandale S6 127 E8
Sheffield S7 140 E6
Wood Syke S75 54 A7
Wood Terr S60 115 D3
Woodthorpe Cres S13 142 C8
Woodthorpe Prim Sch S13 142 C7
Woodthorpe Rd S13 142 C7
Woodvale Cl S75 32 E4
Woodvale Flats S10 128 B1
Woodvale Rd S10 128 B1
Woodview DN5 61 B1
Wood View
4 Askern DN6 22 B8
Barnsley S70 75 F5
Branton DN3 64 E1
Conisbrough DN12 81 E1
Hoyland S74 77 A5
Maltby S66 119 B5
New Edlington DN12 82 C2
Wood View Ho S21 155 C3
Woodview La S75 33 B3
Wood View Pl S60 115 D3
Woodview Rd S6 128 C7
Woodview Terr S10 139 E8
Woodway The S66 117 B7
Wood Wlk
Mexborough S64 79 F6
Royston S71 15 C5
Woofindin Ave S11 139 E7
Woofindin Rd S10 139 D7
Wooldale Cl S20 143 A2
Wooldale Croft S20 143 A2
Wooldale Dr S20 143 A2
Wooldale Gdns S20 143 A2
Wooley Ave S73 56 C2
Woollen La 3 S6 128 E5
Woolley Colliery Rd S75 13 E2
Woolley Edge La WF4 13 E6
Woolley Hall Gdns WF4 14 A7
Woolley Ho 6 DN1 62 C1
Woolley Low Moor La WF4 13 D8
Woolley Park Gdns WF4 14 A7
Woolley Rd S36 73 A1
Woolley Wood Rd S5 113 F7
Woolley Wood Sch S5 113 E6
Woolstocks La S75 31 E3
Wootton Ct S65 98 E2
Worcester Ave DN2 63 A7
Worcester Cl S10 127 B1
Worcester Dr S10 127 B1
Worcester Rd S10 127 B1
Wordsworth Ave
Dinnington S25 147 A8
Doncaster DN4 83 B6
Norton DN6 4 C1
Penistone S36 51 C2
Sheffield S5 112 E5
Wordsworth Cl S5 112 E6
Wordsworth Cres S5 112 E4
Wordsworth Ct S36 51 D4
Wordsworth Dr
Bentley DN5 61 F4
Rotherham S65 116 A6
Sheffield S5 112 E4
Wordsworth Rd
Barnsley S71 34 B4
Wath u D S63 78 C7
Work Bank La S36 51 B4
Workhouse La S3 161 A4
Worksop Rd
Aston S26 144 E7
Sheffield S9 130 A6
Thorpe Salvin S80 158 E7
Tickhill DN11 120 F6
Todwick S26 145 C7
Woodsetts S81 147 D2
Woodsetts S81 147 F3
Wormley Hill La DN14 8 D5
Worral Ave S60 131 E4
Worral Cl S70 54 F6
Worral Ct 3 DN3 43 A2
Worrall Dr S35 111 D5
Worrall Rd
Chapeltown S35 94 F7
Oughtibridge S35 111 E3
Sheffield S6 111 E3
Worry Goose La S60 116 D2
Worsbrough View S75 75 D6
Worsbrough Bank End Prim Sch S70 55 C6
Worsbrough Common Prim Sch S70 54 F6
Worsbrough Ctry Pk* S70 54 E3
Worsbrough Rd
Barnsley S70 54 F1
Hoyland S74 55 D1
Worsley Cl S70 55 B6
Worsley Pl DN6 20 F2
Worthing Cres DN12 81 D2
Worthing Rd S9 129 E5
Wortley Ave
Conisbrough DN12 81 A2
Swinton S64 79 D3
Wombwell S73 56 B4
Wortley Ct S35 94 D7
Wortley Dr S35 111 E7
Wortley Hall Gdn* S35 74 E3
Wortley Mews S61 95 E4
Wortley Pl WF9 17 C7
Wortley Rd
Chapeltown S35 94 D8
Rotherham S61 114 F8
Stocksbridge S36 74 A1
Wortley St 7 S70 33 E1
Wortley Top Forge Mus* S35 74 B4
Wortley View S74 55 D1
Wostenholm Rd S7 140 F8
Wragby Rd S11 140 A8
Wragg Rd S2 129 E2
Wrancarr La DN6 23 A6
Wrancarr Wood La DN5 22 F5
Wrangbrook La WF9 19 D7
Wrangbrook Rd WF9 19 D8
Wreakes La S18 152 F2
Wrelton Cl S71 15 B3
Wren Bank S2 129 E2
Wren Park Cl S12 154 E8
Wrens Way S70 75 F8
Wright's Hill 2 S2 140 F8
Wright Bsns Pk DN4 62 A1
Wright Cres S73 56 D2
Wrightson Ave DN4 82 C5
Wrightson Terr DN5 62 B6
Wright St S25 146 E6
Wroot Rd DN9 87 B6
Wroot Travis Charity CE Prim Sch DN9 67 A2
Wroxham Cl S66 117 E5
Wroxham Dr S66 117 E5
Wroxham Way
Bentley DN5 61 E5
Rotherham S66 117 E6
Wulfric Cl S2 141 F8
Wulfric Pl S2 141 F8
Wulfric Rd
Eckington S21 155 C3
Sheffield S2 142 A8
Wyatt Ave S11 140 C6
Wybourn Com Prim Sch S2 129 E3
Wybourn House Rd S2 129 E3
Wybourn Terr S2 129 E3
Wychwood Cl DN4 82 F4
Wychwood Croft 8 S20 144 A2
Wychwood Glen 7 S20 144 A2
Wychwood Gr 9 S20 144 A2
Wycombe St S71 34 E2
Wyedale Croft S20 143 F4
Wyming Brook Dr S6 126 B2
Wyndthorpe Ave DN4 84 E7
Wyndthorpe Ct S60 116 C4
Wynford Dr WF9 19 A3
Wyn Gr S73 78 A8
Wynlea Dr S81 136 F6
Wynmoor Cres S73 78 A7
Wynyard Rd S6 112 B1
Wyvern Gdns S17 151 E6

Y

Yarborough Terr DN5 62 B5
Yardley Sq S3 160 B4
Yarmouth St S9 114 B1
Yarwell Dr S66 118 E6
Yates Cl S66 117 A3
Yealand Cl DN6 40 B6
Yearling Chase S64 79 B3
Yeomans Rd S6 128 E5
Yeomans Way S25 146 D4
Yewdale S70 55 B5
Yew Greave Cres S5 112 F7
Yew La S5 112 F7
Yewlands Sch Tech Coll S35 112 E7
Yews Ave S70 55 B5
Yews Cl S35 111 D4
Yews Hospl The S35 111 E4
Yews La
Sheffield S6 126 D8
Worsbrough S70 55 B6
Yews Pl S70 55 B7
Yews The S65 115 F7
Yew Tree Ave S25 146 F5
Yew Tree Cl S66 133 F7
Yew Tree Cres DN11 85 A2
Yew Tree Ct DN6 21 C8

Yew Tree Dr
Bawtry DN10 . . . . **122** F7
Killamarsh S21 . . . . **156** C5
Sheffield S9 . . . . **114** F1
Yew Tree Rd S66 . . . . **118** D6
Yewtrees La S36 . . . . **92** B5
Yoredale Ave S35 . . . . **94** F6
York Bldgs DN12 . . . . **82** B3
York Cl WF9 . . . . **19** A4
York Gdns
Doncaster DN4 . . . .**63** D1
Wath u D S63 . . . . **78** D7
York La S66 . . . . **133** B8
York Mews S63 . . . . **58** E8

York Pl S81 . . . .**159** F7
York Rd
Bentley DN5 . . . .**61** E7
Doncaster DN5 . . . .**62** B4
Harworth DN11 . . . . **122** A4
Hatfield DN7 . . . .**44** A8
Rotherham S65 . . . . **115** E7
Sheffield S9 . . . . **130** C5
Stocksbridge S36 . . . .**73** B1
Tickhill DN11 . . . . **121** B7
York Rise S26 . . . . **144** C7
Yorkshire Sculpture Pk★
WF4 . . . .**12** E7
Yorkshire Way DN3 . . . .**64** E7

York Sq ▣ S64 . . . .**80** A4
York St
Barnsley S70 . . . .**33** E1
Cudworth S72 . . . .**35** B6
Hemsworth WF9 . . . .**17** E5
Hoyland S74 . . . .**76** E7
Mexborough S64 . . . .**79** F5
Rossington DN11 . . . .**84** E2
Sheffield S1 . . . . **161** A4
Thurnscoe S63 . . . .**37** F1
Wombwell S73 . . . .**56** D3
York Way DN12 . . . .**81** E3
Youlgreave Dr
S12 . . . . **142** D5

Young St
Doncaster DN1 . . . .**62** D3
Sheffield S3 . . . . **160** C1
Yvonne Gr S73 . . . .**56** B3

Z

Zamor Cres S66 . . . .**133** E5
Zenith Pk S75 . . . .**33** A4
Zetland Rd
Doncaster DN2 . . . .**63** A4
Hoyland S74 . . . .**77** B5
Zion Dr S75 . . . .**14** B1

Zion La S9 . . . . **129** F6
Zion Pl S9 . . . . **129** F6
Zion Terr S70 . . . .**55** E7

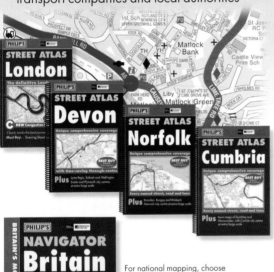